ANDREW JACKSON
THE POLITICS OF RESENTMENT

CHRISTOPHER ADAMO

Andrew Jackson: The Politics of Resentment
Copyright © 2025 by Christopher Adamo.

All rights reserved. No part of this publication may be reproduced, distributed, or transmitted in any form or by any means, including photocopying, recording, or other electronic or mechanical methods, without the written consent of the publisher. The only exceptions are for brief quotations included in critical reviews and other noncommercial uses permitted by copyright law.

MILTON & HUGO L.L.C.
4407 Park Ave., Suite 5
Union City, NJ 07087, USA

Website: *www. miltonandhugo.com*
Hotline: *1- 888-778-0033*
Email: *info@miltonandhugo.com*

Ordering Information:
Quantity sales. Special discounts are granted to corporations, associations, and other organizations. For more information on these discounts, please reach out to the publisher using the contact information provided above.

Library of Congress Control Number:		2025920854	
ISBN-13:	979-8-89285-613-3	[Paperback Edition]	
	979-8-89285-614-0	[Hardback Edition]	
	979-8-89285-615-7	[Digital Edition]	

Rev. date: 08/25/2025

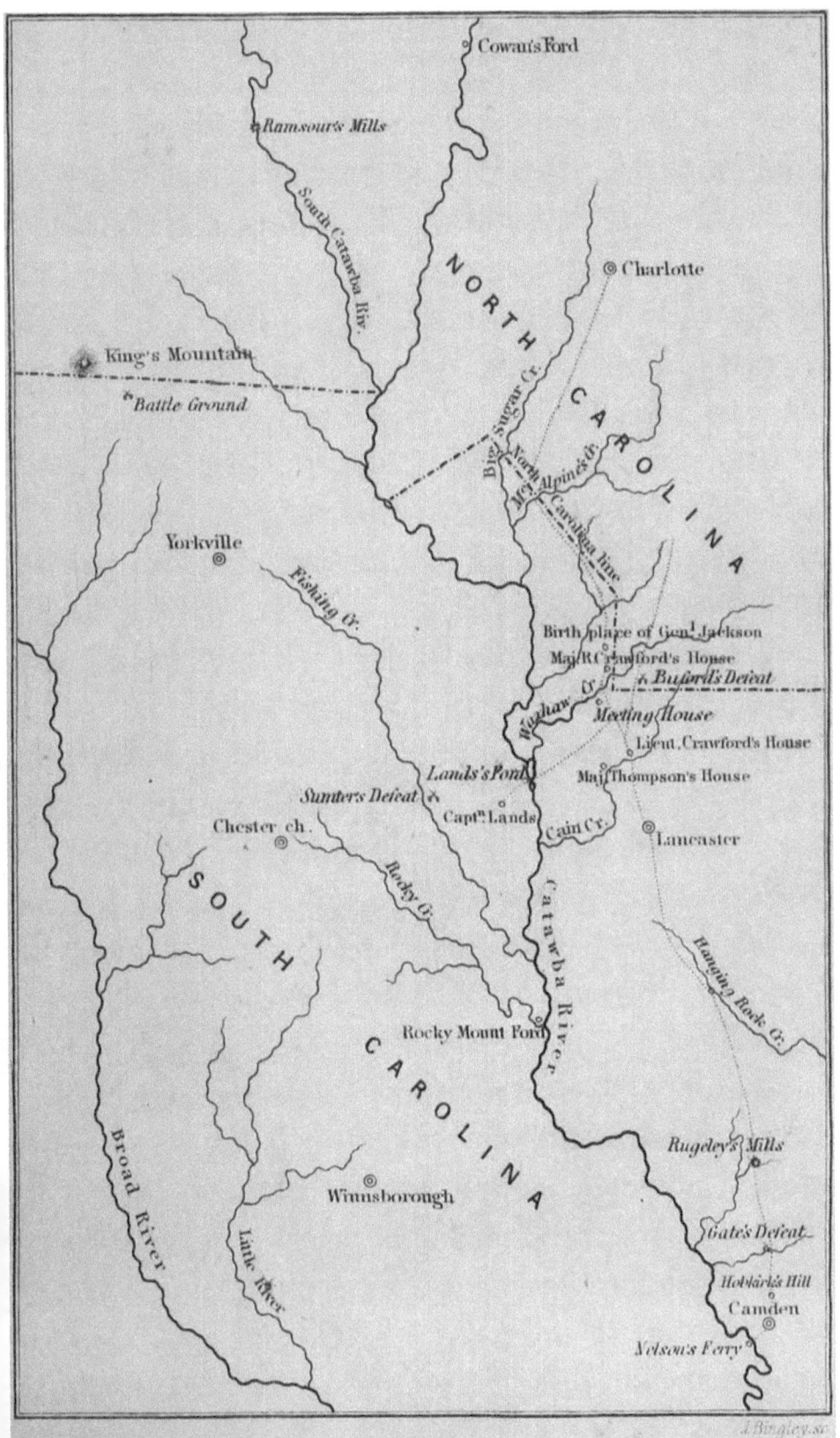

NEW YORK, HARPER & BROTHERS.

FOREWORD

In our contemporary era of stark political divisions and populist movements, few historical figures offer more relevant insights than Andrew Jackson, America's seventh president. This comprehensive examination of Jackson's life and legacy arrives at a crucial moment when Americans once again grapple with questions of democratic representation, political polarization, and the nature of leadership.

This work delves deep into the paradox of Jackson's presidency - a man who simultaneously expanded democratic participation while enforcing policies that led to the displacement and suffering of Native Americans. Through meticulous research and analysis, I have sought to explore how Jackson's brand of populism reshaped American political discourse and institutional structures in ways that continue to reverberate today.

The parallel between Jackson's era and our current political climate is striking. Just as Jackson's presidency marked a fundamental shift in American democracy, introducing a more direct relationship between the president and the people, we now witness similar transformations in political communication and voter engagement. This book argues that Jackson's presidency was not merely a chapter in American history but a crucial turning point that established patterns of political behavior and institutional tensions that would eventually contribute to the Civil War and beyond.

By examining Jackson's complex legacy - from his role in expanding suffrage for white males to his implementation of the Indian Removal Act, from his war against the Second Bank of the United States to his assertion of executive power - we gain valuable insights into current political dynamics. The "politics of resentment" that characterized Jackson's era bears remarkable similarities to contemporary political movements, making this historical analysis particularly relevant for understanding our present moment.

In writing this book, I have sought to challenge readers to consider whether Jackson's influence on American political development has been underestimated, particularly in relation to the sectional conflicts that led to the Civil War. More importantly, it invites us to reflect on how historical patterns of populism, political polarization, and institutional conflict continue to shape our democratic experiment.

The historical parallels between Andrew Jackson's presidency and contemporary political movements, particularly those associated with Donald Trump's political career, offer fascinating insights into the enduring nature of populist politics in America. This essay focuses on the life of Andrew Jackson but explores the concept of the "politics of resentment" during the Age of Jackson, so that readers will consider the dangers of decision-making through resentful motives that we continue to see today. Although separated by nearly two centuries the eras are connected by similar political approaches and voter appeals.

Jackson's presidency (1829-1837) marked a significant shift in American political culture, characterized by his appeal to the "common man" and opposition to what he termed "elite establishments." His political strategy centered on mobilizing rural and working-class white voters who felt marginalized by the political establishment. Jackson's populist approach, which included attacks on the National Bank and support for Indian removal policies, resonated with voters who harbored resentment against perceived coastal elites and established institutions.

Similar patterns emerged during Trump's political ascendancy. Like Jackson, Trump positioned himself as an outsider fighting against established political institutions. Both leaders mastered the art of channeling public grievances against perceived elite groups, whether they were nineteenth-century bankers or modern-day political establishments. Their communication styles, though products of different eras, shared common elements: direct appeal to supporters, criticism of traditional media, and the ability to transform complex political issues into simple narratives of "us versus them."

The "politics of resentment" framework helps explain how both leaders successfully mobilized voters who felt economically or culturally marginalized. Jackson's supporters resented the influence of Eastern banking interests and urban elites, while Trump's base often expressed frustration with globalization, immigration policies, and perceived coastal elite dominance in cultural and political spheres.

Both presidencies challenged institutional norms. Jackson's use of the veto power and his conflict with the Supreme Court parallels Trump's executive orders and challenges to traditional governmental processes. These similarities reflect how populist leaders, galvanized by widespread popular support, often test the boundaries of presidential authority when confronting established institutions.

Understanding these historical parallels provides valuable context for analyzing contemporary political movements. While historical circumstances differ significantly, the underlying dynamics of populist appeal and the politics of resentment remain remarkably consistent, demonstrating the cyclical nature of American political movements and the enduring influence of Jacksonian democracy on modern political discourse.

This connection between past and present highlights how certain political strategies and voter appeals persist throughout American history, adapting to new circumstances while maintaining core characteristics that resonate with segments of the electorate feeling disconnected from traditional power structures.

As we navigate our own period of political transformation and social change, understanding Jackson's era becomes not just an academic exercise but a crucial lens through which to view our present challenges. This work offers both a warning and a guide for those seeking to understand how democratic institutions can withstand the pressures of polarization and populism while striving to create a more perfect union.

CHRISTOPHER ADAMO

Andrew Jackson in the 1840s

This work is dedicated to my family.

CONTENTS

Foreword vii
Chapter 1   Fallen Patriarch 1
Chapter 2   No Quarter 18
Chapter 3   Post Mortem 30
Chapter 4   War is Hell 40
Chapter 5   On His Own 54
Chapter 6   To the Bar 64
Chapter 7   Go West, Young Man! 78
Chapter 8   New Arrival 88
Chapter 9   O, Cumberland River 99
Chapter 10 Introducing the Attorney General 110
Chapter 11 Intrigue 119
Chapter 12 Our Federal Union 129
Chapter 13 Natchez Nuptials 139
Chapter 14 Heading Home 150
Chapter 15 Statehood 163
Chapter 16 Revolutionary Changes 172
Chapter 17 Mr. Jackson Goes to Philadelphia 181
Chapter 18 Jackson versus Nolichucky Jack 198
Chapter 19 Not for the Legislative Life 211
Chapter 20 Home Again 222
Chapter 21 Militia Man 233
Chapter 22 A Man on his Own 246
Chapter 23 The Merchant and the Horseman 262
Chapter 24 Blood on the Red River 279
Chapter 25 A Burr in My Side 288
Chapter 26 Choose your Friends Wisely 298
Chapter 27 The Chesapeake Affair 310
Chapter 28 War! 317
Chapter 29 The War Comes South 327
Chapter 30 Jackson vs. Himself 342

Chapter 31	The Creek War	353
Chapter 32	Raiding the Red Sticks	362
Chapter 33	Horseshoe Bend	372
Chapter 34	Sharp Knife	389
Chapter 35	The British Monster Comes South	399
Chapter 36	New Orleans	409
Chapter 37	Crescent City Clash	423
Chapter 38	The British are Coming	432
Chapter 39	Villeré's Plantation	442
Chapter 40	The British Hold the Cards	451
Chapter 41	The Dawn of a New Year	466
Chapter 42	The Eighth of January	477
Chapter 43	All Hail, the Savior	488
Chapter 44	The Aftermath	505
Chapter 45	A Hero is Born	519
Chapter 46	A Man for the Ages	532
Chapter 47	Jackson versus the City of New Orleans	540
Chapter 48	Peace	551
Chapter 49	National Hero	571
Chapter 50	Fame Game	581
Chapter 51	Removal	595
Chapter 52	And Now for the Seminole	603
Chapter 53	A Dangerous Man	616
Chapter 54	Growing Pains	627
Chapter 55	The Life of a Planter	637
Chapter 56	The Governor	646
Chapter 57	Home Again	655
Chapter 58	The Presidency Route	665
Chapter 59	Era of Shady Dealings	673
Chapter 60	What Does Jackson Stand For?	682
Chapter 61	A Corrupt Bargain	694
Chapter 62	Revenge	704
Chapter 63	Mudslinging	719
Chapter 64	Weathering the Storm	731
Chapter 65	A Tragic Victory	743
Chapter 66	King Mob	750
Chapter 67	The Petticoat Affair	766

Chapter 68	America: Federal vs. State	773
Chapter 69	The Hated Tariff	782
Chapter 70	The Fall of Calhoun	797
Chapter 71	A Second Cabinet	806
Chapter 72	Executive Struggles	815
Chapter 73	That Abominable Tariff	824
Chapter 74	The Question of Removal	836
Chapter 75	Enforcement Matters	855
Chapter 76	The Monster Must be Killed	872
Chapter 77	Mandate of the People	883
Chapter 78	Pet Banks	891
Chapter 79	Planting the Seeds of Recession	904
Chapter 80	We Must Have Texas	917
Chapter 81	Texas Revolution	929
Chapter 82	Legacy & Family	952
Chapter 83	A Tragic Loss	960
Chapter 84	Retirement at Last?	975
Chapter 85	A Mixed Mourning	991
Epilogue		997
Index		1003

CHAPTER

1

FALLEN PATRIARCH

> "They call themselves Scotch-Irish,–ignavus pecus,–and the bitterest railers against the church [of England] that ever trod upon American ground."
> – Rev. George Ross

A vibrant springtime sun pierced the morning mist, casting a warm, honeyed glow as it filtered through the tall pines, painting the rolling hills of the Waxhaws in brilliant hues of amber and green. It was 1775, and the morning dew still clung to the tall grass that surrounded the shabby wooden schoolhouse where young Andrew Jackson, aged eight, sat restlessly on his bench. Further north, there was trouble brewing, but in the remote and dense forests of the Piedmont, a sweet and blameless ignorance resonated across the border between North and South Carolina. The morning air was sweet with the scent of honeysuckle and wild roses that grew haphazardly in the rough-hewn settlement, a place where Scotch-Irish immigrants like the Jacksons had made their home. Birds chirped their morning songs as they flitted between the towering pine trees that surrounded the Waxhaw schoolhouse, and all young Andy could think about was being outside, galloping with his brothers through the fields on horseback. Instead, he was stuck inside this dank wooden, windowless classroom, and he didn't like it.

During the morning lessons, Andy struggled with his reading assignment. Never the best student, his thick frontier accent made pronouncing certain words even more difficult, and when he stumbled over a particularly challenging passage, several of his classmates snickered. His face turned as red as the clay soil of the Waxhaw region. The feisty Andy wasn't one to take mockery lightly. He stood up abruptly, the wooden bench scraping against the rough-hewn floor. His fierce blue eyes blazed as he turned to face his classmates, his fists clenched at his sides.

"Laugh again," he challenged, his voice trembling with both embarrassment and anger, "and I'll thrash every last one of you!" The classroom fell silent. Even at his young age, Andrew Jackson's reputation for being quick-tempered and determined was well known. His peers had seen him fight before, and none wished to test his resolve. The teacher, hiding a knowing smile, called the class back to order.

But not to be cowed by some young upstart, some of the older boys made a note of the gaunt, red-headed Andy's sensitivities, and as children through the ages are wont to do, sought another opportunity to see what fun might come from getting hot-headed Andy worked up again. Sure enough, it did not take long. Knowing as they did how competitive and overbearing Andy could be, one day after school-hours, the boys handed him a gun, loaded to the muzzle. They knew that if they dared him to fire it, he would surely do it, and the thought of him thrashing about in the dirt was just too much to resist. Andy Jackson was never one to resist a challenge, and this was no exception, as expected. Grabbing the gun as soon as it was offered, he fired it without a second thought, only to have the recoil immediately throw him to the ground in a thud, sprawled in a heap. Outraged by the prank the boys had played on him, Andrew, in a tizzy, squirmed to his feet, and then screamed in a furious rampage, "By God! If one of you laughs, I'll kill him!" The boys saw that the lad had fire in his eyes, and suddenly the raucous laughter ceased. Not a sound could be heard; sensing the fury in the boy's unsettling demeanor and his fiery blue eyes, no one was laughing. [1]

That day, no one dared laugh at Andrew Jackson, and very few ever did from that day forward, at least not to his face, and not unless they were expecting a firestorm of reaction. Even as a boy, he displayed the fierce pride and determination that would later characterize his life as a military leader and the seventh President of the United States.

---

[1] Jackson, *Correspondence*, Volume III. Pg. 265

ANDREW JACKSON: THE POLITICS OF RESENTMENT

What was it about Andrew Jackson that caused him, by the 1830s, to be so loved by so many Americans that many not only held him above all other Americans, living or dead, but some even voted for him for president some fifteen years after his death? No other American president, not even Washington, Jefferson, or Lincoln dominated an era so entirely that his influence carried on long after his death and ultimately spanned decades.

No other individual in the first century of the nation's history had such an astounding impact, not only on the era itself, but on the nature of American democracy in general. Andrew Jackson virtually held the country in the palm of his hands for a period of time that extended beyond his two terms as president. Whether you supported him or not, he got a reaction; Jackson caused you to have an opinion about him, one way or another. That opinion was usually either fierce love, or loathing hate, there was rarely any middle ground. That a man of such immense influence, towering achievement and colossal popularity began his life in dirt poor obscurity, from one of the most rural, economically backward regions of the country, orphaned by age 14, only added to his fascinating legacy. Jackson was, essentially, a character ripped right out of a Dickens novel, but someone who was as real as you and me. His life was a movie script, and one that you just had to get the rights to. The life of Andrew Jackson offers proof to all those who knew him, that, time and again, like Mark Twain once said, 'Truth is stranger than fiction.'

The story of Andrew Jackson began quite humbly in a quiet coastal town in Northern Ireland. The year was 1765, and four hearty sons of the reasonably well-off Ulster linen weaver Hugh Jackson, were busy following in the Jackson family tradition, raising large families of their own, farming the land, working in the mill, and paying the usual rents to the "Lord High Steward," the First Baron Thomas Wyndham.

The Jacksons were of Scotch-Irish descent. Previous generations of the family had crossed from Scotland to Northern Ireland after William III's forces defeated the army of King James II in 1690, at the Battle of the Boyne. Though born in Northern Ireland, the Jackson sons still spoke in the brogue that betrayed their Scottish roots. By all accounts, the four brothers were a tight-knit clan, proud of their heritage as lowlanders, which they continued to preserve.

Andrew Jackson, Senior, Hugh's youngest son, lived in the small vibrant town of Castlereagh, only a couple of miles down the road from the bustling city of Belfast, on Northern Ireland's eastern coast. Only a year before, Andrew had married Elizabeth Hutchinson Jackson, who had since bore him a son, one year old Hugh, and was pregnant with another, soon to be son number two, baby Robert. Encouraged by his wife's sisters, and an uncle who had served in America during the French and Indian War, Andrew and Elizabeth had made a life-changing decision: they were packing up and leaving behind the only life they had ever known. With their son, and all of the meager possessions they could afford to bring, the young couple was starting a new life, having booked passage for the voyage to the American colonies. It was a budding springtime, and the Jacksons set sail from the port of Carrickfergus, and were on their way, in search of a better life in America.

The competition over the lush, vast lands of the future United States of America began long before the birth of Andrew Jackson. The battle for the Americas dates back to the arrival of human beings who ventured across the Arctic plain from Asia some 12,000 years ago. Thus began, via a land bridge (according to most accounts), the human history of the North American continent. Some thirty-five thousand years ago, the Ice Age congealed much of the world's oceans into massive ice-packed glaciers, lowering the level of the sea. As the sea level dropped, the land bridge that provided passage for these early intrepid explorers (into what we now know as Alaska) was created. The bridge connected Eurasia with North America in the area of the present-day Bering Sea between Siberia and Alaska. Across that bridge, probably following migratory herds of game, ventured small bands of nomadic Asian hunters–the ancient ancestors of the tribes of Native Americans that European explorers would encounter thousands of years later.

Oral tradition and archaeological evidence reveal that warfare among North American tribes was common, fueled by competition for resources. The vast forests, rivers, and fertile lands were the prizes to be had if strong tribes could expand their territories. This endless competition led inevitably to a cycle of decline for weaker communities, and the rise of new confederations of clans. Diplomacy played a role as well, notably by five nations who came together to create the Iroquois

Confederation, or Haudenosaunee, formed around the year 1200 in the Northeast, under the "Great Tree of Peace." [2]

The arrival of Europeans in North America introduced new dynamics to the indigenous peoples of the continent. Europeans brought advanced weaponry, including steel tools and firearms. They brought new animals, including horses, pigs, and cattle. But their greatest impact was through disease. The most notorious of these European diseases introduced among the natives of the Americas was smallpox, which decimated populations who lacked immunity to the deadly strains. All told, smallpox would devastate entire indigenous nations, wiping out populations nearly wholesale, with losses as high as ninety percent in some areas.

Initially, many Native American nations welcomed the Europeans, attracted by new trade goods, as well as simple curiosity. However, as European settlement expanded, conflicts intensified. In the 1670s, the son of Chief Massasoit of the Wampanoag, the aging sachem Metacom, who the English called 'King Philip,' led a coalition against English settlers in New England which resulted in violent confrontations and Metacom's eventual execution. After three years of devastating warfare in what became known as King Phillip's War, those who had followed Metacom were driven out of the region, but not before a wave of attacks against white settlements nearly brought an end to English colonization in New England.

As time went on, Native American resistance evolved, as tribes recognized the divisions among European powers, particularly during the French and Indian War (1754-1763). This conflict saw tribes, such as the Delawares and Shawnees ally with the French against the English, leading to incidents of extreme violence against British settlements. The degree to which these desperate tribes ravaged English colonial communities brought further violence, in the form of retributive attacks, and for nearly a decade, violence and bloodshed characterized the frontier. The war concluded with the French ceding their territories, leaving frustrated Native Americans vulnerable to British expansion.

---

[2] William Nelson Fenton (1998). *The Great Law and the Longhouse: A Political History of the Iroquois Confederacy.* University of Oklahoma Press.

Pontiac, an Ottawa chief, emerged as a key figure in resisting British dominance. Following the French defeat, he united various tribes against the British, launching a successful campaign that included the siege of Fort Detroit. His strategies relied on surprise attacks, such as the ambush at Fort Mackinac, in modern-day Michigan. Despite initial victories, the British retaliated, employing brutal tactics that defied description for their capacity to devastate tribes. Soon, the British upped the ante even further. Facing depleted resources and manpower in the extended struggle, they resorted to biological warfare, distributing smallpox-infested blankets to weaken Native resistance.

The ensuing conflicts resulted in significant casualties among Native Americans and settlers alike. Although Pontiac's coalition initially conquered vast territory, the British military response and subsequent smallpox epidemic turned the tide against them. On July 25, 1766, Pontiac and the British Superintendent of Indian Affairs negotiated an end to the war. Though "Pontiac's War" was unable to kick the British out of the Great Lakes region, the uprising demonstrated the viability of pantribal cooperation in the struggle against European American colonialism. The British government sought peace, and a temporary status quo ensued; one that did little to alleviate the fears of American colonists, who saw Indigenous Nations as a persistent threat.

Amidst this conflict, the struggle for land and survival shaped the relationships between Native Americans and European settlers. The narrative of Pontiac's War highlighted the devastating effects of colonial expansion on Indigenous communities and the complexity of alliances and enmities that characterized the period. The outcome reinforced the perception of Native Americans as a danger to settlers, setting the stage for future conflicts over land, and ultimately, for survival.[3]

The destructive French and Indian War in North America, along with its related European theater, the Seven Years' War, had been settled for just two years at the time the Jacksons made their ocean crossing. The year 1765 was to be marked by a sharp increase in conflict between the colonies and the mother country, particularly with the war-weary British enacting the hated Stamp Act. The once peaceful, semi-autonomous

---

[3] Dowd, Gregory Evans (2002). *War under Heaven: Pontiac, the Indian Nations, & the British Empire*. Baltimore: Johns Hopkins University Press, p. 117.

thirteen colonies were now in the throes of resistance to new and tighter imperial controls by his majesty George III's government. Faced with a mountain of debt from the costly and prolonged nine-year struggle to subdue the French in their efforts to wrest control of the Ohio River Valley and saddled with the added cost of subduing the frontier in response to Pontiac's War, the British parliament shifted policy and despite some opposition, chose to tax the colonies directly for the first time.[4]

Amid this turmoil, the Scotch-Irish were immigrating to America in ever increasing numbers by the 1760s. Drawn by the promise of a new life, frustrated with the limitations of their old life, and inspired by the chain migration of so many of their countrymen before them, they crossed the Atlantic in droves. Arriving in every port they could find passage to, the resilient Scotch-Irish fanned out into the interior, many finding opportunity for land only in the higher elevations beyond the fall line.

In April of 1765 this group of Scotch-Irish emigrants boarded a ship, sailing West. Leaving behind the past and their old lives behind forever, they said goodbye to those they left behind, and settled in for the long and difficult crossing, bound for the teeming shores of America. They had made the ultimate gamble. There was no turning back. Watching Ireland's mystical mountains recede in the haze and the waves behind them, the Jacksons must have surely felt a range of emotion.

While the documentation for the Jacksons' journey is sparse, it is very likely that they and their Crawford neighbors landed first in Pennsylvania, although the number of various theories existing among historians as to the exact location of the Jacksons' arrival is astounding. Regardless of the point of entry for the newly arrived Jackson immigrants, the destination was largely the same, somewhere in the backcountry among their own countrymen was the choice among ultimate destinations. Seeking religious freedom, to practice their Presbyterian faith without fear of persecution, they thanked God for their safe passage.

With the promise of land and opportunity in America, the group would slowly make their way south. The former linen-weavers, the

---

[4] Anderson, Fred (2006). *The War That Made America: A Short History of the French and Indian War.* Pg. 10

28-year-old Andrew and his 25-year-old wife of just three years, Elizabeth Jackson, peered wondrously over the bulwark as the weathered ship entered cautiously into the turbulent waters of the Delaware River. As if an ocean crossing with an infant wasn't difficult enough, "Betty" gave birth during the weeks at sea, and a pale but hearty baby boy, Robert, was the newest addition to the Jacksons' growing brood. After weeks of treacherous sea travel, in the turbid waters of the Atlantic Ocean, their grueling voyage nearly complete, the Jacksons, now with another hungry mouth to feed, eyed the sprawling, lush shoreline of America.[5]

Nearly a century old by 1765, the city of Philadelphia had been carved out of the forests of Pennsylvania by groups of enterprising Quakers, eager to have a city of their own to call home. The Jackson couple, with young Hugh in hand, and the swaddled baby Robert strapped onto his father's back, took in the land they had heard so many fanciful stories about, a multitude of contrasting and lurid descriptions by kinsfolk and others in Ulster and Castlereagh. Their long-awaited arrival in this land of plenty was now in front of them, and one wonders about the thoughts going through the minds of young Andrew and Elizabeth. Had they any inkling on that timorous day on the shores of an unknown land, that one day, a child of their very own would grow up to become the seventh president? Could they imagine that a child of their own, not yet conceived was to become revered by so many Americans as the savior of their country?

Upon disembarking from the vessel, amidst the unfamiliar and vibrant tapestry of this bustling port city, the group immersed themselves in a search for horses, and a sturdy wagon, to carry them into the wild heart of the backcountry. Their plan was to make it south to join up with the Crawfords in South Carolina, Betty's family. Eyeing the large estates, the two-story brick and stone houses that dotted the shores of the Schuylkill River, the Jacksons may have felt mixed emotions. They were to head South, destined for the Waxhaws, a region of South Carolina named for an extinct local indigenous nation (originally called the Wysacky) who once lived in the area. The Crawfords had found

---

[5] Brands, H. W. (2005). *Andrew Jackson: His Life and Times*. New York, NY: Knopf Doubleday Publishing Group.

some relative success there, scratching out a farmstead. Having sent Andrew and Betty letters full of possibilities, the Crawfords offered a welcoming base. The Jacksons hoped to find the kind of prosperity that their relatives had described.

By the time the Jacksons arrived, the steady influx of Europeans into the crowded Pennsylvania counties of York, Chester and Lancaster, had made affordable land scarcer. Those who were unable or unwilling to pay the exorbitant prices for land had another alternative. Available land in the western portions of Virginia, the Carolinas and Georgia were advertised in newspapers such as Ben Franklin's *Pennsylvania Gazette*.[6] Like so many others who had followed their kinsmen south, family relations would be the draw that would take the Jacksons to the Waxhaws. For those intrepid pioneers who populated the backcountry, a community of related families made the whole more self-sufficient and also provided security from the ever-present threat of Indian attack.

While there are no surviving records of the Jackson's journey south, one can assume their experience was not much different from the multitudes of others who had sought the cheaper land of the "Southern Plantations" since the early days of Jamestown. With the most recent addition, the colony of Georgia, founded as recently as 1733, the availability of land at a cheap rate was at a premium. Reverend Hugh McAden, a Presbyterian minister who accepted a call from the Hanover Presbytery to preach from Virginia to Georgia made these comments in 1759, "Alone in the wilderness, sometimes a house in ten miles, and sometimes not that." Near Augusta Courthouse he "stayed for dinner" at Mr. Poage's, "the first I had eaten since I left Pennsylvania." Also in Augusta County in 1752, Bishop August Spangenberg remembers, "there the bad road began. It was uphill and down, and we had constantly to push the wagon, or hold it back by ropes that we fastened to the rear." This journey could take as long as six weeks.[7]

Organizing a trip down the Great Philadelphia Wagon Road in 1767 was not for the faint of heart. Ahead of the Jacksons lay hundreds of miles of untamed wilderness, sometimes hostile Indians, the elements,

---

[6] Franklin, Benjamin, and David Hall, publishers. *The Pennsylvania Gazette*, [May, 1731]. American Antiquarian Society.

[7] Journal of Bishop August Gottlieb Spangenberg's Voyage to North Carolina to Establish a Moravian Settlement. Volume 5, pgs.7-9

and wild animals. The first order of business was to acquire a pack animal or two to carry supplies such as tools or extra clothing, or generally whatever they had brought with them from home. A weapon was a necessity. The York, Chester and Lancaster areas in Pennsylvania were well stocked with German gunsmiths who had brought their trade from overseas. Once a person was properly equipped he could then set his sights southward.

Andrew and Elizabeth Jackson and their young brood would have found their southern travels long and grueling. After months on the road, they would have reached the upper Piedmont area of North Carolina, and likely stayed with relatives in Guilford County, as would Elizabeth, Andrew Jr. and Robert later on as refugees during the Revolution. By 1772, there would be a thirty-mile, north-south section of land, which was deeded to South Carolina. It was called the 'New Acquisition' and ran from the Catawba River, just south of Charlotte Town, all the way west into the lower Cherokee towns. The low country gentry of South Carolina who lived in the beautiful estates of Charles Town and the rice planters all along the coast of the southern Carolina province, sought a buffer between them and the Cherokees and other warring tribes such as the Catawba, who might disrupt the peace. The thought was that if more Indian land was opened to settlers, then the safer they would be in their luxurious estates.

Thus, the South Carolina government began issuing land grants to all who wanted them. In 1767, while the New Acquisition would not be officially created for another five years, this is the environment the Jacksons would have encountered when they reached South Carolina.

In this vast land of towering hardwoods and sparklingly clean water, it would seem like a dream that only after a few months of being in America, the family could become landowners with a successful farm of their own. With a lot of pluck and even more luck, the Jacksons would be on the rise in a country that had no ceiling to those hardy individuals willing to work for it. For early pioneers of the Carolina Piedmont, families lived in constant fear of indigenous attack. The Cherokee, Catawba, Shawnee, and other tribes were outraged that scores of white families continued to arrive in droves, occupying and settling upon their ancient hunting grounds. By the time of their arrival in the settlement of the Waxhaws, indigenous tribes had largely been forced west, either from disease or white encroachment, to the upper settlements of the mountains and beyond. [8]

In those first days in the Carolinas, however, the Jacksons would have found a very different environment from what they had experienced in Ireland. If they were lucky enough, they would have arrived in the spring. Most likely, however, they reached the Carolinas in the sweltering heat of summer, which meant that the Jacksons had to have been beaten down by the subtropical temperatures as they made their way to the Waxhaws, in the last leg of their long, tiresome journey. The dirt road they were to follow was a long one, surrounded by little in the way of habitations, just woods, swamps, and a few isolated farms along the way. As they moved south, the Jacksons must have grown weary of the isolation. The distance between towns was vast, and the towns themselves small. Charlotte, the nearest city to the Waxhaws, was still but a small inland trading village, only established fourteen years prior, in 1753.[9]

Andrew and Betty would persevere, nonetheless, and after several weary days and nights, would arrive among their kinfolk in the rolling hills of the Waxhaws. With its many hardwood forests, lush farmland and numerous creeks and rivers running through it, Andrew and his wife must have felt a sense of satisfaction having arrived in a land of such promise. They would soon seek to fulfill their lifelong dream, having land of their own on which to raise a family.

Waiting to greet the weary travelers upon their arrival was the James Crawford family. Betty's closest sister, Jane Hutchinson, was married to James Crawford, and after Jackson's father's death, his mother and children would live with the Crawfords. In the area, as well, was another Hutchinson sister, who had recently married into the George McCamie family. Two other Hutchinson sisters lived in the area as well, both married into the Leslie family. This would have been a joyous reunion for the sisters in the pine forests of the Waxhaws, and a welcome embrace for the newly arrived family, having crossed an ocean, and traversed a wild frontier.

---

[8] Museum of the Waxhaws. 2024 Andrew Jackson Historical Foundation, Inc.
[9] *"The Charlotte-Mecklenburg Story: History Timeline: Founding a New City"*. cmstory.org Web Site. Public Library of Charlotte and Mecklenburg County. Archived from the original on May 18, 2015. Retrieved September 25, 2015.

Like many other colonists before them, Andrew and Betty Jackson would purchase a small farm of their own near their Crawford relatives in the piney forests of the Waxhaws. But unlike the Crawfords, the Leslies, the senior Andrew Jackson would choose an area much more northerly than their relatives. While the Crawfords arrived with quite a bit more capital and could afford land on the fertile side of the creek, Andrew Jackson struggled to find land that he could afford. Having to leave the near vicinity of their relatives, and search another branch of the Catawba, the Jacksons sought to find some promising acreage. Their search landed the family on the more rugged northern side of the relatively undefined border separating the two Carolinas. It was therefore in North Carolina (by most accounts) where they would finally find some land of their own. While it was not the most promising two hundred acres, it was all the Jacksons could afford. Here they would begin to carve out a homestead located on what was referred to as Ligget's Branch, near the headwaters of Twelve Mile Creek. [10]

This would have later importance later, as the state of North Carolina, based on the Jackson property being on the northern side of the border, would later claim Jackson as one of their own, although where baby Andrew was actually born remains in dispute.

In question as well is whether the Jacksons squatted on the land along Twelve Mile Creek, or if a purchase was legally rendered. This remains a source of uncertain controversy. In any event, at near subsistence levels, the Jacksons would begin their new life, scraping and clawing to eke out a living. After a modest log cabin was built, and seeds planted in the partially cleared fields around it, the family's daily lives were absorbed in toil. Within two years of their arrival, and with his wife now pregnant with their third child, the clearing of this forested land became more necessary than ever for the struggling farm family. This, however, would prove to be backbreaking labor. Resolute nonetheless, in their efforts to plant roots and establish a successful farm for their young family, the Jacksons pushed on day after day alongside the wide, deep Catawba River. With soon another mouth to feed, they toiled tirelessly around

---

[10] Howard, Jeffrey Allen. "Andrew Jackson Birthplace," NCPedia.org, (accessed January 16, 2017)

the clock to clear the fields and somehow turn those barren clay fields into a profitable farm.

But fate had other plans for the Jacksons. In the cold of February 1767, tragedy struck. Elizabeth, pregnant with Andrew Junior, received devastating news. Just weeks away from giving birth, a neighbor rushed out to alert Elizabeth back at the cabin. Her young husband, determined to have a crop in the ground before the end of the planting season, had suffered a logging accident while clearing his fields. Most likely straining to lift a heavy tree trunk, the twenty-nine-year-old likely suffered a heart attack and was now dead.

Just three weeks later, the grief-stricken Elizabeth would give birth to her third son. Named in memory of his father, young Andrew Jackson, Junior was born on March 15, 1767 in the home of Betty's sister Jane Hutchinson Crawford, and her husband James Crawford. Some controversy exists over the exact location of baby Andrew's birthplace, as others have claimed that it took place North of the border closer to the Jackson property, in the home of Betty's sister Margaret McCamie. In later years, Jackson himself would insist that it was in the Crawford home that he came into the world. Regardless of the dispute over location, Andrew Jackson, Jr. was born into tragedy, with a bereft family and a difficult financial situation. The loss of the breadwinner Andrew Sr. meant that the young Andrew would be brought up without the guiding hand of a father. The newborn Andrew, his widowed mother Elizabeth, and his two brothers Hugh and Robert would have no easy road ahead.

As if the loss of her husband wasn't tragic enough, the story of Andrew Jackson Senior's final journey was one of bizarre and unforeseen events that probably caused Elizabeth no small amount of added distress. According to those who witnessed it firsthand, the body of the deceased Andrew Senior was placed on a wagon to be taken to the Waxhaws Presbyterian Church (in what is today the town of Mineral Springs, North Carolina) for burial. Two men who were assigned the task of leading the wagon, instead of going directly to their destination, decided to stop at several homes along the way. At each stop, the men were offered peach brandy, a popular local beverage at the time, and they drank to their heart's content. By the time they arrived at Waxhaw Creek, they were so inebriated that they lost control of the wagon, and Andrew Jackson Senior's body rolled off into the water. In their drunken state, the men were unable to find the body. Miraculously, they eventually stumbled upon the body in Waxhaw Creek and were able to continue on their way to the church for the burial.[11] Was the fallen Andrew, Senior's odd misadventure somehow foreshadowing of the political future that lay ahead for his youngest child? Time would tell.

Yet despite the mishaps on the way to the church, Andrew Jackson, Sr.'s legacy lived on, especially for those he left behind. And although "Andy Jr." never knew him, it is very likely that the early loss of his father had a significant impact on Andrew Jackon's life.

There are competing versions as to the exact location where the future seventh President of the United States was born. The claims vary depending on who was asked. Some say it was on the farm of Elizabeth's sister Margaret McCamie, which was on the North Carolina side of the border. But many, including Andrew Jackson himself, believe that it was at the home of her sister, Jane Crawford in South Carolina. In a letter dated August 11th, 1824, Jackson, then a candidate for the Presidency of the United States, wrote in a letter to J. H. Witherspoon "I was born in South Carolina. As I have been told at the plantation where James Crawford lived about 1 mile from the Carolina Road of the Waxhaw Creek. I left that state in 1784."[12]

At any rate, regardless of his place of birth, baby Andrew's family soon took up residence at the Crawfords shortly after his father's death. It was with the Crawfords that many facets of the man that would later become known as "Old Hickory" would be forged. Most particularly among these aspects, a bitter hatred of the occupying British forces would take root.

At least two of Jackson's uncles experienced success in the Waxhaws. One, Robert Crawford, owned a large house, a significant tract of land, and several slaves, holding prominent positions within the larger community. James Crawford, not as prosperous as his brother, still owned several hundred acres of land, and it was on this land that the three sons of Andrew Jackson, Sr. would spend their childhood. They and other

---

[11] "The Strange Tale of Andrew Jackson Sr.'s Final Journey," Museum of the Waxhaws, May, 2023.

[12] Jackson Papers. AJ to JH Witherspoon. Aug. 11, 1824. Jackson, *Correspondence*, Volume I.

relatives provided a kinship network of support for Jackson's immediate family when it faced its many daunting challenges.

The center of the Waxhaws region was known as the Waxhaw Settlement, consisting of the general area of Lancaster County south of Twelve Mile Creek and north of Cane Creek. The actual boundaries of the Waxhaws, however, are hard to define. Most authors agree that land in Chester and Lancaster Counties makes up what was once the domain of the Waxhaws, so this area still retains the name. The Waxhaws area was largely settled by the Scots Irish who came from Virginia and Pennsylvania. They brought the Presbyterian faith with them and founded Old Waxhaw Church, the oldest in the upcountry, around 1750. This church became the center of Presbyterian influence in the backcountry, and with the founding of the Waxhaw Academy, it became the intellectual center as well. The area was a stronghold of patriot sentiment during the Revolutionary War. The Battle of the Waxhaws (May 29, 1780) would be fought here, while the Battle of Hanging Rock (August 6, 1780) would take place just south of the Waxhaws. It was here that future president Andrew Jackson would first see combat. [13]

By 1767, the Thirteen Colonies were ablaze with rising revolutionary fervor, especially in areas affected by that year's Townshend Acts, and even more strenuously, by the Stamp Act passed by the British Parliament just two years before. For rural North and South Carolinians, however, much angst was brewing over the various economic and governmental missteps the colonial governments of both colonies seemed to commit on a consistent basis. The factors behind settlers' frustrations ranged from lawlessness in areas such as Waxhaw, to oppressive government corruption often stemming from Crown-appointed officials, especially notable in Alamance County, North Carolina. Many of these strains could be traced back to a response to tighter British controls that began with the end of the French and Indian War just four years before baby Andrew's birth. While Elizabeth Jackson struggled to raise her three boys without her deceased husband, the rural Carolina backcountry still sought to recover from the Cherokee War, which had ravaged much of the region throughout the period.

---

[13] Parton, James. *General Jackson*. New York. D. Appleton & Company. 1893. Pg. 7.

This devastating conflict, also called the Cherokee Uprising or Rebellion, was an outgrowth of the larger conflict between France and Great Britain that began in 1754. This war was part of the French and Indian War and was fought between British (and colonial) forces and the several bands of the Cherokee. The war began in Virginia in 1758 when settlers attacked and killed several Cherokee warriors returning from battle against the French. In the spring of 1759, the Cherokees retaliated in North Carolina, where tensions between the tribe and European settlers had long been on the rise. The conflict soon spread southward and would last well into the 1760s. Although the conflict with the Cherokee would have concluded by the time of Andrew's birth in 1767, it is very likely that the community where he grew up harbored deep-seated resentment against the Cherokee Nation as a whole, which no doubt had a lasting impact on the future President.

After the Cherokee War, large numbers of newly arriving settlers poured into the South Carolina backcountry. Although peace was achieved by 1763, by 1765, as a result of the war, bands of outlaws and marauders began to operate in the area. Since no assistance was received from the government in Charles Town, nearly 200 miles away, the local settlers formed vigilante groups to attempt to drive out this dangerous criminal element on their own. Additionally, the settlers in the backcountry had long felt under-represented in the South Carolina Assembly, although they paid large sums in taxes. Generally, the region received little support of any kind from the colony's government. As a result, this newly-organized group of vigilantes would form an anti-government group called the Regulators. The backcountry farmers who made up the Regulators demanded equal representation in the colony's government, as well as the benefits of law enforcement, courts, jails, roads, schools, and judicial districts. [14]

The actions and demands of the Regulators would finally bear fruit by 1768. It was in July of that year that the South Carolina legislature in Charles Town agreed to the Circuit Court Act. Activated by 1769, this act provided for local courts that would serve the backcountry for the first time. While this did much to avert civil war in the region, the

---

[14] Bassett, John Spencer (1867–1928) (1895). "The Regulators of North Carolina (1765–1771)". Washington: Govt. Print. Off.

growing colonial discontent in other parts of the colonies over British actions would take the settlers of all thirteen colonies down a road to revolution the likes of which the world had never before seen. And it was in this turbulent environment that young Andrew Jackson was reared. Like so many others of the time, the rebellious passions that perpetuated the American Revolution would directly impact the Jackson family more fully (and devastatingly) than anyone at the time could possibly imagine.

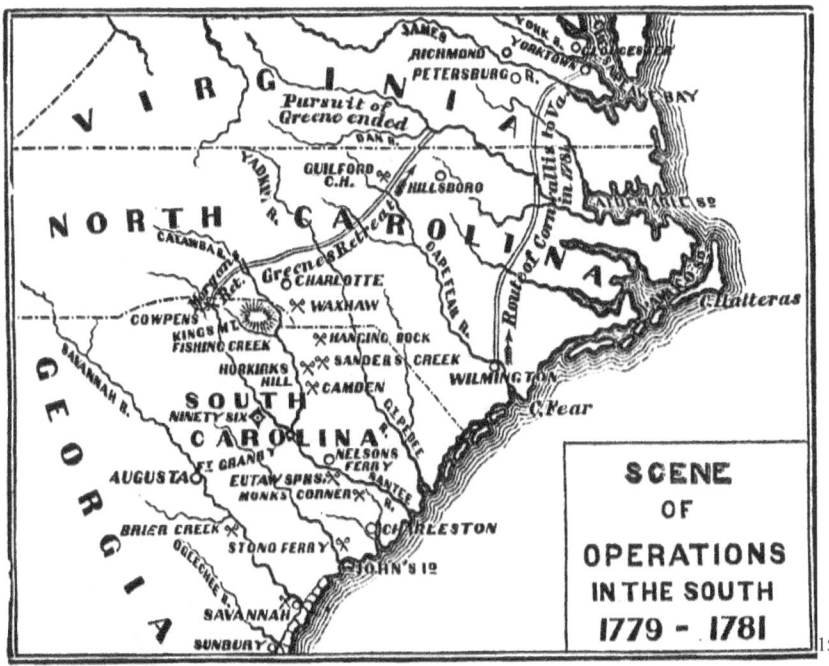

---

[15] Map Credit: Waxhaw'

CHAPTER 2

NO QUARTER

"Andy will fight his way in the world."
-Elizabeth Jackson

Although written records of young Andrew Jackson's childhood are minimal, in David S. Heidler's 2003 book "Old Hickory's War," the author explains: "Uncles and cousins taught him and his brothers the skills essential for the frontier, such as how to hunt, farm, and handle firearms." Jackson exhibited, early on, a volatile temper and a streak of stubborn independence. His anger was easy to trigger, and his acute sense of honor made him alert for slights. He seems to have suffered from sialorrhea (hypersalivation), and the symptomatic drooling invited playful jibes and outright insults. Jackson reacted to both as affronts, and almost all his boyhood companions had memories of violent episodes with windmilling fists and ear-biting tussles.[16]

Young Jackson grew tall but never stout, and his lithe frame made him an easy match for larger boys. Most of his peers soon learned not to cross him, however. Jackson not only fought anyone regardless of size but also refused to stop fighting when losing. According to those who knew him as a child, Andy wasn't the toughest kid on the block, just the most persistent. One of his schoolmates had once said, "I could throw him three times out of four, but he would never stay thrown. He was dead game and never would give up." Both the touchiness and the

---

[16] Remini, Robert V. (1977). *Andrew Jackson and the Course of American Empire, 1767–1821.* New York: Harper & Row.

tenacity never changed throughout his long life. Over the years, most seemed to discover that challenging Andrew Jackson was more trouble than it was worth.

The year was 1776, and up north in the colony of Pennsylvania, the delegates at the Continental Congress were in the process of writing up a document that was to declare the true meaning of the Revolution: Independence. Yet, despite the frenzy and excitement most young boys of the colonies felt, especially over the prospect for adventure war offered, Andy Jackson would not be fighting in it, at least not if Betty Jackson had her way. She had big plans for her cherished youngest son and having him go off to die in a war was not part of those plans. And most certainly not at the ripe young age of nine, which the tall, gaunt lad became in 1776. Instead, Andy was sent to live with his uncle, Captain Robert Crawford, at the big log house near Waxhaw Creek.

The boy was to attend a new school, an academy where Latin and Greek were taught. After all, these subjects were the gateway to higher education, and along with mathematics, meant serious learning. It had not been easy for Betty to get her son accepted into the school, designed for the best and the brightest lads in Waxhaw. Some strings were pulled between Betty as well as Robert Crawford, but they had gotten him in, and Betty could not be happier. The new school was called the Waxhaw Meeting House, also known as the Waxhaw Academy, just three miles from his Uncle Robert's house. He would attend with his cousin, Will Crawford. They would stay at their uncle's, along with a third boy. Neither of the two other Jackson boys would attend.

Elizabeth Jackson would not be accused of playing favorites among her sons, in fact, she would not be accused of anything, for she was a hard-edged woman who instilled a toughness in her boys. "Do not let me see you cry again," she'd say, Jackson later recalled. "Girls were made to cry, not boys." Yet, she was also a caring mother who had especially high hopes for young Andrew. Hopes for Andy becoming the most powerful man in the country probably never entered her mind. Instead, she dreamt of her youngest son one day becoming a Presbyterian minister.[17]

Having previously enrolled Andy with the local log-cabin "common" school that Waxhaw offered, Elizabeth was determined to get him

---

[17] Wilentz, Sean. *Andrew Jackson*, New York, NY: Henry Holt and Company, 2005.

onto a better path educationally. In this backcountry region of devout, hard working Scotch-Irish immigrants, most children learned enough at local "common" schools to read the Bible and run their farms. But, for ambitious parents like Andrew's mother, a higher road of learning was a must-have. The widow Betty Jackson, never one to forget the importance of frugality, paid a local schoolmaster for advanced classes at the Waxhaw Academy, probably the area's most prestigious school. Here Andy and his classmates would study the humanities courses the school offered, as preparation for careers in law, medicine, or the church.

However, the young, brash Jackson quickly dashed his mother's ecclesiastical hopes before they even began to take root. With his consistent lack of focus, often showing inattention during lessons, Betty had to grapple with the fact that a career in the faith was not in the cards for her youngest son. As time went by, with this growing propensity for pranks, cursing and fighting, young Andy developed a reputation for trouble. Jackson's own words about his youth may help clarify the degree to which he was not the ideal candidate for the cloth: "I was born for the storm, and a calm does not suit me." More broadly, one can say that though Andy "learned his letters, as the saying went, the idea of reading for knowledge or entertainment never really took hold in his mind."[18]

Although Jackson showed very little interest in schoolbooks as a youth, he would one day develop an interest in history. It is no surprise that he always considered William Wallace the "best model for a young man…we find in him the truly undaunted courage, always ready to brave any dangers, for the relief of his country and his friends." [19] In some ways, Jackson's courage and ability to lead would mirror that of the charismatic Wallace, but in the 1770s, any such dreams seemed a long ways away, and far distant from reality.

Elizabeth's dreams of a brighter future for Andrew were not to be easily realized. Jackson also struggled to make friends in his early days at the Waxhaw Academy, a log schoolhouse next to the Meeting House where boys studied under the direction of the minister William Humphries and later Reverend James White. Established in 1759 by Presbyterian clergyman William Richardson, for nearly a century a

---

[18] AJ to AJ Donelson. Jackson, *Correspondence*, III
[19] Booraem, Hendrik (2001). *Young Hickory: The Making of Andrew Jackson*. Lanham, MD: Taylor Trade Publishing.

series of trained ministers taught the young men of Waxhaw. Along with Jackson, other notables to attend the Academy include later South Carolina Governor Stephen Miller, U.S. Senator and judge William Smith, and Reverend John Brown, who later became a President of the University of Georgia. According to the Boy of the Waxhaws marker, erected in 2009, the inscription states that Jackson was "born among the red clay hills of our county and here he spent the formative years of his life, his first seventeen, riding horseback, wrestling, cock-fighting, and gaining the best education the frontier had to offer: instructions from the Presbyterian minister at the Waxhaw Meeting House." Although Jackson would gain a "smattering of higher education," the seduction of the frontier lifestyle would ultimately capture Jackson's passions. Set in the context of a growing conflict that would soon engulf the colonies, the young mind of Andy Jackson would be drawn towards a future that would put him on a collision course with destiny.

But far to the north, in the colony of Massachusetts, the Battle of Lexington and Concord in the spring of 1775, and the "shot heard round the world" would resonate through the Thirteen Colonies with the force of a thousand volleys. Andrew Jackson was just eight years old when the first shots were fired on the Lexington Green, but like most colonists of the time, his life would be touched by the conflict in irrevocable ways.

Three years later, by 1778, the British high command, in an effort to regain the upper hand in a frustratingly dissatisfying rebellion against the upstart Continental Army, led by the ever-elusive General George Washington, settled upon a new approach. Known as the Southern Strategy, the British fleet would be sent as far as Georgia, and would work their way up the coast, determined to remove any options for retreat, and recruit was many Loyalists as they could along the way. Following the failed Saratoga Campaign of 1777, in upstate New York, in which British General "Gentlemen Johnny" Burgoyne's army was forced to surrender at the hands of the ragtag colonials under the direction of Horatio Gates and Benedict Arnold, British leadership was compelled to reevaluate their approach to the war in North America. Viewing New England as the central source of rebellion, they believed that resistance to their rule was merely a local problem and did not represent the true feelings of the rest of the colonies. But, having failed at efforts to isolate New England from the other colonies, they recognized the need for a new strategy to maintain control over the whole of the American territories.[20]

The southern campaign was to be led by General Sir Henry Clinton, who had built up more than four years of prior experience leading elite British troops in North America, engaged in battles since the start of the war. The hopes for the plan hinged upon gaining control of the southern colonies by concentrating their forces there, believing that a large Loyalist population in the region would rush to their side to support them. According to British Undersecretary Charles Jenkins, the mastermind behind the new strategy, the ploy would allow the Redcoats to weaken the Patriot cause up north, to stem the tide of reinforcements arriving daily, and potentially turn the tide of the war in their favor.

This strategy involved leveraging the South's agricultural resources and strategic ports, but it was doomed from the start. With strong Patriot resistance in every colony by 1778, the British had overestimated the number and the ability of Loyalists to support their cause. After capturing Savannah, Georgia, marking the British's first military presence in the Southern states during the Revolution, Clinton aimed to gain Loyalist support and cut off aid to the rebellion by advancing into South Carolina, targeting Charles Town.

Having failed to take Charleston in 1776, this time around, the British steadied their formidable armaments for a renewed and more determined effort to take the South's largest port city. To the people in the Waxhaws, less than two hundred miles from Charleston, word of the British threat caused more than a little alarm. Clinton's army had already taken control of Georgia and was now expected to advance on South Carolina by land and sea. Several militia companies set out from the Waxhaws to help defend the capital. Most went by horseback, as they were reluctant to march, as were most backcountry men. Captain Robert Crawford led one company, and at least two other companies joined his troops on the journey. Most of the Crawford men went along, muskets in hand.

---

[20] Leckie, Robert. *George Washington's War: The Saga of the American Revolution*. 1992. pp. 496, 507–517

Around the same time, William Richardson Davie, fresh from his law studies in North Carolina, reappeared in the Waxhaws. Now, a lieutenant, Davie was in command of a North Carolina unit sent to defend Charleston. Hugh Jackson, sixteen or seventeen at the time and eager to fight, had not yet joined the militia, but now got his mother's permission to join Davies's company. On a borrowed horse, Andrew Jackson's eldest brother 'Huey' headed down the road to Charles Town with the other cavalrymen, with a brave wink and a confident smile. Little did his mother and brothers know it would be the last time they would ever see him.

For the next several weeks, through April and May, Waxhaw residents anxiously awaited news of the battle, desperate for any word on the fate of their husbands, brothers and sons. Betty Jackson and other women of the area scoured the Camden Road for travelers and news of the campaign. News was slow in coming, and what rumors did make their way to the Waxhaws often contradicted previous reports. Finally, in the middle of June, one of the Waxhaw companies rode in with the latest news. There would be no fight, he said, the British, camped on an island near the coast, were planning to head back to Georgia.

Towards the end of the month, however, Crawford's company returned with a very different report. American forces, led by Major General Benjamin Lincoln, had attacked the British on John's Island. On June 16, 1779, Prevost began evacuating his troops from the island on the outskirts of Charleston, leaving some to cover the withdrawal, when they were attacked by the Americans. The ensuing battle occurred in a place called Stono Ferry, and it could hardly have gone worse for the Americans. Silas Barr from Gill's Creek was dead, as were many others. Lieutenant Davie himself was wounded, and worst of all for the Jacksons back home, Huey Jackson was dying. He had been sick, and Davie had ordered him to stay out of the engagement, but he had foolishly, but courageously, gone into battle anyway. Making it out alive, he collapsed from exhaustion as soon as it was over. Having barely made it home, he died almost at once, amid the tears of his family. Hugh Jackson, aged 17, was buried in the churchyard. [21]

---

[21] Parton, James, *General Jackson*, Pg. 6.

In this relatively insignificant American attack, repulsed by British and Hessian troops on the outskirts of Charleston, Private Hugh Jackson met his death. Yet he had died fighting for a cause he believed in, and one that had not been entirely in vain. For although the British overcame the Americans at Stono, they continued their retreat into Georgia. In the end, the failed American offensive lasted no more than an hour, and along with the felling of Hugh Jackson, led to the deaths of 33 other Americans, and 26 British soldiers. Betty's oldest had been heavily relied upon around the farm back home, and was now gone, a brave teenager determined to fight despite his illness. Exhausted and weak, fatigued and inexperienced in the heat of battle in the muggy swamps of Stono Ferry, young Huey had managed to survive his one and only battle, and afterward still clung to life. Determined to make it home, the boy hung on steadfast throughout the several days journey. Historian Hendrik Booraem puts it well in his book *Young Hickory: The Making of Andrew Jackson*, "The circumstance of his death suggests a determination and boldness like that of his famous youngest brother." [22]

Devastated by the news of his fallen eldest brother, young Andy Jackson had now tasted the sour bite of grief that war so often brings. It was a bitter, acrid taste that, much to the chagrin of young Andrew Jackson, he would soon grow more familiar with. For now the grieving residents of Waxhaw settled down for a tough winter.

After what seemed an eternity, spring returned. Soon, a chain of events began that would once again throw the lives of nearly all Waxhaw citizens into disarray. The events began on April 10th, 1780, and for Andy Jackson, the tide of war was about to engender the most agonizing weeks in the boy's already turbulent life. Thomas Sumter, the "Fighting Gamecock", who had been so heroic in thwarting the enemy early in the war, was once again raising troops in the Waxhaws. The rumor mill had been rampant with talk of General Nathanael Greene's branch of the Continental army coming to South Carolina. Having led Cornwallis in a game of cat and mouse throughout much of the North Carolina piedmont, Greene now sought to retake control of Camden, South Carolina while Cornwallis rested his troops in Wilmington, on the coast. The Quaker General, Greene had proven his mettle fighting

---

[22] Booraem, Hendrik, *Young Hickory*, the Making of Andrew Jackson. 2001. Pg. 47-48

under Washington in the north, and now Sumter and his partisan bands were in a frenzy over this new opportunity for revenge.

By this period, Andrew and Robert Jackson had developed a reasonable familiarity with the "manual exercise" and possessed a basic understanding of the various formations on the field, as their mother had reluctantly agreed to allow her sons to participate in local drills and community musters.[23] The American forces, recognizing their numerical inferiority and lack of discipline, had retreated into the interior of North Carolina. However, upon hearing the news that Lord Cornwallis and his Redcoats had crossed the Yadkin River, they began to return in small groups to their home state. Upon their return, they discovered that a Cornwallis Lieutenant, Lord Rawdon, had taken control of Camden, leaving the surrounding region in a state of devastation.

The respite from British attack had not lasted long for the people of South Carolina. The vainglorious effort by Lincoln, poorly conceived, and badly executed, had resulted in significant American and British casualties, and while the British failed to secure Charles Town, they gained valuable intelligence for future operations. This skirmish ultimately influenced the British strategy for successfully attacking Charles Town in the spring of 1780, despite the initial setback. The British would return with both land and sea forces of colossal proportions. The desperate call for volunteers once again went out throughout the Waxhaws, and again the men of the region responded in full. This included the men of the Crawford family. Robin and Andy Jackson most likely pleaded with their mother to allow them to join the cause, but Betty Jackson would have none of it. Having lost her eldest son, she was adamant that the boys remain home. Besides, she argued, they were too young, Andy had just turned thirteen, and Robin was no older than sixteen. To Elizabeth, allowing the boys to defend their homes was one thing, but heading off to battle miles away in Charles Town was another.

As it turns out, it was fortunate for the Jackson boys that they did not make the trip to Charles Town, as this time, for the enemy was too formidable for the Carolinians. By early April, British forces

---

[23] Eaton, John Henry, and Reid, John. *The Life of Andrew Jackson, major-general in the service of the United States: comprising a history of the war in the South, from the commencement of the Creek campaign, to the termination of the hostilities before New Orleans.* Philadelphia. 1824. p. 10.

had successfully surrounded the Americans in the beleaguered city. To make things even worse for the defenders, British warships managed to slip past Fort Moultrie at the entrance to Charleston Harbor, cutting off General Lincoln's position and blocking any chance for escape or reinforcements. The situation tightened further as more British troops gathered in the Charleston area, bombarding the Americans' hastily built defenses.

On April 21, in an effort to save his army, General Lincoln proposed to surrender the city if his men could leave safely. Clinton, however, rejected this offer and quickly resumed the artillery attacks. Over the next two weeks, the British forces drew closer to the American lines. By May 8, the two armies were only a few yards apart. Clinton demanded that Lincoln surrender without conditions. When Lincoln refused, Clinton ordered the city to be bombarded with heated cannonballs. As Charleston went up in flames, Lincoln had no choice but to face the reality of the situation.

The siege of Charleston finally ended on May 12, 1780. With General Lincoln's surrender, an entire American army of about 5,000 men was lost. Those who had survived would be paroled, on the promise to never again take up arms against his majesty, George III. The recently promoted Major Robert Crawford was among those who had been forced to take the oath. Lord Cornwallis would soon extend his control over the entirety of South Carolina. The men of Waxhaw were headed home. But the terror for the people of the Waxhaws had only just begun.

On Sunday night, May 28th, frantic news reached the Waxhaws that a British cavalry force of several hundred troops were headed rapidly to the region, reportedly in pursuit of a retreating Continental army headed for North Carolina. To James Crawford and his fellow Whigs, this was disheartening news. Already marked as enemies of the British, and uncertain about the designs of the armed men headed their way, Crawford and his band of loyal Whig Patriots headed for the cover of the woods. Andy and Robin joined them. Betty Jackson had once again relented, frightened by rumors that the British had taken up a practice of kidnapping young boys and forcing them to serve in the army.

The next day, just miles from the Crawford property, British forces under the fiendish Banastre Tarleton would surprise American forces at the Waxhaw's Settlement, killing over 100 soldiers and destroying the settlement almost entirely. Many survivors of the battle told shocking stories of British soldiers who massacred patriots attempting to surrender. The scene was one of such slaughter that it garnered the name 'Waxhaw's Massacre,' also called 'Buford's Massacre,' and it sparked outrage throughout the colonies. In the attack of May 29th, the now infamous and hated British commander Banastre Tarleton had engaged and overwhelmed the Patriot force at Waxhaw under the command of Abraham Buford in a dreadful, one-sided defeat for the Patriots. Rather than accepting that all hope was lost, however, the defeat actually rallied the Americans in its cruelty. The ever-plucky Continental forces in the South would turn this stunning defeat into a propaganda victory, stirring up passionate anti-British sentiment throughout the colonies.[24]

On the following day, May 30th, the teen-aged Andy Jackson, mounted, armed and ready, spotted a troop of green-jacketed British dragoons coming through the woods. With a sharp eye, he recognized their leader, the notorious Colonel Tarleton. Tarleton and his men, fresh from the defeat of the retreating Continentals at Buford's Massacre, were now turning their attention to forming an alliance. The Tarleton cavalry moved towards the land of the nearby Catawba nation, eager to enlist the tribe in their cause. Years later, Jackson would recall that "Tarleton passed to within a hundred yards from where I was. I could have shot him." [25]

Once Tarleton and his dragoons had moved on, their business concluded, the Whig forces of the Waxhaws were free to come out of their hiding. The women of the region, which undoubtedly included Betty Jackson, hitched up their wagons and made the journey to the site of Tarleton's devastating attack on the retreating Americans. Some twelve miles east of the Salisbury Road the women encountered terrified survivors fleeing through the woods, who described the affair as that of a bloody slaughter. Once the women arrived on the field, a slaughter is indeed what they encountered. "Mass graves held the bodies of over one hundred dead, and another one hundred and fifty men lay dead on the

---

[24] Piecuch, Jim. *"The Blood Be Upon Your Head": Tarleton and the Myth of Buford's Massacre*. 2010. Kennesaw State University.
[25] Jackson, *Correspondence*, LOC; Booraem, Hendrik, p. 49

field."[26] Most of the agonized wounded suffered from horrific cuts from British sabers, deep gashes, severed limbs, and even a decapitation.

In his official papers, Banastre Tarleton described the engagement, which would forever come to be known as Buford's Massacre: "I have cut 170 Off'rs and men to pieces." The survivors of the gruesome affair would insist that Tarleton's forces had overpowered them, and the American commander, Colonel Abraham Buford, in an attempt to surrender, had asked for quarter. No quarter would be given however. Tarleton's cavalry, after a short pause, resumed the attack on the American troops, again under a flag of truce, killing several more. "Tarleton's Quarter" and "Bloody Tarleton" became the phrases that rang through the American South. From this day in late May of 1780 on, in the hearts and minds of Americans, the name Banastre Tarleton would forever incite fear, hatred and cries of vengeance. Tarleton became a public enemy, a butcher, and the engagement became a battle cry for Patriot forces citing "Remember the Waxhaws!" in the Southern theatre. [27]

In the wake of the Buford Massacre, better known as the Battle of Waxhaws, the anxious, grief-stricken citizens of the region were awarded very little time to mourn or reflect, as shortly after the tragedy, more distressing news arrived in the Waxhaws. An even larger contingent of Redcoats, led by Lord Rawdon, was charging toward the area, determined to ravage the region until every resident vowed never to participate in the war again. Elizabeth Jackson, her sons, the Crawfords, and most of their neighbors abandoned their homes rather than pledge their allegiance. They journeyed north, hoping to hold out until the enemy departed. A back-and-forth struggle soon ensued: the people of the Waxhaws retreating northward each time the British advanced upon them. During the summer of 1780, there were so many alerts regarding troop movements by "malevolent Tories" that the inhabitants of the Waxhaws lived in constant terror, prepared to escape the area at a moment's notice to avoid the impending wrath.

The threat and the terror that this constant strain of attack placed on the adults of Waxhaw was most assuredly a crippling psychological agony.

---

[26] Wilson, David K (2005). *The Southern Strategy: Britain's Conquest of South Carolina and Georgia, 1775–1780*. Columbia, SC: University of South Carolina Press, p. 260.

[27] Piecuch, Jim. *"The Blood Be Upon Your Head": Tarleton and the Myth of Buford's Massacre.* 2010. Kennesaw State University.

Consider then the toll the many months would have inflicted upon the children of the besieged region. For Andy Jackson in early 1780, he had just turned thirteen on the Ides of March. For the previous five years, his country had been at war against the world's most hegemonic power, and now perpetual warfare had become the normal state of his neighborhood. Neighbors who seemed friendly by day could turn deadly predators by night. Keeping up a constant vigil for a lad not yet fully comprehending the meaning of the struggle would surely impact Jackson's personality for the remainder of his days.

CHAPTER 3

POST MORTEM

"The period of debate is closed. Arms, as the last resource, decide the contest...the blood of the slain, the weeping voice of nature, cries "tis time to part."
—Thomas Paine

The remaining war-weary Jackson family, along with their Crawford relatives had somehow endured through the arduous British invasion of the western Carolinas in 1780-81. Having been forced to flee the Waxhaws on numerous occasions throughout the war, the family now sought mere survival. Often beset by sorrow amid the stark, glaring absence of eldest son Hugh Jackson, the family grief must have most assuredly known no bounds. Surely the young Andy and Robert ached for vengeance against the hated enemy who had robbed them of the loss of their big brother. Yet, despite the shadow his loss placed over their lives, there was no time to mourn his loss. What with the turmoil of war in the Waxhaws constantly surrounding them, survival was their needed distraction. Perhaps this was why Andrew Jackson, throughout his life, could not sit still for long.

Betty Jackson, no longer able to prevent her youngest son from joining the fight, would now relent entirely. It was indeed time for all hands on deck, for the British were coming, and their Tory allies smelled blood in the water. Undoubtedly, Elizabeth's motivation to allow the boys to take part in the war was rooted in a pragmatic necessity as well as pride. More significantly, it stemmed from a deep-seated animosity towards the British. This resentment had persisted for many years and had only escalated with the passing of her Huey the previous year. During chilly winter nights, Betty would gather her sons around the hearth and tell them tales of their grandfather's hardships at the Battle of Carrickfergus in 1760, back in the old country, and the oppression inflicted by the Irish aristocracy on the working class across Ireland. She reminded her boys that their foremost obligation would always be to defend and uphold the family, along with the rights of humanity. Thus, young Andrew developed a lasting, almost indelible loathing for the British, shaped not only by his mother's teachings but also by his own experiences in war.[28]

Since the May 12th capture of Charleston, the South's preeminent port city, the situation in the Carolinas looked bleak for the Patriot cause. Groups of British soldiers, along with their Tory sympathizers, pillaged the South Carolina countryside. As the Tories wreaked havoc in the Waxhaws, committing acts of murder, arson, and looting, the cries for resistance grew louder. As a result, the hazy summer of 1780 was marked by intensifying partisan resistance to the British. Lord Charles Cornwallis' string of garrisons built in and around the Charleston area were the first targets. The Patriots had become increasingly bold in their attacks on these outposts, particularly after guerilla detachments defeated a British force commanded by Captain Christian Huck on July 12th.

Finally, help arrived from the north in the form of Colonels William R. Davie and Thomas Sumter, two of the most skilled light-horse leaders fighting for the Patriot cause. Shortly thereafter, Patriot leaders from across the Carolinas, rallied by the return of Davie and Sumter, met to decide on their next strike. Fueled by a desire for vengeance, particularly against the infamous "Butcher Tarleton," their return rallied the local Whigs to join the fight. Set on achieving a real measure of revenge and turning the tide of morale that had gone against the region, they came close to succeeding. It was determined that regular Continental units, along with partisan troops, would focus their efforts on British outposts in the Catawba River Valley. The northernmost of these outposts,

---

[28] Remini, Robert V., *Andrew Jackson and the Course of American Empire*. 1977. P. 17.

Hanging Rock, guarded the Camden-Charlotte Road. It was here that Davie, along with General Sumter, would strike.

Near present-day Heath Springs, South Carolina on August 6th, 1780, patriot forces did just that, striking a bold, multi-pronged blow upon the British in an effort to regain ground in the Southern colonies after the loss of Charleston. The Battle of Hanging Rock, as it became known, was part of Davie and Sumter's overall campaign goal: to disrupt British outposts in the South Carolina backcountry following the capture of Charleston in May, 1780. The Americans, under Sumter, attacked a less fortified British post, hoping it would be the start of many such victories that would weaken British control of the South. While the enemy suffered heavier casualties, and the Americans successfully seized supplies and horses, the battle is considered indecisive for one reason: Sumter's withdrawal. However, overall the battle was helpful for a number of more positive reasons: it improved morale, it sent Tories back into hiding, and it loosened the British hold on the region.

The victory might have been more complete had things not gone awry for Sumter's men. American forces initially made some gains at the outset. Startling the British troops upon first contact, and forcing them back, the victory slipped away from the Americans. Seizing some British rum upon first running off his majesty's troops, the worn and thirsty Americans indulged in this contraband they had seized from the enemy on that tumultuous summer day. Colonel Sumter had devised a plan for his troops to charge on horseback towards the enemy and then dismount to continue the attack on foot. Unfortunately, the plan fell apart, largely due to the effects of the rum.[29] As the battle commenced, the inebriated Americans, startled by the first shots fired, began to scatter in every direction, tipsy and frantic. The ensuing retreat was a rather sad yet somewhat humorous spectacle.

Davie's and Sumter's forces suffered heavy losses in this first fray. Lieutenant James Crawford was among the badly wounded. Crawford was thought to be on the brink of death and was brought to a riverbank to die in peace, with a folded coat placed under his head for comfort. The next day, his friends discovered him there, still alive, but unfortunately,

---

[29] Scoggins, Michael C (2005). *The Day It Rained Militia: Huck's Defeat and the Revolution in the South Carolina Backcountry, May–July 1780*. Charleston, SC: The History Press.

his coat had been stolen by Tory looters. The 51-year-old, despite his injuries, was then taken back home to recover.

The Battle of Hanging Rock would be the Jackson boys' "first field." Andy and Robert, now war-hardened from the many brushes with combat, were to tend the Patriot's horses, ensuring they would not bolt upon the sound of the first volleys. Andrew also rode with Colonel Davie in the role of courier, and he had the opportunity to learn from the commander as he led the campaign.

Colonel Davie, as the future General Jackson often would in years to come, exhibited bold courage in his leadership. Combining strategic maneuvers and decisiveness with a prudent demeanor, Davie's vigilance was unceasing. His industriousness was relentless throughout the fight. In later years, Andrew Jackson would frequently acknowledge Davie as one of his most significant military mentors, and contemporary historians widely regard Davie as a pivotal influence on Jackson's early military development.

Although the relatively inexperienced patriots fought courageously, their eventual withdrawal cost them in their efforts to regain control of the state. Yet, despite suffering twelve deaths, with forty-one men wounded, patriot forces would inflict over two-hundred British casualties. In the end, Hanging Rock was considered a Patriot victory, if not an overwhelming one. While the American forces regrouped, they took satisfaction in what they considered a moral victory, which served to further embolden Patriot efforts to dislodge the British in the South. Lieutenant John Adair, who had been in the 3rd South Carolina Rangers when Charleston fell and served in fourteen battles during the American Revolution, concluded, "This I believe was the hardest fought battle during the war in the South."

The Battle of Hanging Rock felt like a victory for most of Sumter's men. They had bloodied the British and made off with plunder aplenty. "About one hundred horses, two Hundred & Fifty stand of arms, and other articles of Considerable Value" Sumter wrote proudly in a letter to Horatio Gates, who had taken over command of the Continental forces marching to meet up with the British. But Sumter well knew, as did much of the Patriot brass, that this was an incomplete victory. They had failed to drive the British out, had abandoned the field and left the

British with it still in their possession. Sumter would blame the failure on "want of led."[30]

For William Davie, it was clear that, in local militias like Sumter's, following orders from an immediate commander, usually a kinsman of most of the soldiers, was not a problem for most men. However, he noticed a fundamental flaw, in that any orders given from a general commander were all too often ignored. Only a professional army, disciplined and drilled, would be able to match the British in the open field.

For many, the battle brought mixed emotions. Numerous families had lost loved ones. Jim Crawford had taken a bullet and was left for dead, but had somehow survived, although he would never fully recover. Others had lost horses, weapons, and property. For the young Jackson boys, their first encounters with battle must have been a truly riveting experience, and the many lessons Andy learned on that steamy August day would not soon be forgotten.

After the Battle of Hanging Rock, Andrew and Robert reunited with their mother in the Waxhaw settlement. It was harvest season, and there was work to do on the Crawford farm. As Sumter's men settled back into camp on Cane Creek, the Jackson boys busied themselves aiding in the gathering of peaches for the stills, carrying corn to the mill, helping load the grains into the grinder. While the ear corn was roasting over the fire, the boys joined in to the "scuttlebutt" of what the war's next tribulations would bring. As if blown in on the southern winds, the rumors, news and questions flew throughout the settlement, spreading like wildfire. When would General Gates arrive in Camden with his Continental troops? What would be Lord Rawdon's next move? What of Tarleton?

Meanwhile, the boys would slip off as often as they could to Sumter's camp, admiring the horses confiscated from the British. Regaled by the tales and war stories the men told around their smoky campfires,

---

[30] Sumter, Thomas. *Letter from Thomas Sumter to Thomas Pinckney*. August 9, 1780. Volume 14, pp. 540-543

the songs they crafted about the heroics of their commander, set to traditional Irish ballads, ran through the boys' heads:
"When we were first in banishment, old Sumter took command,
And on the borders of our state, we did take a stand,
For to subdue the English and keep down Popery
Huzza for General Sumter! Huzza for liberty!" [31]

Yet the merriment did not last long, and soon it was time to get back to business. On August 12th, Captain Fred Kimball came galloping back to camp. Sumter had sent him with instructions to deliver a letter for General Gates. Now he returned, breathlessly delivering the news that Gates and 3,000 of his troops were only a day away. The camp quickly buzzed into action. Gates was to be coming in from the east by the way of the Cheraws, and his instructions were for Sumter and his men to commence harassment of British supply routes without haste.

This would have been welcome news for Sumter's men, who were eager for action, and low on food rations. Setting out the next day, they crossed Land's Ford and headed south. Out of necessity, Robert Crawford had now been made a field commander. His brothers, sons, and nephews would join him in the coming fray. Young Andy would not be permitted to go along on this encounter, but by all accounts, his brother Robert did take part. What little evidence has survived about the activities of the Jackson family in these sweltering August days of 1780 include no mention of "Robin" (Robert.) The record appears eerily quiet from the time Sumter and his men rode away from camp heading toward Camden. Those who remained behind kept an ear to the ground in hopes of hearing any clue of what was happening with the armies. On August 15th, William R. Davie and his men passed through from North Carolina on their way to Camden.

On the morning of August 16th, the family was alarmed by the sudden surge of traffic on the Camden Road. Men, horses, wagons, were in full retreat. Indeed, the news could not be worse. The Continental forces under General Horatio Gates were routed at Camden, in a true show of British might. The dismayed Waxhaw residents out on the road, reveling at the sight of so many defeated soldiers' flight, would soon

---

[31] Booraem, Hendrik. 2001. Young Hickory. P. 69.; Also, printed in Gregorie, Anna King, Biography of General Thomas Sumter, published in 1931. Pp. 143-144.

encounter a somber General Gates himself, as he hurriedly stopped to change out his horses on his way through, hell-bent for Charlotte.

Over the next few sweltering days, Waxhaw residents, eager for more information on what exactly happened in Camden, did their best to accommodate the many weary and despondent Virginians, Marylanders and North Carolinians passing through on their way north. Desperate for food and water, the retreating soldiers told of a defeat even more one-sided than was first conveyed. British troops chased fleeing Continentals more than 20 miles up the road before turning back, with the Butcher Tarleton leading his cavalry, bloody sabers and all. Davie and a few other troops led what seemed to be a successful rear guard action to protect the wounded stragglers in the rear, believing the British had turned back against their resistance.

However, just as the Americans were finally allowed a moment of breath, the news got worse. On the 18th, word arrived that Tarleton had not given up the chase entirely. Crossing the river, he and his notorious cavalry surprised Sumter's men, who were resting on the bank of Fishing Creek. Several of the men were bathing in the river when Tarleton's men "burst upon them without warning." Major Crawford managed to swim to the far side of the river to escape, but having passed out from exhaustion and a bottle of whiskey the night before, he would receive much of the blame for the defeat. Sumter himself also managed to escape, but many local men were either killed, wounded or taken prisoner. The malice of the enemy incited abject terror in the hearts of those who remained in the Waxhaws, as now there appeared to be no one left to defend them.

The worst Patriot defeat of the Revolution, the rout of Gates' army caused disarray for the Southern Continental army. The hero of Saratoga, Horatio Gates, was not only humbled, but had abandoned his army after the humiliating trouncing. Lord Cornwallis, flush with victory, now directed his army towards the Waxhaws. Once again, the inhabitants of the region panicked, and many took to the road northward to escape the encroaching and rejuvenated British army.[32]

---

[32] Buchanan, John (1997). *The Road to Guilford Courthouse*. New York: John Wiley & Sons. pp. 26, 71, 80.

On a late September afternoon, at a spot about five miles south of Charlotte, a 14-year-old Susan Smart, peering out the window of her home, keeping an eye out for travelers on the road nearby, spotted a sight that caught her eye. With the war heating up in the area, it was her job to greet anyone passing by and ask for news, especially about the regiment where her father and brother were fighting. On this hazy summer day, with the fading sun poking through the tall pines, casting shadows over the dusty lane, Susan peered out to spot a tall, lanky young man riding a short pony. His legs were so long that they nearly touched the ground. He wore a weathered yellow hat that flopped over his face, looking utterly worn out and dusty. To Susan, he seemed like "the forlornest apparition" she had ever seen. She rushed outside to approach the weary boy, hoping he had information about her father's regiment.

"Where are you from?" she asked, her anxiety evident.

"From below," he replied.

"And where are you headed?" she continued.

"Above."

"Who are you with?" Susan asked cautiously.

"The Congress," he answered.

"What are you doing down here?" she probed.

"Oh, we are popping them still," said the boy.

Susan couldn't help but think that if someone as thin and ragged as he was involved, the 'popping' probably wasn't going very well. Finally, she asked, "What's your name?"

"Andrew Jackson," he answered promptly.[33]

To this youngster Andrew Jackson, Susan inquired about the army and her father's unit, and Andrew shared what little he knew, most of it grim. He mentioned that Gates' army was in disarray, with many soldiers fleeing. He also noted that Lord Rawdon had taken over Robert Crawford's home in the Waxhaw area. Robert, who was the brother of James Crawford, owned a large piece of land at the head of Waxhaw Creek, which was now serving as headquarters for the commander-in-chief.[34]

---

[33] Parton, p. 73-74.
[34] Remini, p. 19.

Andrew and his lean pony would continue on to the Wilson home near Charlotte to rejoin his mother and relatives until it was safe to return to the Waxhaws. He would board with the Wilsons (Mrs. Wilson was a distant relative of Elizabeth's) for several weeks, doing small chores around the farm. He helped feed the chickens, pulled fodder, and would frequently head to the town shops for a sharpening of the farm tools. One Wilson boy recalls that Jackson "never returned to the farm without some sort of new weapon with which to kill the British." Once he affixed a scythe to a pole, slashing the weeds around the Wilson house with fury, chanting: "Oh, if I were a man, how I would sweep down the British with my grass blade!" Mrs. Wilson's most indelible memory of the young Andrew was his willingness to go into the garden and help her pick beans for dinner. Believing the young man did this out of gratitude for the Wilson's hospitality, she added, "He did like his corn and beans, though." [35]

---

[35] Kendall, Amos, *Life of Andrew Jackson: Private, Military, and Civil*, 1843. Pp.34-36

Waxhaw Birthplace marker: (Image Source: TheHermitage.com)

CHAPTER

4

WAR IS HELL

"The time to guard against corruption and tyranny, is before they shall have gotten hold on us. It is better to keep the wolf out of the fold, than to trust to drawing his teeth and talons after he shall have entered.
  -Thomas Jefferson, 1782, Query XIII, "Constitution"

After an extended stint in Charlotte, by February 1781, all three of the Jackson family members were back in the Waxhaws. Lord Cornwallis and his massive force had been expected to head directly into the Waxhaws after their thorough rout of the Continentals at Camden. Yet, they had lingered and stayed for three weeks, resting and relishing the spoils of victory. As a result, Betty Jackson and her youngest son were compelled to extend their stay away from their home. Reluctantly, she realized she could not keep Robert from joining his Crawford relatives in the fight, and so a tearful separation came about from her older son. By winter, Betty missed him greatly, along with her home, particularly the Conocochegue peach trees, whose fruit was ripening behind the Crawford house. Betty sat at the spinning wheel most days with her kinfolk, turning out fine flaxen yarn ("some of the finest you ever saw", according to Susan Smart) and lamented to the other women over the death of Hugh, and voiced her fears of the various enemy threats that ranged from the British to the Cherokee to the "heathen Hessians." There were even such sordid rumors of the Hessian mercenaries kidnapping children and taking them back to Germany with them.[36]

For Andy Jackson, in his time as a refugee in Mecklenburg County, many of his hours were spent at the local smithy, listening to the latest news from the men who stood around the big iron forge. Andy listened for the latest updates about the fighting, no doubt curious as to the status of his brother, who was still off somewhere with the Crawford men. The British, though, would not move until September, and the word of the latest British maneuvering would reach Charlotte before long. By the second week of the month, Cornwallis and his men had finally decided to push on, headed down the Camden Road to the Waxhaws, where he would indeed commandeer Robert Crawford's house as his headquarters. Soon, the British were grinding their grains at Blair's Mill, slaughtering the Crawfords' animals, seizing for their own use whatever could be consumed. They would rest there for nearly two weeks.

In the meantime, William R. Davie decided the time was ripe to strike back. He and his North Carolina cavalry had planned an ambush, and their execution was nearly flawless. Davie and his troops pulled off the element of surprise, attacking the British in Waxhaw suddenly, and precisely, bringing cheers among the remaining Waxhaw holdouts still in the settlements. Davie was now their lone protector after the defeat of both Gates' and Sumter's forces. While the battle was not a massive engagement, it raised the morale of the Carolinians, and bought time for the Continentals, whose Congress in Philadelphia was working to redirect troops down to the Carolinas to counter Cornwallis.

As Davie was often inclined to do, he struck a band of Tories, instead of the regular Redcoat army directly. The group he attacked was led by the Tory renegade Captain Christian Huck and his band of thieves (as they were derisively referred to by local Whigs who had been victimized by their ambushes). Huck's strategy had been to trail behind Cornwallis' troops, using them as cover to murder and pillage, mostly in search of whatever treasure they could find. For example, they had struck Baron Adair's homestead in Waxhaw previously, accosting his wife, and "stripping the rings from her hand, the silver buckles from her shoes,

---

[36] Baer, Friederike, Penn State Abington, *Hessians: German Soldiers in the American Revolutionary War*.

and the lace handkerchief from her neck." [37] The band then proceeded to Hugh McCain's farm, who was rumored to have considerable money hidden somewhere on his property. The Tories suspended McCain from a walnut tree, and they would have killed him for not revealing the location of his stash had his slaves not intervened and run the rogues off. At the nearby farmstead of James Walkup, the notorious bandits hung his young son by the thumbs in an effort to pry the whereabouts of his father's pot of gold coins out of him. In the meantime, Margaret Walkup and her other children, along with two others sets of mothers and children, were being held hostage inside the family cabin.

The Walkup farm was where Davie chose to strike the marauders, as one of his men who would co-lead the attack was its owner, Captain Walkup himself. Surrounded by cornfields, the cabin was off the main road, and on the early morning of September 21st, Davie led a group of his cavalry cautiously down the lane, while Walkup led a group on foot through the fields. Many of the Tories were still asleep, and the Whig forces achieved complete surprise, killing more than 15 of them, and wounding some 40 others. Allegedly, Walkup kissed his wife and children, releasing his eldest son from his agonizing torture before escaping with more than 90 horses, and over a hundred stand of arms. Angered by the news, the recently ill Banastre Tarleton and his notorious legion, who had been camped nearby, arrived at the scene too late, unable to prevent the successful Davie from adding to his legacy. To the young Andrew Jackson, who would revel in the brains behind Davie's stealthy tactics, this was more proof that the college educated officer was his ideal commander.

Nevertheless, while the exploits of William R. Davie and his men probably soothed some of the pains of the Waxhaw populace, these raids were, after all, only minor victories. The monolithic Cornwallis army, led by the fierce Tarleton cavalry, still held the upper hand, and they now left the Waxhaws, heading for Charlotte and the lush farms of North Carolina. When word of the British movement reached the Jacksons, Betty chose to flee the area once again. This time packing up the few possessions she and Andrew could carry.

---

[37] Booraem, 2001. Pp.27-28

Accompanied by the McCamie women, they would travel up the Great Wagon Road through the piney forests toward the northeast. For unknown reasons, their destination on this journey would be Guilford County, North Carolina. Perhaps Margaret McCamie had relatives in the area, or the group simply thought this would be the safest refuge. At any rate, by February 1781, with the British forces having now evacuated the area, the three remaining Jacksons, Betty, Andrew and Robert would be reunited in the Waxhaws once again. The countryside now calmed, the settlers sought to repair the damage done by the occupation.

By the spring of 1781, Nathanael Greene readied plans to strike against the remaining British troops at their post in Camden, knowing that the addled Cornwallis army had limped and staggered away after their costly victory at Guilford Courthouse. Cornwallis withdrew his army first to Ramsey's Mill and then to the British base at Wilmington, where he resupplied, and rested his battered and weary troops. Greene had dictated the terms of Cornwallis' pursuit all winter and spring, and had led masterfully, keeping Cornwallis chasing fruitlessly until he, Greene, was able to reinforce his army, and choose a prime location to turn and take on the Redcoats. Guilford Courthouse had been that ideal spot, and his troops had pushed the more seasoned British troops to the brink. The British had only claimed the field after having to fire artillery onto their own troops, engaged in fierce hand to hand combat. The ploy did the trick, forcing Greene's men to retreat, and for the British to hail it a victory in the end. Back in London, upon hearing the news of the battle that had cost Cornwallis a quarter of his army, British Parliamentarian Charles James Fox told the House of Commons ruefully, "Another such victory would ruin the British army." [38] Now Greene sensed the time was right to regain Camden while Cornwallis rested his men in Wilmington. Colonel Sumter soon rallied his men to join him.

Sumter was pleased to have a clear goal in mind for this new mission. Many of his men had been deserting his command, seeking opportunities to engage in the ever-intensifying conflict with the local Tories. By 1781, the Tory War, as it would become known, was increasing rapidly in viciousness and bloodshed. It had become a war of terror, often between former neighbors, Loyalists versus Patriots, Tories versus Whigs. Sumter

---

[38] Baker, Thomas E., *Another Such Victory*. 1999.

was often confounded, finding it more and more difficult to rein in his men, angered by Tory raids, and eager for vengeance. This he explained in a letter to Greene; his troops were "Imprudently Going upon private and Disgracefull business."[39] Frequently, many of his more undisciplined soldiers would sneak away from camp to engage in raids against certain Tories, more often less strategic efforts than attacks on people with whom they had personal differences.

Such was the tenor of the Tory War. The nobler, more focused cause, to which so many had professed in earlier days of the Revolution, now degraded into motives of greed, and vendettas. Taking advantage of the situation, some had sunk to unfounded accusations of the disloyalty of others, simply to rob them of their possessions. Sumter went on to write that while "no cases of this sort were reported from the Waxhaws ..... there were many outrageous examples from Camden and elsewhere in the backcountry."[40]

This recruitment of fresh blood for the "Whig" cause would sweep young Andy Jackson directly into the fray of the combatant armies. The plan was for the Whig fighters to rendezvous at the Waxhaw meeting house on the afternoon of April 10th, 1781. In response to the return of many Waxhaw settlers who had fled the area, the British commander, Lord Rawdon, upon receiving word of their movements, promptly dispatched Major Coffin with a unit of light dragoons, an infantry company, and a significant number of Loyalists to capture and eliminate them. Anticipating this advance, the settlers swiftly designated the Waxhaw meeting house as their gathering point to better consolidate their dispersed forces.

On April 9th, Andy, his brother Robert, and cousins Tommy and Jim Crawford sat on horseback in the shelter of the trees outside the meeting house, surrounded by several other Whig partisans. Sitting in the cover of the pines towering above them, they awaited Captain Billy Nesbitt of the Kershaw regiment, who was to lead the boys to their meeting place with Sumter and his men. It was a rainy spring day, and looking down through the mist, the boys thought they spotted Nisbett and others coming down the road towards them. However, as the riders

---

[39] Sumter to N. Greene, 1780. Sumter Papers, LC
[40] Booraem, 2001, Ch.5

drew closer, the men in front moved aside and revealed the identity of the approaching party. It was not Nesbit at all but a troop of uniformed British dragoons. They had placed some Tories in front, dressed in ordinary backcountry homespun, to act as a screen. The dragoons, sabers held high, charged at Andy and the crowd of Whigs before anyone had time to react. [41]

Trembling with fear, the Jackson and Crawford boys spurred their horses through the woods behind the meeting house at full speed, down into the valley of Cane Creek, with a couple of dragoons hot on their heels behind them. At the crossing of the flooded creek there was a patch of mud where Jim's horse got stuck. The others, looking back, could see him being overpowered by one of the dragoons with a blackjack (a club of leather filled with lead). They went on past a secret bend in Creek Valley where they found a hiding spot. They dismounted and took cover, listening, waiting. Leaving the horses saddled, prepared to leave again if necessary, they heard nothing. They waited anxiously, hearts still pounding without mercy, terror-stricken by the sight of Jim's clubbing.

It grew dark, and the boys were edgy. Suddenly startled by a loud roar, they spotted an orange glow through the trees and recognized the ghastly sight of the meeting house going up in flames. What had been their community house was now in British hands, and they were powerless to do anything but stay hidden and cowering under the trees. Finally, the three cleared themselves spots on the creek bank, lay down, and sank into a troubled sleep. [42]

The next day, however, the boys' luck was to run its course. Having survived their frightful encounter the night before, the Jackson brothers packed up and headed to a neighbor's house with the hopes of food and sustenance. But it was here that suddenly, without warning, enemy British dragoons swarmed upon the house. Coffin's dragoons had gotten word of their whereabouts and now broke into the house with a huge thud, and a crashing in of the front door. Coffin's men had been on patrol, sweeping the area in search of rebels.

Very likely, it was a Tory neighbor, loyal to the British who spotted the boys' horses and gave their location away. The doors were sealed

---

[41] Eaton and Reid., p.12
[42] Parton, p.10

and a violent search of the home ensued. The boys were seized and held prisoner by the invaders, who then ransacked the home with abandon. Glass was shattered, the handmade furniture slashed and destroyed, clothes were ripped and tossed about as the soldiers vented their hatred of the upstart Patriots.

In an effort to humiliate his captives before him, the dragoon commander then approached the younger of the two prisoners. Looking down at the swamp mud he had tracked in, he ordered, "Boy, clean my boots!" The 14-year-old Andrew drew himself up to his full height, looked the officer in the eye, and replied, "Sir, I am a prisoner of war, and claim to be treated as such!" At that moment, an obstinate temperament mixed with violent disdain for the British caused a defiant Andy Jackson an enduring punishment. Faced with Jackson's refusal, the furious officer raised his sword and swung it at Andy, who held his hands up in a defensive manner. The sword tore into flesh, cutting his forearm to the bone and a long gash in the boy's forehead. Jackson was lucky to not have been decapitated. Blood gushed from both searing wounds. His forehead and hand would be scarred for life as a result of this incident. [43]

The officer, still outraged, then turned to Andrew's brother Robert. "Then you clean my boots!" When, like his younger brother, Robert refused to be humiliated by giving in to such a demand, the sword sliced through the air once again. This time, the officer used the flat of his sword, which struck Robert's head, nearly knocking the boys unconscious. Their wounds then left untreated, the boys, along with twenty other captives from the Waxhaws were chained and marched roughly 40 miles to a British prison camp in the town of Camden, where they were then housed with close to 250 other prisoners.

Locked up in the rudimentary camp, in drafty, disease-infested quarters, with no beds, scarce food, and no medical care, the prisoners suffered immensely. Their British jailers did not bother with such details as treating wounds or addressing the prisoners' illnesses. As a result, diseases such as smallpox ran rampant in the ill-fated camp, and those who did not contract the deadly disease faced the dangers of dysentery and malnourishment. Young Andrew's fourteenth birthday passed to the sounds of pleading and the desperate cries of the men around him who

---

[43] Reid and Eaton, Jackson. p. 16.

were beyond hope. Unfortunately, it soon became clear to Andrew that Robert was among the gravely ill. Adding to the infection that spread from his untreated head wound, Robert soon contracted smallpox as well.

Soon, Andrew himself would be stricken with the deadly fever that usually marked the first sign of smallpox. Before long, the flat red bumps would appear on both boys' faces, filling in with the deadly pus that would begin to crust over. Yet, a ray of hope would appear by late April, when Continental Army General Nathanael Greene's forces made camp on nearby Hobkirk's Hill, within view of the prison, and within sight of the prisoners. That sense of hope would vanish quickly, however, on April 25th, when the British surprised Greene's small force of rebels and over-ran the hill. Robert was, by this time, staring death in the face, and young Andrew was facing a similar fate. Something would have to happen, and soon or both boys were to end up with the same demise as their brother Hugh, young casualties of the Revolution.

Fortunately, fate had different designs for the Jackson boys. It was the appearance of Elizabeth Hutchinson Jackson, their mother, that would save the day. The British had agreed on a prisoner exchange, offering to free the American captives for thirteen of their soldiers held by the Patriots. Betty had learned of the location of her two remaining sons and had traveled to Camden to check on their well-being. She was shocked and unprepared for what she would find: Her two once virile boys appeared as emaciated and gaunt as living skeletons: malnourished, pale, and suffering from the infections of the untreated wounds the officer's sword had rendered weeks earlier. Elizabeth acted quickly and resolutely, successfully arguing for their release.[44]

Reunited, mother and sons began the journey home. Robert was so ill at this point that he was not able to sit up on horseback without support, and his mother was forced to keep him propped up in the saddle. Barefoot and with no overcoat, Andy walked the full forty-five miles by his mother's side. As if to test the Jacksons further, a violent rainstorm hit, saturating the traveling refugees. This downpour may have been the final death knell for young Robert Jackson. While he would

---

[44] McLaughlin to Kendall, Jan. 1843. Jackson Papers, LC.

manage to make it back to their home in Waxhaw alive, two days later, tucked into bed, he would breathe his last.

Young Andrew fared only a little better than his brother. For weeks the third of the Jackson brothers remained in critical condition. By all appearances, he was soon to become the latest Jackson casualty of the War for Independence. Delirious for weeks, not much more than an invalid for months, the boy held on for dear life. Thanks to Betty's care, however, his condition slowly began to improve. By the fall, the immediate danger of death would subside, and he would begin to recover.

With her son Andy now out of danger, Betty, moved by what she had witnessed at Camden, now became focused on the harrowing experiences of young boys suffering fates similar to her sons. The mother who had once regaled her sons with stories of the battle for freedom in her native Ireland, including tales of their grandfather fighting the British in Ireland and his participation in the siege of Carrickfergus, had now grown weary of war and all of its suffering. Having lived through the death of two of her beloved sons, seeing a third son nearly destroyed by disease, and having endured the suffering of the Waxhaws' Massacre, the stout Scotch-Irish Betty could no longer stay inactive. Hearing news of two of her nephews, William and James Crawford's imprisonment in Charleston, Betty joined several other patriot women in the Waxhaw area in the one hundred-sixty mile journey to provide for their aid.

It is a mystery that remains unsolved as to why Andrew Jackson's mother left her son behind. Andy, recently near-death from smallpox, malnutrition, and the various other ailments, said goodbye to his mother, who set out for Charleston to look after her nephews. Perhaps it was based on loyalty to the Crawford family that had taken her and her boys in. Most likely, Betty assumed that Andy had made a full recovery and no longer needed her care; that he would soon be headed off on his own back to the war. Unbeknownst to either of them at the time, however, they would never see each other again.

By this time, the war had raged on for more than six and a half years, but, at long last, it was slowly starting to turn in favor of the patriot cause. The new United States of America, with the help of France, were poised on the brink of the impossible: defeating Great Britain, the world's most powerful empire. However, to Elizabeth Jackson and the other women of Waxhaw, it was clear that many of the poor, malnourished, imprisoned souls in Charleston and elsewhere would not live to see the new nation they had paid so dearly to help create.

Upon arriving in Charleston Harbor, Betty and the other women gained access to the crowded prison ships that lined the oceanfront. Despite doing their best to nurse the ailing prisoners back to health, for many it was too late. Cholera had recently struck the ship where the Crawford sons were held, and soon Elizabeth would contract the deadly disease herself. Shortly after General Cornwallis would surrender at Yorktown, Virginia in October of 1781, Elizabeth Hutchinson Jackson was dead.

Elizabeth Hutchinson Jackson, known affectionately as Betty, died on November 2nd, 1781, in Charleston, South Carolina. She was forty-one years old. Just prior to her passing, Elizabeth wrote a letter to her son to express her parting words of advice for the young man:

> "Andrew, if I should not see you again, I wish you to remember and treasure up some things I have already said to you. In this world you will have to make your own way. To do that you must have friends. You can make friends by being honest and you can keep them by being steadfast. You must keep in mind that friends worth having will, in the long run, expect as much from you as they give to you.
>
> To forget an obligation or be ungrateful for a kindness is a base crime, not merely a fault or a sin, but an actual crime. Men guilty of it sooner or later must suffer the penalty. In personal conduct be always polite but never obsequious. None will respect you more than you respect yourself. Avoid quarrels as long as you can without yielding to imposition. But sustain your manhood always.
>
> Never bring a suit in law for assault and battery or for defamation. The law affords no remedy for such outrages that can satisfy the feelings of a true man. Never wound the feelings of others. Never brook wanton outrage upon your own feelings. If you ever have

to vindicate your feelings or defend your honor, do it calmly. If angry at first, wait till your wrath cools before you proceed."⁴⁵

The young, convalescing Andrew Jackson learned of his mother's death when the matrons who had accompanied her to Charleston returned to the Waxhaws, without her, later in 1781. As a notice of her death, relatives sent a small pile of Elizabeth's belongings to Andrew, whose entire immediate family was now dead from war-related hardships. These hardships the 14-year-old Andy blamed on the British, and a deep-seated resentment welled within him, one that he would never fully shake. It is unclear as to how Jackson felt about the passing of his mother. In his 1991 book, *Fathers and Children*, Michael Paul Rogin asserts that Jackson hated his mother for abandoning him in his hour of need.⁴⁶ Most other sources have instead cited Jackson's deference for the memory of his mother. Betty had been the most significant figure in her son's life—the one who had guided him, admired him, supported him, and shielded him from adversaries. No one else in the Waxhaws could fulfill those roles. He would honor her memory and refer to her as a source of wisdom for the rest of his days.

As most historians who have covered Jackson's life over the years have written, the loss of Jackson's family during the American Revolution had a profound impact on his emotional development. He apparently spoke of his mother often throughout his life and recalled the harsh lessons she had instilled in him during childhood, but also the love and support she had shown him. He cherished her memory forever. Jackson later felt much regret that he was unable to ascertain the location of Elizabeth's grave, and could not honor her remains with a proper memorial.

Years later, in August of 1824, Andrew Jackson, (then a famous war hero and candidate for the Presidency) while residing at his home in Nashville, Tennessee, received a letter from a stranger in the old Waxhaw community of South Carolina. According to the Charleston County Public Library's *"Moving Memorials to Elizabeth Jackson,"* the writer was James Hervey Witherspoon (1784–1842) of Cane Creek, Lancaster County, who informed the presidential candidate that he had

---

⁴⁵ James H. Witherspoon to AJ, April 16, 1825 in Jackson, *Correspondence*, III, 282-283.
⁴⁶ Rogin, *Fathers and Children*, pg. 46

"just named his newborn son Andrew Jackson Witherspoon to honor the man he considered an American hero. General Jackson was still fondly remembered in the neighborhood, but the writer asked if the general could confirm whether he had been born in North or South Carolina. Old Mrs. Barton, at whose home Elizabeth Jackson had died in 1781, still lived in the Waxhaw neighborhood, said Mr. Witherspoon, and they all wished him well." [47]

This brief mention of Jackson's mother and the survival of a woman who witnessed her death sparked immediate interest in Nashville. The general composed a short reply on August 11th, 1824, which survives among Jackson's papers at the Library of Congress and was published in the early twentieth century. Because this letter contains details of great importance to this story, here are a few lines of Jackson's reply:

> "I knew she died near Charleston, having visited that City with several matrons to afford relief to our prisoners with the British – not her son as you suppose, for at that time my two Elder brothers were no more; but two of her Nephews, William and Joseph Crawford, Sons of James Crawford, then deceased. I well recollect one of the matrons that went with her was Mrs. Barton. If possible, Mrs. Barton can inform me where she was buried that I can find her grave. This to me would be great satisfaction, that I might collect her bones and inter them with that of my father and brothers."

Jackson recounted to friends in later years that he had gone to Charleston shortly after the British evacuation (December, 1782) and spent "many reckless weeks betting on horse races and games of chance."[48] Whether or not he searched for his mother's grave during his time in Charleston is unclear, but the mystery surrounding her final resting place haunted him for many years.

James Witherspoon wrote back to Jackson that Agnes Barton lived within one mile of him and that he had interviewed her. Mrs. Barton could not tell him exactly where the gravesite was located but said that as

---

[47] Kendall, *Jackson*, p. 58
[48] Jackson, *Correspondence*, III

well as she could remember it was "in the suburbs of Charleston, about one mile from what was then called the Governor's Gate, which is in and about the forks of the Meeting and Kingstree Roads." In recent times, according to newspaper articles, the spot where Elizabeth Jackson was buried is said to be on the old campus of the Citadel. Agnes Barton had come to the Waxhaws when Andy Jackson was just two years old, but during the Revolutionary War, she and her husband went to Charleston and settled just outside of the city, in Charleston Neck. When Elizabeth Jackson became ill, she was taken into Mrs. Barton's home and nursed. When she died, Mrs. Barton dressed the corpse in her own best dress, while Mr. Barton built the casket. They buried her on a hill in a simple unmarked grave.

Andrew Jackson never fulfilled his wish to find the bones of his mother and place them beside his father's and brothers' graves. Not until 1949 was there a marker to Elizabeth Jackson placed in the Old Waxhaw Presbyterian Cemetery, alongside the graves of Jackson's father and brothers. The cemetery is located in upper Lancaster district, near Jackson's birthplace.

With Lord Cornwallis' surrender at Yorktown, Virginia in October, 1871, after nearly seven years, the War for Independence was finally over, or at least as far as the British were concerned. Americans cheered up and down the thirteen former colonies, now the United States of America. George Washington emerged as the war's greatest hero, and Andrew Jackson's country was free from British tyranny. Yet, he and so many others had paid an astounding price. The lessons of the war, so emblazoned in the young man's mind, would never be forgotten.

As a result of having experienced firsthand the horrors of war at such a young age, along with the trauma of loss, he shared a deep sense of fearlessness with many young men from the backcountry who had survived, especially those orphaned by the war. They felt a fatalistic belief that the worst had already happened, leaving nothing left to fear. This mindset contributed to a significant increase in crime and violence in interior South Carolina in the years following the war,[49] even as the wartime atmosphere began to fade. However, the underlying feeling of dread never truly disappeared. As a boy, he had pretended to be

---

[49] Booraem, Hendrik. *The Making of Young Hickory*, 2001. p.111.

fearless, embodying that attitude in his words and actions. But in the postwar period, it was as if he did not have to pretend any longer. Having lost everything dear to him and still survived, he believed he could endure anything. Situations that once seemed threatening no longer intimidated him; in fact, drawing from the experiences of some 20th-century survivors, they might have even given him a thrill. In his teenage and adult years, he displayed a calm, almost detached willingness—an eagerness—to take risks, both physical and personal. This made him formidable to his opponents and magnetically attractive to his friends.

The scars he bore on his hands and face (and certainly within his mind and heart,) he would carry for the rest of his life. Jackson would wear the scars with pride, as his own badge of freedom in this free land of America. As he set out on his own to "make his own way," a fierce determination would take a tight grip on his spirit. And with a single-minded resolve, he would hold tightly to his course moving forward, as though in place of his family, which was no more.

CHAPTER

5

ON HIS OWN

"The greatest and completest revolution the world ever knew, gloriously and happily accomplished."
                                   –Thomas Paine, *The Crisis*

Now an orphan and a hardened veteran of war, as well as a veteran of personal suffering and trauma, the fourteen-year-old Andrew Jackson had only distant relatives left to turn to for guidance. The only father-figure Andy and his brothers ever had, their Uncle James Crawford, had also died as a result of a Tory raid the year before. More thoroughly on his own than he had ever been, still suffering from the remnants of his injuries and illnesses, embattled by grief and a severe depression only occasionally relieved by fits of anger, Jackson pushed onward. Taken in by another relative, Major Thomas Crawford, Andrew would prove to be difficult to handle. The living arrangement that the boy found himself in was not harmonious, by any stretch. The bitterness that the boy felt seemed to fester from the devastation of the war, and it consistently boiled over, often at the slightest provocation. [50]

An instance that stands out as very emblematic of young Jackson's state of mind in this difficult postwar period involved another soldier also living at the Crawford home at the time. This other soldier, one Captain Galbraith, whom Jackson later remembered as having a "very proud and haughty disposition," took offense at something Jackson said and threatened to "chastise" the young man. As Galbraith raised his

---

[50] Remini, 1977. p. 26

hand to strike, Andrew reportedly unleashed a torrent of obscenities at Galbraith. His wild outburst shocked Galbraith. Jackson went on to swear that if he were to strike him, Galbraith was a dead man. Retelling the story with a biographer years later, Jackson recalled: "I had arrived at an age to know my rights, and although weak and feeble from disease, I had courage to defend them, and if he attempted anything of that kind I would most assuredly Send him to the other world."

Whatever true homicidal tendencies Andrew Jackson felt towards Captain Galbraith aside, the threat brought the desired response: the Captain backed down. Yet, the discord between the two would continue to such an extent that it was soon decided that Jackson would have to leave Major Crawford's home. He instead went to live at the home of Mr. Joseph White, an uncle of Thomas Crawford's wife, whose son had recently begun a career as a saddler. Soon, the aspiring but troubled young man would take on an apprenticeship with his Crawford cousin.

Andrew Jackson loved horses, having learned to ride at a young age. Still suffering greatly from the residue of his various wartime illnesses, the youth may have been aided by the distraction of the White's saddler shop, as he was naturally drawn to the trade. Helping out "as much as the fever and ague would allow," he later recalled, he managed to pick up a good bit of learning from his experience in the shop. This would be useful down the road, embarking on a military career that would require long hours in the saddle. It was probably this experience that generated Jackson's life-long love of horses, horse-racing and breeding. This period of time, Jackson would later attest, was one of the most difficult of his life, a life full of innumerable trials and tribulations, as the boy struggled to fully grasp the loss of his family. The saddle shop may have done much to provide the necessary redirection the boy needed to help push him through.

While recovering from the loss of his family and doing his best to overcome the pains of his captivity, Jackson was also aided by the social opportunities that the British occupation of Charleston provided. Several socially prominent families, forced out of the city by the presence of the Redcoats, had taken up temporary residence in the Waxhaws. According to David Remini in his book Andrew Jackson and the Course of Empire, "they were a wild bunch, and Andrew fell in with them almost at once….drinking, cockfighting, gambling, mischief-making, he seemed determined to go as far as possible in leading an 'abandoned life.'" [51]

This renegade behavior did not go over well with his relations, who, in their dismay, struggled to rein in the boy. Jackson would later admit that he and this particular branch of his Crawford relatives were never particularly close, and this period of time would soon lead to a permanent rupture of their relationship. When the British evacuated Charles Town in late 1782, and many of his new found friends returned to their homes in the Holy City of Charleston, Jackson, drawn by the excitement their stories foretold, would follow.

The 15-year-old Andy Jackson soon mounted a "fine mare," one that he likely acquired through his work in the saddler shop and made the sojourn to the coast. According to his own recollection, Jackson would "burn up the town," at least as much as a young teenager out on his own could. When his grandfather died in Carrickfergus, Andrew had inherited approximately £400. The boy would soon burn through this small sum however, in a stretch of fast-living and hobnobbing in Charleston with his newfound friends, a much wealthier crowd. Their far higher standard of living meant spending, and the money quickly dissipating in the spree.

Heading for financial ruin, Andrew took part in a game of craps known as "rattle and snap." Played with beans and a snap of the fingers, one of the players challenged Jackson to a wager of $200 for Jackson's horse. Recognizing the risk, Andrew accepted the offer, picked up the dice, probably whispering a quiet prayer to the heavens and 'rattled and snapped.' In the face of financial devastation, the boy won. Very possibly, this near miss of total ruin may have jolted the boy out of his wild ways, for soon after, the teenage Jackson made good on his debts, packed up his belongings, and headed home. Years later, Jackson attested, "My calculation was that, if a loser in the game, I would give the landlord my saddle and bridle, as far as they would go, ask a credit for the balance, and walk away from the city; but being successful, I had new spirits infused into me, left the table, and from that moment to the present time, I have never thrown dice for a wager." [52]

---

[51] Remini, 1977. p.27
[52] McLaughlin to Kendall, Feb. 14, 1843, Jackson Papers, LC; Kendall, *Jackson*, p. 68; Parton, *General Jackson*, I, 98.

Andrew Jackson's departure from the city marked a turning point in his life. Perhaps it was his successful 'winner take all gamble' that altered his tide of fortune. Or maybe it can be attributed to the near brush with financial ruin that had awakened him. Either way, with money in his pocket, sanguine hopes of his ambitions rising, Jackson seems to have reached a crossroads, and he chose to make a break from the wayward life. The demons within the young man were still there, but he seems to have decided at that crucial moment in his young life, that it was time to tamp them down, and decide what it was he wanted to do with his life. Having nearly lost everything, he now began to think bigger than he ever had before. With an obstinate determination to not only survive, but to thrive, hardened by war and death, the teenaged Andrew Jackson would move forward into a life and a future that remained entirely unwritten.

When 17-year-old Andrew Jackson returned to the Waxhaws on his fine mare after his escapades in Charleston, he sought to continue his education. However, the old Waxhaw Academy was no more, burned to the ground, another casualty of the Revolution. Undeterred, Jackson would seek out his former mentor Robert McCulloch, who now ran a school known as Bethel Academy in the "New Acquisition," the strip of land that South Carolina had acquired from North Carolina when the boundary was redrawn just before the war. The location of the school was unique in that it was not beside the Bethel Church, as most academies were, but about 2 miles down from a large ironworks company owned by one Billy Hill, known as Area Works. Hill's business had been shut down by the British during the war, but now Hill had reopened it, his operation humming along prosperously. The ironworks company drew families into the New Acquisition, including some who sent their sons to Bethel Academy. Here, Andrew would resume his studies, dividing his time between courses on language and a "desultory course of studies." Jackson seemed determined to emulate his military hero, and follow the course William R. Davie had followed, in order to get the education of a minister, and use it to become a lawyer.[53]

The air around the Bethel Academy was perpetually filled with the scent of wood smoke emanating from the Hill furnaces, which operated around the clock. The landscape was marked by extensive patches of red clay and scattered tree stumps, evidence of the vast tracts of forest cleared to sustain the forges. Along the road to Salisbury, wagons clattered by, laden with an assortment of Hill's iron products destined for trade with merchants in the area. Colonel Hill, characterized by his lean frame, lively demeanor, prominent nose, and somewhat disheveled attire, was a familiar figure around the meeting house and the academy. It is believed that some of his children, including Billy, Jr., who was roughly the same age as Jackson, may have received their education under the tutelage of McCulloch.[54]

Andrew Jackson's tenure at Bethel Academy was likely brief. His primary motive for enrollment was to enhance his proficiency in English and Latin—the languages predominant in legal discourse—thereby increasing his likelihood of passing the bar exam. In addition to his studies, he occasionally appraised horses for claims related to the Revolutionary War and took on the role of a teacher at a school for young children. This school was situated a few miles north of Waxhaw Creek, in an area populated by many of Jackson's former neighbors, including the Porters and Millers. Both families entrusted their children to his care, allowing Jackson to take center stage as an educator.

For more than a year, Jackson taught classes, learning as he went along, preparing lessons and teaching young students near the Waxhaw Methodist Episcopal Church in South Carolina. For the first time, Jackson was a leader, one who commanded respect in the classroom. Students would stand and bow upon his arrival, addressing him with deference as he guided them through their lessons. He actively intervened during disputes, enforced discipline for misbehavior, and instructed them in proper penmanship. With his dynamic personality, Jackson effectively maintained order among the children, and the financial support from the parents of his pupils proved beneficial during his later pursuit of

---

[53] Reid and Eaton, *Jackson*, p.14; Arda Walker, The Educational Training and Views of Andrew Jackson," *ETHSP*, 1944. No. 16, p.22

[54] Booraem, pg. 134.

his legal studies. Ultimately, Jackson's choice to teach was likely driven by a desire to demonstrate his intellectual growth to the community. He was no longer merely the hot-tempered saddler and cockfighter. Andrew Jackson, while not yet the epitome of a gentleman, had indeed transformed into a man of considerable change.

Yet the ambition that Jackson held would soon outgrow the limitations of the teaching profession, and the young man would seek opportunities elsewhere. Nonetheless, the idea of the young "cracker" (as most backcountry men would have been called by the high society Charleston crowd) who had been so uncultivated in manner just a few years before, now teaching school and aspiring for more, suggests that young Andrew had undergone a startling transformation in a rather short period of time.[55]

One does wonder as to the root cause of this transformation. There is some evidence on the historical record that shows Jackson having made not one, but two lengthy visits to Charleston (officially renamed as such in 1783 from its previous moniker Charles Town.) He had traveled to the Holy City once with Major Crawford, and once by himself. This was quite an undertaking for a man so young. Charleston was renowned throughout the American South for its refined manners, its high society culture. For most backcountry orphans, contact with this glamorous Charleston sect would have been impossible, but it seems that Andrew had not only found acceptance by many of the Charleston refugees he had become acquainted with in the Waxhaws, but even admiration. Perhaps it was Jackson's earnest spirit and fortitude amid such adversity and personal loss. Or perhaps it was his self-confidence, his articulate speech. Whatever it was that drew the respect of many of the wealthier young men of Charleston, Jackson was accepted by these well-to-do low country friends. In return, Jackson seems to have resigned himself completely to the pleasure of their company. This just might have been the influence that pushed the young man to envisage a life of more than mere frivolity. Jackson began to envision himself in the life of a gentleman.

---

[55] Walker, Alexander. Jackson And New Orleans: *An Authentic Narrative of the Memorable Achievements of the American Army, Under Andrew Jackson, Before New Orleans, In The Winter Of 1814-15*. (1856)

In 1784, during part of this period, Jackson resided in the Waxhaws, either with Major Crawford or the McCamie family. But he was not destined to stay long. The now seventeen-year-old Jackson would soon move forward even further to act upon his vision for himself as a man of means, someone that those around him would admire and respect. After all, in the 1780s, it was the profession of attorney-at-law that set a man on a road to gentility. Becoming a lawyer offered a way out of the laboring class. As Charles Brockdon Brown wrote: "An usher! A clerk! A taylor! Whenever these images occur, some emotions of contempt are sure to bear them company....I am a student of law, whereas they are servile mechanics."[56] Despite appearances or past circumstances, Jackson's time among the genteel of Charleston had settled one thing for certain in his mind: he was destined to be a gentleman, and he would find a way to live like one. In short, the teenaged Jackson had found something intrinsic within himself: a driving need to succeed.

With all these influences stirring an ever-rising tide of ambition within the rangy, ambitious Jackson, he would set out to make his dream a reality. The seventeen-year-old packed up his belongings and headed up the road to Salisbury in December of 1784, the seat of Rowan County, North Carolina. The town of Salisbury had grown in importance due to its location on the Great Wagon Road, the 800-mile trail that ran all the way from Pennsylvania to Augusta, Georgia. The town where William R. Davie himself had learned to master the law would be Jackson's chosen setting for his continuing rise.

With a farewell to the past, Andrew Jackson was never to return to the place of his birth. Entering Salisbury, the ambitious seventeen-year-old felt a sense of hope and promise. Established as the Rowan County seat in 1755, the town's advantageous location meant that it was an ideal spot for the prominent and the ambitious. In 1781, Salisbury had served as the temporary headquarters for both the British and American armies before the Battle of Guilford Courthouse. Thus, like so many other towns impacted by the war, much change was afoot by the time Andrew Jackson would begin to make his mark there.

Yet, before the assiduous Jackson ultimately chose Salisbury as his educational setting, he made a surprising decision to travel roughly sixty

---

[56] Lee, Carter. Andrew Jackson Papers. Pg. 5-6.

miles west to Morganton, North Carolina. His reasons for this sudden change of plans are unknown. Perhaps at just seventeen, Jackson couldn't foresee the potential that Salisbury held, despite the presence of his cousin Will Crawford also training for the legal profession there. Or perhaps he preferred to find a pathway of his own, without the support of any of his relations. At any rate, upon reaching Morganton, he located the home of a well-known lawyer, Colonel Waightstill Avery, famous for having one of the finest law libraries in North Carolina. Andrew sought learning and guidance within the field, and hoped to stay at Avery's home, so he knocked on Avery's large wooden double-doors.

Unfortunately for Jackson, the Colonel informed the boy that there was no space available, and his request to train there was denied. Reluctantly, the frustrated Jackson was forced to head back to Salisbury, down but not yet out. This time, he would stay in Salisbury, despite whatever reservations he had held previously. And it was here, this time, that he would finally find a pathway for his legal aspirations.[57]

The decision to head towards Salisbury for his legal training probably had much to do with his cousin Will Crawford. His knowledge of the town goes back to a visit he took only a year or so before. During Jackson's tenure as a teacher in the Waxhaws, he undertook a journey to Salisbury for business purposes. According to family lore, Major Robert Crawford found himself in financial difficulty, grappling with debts amassed by his son Will during the war. Will, who had also experienced challenges with the duplicitous Colonel Gallbraith, was residing in Salisbury at the time. To alleviate his financial burden, the Major resolved to sell a few slaves, recognizing that Salisbury, as the hub of the backcountry, would yield higher prices than Charleston. The Major requested that Jackson undertake the journey to handle the sale, instructing him to seek Will's assistance should any legal issues arise. Thus, the seventeen-year-old Jackson, dressed in his Sunday best and armed with a pistol, embarked on an eighty-mile trek along the dusty Wagon Road, driving the Crawford slaves to Salisbury.

That Major Crawford would trust the seventeen-year-old Jackson to take on such a daunting task as a slave trade in Salisbury says much about the lengths that the boy had matured in such a short time since his days

---

[57] Reid and Eaton. p.15

of trouble and high-living just after the war's end. Yet, there is no record of whether this maturity led to any moral concerns that may have swirled in the mind of the teenage teacher-turned-slave-trader, Andrew Jackson.

Upon reaching Salisbury, having successfully completed the sale without incident, Jackson had the opportunity to engage Will Crawford in discussions regarding legal studies, the potential for practicing law in North Carolina, and living expenses. It is likely that Will encouraged Jackson to consider relocating to Salisbury, which, due to its geography on several thoroughfares, presented a wealth of legal opportunities. Additionally, Jackson learned that the town was home to several esteemed families known for their refinement. Another of Salisbury's distinguishing features that likely appealed to the gregarious Jackson was that the town was celebrated for its vibrant social scene, including parties, dancing, and various amusements. Will would have certainly stressed this to his gregarious cousin. Ultimately, this pivotal conversation with Will Crawford would play a significant role in Jackson's eventual decision to move to Salisbury. It was also likely that it was, in fact, his cousin Will who suggested the office of Spruce McCay as a viable option for his legal training.

In 1783 Spruce McCay purchased lots 19 and 27 in the western square of Salisbury where the stately Rowan Public Library now stands. The son of the former Rowan County sheriff, and a graduate of what is today Princeton College in New Jersey, McCay would go on to become a prominent judge in the state. In the purchase, he acquired a small law office and a home that previously belonged to Adlai Osborne, former clerk of the Rowan court and of the Committee of Safety. It was in this little office that McCay would soon take on the tutelage of the young, aspiring Andrew Jackson. McCay was destined to become the legal instructor for his young pupil, the future president, in the field of law from 1784 to 1785.[58]

Law students often engaged in a considerable amount of copying as part of their clerical responsibilities, creating hand-written duplicates of documents that circulated through their instructor's office. His cousin Will was building a growing legal practice in Salisbury, managing more

---

[58] Brawley, James. 1991. Revised by SLNC Government & Heritage Library, December 2022. from the *Dictionary of North Carolina Biography*, 6 volumes, edited by William S. Powell. Copyright ©1979-1996 by the University of North Carolina Press.

paperwork than he could probably handle. Jackson had a neat and legible handwriting style, which would have made him a good candidate to assist Will in his workload. All the while, he would learn the structure of legal documents by transcribing writs and deeds for his cousin. Once having begun this clerking opportunity, it likely didn't take him long to become proficient in this area of law, and he soon progressed to reading legal textbooks.

Even in the late 18th century, prior to the outpouring of extensive state and federal reports in the American court system, when most state laws were relatively few and straightforward, there was a substantial amount of literature that aspiring lawyers needed to familiarize themselves with. The legal library in Spruce McCay's office illustrated the wealth of legal literature available at the time; it contained fifty-two legal works, many of which were part of multi-volume sets—such as *Blackstone's Commentaries*, which spanned four volumes, *Bacon's Abridgement of the Laws* in five volumes, the *Statutes at Large*, along with several other essential texts. Some items in the collection were aimed specifically at novice lawyers, while others were fundamental references that every lawyer, regardless of experience level, frequently consulted.

Thus commenced the legal education of Andrew Jackson. The tall, awkward seventeen-year-old worked diligently to unravel the complexities of the profession. Over a span of two years, Jackson devoted himself to various tasks: meticulously copying documents, running errands, maintaining the office's cleanliness, perusing law books, and fulfilling any request made by McCay. His efforts were driven by a singular ambition—to one day gain admission to the bar.

The extent of Jackson's legal knowledge remains a subject of debate. Historically, he was not recognized as the most adept student in any discipline; nevertheless, he exhibited a strong commitment to his studies. It was in his nature to undertake whatever was necessary to meet his needs. In this regard, he proved to be a successful student, extracting the essential knowledge he required from his legal training.

By no means was the twenty-year-old Andrew Jackson prepared to take on the legal magicians of the courtroom, but for the pragmatic young man without a family, the job at hand was to do whatever he needed to do to become a practicing attorney, and his determination in this matter was unbending.

CHAPTER

6

TO THE BAR

"The study of the law is useful in a variety of points of view. It qualifies a man to be useful to himself, to his neighbors and the public."

—*Thomas Jefferson, 1790*

Inexperienced, but with no shortage of self-confidence, seventeen-year-old Andrew Jackson traveled to Salisbury, North Carolina in 1784 to gain a legal education, and to reach the goal he was certain was necessary for the life he envisioned for himself: to become a practicing lawyer. He seems to have attached himself fairly closely to his cousin, Will Crawford, over the next two or three years. While there is not a lot of documentary evidence for this period in Jackson's life, it has been established that shortly after establishing himself in Salisbury, Jackson would begin instruction with the law firm of Spruce McCay.

Ultimately, Jackson realized, the most prudent course of action was to align himself with a seasoned practicing lawyer who could provide guidance in navigating the complexities of legal literature. He had tried to learn solely on his own, after all, as confident a boy as he was becoming, he figured that all he would have to do is to know enough to pass the bar. But, in his pursuit of legal knowledge, Jackson found himself in need of access to legal texts, or as those in the legal profession of the 1780s called them, 'legal authorities.' These complicated writings necessitated a slow and deliberate approach to reading. His cousin, Will Crawford, a novice lawyer with merely a year of experience himself, could offer little assistance in this endeavor. With his limited collection of law books, Crawford was not equipped to support Jackson's ambitions.

Recognizing the potential benefits of a better-supplied mentor, Jackson next sought the companionship of Charles Bruce, a prosperous landowner from Guilford County, who possessed a modest library of legal texts. It is likely that Jackson became acquainted with Bruce through his time in Guilford during the war. Regular access to the resources Bruce owned would have greatly aided Jackson's legal education and training. Evidence shows that during the course of Jackson's previous extended stays in Guilford, he managed to acquire some of Mr. Bruce's vast array of law books. The complex legal authorities though, would require some serious explanation for the young novice. [59]

Law books, dense and challenging, especially for a novice, required the mentorship of someone experienced in the field, someone who could explain the jargon. After grappling with the texts from Bruce's library, Jackson likely concluded that he would gain more benefit from formal instruction. This led him to approach McCay, a respected figure in the Salisbury legal community. The influence of Jackson's old friend, the charismatic John McNairy—who had previously studied under McCay and was now running a successful law office in town—likely played a role in persuading McCay to accept Jackson as a pupil. Thus, under McCay's tutelage, Jackson was poised to embark on a more structured journey into the legal profession. In the meantime, he chose to take up residence in the famous Rowan House.

Built in 1772, according to the 'Heritage of Rowan County,' the Rowan House was built in 1772 by carpenter Joseph Atkins for Henry Hughes. Legend has it that while Jackson studied at McCay's firm, he often played cards with Mr. Hughes in the basement for his room and board. When Jackson left, he reportedly owed Hughes a considerable sum of money, but after the Battle of New Orleans, Hughes marked the bill "Paid in Full."

In the vibrant and spirited life of Andrew Jackson, the daily responsibilities of a law office could hardly contain the boundless energy that characterized his youth. Residing at Rowan House alongside fellow law students, Jackson immersed himself in a life filled with exuberance

---

[59] Walker, Arda, *ETHSP*, p. 23

and camaraderie. Reports indicate that he engaged in such frequent and varied escapades as those of his earlier mischief with his Crawford relatives, or during his time with the Charleston elite in Waxhaw. However, this phase was distinct; it was not merely a descent into chaos or an expression of suppressed anger, but rather a release of pent-up energy following the tedious hours spent at McCay's legal office. Now Jackson was blowing off steam while maintaining his position at McCay's and keeping eyes on the prize.

To say this period in Jackson's life was marked by youthful exuberance is putting it mildly. Some of the antics of he and his fellow lawyers-in-training bordered on recklessness. After long days of legal work, Jackson and his companions sought entertainment in the most uninhibited ways possible. Before long, Jackson earned a reputation as the leader of this group of hooligans. A local resident later remarked that Jackson was "the most roaring, rollicking, game-cocking, horse-racing, card-playing mischievous fellow that ever lived in Salisbury." His focus on law was reportedly minimal, as he was "more in the stable than in the office," often prioritizing his interests in horses and socializing over his legal studies.

Whether it was horses, or the pursuit of feminine flirtations, Andrew Jackson found ways to enjoy himself. He was often away on "parties of pleasure" and became "quite a beau in the town." His love of card-playing, dancing and merry making, cultivated from his days in post-war Charleston, now began to include pranks, practical jokes, as well as long hours of drinking and card-playing. With one eye on his professional aspirations, Jackson was "A lively fellow, fun-loving, a sport with the young ladies, he was ever careful, however, not to provoke a scandal that might lead to social disgrace. One of his favorite pastimes for laughs was to relocate outhouses to remote places. Others included stealing gates and signposts. [60]

This less formalized Southern education complemented the rowdy lifestyle Jackson and his like-minded peers maintained. Engaging in cockfighting, horse-racing, drunken revelry and pranks throughout Salisbury, he and his "associates" had gleefully created their 'new normal.' A far cry from the tragic war-torn days of just a few years earlier, and

---

[60] Remini, 1977, p.30

perhaps as a result of those difficult times, Jackson was never far from chicanery. On one occasion, after concluding dinner at a local tavern, the young men decided it would be a fine idea to smash the dining ware they had used. "They made good on their feelings by shattering the plates and glasses. Then they broke the table in two, battered the chairs and other furniture into splinters, heaped it all into a pile and set the pile ablaze."[61]

In these early years of Andrew Jackson's professional life, some of his indiscretions, while not overtly destructive, garnered considerable scandal. A notable incident occurred during a Christmas ball held at the local dancing school in Salisbury. In a move that ruffled the feathers of many a Salisbury citizen, Jackson extended invitations to two 'women of ill repute,' commonly known throughout the town as prostitutes. Their appearance at the festivities caused widespread shock among the 'respectable' attendees of the ball, and a moment of social awkwardness ensued, one that lingered in the memory of many who witnessed the scene. Jackson's prank did not go over well, and some saw it not only as inappropriate considering the occasion, but a cruel jest, prompting Jackson to extend apologies to the women present at the ball. However, it remains unclear whether he ever offered a similar apology to the two women he had invited.

If Spruce McCay's young wife was among the offended women, and there is every reason to believe she was, this would help clear up the mystery as to why Jackson suddenly left town in the middle of his law study at McCay's firm. It seems clear that Jackson soon departed Salisbury to study with seasoned attorney John Stokes, who lived in the adjoining county of Montgomery, although he practiced in Salisbury. Jackson left Salisbury in the winter of 1787, as the matron at the Rowan house recalled later, and that at some point Jackson and his cronies, self-dubbed "The Inseparables" gave up their room, not having paid their bills, and that some or all of them left town altogether. The historical record consistently shows that Jackson left McCay's to study with Stokes, and those biographers who have connected the change with the incident at the ball may well be right.[62]

---

[61] James, Marquis – The Life of Andrew Jackson: The Border Captain; Portrait of a President – Bobbs Merrill, 1937
[62] Aunt Judy's recollections: Parton, I: 106; Reid and Eaton, p.14; Brawley, *Footnotes to History*, Salisbury Post, July 22, 1962; Eli Brown, 320.

Despite these youthful distractions and social missteps, there is evidence to suggest that Jackson approached his legal studies with sincerity and dedication. As noted by early biographer James Parton in his 1860 work, "Life of Andrew Jackson," Jackson's commitment to his education hinted at a deeper ambition beneath his youthful antics. Yet, could one look at this time of youthful 'devil-may-care' attitude as a warning sign of excessive constitutional liberties that Andrew Jackson would one day take as the commander in chief? Could pushing aside norms, mores and legal limitations as a youth have been the red flag for later indiscretions as president, so long as his ends were achieved? One could make the connection, but much time would pass before the unharnessed power of absolute authority would present itself so amply in the worn hands of Old Hickory.

In the meantime, by all appearances and despite his wild ways, Andrew Jackson was a popular figure in Salisbury. With his tall, stately bearing and penetrating blue eyes, he bore a commanding and charismatic presence to most observers, even in those years. As a youth, he had the opportunity to observe some of Carolina's leading men in their social graces, manners, and comportment. The war had placed dynamic men into the thrust of young Andy's orbit, and having spent considerable lengths of time, with men of such stature as William R. Davie, Thomas Sumter, and Major Robert Crawford, the boy had learned much about the power of "presence." The inherent quality that cannot be imparted through instruction, that of charisma, was a trait that many observers would later affirm Jackson held in abundance.

The ever-present struggle, which remained a dominant theme throughout Jackson's life, ingrained in him both relentless ambition and fierce determination. This inner drive; this focus on the 'means to an end,' may well have fueled the budding attorney and social dynamo. Despite appearances, however, Jackson was also developing the means to rein in his aggressions, learning how to keep a steady eye on his manners, grace and bearing. In search of the respect and status of a gentleman, the pathway to achieving these lofty ambitions remained foremost on Jackson's mind.

Fortunately for Andy Jackson, a commanding presence, and an unquestioning self-confidence were his natural endowments. As David Remini puts it in his 1977 book, *Andrew Jackson and the Course of Empire*,

"There was a quality about him that commanded attention, respect, awe and occasionally fear. Whenever something happened, he was invariably a prime mover. His leadership of the law students on the nightly prowls and hijinx was only one example." [63]

Despite his best efforts, according to William Garrott Brown, in his 1900 biography *Andrew Jackson*, the young barrister in training "was not overfond of study, and never acquired any great knowledge of the law...but distinguished by considerable grace and dignity of manner; an exquisite rider and a capital shot; of an extraordinarily passionate temper, yet singularly swift, even when his anger was at white heat, to seize upon the right means to protect himself or discomfit an adversary."[64]

During his Salisbury period, as long-time Tennessee friend William B. Lewis would attest, Jackson became aware of the power of his anger and had enough control over it to use it to his advantage. "No man knew better than Andrew Jackson when to get into a passion, and when not." In moments when he allowed his passions to surface, the consequences were often catastrophic, instilling fear in all who could hear his voice. This ability would prove invaluable in the numerous military and political struggles that lay ahead. However, by all accounts, Jackson was adept at maintaining shrewd control over his emotions, at least to the degree he wished to display. At his core, he was a conservative, prudent individual, whose ambition and resolve to achieve shaped every action and word he expressed.

Even at this early point in his life, Andrew Jackson had become a leader, and he seems to have already established an intense pattern of operation to have his way. While honing his natural gifts of leadership, Jackson, in his late teens, seems to have begun to master the unquestionable art of command. Whether it was command over other men, or command of his own condition, he was steadfast in its direction. After having learned enough from Spruce McCay's law firm, or perhaps embarrassed by his misconduct, Jackson was ready to move on to the next chapter of his young life. Believing he gained as much law knowledge as was necessary to generate a profession and all that came with it, and no more, Jackson moved forward. Financial need likely drove Jackson out

---

[63] Remini, 1977. p.31
[64] Brown, William Garrett. *Andrew Jackson*. The Riverside Biographical Series. 1900.

of Salisbury as well after just two years in the town. Not much is known about the next brief period in his life prior to his passing of the bar exam in 1787, but by 1787, the nineteen-year-old then made his way east to the law office of John Stokes in Montgomery County.

For the next six months, Jackson would immerse himself in the firm of the esteemed Stokes, a figure widely regarded as one of the finest attorneys in North Carolina. Stokes, who also served as a state senator representing Montgomery County, was a courageous soldier in the Revolutionary War. He had tragically lost a hand during the brutal encounter with Tarleton's brigade at Buford's Massacre. It is believed that he may have even been cared for at the Waxhaw Meeting House by Betty Jackson and her sons during his recovery. In lieu of his lost hand, Stokes utilized a silver knob, which he would emphatically strike against the table during his courtroom arguments to underscore his points. Amidst the scenic confluence of the Yadkin and Uwharrie Rivers, Andrew Jackson honed his legal skills under the guidance of this learned yet unconventional mentor.

On September 26th, 1787, only days after the 55 delegates in Philadelphia had framed a brand-new Constitution for the young republic, Jackson would appear for examination before Samuel Ashe and John F. Williams, two judges of the Superior Court of Law and Equity of North Carolina. Along with Judge Williams, Judge Ashe, who would go on to become the governor of the state in 1795, and for whom the city of Asheville would be named two years later, found Jackson to be a young man of "unblemished moral character," and competent enough in his knowledge of the law. Thus, the court authorized Jackson to begin practicing as an attorney.

Jackson was given the go ahead to begin adjudicating in the courts of pleas and quarter sessions within the state, but it seems that, at least at first, Jackson chose to drift instead, somewhat sporadically, with his cronies from Salisbury. Only nineteen, and not yet ready to give up the party lifestyle, for a year or so Jackson did very little that has been recorded, with the exception of one adventurous evening in the late fall season of 1787. It is not clear as to the exact details that got Jackson and his friends into trouble, but it is known that Hugh Montgomery, William Cupples, Daniel Clary, Henry Giles and himself, all Salisbury colleagues and veterans of many a merry prank, were caught trespassing.

They were to appear in court for unnamed damages that came to the sum of 500 pounds and were bound to Sheriff Lewis Beard of Rowan County. Their bond was to be put at 1000 pounds "by which they were guaranteed to appear at the courthouse on the first Monday of November, 1787, and thare to answer Unto John Ludlo & Andrew Baird on a plea of Trespass on a Case, etc." [65] This was quite in contrast to having been found a man of "unblemished character" by the future governor of the state just a month before.

While the outcome of the case remains uncertain, it is clear that a resolution was reached that satisfied all parties involved. Jackson likely gained valuable insights from this experience, reflecting on the consequences of his previous misadventures. Following this episode, he found it was indeed to give Salisbury a final adieu. Jackson relocated to the small town of Martinville, North Carolina, situated in Guilford County. However, an interesting description of the group's final celebratory evening at the Rowan House just prior to Jackson's exodus survives and provides a colorful glimpse into the raucous atmosphere that the young men had enjoyed over the previous two years. Historian Alfred Henry Lewis, in his book *When Men Grew Tall Or the Story of Andrew Jackson*, writes:

> *"The foppish, horse-faced Andy strides into the Rowan House. In the long-room he meets mine host Brown, who has fame as a publican, and none as a sinner, throughout North Carolina.*
>
> *"Supper in my rooms, Mr. Brown," commands our hero; "supper for three. Have it hot and ready at sharp seven. Also let us have plenty of whisky and tobacco."*
>
> *Mine host Brown says that all shall be as ordered.*
>
> *The foppish Andy, with that grave manner of dignity which laughs at his boyish twenty years, explains to his landlord that he will call for his bill in the morning.*

---

[65] Heiskell, S.G. *Andrew Jackson and Early Tennessee History*. Nashville. 1918

"Have my horse, Cherokee," he says, "well groomed and saddled. To-morrow I leave Salisbury."

"Going West?"

"West," returns Andy.

"As to the bill," ventures mine host Brown, "would you like to play a game of all-fours, and make it double or nothing?"

Andy the horse-faced hesitates.

"You have such vile luck," he says, as though remonstrating with mine host Brown for a fault. "It seems shameful to play with you, since you never win."

Mine host Brown looks sheepishly apologetic.

"For one as eager to play as I am," he responds, "it does look as though I ought to know more about the game. However, since it's your last night, we might as well preserve a record."

Andy the horse-faced yields to the rabid anxiety of mine host Brown to gamble. The game shall be played presently; meanwhile, there is an errand which takes him to his rooms.

Andy goes to his rooms; mine host Brown, after preparing a table in the long-room for the promised game, saunters fatly—being rotund as a publican should be—into the kitchen, to leave directions concerning that triangular supper. There he encounters his wife, as rotund as himself, supervising the energies of a phalanx of black Amazons, who form the culinary forces of the Rowan House.

"Young Jackson leaves in the morning, mother," observes mine host Brown to Mrs. Brown, whom he always addresses as "mother."

"For good?" asks Mrs. Brown, who is singeing the pin feathers from a chicken of much fatness, and exceeding yellow as to leg.

"Oh, I knew he was going," returns mine host Brown, rather irrelevantly. "Spruce Mc-Cay told me that he was about to advise him to emigrate to the western counties. Spruce says the Cumberland country is just the place for him."

"And now I suppose," remarks Mrs. Brown, "you'll let him win a good-by game of cards, to square his bill."

"Why not?" returns mine host Brown. "He's got no money; never had any money. You yourself said, when he came here, to give him his board free, because you knew and loved his dead mother. Now the Christian thing is to let him win it. In that way his pride is saved; at the same time it gives me amusement."

"Well, Marmaduke," says Mrs. Brown, moving off with the yellow-legged fowl, "I'm sure I don't care how you manage, only so you don't take his money."

"There never was a chance, mother. He never has any money, after his clothes are bought."

The game of all-fours is played; and is won by Andy of the horse face, who thereby rounds off a run of card-luck that has continued unbroken for two years.

"It looks as though I'd never beat you!" exclaims mine host Brown, pretending sadness and imitating a sigh.

"You ought never to gamble," advises the horse-faced Andy solemnly.

Mine host Brown produces his bill, wherein the charges for board, lodging, laundry, tobacco, and whisky in pints, quarts and gallons are set down on one side, to be balanced and acquitted by divers sums lost at all-fours, the same being noted opposite.

"There you are! All square!" says mine host Brown.

"But the charges for to-night's supper?"

"Mother"—meaning Mrs. Brown—"says the supper is to be with her compliments."

Steaming hot, the supper comes promptly at seven. It is followed, steaming hot, by unlimited whisky punch. Pipes are lighted, and, with glasses at easy hand, the three boys draw about the fire. The punch, the pipes, and the crackling log fire are very comfortable adjuncts on an October night.

"And now," cries Crawford, who is full of life and interest, "now for the news and the proposition!"

McNairy nods owlish assent to the words of his volatile friend. He intends one day to be a judge, and, while quite as lively as Crawford, seizes on occasions such as this to practice his features in a formidable woolsack gravity.

"First," observes Andy, soberly sipping his punch, "let me put a question: What is my standing in Rowan County?"

"You are the recognized authority," cries Crawford, "on dog fighting, cockfighting, and horse racing."

McNairy nods.

"Humph!" says Andy. Then, on the heels of a pause: "And what should you say were my chief accomplishments?"

Again Crawford takes it upon himself to reply.

"You ride, shoot, run, jump, wrestle, dance and make love beyond expression."

McNairy the judicial nods.

ANDREW JACKSON: THE POLITICS OF RESENTMENT

"Humph!" says Andy.

The trio puff and sip in silence.

"You say nothing for my knowledge of law?" This from the disgruntled Andy, with a rising inflection that is like finding fault.

"No!" cry the others in hearty concert.

"You wouldn't believe us if we did," adds McNairy of the future woolsack.

"Neither would the Judge," returns Andy cynically. "The Judge" is the title by which the three designate their master, Spruce Mc-Cay. Andy goes on: "The news I promised is this. To-morrow I leave Salisbury. The Judge has recommended my admission to the bar, and I shall take the oath and get my license before I start. I shall transfer myself to the region along the Cumberland, where I am told a barrister of my singular lack of ability should find plenty of practice."

"Why do you leave old Rowan?" asks woolsack McNairy, beginning to take an interest.

"Because I have no education, less law, and still less money. It seems that these are conditions precedent to staying in Rowan with credit."

"Well," cries McNairy the judicial, grasping Andy's long bony hand, "you have as much education, as much law, and as much money as I. Under the circumstances I shall go with you."

"And I," breaks in the lively Crawford, "since I have none of those ignorant and poverty-eaten qualifications you name, but on the contrary am rich, wise and learned—I shall remain here. When the wilderness casts you fellows out, come back and I shall welcome you. Pending which—as Parson Hicks would say—receive my blessing."

> *The evening wears on amid clouds of tobacco smoke and rivers of punch. At the close the three take hold of hands, and sing a farewell song very badly. Then, since they look on the evening as a sacred one, they wind up by breaking the pipes they have smoked and the glasses they have drunk from, to save them in the hereafter from profane and vulgar uses. At last, rather deviously, they make their various ways to bed.*
>
> *The next day, young Andrew Jackson, barrister and counselor at law, with all his belongings—save the rifle he carries, and the pistols in his saddle holsters—crowded into a pair of saddlebags, rides out of Salisbury on his bay horse Cherokee. He will stop at Martinsville for a space, awaiting the judicial McNairy.*[66]

While this Lewis version is written with a flair for the theatric, some creative license, and a shaky chronology, the portrait he paints of the raucous young attorneys' exuberant zest for life, camaraderie and humor tell us much about this period in Jackson's life. His time in Salisbury would be remembered for generations, especially after Jackson's rise to fame. For some residents of Salisbury, Jackson's potential as a serious leader was not what came to mind first when they recalled the tall youngster's rowdy ways. As Margaret L. Coit wrote in her 1965 biography of Jackson, the future president had been "the recognized leader of the town–in cockfighting, horseracing, dancing and drinking. "Jackson for president?" …Jackson?" recalled one old lady, "Well, if Andrew Jackson can be President, anyone can!"[67]

During his time in Martinville, Jackson would, for a time, reside with two acquaintances, Joseph Henderson and Bennett Searcy, who operated a country store in the area. To occupy his time, Jackson assisted his friends in managing their business, thereby acquiring another skill to add to his growing repertoire of trades. Additionally, there is evidence suggesting that Jackson obtained a commission as a constable, a role that would later prove advantageous during his tenure in Tennessee. The

---

[66] Lewis, Alfred Henry, 1907., *When Men Grew Tall or the Story of Andrew Jackson.*
[67] Coit, Margaret L. *Andrew Jackson.* Houghton Mifflin Company, Boston, 1965. Pg. 9.

specific duties and scope of this commission, however, remain largely undocumented.

Jackson began officially practicing law during this meandering period. He received his license in Guilford County on November 20th, 1787. By January of 1789, he would acquire licenses for five counties in North Carolina, and three in the western territory of Tennessee. He was practicing law in a circuit more than a hundred miles long. As he journeyed across the state, taking part in some modest gambling, and mingling with various influential North Carolinians, he took time to participate in one of his passions, horse racing. While there is little evidence as to his success in these early races, the competitive, adventurous Jackson held a life-long passion for horses, and horse-breeding.

The various adventures of this exploratory period mingled well with the traveling circuit of a young barrister, and soon, when an exciting new opportunity came knocking, Jackson answered the call.

John McNairy, Source: Tennessee Portrait Project

CHAPTER

7

GO WEST, YOUNG MAN!

"Westward lay the march of American Empire."
-Winston Churchill

In 1785, the North Carolina Assembly, responding to the demands of western settlers, created a superior court in Davidson County, far beyond the mountains in the recently established "Cumberland Settlements." Following the Revolution, western pioneers, eager to exploit the lands the war had opened up, began to fill in the vast rolling hills of what would become the state of Tennessee. The first appointment the government of North Carolina offered for this position went to an unnamed man who resigned the commission before making the journey to the territory. In other words, this was not a highly desired post, and as a result, the position remained vacant, with few clamoring to offer up their services. The venture was certain to carry with it reward, but there was no small amount of risk involved as well, to be sure.[68]

The area beyond the Appalachians was still a rugged wilderness, and not many established lawyers wished to take on such a gamble. The appointment was ideal, however, for a young, single lawyer willing to travel long distances through largely uncharted territory. And, after all, the judgeship would bring respectability and good pay. More importantly, it would put the holder of the office in a position to purchase large amounts of land in the new settlements, at prices the individual could

---

[68] Haywood, John. *The Civil and Political History of the State of Tennessee.* Nashville. 1915. 211-212, 243.

dictate on their own. At some point, Andrew Jackson's former gaming companion and fellow law student at McCay's, John McNairy, would be made aware of this position, one he felt he was perfectly suited for. McNairy threw his hat into the ring.

John McNairy's legal career had been bolstered by the mentorship of Alexander Martin, a former neighbor and two-time governor of the state, who guided him through the intricacies of the law. McNairy obtained his license to practice in 1783 and, like Jackson, honed his skills at the McCay firm for approximately two years. This foundation paved the way for a profound and enduring friendship between the two. By late 1787, Jackson learned of McNairy's intriguing new opportunity. McNairy began his efforts to obtain the position that autumn, sensing the potential of the new Cumberland settlements. If he should receive the appointment, McNairy had offered his talented and charismatic friend Andrew Jackson a job; McNairy wanted Jackson alongside him.

Yet, McNairy had now been waiting months to hear word of the legislature's decision. Beginning to think the post would not materialize, in December of 1787, McNairy finally got the nod. By this time, Jackson and McNairy both resided in the latter's story and a half log home just outside Martinville, engaged in circuit riding with the court, acquiring invaluable experience in courtroom procedures and legal matters. As it turns out, in true early North Carolina fashion, the votes for the western judgeship had been counted four months before, in favor of McNairy, but no one had bothered to tell him the good news to that point. The news finally arrived just in time for the holidays, and the long-awaited news must have certainly led the new judge and his friends to toast a drink or two in celebration.

The state of North Carolina, recognizing the twenty-five year old McNairy's potential, (and indubitably swayed by the influence of Governor Martin) officially elected the energetic young man to serve as a superior court judge for the Western District of North Carolina, more specifically for what would soon be named the "Mero District" in Davidson County, today's eastern portion of the state of Tennessee. With this new appointment, like that of his district he would preside over, McNairy's authority now stretched clear to the banks of the Mississippi River. Additionally, McNairy was given the power to appoint the public prosecutor for the district, or the job of Solicitor, and, as promised, he offered that post to his old friend Andy Jackson. Jackson did not take long to consider the offer, envisioning the potential of an intriguing future in the untamed west.[69]

The wilderness of Tennessee promised not only adventure but also the potential for significant rewards. McNairy and Jackson would be getting in on the ground floor, and they knew it. The burgeoning territory was witnessing an influx of settlers crossing the mountains, and the environment was ripe with legal opportunities. To that point, lawyers were a rarity on the frontier, where the need for establishing law and governance would be in high demand. As Tennessee approached its admission as the sixteenth state in the Union, (by 1796) the prospects for a young and ambitious attorney like Jackson were abundant. Considering the risks of attempting a new start in rough, largely unsettled country, Jackson seems to have shown little hesitation in accepting McNairy's offer. This decision would prove to be the start of a transformative chapter in the twenty-year-old Jackson's life.

The appointment of a man as young and inexperienced as Andrew Jackson to such a significant position may seem surprising at first. Solicitor of the Western Territory was in itself a prestigious position even for a man twice Jackson's age and experience. Yet, taking on a job in unsettled western territory where law and order were non-existent was simply not something that established eastern lawyers took on. This was a job for a young upstart, a man seeking to prove himself; a man with nothing holding him back. That man was twenty-year-old Andrew Jackson.

Understanding the context of Tennessee at that time helps to clarify further. The term "Tennessee" can be misleading because the area where Jackson would move was still part of North Carolina in 1788. In fact, it would remain so six years later, when, in 1794, residents would attempt to separate from the state of North Carolina. Far removed from the government in Raleigh, Davidson County settlers wished to become a separate entity, and attempted to establish their independence as the State of Franklin, named in honor of the esteemed founder Benjamin Franklin, who had passed away just four years before. Franklin had stood his ground in negotiations with France regarding the new United States'

---

[69] James, Marquis. p. 41, 378

possession of these very western lands the French eyed, and therefore Americans in the west held his memory in high regard.[70]

Those involved in the effort to create the separate state of Franklin lived in what is now east Tennessee, the mountainous region in which Jonesborough, which by that time remained a settlement of only about fifty or sixty log cabins, served as the main town. Nashville, some 200 miles further west, was still a fledgling city, having been founded just under ten years earlier by Captain James Robertson in 1779. In 1777, Richard Henderson of the Transylvania Land Company acquired a vast area of land from the Cherokees, which included much of what is now Middle Tennessee. In the spring of 1779, Robertson and a small group of settlers, representing Henderson's claim, traveled to a location along the Cumberland River called French Lick. They chose a spot for a new settlement and, later that year, Robertson returned with more men to build temporary shelters for their friends and family, who planned to join them soon.

On Christmas Day in 1779, Robertson guided a small group of nine men down the partially frozen Cumberland River, bringing their cattle along. After crossing the river, they discovered an ideal spot along a bluff, where they built simple cabins to shelter them for the winter. From this vantage point overlooking the river, they established a fort, naming it Fort Nashborough in honor of Francis Nash, who had fought alongside Robertson in the Regulators' battle of Alamance in 1771.

The following year, Colonel John Donelson arrived from Virginia with a larger group of 120 men, women, and children to join Robertson, his fellow Virginian. The name Donelson would soon be significant in the life of Andrew Jackson. This group included many families, as well as Donelson's own large family—his wife Rachel Stockley, their children, and about thirty African American slaves. Among the travelers was Donelson's thirteen-year-old daughter, Rachel, who would later become Jackson's wife. Also part of this expedition were James Robertson's wife, Charlotte, and five of their eleven children.

To call Colonel Donelson's journey remarkable is something of an understatement. He and his resilient group traveled in flatboats, canoes,

---

[70] Mielnik, Tara Mitchell. "Campbell, Arthur". *Tennessee Encyclopedia of History and Culture*. Retrieved January 17, 2023.

and dugouts, first navigating the Holston River, then the Tennessee, into the Ohio, and finally up the Cumberland River to Nashville. During the four-month voyage, the hardy pioneers suffered Indian attacks, a smallpox outbreak, hunger, exhaustion, extreme cold, swift currents, and treacherous shoals.[71] Donelson's boat, the Adventure, carried several families along with household goods and necessary supplies for establishing a settlement in this rugged, new land. At the mouth of the Clinch River, another group of emigrants joined Donelson's party on their expedition. All told the flotilla included over 30 vessels packed to the tipping point.

Donelson kept an account of his historic journey and of the hardships they endured. On December 22 he made his first entry in his "Journal of a Voyage, intended by God's permission, in the good boat Adventure, from Fort Patrick Henry, on Holston river to the French Salt Springs on Cumberland River." On April 24, 1780, Donelson's party reached the end of their thousand mile journey and were finally reunited with family and friends at the Big Salt Lick (now Nashville). Within a week of Donelson's arrival, Henderson prepared the Cumberland Compact, of which Donelson was the fifth signer.

By the time Andrew Jackson arrived in Nashville, John Donelson was already dead and buried. He had died under mysterious circumstances, and not of natural causes. If anyone was certain about how he had been killed, they did not reveal the details, instead offering a vague story about an "Indian attack." Nonetheless, Donelson had established his family on a Cumberland farm they named Clover Bottom, for the broad meadow that emerged from the rich, black soil of the flood plain. Just as Donelson and his sons had planted their first corn crop, the river flooded again, destroying the crop and forcing the family to move to higher ground. Struggles with local tribes discouraged them from returning to Clover Bottom, leading the Donelsons to seek temporary refuge in Kentucky.

The family returned to the Cumberland region by 1785, where Donelson, his wife Rachel Stockley and their remaining children settled in a log cabin situated ten miles from Nashville. During the summer months, he worked the farm while taking on various jobs in the winter,

---

[71] Owens, Anne-Leslie, *John Donelson*, Tennessee Encyclopedia. Tennessee Historical Society. 2025.

including surveying land for speculators eager to profit from western lands. Tragically, it was during one of these surveying trips in the woods near the Barren River that he met his violent end. Given their active presence in the area, suspicion fell initially on local tribesmen. However, after an examination of the remains showed an intact scalp, white highwaymen were believed to be the culprits, particularly due to the fact that Donelson's wallet was stolen. Despite the efforts of the family, the perpetrators were never identified, and the case remained unsolved. [72]

A few years later, when Andrew Jackson arrived in Nashville, he found Mrs. Donelson a widow, and her children fatherless. The killing of John Donelson highlighted the precarious nature of the early Nashville settlement Jackson encountered. Native tribes posed a constant threat, incited to attack settlers if not by their own councils, then first by the British and later by the Spanish. The region had been contested among these forces for more than a century. This hostile environment, and the legacy of retributions and death so embedded in frontier life undoubtedly influenced Jackson upon his arrival, shaping the course of American history.

Following her husband's death, Rachel Stockley Donelson, compelled to seek alternative income, transformed her home into a boarding house, soon taking on a half dozen or so boarders. Shortly after the new solicitor's arrival in Nashville, Andrew Jackson became one of them. For a widow of the wild west, which the Tennessee frontier was certainly considered in those days, bringing in boarders brought income along with protection against the threat of Indian attack. Newcomers were arriving in the Cumberland daily, yet the white population still remained too small to guarantee safety and security. According to historical records, during the formative years of 1780 and 1794 within seven miles of Nashville, Indian attacks accounted for an average of one white settler killed every ten days.[73]

During those perilous early years along the Cumberland River, the threat of attack rose to such a level that settlers were often forced to escape to safety, sometimes fleeing the area entirely. On such occasions,

---

[72] Rust, Randal. "Donelson, John". Archived from the original on 2024-11-10. Tennessee Historical Society
[73] Reid and Eaton, *Jackson*, p. 19.

families like the Donelsons sought refuge as far north as Kentucky. Eventually, a unified effort was initiated to bring together frontier forces from both eastern and western Tennessee settlements to drive most of the indigenous tribes out of the area. However, even after this temporary relief, the danger still lingered, and the threat remained a constant worry. The settlers of western North Carolina decided it was time to meet to discuss their issues. They knew they needed a political voice and the consensus was that they suffered because North Carolina did not want the trouble or expense of protecting its western counties. Washington, Sullivan, Greene, Davidson, Sumner, and Tennessee Counties needed protection from Native American attacks as well as help building roads and forts. The national government formed under the Articles of Confederation was too weak to meet the westerners' demands. Westerners were also desperate for the right to navigate the Mississippi River, arguing that commerce in the west suffered immensely without trade access to this crucial waterway.

So it was in 1784, that the settlers of the region, only a year removed from the official recognition of the newly independent United States, were eager to break away from North Carolina, and form a state of their own. As early as 1781, under the hastily created Articles of Confederation, the Confederation Congress in Philadelphia had struggled to maintain unity among the often unruly thirteen states. In order to shore up their authority and create much needed revenue, Congress requested that any state in possession of unorganized western lands cede those lands to the control of the United States for the nation's benefit. In June 1784, the North Carolina government agreed to give up three of its western counties (Washington, Sullivan, and Greene Counties) to the Confederation Congress to help alleviate the significant debt incurred after the Revolutionary War. Upon learning of North Carolina's decision, the residents of these three counties jubilantly gathered in Jonesborough that August to establish their own independent legal state, separate from North Carolina, and the short-lived State of Franklin was born. [74]

However, before the Confederation Congress could act to accept North Carolina's cession decision, the state's newly elected legislature repealed it. The new North Carolina legislators did not like the idea of

---

[74] Williams, *History of the Lost State of Franklin*, p. 30

just giving away land to the federal government, thus they reversed the decision to relinquish control of the counties. Frustrated by conflicts with the state over land grants, and a general sense of their being underrepresented in the distant legislature, the settlers of "Franklin" remained determined to stay the course, and pursue their independence. They chose John Sevier, a hero from the Revolution's Battle of King's Mountain, as their leader. Revered as "Nolichucky Jack," for his exploits against the British, Tories, and their Native allies in the mountains, Sevier was elected as the governor of the unofficial state. In December 1784, they crafted their very own Declaration of Independence and proposed a draft of a state constitution.

In their Declaration, the delegates of the State of Franklin stated, "We unanimously agree that our lives, liberties, and Prosperity can be more secure & our happiness much better propagated by our separation, & consequently that it is our duty and unalienable right to form ourselves into a new Independent State." The provisional constitution from December 1784 was based on North Carolina's constitution. While it retained many of the original features, it lowered the land and wealth requirements for voters and office holders. But immediately, there were disagreements as to how to best operate their new proposed state. An alternative constitution, known as the Houston constitution (backed by Rev. Samuel Houston), proposed different rules. It referred to the state as "Frankland" rather than Franklin and barred ministers, lawyers, and doctors from holding state office, along with those deemed "immoral" or guilty of behaviors such as drunkenness, gambling, and swearing. In November 1785, a General Assembly convened to evaluate the two constitutions and decided to stick with the original version from December 1784.

With these divisions, the effort to establish the State of Franklin struggled to gain traction, and the Confederation Congress turned down Franklin's request to become the 14th state. There were many problems that had prevented Franklin's approval. First and foremost, the Federal government didn't have an actual plan in place of how to create a new state. Lacking this, the Confederation Congress decided it was best to simply give the lands back to North Carolina and would not let Franklin become a state.

Competition for power between the two Johns, leaders John Sevier and John Tipton, created conflicts as well, while residents faced ongoing disputes and fights with the Cherokee. In fact, the internal strains that had prevented Congress' recognition of Franklin soon worked to derail the movement entirely. By 1788, after a slew of quarreling and bickering, the residents of Franklin lost the drive that had originally fueled their effort toward independence, and ultimately decided to renew their allegiance to the "Old North State." Within a year of the movement's beginnings, North Carolina reclaimed control of the three counties. Thus, even though the State of Franklin went on for four years (1785-1788) in the minds of Franklin-ites, it never really became a state.

Although John Sevier faced heavy criticism for his role in what North Carolina labeled an unpatriotic insurrection, he had numerous supporters who rallied behind him, and this led to his election to the upper house of the North Carolina legislature. Despite being discredited among North Carolinians, Nolichucky Jack was allowed to take his seat in the state assembly in New Bern.[75]

As the fifty-five framers of the constitution hammered out the framework of government for the United States of America, the settlers of western North Carolina continued to try to find their footing. In 1788, North Carolina held its ratification convention in Hillsborough to decide whether the state would join in the new Union created under the federal banner. Delegates from Washington County included Colonel Tipton among other leaders of the western settlements, but, ultimately, they neither rejected nor ratified the new Constitution. Anti-Federalists had dominated proceedings in Hillsborough, with their main concern being the absence of a bill of rights in the new Constitution. For those of western North Carolina, then, especially the further western settlements along the Cumberland, the future was in limbo. Where did they stand? Who was to provide the governmental power necessary for the settlements to succeed? Some, in desperation, began to turn their eyes further to the southwest to consider a radical move: an alliance with the kingdom of Spain.

---

[75] DeWitt, John H., ed., "Journal of John Sevier," *Tennessee Historical Magazine* 5 (1919), 6 (1920).

Following the Hillsborough convention, federalists and anti-federalists continued their debate, with federalists advocating for the constitution and anti-federalists expressing concerns about the potential for a strong national government. The election of George Washington and the proposal of the Bill of Rights were significant factors in shifting public opinion in favor of ratification. In 1789, North Carolina chose to meet again to reconsider their stance on ratification, which now promised not only the guarantee of individual rights, but the leadership of the highly regarded Washington as president. Additionally, the state realized it had little choice, the union of the states had already begun under the federal system, as nine of the thirteen states had ratified it. It was either join or die by the autumn of 1789. This time the November convention was to be held in Fayetteville, North Carolina, and not to be outdone by his rival John Tipton, Sevier was chosen to represent the western settlements.

The Fayetteville Convention saw a decisive victory for the Federalists, reversing the previous year's vote, with the Constitution being ratified by a 194 to 77 vote. Following the ratification, North Carolina officially joined the United States, becoming the twelfth state to ratify. Sevier returned home to the applause of his many supporters in the western settlements. These supporters of Sevier would play a significant role in a later chapter of Andrew Jackson's life that would have much importance for the state of Tennessee and the country as a whole. [76]

---

[76] Cavanagh, John C. (2006). "Convention of 1789". *NCPedia*. Retrieved July 23, 2019.

CHAPTER

8

NEW ARRIVAL

"I was born for the storm."
-Andrew Jackson

In 1784, when Nashville, Jonesborough and other western settlements were still part of North Carolina, the Spanish government barred American traders from access to the lower Mississippi River, causing great consternation to political leaders and tradesmen on the frontier. At the request of the citizens of Nashville, four years later, the year Jackson would arrive in the region, the North Carolina legislature named the legal district for present-day Middle Tennessee the "Mero District."[77] As strange as this decision seems now, it was likely equally confusing to many at the time. But early Nashville-area citizens, including James Robertson himself, having failed in other attempts to gain favor with the Spanish governor of Louisiana, decided to try his hand at flattery. In an effort to convince the Spanish government to reopen the lower Mississippi, and especially the vital port city of New Orleans, to American trade, Robertson was willing to appeal to the vanity of the Spanish governor.

So vital to the interests of the region, access to New Orleans would mean lucrative trade profits, and would open up markets for the goods western settlers were desperate to ship. Currying favor through flattery might also, so Robertson hoped, convince the Spanish to cease what many believed the Spanish had been up to for years: inciting Indigenous attacks on America frontier settlements, and providing arms to tribes

---

[77] Carey, Bill. "Remembering the Mero District." *The Tennessee Magazine*. 2021

that were fighting settlers. Thus, in the heat of summer, 1788, the North Carolina legislature approved the measure, combining the settlements around the Cumberland River into one district, which they named Mero (an incorrect spelling of the Louisiana governor, Esteban Rodriguez Miró's, last name.)

Andrew Jackson now turned his eyes and aspirations westward toward this newly created Mero District, shifting his focus and ambitions to the hills of the Great Smoky Mountains and beyond. Having spent the past year wandering throughout the dusty backroads of North Carolina, with his entire immediate family dead and buried, and with no close relations to tie him down, the adventurous Jackson was enticed by the possibilities of the Tennessee wilderness. It was time to explore the potential of this fresh opportunity beyond the mountains. As he would later attest to an early biographer, the decision to make the move west was more experimental than anything. Although relatively successful thus far in his legal career in North Carolina, he was by no means wealthy enough in the state that he was risking his fortune by pulling up stakes. After all, curious, adventurous, young and ambitious, the ever-gregarious Andrew Jackson was not one to shy away from a new experience.

With the issues between North Carolina and its western counties seemingly resolved, the western district of Mero, was destined to receive a brash new group of lively law enforcement officers hailing from the Carolinas, including Jackson, John McNairy, Bennett Searcy, and others. Spruce McCay would have been proud. [78]

Nearing the Christmas season of 1787, however, McNairy had no thought of attempting to make the journey over the mountains immediately, not in the throes of what was already shaping up to be a frigidly cold winter. The rutty, windy dirt tracks across the Great Smoky Mountains, still relatively new and untrodden, were challenging enough in any season. The narrow ascents and descents over sheer rock faces, near vertical inclines up sharp edged bedrock, passes that bristled with obstacles, the fording of rushing rapids, and precarious descents into craggy ravines aside, not to mention the threat of the abundant wildlife of the region: mountain lions, wolves and bears in the sometimes impenetrable forests, he and Jackson were in no rush to move out. Even

---

[78] Owsley, Harriet C., Jackson Papers Project; Remini, 1977.

after crossing the mountain range, the travelers would still be far from Davidson County. Another 200 miles, and another mountain range, the Cumberlands, would still stand in their way. In those days, not even the heartiest of travelers would attempt to make such a journey in the dead of winter, even for an emergency. No, the group would wait until spring and spend their time gathering supplies and information about the new country beyond the hills.

In a general sense, they were already aware of what they would find once they arrived in Nashville. They had heard the stories told for many years: that the land in the mountains was poor for farming; steep, rocky, and infertile; but beyond the craggy soil of the highlands lay a lush haven, a terrestrial Eden, abundant and fertile, unclaimed and untouched by civilization. From a 1749 expedition for the Royal Land Company, Dr. Thomas Walker wrote a glowing report describing the abundance of life along the Cumberland River.[79] In his journal Walker writes of the "fertility of the soil, abundant game aplenty, turkey, deer, elk, buffalo. Abundant rivers, streams and springs teeming perch, Mullets, and Carp in plenty, and the large Sort of Cat Fish. Several thick forests of Beech Trees, large deposits of very good coal and Flint. The water is the most transparent I ever saw, and rapid enough to easily turn a mill …. with Natural springs that blow cool air." Early writers advertised the "Goodness of the Range," and "People flocking daily to it." [80]

Another of the early writers who provided more glowing descriptions of the area was Dick Henderson, the brother of Jackson's long-time Martinville friend Tom Henderson. Writing in 1775, when Jackson was just eight years old, and the Revolution was just commencing, Dick had been one of the first to organize an exploratory trip to the region. Although he died in 1785, he left a vivid account of the Cumberland. Another Henderson brother, Sam, who still lived in Guilford County, had accompanied Dick on his explorations. Jackson probably coaxed him for information on the area during his time in Martinville. According to his brother Tom, Sam had become a capable outdoorsman partially as a result of his Cumberland experience. He was known to revel in his stories of battles, sieges and skirmishes during the Henderson expedition

---

[79] Henderson, Archibald, *Dr. Thomas Walker, and the Loyal Company of Virginia*, p.77.
[80] Booraem, 2001, p.192.

and still loved to regale listeners with tales of his western adventures, including the "Indian manner of fighting." [81]

Jackson envisioned a bright future in the west, but would need money for the journey. So the young attorney spent the winter months working as many cases as he could take on. The remainder of his time that winter was spent caring for his horses, cleaning his rifle and pistols, and hoping for some good luck with his card playing. After the Christmas holiday, he got down to business even further, trying cases at a rapid rate, traveling from one log inn to another, from one rustic courthouse to the next, through the frost, the winds, and the rains of winter. Lugging around his satchel full of legal documents and his copy of *Bacon*, (his go-to legal reference wrapped neatly in calfskin,) enduring the tavern fare and bantering with landlords and horse traders along the way, he would draw up a writ or a deed on the stiff paper he hauled with him for the right price.

There are no surviving court records that prove Jackson's presence in the counties of North Carolina in January of 1788, but there is court documentation of him trying a case in the city of Rockingham in Richmond County in February. This was evidently his first recorded case, and he defended partners Terrant and McClain against a suit by one Peter O'Neal for trespassing. It was a dubious start if it truly was Jackson's first case, for he and his clients would end up on the losing side, outmaneuvered by the prosecuting attorney Nathaniel Williams. According to the trial docket in Rockingham County, Jackson's clients were sentenced to a fine of twenty-nine pounds.

A few weeks later, before leaving for the west, Jackson passed through Richmond County once more, drawing up a promissory note for two local landowners, Edwin Hickman and David Poindexter. According to Jackson himself, who told the story years later, he stopped by Jesse Lester's tavern in Richmond County. He owed Lester some money, and handing him a promissory note, pledged to make good on his debt. Interestingly, according to local tradition, some twenty-seven years later, in 1815, Lester was reported to have taken out the faded promissory

---

[81] Miller, 1988.

note, crossed out Jackson's debt and wrote "Paid in full by the Battle of New Orleans." [82]

By early March 1788, Jackson, alongside McNairy and Bennett Searcy, (a relation of Jackson's friend Tom Searcy from Martinville, who was to become the clerk of the court,) were finally set to embark on their journey, ultimately headed for the newly established town of Nashville, nestled alongside the wide, majestic Cumberland River. Their expedition commenced in Morganton, North Carolina, where they joined a group that included the family of General William Lee Davidson, embarking on an overmountain trek fraught with the perils of the Indian frontier. They set off westward, traveling along the 'Wilderness Trace' through the mountains. Each man, mounted on a horse, carried a small assortment of personal items, "a firearm, and a wallet filled with letters from notable citizens of the old community meant for the settlers of the brand new."[83] Their first stop was to be Jonesborough, the main town of the western settlements (later east Tennessee,) after which they planned to continue on to the Cumberland.

The group traveled in two lines through a region that fortunately was, by this time, mostly free of hostile tribes, as had not been the case in earlier years. Once the realm of the warlike Cherokee and other indigenous nations, through the efforts of "Nolichucky Jack," and his Watauga Association, the region had grown more peaceful, making it a more benign crossing for travelers. Their record of this journey does not show evidence of peril, and the group would arrive unscathed in Jonesborough. Although the exact date is not known as to when Jackson first laid eyes on the town, court records show he received his law license for Washington County on May 12, 1788.

It quickly became clear to the new arrivals that they wouldn't be able to carry on to Nashville to make it in time for the court session, which was to start in just a few days. As a result, they decided to remain in Jonesborough until the fall. Unbeknownst to Jackson at the time, this chance delay in what is today known as "Tennessee's Oldest Town," would nearly cost the 21-year-old his life.

---

[82] Bassett, John Spencer. The Life of Andrew Jackson. Garden City, N.Y., Doubleday, Page & Company, 1911, p.112

[83] Booraem, Hendrik, 2001, p. 195

ANDREW JACKSON: THE POLITICS OF RESENTMENT

When Andrew Jackson, John McNairy and the rest of the new legal team arrived in Jonesborough, they found a "rough hewn village" numbering around 60 cabins. The settlement was nearing just its ninth anniversary but could already take pride in its brand-new courthouse in the center of the settlement, where one could still smell the freshly cut cedar. Legend has it that when Jackson first rode into the town, he trailed behind him a second horse, and a pack of hound dogs.[84] It was as if Jackson were determined to make a grand entrance amid his new surroundings.

Situated nearly two hundred miles east of Nashville, the wide expanse of land between the two settlements was largely inhabited by hostile native tribes, infamous for vicious attacks on whites they considered trespassers. If Jackson and his party had wished to push on to Nashville immediately, they would need to hire a force of several dozen armed men for protection. This seemed to settle the question, the newly arrived group would stay in Jonesborough for the time being and maybe generate some income while they were at it.

Having to find lodgings as a result, Jackson found temporary residence in the Christopher Taylor House not far from the Jonesborough Courthouse. He then began to familiarize himself with the local citizenry. Realizing the opportunity to invent his image anew in his new environment, Jackson seemed determined to instill the belief that he was indeed truly a gentleman. In southern society in those days, gentlemen had servants, and true to form, within days Jackson acquired one of his own, a female slave named Nancy.[85] It is not known whether he purposefully sought out a female slave, or if the eighteen-year-old Nancy was simply purchased as a result of availability. There are also contradictory accounts of whether Jackson paid for the girl himself or if she was considered payment for legal services rendered.[86]

At any rate, this marked Jackson's first step toward the trappings of a Southern gentleman, and his foray into the realm of slave ownership. Having already brokered slave deals, and engaged in slave trafficking, Jackson was now stepping up his activity in the peculiar institution.

---

[84] Allison, John. *Dropped Stitches in Tennessee History*. Nashville, 1897. Pg. 10
[85] Remini, 1977. p. 37
[86] Haywood, John. *The Civil and Political History of the State of Tennessee*. Nashville. 1915. Pg.194

Though, as was evidenced by his later plantation life at the Hermitage, and ever-increasing connection with human bondage, this was but a small step. For young Nancy, however, it was anything but a small step, and one wonders as to the type of relationship Jackson built with the teenaged Nancy, as well as whether he considered the moral implications of his ownership of a slave of his own.

Like most Southerners of the period, given the limited economic opportunity of the region, plantation agriculture was the main aspiration for Andrew Jackson. The planter aristocracy of the South had not yet reached the heights of wealth it would attain during the antebellum period, but in 1788, planters with a large amount of slaves were already some of the wealthiest in the nation. Slaveholding was not only an accepted form of meeting one's labor needs, but was considered by many Southerners, even at that early date, to be the preferred, most efficient option. Soon, Southern planters would argue that the peculiar institution of slavery was not a necessary evil, but a necessary good.

Included within this vein, like most other well to do southern men of the time, Jackson would often frequent the racetrack, not only to spectate, but to participate as well. Horses were not only a Jackson passion since his courier days during the war, but also another layer of the life of a gentleman he emulated. He would soon increase his efforts to breed horses and acquire thoroughbreds of the finest quality. Though Kentucky would later become the premiere state renowned for its horseracing, and its famous Kentucky Derby, at the time Tennessee was the ideal region when it came to racing, breeding, and "gambling on the ponies" at the track.

Unfortunately for Andrew Jackson, another aspect of the gentleman lifestyle he would subscribe to was the infamous 'Code Duello.' The set of rules for dueling was in its heyday by the late 1780s.[87] It was created, among other reasons, as a way to help prevent vendettas between social factions and families. A chivalric gentleman was expected to be honorable and therefore must always be prepared to defend his honor, to the death if need be. The year 1788 would mark the first of many duels that Jackson would fight to defend his own sense of honor, and

---

[87] Wyatt-Brown, Bertram. 1982. *Southern honor: ethics and behavior in the Old South*. New York: Oxford University Press. Pages 167 and 350–351.

ironically, his first antagonist happened to be someone that Jackson had met previously: none other than Waightstill Avery, the same Morganton lawyer from whom Jackson had first requested legal training; that same Morganton lawyer who had turned young Jackson away at his door.

Avery, like McCay, Stokes and others, made frequent court visits to Jonesborough as part of the legal circuit. By 1782, with the incorporation of the town's first court, he had been made the attorney for the state. Having obtained a license to practice law in Jonesborough, Jackson now had a source of income to preoccupy himself with before resuming his trek to Nashville. Soon after his arrival, working out of his room at the Taylor house, located about two miles west of town, Jackson soon began defending clients in the new Washington County courthouse. While trying one of these cases, Jackson came up against Avery as a legal opponent. Going up against the far more seasoned Waightstill Avery was not an easy task, and, as expected, the case was not going in Jackson's favor by any stretch. Before long things got heated, though it is not known exactly what was said to set off the tryst. According to most accounts, Avery made a sarcastic remark at one point to mockingly counter one of Jackson's arguments. It must have been vexing for the state's most respected attorneys to be challenged by the young upstart Jackson, an inexperienced twenty-year-old he had rejected as a student just a few years before. As Jackson fumbled through his weak argument, Avery responded with a quip that mocked Jackson's previous point, generating snickers from those in attendance in the courtroom.[88]

Considering the history between Avery and his younger, once-rejected opponent, any form of mockery coming from his more experienced opponent was too much for the nervy Jackson, who ignited with an outburst of anger. Infuriated, Jackson reportedly scribbled some lines on a note that he tore out of his lawbook and hurled at Avery. It was not revealed as to exactly what the message was, but clearly it was not to thank him for his fine lessons in legality.

Although the two left the courthouse without incident upon adjournment (Avery won the case,) Jackson, seething over the insult and the public humiliation that accompanied it, spent most of that night brooding over how best to redress this grievance. Weighing the

---

[88] Remini, 1977. pp. 38-39

issue into the wee hours as to whether the insult was worth risking his life over, whatever his thought process was, by morning, Jackson had made up his mind that he would demand satisfaction. He may have considered his prowess with a gun, and liked his odds, or perhaps, in keeping with the cultivation of his gentlemanly image, he determined that the circumstances required him to issue the formal challenge. To be a gentleman, one must behave like a gentleman, and this did not include allowing one's honor to be tarnished without reproach; this was not acceptable under the Code Duello.

Most likely what sealed the decision for the newcomer in this frontier environment was that the insult had been public, and in court, and therefore he had no choice but to salvage his reputation as a lawyer and as a man and settle the issue publicly. The following day, Waightstill Avery received this letter, misspellings and all:

Aug. 12, 1788

Sir: When a man's feelings and charector are injured he ought to seek a speedy redress. You rec'd. a few lines from me yesterday and undoubtedly you understand me. My charector you have injured; and further you have Insulted me in the presence of a court and larg audianc. I therefore call upon you as a gentleman to give me satisfaction for the Same; and I further call upon you to give Me an answer immediately without Equivocation and I hope you can do without dinner until the business done; for it is consistent with the charector of a gentleman when he Injures a man to make a spedy reparation; therefore I hope you will not fail in meeting me this day, from yr obt st.

Andw. Jackson
PS: this Evening after court adjourned [89]

Waightstill Avery was a formidable opponent in the oak paneled courtrooms of the Piedmont, but he was no duelist. A 47-year-old family man at the time of Jackson's challenge, first in his class at Princeton,

---

[89] Putnam, A. W. *History of Middle Tennessee.* Nashville. 1895. Pgs. 69-79.

class of '66, with a record of service in the State Congress and a hand in crafting the famous Mecklenburg Resolves against British oppression, Avery was not about to get himself killed over some crazy young upstart's notion of honor. Yet, such was the culture on the frontier. One could not allow a formal challenge to go unaddressed and still hope to save face in the community. Reticent but willing, Avery agreed to meet his young adversary just after dark in a hollow north of town.

Both men and their seconds arrived at the agreed upon time, set the distance, and took their positions, the signal was given and both men fired–into the air. Neither had any intention of getting hurt. Perhaps each man's seconds had already worked out some form of satisfactory solution that had previously settled the matter. Whatever the case, Jackson, his honor restored, reportedly strode up to Avery after the shots, shook his hand, stated that there was nothing more to settle, then turned and walked away into the steamy summer night. The two would later become lasting friends.

Such was the story of Jackson's first duel, destined not to be his last. The nature of the encounter seems out of sorts with the reputation that would be described by so many writers and historians in later years. Yet, it was representative of the personality and character of the man Jackson was. Sensitive about his honor, and the perception of others, Jackson was temperamental, even at times impulsive, but never entirely rudderless or unreasonable. While the 21-year-old prioritized his reputation as a gentleman, he understood the need to balance that concern with a sense of duty, recognition and acceptance. When the sensible solution offered itself, Jackson readily accepted, playing his part for the sake of appearances, but happy to move on without bloodshed. This may not have been the case later on, but at the outset of a new and promising career on a burgeoning frontier, Jackson showed that he could embrace caution and compromise when it served his purposes. Perhaps he held a hidden admiration for the elder, more accomplished Avery, and simply wished to gain the man's respect. As would be evidenced later in his life, Jackson certainly had the capacity for killing, but the motives behind it would need to be of more gravity than this trivial matter with Waightstill Avery. In the end, Jackson felt that his actions had been justified, and that he had proven himself an honorable man.

There were many in Jonesborough who viewed the young newcomer with a growing admiration. It is certain that, by all accounts, Jackson was making a name for himself in the town. Having gone toe-to-toe with a wealthy and influential public figure such as Avery, albeit over a trifling matter hardly worth mentioning, he was young, assertive, and gaining the attention of the town. His actions do beg the question, however, did the risk involved in this flirtation with danger and possible death at the hands of Waightstill Avery ever occur to Jackson? Had the notion of his own mortality entered his mind in those early years of his career? Was he at all concerned about his reputation as a hot head? If the answer to any of these questions was yes, it did not seem to matter to Jackson, or to anyone else on the frontier in 1788, for Jackson's star was on the rise, and for the young solicitor, there was no looking back.

CHAPTER

9

O, CUMBERLAND RIVER

"Forget the former things; do not dwell on the past. See, I am doing a new thing! Now it springs up; do you perceive it? I will make a way in the wilderness and streams in the wasteland."

-Isaiah 43:18-19

Two months later, having survived his first duel, and having gotten his feet wet in the frontier legal trade, Andrew Jackson now packed up his belongings, and moved on to his true destination. Jackson, along with his slave Nancy, John McNairy, Bennett Searcy and a number of other settlers would finally be granted the protective escort required to cross the hostile 200 miles to Nashville. Leaving Jonesborough in late October, they entered into the most dangerous stretch of the Tennessee frontier. They took the Fort Blount Road, which crossed the Cumberland River. Not long into the journey, Jackson would prove his mettle, providing a glimpse of the general and Indian fighter he would become in future years. [90]

According to the story, it was nighttime, amidst the dark woods of the Tennessee frontier. Most of the camp was sound asleep, with the exception of those put on duty as lookouts. Jackson may have been one of them, or perhaps he simply felt it necessary to stay awake and keep an eye out. In any event, as the account goes, Jackson was sitting on the ground, back against a tree, smoking his corncob pipe, when he began

[90] Parton, James. *Life of Andrew Jackson*, I, Kessinger Publishing. 2006. pp.122-124

to doze off some time around 10 o'clock, hardly aware of the hooting of owls nearby. Yet, at some point he did notice the sound, and something about it struck him as off somehow. He didn't remember having seen owls in that part of the country to that point. Then he heard another hoot, only louder, and this time he grabbed his rifle in alarm. Bolting to his feet, he crept cautiously to where his friends were sleeping.

"Searcy," Jackson whispered with urgency, "raise your head and don't make a sound."

His friend, awakening, replied groggily, "what's the matter?"

"The owls, there–there again, isn't that a little *too* natural?"

"Do you think so?" asked Searcy.

"I know it," Jackson replied. "There are Indians all around us. I've heard them in every direction. They mean to attack us before daybreak."

The other members of the group were quickly stirred out of their slumber and hustled to quickly gather up their gear as quietly as they could. Jackson urged that they break camp immediately, and the group flowed swiftly into action. Fortunately for the party, no attack came. Plunging deeper into the woods, they escaped without harm, and were safely on their way before long, seeing no more signs of danger. Incidentally it was reported to them later, a party of hunters who, just hours thereafter, camped in this same location had been murdered by native members of the Creek nation. These were likely the very same tribesmen who had attempted to surprise the sleeping Jackson party. Only one of the hunters managed to escape.

The first in a series of incidents in which Jackson displayed his unflappable penchant for cool-headed command on the frontier, his emergence as a leader in the intensity of battle was being meticulously forged. However inflated the story may have become over time, by all accounts, despite those in the company whose job it was to protect and guide the travelers through this harrowing stretch of country, it was Jackson who rescued the party from their brush with disaster. Was this legendary tale folklore, or propaganda later fabricated by the Jacksonians who wished to see their hero king? Not by the various accounts of those present on the journey through the mountains. The young attorney's reputation for bravery was growing, and Jackson was realizing another facet of his character: He had a penchant for combat.

The remainder of the journey remained uneventful, and Jackson and his companions arrived in Nashville on October 26th, 1788. Nearing the crude outpost settled only a decade or so before, the newcomers laid eyes on the lush, unmilled landscape that was to be their new home, enriched by the flowing waters of the Cumberland River. The possession of this valley of the Cumberland, so abundant in livestock, so fruitful in flora and hardwoods, had been fought over for generations by the Native Americans of the region. Appearing to have exhausted themselves in the competition, the tribes had to feel dismay at the end results, as white men ultimately snatched the land right out from under them, as if to settle the dispute. [91]

When Jackson, McNairy, Searcy and the others arrived on the cedar bluff overlooking Nashville in the fall of 1788, the town contained a population of only a few hundred. In this rugged frontier, where the threat of attack from Native tribes was still very real, settlement unfurled in an even harsher form than what Jackson had known in his years in the Waxhaws. The town boasted a rough wooden courthouse, knobby cabins crafted from coarse, unhewn logs, tents, and a few other unadorned, unmilled and unrefined shelters, huddled around the old, logged fortress of Fort Nashborough. In fact, the refineries that marked the splendor of home interiors in older communities back east were wholly lacking in this new country. "Settlers slept on skins heaped on the floor, and the floor itself might be only rough planks laid on the earth, with snakes sometimes gliding up through the cracks."[92] A few more years would pass before settlers would feel safe enough to spread out further away from their neighbors and begin to build in more isolated outskirts of the settlement. For now, anyone who knew what was good for them, remained in close quarters with the community.

The pioneers who built Nashville and the surrounding area of the soon to be "Volunteer State" were defined by their remarkable resilience and complex nature. Primarily of English and Scotch-Irish descent, these settlers embodied a unique blend of strength, determination, and raw survival skills. As a must, the individuals who dared to take on the challenge of carving out a life on the Tennessee frontier possessed

---

[91] Parton, p.22
[92] Abernethy, T.P, *From Frontier to Plantation in Tennessee, A Study in Frontier Democracy*, Univ. of NC Press, 1932.

exceptional adaptability to the challenges of the wilderness. A prerequisite for any late 18th century pioneer was to have a remarkable instinct for survival, along with an abundant capacity for confronting the unknown, as well as a deep commitment to personal and community survival. While the limitations of Jackson's neighbors were many, their virtues included courage, self-reliance, energy, inventiveness, generosity, honesty and the art of being direct. Andrew Jackson had found his home.

Yet, Jackson must have quickly taken note of the contrast between his new frontier home, and the more settled villages of the North Carolina Piedmont. Goods for settlers were brought to the Cumberland from distant lands, carried hundreds of miles over rutty roads, from as far away as the bustling cities of the east, particularly the industrious city of Philadelphia. Long awaited and growing dearer by the time shipment of goods arrived, delivery was costly, and often risky. As for essentials— food, clothing, and shelter— each family relied on its own handicraft. The population contained a predominance of men, as was the way of the frontier. Yet for the steadfast women who took on the challenge of starting a new life in the west, the common work and hardships of early settlement forged some of the most versatile, capable and heartiest women in the country.

Bearing the weight of life in the wilderness, the challenge of ceaseless labor and the burden of toil to scratch out an existence in an unsettled country right alongside the menfolk, these women of the west were true pioneers in the re-imagining of what it meant to be an American woman. With the need for all hands-on deck in the rough shorn wilderness beyond the mountains, frontier women busted down long entrenched gender barriers. Jackson would soon develop an interest in one tough Tennessee woman that would have long lasting ramifications for the rest of his life.

As Jackson settled into Nashville, and into his respectable position as Solicitor of the district, both his reputation and that of Nashville would flourish. His rise to prominence benefited greatly from his acquaintance with the Donelson family, and particularly his encounter with the widow Donelson's youngest daughter, the vivacious Rachel Donelson.

A contemporary would describe Rachel Donelson as "possessing a beautiful, molded form, with lustrous, black eyes, dark glossy hair, full red lips, and a sweet oval face, rippling with smiles and dimples."

Her beauty attracted many admirers, including her husband, Lewis Robards. Full of energy and only thirteen when the family made its tumultuous journey to Nashville, Rachel was widely considered the most beautiful of the Donelson sisters. In her book *Dames and Daughters of the Young Republic*, biographer Geraldine Brooks describes Rachel as a "true pioneer woman, typical of those found in the early frontier towns of America, known for being a lively, vibrant, spirited and adventurous young woman, an accomplished equestrian, and a delightful companion." This portrayal echoes that of Jackson's biographer, James Parton, who described Rachel as "the best storyteller, the finest dancer, the liveliest friend, and the most daring horsewoman in the western region."[93]

The alluring Rachel met Lewis Robards, nine years her senior, during the Donelsons' stay in Kentucky. Their courtship blossomed quickly, and soon the two married on March 1st, 1785, shortly after Rachel's seventeenth birthday. The wedding took place at Harrodsburg in Mercer County, and was considered an advantageous pairing for both prominent frontier families. When John and the elder Rachel and their other children returned to the Cumberland, Rachel remained with her husband, unaware that she was bidding farewell to her father for the last time.

In the years after John Donelson's death, his children would begin to disperse, but his youngest daughter would return to the nest. Initially, the young couple's relationship went smoothly in the home of Robards' widowed mother, who grew close to her daughter-in-law. However, one account describes Robards as "a rather suspicious-minded and jealous individual, who constantly quarreled with his wife and accused her of all manner of improprieties, some of which he himself was guilty of." Another alleges that Robards "frequented the slave quarters at night"—and as a recent *Smithsonian* article points out, these sexual encounters were with enslaved women "almost certainly without their consent."[94]

Robards was prone to drinking, perhaps scarred from his time fighting as a Captain in the Revolution, which certainly didn't improve the discord of the marriage. From its inception, the marriage was

---

[93] Parton, p.23; Brooks, Geraldine, *Dames and Daughters of the Young Republic*. Kessinger Publishing, 2007.
[94] Boissoneault, Lorraine "Rachel Jackson, the Scandalous Divorcee Who Almost Became First Lady," *Smithsonian Magazine*, June 2017.

ill-fated, as Rachel was a captivating and vivacious young woman—precisely the kind to incite a jealous husband's fury merely by existing as she did. As historian James Parton puts it, in his seminal book, *Life of Andrew Jackson*, she was a "rattle; a high spirited, insouciant, frivolous charmer." [95]

Tensions arose further when the widow Robards took in a boarder named Peyton Short. Short found Rachel appealing, and she enjoyed his attention. It is unknown as to whether Rachel and Short had an affair, but the fracture in the marriage came to a head one evening when Robards caught the two conversing in a way that he felt went beyond standard civility. Taking Rachel's politeness towards Short as excessive, Robards flew into a jealous rage, accusing her of infidelity and Short of "cuckolding" him. Although their interactions may have been mere flirtations, Robards would not be swayed. Despite Rachel's protests of innocence, and pleas from his mother to calm down, Robards would banish his wife from his mother's home. Writing to Rachel's mother in the Cumberland, Robards declared that he could "no longer be under the same roof" as Rachel. Responding to demands that Mrs. Donelson reclaim her daughter, Rachel's brother Samuel was soon dispatched north to fetch his sister, and back home she went.

With her marriage on the rocks, Rachel was back in the Cumberland region once again, returning to Nashville around the same time Andrew Jackson arrived in town. The new solicitor needed accommodation, and upon inquiry, discovered that Mrs. Donelson welcomed a lodger, especially one serving as the Solicitor of the district. She could use the money, and the added protection of an officer of the court was an added bonus. The widow Donelson lived in a blockhouse slightly more spacious than most of the other Cumberland homes. Built more for defensive purposes than comfort, the blockhouse design offered multiple stories along with a separate cabin, and thus, ample room for boarders.

Jackson settled into the small cabin just a short distance from the main house on the Donelson property. Soon after, he would acquire a roommate, John Overton, with whom he would share space in the cabin. Like Jackson, Overton was a lawyer who would later achieve prominence at the Tennessee bar. He had previously been a boarder at the widow

---

[95] Parton, p.24

Robards' house along with Rachel and Lewis Robards. Overton had been on hand to witness the deterioration of the Robards' marriage, Rachel's return to her mother's home, and Robards' subsequent loneliness and regret. He would attest later on that Robards, though of a good family, and undoubtedly in love with his wife, was plagued by an excessively jealous disposition. The widow Robards, distressed by the loss of her daughter-in-law and believing her son had made a mistake, enlisted Overton's help. "The old lady told me he regretted what had taken place and that he wished to be reconciled to his wife," he recounted.[96]

Overton insisted on speaking directly with Robards, who confirmed his remorse and desire to reunite with Rachel, asking him to help restore their relationship. "He requested that I would use my exertions to restore harmony," Overton would attest. He then traveled to Nashville, arriving at the Donelson residence, in the spring of 1789, just weeks after Jackson had moved in. His intervention proved effective. Rachel was nearly as disheartened by the separation as Robards, and wished to give the marriage a second try, paving the way for a potential reconciliation. She may have still loved him, and just as likely, was discouraged by the prospect of a dismal future as an abandoned wife.

Divorce was a tricky proposition in America in the 1780s. To obtain one, a special act of the legislature had to be passed, which required patience, influence and connections. Additionally, the Robards' wedding, having taken place in Kentucky (still a part of Virginia at the time,) would require traveling across the many miles to Richmond, Virginia, crossing mountainous terrain, or else hiring someone on their behalf to make the journey. Likely, the process would take years to complete and would cost more money than Rachel could easily afford. As later events would show, Rachel was unaware of the many obstacles she faced in obtaining a divorce, but she knew the process would not be easy, especially if Robards challenged it. So, when Overton brought the news that her husband wanted to reconcile, she consented.

Robards traveled from Kentucky and arrived in the Cumberland to join his wife. He owned a tract of land on the south bank of the river, several miles from the Donelson home. He and Rachel, he envisioned, would build a home and a family on his property. In the meantime, he

---

[96] Brands, HW, *The Life and Times of Andrew Jackson*. Doubleday Publishing, 2005, Ch.5.

lived with his wife in the widow Donelson's house. He and Andrew Jackson came to know each other during this period, as the Robards, Overton and Jackson all took their meals together at Mrs. Donelson's table. Within a few months, Robards' suspicious ways returned to the surface. "Rachel's spouse harbored often irrational suspicions regarding her flirtatious demeanor and began to conjure various sordid notions about her character." Overton would later attest. Soon, Robards' jealousy would be aimed directly at Andrew Jackson, Overton recalled. He believed his envy was in part an aspect of Robards' paranoia, and "fevered" mind.[97]

John Overton would comment on these observations over forty years later, after a close and enduring friendship with Andrew Jackson. What with Overton's reminiscences on the subject of the Robards and Jackson having been recorded so many years later, along with Overton's devotion to Jackson, his comments can certainly be taken with a grain of salt. Overton's views on the subject were probably not a little unbiased, knowing Jackson's character as well as he did, starting with their time sharing the Donelson cabin together in 1789. As young lawyers roughly the same age, (Overton was just a year older), he and Jackson got along well, and with their hectic schedules on the law circuit, there were few others in the county with whom they associated quite so closely. As Overton put it, "besides sharing, as we frequently did, common dangers, such an intimacy ensued as might reasonably be expected."

Early on in the future Jacksons' acquaintance with Rachel's proprietorial husband, if Jackson was aware of Robards' jealousy, he did not let on. But after a time, there would be no mistaking it. He had made an immediate impression with the Donelson family, along with most of their Nashville neighbors. Mrs. Donelson, as one of the original matriarchs of the Cumberland, was a woman of property, noted for keeping an exceptionally clean house. Jackson had chosen to lodge with the Donelsons in large part for this very reason, and Mrs. Donelson was happy to have the young newcomer, with his impressive countenance and employment. Jackson's presence provided a sense of security for the widow and her daughter, and he possessed just the fun-loving temperament that would have attracted Rachel to him.

---

[97] Brands, HW, *The Life and Times of Andrew Jackson*. Doubleday Publishing. 2005. Ch.5.

Without a doubt, Jackson would have done whatever he could to charm, amuse and ingratiate himself to both mother and daughter. As David Remini points out, "So here was Rachel, a lively, delightful, fun-loving young woman, who liked to dance and ride horses, and tell amusing stories to an appreciative audience, married to an agitated, suspicious, anti-social husband, and here was Jackson, of charm, social standing, and a commanding presence, who could match Rachel's gaiety and bounce, and then spice it with a little wildness of his own--certainly all the ingredients for an explosive domestic quarrel."

Torn asunder by accusations and fierce disputes, the Robards' union was in trouble. Before long, the powder keg erupted, as expected. Time and again, Robards accused Rachel of seeking out conversations with Jackson, and inevitably heated arguments between husband and wife followed. Sometimes the widow Donelson tried to intervene, to no avail. No matter how many denials Rachel would offer, Robards would refuse to believe her. There are contradictory accounts of the level of complicity owed to Jackson in this controversy. On the one hand, he is portrayed as an innocent victim, merely caught up in the tide of circumstance, while on the other, he appears to have goaded Robards intentionally, throwing fuel onto the fire by flirting outwardly with his wife.

One story that stands out in the rising tide of hostilities took place during an afternoon stroll near the Nashville stockade. Robards, conversing with one of the stockade guards, commented on Jackson's "over-friendliness" with his wife. The guard happened to be a friend of Jackson's and soon relayed the comment to him. Jackson was incensed, and threatened Robards, saying he would "cut his ears out of his head." Alarmed and intimidated, Robards reported Jackson's threat to the nearest magistrate. Jackson was soon arrested as a result. Being led to the blockhouse jail, with Robards trailing behind, Jackson somehow convinced his guard to allow him to hold his butcher knife. Swearing to do no harm, the guard (foolishly) allowed Jackson to hold it while he was led along. Jackson fingered the blade, menacingly glaring at Robards as he did so. Unnerved, Robards took off scared, running into the woods. An account from one observer of the parody reported that Jackson got away from the guard and chased after Robards, both disappearing into the brush. Returning a few moments later, Jackson continued on to the magistrate, as if nothing at all had transpired. Robards was nowhere to be found. Upon arriving in front of the judge, since Robards could not be located, the warrant was dismissed.

Another account paints Jackson in a much more innocent light. Once the situation at the Donelson home became more and more intolerable, John Overton suggested that he and Jackson find different living arrangements. Jackson agreed but first wanted to confront Robards directly. Not wishing to leave with his honor in question, Jackson spoke face to face with the disgruntled husband. Never known for his tact, whatever Jackson said to Robards only worsened the situation. The confrontation occurred near the Donelson's orchard fence and started peacefully enough. In a calm voice, Jackson accused Robards of treating Rachel unfairly. As he went on, Robards became increasingly angry, until his ire reached the point of outrage.[98]

Threatening to whip Jackson right there on the spot, Robards' face grew crimson in color. Jackson replied that he "did not have the bodily strength to fight Robards, nor did he want to if he could, because he was innocent of the charges." Adding that he would give Robards "gentlemanly satisfaction" if he insisted on fighting him, Jackson stood his ground. Robards became outraged, but with Jackson uncowed, he did not strike. Instead, he cursed Jackson and Rachel for making him so miserable and swore that he would never live with her again. [99]

A third account seems to be the most likely. According to H.W. Brands in his 2005 biography, *The Life and Times of Andrew Jackson*, "When Jackson was mildly angry, it typically showed in his face and voice, but when something really provoked him, his manner calmed. It did so now."[100] Jackson quietly challenged Robards to a duel, but Robards refused. Damning the two of them, he vowed to have no more to do with either Rachel or Jackson. Soon thereafter, he returned to Kentucky, leaving his wife with her mother.

---

[98] Robert V. Remini, *Andrew Jackson, Volume One, The Course of the American Empire, 1767-1821* (Baltimore: Johns Hopkins University Press, 1998) p. 57.; James Parton, *The Life of Andrew Jackson, Volume III* (New York: Mason Brothers, 1861) p. 148.

[99] Robert V. Remini, *Andrew Jackson, Volume One, The Course of the American Empire, 1767-1821* (Baltimore: Johns Hopkins University Press, 1998) p. 57.

[100] Brands, HW, The Life and Times of Andrew Jackson. Doubleday Publishing. 2005. Ch.5.

As promised to Overton, Jackson did leave the Donelson home and found room and board at Kasper Mansker's Station. But that would certainly not be the end of the story for he and Rachel Donelson Robards. With Robards having fled the scene, Rachel was now available, and Solicitor Jackson, for his part, was smitten with the lovely Rachel. However, there was one problem, Robards was not ready to terminate the marriage, at least not yet.

CHAPTER

10

INTRODUCING THE ATTORNEY GENERAL

"Without Contraries is no progression. Attraction and Repulsion, Reason and Energy, Love and Hate, are necessary to Human existence."

-William Blake

The red-haired, blue-eyed, and rangy Andrew Jackson had made quite an entrance in Nashville. With a lean frame, standing an inch over six feet, the imposing Jackson cut quite a figure on the frontier. With his personal life suddenly smoothed out by the departure of his nemesis, Lewis Robards, Jackson could now focus not only on his passion for Rachel, but on his promising professional life. In this area, Jackson's rise was quite meteoric. His connection to Judge McNairy continued to pay dividends for the young solicitor. Already licensed to practice law in Nashville, McNairy named Jackson the public prosecutor for the entire Mero District. This included Davidson (of which Nashville was the county seat,) Sumner and Tennessee County. While Jackson served without pay, as the law did not yet include a provision for district attorney, the legislature would retroactively reimburse him for his time on the post periodically. On Dec. 21st, 1789, Jackson was officially elected Attorney General of the district of Mero by the state.

As historian Margaret Coit states, "Law and order were unknown quantities in Nashville in 1789, and the demanding and risky job of maintaining order and enforcing the law primarily fell to the local solicitor." It's no surprise that few people eagerly sought the position that Andrew Jackson now filled. On the frontier of the late 1780s, a job such as Jackson's required a commitment that extended to all hours of the day, any given day. Many residents of the Cumberland had left the east suddenly and for good reason, killing was looked upon as murder only if the victim had not had a chance to defend themselves. The one lawyer in town before Jackson arrived had "been engaged by every debtor in the community, and won his cases without opposition. Hence, any man or organization to whom money was owed was on the verge of bankruptcy." [101]

The stubborn resilience and steadfast determination that characterized Andrew Jackson's early life remained a constant theme in his early career in the frontier territories. If there had been any question as to whether the raw, untested Jackson would prove a capable choice as Solicitor in this rugged new environment, he quickly put those doubts to rest. Jackson's professional reputation grew rapidly, and for good reason. Whether dealing with legal disputes involving Native Americans or challenging settlers who attempted to circumvent the law, he maintained an unwavering commitment to his duties. Governor Blount recognized his effectiveness, declaring that Jackson would "certainly ensure that legal offenders were brought to justice."

To the propertied class of the district, Jackson's appointment could not have come at a better time. For the creditors hoping for justice on monies owed, reliance on Jackson would be ample. Prior to the new prosecutor's arrival, debtors had long refused to pay legally obligated fees and had worked together to circumvent the law. A successful effort had been made by this banded group to bribe Jackson's predecessor, hence, his unblemished record of victory in debtors' court, as previously noted. To exacerbate an already broken system, the incompetence of the Davidson County sheriff was almost universally known. Upon Jackson's appointment, creditors, storekeepers, and merchants rushed to the new prosecutor with a deluge of requests to help them collect on their bills. Jackson was eager to assist, building up his reputation as an inexhaustible

---

[101] Coit, Margaret L. *Andrew Jackson*. Houghton Mifflin Company, Boston, 1965. Pg. 9-12

dynamo, issuing seventy writs for delinquent collection within a single month.[102]

As a result of his tireless efforts, Jackson's legal practice soared. The interests of money and capital sought out his services from far and wide. The amount of money owed by the large number of debtors in Davidson County was so great that many had lost track of much of their debts. Jackson pursued them relentlessly nonetheless, often ruffling feathers. This approach invariably led to conflicts. Some of his conflicts were unconventional, including one memorable incident where he reportedly took on a belligerent debtor using a fence rail. Jackson's persistence had so angered the debtor, a rather large frontiersman, that he walked right up to Jackson one afternoon and deliberately stepped on his foot. Jackson ignored this slight at first, but when the man repeated the act, Jackson calmly picked up a fence rail, swung it at the man and knocked him out cold.

Jackson's reputation for firmness had now extended beyond the courtroom. Jackson became known for his willingness to engage in physical confrontations if the situation required, a characteristic typical of frontier life at the time. In short, with his exceptional work ethic, and fearless nature in the face of confrontation, the new Solicitor had established himself as a formidable professional who was not one to back away from a conflict. Business was good.[103]

During the first few years of his arrival, records show that Jackson handled nearly half of all court cases on the Davidson County docket. A single session in April of 1789 shows that he argued all thirteen cases that came before the court, all for debts. Along with debts, Jackson handled cases involving land titles, sales and assault. These cases required extensive travel through the raw backwoods of the region, meaning Jackson was constantly on horseback, traversing the 200-mile court circuit endlessly, all during a time in which the threat of Indian attack stood at an alarming level.

Riding hours in the saddle along the muddy roads of Tennessee, Jackson gained intimate knowledge of the Cumberland and its inhabitants. Not for the faint of heart, the wilderness presented constant dangers, and

---

[102] Remini, 1977.
[103] Remini, 1977. p. 43

navigating these challenges required courage, skill and caution. Often traveling alone, sleeping under the stars, ever-vigilant in the woods, Kentucky rifle close at hand, Jackson learned the ways of the frontier. When he did travel with others, he developed a reputation for bravery and grit on the trail, his foresight and quick thinking saved himself and fellow travelers from potential attacks on multiple occasions.[104]

Knowing the nature of Jackson's irascible and often obstinate character, the fondness he developed for his friends and neighbors in the Cumberland is fitting. Like many backcountry men of the 18th century, the deficiencies of character among Tennesseans often included violent, contradictory and intolerant attitudes, limited cultural understanding including prejudice against foreigners and indigenous populations, and an excessive affinity for sour mash whiskey among other aperitifs. These settlers viewed conflict as a primary means of problem-solving, often preferring personal confrontation over legal resolution. While they generally held reverence for the legal system, the frontier mentality frequently steered them toward vigilante law, taking justice into their own hands.[105]

Social interactions on this early frontier were intense and direct. Typical leisure activities included hunting, horse racing, competitive drinking, physical confrontations, and legal disputes. Despite their rough exterior, they held deep respect for core values: protecting women, honoring their country, and respecting the courageous. Their approach to civilization was less about gentle transformation and more about forceful adaptation, representing a raw, uncompromising approach to westward expansion. These trailblazers of the Cumberland were the architects of a challenging, transformative period in American history—complex individuals who shaped a nation through their extraordinary resilience and unyielding spirit.

Western court records from this period reveal a wild assortment of conflicts - street brawls, physical confrontations, and violent disputes that went far beyond typical legal disagreements. Other disputes followed the more formal protocol of dueling. At just 21-years-old, Jackson faced significant challenges in commanding respect from willful individuals,

---

[104] Brown, William Garrett. Andrew Jackson. The Riverside Biographical Series. 1900.
[105] Brands, HW. 2005. Ch. 6

quick to settle arguments through physical means. This role would require more than just legal knowledge. The young solicitor needed physical courage, quick thinking, decisiveness, an ability to command respect, and survival instincts. The job was a delicate balance. Being too weak minded meant being disrespected, while being too aggressive could create dangerous enemies. One wrong move could literally cost him his life.[106]

In this roughneck environment, Andrew Jackson seemed perfectly suited to the role. Not a stranger to hardship, from a young age Jackson had been hardened more than most. Thrown into the fire of war and death, prison camp, smallpox, the thunder of battle, and heart wrenching loss, Jackson's fierce nature was forged, and he had persevered. Time and again, he displayed an unbreakable will, extraordinary courage, raw toughness, and a remarkable ability to respond to intense situations effectively. His unique qualities made him not only capable of surviving in this challenging position, but potentially excelling in ways others could not.

Court Day in Nashville's early days was a pivotal social event. To escape the monotony of the farm, a day at the courthouse offered a break from the isolation of the plow. These gatherings were more than legal proceedings; they were social epicenters where gossip spread, political debates raged, and public opinion formed. Lawyers and politicians used these opportunities to build reputations, with "stump-speaking" becoming not only a critical method of voter persuasion, but a favored form of entertainment. The close-knit nature of the frontier community meant that the details of personal intimacy often became public knowledge and could significantly influence courtroom proceedings. The frontier society of the Cumberland in the 18th century was characterized by limited capital, petty disputes that frequently turned deadly, and a complex legal environment where personal conflicts were constantly negotiated.

Public prosecutors such as Andrew Jackson played a crucial role in establishing law and order, often a challenging process in the backwaters of the frontier. The concept of "squatterism" emerged, where settlers would occupy property unlawfully, bearing no title to the

---

[106] Fowler, Russell. Clash of the Titans. Tennessee Bar Association. 2020.

land. Challenging existing political jurisdictions and creating tensions between new inhabitants and established authorities, these dynamics were fundamental in shaping early American democratic practices. The prevalence of squatters in the backcountry revealed the often arbitrary legal statutes Jackson had to contend with, as well as the lax approach of frontiersmen to constituted authority.

Jackson's term as public prosecutor in Tennessee carried on through the first several years of his residency in the Cumberland, a role that required exceptional courage, as it put him at odds with criminality on a regular basis. This often-challenging work frequently pitted Jackson against some of the roughest individuals in the area, often in their very worst moments. Yet, Solicitor Jackson also engendered the gratitude of people when he was successful in their cases, fostering loyalty and devotion to him that he could count on for years to come. As lawless as the Cumberland frontier of the Cumberland was in those early days of the nation's infancy, a district attorney faced serious threats. Jackson certainly encountered many "personal difficulties" in this role, conditioning himself in his ability to confront others, and to triumph in these confrontations.

Many years later, as President, Jackson recounted an incident from his early days as a lawyer to a close friend in the White House, who was concerned about facing aggression for his political support of Jackson's administration. "Now, Mr. B.," said the General, "if any one attacks you, I know how you'll fight with that big black stick of yours. You'll aim right for his head. Well, sir, ten chances to one he'll ward it off; and if you do hit him, you won't bring him down. No, sir," (taking the stick into his own hands,) "you hold the stick so, and punch him in the stomach, and you'll drop him. I'll tell you how I found that out. When I was a young man practicing law in Tennessee, there was a big bullying fellow that wanted to pick a quarrel with me, and so, trod on my toes. Supposing it accidental, I said nothing. Soon after, he did it again, and I began to suspect his object. In a few minutes he came by a third time, pushing against me violently, and evidently meaning to fight. He was a man of immense size, one of the very biggest men I ever saw. As quick as a flash, I snatched a small rail from the top of the fence, and gave him the point of it full in his stomach. Sir, it doubled him up. He fell at my feet, and I stamped on him. Soon he got up savage, and was about to fly at me like a tiger. The bystanders made as though they would interfere. Says I, 'Gentlemen, stand back, give me room, that's all I ask, and I'll manage him.' With that, I stood ready with the rail pointed. He gave me one look and turned away, a whipped man, sir, and feeling like one. So, sir, I say to you, if any villain assaults you, give him the pint in his belly."[107]

It hadn't been Jackson's original intention to stay on the Tennessee frontier permanently, but with the prosperity of his professional career ascending rapidly, Jackson sought to plant roots. With his legal practice thriving, and his unbridled love for Rachel in full bloom, he made the decision to remain in Nashville permanently. By the time Tennessee was preparing to become a state, Jackson had accumulated a substantial estate, primarily through land ownership. His success was not achieved by neglecting his professional responsibilities, but through hard work, determination, and an uncompromising approach to his legal and personal challenges.

Despite the violent nature of some of his conflicts—which would be viewed differently by modern standards—these experiences contributed to Jackson's rising prominence in the community. Emerging as an outspoken leader in the early development of the Tennessee territory, embodying the gritty spirit of frontier leadership and personal integrity. Like all men of the frontier in the 1790s, Jackson committed himself to the communal attitude of strength against the threat of Indigenous Nations hostile to White communities.

After an attack by members of the Creek Nation on Robertson's Station in which several whites were killed and wounded, Jackson volunteered to join a twenty-man expedition to punish the "savages." They pursued the attackers to their camp on Duck River, and hid in the cane near their camp, biding their time. At sunrise, they struck, driving the Creeks across the river. Although most of them escaped, Jackson's posse managed to capture their guns, shot pouches and baggage, including their moccasins, leggings, blankets, and skins.[108] This was Jackson's first formal expedition against the Natives of Tennessee, and although he held the lowly rank of private, he was commended by those he served under as "bold, dashing, fearless, and mad upon his enemies." What

---

[107] Parton, James. Ch. XII.
[108] Putnam, A.W., History of Middle Tennessee; Life And Times Of General James Robertson. 2010. Pg. 318. A.W. Books.

Jackson lacked in combat experience, he made up for in enthusiasm, proving irrepressible when it came time to strike, as one contemporary stated, he had a "great ambition for encounters with the savages." and he indulged in this ambition as often as he was able.

In his many years on horseback, riding the legal circuit and traveling the backwoods of Tennessee, Jackson played a vital protective role for others; escorting settlers and enforcing justice in a region that could have easily descended into lawlessness. Jackson rallied volunteer troops, projecting personal strength and creating a powerful and well-known persona. This aura of strength, perhaps more than any particular gift of insight, judgment, or rhetoric, propelled him forward, and rallied others to his side. To his contemporaries, Jackson was a man you could count on.[109]

On a later occasion, Jackson took on a leadership role when he and his traveling party stumbled upon a recently abandoned campsite of a large group of Native Americans. It was clear to Jackson and the others that they were in danger of ambush, and retreat appeared to be their only option. Needing to cross a small, swollen stream, they built a raft out of logs and bushes bound together with some hickory. Jackson and a companion pushed off with the guns and equipment, and headed downstream, only to be seized by a powerful undercurrent. Being pushed rapidly forward, the two were careening towards a waterfall, and Jackson struggled to steer the raft toward the bank. Wrenching one of the oars from its fastening, he braced himself at the stern of the raft. Using his length, he held the oar out to his friends on the shore, who managed to grab it and pull the raft to safety. The close call caused his friends to chide Jackson, who simply laughed and replied: "A miss is as good as a mile, you see how near I can graze danger. Come on and I will save you yet." The party continued down the banks and found a more suitable spot to ford the stream and crossed to safety.[110]

Another legendary tale recounts Jackson tracking through the forest to meet a group of friends traversing the wilderness. Upon arriving late at their meeting spot and realizing that his friends had already departed, he set out on his own to catch up with them. Alarmingly however, he

---

[109] Meacham, Jon, *American Lion: Andrew Jackson in the White House*, Random House, 2009. Ch. 1
[110] Kendall, Amos. *Life of Andrew Jackson: Private, Military and Civil.* Harper. 1843. p. 86

noticed numerous moccasin tracks, indicating a war party likely intent on attacking his unsuspecting companions. With no time to waste, Jackson rushed ahead to warn them of the impending danger.

Fortunately, there was still time; the natives had veered off the road and into the woods, seeking to encircle the group and set an ambush. Driven by fear for his friends' safety, Jackson hurried onward. He reached them as night fell, just after they had crossed a deep, nearly frozen river, where they were drying their clothes. Bursting into their camp, Jackson shouted his warning, and the group hurried to resume their march. They pressed on throughout the night and into most of the next day, not daring to stop or rest. Finally, they arrived at the cabins of a group of hunters. Despite their pleas for shelter, the hunters refused Jackson's party out of fear that they would steal supplies.

Forced back into the cold night, and buffeted by a fierce storm of wind and snow, the group eventually had to halt and rest, utterly worn out and unable to take another step. Jackson, who had gone without sleep for sixty hours straight, wrapped himself in his blanket and collapsed on the ground. The next morning, he awoke to find himself buried under six inches of snow. The hunting party, members of the Chickasaw Nation, continued on the hunt, desperation driving them forward. Upon discovering the hunters' cabins, they rampaged the site, killing the hunters to the last man. Afterward they turned back, allowing Jackson and his friends to proceed unmolested.[111]

The threat of attack on the trail molded the early settlers of Tennessee into a daring and reckless group. According to historical accounts, they placed little value on life, whether their own or that of the Indians, valuing horses and rifles above all else. Yet amidst their struggles and hardships, they managed to find leisure. They played cards, engaged in foot races, pitched quoits, (similar to an early version of horseshoes) and spent hours in "idle chat." They could entertain themselves with the violin, song, and dance, even as the sounds of war echoed above the lively music. Such was life on the frontier.

---

[111] McLaughlin to Kendall, Jackson Papers. March 14, 1843.

CHAPTER

11

INTRIGUE

"Take time to deliberate; but when the time for action arrives, stop thinking and go in."
-Andrew Jackson

The presence of enemies afoot, and the dangers such enemies posed, heavily influenced the early political landscape of Tennessee. The settlers of the Cumberland even resorted to intrigue to protect themselves from attacks. As noted, many continued to court the Spanish along their southern border, hinting at a potential secession from the United States to persuade the Spanish governor in New Orleans to deter Indian aggression. However, others viewed the Spanish with hostility for efforts they believed the Spanish to be guilty of, such as inciting indigenous nations to make war against the Americans. For many, an alliance with Spain was unthinkable.

Despite the agreed upon terms of the 1783 Treaty of Paris, the Spanish did not recognize the southern boundary of the United States, at least not the 31st parallel boundary Americans had been granted as a result of the victory in the Revolution. The Spanish had failed in their attempts to negotiate a U.S. boundary well east of the Mississippi, and the issue still grated at the Spanish. Spain had been in control of New Orleans since the end of the French and Indian War and laid a claim to territory on the east bank of the Mississippi much farther north than the treaty allowed. The Spanish government administered a large area north of the line, including the profitable trade town of Natchez, Mississippi, although it lay well within United States territory, according to the treaty. Natchez was located on the east bank of the Mississippi, and it was there that the Spanish seized the city from the British in 1779, who had taken it from the French twenty years earlier. With both Natchez and New Orleans firmly in Spanish hands, the merchandise of American tradesmen in the west was at the mercy of the Spanish government. Without Spanish approval, Tennesseans were barred from sending their goods to eastern markets. Additionally, the presence of the Spanish blocked American aspirations of expansion to the south and west.[112]

The Spanish government's uneasiness with the growth of the American West was a constant factor in its diplomacy since the beginning of the Revolutionary War. Writing in December 1783, Francisco Rendon, the Spanish agent in Philadelphia reported, in a letter to the Spanish government, that Kentucky had applied to Virginia for permission to form a separate state in conformity with the general principles of the Confederation, and that Connecticut was preparing to make use of the territory claimed by it in the Ohio Valley. These indications of the rapid extension of the American system across the mountains was alarming to the Kingdom of Spain. This concern, amplified by increasing reports of its agents in North America regarding the encroachment of settlements in Tennessee and Georgia, eventually led to action on the part of Spain.

To meet this situation accordingly, José Moñino y Redondo, 1st Count of Floridablanca, Spanish statesman and chief minister under King Charles III, adopted three measures. A royal order was issued closing the Mississippi River to all but Spanish ships; a formal statement was drawn up setting forth Spain's position in regard to the navigation of the Mississippi and the boundary of its possessions on the east bank of the river; and Diego de Gardoqui, the Spanish minister to the United States, was sent to negotiate a treaty with the Americans.[113]

Floridablanca, Guardoqi and the Spanish had failed repeatedly in their efforts to sort out the issue through diplomatic means. In 1788, in a letter to Floridablanca, Guardoqi related some private conversations about the West that he had two years earlier with Dr. James White, a North Carolina Congressional delegate, and former Superintendent of

---

[112] Whitaker, Arthur Preston. *The Spanish-American Frontier, 1783-1795*. Gloucester, MA, 1962

[113] Ibid, p. 80

Indian Affairs for the Southern District. White assured the Spanish minister that the western country would happily sever the connection with the United States and unite with Spain, or their ally, the British were they able to guarantee access to the entire length of the Mississippi. To sweeten the offer, White added a further intrigue, suggesting "that if Spain would open the river to westerners, the Spanish crown would win western allegiance forever. James Robertson supported this idea as well, declaring in similar correspondence, "in all probability, we cannot long remain in our present state, and if the British, or any commercial nation who may be in possession of the mouth of the Mississippi would furnish us with trade, and receive our produce there cannot be a doubt that the people on the west side of the Appalachian Mountains will open their eyes to their real interest."[114]

The degree to which western representatives were willing to engage in such treasonous efforts is indicative of the dire economic straits western settlers faced. The tone of both letters reflects the frustrations of frontier regions at the inept shortcomings of the Confederation Congress in Philadelphia in 1788. Ready and willing westerners vowing to take a knee for the king of Spain for the purposes of trade and protection indicates just how neglected many in the region felt. Yet, Jackson was not among the contingent that looked to secession and a marriage with the Spanish as the best course. Although the future governor of Tennessee, Nolichucky Jack himself, was more favorable to such a marriage. John Sevier, responding to the Spanish invitation to western settlers to migrate into Spanish territory southward, encouraged many of his constituents to consider the offer. Doing so would mean exemption from the fifteen percent duty the Spanish otherwise charged for traveling the Mississippi.[115]

And there was also the issue of hostile Nations to consider, especially the warring Creeks and Chickamaugas. Determined as ever to drive the Americans off their ancestral lands, and not in need of Spain's or Britain's instigation to do so, the tribes increased their attacks. The charismatic Creek leader Alexander McGillivray directed a war that had raged across the southern and western frontier since 1786. James

---

[114] Ibid, p. 81
[115] Samuel Cole Williams, *History of the Lost State of Franklin*, (New York: The Press of the Pioneers, 1933), p. 311.

Robertson had lost a son in the savage fighting, and after two years of bloodshed and loss, he appealed to McGillivray, and through him to the Spanish, to end the fighting. So disillusioned were western settlers like Sevier and Robertson, heartsick and miserable from the conflict, that they were prepared to accept any outcome to ensure peace, even if it meant allegiance to the Spanish crown. In the wake of Shay's Rebellion, and the ineffectiveness of the Articles of Confederation, such a uniting with Spain would also release the westerners from a dependence on an ineffective Congress.[116]

For others, however, especially those who had given so much blood and tears to the cause of American liberty, uniting with a Catholic monarch in King Charles of Spain was out of the question. Jackson professed to be of this mindset himself, although, despite his later denials, he did at times seem open to "intrigues." Evidence of such intrigues begins in the form of correspondence between Jackson and a young French captain, Andre Fagot. Based on the letters exchanged between the two men, it may have appeared to some that Jackson was also in league with the idea of a Spanish alliance.

Fagot, who operated out of St. Louis, arrived in Nashville during this period to engage in trade, as well as to represent Governor Miró of Louisiana in negotiations with Cumberland settlers. Jackson met with Fagot, who had a message from the Spanish governor. Jackson seemed to think favorably of the Frenchman. He arranged for a meeting between Fagot and General Daniel Smith, who was the commanding general of the Mero District Militia. Jackson wrote to Smith:

"Sir, I had the pleasure of seeing Captain Fargo (sic) yesterday, who put me under obligations of seeing you this day. But as the weather seems dull and heavy, it prevents my coming up. But I commit to you in this small piece of paper the business he wants with you: he expresses a great friendship for the welfare and harmony of this country: he wishes to become a citizen and trade to this country, by which means, and through you I think we can have a lasting peace with the Indians. He wishes you to write to the governor (Miró) informing him the desire of a commercial

---

[116] Remini, 1977. p. 47

treaty with that country...he will then importune the governor for the privilege or permit for trade to this country, which he is sure to obtain, as he is related to His Excellency. Then he will show the propriety of having a peace with the Indians for the purpose of the benefit of trade with this country: and also show the Governor the respect this country honors him with by giving it his name: he bears the commission of Captain under the King of Spain, which is an honorable title in that country, and can, in my opinion, do a great deal for this; and hopes you will do him the honor as to see him upon this occasion before he sets out for the Orleans, and I think it the only immediate way to obtain a peace with the Savage. I hope you will consider it well, and give me a few lines upon the occasion by Colonel Donelson, who hands you this, as I have the good of this country at heart, and I hope also if you will do Mr. Fargo the honor as to go and see him upon the occasion, as you go down you will give me a call, as I think I could give you some satisfaction on this subject. This, sir, from your very Humble Servant,

-Andrew Jackson [117]

Fagot was attempting to negotiate his way among the many powers of the region, be it the Spanish, the British, the Americans or Native Americans, all of whom laid a claim to the region surrounding the Mississippi in one form or another. At the time he reached out to Jackson, Fagot's mission was to create a regular network of trade between the Cumberland and Spanish New Orleans. James Wilkinson, who had been appointed as the first governor of the newly acquired western lands of the Louisiana Purchase in 1803, had already shown the potential of the possibility of trade with the Spanish. Fagot hoped to show the people of the Cumberland how lucrative trade between the two regions could be, and as a shrewd and aggressive operator he had already sized up the power circles in the Nashville area to his benefit. Fagot already knew General Smith and was hoping to ingratiate himself more to both he and Jackson for future advantage.

---

[117] Parton, James. pg. 141-142.

Such a trade network would also require some form of acceptance from the many indigenous nations of the region, the Cherokee, Creeks and Chickasaw among others, if it were to be successful. It was here where Jackson's key interest lay, eager to see an end to the killing between the various tribes and settlers on the frontier. Fagot was a persuasive salesman, adept at knowing the words each group wished to hear, whether it was to the benefit of the Spanish, the Americans or the Natives, he spoke a good game to whomever he addressed. As evidenced by the letter Jackson sent to General Smith, Fagot had clearly won him over. To General Smith, Fagot's "esteem for the United States," and that he truly had the country's best interests at heart probably caused a laugh from the general, coming from the young Frenchman who'd hardly just arrived in the country. But Smith believed Jackson, at least, had the interests of the southwest in mind when he wrote the letter, however unwittingly he was at the time as to the true intentions of Fagot.

As events would later prove, no one did more to pacify the frontier region for American trade than Jackson. However, not only had Jackson spelled Fagot's name wrong, he was also mistaken as to the relation between Fagot and Miró. The two were not related, nor did either of them truly have the best interests of America in mind, or the southwestern frontier for that matter. In any event, Jackson urged Smith to meet with Fagot, as "the only immediate way to obtain a peace" with the Indians. Unaware as he was, however, that he was wading into deep water with the Frenchman. Soon, Jackson would regret having ever spoken to Fagot in the first place. [118]

General Smith, who had already become familiar with Fagot from previous interactions, took Jackson up on his suggestions. The blunders in Jackson's letter likely amused him considerably. Smith was aware of the Frenchman's desire to foster "an enduring friendship between Spain and the Cumberland region," as well as his wish to gain U.S. citizenship. Although Smith did not express a desire to unite with Spain, he did reveal to Fagot (who then relayed the word to Governor Miró) that the western region wished to separate from North Carolina and form a state of their own. Upon being given such affirming news from Fagot, Miró seems to have heard a very different message, that Jackson, Smith, and

---

[118] Brands, H.W. Ch. 6

the southwestern region wanted nothing more than to be annexed into the Spanish empire.

Yet, few westerners were ready to eschew their democratic system, and become subjects of the Spanish king, although they were often ingenuine in this regard with representatives of the Spanish. Clearly a lack of candor was present on both sides, as shown by Fagot's intimations toward both Jackson and Miró. By misrepresenting his relationship with Miró, Fagot made Jackson feel confident that a new trade permit with Spain would be easily granted. Smith took Jackson up on his suggestions because he had similar high hopes of the economic benefits the permit would bring. With his friendly conversation with Smith, Fagot left fully convinced that the Cumberland leaders were prepared to secede from the United States in favor of joining the Kingdom of Spain. Both Jackson and Smith had unknowingly encouraged Fagot to misrepresent their intentions, and those of the Cumberland.

Such encouragements to the Spanish could well have led to the indictment of both Jackson and Smith for treason against the United States. With Fagot's exuberant message of affirmation, Miró was prepared to set the process into motion that would be celebrated all across the Iberian Peninsula. Correspondence with Madrid was already underway: The southwestern region of the United States stood poised to join in a confederacy with his government. After all, not only would this improve commerce between both countries, both Fagot and Miró now both argued, but joint action against any hostile tribes would plausibly mean a powerful joining of forces capable of subduing the frontier indefinitely. All the better for those like Fagot who would be at the forefront of the peaceful commerce such a result would create. This potential annexation of the Cumberland region would also heap praise and glory onto the name Miró back on the Iberian Peninsula. For both Fagot and Miró, there was a lot to be gained from a western secession from the United States.

By this time, Jackson was developing an interest in mercantilist endeavors, and like so many others in the region, he had an acute awareness of threats from such hostile tribes as the Creeks and the Chickamauga presented. Yet, Jackson's letter to Smith betrayed no ill will towards the United States nor loyalty to Spain but showed that the people of the Cumberland were simply eager to explore any options that might bring relief from Indian attacks. Jackson recognized the potential of Fagot's trade network to foster a lasting peace on the frontier. By advising General Smith to write to Miró in support of a new commercial treaty, Jackson hoped to improve the value of his own land holdings, as well as those of his region. Fagot was to deliver this letter and seek a trading permit for the Cumberland people.

In his letter to Miró, Smith introduced Fagot as a trustworthy individual, urging the Spanish governor to correspond with him for specific information, stating that, in Fagot, the Cumberland people "have very great confidence . . . and beg leave to refer your excellency to him for a particular intelligence. We have honored our district with your Excellency's name ... and I should look upon myself as much honored by a Correspondence from you."[119] All flattery of Miró aside, the "particular intelligence" to which Smith referred was given to Miró by Fagot directly: in September the Cumberland settlers were to hold a convention to secure a separation from North Carolina. This done, they were to send delegates to New Orleans to arrange a union with Spain.

In response to this vital information, Miró expressed his satisfaction in being honored by having his name attached to the western territory. He conveyed his good wishes for their prosperity, eagerly anticipating the outcomes of their planned convention in September. When the delegates convened on the first day of September, they resolved to North Carolina that it should immediately cede its western lands to Congress. However, no motions were made to select delegates for a union with Spain, as no such union was ever intended. On September 2nd, Miró was informed by James Robertson that the convention had taken place and that the Cumberland people were seeking separation from North Carolina. He noted that, despite feeling "unprotected" and desiring a "more interesting connection," they would remain "obedient to the new Congress of the United States." The settlers expressed their dissatisfaction with the lack of protection from the United States, stating that the district of Mero was frequently raided and its inhabitants killed by Creek and Cherokee tribes. While some in the district did feel a desire to unite with Spain,

---

[119] AJ to Smith, Feb. 13, 1789, in Parton, Jackson, I, 141-142. Jackson, *Correspondence*, I, 7.

neither Robertson, Jackson nor Smith were among them, despite the message Fagot had delivered to Governor Miró. [120]

The Spanish government had long hoped to see more settlement in their territories, but had little success in attracting emigration into this northern outpost of their empire. Miró had previously invited James Robertson to settle in Spanish territory, but in his response, Robertson acknowledged the advantages of Spanish governance but expressed contentment with his current estate, stating that it could not be matched elsewhere. All of this evidence points to one conclusion, that while the Cumberland people were unhappy with the United States for failing to provide protection against Indian attacks, they did not intend to abandon it in favor of Spain. The conflicting principles of Spanish and frontier governance were evident in Robertson's rejection of Miró's invitation. Both parties showed little willingness to accommodate one another's needs. Consequently, Robertson and Smith were not surprised by Miró's ambiguous responses, as he neither promised to use his influence to stop the Indian attacks nor to grant Fagot the trade permit that Jackson sought.

The Cumberland settlers were well aware of the Spanish government's reluctance to offer local governance and religious freedom—privileges they would have expected as Americans had they considered joining a foreign power. They remained focused on their goal to persuade North Carolina to cede its western lands to Congress, which they viewed as their ultimate hope for protection. In fact, Jackson was particularly adamant of an opposite view as to what was relayed to Miró regarding his intentions. To him, along with Smith and many other powerful Cumberland figures, what lands Spain owned should become American.

This notion was further reinforced in a letter Robertson sent to North Carolina Governor Samuel Johnston on the same day he wrote to Miró. Robertson, along with other leaders in the Cumberland used the threat of inhabitants exiting the western district for Spanish territory to pressure the state government to cede its western lands. At the same time, in flirting with the Spanish, the hope was that Miró would use his influence with the Creek and other tribes to lessen their attacks on frontier settlers. Robertson stated to Governor Johnston that the

---

[120] James, Marquis, *The Life of Andrew Jackson*, Bobbs Merrill, 1938, p. 57

ongoing Indian raids were prompting many people to seek safety under the protection of a foreign power. He mentioned Colonel Robert Stark's open desire to lead inhabitants into Spanish territory, noting that many were on the verge of leaving were it not for the discouragement from recent visitors, particularly Dr. White. Robertson requested information on whether there were legal means to prevent Colonel Stark and others from enticing citizens to emigrate so publicly.[121]

The intention behind this letter is clear: Robertson was alerting the governor to the discontent among the Cumberland people, who, feeling abandoned by North Carolina, were in a precarious state. He believed that a cession of the region to Congress would likely alleviate their concerns. Robertson and others employed shrewd and canny strategy, using the Spanish to promote immediate objectives: whether a change in Indian policy, or the opening of the Spanish. Meanwhile by pressuring North Carolina, the goal of expediting a western cession by the state could be achieved. The political mettle of the crafty Cumberland politicos was beginning to gel, as, to a large extent, the intrigues worked, eventually. Miró succeeded in getting the various tribes to lessen their attacks on the settlements, the Mississippi was partially opened, and North Carolina both ratified the Constitution, and ceded her western lands to the new Federal Union.

For now, the Spanish frontier issue was set aside, but by no means would it remain in the background for long.

---

[121] Whitaker, *Spanish American Frontier*, p. 113

CHAPTER

12

OUR FEDERAL UNION

"Our new Constitution is now established, and has an appearance that promises permanency; but in this world nothing can be said to be certain, except death and taxes!"
— *Benjamin Franklin*

When the First Congress of the United States met in New York City in September of 1789, they would draft the first ten amendments to the Constitution, known as the Bill of Rights. This decision was not one that most Federalists desired or felt was necessary, but they fulfilled their promise to those who opposed the new system, nonetheless. Anti-Federalists who feared the centralized authority the new federal constitution seemed to threaten, demanded the guarantee the Bill of Rights promised as a condition for ratification. Over time, the Bill of Rights has been hailed as a key component of American liberty, explicitly protecting fundamental individual freedoms; those of speech, religion, and assembly. These rights listed and drafted by the First Congress are widely seen today as essential to a democratic society.

But throughout much of 1789, not everyone in New York was convinced that a Bill of Rights would benefit the governance of the United States, including many northerners such as Alexander Hamilton, and even some southerners, such as James Madison. But for many Southerners, particularly Thomas Jefferson, Patrick Henry and George Mason, keeping sovereignty in the hands of the individual states was crucial. Andrew Jackson tended to fall more in league with this latter group, although his views would change somewhat by the time he found himself at the head of the national government. Ultimately, although they found the list of rights unnecessary, Federalists relented, compromised, and eventually conceded. Their concession of the Bill of Rights helped secure ratification of the Constitution by addressing Anti-Federalist concerns, particularly about potential government overreach.[122]

The new federal Congress also took stock of western land cessions. When it came to North Carolina's recent cession, Congress acted quickly, and within six months, settlers of the Cumberland became residents of the newly organized Southwest Territory. In late May 1790, Congress established the Territory of the United States, South of the River Ohio, and provided for its governance until it transitioned to statehood. The stipulation included in the Northwest Ordinance of 1787 stated that new territories required appointed officials to administer law and order.

To fill that requirement for the Southwest Territory, President George Washington appointed William Blount of North Carolina as governor, General Smith of the Mero District as Secretary, and John McNairy, Joseph Anderson and David Campbell as the three territorial judges. The ordinance was modeled after the Northwest Ordinance, although, unlike its northern counterpart, it allowed slavery in the territory. The land designated included all territory from the southern border of Kentucky to the northern boundary of present-day Alabama and Mississippi. The Southwest Territory was bordered on the east by Virginia, North Carolina, and Georgia, on the north by the Ohio River, on the west by the Mississippi River, and on the south by Spanish Florida.

The choice of William Blount as territorial governor would have major implications for Andrew Jackson, who would soon become well-acquainted with the North Carolinian. This relationship proved vital, especially considering that another result of the first federal Congress's creation of the Southwest Territory was temporarily sidelining Andrew Jackson from his work. When Congress established the new territory, North Carolina lost its western half, along with Jackson's position as the state's western solicitor. Nevertheless, the work was still required, and someone would have to do it, just under a new name, whether by

---

[122] Berkin, Carol. *A Brilliant Solution: Inventing the American Constitution*, Houghton Mifflin Harcourt, 2003, p. 175.

an employee of North Carolina or the federal government. Recognizing this, the ambitious and recently unemployed Jackson sought to point this out to the newly appointed Governor Blount, whom he had yet to meet.[123]

First and foremost, Jackson would have to ingratiate himself with the new governor. Understanding the importance of first impressions, Jackson used his growing network of powerful connections to arrange an ideal opportunity to get to know the governor of the new territory. It would then be on him to convince the savvy, and often unorthodox politician that he, Andrew Jackson, was right for the job. As with most opportunities that came along in those early days of Andrew Jackson's career, the young lawyer from Waxhaw would find a way, and it would lead to Blount appointing Jackson as the attorney for the Mero district of the Southwest Territory.

Blount was a distinctive figure in the realm of politics, and as a long-time land speculator, his primary motivation was financial concerns, particularly his own. He embodied the traits of an early wheeler-dealer, and a shrewd politician who knew how to achieve his goals, often by the most direct means. He openly campaigned for the position of territorial governor, candidly admitting to his brother that it was "of great importance to our western speculations." In another correspondence, he provided further insight into his priorities in lobbying for the appointment. "The Salary is handsome, and my Western lands had become so great an object to me that I should go to the Western country to secure them and perhaps my presence will have enhanced their value." [124]

Like many men of his generation, William Blount was transformed by his experiences in the War for Independence. It caused him to moderate his initial sense of loyalty to just one class and section, intentionally broadening his attention to the country as a whole, allowing him to become a leader in the westward expansion of the nation. Through this transformation, Blount became a strong nationalist, convinced that only a strong central government could harness the potential for nationhood

---

[123] AJ to James Roberston, 1792, Jackson Papers, LC
[124] Remini, 1977. p. 51; Blount to John Steele, quoted in Alice B. Keith, "The North Carolina Blount Brothers in Business and Politics, 1789-1812," unpublished dissertation, University of North Carolina, 1940.

that he saw around him. To Governor Blount, the future lay in the lands of the those in the West.

Governor Blount utilized several of his influential contacts to obtain the nod from President Washington. For Blount, however, the drawback of becoming the new territorial governor meant that he would have to also take on the role of Superintendent of Indian Affairs in the district. This role meant supervising the four Southern tribes, the Cherokees, Creeks, Choctaws and Chickasaws. This was disagreeable business to Blount, he admitted frankly, but considered the importance of his land dealings outweighing the difficulty of dealing with the "savages."[125]

In order to administer the new territory, Blount was given enormous appointment powers, which he wielded with relished authority. He had absolute control over legal appointments and licenses and boasted about it openly. This time-honored political technique was one that young Andrew Jackson would take careful note of and would follow the governor's example to make use of later on. Several of Jackson's friends in the legal community assisted Governor Blount in his administrative offices, even some who had traveled with Jackson from North Carolina, including Archibald Roane and David Allison, who became the Attorney General in the Washington district, and Roane's business manager respectively. General Daniel Smith would also be given the post of surveyor general for the territory, and both John Sevier and James Robertson were appointed by Blount as brigadier generals in the territorial militia, which were later approved by Congress. With these broad powers of delegation, Blount held near total control over the Southwest Territorial government.

Blount was no newcomer to the political game, and he had honed his skills of getting what he wanted by mastering the art of strategic flattery with his superiors. Naming the territorial capital Knoxville, after Secretary of War Henry Knox, Jefferson County for Secretary of State Thomas Jefferson, and Hamilton County for the Secretary of the Treasury, Blount fortified the support of the top federal brass. His political wherewithal guaranteed that Blount would remain in the driver's seat for quite some time in the political arena of the new territory. Getting in good with Blount would behoove young Cumberland movers

---

[125] Blount to John Gray Blount, Blount Papers, LC., p. 68.

and shakers like Jackson, and in this area, Jackson took advantage of his connections.

Governor Blount's monopoly on territorial power drew many ambitious, like-minded individuals to support him. Without Blount's influence, advancing one's career in Tennessee would be extremely difficult. Jackson had multiple connections to the governor, including McNairy, Smith, and Allyson, who all played a role in facilitating an introduction between Blount and the young lawyer Jackson, who assured the governor of his loyalty and reliability. Jackson also had an impressive track record as a hard-working and successful prosecutor, making it advantageous for the governor to seek the support of such a talented and promising young man.[126]

Eventually, Jackson was introduced to Blount, who assessed him and, on February 15, 1791, offered him the lofty position of Attorney General of the district, which Jackson accepted. The responsibilities of this role were similar to those he had fulfilled as a prosecuting attorney; however, Blount envisioned additional duties for Jackson, particularly concerning the resolution of the Indian issue. He communicated to General Robertson his desire for a recent treaty with the Cherokee to be "preserved inviolate," and if it could not be upheld, he urged that examples be made of the first violators. Blount stated, "It will be the duty of the Attorney of the District, Mr. Jackson, to prosecute on information in all such cases, and I have no doubt that he will readily do it." When Blount learned that several white settlers had breached the treaty, he took action to demonstrate his expectations while expressing further confidence in Jackson as his appointee. He declared, "Let the district attorney, Mr. Jackson, be informed; he will be certain to do his duty, and the offenders will be prosecuted." [127]

This was the beginning of a prodigious professional relationship between Jackson and Governor Blount, and the first step towards the new district attorney becoming a protégé of the 42-year-old Blount, and the recipient of important political patronage including Jackson's later appointment as judge-advocate of the Davidson County militia regiment.

---

[126] Blount to Roberston, January 2, 1792, in *AHM*, (July 1896), III, 280, See also Blount to Roberston, January 5, 1792, ibid, p. 282, and Blount to Robertson, January 18, 1794, in *AHM* (July, 1898), III 280.

[127] Putnam, p. 351

Blount was Jackson's first political patron, and at first glance, he seemed a promising mentor. The oldest of his father's thirteen children, Blount had served in the American Revolution under Horatio Gates. Afterward, he served in the North Carolina legislature, represented North Carolina in the Confederation Congress, and attended the Philadelphia Constitutional Convention. Blount's strong federalist stance in a state filled with Anti-Federalists made him an obvious choice for governor of the new Southwest Territory.[128]

As noted, Blount's interests in the Southwest Territory extended beyond politics; he had heavily speculated in lands along the Tennessee River since the mid-1780s and intended to utilize his political influence to profit from these investments. This was not uncommon in an era when land speculation was a national pastime, and many supporters of the Federal Constitution openly acknowledged that ratification would significantly enhance the value of their speculative interests. Initially, Blount limited his political dealings to negotiations with the Cherokees and other indigenous nations, who were persuaded and coerced into ceding territory to white settlers. As long as Blount's political schemes shortchanged the Cherokee alone, and not his white constituents, Blount remained popular, and some of that popularity rubbed off onto Jackson. Within months of being appointed district attorney, Jackson was honored by being nominated for the Davidson Academy board of superintendents, the first educational institution in the Cumberland region. As the region prospered, its new district attorney prospered right along with it.

With over a million acres of western land within the territory he and his brothers owned, Governor Blount set out to ensure the protection of these vast holdings. Doing so meant driving out the Indians, or at least ensuring their pacification, would be a top priority. Blount was counting on assistance from the Federal government on this suppression, but the regular army had its hands full with the Indians of the Northwest Territory, who would inflict a crushing setback to the army in 1791 at the Battle of the Wabash. As a result, Secretary Knox informed Blount that he was to bide his time when it came to the Southwestern tribes, and could only use the local militia to protect the settlements. Being relegated

---

[128] Masterson, William Henry (1954). *William Blount*. Baton Rouge: Louisiana State University Press.

to a defensive posture would prove challenging to say the least. With the success of Chief Little Turtle at Wabash, and with the replacement of Spanish governor Miró with the more aggressive Baron de Carondolet, who preferred stepping up Spanish efforts to stir up native tribes to attack frontier settlements as more effective policy against American expansion, Blount had his hands full when it came to the protection of his district, and particularly, his cherished land investments.

Much to the annoyance of many in the federal government, Blount badgered Knox's War Department as often as he could to secure support for Southwestern protection, especially in light of the Spanish change of policy. With a renewed Spanish/indigenous threat, Blount saw the ousting of hostiles as an ever-increasing necessity. In a letter to Knox, Blount wrote: "the Creeks, if not the Cherokees, must be chastised by the hand of the Government." Blount's letter to Knox, written from Knoxville on October of 1792, enclosed recent accounts that warned of "the increasing hostility of the Cherokees, from the five Lower Towns and the Creeks, requiring the Militia to turn out with unusual alacrity," and that he hoped to receive Knox's orders "as speedily as possible." Secretary Knox was compelled to report to Congress on the hostile designs among the Indians in and around the Cumberland: "It would appear, that the five Cherokee towns, containing perhaps from three to five hundred warriors, and abetted by a number of individuals of the Upper Creeks, chiefly young men, are disposed for war; and their principal object appears to be the settlements on Cumberland River."[129]

Blount's beseeching of Knox would not bring the desired results the Governor hoped for, and he continued to warn of the consequences of federal inaction. Knox, for his part, did authorize "Storekeeper and Paymaster" David Allison to purchase goods in the amount of $5,784.70 to combat the Indian threat. While this amount would prove insufficient in ending the war, it did result in a temporary truce, after it helped finance a number of successful militia raids against the tribes.[130] Subduing the frontier settlements was an aspect of Blount's administration that coincided with the interests of Jackson, and it would draw the two men together.

---

[129] Senate — Annals of Congress, 2nd Congress, All Sessions (October 24, 1791 - March 2, 1793)

[130] Ibid, p. 299

By the 1790s, Jackson's renown in and around the growing city of Nashville had grown considerably. Widely recognized as a reliable, diligent, and loyal official throughout the region, this strong reputation led to several appointments over the following years, all of which contributed to his career advancement. On September 1, 1792, he was appointed as the judge advocate for the Davidson County cavalry regiment, which was commanded by Lieutenant Colonel Robert Hays, Jackson's brother-in-law, married to Jane Donelson, Rachel's sister. The connection to the Donelsons proved to once again bear productive fruit for Jackson's career. This post marked Jackson's first military role; although it was awarded through family connection more than legal expertise, it initiated a long and important association with the Tennessee militia that significantly influenced his political career.

Soon, Governor Blount's favorable impression of the abilities of Andrew Jackson would grow, and before long the governor became one of Jackson's most outspoken advocates. This would have major implications for Jackson's career. Blount, in turn, came to rely on Jackson's loyalty and support equally as much, and considered Jackson one of his most reliable lieutenants in the Cumberland, willing and able to perform the type of difficult and controversial work that needed to be done. James Robertson was also well-entrenched in the Blount camp, and he too held high esteem for the able and industrious Jackson, who showed a marked vigilance to uphold the law, particularly when it served the purposes of the ever-powerful Blount faction. Between these two extremely influential Tennesseans, Jackson's promotions came regularly and often.

Not surprisingly, Jackson began to accumulate wealth during this period. As his reputation and professional career grew, so did his land holdings, mirroring the success of many westerners seeking investment opportunities. Land was the prime asset for those who ventured west in search of a better life. Savvy investors sought to purchase more land whenever possible, though this came with risks; some who over-speculated ended up wallowing away in the ignominy of debtors' prison. However, this risk did not deter generations of dreamers enchanted by the allure of western lands and open pastures.

Along with maintaining close professional ties to Governor Blount, Jackson found various ways to increase the value of his own estate. Despite the prestige of the political appointments he received, Jackson's responsibilities as attorney for the state and trustee of the Academy did not entirely consume his time, and by themselves would not have allowed for the kind of lifestyle the ambitious Jackson desired. Thus, to fill his free time productively, the young attorney general took on other legal clients, many of whom were financially struggling and unable to pay court fees, often offering land deeds instead. On the frontier, cash was perpetually scarce, and alternative items circulated as currency. Corn, cattle, and horses often replaced hard money, but nothing was as prevalent as paper representing land. As A.W. Putnam wrote in History of Middle Tennessee, it was said of this period: "The amount of silver and gold was very small. Horses and cows, axes and cowbells, constituted the ready 'circulating medium.' To this indispensable yet variable currency was added the military warrants for land." [131]

Jackson remained vigilant for any opportunities to increase his holdings, always with an ear to the ground when it came to land prospects. With the support of influential and affluent westerners, the attorney general participated in a number of largely successful land ventures over the following decade. Some of his land schemes, in fact, raise questions of legality. Yet, much of his legal dealings at the time resulted in fees that were often compensated with land, substituted for currency, on the frontier. Many of Jackson's cases involved large land transactions, which he was hired on to facilitate, thus receiving a portion of the acreage as a commission for his efforts. Over time, prices for goods and services were quoted in acres, with 640 acres representing a square mile. By the mid-1790s, Jackson's land holdings encompassed roughly the size of an entire county if consolidated into a single tract.[132]

By the time Tennessee entered the Union in 1796, Jackson owned an extensive amount of land. The land records of 1794-1797 show the accumulation of property that laid the foundation for the large estate Jackson would eventually acquire. The extent of Jackson's land ownership grew steadily over the course of the 1790s, much of it from his involvement in the land speculation so common on the frontier. Hoping to make a profit, Jackson and Overton created land deeds and titles between themselves that they often exchanged for small sums from one

---

[131] Putnam, A.W., p. 177-242
[132] Brands, H.W., 2005. Part 1. (1767-1805)

to the other. To call the legality of many of these transactions 'suspect' would certainly not be overstating it, especially considering much of the land went beyond the "Land-Grab" territory allotted to white settlers in treaties with indigenous nations from previous agreements.

Jackson's land strategy, like most on the frontier in those days, was to buy up the land, or acquire it, as he often did, at rock-bottom rates, and wait for immigration to push the value up. With this time-honored approach, the future president profited more and more with the nation's ever-increasing natural rate of westward expansion. By supporting policies that promoted expansion, he, Blount and other important leaders of the territory inevitably profited. Ultimately, by these means, Jackson became one of the largest landholders in the Southwest Territory. A record of a land deal sold by Jackson to a land company in Philadelphia reflects the type of transactions with which Jackson became adept. Purchasing the tract for six thousand dollars on behalf of a client, Jackson was left with several thousand more acres still in his possession. He would utilize the wealth these types of transactions generated to begin to build his own lavish estate. Before long, Jackson would establish the home he had long promised Rachel; their 'Eden and prized possession, the cotton plantation known as the "Hermitage," which they would buy in 1804.

Records show that Jackson paid cash in the amount of eight hundred dollars–a high price in those days–for the six hundred and fifty acres of land that would become the Hermitage. First, however, Jackson and Rachel purchased a more modest estate, 'Hunter's Hill,' in 1796, about thirteen miles from Nashville, not far from Rachel's brother, John Donelson. The two would reside on this plantation for eight years prior to making the move to the Hermitage. In small but deliberate steps, Jackson would reach the heights he had dreamed of since his Charleston days, that of membership into the fabled planter class.

CHAPTER

13

NATCHEZ NUPTIALS

"Love to faults is always blind, always is to joy inclined. Lawless, winged, and unconfined, and breaks all chains from every mind."

-William Blake

Thomas Jefferson envisioned the West as a limitless horizon of cheap, abundantly fertile lands where self-sufficient yeoman farmers could till the earth; where their livestock could roam, free from government interference. Jackson shared this mentality, drawn more to the buying and selling of western land as much as the farmer's life. Like many ambitious frontiersmen, the quest for such wide open, unclaimed lands fueled negative perceptions of Native Americans, the Spanish, and the English, who were all perceived as obstacles to Americans' land acquisitions, and impediments to American wealth. This drive for westward expansion significantly shaped the individualistic spirit embedded in republican institutions and the democratic attitudes of Americans. Jackson was not immune to such sentiments.

Yet, business in land was not Andrew Jackson's only egg in the basket. When the Spanish moderated their approach to attracting American settlers into their northern territories, Jackson was one of the first westerners to take advantage of the business opportunity this presented. By 1789, Jackson had become intimately familiar with the bustling trade city of Natchez, having made several visits to the Spanish-held port city on the Mississippi, as part of his legal circuit. Through his travels, Jackson made several important business connections there and soon established a profitable trading network of his own. Many of his contacts in Natchez were American emigrants and successful entrepreneurs. Included in this group were the brothers Abner and Marston Green, Melling Woolley and John Potter.[133] Jackson would provide these merchants with the products of the Tennessee frontier, furs, cotton, skins and feathers in exchange for bedding, pork, beef, lime, boats and even slaves. With such a lucrative trade operation, Jackson invested in a partnership with a Donelson brother-in-law as part owner of a general store in Nashville.

Jackson frequently engaged in slave-trading in and around the Natchez Trace area as well. Similar to his first venture to Salisbury, where the teenage Jackson had carried a slave transaction for his uncle, Jackson transported slaves to Natchez as a courtesy to friends and even helped return a runaway slave to the Natchez governor Manuel Gayoso de Lemos for James Robertson. Perhaps it was this familiarity with the buying, selling and exchanging of enslaved human beings that drew Jackson to increase his own slave holdings, as his wealth began to increase. Jackson was not one to debate on the moral implications of slavery; there is little evidence that he ever considered it anything more than an accepted fact of life. There are no written records that demonstrate his opinion on the issue during this period. His slave holdings would continue at a steady rate throughout this time period. In a document from 1790 that lists Jackson's slave ownership, signed and approved by David Allison, it shows him owning five slaves between the ages of 32 and two years old. This number would grow exponentially over the next half century. [134]

Andrew Jackson seems to have viewed slavery as a practical necessity and had no qualms about continuing to accrue slaves throughout his long career. Between 1790 and 1794, Jackson made a number of purchases of human flesh as he made steady increases in his economic security. By the mid-1790s, Jackson owned as many as 16 slaves, and that number increased regularly with each passing year. As noted, no evidence exists

---

[133] Remini, 1977. p. 56
[134] Cheathem, Mark R. (October 2012). *The Evolution of the Enslaved Community at Andrew Jackson's Plantations, 1790s–1840s* (PDF). 2012 BRANCH (Association of British American Nineteenth Century Historians). p. 3.

that Jackson, unlike Jefferson before him, ever questioned the morality of slavery. But there is also no record of writing from Jackson that seeks to defend slavery as a moral good. Like many other Southerners during the period especially after the turn of the century, Jackson's participation in the institution of slavery is all one can go on, and within that realm, Jackson not only showed no opposition to the peculiar institution but profited handsomely off it throughout his life.

Despite the unfortunate business of Jackson's involvement in human bondage, he had established himself effectively in the realms of early Tennessee law and business. Yet, for all Jackson's hard work and business pursuits, he was never one to be accused of "all work and no play," for he continued to pursue his love of sport and spirits. Never one to turn down a good time, he took part in the horse business in Natchez, whether it was interest in horse trading, racing or breeding. Horses would continue to be one of his strongest passions, as would be shown later on. Among his other passions, reminiscent of his Salisbury days, was the liquor that flowed through Natchez like the waters of the nearby Mississippi. Jackson was reportedly a frequent patron of the friendly retreat known as "Bayou Pierre," where he was known to spend "many agreeable hours" among friends.[135]

In the autumn of 1790, a rumor circulated through the Cumberland that Lewis Robards intended to return to the area to reclaim his wife and take her back with him to Kentucky. Upon receiving the troubling news, Rachel Donelson Robards became filled with anxiety, and not a small amount of irritation. Ominously, Robards had warned her that he intended to "haunt her for the rest of her days." Convinced that living with him was not only impossible, but highly undesirable, she made the decision to leave Nashville, or so many claimed. Or was an escape to Natchez Jackson's idea? It is not clear whether Rachel came to the decision on her own or was encouraged to leave by those close to her,

---

[135] Remini, 1977. p. 55.

particularly Andrew Jackson. For by this time, there was no going back, the two had fallen madly in love with each other.[136]

One account posits that upon hearing the news of Rachel's plans to depart, Jackson was said to be "filled with deep sorrow."[137] As noted by John Overton, believing he was the reason for Rachel's difficult situation, Jackson resolved to accompany her to Natchez, regardless of appearances. If he and Rachel were to be together, it couldn't be in Nashville—not yet, at least. Too many people were aware that Rachel was still married to Robards. Natchez, being far away, was beyond the reach of Robards, who might have sought to return. It was also out of sight of judgmental neighbors and beyond the jurisdiction of American law. In Natchez, Jackson and Rachel could live as husband and wife without interference. If Robards learned of their elopement, he might divorce Rachel, which would be advantageous for them. In fact, some speculate that this premature decision was a strategic move to provoke Mr. Robards into hastening the divorce proceedings, thereby freeing Rachel to marry Jackson.

Colonel Robert Stark, the aforementioned proponent of collusion between the Cumberland and Spanish Natchez, was a frequent traveler along the route between the two settlements. A respected elder and friend of Mrs. Donelson, Stark had already agreed to escort Rachel to Natchez, on the banks of the Mississippi River. It seems that either Jackson persuaded Stark to allow him to join the travelers, or Stark invited him for the added protection he could provide through hostile territory. Most likely, knowing where Jackson's heart was, he insisted on going along. Regardless of how it came about, Jackson's involvement surely confirmed Mr. Robards' suspicions of Jackson, and further damaged Rachel's reputation, at least among those in the Robards camp. With several male relatives who could have provided Rachel's protection on the journey instead of Jackson, Robards had plenty of ammunition that he had been intentionally made the cuckold.

As a serious suitor of Rachel and well-received within the Donelson family, Jackson may have already sought permission from the widow Donelson to marry her daughter, which would have legitimized their

---

[136] James, *Jackson*, p. 803.
[137] Remini, 1977. p. 58; Ibid.

journey to Natchez together, at least to some degree. According to one account, Jackson did ask for Mrs. Donelson's permission to propose to Rachel, to which she reportedly responded, "Mr. Jackson, would you sacrifice your life to save my poor child's good name?" Jackson's reply was, "Ten thousand lives, Madame, if I had them." If such a passionate reply was indeed true, Jackson's dramatic flair for the romantic even at the ripe age of twenty-four is clearly evidenced, as well as his early determination to marry his love, despite any challenges or appearances. Whether this was the case or not, Jackson's choice to accompany Rachel would later be cited as evidence of his moral failings and would continue to haunt both he and his beloved.[138]

Jackson faced a torrent of criticism for his involvement with a married woman, and he may have deserved the backlash. However, it seems unlikely that he was indifferent to the impact on Rachel's reputation, as evidenced by his visceral reaction on other occasions when confronted with any slander of her character. Characteristically, he probably felt compelled to protect her, given the tumultuous relationship she endured with Robards, or he could have simply felt such powerful infatuation for Rachel that he couldn't bear the thought of her being far away. The deep devotion to each other, and the piety that the young lovers later exhibited, has often been cited as evidence of the remorse they harbored for the illicit love affair, in light of adultery accusations. Rachel particularly suffered due to her relationship with Andrew Jackson, although neither could have known the extent of what they were in for at the time.

The decision to leave Nashville occurred in January of 1791, according to the official account written by John Overton in 1827. This date is significant as Overton would later cite it in his defense of the Jacksons as not guilty of adultery or bigamy, as Robards would later claim. According to Overton, it was during the winter of 1790-1791, nearly six months after Rachel learned of Robards' intentions, that Jackson, Rachel, the widow Donelson, and Stark (along with Stark's family) traveled downriver to Natchez.

The soon-to-be-wed Jacksons embarked on their riverboat journey heading first down the Cumberland River, continuing to the Ohio, and ultimately to the Mississippi. The journey took several weeks. They

---

[138] Richey, Clark, "The Jackson's Mississippi Honeymoon," *Talk of the Town*, Dec. 8, 2020

floated south until reaching Natchez, where Jackson ensured that Rachel and her mother were settled safely with friends (Rachel and the widow Donelson took up residence with the families of Colonel Thomas Green and Colonel Bruin in Natchez.) After delivering his charge, Jackson returned to Nashville to manage his responsibilities in the prosecutor's office by April 1791. Court records show Jackson back in Nashville's superior court by May.

According to John Overton's account years later, it was at or about this time that Jackson heard news that Lewis Robards had obtained a divorce through the Virginia courts. Unbeknownst to Jackson, however, (or so it was later claimed,) Robards had not been granted a divorce, but only an enabling act by the court. This permitted Robards to commence a suit for divorce in a Kentucky court. The Virginia records show that the court believed there was enough proof of adultery for Robards to file the suit in the Kentucky court, yet Robards, as it turns out, would let the matter sit for two years. Having heard the news of the granting of Rachel's divorce, (but making no effort to confirm its validity) Jackson hastened back to Natchez to marry his beloved at long last. Overton's account states that they were wed in August 1791, in the still-standing home of Thomas Marston Green, Jr., known as "Springfield." [139]

After their long and illicit courtship (that may or may not have been quite so long), the two were officially married. Or were they? As evidence later proved, Overton's memory was inaccurate by a year; Spanish records indicate that Jackson and Rachel actually arrived in Natchez during the winter of 1789-90. Furthermore, Jackson was not a late addition to the traveling party, as he had been in Natchez earlier that year to explore trading opportunities. Taking the entire trail of facts together, it seems most likely that Jackson and Rachel actually ran off together to Natchez (by riverboat, or possibly overland via the Natchez Trace) sometime between July 1789 and returned to Tennessee in July 1790.

Whatever the exact dates, Natchez was still under Spanish rule throughout the late 1780s, early 1790s, so all marriage proceedings would have to be performed by the Catholic Church. Jackson and Rachel were not only both Protestant, but no Catholic priest would have knowingly married a woman whose former husband was still alive. Furthermore,

---

[139] Overton, John. *United States Telegraph*, June, 1827

there is no official record of the wedding having taken place. All that is left to go on is word of mouth.

Although Natchez was officially Catholic, and only Catholic marriages were permitted, Protestant ministers did live in the district, and they did on occasion perform marriage ceremonies (for which they frequently got into trouble.) On the whole, the Spanish pursued a liberal policy toward non-Catholics as part of their effort to attract Americans to the district. Protestants were neither persecuted nor required to convert to Catholicism; they were not disturbed in the practice of their religion, unless they attempted to preach in public. But, a marriage performed by a Protestant minister would, in the eyes of the Spanish, be illegal. The situation was regularized in 1792 when a royal decree required the Catholic priests to officiate at all baptisms and marriages, including those of Protestants. For a Protestant couple to be legally married in Natchez in the 1790s without the benefit of a Catholic priest, they would have to leave the district and have their marriage solemnized in the United States.

It is possible that a Protestant minister in Natchez did in fact marry Jackson and Rachel. Such a marriage would've been considered perfectly legal in frontier communities where jurisdictions were sometimes so confusing that no one could tell where legal authority officially resided. A theory has been advanced that Rachel and Andrew were married by Colonel Thomas Green Senior, acting as a magistrate of Georgia, as they were reportedly at his son's home. But, if such a ceremony was performed, it too was illegal.[140]

The state of Georgia claimed the Natchez area in the mid-1780s as within her legal boundaries and attempted to exercise sovereignty over the district by forming it into the county of "Bourbon" and assigning justices of the peace to administer it. Several members of the Green family received appointments in this county, much to the distress of the Spanish. At one time, locked up in a Spanish jail, Colonel Green was forced to transfer his property to his sons before being exiled. In 1788, Georgia abandoned the Bourbon County plan, which effectively ended the authority of all its officials. In 1789, the Spanish government allowed the Colonel to return to Natchez on the condition that he renounce

---

[140] Remini, 1977. p. 60.

any ties to the Bourbon scheme and take an oath of loyalty to Spain. Following this, he was permitted to live with his sons. Consequently, it is highly improbable that Green conducted a wedding ceremony. If he did, it would have jeopardized his loyalty oath, making his actions illegal.[141]

Whatever truly happened in Natchez, Jackson revisited his business interests while there. Utilizing his many connections, he and Rachel acquired a tract of land near the Green's property in Bruinsburg, where the Mississippi River intersects with the Bayou Pierre. The land was located about 25 miles north of Natchez. This may have been land that Rachel had inherited from her relatives. Regardless of how they managed to acquire the property, Jackson constructed a log house on it that overlooked both the bayou and the river.

A now happily married young man to the "most beautiful woman in Nashville," full of dreams and ambitions, Jackson, a lover of horse racing, dreamed of building a racetrack on his property, a topic he frequently discussed with his wife and others. The happy couple spent their honeymoon on their new riverfront property. A visitor to the Jackson's Mississippi home later remarked, "I cannot [ever] lose the remembrance of the agreeable hours at Bayou Pierre."[142]

However, peace and serenity were short-lived around the ambitious future president. It would be just three years later, when the Jacksons received the shocking news that Robards and Rachel were not granted a divorce in 1791, (or 1790) after all. Officially, the Robards' ill-fated marriage would not be terminated until September 27, 1793, by a Mercer County court in Harrodsburg, Kentucky. By that time, Rachel and Jackson had been living together for at least two years, and probably more likely three. The jury had no difficulty concluding that the marriage between Rachel and Robards should be dissolved, stating, "Rachel Robards hath deserted the plaintiff, Lewis Robards, and hath and doth, still live in adultery with another man." In an age when a woman's reputation was everything, Rachel was officially deemed an adulteress by a court of law.

It is unclear as to why Lewis Robards waited so long to obtain the divorce from Rachel. Perhaps he hoped for property from the Donelson

---

[141] James, *Jackson*, p. 67 and 804

[142] Cochran, George, April 15, 1797, Jackson Papers, LC; Rowland, Erin, "Marking the Natchez Trace," *Publications of the Mississippi Historical Society*, 1910. XI, 355-356.

estate, or he simply wished to exact a measure of revenge against Rachel and Jackson by dragging out the process. At any rate, the damage was done, although the price of the delay would not be paid more fully until more than three decades later. For Jackson's part, having heard the news from John Overton, and being advised by his friend to secure the marriage legally, Jackson finally relented. On January, 27th, 1794, he and Rachel were married by the Davidson County justice of the peace, who happened to be Rachel's brother-in-law Robert Hays. Those were the facts that were presented to the American people in the 1820s when Jackson was the leading contender for the Presidency.

The historical timeline is clearly off, however, as posterity has shown. Jackson's supporters later claimed that upon learning Robards had initiated divorce proceedings, Jackson returned to Nashville in the fall of 1791 and presented himself as Rachel's husband. Controversially, documents related to John Donelson's estate, dated January 1791, list Rachel as Rachel Jackson, indicating they were back in Nashville that spring. The claim that they married in Natchez is also disputable, as no records or witnesses of the ceremony have been found. The most likely scenario is that Jackson and Rachel, frustrated by legal obstacles, eloped to Natchez and began living together. Their long-term plans were uncertain, perhaps even to themselves.

Like many young lovers, Andrew Jackson and Rachel Donelson Robards were caught up in their infatuation, unaware that Jackson would eventually become a presidential candidate needing to justify his actions. At that time, he was but twenty-two years old, with nothing tying him down. He was deeply in love with Rachel, whom he considered the most important part of his life. He was willing to eschew all other concerns to be with her. The couple were not overwhelmingly concerned about scandal, or they figured whatever the consequences of an elopement, they would be short-lived; Robards would divorce Rachel, and upon their return to Nashville, the community would find other scandalous gossip to chat about over the neighboring fence. Certainly, Jackson had no idea at the time he would one day be a leading contender for the Presidency of the United States, where every past action is suddenly examined under the microscope.

While there have been varying accounts of the union between Mr. and Mrs. Andrew Jackson and its details, one thing is certain: the couple was not ostracized by the Nashville community upon their return. In fact, the record seems to indicate quite the opposite. Within the next few years, the people of the state conferred a number of honors on Jackson, which they would not have done had they believed he had acted improperly. As a neighbor of Jackson's in Nashville would later write "I would ask how it is possible that any man could be held in such estimation by a whole community if he acted as has been alleged? ...the thing is impossible and the mere supposition of its possibility is a vile slander upon the whole population of the state."[143]

Jackson was, as noted, chosen to serve on the board of Davidson Academy in 1791, which later became Nashville University. He would serve in this role until 1805. Such a prestigious honor would not likely have been granted to a person shaded by community scandal. Not to mention that Jackson was the attorney general of the Southwest Territory, and highly regarded in the highest political circles of his chosen region. If there was scandal, it does not seem to have been an epidemic.

Whatever the circumstances of their marriage, the union between Rachel and Andrew Jackson provided a sobering, calming and peaceful effect on both. Rachel was the one constant in Jackson's tumultuous and often violent world. Jackson's considerable temper dissipated over the years, as tenderness and affection for his wife softened his edges. As H.W. Brands writes "Having been fatherless since birth and motherless since his early teens, with no surviving siblings or close cousins, Rachel became the emotional center of his life."[144] Their marriage was characterized by a deep love and devotion that endured throughout their lives. In their many years together, Rachel Jackson was much beloved by her husband (he referred to her as "My Dearest Heart" in his correspondence to her.) In a letter Jackson wrote to Rachel when work took him away, his devotion is evident: "My dearest heart, it is with the greatest pleasure I sit down to write you. Though I am absent, my heart rests with you. With what pleasing hopes I view the future period when I shall be restored to your arms, there to spend the rest of my days in domestic sweetness with you, the dear companion of my life." [145]

---

[143] Parton, James, p. 146
[144] Brands, H.W. 2005, Part I
[145] Brands, H.W., 2005. Part I

ANDREW JACKSON: THE POLITICS OF RESENTMENT

Throughout his lengthy public career, Jackson's many enemies made every manner of accusation against him over the years. Yet, among all the hostility, no one could ever question his loyalty and devotion to Rachel. The boy without a home since the age of fourteen now had a warm, familial hearth to return to. By all accounts, Jackson became more tender and affectionate towards Rachel as the years passed. As time passes, sheer, unbridled love gave way to a deep and affectionate companionship, possibly strengthened ever more by the guilt both may have felt for having "caused" each other anguish and scandal. As the years went on in their union, those who observed their love and respect for each other were moved by the maturation of their affection, and the respect shown between them. For all of Jackson's faults, dishonoring his wife was never one of them.

CHAPTER

14

HEADING HOME

"Oh Tennessee, my Tennessee."
-William P. Lawrence

About a month after their "marriage," the couple decided it was time to head home. Land deals and legal concerns necessitated a return trip to Nashville for the newlyweds. They were to travel north up the Natchez Trace alongside approximately one hundred others, united by a common belief in "safety in numbers." Although no attacks were reported on the riverboat journey to Natchez, the return trip was to be made overland through this dangerous country. The Natchez Trace was notorious for its hazards, with small groups often targeted by robbers, murderers, and hostile tribes. The Chickasaw and Choctaw were generally friendly, but the perpetually aggrieved Creeks sometimes caused travelers trouble, prompting Jackson to opt for traveling in a group, especially considering his beloved Rachel accompanied him.

Among the hundred frontier citizens making the journey up the Natchez Trace in September 1791, only three names are known: Andrew and Rachel Jackson, along with a Kentucky soldier and Indian fighter named Hugh McGary. McGary had pioneered Kentucky with Daniel Boone and settled in Boonesborough, traveling with Boone on his second expedition through the Cumberland Gap. Loud and domineering, McGary had a fierce temper that proved useful in battle but often alienated him from others in daily life. Nonetheless, he was just the type of added protection necessary for the often-tempestuous journey through the perils of the frontier trail.[146]

By the time the forty-seven-year-old McGary journeyed toward Nashville with the Jacksons, he had been dismissed from military command, court-martialed, and found guilty of murdering a Shawnee sachem. He had a contentious history with Boone and was known to have killed another Shawnee combatant during a skirmish in Kentucky. McGary's volatile nature was well-documented. It was noted that McGary was "void of humane and gentle qualities" and "a quarrelsome and unpleasant man in civil life." Ironically, his wife Mary is said to have brought the first Bible into Kentucky, though she was not on this trip.

Along with McGary, Andrew Jackson, never one to be accused of a dispassionate temperament himself, traveling north on the Natchez Trace in the humid fall air of Mississippi with the love of his life, trouble was surely brewing.

In 1791, the Mississippi Territory, through which the Natchez Trace ran, was acknowledged by the United States government as being under the control of the Choctaw Indians in the south and the Chickasaw Indians in the north. Both tribes maintained friendly relations with the U.S. and played significant roles in peace treaties signed in Nashville in 1783 and in Hopewell, South Carolina, in 1786. Encounters between Chickasaw and Choctaw Indians and travelers on the Natchez Trace were common during the 1790s and were generally peaceful. Negative interactions between settlers and either the Chickasaw or Choctaws often stemmed from trading exchanges or friendly visits among individuals who had likely met before.

However, a conflict arose during the journey between Jackson and Hugh McGary concerning a perceived "Indian attack." The specifics of the potential conflict involving the Indians are unclear. It is evident that Jackson and McGary quickly adopted opposing responses to the potentially incendiary situation.

Given McGary's known bombastic nature and the fact that Jackson was traveling with his new bride, it is reasonable to speculate that McGary pushed for confrontation while Jackson, acting as a protector, advised against it. Jackson may have highlighted McGary's history of poor

---

[146] Richey, Clark, "Jackson v. McGary," *Talk of the Town*. 2020.

decisions to the other travelers, who likely understood that no credible threat from the Chickasaws or Choctaws existed. There were no reports of the more hostile Creeks at the time of this particular incident either. Ultimately, whatever threat was perceived faded without incident, and the Jacksons, McGary, and the other travelers safely reached Nashville in October 1791.[147]

This conflict marked the beginning of a lifelong enmity, however, between McGary and Jackson. John Overton later explained that the origins of their feud occurred as a result of their disagreement over the perceived attack on their return trip: "Circumstances then occurred calculated to excite in McGary a strong feeling of dislike toward General Jackson, which it is unnecessary to detail as they related solely to a meditated attack by the Indians." As a result of some unspecified grudge toward Jackson, McGary sought revenge. Perhaps his authority, McGary felt, had been undermined by Jackson in such a way that he was made to look foolish. Unfortunately for Rachel and Andrew Jackson, an opportunity for McGary to act vengefully soon arose.[148]

In the fall of 1793, when Lewis Robards finally brought his case before a jury to culminate the divorce suit, he brought along a star witness for the proceedings, Hugh McGary himself. McGary testified before the court that on the return trip from their Natchez "honeymoon" Andrew and Rachel Jackson had "slept under the same blanket." Consequently, the jury ruled as they did in favor of Robards due largely to McGary's testimony; he had achieved his revenge.

Rachel Jackson could never fully escape scandal, which was fueled by McGary's testimony. McGary passed away in 1806, but his vendetta would persist and rear its ugly head once again years later.

And so it transpired. Whether they arrived in Nashville in spring or autumn of 1790 or 1791, they did so as husband and wife after the news of Robards' divorce. No one asked to see a divorce decree or marriage license. The Donelson family welcomed Rachel and her new husband, viewing him as a significant improvement over the previous one. Despite the irregularities of their union, it provided Jackson with an emotional security he had never experienced.

---

[147] Richey, Clark, "McGary's Untempered Bravado." *Talk of the Town*. 2020.
[148] Richey, Clark, "McGary's Untempered Bravado." *Talk of the Town*. 2020.

Andrew and Rachel Jackson were both twenty-four years old at the time of their Natchez wedding, and upon their return from the Mississippi town, the happy couple would spend the next two years residing with Rachel's mother. But with Jackson's fortunes as a savvy land-dealer and attorney on the rise, the move into their own home was the obvious next step. To provide Rachel with a suitable home, records show that Jackson purchased a 330-acre property in Jones Bend from her brother, John Donelson, in February 1792. The deed, on file at the Davidson County Courthouse, identifies the property, Poplar Grove, as running east from the river 329 poles, or just over a mile. No description is left of the house Jackson had built, or any record as to whether John Donelson constructed it, nor whether Jackson himself was the builder. It seems probable that, since the property does not mention any "improvements," which was the usual designation of buildings already erected, that it was built for the Jacksons. No doubt it was made of logs, as were most of the frontier homes of the period. It got its name from the fine poplar trees that grew around it.

As the Jacksons were becoming ensconced in their new home at Poplar Grove in late 1793, the happy couple soon received stunning news from John Overton. During a working visit to Jonesborough, Jackson was embarrassed and dismayed to discover that Lewis Robards' divorce from Rachel had only just been finalized. Robards had begun the process over two years earlier but had only completed it now. This disconcerting news not only revived questions about Jackson and Rachel's elopement but also indicated that their marriage was, in fact, illegal. Overton suggested a quiet wedding ceremony to resolve the matter, to which Jackson declined, adamantly insisting that he and Rachel were already legally married. Opposing Overton's suggestion, Jackson felt that a renewed wedding ceremony could be seen as a concession that would vindicate Robards, and appear as if the Jacksons had been aware all along of their illicit coupling. He and Rachel would not "remarry," Jackson firmly asserted, because their initial wedding before God was legitimate in the eyes of the public, and doing so would be an admission of guilt. Overton reminded Jackson, however, that the courts had their own requirements.

As noted, Jackson finally and reluctantly accepted Overton's reasoning, and followed his friend's to marry Rachel legally in the eyes of the law. With these proceedings completed, the issue remained settled for several years, and they nearly forgot it had ever been a concern. However, Andrew Jackson, as a high-ranking official of the court system, should well have known better. And, by no means would this be the end of the issue. [149]

Most of Andrew Jackson's adult life would be spent close to what is now the Village of Old Hickory, named after the famous General. He would never venture far; with the exception of times in which service to his country compelled him, whether in war or as commander in chief, Jackson would always hang his hat near the quick-flowing Cumberland River. Some of the Jackson couple's happiest years would be spent in the first home he and Rachel built together at Poplar Grove, surrounded by pine forests, just a few miles northeast of downtown Nashville, on the banks of the Cumberland River.

The completed home was first occupied by the Jacksons no later than May 16, 1794, based on a letter that survives to this day, bearing that date, written from there by Jackson to friend John McKee. Jackson referred to his estate also as "Poplar Flat" as indicated by a letter he wrote to John Overton, headed "Poplar Flat, June 10, 1795." Jackson's well on the property is a last remnant of the life the young couple built on their riverside estate. They would remain in the home until Jackson sold it to another Donelson in-law in 1797, prior to their move to nearby Hunter's Hill.

Despite its difficult beginnings, the marriage into the Donelson family significantly elevated Andrew Jackson's social standing. No family in western Tennessee, aside from James Robertson's, had greater distinction. His connection to his Donelson in-laws opened the doors to opportunities that would have likely been denied to Jackson. His union with Rachel not only enhanced his social stature, which Jackson valued greatly, but also provided him with a crucial partner in managing the growing Jackson estate. Away frequently on business matters, Rachel skillfully managed their Poplar Grove "farm," (really a plantation) a substantial undertaking. Jackson later credited her with the plantation's success, declaring that, without her, it would have fallen into disrepair

---

[149] Ibid; Marriage License, Miscellaneous Jackson Papers, HUL; Robison, Dan M., "Robert Hays, Unsung Pioneer of the Cumberland Country," THQ (Fall 1967), XXV, 263-278.

and ruin. Historians, too, have recognized Rachel's exceptional administrative abilities as key to the plantation's steady prosperity.

Jackson's perspective on marriage is evident in a letter to a younger relative, where he advised, "A man must have more than romance on his mind when he seeks a wife. Seek one who will aid you in your exertions in making a competency and will take care of it when made, for you will find it easier to spend two thousand dollars than to make five hundred. Look at the economy of the mother and if you find it in her you will find it in the daughter. recollect the industry of your dear aunt (Rachel), and with what economy she watched over what I made, and how we waded through the vast expence of the mass of company we had. nothing but her care and industry, with good economy could have saved me from ruin. If she had been extravagant the property would have vanished and poverty and want would have been our doom. Think of this before you attempt to select a wife." In his later years, Jackson reflected on how much he owed his beloved wife for his success.[150]

The fortunes of the public prosecutor, slave owner, mercantile store owner, land dealer, and sometimes slave trader Andrew Jackson continued to improve in his and Rachel's happy years at Poplar Grove. Steadily, a degree of regional notoriety and fame would grow even further throughout the 1790s. Well-known throughout the Cumberland Settlements, Jackson prospered in Nashville, despite his early conflicts with Lewis Robards. He built a legal practice, entered into trading ventures, eventually sold his general store before it went under, and continued to increase his holdings in both land and slaves. His land transactions began to bear fruit with the rush of settlement beyond the mountains that continued to increase throughout the 1790s, as the population of Tennessee tripled between 1790 and 1800.

In the 1790s, however, the people of the Cumberland Region faced the persistent "Indian Problem" that had long hounded American frontier families. Despite treaties and various punitive measures taken by settlers against tribes such as the Creek, Chickamauga, Cherokee

---

[150] Jackson, *Correspondence*, V, 60.

and Choctaw, violence continued. The persistent problem, as was the case in other regions on the American frontier, was constant white encroachment on indigenous lands, far beyond the provision of previous treaties. These encroachments often brought retributive attacks by tribal forces. Leaders such as Jackson, Governor William Blount, General James Robertson, and other key figures expressed frustration over the Federal government's inaction. With mounting pressure from his constituents to take decisive action on the one hand, and instructions from the Washington administration to avoid any military offensives on the other, William Blount faced a recurring and frustrating dilemma.

During the Revolutionary War, the Cherokee band of Chickamauga conducted ongoing raids against American settlers, often with assistance from British and Spanish forces. After the war, they moved west of Lookout Mountain and used Nickajack Cave as a stronghold. Violence between the Chickamauga and western frontiersmen persisted for decades. Despite the December 1791 Treaty of Holston between Governor Blount and most Cherokee bands, settlers in the Cumberland Region, particularly around Nashville, remained fearful. Frequent raids by the Chickamauga and their Creek allies had brought increased tensions to the frontier. In 1792, Blount engaged in continued peace negotiations with the various tribes. However, when the Chickamauga launched an attack against the Mero District in September 1792, which was thwarted at the Battle of Buchanan's Station, negotiations collapsed, leading to two more years of defensive engagements.

Andrew Jackson, with his growing political prestige, and reputation as a brave frontier traveler and Indian fighter, summed up the feelings of many in the Cumberland in a letter, "I fear that their peace talks are only delusions," he wrote in 1794, "and in order to put us off-guard; why Treat with them, does not Experience teach us that treaties answer no other purpose than opening an easy door for the Indians to pass through to Butcher our citizens. What motives Congress are governed by with respect to their pacific disposition towards Indians I know not; some say humanity dictates it; but certainly she ought to extend an equal share of humanity to her own citizens...[151]"

---

[151] Jackson, Correspondence to McKee, pg. 12-13.

The Cumberland settlements remained prime targets for the Chickamauga bands, leading to both physical and psychological damage to the local population. The settlers continued to insist on governmental action, arguing that American lives were being sacrificed due to the federal government's indifference. The Chickamauga allied with the more hostile Creek tribes, conducting a series of raids on the lower towns near Chattanooga. Villages were burned and pillaged throughout the region, in a desperate attempt to drive settlers away. However, a strong defense was mounted, and white settlers, vowing retribution against the outraged tribes, struck back even more violently. The Chickamauga's resistance against encroachment into their territory would culminate in a bloody confrontation that forever tipped the balance of power in the region in favor of the whites.

Earlier incidents of bloodshed against settlers were the catalysts for the ultimate military campaign against the Chickamauga. Just under forty miles northeast of downtown Nashville today is a town known as Castilian Springs, a salt lick and sulfur water spring formerly known as Bledsoe's Lick, it was first "discovered" by Col. Isaac Bledsoe, while hunting in 1772. Bledsoe reported that he saw such a large herd of buffalos by the springs that he was afraid to get off his horse for fear he would be run over and trampled to death. He returned with settlers in 1780 and built a station near the spring. In 1779, in order to help protect the growing settlement, Bledsoe built a fort on the hill south of the springs and about three hundred yards west of where Bledsoe Academy is located today. Isaac's brother, Col. Anthony Bledsoe came about two years after the fort was built, and he built a nearby fort of his own to reinforce the family's protection. [152]

However, while visiting his brother Isaac's fort in Bledsoe's Lick, Anthony Bledsoe was killed by the Indians on July 20th, 1788. The attack occurred in the dead of night and was the first violence since a recent treaty. The circumstances of the killing were these: Col. Anthony Bledsoe had left his fort at Greenfield and moved in one end of the double cabins on the property. A lane came down at right angles to the fort, with the mouth of it being about thirty yards from the Nashville Road. The attackers, a band of young Chickamauga warriors, prowling during the

---

[152] 2025 Bledsoe's Lick Historical Association

day, had lay in wait, ready to strike at the most opportune moment. By nightfall, with a bright moon in the sky, they posted themselves in the fence corners fronting the passage between the two cabins. To distract the men in the fort, the warriors mounted a small party on horseback and galloped loudly past the fort, hoping to attract the persons into the passage through which the moonlight poured in full splendor. The plan succeeded: for at the sound of the horses feet, Col. Anthony Bledsoe and his servant, Campbell, both jumped to their feet and ran out into the passage. The Chickamauga lying in wait had a clear shot, and both men were gunned down.

Col. Anthony Bledsoe died the next morning and the servant Campbell the morning after. The trouble, however, was not over. Another officer, General James Hall had also been asleep in the fort's cabin, and being aroused by the firing of the guns, jumped up and went to the portholes with the other men in the fort. The men stayed on the lookout until daylight. In the morning the Chickamauga warriors had disappeared. The men in the fort, thinking the bloodshed was over, then found a neighbor, Mr. Walters shot to death on a creek not far from the fort, where Branham's Mill now stands.

During the winter, 1788-89, Charles Morgan and John Gibson were killed as they were going from the fort at Bledsoe's Lick to the house of General Hall. Again, there was evidence that their deaths were at the hands of the same Chickamauga band. Not long after the killing of Col. Bledsoe, the men of the fort were in the cabin that had been occupied by the deceased Bledsoe. A school master by the name of George Hamilton was entertaining the men as they sat in front of the fire, singing at the top of his voice. Another band of warriors, again lying in wait around the house, found a crack in the back of the chimney and pointed a gun through the crack, firing on Hamilton. The bullet hit Hamilton's chin, breaking his jawbone. Somehow, Hamilton survived the attack.

Despite the danger, Colonel Isaac Bledsoe and another brother, Jesse, still remained in the fort close to five years later when, on April 23, 1793, the elder Bledsoe was killed in the field three or four hundred yards west of the fort. This time the attack had been at sunrise as the Colonel and his servants were going out to tend to some log heaps that they were burning in the clearing. The following year, a son of Anthony Bledsoe and a nephew of Anthony and Isaac (also named Anthony) were both ambushed and killed near Rock Castle at what is now Hendersonville. Again, white settlers identified the Chickamauga as the culprits and vowed continued revenge.

Yet, to many settlers of the Cumberland, the final straw occurred when, on the morning of July 9, 1794, when the well-respected Major George Winchester, Revolutionary War veteran, and commander of the local Militia, was on his way from Bledsoe's Lick to a meeting of the Sumner County Quarterly Court, of which he was a member. As George, the brother of militia general James Hamilton neared the town of Gallatin, at the junction of present-day Hartsville and Scottsville Pikes, he was ambushed, killed and scalped. "He was the last, but by one, to be thus killed," according to Colonel William Martin, who described him as "...a superior man in every way to the General. They [the Indians] killed Major Winchester, near the site of Gallatin, while he was on his way to court. He was an excellent man, and we suffered a great loss in his death." [153]

The deaths of both Colonel Anthony Bledsoe's and Major General George Winchester's sons by 1794 prompted Governor Blount to finally sanction military action. Andrew Jackson, fueled by anger and resentment from the killings, emerged as a prominent figure advocating for the Chickamauga's removal. His letters expressed strong sentiments against what he referred to as the "red men" and their actions. Encouraging the government to act in retribution Jackson wrote, "in doing this Congress would act justly and punish the barbarians for murdering her innocent citizens.....they (the barbarians) ought to be Scurged for the infringement of the Treaty. I dread the consequence of the ensuing summer. The Indian appears very Troublesome the Frontier discouraged and breaking and numbers leaving the Territory and moving to Kentucky, this Country is Declining fast, and unless Congress lends us a more ample protection this Country will have at length to break or seek protection from some other Source than the present." [154]

Despite explicit federal orders to refrain from military action, the leaders in the Cumberland devised a plan. Frustrated with the federal government's inaction, General Robertson took charge and orchestrated

---

[153] Carr, John, *Early Times in Middle Tennessee*, Chapter 4, 1857.
[154] Jackson to McKee, *Correspondence*, pg. 12-13.

an attack against the Chickamauga towns. Major James Ore was appointed to lead the militia troops in September 1794. In a letter from Robertson from Nashville to Major Ore on Sept. 6th, 1794, Robertson orders, "The object of your command is to defend the District of Mero against the Creeks and Cherokees of the lower towns, who I have received information are about to invade it, as also to punish such Indians as have committed recent depredations. For these objects, you will march, with the men under your command, from Brown's Block House on the 8th instant, and proceed along Taylor's Trace towards the Tennessee; and if you do not meet this party before you arrive at the Tennessee; you will pass it and destroy the lower Cherokee towns, which must serve as a check to the expected invaders; taking care to spare women and children, and to treat all prisoners who may fall into your hands with humanity, and thereby teach those savages to spare the citizens of the United States, under similar circumstances. Should you in your march discover the trails of Indians returning from commission of recent depredations on the frontiers, which can generally be distinguished by the horses stolen being shod, you are to give pursuit to such parties, even to the towns from whence they came, and punish them for their aggressions in an exemplary manner to the terror of others from the commission of similar offenses, provided this can be consistent with the main object of your command, as above expressed, the defense of the District of Mero against the expected party of Creeks and Cherokees. I have the utmost confidence in your patriotism and bravery, and with my warmest wishes for your success."[155]

Although Governor Blount gave Robertson explicit orders to stay in compliance with federal regulations, and only employ troops for defensive tactics, Robertson seems to have taken those directives with a grain of salt. The expedition successfully reached Nickajack Town in mid-August, but found only a small number of warriors present, as many villagers had fled to Running Water Town. As the American soldiers pursued fleeing villagers, they encountered the returning Chickamauga warriors. The ensuing battle at "the Narrows" along the Tennessee River resulted in a disastrous defeat for the Chickamauga, who managed to wound only three Americans and suffered significant losses, with 70

---

[155] Robertson to Ore, Sept. 6, 1794, Robertson Papers, LC.

of their own dead. The battle also resulted in the destruction of both villages.

In response to "provocation beyond endurance from the Indians," General Robertson and his expedition sent a powerful message by inflicting such severe losses on the Chickamauga, who were thus forced to leave the Cumberland settlements in peace once and for all. This conflict, known as the "Nickajack Expedition," marked a turning point in the long-standing struggle between Robertson's frontiersmen and the Chickamauga Cherokee. To many, the ends justified the means, as the settlements were provided with a period of relief from attack. Robertson, however, was forced to resign his military commission as a result of his disregard for governmental orders, despite Robertson's written plea to Blount expressing his regret for his "high-handedness." Robertson's punishment was ultimately a small slap on the wrist, as the General was close to retirement as it was. By his remorseful words, and his insistence on his desire for right-minded citizenship and obedience to the law, Robertson managed to retain his political standing with the Governor. To Andrew Jackson, Robertson's actions were to be commended, and his example of how to mete out frontier justice, when it came to subduing the indigenous, was absorbed. [156]

The Nickajack Expedition became infamous as the "Last Battle of the Cherokee." Following this defeat, the Cherokee tribe agreed to yet another treaty, ceding more of their ancestral lands. Following the Cherokee defeat at Nickajack and Running Water towns, American military victories had subdued the once formidable Cherokee Nation. Ultimately, thirty-nine Cherokee leaders, including those from the Chickamauga, signed the 1798 Treaty of Tellico, ceding a large portion of land in East Tennessee to the United States.[157]

Earlier treaties honored by the Washington administration may have delayed such actions, but by the fall of 1794, the opportunity to end the Cherokee threat outweighed concerns for indigenous rights. Overall, the federal government did not seem inclined to discipline their generals on the frontier any more than Blount had been. After

---

[156] Roberston to Blount, October 1, 1794, in *AHM* (October 1898), III, 361.
[157] United States (1846). "A Century of Lawmaking for a New Nation: U.S. Congressional Documents and Debates, 1774 - 1875". *Statutes at Large*. Boston: Charles C. Little and James Brown. pp. 62–65. LCCN 98660545. Retrieved May 17, 2011.

being forced to resign his commission, when no replacement officer was named, Robertson continued to go about his duties as though nothing had happened. The end result was clear to other frontier officers from Robertson's example: that orders from the federal government, when it came to Native Americans, were subject to discretion, and these orders could be ignored when one felt the need.

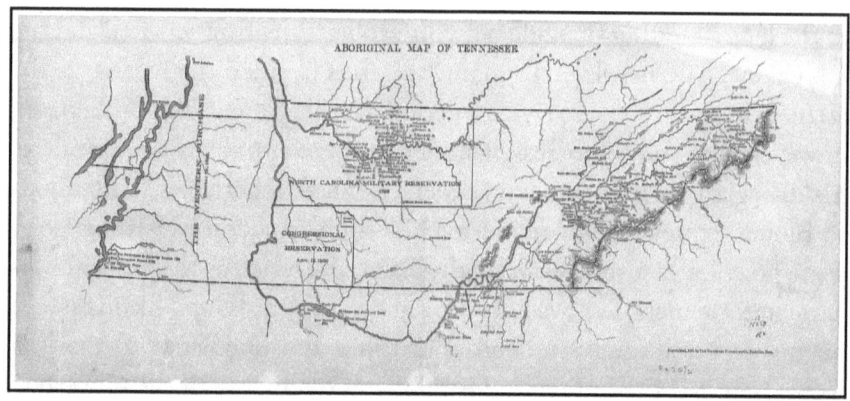

Aboriginal Map of Tennessee, Source: Library of Congress

CHAPTER

15

STATEHOOD

"Westward, ever westward."
-Henry Wells

Following the Nickajack expedition, settlers began to pour into the Cumberland settlements. Putnam's *History of Middle Tennessee* describes the influx as follows, "On the last summer, a good wagon road was cut across Cumberland Mountain, and it was passed by thirty or forty wagons in the fall. The late friendly conduct by the Cherokee Indians, in consequence of a long talk with Governor Blount, and the amicable disposition of the Spanish government, has greatly altered the condition for the settlers on the Cumberland River, and made them perfectly happy. Several thousands crossed the Cumberland in September, October, November last, in detached families, without a guard and without danger. The Indians treated them with kindness, visited their camp at night, and supplied them plentifully with venison."[158] This report brought more settlers into the region.

The dark clouds that portended trouble on the frontier had begun to dissipate by the mid-1790s, replaced by luminous blue, sunny skies. The economy, while still in its adolescence, had grown out of its infancy, and had begun to flourish, with new manufactories along its key rivers. Pushing to the banks of the mighty Mississippi, the crowded east could now point its ever-growing population west, to the hills beyond the Smoky Mountains, which joined Kentucky and the new Northwest

---
[158] Putnam, A.W., *History of Middle Tennessee.* P. 351.

Territory as "safety valves" to relieve the density of the Atlantic Seaboard. With these developments, a new generation of Americans pushed west, with high hopes for a continued prosperity.

With the rising population, Governor Blount now decided the time was ripe for bold action by the Southwest Territory. Having temporarily silenced the noise of his constituents regarding internal threats, Blount used the reprieve to take a bold and decisive step. He would petition the government to accept the admission of the new state of Tennessee into the Union. Blount was well aware of the benefits of statehood, as with it, he and the government could manage its "Indian problem" any way it chose. Traditionally opposed to increased forms of representation by the people within his district, efforts to push for statehood represented an about face for the previously semi-dictatorial Blount, who had long viewed representative government as a means to undermine his control of the territory. But as more people entered the region, any delays for added representation threatened the governor's popularity, thus, Blount was forced to relent.

Reluctantly, in late 1793, Blount ordered the election of thirteen men to form a House of Representatives for the Southwest Territory. This body met at Knoxville, nominating ten men, of which President Washington chose five, to serve as the upper house of the legislative Territory. Ironically, most of these five were associates of Blount's land speculation, and they included John Sevier, Stokely Donelson (Jackson's brother-in-law), James Winchester, and Griffith Rutherford. Rutherford was chosen as presiding officer of the legislature, and Dr. James White was sent off to Washington as representative for the Southwest Territory in Congress.

A territorial legislature was one thing, but relinquishing control of his territory was another matter entirely. More than two years later, William Blount had yet to take any action that might compromise his authority. However, as he began to recognize the advantages of statehood for Tennessee, his perspective began to shift by mid-1795. For instance, the governor realized a bonus of statehood was that he would no longer have to bear the added burden of serving as Indian Commissioner, forced to confront the challenges posed by Native Americans himself. Furthermore, Blount's land holdings stood to gain significantly from such a move, enabling him to hand off the responsibility of protecting such lands to more qualified individuals: prominent frontier fighters like "Nolichucky Jack" himself, John Sevier was to be recruited for such purposes. Another factor likely influencing Blount's change of heart involved the threat to his own power Sevier's popularity posed, whose pursuit of higher office had become a concern, as Sevier's wide support base meant Blount was likely to be supplanted as power broker by Nolichucky Jack. Statehood would alleviate this issue, as Blount envisioned himself securing the new senatorial seat that would accompany statehood, while allowing Sevier to assume the governorship. Blount could not only escape Knoxville for Philadelphia but would have even more access to national resources and decision-making power.[159]

William Blount was known for his adept political maneuvering, and his management of the Tennessee statehood process showcased his skills remarkably. He first communicated his intentions through his favored outlet, the *Knoxville Gazette*. On August 25, 1794, the *Gazette* published an article aligned with Blount's wishes, urging the legislature to "take measures that this territory may, as speedily as possible, become a member state of the federal union." Blount subsequently informed his most trusted circle of his plans and promised them a share of the rewards. In a letter to James Robertson, Blount expressed his desire to address the Cherokee issue, which Robertson was eager to tackle. This offered a compelling way to gain the community's support by proposing a solution to the looming threat of Indian attack, and Robertson was persuaded.[160]

In order to expedite this process, Blount went right to work. First, he pushed a bill through the General Assembly to conduct a census aimed at determining the population total required for statehood. The minimum requirement was 60,000, and upon completion, the census revealed the Southwest's population exceeded 77,000. Confirming the count, Blount then reached out to Congressman White to explore the fastest route for Tennessee's admission into the Union. This initiative was unprecedented, as no territory had yet achieved statehood. However, the Northwest Ordinance of 1787 outlined a procedure for this purpose, and Tennessee would be the first to utilize it.[161]

---

[159] Blount to John Gray Blount, Oct. 1794, in Blount Papers, II, 449.
[160] Archives of the Knoxville Gazette, 1794.; Keith, Alice Barnwell, *The North Carolina Blount Brothers*, p. 412.
[161] Ramsey, J.G.M., *Annals of Tennessee*, p. 653.

White informed Blount that the initial step was to hold a vote among the citizens for statehood. Next, an application would need to be submitted to Congress, along with the drafting of a state constitution by an elected assembly. Blount initiated the voting process, and as anticipated, the majority of citizens favored the proposal, which passed with a vote of 6,504 to 2,562. Part of the appeal to many of the voters came about as a result of another shrewd move by the orchestrator Blount, who initiated an economic survey to be conducted on the territory. Blount's purpose of this was to demonstrate to Congress the economic health of the Southwest territory, thereby convincing the representatives in the House of the merits allowing Tennessee into the Union would bring. The results of the financial report were so favorable that Congress recommended a tax reduction at the first state assembly. This helped convince the public to vote in favor of statehood.

Blount continued his rapid political orchestrations with aplomb. The governor then convened a constitutional convention in Knoxville, where delegates from various counties developed a model state constitution and a democratic bill of rights. The Tennessee Constitution drew inspiration from both the United States Constitution as well as that of the state of North Carolina's. It permitted free males aged 21 or older who owned land to vote, regardless of race. Thus, both white and free Black men meeting the criteria could participate in elections. As Blount had foreseen, the voters selected John Sevier as governor. The speed at which all of this was handled was remarkable; the legislature met in Knoxville for only a few weeks.

As the Southwest Territory was the first Federal territory to seek statehood, Congress faced uncertainty regarding the process. Members of the Federalist Party opposed statehood for Tennessee, fearing that Tennessee voters would favor their adversaries, the Democratic-Republicans. Senator Sedgwick of Massachusetts led the Federalist opposition. Ultimately, the opposing Federalists lost in a narrow vote. Congress approved Tennessee's admission as the sixteenth state of the Union on June 1, 1796, with a final tally of 43-30. Knoxville was designated as the first state capital.

Following the advice of his mentor, Governor Blount, Jackson was among the many Tennesseans who favored statehood, despite the fact that a large percentage in his home county did not. Part of the reason for so many Davidson County citizens' hesitance was likely their resentment of the eastern counties' domination of the territory. But Jackson saw opportunity with the transition to statehood, and by ensuring a close relationship with Blount, Jackson was rewarded, singled out as one of the more promising young men of the district by those in Blount's camp. Jackson's standing among this influential group is evidenced in a letter from Joseph Anderson, one of the five appointees by President Washington to the territory's upper house, offering Jackson a post as one of the new state's Congressmen. "We would be entitled to Two representatives in Congress. My choice, as well as a number of others, for one of these posts, is yourself." [162]

Jackson's political career in Tennessee progressed with speed and alacrity. He was first chosen as one of just five Davidson County delegates at the state constitutional convention in 1795. As soon as the convention got underway, two delegates were chosen from each county to draft a preliminary constitution. Two of the most learned and able men were chosen from each county, and both John McNairy and Jackson got the nod for Davidson County. The various deliberations of the convention were not recorded for posterity, so there is no definitive way to determine the amount of influence the Davidson County delegates had in the creation of the state constitution, but those present attested to the moderation and harmony of the proceedings. Governor Blount had been instrumental in choosing a majority of the candidates himself through a variety of means to ensure pro-statehood representation, which ensured the proceedings were much less divisive. This also assured the pro-Blount partisans a large measure of control over the outcome. The convention took 27 days all told, in the little building in Knoxville that later became a schoolhouse.

By all accounts, Jackson made a strong showing at the Knoxville convention among the delegates. Hesitant to appear to be the orchestrator of motions on the floor, he played a more reserved role, appearing more subordinate and behind the scenes than he really was, influencing older members of his delegation to propose bills which he would subsequently second, and argued vociferously in favor of. While he refrained from taking the lead, his engaging speeches and respectable arguments

---

[162] Anderson to AJ, Jackson Papers, LC, p. 15

enhanced his stature among the other delegates. This showing at the convention did much to establish Jackson as a prominent figure in the western community.

By the conclusion of the convention on February 6, 1796, Jackson had gained a large degree of respect within the Blount circle, proving himself a reliable supporter of the territory's land interests. On another issue, Jackson won points by supporting Blount as a proponent of a two-house legislature, against a rival faction pressing for a unicameral body. Jackson's support in favor of Blount's proposal helped the motion pass, and Tennessee's constitution called for both a state House of Representatives and a state Senate. Blount grew in his appreciation of Jackson as a result and sought to promote the young Tennessean when the opportunity arose.[163]

Jackson's activity, energy and decisiveness throughout the convention impressed not only the Blount clique, but many of the county delegations throughout the convention. Participating actively in debates supporting proposals that showcased his growth as a credible politician, Jackson established himself more fully as a key figure in western Tennessee. A legend has it that it was Jackson who came up with the name of Tennessee for the new state, although this turned out to be proven false. The name was actually derived from Tinnase or Tenase, the name of a Cherokee chief, and of course the name Native Americans used for the Tennessee River, as well as the short-lived Tennessee County. The name was already in general use at the time, largely as a result of the book by General Daniel Smith entitled *Short Description of Tennessee's Government*, published in 1793.[164] Nonetheless, Jackson and others liked the name for its smooth, attractive sound that, they declared, captured the beauty of its landscape. Better yet, the name sounded American, not like so many previous state names that reflected the English monarchy. This would have most certainly appealed to the intense anglophobe Jackson, with his distaste for all things British.

Before the finalization of the original version of the Constitution, a debate arose concerning the Presbyterian tradition of delegates taking an oath. This oath was intended to be a declaration of faith required

---

[163] Ibid, p. 654
[164] Smith, Daniel, *Short Description of Tennessee's Government*, 1796, pp. 2-36.

from all officeholders, affirming their belief in God, an afterlife, and the divine authority of the holy scriptures. Jackson opposed this motion, and ultimately, the opposition prevailed. The original Constitution also contained a provision that prohibited clergymen from holding civil or military office or any position of trust within the state. Jackson opposed this exclusion and voted against it, which resulted in the overturning of the provision.

Interestingly, Jackson, the later champion of the Common Man, supported a requirement that candidates for the General Assembly be required to possess at least 200 acres of property. His stance reflected the views of many frontiersmen of the time, who were generally conservative on issues of property rights and slavery, resisting governmental interference in these matters. However, when it came to the issue of government responsibility for protection against Indian attacks, he strongly advocated for the full utilization of state resources.

Despite the fact that most voters in the Nashville area were against statehood, Jackson saw the impracticality of creating a separate state for the western counties. The western half of the state held just under 12,000 people at the time, and therefore the Cumberland settlers would have to wait years to gain the required 60,000. As a result, Jackson understood that aligning with the eastern counties was essential for gaining statehood, and he voted accordingly, putting him in league with Governor Blount. While Jackson sided with Blount in recognizing the necessity of statehood for Tennessee as a means of protecting their land speculation, as well as their local interests, the problem for these eager Tennesseans at the Knoxville Convention was that none of these efforts had been done with federal approval from Congress. Blount, in his haste, had only sought the logistics of the process from Congressman White. By initiating the statehood proceedings, Tennessee had acted alone. In response, an offended Congress was unwilling to accept the actions of what they viewed as a hasty territorial government.[165]

The political tug of war between Tennessee and the national government was further complicated by the impending presidential election, with concerns that Tennessee's admission would benefit

---

[165] Williams, Charlotte, "Congressional Action on the Admission of Tennessee into the Union." *THQ*, Dec. 1943, II, 291-315.

Thomas Jefferson's campaign against the Federalists. Opposition within Congress, especially among New England Federalists, argued that Tennessee's statehood lacked proper congressional initiative and that its constitution was flawed. Nonetheless, supporters in Congress argued for the people's right to statehood, and a favorable report on the admission bill was submitted.

On April 12, 1796, after considerable debate, the House of Representatives passed the bill for Tennessee's admission by a vote of 43 to 30, with substantial support from the Republican majority. The Senate initially opposed the bill, led by future presidential candidate Rufus King, who cited the inaccuracy of the census count as their reasoning. Eventually, however, they agreed to a compromise that allowed for immediate admission while reducing Tennessee's representation temporarily. The delay by the Senate was decried by the Jeffersonians as a ploy to deny the Republican campaign the original representation Tennessee would have been granted, which would have surely gone to Jefferson. The Federalist tactic worked out well for their candidate Adams who won the election by a majority of three votes. Nonetheless, statehood was granted, and President Washington signed the bill on June 1, 1796, making Tennessee the 16th state.[166]

After admission, the Tennessee legislature quickly re-elected its senators and adjusted their electoral votes, frustrated with Congress over representation and inaccurate taxation. The Federalist opposition to statehood destroyed the party's strength in Tennessee, with many key leaders, including William Blount, shifting political allegiance to the Republicans. Blount, who had run an efficient territorial government, threw his support behind Andrew Jackson in his bid to become Tennessee's representative in Congress. Jackson, having established his popularity and connections among the delegates at the Convention, was elected to become Tennessee's first Congressman at the age of twenty-nine, without serious opposition. The orphan Andy was on his way to the nation's capital.

However, it had become clear to both Blount and Jackson that the political dynamics in Tennessee were shifting. Signs of emerging

---

[166] Williams, Samuel C., "The Admission of Tennessee into the Union," *THQ*, Dec. 1945, IV, 291-319.

opposition to the Blount faction were rearing its belligerent head by the end of the Knoxville convention, particularly from the supporters of new Governor John Sevier, who seemed to resent being overshadowed by Blount's political maneuverings. The new state of Tennessee was already divided, as growing tensions between eastern and western counties, state and federal authority factions, the struggle for local representation, and the competition among emerging political leaders, all of which would shape the future of the state and its governance.

Years later, Jackson's political acumen would draw the attention of keen observers who speculated about his earlier influences. Although not crediting anyone explicitly, it is reasonable to assume that he modeled much of his political approach on the cunning William Blount, whose controversial political methods were undeniably effective. Blount appreciated Jackson's strong western views, which resonated with many Cumberland settlers. Jackson was outspoken about the actions of Native Americans, the Spanish, and the British, gaining wide support in western Tennessee for their "criminalities." In Jackson's frequent criticisms of the ineffectiveness of Congress, the new Congressman was especially cheered. [167]

---

[167] AJ to Macon, Nathaniel, Oct. 4, 1795, Jackson, *Correspondence*, I, 17-18.

CHAPTER

16

REVOLUTIONARY CHANGES

"Your people, sir, is a great beast.... The people are turbulent and changing; they seldom judge or determine the right."
-Alexander Hamilton

On July 14, 1789, a riotous mob of Parisians–overtaxed, overworked, and unfairly imprisoned—revolted against King Louis XVI of France. They did so in intemperate fashion, by storming the Bastille–a dank prison described by the Marquis de Lafayette as France's "fortress of despotism"[168]---killed several soldiers and then paraded the severed heads of its commanding officer and the mayor of Paris throughout the city. This marked the beginning of the French Revolution, and its bloody launch was a sign of things to come.

The unexpected intensity of the events in France shocked Europe, and its effects would resonate powerfully across the Atlantic, deeply affecting the young United States. The ideals of liberty, equality, and fraternity; the initial rallying cries of the French Revolutionaries, and the fervor of the Revolution's ideals, rang far and wide. Inspired by the American Revolution, the turbulent events in France would play crucial roles in shaping the nation. The French Revolution, which would rage on for most of the 1790s, reshaped not only France, but impacted much of the world.

---

[168] Kennedy and Cohen, *The American Pageant*, Wadsworth, Cengage Learning Distributor, 2013. pg. 190.

As the revolution unfolded, American citizens watched closely, stirred by a connection to the French struggle against monarchy and oppression, so reminiscent of their own struggle against British rule. Indeed, the roots of the two revolutions were closely intertwined. The efforts made by France to aid the rebellious Americans a decade earlier had forced the French government to seek new revenues, lighting the fuse that led to the political explosion in Paris in 1789.

The democratic ideals that fueled the Revolution resonated with the American spirit, reigniting debates about governance and individual rights from the Atlantic to the Mississippi. The causes of the French Revolution were many, including King Louis' extravagant spending, the country's involvement in the American Revolution, and economic hardship. On July 14th, a crowd of Parisians, disgusted with the aristocracy and the king's economic policies, stormed the Bastille, a fortress prison in Paris. Overpowering the guards, the mob gained control of the fortress, a symbol of the monarchy's oppressive power.

The storming of the Bastille, led by members of the Third Estate, France's oppressed lower class, was the pivotal moment that marked the start of the revolution. Bastille Day is still celebrated as France's national holiday, just as Americans celebrate the Fourth of July. Six days after the Bastille, the exhilarated revolutionaries took the Tennis Court Oath, vowing not to separate until a written constitution was established for France. Within a few years, the king, along with most of the members of the French royal family, faced execution, leading France into a tumultuous period known as the 'Reign of Terror,' which, along with the guillotining of the king and queen, included the execution of some forty thousand Frenchmen, as well as preemptive attacks on neighboring countries. The French revolutionaries stripped the Catholic Church of its property and privileges, briefly experimented with a new state religion called the 'Cult of Reason,' and eventually conceded supreme power to a brash young general from Corsica, Napoleon Bonaparte, who shook all of Europe in the name of "liberty, equality, and fraternity." [169]

Initially, many Americans celebrated the French Revolution, inspired by the support of their former ally in their own fight against

---

[169] Greer, Donald, *The Incidence of the Terror during the French Revolution : A Statistical Interpretation*. Cambridge: Harvard University Press, coll. Harvard historical monographs, 1935, (no VIII). pp. 26–37.

Great Britain. As the American revolutionary Thomas Paine remarked to George Washington, "The principles of America opened the Bastille."[170] However, as conditions in Paris deteriorated and the situation became marred by blood and violence, many Americans became disillusioned with what was happening in France. The Revolution soon evolved into both a civil war and an international conflict.

However, the French Revolution also caused divisions among Americans, who, whether they wished to support the revolution or not, began to take sides. While many supported the revolutionaries, others feared the chaos and violence that accompanied it. After the democratically idyllic first days of the Paris events, the ensuing rise of radical factions in France led to debates throughout American towns and cities, whether to support the revolutionaries or remain neutral. Hadn't the British just been the enemy of all Americans just a few years earlier? Hadn't the French been our trusted allies? Did the United States have an obligation to assist France in its struggles? But could Americans take the risk of such revolutionary violence threatening to bring down entire American institutions still in their infancy?

This conflict of opinions played out in the political landscape of the early 1790s, eventually influencing the formation of the first two political parties. Despite President Washington's warnings to remain neutral, Secretary of State Thomas Jefferson and his supporters (including the Anglophobic Jackson) leaned towards France, while Secretary of the Treasury Alexander Hamilton favored Great Britain. Jefferson, the author of the Declaration of Independence, argued that American honor and necessity required support for France, given their crucial alliance in the American struggle for independence. "My own affections have been deeply wounded by some of the martyrs to this cause, but rather than it should have failed, I would have seen half the earth desolated," Jefferson wrote in 1792. Conversely, Hamilton contended that, "whatever the initial merits of the French Revolution… have been washed away in the blood of the terror."[171]

---

[170] Kennedy and Cohen, *The American Pageant*, Wadsworth, Cengage Learning Distributor, 2013. pg. 191.
[171] From Thomas Jefferson to William Short, Jan. 3, 1793. *Founders Online*. University of Virginia Press.

The divisions not only split the nation politically but also emotionally, as responses to the chaotic events in France varied widely among Americans. The fissures the revolution created in American society reflected larger political points of view regarding equal rights, social class, centralized authority, and economic opportunity. The divisions became more stark as the revolution evolved, and were often demarcated along regional lines, as well as social class. The rift even threatened to fracture the federal government itself. While it created divisions among Americans regarding support for the revolution, it ultimately contributed to the shaping of a new political identity in the nation, rooted in the revolutionary ideals of liberty and equality.

As tensions within Washington's cabinet escalated, Secretary of State Jefferson grew increasingly disillusioned with Washington and Hamilton's pro-British leanings, leading to his eventual resignation from the cabinet. Hamilton's influence, along with the vacancy Jefferson left behind, swayed President Washington increasingly towards the Federalist perspective. When John Adams won the presidency in 1796 over Jefferson, the country's foreign policy shifted towards a Federalist alignment favoring Great Britain. It would be this very debate, France or Britain, rule by the elite, or trust in the common man, that would define much of the political debates of the last decade of the 18th century.

The passion of the French revolutionaries inspired Americans throughout the nation, even those far removed from the cosmopolitan cities of the Atlantic seaboard. On the Tennessee frontier, the impact was profound. As in many frontier communities, Tennessee settlers largely embraced the democratic ideals France evoked. The Cumberland region, characterized by its rugged terrain and independent spirit, saluted the emergence of leaders who would champion these new ideas, not least of all the bright, educated and charismatic Andrew Jackson. Jackson, at the ripe age of 22, was by no means immune to the revolutionary fervor of the times. On the contrary, he might have been even more impassioned than he had been eight years earlier, when the teenage Andrew and his family swore allegiance to the Patriot cause.

As evidenced later in his career, Jackson championed the rights of the common man and advocated for their participation in government, reflecting the revolutionary spirit that was sweeping across the Atlantic. Jackson and other leaders would work to establish a sense of community and governance that reflected the democratic ideals inspired by the French Revolution. They sought to create a government that represented the voices of ordinary people, moving away from the elitist structures that had dominated European societies. The obvious exception, of course, was that for most white frontiersmen of the 1790s, those deserving of equal rights were a limited group, confined only to white males. Yet perhaps, it was the undercurrent of the French Revolution that ignited broader discussions about equality for those who had never before enjoyed the pleasure of its succor.

As the French Revolution spread by the early 1790s, the ideals the revolutionaries clamored for so outspokenly seemed to threaten the very existence of monarchies across the European continent. When the revolutionaries succeeded in executing King Louis XVI, the British decided it was time to put a stop to the Revolution altogether, lest its damaging ideals should penetrate English shores. Thus, in 1793, Great Britain and France entered into war, and America suddenly found itself caught in the middle.

President Washington acted quickly, announcing emphatically that the United States would maintain a stance of neutrality.[172] Although the young nation aimed to engage in free trade with both sides, it ultimately, and almost inevitably, became embroiled in the conflict. American trading ships heading to Europe were captured on the high seas and taken by the navies of both nations, but particularly by the British, whose massive navy exerted more control over the world's oceans.

Jeffersonian-Republicans, angered by British attacks at sea, and led by James Madison (who, influenced by Jefferson, had undergone a departure from his Federalist views of 1787,) aimed to impose economic sanctions on Great Britain through higher tariffs on British ships. Some in Congress even called for another declaration of war against the Redcoats. However, President Washington opted for diplomacy over force of arms, sending Chief Justice John Jay to London to negotiate with Britain.

Jay, one of the authors of the Federal Papers along with James Madison and fellow Federalist Alexander Hamilton, was the Chief Justice of the

---

[172] Hamilton, Alexander and James Madison. *The Letters of Pacificus and Helvidius on the Proclamation of Neutrality of 1793*. Washington, D.C.: J & G.S. Gideon, 1845.

United States Supreme Court, and a keen negotiator familiar with the British based on prior experience. Washington, therefore, responding to the increasingly alarming tensions with the former mother country, sent Jay, olive branch in hand, to avoid war with the mighty British. [173]

The treaty negotiations were specifically designed to address unresolved issues still festering from the American Revolution, and to promote peace and commerce between the two nations. Its primary goals were to maintain U.S. neutrality, with an eye on providing time for the nation to strengthen its military. Key provisions of Jay's treaty included free border crossings for U.S. and British citizens, granting the U.S. "most favored nation" status in trade, and the removal of certain British military outposts from the Northwest Territory. The obvious omission of course, was the issue that most preempted such negotiations in the first place, that of British "impressment" of American ships. By refusing to address this issue, Jay, and by association, Washington, would face severe criticism.

Despite being well received by the British, Jay secured only limited concessions, and failed at some of the most important objectives. The negotiations were, however, successful in one main aspect; it kept America from having to go to war against the British. Largely as a result of the inferior position the United States held due to its military weakness, the British held the upper hand, and they knew it. The United States, although on the rise since the ratification of the new federal Constitution, was still a military weakling since the end of the Revolution twelve years earlier, having largely downsized its military strength. The British on the other hand were the world's premiere military power.

For their part, the British agreed to withdraw from northwestern posts and promised reparations for past seizures of American ships but made no promises to ensure against future seizure. In exchange, the U.S. granted Britain most-favored-nation status, relinquishing its right to impose tariffs and committing to repay pre-Revolutionary war debts, while largely accepting British interpretations of neutral rights and contraband. Ultimately the lack of British recognition regarding American shipping was the death knell of the treaty, and Jay would be welcomed home with derision.

---

[173] John Jay's Treaty, 1794-1795, Foreign Service Institute, Office of the Historian.

Despite his best efforts, and the several concessions between the two nations he did manage, Jay was lambasted by Americans from New England to the southern frontier. The resulting treaty disappointed many Americans, but particularly Jeffersonian-Republicans, mainly due to its failure to address the worst of the British crimes: their violations of America's neutral rights, especially their attacks on American shipping and impressment of sailors. Upon receiving the treaty in March 1795, Washington, aware of its limitations, withheld it from the public due to his own dissatisfaction, and the anticipated political backlash it would ignite. As Washington predicted, the treaty, despite its importance, faced vehement backlash from the American public, particularly among Democratic-Republicans, who insisted that it favored the Federalist Party, and was an insult to our former ally France.

Nevertheless, President Washington supported the treaty, understanding its necessity for preserving peace with Britain, and avoiding the calamity of another war against the superpower, one he knew the United States was very ill-prepared for. Another legacy of the Jay Treaty, and one that outraged Democratic-Republicans, includes the establishment of "executive privilege," allowing the president to withhold information from Congress when necessary. Initially, the Jeffersonian-Republicans appeared to have enough votes to obstruct appropriations, but the Federalists successfully garnered public support for the treaty through meetings and petitions.

Massachusetts Federalist Fisher Ames delivered a powerful address in the House, warning that rejecting the treaty could lead to war with Great Britain and trigger an economic decline. His speech represented the peak of a prolonged and ultimately successful ten-month effort by Federalists to garner public support for the Jay Treaty. Throughout his address, Ames reiterated key positions and arguments that Federalists had presented during the public debate, echoing concerns raised since the previous summer. He effectively highlighted the potential dangers and calamities that would arise if the treaty were not ratified, encapsulating the essence of Federalist viewpoints. In essence, Ames' speech resonated both emotionally and intellectually, serving as a conclusive statement of the Federalist campaign for the ratification of the Jay Treaty.[174]

Ultimately, in July 1795, the Senate narrowly approved the treaty along party lines, with Federalists in favor and Jeffersonian-Republicans against, also removing Article XII, which limited U.S. trade in the British West Indies. As Ames pointed out in his celebrated speech, national honor compelled the House to uphold the treaty after the Senate and President had duly ratified it. If the House refused, "we greatly fear it would be deemed, by other nations, a stain on our honour as a people, and a bar to all future negociation." Baltimore citizens, sending instructions to Congressman Samuel Smith to vote for appropriations, warned that "the national honor, peace, and welfare are implicated in the decision to be made by the House of Representatives."[175]

When a senator leaked the treaty to Benjamin Franklin Bache's Jeffersonian-Republican newspaper, the Philadelphia Aurora, in July 1795, it sparked nationwide outrage. Madison noted the reaction was "like an electric velocity" throughout the Union. During Independence Day parades that same month, crowds burned the treaty and John Jay in effigy, prompting Jay to comment that he could "walk the eastern seaboard by the light of the flames." In New York, Hamilton faced an angry mob that pelted him with stones in an attempt to defend the treaty. Jeffersonian-Republicans were particularly outraged, viewing the treaty as a disgraceful capitulation that restored the U.S. to a colonial status under monarchical Great Britain. They believed it reinforced the idea that Federalists favored monarchy, while Madison criticized the treaty for its "shameful concessions" and "mock reciprocities," claiming it could be detrimental to the interests and liberty of the United States.

As a committed Jeffersonian, and an opponent of all things British, Andrew Jackson was outspoken against the Jay Treaty, especially its secrecy, which to Jackson smacked of aristocratic rule. Upon learning of the treaty, Jackson expressed his outrage in a letter to Nathaniel Macon:

---

[174] Estes, Todd, "Shaping the Politics of Public Opinion: Federalists and the Jay Treaty Debate," *Journal of the Early Republic* 20. Fall 2000. 393-422.

[175] Grand Jury Resolution, Allegheny County, Pennsylvania, *The Pittsburgh Gazette*, March 12, 1796; Letter to Samuel Smith by citizens of Baltimore, Claypoole's *American Daily Advertiser*, April 27, 1796. See also *Albany Gazette*, April 25, 1796 and Columbian Centinel, April 27, 1796.

"What an alarming situation, with the late Negciation of Mr. Jay with Lord Greenvill, (for a treaty of commerce it cannot be properly called, as it wants reciprocity), being ratified by the two-third of the Senate & president has plunged our Country in; will it end in a Civil Warr, or will our Country be relieved from its present ignominy by the firmness of our representatives in Congress (by impeachments of our Constitutional rights) have the insulting Cringing and ignominious child of aristocratic secracy removed Erased and obliterated from the archives of the Grand republick of the united States."

In this moment, the feral Jackson emerges as a fierce, menacing nationalist, threatening civil war and calling for impeachment in response to perceived threats to the "Grand republick." His passionate demands for action, driven by a strong sense of national pride, positioned him as a potentially dangerous force on the frontier, especially with his proximity to the "Spanish Dons" and their native allies. Jackson deemed the Jay Treaty unconstitutional.

Adamant in his insistence that the President required prior Senate approval before the formation of any treaty, Jackson was keen to point out that Washington had not met this requirement. He went on to criticize the treaty as inconsistent with international law, reminding Macon that the president should act only in ways that reflect the will of the American people. His views reflected a narrow (or strict) interpretation of the Constitution and showcased his contempt for Congress, particularly the Senate, which he referred to dismissively as a group of "Neebobs."[176]

Jackson, shaped by his background as a frontiersman, embodied frontier ideology, heavily in favor of strong states' rights while viewing the federal government as distant and disconnected when it came to local issues, such as attacks by native tribes. His writing style, characterized by using "States" with a capital 'S' and "united" with a lowercase 'u,' while it may have been simply in keeping with his characteristic struggles with spelling and punctuation, nevertheless hinted at his prioritization of state interests over federal authority.

---

[176] Jackson Papers, LC.

CHAPTER

17

MR. JACKSON GOES TO PHILADELPHIA

"We have land to labor then, let us never wish to see our citizens occupied at a work-bench, or twirling a distaff.... For the general operations of manufacture, let our workshops remain in Europe.... the mobs of great cities add just so much to the support of pure government, as sores do to the strength of the human body."

—Thomas Jefferson

When Andrew Jackson arrived in Philadelphia, the nation's capital, in the fall of 1796 to participate in the deliberation of the fourth Congress, second session, it was not his first trip to the great city. In March 1795 he had come to Philadelphia to sell a large tract of land in Tennessee--and here begins the strangest, most convoluted, most potentially dangerous sequence of events in Jackson's long, complicated, sometimes hidden personal history. This is the story of Jackson as land speculator, an experience that nearly landed him in prison.

The surrender, or ceding, of western land by individual states to the national government at the time of the adoption of the Articles of Confederation began a process in which the state North Carolina had to be prodded to cooperate. The leaders of the Old North State would eventually relent, but not before the state passed a Bonus Act that set aside a military reservation in Tennessee, from which veterans of the Revolutionary War could be paid in land for their service. The land grants rose on a graduated scale from 640 acres per section for a private soldier to 12,000 acres for a brigadier general. Between 1784 and 1799 some 5,312 military warrants were issued for eligible veterans, although fewer than 1/4 of this number were redeemed by the veterans themselves.[177] In 1783, North Carolina also passed the infamous Land Grab Act, largely at the behest of William Blount and his brother John Gray Blount, which opened all of the Tennessee land for purchase, even though Indian claims had not yet been extinguished. The Blount family became the largest beneficiary of this act, gaining possession of millions of acres of land stretching from South Carolina to Arkansas, though most of it lay within Tennessee.[178]

Allies of the Blounts also benefited from the land grab. One of them, John Rice, obtained a choice grant in the western District of Tennessee that included the Fourth Chickasaw Bluff, the site of present-day Memphis. In 1792, Rice was killed, and in the settlement of his estate, John Overton emerged with a considerable amount of the Rice Grant, including the Fourth Chickasaw Bluff. At approximately the same time, on May 12, 1794, Overton and Andrew Jackson signed an agreement to establish a partnership for the purchase and sale of land "within and without" the military reservation. It is unclear as to whether Jackson bought into Overton's holdings of the Rice Grant or was Overton's partner at the time the grant was acquired. In any event, by 1795 Jackson and Overton shared 50,000 acres of land, part of which was the Rice Grant.

Other allies shared in the land grab as well. David Allison, a Blount appointee as business manager for the family, was one of them. In the latter capacity, he took up residence in Philadelphia, where he became a partner in the firm of John B. Evans and Company, a mercantile establishment that conducted a substantial amount of business with the settlers of the Cumberland. So good were Allison's business connections in Philadelphia that Tennessee acquaintances had little difficulty establishing credit with mercantile firms in the capital. But it was land speculation rather than mercantile goods that engaged Allison's real

---

[177] Office of the Historian, Foreign Service Institute, United States Department of State Records
[178] Remini, 1977. p. 135.; Smith, Sam R., ed. *Jackson Papers Project*, "Andrew Jackson and Land Speculation." P. 1-3.

interest. Together with William Blount, he bought and sold hundreds of thousands of acres.[179]

Andrew Jackson, who probably immersed himself in land speculation almost on his arrival in Tennessee, found land to be the shortest and quickest way to riches in the West. Jackson may also have partnered with Thomas Green in the Natchez district to acquire land in the Bourbon County conspiracy. Unquestionably Jackson was a willing participant in any land scheme that seemed promising; however, it is difficult to follow his business transactions in this regard because the documentation is incomplete. But it is no exaggeration to suppose that, at the age of 30, Jackson's speculating interests included hundreds of thousands of acres of land.[180]

When Jackson traveled to Philadelphia in 1795 it was for the purpose of selling 50,000 acres held jointly with his partner, Overton, and another 18,750 acres he had been commissioned to sell by a member of the Rice family. Shortly after arriving in Philadelphia, Jackson received a note from Overton with explicit instructions. "Be candid and unreserved with the purchasers," Overton wrote."If you sell lands and get money that you can spare, it will be best that you purchase, somewhere in the lower part of the eastern states such Negroes we may want for rice, and also a likely Negro boy which I want for a servant… If you purchase Negroes in any of the northern states, be careful in so doing not to subject yourself to the penal laws of the state." This prudent advice the cautious Overton felt obliged to remind his sometimes-reckless friend, Andrew Jackson. He also warned Jackson against taking goods in payment for their land. [181]

Having arrived in Philadelphia, Jackson soon encountered unexpected problems. First off, no one was very interested in his property. He presumed he could easily dispose of the land holdings, and yet, one day followed another without finding a buyer. For twenty-two days he fumed with anxious apprehension. He went "through difficulties, such as I never experienced before," he told Overton.[182] At this point of near

---

[179] Smith, *Andrew Jackson and Land Speculation*, p. 6-7.
[180] The Jackson Papers Project. University of Tennessee.
[181] "Memorandum for A. Jackson in Phila," from John Overton, March 8, 1795. Jackson Papers, LC.
[182] AJ to Overton, June 9, 1795, Claybrooke and Overton Papers, *THS*

desperation, Jackson met up with his old acquaintance from the Blount faction, David Allison.

Allison was prepared to buy the property and offered 20 cents per acre. Under the circumstances, Jackson jumped at the offer. His directive from Rice with respect to the 18,750 acres was that he must not sell the land for less than 12 1/2 cents per acre for which he would receive a 10% commission. With Allison's offer well over that figure, Jackson agreed to sell both the 50,000 acres and the Rice property, and in exchange he accepted three promissory notes from Allison.[183]

Jackson had been running a trading operation from Tennessee north to Kentucky and south to Natchez, Mississippi, and he planned to open a regular store on the Cumberland River to consolidate these activities and place them on a more business-like footing. In preparation for this, he took his brother-in-law, Samuel Donelson, on as a partner.[184] His brief experience as a storekeeper in North Carolina encouraged him in this venture almost as much as his need to consolidate his business operations. Thus, Jackson now functioned as lawyer, land speculator, government official, and now storekeeper.

To stock his store, Jackson made purchases from Meeker, Cochran and Company, a Philadelphia firm, and presented Allison's notes, which he endorsed in payment. Allison also took Jackson to John B. Evans and Company, where Allison was a partner, to purchase additional supplies. With Allison's voucher Jackson was allowed to "have goods to any amount I thought proper to take out."[185] When the invoice was presented, Jackson again offered Allison's notes, which Evans accepted after they had been properly endorsed. Later, Jackson admitted he did not realize at the time that in signing the notes he "stood security for the payment" of them," or that Mr. E. expected me to do so, or even contemplated such a thing."[186]

In admitting to this, Jackson's naïveté in such financial matters was made evident. For a man of business, let alone a lawyer, to enter into financial transactions involving thousands of dollars without knowing

---

[183] "Memorandum for A. Jackson" from Overton, March 8, 1795, Power of Attorney Joel Rice to AJ, April 5, 1795
[184] Account book located at the Hermitage, LHA.
[185] The Allison Transaction, undated, Jackson Papers, LC.
[186] Ibid.

his responsibilities and the degree of his involvement was indeed a head-scratcher. Sometimes the young Jackson's foolishness was remarkable. He lamely excused himself to Overton by blaming the situation on unforeseen circumstances.[187] Nevertheless, Evans informed him that, by rights, the notes must be redeemed or he would bring suit. When Jackson returned to Tennessee, his exhaustion bordered on depression from the experience. He said he was "fatigued even almost unto death."[188]

But his struggles in this matter were just beginning, and the real blow came two months later. Jackson had no sooner set up his trading post on the Cumberland when he received a short business letter from Meeker, Cochran and company: "We are sorry so soon after your departure, to follow you the advice, that any notes or acceptances of David Allison's now following due, are not generally or regularly paid, and that there is little reason to expect he will be more punctual here after, as his reasons no doubt must suffer, in his want, of punctuality. We take this early opportunity to make known to you that we have little or no expectation of getting paid from him, and that we shall have to get our money from you, which we shall expect at maturity, as the original credit was longer than we usually gave, assuring you of your perfect regard, we remain, dear sir, your very obedient servant."[189]

The news of Allison's bankruptcy shocked Jackson to the core. And the shock was repeated a few months later when he received another letter, this one from John B. Evans and Company, stating that Allison's notes, endorsed by Jackson, were due on February 13, and, since Allison could not meet them, Jackson was responsible. Having had enough, Jackson immediately sold his store to Colonel Elijah Robertson for 33,000 acres of land, realizing a slight profit. Glad to have washed his hands of the mercantile business, Jackson dashed over to Knoxville and sold the land to James Stewart for $.25 per acre, of which $2,800 was to be paid within 60 days to Jackson's Philadelphia creditors and the remainder within two years. This happened at the time Jackson was attending the Tennessee Constitutional Convention, and he probably

---

[187] AJ to Overton, June 9, 1795, Claybrooke and Overton Papers, *THS*
[188] Ibid.
[189] Meeker, Cochran and Co. to AJ, August 22, 1795, Jackson Papers, LC

offered the land to Stewart through William Blount, who served as Stewart's agent.[190]

In February 1796, Jackson and Overton revalidated their partnership and took protective action against their liability by agreeing to bear an equal share in any loss incurred in the Allison transaction "under penalty of $100,000 each." The following month, Jackson began picking up large parcels of land all over Tennessee, from Powell's Valley in the eastern District, to the Obion river in the western District. Much of this land was probably intended for sale in Philadelphia. At this time, he also purchased the Hunters Hill plot, 640 acres on the south side of the Cumberland River, formerly owned by Lewis Robards (painful news to Robards, no doubt, as this was the property he had purchased originally to begin his married life with Rachel, but which he was unable to occupy because of the Chickasaw menace.) Over a period of two months in the spring of 1796, Jackson obtained 29,228 acres of land for sale in Philadelphia, of which 11,760 acres was purchased from Stockley Donaldson and 5,000 at a sheriff's sale.[191]

When Jackson arrived in Philadelphia in June 1796, he met with William Blount, his political mentor, and James Stewart's agent. According to the terms of the land sale to Stewart, the first payment was due in Philadelphia within 60 days. But the cash could not be scraped together. Instead, Blount agreed to assure the amount Jackson owed his creditors, and Jackson, in turn, deducted this amount from the price of the land sale. Twenty-four years later, Jackson noted, with a touch of chagrin, that the land he sold Stewart was worth $200,000.[192]

Jackson had nearly 30,000 additional acres for sale when he reached Philadelphia in June 1796. Again, he had trouble finding a buyer. And again, incredibly, he turned to Allison and Blount. He sold 28,810 acres to the two, taking two notes from Allison for $5,000 and $676.73 and one note from Blount for $4,539.94. Blount promised this money plus interest within two years.

---

[190] Blount to Stuart, April 5,6, 1796, Stuart to Blount, April 5, 1796, Stuart to AJ, April 17, 1796, Jackson Memorandum, Allison Affair, July 15, 1801; Jackson Papers, LC.
[191] Davidson County and Knox County Deed Books, C and D, pp. 492-496, NC Land Grant Book, Vol. 88, p. 328
[192] Remini, 1977. p. 90

With Blount's security, Jackson was out of immediate danger, but the problem remained of what to do about Allison, who owed him the price of the original land sale—which, with interest, Jackson later estimated came to twenty-thousand dollars. Moreover, on May 13, 1795, Allison gave Jackson an additional note for $1,101. 27 Allison was deeply in debt to the young congressman and going deeper each year due to the interest. But there was nothing Jackson could do to get his money but wait and hope that Allison would soon set his financial house in order.[193]

Such a scenario was not to be. The Allison affair dragged on for several more years and almost ended with Jackson sitting in debtor's prison. Having accepted notes from Blount and Allison, Jackson purchased $4,800 worth of merchandise in Philadelphia (probably for resale in Tennessee) and returned home. A few months later, he obtained another 1,000 acres in Sumner County from Elisha Rice. So the process of buying and selling land went on, year after year. Even as Jackson headed for Philadelphia to begin his career as a member of Congress, his brother-in-law, Stockley Donelson signaled him about further land sales. "I should've written to you before this, but heard you were elected a member of Congress and was on your way there," Donelson wrote, "I want to purchase yours and brother Samuel's right of land on Duck River that you purchased of William Purnell… I want you to make inquiry and get all the military land survey that you possibly can… I will make it worth your trouble."[194] No matter what Andrew Jackson had going on, land speculation was a constant concern.

Heading for Philadelphia in 1796, Jackson was on the cusp of a period of long absences from home. These absences meant family separation for extended periods of time, which would be very difficult for him—and more so for Rachel. Frequently he wrote her long, fond letters that show a side of the man seldom seen. One of the earliest letters that survives, written in 1796, conveys a tenderness quite remarkable for Jackson:

"I have this moment finished my business here which I have got in good train and hope to wind it up this Touer, and will leave this tomorrow morning for Jonesboro, where I hope to finish

---

[193] Remini, 1977. p. 90-91;
[194] Donelson to AJ, June 16, 1796, *Jackson v. Andrew Erwin, et al*, Case Record; copy JPP.

it, and though it is now half after 10 o'clock, could not think of going to bed without writing you. May it give you pleasure to receive it. May it add to your contentment until I return. May you be blessed with health. May the goddess of slumber every evening light on your eyebrows and gently lull you to sleep and conduct you through the night with pleasing thoughts and pleasant dreams. Could I only know you were contented and enjoyed peace of mind, what satisfaction it would afford me whilst traveling the lonely tiresome road. It would relieve my anxious breast and shorten the way--may the great "I am" bless and protect you until that happy and wished for moment arrives when I am restored to your sweet embrace, which is the nightly prayer of your affectionate husband,

–Andrew Jackson.[195]
-PS my compliments to my good old mother, Mrs. Donelson, that best of friends. Tell her with what pain I reflect upon leaving home without shaking her by the hand and asking her blessings."

The painful separations due to "public life" could not be avoided, and in late 1796, Jackson began his new career as a member of Congress in Philadelphia. For the second time in just over a year, he undertook the 42-day journey, exhausting two horses along the way before arriving on a third horse (which he kept for many years.) Philadelphia, with a population of 65,000, was a hub of elegance and civility. For a young and ambitious westerner like Andrew Jackson, the cosmopolitan city must have been a wonder. Jackson no doubt recognized the unique opportunity Philadelphia presented. He lived with a Congressman Hardy, who had extensive local connections, likely enabling Jackson to enjoy a vibrant social life.

Albert Gallatin, the French accented Swiss-born politician, diplomat, ethnologist and linguist, recalled seeing Jackson upon his arrival. He described Jackson as "a tall, blank uncouth-looking person, with long hair hanging over his face and a queue tied with eel skin; his dress was singular, and his manners and deportment those of a

---
[195] AJ to Rachel Jackson, May 9, 1796, Jackson Papers, LC.

rough backwoodsman." Gallatin never was a Jackson supporter, and his portrayal was probably an exaggerated distortion. Although Jackson may have had rough edges in 1796, he was familiar with how gentlemen dressed in eastern cities. As Tennessee's first representative, he would not risk entering Congress inappropriately attired, as noted by an early biographer who stated that Gallatin's negative description was unrecognizable to Jackson's friends.[196]

Jackson arrived in Congress in early December for what was then known as Congress' "short session." Unlike many colleagues, Jackson was present on the House floor on Congress's opening day, and he remained present and punctual throughout the short session. He served alongside several notable statesmen, which included the likes of James Madison, Albert Gallatin, and Nathaniel Macon. Both houses of Congress awaited a Senate quorum before commencing business. Just months earlier, President Washington had called for a gradual navy buildup for protecting American commerce, suggested government aid for manufacturers, proposed a national university and military academy, condemned French attacks on American ships, and expressed hope that the government would protect American liberties indefinitely.

He arrived in time to hear President Washington's farewell address, which warned against the perils of partisanship and foreign entanglements. "It is our true policy to steer clear of any permanent alliances with any portion of the foreign world." While Jackson agreed with these sentiments, he took the highly unusual step of joining others within his party in a protest of the address. In the past, Congress had responded to the President's message with a simple, pro forma voice vote, but the contentious atmosphere surrounding the campaign for Washington's successor inspired several Republicans to contest this tradition. Jackson joined eleven others in voting against accepting Washington's speech.[197]

Jackson disagreed with Washington on certain points of substance, disagreeing with the President's suggestion that the British posed no harm. Citing numerous crimes against American neutrality at sea, Jackson pointed out that as far as he could see, British actions against American

---

[196] Parton, *Jackson*, I. 196.
[197] *Annals of Congress*, 4th Congress, 2nd Session, p.1668.

commerce were significant, outnumbering French grievances some 20 to one. It seemed to the freshman Congressman that Washington spoke only of French violations, excusing the British altogether. This seemed to validate Jackson's feelings that the Washington administration leaned far too Federalist, far too anti-French, and far too aristocratic. These sentiments put Jackson in good favor with the many Jeffersonians in Congress. [198]

A House committee was formed to draft a formal reply to the President's address, filled with praise for Washington. On December 11, this reply was debated for two days, revealing discord amongst the members of the House. Thomas Blount of North Carolina called for a recorded vote to show that not all members approved of the lavish tribute. Posterity has kindly forgotten Thomas Blount—but not all of the representatives who voted nay. Among those who rejected the salute to Washington were Edward Livingston, Nathaniel Macon, and Andrew Jackson.[199]

Years later, when Jackson himself ran for the presidency, this vote was remembered and used against him by his rivals, which caused Jackson great embarrassment. By that point in time, the legacy of the great Washington had grown to such a point that anyone appearing to display the slightest disrespect to the founding father's legacy was considered practically a traitor to the nation itself and was certainly one who did not deserve to follow Washington into the White House. But the bold young Congressman Jackson stood his ground.

To Jackson and other dissenters, the President's address to Congress too closely mirrored the British tradition of monarchical addresses. Thomas Jefferson later shared these views and was the first to discontinue the practice of direct Presidential addresses, a tradition not revived until Woodrow Wilson in the early 20th century. This decision by Jackson, a freshman Congressman, required considerable courage and independence, though it could be seen as lacking in courtesy and judgment. Jackson disdainfully viewed the Jay Treaty with Great Britain, established by the Washington administration, and approved by the

---

[198] AJ to Hays, Dec. 16, 1796, Jackson Papers, LC; Remini, p. 93.
[199] AJ to John Donelson, Jan. 18, 1797, in the *Kentucky Yeoman*, November, 5, 1847, copy JPP

aristocratic Senate, as a disgrace to the republic. He, like many others, believed that Washington warranted no gratitude for it.

Generally, Jackson was frustrated with the administration's apparent sympathy towards Britain over France, as revealed in a letter to his brother-in-law, Robert Hays, in which he noted that the President's supporters sought a friendship with Britain, potentially at the cost of conflict with France. Jackson's disdain for Britain was more a product of his revolutionary experiences and his suspicions of British and Spanish intentions than by Jefferson's pro-French ideology. Jackson was also critical of the current administration's tolerance of massacres and atrocities committed by indigenous nations in Tennessee, having responded to frontier pleas for assistance largely with silence. Surrounded by England and Spain, the United States faced barriers to expansion and frontier families were frequently subjected to indigenous attacks instigated by these powers.

Several of Jackson's letters during the session expressed these concerns. He wrote of the removal from office of individuals who professed "Republican principles," if they did not align exactly with the executive. He stated, "If a man cannot be led to believe as the president believes in politics, he is not to fill an office in the United States. This, sir, in my view, is more dangerous than the establishment of religion," (which is notable considering Jackson's own actions as president three decades later.) In another letter to John Overton, Jackson writes "the executive of the Union has ever since the commencement of the present government, been grasping after power, and in many instances, exercised powers not constitutionally vested in him," reflecting further criticism of President Jackson. Further criticism that would come back to Jackson in spades during his Presidential campaign.[200]

In voting against the reply to Washington, Jackson joined several other congressmen committed to a more conservative government philosophy. Interpreting the Constitution narrowly, Jackson and the other dissenters prioritized state privileges, and opposed unnecessary appropriations by the central government. To them, less government was better government. By aligning himself with figures like Nathaniel Macon of North Carolina and Henry Tazewell of Virginia, Jackson

---

[200] AJ to Overton, Feb. 24, 1797, Hurja Collection, THS.; Remini, p. 94.

reinforced his own conservatism, mirroring western concerns for states' rights and sovereignty. The conservative members of Congress welcomed Jackson in, and many maintained regular correspondence with him.[201]

"A month after the session began, Jackson noted, 'the legislature of the Union progresses slowly in business. Much of the time has been consumed in committee preparing for the House. There is much discussion about increasing government salaries and imposing a direct tax, neither of which I hope will occur. The necessity for a direct tax is strongly urged, as indicated by the secretary's report, which suggests raising an additional $1,200,000 for the next year to meet government exigencies." [202]

True to his word, Jackson voted against the direct tax during the final legislative action and opposed an appropriation to aid the victims of a devastating fire in late November that nearly destroyed Savannah, Georgia, wiping out two-thirds of the city's homes and buildings. Aside from his lack of empathy for the Georgians, these votes highlighted his commitment to conservative states' rights. Although he largely remained a quiet freshman congressman, he tended to follow the lead of more established conservative colleagues. However, when a petition from Hugh Lawson White sought compensation for his services in an offensive attack against the Catawba led by General Sevier in 1793, Jackson became engaged.

President Washington had refused to honor the petition, stating he required special Congressional authorization. On December 29, 1796, the committee of claims presented the petition to the full House, reporting that tribal forces had significantly harassed Tennessee settlers through theft and murder. The committee asked the House to determine whether these aggressions constituted imminent danger, noting that the attack had been undertaken without presidential approval and contrary to orders to refrain from war unless attacked. The War Department certainly held the same view, as shown by their immediate objection to the petition. These objections angered Jackson, as it implied improper conduct by Tennessee settlers and seemed to sympathize with the indigenous. [203]

---

[201] Letters of Tazewell, Macon, and Stevens Mason of Virginia, Jackson Papers, LC.
[202] AJ to Hays, Jan. 8, 1797, Jackson, *Correspondence*, I, 24.
[203] AJ to Sevier, Jan. 18, 1797, Jackson Papers, LC.

A hostile Jackson took the floor once again, arguing that the expedition was both just and necessary, pointing out that "As an inhabitant of the Country" he carried a good amount of knowledge on the matter, unlike the far-removed politicians he now addressed. When war threatened the state, he asserted, with women and children in peril from the "knife and tomahawk" held over them, resistance was imperative. He disputed several points made in the Secretary of War's report, claiming inaccuracies, particularly regarding the nature of the Sevier expedition. Jackson maintained that the militia *had* acted defensively until they were suddenly attacked by over 'twelve hundred Indians.' In such a precarious situation, he contended, the acting secretary had no choice but to pursue the enemy, making the expedition necessary and White's claim legitimate.

Jackson was just getting warmed up. He argued that the question of whether the expedition was necessary cut right to the heart of soldier subordination. The troops, he argued, had been called out by a superior officer and had no grounds to question his authority. "If we accepted the contrary doctrine," he stated, "it would undermine the very foundation of subordination." He emphasized that allowing soldiers to question the legality of their orders before obeying would permit them to refuse service until satisfied with the legality. This is madness, Jackson said. No one can act on such a principle, certainly no army. They participated in this perilous campaign with "full confidence that the United States would pay them, believing that they had appointed such officers, as would not call them into the field without proper authority." Even if the expedition was "unconstitutional,"—which he did not believe for a moment, "it ought not to affect the soldier, since he had no choice in the business, being obliged to obey his superior." [204]

Jackson insisted that since the expedition was just and necessary, expenses for everyone involved, not just White's—should be paid by the government. Jackson may have been unsympathetic and miserly with the victims of the Savannah fire, but with the Tennessee expeditionary heroes, he was generous to a fault. And his motion, an expression of his own heartfelt sentiments, was one that was certain to spark gratitude and appreciation in Tennessee.

---

[204] Remini, 1977, p. 95

There was considerable debate over the original committee report, and several representatives argued that the entire matter should go back to the committee for further consideration. To this, Jackson jumped to his feet again, protesting that sending the petition back to committee would temporarily dispose of the issue, perhaps pushing it to the back burner permanently. Jackson declared that though he did not know the rules of the House very well, "it was a very circuitous way of doing business."[205] Why refer the matter back to committee, he asked, when all the facts were known, and there was nothing further the committee could learn? The House, however, did not arrive at a decision immediately, and adjourned for the day without taking action on the report. These were brave actions from a newcomer in the vaunted halls of Congress.

When the session reconvened the next afternoon, Jackson quickly returned to the issue and was recognized. He then presented a petition from George Colbert, a chief of the Chickasaw nation, regarding the government's failure to fully compensate the tribe for supplies provided to a detachment of Tennessee volunteers led by Colonel Mansker. Jackson later wrote, "I mentioned the actions I took to address the matter of Colonel Mansker's troops marching to the Chickasaw nation by submitting a petition in the name of G. Colbert, seeking payment for the provisions and to relieve Captain David Smith, but I believe the claim will be denied." The House referred Colbert's petition to the committee of claims and then revisited Hugh Lawson White's petition. Jackson's earlier resolution was read again, and he requested to address the full House.

The tall, whip-thin Jackson rose to address the hall. Though no orator, he commenced his speech with passion and volume, his wiry hair slightly askew. Reminding his audience that the rations for the expedition had already been paid for by the Secretary of War, he saw no valid reason against covering the full cost of the expedition. He argued that partial payment implied an obligation for the whole. General Sevier was bound to obey the orders he received to undertake the expedition; so too were the officers under him.

For a freshman congressman, the speech was nearly outstanding, earning him a measure of respect from his colleagues at the outset

---

[205] Sevier to AJ, Dec. 12, 1796, Sevier Papers, TSL.

of his congressional career. He had done his part to honor the heroes of Tennessee, generating enthusiasm at home—if his resolution was approved. The speech contained principles that were central to Jackson's life, later reinforced during his military career, including authority, responsibility, discipline, and loyalty. Jackson's strict views left no room for compromise: soldiers were to obey authorized orders, and governments were to support their soldiers regardless of cost or risk.[206] The constitutionality of the campaign, Jackson argued, was irrelevant.

In the ensuing deliberation, it was noted that the petition before the House came from a single individual (White), while Jackson's resolution sought compensation for the entire expeditionary force, raising a question of whether to act on the petition or ignore it in favor of Jackson's resolution. This prompted Jackson to regain the floor once again, pointing out that the committee report indicated that accepting White's petition would set a precedent for the entire militia involved in the campaign. If White's petition was valid, so were those of all the expedition's men, negating the need for individual applications.[207]

A lengthy debate followed. Representative Robert Rutherford of Virginia noted that Jackson had presented the matter so clearly that further discussion seemed unnecessary. James Madison of Virginia supported Jackson's stance, asserting that the government had a commitment to all who served. The issue was then referred to a select committee, which included Jackson and members from several states.[208] After a month of deliberations, the committee issued a clear report, stating two key questions: Was the expedition essential for frontier defense? Did the governor have the authority to compel militia obedience? The committee answered yes to both and recommended full compensation for the militia. The House approved the recommendation without debate, forwarding it to the committee of ways and means for inclusion in the federal appropriations for 1797, granting $22,816. 51

In just his first month in Congress, Jackson had achieved a noteworthy outcome for Tennessee. He not only secured compensation for a group of soldiers, but also claimed a victory over the national government, advocating for westerners facing challenges on the frontier. Even more

---

[206] AJ to Robert Hays, Jan. 8, 1797, Jackson, *Correspondence*, I, 24.
[207] *Annals of Congress*, 4th Congress, 2nd Session, p. 1737; Remini, p. 96.
[208] Ibid.

remarkable, the end result was a cash settlement, the clearest, most tangible sign of his success, and the surest way to please those at home. His achievement would greatly increase Jackson's chances of reelection should he seek a second term in the House. The paramount lesson of attentiveness to one's constituents was clearly not lost on Jackson, who seemed to understand that his political longevity depended on it.

In a letter after his initial victory, he noted, "I am the only representative from the state. Consequently, all the business of the state in the House of Representatives evolves on me... I have not much time to waste, and I am well convinced that my constituents would rather have justice done than receive letters from me."[209]

While addressing his constituents' needs, Jackson did not forget his family and friends as well. He informed his brother-in-law, Robert Hays, that he would likely be appointed marshal but was uncertain about the district court judge position, suggesting John Rhea might be favored. Washington later appointed Hays as Marshal and John McNairy as judge, both confirmations occurring swiftly. Understandably proud, Jackson notified Governor Sevier that he and his army would be compensated for their 1793 services against the Indians. He expressed concern over a proposed direct tax, predicting it would be unpopular in Tennessee due to the current state of American commerce. He criticized the administration's pro-British stance, lamenting the implications for France, stating, "I am sorry to see our country... involved in such a situation with the Republic of France... we ought to wish them success if we could not aid them."[210]

In the same letter, Jackson expressed his commitment to states' rights, a position "I long entertained," he asserted, which was "founded on mature deliberation." He believed first and foremost in the sovereignty of the state, supported by constitutional principles and international law, writing that only the "strong hand of power" could take away that right. This, as much as any other Jackson letters of the period, articulated his "philosophy of government" throughout his early political life. A consistent emphasis on states' rights can be seen in his thoughts and

---

[209] Ibid.
[210] Ibid, p. 2155

writings throughout his career, even as many of his presidential actions contrarily enhanced the power of the central government.[211]

Jackson diligently represented Tennessee in Congress, attending nearly all roll call votes. He supported the construction of Navy frigates and opposed bribing pirates in the Mediterranean, reflecting his strong patriotism.[212] Jackson voted against funding for presidential mansion furniture and resisted lifting restrictions on public expenditures. Although he generally favored fiscal conservatism, he occasionally compromised his principles, especially when it meant benefits for those of his home state. For example, he reversed his opposition to a pay boost for the Secretary of War (not surprisingly) but advocated for a higher salary for a Tennessee district judge, citing the high cost of living on the distant frontier and travel dangers, but ultimately failed to prevent a salary reduction.[213]

At the end of his first session in Congress, the record of Andrew Jackson's debut performance could well be described as modestly successful, marked by solid contributions including committee work, speeches, and a majority voting record. He demonstrated diligence and a strong commitment to his constituents and state interests, while also showing pragmatic flexibility in his voting, when it served his purposes. After Congress adjourned on March 3, 1797, Jackson returned home, becoming engrossed in the political tensions in Tennessee, made all the more pronounced in his absence, particularly the rivalry between the Sevier faction and the Blount clique.[214]

The young Congressmen returned as though a prodigal son, having made a name for himself in the big halls of Congress. But Jackson was returning to a Tennessee that was in flux, and one where bitter resentments at the highest levels of an ever-evolving state government were about to turn ugly.

---

[211] "The Payment of Sevier's Expedition," William C.C. Claiborne wrote to Jackson in July, 1797, Jackson Papers, LC
[212] AJ to Daniel Smith, Dec. 18, 1796, Jackson Papers, LC.
[213] AJ to Sevier, Jan. 18, 1797, Jackson Papers, LC.
[214] AJ to Hays, Jan. 8, 1797, Jackson, *Correspondence*, I, 24.

CHAPTER 18

JACKSON VERSUS NOLICHUCKY JACK

"A Military ardor & Spirit Warmly diffuses itself throughout the State of Tennessee...... Who are composed of such men, as Would in My opinion do honor to any Army in the Universe."
-John Sevier

John Sevier became a legendary figure on the frontier from his wildly successful offensive against the Cherokee during the Revolutionary War. Carolinians faced a dire situation in the late 1770s, with the British on the warpath throughout the lower southern colonies, and the Cherokee, allied with the British, terrorizing the frontier. But in this treacherous atmosphere, John Sevier emerged heroically. With just 150 men, Sevier relentlessly pursued over a thousand Cherokee warriors through the rugged Smoky Mountains, ultimately breaking their resistance and earning hero status. He also led his mountaineer militia against the British forces under Lord Cornwallis. His legend was established, and John Sevier would forever after be remembered as the great "Nolichucky Jack."[215]

During the British Carolina offensive, Major Patrick Ferguson threatened Sevier's "Over-Mountain Men," as they became known, warning them to lay down their weapons or face destruction. Calling out the masculinity of these Over-Mountain Men, Ferguson became

---

[215] Faris, John, T., *Nolichucky Jack: A Thrilling Tale of John Sevier*, 1999.

a marked man. His insult spurred Sevier and Colonel Isaac Shelby to take the fight to Ferguson and his Loyalists themselves. They joined forces with William Campbell, crossed the Smokies and Blue Ridge Mountains, and caught the Tories at King's Mountain, not far from Jackson's Waxhaw region, in October of 1780. Expecting a bayonet charge, the British were instead met with a relentless rifle assault from Sevier's men, resulting in the deaths of about 230 British and Loyalist soldiers, including Ferguson, as well as the capture of around seven hundred men. The rebels suffered only twenty-eight killed and approximately sixty wounded. [216]

By shoring up Patriot control of the western Piedmont region, King's Mountain is celebrated as an important rebel victory in the Revolutionary War. Theodore Roosevelt later highlighted the Battle of King's Mountain in his book, "The Winning of the West," writing of the importance of this group of western men in providing crucial support to their fellow Patriots during a dire time, striking a decisive blow against Cornwallis's forces.[217]

Sevier gained immense fame from this victory, becoming a prominent leader in the western district and as noted, was elected as the first governor of the State of Franklin. His popularity grew, leading to his election as a North Carolina Congressman. After North Carolina ratified the new federal Constitution in 1788, he became the first member elected to Congress from west of the mountains. However, he served only a few months in Congress due to the cession of western territory to the United States, cutting his term short.[218]

Later, President Washington appointed Sevier brigadier general of the Tennessee militia. Sevier was active in the politics of the Southwest Territory and forged a business alliance with William Blount's brother, James. This partnership led to Sevier being elected the first governor of Tennessee upon its admission to the Union, although, as previously mentioned, soon a rift would arise between the two Blounts and Sevier.

---

[216] Ibid.
[217] Roosevelt, Theodore, *The Winning of the West, Volume I, From the Alleghanies to the Mississippi, 1769-1776*, Bison Books.
[218] Michael Toomey, "Southwest Territory," *Tennessee Encyclopedia of History and Culture*, 2009. Retrieved: July 22, 2012.

This rift would inevitably lead to Jackson and Sevier in each other's crosshairs.

As John Sevier, with a growing faction of his own, now at odds with William Blount's powerful western faction, Jackson's loyalty to the Blount faction now became an issue with Governor Sevier. As Tennessee state politics heated up, Sevier's and Blount's respective regional factions became more divided. As governor, Sevier, who had previously gotten along well with Andrew Jackson, soon encountered his first conflict with the irascible Congressman, despite Jackson's success in gaining compensation for Sevier's militia expedition. Jackson's ambitions, heightened by his pursuit of the position of major general of the Tennessee militia in 1796, would put him on a collision course with Governor Sevier.[219]

As the talented military minded Sevier was set to take on his new position as the first governor of the newly created state of Tennessee, the militia command Sevier held was soon to become vacant. By rights, Sevier could not serve in both capacities, and Jackson eyed the generalship for himself, although he had no formal military experience. Sevier relinquished the post, but prepared to secure his own chosen successor, one of his most trusted lieutenants, George Conway, a man of lengthy military service in the Southwest Territory and the state.[220]

Governor Sevier aimed to ensure the position for Conway by prematurely commissioning junior officers who favored his candidate. Unbeknownst at the time, this would mark the start of a tumultuous and mercurial relationship marked by both alliance and rivalry between Sevier and Jackson, as they each sought to serve the public and improve their economic status on the frontier.[221]

The rank of major-general of the Tennessee militia was one that Sevier held since 1791. Jackson's work as judge advocate with the militia had piqued his interest in a military career. Perhaps recalling his Revolutionary experience as a young courier, and the example set by his early mentor, William R. Davie, the honorable position was one that Jackson highly desired. Not only did he feel military command suited his temperament much better than as a legislator, but he envisioned the glory

---

[219] AJ to Sevier, May 10, 1797, Jackson, *Correspondence*, p. 35-36.
[220] Remini, 1977. p. 101
[221] AJ to Sevier, Jan. 18, 1797, Jackson Papers, LC.

of military success as well. Always the passionate frontier fighter and protector, head of the militia would put him at the forefront of defense against Native American attack, a cause very dear to him. To Jackson, this was a position he could excel in, and one that would bring greater reward, enhancing his reputation and popularity among Tennesseans.[222]

Elections in the Tennessee militia were operated by a democratic process for selecting commanding officers within its three militia districts, including Mero, which had a brigade, county regiment, and cavalry regiment. Officers at the regimental and company levels were elected by militia members, while brigadier generals were chosen by field officers, who also elected a major general to oversee the state's militia, with the governor casting a tie-breaking vote if necessary. But Sevier, in determining that Conway should win the post, was inexhaustibly active behind the scenes. [223]

In November 1796, brigadier generals and field officers voted in their districts, during which Sevier sent blank commissions for appointing preferred cavalry officers, whom he had instructed to cast their vote for Conway for major general. Sevier also included a recommendation in favor of Conway. Jackson became privy to this when he attended the Mero election in Nashville, where Sevier crony Joel Lewis read a letter from Sevier in Jackson's presence. Citing the letter, Lewis spoke against Jackson's candidacy in favor of Conway's.

Jackson, professing to be stunned that the governor would stoop to an "interference with free elections," voiced his opposition to Sevier's tactics, which he felt "exceeded constitutional authority." Attempting to put a stop to it, Jackson, never one to shy away from confrontation, even with high-ranking individuals, expressed his feelings in a letter to Sevier. "Viewing Sir with horror," he wrote Sevier, "in a private letter from the executive of the state induced to influence the officers, to do that which in my opinion was an unconstitutional act and which would establish a precedent dangerous to the rights of the people I proceeded to reply to Mr. Lewis with some warmth." [224]

Perhaps Jackson was truly horrified by what he considered a dangerous precedent, but there was obviously much more to Jackson's objections,

---

[222] Ibid.
[223] Ibid.
[224] Ibid.

particularly his desire to win the election himself. Reacting angrily, Jackson chose to express his distaste at Sevier's "high handed tactics" and his use of blank commissions. But Jackson's anger seemed to also stem from what he perceived as Sevier's personal attack against his character. Word of Jackson's furious reaction eventually reached Sevier, who, rather than defusing the situation diplomatically, dismissed Jackson as a "poor pitiful, petty fogging lawyer." Sevier dismissed Jackson's comments as "scurelous."[225]

Word of Sevier's insults made their way back to Jackson, who later accused Sevier of purposefully undermining him, having been aware of Jackson's aspirations, and preventing his ascension to the post. Angered not only from ultimately losing the election to Conway, but bitter at Sevier's role in his defeat, Jackson stewed. Thus, the tensions continued on and led to a bitter exchange of letters between the two men. In one correspondence, Jackson confronted Sevier about the attack on his character, to which Sevier downplayed the remarks, attributing them to a misunderstanding and asserting his lack of malicious intent.

Although driven by furious emotions (very likely Jackson wished to challenge Sevier to a duel), a conflict with as esteemed a figure as Sevier risked damaging Jackson's reputation within Tennessee politics, something he could ill afford to do. So, the young Tennessee upstart accepted Sevier's explanation, and the incident passed. But this would not be the last battle between the two powerful Tennesseans.

Jackson's decision to let cooler heads prevail in this first confrontation with John Sevier showed his maturation in his understanding of Tennessee politics. The defeated yet cagey Jackson may have lost the election as major general, but he had learned a valuable lesson: before pursuing higher rank in the militia, he would have to bolster his strength among the militiamen. He subsequently became more involved in militia elections over the next few years, slowly and steadily building his political power.[226]

Jackson did not forget Sevier's meddling in the militia election, nor did he appreciate Sevier's opposition to his campaign and perceived slight against his character. Fortunately for Jackson, an opportunity

---

[225] Sevier to AJ. Jan. 19, 1797, Sevier Papers, LC.
[226] James, *Jackson*, p. 19

for a measure of revenge came not long after the start of their feud. In 1797, as Jackson was headed to Philadelphia for a congressional session, he met Tennessee politician John Love along the way. Love dropped a potentially lethal bomb on Jackson, informing him of a remarkable land fraud in which a company of speculators in Tennessee were forging North Carolina land warrants and selling Tennessee lands, to which they held no right. [227]

This was the first Jackson had heard of the corruption, and when he uncovered the names of those involved, he was shocked to find the degree of scandal he was uncovering. Upon further digging, Jackson recognized the names of many of the speculators involved who had forged North Carolina land warrants. Much of the fraud operated through the office of James Glasgow, Secretary of State for North Carolina. At first, Jackson did not know the extent of the conspiracy or all the names of the principal agents. But he was soon to find out and would be further stunned to learn of several very influential individuals who could be implicated, and to the extent they were, including both friends and family members. [228]

Gathering information through various personal connections (and in some cases through intimidation), Jackson found to his dismay that he was well-acquainted with several of those involved in the scheme, including Rachel's brother Stockley Donelson. Despite the damage it would do to his brother-in-law, Jackson felt compelled to expose the fraud, and thus he reported it to North Carolina's Governor Samuel Ashe on March 24, 1798. Reportedly, Jackson was not yet aware that the trail of corruption led all the way to the top of Tennessee politics, pointing directly to Governor Sevier himself.

An investigation, now in the hands of the North Carolina government, revealed that the conspiracy involved over 4 million acres of land, defrauding not only the state, but veterans of the Revolutionary War as well. A concerned Governor Ashe wrote to Governor Sevier, seeking the extradition of several of the implicated individuals, but to Ashe's dismay, Sevier refused. Soon, it became clear to Jackson that Governor Sevier himself was not only involved in the scheme but may have been its mastermind.

---

[227] AJ to Sevier, May 10, 1797. Jackson Papers, LC.
[228] AJ to Sevier, October 9, 1803. Jackson, *Correspondence*.

To the cagey Jackson, though Sevier's involvement was clear, and he soon had the evidence to prove it, he chose not to reveal Sevier's involvement to Governor Ashe. He chose instead to sit on his proof, which included evidence that Sevier had acquired land warrants under the Confiscation Act of 1779, aiming to profit by inflating land prices. Why he didn't expose Sevier's involvement is unclear, especially in light of the first round in their feud over the militia election. Whether his decision was based on the truce the men had agreed to or was primarily calculated to maintain Jackson's political connection to the governor is not entirely known.[229]

Probably Jackson's discretion was strategic. Sevier had not opposed Jackson's election to the Senate, and perhaps Jackson saw the value of continuing to foster a cooperative relationship with the governor, whether it compromised the ethics of public office. Ultimately, although shocked to find that Sevier himself was involved in the scandal, his decision not to expose this scandalous secret ensured he and Sevier could remain in their truce, however tentative it was since the day Jackson lost to Conway. Sevier, Jackson knew, held considerable influence in Tennessee, particularly in the eastern part of the state, and Jackson was cautious not to confront that power, at least for the time being.

For now, it was a savvy political move for Jackson to cooperate with Sevier as much as possible. More crucially, Jackson did not give up on his most desired prize: the rank of major general in the militia, and this may have been part of his decision to not out Sevier. This ambition of commanding the Tennessee militia still burned passionately within Jackson, having nearly won the post previously. Since his loss to Conway five years earlier, Jackson was building his coalition within the militia. The one individual who could effectively obstruct his path, as illustrated in the last election, was John Sevier. Perhaps next time, if Sevier chose not to intervene, Jackson might prevail.

By keeping this scandalous information confidential, Jackson also held a potential advantage that he could leverage against the governor whenever necessary. Essentially, he had the trump card he could use against Sevier any time he needed. Most likely, Jackson strategized that

---

[229] Boonshoft, Mark, *Dispossessing Loyalists and Redistributing Property in Revolutionary New York*, September 19, 2016.

waiting was his best option, and this advice may have been given by William Blount, still Jackson's key political mentor. In the meantime, he would maintain cordial relations with the governor for his own benefit. He even went so far as to indicate his willingness to assist with any needs in the Mero district that the governor might have. For Jackson, this was more about personal gain than serving the public good, at least for the time being. [230]

Still, the rivalry between two of the leading men of Tennessee would only worsen. Later that same year, their relationship deteriorated further after Jackson's return from Philadelphia. The mistrust Jackson could not help but feel towards Sevier led to a third encounter between the two men, as a series of angry letters were hastily exchanged back and forth.[231] Although tensions calmed with the intervention of General Robertson, and other mutual friends, they continued to harbor suspicions about each other's intentions.

The Jackson-Sevier rift had its roots in the rival factions each supported, with Sevier's representing eastern Tennessee, and Jackson's support of the Blount faction representing the West. Despite their attempts to publicly reconcile through conciliatory letters on the part of both of the men, the mutual wariness persisted. In one letter, Sevier attempted to calm the waters by insisting that he was not Jackson's enemy. Jackson, in reply, acknowledged (whether convincingly or not) no malicious intent on Sevier's part. But the tensions remained, and as an offshoot, their rift eventually strained Jackson's relationship with his old friend Judge McNairy, whom he perceived as too supportive of Sevier.[232]

Despite Jackson's trouble with Sevier's eastern Tennessee syndicate, the Blount faction could not have been more pleased with their young congressman and his political development over the past year. Praising his protege's bold challenge of the popular and powerful Sevier for the position of major general, Blount also commended Jackson on his performance in Congress, which earned him further praise from figures such as Tennessee Senator William Cocke and others, placing his political career on firm footing. 71 Blount, who had been a strong

---

[230] Remini, 1977, p.118.
[231] Goodpasture, A.V., *Genesis of the Jackson-Sevier Feud*.
[232] Bassett, Spencer. *The Life of Andrew Jackson*, V.I., p. 58.

supporter of Jackson, suggested backing him for a Senate seat in the upcoming election. [233]

The opportunity to send Jackson to the Senate had arisen due to a conspiracy that led to Blount's ousting from the senatorial halls. It all began when word leaked out that Spain had agreed to return part of Louisiana to Napoleonic France. The Pinckney Treaty (1795) had only recently been signed between the United States and Spain, opening the entire Mississippi River to American trade, at long last. But now, the potential return of the French to the lower Mississippi Valley posed a significant threat, as it shifted the conflict from Spain, a shell of its former self, to a more formidable adversary, Napoleon Bonaparte of France.

The Corsican Napoleon's imperialistic ambitions seemed to know no bounds, and by his countrymen supplanting the Spanish in the vital port city of New Orleans, the Pinckney Treaty would have been all for naught, as Napoleon and the French were not a part of it, and would certainly not be bound by its restraints. Concerns over potential French control of the Mississippi and their acquisition of New Orleans renewed the threat to American trade once again, just when American rights of deposit in the "Crescent City" had finally been secured. Blount and others in Tennessee feared these hard-won rights were on the verge of disappearing. It was time to act. [234]

Falling land values exacerbated by fears of French intervention in the Southwest combined to spell trouble for the Blount brothers, whose financial difficulties prompted the elder Blount to turn to the only power on earth who could keep Napoleon at bay, Great Britain. Blount believed that, with England at war with Spain and France, an alliance would benefit both America and the British. The British could support American land speculation by financing campaigns against Florida and Louisiana, led by Tennesseans.

This change in perspective, driven by William Blount's own economic interests, was also fueled by hopes of guaranteed access to the Mississippi River for all westerners. Blount reasoned that, in the 1783 Treaty of Paris, the British had guaranteed free navigation, after

---

[233] Ramsey, J.G.M, *Annals of Tennessee*, p.677. LOC.
[234] Remini, 1977. p. 105.

all, as well as concessions in the west. In exchange for Blount's forces doing the grunt work, England would offer large land grants and ensure free navigation of the Mississippi, or so Blount proposed. This would enhance his financial standing and benefit western land interests to boot. Expelling Britain's enemies altogether, both Spain and France, would boost land values for all involved, Blount explained.

Unfortunately for William Blount, his unlawful scheming was soon to become public knowledge. After an incriminating letter written by Blount to fellow conspirator James Carey was intercepted, it ended up in the hands of the Adams administration. The letter was then turned over to the Senate, after which a House committee launched an investigation, ultimately concluding that Blount conspired to launch a military expedition against Florida and Louisiana for Great Britain. [235]

Following the committee's report, the House adopted impeachment charges and requested Blount's seat be "sequestered." The Senate expelled him instead, preventing a trial. That Blount's conspiratorial wherewithal was apparently not as sharp as his political acumen became clear. In his rather foolish, blunt, and candid letter to Carey, Blount laid out his scheme in language that was all too clear as to his culpability. With the conspiracy entirely revealed, the Tennessee senator was soon out of a job.

Blount, for his part, did not attempt to dispute the charges against him. His silence, however, was taken as an admission of guilt by the committee. The deliberate pace of the House Committee's investigation, and their clumsy handling of the trial highlighted Congress's inexperience with impeachable offenses. Despite the ongoing charges, Blount acknowledged the implications of his letter while hoping that western citizens would view his actions favorably, capitalizing on the regional resentment towards eastern attitudes regarding western aspirations.

While some back home were reluctant to show their support for Blount, Jackson's loyalty never wavered for a moment.[236] Committed wholeheartedly to the motives behind the conspiracy against the Spanish in Florida and Louisiana, Jackson loyally defended his political mentor at every opportunity. He justified the conspiracy by emphasizing its benefits for western expansion. The West required control of the Mississippi and

---

[235] *ASPFA*, II, 72-74, *Annals of Congress*, 5th Congress, 1st Session, 72-74.
[236] AJ to Willie Blount, Feb. 21, 1798, Blount Collection, LC.

New Orleans, along with the removal of any obstacles, including foreign powers and indigenous peoples, to ensure economic progress along the frontier. Jackson›s loyalty to his political mentor solidified his bond with Blount, and in return, Blount made sure that Tennesseans understood that it was surely Jackson who was just the man to replace him in the federal Senate.

Like Aaron Burr's later conspiracy with James Wilkinson, the Blount conspiracy was unsuccessful in large part because it was more unilateral and driven by individual aspirations. Jackson's later "conspiracy" in Spanish Florida was different in that it took into account the necessary and important presence of the United States. To be sure, Jackson's "conspiracy" served the economic ambitions of western Americans; but it also served the expansionist and imperial ambitions of the entire people of the United States.[237] At the time of Jackson's high-handed exploits in Spanish Florida in 1819, he was, after all on a federally sanctioned campaign, and his control of the military was certainly in his favor. This guise of national defense set his efforts much more on the road to success.

Jackson gained support in Tennessee (especially within the Blount faction) by his outspoken defense of his mentor's conspiracy, and in his articulation of the potential achievements for the West had it succeeded. While Blount became a casualty of political bias fostered by the Adams administration, Jackson argued, in Tennessee, he and many others felt strongly that Adams, who enforced Washington's Indian policy and displaced white settlers from Indian lands, harbored a hatred for the West.

Blount could have sought reelection to the United States Senate to assert the influence of westerners against eastern opposition but instead opted to pursue the governorship of Tennessee following Sevier's planned resignation. Sevier hoped to lead a potential military effort amid rising tensions with France. A war with France ultimately did not materialize, (although a Quasi-War at sea did,) so Sevier remained governor. Blount was instead elected to the Tennessee State Senate. Despite impending impeachment charges, Blount's defense in the Senate trial argued that he could not be tried as he was no longer a senator, leading to the Senate's

---

[237] Abernethy, Thomas P., *The South in the New Nation*, 1789-1819, Baton Rouge, 1961. pp. 169-191.

dismissal of the case on January 11, 1799, citing lack of jurisdiction, even as serious allegations against him, including conspiracy to violate American neutrality, went unaddressed. The Blount case marked another key aspect in the evolutionary process of the U.S. Constitution that Americans still needed ironed out. [238]

With the departure of Blount from the United States Senate and his decision not to seek reelection, a replacement was needed. The Blount faction also chose to remove William Cocke from the Senate as a consequence of Cocke's vote to expel Blount, signaling his split from the group, as he sought new political alliances. Joseph Anderson was elected unopposed to fill Blount's seat, while the Blount supporters turned their attention to finding a candidate to oppose the disloyal Cocke in the upcoming election. They nominated Jackson, highlighting his strong performance in the House of Representatives and his commitment to Tennessee's interests. Blount endorsed Jackson, predicting Cocke's defeat and heralding the abilities of Jackson in the *Knoxville Gazette*. [239]

The election in the fall of 1797 resulted in a victory for Andrew Jackson, who received twenty votes from the Tennessee legislature compared to William Cocke's thirteen, a development that pleased Blount greatly. Following this, fellow Republican William C.C. Claiborne was chosen to replace Jackson in the House of Representatives. However, tensions escalated between Jackson and Cocke after the election due to a personal dispute regarding a private letter, which Jackson had written in confidence to Cocke, who then revealed some of its private contents to others, portraying Jackson in an unfavorable light. Jackson's outrage nearly resulted in bloodshed.

> In a letter to Cocke dated November 9, 1797,
> "Your sacrificing all private confidence by making publick my private letter merits, and receives my utmost Indignation, Sir, the baseness of your heart, in violating a confidence proposed in you in an hour of intimate friendship, should as I conceive it was between you and me, by the most solemn obligation will bring down the indignation of the thinking part of mankind upon

---

[238] Annals of Congress, 5th Congress, 1st Session, I, 947.
[239] Blount to John Gray Blount, Nov. 7, 1797, *Blount Papers*, III, 175.

you and the thunderbolt you were preparing for me will burst upon your own head, it will occasion that part of mankind, that here to for viewed you worthy of public confidence to pause a moment and reflect how far a man is worthy…who has violated all kind of private at the shrine of malice occasion by you to disappointment, the western world will think for themselves like free men as they are and view the man who has made such sacrifice as you have done, capable of betraying all public confidence to private interest." [240]

Six months after their conflict, Jackson, determined to clear from his name the false accusations, insisted on a public declaration of his innocence. The only alternative, Jackson offered, was to meet Cocke for "satisfaction." Both men, however, each believing the other had received misleading information, ultimately agreed to resolve their dispute through arbitration by a respected panel. This decision averted a duel, as the panel ultimately concluded that false information inspired by hearsay was the source of their animosity, intensified by the heated nature of the recent election, particularly affecting Cocke after his defeat. The resolution appeased Jackson, allowing both men to avoid a violent confrontation, and very possibly their deaths. There would be more time for duels later.

---

[240] AJ to William Cocke, November 9, 1797, Jackson Papers, LC.

CHAPTER

19

NOT FOR THE LEGISLATIVE LIFE

"It is to be regretted that the rich and powerful too often bend the acts of government to their selfish purposes."
                                        -Andrew Jackson

The biting wind whips through the cobbled streets of Philadelphia, carrying with it the scent of coal smoke and the distant rumble of carriages. The air itself weighs heavy with discontent. Inside a sparsely furnished room, lit by the flickering glow of a single candle, Jackson sits hunched over a desk, his brow furrowed in a familiar frown. The very ink with which he writes seems to reflect the darkness that has settled over his spirit this winter.

The long journey from his beloved Rachel, back home in Tennessee, has taken its toll. The letters he has come to rely so heavily upon are a constant reminder of the miles that separate them. Each missive brings a fresh wave of melancholy, a potent brew of sadness that threatens to consume him. The halls of Congress, once a place of ambition and purpose, now feel like a gilded cage, trapping him in a velvet prison to which there seems to be no escape.

He picks up a quill, dips it into the inkwell, and begins to write, the words flowing out like a torrent of pent-up frustrations. Jackson has reached the end of his rope, and his words are a testament to his state, a reflection of his unhappiness with life in Philadelphia. He writes of his impatience with the legislators he has to associate with on a daily basis;

as well as his anger, his distress over the maddening hours of political gridlock and debate; the constant infighting over the Quasi War, the Adams administration, the Federalists who refuse to see things the way the Jeffersonians do, and the difficulty he has in mastering his temperament. The absence of Rachel is a constant ache, a wound that refuses to heal. He cannot find the right words, which has been his constant weight.

He knows that Rachel, too, is suffering. He has read her letters, filled with her own loneliness and longing. The distance has cast a shadow over her as well, and her unhappiness mirrors his own. He is trapped in a cycle of despair, a prisoner of circumstance amid the vast, unforgiving expanse that separates him from the one person who can bring him solace. He reads her words from Tennessee, "The snow falls outside, a cold, relentless curtain. Inside, the fire struggles to ward off the chill, but it cannot reach the depths of my soul. Another letter arrives, another reminder of the chasm that yawns between us." Rachel's words, though filled with love, are laced with the same weariness that plagues his own heart. The weight of these absences, the endless days and nights apart, threatens to crush the lost thirty-year-old. How long, Jackson thinks, must I endure this torment?"

During the winter of 1797-98, Andrew Jackson's letters portray the depression he was clearly feeling and had been for some time. His unhappy emotional state throughout the depressing winter, far from home, and a mood tainted by his discontent with life as a Congressman in Philadelphia is marked by anger and distress, particularly regarding the long absences from his wife. Jackson's writing betrays his increasing difficulty with attempts to master his temperament effectively. Added to Jackson's unhappiness were the letters he read from an equally disheartened Rachel, who was also unhappy with his long, extended absences.

The extreme sadness and guilt seemed to torment Jackson throughout this dismal period, and his regret over leaving Rachel in tears upon his departure takes its toll. Fearing her prolonged somber state, which overshadowed his own well-being, his bleak mood persists throughout his brief term as United States senator, which may well have been a cause for the negative impression Jackson made on Vice President Thomas Jefferson. Jefferson, as president of the Senate, would famously remark on his first impressions of the young Tennessee Senator Jackson, whose volatile temperament, Jefferson stated, stood out more than any other characteristic. Having witnessed him often as presiding officer of the Senate, Jefferson noted that Jackson's anger would cause him to repeatedly struggle even to speak on the Senate floor. Due to Jackson's overwhelming rage, Jefferson recalled his impressions of the young Senator as "a dangerous individual."[241] Retaining this image of Jackson years later, Jefferson commented during the General's victorious post-New Orleans period that, despite his eventual emotional cooling over time, Jackson remained a danger to the country.

There is justification for taking Jefferson's words with a grain of salt, expressed a quarter-century after the events in question, during the contentious, negative campaign for the presidency between Jackson and John Quincy Adams. Massachusetts Congressman Daniel Webster, a supporter of Adams, sought to persuade Jefferson to publicly denounce Jackson's candidacy, to which Jefferson readily agreed. "I am quite alarmed at the possibility of General Jackson becoming president. He is among the most unsuitable individuals I am aware of for such a position. He shows very little regard for laws or constitutions. He poses a significant threat."[242] First impressions mean a lot, and unfortunately for Jackson, Jefferson's first impressions of him as a young senator came during one of the unhappiest times in Jackson's life.

Besides the extended absences from his hearth and home, much of Jackson's distress during 1797-1798 concerned his ongoing financial difficulties. During the winter, Jackson faced significant money problems, primarily stemming from financial troubles linked to David Allison. Jackson's connections to the unreliable Allison haunted Jackson, and they were marked by a series of financial grievances, culminating in Allison's imprisonment in Philadelphia. Allison, who became deathly sick in prison, would die in his cell just a year later. Despite Allison's untimely demise, Jackson remained furious, expressing his frustrations to John Overton regarding Allison's lack of integrity and the financial burden he placed on him, who had acted as security for Allison's debts.

---

[241] Parton, *Jackson*, p. 219.
[242] Ibid.

Jackson's hopes for recovery were dashed when he learned that his usual source of bailout, William Blount, was unable to assist him. The former governor of the Southwest Territory had also been entangled in financial difficulties due to his dealings with Allison, and now Blount's legal troubles, derived from his conspiratorial charges, had also had deleterious effects on his financial standing. Without Blount's financial backing, Jackson began to feel the squeeze more fully than ever before. [243]

In addition to his financial woes, Jackson's political performance suffered during this period, certainly both a cause and effect of his woes. His record in the Senate was notably sparse, with minimal participation in debates and only a handful of votes in favor of the majority. He notably opposed key nominations, including General Arthur St. Clair for governor and John Quincy Adams for commissioner to Sweden. His actions during impeachment proceedings demonstrated his partisan stance, as he consistently voted against the reports and motions related to the impeachment, further illustrating his disengagement from his senatorial responsibilities.

Clearly Jackson was not cut out for the Senate, at least not at that time. Far younger and less experienced than the nationally renowned figures that debated policy in the Senate chamber, including the renowned Rober Morris and Thedore Sedgwick among others, Jackson lacked the confidence to be able to contribute effectively. If what Jefferson had said was true, with Jackson nearly choking with anger but unable to articulate his feelings in discussions, his frustration must have been palpable.

To Jackson's credit, he continued to show up for the job despite his unhappiness, his strong sense of duty compelling him on. He was not only present for all sessions in the Senate chamber, he stayed informed on national issues, and kept friends back home informed of them in his correspondence, as well as his opinions on the key issues. Amid tensions with France, many impassioned congressmen favored a war policy and pushed President Adams to defend American honor. Jackson believed, however, that a treaty would ultimately be reached, holding firm to the hope that France's focus would shift toward continued animosity with Great Britain.

---

[243] AJ to James Jackson, Aug. 25, 1819, Jackson, *Correspondence*, II, 427.

Jackson, and other Senators of his party, speculated that if Bonaparte landed in England, a revolution and the rise of a republic could well follow. This belief sheds light on both Jackson's admiration for Napoleon and his longstanding animosity toward the British. "France has finally concluded a treaty with the emperor and the king of Sardinia," he told James Robertson, "and is now turning her force toward Great Britain. Bonaparte, with 150,000 troops (used to conquer), is ordered to the coast, and called the army of England. Do not then be surprised if my next letter should announce a revolution in England. Should Bonaparte make a landing on the English shore, tyranny will be humbled, a throne, crushed, and a republic will spring from the wreck, and millions of distressed people restored to the rights of men by the conquering arm of Bonaparte." These were high hopes indeed. [244]

To say that the French were not happy with the United States in the second half of the 1790s would be an understatement. Outraged by Jay's Treaty, viewing it as a betrayal by their former ally, and a step towards an Americans alliance with Britain, the seizure of close to three hundred American merchant ships by French frigates began in the fall of 1796. By mid-1797, French privateers began attacking all merchant ships in American waters, regardless of nationality. [245]

In response to the escalating tensions, Adams sought to maintain peace by appointing a diplomatic commission to negotiate with France. The diplomats Adams sent included the future Chief Justice of the Supreme Court, John Marshall, who hoped to meet with the crafty French foreign minister, The Prince of Talleyrand, Charles Maurice de Talleyrand-Périgord. However, the American envoys were instead approached by three intermediaries of Talleyrand, later referred to as X,Y, and Z to the American public. These agents, sent as go-betweens, met the Americans with demands for a substantial bribe and an unneutral loan, which were deemed unacceptable by Marshall and the other negotiators. As a result, the talks fell apart before they had even begun, and it ignited a wave of war hysteria across the United States when it reached American shores, prompting significant military preparations

---

[244] AJ to Robertson, Jan. 11, 1798, Jackson, *Correspondence*, I, 42.
[245] Allen, Gardner Weld (1909). *Our Naval War With France*. Boston and New York: Houghton Mifflin.

even among traditionally pro-French Jeffersonians, who now felt shame over France's actions.[246]

To Adams's credit, he stood firm against the mounting pressure and demands for war. Recognizing the nation's vulnerability, the President opted for diplomacy. In 1799, he submitted the name of a new minister to France, aiming for peace. But, in November of that year, Napoleon Bonaparte rose to power in France following a coup d'état known as the Coup of 18 Brumaire. This event overthrew the French Directory, replacing it with a three-member Consulate, with Napoleon as First Consul, effectively making him the leading political figure in France. [247]

By early 1800, with Napoleon in power, the political climate had shifted, and the new French leader now sought to resolve the American conflict in favor of a focus on European ambitions. This led to the signing of the Convention of 1800, in which France annulled their previous alliance with the U.S. in exchange for the United States agreeing to compensate French shippers. While the convention addressed many issues, it did not settle the question of compensation for American ship owners who had suffered losses during the Quasi-War. This issue would be a point of contention later on.

Adams's efforts not only averted war but also set the stage for the future acquisition of Louisiana, solidifying his legacy as a peacemaker despite the initial backlash against his decision. Were it not for Adams's use of diplomacy instead of force, Napoleon likely would have rejected Jefferson's 1803 offer to purchase Louisiana. While the memory of the Adams administration is often clouded by the controversies surrounding the Alien and Sedition Acts that he and the Federalists in Congress sanctioned in 1798, Adams deserves credit for more than is often attributed to his legacy.

Senator Andrew Jackson, however, was highly critical of President Adams's administration for many reasons. One criticism, ironically, involved Adams's patronage system, which Jackson likened to Washington's, calling it "execrable." Jackson and his Tennessee colleagues were also frustrated by Adams's Indigenous policy, demonstrated particularly by a letter denouncing the military's treatment of Judge

---

[246] Ibid.
[247] DeConde, Alexander (1966). *The Quasi-War: The Politics and Diplomacy of the Undeclared War with France, 1797–1801*. Charles Scribner's Sons.

David Campbell, accused of violating the Administration's Indian Policy. Jackson and his Tennessee colleagues deemed this an unlawful violation of Campbell's civil liberties. Although Adams eventually responded satisfactorily with a revised Indian treaty, Jackson remained disillusioned with the administration.

Struggling with his role as a senator, Jackson, too young and inexperienced for the position, managed to meet the minimal Senatorial requirements with a large degree of indifference. Clearly not fully invested in his office, and not matching the level of attention and effort the job required, the thirty-year-old Senator considered quitting altogether. A fall on the ice that winter only made matters worse, as Jackson was then confined to his chair for weeks. Ultimately, his moodiness, debts, and dissatisfaction led him to ask for and receive a leave of absence from the Senate after just one session.

Ultimately, Jackson had become disenchanted with life as a legislator. As historian A.W. Putnam explains, "To be a member of Congress, at that day, from a State so remote as Tennessee, (six weeks' journey from Philadelphia) absorbed nearly the whole year; and this alone would have rendered such a man as Jackson, formed for activity and keen in the pursuit of fortune, averse to filling the office. Nor was there ever a man less inclined than he to pass the best hours of every day for seven successive months, quiescent in a red morocco chair, playing Senator..."[248] Taking action came instinctively to him, while patience was a lifelong struggle.

By late spring, 1798, Jackson packed his few belongings and returned to Nashville. Upon his return to Tennessee, he promptly, and without much explanation or remorse, resigned from the office altogether, rejecting the role he did not wish to fulfill. Jackson, in fact, had serious doubts as to whether or not he was best suited to the offices of a politician. He was especially unhappy with the distance from home, and length of time spent away from his wife. Frustrated by the wrangling political scene in the nation's capital, Jackson sought active employment closer to home, in a position that would offer fulfillment, and would be much more to his liking.

---

[248] Putnam, A. W. *History of Middle Tennessee*, p. 174.

After just one year as a Senator, Andrew Jackson, having promptly resigned from the Senate formally upon returning home, also submitted, or so he stated at the time, his resignation from public life. The man he felt was most suitable to replace him was Tennessean Daniel Smith, who, Jackson later stated, could serve the Senate better than he could. Viewing the legislature derisively, Jackson refused to waste his time on "sticks and spittle"[249] as he would describe the minor disputes he witnessed in the Senate chamber.

It was becoming clear to Jackson, and probably to those who knew him best at that time, that the legislature was simply not the right fit for his temperament. His natural disposition did not lend itself to negotiation. The proper course of action for the decisive and firm Jackson, in whom firm action came much more naturally than discussion and compromise, was to take the helm with two hands. With that said, Jackson chose to walk away from the Senate, but not from politics entirely. Confident in his own judgments, he much preferred to lead, and if he was to stay in politics, he needed a position more suited to this mold, one that he had not yet found.

Jackson thus returned to hearth and home and to the love of his wife, closing out the first chapter in his political career. In retrospect, it was a chapter that can be seen as a proving ground, one that helped shape his future as a national figure and define the dogged leader Jackson would become. Characterized by the challenges of land speculation, financial troubles, conflicts with political rivals, and a commitment to representing the interests of Tennessee, his experiences in both houses of Congress introduced Jackson to the complexities of American politics. A training ground for the politician Jackson would later become, this period taught the Tennessean the aspects of life in the capital that he abhorred: the laborious legislative process, the endless debates, the constant social posturing. Jackson emerged from this period with a clearer idea of what he did not want from politics. His response to his experiences and actions laid the groundwork for his later presidency and the controversies that would define his legacy.

---

[249] AJ to Robertson, March 7, 1798, Jackson Papers, LC.

From the correspondence that survived the years, including a later Hermitage fire that destroyed much of his letters to Rachel, Jackson's love and affection never wavered. His letters displayed his consistent devotion to his wife. As early as 1796, when public business took him away from home for an extended period he wrote to Rachel, "I mean to retire from the business of public life, and with you alone in sweet retirement, which is my only ambition and ultimate wish. May it give you pleasure to receive it, may it add to your contentment until I return, may you be blessed with health."[250] Jackson's yearning for his wife was surpassed only by Rachel's sorrow over his absences. Her distress at Jackson's frequent departures often carried with it physical ailments, which only made her emotional state worse. His wife's welfare was a foremost concern that Jackson fretted over during his time away. Yet, regardless, Jackson would continue, throughout his life, to pursue opportunities that took him away from home.

Rachel's letters indicate how greatly she missed Jackson and worried for his safety. "What a vacuum is in my soul [when] you are absent," she wrote in one letter, and in another, "You have been gone a long time, six months, in all that time what has been your trials, dangers and difficulties, hardships, oh lorde of heaven how can I bare it. . ." She wrote of her misery without him and that she suffered from "sick headaches and sometimes could not sleep for crying."[251] Adding to Jackson's anxiety was the constant threat of Indian attack on the frontier, too near to Rachel's vicinity for his comfort. These factors clinched the decision for Andrew Jackson, who longed for the familiarity of home, the ability of an honest man to do real work for the good of his wife. Philadelphia was not the place for him, Nashville and Rachel were his true home.

Jackson had special reasons to shield Rachel from "the abuses of the world." He had been her protector since the beginning of their relationship, "rescuing her" from the oppressive Robards. Their elopement had brought its own issues, both legal and social, (issues that kept stubbornly reemerging over time), intensifying his desire to protect her. Although Nashville was a safer place than it had been ten years

---

[250] Brands, H.W., 2005. Part 1.
[251] Jackson, Rachel, The Hermitage Collection, 2021.

before, threats remained, particularly from indigenous attacks. Both Rachel and Jackson worried for each other during his travels.

During an extended absence, Jackson wrote to Robert Hays, Rachel's brother, asking him to care for his sister. "I now beg of you to look after Mrs. Jackson, as the state I left her in fills me with woe, more painful than any event in my life." He frequently inquired with friends in Nashville about her well-being and grew impatient when updates were scarce. "It is such neglect that I feel it sensibly," he expressed. When news arrived, especially good news of her improved spirits, he felt grateful. "I hold myself much indebted to him for his letter," he mentioned regarding a friend's updates on Rachel.[252]

If Jackson had felt his work in Congress was essential, he might have been able to set aside his concerns for Rachel. However, witnessing politicians bicker over trivial matters, he concluded that he could do more good for his wife back home than he could do for the state of Tennessee in Philadelphia. Back in Nashville, Jackson returned to familiar work, including land dealings and farming. It was time indeed to grapple with his personal affairs. This would be no easy challenge, for Jackson's head was just barely above water in that respect. The ledger at Hunter's Hill showed a small profit, but Jackson was determined to increase it. Ever willing to try, he attempted commerce again due to the need for supplies and crop sales in a cash-scarce market. He wrote to a Philadelphia merchant about a barter arrangement, explaining his intention to purchase goods in exchange for cotton and land.

Done with legislative failings, and at home once again, Andrew Jackson began a new chapter in his life. While his political rise had been satisfying to the once penniless young man, his financial standing still remained all too precarious. For Jackson, now toting the added burden of a devoted wife to support, his lifelong mission to lead the life of a gentleman reoccupied his time and attention. Politics would have to wait.

---

[252] Jackson to Hays, Jackson, *Correspondence*, March, 1798.

ANDREW JACKSON: THE POLITICS OF RESENTMENT

Lithograph of the Hermitage, 1848, by James S. Baillie

CHAPTER

20

HOME AGAIN

"All the rights secured to the citizen under the Constitution are worth nothing, and a mere bubble, except guaranteed to them by an independent and virtuous judiciary."
-Andrew Jackson

In the summer of 1798, Andrew Jackson returned to private enterprise. The former Senator from the state of Tennessee now resumed his familiar occupations, particularly his land dealings, and his farming operations. He even reconsidered his commercial ventures once again, largely due to his need for costly farm supplies of seed, machinery, and livestock. Jackson decided that in the difficult frontier marketplace, so void of real cash, bartering for his needs would be most effective. Mired in these necessities, controlling an aspect of the supply chain made the most sense to Jackson. Thus, he would soon embark upon a return to the mercantile business as a partner in a dry goods store with a brother-in-law. He would even tried his hand for a time in running a riverside boatyard.[253]

His rough frontier home grew, from the Poplar Flat property, which Jackson sold in the autumn of 1797, to a 640-acre property on the Cumberland River called Hunter's Hill. Before the age of 40, Jackson would now become a prominent trader and planter and continue to add to his property. Soon his estate would be worked by dozens of slaves. His

---

[253] Bassett, John Spencer. *The life of Andrew Jackson*, Garden City, N.Y., Doubleday, Page & Company, 1911, p.32

enterprises were ever-expanding, and his personal wealth grew steadily from year to year throughout the turn of the century.

Yet, once again, Jackson faced personal discontent. The life of a farmer and trader simply did not fulfill his lofty ambitions. As a result, Jackson was always on the lookout for the next step forward professionally. In this capacity, a new occupation would soon happen upon him, one that could potentially rekindle his political aspirations. Despite his insistence that he was done with public life, Jackson could not resist the call of the political arena.

Another reason for Jackson's decision to resign from the Senate was not based on a disdain for the political system entirely, but instead on the possibility of a different public office, one more suited to his wishes. Desiring a more convenient situation politically, he sought a post that would keep him close to his interests in Tennessee without requiring him to leave the state for months on end. Meeting this requirement, he would take on a position only if he was still able to fulfill his financial requirements. Soon, such a job materialized, and not just any job; one that would pay more than any other office in the state, with the exception of the governorship, and one that would advance his political and military ambitions by taking him to all parts of Tennessee, and bringing him into contact with the people and the leaders of the various sections of the state. [254]

An offer such as this may well have seemed too good to be true for the busy Jackson. Especially a post that would allow the degree of autonomy he lacked as a legislator. Yet, like manna from heaven, such a job would soon offer itself up for the former legislator to grab, and it checked all the boxes. Only a few months after Jackson's return from the nation's capital, a state judgeship arose that fit these requirements. This was not just any judgeship, but a seat on the Tennessee Superior Court.

This new opportunity would allow Jackson to remain in Tennessee, and with its lofty rank it came with the prestige and respect Jackson craved. He may have walked away from the United States Senate, but his interest in politics certainly did not wane entirely, nor did his lifelong desire to burnish his image and professional reputation, while accepting the gratitude of the public and the prestige that came with it. Even as he refocused his efforts back home, on his beloved wife, his business

---

[254] Remini, 1977, p. 113

affairs, and his estate, Jackson's political interests, and desire for public acclaim carried on.

Although Jackson's role in Congress had been undistinguished, his reputation in Tennessee remained strong, and it was this reputation that helped him land the job on the judiciary. Soon after returning, he received a letter from Governor Sevier appointing him to "The Superior Court of Law and Equity," commonly referred to as "The Supreme Court" of Tennessee. This set of judges formed the state's highest appellate tribunal court, overseeing appeals from decisions made by judges acting individually as the Superior Court and from county courts. Jackson accepted the offer without much deliberation.

But why had John Sevier appointed Jackson? The reasons are unclear, particularly since Jackson remained a political rival of the governor, and Sevier was aligned with the faction opposing Blount. It is possible that Sevier hoped to diminish Jackson's political influence by placing him on the bench. At any rate, Jackson's interim commission was signed on September 20, 1798, and he was elected by the General Assembly on December 20, at the age of 31, to serve "during good behavior," effectively granting him a life appointment.

Once again, Jackson's powerful connections within the state paid off. William Blount had previously communicated with the Governor, indicating the western portion of the state's desire to see Andrew Jackson appointed to the post. Blount had then informed Jackson the job was his if he wanted, indicating that many in the state wished for him to accept if appointed, and Jackson obliged. On September 20th, 1798, Jackson's commission was signed by his former rival, to become an interim judge of the Superior Court (now the Tennessee Supreme Court). [255]

It remains unclear if Jackson initiated this move, or was approached by others, but he was soon elected to the Court on a permanent basis, without opposition, at the age of 31. Thanks to his stern reputation, and his connections with the Blount faction, along with the support of other influential friends, he had reached the pinnacle of the Tennessee law profession. Barring impeachment, Jackson now held a prestigious job for life. The six-hundred-dollar salary was only slightly less than that of

---

[255] Remini, 1977, p. 114; Blount to Sevier, July 6th, 1798. In AHM (January 1900), V. 121-122.

the governor, making it the second highest paid government position in Tennessee.

Jackson's speculating, farming and trading enterprises were proving to be lucrative enough to keep he and Rachel content, but not so profitable (or demanding) that it prevented a return to public service. Additionally, Jackson desired the respect that would come with his position on the highest court in Tennessee.

For the next six years, he rode the law circuit over the state and became both well-respected by many for his stern, decisive demeanor on the bench and hated by others for the same. Yet, Jackson's years as superior court judge are often overlooked when historians consider the formative experiences that led to Jackson's dynamic rise. Serving as a judge requires not only an even-keel temperament, but a deep understanding of the law and legal principles.

Not naturally suited to the legislature, Jackson had only a rudimentary grasp of legal interpretation. His training in the law had been minimal, and he lacked the inclination to study jurisprudence deeply. Furthermore, his legal library had not grown tremendously over the years. His temperament, contrary to the impartiality expected of a judge, was driven by a strong sense of right and wrong. It also requires strong analytical skills to interpret laws and apply them to specific cases. To be effective on the bench, an ability to communicate complex legal issues in clear and understandable language is a must. Did Jackson possess these qualities?

We know of Jackson's hot temper, prickly sense of honor, and sensitivity to insults which would continue to embroil him in conflict throughout his life. His penchant for conflict, in fact, including physical confrontation, would nearly cost him his life. Even though his career involved making, interpreting and enforcing the law, it was not his highest calling. When it came to the law, if it contradicted his sense of justice, he would prioritize justice. He prioritized matters of honor, as well, over that of legality. This type of approach would not go over well in the hallowed chambers of the United States Supreme Court back east, but this was the Tennessee frontier.

Although Judge Jackson did not fit the traditional magistrate's mold, his firm decisiveness, along with his sense of honor and justice, resonated with the more practical-minded westerners of his time. As John S. Bassett concluded in his 1911 Jackson biography, "He had many qualifications of a good judge. He was, no doubt, but little versed in the law. But he had common sense, integrity, courage, and impartiality." [256] James C. Curtis declared that Jackson provided a "crude, but fair, brand of justice." [257] Yet, by most accounts, Judge Jackson proved to be an effective judge in his six years on the bench, reinforcing the growing belief that Jackson could be a calculated master when it came to controlling his temperament, using it for martial purposes when necessary, and managing it for the betterment of himself, his career, and the public good as he saw it to be.

Known for his dedication and popularity, Jackson handled a wide array of cases efficiently, maintaining courtroom decorum, not an easy task on the rough Tennessee frontier. Despite his unscholarly law background, Jackson appears to have excelled on the court. He built a collection of law books and was regarded as the most knowledgeable judge on the court (which tells us much about his fellow justices.) Praised for his authority and generally sound judgments, all despite his informal style, Jackson balanced adherence to a strict code with compassion, as seen when he advocated for a young offender's pardon. As Judge Jackson (as he preferred to be called even after his judgeship) wrote William Blount, "A good judiciary lends much to the dignity of a state and the happiness of a people. When on the contrary a bad judiciary involved in party business is the greatest curse that can befall a country." [258]

Jackson proved to be an effective judge, whose years on the bench were critical not only to the advancement of his career, but also to the development of Tennessee's infant judiciary. Despite his limited legal knowledge at the outset, Jackson developed a surprisingly respectable reputation and record as a jurist. Several factors contributed to his success on the bench. Firstly, Jackson was widely regarded as a judge of the highest integrity, known for making swift and decisive rulings free from discrimination or bias. Judge Jackson displayed courage in his decisions and spoke with confidence, commanding authority in his courtroom where instances of contempt were rare. His strong sense of justice, though at times misguided, helped him maintain impartiality in most situations.

---

[256] Bassett, 1911. p. 32.
[257] Curtis, James C., *Andrew Jackson and the Search for American Vindication*. 1st Edition. Pearson. p. 22
[258] AJ to Blount, 1799, Jackson Papers, LC.

While he may not have been a judicial Blackstone, Jackson's decisions were generally sound. According to the testimony of his contemporaries, the people of Tennessee were well-served by him, regardless of his lack of legal frills. Perhaps Jackson may not have been deemed so effective a magistrate back east, but on the Tennessee frontier, where justice was perhaps less letter-of-the-law, Jackson was well-suited for his robes.

In Tennessee, where formal recordings of judicial rulings did not become standard practice until after Jackson left the bench in 1804, only five of his written decisions survive, each co-signed by Jackson and other Superior Court members. Nonetheless, to say that Jackson's court was based solely on arbitrary measures would be inaccurate. Frontier justice stereotypes notwithstanding, judicial proceedings during this period in Tennessee were neither rudimentary nor improvised. Early judges were committed to establishing proper courtroom practices and decorum, enforcing strict adherence to accepted procedures. Disrespect for the law, unruly behavior, and legal misconduct faced severe penalties.

Jackson understood the expectations of his role, donning a judicial gown in court—perhaps reflecting his enormous sense of dignity and self-importance or an acknowledgment that the position warranted such attire. By all accounts, Jackson raised the bar by setting for himself and others within and around his courtroom, an expected level of professionalism that the important role of jurisprudence merited. Overall, he performed his duties with distinction and seemed to revel in the robes of a judge.

As a judge of the Tennessee Superior Court for six years, Jackson displayed his commitment to frontier justice and was ever-increasing in his knowledge of the law. Most of all, Jackson ran an efficient courtroom. It was commonly said that the Jackson court never faced a backlog. Cases were resolved with remarkable speed under his watch, astonishing more experienced jurists. In just 15 days, Jackson processed 50 cases. The role of a superior court judge involved traveling to various towns, and a story circulated about one occasion when Jackson was interrupted while dispensing justice at a crossroads. Here, while presiding over court in a small village and "dispensing justice in large and small doses," in one of his trials, Judge Jackson dealt with a case involving a man named Russell Bean, a veteran of the Battle of Kings Mountain, who had been indicted for a serious crime: cutting off the ears of his wife's baby, which was fathered by another man. In front of Jackson's bench, Bean threatened to kill Jackson, the jury, and everyone else present in the courtroom before storming out.

When a local sheriff, ordered to bring Bean back into court, found Bean outside the courthouse inciting a crowd, he reported back to Jackson that Bean was too dangerous to apprehend. The sheriff expressed his fear of Bean, who, he said, refused to appear in court. He reported to Jackson, "Russell Bean would not be taken." Dismayed, Jackson insisted that the culprit be arrested and informed the sheriff that he had the right to summon a 'posse comitatus' to assist in the law's execution. The sheriff did just that, but Bean's intimidation frightened them away too, threatening to "shoot the first skunk who came within ten feet of him." After a time, the sheriff returned again to Judge Jackson's court, informing him that Bean still managed to resist being brought in. Astonished, the exasperated Jackson, firmly informed the sheriff that such a result "was an absurdity, and could not be received."

The sheriff then requested Jackson's presence in the posse, and Jackson agreed, calling a ten-minute recess. Determined to take action himself, he removed his judicial robe, armed himself with a pistol, his ire now fully raised. He then stated to the sheriff "Sir, since you will not arrest him, I will attend you and see that you do your duty." They proceeded out of the courtroom, onto the courthouse steps, where they found Bean, standing a short distance away, armed with a dirk and a brace of pistols, still causing chaos in the street, cursing and inciting the crowd around him with threatening epithets, vowing death and damnation to anyone who might attempt to molest him. Waving a pistol, Bean taunted all around him, boasting loudly about his superiority to the law. Upon seeing this, and irate Jackson marched directly up to the ruffian. Pointing his gun at Bean, the Judge commanded, "Now surrender you infernal villain, this very instant, or I'll blow you through!"

The suddenly startled Bean stood perfectly still, watching Jackson's blazing eyes. Then, recognizing the seriousness in the judge's face, Bean complied. Unnerved by Jackson's firm advance and formidable presence, he placed his pistol on the ground, and surrendering to Jackson, stated, "I will surrender to you, sir, but no one else." When he was later asked how one man was able to bring him in, when an entire posse could not, Bean replied, "Why, when he came up, I looked him in the eyes and I saw 'shoot.' There wasn't shoot in nary other eye in the crowd. So I says to myself, says I: Hoss, it's about time to sing small, and so I did." [259]

Perhaps this is what truly occurred, though it is likely the story was embellished over the years, especially as the legend of Jackson grew. At any rate, this captures the essence of what made Jackson an effective backwoods judge. Although he could most certainly be touchy and unreasonable, this episode in Tennessee highlights the faith others placed in him during perilous times and the respect his bravery commanded, even from foes. By projecting personal strength, Jackson created a persona of power. It was this aura perhaps more than any particular gift of insight, judgment or rhetoric that propelled him forward. [260]

Jackson once told Rachel, "When danger rears its head, I could never shrink from it." Jackson did what others would not or could not do, and in a world filled with threats, his willingness to confront danger, to throw that first stone, established him as a hero and a central figure whom people could rely on.[261] Regardless of the Bean story's accuracy, Judge Jackson's reputation was well on its way to becoming larger than life by this time, and his renown as a formidable figure was spreading.

Meanwhile, Jackson devoted himself to maintaining the utmost dignity and integrity of his courtroom. A lifelong indignance to being questioned, Jackson ran his courtroom as a reflection of his personality. When a man allegedly questioned his honesty, Judge Jackson confronted him directly. Although the man denied the accusation, Jackson insisted on having a written statement. He required the man to sign an affidavit affirming that his accusation was false. In similar situations in the past, Jackson might have sought retribution by demanding "satisfaction." However, now a member of Tennessee's highest court, the former combatant seems to have learned the first steps in personal restraint by this time, harnessing his anger when the situation required it.

As a judge, an awareness of the need to avoid "unseemly" duels in order to uphold his respectable reputation (unless absolutely required) was paramount. Taking the law into his own hands to such an extent was not something a Superior Court judge could stoop to, and even Judge

---

[259] Parton, Jackson, I, 228-299. McLaughlin, James A. to Kendall, Jan. 8, 1843, Jackson Papers, LC; Kendall, Jackson, pp. 102-103.

[260] Meacham, Jon, *American Lion: Andrew Jackson in the White House* (2008). Chapter 1.

[261] Ibid.

Jackson adhered to this principle. Increasingly, as time went by, Jackson showed a growing mastery of his mercurial temperament, knowing full well the effectiveness of its release, should the situation require it.

As noted, the Superior Court bench seat was a lifetime appointment, should Jackson choose to stay on. But, while he valued the respect the position brought with it, the conditions proved, ultimately, to be less than ideal. First off, Jackson had underestimated the travel costs associated with the circuit, and he and his fellow judges often lacked reimbursement from the state for their expenses. "I sink money. The salary is too low, and the judiciary barely spares my expense," Jackson noted. Additionally, many of his colleagues in the court were even less knowledgeable about the law than Jackson. He often lamented on how frequently he faced the burden of deciding difficult cases without true legal experts around to assist him. On the plus side, the judgeship did not require a full-time commitment, which allowed Jackson to focus concomitantly on his land speculation/farming/mercantile enterprises, the latter of which he had less of a hands-on role than his partners.

Still, Jackson frequently contemplated retiring from the bench. In this regard, if the opinion of others is any reflection as to his job performance as a judge, Jackson performed well. In mentioning thoughts of retirement to friends and supporters, he was often urged to reconsider. In a letter to Jackson, James Robertson wrote a persuasive letter to his friend, recalling in his travels through Tennessee the many people he encountered who "expressed their desire to see you remain with the court, that your experience and leadership qualify you better than anyone else." Nearly the entire Tennessee House of Representatives and several state senators sent Jackson a statement that expressed their wishes to see him stay on, "Talents like yours are for the public good. We hope at this momentous crisis, when party rages at an extraordinary manner, you will not retire from the services of your country." Robertson may or may not have been aware, however, that party ragings were no more extraordinary than any other time in American history. Nonetheless, the point was the same, Jackson was heavily valued on the Tennessee court.[262]

Jackson acknowledged the public sentiment, explaining, "Retirement to private life has been for some time a very desirable event. But you have

---

[262] Robertson to AJ, 1804. Robertson Papers, LC.

said my further services as a judge will be useful. When my services are called for, they belong to my country, and your voice is obeyed," As capable as Jackson was as a judge, many friends urged him to consider a return to Congress and the pursuit of a more active political career. "I have been importuned," he wrote to Robert Hays, "Nay, I may say pressed by some to allow my name to be put forward for Congress."[263]

Yet, at the same time, encouragements to remain on the bench continued. "On the other hand," Jackson wrote, "I am Pressed by the Barr to remain on the bench, One event has taken place that I believe will determin me to remain where I am, and you may believe me when I Say it is motives of Publick good." Hugh Lawson White, an exceptionally skilled lawyer who was soon to be elected to the bench, urged Jackson that his own election depended on him not leaving the judiciary. Jackson noted that White's election "should be the wish of every citizen—and nothing can be of greater importance to the state. To have this done is my greatest wish—and if my staying in my current position will help achieve that goal, it is a duty I owe to my country." [264]

Jackson did add one caveat to remaining with the court, "If health will permit me." Although generally healthy, Jackson faced many of the common ailments of the time. Infectious disease was a constant threat: rheumatism, typhoid fever, and yellow fever frequently devastated populations in those days of primitive medical knowledge. With a less-dense frontier population, the threat of epidemics were somewhat mitigated. But frontier life posed other health challenges, such as long hours in the saddle that strained the spine. Jackson frequently complained of bouts of rheumatism, and his fall on the Philadelphia ice caused knee pain that especially acted up during cold weather.

Time and again throughout his lifetime, Jackson found a way through ill health, despite many instances in which his ailments could well have been life-threatening. One instance that stands out during this period involved a stable fire in Jonesborough, which roused him from his bed in the famous Chester Inn, causing a cough that lingered for weeks.[265] As was the uncertain nature of colds in that era, there was always the fear that it might lead to something worse. Pneumonia and tuberculosis were

---

[263] AJ to Hays, Jackson, *Correspondence*, 1803.
[264] Remini, 1977, p. 116.
[265] Historic Jonesborough, Tennessee, https://www.jonesboroughtn.org/about/history/

constant threats and could turn deadly in a moment's notice. As a result, life expectancies were much lower than today, partly due to high infant mortality rates. Surviving the first five years of childhood provided some hope for a longer life, but accidents and epidemics still claimed many lives, often in heartbreakingly devastating fashion.

Jackson's knee pain eventually subsided, though it still stiffened in cold weather. His cough, acquired from attempting to rescue the horses during the stable fire, eventually went away, and overall, he managed to remain free of serious illness. Yet, Jackson knew good health was a precious gift, not a guarantee. For the orphan whose parents and brothers had all died young, Jackson was particularly mindful of his health, and probably pretty certain he did not have a long life ahead of him. At age 35, and with a family to support, he needed to be vigilant about his well-being.

When it came to Jackson's family, August 25, 1799 was an important date for Judge Jackson and his wife Rachel. For it was on this day that Andrew Jackson Donelson was born. The son of Rachel Jackson's brother Samuel and Mary Smith Donelson, he would soon move to the Hermitage as a small child, after the death of his father and remarriage of his mother. A ward who became like a son to the Jacksons, Andrew Donelson would go on to serve as an aide-de-camp to Major General Jackson during the Seminole War and accompany Jackson to Washington in 1829 as his personal assistant. With another mouth to feed, Judge Jackson continued to seek ways in which he could increase his personal fortune.

Although Jackson agreed to stay on as Supreme Court justice of Tennessee, the challenges that caused him to consider retirement persisted.[266] During his long circuit rides with the court, travel kept him away from Rachel, and both wondered how long they could manage the strain. With his costly travel schedule, Jackson obsessed over ways to improve his income and escape his ever-present financial woes. By mid-life, with his political aspirations beginning to wane, he began to increasingly shift his focus toward his other endeavors, particularly, his continued interest in commanding the militia. It was this transition that would once again place Jackson and John Sevier onto a collision course, and the next chapter of their seemingly interminable feud.

---

[266] Kendall, p. 103

CHAPTER 21

MILITIA MAN

"Give me a thousand Tennesseans and I'll whip any other thousand men on the globe!"
—Andrew Jackson

While serving as judge in 1802, Jackson clashed, for a third time, with Tennessee governor John Sevier, and as in the first instance, the source of the conflict would be the position of major general of the state militia. Sevier, a veteran and an established politician, was over twenty years older than Jackson, with more military experience in one finger than Jackson had in his entire body. Yet, when both men put their names down for election to the position of Major General of Tennessee, Jackson won, despite the odds against him. Sevier's outrage at this insult would culminate in a new round of conflict between the two ambitious Tennesseans. This time the confrontation would play out on the streets of Knoxville, and would escalate to a duel, the second such affair of Jackson's already contentious life.

The opportunity arose in early 1802 when the commanding general position of the Tennessee militia became vacant, Jackson went after it for a second time, more prepared and determined to capture the position he had longed for. To be named Major-General of the Tennessee militia was a true prize, one that offered the respect and prestige Jackson craved. Importantly as well, it paid far better than his judgeship. According to his interpretation of the Tennessee Constitution, which he helped write, he could hold both roles without violating the separation of powers.

Could this be Jackson's way out of his longstanding money troubles? He certainly thought so. No one challenged Jackson about the possible issues of legality, or conflict of interests, of him holding both roles for the state. But there would be one familiar Tennessean standing in his way, and once again, that man was John Sevier.[267]

After serving three consecutive two-year terms, by 1801, Sevier was no longer in the Governor's House. The state constitution stipulated that no governor could serve more than three consecutive terms without sitting out at least one term. Thus, Sevier would have to wait until 1803 to recapture the top executive position. Yet, like Jackson, he eyed the vacant militia command that the death of General Conway had created. Desiring a return to the prestigious command he once held, Sevier coveted the post and was a frontrunner for the highly sought-after position. Jackson was Sevier's main contender, pitting the two hot-blooded frontiersmen head-to-head, in direct competition. The tentative truce between them, bitterly agreed to in 1796, dissolved quickly. Their rivalry not only intensified as they both campaigned for the position but would now increase to unprecedented heights.

In the militia election of February 5, 1802, Jackson tied with Sevier for the position of Major General, both receiving 17 votes. While Jackson firmly held support from his own district, Sevier secured the votes of the eastern regions, his home base. When election day arrived, the votes were counted, and both Jackson and Sevier received an equal number. The tie prompted Sevier to immediately propose a second ballot, which Jackson rejected, insisting the decision should go to the governor.

According to the state constitution, which he helped write, Jackson was correct. In such situations, the governor of the state, who served as the commander-in-chief of the militia, had the deciding vote. Governor Archibald Roane had replaced Sevier as governor just a year before, and the two men were not friends, as Roane, like Jackson, was a member of the Blount faction. To make matters worse for Sevier, Governor Roane, as it happened, was Jackson's close friend since the two young lawyers received their attorney license on the same day, in the same Washington County, North Carolina courtroom. Roane also stood to

---

[267] Remini, 1977. p. 117.

gain politically by voting against Sevier, and especially by exposing the former Governor's wrongdoing.

According to some accounts, it was during this period that Jackson chose to finally expose Sevier from his involvement in the 1797 land fraud evidence that Jackson had been sitting on, biding his time for the right moment. Jackson decided it was time to out Sevier for his role in the scheme, and he made his long-held secret of Sevier's involvement public knowledge. He had found that long awaited moment, guaranteeing his victory over Sevier. Without hesitation, Roane cast his vote for Jackson, resulting in Jackson's appointment as Major General, which became official on April 1, 1802, much to the frustration of John Sevier.[268]

Jackson's political maneuvering and relationships with younger militia officers contributed to this outcome. He had spent the previous years determined to do the leg work necessary to win the job, having learned from his loss to Conway five years earlier. Unlike 1796, Jackson had prepared his way, shoring up support among the militia officers of the Cumberland and the surrounding regions, knowing that, as before, it would be they who would choose their new commander.

Command of the Tennessee militia now belonged to Andrew Jackson, and the victory over Sevier had to feel good. Now regarded as the first warrior of Tennessee, Jackson was largely free to dictate the course for the defense of Tennessee, and the western frontier. The rank of major-general of the Tennessee militia in 1802 meant more than mere titles, uniforms, and impressive displays during general muster days. The prestigious rank meant that whoever held it was the chief, unquestionably in charge of defending the state and every mother, wife and child therein. Defending the homeland from invasion, whether it be from hostile tribes, or the ongoing threats of war with either France or England, was to a fighter like Jackson, the ultimate opportunity.

The advantages of Jackson's new position caused grudging resentment from Sevier, who had good reason to feel he should have been returned to the command, based on his impeccable record of battlefield experience. He was the legendary "Nolichucky Jack," after all, the most successful Indian fighter the southwestern region had ever seen. What had Jackson done to merit command of the heralded Tennessee militia? Sevier's

---

[268] Driver, Carl S., *John Sevier, Pioneer of the Old Southwest*, Chapel Hill, 1932, p. 146.

frustration grew when he launched a campaign, a year later, to reclaim the governor's house. With Sevier facing off against the incumbent Governor Roane, Jackson, not surprisingly, endorsed his friend over his rival, publicly throwing his support in favor of Roane.

As tensions rose, Sevier announced his candidacy for governor in 1803. In retaliation to Jackson's allegations of fraud, which had been published in the *Knoxville Gazette*, Sevier's supporters aimed to diminish Jackson's command by creating two militia districts. Unfortunately for the Sevier faction, who sought to destroy Jackson's reputation, the increasingly popular Jackson showed a respectable boldness facing a mob plotting against him, ultimately furthering a solid reputation as a firm and unbreakable leader. [269]

East Tennessee was filled with Sevier's supporters, who, during the campaign, developed a strong opposition to Roane for his role in the militia vote of 1802, and his membership in the Blount faction. When Sevier leveled corruption charges against Roane, Jackson came to his friend's aid to, "exonerate Mr. Roane from the implications circulated against him." Jackson revived accusations of fraud against Sevier, and the bitterness escalated.

Jackson chose the *Tennessee Gazette* as his organ for exposing Sevier. He claimed that Sevier had plotted to destroy the original land ownership records and replaced genuine entries with forged ones. He further alleged that Sevier had engaged in bribery to ensure the replacement remained undisclosed. Jackson presented letters and affidavits that supported his accusations, including a dubious offer from Sevier involving three parcels of land. With Jackson's accusations against Sevier, particularly the notion of the governor using his office for personal gain, Sevier responded by publicly accusing Jackson of defamation of character[270].

Despite Jackson's efforts, Tennessee voters simply could not believe that their hero could be involved in such a dishonest scheme, and Sevier won the election. Tensions in the long-standing Jackson-Sevier feud, Despite Jackson's efforts, Sevier returned once again to the Governor's House, reflecting eastern Tennesseans undying loyalty to their hero. The scandal impacted Jackson's reputation more significantly, leading to

---

[269] Copy in AHM, Jan., 1889, IV.
[270] Parton, *Jackson*, I, p. 164.

a perception of him as politically aggressive, leading to both praise and enmity, depending largely on the region.

The rivalry between Jackson and Sevier marked the beginning of a long-standing political division in Tennessee, with Jackson emerging as a leader of the western faction, while Sevier maintained control in the east. Only on the frontier would two of the most powerful politicians of a state end up fighting each other on the street in broad daylight. And that is precisely what happened one afternoon on the steps of the Knoxville Courthouse.

In the early 1800s, despite being the state capital, Knoxville was very much a small town, and it was inevitable that the two rival combatants would run into each other sooner or later. Jackson's court work regularly brought him to the capital, where Sevier resided. Inevitably, the expected confrontation presented itself. On Oct. 2nd, 1803, when the two men happened to meet on the steps of the Old Knox County Courthouse, the day had arrived for their face to face.

Taking a break from his caseload, Jackson emerged from the Knoxville courthouse. Stepping out onto the steps, Jackson spotted Sevier and a crowd of people standing directly out front, in the town square, as though waiting ominously for Jackson to appear. As Sevier spoke to the large crowd, he spotted Jackson coming out of the courtroom and quickly began to attack him verbally. Jackson responded in kind, and as onlookers gathered around, the voices of the two prominent men rose as their emotions engaged, trading heated words back and forth in verbal confrontation. Hurling insults and accusations, Governor Sevier soon went so far as to brandish his sword, challenging Jackson, daring him to draw arms.

According to witnesses, since Jackson was armed with only a cane against Sevier's sword, the younger man declined. Sevier then began to taunt Jackson further, alluding to his inexperience on the battlefield before becoming major general. This seemed to stump Jackson into a rare moment of hesitation, before stammering a defense of his services to the state. To this, Sevier infamously responded, "Services? Why, I know of no great service you have rendered the country except taking a trip to Natchez with another man's wife!"[271]

---

[271] Remini, 1977. p. 121.

Like Sevier had dropped a bomb, a hush enveloped the courthouse square. Sevier's comment had silenced the stunned crowd. It was as clear as the hot Tennessee sun above them that Sevier had crossed a line. This was sacred ground to Andrew Jackson, and most everyone knew it. Although most knew of the circumstances surrounding Jackson and Rachel's early days, out of respect for Mrs. Jackson, if not for Jackson himself, most had kept the common knowledge quiet. After a moment of stunned silence came the outraged Jackson's celebrated reply: "Great God!" Jackson roared, "Do you mention her sacred name?!?"[272]

Jackson, enraged by the insult to his wife, lunged at Sevier. The crowd intervened, separating the two men. Words and emotions rapidly accelerated from there, and no doubt egged on by the crowd, both men threatened to kill the other. Jackson may have fought it out right then and there if he had been armed. Yet, according to the recollection of Isaac Avery, an eyewitness to the scene, "several shots were fired in the crowded street." (Although it is not clear who shot them.) One man was grazed by a bullet and many onlookers screamed in terror. Luckily, no one was seriously injured. Avery would go on to add that Jackson's exclamation "Great God!" became a popular phrase among the young men of Knoxville for some time. [273]

By the following day, Jackson's emotions had cooled enough for him to pen a letter to Sevier, dated October 2, 1803. Jackson wrote Sevier, accusing him of ungentlemanly conduct and demanding satisfaction for the perceived slights. He requested a duel, stating that both he and his friend would be armed with pistols. Even with a day's passing, the bitter resentment is still very much present in Jackson's words:

"The ungentlemanly Expressions, and gasgonading conduct of yours relative to me on yesterday was in true character of yourself, and unmask you to the world, and plainly shews that they were the ebulations of a base mind goaded with stubborn prooffs of fraud, and flowing from a source devoid of every refined sentiment, or delicate sensation. But sir the Voice of the people has made you a Governor. This alone makes you worthy of my notice or the notice of any Gentleman. To the office I bear respect, to the Voice of the people who placed it on you I pay respect, and

---

[272] Ibid, 121.
[273] Ibid, 121.

as such I only deign to notice you, and call upon you for that satisfaction and explanation that your ungentlemanly conduct & expressions require, for this purpose I request an interview, and my friend who will hand you this will point out the time and place, when and where I shall Expect to see you with your friend and no other person. My friend and myself will be armed with pistols. You cannot mistake me or my meaning." [274]

Sevier responded by mocking Jackson's challenge (while maintaining proper spelling,) asserting that Jackson's actions had revealed his true character. He accepted Jackson's challenge but stipulated that the duel take place outside Tennessee. Though Sevier did not wish to duel the younger man (twenty-two years his junior) whom he considered a mere greenhorn, a "Johnny Come Lately" not worthy of his time. As governor of the state, and a living legend on the frontier, Sevier did not feel he had anything to prove to anyone. Not to mention as the chief enforcer of Tennessee law, which banned dueling, how would it look to his voters? Yet, knowing the climate in which he lived, could he afford to ignore such a direct affront, even with the lofty status he had earned in the Indian Wars? Despite his reluctance, it did not take long for Sevier to respond, and he did so by mimicking many of Jackson's words in his letter:

"Your Ungentlemanly and Gasgonading conduct of yesterday, and indeed at all other times heretofore, have unmasked yourself to me and to the World. The Voice of the Assembly has made you a Judge, and this alone has made you Worthy of My notice or Any other Gentleman, to the office I have respect and this Alone makes you worthy of my notice....I shall wait on you with pleasure at any time and place not within the state of Tennessee, attended by my friend, with pistols, presuming you know nothing about the use of any other arms. Georgia, Virginia, and North Carolina are all within our vicinity.... you cannot mistake me and my meaning."[275]

Letters with details and proposals went back and forth, each man either ignorantly or willfully misunderstanding the suggestions of the other. As if play-acting in a comedy, while the two antagonists declared their mutual willingness to square off, they could not agree on a time or

---

[274] AJ to Sevier, Oct. 2, 1803, Jackson, *Correspondence*, I, 71.
[275] Sevier to AJ, Oct.3, 1803, Miscellaneous Papers, *THC*.

a place for the duel. Sevier eventually concluded the correspondence by agreeing to meet Jackson at any time or location he suggested, as long as it was outside the state of Tennessee (in a nod to the laws of the state.) This, Jackson viewed as cowardly avoidance and accused Sevier of having "squeamish fears." Yet, Sevier still dragged his feet. He instructed his friend to communicate to Jackson that he could meet for the "interview" in five days, but no sooner. Jackson was furious. He decided to make good on his threat to go public with his accusations.

He announced his feelings in the *Gazette* as to the cowardice of the governor, "To all whom Shall See these presents Greeting—Know yea that I Andrew Jackson, do pronounce, Publish, and declare to the world, that his Excellency John Sevier Esqr. Governor, Captain General and commander in chief, of the land and Naval forces of the State of Tennessee—is a base coward and poltroon. He will basely insult, but has not the courage to repair the wound."[276]

To this, Sevier felt compelled to answer once again. "I am again perplexed with your scurelous and poltroon language. I have constantly informed you that I would cheerfully wait on you in any other quarter and that you had nothing to do but name the place, and you should be accommodated. I am now constrained to tell you that your conduct during the whole of your pretended bravery shows you to be a pitiful poltroon and coward….If you wish the interview, accept the proposal I have made you, and let us prepare for the campaign."

Jackson insisted originally that since the insult in which Sevier had taken "the name of a lady into your polluted lips," occurred in Knoxville, then that was where the duel should be held. Yet, to ensure satisfaction, he finally relented on this point, agreeing that they should cross to the "nearest part of the Indian boundary line," Indigenous lands held no restrictions against dueling, and there they could legally settle their differences. Jackson wrote, "I shall expect an answer in the space of one hour." Sevier accepted this proposal, "I am happy to find you so accommodating. My friend will agree upon the time and place of rendezvous."

Eventually, and after much debate, the two finally managed to settle on the time and place for their much-anticipated duel, Southwest Point,

---

[276] Parton, Jackson, I, pp.234-235.

Virginia, not far from the Cumberland Gap, about a one-day journey from Knoxville. Jackson quickly headed for the location, but Sevier, still hesitant to stoop to dueling the younger upstart, remained in Knoxville for two more days. Jackson waited impatiently at Southwest Point, his fury mounting, until finally, he had enough. Starting to turn back for Knoxville, Jackson was convinced that Sevier really was the exact brand of coward and poltroon he had accused him of being.

Riding with his second along the Kingston Road about forty miles west of Knoxville (near the town of Kingston, Tennessee) Jackson soon spotted Sevier approaching, with his son, James, riding alongside. It was customary in a duel for each combatant to have, present with him, an assistant, properly called a "second." It was the second's duty to ensure that his man was not ambushed by the other party, that the rules of the duel were agreed upon and followed, that pistols or cutlasses were available, and sometimes the second simply stood by and held the horse.

Jackson dismounted, brandishing his pistols. Walking aggressively towards Sevier, who upon seeing Jackson approach, dismounted as well, though leaving his pistols strapped to the saddle. Sevier held only his sword in his hand, according to his account. Jackson began a round of renewed name-calling at Sevier, and then demanded that they settle their dispute immediately, once and for all. Sevier then called back to Jackson that he would not fire, and that he did not wish to be assassinated. Jackson assured the governor that this would be no assassination.[277]

Jackson then sent his second, Dr. Thomas Van Dyke, to deliver a letter detailing Sevier's alleged offenses, which Sevier refused to accept. This sent Jackson into a tirade, prompting Van Dyke to suggest that both men ready their pistols and "meet in a proper manner on the field of honor." Jackson agreed to do just that, but Sevier again refused. After another round of profane epithets between the two men, Van Dyke urged the men to holster their pistols and remount their horses. Both men accepted this suggestion and got back on horseback, but the still enraged Jackson declared that there had been "too much low abuse made use of," and that he would "correct him." Van Dyke continued his recollections, "General Jackson then brandished his sword, cane and pistol and rode up to General Sevier. General Sevier then drew his sword in response,

---

[277] Kendall, *Jackson*, p. 107.

dismounted and let the horse loose. At that point, according to Van Dyke, "General Jackson pursued him around us (he and two passersby who had stopped to observe the waggish scene) as we sat upon our horses, several times. Young Mr. (James) Sevier drew his pistol on General Jackson. On which I immediately drew mine, and observed that I should protect Mr. Jackson."[278]

One of the two passersby told his account of the tale differently "Judge Jackson swore that he would cane him, and as Jackson advanced toward him, the governor drew his sword, which frightened his horse, which ran away with the governor's pistols. Judge Jackson immediately drew his pistol, and advanced again, at which the governor went behind a tree and damned Jackson. "Did he want to fire on a naked man?" On which his son drew his pistol and advanced toward his father. Dr. Van Dyke immediately drew his pistol, and advanced toward the governor's son."[279]

In James Parton's version of the comedic affair, the encounter played out as follows, "Jackson rode slowly toward the governor's party until he was within a hundred yards of them. Then, leveling his cane, as knights of old were wont to level their lances, he struck spurs into his horse, and galloped furiously at the governor. Sevier, astounded at this tremendous apparition, and intending, if he fought at all, to fight fairly (and on terra firma), dismounted; but, in so doing, stepped upon the scabbard of his sword, and fell prostrate under his horse.

Jackson, seeing his enemy thus vanish from his sight, reined in his own fiery steed, and gave time for the governor's friends to get between them and prevent a conflict. Through the efforts of some gentlemen in Sevier's party who were friends of both the belligerents, the affair was patched up on the spot, and the whole party rode toward Knoxville together in relative amity. Nor was there any renewal of the combat." [280]

In yet another version of the story, written much later on, the details are even more varied: "Somewhere on the Kingston Road, Jackson and Dr. Van Dyke encountered General Sevier and his son James. The Seviers had brought pistols, but tempers flared and the horses spooked and ran

---

[278] Brands, HW, 2005, Ch. 7
[279] Many of the details of the fight are taken from the affidavit of Andrew Greer, Oct. 23, 1803 in *AHM*, V. 208,
[280] Parton, *Jackson*, p. 235.

off when Jackson began yelling and swinging his sword around. Without pistols, Sevier hid behind a tree. James Sevier aimed his pistol at Jackson, which forced Dr. Van Dyke to take aim at James and General Sevier.[281]

The horses watched from the distant forest, probably wondering which one of the fools was going to get shot first. For several minutes, the situation was critical as threats, insults, and challenges were hurled across the Kingston Road. Somehow, due to the circumstances, the men finally agreed to part and resume the conflict at another time. But time passed and no such action was taken. Their anger and hatred would always remain, but the duel never came about again."[282]

In yet another account of the slapstick confrontation, the details are slightly different once again and suggests that history can often be told in innumerable ways depending on who's doing the telling. In this version, during the chaos of Jackson's pursuit of Sever, the governor fell from his horse while fumbling for his sword, which broke during the fall. "Satisfied, Jackson considered the matter closed, and both men and their followers then rode back into town, no longer at odds, but certainly not friendly with each other."[283]

It is interesting to compare the various historical accounts that have survived the centuries since this infamous encounter, and how differently people can view the "truth" of any given situation. Whichever account is more accurate is difficult to say, but most end in a similar fashion, with the two adversaries retrieving their horses after the ruckus, and riding off, each cursing the other, but apparently feeling that there was no more need for a renewal of hostilities.

Back in Knoxville, each side relayed their versions of the confrontation to their respective supporters, who then magnified their understanding of the incident to the local papers for months afterward, the absurd truth of what "really happened." The debates evolved as to who actually was the "poltroon," in the affair, which was then discussed and fought over among the Tennessee populace for the months and years to come.

James Parton adds, "The anger of the antagonists and their friends found vent in newspaper statements, and after a brief paper war, exhausted itself. Ultimately, with their tempers cooled, they each went

---

[281] Ibid, p. 234-235
[282] Guy, Joe. "Duel on the Kingston Road." *Hidden History*. McMinn Co., TN.
[283] Ibid.

their separate ways, considering the matter resolved. Nonetheless, the animosity between Sevier and Jackson remained until Sevier's death in 1815." Sevier's final conclusion about Judge Jackson was that he was "One of the most abandoned rascals in principle my eyes ever beheld." [284]

However it went down, the awkward and farcical scene between these two otherwise respected leaders seemed to douse any remaining urge to act on their disdain for each other. Despite his efforts, Jackson was unable to keep Sevier out of the Governor's mansion, nor was he able to prove his guilt in the fraud charges. Jackson's later attempts to have the governor impeached failed as well.

The duel with John Sevier had deleterious effects on Jackson's image in the eyes of Tennesseans, and it would take the judge years to rebuild his standing. In retrospect, one could argue, Jackson came out as the villain in his recurring encounters with John Sevier. His popularity and esteem took a hit, especially in eastern Tennessee, and with those close to Governor Sevier, but even for a time among some of his own Cumberland neighbors. Sevier, on the other hand, went on to win another three consecutive terms as head of the state, and remained a powerful force in Tennessee politics until his death.

Andrew Jackson, through his antics, tarnished his image among some of the people who had once supported him, and while his list of friends would continue to grow, so would his list of enemies. Jackson faced challenges from rival factions, including the Blount faction, which limited his political ascent during Sevier's continued governorship. Ultimately, Jackson's election as major general and the onset of the War of 1812 shaped his military career, and while he possessed ambition and talent, his rise was also influenced by some degree of luck and fortunate circumstances.

The conflict with Sevier strained Jackson's relationships, particularly with Judge John McNairy, who was at the time more aligned with Sevier than Jackson, thus marking another casualty of this period. Jackson and his friend (and original political benefactor) McNairy had become estranged since the Knoxville Convention, when rumors (later believed to be false) had reached McNairy that Jackson opposed his nomination as a delegate to the convention.[285] The two former North Carolinians had

---

[284] Sevier, John, *AHM*, 1899.
[285] AJ to McNairy, May 9, 1797, McNairy to AJ, May 12, 1797 and AJ to McNairy, May 9, 1797, in Jackson, *Correspondence*, I, 34-37.

also ended up on different sides of the political battlelines on more than one occasion, with one example being McNairy's role in the removal of James Robertson from the Chickasaw Indian Agency, which generated Jackson's outrage at McNairy, creating a permanent rift.

John McNairy would not be the last friend to reconsider his impressions of Andrew Jackson, nor would he be the last man Jackson would rub the wrong way. Yet, Jackson was not a man who stayed up at night concerned over the feelings of those who went against him. Besides, he had other important matters on his mind. With the death of William Blount in 1801, and despite his "ungentlemanly conduct" at times, Jackson still managed to accede to the position of leading man in western Tennessee, at least in the estimation of most Nashville political circles. An alliance with the influential Senator John Tipton had helped him overcome, for the most part, the fallout from the foolishness that was the Sevier tiff. Tipton himself was another of Sevier's earliest rivals, which behooved Jackson in solidifying a bond between himself and Tipton.[286]

Willie Blount is another example of those who helped Jackson avoid a loss of face entirely from the Sevier rivalry debacle. William Blount's half-brother Willie managed to build a moderately strong political faction himself by 1809, thereby recreating some of the Blount prestige William had created. This enabled Willie (pronounced Wiley) to serve two terms as governor of the state. This kept Jackson in good standing politically. Nonetheless, though Jackson was certainly not without talents and ability, his behavior during the Sevier feud hurt his political fortunes in the period before the War of 1812 and could have had far worse consequences for his career, were it not for a little bit of luck, and the help of loyal friends.[287]

The two most significant events in Jackson's military career—his election as major general of the militia and the beginning of the War of 1812—occurred during a period when Sevier was out of office, placing the state's administration in the hands of Jackson's political allies, allowing him to preserve his image as a credible political leader, in Tennessee, to no small degree.

---

[286] Driver, *Sevier*, p. 98.
[287] AJ to Willie Blount, Jackson Papers, 1802.

CHAPTER

22

A MAN ON HIS OWN

"Live within your means, never be in debt, and by husbanding your money you can always lay it out well. But when you get in debt you become a slave. Therefore I say to you never involve yourself in debt, and become no man's surety."
—Andrew Jackson

The fact that Andrew Jackson had a quick temper was no secret. The planter, former Congressman, Senator, Supreme Court justice of Tennessee, and Major General of the Tennessee militia was renowned for his capacity to "go off the handle." That his quick temper thrived on conflict was also becoming common knowledge. Whether or not Jackson actively sought out confrontation is uncertain, but he seemed entirely in his element when it found him. One could argue as well that he slumped when conflict was absent.

In the fall of 1803, Andrew Jackson embarked on a journey from Nashville to Jonesborough. His purpose was to preside over a court session. During his travels, Jackson encountered a friend on the road. This friend delivered a crucial warning: a group of individuals planned to confront Jackson upon his arrival in Jonesborough. Despite his weakened state and the looming threat, Jackson pressed onward. He urged his horse forward, determined to reach Jonesborough.[288]

At the time, Jackson was battling an intermittent fever. This illness had significantly weakened him, making it challenging for him to endure

---
[288] Meacham, *American Lion*, Ch. 1

the rigors of travel, particularly the strain of remaining in the saddle for extended periods. But ever the warrior, Jackson continued on, refusing to miss his deadline. Upon arriving in Jonesborough, Jackson, burning with fever, was utterly exhausted. He was so fatigued that he required assistance to dismount his horse. The fever continued to rage within him. He immediately sought rest and lay down on a bed in a tavern.

Moments later, a friend entered and informed him that Colonel Harrison and a "regiment of men" were gathered outside the tavern, intending to tar and feather him. His friend suggested he lock the door for safety. Instead, Jackson abruptly got up, flung open the door, and declared, with a commanding presence that had won him many a verbal battle over the years, "Give my compliments to Colonel Harrison, and tell him my door is open to receive him and his regiment whenever they choose to come and see me! I hope the Colonel's chivalry will inspire him to lead his men, rather than follow them!" [289]

Speechless and startled by Jackson's unexpected aggression, the regiment, either out of shame for confronting an ill man or fear of facing a determined one, reconsidered their intentions and gradually dispersed. Judge Jackson recovered from his illness, proceeded with his court schedule as planned, and heard no further threats while in Jonesborough. [290]

Even stricken with fever, Jackson itched for confrontation. To scratch that itch, and to satisfy that long held urge for battlefield glory, all that the Major General lacked was a campaign in which to lead his Tennessee militiamen. After the fallout from his conflict with Governor Sevier, Judge Jackson, who was never satisfied with his position on the Superior Court, which he believed he was ill-suited for, grew increasingly discontented. He yearned to trade his judicial robes for a position that required less confinement and offered more opportunities for action.

Yet, during the early years of Jackson's military career, there were few opportunities to prove his mettle on the battlefield. A potential threat, however, began to slowly materialize after all, and seemed likely to result in action for Jackson and his troops at long last. It arose in 1803, shortly after President Jefferson's heralded purchase of Louisiana. The dangers

---

[289] Kendall, *Jackson*, p. 105-106.
[290] Parton, *Jackson*, Ch. 3

of Napoleon's ambitions, combined with the pressure from westerners to secure control of New Orleans, pushed the federal government's concern over intrigues, conspiracies and treasonous acts to unprecedented heights.

In this climate of uncertainty over Louisiana's transfer, there were many alarming questions being asked. First off was the question of the Spanish authorities in Louisiana. Would they submit to either French or American control of the territory, and walk away peacefully? Would disgruntled Americans plot to wrest control of the vast lands for their own gain? Could a combination of the two come to pass?

"There is one single spot," Jefferson wrote to Robert Livingston, American envoy to France, "the possessor of which is our natural and habitual enemy. It is New Orleans, through which three-eighths of our territory must pass to market. The day that France takes possession of New Orleans, from that moment we must marry ourselves to the British fleet and nation." [291]

Jefferson's words impart the danger Americans believed Napoleon Bonaparte and the erratic French nation posed. Coming from the francophile Jefferson, these words were even more telling and truly represent the concern in which these fears were based. They were spoken when the deal to acquire Louisiana was not yet finalized. Livingston and James Monroe were in France at that very time, with instructions from the President to push the purchase through.

Fortunately for the United States, the mercurial Napoleon needed the money, as his ever-widening European war was bankrupting the French Republic, and the ongoing Haitian Revolution was dousing Bonaparte's dream of a renewed French empire in the Americas. Ridding himself of Louisiana had become a necessity, although by selling it to the United States, Napoleon broke an earlier promise to the Spanish never to transfer ownership of the city to anyone else with the exception of Spain. Not only would he sell New Orleans to the Americans, but the entire Louisiana Territory.

Jefferson, through Livingston and Monroe, could not pass up the $15 million offer the French proposed, and gave them the green light. Jefferson knew, as the leader of the Republican view of strictly interpreting

---

[291] Jefferson to Livingston, April 18, 1802, P.L. Ford, ed; Writings of Thomas Jefferson, 1935. Washington, VIII, 134-137.

the Constitution, that this was sure to set off a firestorm of Federalist accusations of hypocrisy. But was this an unconstitutional act by the president? Jefferson was not sure, and the criticism could well derive from many within his own party for that matter. In truth, Jefferson himself held grave doubts as to the constitutionality of the purchase. Yet, his vision of an agrarian, utopian America, with its growing population, and demand for farmland left him no choice. At least, so he felt.

To his opposition, the purchase was an unconstitutional expansion of power, motivated by a desire to strengthen the southern states and weaken their own political influence. Hamilton, though no longer in office at the time, argued that the vast new territory would be difficult to govern effectively; that it would spread the population too thin across the vast area, incapacitating the federal government. Some even threatened secession over the perceived imbalance it might create within the Union.

Federalist leader Rufus King, in a letter to fellow Jefferson detractor Thomas Pickering reflects these frustrations, "According to the Constitution, Congress may admit new states. But can the President sign treaties forcing Congress to do so? According to the Louisiana Treaty, the territory must be formed into states and admitted into the Union. Will Congress be allowed to set any rules for their admission? Since slavery is legal and exists in Louisiana, and the treaty states that we must protect the property of the inhabitants, won't we be forced to admit the new states as slave states? Doing so will worsen the problem of unequal representation from slave and free states." [292] The prospect of more western land inhabited by more western farmers certainly did not appeal to the Federalists.

But Jefferson viewed the alternative as even more troubling: a more formidable, and unpredictable foreign power controlling New Orleans, the instigation of rebellion or treason it might well spark among the restless western population, already frustrated with the government's failure to ensure free trade on the Mississippi River and in the Crescent City. Regardless of constitutional concerns, he believed that the safety of the Union required him to act, and thus, the deal was finalized on

---

[292] Rufus King. "Letters Protesting the Louisiana Purchase", Letter, March 04, 1804. From Teaching American History. (accessed June 28, 2025).

April 30th, 1803. Although France would not officially transfer its claim to the territory until the following March.

Jefferson got more than he bargained for. The purchase of the entire Louisiana Territory doubled the size of the United States. Although a bargain-rate purchase, the deal cost the country $15 million for 828,000 square miles of land west of the Mississippi River. As some Federalists in New England declaimed critically, however cheap the deal was, it was still "more money we don't have, for more land we don't need." The purchase had a number of impacts, regardless, including strengthening the country's material and strategic position, stimulating westward expansion, and confirming the federal Constitution's doctrine of implied powers. The greatest land deal in the nations' history took the young United States across the Mississippi River and propelled its westward expansion.

But there was one problem, the presence of the Spanish still remained. Though the treachery of Napoleon had squeezed them out of their rights to Louisiana, they were even more determined to remain entrenched in the Floridas, Texas, and the American Southwest. Even as the United States' population growth accelerated, (doubling in just twenty years since the end of the Revolutionary War) and the Spanish population in North America remained infinitesimal in comparison, the Spanish showed no signs of relinquishing their territories. To many leaders of western cities, it was the presence of the Spanish and their machinations that stirred up indigenous tribes to resist American expansion. Many also held the belief that it was ultimately Spanish officials who were at the heart of conspiracies among American westerners to engage in treasonous intrigues. And to westerners in general, such allegiance to Spain was not necessarily an uninviting prospect, if it meant better conditions on the Mississippi and in the Gulf of Mexico.

Although Napoleon and France had forced Spain to cede Louisiana, the French never physically occupied the territory themselves, but instead had the Spanish continue to administer the lands in the name of France. This meant that the Spanish officials who had long held posts in New Orleans, Natchez and the like could potentially either refuse to accept the treaty or decline to hand over their authority when the time came. This concern caused many, including Jefferson, anxiety. To prevent such a scenario, the president sent the order to western Tennessee for Jackson's command to be prepared to march. If it became necessary to use force to remove the Spanish presence from Louisiana, it would be General Jackson's campaign to lead.

Jackson, excited for this potential opportunity, did not hesitate to alert his troops, and on August 7th, 1803, he sent out his "General Order to the Militia as to Spanish Threats." The tone of his orders display how seriously Jackson took the Spanish menace. "The late conduct of the Spanish government, added to the Hostile appearance and menacing attitude of their Armed forces already incamped within the limits of our government, make it necessary that the Militia under my command should be in complete order and in a moment's warning ready to march."

Jackson's order went on to list the various accusations against the Spanish government in Louisiana. This included the unlawful arrest and extradition of five Americans to Spain for trial, and of forcefully removing the American flag from flying in New Orleans. Jackson expressed his outrage at the Spanish ordering of Americans off the Red River, despite these surveyors' federal mandate to explore the region. He concluded the list of grievances by pointing out Spain's unjustifiable position east of the Sabine River, well within the boundaries of New Orleans, now the property of the United States. Condemned these actions as insulting and degrading to the nation's character and constitutional rights, the Major General emphasized to his men that the perceived offenses provoke natural resentment and "demand prompt satisfaction." While his words almost come across as sound as though Jackson is challenging Spain to a duel, the language and tone were clearly intended to strike at the heart of longstanding western dissatisfaction with Spanish offenses.[293]

The long-awaited opportunity for action in the field might finally be at hand, and Jackson expected his troops to be ready should the order come. On October 31st, the secretary of war, Henry Dearborn, ordered him to procure enough boats to convey 1,500 men from Tennessee by December 20th, at the latest. Although General Jackson had little experience as a commander, his tone reflects the confidence he possessed in himself when it came to the prospect of leading troops into battle, and his ability to inspire that confidence in his men was already beginning to show.

---

[293] Jackson, *Correspondence*, I, 68.

Fortunately (or possibly unfortunately from Andrew Jackson's perspective,) as it turns out, the Spanish respected the treaty signed by Napoleon and chose not to test the Americans. Jackson and the militia, therefore, were forced to stand down, and would not be needed to hasten the Spanish departure. The news came as a long-awaited sigh of relief for westerners, who would finally be unobstructed in their use of the Mississippi, and of their right of deposit in New Orleans. The boost this would give the economy tremendously lifted the spirits of Tennesseans, although Jackson regretted missing a chance for some retribution against "The Hated Dons," as he referred to the Spanish.

Nevertheless, the Major General expressed the celebratory sentiments of his state in a letter of thanks to Jefferson, "All the Western Hemisphere rejoices at the Joyfull news of the cession of Louisiana, an event which places the peace, happiness and liberty of our country on a lasting basis, an event which generations yet unborn with each revolving year will hail the day, and with it the causes which gave it birth."[294] Federal troops would be sent down the Mississippi shortly thereafter, and soon the American flag was hoisted proudly over the Crescent City of New Orleans.

With the Spanish threat past, Jackson and the militia resumed their inactivity. The judge returned to judicial proceedings, and to his business interests. Yet, like many southerners, he continued to ponder the possibilities Louisiana offered. The new territory would need law and order, and a strong hand to guide the lands firmly into the American system of government. Jackson felt he was just the man for the job. Increasingly, therefore, he sought a means to ensure that he receive the appointment as governor of the Louisiana Territory. But how to go about it?

Previous political appointments had often come at the hands of William Blount. But Blount was no more, having died of a fever in 1800, and Willie had yet to firmly revive the Blount political machine. Yet, Jackson had learned quite a bit from his political mentor, the elder Blount, especially a reliance on the support of one's network of loyal and influential contacts. Thus, Jackson's first move was to engender the support of the Tennessee delegation in Washington.

---

[294] AJ to Jefferson, 1804, Jackson Papers, LC.

Although facing some resistance initially, largely a byproduct of the Sevier feud, they eventually relented, some enthusiastically, and Jackson received the support he sought. The representatives sanctioned Jackson's appointment to Jefferson in a petition to the President, knowing the Major General's commitment to the interests of Tennessee, the firm hand he would surely provide to prevent indigenous attack, and to prevent any further Spanish offenses.

Jackson did not stop there. He turned next to his compatriots within the ranks of the Republican party, the very same men who had been indispensable in Jefferson's rise to the Presidency. Many of these men Jackson had built coalitions with during his days in Congress, particularly Matthew Lyon, one of the victims of Adams' Alien and Sedition Acts of 1798. Lyon had become renowned in Republican circles and hailed as a martyr after his arrest for "violating" the controversial Federalist acts. Imprisoned by the Adams administration for sedition, the Irish-born Connecticut Congressman Lyon was therefore heroic to most Republicans, including Jefferson.

Jackson arranged for a personal appeal from him to the President, which Lyon was happy to provide. With all this working in his favor, Jackson headed to Washington prepared to meet with the President, hoping Jefferson might wish for a face to face. But, upon arriving in the capital city, and receiving no invitation from Jefferson, Jackson could not suffer the humiliation of prostrating himself before the President. Writing to John Coffee, Jackson feared such a solicitation of the President "might be construed into the conduct of a courteor." [295]

Jefferson ultimately passed on appointing Jackson, and instead gave the nod to W.C.C. Claiborne, who had accompanied General Wilkinson and the federal troops to New Orleans already. Although Claiborne was, to Jefferson, the obvious choice for the role, Jackson felt humiliated, and seemed to take the slight personally. Claiborne was younger than Jackson and had been his replacement in the House of Representatives when Jackson filled the Senate seat, therefore making Claiborne his subordinate in Tennessee, at least in Jackson's eyes. Jefferson probably never realistically considered appointing Jackson for a moment, knowing what he knew of his horrendous performance in the Senate. But to

---

[295] Parton, *Jackson*, I, p. 29.

Jackson, it was galling to be rejected, and his loyalty and support of Jefferson vanished in an instant. [296]

Instead, Jackson gravitated toward the more conservative wing of the Republican party, the faction that favored states' rights more heavily than moderates. This began a trend in which Jackson became increasingly anti-Jefferson as time went on, favoring instead stout conservatives such as Nathaniel Macon of North Carolina, with whom he would build a close connection. Despite the failed campaign for the Louisiana appointment, Jackson's deft maneuverings displayed the degree to which his political skills had evolved. Through experiences in Congress, his connection to the Blount family, and his command of the Tennessee militia, he had gained real acumen in the political arena, driven by an ambition that propelled him toward recognition and advancement. Jackson often claimed that he did not pursue office; rather, it pursued him, due to his service to the republic. To some extent, this was true. On July 24th, 1804, Jackson officially resigned his judicial position with the Superior Court, citing health concerns. While his health was a partial cause, it did not tell the whole story. Another motive was financial; Jackson could no longer afford the costly judicial travel circuit, with its many expenditures the state so infrequently reimbursed. This had left his financial situation in a deteriorated state, necessitating a refocus on personal affairs.

There was a third reason for his resignation however, and not one to be taken lightly: Jackson faced potential embarrassment in court, and possible fraud charges of his own. Several land fraud cases threatened to come up on the docket that may have implicated him. One of these threatened to cause Jackson severe financial trouble, and possible ruin, and once again it revolved around his dealings with the late David Allison.

In 1794, Jackson became involved in a land transaction where 85,000 acres were sold to Allison, who later mortgaged the property to a Philadelphia merchant named Norton Pryor. After Allison's death, Jackson, constrained by his role as judge, appointed John Overton to handle the foreclosure suit. The land was sold in 1802, resulting in substantial

---

[296] AJ to Coffee, April 28, 1804, Coffee Papers, *THS*.

profits for Jackson, who eventually sold his share at a significant markup. By 1810, Jackson learned that the original court decision regarding the Allison land was potentially invalid due to jurisdiction issues. (It had been tried in a federal court, and since Tennessee was now a state, the court's decision was no longer valid.) Alarmed, he quickly made his way to Georgia to seek out the Allison heirs to secure their rights to the property. In exchange for forgiving their father›s debt, (and offering them a $500 settlement), Jackson persuaded them to sign over their rights, thus securing a legal claim to the land.[297]

Despite his attempts to negotiate with Andrew Erwin, who had purchased the land from Pryor, Jackson faced refusal. Erwin, a political rival within the state, was unwilling to give Jackson even a penny. Yet, shrewdly, Jackson bided his time, as well he would need to, as the lengthy legal battle that ensued lasted a decade. During those ten years, Jackson's reputation grew as a national hero, which certainly did not help Erwin's side in the case. The suit finally culminated in a settlement where Erwin agreed to pay Jackson $10,000, which, after Erwin's wife pleaded with Jackson, he ultimately forgave. This benevolent decision in the name of the teary-eyed Mrs. Erwin exhibited the interesting dichotomy of Jackson's personality; extreme vindictiveness at times combined with generosity to a fault at others, especially toward women.

The court costs for the long, drawn-out process set Jackson back some $2,000 alone, not counting in the cost of travel, as well as the opportunity cost of ten years' worth of legal haggling. By forgiving Erwin's debt in the end, Jackson was left with only the tearful gratitude of Mrs. Erwin, and her family. [298] Although his gracious act would pay at least some dividends in that it helped defuse any political animosity between he and Erwin, which would come in handy down the road.

Financially, this was another loss for Jackson, although, it was a near miss from the total calamity that it might have been, and one that may well have forever changed the course of American history. Total financial ruin could easily have been the result of the case for Jackson, which would have likely forced him out of the political game altogether. Would such a fiscal disaster have driven Jackson out of the militia as well, in

---

[297] Smith, *Andrew Jackson and Land Speculation*, p. 19.
[298] Bedford County Deed Book. AAA. pp. 362-365.

order to concentrate on more lucrative money-making opportunities? Or, by exposing any potential corruption in connection with David Allison, which some shadier contracts between Jackson and Overton's land acquisitions seem to allude to, thus bespotting his reputation, Jackson may well have lost his standing among his militia soldiers, thus preventing his reelection as major-general. Cutting off the path to Jackson's meteoric rise as a general would have also prevented Jackson's route to national fame, prestige, and eventually, the presidency. A close call; but one that Jackson's resourcefulness and quick, decisive action allowed him to avoid. The fallout from the Allison deal instilled in Andrew Jackson a deep-seated aversion to debt and banks; one that would last a lifetime. Andrew Jackson was fundamentally opposed to anything financially complicated, particularly debt, which he detested. Around the year 1804, he decided to simplify his life and start anew, shifting his focus to rebuilding his fortune, selling his large farm at Hunters Hill. Having not actually tried a case himself since 1796, and no longer able to rely on his judge's salary, he also sold approximately twenty-five thousand acres of his undeveloped land in other areas of the state.

Continuing to alter his lifestyle, Jackson purchased a 425-acre farm from his neighbor Nathaniel Hays on July 5, 1804. Called "Rural Retreat," he eventually renamed the property using the French term "Hermitage." Starting over, Jackson relocated himself, his wife and slaves, to the Hermitage, where he and Rachel returned to life in a rough-hewn log cabin, a blockhouse of three rooms on the property. Beginning anew at the Hermitage, Jackson aimed to regroup financially and then consolidate his wealth.[299]

This frugal decision was pragmatic, and Jackson's minimalism paid off. By doing so, he was able to clear his debts. The Jacksons would slowly but steadily expand the Hermitage land into a plantation with a chief goal in mind: To produce cotton as a money-making enterprise; to become a profitable planter and to achieve financial success. This, Andrew Jackson believed, would be the final avenue to the life of the gentleman planter he had for so long avidly sought.

Whether for business reasons or military endeavors, there were times over the years when Jackson was forced to be away from the

---

[299] AJ to Andrew Donelson, 1844. Private Collection, LC.

Hermitage for long stretches. Nonetheless, the estate continued to thrive. Despite Rachel's ever-vigilant longing for Jackson's return, her steady management of the growing plantation never wavered, and the Hermitage produced profitable cash crops of cotton and corn. The Jacksons' estate soon became the envy of his neighbors. Willie Blount, after a visit to the Hermitage in the post-war period remarked,

"Although I have ever considered him to be among the most industrious men of my acquaintance, both in public and private life, I was really surprised to find his farm in such excellent order and so very productive, under all circumstances relating to his absence from home, attending the public relations during the late war and since. His farming land is, as you know, very fertile, very beautiful and eligibly situated for comfort. It is largely improved, handsomely arranged, with gratifying appearance to the visitors at his most hospitable house, open to all who have the pleasure of his acquaintance and who travel through his neighborhood, none of whom pass that way without calling on him for social intercourse, viewing him to be the polite gentleman at home and abroad and the friend of man everywhere. His every arrangement for farming on an extensive scale delights the man of observation; his fields are extensive and nicely cultivated as a garden; his meadows and pastures are extensive and neatly kept; his stock of horses, cattle, sheep, and hogs are of the best kind and all in excellent order."[300] Blount makes no mention of the ever-increasing number of enslaved human beings who toiled daily in the fields to ensure such a pleasant farming operation for the Jackson family.

Although the Spanish had grown cotton in America as early as 1556, it didn't have much of a role on the continent until the 1790s. The leaders of the new nation, desperate for capital, were bent on finding a product that could tip the trade deficit in their favor. Their scanty exports revolving largely around naval stores, fish and tobacco, were insufficient for real economic success, and the founders knew it. After a series of technological breakthroughs in England's textile industry, (the spinning Jenny for example) the answer revealed itself, and the nation's new economic path was suddenly clear: the South would grow the crop,

---

[300] James, Marquis. *Andrew Jackson: Portrait of a President*.1938. Ch. 1.

and the north would manufacture it, and then ship the cloth to markets far and wide.

Before that vision could become a reality, however, someone had to figure out a way to produce cotton on a large scale. The practice of extracting cotton seeds from its fibers was slow, laborious and painful, that is until Eli Whitney came along. Whitney, a young Yankee tinkerer living in Georgia in 1793, revolutionized the cotton game by inventing the cotton gin. His idea wasn't new. The Hindus had used a hand-cranked apparatus for hundreds of years, called the churka, to extract cotton seeds, and American planters had made improvements on the design since the 1740s. But Whitney, secreted away in a basement room in the house of Nathanael Greene's widow in Greene County, Georgia, greatly advanced the concept.

Fresh out of Yale University, Whitney had taken a job as a private tutor when he met up with Catherine Greene, who invited him to her Georgia plantation. Whitney was soon sucked in by the foremost problem confronting area planters: the time and effort required to produce cotton on a large-scale. Whitney became inspired, as the story goes, by watching a plantation cat claw at a chicken carcass through chicken wire. The cat came away with a paw full of clean feathers. Whitney's boxy gadget used a spike cylinder and a series of brushes, to tear away the cotton lint and a slotted iron breastwork to segregate the seeds. Previous to Whitney's invention, a good picker could produce one pound of seed-free fiber per day. Now, the amount skyrocketed, to fifty or more pounds daily.

Unfortunately, Whitney's cotton gin significantly amplified the institution of slavery in the United States. While it reduced the labor of separating cotton fibers from seeds, it simultaneously increased the demand for cotton, which in turn fueled the expansion of plantations and the need for more enslaved labor. This led to a dramatic rise in the enslaved population and set the stage for the economic and social divisions between North and South. "Furs, cattle, oil, gold, wheat, corn, railroads—the tale of all these… excites the imagination as one perceives with what courage and adventurousness men have bent the resources of nature to their use," one historian has written, "But it is the melancholy distinction of cotton to be the very stuff of high drama and tragedy, of bloody civil war and the unutterable woe of human slavery." [301]

Soon, Greene County, Georgia was producing unprecedented amounts of cotton and was regarded by the 1830s as one of the most lucrative cotton areas in Georgia, having produced two of the state's first three cotton millionaires. Slaves soon constituted two-thirds of Greene's population and picked 12,000 bales each year.[302]

Not to be out done, Jackson, like so many others in the South, was determined to cash in on the wealth of the cotton kingdom. As a result, his own initially modest plantation workforce did in fact grow steadily over the years, with Jackson acquiring numerous enslaved men, women and children via the domestic slave trade, eventually accumulating one hundred and fifty slaves at the Hermitage alone by the time of his death. Jackson's views on slavery were complex, though some have described him as a benevolent slave owner in comparison with many of his contemporaries. At times, the record belies such benevolence. Jackson demanded obedience among his slaves and could be especially merciless toward runaways.

By most accounts, both Jackson and Rachel maintained a level of decency toward their slaves, advocating for humane treatment with the overseers the family hired. But there are examples of cruelty. Jackson is known to have resorted to ordering severe whippings when he deemed it necessary. In 1804, placing a newspaper advertisement for a runaway slave named Tom Gid, Jackson offered "ten dollars extra for every hundred lashes any person will give him, to the amount of three hundred" if Tom was captured outside of the state. (Tom does not appear to have been captured.) Historical accounts indicate that punishments exceeding 200 lashes were often considered extremely dangerous and sometimes fatal. In at least one case, two enslaved individuals died after receiving 300 lashes.[303]

---

[301] Arax, Mark & Wartzman, Rick, *The King of California, J.G. Boswell and the Making of a Secret American Empire*, Public Affairs, New York, 2003, p. 26.
[302] Arax & Wartzman, pp. 26-27.
[303] Hopkins, Callie, *AU Fellow 2018-2019; "Inventory of Hermitage Slaves and Property,"* in *The Papers of Andrew Jackson, Volume VII:* 1829, Knoxville: University of Tennessee Press, 2007), ed. Daniel Feller, et al., 8.

In the case of a repeat offender named Gilbert, running away ultimately cost him his life. In August 1827, Jackson's overseer, Ira Walton, decided to whip Gilbert in front of the other slaves to send a message; however, the slave fought back and ended up dead from a knife wound. This incident would return to haunt Jackson just two years later in his bid for the presidency, as will be discussed.

Female slaves were also subjected to violence at the Hermitage. In 1815, one of Jackson's nephews informed him that "[y]our wenches as usual commenced open war" against the overseer. This behavior ceased after the slave women were "brought to order by Hickory oil," referring to whippings with the lash. In 1821, while the Jacksons lived in Florida during Andrew's tenure as territorial governor, Rachel wrote to her husband about her slave, Betty, that she "has been putting on some airs, and been guilty of a great deal of impudence." Betty's offense was washing clothes for individuals in the neighborhood without Rachel's "express permission." Jackson instructed several men in their Pensacola household to punish Betty with fifty lashes at "the public whipping post" if she refused to obey his wife. He wrote to one of the men that Betty was "capable of being a good & valluable servant," but to achieve this, "she must be ruled with the cowhide." [304]

According to the evidence, a conclusion that can be drawn on Jackson's views about slavery is rather one-dimensional. Jackson did not seem to question the system, he had grown up around slavery in the Waxhaws, though on a smaller scale, so Jackson likely viewed the system simply as something he had always known and was therefore a normal part of life. It does not appear Jackson gave the morality issues involved with slave ownership much consideration. His main concern in his desire to own slaves was to maintain his social status and remain wealthy. If he spent time considering whether owning slaves was right or wrong, he did not leave much evidence of those thoughts. He expressed no qualms, and asked no questions about the institution publicly, despite being a significant slave owner. One could argue that Jackson did all he could to not only maintain the system of slavery but allow its extension into further western territories.

---

[304] Cheatham, *Andrew Jackson, Southerner*, 2013. Part I.

One wonders what Jackson's legacy might have been had he lived just twenty years later. Alas, the answer to that question can never be known. As for the United States, the road that was developing was not yet clear when it came to such questions as the morality of slavery, human beings as legal property, and the status, slave or free, of future lands in the west. But all too soon, like a dark dust cloud on the horizon, the country would find itself traveling on such a road, irrevocably, with no signs of exit as far as the eye could see.

CHAPTER

23

THE MERCHANT AND THE HORSEMAN

"In a bet there is a fool and a thief."
– Old Proverb

The year 1803 marked a turning point for Andrew Jackson. Among other reasons, the abrupt end of a fraying business partnership with Thomas Watson, which came about on August 6, signaled a new chapter for Jackson's mercantile interests. Driven by ambition and opportunity, this split set the stage for new ventures and a shifting landscape of alliances for the profit-minded Jackson. Wasting no time in quickly reshaping his business dealings, he attempted to realign the groundwork for future monetary success. Blood and business intertwined often in the life of Andrew Jackson, and as he sought to adjust and expand his mercantile interests, family ties played a crucial role, shaping his partnerships and influencing his path to prominence. The disagreement between the two revolved around the amount of cotton received and invested for the years 1802 and 1803.[305] No longer content with a passive role in store ownership, he plunged more fully into the world of commerce, forging new partnerships and solidifying his position in the burgeoning Tennessee economy. From the cotton fields to the counting house, Jackson's ambition continued to take root.

---

[305] AJ to Watson, Jan. 25, 1804, Jackson Papers, LC.

Jackson soon supplanted Thomas Watson with a nephew of Rachel's named John Hutchings. Known as "Jackey," Hutchings was the son of Rachel's older sister Catherine. Before long, Jackson was in business with John Coffee as well, and the partnership was known as Jackson, Coffee & Hutchings.[306] Coffee had previously been engaged in business in a nearby town, and was soon to marry Rachel's niece, Mary Polly Donelson, in 1809.

The store operated by Jackson, Coffee & Hutchings was in a blockhouse on Stone's River at a site called Clover Bottom, just three miles from the Hermitage and eight miles from Nashville. The trio turned the blockhouse into a fine general store that initially prospered. Their establishment provided a diverse range of goods primarily imported from Philadelphia. Their inventory included items such as cloth, blankets, calico, and various dry goods, with prices in the Cumberland region significantly inflated—often three times those in Philadelphia. For instance, broadcloth priced at five dollars per yard in Philadelphia sold for fifteen dollars in their store. Besides fabric, they also offered salt, grindstones, hardware, gunpowder, cowbells, and essential items for the local populace.

Instead of cash transactions, the store engaged in trade for local produce (with cash being in such short supply in the west) including both ginned and unginned cotton, wheat, corn, tobacco, pork, skins, and furs. This produce was transported via flatboats along the Cumberland, Ohio, and Mississippi rivers to Natchez, where it was sold for the New Orleans market. Additionally, the firm constructed boats for fellow traders, leveraging their choice location along a branch of the Cumberland River. Before Coffee joined the firm, Jackson and Hutchings managed a branch store in Gallatin, Tennessee, as well, which was twenty-six miles from Nashville. It was followed by stores in Lebanon and at the Cantonment on the Tennessee river (a military establishment about 300 miles north of Mobile and close to Muscle Shoals.)

With expensive shipping costs to bring merchandise from faraway eastern sources, prices remained high, with broadcloth selling for fifteen dollars per, in Tennessee. The store traded rifles, skillets, grindstones,

---

[306] Chappell, Gordon, "The Life and Activities of General John Coffee," March 1942, *THQ*, I, 128.

salt, coffee, calico, and allspice for cotton, tobacco, pork, pelts, and slaves, which Jackson and Hutchings intended to sell for cash in New Orleans. Despite a sluggish market and minimal cotton cultivation, Jackson remained hopeful. However, by spring 1805, Jackson's focus began to shift away from the store. He became engrossed in new ventures, particularly after receiving news of a lead mine discovery on nearby White River. [307]

Meanwhile, Jackson also began to grow dissatisfied with the cotton trade, which was becoming too convoluted for his liking, and "overwrought with middlemen." As meticulous as Jackson typically was in his business dealings, he vehemently resented any accusation he believed to be unfair. "I am truly sorry," Jackson wrote, "that any of our cotton has been directed to Liverpool… The costs will eat up the profits." This particular transaction had been conducted in New Orleans by John Hutchings, who Jackson believed sometimes lacked the business sense necessary for such long-distance trade.

Jackson, Coffee & Hutchings's primary agents were Boggs, Davidson & Company, a well-known cotton brokerage firm in Philadelphia, who also had a junior partner in New Orleans that Hutchings dealt with. Upon further investigation, Jackson accused this partner and Davidson of misleading Hutchings into shipping 100 bales to England. However, 133 bales had been sent "in the brigg Maria" to Philadelphia, as Jackson requested. Unfortunately, the invoice detailing their status upon arrival at Clover Bottom indicated that two bales were missing, and further deductions for insurance, interest, and commissions (which Jackson deemed excessive) reduced the amount further. Frustrated by these losses, Jackson confronted Davidson, asserting, "you are regardless of truth… and… we shall meet." [308]

The situation embodied much of the frustration Jackson and his partners experienced in the mercantile trade, and despite experiencing some initial success, Jackson, Coffee, & Hutchings ultimately saw their firm fail. Several factors contributed to this downfall, not least of which was a severe regional depression, along with bad debts, and a breakdown in communication between Nashville and the lower country nearer the

---

[307] Parton, *Jackson*, I, p. 249.
[308] Parton, *Jackson*, p. 250.

Mississippi. This communication failure hindered the trio's ability to determine prices and transportation costs effectively. All too frequently, the firm's boats arrived in a saturated market, and inevitably, substantial losses followed. The high costs associated with transporting goods from Philadelphia consumed large amounts of cash, which significantly reduced profit margins. As the store began to struggle, Jackson made the decision to exit the business by selling his share to Coffee, accepting notes payable over extended periods.[309]

Jackson therefore sought new opportunities and always had his ear to the ground in search of new adventures. It did not take him long for him to find one then, and it was one that was dear to his heart. Jackson's new adventure was in fact ideal, it lay close to home, and was centered around horses, a long-time love of his since childhood. Two nearby acquaintances, William Preston Anderson and his brother Patton, had started constructing a racehorse track on a picturesque oval meadow, just a few hundred yards from Jackson and Hutchings' establishment, the very land where Rachel Jackson's father had camped with his large family at the end of their epic journey in the *Adventure*.

It seems the Andersons had gotten in over their heads financially in this ambitious venture, and as a result, out of necessity, Jackson and Hutchings would soon take over a two-thirds interest in the racecourse. True to Jackson's nature, the majority owners expanded the project significantly. A small army of workers was soon hired on, and began building a tavern, stalls for vendors, and a keelboat yard, ensuring entertainment and easy access for racing fans far and wide. Jackson was galvanized, energized, and back in the game.

—⚘—

Andrew Jackson›s public life was characterized by his challenge to the notion that birth and breeding were necessary for success. However, in his personal life, it was a different story. Similar to the most snobbish of European aristocrats, Jackson valued bloodlines and pedigree more than he would ever admit. Recall his infatuation with the well-heeled Charleston crowd to which Jackson aspired as a young man.

---

[309] Ibid., 251.

Jackson's love for horse racing began even before he fell in with that set, beginning in his youth in Waxhaw, where he tested his equestrian skills against the other boys of the backwoods. The "Sport of Kings" would therefore always remain a passion with Jackson. Developing a special connection to horses, and a gentle manner with them from the start, by fifteen, the youngster had not only proven his worth on horseback as a speedy courier in the heat of battle, he was considered an excellent judge of horseflesh, and a savvy horse trader to boot. Jackson had enjoyed the races especially during his carousing Charleston days as a teenager, which quickly consumed his modest inheritance at the city's horse racing tracks. By 16, he was an authorized appraiser of horses, with his first known signature on a 1783 appraisal of a horse valued at 150 pounds.[310]

After the Revolutionary War, Jackson shifted his focus westward. As an apprentice lawyer, he struggled financially but remained involved in the vibrant Nashville racing scene, eventually becoming a prominent figure throughout Tennessee within the sport. With his financial struggles, the chance to strike it rich on one good gamble always appealed to Jackson, and soon, betting on his horses would become one of his important revenue streams. [311]

A love of gambling was long one of Jackson's vices, as evidenced by his frequent involvement in cock fighting as well. Jackson loved cock fighting and frequently took his birds to the cockpit in the public Square near the old Nashville Inn. He would cheer on his favorite birds with wild cries and demands for bets. "Hurrah! My Dominica! $10 on my Dominica!" or, "Hurrah! My Bernadotte! $20 on my Bernadotte! Who will take me up? Well done my Bernadotte! My Bernadotte forever!"[312]

But it was horse racing that took up much of Jackson's leisure time. Soon it became more than just a hobby. While originally reserved for the elite of the Northeast, Democrats had begun to gain control of horse racing in America. With its foundations on Long Island, by a 17th Century British colonel named Richard Nicholls, it had shifted to the warmer climates of the South by the mid to late 18th century, where

---

[310] Remini, 1977, p. 134.
[311] AJ to P. Anderson, 1805, Jackson Papers, LC.
[312] Parton, *Jackson*, I, p. 253.

wealthy planters fostered connections with British aristocrats through horse racing and breeding.

The Revolutionary War interrupted these ties, and while efforts were made to restore them after 1783, the relationship was changed permanently. The settlement of the southwestern states of Kentucky and Tennessee introduced new lush and affordable green pastures for racing. Tennessee soon became a hub for serious racers and breeders during Jackson's time, only later surpassed by Kentucky in the twentieth century. Horse racing in Tennessee began in a more casual fashion until Jackson's time, when it soon began to draw more eager patrons, reflecting a deep-rooted culture that became a significant part of the region's identity.

By 1906, however, the Tennessee General Assembly prohibited gambling, which effectively ended Tennessee's reputation as one of the premier breeding and training grounds for racehorses in the nation. But in the first decade of the 1800s, Tennessee thrived as a hub for exceptional thoroughbreds. The first race with a prize purse took place in Gallatin in 1804, and soon horse racing was among the earliest significant sporting events in the region. Andrew and Rachel Jackson attended the race, in which Jackson ran his horse Indian Queen against Dr. R. D. Barry's horse Polly Medley.[313] Tennessee horse racing was a growing social scene in those days, enhanced by actual formalized racetracks. (Previously, if a horse race was to be run, it was simply marked out by the participants on an open field.)

As popular as horse racing was, it could arguably be outstripped by the thrill of gambling. Andrew Jackson not only raced horses himself but also loved to place bets on them. From the moment he settled in the Cumberland area, Jackson participated actively in breeding, training, and racing "the ponies." For years since, he continued in the breeding process, which soon extended to cows and mules as well. But specifically, the breeding and training of horses became one of Jackson's greatest talents. His renown grew in this field, and it became widespread knowledge that Jackson possessed a knack for recognizing a fast, well-bred horse. This soon became part of his inventory of wealth, as here,

---

[313] Mielnik, Tara Mitchell, "Early Horse Racing Tracks," *Tennessee Encyclopedia*, Oct. 8, 2017.

too, Jackson discovered the spirit of the speculator, betting on his own thoroughbreds. This sometimes earned him thousands of dollars, but at other times cost him just as much, placing he and Rachel precariously on the brink of ruin.

His prized horse, Indian Princess, was regarded as the fastest in the country and had defeated all competitors, until the impressive horse Greyhound came along. Jackson, who was strapped for cash at the time, (as he often was) and hoping to turn his luck around, arranged a race with the unbeaten competitor, a gelding owned by a neighbor, Lazarus Cotton. In a heavy blow to Jackson's pride and to his wallet, a triumphant Greyhound won all three heats. Cotton's stallion also won a race against a stud Virginia thoroughbred named Truxton, whose reputation preceded him into Tennessee. This loss practically bankrupted his owner, one John Verrell, and the big bay was his last asset, about to be seized to pay his debts.

After Indian Queen's losses, Jackson was nearly bankrupt himself, but he embarked on an extensive tour of Virginia anyway, determined to purchase Truxton, who was legendary throughout the region, and if not, then an improved breed at any rate. On a mission to find the horse that could win him back his lost fortune, Jackson tracked down Verrell and Truxton, eventually locating Verrell's plantation in Chesterfield County, Virginia. After first having seen him race in Tennessee, coming across the exquisitely built stallion again, Jackson decided he had to have him.

As luck would have it, the timing was just right. Verrell, still reeling in financial straits from his losing bets against Greyhound was ready and willing to sell his most prized cash horse. Jackson offered him $1500 for Truxton, plus three geldings and a promise of two more, should Truxton "win a purse" next fall. In return, Jackson would pay off Verrell's debts, totaling $1170. Verrell agreed, and Jackson returned from Virginia with the beautiful Truxton, who stood at 15 hands 3 inches high.

At six-years-old, Truxton was a handsome stallion, well-formed with powerful haunches and white hind feet. His pedigree was impeccable, sired by a champion British horse, Diomed. Jackson felt certain that with better training, the horse could outpace Greyhound in time. Once Truxton was his, Jackson wasted no time, soon entering him in a return match with Greyhound – for a side bet of $5000.

According to Marquis James, a nineteenth century Jackson biographer, "How Jackson raised five thousand dollars at this critical juncture is a point the present reviewer is unable to clarify."[314] Other biographers have inferred that debts and gambling never seemed to interfere with Jackson's efforts to move his finances forward. Verrell made his way to Tennessee to assist Jackson in Truxton's training, determined to cash in on Jackson's investment himself. Jackson and Verell worked together to train the horse to their purpose, along with a hired trainer, Captain Samuel Pryor. It is said that the Truxton faced a harsh training schedule, and that the men pushed the horse to the limit of endurance. That is easy to believe knowing Jackson.

However it was accomplished, Truxton seems to have been instilled at that time with an iron will to win – not unlike the character of Jackson himself. Ultimately, the efforts of all involved in the training of the prize horse would pay off handsomely, as the thoroughbred would go on to become one of the greatest racehorses he ever owned, and Jackson took great pride in this acquisition. This period of all things horse-related fueled a lifelong passion for horses in the heart of Andrew Jackson.

The match race between Truxton and Greyhound was the last race of the 1805 season – and nearly everyone from miles around was in attendance, including many of the men's wives in their finest attire. Anyone who was anyone in the Cumberland region seemed to be in attendance that day. Jackson had intensively trained and raced his new prize horse at Clover Bottom, just a stone's throw from his store, gearing up for the big faceoff. Greyhound was the favorite, based on his previous wins, plus the ongoing gossip that Jackson had exhausted Truxton in training. Betting was heavy. Not only was cash wagered, but according to Congressman Baliey Peyton, who had heard the story from Jackson himself, numerous 640-acre tracts were staked. Plus, several wagers in "wearing apparel." Patton Anderson, Jackson's 125-pound jockey, bet all his worth on Truxton – plus, it is said, he wagered a few other horses that did not even belong to him, including a few with "ladies' saddles on them."[315]

---

[314] James, Marquis, p. 106.
[315] James, Marquis, p. 106.

On the day of the race, Truxton, proving the gossip false, showed the pay off of his intense training regimen. Jackson's new prize horse whipped Greyhound soundly. To celebrate, the ecstatic jockey Anderson treated his co-winners to a barrel of cider and a basket of ginger cakes. The winnings paid off all John Verrell's debts and made a small fortune for Andrew Jackson. The hats and belts won helped replenish his wardrobe by no small degree. After having defeated Greyhound, Jackson bought him immediately from a depressed Lazarus Cotton and added him to his stable at the new Clover Bottom Racetrack.

Jackson, now having acquired both Truxton and Greyhound, placed bets on them that would have caused stress for even the most renegade gamblers. Large amounts of cash and land deeds exchanged hands, leading to either a windfall, or financial ruin for men and their families, with significant farms gained or lost, sometimes based on a single race. Truxton alone won more than twenty thousand dollars in early 1800's prize money. Eventually, like all fine racehorses, Truxton was put to service, and went on to sire some excellent foals, earning Jackson a considerable amount in stud fees.

The ponies Truxton sired grew to become legendary racehorses in their own right. By the time Jackson became President in 1829, Truxton was an old horse, but Jackson was still an avid horse owner-racer. He brought a string of fine horses to an already crowded White House stable and convinced Congress to approve another $3,500 for additional renovations. Legend has it, his beloved Truxton lived there, although he would have been past thirty – very old for a horse, even one owned by Andrew Jackson.

However, it would be this love of the ponies, and the thrill of the race that would lead Jackson down a road that nearly cost him his life, and one that would ultimately culminate in pain and bloodshed. In just a year after the epic race between Truxton and Greyhound, in the spring of 1806, Jackson arranged another high-stakes race, this time between his prize horse Truxton, and Captain Joseph Ervin's mighty stallion, who went by the name of Plowboy.

The race was a very big deal in Nashville, as both horses were touted as the fastest in the west. The frenzied excitement among the Nashville socialites grew in anticipation of the colossal matchup. The wagers placed amounted to an all-time high. Horse fever raged among the warm winds of spring in the Cumberland. But for one horse lover, the fiery twenty-five-year-old Nashville attorney, Charles Dickinson, all that was about to change. [316]

Jackson and Ervin had agreed that should either side feel the need to forfeit the race for whatever reason, there was to be paid a fee of $800. As it turns out, just prior to the day of the race, Plowboy went lame, and Ervin was forced to pay Jackson the forfeit fee. The promissory notes that could be accepted for the fee had been agreed upon initially at the time of the wager.

On the frontier in those days, with real cash in such scarce supply, promissory notes often substituted for money. Some promissory notes were much more reliable than others, and with the still existent residue of Jackson's dealings with David Allison, he was especially careful when it came to such agreements. Ervin originally offered Jackson a variety of notes to pay him the fee, but the notes were not on the previously agreed upon list. Jackson refused to accept these as a result, reminding Ervin of the agreement. The list of notes the men had agreed upon was in the care of Ervin's son-in-law, Dickinson, who then provided the list to Ervin. Ervin then made a selection of notes that Jackson would accept, and the matter was settled, presumably.

To many young men of the times, a challenge to a more prominent and established individual such as Andrew Jackson could make one's name known, provide standing, and a reputation as a gentleman to take note of. Jackson was certainly a prominent figure whose reputation had been made in a similar fashion in affairs of honor against the likes of Waightstill Avery and John Sevier.

To Charles Dickinson, the matter of the promissory notes seemed to provide him just such an opportunity against the mighty former Senator, Judge, and Major General, Andrew Jackson. Dickinson had taken offense to Jackson's rejection of the promissory notes Ervin had originally offered him to pay the forfeit fee, as the notes were signed by the attorney Dickinson himself. Dickinson felt his integrity had been questioned, and rumor had it that while drinking in a local tavern, he had denigrated Jackson derisively.

---

[316] Kendall, *Jackson*, p. 115.

The news was relayed back to Jackson that Dickinson had taken the "sacred name" of Rachel into his "polluted mouth," referring sarcastically to her questionable matrimonial history. Once again to Jackson, these were fighting words. This would mark the start of escalating trouble between Jackson and Dickinson, a young man known for having a wild side, one that sometimes devolved into outright recklessness. [317]

An angry Jackson sought out Charles Dickinson and confronted him face to face. Dickinson denied the charge, stating that if he had said something of the sort then he didn't recall, and that he was likely drunk. Jackson, now older and chastened somewhat by the harmful effects of previous duels, wanted no part of an encounter with the young upstart, and accepted the explanation. But the matter did not end there. Jackson soon heard of Dickinson repeating the defamation of Rachel, and this time he turned to Dickinson's father-in-law, requesting Ervin to restrain his daughter's unruly husband. "I want no quarrel with him," Jackson told his old acquaintance Ervin, claiming that Dickinson was "being used by my enemies," referring to the Sevier faction. [318]

A short while later, a friend of Dickinson's, and fellow cub lawyer even less established, named Thomas Swann, inserted himself into the affair. One afternoon, Swann happened to be present when the jockey Patton Anderson was entertaining acquaintances at a gathering at George and Robert Bells' store in Nashville. Anderson, shameless when it came to gossip, was relating the details of the misunderstanding regarding the promissory notes between Jackson and Ervin. Apparently, Anderson did not have his facts straight on the details, which Swann later relayed to Dickinson. Offended for a second time, Dickinson corresponded with Jackson for clarification of the matter, and Jackson, who disagreed with Swann's version of what was said, replied that Swann was a "Damned Lyar."

It is remarkable, in hindsight, that tragedy could ultimately result from such trivialities of hearsay and wordplay.[319] But more often than not, this level of adolescence was common in that period when it came to duels on the frontier. At any rate, Swann had now taken on the role of go-between and soon became caught in the crossfire himself. When

---

[317] Bassett, *Jackson*, p. 61.
[318] James, *The Life of Andrew Jackson*, p. 108.
[319] Kendall, *Jackson*, pp. 115-116.

Dickinson related to Swann Jackson's accusations of Swann's dishonest character, he too grew indignant. The twenty-three-year-old Swann fired off an angry letter to Jackson, dated Jan. 3rd, 1806, demanding an explanation. "The harshness of this expression has deeply wounded my feelings; it is language to which I am a stranger, which no man, acquainted with my character, would venture to apply to me, and which, should the information of Mr. Dickinson be correct, I shall be under the necessity of taking proper notice of." [320]

The wording of the letter seemed to imply a challenge, but Jackson did not consider Swann to be worthy of a duel. Instead, Jackson sought to soothe the young Swann's feelings in his reply, explaining that no offense had been intended. "If incautiously I inflict a wound, I always hasten to remove it." In his response, however, Jackson included a charge against the character of the thin-skinned Dickinson, claiming that Swann was being used as a catspaw by his friend, and that "The base poltroon and cowardly talebearer will always act in the background. You can apply the latter to Mr. Dickinson. I write it for his eye." [321]

This missive soon ignited a firestorm of indignation and hurt feelings. In short order, word of not one, but eventually, three separate challenges of honor would be demanded against Jackson. First came Dickinson's letter, which insisted that Jackson was a cowardly equivocator, and that an answer to his offenses was required. Dickinson however, was soon off to New Orleans on business, sparing Jackson the need to reply to him, and he hoped the time away might defuse Dickinson's outrage. In the meantime, Swann's letter arrived, also demanding satisfaction for Jackson's base accusations, "Think not I am intimidated by your threats. No power terrestrial shall prevent the settled purpose of my soul...My friend, the bearer of this is authorized to make complete arrangements in the field of honor."[322] Swann was clearly spoiling for a fight, but Jackson chose instead to confront the young man in person.

Wasting no time in tracking down the young and impetuous Thomas Swann, Jackson found him drinking with friends at the popular Winn's Tavern in Nashville. Marching up to Swann, Jackson began, after a few words, when it appeared Swann was going for his gun, Jackson began

---
[320] Swann to AJ, Jan. 3, 1806, Jackson Papers, LC.
[321] Ibid, p. 139.
[322] Ibid, p. 140.

beating the younger man over the head with his cane. The caning had a devastating effect and would have had more until Jackson apparently tripped and nearly fell into the tavern's fireplace, ending the assault. [323]

Jackson and his friends hoped this intimidating attack might put an end to the quarrel once and for all, but alas, at this they were disappointed. Soon, a third antagonist entered the fray, in the person of John McNairy's younger brother, Nathaniel McNairy. The younger McNairy soon presented himself to Jackson on behalf of Swann, demanding satisfaction for the attack on his friend. Jackson replied that since Swann was no gentleman, he would not take part in a duel of honor afforded only to those of such rank. Instead, he informed McNairy, he would meet Swann at a place of his choosing, and shoot it out, as long as he understood it was to be no duel. McNairy went away with no promises of ending hostilities. Additionally, word soon arrived that Dickinson, on his way south, was passing his time practicing his accuracy with a pistol. [324]

The matter now intensified further. Swann, humiliated by the incident at Winn's Tavern, now took his fight to the newspapers, making the scandal public. On March 1st, 1806, Swann charged Jackson, in Nashville's only newspaper *The Impartial Review and Cumberland Repository*, that the general was a falsifying coward. By calling Jackson out to the public, Swann had raised the stakes irrevocably. Now, Jackson was no longer able to walk away from the affair without significant damage to his reputation. Never one to allow any tarnishing of his name, Jackson soon responded to Swann's charges using the same newspaper. His reply stated that Swann was no gentleman, but merely a pawn in the hands of Dickinson, the true "worthless, drunken, blackguard scoundrel." [325]

In the column, Jackson also referred to young McNairy as a meddler, who fired off a published reply. McNairy referred derisively to Jackson's trusted partner and friend John Coffee, who now became involved in the conflict despite his agreeable demeanor. Coffee now challenged McNairy to a duel, and the two soon squared off just across the Kentucky state line. At their meeting, however, McNairy fired before the agreed upon

---

[323] John Coffee's statement, in Jackson, *Correspondence*, I, 130.
[324] Parton, *Jackson*, I, p. 275.
[325] AJ to Swann, Jackson, *Correspondence*, 138.

count of three and hit Coffee in the thigh. Once the seconds of both duelists argued it out, a peaceful settlement was reached, but not until McNairy offered to give Coffee a second shot. To Coffee's credit, he did not take up McNairy's offer, accepting that the shot was an accident. The parties reached an agreement and the affair was settled.[326]

In the meantime, the long-anticipated race between the mighty Truxton and his top contender, Plowboy, was rearranged, and the feelings of both factions for the rival stallions were more intense than ever, as was the public excitement. The announcement in *The Impartial Review* reflected the hullabaloo, "On Thursday, the 3d of April next will be run the greatest and most interesting race ever run between General Jackson's horse TRUXTON, 6 years old carrying 124 pounds, and Capt. Joseph Ervin's horse PLOUGHBOY, 8 years old carrying 130 pounds... for the sum of 3,000 dollars." [327]

The buzz over the event was electric, and the people came out in droves. On the day of the race, the roads to Clover Bottom were so lined with carriages that it prompted Jackson to swear that it was "the largest concourse of people I ever saw assembled, except in an army." But around Truxton's stall, Jackson's face was grave. Truxton had suffered an injury to his thigh in training, and it had swollen considerably. Thus, it was not clear if the horse would be able to go. The Truxton team was entirely against the idea of their horse risking worse injury by racing on that day, with the exception of Jackson. The general strode over to his horse, stroked his nose, whispering in his ear. A few moments later he returned to the team, a buoyed expression on his face, and stated calmly. "Truxton will race."[328]

Hearing the news of Truxton's injury, the Ervin side was ecstatic, and the bets in favor of Plowboy rolled in. The Truxton supporters were less enthusiastic in their wagers in favor of Jackson's horse. Ultimately, many still put up their money, assured by Jackson of Truxton's health, but only about half the draw that a healthy Truxton would have inspired. The horses were led out to the track as the sun began to drop in the sky. The race was to be two-miles in length, and there would be two heats. At the sound of the gun, the horses dashed out for the first go around,

---

[326] Parton, *Jackson*, I, p. 288.
[327] James, p. 111.
[328] Ibid, 111.

and despite Truxton's slow start, the hobbled horse showed his mettle, slipping into the lead past Plowboy and holding it through to the finish line. But it was a hard-earned victory, and now both the front and hind legs seemed to be giving the horse pain. It did not appear Jackson's stallion would be able to run the second heat.

Next, a hard rain soaked the track, but the horses were led to the starting gate, anyway, the dense crowd straining to see through the downpour. The drums tapped, and the angular body of the favorite, Truxton, sprinted ahead of Plowboy with effortless ease, and ran away with the victory. The Ervin camp was dumbstruck, Truxton had defeated their horse in a clean sweep "without whip or spur by sixty yards." Jackson and his partisans were jubilant, and the crowd roared, their spirits elated by the indescribable and indestructible Truxton.

Truxton's win over Plowboy, however, only exacerbated the affray between Jackson and Joseph Ervin's capricious son-in-law. When Dickinson returned from New Orleans in May, his anger at Jackson had not subsided. In fact, it appeared that his wounds had festered during his sojourn south. Dickinson, as if to make up for lost time, hastened almost immediately to the *Repository* to get his still-bruised feelings out to the general public. On May 21st, he handed a card to the editor of the *Review*, Thomas Eastin, whose next publication was to go out on the 24th. But, before publishing it, Eastin handed the note to Thomas Overton, John Overton's brother, and a brigadier general in the militia. Overton was also a friend of Jackson's, and having read Dickinson's defamatory accusations, he rode out to the Hermitage with Dickinson's letter in hand. "General," Overton said, "it's a piece that cannot be passed over, you must challenge him." [329]

Jackson insisted on reading the article for himself before making any judgment on it, and headed down to Eastin's office to read the piece himself. In it, Dickinson referred to Jackson, among other choice descriptions, as a "poltroon, coward, and a frivolous, worthless scoundrel." This was too much for Jackson to let pass. Despite pleadings from many of his friends and supporters (particularly the venerable James Roberston) not to engage with Dickinson, Jackson's mind was made up. This would

---

[329] Ibid, 113.

have to be settled exactly as the hot-headed Dickinson wished, on the field of honor.

Jackson could have agreed to square off with any of the three accusers who had challenged him; but Swann was, to Jackson, a nobody, and McNairy was too young and naive to be worth a mention. Dickinson was the only one of the three with any standing in Nashville, in light of his recent publication slandering the major general/supreme court justice, Jackson therefore decided it was he that he must "demand satisfaction" from.

Within the hour, Thomas Overton delivered Jackson's letter to Dickinson. In a tone of exasperation at the younger man, Jackson wrote that Dickinson's conduct had been "So insulting, that it requires and shall have my notice. Insults may be given by men, and of such a kind that they must be noticed and treated with the respect due a gentleman, altho (as in the present instance) you do not merit it. I hope sir your courage will be ample security to me that I will obtain speedily that satisfaction due me for the insults offered, and in the way my friend who hands you this will point out, he waits upon you for that purpose, and with your friend you will enter into immediate arrangements for this purpose."

Before the day was out, Jackson received a reply to his challenge from Dr. Hanson Catlett on behalf of his adversary. Dickinson's response to Jackson is dated May 23rd, 1806: "Gen. Andrew Jackson, Sir, your note of this morning is received, and your request shall be granted. My friend who hands you this will make the necessary arrangements. I am, etc. -Charles Dickinson" [330]

After the long and winding road of back and forths, the insinuations, and tomfoolery, the duel was finally set. Each party's seconds quickly conferred, and the time and place was agreed upon. Jackson, eager to be done with Dickinson, agreed to meet on Friday, May 30th in Logan County, Kentucky on the banks of the Red River. Jackson was glad that the Dickinson side had agreed so quickly, but he chafed at having to wait a week for the interview. Nor was he in favor of riding forty miles to Kentucky solely out of regard for Tennessee's unenforceable statute against dueling. He did not wish to wait a week, and travel

---

[330] AJ to Dickinson, 1806, *Correspondence*, pg. 141.

afar for something that could be done in a few hours in a nearby field. Dickinson's party asked for the delay so that he could borrow a set of pistols. Jackson's second, Thomas Overton, offered the use of Jackson's guns, the same ones used in Coffee's duel with McNairy.

Disgusted with the delay, Jackson prompted General Overton to write the following note to Dickinson's second, Dr. Catlett: "Sir, the affair of honor to be settled between my friend General Jackson and Charles Dickinson, Esq., is wished not to be postponed until the 30th instant (say Friday) agreeable to your time appointed, if it can be done sooner. In order that no inconvenience on your part may occur, if you can not obtain pistols, we pledge ourselves to give you choice of ours. Let me hear from you immediately." No answer came that night, nor early the next morning.[331]

The impatient Jackson urged Overton to write a second note to his adversary's second: "Sir, I pressed you in favor of my friend General Jackson for immediate satisfaction for the injury that his feelings had received from a publication of Charles Dickinson. You replied that it might not be in your power to obtain pistols. In my note of yesterday, in order to remove any obstacles as it respected pistols, I agreed to give you choice of ours, the other we pledged ourselves to make use of. For God's sake, let this business be brought to an issue immediately, as I can not see, after the publication, why Mr. Dickinson should wish to put it off till Friday." To Jackson, this trivial feud with a hot-headed and upstart youngster and his cronies had gone on long enough. It was time to settle the matter. Jackson would have satisfaction.

---

[331] AJ to Dickinson, May 23, 1806, Jackson, *Correspondence*, I, 143-144.

CHAPTER

24

BLOOD ON THE RED RIVER

"I thoroughly disapprove of duels. If a man should challenge me, I would take him kindly and forgivingly by the hand and lead him to a quiet place and kill him."
                                                    -Mark Twain

In the quaint town of Adairville, Kentucky, nestled within the heart of Logan County, a solemn marker still stands to this day. It tells a story of runaway pride, of unbridled emotions and of the bitter consequences of the Code Duello, that plagued southern culture long ago. And it marks the spot of a duel that would alter the course of history, particularly in the early days of the state of Tennessee. This unassuming site, now a tranquil set amid a break in the poplar woods beside the Red River, once bore witness to a fateful encounter between two ambitious, resolute, and volatile men: the respected judge, planter and militia general Andrew Jackson and the young, brash, fiery, and ambitious Charles Dickinson.

The heart of the matter lay in a tangled web of personal affronts. Dickinson had accused Jackson of insulting his honor, and on Jackson's end, Dickinson's audacity, gaul, and most problematically, his crossing of that sacred line, aiming his invectives at Jackson's beloved wife, Rachel. Indeed, the lifelong snag of Rachel's past remained a lingering specter over the Jacksons' lives, and it would not be the last time that the Robards issue would rear its unsightly head.

Despite the efforts by Jackson and Thomas Overton to expedite the duel, the Dickinson camp stood firm on the date, not giving a reason as to why they could not accept their adversary's counteroffer. So, a full six days of waiting, it would have to be, before the affair of honor would finally culminate once and for all. Jackson bided his time. Meanwhile, nearly all of Nashville had been made aware of the approaching duel, and many a wager was placed, most of which figured against Jackson, as the younger man, Charles Dickinson was known, if not for much else, to be a crack shot.[332]

So it was on the eve of May 30, 1806, when the crisp spring winds off the Red River rustled the green poplar leaves, as the combatants rode up onto the agreed upon location. The evening air crackled with the strains of agitation as the two adversaries took their positions on the sprawling grounds of the Jeff Burr farm.

Their animosity had only hardened over the course of the months since their first encounter, inured by angry letters, harsh words, barbs and insults. The sacrilege that Dickinson had committed, by uttering the sacred name of Rachel Jackson, in such malignant fashion, could not go unanswered. Dickinson, assuredly justified in his cause, emboldened by the concept of personal honor in labeling Jackson a coward and a scoundrel, cut deep into the extreme sensitivities of the principled and sentient Andrew Jackson.

Jackson had awakened at five that morning. He and Overton left Miller's Tavern and arrived on the field before sunrise. Waiting quietly for the Dickinson party, Jackson stood somber and reflective, pistol in hand. His party included John Overton, a surgeon, and a few other unnamed supporters. "How do you feel about it now, General?" asked one of the party as Jackson turned to go. "Oh, all right," replied Jackson, confidently, "I shall wing him, never fear." [333]

Dr. Catlett won the coin toss for choice of position, perhaps a bad omen. With the darkness of pre-sunrise, however, choice of position did not matter much. Overton won the right to call, and the positions were marked off. Jackson stood tall in his long frock coat, staring intently at his enemy. Overton then called out, "Gentlemen, are you ready?

It was later reported that Charles Dickinson had been in high spirits leading up to the affair, perhaps from the overconfidence of youth. It is

---

[332] Parton, *Jackson*, I, p. 295.
[333] ibid, p. 298.

said that he, too, had placed a wager in his favor that he would strike down Jackson on the first shot. Did it ever occur to him that May 30th could well be his last day on earth?

Jackson knew what he had to do, and it certainly did not involve haste. The older man did not get where he was by rushing; he would not act rashly, no hasty quick fire, no hurried panic shot from his pistol. It was decided, he would allow Dickinson the first shot, despite having heard plenty about Dickinson's marksmanship. Realizing he would likely be shot, perhaps badly, Jackson had prepared himself; he accepted that he may have to absorb the pain of a bullet. But, even if it was the last act of his life, he felt confident that he would have the will to regain his balance, stand calmly, aim carefully and fire straight.

Jackson guessed correctly, although it nearly cost him his life. The two men stood face to face, their intentions clear, their fates wholly uncertain. On the word fire, Dickinson pulled the trigger almost immediately, and a fleck of dust rose from Jackson's dark blue coat, his left hand clutched at his chest. He later reported that for an instant or two, he thought he might be dying. But he regained his composure and raised his pistol. Standing straight, teeth clenched, Jackson took aim and fired. Dickinson, shocked at the sight of Jackson still standing, took a step back from his position, and cried out incredulously, "Great God, have I missed him?!?"

"Back to your mark, sir!"[334] Overton cried out, aiming his pistol at young Dickinson.

Dickinson regained his composure, stepped back to his mark, and waited for the return shot from his opponent. General Jackson aimed carefully and pulled the trigger, but the pistol didn't fire. He checked the trigger and saw it was stuck at half cock. After resetting it, he aimed again and fired. This time the shot rang out, a firebell in the early Kentucky morning that rattled the trees all around the forested scene. Dickinson's face went pale; he staggered, his friends rushing to him, gently lowering him to the ground against a bush. His trousers quickly went red with blood. The Dickinson party removed his clothes and found blood pouring from his side. Unfortunately, the bullet was lodged above his opposite hip, just beneath the skin, having passed through his body

---

[334] ibid, 299.

below the ribs. Like that of Hamilton just two years before, it was a fatal wound.

Overton approached to check on Dickinson's condition, then returned to Jackson, his face solemn. "He won't be needing anything from you anymore, General," and led Jackson away. They had gone about a hundred yards, with Overton on one side of Jackson and the surgeon on the other, neither spoke a word until the surgeon noticed Jackson's shoe full of blood. "My God! General Jackson, are you hit?" he exclaimed, pointing at the blood. "Oh, I believe he just nicked me a bit. Let's take a look, but let's not mention it there," Jackson replied, indicating the house. He opened his coat. Dickinson's aim had been accurate; he hit where he thought Jackson's heart was. However, due to Jackson's slender build and loose coat, the bullet broke only a couple of ribs and grazed the breastbone. It was painful and looked worse, but it wasn't severe or life-threatening, and the judge was able to ride to the tavern with little trouble.

When Jackson and his party reached the house, they approached a woman busily churning butter. Lightheartedly despite his condition, Jackson asked if it was ready. She replied it was just about done. He requested some buttermilk. As she was getting it, she noticed him open his coat, checking inside it. She noticed then that his shirt was soaked with blood, and she stared in shock. Catching her eye, he quickly buttoned his coat again. She filled a quart measure with buttermilk and handed it to him. He drank it in one go, then went inside, removed his coat, and had his wound examined and treated. Afterward, he sent one of his attendants to Dr. Catlett to ask about Dickinson's condition and to offer assistance from his surgeon.

A polite response came back, stating that Dickinson's case was beyond surgical help. Later that day, Jackson sent a bottle of wine to Dr. Catlett for Dickinson. However, there was one thing Jackson couldn't grant him even in such dire circumstances. An old friend of General Jackson remarked, "Although the General had been wounded, he wanted to keep it a secret until he left the area, so he initially concealed it even from his friends. His reason was that since Dickinson prided himself on being the best shot in the world and was sure he would kill him with the first shot, Jackson didn't want Dickinson to have the satisfaction of knowing he had hit him."[335]

Charles Dickinson was bleeding to death. They had managed to slow the bleeding to a certain extent, but it couldn't be stopped entirely. He had been taken back to the Harrison house, where he had spent the night, and was laid out on a mattress, which was soon soaked with blood. The wounded Dickinson's pain was excruciating, and he had cried out in agony throughout the day. At nine in the evening, he suddenly asked why the lights had been turned off. The doctor realized then that the end was near. His wife, who had been called in the morning, wouldn't make it in time to say goodbye. He finally succumbed to his wounds, and died five minutes later, reportedly cursing the bullet that had struck him. His wife rushed to the scene after hearing he was "dangerously wounded" and encountered a procession of silent horsemen leading a rough wagon carrying her husband's body. Charles Dickinson was but twenty-five-years-old.

Though Jackson emerged from the duel with his own wound, one that would continue to cause pain for the rest of his days, he emerged the victor. But at what cost? For more than a month, Jackson could hardly move, as the bullet had broken two of his ribs. The trajectory of the bullet had been so close to his heart, that it was determined that it could not be removed. The lead that the bullet contained caused considerable illness over the years. The wound did not heal properly, and Jackson's discomfort would continue for the remainder of his life.[336]

Not only did the Dickinson affair result in lifelong physical pain for Jackson, but as his venerable friend James Robertson had warned, even a victory in this affair would be pyrrhic at best. Jackson's reputation suffered tremendously from his actions, and the harm done did not easily subside. The people of Nashville were dismayed at the news of the killing, especially upon hearing of how poor Dickinson was made to stand defenseless, waiting for the vengeful Jackson to massacre him. Dickinson's emotion-filled funeral brought out a large mass of mourners (particularly among the area's Sevier supporters), as the newspaper reported,

---

[335] Parton, *Jackson*, pp. 299-300.
[336] ibid, 303.

"On Tuesday evening (or afternoon) last," the *Impartial Review* of the following week reported, "The remains of Mr. Charles Dickinson were committed to the grave, at the residence of Mr. Joseph Ervin, attended by a large number of the citizens of Nashville and its neighborhood. There have been few instances in which stronger impressions of sorrow or testimonies were evinced than on the one we have the unwelcome task to report. In the prime of life, and blessed in domestic circumstances, with almost every valuable enjoyment, he fell a victim to the barbarous and pernicious practice of dueling. By his untimely fate the community is deprived of an amiable man and a virtuous citizen. His friends will long lament with particular sensibility the deplorable event. Mr. Dickinson was a native of Maryland, where he was highly valued by the discriminating and good; and those who knew him best respected him most. With a consort that has to bear with this, the severest of afflictions, and an infant child, his friends and acquaintances will cordially sympathize. Their loss is above calculation. May Heaven assuage their anguish by administering such consolations as are beyond the power of human accident or change."[337]

And the situation only became worse for Jackson. Charles Dickinson had many friends in Nashville, while Andrew Jackson had an ever-growing number of adversaries. The events of the months leading up to the affair, and the circumstances surrounding it caused horror and repulsion in many. An informal meeting was arranged among the deceased's friends and family, and they agreed to petition the newspaper, requesting that its next publication be dedicated as tribute to his memory. The petition was signed by seventy-three of the most prominent citizens of Nashville,

> "The undersigned, citizens of Nashville and its vicinity, respectfully request Mr. Bradford and Mr. Eastin to mourn Mr. Charles Dickinson in the next edition of their paper as a tribute to his memory and a demonstration of regret for his untimely death."

---

[337] ibid, 304

Mr. Eastin readily agreed to fulfill the request, much to the annoyance of the convalescing General Jackson. While at his residence, Jackson learned of this effort, and wasted no time, despite his wounds, in having a message of his own dashed off to the editor: "Mr. Eastin: I have been informed that at the request of various citizens of Nashville and its vicinity, you plan to adorn your paper in mourning as a tribute to the memory of Charles Dickinson and to express regret for his untimely death. Your paper serves as a public platform and is generally perceived as the public will, unless stated otherwise. Assuming that the public is not in mourning for this event, it is only fair and just to disclose the names of those citizens who made this request, so that the public may determine whether the true intentions of the signers were indeed a tribute of respect for the deceased, or if there lies something else that may not be immediately apparent."[338]

Eastin, caught in the crosshairs, sought to appease all parties involved. For the Dickinson faction, he agreed to place his paper in mourning, publishing the memorial. But he also published Jackson's letter, and he added the following: "In answer to the request of General Jackson I can only observe that, previously, the request of some of the citizens of Nashville and its vicinity had been put to type, and as soon as it had transpired that the above request had been made, a number of the subscribers, to the amount of twenty six, called and erased their names. Always willing to support, by my acts, the title of my paper—always willing to attend to the request of any portion of our citizens when they will take the responsibility on themselves, induced me to comply with the petition of those requesting citizens, and place my paper in mourning. Impartiality induces me also to attend to the request of General Jackson." Yet, forty-six others stuck firm to their position, despite their names being publicized. This group included some former Jackson supporters, including one of the Robertson clan, Dr. Felix Robertson, the son of Nashville's founder.

The duel was a tragic scandal in the minds of many throughout the Cumberland who viewed the shooting of Dickinson as a brutal, cold-blooded killing. Jackson's reputation was considerably damaged, especially coming on the heels of the Sevier feud. The general, once so

---

[338] AJ to Thomas Eastin, Jackson Papers, *TSL*.

revered in Nashville, was now, at least for the time being, viewed as a vindictive and volatile man, especially among Dickinson's friends. While the slaying was not entirely viewed as murder, many felt that Jackson's actions were indeed criminal, and that there had been no need to shoot to kill.

For Jackson's friends, however, the decision to kill Dickinson was justifiable considering that the General had just been shot nearly to death. The bullet had barely missed his heart, and in those moments of fighting for his life, they argued, fearing that his wound might be fatal, he had a right to exact revenge. And, as many of his supporters insisted during those emotional weeks just after the duel, the anger towards Jackson would subside. And with the passing of time, and its soothing effects on the public passions, this did eventually come to pass. These were still the days of the Code Duello after all, even if it was beginning to be phased out, as this tragic result, combined with the Hamilton-Burr duel, did much to expedite.

Tennesseans still believed that a gentleman was entitled to satisfaction, particularly one who had just taken a bullet inches from his heart. It was also soon common knowledge how badly Dickinson wished to kill Jackson. He "marked the gen'l on a tree and boasted how often he had hit him, and when Setting out to meet the gen'l left 300$ with Mr. Wagaman to bet he would kill the gen'l." [339]

Nonetheless, for the next few months, Jackson was anything but popular, and while he recovered from his bullet wound, he remained largely ostracized by many in Nashville society. If he had been hoping for a political opportunity during the years leading up to the war in 1812, it is highly unlikely that the Tennessee populace would have elected their Major-General to any post. But, as the years passed, Jackson's reputation would revive. As for Dickinson, he found his final resting place at Old City Cemetery in Nashville, a silent testament to the tragic rivalry that shaped the destinies of both men. The marker in Adairville stands not just as a reminder of a duel, but as a poignant reflection of the fierce passions that drive men to the brink, forever altering the course of history.

---

[339] ibid

ANDREW JACKSON: THE POLITICS OF RESENTMENT

CHAPTER

25

A BURR IN MY SIDE

> *"Never do today what you can put off till tomorrow. Delay may give clearer light as to what is best to be done."*
> —*Aaron Burr*

For several years following the Dickinson incident, Jackson struggled through some of the most difficult times since his youth. In constant pain from his bullet wound, struggling with political, social, and financial challenges, he might well have fallen into the throes of a gloomy depression. But not Andrew Jackson. Although his reputation in Nashville had taken a hit, sharply contrasted from his earlier meteoric rise amongst his Cumberland acquaintances, the resilient Jackson was not one to dwell on the negative. Any guilt he may have felt regarding Dickinson's death or his diminished standing in the community, he made up for by, of all things, throwing parties.

Despite his actions, Jackson's network of friends was still strong. He always had his home life, which was his rock and his salvation. Rachel remained his most cherished companion, and his efforts to transform his acreage into a plantation suitable for a gentleman farmer were coming along substantially. This provided comfort for Jackson, and a buoy even in hard times. She was the rudder he needed to stay the course.

Although Jackson had not yet constructed the grand mansion that currently stands on the expansive Hermitage property, he built a second house just twenty feet away from the three-room blockhouse he and Rachel called home. This new house was smaller than the original, but a covered passageway was constructed, connecting the two. With the increased space, Jackson and Rachel stepped up their efforts to entertain. The Jacksons became frequent hosts, inviting friends and relatives to the Hermitage, and entertaining them with grand soirees.

The Hermitage became the place to be, well-known for its festive gatherings of family, friends and dignitaries. Attracting visitors from nearly every social class in the Cumberland and beyond, the Jacksons became renowned for their parties. Jackson was as friendly and animated in conversation as he was generous towards his guests. With his fast-talking charm and colorful storytelling, he entertained well into the wee hours of the night, yet throughout the evening, still maintained a dignified composure. "His house was the seat of hospitality," wrote Thomas Hart Benton, at the time still a young militia officer under Jackson, "the resort of friends and acquaintances, of all strangers visiting the state."[340]

Perhaps Jackson was intent on reviving his image, beset by the fall from grace his temperament had caused. Whatever the case, the house of the General became known for conviviality, fine dining, an interesting conversation around the fireplace, Tennessee whiskey, and a good smoke in the parlor. Friends of the Jacksons attended their galas as often as they could to revel in the camaraderie, and to hear Jackson "spin a yarn." He preferred a seat not at the head of the table, but in between two ladies with whom he could converse, while always keeping an ear on the other end of the table in case something piqued his interest. When it did, he didn't miss the opportunity to offer his opinion, or to crack a joke, with the bearing at all times that his position as judge and major general required.

A frequent female visitor at the Hermitage in those days commented "the General was the prince of hospitality; not because he entertained a great many people; but because the poor, belated peddler was as welcome as the President of the United States and made so much at his ease that he felt as though he had got home."[341]

While Jackson sought to revive his social standing in Nashville by playing the gracious host, another leading man up north, who had

---

[340] James, *The Life of Andrew Jackson*, p. 111.
[341] Reid and Eaton, John Henry, *The Life of Andrew Jackson: Major-General in the Service of the United States*, 1824, pp. 11-12.

also experienced a recent fall from favor, would soon make his way to Tennessee. In Weehawken, New Jersey, in the heat of July, 1804, on the west bank of the Hudson River, this friend of Jackson's had finally dealt with his long-time associate-turned bitter rival, ending a festering feud that had been on a slow-cook for years. Indicted for murder, he took refuge on the coastal Georgia island of St. Simon's, spending the hot summer days writing fond, playful letters to his daughter, Theodosia. He spoke of how much he missed her, but also alluded to mysterious intrigues, and bold plans for their future.

Aaron Burr's legacy as a founding father is both enigmatic and complex. Born on February 6, 1756, in Newark, New Jersey, Burr lost both parents by age two and was raised by his uncle Timothy Edwards, who provided his education. At 13, he was accepted into Princeton, studying theology before shifting to law. Inspired by colonial protests, he joined the Continental Army after the battles of Lexington and Concord in 1775.

Burr's military career was notable; he served under Benedict Arnold in the failed Canadian invasion of late 1775 and became a hero after General Richard Montgomery's death at the Battle of Quebec, when he attempted to retrieve the fallen General's body. He was promoted to lieutenant colonel and played key roles in the American retreat from New York and defending Valley Forge, before resigning in 1779 due to health issues.

After becoming a successful lawyer, Burr entered New York politics, serving in the State Assembly and as Attorney General. He became a senator in 1791, but his presidential aspirations in 1796 and 1800 fell short. In 1800, he tied with Thomas Jefferson in electoral votes, leading to a contentious decision by the House of Representatives, where Burr's silence raised suspicions. Some accused Burr of attempting to steal the election from Jefferson, and while Burr served four years as Vice President under the third president, he was summarily ushered out of the Republican party.[342]

Ambitious for the governorship, he faced a fierce opposition campaign led by Alexander Hamilton, culminating in the infamous

---

[342] Taylor, Joe Gray, *The Aaron Burr Conspiracy*, The West Tennessee Historical Society Papers, 1947, I, 81-90.

duel at Weehawken on July 11, 1804. Following the duel and losing the gubernatorial election in the autumn, Burr was downtrodden. Facing a political snub by many, even in his home state, he laid low for a time. In December 1804, as Congress convened, Burr emerged from hiding and seamlessly resumed his duties as Vice President of the United States, as though nothing at all had changed.

The Senate had never had a more polished and judicious presiding officer, and during this session, the trial of Supreme Court Justice Samuel Chase made the role especially significant. Even the most obdurate critic would have been hard pressed to find objections to Burr's flawless management of this trial, in which, by all accounts, the former Vice President displayed a dignified and impartial aplomb, despite Jefferson's pressure to be less even-handed. His abilities in the trial brought forth a spectator's praise for its "angelic impartiality and devilish cunning." [343]

Burr left for the West in 1805, cementing his transition from revered hero to controversial figure in American history. After President Jefferson excluded him from the 1804 ticket, Burr's political fortunes declined. Faced with the general status of a social pariah, along with the annihilation of his political career, he sought out someone he knew would understand. Who better to relate to a loss of face from a tempestuous duel than Andrew Jackson. Thus, Burr headed west, but with more than just mere visitations on his agenda.

On his first tour west of the Appalachians, the former Vice President traveled to New Orleans, stopping in Tennessee on his way back east. On May 29th, he arrived in Nashville, where Andrew Jackson and the leading men of the Cumberland held a dinner in his honor. Jackson brought Burr home afterwards, and the two men discovered some common interests, including that of horsemanship. Burr, in fact, loaned Jackson his best horseman.

Former Vice President Burr was quite popular in conservative Republican Nashville, and was quite well-received as a result, a stark contrast to his ignominy back East. Abhorred by the Federalists, who were livid over the death of their champion Hamilton just thirteen months before, the spurned Burr's home state of New York was no longer the welcoming base it had long been. But in Tennessee, Burr

---

[343] James, p. 102.

faced no such difficulties. Alexander Hamilton had been odious to western Republicans, and no one in Nashville held his death against Burr. Tennesseans certainly understood the culture of dueling. Honor was honor, and to the Republicans of the west, the fewer Federalists, the better. Burr's standing in Nashville, therefore, was secure, and in fact, throughout the frontier, particularly among Republicans, Burr's good standing had been restored.

There were several other reasons why Aaron Burr was well-received among Tennesseans. In 1796, he had stood behind the cause of Tennessee statehood, advocating for the state's admission during his time in the Senate. The people of Nashville remembered his efforts at the polls in 1800, voting wholeheartedly for the Jefferson-Burr ticket. The recently elegant and moving farewell speech given by Burr on his final day as president of the Senate, just then circulating in the newspapers, was also exceedingly admired, especially by a Tennessee public that could certainly relate to feelings of neglect from the East.

The Promethean mind of Aaron Burr was constantly active, and since his much-publicized scandal back home, he actively sought to ennoble himself among westerners. Burr knew well the frustrations of frontiersmen over the federal government's apathy towards their interests, and their exposure to attacks by outside forces. This vulnerability to intrigues by foreign enemies provided opportunities for someone as keen as Aaron Burr to be taken advantage of. The savvy Burr aimed to capitalize on these opportunities in a truly unprecedented way.[344]

Formulating a daring and almost fantastical plan, Burr set out on a true wild west adventure that could revive his dwindling fortunes in outrageous fashion. Before departing Washington, he examined the situation: the expansive territory of Louisiana, currently in conflict with England, Spain, and many of its own inhabitants; Kentucky and Tennessee, recently caught up in a secession plot. While in Washington, he had quietly confided in the British and Spanish ministers about a scheme to detach the Mississippi Valley from the Union. Recognizing the danger, however, neither representative of the European powers took

---

[344] ibid. p.102-103.

the bait. However, the ambassadors' responses could be characterized, neither the English nor the Spanish were willing to fund his ventures.[345]

Burr then engaged in discussions with a group of dissatisfied Creoles, relying on only one significant ally, Brigadier General James Wilkinson. Wilkinson, a Marylander by birth, and a former colonel in the Continental Army, had a dubious reputation, having become a key figure in the old Spanish conspiracy and ultimately a secret agent for the Spanish crown. Following the acquisition of Louisiana by the United States, Wilkinson returned to military service under President Jefferson, maintaining his standing with Spain throughout. Wilkinson was Jefferson's selection as the first governor of Louisiana and the man who'd had the dubious honor of ceremoniously raising the American flag over New Orleans, surrounded by his troops at the outset of American possession of the Crescent City.

Colonel Burr faced a dilemma regarding transparency over the failures of his recent fundraising efforts. He could not fully reveal the President's suspicions or the precarious nature of his situation. To each party, therefore, Burr offered a slightly varied interpretation of his ambitious plans, and he argued that without their intervention, westward expansion would not be possible. Essentially, Burr's plan was to recruit settlers for a tract along the Ouachita River in Louisiana, which most, except the very naive, regarded as a cover for a military invasion of Texas, a move entirely consistent with the spirit of the West. Burr aimed to assess conditions and gauge local reactions, with aspirations to establish his colony as a launching point that could ultimately lead to a potential capture of Florida as well.[346]

Sojourning down the Ohio River, Cincinnati and Louisville welcomed the famous traveler. In Frankfurt, he was hosted by United States Senator John Brown, and met many of Kentucky's most influential figures, particularly those involved in the old Spanish plot. The specifics of his intentions, however, were shrouded in ambiguity. Shrewdly, Burr tailored his narratives to match the personalities and characters of those he spoke with, perhaps revealing his own uncertainty and a willingness to adapt his plans as he went along. Though never openly admitting to

---

[345] Abernethy, *The Burr Conspiracy*, p. 28
[346] ibid.

treasonous intentions, he hinted at various enticing possibilities that appealed to many westerners, whose rich history of plotting against foreign powers and their own government were well known. Any scheme that promoted western land and trade interests was often justified, especially if it involved displacing native peoples and Spanish settlers.

Whether England supported him or not, and whether Spain was a certainty or an impossibility, depended on the immediate needs of the moment. However, Burr misread the feelings of westerners, and therefore the funding he hoped to raise did not materialize. He aimed to seize Mobile or West Florida, Texas, or even all of Mexico[347]—anything to gain favor or secure promises of men and money. The precise goals of such a flexible scheme remain unclear to this day, but the conquest of Mexico, along with the potential annexation of the lower Mississippi Valley to create an empire over which Aaron Burr would reign as king, was a vision that was more than mere fanciful imagination.

For all Burr's trickery, his grand plans proved transparent in motive. It was too clear to many who heard his pitch that this was about personal gain, for himself and the Burr name, rather than a cause more closely linked with the broader ambitions of western settlers. This marked a critical miscalculation on the part of the former Vice President. Had he crafted a vision that resonated with the prevailing sentiments of the time—similar to Andrew Jackson's later endeavors—Burr might have emerged as a celebrated hero rather than pursuing a path driven so manifestly for his own benefit.

From Kentucky, Burr sent Andrew Jackson $3,500, (the origins of this sum however unclear) commissioning him to construct and supply five riverboats. Eager and ready to assist, Jackson responded quickly, recruiting his associates and activating the mission. John Coffee initiated the riverboat task at Clover Bottom, while Patton Anderson organized a squadron of militia troops for the expedition. On October 4, 1806, Jackson prepared the Tennessee militia for military readiness, citing Spanish hostility. Jackson's message to his troops was verbatim what he had announced to his men five years before, when Jefferson had

---

[347] Ranck, James B., "Andrew Jackson and the Burr Conspiracy," *THM*, Oct. 1930, 2nd Series, I, 17-28.

requested their preparedness against any potential Spanish resistance to the American possession of Louisiana.

Amidst this flurry of activity, an unfamiliar visitor arrived at the Hermitage, a well-dressed young man who introduced himself to Jackson as Captain Fort, claiming to be traveling from New York to join Burr's efforts. He spent the night discussing the Burr project, which he indiscreetly described as a scheme "to divide the Union." In an effort to feel out the intentions of the young captain, Jackson pressed him about the specifics of this plan. Fort suggested that the strategy involved seizing New Orleans and controlling the bank, effectively halting trade and conquering Mexico to unite the western territories with the newly acquired lands. When Jackson inquired how this ambitious endeavor would unfold, Fort mentioned the involvement of federal troops led by General Wilkinson.

Jackson viewed Wilkinson with deep suspicion, aware of his contentious history and questionable loyalties. When Jackson probed Fort about the source of his information, the captain deflected, claiming to have heard it from Colonel Swartwout in New York, one of Burr's lieutenants. It became evident to Jackson that Fort had inadvertently revealed too much. The realization struck him with clarity: the treasonous plot Fort discussed aligned with the conspiracy in which he believed Burr was engaged, the very same one in which he, Jackson, could now be implicated.[348]

Without delay, an alarmed Jackson hurried to his desk and began drafting letters, warning others of the conspiracy, and its potential threat to the Union. Still not certain of his plans regarding New Orleans, he penned a letter to Burr, informing him succinctly that there would be no further association until his suspicions were thoroughly addressed. A master of equivocation, Burr deflected Jackson's concerns. Renowned for his artistic powers of persuasion, Burr combined ambiguity with plausibility better than most, and he was just wily enough to stay always a step ahead of any contradictions in his story. This left Jackson, charmed by Burr since the outset, uncertain as to exactly what he was about.

Keenly aware of the threats posed by nearby Indian tribes, their Spanish allies, and particularly the British, Jackson would have been

---

[348] AJ to George W. Campbell, January 15, 1807, Jackson, *Correspondence*, I, 168-169.

exceedingly compliant in efforts to potentially unseat the foes of the Tennessee frontier. Eager for action, this left him open to intrigues, and Burr, aware of this, had his mark. But Jackson was no fool, and he now distanced himself as best he could to avoid any accusations of treason. While publicly promoting aggression against Spain, he remained loyal to the United States above all else, refusing to engage any further in a plan that would jeopardize the bond of union. Although increasingly frustrated with Presidents Jefferson and Madison's inability to address British violations of American sovereignty, Jackson was a Unionist through and through, and treason against his country was simply not his bag.

Yet, despite his suspicions, Jackson refrained from accusing anyone outright. Until he gathered more evidence, he would seek only to protect himself. In order to stem any future accusation against his own involvement, Jackson became proactive. In a letter to President Jefferson, Jackson reaffirmed his loyalty to the administration and offered support against possible aggression on the nation's borders. This prompted a confused Jefferson to respond to the strange letter with a call for peace while acknowledging the need for military action only if provoked. Aaron Burr may have shown his cards, revealing a readiness to betray the United States for personal gain, but he and Wilkinson would have to find another crony. It would not be Andrew Jackson.

Jackson composed another lengthy letter to Daniel Smith,[349] his successor in the United States Senate, informing him of his concerns regarding Spain. His words made clear that a Spanish effort to capture New Orleans and Louisiana was being concocted, with the goal of dividing the Union. The letter did not mince words. First and foremost, Jackson informed Smith that there was discord between the U.S. government and Spain, with their minister openly at odds with the American executive. Secondly, a scheming individual was believed to be colluding with the Spanish to reclaim territory, and that Spanish forces were positioned near New Orleans under the pretext of defending their frontier, while the governor of New Orleans was organizing the militia. Lastly, at that critical moment, the commanding general, stationed in Louisiana, ordered the militia to return home.

---

[349] AJ to Daniel Smith, Nov. 12, 1806, Jackson Papers, LC.

The conspiracy, Jackson further elaborated, involved a descent from the Ohio and upper Louisiana towards New Orleans, where a significant portion of the population was believed to be in cahoots. If successful, the city would fall easily to the attackers, who would then shut the port and invite the western world to join in lucrative trade. By ceasing all communications, the conspirators aimed to keep Washington in the dark until it was too late. Jackson urged Smith to advise Jefferson to act swiftly to monitor the general and give orders for the defense of New Orleans.

Instead of waiting for the president's warning to reach New Orleans, Jackson directly wrote to Governor Claiborne, expressing fears of treachery and urging him to prepare his defenses against a possible Spanish attack. With subtlety, Jackson also recognized Governor Claiborne as a potential ally in the Burr plot aimed at subjugating Mexico. He stated his love for his country and government, expressing a willingness to see Mexico subdued but emphasizing that he would die before allowing the Union to be divided.

On November 3, 1806, the same day Jackson received orders to build flatboats, U.S. District Attorney Joseph Hamilton Daviess petitioned the federal court in Frankfort, Kentucky, to arrest Aaron Burr for treason. The presiding judge, Harry Innes, who had alleged connections to Wilkinson and Spanish plots, denied the motion but agreed to summon a grand jury to consider evidence against Burr. On November 12, as Jackson was busy writing letters, the courtroom was crowded with people eager to hear the proceedings. Burr appeared alongside his attorney, young Henry Clay, who also represented Jackson's trading house in Kentucky.

To everyone's surprise, Daviess requested the dismissal of the jury, revealing that his chief witness had fled to Indiana. The courtroom erupted in laughter at Daviess's predicament, while Burr received cheers. During this time, Burr sent a letter to Jackson, making "the most sacred pledges" that he held no hostile intentions towards the United States. Both Jackson and President Jefferson were puzzled by Burr's assurances, as Jefferson had been receiving reports about Burr's designs for months. Despite their suspicions, neither could pinpoint any concrete evidence.

Amid smoke and mirrors, Aaron Burr, always calculating, had slithered his way out of another precarious political pickle, or had he?

CHAPTER

26

CHOOSE YOUR FRIENDS WISELY

"I have accustomed myself to receive with respect the opinions of others, but always take the responsibility of deciding for myself."

-Andrew Jackson

General James Wilkinson faced a dilemma: whom should he betray for the greatest advantage— the United States, Spain, or Aaron Burr? On October 8, 1807, in Natchitoches, Louisiana, the feisty fifty-year old Marylander received a message from former Vice President Aaron Burr, which he spent the night decoding. The following morning, he made his choice, he would betray Aaron Burr. It took twelve days for Wilkinson to send a cunning letter to Jefferson, while simultaneously demanding a payment of $110,000 from Mexico City for his services. On November 26, Jefferson proclaimed the existence of a military conspiracy against Spain, warning "faithful citizens" to avoid it and ordering authorities to seize boats and apprehend the unnamed culprits. Daviess made another appeal for Burr's arrest, but once again, witnesses failed him, allowing Burr to leave the courtroom unscathed, instead attending a ball in his honor.

It was not long before confusion spread among Burr's camps in Ohio. Responding to the president's proclamation, the governor of Ohio ordered the seizure of Burr's boats at Marietta. Most adhered to the call for caution except for some thirty men led by Harmon Blennerhassett, who fled down the river. Burr reached Nashville on December 17, where the *Impartial Review* noted his arrival. General Jackson was absent during Burr's visit to the Hermitage, and Rachel received him coldly, not inviting him to stay. Burr lodged at the Clover Bottom Tavern, where Jackson paid him a stiff visit, taking John Coffee as a witness.[350]

After much vehement denial, Burr assured Jackson that his intentions had come with the blessing of the government, and presented a blank commission signed by Jefferson. Jackson's suspicions were somewhat alleviated, and he allowed Burr to take two boats, which was all he desired, and permitted Rachel's 17-year-old nephew, Stockley Hays, to board one of them to continue his education in New Orleans. However, Patton Anderson's military company remained behind, and Hays was sent with explicit instructions to carry confidential letters to Governor Claiborne.[351]

Burr and his boats departed at dawn on December 22. They had traveled too far to be intercepted when Jefferson's proclamation arrived, however. Dealing with treachery, Jackson learned, required caution. On January 3, the *Impartial Review* reported the burning of Burr's effigy, with citizens who once admired him now vocally decrying his actions. The panic spread beyond Nashville as well. In Pittsburgh, Pennsylvania, Captain Reed informed the War Department that a Tennessee army, with Andrew Jackson at the helm, was marching to join Burr. *The Richmond Inquirer* reported that while General Wilkinson was deemed to have been tampered with unsuccessfully, it lacked clarity on the identity of the militia general in Tennessee.

As frightened friends rallied around a fire in the courthouse square, Jackson moved swiftly to confront the perceived threat to the Union, and to his reputation. On New Year's night, he received a communication from Secretary of War Henry Dearborn, which he described as "a milk and water thing... the meanest old woman you ever saw." The letter was dated December 19, 1806, and in it, the Secretary of War acknowledged Jackson's suspicions, "It appears that you have some reason for suspecting that some unlawful enterprise is in contemplation on the western waters." Dearborn admonished Jackson to be prepared and do his utmost to counter these conspiracies. The letter not so subtly pointed out that back

---

[350] AJ to Campbell, Jan. 5, 1807, Jackson, *Correspondence*, I, 169.
[351] Whitaker, Arthur P., *The Mississippi Question*, p. 241

East, reports were circulating about Jackson being involved in Burr's plans. Jackson took umbrage to the Secretary's insinuations and sought to clarify his position. He acknowledged the secretary's letter, but he stressed the soldier's duty to protect the country while also defending his honor against what he perceived as unfair and unfounded accusations. The entire scandalous affair had General Jackson up in arms, and he would be heard. [352]

Believing that Secretary Dearborn wanted Burr apprehended, Jackson mobilized two brigades and called for volunteers. He dispatched Lieutenant Jack Morrell to Captain Bissell at Fort Massac on the Ohio to intercept the armed boats and request reinforcements if necessary. As the flames of panic faded, the men of Nashville soon came to the realization that supporting Jackson, rather than accusing him, might be a better way to prove their loyalty. Old General Robertson even went so far as to offer the services of Revolutionary veterans, the famed "Corps of Invincibles."

Jackson's opportunity to claim his title as protector of the Republic soon went by the wayside, however, as the military aspect of Burr's expedition had been wholly exaggerated. The Volunteers of Tennessee may well have become the stuff of legend in that moment, chasing down the fugitive Burr, but, ultimately, that proved unnecessary. Morrell returned with a report from Captain Bissell that Burr had passed down the river with boats unarmed, as it turns out. Thus, there was no reason to detain him.

Unbeknownst to Burr, tensions were mounting as Wilkinson prepared to betray his co-conspirators and undermine Burr's plans. Wilkinson sent a message to federal authorities and President Jefferson that Burr intended to entice the western states to leave the Union and join with him as he colonized new lands – with the support of England. He convinced the President that Burr alone was guilty by providing a secret letter that was written by Burr to Wilkinson. However, Wilkinson had altered the letter to clear his own name, and his ploy worked like a charm. A vindicated Jefferson alerted Congress about Burr's plan, and he ordered his arrest.[353]

---

[352] Bassett, *Jackson*, p. 52.
[353] Malone, Dumas, *Jefferson the President, Second Term*, pp. 215-371.

The crafty Aaron Burr, never one to be outsmarted, soon caught on, and he deserted his boats and slipped into hiding. As the imagined threat to the nation dissipated, Jackson turned his attention to his own defense. Despite his usual nature of writing in a stream-of-consciousness approach, full of firm decisiveness without a second thought, Jackson found himself, on this occasion, repeatedly dissatisfied with his drafts. He wrote to Secretary Dearborn, expressing that, while he had treated Burr with hospitality, he would cut his throat if proven to be a traitor. "Mr. Dearborn, Sir, Col. B received all the hospitality that a banished patriot was entitled to…But sir, when proof shews him to be a treator, I would cut his throat with as much pleasure as I would cut yours on equal testimony." [354]

After several drafts, Jackson sent the pointed letter to Dearborn, accusing him of dishonor for implying that Jackson was somehow involved in the conspiracy. He demanded accountability for the implications made against him. Likely Dearborn contemplated Jackson's loaded claim, deciphering its thinly veiled meaning, with a quizzical expression and a sweaty palm to his throat. Wisely, Dearborn remained silent and offered no defense, however, and the correspondence concluded without further comment from either side regarding Jackson's relationship with Burr.

Jackson continued his efforts to uncover the truth behind Burr's actions. He remained convinced that other officials were also entangled in this sordid web of conspiracy, particularly Wilkinson. But, for Aaton Burr, the damage was done. "Jefferson himself never doubted that Burr was a traitor. Indeed, on January 22, 1807, he had pronounced Burr guilty of treason to Congress and the entire nation—without a grand jury indictment," writes historian Kent Newmyer, in his book "The Treason Trial of Aaron Burr: Law, Politics and the Character Wars of the New Nation."[355]

"In Jefferson's morally dichotomous calculus, Burr was a danger to the republic; in Jefferson's personalized view of the presidency, it was his responsibility to eliminate the danger, even if it meant breaking the law.

---

[354] AJ to Dearborn, 1807, Jackson Papers, LC.
[355] Newmyer, Kent, *The Treason Trial of Aaron Burr: Law, Politics and the Character Wars of the New Nation*, Cambridge University Press, 2012.

Burr brought out the worst in Jefferson, and Jefferson brought out the worst in Burr," said Newmyer.[356]

Chief Justice John Marshall, a long-standing political rival of Thomas Jefferson (and interestingly, also his distant cousin), presided over Aaron Burr's treason trial as the federal judge for the U.S. Circuit Court for Virginia. During the trial, which was held in Richmond, Marshall took the unorthodox step of issuing a subpoena to President Jefferson, requiring him to provide documents that Burr had requested for his defense. However, Jefferson only submitted parts of the letters to the court and did not acknowledge the subpoena. More significantly, testimony revealed that Burr was actually 100 miles away from Blennerhassett's Island on the Ohio River, which was the site where the government alleged Burr was planning an overt act of treason.

Marshall instructed the jury to limit their analysis to the evidence regarding actions taken on Blennerhassett's Island. He referred to a previous case involving Burr, known as Ex parte Bollman, which had already narrowed the definition of what constituted an act of war against the United States. He stated, "No testimony relative to the conduct or declarations of the prisoner elsewhere, and subsequent to the transaction on Blennerhassett's Island, can be admitted; because such testimony, being in its nature merely corroborative and incompetent to prove the overt act in itself, is irrelevant until there be proof of the overt act by two witnesses. This opinion does not comprehend the proof by two witnesses that the meeting on Blennerhassett's Island was procured by the prisoner."[357] The trial had devolved into a political duel between the two prominent Virginia cousins, Jefferson and Marshall.

Andrew Jackson's role in the unfolding melodrama would soon continue. As requested by Burr's defense team, Jackson traveled to Richmond to serve as a witness. Set to testify in Burr's defense, Jackson regaled the crowd on the steps of the courthouse by railing against President Jefferson. Jackson's vitriolic language against the administration prompted Burr's defense team to opt against putting him on the stand, fearing his volatility might work against Burr's case. Having said his piece against Jefferson, Jackson headed back to Nashville, outraged by being

---

[356] ibid.
[357] Roberston, David, *Report of the Trials of Aaron Burr*, New York, 1875, I, 312.

denied the chance to expose General Wilkinson on the witness stand. Any whisper of Wilkinson's guilt was quickly dismissed by Jefferson, fueling Jackson's suspicions that something was amiss.

Frustrated and repulsed by Wilkinson's obvious culpability, and the cover-up by the Jeffersonians, he maligned both the General and the President all the way back to Tennessee, but to no avail. The vociferous denunciations reached the Jefferson administration's ears, harming Jackson's standing with the Secretary of State, James Madison. Madison would not forget Jackson's offensive words several years down the road when he would intentionally pass over Jackson in his search for generals to take on the British in 1812. Jackson was twice recommended by others to President Madison for a commission in the regular army, and Madison rejected him both times.

As for the fate of Aaron Burr, when the court was made aware of Wilkinson's evidence tampering, the jury quickly reached a verdict, acquitting Burr of all charges. "We of the jury say that Aaron Burr is not proved to be guilty under this indictment by any evidence submitted to us. We therefore find him not guilty." [358] Following the news of the verdict, it was reported that an angered Jefferson blamed John Marshall for his "mishandling" of the trial. The President sought to have the House bring impeachment charges against Marshall, but nothing came of this effort.

Despite Jackson's whistleblowing against James Wilkinson, the general would defy justice till the end. Wilkinson's treasonous activities would not be fully exposed until after his death in 1825. His conduct at the Burr trial, however, caused President Madison to court-martial the commanding American general in 1811, but the slippery Wilkinson was acquitted of any wrongdoing yet again.

The checkered political career of Aaron Burr was now over, while that of Jackson's had still barely begun. But both men dodged a potentially mortal bullet. Wisely, Burr went into a brief exile, leaving the United States to live in Europe for a time. He returned in 1812 and resumed practicing law in New York City, where he would live out his remaining years, still grappling with his past. Finally, having out-lived his rival

---

[358] Bomboy, Scott, ed. "Aaron Burr's Trial and the Constitution's Treason Clause," *National Constitution Center*, Sept. 2023.

Hamilton by 32 years, but never fully able to outrun his demons, Aaron Burr died on September 14, 1836.

Chastened and frustrated by the Jefferson-Madison team, Andrew Jackson returned home after the Burr conspiracy having learned some hard lessons. Never able to entirely escape suspicions that he had conspired with Burr to break up the Union, the damage to his reputation further deepened the scorn in the eyes of his enemies. To make matters worse for the Major General, having lost faith in Jefferson for his attacks on Aaron Burr, Jackson's antagonism was only exacerbated by the President's unwillingness to confront the British. This animosity extended to Madison as well, by association, and Jackson led a faction in Tennessee that backed James Monroe for President in 1808, but to no avail.

Nonetheless, Jackson remained committed to the belief that there was a strong need to oust the Spanish from the Southwest, and that the British, too, must be dealt with, despite whatever apathy the administration in Washington displayed. Believing now, more than ever, that any forced removal of the Spanish could not originate from the people themselves, but from the armed forces of the nation under proper direction, Major General Jackson was determined to provide that direction when the opportunity arose.

But with his visions of military heroism dashed for the moment, Jackson returned to his farm, and the management of his estate. By bearing down more closely on financial matters, he managed to enjoy a period of economic viability like never before. With Truxton bringing in as much as $20,000 worth of prize money, and siring colts that would go on to bring in further rewards, the Jacksons were finally able to gain a sense of financial security. Combining some judicious land speculations, and a series of successful cotton harvests, the Jacksons' standard of living rose to new heights. If he didn't know better, he might have been able to relax a little, having finally overcome the setbacks of the Allison debacle. But Jackson was never one to rest when it came to his finances, despite commencing a period of life as a relatively well-to-do planter.

This rising affluence came at a good time for the Jackson family as well, as it was about to grow considerably. In December of 1809, the Jacksons adopted the infant son of Rachel's brother Severn Donelson, and his wife Elizabeth Rucker Donelson. Elizabeth's pregnancy had been difficult, and she was left weak and unwell. Two baby boys, it was decided, would be too much for her to handle. The decision was made to allow Rachel the opportunity of motherhood she had long dreamt of but had been unable to produce for herself. The Jacksons named the baby Andrew Jackson, Jr. Rachel was overjoyed, as was Jackson, as their frustrations at not having a child of their own had taken a toll. Bouncing baby boy Andrew Junior would be theirs to raise on their own, and Rachel, who had longed for a sense of family, settled pleasantly into motherhood. [359]

This was not the Jacksons' first foray into the rearing of children. Donelson nieces and nephews were constantly being cared for at the Hermitage for both long and short visits, filling the halls with laughter and merriment. The Jacksons loved children, and on several occasions, the General and Rachel served as guardians for the offspring of family friends whose fathers had died. Following the death of Edward Butler in 1804, Andrew Jackson became the guardian of Butler's children. John Samuel, Andrew Jackson and Daniel Smith Donelson were the sons of Rachel's brother, Samuel Donelson, and wife, Polly Smith Donelson. Since their mother was still alive after Samuel died, the boys lived part-time at The Hermitage.

Andrew Jackson Hutchings was a grandnephew. His father, John Hutchings, was the son of Rachel's sister Catherine Donelson and Thomas Hutchings, Jackson's longtime friend and store partner. Both Thomas and Catherine died by the time young John was five in 1817. His nickname was "Little Hutchings," and he lived at The Hermitage. William Ferdinand, Mary and Micajah Claiborne were the children of Thomas and Sarah Lewis Claiborne. Sarah was a daughter of Jackson's friend William Terrell Lewis. Margaret and Jane Watkins' parents were Jacob and Sally Williams Lloyd Watkins. The family moved from Virginia to Tennessee in 1806 and were neighbors of the Jacksons. They died soon after arriving, and their six children were raised by various neighbors. Jane Hays was the daughter of Nathaniel and Elizabeth Hays, who sold the property the Hermitage sits on to Jackson in 1804. After her parents died, the Jacksons offered to care for her.

---

[359] Andrew Jackson: Family History. LOC.gov/collections.

In general, the Jacksons felt a unique bond with the children they were fortunate enough to care for, and the addition of Andrew, Jr. brought joy to the family. This was especially true for Rachel, who resented the long separations from her husband his public commitments so often caused. She had now found a measure of comfort and joyous purpose in caring for a son of her own. It filled Jackson with joy as well and harkened back to memories of growing up with his brothers in the Waxhaws, and the love his mother had provided. As Rachel embraced her role as a mother, Andrew Jackson continued to face off with his perpetual financial challenges, but the Major General continued to grow as a father, while maintaining his prominent position in the Nashville community. Cherishing family life, Jackson believed that it was the foundation of society. With Rachel, their newborn, and the Donelson kin by his side, Jackson navigated the complexities of personal and public life, attempting to balance his lofty ambitions with fulfilling responsibilities to those he loved.

While fatherhood softened Jackson's edges, he still struggled with his temper. Despite frequent episodes of intense anger, he could also display remarkable tenderness. Observers frequently noted that there were two sides to Jackson: one that was fierce and militant, and another that was compassionate and generous. A story that Thomas H. Benton told in Congress about Jackson reflects the dichotomous personality of the man who would become "Old Hickory." In 1812, Benton was a young lawyer in Nashville and a militia officer under Jackson, rode to The Hermitage one evening to find the general, "and came upon him in the twilight, sitting alone before the fire, a lamb and a child between his knees. He started a little, called a servant to remove the two innocents to another room, and explained to me how it was. The child had cried because the lamb was out in the cold and begged him to bring it in — which he had done to please the child, his adopted son."[360]

In fact, his dual nature often surprised observers, especially the speed at which he could flip from one to the other. One day, after an incident involving a careless wagon driver, who, in passing, bumped into Jackson's carriage, giving Rachel a violent lurch. Jackson's anger erupted, and he let loose a torrid of profanity and oaths that would have done the saltiest

---

[360] Benton, Thomas Hart, *Thirty Years View*, New York, 1854, I, 736.

sailor proud. The offending wagon riders were some rough individuals according to those in observance, but nonetheless, they slinked away quietly in the face of Jackson's rage. Yet, Jackson's tantrums were often revealed to be more for show than genuine rage. He became adept at using intimidation to achieve his ends, as seen when he vowed revenge against David Magness, who had killed his friend Patten Anderson.

Jackson and Patten Anderson had been close friends since Jackson bought Clover Bottom from the Anderson brothers several years before. In 1810, however, Anderson was shot to death in Shelbyville by one David Magness during a dispute over land titles. Jackson vowed that Magness must be punished severely, even though Magness had shot Anderson after witnessing him attack his father. The trial lasted two weeks and featured some of the best lawyers in the state: Felix Grundy for the defense and Thomas Hart Benton for the prosecution.

In a drunken state, Jackson rode into town and delivered a slurred, passionate (and very profane) speech in the public square, claiming that Magnus was a coward and had assassinated Anderson in cold blood. In utter disbelief, someone in the crowd exclaimed "Pshaw!" to which Jackson heard, and indignantly yelled out "Who dares to say pshaw at me?" In receiving no response, Jackson threatened "By God! I'll knock any man's head off who says pshaw at me." In response to this outburst came more silence, and quietly, the individual slinked away.

Jackson then entered the courtroom to testify against Magness, and to "remind the jury of its duty." However, his arrogant demeanor had the opposite effect of what he intended. The clever Grundy took advantage of the situation and pressed Jackson to admit that Anderson was a troublemaker. "Had not Anderson frequently been in 'difficulties'?" Grundy pointedly asked. Jackson could not deny this but recognized the lawyer's tactic. "Sir," the general replied, adopting his most irate Jacksonian demeanor, "my friend Patton Anderson was the natural enemy of scoundrels!"[361] The jury did not appreciate Jackson's arrogance, and ultimately found Magness guilty of manslaughter—a lighter verdict than expected—and sentenced him to be branded on the hand. Infuriated by

---

[361] Parton, *Jackson*, p. 340.

what he perceived as a miscarriage of justice, Jackson shook his fist under the nose of one of the jurors.[362]

At age 43, Rachel Jackson had become a rather plump woman, but she still possessed youthful grace, along with those dark, youthful eyes that had captivated Jackson upon first sight. Although she had a carriage, she preferred riding horseback, and not in the usual side-saddle manner that was expected of women. Despite Nashville's growth, Rachel held on to her old-fashioned frontier roots; this was embodied by her more traditional fashion choices, which sometimes caused some ridicule among the 'chic' ladies of Nashville. Her life was marked by years of piety, generosity, and kindness. Yet gossip about her past lingered amidst the proper ladies of Tennessee, who often whispered criticisms of Rachel Jackson, and thumbed their noses at her.

Jackson's reputation as a man who could handle men was well established, but when it came to handling attacks from women, he faced difficulties, even when it came to defending his beloved. When rumors circulated that some of the women around town had been speaking derisively about Rachel, he tasked John Hutchings' wife to investigate the situation. When Mrs. Hutchings returned with news that the rumors were proven unfounded, Jackson was at a loss. The past continued to haunt the Jacksons, and the pain that it caused Rachel was a constant source of frustration for her husband, whose ambition and rising fame often came at the cost of his domestic happiness. Determined to change his circumstances, Jackson contemplated leaving Tennessee for a quieter life elsewhere, hoping to restore peace for himself and Rachel. Jackson's nephew was sent to inspect the new Mississippi Territory, where he reported on the land and its people. The couple considered moving to Washington County, Mississippi, recalling fond memories of their honeymoon in Natchez. As fate would have it, and unbeknownst to the Jacksons, a pending war was soon on its way, which would disrupt any plans of a new life in Mississippi.

Jackson's reputation for vengeance was further illustrated when he intervened in the affairs of Silas Dinsmore, a United States agent to the Choctaw Indians. Dinsmore's actions against runaway slaves drew Jackson's ire, mainly because Dinsmore's "crimes" seemed to favor the

---

[362] ibid, 344.

slaves more than the slave owners. Jackson sought to teach the agent a lesson about his duties, and his public outcry against Dinsmore garnered support, leading to the agent's eventual removal. When Dinsmore later sought to restore a friendship with Jackson some years later, he was met with an icy and unforgiving stare from the General.[363]

But if Jackson was a terrible enemy, he was also the most faithful of friends. Men both feared and hated him; many also loved him, and Jackson would go to the same extended lengths to help a friend as he would to destroy an enemy. In social settings, Jackson's loyalty was well-known. Once, at a large outdoor banquet, he demonstrated both his willingness to come to the aid of a friend and his legendary impulsiveness. While conversing at one end of a long and crowded dinner table, Jackson heard what sounded to him like a friend being attacked on the opposite end of the table. Rather than pushing through the crowd around it, Jackson dramatically jumped on top of the table and made his way toward his friend in need. While the party came to a screeching standstill at the sight of the lanky Jackson careening across the dinner table, food, dishes, and silverware flying in every direction, the General reached into his coat pocket. The crowd's audible gasp was palpable, and several bystanders could be heard pleading with Jackson, "Don't fire! Don't fire!" Jackson, realizing that his friend was not under attack, seemed to catch himself at that moment. Realizing it was a false alarm and recognizing the many eyes gawking at him in fear, Jackson reached his hand out from his coat pocket slowly, pulling out his tobacco tin, and then quickly snapping it closed with a loud click. He then returned to his seat at the table as though nothing had happened. [364]

---

[363] Grundy to AJ, Feb. 12, 1812, Jackson Papers, LC.
[364] Parton, *Jackson*, p. 357, 358.

CHAPTER

27

THE CHESAPEAKE AFFAIR

"The affair of the Chesapeake put war into my hand. I had only to open it, and let havoc loose."
-Thomas Jefferson

When it came to foreign affairs, it took an explosive event to jolt the young nation from its complacency. Whether out of fear or reluctance to confront its old nemesis, the United States seemed unable and unwilling to deal with Europeans powers, particularly the British. That is until the summer of 1807, when fate delivered just that–an explosion. It came on June 22nd, just off the Virginia coast; a British attack in the nation's own backyard, and one that infuriated an American public sick and tired of being pushed around; a nation fed up with the humiliations at the hands of the bully across the Atlantic.

By 1807, The Napoleonic Wars had raged between Great Britain and France for over four years. A struggle of colossal proportions between Napoleon's French Republicans and British defenders of monarchy, embroiled nearly all of Europe, disrupting global trade routes and posing insurmountable obstacles for neutral nations, not least of which was the United States of America. The two warring nations sought to weaken each other by striking at the commerce of their enemy, which placed a very clear target on American ships, accompanied by a thorough disregard for the neutral shipping rights of the young nation. Heavily reliant on maritime trade, the United States found its vessels caught in the crossfire, time and again. Most infuriating was the British practice of impressment, seizing sailors off American ships in search of deserters of the Royal Navy. Outraged by this practice, concerned Americans wondered just how long it would be before the nation was drawn into the struggle.[365]

At roughly 3:30 pm on a paltry summer afternoon, amid the fervor of the highly publicized Burr trial, the broadside guns of the *HMS Leopard* unleashed chaos upon an American frigate, *the Chesapeake*. From a distance, the double-decked *Leopard* and the frigate *USS Chesapeake* had seemed the picture of serenity as they rode the gentle swells off Cape Henry on the afternoon of 22 June 1807. On the decks of the two warships, however, it was a different story. [366]

As his Royal Navy vessel patrolled off the coast of Virginia, Londoner and former tailor Jenkin Ratford, along with four other crewmen, decided to steal a boat and desert to the shores of Norfolk. Ratford later boasted about his escape to the "land of liberty" in the streets of Norfolk, which earned him the ire of British authorities, when word reached them. They vowed to make an example of the audacious Englishman, who subsequently joined the crew of the American frigate, the USS *Chesapeake*.

At 6 am on the 22nd, the *Chesapeake* set sail from Norfolk for the Mediterranean. With its decks cluttered with cargo and its guns carelessly stowed, the vessel became an appealing target for the crew of the fifty-gun HMS *Leopard*, who intercepted it off the coast of Norfolk. When the British commander requested permission to search the ship for deserters, American commodore James Barron refused to muster his crew for inspection. Moments later, the captain of the *Leopard* retaliated with a barrage of broadsides, The *Leopard*'s cannon fire ripped through her sides, crashed into the U.S. ship some 50 yards away, tearing away her rigging and sending lethal wooden splinters in all directions. resulting in the deaths of three American sailors, and wounding eighteen more. British officers then boarded the damaged *Chesapeake* and seized what they sought: a handful of suspected deserters, including Jenkin Ratford. The other three men carried off were American citizens.

This humiliating encounter enraged the American public. Had this occurred far off the coast, the attack would have still been lamented,

---

[365] Horsman, Reginald, *The Causes of the War of 1812*, Philadelphia, 1962, Ch.1-3.
366 Cooper, James Fenimore, *History of the navy of the United States of America*. Stringer & Townsend, New York. 1826, p. 226.

but that it happened off the Hampton shore, in plain sight of those on the Virginia coast, Americans were even more provoked. The coup de grâce to the affront was the nonchalant manner in which the *Leopard* then remained in American waters, brazenly anchoring at the mouth of the Chesapeake Bay, as though perched for its next target. The incident incensed Americans, as the British had clearly violated the nation's sovereignty. The men on board the *Leopard* had used force, fired upon the American flag, and destroyed American life and property. Even the staunchest pacifists could not contain their outrage in the face of such blatant disrespect. Surely President Jefferson would demand retribution; or would he? [367]

War fever swept across the United States, as news of the affair spread, prompting the Washington Intelligencer's headlines the next day, "British Outrage!" Mass indignation of the American public pressured the Republican administration in Washington into action. President Jefferson asserted, "Never since the Battle of Lexington have I seen this country in such a state of exasperation as at present, and even that did not produce such unanimity." [368] With both Republicans and Federalists demanding action, war between Britain and the U.S. seemed inevitable.

For many, particularly Andrew Jackson, the attack on the Chesapeake was an affront to American pride, and an insult to American honor. Long exasperated by Jefferson's inaction to British injuries, and the government's general malaise regarding British impressment, Jackson expressed his outrage in a letter to a Virginia friend, "The degradation offered to our government ... has roused every feeling of the American heart, and war with that nation is inevitable." To Jackson, the attack by the HMS *Leopard* warranted, no, it demanded, a military response. However, while Jackson stewed, America waited, and the losses at sea mounted. Despite the outrage, there seemed to be little likelihood of the Jefferson-Madison tandem answering the demand for war. Nor

---

[367] Perkins, Bradford (1974) [1968]. Levy, Leonard (ed.). *Embargo: Alternative to War, Chapter 8: Prologue to War: England and the United States, 1805–1812* (Essays on the Early Republic 1789–1815 ed.). Dryden Press. p. 315

[368] Jefferson, Thomas (July 14, 1807). "From Thomas Jefferson to Pierre Samuel Du Pont de Nemours, 14 July 1807". *founders.archives.gov*. US National Archives. Retrieved September 1, 2020.

were there any signs that the British planned to change their policy of impressment.[369]

In truth, there was little President Jefferson could do militarily to respond to the British incident, and he knew it. America's small navy, already deployed in the Mediterranean addressing the Barbary pirates, would be no match for the powerful Royal Navy, hardened by years of war against Napoleon's fleet. The army had been significantly reduced by Republicans eager to cut government spending. As Jefferson waited for war fever to subside, he opted for economic coercion as an alternative to military action. The President endorsed an embargo on foreign trade, in the hopes that by denying British access to American goods, the economic pressure would entice Parliament to respect American neutrality.

After much debate, the Tenth Congress approved the Embargo Act in December, and American ships were sidelined, and ports were shut down.[370] As Jefferson assured the American people, "To the Senate & House of Representatives of the United States: The communications now made, shewing the great & increasing dangers with which our vessels, our seamen and merchandize are threatened, on the high seas & elsewhere, from the belligerent powers of Europe, and it being of the greatest importance to keep in safety these essential resources, I deem it my duty to recommend the subject to the consideration of Congress, who will doubtless perceive all the advantage which may be expected from an inhibition of the departure of our vessels from the ports of the United States. Their wisdom will also see the necessity of making every preparation for whatever events may grow out of the present crisis."[371]

Despite what Jefferson had hoped, the effects of the Embargo Act were almost entirely negative for the United States. Although the embargo was successful in preventing war, it was especially devastating to the economy of New England. There, American merchants and farmers suffered; their goods sat unsold, crops rotted in warehouses. While the American economy faced stagnation, the Act had very little

---

[369] Kilmeade, Brian and Yeager, Don, Excerpted from *Andrew Jackson and the Miracle of New Orleans*, Sentinel, an imprint of Penguin Publishing Group, Penguin Random House LLC. 2017.

[370] Acts of the Tenth Congress, Statute 451, Dec. 22, 1807.

[371] Thomas Jefferson Address to Congress, Dec. 17, 1807, RG 46—Records of the U.S. Senate.

effect on the British. British trade did not suffer to the extent the framers of the embargo had intended. There was an initial effect on the price of goods in Britain, but the Britons quickly adapted to the altered prices. Lacking access to American trade, the British simply found goods in other markets, and other ways to meet their needs, supplementing their decreased North American trade with South American commerce. Items that could not be replaced via other trading partners were not goods that were vital to the survival of the country. The other country in question, France, seemed to welcome the American embargo because it supported Napoleon's Continental System.

In the meantime, the Embargo-fueled depression exacerbated tensions in New England, as well as other parts of the country. Economic opportunity waned; Americans were thrown out of work, and widespread protests threatened to turn violent. Warnings were sent to Washington that New England was prepared to resist the Act with arms. "Where is the Yankee," asked the Newburyport Herald, "who could bear to be abused and ridiculed by Virginian boys?" Laws passed by slave-owning southerners were not to be tolerated, and if New England protests went unheard "a spirit, daring and uncontrollable, will burst out in a just and powerful resentment" Behind these threats lay the ominous specter of a shattered Union.[372]

The Embargo Act's negative consequences forced President Jefferson and Congress to consider a repeal of the measure. But Jefferson was nearly out of office, coming to the end of his second term by early 1809. Just days before the diminutive James Madison was to be sworn in as the new commander in chief, Congress chose to repeal the Embargo Act after nearly two years. New Englanders everywhere breathed a sigh of relief, as the hated embargo was lifted, at least partially. Congress voted to replace it with the Nonintercourse Act, which allowed commerce to resume with all foreign nations, with the significant exception of Britain and France. A caveat was also added as an enticement to the warring powers: the ban on trade would be lifted with whichever power began respecting American shipping rights.

His replacement and closest fellow Virginia associate, the brilliant but indecisive James Madison, was inaugurated on March 4th. Madison,

---

[372] Benjamin W. Labaree, *Patriots and Partisans: The Merchants of Newburyport, 1764–1815*, Cambridge, Mass., 1962, p. 166.

looking wan but dapper in a woolen blue suit entirely American-made, took stock of the national crisis. Not only was the American economy suffering, but American morale was also at an all-time low. Moreover, goods continued to reach Great Britain through illegal shipments and smuggling. Speaking softly at first (with an obvious tremble) but gaining momentum in front of the packed Senate chamber as he spoke, the new president stressed the country's desire for peace and positive relations with all foreign nations, especially with belligerents. In honor of his predecessor, he emphasized his wish to see the nation remain a neutral country, as Americans progressed and built their nation. The new president spoke clearly on one point, the U.S. had one too many bloody and wasteful wars. "It has been the true glory of the United States to cultivate peace by observing justice."[373]

These were nice words, but not the words angry Americans wanted to hear. Peaceful attempts to resolve issues with the British had ended in near economic ruin, and the nation stood on the precipice of disunion. Madison would have to act, and act quickly before the crisis grew worse. But the new President faced difficult questions. What was the best course of action? The embargo had failed, just as the earlier Non-Importation Act had, passed by Congress in 1806, which forbade imports on certain British goods. In a coercive effort to coax the British to end impressment, attempts to respond economically, instead of militarily, remained ineffective. The Napoleonic Wars still raged on, and the powers of Europe continued in their steadfast determination to harass American trade at any cost, if it would help the cause, or harm that of the enemy.

The Non-Intercourse Act of 1809, along with the subsequent Macon's Bill No. 2, as it was known, passed just over a year later, and these were steps in the right direction, but it did not do enough to resolve the economic crisis that had beset the nation. In the meantime, relations with the British continued to deteriorate. Under the authority of the British Orders in Council, decreed in 1807, the British Royal Navy seized some 400 American merchant ships and their cargoes between 1807 and 1812. Press gangs, in efforts to target British subjects for naval service, swept up American sailors by the thousands by 1812, pressing them into the crews

---

[373] *"The First Inaugural Address of President James Madison"*. The University of Oklahoma College of Law. Archived from the original on 21 October 2016. Retrieved 11 November 2016.

of British ships. In fact, British ship captains, facing the ever-expanding Anglo-French war, had been given strict orders to supplement their crews by whatever means necessary. Some of the impressed sailors were born in British possessions but had migrated to the United States, while many others had attained citizenship that was either in question or simply could not be documented. Some were simply mistaken for British sailors despite having never stepped foot on British soil.[374]

Despite both legislative and diplomatic attempts to resolve the crisis during Madison's first term, many of the kidnapped sailors were either held on British ships against their will or were languishing in Dartmoor prison on the English coast, half-starved and homesick. American families of the kidnapped sons, brothers and husbands appealed to federal authorities, but to no avail. The British government ignored diplomatic efforts to aid the impressed, and as long as the French man-of-wars continued to roam the waters of the Atlantic and the Mediterranean, the Crown displayed no signs that his majesty's fleet would alter its policies regarding American shipping. In fact, out of desperate need for manpower, the British crown authorized the recruitment of press gangs from some of the poorest city streets in the kingdom, sweeping clean the idle "dregs" of British society to fill the ranks. As Winston Churchill later wrote a century later, British naval life could be described as "Rum, buggery and lash."[375]

Efforts to placate the British led to further losses in the American West, where British agents stirred up tensions among Native American tribes. The Five Civilized Tribes—Cherokee, Chickasaw, Choctaw, Creek, and Seminole—had maintained peace with European settlers, but increasing white settlement led to rising tensions and conflicts. Fear pervaded daily life for frontier families, as horror stories circulated of settlements coming under attack. How long would the federal government remain idle and allow the loss of American security? Would the repeated insults to American honor go unpunished? The questions remained for those on the American frontier. [376]

---

[374] Holmberg, Tom. "The Acts, Orders in Council, &c. of Great Britain (on Trade)," 1793–1812", *The Napoleon Series Archive, 2003*.

[375] Churchill, Winston, *A History of the English-Speaking Peoples*, Book IX, Volume III, *The Age of Revolution*.

[376] H.W. Brands, 2005. Part 1.

CHAPTER

28

WAR!

"Of all the enemies to public liberty war, is, perhaps, the most to be dreaded because it comprises and develops the germ of every other."
—*James Madison*

Finally, the time had come. In June of 1812, the United States of America declared war. In response to the repeated grievances that had undermined American sovereignty and wreaked havoc on the nation's economy, Congress approved the first official declaration of war in the nation's history. Passed on June 18th, after months of heated debate in the halls of Congress, the United States was going to war against their mother country for a second time. "Mr. Madison's War," as the anti-war Federalists derided it, passed in a close Senate vote of 19 to 13.[377] Cries of restoring America's honor won the day in the House as well, led by a group of young and boisterous new Congressmen known as War Hawks. At the head of this brash new generation, largely fronted by members of the Democratic-Republican Party, were the likes of Henry Clay, John C. Calhoun, and Jackson's Tennessee associate Felix Grundy. Truculent and hungry, fed up with British arrogance, and insults to American prestige, the War Hawks had pressured Madison to address the crisis head on.[378]

---

[377] *Connecticut Mirror*, June 22, 1812, USS Constitution Museum Collection.
[378] McNamara, Robert. "War Hawks and the War of 1812 Explained". *ThoughtCo*. Retrieved 9 January 2024.

With their constituencies largely from the South and West, the bellicose War Hawk faction overpowered the heavy resistance of New Englanders. To the Federalist dominated northeast, with its reliance on shipping and trade, a war against the world's premiere economy would spell further devastation to the region's already battered commercial interests. But the War Hawks would have their way, and fellow Republican Madison, despite his reservations, could hold them off no longer. Federalist outrage notwithstanding, the United States of America had its first declaration of war against a foreign power, and a crucial moment now arrived for the young nation at a crossroads. Just 29 years following the Treaty of Paris, which officially concluded the Revolutionary War, the United States found itself once again in confrontation with the leading military and economic power in the world, the empire of Great Britain, upon which the sun never set.

Yes, it had been nearly thirty years since the colonists' improbable victory in the Revolutionary War, yet the British had continued to disregard American sovereignty throughout. Under President James Madison's leadership, the wounded pride of the nation had finally become too much, and Americans reached its breaking point. Showing restraint as long as he could, Madison's frustration with the prolonged crisis led him to address Congress gravely on June 1st, 1812. "Such is the spectacle of injuries and indignities which have been heaped on our country, and such the crisis which its unexampled forbearance and conciliatory efforts have not been able to avert." Determined to send a message to England and the world, Madison urged Congress to declare war, articulating four significant grievances that underscored the necessity for such action. The first of these indignities was the infuriating practice of impressment, akin to slavery in the minds of many outraged Americans. The second highlighted the issue of illegal blockades that hindered American trade and maritime rights. Thirdly, the British Orders in Council, which restricted American commerce, were cited as a direct affront to U.S. sovereignty. Lastly, Madison pointed to British complicity in exacerbating conflicts with Native American tribes in the northwest, reigniting hostilities that threatened American frontier security, made life increasingly difficult for America's second-generation citizens, particularly those pushing westward.[379]

Amidst these pressing concerns, the President contended that a de facto state of war had already been established. Overlooking these grievances, Madison argued, would not only betray the nation's principles but also implicitly endorse British actions that undermined the sovereignty of the United States, as well as destroy American prestige abroad. Having forced a cessation of attacks from the pirates off the North African coast, for the time being, the successful culmination of the Barbary Wars had added marginal credibility to America's image militarily, but it was tentative at best. This critical juncture in American governance, Madison contended, reflected the urgent need to assert national rights and confront the challenges posed by British aggression.

Anxious to prove to their fathers, uncles and grandfathers, Revolutionary War veterans who'd long boasted of victory over British authority thirty years earlier, and critical of this new generation's "spinelessness," the majority of Congressmen agreed with Madison. Eager to display American might, the War Hawks argued that an invasion of Canada would serve as rightful payback for British arrogance and insults. A takeover of Canada would add the great St. Lawrence River valley to the nation, and the combination of that important waterway with the Great Lakes held the potential for unimagined economic opportunity for the nation. "I should not with to extend the boundary of the United States by war," Representative Richard M. Johnson of Kentucky said, "if Great Britain would leave us the quiet enjoyment of independence; but considering her deadly and implacable enmity, and her continued hostilities, I shall never die contented until I see her expelled from North America, and her territories incorporated with the United States."[380] Excited for the opportunity to turn the tide of the nation's psyche, many Americans would refer to the renewed conflict as the "Second War of Independence."

Though reluctant to jeopardize the new nation's liberty, Madison was determined to send a message to England and the world: the United States would not tolerate bullying. The pressing question, though, was

---

[379] June 1, 1812: Special Message to Congress on the Foreign Policy Crisis -- War Message | Miller Center". *millercenter.org*. 20 October 2016. Retrieved 9 January 2024.
[380] Quoted in Dangerfield, George, *The Era of Good Feelings* (New York, 1952), p.39.

whether America could actually win the conflict. Less than 30 years after the last war, with virtually no national army, and a minuscule navy, could Americans defend themselves against Britain, this time without France's assistance? Madison was not certain, and his reluctance prior to his address had reflected this uncertainty. After counsel from his cabinet, however, he gambled that the British, with their hands full battling Napoleon in Europe, would be hard-pressed to focus on the conflict in North America. Would King George III and Parliament be able to manage two costly wars simultaneously? The world was about to find out.

Despite the War Hawks' enthusiasm, many Americans opposed a war against the British outright. Not only did such opposition pose a lethal threat to national unity, but it would hamper the effectiveness of the campaign. The Federalist Party, primarily representing northern interests reliant on British trade, unanimously opposed the declaration. While even moderate New Englanders favored peace with Britain, some took a more extreme position, even threatening to leave the Union altogether, in order to avoid a war. When it came time to muster soldiers along the Canadian border, many New Englanders refused the call. Editors expressed their outrage. A newspaper from New Bedford mourned the "awful calamity." A headline from the Portsmouth, New Hampshire Oracle proclaimed, "THE DIE IS CAST." The editorial decried that the "Horrid WAR" caused every local citizen to rush "from his house, as if it was on fire," and gather "with his neighbor at the corners of some street, trying to derive comfort from his friends — the trembling lips, the broken voice and the faltering tongue, give answer to eager enquirers, 'THERE IS WAR'." [381] In Boston, a Federalist-leaning newspaper expressed: "The overwhelming calamity — so much dreaded by many — so little expected by the community at large — but so long considered inevitable by a few — has befallen OUR COUNTRY."[382]

Belligerent Democratic-Republicans lambasted the anti-war Federalists as unpatriotic and cowardly. Yet, even to many even outside of New England, a war against the British was unnecessary and foolhardy. Favoring the continuance of diplomacy as the rightful solution, many

---

[381] Ellis, James H., *A Ruinous and Unhappy War: New England and the War of 1812*, 1932, Algora. Publishing. P. 16

[382] ibid, 17.

shuddered at the thought of a new generation of young men sent to the slaughter in the face of superior British weaponry.

But for most westerners, the Declaration of War was well overdue. Driven by a desire to overcome the seemingly endless period of inactivity that had left many feeling disgraced and exasperated, the declaration of war brought particular joy to the people of West Tennessee. Spain's close alliance with England suggested that she would likely be drawn into the conflict, and such an involvement offered the long-awaited opportunity to seek retribution for numerous grievances against the Spanish on the frontier. While more northerly War Hawks spoke of seizing Canada, to westerners like Jackson, the rallying cry was Florida, with its tropical climate and sandy beaches. Defeating Spain and ousting them from the Southwestern frontier once and for all would be a dream come true.

However, westerners would be dismayed in these hopes. Congress proved cautious about involving Spain in the war. Engaging in an invasion of Spanish territories would have strained the nation's already thin military capacities, so the argument went. At the same time, King Ferdinand of Spain was unwilling to jeopardize his control over Florida by entering a conflict that would provide him with little to no military support. During the period leading up to 1812, preoccupied with its own internal challenges and conflicts, the Spanish Empire was in the midst of significant political instability. This was particularly due to the six-year Peninsular War that began in 1808, where Spain was embroiled in a struggle against Napoleonic France. This conflict consumed much of Spain's military resources and attention, leaving little capacity or interest in engaging in a war across the Atlantic.

But for Jackson and the Tennessee militia, long held in reserve, the thought of being unleashed at long last brought jubilance. On February 6, 1812, anticipating conflict, Congress authorized the enlistment of fifty thousand volunteers. This news ignited enthusiasm among the people of Tennessee, who had petitioned for military action in town meetings and through the legislature. On March 7th, Jackson issued a passionate call for volunteers to his division. In fiery prose, he urged his fellow citizens to prove their commitment to the cause they had long demanded by stepping forward to serve. The response exceeded his expectations; on June 25th, just a week after Congress declared war, he offered the President twenty-five hundred volunteers.

But the administration was not keen on promoting Andrew Jackson to the field. So, Jackson was forced to sit on his hands. Not until the fall of 1812 was Governor Willie Blount asked to provide volunteers to support General James Wilkinson in a newly-proposed defense of New Orleans. Although the administration saw the importance of protecting the country against a possible invasion of the south, Madison also hoped to assemble a force to seize east Florida. Since the administration had not ordered Blount specifically to exclude Jackson, the governor felt authorized to appoint the most qualified commander, and he chose Jackson without much hesitation, filling his name in one of the seventy blank commissions that Washington had forwarded. This was an important decision as it meant that Jackson was not a Major-General of United States volunteers, not just those of Tennessee. [383]

Taking stock of the situation for the people of the Southwest, Major General Andrew Jackson assessed the threats his militia faced. The British presence was minimal on the southwestern frontier, despite their influence in the Great Lakes region. The Spanish, despite the conspiracies, intrigues and subtle subversion efforts against their American neighbors, were not committed to war. Jackson accurately viewed a growing confederacy of Native American tribes, therefore, as the primary threat to American security in the western lands. The situation had escalated with a major Shawnee uprising in 1811, leading to reports of British support for Native American raids against American settlers. Jackson, disturbed by an attack not far from Nashville, suspected British involvement. Evidence of British collusion was provided in the hands of many of the perpetrators, who held British carbines during the assault that had left many frontier families dead.

Two years prior to the outbreak of war, Native Americans in the West sought to form a strategic coalition to defend themselves against encroaching American settlers. While the British offered guidance for such an effort, Northwestern tribes, marginalized and decimated, needed no such persuasion. The movement was intrinsic and led by the charismatic fifty-three-year-old Shawnee chief and warrior, Tecumseh, and his magnetic younger brother, Tenskwatawa, better known as "The Prophet." The two fierce, beguiling brothers sought to achieve what the indigenous

---

[383] Eustis to Blount, Oct. 21, 1812, Jackson, *Correspondence*, I, 240, note 5.

peoples of North America had long struggled to do: unite the tribes of both the northwestern and southwestern regions into a powerful confederacy. [384]

The threat of a united front among Native American tribes, led by a powerful and inspiring leader such as Tecumseh, caused alarm all along the frontier. So much so that it prompted the Indiana and Kentucky militia, led by Indiana governor William Henry Harrison, to act swiftly. Rather than waiting to be attacked, Harrison took the fight to the northwestern tribes in 1810, marching up the Wabash River. Setting up camp near Tecumseh's settlement. While Tecumseh was away recruiting Southern tribes such as the Creeks into his confederacy, the Prophet mistakenly attacked Harrison's camp. Harrison's larger force repelled the attack and forced a Shawnee retreat. Burning the village to the ground, Harrison's forces inflicted a resounding defeat at what became known as the Battle of Tippecanoe. The Prophet Tenskwatawa was so decisively defeated that it caused many of his supporters to abandon him. Having lost his prestige, and his followers dispersed, he fled to Canada and ceased to be a factor in Tecumseh's plans.[385]

The success of Harrison's troops captured the attention of many in Tennessee, including Major General Jackson. When reports indicated that Harrison faced challenges, Jackson offered the assistance of five hundred West Tennessee volunteers. Unfortunately for the Volunteers eager for action, fate had other designs. The spirit of war remained strong in the West and continued to gather strength. The call for action was evident in Congress, with western representatives taking the initiative to actively organize military action. Even before hostilities were officially sanctioned, Jackson had sensed that conflict was on the horizon. Six months prior, he began actively seeking every possible avenue to secure leadership in a campaign for his loyal militiamen. He wrote to Governor Willie Blount, promising the mobilization of four thousand men with just ten days' notice, promising to reach Quebec with two thousand five hundred troops within ninety days. The governor took Jackson's claims seriously and relayed the information to the Secretary of War John Armstrong, vouching for Jackson:

---

[384] Coles, Harry, *The War of 1812*, Chicago, 1965, p. 192.
[385] ibid.

"He loves his country, and his countrymen have full confidence in him. He delights in peace but does not fear war. He finds a unique satisfaction in confronting his enemies; for him, the greatest joy is to meet them on the battlefield. During this critical time, he feels a profound commitment to the welfare of the United States, and at no point in his life has he felt differently. His understanding and integrity can be trusted. He possesses an independent and generous spirit, and his habits and manners are open and welcoming. He should be in command of his volunteers."[386]

Perhaps Armstrong can be forgiven for sensing some embellishments in Blount's description of Jackson's "open and welcoming manners," for he, like Madison, remained reticent to place trust in the hands of Andrew Jackson, whom the administration perceived as a potentially volatile loose cannon. Despite frustrations among westerners, Jackson especially, their influence in Washington was limited at best. The main decision-makers hailed mostly from Virginia, or New England, and they showed little sympathy for their western counterparts, whose lifestyle and habits were often the butt of the joke. The dangers faced by families on the frontier were foreign to most eastern politicians, who faced no such threats. Dismissing calls for retaliation, and ignoring western pleas for assistance, eastern politicians showed ambivalence, if not outright apathy to the interests of the frontier.

However, as the nation's population grew, political dynamics began to shift. With the rise of the militant War Hawks, the West gained a much more vocal and dynamic representation in Congress, particularly that of the talented Kentuckian Henry Clay. Clay and his ilk did all they could to rouse Congress out of its passivity regarding England. Viewing British attitudes as a threat to American liberty, and recognizing the need for westward expansion, the War Hawks exerted pressure on the Madison administration. Pointing to Canada, which they insisted should be in American hands, Clay led the charge with fiery speeches in Congress, extolling the remaining presence of the British in Northwestern forts that they had long ago been required to vacate.

The declaration of war thrilled the War Hawks and Jackson alike. Jackson, who had long harbored a festering hatred of the British and a

---

[386] Blount to Armstrong, 1813, Blount Papers, LC.

desire for revenge, was eager to defend his nation's honor. In memorial to his fallen family members so many years ago and having adopted America as his family with the death of his mother and brothers, Jackson had for years dreamt of the opportunity for redemption. Having stood at the ready since his election as major general of the militia in 1802, he had prepared his men for pending action on three previous occasions but had been forced to stand down with each false alarm. This time it would be different. Jackson's forceful leadership style resonated in the hearts of his men, who trained with added vigor. The Tennessee Volunteers appreciated their commander's unbridled, outspoken nature and his steadfast commitment to their rights. Motivated and loyal to their leader, they had reelected him time and again as Major General. As rumors of war grew, Jackson prepared to rally westerners in defense of American liberty.[387]

In a call to action, Jackson urged citizens to recognize their identity as free-born sons of America, rejecting foreign oppression. He understood the critical importance of securing New Orleans as a strategic point for victory in the West. He stressed that the defense of the lower Mississippi and the city of New Orleans was a natural obligation for all Tennesseans. Reminding his men of the importance of the Crescent City as the vital gateway for the nation, without it, Jackson urged, the economic lifelines of western farmers and merchants would be lost. The British questioned America's ownership of the Louisiana Territory in general, and they 'licked their chops' at the potential opportunity to disrupt American expansion at this seemingly vulnerable location. Jackson's awareness of this position, as he reminded his troops, made defending New Orleans imperative. Any British victory there would give the enemy command of the Mississippi, significantly hindering the American experiment.

With war declared, however, difficult questions loomed in Washington. Differences of opinion on strategy and leadership carried the day. The nation stood at a pivotal moment, poised on the brink of ruinous defeat, or a glorious victory that would define a generation, and place the young nation firmly at the head of a new world order. Would Republicanism survive, or would monarchy crush the American dream once and for all?

---

[387] Parton, *Jackson*, p. 388.

Andrew Jackson in 1812   *James Madison*   *Tecumseh*

After four years of commercial warfare and economic depression for American merchants, and no shift in British policy, Madison seeks a declaration of war. Source: https://www.loc.gov/static/collections/james-madison-papers/images/john-bull.jpg

CHAPTER

29

THE WAR COMES SOUTH

"So live your life that the fear of death can never enter your heart. Trouble no one about their religion; respect others in their view, and demand that they respect yours. Love your life, perfect your life, beautify all things in your life. Seek to make your life long and its purpose in the service of your people."

—*Tecumseh*

His real name was Tekoomsē, which translates to "Shooting Star" or "Panther Across the Sky" in the Shawnee language. Tecumseh was born in a Native American village near what is now Xenia, Ohio. His father was tragically killed by white settlers in 1774, when the young boy was just six years old. When Tecumseh was just seven years old, his mother, a member of the Muskogee (Creek Confederacy), left him to travel with part of her tribe to Missouri, and her fate became unknown. Left without his parents, he was raised by his older sister, Tecumapease, who taught him the strict Shawnee values of honesty. His older brother, Cheeseekau, taught him the essential skills of hunting and woodcraft. Tecumseh was soon adopted by the Shawnee chief Blackfish, where he grew up alongside several white foster brothers who had been captured by the tribe.[388]

---

[388] Horsman, Reginald, *British Indian Policy in the Northwest*, 1807-1812, *MVHR*, April, 1958, XLV, 51-67.

As Tecumseh grew older, the violence and invasion of Shawnee lands deepened his hatred for whites, a loathing instilled in him by his mother. When he was about 14, during the American Revolution, he joined Blackfish in attacks against American settlers on the frontier. However, Tecumseh also had a moderating compassion, and he recognized the cruelty in some of his fellow Shawnees. After witnessing an appalling act of torture during a raid, he spoke out passionately against such brutality, realizing that his words could be just as powerful as his weapons.[389]

After the war, Tecumseh spent several years fighting small skirmishes against whites and aiding the Cherokee in the South. After the death of his brother Cheeseekau during a failed raid near Nashville in 1792, he fell into a dark depression. Yet, he struggled on and was soon recognized as a standout among his peers. Despite being the youngest of his group, Tecumseh was chosen as their leader, and through his force of personality, he was soon building alliances with tribes like the Creeks. When Shawnee chief Bluejacket called for a united front against U.S. forces led by Major General Anthony Wayne, Tecumseh returned to Ohio. He directed an unsuccessful attack on Fort Recovery in June 1794 and witnessed another brother, Sauwaseekau, killed at the Battle of Fallen Timbers.[390]

At a gathering of Old Northwest chiefs called by Wayne in Greenville, Ohio, Tecumseh chose to remain distant. When the Treaty of Greenville was signed in August 1795, he refused to recognize it, criticizing the "peace" chiefs for giving away land that he believed belonged to all Native Americans. He argued that land was a shared resource, similar to air and water, which later became a central part of his beliefs.

Thanks to his exceptional oratory skills, which were compared to those of rising political figures like Henry Clay, Tecumseh emerged as a spokesperson for Native Americans in councils held in Ohio in 1799 and 1804. During this time, he studied treaties and sought peaceful solutions in Ohio and Indiana. Around 1808, Tecumseh and the Prophet settled in present-day Indiana due to Tenskwatawa's spiritual claims. Together, they encourage fellow First Nations to reject white customs and unite

---

[389] Sugden, John, *Tecumseh: A Life*. New York: Henry Holt and Company. 1997. P. 167.
[390] Sugden, pp. 87-90.

against encroachment. The Prophet's ideas resonated with many, leading to a surge of followers.

With relentless energy, Tecumseh worked to create an Indian confederation to resist white expansion. He traveled extensively, from the Ozarks to New York and from Iowa to Florida, gaining support, especially among the Creek tribes. The influx of settlers had devastated the Indian economy, leading to a desperate need for unity. After the devastation of the Battle of Tippecanoe, Tecumseh assembled his followers and joined the British forces at Fort Malden on the Canadian side of the River. As tensions mounted, Tecumseh rallied his followers, assembling one of the most powerful Native American forces, playing a crucial role in the capture of Detroit and the defeat of 2,500 U.S. soldiers in 1812.

Fired with the promise of triumph after the fall of Detroit, Tecumseh departed on another long journey, this time heading south in an effort to arouse the tribes of the Southwest. Speaking to a council of chiefs, Tecumseh spoke with emotion. "Brothers — My people wish for peace; the red men all wish for peace; but where the white people are, there is no peace for them, except it be on the bosom of our mother. Where today are the Pequod? Where are the Narragansett, the Mohican, the Pokanoket, and many other once powerful tribes of our people? They have vanished before the avarice and the oppression of the White Man, as snow before a summer sun. Will we let ourselves be destroyed in our turn without a struggle, give up our homes, our country bequeathed to us by the Great Spirit, the graves of our dead and everything that is dear to us? I know you will cry with me, Never! NEVER!"[391] Although moved by Tecumseh's words, the Chickasaws and Cherokees rejected his call, but a band of Alabama Creeks rose in rebellion in response to "The Prophet's" inspired oratory. The marauding band, driven by promises of land, attacked a settlement along the mouth of the Duck River in the spring of 1812. The violent raid left six settlers dead. The Creeks took a woman hostage as well, all just a hundred miles from Jackson's home.

Tecumseh returned north to collaborate with British General Henry A. Procter in an invasion of Ohio. Together, they besieged Fort Meigs, but their plans were thwarted by Oliver Hazard Perry's victory in the

---

[391] Tecumseh's Speech to the Osages, Winter 1811-12. *History Is a Weapon.*

Battle of Lake Erie, leading to their retreat. At the Thames River in southern Ontario on October 5, 1813, Tecumseh fought bravely but was ultimately killed in the battle. His body was buried in secret, and the exact circumstances of his death remain unclear.[392] Procter abandoned Tecumseh at the Battle of the Thames against his old enemy, Harrison. His death dashed any hopes of reviving his movement against further white settlement in the area. Tecumseh's passing marked the end of organized Native American resistance in the Ohio River Valley and much of the Midwest and South, leading to the forced relocation of tribes beyond the Mississippi River. But Tecumseh's memory and message lived on, and his words resonated with indigenous peoples through the ages. "When your time comes to die, be not like those whose hearts are filled with the fear of death, so that when their time comes they weep and pray for a little more time to live their lives over again in a different way. Sing your death song and die like a hero going home."[393]

Meanwhile, Major General Andrew Jackson ramped up his efforts to ignite an inspired cause among the people on the Tennessee frontier. "Citizens!" Jackson wrote in a broadside. "Your government has at last yielded to the impulse of a nation.... Are we the titled slaves of George the Third? The military conscripts of Napoleon the great? Or the frozen peasants of the Russian czar? No—we are the free-born sons of America; the citizens of the only republic now existing in the world." [394]

Having lived along the southwestern frontier for more than two decades, Jackson understood the importance of defending the lower Mississippi, and particularly the city of New Orleans. The British still questioned the legitimacy of American ownership of Louisiana, which many in Europe believed remained rightfully a possession of Spain. Aware of previous Spanish intrigues to retain their hold on the Mississippi altogether, Jackson feared that this sort of thinking could well provide the British with the motivation to capture New Orleans. Such an outcome would be the ideal way to disrupt American expansion westward, perhaps permanently, and it was an outcome that motivated Jackson and his men to resist.

---

[392] Swaminathan, Nikhil, "Lost Tombs," *Archaeology Magazine*, July/August, 2013.
[393] Eckert, Allan, *A Sorrow in Our Heart: The Life of Tecumseh*, 1993, p.528.
[394] Jackson, Andrew, March 7, 1812, Jackson Papers, LC.

Both Jackson and Governor Willie Blount recognized the threat of the Creeks that Tecumseh had rallied onto the warpath. Jackson and Blount kept close counsel, and Jackson communicated to the governor that he was prepared to defend the state. "The safety of our whole frontier requires, a speedy stroke against the Creeks, and with or without orders ... I shall penetrate the Creek Towns, untill the Captive, with her Captors are delivered up, and think myself Justifiable, in laying waste their villiages, burning their houses, killing their warriors and leading into Captivity their wives and children, untill I do obtain a surrender of the Captive, and the Captors." [395]

But Jackson's 2,500 volunteers would have to wait. Despite his offers to Washington, no orders arrived throughout the entire summer and much of the fall. Jackson bided his time at home with Rachel but was soon beside himself. Frustrated by the "old grannies" in the War Department, Jackson was given no orders, receiving only a polite but perfunctory response from the President, who accepted Jackson's offer, but sent no marching orders of any kind. Jackson was dismayed and confused but soon became convinced of the reason for Madison's brush-off: his association with Burr five years earlier, along with his lack of support for Madison as President. Madison had not forgotten the disloyalty he perceived from Jackson, who was now paying the price by not being favored with an active command. Troops were being sent into Quebec, including two regiments of Jackson's men, but they were to be led by Henry Dearborn, and Brigadier-General James Winchester, not Jackson.

Meanwhile the campaign to wrest Canada away from the British was off to a disastrous start. In early 1812, the territorial governor of Michigan, William Hull, ventured to Washington. His purpose was to lobby the Madison administration for command of the expected American invasion of Canada. Having distinguished himself in a number of Revolutionary War battles, many saw Hull as a natural choice. Unlike the "disloyal" Jackson, Hull's offer was accepted. But it would prove to be an egregious choice. The strategy for invading Canada centered on capturing the vital city of Montreal. Yet, Hull instead proposed an invasion from the west, using Fort Detroit as a base. Hoping for a quick

---

[395] Jackson to Willie Blount, July 3, 1812, Jackson Papers, LC.

and decisive knockout blow, President Madison endorsed Hull's bid. Embracing Hull's plan for invasion would have enormous consequences for both the American and British sides and had huge influence on the early course of the war.

Hull reached Fort Detroit in July and crossed into Canada proclaiming "I come to find enemies not to make them. I come to protect and not to injure you."[396] Initially, Hull's declarations appealed to the ambivalent population, and 500 Canadian militia deserted. Facing a prevailing sense of defeatism among his forces that threatened his ability to oppose the invasion, British General Isaac Brock fortified Canadian resolve by improving the militia's capabilities, tightening up compulsory requirements for service, and aggressively courting allies among the Shawnee, and this included the great warrior chief Tecumseh. Hearing word of these preparations, and haunted by the threat of Native American atrocities, Hull began to lose his nerve for the invasion. In August, he ordered his forces withdrawn from Canada back to Fort Detroit. Some of Hull's dispirited men began to lose confidence in their general. One officer declared, "He is a coward...and will not risk his person."[397]

Sensing fear, Brock pursued the Americans, parading his Native allies around Fort Detroit for psychological effect. He later called for Hull's surrender with this unnerving message: "It is far from my intention to join in a war of extermination, but...the numerous body of Indians who have attached themselves...will be beyond control the moment the contest commences."[398]

On August 16, a terrified Hull surrendered Fort Detroit, along with his 2,500 men. It was an inspiring victory for Brock and Canada, and it was accomplished without a shot fired. America's humiliation continued, and Hull's name was cursed far and wide.

The cowardice of William Hull added further insult to Andrew Jackson, still sidelined at the Hermitage, and railing against the government for their incompetence. No general of any real prowess had yet to be commissioned. Yes, Jackson was unproven at this point in his

---

[396] Laxer, James, *Tecumseh and Brock: The War of 1812*. House of Anansi Press. 2012, p. 131.
[397] Papers of Captain Thomas Jessup, August 1812.
[398] Laxer, p. 132.

career, but those who served under him in Tennessee recognized his ability. To them, not summoning Jackson to the field was tantamount to risking the safety of the nation, especially in light of General Hull's abysmal efforts in Detroit. The frustrated Jackson did not stay quiet. Reacting to his omission as a commander in the field, Jackson spoke as often and as loudly as he could, announcing publicly of how he would rain down destruction not only upon the Creeks, but on the conquest of West Florida, as well, and the capture of Spanish-held Mobile. Tennesseans cheered these words joyously, envisioning the fruits of this effort that would give westerners access to the Gulf of Mexico.

Jackson was aware, however, particularly from having come so close to ruin with his proximity to the Burr conspiracy, that acting militarily without legal authority was a sure road to a court-martial. So, Jackson could do little but wait and hope. It was not until October 1812, that Governor Blount sent word that the President requested that 1,500 Tennessee Volunteers be sent as reinforcements to assist General Wilkinson in the defense of New Orleans. The administration wished to not only shore up fortifications against a potential British attack there, but also to utilize the extra manpower for a combined strike against East Florida. The opportunity to finally rid the nation of Spanish control of Florida was too tempting for Madison and the War Department to pass up.

As noted, while the Madison cabinet had implied to Governor Blount that they could do without Andrew Jackson in the war effort, they had not explicitly denied the commissioning of Jackson in writing. After checking as to the legality of Jackson's commission as major general of the regular army, Blount took it upon himself to ensure that Jackson was finally given his marching orders. He was to lead the Volunteers to New Orleans. Jackson was finally to have his chance at military glory, at long last. Major General Jackson, United States Army, was overjoyed.

The only issue that Jackson now faced was that he would be serving under James Wilkinson. Blount did not have much trouble urging the eager Jackson to accept his mission nonetheless, despite his reservations. Chomping at the bit to finally see action, Jackson accepted. "It is a duty of every citizen to do something for his country."[399] Still, it bothered

---

[399] Jackson to Willie Blount, Nov. 11, 1812, Jackson, *Correspondence*, 238-239.

Jackson that he would be forced to serve under a man he neither trusted nor respected, and it confirmed his suspicions that the Madison administration wished either to leave him out entirely or condescend him to serve under Wilkinson. More likely Madison's reluctance had been due to the prospect of two men serving together who clearly held such enmity for each other.

Recognizing there was little time to waste, in a fervent appeal, Jackson rallied a diverse assembly of farmers, planters, and businessmen—many of whom were descendants of veterans from the Revolutionary War—who flocked to Nashville. These volunteers, soon to be known as Jackson's Volunteers, were driven by an ardent desire to defend their homeland, safeguard their families, and serve under the leadership of General Jackson. But the immediacy of the orders meant that Jackson had limited opportunities to organize and train his newly assembled forces before their march toward New Orleans commenced in January 1813.

Blount's orders called for Jackson to have two divisions ready for transport by December 10th. Since they were to head downriver, they would need boats, camp supplies, and provisions, all of which were to be requisitioned by Jackson. The men would need to supply their own weapons, but the government promised to provide rifles for any soldiers who had none. Jackson told the men to pack warm clothing for the winter and spring, and that the expedition would require the men to be away from their homes for six to seven months.

On January 7th, 1813, Major General Jackson was finally on the move at long last, leaving Nashville for Natchez with the West Tennessee militia. A fleet of 30 boats carried Jackson and over 2,000 men down the Cumberland River. Their journey, however, was soon beset by difficulties. A sudden cold snap encased the river in ice, resulting in a four-day delay for the troops. The harsh winter weather compounded their struggle, as relentless rain, hail, and snow created a miserable environment for the soldiers. Amidst these challenges, Jackson himself suffered from severe pain in his neck and head, though he managed to recover. Once the ice finally melted, the boats resumed their journey, albeit not without mishap. All told, it would be five weeks before the troops would reach Natchez, having lost one boat, and three lives.

Upon finally reaching Natchez and making camp, Jackson received word from the irrepressible General Wilkinson that they were to remain where they were. Jackson was dismayed: why stay in remote Natchez when the orders had been to proceed without haste to New Orleans? However, Wilkinson detested Jackson and wished to keep him away as long as possible. "It becomes my duty to request you to halt in that vicinity."[400] Wilkinson wrote, listing as reasons a lack of provisions and horses for Jackson's men. Wilkinson wrote the War Department complaining of Jackson's lack of communication with him on his command. In short, Wilkinson did not wish to work with Andrew Jackson, and that meant Jackson, the subordinate officer, was forced to stand down.

Although U.S. troops had improved the Natchez Trace since 1801, it wasn't until 1812 that the military was able to capitalize on their efforts. The popular path through Choctaw and Chickasaw lands became a vital thoroughfare when it was believed British ships threatened the Gulf Coast. That winter would prove to be one of the most frigid on record, and at some points along the Natchez Trace, the snow was a foot deep. The firewood that Jackson's quartermaster, William Lewis, brought along for the journey was burned up on the first night. Jackson and Lewis spent most of the wee hours hauling those passed out from liquor closer to the fire. When Jackson was finally able to head to a nearby tavern to sleep, it was nearly six in the morning. Upon entering, the General overheard a civilian grumbling over the "stupidity of the government" in exposing the men to the brutal elements while officers were accommodated with warm beds in taverns.

The weary Jackson cut the griping civilian off before he could finish. "You damned scoundrel! Sowing disaffection among the troops. Why, the quartermaster and I have been up all night, making the men comfortable. Let me hear no such talk or I'm damned if I don't ram that red hot handiron down your throat!"[401]

A few days later, the weather improved, and the reorganized troops were readied to march. Jackson had spent the time assigning positions with his general staff. Besides the quartermaster Lewis, Jackson appointed the Pennsylvanian William Carroll as brigade inspector. The young and able attorney Thomas Hart Benton was chosen as first aide-de-camp. Benton's friend, the able Virginian John Reid was picked as

---

[400] Wilkinson to AJ, January 22, 25, February 22, March 1, 8, 1813, Jackson Papers, LC.
[401] Parton, *Jackson*, I, p. 368.

second aide-de-camp, and Jackson's Secretary. Command of the cavalry was given to Jackson's business partner John Coffee, a big brute of a man at well over six-feet tall and broad shoulders. Coffee became Jackson's most trusted officer and proved to be an able commander.

While in camp, Jackson took the opportunity to drill his troops, turning them into a disciplined fighting force. The men cleaned and tested their weapons, packed and unpacked their kits, ready to march and fight in a moment's notice. The men were being told that the British were bearing down on New Orleans, and Jackson's troops were eager to contribute to the city's defense. But, alas, they would soon be disappointed.

On the 15th of March, a stunning message was received from the War Department. Jackson and his staff had been anticipating word from Secretary of War William Eustis that it was time to embark downriver to New Orleans. But the message was quite the contrary, and it caused Jackson's humiliation and immediate infuriation, as well as that of his troops. Secretary of War William Eustis, the letter informed the General, had been replaced by John Armstrong, who had decided to scrap all of Eustis's strategic planning. Instead of focusing on New Orleans, Armstrong had decided that the East Coast was where the greatest threat lie. As for Jackson's troops, they were now being told simply that "on receipt of this letter, consider your Corps dismissed from public service."[402]

Jackson was perplexed and dismayed by the letter. Could the Secretary of War really mean for his men, five hundred miles from home, to disperse, and make their way home on their own? The brief orders had left no room for interpretation, and no explanations. Jackson's Corps were simply dismissed from service. But what of New Orleans, the strategically vital gateway to the Mississippi and the Gulf? Who was to protect the city, and the West? Jackson was at a loss of what to do. Not that he was unhappy to be allowed to return home. He always kept a portrait of Rachel with him, and he missed her and four-year-old Andrew, Jr. terribly. He would love nothing more than to be reunited with his family after months away, but he'd envisioned a return under much different circumstances.

---

[402] John Armstrong to AJ, Feb. 1813, Jackson, *Correspondence*, 275-276.

Since the outset of the war, Jackson had argued vehemently that to defeat the British; control of the Gulf Coast was vital. He had believed the brain trust in Washington saw eye to eye with him on this point. The Spanish still controlled much of the ports on the Gulf, and the British had courted the Spanish as their ally. Using these deep-water harbors for their ships and having the ability to control the Mississippi River would give the British an almost insurmountable advantage. Yet, Secretary Armstrong had given no battle orders, and had disbanded Jackson's army. To make matters worse, the Secretary's orders were for Jackson to "confiscate his men's weapons and take measures to have them delivered" to General Wilkinson in New Orleans.[403] What Armstrong was requesting was, in essence, to have Jackson's men disarmed and ordered to find their way home as best they could. No pay, no supplies. This Jackson simply could not do. [404]

In a letter to Rachel, Jackson expressed his frustration, "I hope to order the line of march in a few days, my duty my feelings, and Justice to those brave fellows who followed me at the call of their country, deserve more from their Goverment, than what they have recd. They at least deserved, by the orders of their goverment, to have recd. every necessary comfort for the sick, convayences that would insure them a safe return to their family their country and their homes. This has not been the case, it is only by and through me, that these things can be the sick shall be taken back as far as life lasts, and supplies shall be had, altho their Patriotism has been but illy rewarded by an ungratefull officer, (not Country) it is therefore my duty to act as a father to the sick and to the well and stay with them untill I march them into Nashville."[405]

Jackson had a difficult time not taking this dismissal as a personal attack. He felt certain there was some hidden enemy behind it, always lurking, trying to undermine him. On this occasion, Jackson had no doubt, that enemy was Wilkinson. The reality was the administration discovered that Congress was opposed to an invasion of East Florida, for fear of a war with Spain. Since Spain had an alliance with Russia, and the Czar to play the role of mediator between the US and Great Britain, the administration chose to drop the plan for fear of stirring up further

---

[403] ibid, 276
[404] AJ to Armstrong, March 13, 15, 1813, Jackson Papers, LC.
[405] AJ to Rachel, March 15, 1813, Jackson Papers, LC

international enmity. As a result, Secretary Armstrong chose to dismiss the force that was supposed to carry out the attack. Jackson was unaware of all of these machinations, and he continued to stew in personal affront.

However, Congress did approve the seizure of what remained of West Florida. By spring 1813, American forces easily captured Mobile and forced the Spanish garrison to retreat to Pensacola. Jackson was unaware of any of this too. All he knew was he'd been given an order for his men to go home, which angered him to no end. He called in his aide Thomas Hart Benton and declared that Armstrong's order was not to be followed; he would not dismiss his volunteers and leave them to struggle on their own.[406] Instead, he would personally lead them back to Tennessee, even if he had to use his own finances to fund the journey. In a letter to Armstrong, he informed the Secretary, "I mean to commence my March to Nashville in a few days, at which place I expect the troops to be paid and the necessary supplies furnished by the agents of government...after which I will dismiss them to their homes and families."[407]

Some of Jackson's letter to the Secretary was drafted in harsh tones, but, with the encouragement of his aides—who also wanted to keep the army together and march back to Nashville—he decided to tone it down. Still, he made it clear to Armstrong that "these brave men deserve a better fate and return from their government." He reminded them that they had rallied around their country's flag when it was insulted and followed him into battle; therefore, he would ensure they returned home safely. Despite his aide's editing, Jackson was less gracious to the Secretary of War than in his letter to Rachel, and not so subtly betrayed his sarcasm, "If it was intended by this order that we should be dismissed eight hundred miles from home, deprived of arms, tents and supplies for the sick–of our arms and supplies for the well...and be sacrificed. Those that could escape from the insalubrious climate, are to be deprived of the necessary support and meet death by famine The remaining few to be deprived of their arms pass through the savage land, where our women children and defenceless citizens are daily murdered–Yet thro. that barbarous clime, must our band of citizen soldiers wander and fall

---

[406] Parton, *Jackson*, I, p. 378.
[407] AJ to Armstrong, March 1813, Jackson Papers, LC.

a sacrifice to the Tomahawk and scalping knife of the wilderness our sick left naked in the open field and remain without supplies without nourishment or an earthly comfort."[408]

Jackson did not stop the correspondence there, turning to the government to vent his frustrations. He wrote to his Congressmen, Parry Humphreys, vowing "as long as I have funds or credit I will stick by my volunteers. I shall march them to Nashville, or bury them with the honors of war--should I die I know they will bury me."[409] He then took his appeal all the way to the top, writing a measured letter to President Madison, expressing his disappointment over the past month and the impact it had on the country and its military reputation. He emphasized the need for every effort to support the ongoing conflict and hoped there would be funds in Nashville to pay his troops when they got there. Speaking candidly, Jackson questioned whether this was the reward a virtuous administration offered its patriotic sons, or if it was the result of a wicked scheme motivated by "political villains" who would sacrifice the best of their country for their own selfish interests.[410]

As badly as Jackson wished to continue on to New Orleans and drive the British into the ocean, as he had promised his men, he and the Volunteers were forced to follow orders. They packed up camp and began the long march home. Without steamboat services to transport his army upstream against the current, Jackson and his Tennessee volunteers faced a tough journey across 500 miles of rugged terrain, much of it through hostile Indian territory. On March 25, 1813, they set out on the one-month march back to Nashville, fighting the cold, and the illness that soon spread through the ranks. The men were lacking supplies, wagons and horses. Jackson and his other officers soon gave up their mounts so that the sick could be conveyed.

There were soon 150 men on the sick list, with 56 of them so ill that they could not sit unassisted. Jackson managed to commandeer eleven wagons, but it was not enough. The going was slow, about eighteen miles a day. Jackson insisted on order and discipline, as he walked alongside his men, urging them onward. Once the march commenced, it progressed steadily, with Jackson gently urging the men forward. When a delirious

---

[408] Parton, *Jackson*, I, p. 384.
[409] AJ to Humphries, March 15, 1813, Jackson Papers, LC.
[410] AJ to Madison, March 15, 1813, Jackson, *Correspondence*, 292-293

soldier in a wagon lifted himself and asked about their location, Jackson replied, "You're on your way home!" prompting cheers from the soldiers. As the army advanced, Jackson was present throughout, moving along the ranks, attentive to any incidents needing his focus, overseeing the distribution of supplies, and motivating his men to keep pressing on. When a recruiting officer from General Wilkinson was spotted lingering around the camp, Jackson directed one of his famous glares at him and warned that any attempt to entice the Volunteers would result in being drummed out of the camp in front of the entire corps.

Jackson led by example, showing no signs of fatigue, while at the same time showing concern for his men's safety and comfort. For many of the soldiers that had not known their General long but had heard the stories of his renowned volatile temper, they were finding instead a firm but humane and compassionate leader. "There was not one belonging to the detachment but what loves him," one of his men reported. As word got out that Jackson was defying orders to ensure their safe return home and even footing part of the bill for their provisions, respect from the men soared. The general's stoic resilience soon earned him the nickname 'Hickory,' which would later evolve into the affectionate title 'Old Hickory' for the toughness his men came to admire in their commander. Although denied the chance at battlefield glory, Jackson was forging his legend.

The fatigued but intact army arrived in Nashville on April 22nd, 1813. Hoping for renewed orders to move his army elsewhere to defend the nation, Jackson would be disappointed once again. It would be five months before the Second Division again received notice that they were to march again. So, in the meantime, Jackson waited, happy to be back with his family, ensuring that business matters were running smoothly at the Hermitage. While the journey to Natchez had been frustrating and far from satisfying militarily, it would prove to be beneficial to Jackson's reputation among the Nashville community. "Long will their General live in the memory of the volunteers of West Tennessee," crowed the Nashville *Whig*, "for his benevolence, humane and fatherly treatment to his soldiers…" [411]

---

[411] Parton, *Jackson*, pp. 384, 486.

ANDREW JACKSON: THE POLITICS OF RESENTMENT

Coming out of a period in which Jackson's public image had taken a hit, viewed as the man who had killed Charles Dickinson, the man who had abetted Aaron Burr, Jackson now took on the air of a more respected, fatherly figure around the local community. His soldiers appreciated their commander, who had fulfilled the promise that no man would be left behind. And more than that, what his men saw in Jackson was what might have always been there, sheer, unyielding willpower. Perhaps it was forged when, sick with fever and smallpox, the 14-year-old prisoner of war walked the forty-mile trek back home, with his mother struggling to hold his dying brother aloft in the saddle. Molded in the fire of war, war was bringing that iron will to life once again, and it inspired the soldiers around him to go to any length for Old Hickory.

Unfortunately, Andrew Jackson was still Andrew Jackson, and therefore, the garnered respect his tenacious and triumphant return had earned him would not last long. In fact, it would all nearly come to an end entirely in what amounted to a summer brawl gone wrong. More foolishness for Andy Jackson, and this time around, he would never be the same.

CHAPTER

30

JACKSON VS. HIMSELF

"Peace, above all things, is to be desired, but blood must sometimes be spilled..."

-Andrew Jackson

Although Jackson's courageous leadership had won him the respect of the multitudes in and around Nashville, Tennessee, his suddenly heroic image did not remain untarnished for long. Having returned from Natchez to the cheers of Tennesseans far and wide, General Jackson was, almost overnight, "the most beloved and esteemed of private citizens in western Tennessee."[412] What a conversion for the man now seen as the "guardian of the frontier."[413] But as Jackson would often do throughout his life, he found ways to batter his own image in the eyes of the public. As always, Jackson was a victim of his own resentments. In 1813, as the great historian Robert V. Remini describes it, Jackson now allowed himself to be drawn into "an unseemly affair of honor that had people shaking their heads in wonder over the fearful, unseemly qualities fused within his singular personality."[414]

Viewed from any perspective, the Jackson-Benton affair served to tarnish the reputations of its participants rather than glorify them. This incident unfolded shortly after General Jackson had successfully returned his troops to Nashville. Quite imprudently, Jackson agreed to serve as

---

[412] Parton, *Jackson*, I, p. 486.
[413] ibid.
[414] Remini, 1977. p. 180.

the second for William (Billy) Carroll in a duel against Jesse Benton, the younger and impulsive brother of Lieutenant Colonel Thomas Hart Benton. At the time, older brother Thomas was away, preoccupied with settling accounts related to Jackson's campaign expenses in Washington. Carroll and Jesse Benton had served together under Jackson on the fabled march to Natchez, but now, petty jealousies devolved into an affair of honor, and Jackson, who should have known better, was caught up in its unbecoming tide.

Carroll, a delicately built Pennsylvanian, faced resentment from rougher pioneer types, including Jesse Benton, also an officer in Jackson's Corps. Benton harbored grievances against Carroll, whose favored position as a brigade inspector during the arduous march from Natchez to Nashville seemed to ignite jealousy among junior officers. Following a series of perceived slights, Benton challenged Carroll to an "affair of honor." Carroll, in turn, requested Jackson's support as his second in the duel. Despite Jackson's initial reluctance, "I am not the man for such an affair," he told Carroll, "I am too old."[415] But Carroll appealed to the General's sense of vanity and paternalism, claiming that Jackson's attention had incited jealousy within the ranks. Thus, Jackson reluctantly agreed to intervene.

Attempting to defuse the conflict, Jackson spoke with the younger Benton, but his efforts proved ineffectual. Ultimately, he consented to serve as Carroll's second. The duel itself, held on June 14th, was a dismal failure. The two opponents stood merely ten feet apart—this distance was a concession to Carroll's lack of marksmanship. At the signal, Jesse Benton shot first and then crouched down to make himself a smaller target for Carroll, who had sustained a thumb injury. Carroll returned fire, hitting Benton's exposed backside; while the injury was embarrassing, it was not life-threatening.

Following the duel, Thomas Hart Benton returned from Washington to learn of his brother's humiliation. Despite possessing far more self-control than Jesse, Thomas immediately inserted himself into the controversy. Soon, both Bentons publicly blamed Jackson for the duel and Jesse's humiliating injury. Thomas decided to address Jackson directly in a letter dated July 25. In this correspondence, he outlined

---

[415] Parton, *Jackson*, I, p. 387.

four perceived errors on Jackson's part regarding the duel. First, he argued, it was inappropriate for a man of Jackson's age and standing to be involved in a duel over trivial matters between young men who had no real grievances. Two, that Jackson had acted dishonorably by delivering a "bullying note" from Carroll to Jessie, leaving him with no choice but to engage in a duel or face disgrace. Thirdly, he attested, if Jackson could not prevent the duel, he should have at least ensured it was conducted fairly and equally, but instead, Benton argued, the affair was conducted in a "savage, unequal, unfair, and base manner."[416]

Jackson was incensed by the language Benton used, which pressed all the right nerves to set the General off. Still relishing his newfound celebrity (and perhaps believing himself invincible as a result), Jackson reacted to Benton's words with outrage. What really infuriated Jackson was that Benton's accusations had been repeated in a public format. Seeing the accusations as an assailment of his character, the General sought immediate retribution. Stopping short of issuing a direct challenge, however, Jackson stated, "I shall neither seek nor decline a duel with you."[417] Benton's argument that Jackson should have distanced himself from the conflict between the younger men was valid, and indeed Jackson should most certainly have not lowered himself to such a role in this young men's spat. But, at the same time, Benton's own intervention, and the heated manner in which he came after Jackson, only worsened the situation.

On August 4, Jackson replied to the older Benton with a measured indignation, recounting his attempts to mediate the dispute and defending the duel's legitimacy. He concluded, echoing Benton's stance, that he neither sought nor shied away from a challenge: "I have fully and frankly explained the circumstances of this affair to you. If satisfactory, I shall be gratified, but if otherwise, I am always amenable to the process of honorable men." Yet there was not much honor to be found about a month later, when these both men found themselves embroiled in reckless violence in a very public setting.

After sending his response, Jackson learned that Benton continued to publicly criticize the General for his handling of the duel. Driven by

---

[416] Benton to AJ, July 25, 1813, Jackson, *Correspondence*, I, pp. 312-313.
[417] ibid. pp. 388, 486

typical Jacksonian passions, in this case his burning desire to protect his honor, Jackson declared his intention to "horsewhip" Thomas Hart Benton upon their next encounter.

Both Bentons arrived in Nashville on September 3, seemingly intent on avoiding Jackson by staying at the City Hotel, a place the General did not normally frequent. That evening, however, Jackson and his companion John Coffee rode into town, ostensibly to "collect their mail," and checked into the Nashville Inn. The following morning, armed with a whip and a small gentleman's sword, Jackson strolled to the Post Office, passing the City Hotel where Thomas Benton stood defiantly at the entrance. After collecting their mail, Jackson and Coffee took the sidewalk route back to their inn, "accidentally" crossing paths with Benton. As Jackson approached, he brandished his whip, staring menacingly at Benton. "Now you damned rascal," Jackson declared, "I'm going to punish you. Defend yourself!" Benton appeared to reach for a firearm, prompting Jackson to draw his pistol and back the older Benton brother into the hotel.

As the confrontation escalated, Jesse Benton suddenly emerged, firing a shot that struck Jackson in the left shoulder, with a second bullet penetrating his left arm. Coffee rushed inside upon hearing the gunfire, firing at both Bentons, but missing. Thomas Benton, having stumbled down a flight of stairs, narrowly escaped unharmed, while Jesse sustained only minor injuries from an altercation outside the hotel, in which Jackson's nephew, Stockley Hays, rushed to the support of his uncle brandishing a dagger.[418]

Jackson most certainly came out of the fight the worst off. He was quickly taken back to the Nashville Inn, where he allegedly bled through two mattresses and managed to persuade the several doctors not to amputate his severely injured arm. "I'll keep my arm," he managed to say just before losing consciousness, and the respect and fear the old judge and general held carried the day, and none of the doctors went against his order. The bullet remained lodged near the bone for years, however, causing Jackson steady and consistent pain for years, only to be removed in 1832. Rachel soon made her way to Jackson's bedside, and for many

---

[418] Benton's Account of the Duel with Jackson, Sept. 10, 1813, Jackson, *Correspondence*, 318.

days, the General's life hung in the balance. He remained confined to his bed for more than two weeks, unable to rise.

In a public display of contempt, Thomas Hart Benton condemned Jackson as an assassin and destroyed the sword Jesse had abandoned during the chaos. Though the Benton brothers appeared to have gained the upper hand, they soon found themselves fearing for their safety. On September 10, Thomas Benton issued a statement on a broadside outlining their side of the story, asserting that they had sought alternative accommodations to avoid Jackson and claiming the General initiated the confrontation. Benton insisted that these facts were sufficient to sway public opinion in their favor, although this was not the case. The public sentiment in Nashville turned against the brothers, with many citizens calling for Thomas's blood. Feeling endangered, Thomas Hart Benton returned to Franklin, Tennessee. After completing his service in the War of 1812, Benton moved to Missouri, where he would begin his political career anew.

Thomas Hart Benton and Jackson did not cross paths again until 1823, when both became United States Senators. They realized it was politically advantageous to bury their old animosity. A simple handshake marked the end of a decade-long feud and the start of a political alliance. In contrast, Jesse, Thomas's brother, never forgave General Jackson. He held a grudge against both Jackson and Thomas for his later actions against the enemy, taking his resentment to the grave.

This marked the conclusion of Jackson's gunfights. Like the others, it had a trivial aspect to it. None of Jackson's adversaries truly elevated his status; instead, they all served to discredit him. Would the once-revered General Jackson manage to recover from this?

Meanwhile, the war raged on, and despite the bloodshed, neither side seemed able to gain much of an advantage. The United States had failed miserably in its attempts to seize Canada, and most of New England refused not only to support the war, but even to acknowledge its existence. In Washington City, James Madison, growing grayer by the minute, wrung his hands in desperation.

During the recovery period following his gunfight, while Jackson was being cared for by the able hands of his devoted wife, alarming news reached Tennessee. Hundreds of settlers had been killed in a massacre of tragic proportions at the hands of a renegade band of Creeks, known as the Red Sticks. The attack occurred on August 30th, in the Mississippi Territory, at Fort Mims, some four hundred miles from Nashville, in what is today part of the state of Alabama. The news of the brutal assault spread rapidly, and was immediately dubbed "Massacre at Fort Mims," igniting fierce and angry resolve throughout the southwest.

As further news of the atrocities at the fort came in, shockwaves of fear and anger reverberated throughout the western states. Fearing an imminent attack closer to home, Tennesseans instinctively turned to Jackson for protection, imploring him to act swiftly to prevent another horror of this sort. Early estimates of hundreds of dead men, women and children at Fort Mims were followed by furious calls for the destruction of the entire Creek Nation. It marked the beginning of the Creek War, a conflict that ultimately set Jackson on the path to national prominence.

Just two weeks after the Benton affair, Jackson, though in pain and bed-ridden, was nevertheless desperate to take the field and rid himself of the previous year's humiliation and its accompanying frustrations. He understood that his long-awaited shot at military distinction had finally arrived, and he knew he couldn't pass it up. Feeling compelled to lead a campaign of retribution, he resolved to act, even without formal authorization, confident that Governor Blount would ultimately support him. He correctly guessed that the process of mobilizing troops would soon be accompanied by official orders to take the fight to the Creeks.

The Fort Mims Massacre escalated an existing civil war among the Creek Indians, into a broader American war of retribution against the Creeks. As the war unfolded, the Creeks displayed a range of responses; some chose to remain neutral, while others allied with white forces against their own people. This complex dynamic would shape the course of the Creek War and its aftermath.

The Creek Indians referred to themselves as the Muskogee nation,[419] but European settlers labeled them as "Creeks" due to their frequent

---

[419] Horsman, Reginald, *Expansion and American Indian Policy*, East Lansing, Michigan, 1967, pp. 160-164.

movements along numerous streams and rivers. Their territory spanned from the Atlantic coast to the Tombigbee River, encompassing areas in present-day Florida, Georgia, Alabama, and Mississippi. When Colonel Benjamin Hawkins was appointed as the agent for the Southern tribes, he endeavored to encourage the Creeks to assimilate into white society by teaching them modern agricultural and industrial practices. Many Creeks, particularly those in the lower region of East Alabama and West Georgia near the Chattahoochee River, embraced these changes, recognizing the benefits of coexistence with white settlers. However, younger members of the Creek tribes, especially those residing in the upper Creek region of central and southern Alabama along the Coosa and Tallapoosa rivers, resisted integration and sought to preserve their traditional culture, even if it meant a fight to the death.

Throughout the Southwest territories lived approximately 60,000 native peoples--mainly Cherokee, Choctaw, Chickasaw, Chickamauga, Seminole, and Creek--bound by treaties with the federal government. Unlike the situation on the Northern front, most of these tribes supported the United States, in hopes that such loyalty might alleviate their diminishing status. Some tribes hedged their bets, however, and allied with the British. The strongest support for the Crown came from Tecumseh's Confederacy, mainly from the Old Northwest and the lower Great Lakes region. North of the Great Lakes, the Mohawks aided the British in Quebec and Ontario. and in the South, the lone convert, inspired by Tecumseh's words, were the militant Red Sticks.

The struggles of the Creek Nation had been arduous and painful. Having suffered through devastating epidemics that cut down four-fifths of the Creek population, a civil war among the Creeks had raged since 1812. Both the Upper and Lower Creeks harbored significant grievances against American expansion. Central to these grievances was the relentless encroachment upon their ancestral lands. The loss of their lands split the Creeks into two factions. The Red Sticks, or Upper Creeks, had chosen to break from their brethren, the Lower Creek, whom they criticized for their submission to whites. Favoring the technology and trade whites brought in, the Lower Creeks had not only assimilated but had ceded much of their lands to the United States. The Red Sticks referred to this more conciliatory faction derisively as "White Sticks." Choosing peace with the settlers who continued to flood onto their lands, the White Sticks sided with the United States in the War of 1812. [420]

The Red Sticks did not. Led by the Chief Red Eagle, they refused to assimilate and instead remained actively insurgent against American settlement on Upper Creek lands. The remarkable, charismatic Chief Red Eagle was born William Weatherford, the son of a Scot father and a Creek mother. Renowned for his fierce antagonism to white settlement, and superb fighting skill, Weatherford remained committed to traditional ideology, determined to preserve traditional Creek culture and communal land ownership. The Red Sticks' militant stance against white settlement had intensified with Tecumseh's charismatic presence two years earlier and had reached feverish heights in the atmosphere of war. [421]

The Spanish, seeking to destabilize American interests, provided support to the Creeks in Florida, promising arms and supplies in exchange for their commitment to resist American encroachment through warfare. As the United States government initiated the construction of roads connecting Georgia to settlements in the Mississippi Territory (Alabama), an influx of white settlers streamed into Creek territory. This was more than enough reason for the Red Sticks to commit themselves to resist, as the collision of distinct cultures rendered conflict not only probable but inevitable.

Violence first broke out between the Upper Creeks and the United States earlier in the summer of 1813. A territorial militia in southern Alabama attacked an armed band of Red Sticks returning from Spanish Florida, where the British had supplied them with weapons. This became known as the "Battle of Burnt Corn," and although the Red Sticks prevailed, both sides suffered two dozen combined casualties. These victorious Upper Creeks, led by Weatherford, soon became marked men among Southern whites.

August 30th,1813 began as an ordinary summer day, as hot and muggy as any other late August day in Alabama. As care-free children played within the confines of the wooden stockade, soldiers leisurely sauntered about Fort Mims. Samuel Mims, a prosperous merchant, had

---

[420] Ibid, 164.
[421] Coles, Henry, *The War of 1812*, Chicago, 1965, p. 192.

established the stronghold approximately 40 miles north of Mobile, purchasing an acre of land enclosed by upright logs, fortified with two heavy gates and 500 portholes positioned 3 and a half feet above the ground. The stockade was defended by one-hundred and twenty militia men under the command of Major Daniel Beasley, a lawyer from the Mississippi Territory with limited military experience. Alongside the militia, nearly three-hundred settlers, including whites, mixed-blood individuals, and friendly Native Americans, occupied the fort, with an estimated equal number of Black slaves held within its walls. This location had become a refuge for American settlers and numerous Creek families seeking safety. [422]

At noon, the beat of a drum within the fort summoned the soldiers to dinner, prompting them to set aside their weapons. However, this drum signal masked a more ominous message. With the first beat, a force of at least 700 Creek warriors surged from the nearby forest, charging across the open fields towards the fort's gates. Major Beasley, in a desperate effort, raced to secure the gates, but the Creeks breached the defenses, overpowering him and clubbing him to death before moving on to the unsuspecting inhabitants. Despite a valiant defense, the settlers faced systematic slaughter.

The swift and overwhelming assault shocked the Mississippi volunteers. The engagement proved disastrous. Reports indicate that nearly two hundred and fifty people were murdered, with the scene described as one of horrific violence—blood and brains splattered across the ground. The death toll included a tragic loss of life among women, children, and enslaved African Americans. Most of the enslaved were spared, but were taken away to serve the Red Sticks. A U.S. army major present at the scene days later described the slaughter, "Indians, Negroes, white men, women and children…in one promiscuous ruin. The main building was burned to ashes, which were filled with bones. The plains and the woods around were covered with dead bodies."[423]

The Creek warriors not only murdered women and children but committed unspeakable atrocities. The Red Stick warriors reportedly engaged in a systematic butchering "in the quickest manner…children

---

[422] Parton, *Jackson*, I, p. 388.
[423] Griffith, Benjamin W. *McIntosh and Weatherford: Creek Indian Leaders*. 1988. Pg. 111.

were seized by the legs and killed by batting their heads against the stockading. The women were scalped and those who were pregnant were opened, while they were alive, and the embryo infants let out of the womb." Weatherford attempted to halt the brutality but was forced to retreat to save himself from his own angry warriors, worked up into an unconscionable frenzy. Many of the victims were burned alive in the buildings in which they hid.[424]

The massacre at Fort Mims spread panic throughout the frontier. After the bloodbath, parties of Indians roved about the country rioting in plunder. The Red Sticks' shocking victory brought a quick response from President Madison in Washington. Word arrived just a few days after the attack that the various militias of the region were to be called into service, including Tennessee, Georgia and the Mississippi Territory. Southerners, including Jackson and Governor Blount were concerned of a British alignment with the Native tribes to attack the entire frontier.

Nashville residents, angry and frightened by the senseless violence at Fort Mims, assembled a town meeting on September 19th to discuss the event. It had been eighteen days since the massacre. A committee, including Colonel Coffee, was formed to consult with Governor Blount and General Jackson and report back the next day. Resolutions were passed urging immediate aid for southern settlers, with Governor Blount supporting this measure. The committee expressed regret over General Jackson's condition but remained confident in his recovery to lead the Tennessee volunteers against the enemy. "We have to regret, said the committee, the present indisposition of our brave and patriotic General Jackson; but we have the utmost confidence, from his declaration and his convalescent state, to announce that he will be able to command as soon as the freeman of Tennessee can be collected to March against the foe." [425]

On September 25, the Tennessee Legislature empowered Governor Blount to call for 3,500 volunteers for a three-month tour of duty, in addition to 1,500 already enlisted regulars, with the state guaranteeing their pay if the federal government did not. They allocated $300,000 for immediate expenses. Blount was counting on his militia generals to repel the impending invasion and provide aid to the suffering citizens

---

[424] Pickett, Albert J. *History of Alabama*. Charleston. 1851. Pg. 275.
[425] Shapiro, *Encyclopedia of Alabama*, pg. 9

of the Mississippi Territory. The East Tennessee militia, commanded by Major General John Cocke, was also dispatched against the Creeks. The influential John Sevier was absent, away serving in Congress; otherwise, he might have been called to lead the operation.

Blount summoned General Cocke and together they paid a visit to Jackson, who they found still bed-ridden and weak from the Benton affray, but on the mend. Blount had ordered Cocke to gather 2,500 East Tennessee troops at Knoxville and was ready to do the same for Jackson if he could lead. Jackson indicated he would be ready by the time the troops assembled, and they discussed the need for provisions in East Tennessee for both divisions, emphasizing the importance of supplies for a moving army.

Prior to the Fort Mims tragedy, Jackson recognized the necessity to address frontier raids by engaging the Creeks before they could receive support from their British and Spanish allies. His earlier appeals to Governor Blount for authorization went unacknowledged, leaving the settlers exposed to the consequences. Jackson, his wounded arm propped awkwardly in a sling, now swung gingerly into action. In a call to arms meant to reassure the citizens of Tennessee, Jackson issued general orders for his militia to gather at Fayetteville for immediate deployment against the Creeks. Planning to mobilize his volunteers quickly, Jackson addressed them on September 24th. "The late attack of the Creek Indians calls loudly for retaliatory vengeance. Those distressed citizens of the frontier have employed the brave Tennesseans for aid.... They are our brothers in distress, and we must not await the slow and tardy orders of the general government." Employing his most provocative language, he rallied the men into purposeful action. To ensure confidence in his abilities to his men, despite his wounds, he wrote as though a miraculous healing had taken place, "The health of your General has been restored—he will command in person."

With fear of missing out as a primary motivator, the frail, convalescent Andrew Jackson, still a shell of his former self, was determined to lead the Tennessee Volunteers against the mighty William Weatherford and the Red Sticks. Lead, he would, no matter the cost. Bidding farewell to his wife and children, Jackson tightened up his sling and mounted his horse. With daylight fading, southward down the dusty Cumberland road he went, into a setting sun.

CHAPTER

31

THE CREEK WAR

*""General Jackson, I am not afraid of you. I fear no man, for
I am a Creek warrior."*
-William Weatherford, Chief Red Eagle

A month to the day after the City Hotel gunfight, the first group of Tennessee Volunteers headed south without their ailing leader, General Andrew Jackson, still too injured to make the trip. The tall, well-built John Coffee, now a brigadier general, led the troops south into the Mississippi Territory. Although Jackson was still recovering, he would not be far behind, and he wished to ensure his presence was felt among his men. Sending a message through Coffee that was read aloud to the soldiers, Jackson reminded them, "The blood of our women and children, recently spilled at Fort Mims, calls for our vengeance. It must not call in vain." [426]

Riding out three days later, Jackson sought to catch up with Coffee and his troops. Pale and wan, Benton's bullet still lodged in his arm, he caught up with the Volunteers, and entered Creek country, undeterred. Eager though he was for action, Jackson carefully considered the intelligence of the enemy he had received from friendly Creeks, Choctaws, and Cherokees. Urging his commanders to form alliances with the tribes in the Mississippi Territory, including the White Sticks, Jackson, though lacking battlefield experience, recognized the invaluable

---
[426] Reid and Eaton, *The Life of Andrew Jackson: Major-General in the Service of the United States*, Kessinger Publishing, pg. 33.

necessity of intel on the enemy. Setting aside his traditional distrust of Native Americans, as he would continue to do throughout the war, was another step in his maturation as a commander. Against pressures from the Red Sticks, Jackson urged White Creek Chief Chenabee, "Hold out obstinately, if one hair of your head is hurt, or of your family or anyone friendly to the whites, I will sacrifice a hundred lives to pay for it. Be of good heart and tell your men they have nothing to fear."[427] The threat was still very real, however, to those nations that showed support for the cause of the whites.

Devising a strategy to penetrate the Creek nation, Jackson and his men would create a pathway through the wilderness to reach Mobile on the coast. This march would serve a dual purpose: it would establish a vital route for future American settlers while dismantling Creek power in the region. Jackson aimed to strike "at the root of the disease" by invading Spanish Florida to capture Pensacola, effectively eliminating the Creeks' capacity for warfare. In one decisive operation, he envisioned the destruction of the Creeks, the establishment of a crucial communication line for western settlers, and the expulsion of Spanish influence from the American continent. Jackson was resolute in his belief that the eradication of both Spanish and British influence in the area was essential for resolving the ongoing "Indian problem."

A fragile and visibly weakened Jackson moved his force south to Fort Deposit, a supply storehouse (southwest of where Montgomery now stands) that Jackson had built for the campaign. They arrived on Oct. 24th, but the going had been rough, as Jackson wrote to one officer, his troops had "encountered every difficulty that can possibly arise from the want of Supplies & from ruggedness of mountains." [428] During the first week of November, Jackson mobilized his troops again, establishing Fort Strother on the banks of the Coosa River, about ninety miles south of Huntsville. When spies reported a large enemy force twelve miles south of his camp, he gave the order to John Coffee's cavalry and mounted riflemen to attack a Red Stick island community just to the east, known as Tallushatchee. The village, Jackson was told, housed two hundred warriors.

---

[427] AJ to Chief Chennabee, Oct. 19, 1813, Jackson Papers, LC.
[428] Jackson Papers, II, 441.

Coffee's force of 900 men attacked the village on November 3rd. They outnumbered the Creeks nearly five to one, and although the Red Sticks fought fiercely, it quickly turned into a massacre. In all, 186 Red Sticks were killed, ("not one escaped to carry the news," Coffee reported) including a number of women and children. The remaining women and children were taken prisoner. Coffee's troops, by contrast, suffered only five killed and 41 wounded.

One soldier, Richard Keith Call, a Virginian and a future governor of the territory of Florida recollected the carnage of the scene after the "hour of danger had passed." Call described the gory scene including individual cabins where they found up to ten dead bodies, including dead mothers clasping their dead children to their breasts. Call wrote of the heat of battle, where passion and vengeance could make "demons out of men," to that of the tears shed for the carnage afterwards.

Call wrote in his journal: "I remember an instant of a brave young soldier, who after fighting like a tiger until the engagement was over, fainted at the sight of the blood he had helped to spill." Call wrote of his memories of the battle years later, with images as vivid as the day it was fought, "The next morning after our march we entered the Indian village, and here I first saw the carnage of the battlefield. I saw it in its worst aspect – when the hour of danger had passed, when I could excite no feeling or passion in my breast, to control my sympathy and sorrow for human suffering. It was to me a horrible and revolting scene – the battle had ended in the village, the warriors fighting in their board houses, which gave little protection against the rifle bullets or musket ball. They fought in the midst of their wives and children, who frequently shared their bloody fate. They fought bravely to the last, none asking or receiving quarter, nor did resistance cease until the last warrior had fallen. Humanity might well have wept over the gory scene before us."[429]

The famous frontiersman Davy Crockett also served at the Battle of Tallushatchee under John Coffee. He was a member of the 2nd Regiment of Volunteer Mounted Riflemen. Crockett described a heart wrenching scene of confronting dozens of Creeks packed into a single dwelling, "We

---

[429] Richard Keith Call Journal, quoted in Herbert J. Doherty, Jr., *Richard Keith Call: Southern Unionist*, Gainesville, 1961, p. 6

now shot them like dogs; and then set the house on fire and burned it up with the forty-six warriors in it."[430]

Jackson arrived to inspect the carnage amid the smoking ruins of Tallushatchee. He determined that Coffee's forces had taken over eighty of the women and children as prisoners, avoiding accusations that the Volunteers had engaged in the type of wholesale slaughter the Red Sticks had committed at Fort Mims. Jackson wrote to Rachel informing her of Coffee's success in destroying the village "in elegant stile." He also wrote of other news; he had sent a "little Indian boy" north to be raised at the Hermitage. Jackson's interpreter, an Indian trader fluent in the Creek language, brought a Native American infant to the General. The 10-month-old infant had somehow survived the attack and had been found in the embrace of his dead mother. His name was Lyncoya, and he was one of two Creek children from the village who were taken by the militiamen. "Charity and Christianity says he ought to be taken care of," Jackson wrote.[431] (Lyncoya was one of two Creek wards in the Jackson family. Another, named Theodore, died as an infant.) Having been orphaned by war himself, Jackson was moved by the orphan boy, and shortly after the battle was found feeding the tiny child, coaxing him with a mix of brown sugar and water. Jackson later adopted Lyncoya, hoping to send him off to West Point one day.[432]

Less than thirty miles from Jackson's encampment on the Coosa River stood Fort Leslie, in the village of Talladega. This small fort became a refuge for a group of one hundred fifty-four friendly Creeks who sought safety from the conflict. In making alliances, Jackson vowed to safeguard the friendly tribes, which also included the Cherokees and Choctaws. His opportunity to fulfill his promise to the friendly Creeks arrived at sunset on November 7, when an express rider appeared. He delivered alarming news: approximately one thousand warriors had surrounded Fort Leslie, led by William Weatherford, Chief Red Eagle, along with one thousand of his Red Stick warriors. The Red Sticks had effectively sealed off the fort and were preventing any escape. The White Creeks feared the same devastating fate as the settlers at Fort Mims.

---

[430] Davy Crockett, *Life of Davy Crockett*, New York, 1854, p. 75.
[431] AJ to Rachel, Dec. 29, 1813, Jackson Papers, LC.
[432] Kendall, *Jackson*, p. 201.

As days passed, the situation for the besieged Creeks grew increasingly desperate and the White Creeks were on the brink of starvation.

The messenger, a brave chief, had crawled through the Red Stick lines, disguised under a hog's skin, complete with head and hooves. Remarkably, he managed to move through to safety by mimicking the animal's movements. Once he was out of danger, he removed his disguise and set off towards Jackson's camp, arriving late the following evening, just four days after the events at Tallushatchee. General Coffee's cavalry was still celebrating their victory, when the news reached their camp.

Recognizing the importance of rescuing his allies, Jackson rushed into action, fearing that their massacre could intimidate other allied tribes and unify them against the United States.

But this effort would pose a significant test of the General's endurance, for Jackson was not in peak condition to respond. He still struggled with the wounds to his left arm and required assistance to mount his horse. Even unfolding a map proved to be a daunting task due to a severe case of dysentery. For years, he had endured various intestinal issues, but the current discomfort was unbearable, making it hard for him to sit upright. Despite this dire situation, he refused to let pain hinder his resolve. Slumped against a tree, he quickly devised a strategy. By midnight, Jackson and his men were on the move.[433]

As he rode towards Talladega, Jackson did his best to lean forward in the saddle, trying to ease the stabbing pain in his abdomen, and not aggravate his ailing left arm. The journey stretched over twenty-five miles, but by sunset the next day, Jackson's army, comprising 1,200 foot-soldiers and eight hundred mounted men, established camp near their objective. Again, Jackson did not rest, instead questioning his scouts about the terrain while crafting a battle plan. At 4:00 AM on November 9th, he ordered his men to wake up. By dawn, Jackson's men deployed to within a half mile of the Red Sticks besieging Talladega. His battle orders, described in a letter to Governor Blount, instructed the infantry to advance "in three lines—the militia on the left, and the volunteers on the right. The cavalry formed the two extreme wings and were ordered to advance in a curve." [434]

---

[433] Brannan, *Official Letters*, p. 265.; Jackson to Blount, Nov. 15, 1813, Jackson Papers, LC.
[434] ibid.

With a significant portion of his forces in position, Jackson commanded three mounted rifle and musket companies to move forward. He anticipated that the enemy would engage this vanguard, allowing them to feign a retreat. This would lure the smaller force into the range of his larger force, where his cavalry could ensnare them in a deadly crossfire. The battle erupted with a barrage of gunfire as Weatherford's Red Sticks, adorned with only red war paint, surged from the thick brush. The Red Stick warriors numbered less than seven-hundred, and the Volunteers' numerical superiority overwhelmed the enemy, although the victory was far from perfect. Davy Crockett described them as being "like a cloud of Egyptian locusts, screaming like all the young devils had been turned loose, with the old devil of all at their head."[435]

The plan unfolded as intended, Jackson's men drew the Red Sticks to charge into the field where they fell directly into the trap. The Tennesseans moved in, firing away at point blank range, as the two curving arms of troops swung around. A hail of bullets inflicted severe casualties, even though the Creeks, some armed with guns and many with bows and arrows, fought back fiercely. Jackson's ploy had worked so well that the Volunteers had surrounded the enemy, and escape seemed impossible. Weatherford's entire force might well have been destroyed in that moment, when suddenly and inexplicably, the right flank of the infantry retreated instead of advancing, allowing Weatherford and a substantial group of Creeks to break through the gap in the line. The mistaken withdrawal was most likely the result of a confusion of orders amid the battle's chaos, and although brief, hundreds of Red Sticks took advantage and exploited the gap. Bolting through the gap, with some of Jackson's men pursued them, many of the fleeing Red Sticks escaped to safety.

John Coffee recalled: "We had nearly surrounded the Indians when they broke through an opening.... that had not been closed, through which many of them escaped. We pursued them three or four miles, killing or wounding as they ran. We have counted two hundred ninety-nine Indians dead on the ground, and it is believed that many have not

---

[435] Crockett, p. 92

been found that were killed dead; but the battle ground was so very large we had not time to hunt them up."[436]

The victory at the Battle of Talladega marked a successful fall campaign for Jackson and his men, although, regrettably, the break in the line had one very negative consequence. The mistake allowed the escape of some 700 Red Sticks to fight another day. Nonetheless, it had profound implications. When the casualties were tallied, Weatherford had indeed lost 300 men, while Jackson had lost only 15. The successful rescue of the White Creeks at Fort Leslie solidified the alliance between the Creek Nation and the United States against the Red Stick faction. Furthermore, the combined losses at Tallushatchee and Talladega, which left over 1,000 Red Stick warriors dead, wounded, or missing, significantly weakened their numbers ahead of the upcoming Battle of Horseshoe Bend, which would ultimately determine the fate of the Creek Nation in Alabama.

Following the Battle of Talladega, after burying the dead and gathering supplies, Jackson's men experienced a notable pause in hostilities. It is during this respite that Jackson earned a new title; to the Red Sticks, General Jackson became Sharp Knife.[437] Despite his challenges, including a useless left arm and a body weakened by dysentery, the inexperienced general had orchestrated his first significant battle and led his troops to victory. Yet, unbeknownst to Jackson and his men, the outcome at Talladega would mark the last piece of good news for many weeks ahead.

Jackson led his army back to Fort Strother, anticipating reinforcements and provisions. Immediately upon reaching the fort, however, Jackson and his men were met with a tumultuous situation. He had planned, as he told a Scotsman licensed to trade with the Creeks, to assemble enough supplies "to enable me to carry a war of destruction through every part of the Creek Nation that remains unfriendly." [438] He had expected to find a shipment of long-awaited supplies delivered from Nashville upon his return. Instead, he found nothing. The supplies had not arrived, though the shipment was supposed to have been delivered weeks ago.

---

[436] Coffee to AJ, Jackson Papers, III, 179-180.
[437] Moore, Ethan, *Spring, 1814: The Battle of Horseshoe Bend*, University of North Carolina at Greensboro, nps.gov. 2017.
[438] Jackson Papers, II, 457.

The sick and wounded who had been left behind when Jackson left for Talladega had consumed nearly all the provisions that remained. Jackson's private stores, brought at his own expense, were also gone. They had been given permission to take the stores; Jackson had ordered the surgeons to distribute his provisions during his absence, should it become necessary. Apparently, it was indeed necessary. Now, however, the army had only a few dozen biscuits and a small supply of meat. So, the remaining cattle were slaughtered and distributed among the troops. What remained were only a few dozen biscuits and a small amount of meat. The decision was made to slaughter the remaining livestock and distribute it to the soldiers. Jackson and his officers made do with the offal.

But the days dragged on without the supplies, and many of the men had not eaten a full meal since before the battle. Some grumblings of desertion began to be heard. In the face of losing his command, Jackson, recognizing the need for solidarity, urged his officers to stay loyal. Using his most persuasive language, he reminded the men of their patriotism and the recent victories they had achieved. He promised that relief was on the way and warned of the dire consequences of retreat. Jackson reassured them, saying, "I have no wish to starve you or deceive you," and promised that if supplies did not arrive in two days, they would all march back together and assign blame appropriately. This stirring appeal convinced the officers and men to wait a bit longer.

When two more days passed without relief, however, the troops insisted that Jackson keep his word and allow them to return home. Desperate at the thought of leading a retreat, Jackson stood his ground, "If only two men will remain with me, I will never abandon this post." A Captain Gordon stepped forward, "I am with you, General, let's see if we can find any others." [439] Soon over a hundred others stepped forward as well and volunteered to stay at Fort Strother. Renewed in hope, Jackson adjusted his plans and prepared to leave with the main army to meet the supply train.

On November 17, the order to march was given. The weary men marched steadily, praying for supplies. To their surprise, and Jackson's delight, they encountered 150 cattle and nine wagons of flour just

---

[439] Reid and Eaton, p. 68.

12 miles from their destination. The men feasted on the food, finally alleviating their hunger, and were then ordered to return to camp.

Jackson and his troops, satiated for the moment, continued the struggle through the winter months. One story often repeated and later published in the newspapers told how a soldier who was nearly starving approached Jackson and asked for something to eat. "I will most cheerfully divide with you what I have," said Old Hickory. With that he put his hand in his pocket and drew out a few acorns. "This is the best and only fare I have."[440] With the lack of food, and the three-month enlistments ending, soldiers began to desert Jackson's army in droves. By December, the Tennessee forces dwindled to less than five hundred.

---

[440] Kendall, *Jackson*, p. 207.

CHAPTER

32

RAIDING THE RED STICKS

"The quality of decision is like the well-timed swoop of a falcon which enables it to strike and destroy its victim."
—Sun Tzu, *The Art of War*

In the bitter December of 1813, amidst the tensions of the Creek War, critical moments unfolded that would forge the mettle of General Andrew Jackson's leadership. Jackson's army faced many challenges as the winter of 1813-14 approached. In the back of his mind was the worry about a British advance on New Orleans. In fact, there was talk of just such an invasion among British naval officers, though they had not yet acted upon the idea. Much more immediate concerns occupied Jackson's attention, however.

Days passed, but still no supplies had arrived to feed his hungry men. With the shipments delayed, Jackson felt the frustrations of his starving troops, growing increasingly restless with each passing day. His volunteers had little food and no feed for their horses. With remaining supplies all but non-existent, hunger and anger mounted, as did hushed talks of mutiny.

Jackson, himself starving and ill with dysentery, railed at the contractors who could not get him provisions. Yet, Jackson had brought his army much further than his supply lines could easily reach, in his haste to see action, and along with the typical logistical problems of nineteenth century frontier warfare, near calamity was the result.

Jackson seethed at his army's situation, and he now felt a renewed hostility toward General Cocke, of the East Tennessee militia, whom he believed was guilty of sabotaging the campaign. Prior to Jackson's army's set out for Talladega from Fort Strother, General James White, who led the advance of General Cocke's army in East Tennessee, was on his way to the fort to rest his men before the remainder of Cocke's army arrived.[441] But in the midst of their march, White received new orders to rejoin Cocke, who was reluctant to have his troops come under Jackson's command. News of these orders infuriated Jackson, who had counted on General White's presence to ensure good order at the fort while he was away. Now, with no supplies, and waning troop discipline, Jackson's ire at Cocke's intervention grew all the more intense, and the situation at the fort deteriorated further.

To add to Jackson's immense frustration, the enlistments of hundreds of men under his command were near expiration. A February 1812 law defined the term of service for volunteers as being a 12-month enlistment, unless dismissed earlier. Jackson's field officers had met and drafted a petition suggesting that the soldiers be permitted to return home. They were starving and were forced to subsist on little to no rations--they had eaten less than two meals the previous five days. Their efforts, the petition argued, had rendered the frontier safe, and therefore, the men should be permitted to return home for a time to regroup, tend to their families, and pack winter clothing. The petition was not irrational, nor was it demanding. The men had made a valid, and respectful case for their temporary dismissal; clearly the army was in a frightful state, and Jackson was simply being asked to allow the men to return to Tennessee before the situation worsened. Were Jackson not who he was, if he were more sympathetic, or less anxious for military glory, he would've heeded the plea. But that was not the way of Andrew Jackson. He stubbornly rejected the officers' plea with condescending scorn, reminding his men what was expected of them as soldiers and frontiersmen.

With the air thick with talk of desertion, discontented soldiers, weary from months of combat and dwindling supplies, the soldiers decided to act. On December 4, Colonel William Martin informed Jackson that his regiment of Volunteers intended to "claim their discharge as a

---

[441] Cocke to White, November, 1813, James White Papers, LC.

matter of right" and return to Tennessee in six days. This announcement infuriated Jackson. Two days later, he replied in a lengthy and somewhat befuddling manner, asserting that their terms of service were not yet fulfilled. He combined a paternal tone with threats, stating that "a father never deceived his children," and declaring that "mutiny and desertion shall be put down, so long as I retain the power of quelling them." This led to a typical Jackson standoff. On December 9, General William Hall notified Jackson that his first brigade of infantry planned to secretly leave camp that evening. Jackson would have none of it; he positioned troops and artillery along the road to block the brigade's exit and threatened to take severe action against anyone attempting to return home.[442]

As one soldier recorded in his journal, Jackson then mounted his horse, rode along the line and "addressed the evacuating troops by companies, in a strain of impassioned eloquence. He feelingly speciated on their former good conduct, and the esteem and applause it had secured them; and pointed to the disgrace which they must heap upon themselves, their families, and country, by persisting, even if they could succeed, in their present mutiny. But he told them they should not succeed, but by passing over his body."[443]

Another soldier's account adds that Jackson, confronting the potential deserters, positioned his horse in their path. With his left arm still in a sling, he rested his musket on the horse's neck. Aiming down the barrel at the rebellious men, he issued a stern warning. "You say you will march. I say by the eternal God, you shall not march while a cartridge can sound fire!" [444]

General Coffee and Major John Reid, understanding the gravity of the situation, strategically positioned themselves on either side of their commanding officer, General Jackson. The three men stood like immovable sentinels, their presence a silent challenge to any who dared break ranks. What followed was a masterclass in military psychology and leadership. The unwavering stance of these three commanders, particularly Jackson's fierce determination, began to affect the restless troops. A few companies of loyal soldiers, moved by their leaders' resolve, stepped forward to stand behind them. Their action triggered a cascading

---

[442] AJ to Coffee, Dec. 9, 1813, Jackson Papers, LC.
[443] Reid and Eaton, p. 84.
[444] Cooper, Owsley, *Struggle for The Gulf*, Ch. 4.

effect - volunteers who, moments ago, had been set on desertion found themselves drawn back by a mixture of respect, fear, and perhaps shame. The potential mutiny dissolved as more soldiers fell back into formation, and Jackson's fighting force remained intact. Jackson had won, for now.

General Cocke and his East Tennessee Volunteers were the hopeful topic of discussion. Jackson assured the men that those whose service was ending could leave upon Cocke's arrival. Three days later, Cocke arrived at Fort Strother with 1,500 men. But this did not solve the dilemma, as their short three-month enlistment was nearing its end as well. Regardless, Hall's brigade promptly departed anyway. A frustrated Jackson wrote to Rachel at the end of the month "I have been much pestered and invested with the shameful retrograde of the volunteers... At half-past eleven o'clock at night, the shameful desertion from their posts of the Volunteer infantry...and the apathy displayed in the interior of the state by the fireside patriots. And with the still more shameful condolence of the contractors, in not supplying us with provisions..." Yet, Jackson's derision and finger-pointing couldn't hide the fact that he had overstepped. By ignoring his men's enlistment terms and venturing too far into inaccessible areas, he increased skepticism among his critics at the War Department in Washington.

Yet, Jackson was by no means ready to give up the cause amidst his frustrations, as he wrote to reassure Rachel, "But be not uneasy, if I have trials and perils, God has fortified me with the fortitude to do my duty under every circumstance."[445]

Jackson continued his letter-writing in the dead of night on December 29, writing a lengthy letter to Governor Blount in a desperate attempt to revive the governor's spirit and courage. Explaining in harsh words that the Indians needed to be "exterminated or conquered" and challenged the governor, "are you, my dear friend, sitting with your arms folded? Give me a force for six months in whose terms of service there is no doubt...and all may be safe, withhold it and all is lost." The words were sharp, and the tone was bitter; nevertheless, he believed Blount would understand his feelings of "personal regard and public good."

"Is the campaign over?" he inquired. "Is protection provided to the frontiers of the Territory as envisioned by the act of assembly? Is the

---

[445] AJ to Blount, Jackson, *Correspondence*, Dec. 29, 1813.

Creek nation exterminated or conquered? ...the answer is clear, isn't it? .... you are suggesting I retreat to appease the whims of the populace and wait for further orders from the Secretary of War. Let me tell you, it is imperative upon you and me to fulfill our duty regardless of the consequences or the opinions of these armchair patriots, those sycophants or cowardly individuals who, despite their bravado, would flee home and leave thousands to fall victim to my retreat."[446]

Jackson spoke frankly. He told Blount outright that it was the governor's responsibility to keep 3,500 men in the field until the Creeks were either "exterminated or conquered." "It is your duty, and whenever the number falls below that level, the state's militia should be called out. President Madison believes—and he has every right to believe—that 5,000 men serving for six months are necessary to protect the frontiers of Tennessee and the Mississippi Territory. If this is not done, the Cherokees, Chocktaws, and Friendly Creeks will join forces with Red Eagle and the Red Sticks. The Chocktaws are wavering, and in these circumstances, I am advised to retreat."[447]

It was a powerful letter, typical of Jackson. It resonated with his resolve to protect the frontier and the nation, at whatever cost. It embodied many of Jackson's sentiments: relentless patriotism, the energy to confront adversity, and the will to succeed. The language struck hard and poignantly. With all his faults—and they were numerous—he was a tenacious, courageous, and formidable man.

Then came a series of devastating setbacks that nearly ended Jackson's military career. Blount aligned himself with the militia in their interpretation of their service terms. The Secretary of War agreed and ordered their honorable discharge. Additionally, Blount advised Jackson to abandon Fort Strother and retreat to the Tennessee frontier. There, Jackson had two options: either wait for orders from the national government or stand by until Blount felt authorized to assemble a new force. Blount suggested that retreat was the wisest course of action, considering the recent events affecting Jackson's army. Blount had already mustered all the troops authorized by Congress and Tennessee's legislature; there was nothing more he could do for the time being.

---

[446] AJ to Blount, 1813, Jackson Papers, LC.
[447] ibid.

Jackson was incredulous. His only significant ally had abandoned him. Throughout his conflicts with the administration over his efforts to sustain an army and protect the frontier, he had relied heavily upon Governor Blount's support. Now, that support seemed to have evaporated. Yet, despite the chaos surrounding him and his disintegrating army, Jackson appeared to draw inner strength from his misfortunes. He was one of those extraordinary individuals who seemed to revel in adversity. The more he was challenged, the more resolute he became. A strong, stubborn determination surged within him whenever his situation looked bleak. His emotional and physical stamina came from remarkable reserves of pent-up desperation.

While his letter was en route to Blount, Jackson informed his troops of the governor's recommendation, giving them the choice to either remain with him and complete the campaign or return home. To his dismay, they opted to go home. As they departed, Old Hickory wished each of them "a smoke tail in their teeth, with a petticoat as a coat of mail to pass down to their offspring."[448] This was his way of branding them all as cowards.

The fort was now nearly deserted. Only one regiment stood between Jackson and the fierce Red Sticks just a few miles away. On January 14, 1814, the term of service for this regiment would end, leaving him alone.

Unbeknownst to the General, however, Governor Blount was not sitting with arms folded, quite the contrary. The recent successes in the Creek campaign had improved recruitment back home. Blount had given orders to a new group of 2,500 conscripts to join Jackson, although it would not be until late February when the full force would arrive. But, new enlistees unexpectedly soon arrived in camp on January 14, 1814; a draft of 900 raw recruits. Seizing the opportunity, Jackson responded to the situation in his usual way, he acted. He quickly organized this inexperienced force, whose enlistments were limited to sixty days. On January 17, determined to get the most fight out of the green recruits, he left Fort Strother and advanced south with the sixty-day enlistees to engage the Creeks at Emuckfaw and Enotachopco. However, these battles were indecisive at best, and Jackson's reduced army, facing superior numbers, returned to Fort Strother with nearly one hundred casualties.

---

[448] AJ to Coffee, Dec. 31. 1813, Jackson, *Correspondence*, I, 431.

Jackson himself was nearly killed when he rode head-long into the battle. "In the midst of showers of balls, of which he seemed unmindful," one officer wrote, "he...[rallied] the alarmed, halting them in their flight, forming his columns, and spiriting them by his example."[449]

It was a near catastrophe, and although Jackson was unaware, he had not needed to act so hastily. Soon the bulk of Blount's recruitment efforts began to arrive and by the end of February, Jackson commanded close to four thousand troops, including several hundred U.S. regulars, who did much to improve the tone of Jackson's army. This marked the first time Jackson would lead regular, non-militia troops. Many of these regulars had caught wind of Jackson's growing reputation and were compelled to fight under Old Hickory.

However, during this time, Old Hickory was anxious. Perhaps his previous struggles with enlistments and desertions were the cause, or perhaps it was the frustrations with the governor, the War Department, delays with supplies. Whatever the cause, Jackson was ill at ease and determined to assert his authority during this period, particularly with the many fresh faces in his ranks. Ordering several court-martials in February and March, Jackson included one for his rival and cohort, General Cocke. Infuriated by reports that Cocke had spread allegations that Jackson ignored the legal enrollment terms for his soldiers, which Cocke claimed had caused desertion, Jackson demanded Governor Blount arrest the East Tennessee general under the law against enticing soldiers to desert. Blount wisely declined to intervene, but Jackson arranged for Cocke's arrest on his own, leading to a court-martial in Nashville. Cocke was ultimately acquitted, despite, as he wrote, facing a tribunal "composed of my bitterest enemies and General Jackson's most devoted, personal friends." [450]

Meanwhile, Red Eagle's renown continued to spread throughout the South. Back on December 23rd, when Jackson was down to just 130 soldiers, and struggling to keep his army together, the Red Sticks encountered a large force of Mississippi Volunteers, led by General William Claiborne, in the village of Oconochaca. Surprised by Claiborne's troops, and facing superior numbers, Weatherford and his

---

[449] Reid and Eaton, pg. 136.
[450] Hickey, p. 406.

men did what damage they could to the Mississippians and then fled. Weatherford, racing along a bluff high above the Alabama River on Arrow, his prized gray horse, escaped using the only option he had, by urging his horse to make a legendary jump off the bluff into the river far below. The stunned militiamen fired at the river, raining a hail of bullets down upon the water, but Red Eagle and his horse emerged further downstream, unscathed. Riding onto the bank, Weatherford dismounted and checked his horse for any signs of blood. Finding none, the indomitable Chief Red Eagle Weatherford rode off into the thick Alabama woods.

Spies had reported that Chief Red Eagle and approximately 3,000 warriors were encamped in a village about one hundred miles away, at a location known as Tohopeka, or Horseshoe Bend, along the Tallapoosa River. Recognizing that another risky engagement like the one at Emuckfaw could not only decimate his raw troops but also cause his allied tribes to wish to rejoin their brethren under Red Eagle, Jackson was determined to make the location the Red Sticks' last stand. Yet, while both Emuckfaw and Enotachopco had been indecisive, Jackson's militia had caused further losses for the already depleted Red Sticks. These casualties and reduction in their forces required that Weatherford's warriors abandon their aggressive policy and retreat more cautiously back into their fortress at Horseshoe Bend.[451] Jackson was learning that with the success of the previous fall, enlistments were increasing, and with that he recognized, time was now on his side. He would wait until conditions were ideal for the final thrust against the enemy.

Jackson had reports from his scouts–the young Davy Crockett among them, the details on the Creek camp at Horseshoe Bend, its location and details. The intel gave the officers a clearer picture as to the best route into Creek country. The location the Red Sticks had chosen was aptly named. The great U-shaped curve in the river was being used as a moat of sorts to protect the Creeks on three sides. The Red Stick warriors, along with a few hundred women and children, inhabited huts on the hundred-acre peninsula, toward the south end. A thin neck to the north was the only entryway onto the peninsula, but, the spies reported, there the enemy had erected a formidable barrier of log breastworks.

---

[451] Bassett, Jackson, p. 114

With the knowledge of the Red Sticks' location, and the best route to find them, Jackson's spirits lifted. Despite the struggles militarily, his confidence as a commander had grown as a result of the raids at Emuckfaw and Enotachopco. He had proven to himself and his men that he could lead an army and preserve it, even in the face of defeat. His outlook was boosted as well from the growing confidence the Madison administration began to show in his abilities. General Thomas Pinckney, his superior, wrote to the Secretary of War, praising Jackson's successes, "Without the personal firmness, popularity and exertions of that officer, the Indian War, on the part of Tennessee, would have been abandoned at least for a time. If government think it advisable to elevate to the rank of general other persons than those now in the army, I have heard of none whose military operations so well entitle him to that distinction." [452]

---

[452] Pinckney to James Madison, Jan. 29, 1814, Jackson, *Correspondence*, I, 452

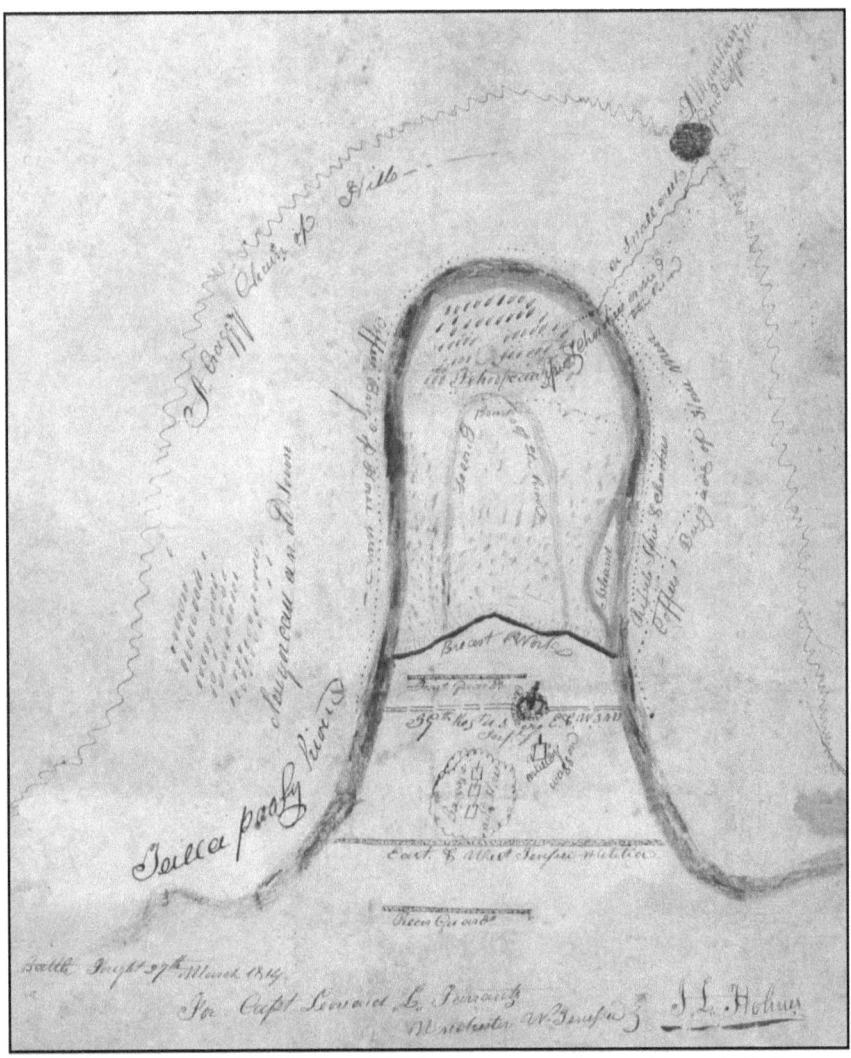

This map by Indian agent Leonard Tarrant shows the Creek encampment and barricade (the Breast Work) at Horseshoe Bend and the positions of American forces, including the Thirty-ninth U.S. Infantry and East and West Tennessee Militia, and the Cherokees and members of Gen. John Coffee's brigade who were deployed along the river. *Courtesy of Alabama Department of Archives and History*

CHAPTER 33

HORSESHOE BEND

"War is a blessing compared with national degradation."
-Andrew Jackson

Jackson himself was pleased with the outcome of the raids at Emuckfaw and Enotachopco. These were not decisive victories by any stretch, but even with raw recruits and a smaller force, his army had proven their mettle. Morale was high, and upon the men's return to Fort Strother, they were met by a large number of new recruits, eager and ready to fight for the talk of the town, General Jackson. The new additions to the army sensed victory in sight, and had rushed to enlist in a winning cause, eager for a share of the glory. The hard work of the fall campaign was beginning to pay dividends.

The General was growing as a commander and had learned from his mistakes of the previous encounters. With all the new faces, Jackson understood that discipline from the outset would be key. This had been proven at Enotachopco in January, and he would tolerate nothing less than a full commitment from every man. Anything less than their absolute best would be met harshly and punished severely.

Jackson wrote home to share the good news with Rachel, but in reply he found her tormented and in near hysterics. Having lost her nephew Alexander Donelson in recent days, Rachel was distraught with grief, loneliness, and anxiety over her husband's safety. Her letter was full of pleas for Jackson to return home. As concerned as he was for his wife, there was no chance Jackson was coming home any time soon. He had a war to win, and he would not leave until the job was completed in full. To ease her distress, he wrote to his wife to reassure her of how close they were to completing the mission.[453]

With nearly 5,000 troops under his command by March, Jackson bore down on training his men, determined to turn them into a professional army. With iron will he drilled his men daily and instilled in them the importance of every detail. "There never was so thorough going a man, nor one who so well knew how to inspire his men with ardor & enthusiasm as our General." wrote one officer, "had he been appointed for the command of the armies in the North I am well assured the war had long ago been at an end. He will not be delayed or trifled with by the contractors...he *makes* them do their duty...indeed every officer and every soldier–every man connected with the army, is here, compelled to the strictest observance of whatever appertains to his duty." [454]

Drumming the importance of sacrifice into his men, Jackson required his officers to rise at three in the morning, soldiers by 3:30. This early start was enforced by Jackson to prevent surprise attacks, as the Creeks often tended to strike at dawn. He tasked his troops with improving the road between Ford Deposit and Fort Strother, banning the transport of whiskey and other non-essential items.

When Generals Cocke and Isaac Roberts opposed his strict discipline and attempted to undermine it, Jackson had them arrested and sent home. He was particularly frustrated with General Roberts, who tried to limit his men's service to three months. When soldiers began to march home, Jackson declared them deserters, although he would later promise pardons for those who returned to duty, and most did.

However, in Jackson's resolution to maintain the strictest military discipline, especially after the troubles of desertion earlier in the winter, an incident occurred that would haunt Jackson's military and political career for years to come and solidify his reputation as a ruthless and inflexible commander. The incident involved a young soldier named John Woods, an 18-year-old militiaman, who had been charged with leaving his post during guard duty. Woods was a member of a company that

---

[453] Rachel to AJ, Feb. 10, 1814, Jackson Papers, LC.
[454] John Reid to Nathan Reid, Oct. 17, Nov. 6, 1813, Reid Papers, LC.

had become known for disciplinary issues, although it appears Woods himself had not been one of the troublemakers.

One cold February morning, after receiving permission to leave his post to get a blanket from his tent, Woods found that his fellow infantrymen had left him breakfast. Hungry and tired, Woods sat down to eat rather than returning immediately to his post. When another officer happened upon his tent and began admonishing Woods with abusive language, he ordered him back to his post. Woods, feeling wronged by the tongue-lashing, angrily refused. An argument ensued, leading to an order for Woods' arrest. In a fit of rage, he threatened to shoot anyone who approached him.

Upon hearing of the mutiny, Jackson rushed from his tent, demanding to know who was responsible, shouting, "Where is the rascal? Shoot him! Shoot him! Shoot ten balls through the villain's body!"[455] Fortunately, Woods was eventually persuaded to surrender his weapon and comply with the arrest.

The teenage Woods was then detained and ordered to appear for a court-martial tribunal. The military court was brief but formal. General Jackson presided over the proceedings. Despite pleas for mercy based on Woods' youth and his previous good conduct, the verdict was swift: guilty of desertion in times of war, punishable by penalty of death. Jackson, though known for his battlefield ferocity, struggled with this decision, according to the accounts of his officers. Remembering the loss of his own brothers during the Revolutionary War, he understood the weight of military sacrifice. However, he believed that discipline was essential for an army's survival. "The law must be enforced," he wrote in his field journal, "lest the entire army dissolve into chaos."[456]

Woods had enlisted in the Tennessee militia for the chance to defend his country, driven by the patriotic fervor that swept the nation. However, the harsh realities of military life -- the endless marches, scarce food, and constant danger -- proved overwhelming for the young soldier. As part of his defense, Woods argued that his violent reaction and insubordination was the result of having read news of his ill mother back home. This, however, did not change the mind of his commander.[457]

---

[455] Parton, *Jackson*, I, p. 508.
[456] Parton, *Jackson*, I, p. 508.
[457] Jackson, General Order, March 12, 1814.

ANDREW JACKSON: THE POLITICS OF RESENTMENT

On the day of his execution, in the crisp morning air of March 14, 1814, the solemn scene unfolded. The scared eighteen-year-old stood before the firing squad. By all accounts, Woods faced his fate with remarkable composure. He had been permitted to write a final letter to his mother, apologizing for both deserting his post and bringing shame to his family. As the sun rose over the Alabama sky, the young soldier was executed by firing squad. [458]

Years later, when Jackson sought the presidency of the United States, the circumstances surrounding Woods's death were highlighted in newspapers nationwide to portray Old Hickory as a butcher who could have shown mercy, chosen a milder sentence but instead chose to take the life of a young volunteer. The punishment was severe. Although Jackson might have been more lenient under different conditions, he offered no defense of his decision. Historians have argued that his experiences from the previous December and January had hardened him, causing him to be extremely strict in discipline matters. He had maintained a force in the field despite immense desertions and hardships, shaping him into a relentless General, focused entirely on defeating the enemy.

Not one to dwell on others' perceptions of him, Jackson moved forward, as did his militia, finally back to full strength. Hardened from the adversity of the winter, the army set out on the same day Woods was executed, March 14. Jackson began the campaign aimed at annihilating the Red Sticks and ending the Creek War once and for all. His plan involved moving southward along the Coosa River and then eastward toward Emuckfaw, anticipating a gathering of Creek tribes. After dismantling this confederacy, he intended to march to Hickory Ground, the sacred center of the Creek Nation, which they believed was protected by deities. Jackson began the march early that morning, leaving four-hundred and fifty men behind to protect Fort Strother, while sending Colonel John Williams and his 39th Regiment downriver to establish an advance post, later named Fort Williams.

Jackson's troops arrived at Fort Williams, where he stationed a strong force before proceeding on towards Horseshoe Bend. Initially cautious, Jackson became more confident after assurances from General Pinckney about reinforcements from Mobile. He then directed a contingent of

---

[458] Reid and Eaton, pp. 142-143.

over three thousand soldiers toward Horseshoe Bend. His force included militia men, regular troops, Cherokee and Lower Creeks. They departed Fort Williams on March 24th, headed for the Tallapoosa by way of Emuckfaw. They would arrive at their destination in just two days, pushing through the Alabama brush, setting up camp near the Red Creeks location at the village of Tehopeka (on Horseshoe Bend) on the night of March 26. That evening, Jackson and his men rested just six miles north of Horseshoe Bend, where intelligence revealed over a thousand braves and nearly 300 women and children were prepared for his attack.

The following morning, at around 10:00 AM on March 27, Jackson arrived at the Bend. He was flabbergasted by what he saw. The Red Sticks were nearly encircled by the river and had reinforced their camp with a breastwork of logs, standing five to eight feet high, featuring a double row of portholes for defense. Chief Menowa had directed the building of the nearly impregnable fortress, which was brilliantly designed, and which made a frontal assault all but impossible. Jackson later described the challenge of the breastworks, "It is impossible to conceive a situation more eligible for defense than the one they had chosen and the skill they manifested in their breastwork was really astonishing."[459]

Jackson launched the attack on Tehopeka from two directions. Knowing he couldn't attack the breastworks head on, he devised a plan. He would divide his force in a two-pronged attack; he would bombard the front of the breastworks with artillery, and he would have General Coffee direct some of the men to swim across the river and create a diversion, in order to force the enemy to another part of the peninsula. The plan was to contain the Creeks inside their fortress, where Jackson would smash through the breastwork to overpower and destroy them.

First, Jackson planted his artillery, a 16 pounder and a 13 pounder, on a small hill between eighty from the closest and two hundred and fifty yards from the furthest point of the breastwork. At 10:30 AM he opened fire. The balls flooded harmlessly into the thick logs or whistled through "the works without shaking the wall." [460] Whenever the Indians peaked over the breast work to fire at the gun crews, Jackson raked to them with

---

[459] Horseshoe Bend, American Battlefield Trust, 2023; AJ to Blount, March 31, 1814, Jackson, *Correspondence*, I.
[460] Reid to Nathan Reid, April, 1814. Reid Papers, LC.

musket and rifle fire. For two hours, the firing continued, the artillery pounding the defenses without inflicting appreciable damage, and the sharp shooters futilely searching the wall for targets. As they watched the frustrated whites attempting to rupture the line of defense, the Indians whooped mockingly. Several medicine men, their heads and shoulders, decorated with the plumage of many birds, danced and howled their incantations to the sun to bring death and damnation to the invaders.

Several hours earlier Jackson had detailed Coffee and his cavalry, along with his companies of spies and the entire force of the friendly Cherokees, to occupy the side of the river opposite the Bend to prevent the Red Sticks from escaping. In addition, General Coffee was told to make some feint or maneuver to divert the enemy from the principal point of attack. Coffee and over thirteen hundred militiamen, Lower Creeks and Cherokee would commence a wide flanking maneuver that would cross the Tallapoosa River and surround the Red Sticks. As directed, some of Coffee's men dutifully swam across the river to the far bank, where they set about seizing the Red Sticks' canoes. Once the canoes were secured, Coffee ordered Colonel Gideon Morgan's Cherokee regiment to cross the river, attack the town itself, and then set fire to the back part of the breastworks.

While Jackson continued to direct the shelling of the breastworks, the sound of small-arms fire could be heard from the back of the fortress, where dark plumes of smoke rose high into the air. By setting the breastworks on fire, Coffee's men had created the diversion Jackson needed. Without pause, he ordered his most elite unit, the 39th U.S. Infantry, on a bayonet charge. The order brought a shout from the men, and Colonel John Williams led the charge under a brutal shower of bullets and arrows. The soldiers reached the rampart and thrust their rifles through the port holes. The soldiers fought at point blank range, shooting muzzle to muzzle, "in which many of the enemy's balls were welded to the bayonets of our musquets."[461]

Major Lemuel P. Montgomery was the first to reach the breastworks. Leaping onto the wall, he turned to call for his men to follow, when a bullet struck him square in the head, and he fell to his death. Undeterred, the 39th kept coming, and at the front of the charge was the young Ensign

---

[461] ibid.

Sam Houston, future governor of Texas. Houston and the 39th mounted the wall, renewing Montgomery's cry. An arrow ripped into Houston's thigh, but he jumped into the fortress anyway. His fellow regulars poured over the wall, followed by a continuous stream of Americans. The breastworks had been breached, the fort was fully penetrated, and a massacre ensued.

The stunned Red Sticks backed away at the sight of hundreds of Jackson's men pouring into the fort and attempted to hide in the thick brush that covered the ground. But the army was upon them, and the killing became savage. The Red Sticks fought on, however; not one of them asking for quarter. They continued to fight on despite being hopelessly outnumbered. "The carnage was dreadful,"[462] Jackson reported. Women and children were not exempt from the carnage and more than 200 fleeing Red Sticks continued to be shot down as they fled. Many headed for the canoes, only to run directly into Coffee's contingent of men. Some of the fleeing Red Sticks leaped down the river bluff, and attempted to hide in the cliffs and tangled brush of fallen trees. As the shooting continued, the remaining Red Sticks jumped wildly from place to place, as the systematic slaughter continued.

Yet, the Red Sticks fought on, despite the withering fire, refusing to surrender. The fighting continued throughout the afternoon. Hoping to end the carnage, Jackson sent a flag of truce and an interpreter to their last stronghold on the bluffs to ask them to throw down their weapons, but they were met with a blast of gunfire that killed one member of the party. At that Jackson leveled his artillery at them, pounding the cliffs with cannonballs, but to no effect. The Indians would not surrender. Jackson then ordered lighted torches thrown down the cliffs. The brush and fallen trees quickly caught fire; the area became an inferno. As the Indians dashed from their hiding places, the soldiers picked them off one by one. The killing continued through the late afternoon and into the evening; it stopped only when the light disappeared, and the soldiers could no longer see their targets. By nightfall, only a few warriors had managed to escape across the river. Jackson counted over 500 dead on the battlefield and estimated an additional 300 drowned in the river.

---

[462] AJ to Rachel, April, 1814, Jackson, *Correspondence*, I.

However, their leader, William Weatherford, was not at the Horseshoe Bend.

The next day, Jackson ordered a count of the dead. Some 557 Indians were found on the ground; Coffee estimated as many as 300 creeks dead in the river; and a few dozen bodies were later discovered in the woods—a total of approximately 900 Indians killed. William Bradford, an infantry officer who remarked successfully "the river ran red with blood." Duncan McCullough, a West Tennessee militia man at Horseshoe Bend affirmed Bradford's observation, "The Tallapoosa might truly be called the river of blood, the water was so stained that at ten o'clock at night it was very perceptively bloody, so much so that it could not be used."[463] Few warriors escaped the carnage; Jackson figured that no more than 15 or 20 Braves got away, but the number may have been higher. As they counted the slain hostels, the soldiers cut off the tips of each nose of the enemy, in order to keep the count accurate. Many also cut long strips of skin from the bodies of the dead Indians to make bridle reins.

As the counting progressed, an 18-year-old Red Stick was brought before Jackson. He had been severely wounded in the leg, and a surgeon was summoned to dress the wound. While the operation progressed, the proud Indian looked at the general and asked, "Cure 'em, kill 'em again?" Jackson assured him he would not be killed. He was so struck by the youth's "manly behavior" that he sent him to the Hermitage, and after the war bound him out to a trade in Nashville, where he married a free black woman and established himself in business. [464]

In picking over the dead, the soldiers discovered three prophets, one of whom was the famous Monahoee, "shot in the mouth by a grape shot," reported Jackson, "as if heaven designed to chastise his imposters by inappropriate punishment."[465] Yet, the absence of Chief Red Eagle was a grave disappointment, and it troubled the Jackson command.

In all, three hundred captives were taken, all of them women and children. Jackson said he regretted learning that two or three women and children were accidentally killed. [466] He never "made war on females, only the base and cowardly do that," he said. His own casualties amounted to

---

[463] Harbert and Hall, *Creek War*, pp. 276-277.
[464] Kendall, *Jackson*, p. 282.
[465] AJ to Blount, March 31, 1814, Jackson, *Correspondence*, I, 491-492.
[466] ibid.492.

47 dead and 159 wounded, along with an additional 23 friendly Creeks and Cherokees killed and 47 wounded.[467]

In the immediate aftermath of the battle, Jackson wasn't sure exactly what he'd won. Jackson was not satisfied with, nor was he fully aware of his unparalleled victory. He wasn't even sure he had entirely defeated the Red Sticks. In tallying the carnage "what effect this would produce on those infatuated and deluded people, I cannot yet say." [468]Jackson wrote to Rachel. For all the hostile Creeks killed at Horseshoe Bend, others remained at large, stubbornly refusing to lay down their arms. Jackson had no choice but to steel his troops for more fighting. He congratulated them on what they had accomplished, nonetheless. He was saddened by the loss of Major Montgomery, however, and he regretted something else: William Weatherford, Chief Red Eagle, had escaped him. The ferocious chief was away from Horseshoe Bend on the day of battle, and Jackson desperately wanted his head as tribute for the massacre at Fort Mims. Nevertheless, the power of the Red Sticks was irreparably broken. Jackson expected the tribesmen to sue for peace immediately. "Should they not," he told his wife, "I will give them, with the permission of having the final stroke at the Hickory ground." [469]

The magnitude of the victory was enormous for the morale of the nation, and it put an end to the Creek War. Militia soldier William Carroll, who later became the fifth governor of the state of Tennessee, was immediately aware of the accomplishment of Jackson's troops. Carroll wrote just after the battle, "I think it the most complete victory that has been obtained over the Indians in America."[470] Carroll didn't know it, but in fact, this was not only the most lopsided victory in American history, over Native Americans to that point, but it remains so to this day. It was also the decisive victory in the southwest throughout the War of 1812. It represented Tecumseh's last great hope of the offensive of which he had prophesized, of the final phase of the contest for the dark and bloody ground of the old Southwest.

---

[467] Coffee to Mary Coffee, April 1, 1814, Coffee Papers, *THS*.
[468]
[469] AJ to Rachel, April 6, 1814, Jackson, *Correspondence*, I.
[470] Phillip Langsdon, *Tennessee: A Political History* (Franklin, Tenn.: Hillsboro Press, 2000), pp. 59–63, 78–80, 91–93.

Jackson was forced to sink his dead in the river to prevent their being scalped by the enemy. Then he collected his wounded and returned to Fort Williams, burning and destroying Red Stick villages as he went. "At my approach," he informed Rachel, "the Creeks fled in all directions... I have burnt the Verse town this day that has been the hot bed of the war and have regained all the scalps taken from Fort Mims."[471] The destruction of the Creek food supply had been so systematic over the last year that the indigenous population, friendly or not, now verged on starvation. With outright starvation a genuine threat, many Red Sticks laid down their weapons or fled to Florida.

On his return to Fort Williams, Jackson gathered his army on parade and published a short address praising his men's courage and the magnitude of their victory. They had redeemed the character of the state, he said, and were entitled to the gratitude of their country. They had destroyed the Creek confederacy, and consequently the "fiend of the Tallapoosa "Would never again disturb the quiet of the frontier or "murder our women and children. Never! By their yells, they had hoped to frighten us, and with their wooden fortifications to oppose us. Stupid mortals! Their yells, but designated their situation, the more certainly; Whilst to their walls became a snare for their own destruction. So will it ever be, when presumption and ignorance contend against bravery and prudence." [472]

While at Fort Williams, many more Creek chiefs surrendered to Old Hickory, agreeing like the others to removal. But where were the remaining chiefs? Jackson asked. Where was William Weatherford? He was told that many of the Creeks had fled to Pensacola to seek the protection of the Spanish. Weatherford too? They could not say. To test their goodwill, Jackson directed the chief to bring Weatherford to his camp, tied as a prisoner, so that he could be dealt with as he deserved.[473]

Weatherford spared the chiefs the further humiliation of turning him in. A few days later, he walked into Jackson's camp carrying a flag of truce and calmly claimed the protection that had been extended to the other chiefs. At the same time, the proud Red Eagle, now stoic and defeated, expressed his desire for peace for himself and his people.

---

[471] ibid.
[472] Reid and Eaton, *Jackson*, 156-157.
[473] ibid, pp. 164-165.

Jackson, 'The Iron General,' surprised at the sudden appearance of his foe, and astonished at Weatherford's gall, informed him that the only way there could be peace was if the remainder of the Red Stick army laid down their weapons, and settled themselves north of Fort Williams, where they would be cut off from Florida and British and Spanish assistance, and where they might more easily become wards of the United States. Staring at his presumption of asking for protection after what he had done at Fort Mims, Jackson stated, "I had directed that you should be brought to me confined," growled Jackson; "had you appeared in this way, I should've known how to have treated you."

When the Red Sticks relocated, they would learn Jackson's final terms for ending the war and establishing peace. Lacking any choice, Red Eagle stoically consented, assuring the General of his desire for friendship and a desire to end the war and live in peace. "I am in your power," replied Red Eagle, "do with me as you please. I am a soldier. I have done the white people all the harm I could; I have fought them and fought them bravely; if I had an army, I would yet fight and contend to the last: but I have none; my people are all gone. I can now do you no more than weep over the misfortune of my nation." [474]

The speech deeply impressed Jackson, who struggled to remain stoic, grave and solemn. He could not hide the admiration, however. Despite the animosity he should have felt, Jackson instead was moved by the courage the chief showed by walking so brazenly into a camp swarming with the enemy, knowing their one desire was to torture and kill him. Still, Jackson had a role to play as commander and conqueror; no amount of admiration could change that. "The terms on which your nation can be saved," Jackson said, "and peace restored, have already been disclosed; in this way, and none other, can you obtain safety." If Red Eagle wanted a continuation of the war, Jackson and his army would fight on.[475]

Weatherford replied quietly. His voice was low, but strong and his pride resonated with every word. So that his nation might be relieved of their sufferings, and the women and children saved from destitution and death, the Red Sticks desired peace. "There was a time," he continued, "when I had a choice, and could've answered you: I have none now--even

---

[474] Royall, Anne, *Letters from Alabama*, Tuscaloosa, 1969, pp. 91-92.
[475] Reid and Eaton, *Jackson*, p.166.

hope has ended. Once I could animate my warriors to battle; but I cannot animate the dead. My warriors can no longer hear my voice: their bones are at Talladega, Tallahatchie, Emuckfaw, and Tehopeka. I have not surrendered myself thoughtlessly, whilst there were chances of success, I never left my post, nor supplicated peace. But my people are gone, and I now ask it for my nation, and for myself. As the misery and misfortune sprout upon my country, I look back with deepest sorrow and wish to avert still greater calamities. If I had been left to contend with the Georgia army, I would've raised my corn on one bank of the river and fought them on the other; but your people have destroyed my nation. You are a brave man: I rely upon your generosity. You will exact no terms of a conquered people, but such as they should accede to; whatever they may be, it would now be madness and folly to oppose. If they are opposed, you would find me amongst the sternest enforcers of obedience. Those who would still hold out can be influenced only by a mean spirit of revenge; into this, they must not and shall not sacrifice the last remnant of their country. You have told us where we might go and be safe. This is a good talk, and my nation ought to listen to it. They shall listen to it." [476]

The conversation between the two warriors ended. Though Jackson respected Weatherford's courage, and was greatly moved by his words, he knew he had to do what was expected of him. He made it clear, therefore, to the man before him, that if peace—true peace---were to commence Weatherford and his people would have only one chance to follow his conditions to the letter. Red Eagle, for his part, promised to do whatever he could to convince the remaining Red Sticks still holding out to surrender. A few days later, he set out to do just that, leaving the camp with several followers to take up residence in the location Jackson suggested. Working to persuade the remaining holdouts to surrender, effectively bringing the Creek War to an end, Weatherford was later pardoned by Jackson and subsequently became a prominent citizen and wealthy planter in Monroe County, Alabama. William Weatherford, the legendary Chief Red Eagle, fought no more. [477]

With the defeat of the Red Sticks, Jackson finally had a moment to breathe. After resting his army briefly, he and his men set out again on

---

[476] ibid, p. 167.
[477] Debo, Angie, *The Road to Disappearance*, Norman, Oklahoma, 1967, p. 82.

April 5, headed for the Hickory Ground at the juncture of the Coosa and Tallapoosa Rivers. Their mission was to destroy whatever remained of any Creek resistance. Jackson also sought to connect with the Georgia and North Carolina militia, both of which General Pinckney was sending his way to strengthen his forces. But for all intents and purposes, the Creek War was over.

Preceded by a detachment of troops sent to scour the country and flush out any and all remaining hostiles, Jackson continued his march toward the Hickory ground. On April 18, he raised the American flag over the old Toulouse French fort, which was rebuilt and renamed Fort Jackson after the commanding general. The French built Fort Toulouse in 1717 to serve as the eastern-most outpost of their Louisiana colony. The French intended to secure the friendship of the Creek Confederacy and make French policy known, while keeping out the soldiers and interests of the British Empire. Now it was to be the stronghold of the United States, and rather than friendship with the Creeks, the demand was submission.

Jackson did not depend on Weatherford to conclude the Creek War; it was his army's responsibility to handle the mopping-up operations. He regularly dispatched detachments to scour the Coosa and Tallapoosa River basins, aiming to "scatter and destroy any who might be found concerting offensive operations." He also employed spies and emissaries to inform the Indians that those who did not retreat north of Fort Williams would be treated as enemies. Jackson noted, "Every hour brings in more" Creeks, all grudgingly accepting of unconditional submission. On April 18, he informed Governor Blount that the campaign was over. [478]

The Battle of Horseshoe Bend was one of the major engagements of the War of 1812. Apart from the incredible number of men killed, Jackson and his men had crushed the will and capacity of the Red Sticks to incite war. This result came just in time, as the British were on the verge of landing troops in the South and providing the tribes of the Upper Creeks with an enormous supply of arms and ammunition. Had the Creeks not been defeated so decisively they would've become a force of incalculable danger to the entire southern half of the United States.

---

[478] AJ to Blount, April 18, 1814, Jackson, *Correspondence*, I, 503.

The battle finally broke the backs of the Red Sticks and the Treaty of Fort Jackson was signed. The treaty ceded 23,000,000 acres of land to the United States, including much of southern Georgia and over half of the state of Alabama. It opened the floodgates of white settlement into Alabama, to the dishonor of the White Stick Creeks, who lost much of their land despite their heroic efforts at Horseshoe Bend.

The aftermath of the battle is controversial, and the story divides along two camps. One view is that Americans were imperialistic and brutally stole lands from the natives, the other perspective defends American motivations as justifiably seeking to provide a buffer zone between Alabama and Spanish Florida. Ultimately, the answer lies in a combination of the two. Such was the reality of the southwestern American frontier in 1814.

Throughout the Creek War, Jackson had led his way. He compromised only when he felt he had to. As badly as the war had gone elsewhere, Jackson's leadership came at a crucial time. As historian Henry Lee points out, "Jackson's gallantry and enterprise were always conspicuous, attracted the confidence of the whites, and inspired honor and respect among the Indians."[479] Jackson now began to garner the respect of a grateful administration in Washington, and a grateful nation, desperate for a victory. But his best was yet to come.

So, by April 1814, troubles with the enemies of the United States, at least among Native American tribes in the southwest, appeared settled. Jackson and his resilient army were to thank for this, and so the Secretary of War appointed General Pinckney and Benjamin Hawkins as commissioners to arrange a peace treaty with the Creek nation. [480] The top priority the two were given was to ensure restitution for the cost of the war. Otherwise, Pinckney was given carte blanche as to the terms of the treaty. Many westerners, however, were unhappy with the selection of these two men as commissioners, especially Hawkins, who was viewed as too benevolent with the tribes. Protests poured into Washington from those who believed the peace terms would not be sufficient punishment for the horrors committed by who they called "savages." Compounding

---

[479] Lee, Henry, *A Vindication of the Character and Public Services of Andrew Jackson*. 1828.
[480] Owsley, *Struggle for the Gulf*, Chapter 7.

Madison's troubles, the West promised more outcry if anything short of a huge cession of land from the Creeks came about.

Jackson, recovering physically from the ailments of the campaign, agreed wholeheartedly with the views of his community on the frontier. In fact, he was their principal spokesman, advocating for the removal of all Creeks from all lands west of the Coosa and north of the Alabama rivers to ensure their complete separation from the Spanish in Florida. On this position, Jackson would stake his claim. With the Creeks defeated, Jackson now seemed to view the Tennessee Valley as his personal domain. He was certainly in the school of thought, like so many conquerors of old, that indeed 'to the victors go the spoils.' The victors, in this case, would exploit the defeated if Jackson and his constituents had something to say about it.

In the meantime, the General continued to quell any lingering conflicts with the remaining combatants in the Southwest while directing the rebuilding of Fort Jackson, which established a protective line through Creek country in Alabama. On April 20, General Pinckney arrived to command the area and negotiate with the Creeks, praising the Tennessee troops and their commander. He celebrated Jackson's victory with banquets, as though it was his own. Once the toasts to the Tennesseans concluded, Pinckney ordered Jackson to return home and discharge his troops. [481]

Although the War of 1812 continued and the remaining British and Spanish presence in the South were still very much in existence, Jackson did not dispute a return to Nashville with his victorious army. A return trip home would be met with glory and honor, but more importantly, Jackson's willingness to release the volunteers after their great victory was sure to improve his reputation regarding soldiers' rights. After all, even the Iron General recognized that he had been obstinate and demanding long enough, it was time to follow orders and allow his men to go home. Within two hours of receiving Pinckney's order, Jackson gathered his troops, and three days later they reached Fort Williams, sixty miles away, where he delivered a farewell address to his soldiers.

Jackson relished every opportunity to deliver speeches directly to his men, crafting addresses that reinforced his connection to the ordinary

---

[481] AJ to Pinckney, May 18, 1814, Jackson, *Correspondence*, II, 1-2.

soldier. The General spoke with obvious pride in his men's bravery, loyalty, and resilience. The troops responded with cheers, and there seemed to be an overall feeling among the men for their commander; that Jackson understood their struggles and would share their sacrifices with the world. Although phrases that included "your General is pleased with you," and "he salutes you" may have come across to the men as patronizing or too fatherly in his approach, the effort hit home, and the men not only delighted in their victory but hailed their chief. For the moment, Jackson's reputation swelled among his beleaguered troops.[482]

Before departing Fort Williams, Jackson addressed the men's bravery, "Within a few days, you have annihilated the power of a nation that, for 20 years, has been the disturber of your peace. Your vengeance has been flooded. Wherever these infuriated allies of our arch enemy assembled for battle, you pursued and dispersed them. The rapidity of your movements, and the brilliancy of your achievements, have corresponded with the valor by which you have been animated. The bravery you have displayed in the field of battle, and the uniform good conduct you have manifested in your encampment, and on your line of march, will Long be cherished in the memory of your General, and will not be forgotten by the Country you have so materially benefited."[483]

With that, Jackson's army headed north, and the heroes were applauded and celebrated all along the route back to Tennessee. News had spread quickly, especially about the glories of General Jackson, who was greeted as the hero who not only defeated the mighty Red Sticks but guaranteed the future security of the region. The army reached Fayetteville, and the men of the victorious Tennessee army were finally home. But before the men were dismissed, Old Hickory got in one final address to his troops, and he saved his best for last.

Again, praising their bravery and their devotion, the General nearly brought himself and his soldiers to tears with his words. In florid prose, Jackson expressed how much it meant to him that this group of men, made up mostly of volunteers, had performed so heroically, and with such self-sacrifice for the good of their country. Standing in front of his ragged, wearied, but victorious men under the tall pines of Alabama,

---

[482] Reid and Eaton, *Jackson*, pp. 173-174.
[483] ibid, 174.

Jackson parted with these final, lasting words before finally dismissing his army: "He would never forget them."[484]

With that, Andrew Jackson was headed home to Nashville, and to a happy reunion with his family. Little did he know the degree to which he would now be embraced as Nashville's favorite son.

---

[484] ibid, 173-174.

CHAPTER

34

SHARP KNIFE

"If they do not come in and submit... a sudden and well directed stroke may be made, that will at once reduce them to unconditional submission."
—Andrew Jackson

As Old Hickory, the conquering hero Andrew Jackson returned to his stomping grounds of Nashville, Tennessee, an excited, near-frenzied crowd waited to greet him, as though he were the prodigal son. The crowd flooded the streets of Nashville and was electric in their exuberance for the man who had quelled the frontier.

Eager to celebrate victory, and his army's vanquishing of the "barbarians," the jubilant crowd hailed Jackson all along the route, as an arrangements committee escorted him to the courthouse. There, Felix Grundy, who then served on the House of Representatives' Foreign Relations Committee, expressed the community's joy in finding a commander capable of eradicating the scourge of the frontier, pacifying the terrifying Chief Red Eagle and subduing the menace of the Red Sticks.

A state banquet at the Bell Tavern followed, and as Jackson was receiving his ceremonial sword, the crowd called out for a speech. Jackson obliged, praising his officers and men, acknowledging the suffering endured and the significant accomplishments his army achieved. "The success which attended our exertions has indeed been very great. We have laid the foundation of a lasting peace to those frontiers which had been so long and so often infested by the savages. We have conquered, we have added a country to ours, which by connecting the settlements of Georgia to those of the Mississippi Territory, and both of them with our own, will become a secure barrier against foreign invasion, or the operation of foreign influence over our red neighbors in the South and we have furnished the means not only of defraying the expenses of the war against the Creeks, but that of which is carrying on against their ally Great Britain." [485]

Jackson spoke in a commanding voice. He was in his moment, and it showed. His speech was one of his best, and it showed not only his growth as a commander, but his evolution as a budding politician as well. His speech featured the results of the Creek campaign: the establishment of lasting peace on the state's frontiers and the expansion of territory connecting the southwestern states with the Mississippi, which would secure against foreign invasion. He concluded by honoring the memory of fallen Tennesseans, calling them true "descendants of the desires of the revolution."[486]

The crowd erupted in applause and appreciation for his words, and for what Jackson and his army had accomplished. At Bell's Tavern, a legend was being forged right before their very eyes. It was a crowd that had suffered from the loss of loved ones, some of which were the very fallen heroes Jackson referred to. Tennesseans, like all Americans in early 1814, thirsted for something to celebrate; a sense of victory and security after the frightful and depressing news of the previous two years. And, to this audience at Bell's Tavern, that it came from one of their own was the crowning stroke.

Andrew Jackson had come a long way in a short amount of time. Less than a year before he had struggled out of a sick bed after a disgraceful gun fight and by sheer willpower and resolve he had forged an army and kept it in the field, even while suffering from bullet wounds that nearly killed him. Throughout the campaign, he had endured enemies on all sides, who did not miss an opportunity to slander his reputation. Now those who still harbored a distaste for Jackson either kept to themselves or joined in on the bandwagon of praise for Old Hickory.[487] Even some

---

[485] John Reid to Nathan Reid, June 15, 1814, Reid Papers, LC.
[486] ibid.
[487] Overton to AJ, May 8, 1814, Jackson Papers, LC.

of the old Sevier faction spoke of Jackson "with affection "and went so far as to mention him as the next governor. The state was prepared to give him whatever he required, so universal was the approval. Orphan Andy had to be pinching himself and wondering how high the tide would rise.

America loves a winner, especially in down times. And the year 1814 had been a down time indeed for the young nation. The bleakness of a war the nation seemed to be losing meant that wins, and winners, were hard to come by. In this context, Jackson was lauded far and wide, farther and wider than he may have otherwise been. His tactics had been nothing special, the foe had not been Herculean, but Jackson's ability to lead his inexperienced army through the hardships of a lengthy frontier were shown to be unmatched.

Not only was General Pinckney effusive in his praise for the Tennesseans and their commander, Jackson was celebrated even in places where he had been loathed just a few months before, particularly in Washington, where even the top brass had to admit that General Andrew Jackson was just what the country needed. For those in charge of the war effort, the victory at Horseshoe Bend could not have come at a better time. Victories had been so few and far between that morale had fallen to devastating lows. Jackson's successes were applauded across the country, at a time when Mr. Madison's War had otherwise been largely disastrous.

Much of the war in the north had been devastating, in fact. With the exception of Oliver Hazard Perry's naval victory at Lake Erie the previous September, few truly heroic Americans had emerged. Having vanquished a foe in Chief Red Eagle, whose legend as an almost godlike supervillain had reached epic proportions, Jackson's status was solidified. And this unprecedented celebrity would soon pay off for the militia general in the form of an offer of high rank in the regular United States Army.

Although Jackson deserved recognition for his leadership in the Creek War, realistically, the universal adulation Old Hickory received seems to outweigh his accomplishments. As a general, he had not yet proven any extraordinary military skill; his better-armed force had defeated the less organized and outnumbered Red Sticks, only one part of the Creek Confederation. Perry's victory on Lake Erie was arguably of more strategic importance in the overall war effort, allowing the Americans to regain control of Detroit, significantly hampering British operations in the Northwest. And while Horseshoe Bend mainly secured American territory from Creek resistance, the British (and possible Spanish) threat to the South remained unaffected. Perry's victory at Lake Erie is seen as the major turning point in the War of 1812, up to that point, whereas Horseshoe Bend, while a significant victory within the Creek War, was a smaller conflict occurring alongside the larger war.

Yet, in light of the numerous setbacks experienced by American generals in the war to that point, particularly those supported by the administration in Washington, it was encouraging to witness a general demonstrate the ability to effectively engage in combat and secure victory on the battlefield. Jackson's key distinction was his ability to command and maintain an army effectively in the field, over a period of several months. Even in the face of severe supply and desertion issues, Jackson nevertheless emerged having earned the confidence of his officers and his enlisted men, driven by his determination to achieve victory. Like many aspects of his run of glory in the War of 1812, Jackson was a beneficiary of good timing, and luck. Horseshoe Bend could not have come at a better time. A dearth of victories had just become palpable throughout the country. Additionally, the impact of defeating imposing Native Americans in the West resonated not only with Westerners' desire for land, but their affinity for bravery, resolve and manliness in the face of frontier hardship, a recurring fear embedded in American culture. Jackson emerged as an iron-willed, unique and fearless figure to the frontiersmen, solidifying his reputation through the Creek War, a reputation he would never relinquish.

Grudgingly, even the Madison Administration recognized that, in Andrew Jackson, they finally had a man who stood out on the field of battle, where others had failed miserably. Secretary of War Armstrong soon recommended that something be done for the hero. Thus, when General Wade Hampton resigned from the army on April 6, 1814, the administration offered Jackson a brigadier generalship in the US Army, with the brevet of major general and command of the Seventh Military District, which included Louisiana, Tennessee, the Mississippi territory, and the Creek nation. The blunders Wade committed on the northern front had caused a firestorm of criticism, primarily due to his failed attempt to capture Montreal, which resulted in a significant defeat at the Battle of Chateauguay.

For most militia commanders, a promotion such as this would have been cause for celebration, and graciously received with satisfaction, humility and honor. But such was not the case with Andrew Jackson. Although having long been passed over by the federal government in the past, such belated recognition, in fact, vexed Jackson. Filled with supreme confidence after such laudatory recognition in Nashville, the General had anticipated a higher rank. He expected to be a made a major general--the rank he held in the militia. Secretary of War John Armstrong tried to soothe the General's bruised ego, explaining that given the current situation militarily, it was the best the administration could do. [488]

Although feeling slighted once again by those back east, he was officially a general in the regular United States Army after all, which was of no small value. With fortune seemingly in his favor more and more since Horseshoe Bend, Jackson soon got more good news. General William Henry Harrison soon resigned in frustration with the War Department, leading Armstrong to offer the vacant major generalship to Jackson, and he accepted the promotion on June 18, 1814. Here, we see another example of Jackson's run of good luck, not only were Harrison and Hampton now out as generals, so too was James Wilkinson, sent North. General Thomas Flournoy had resigned in the spring, and his successor, General Benjamin Howard of Kentucky had died before reaching his post. Jackson, therefore, was now the top commander in the South.

Although the Madison administration underestimated its worth, not seeing the likelihood of a British invasion of the South, Jackson now had a first-class rank and a valuable command. His base pay was $2500 a year, totaling $6500 with allowances, providing him with significant financial benefits during the war.

Jackson's health, however, had been severely worsened by the war, to that point. The newest Major General of the regular United States Army was now suffering from both chronic diarrhea and dysentery. The harsh conditions of the many months in camp, particularly the

---

[488] Armstrong to AJ, May 22, 1814, Jackson Papers, LC.

lack of nutrition from near famine, had been very much to blame for his ailments, but Jackson's own neglect of his suffering had not helped. Though in physical agony from his gunfight wounds, he had endured and persevered, believing his body would respond to his will. But, by the end of the long Creek campaign, things had only gotten worse; his health was greatly compromised, although his willpower had intensified to monumental proportions. Yet the iron-willed Jackson pushed on, undeterred, as always. Having accepted the appointment, his immediate orders from Armstrong were to negotiate a peace treaty with the Creek Nation. [489]

The negotiations having already been concluded by Pinckney and Hawkins, Jackson was ordered to facilitate the signing of the agreement to conclude the treaty. Jackson was guided by the administration's instructions and those given by General Pinckney: that a guarantee in land equal to the government's expenses, a clause giving the United States the legal right to open roads through the Creek country, the cessation of any further communication with the Spanish, and the surrender of any remaining Creek prophets who had instigated the war should all be part of the treaty. Armstrong also suggested that the treaty should include a "capitulation" from the Creeks.

As most everyone in the West suspected, Pinckney and Hawkins provided lenient terms to the Creeks, as directed by Washington. After the outcry from land-hungry Westerners who demanded better representation, after Jackson replaced the two and took charge of the peace negotiations, he ensured the results he and his region demanded. Concerned about the Spanish threat in Florida and its influence on the natives, and with the recent arrival of the British along the coast to initiate attacks against the United States, the hostile Creeks, he felt, would never submit to American domination. Many Red Stick Chiefs sought refuge in Florida, safe from the pursuit of American forces. Jackson, as always, was determined to eradicate Spanish power in Florida once and for all, insisting to Armstrong that resolving the Indian issue required removing all foreign influence. With that, he sought official permission to invade Florida and expand American territory, remembering the implications of Aaron Burr's actions.

---

[489] Armstrong to AJ, May 24, 1814, in *ASPMA*, III, 785.

"Query--if the hostile Creeks," Jackson wrote to Armstrong, "have taken refuge in East Florida, fed and armed there by the Spaniards and British... Will the government say to me... Proceed to _____ and reduce it. If so, I promise the war in the south will have a speedy determination and British influence forever cut off from the Indians in that quarter."[490]

Yet, Jackson waited, and waited, but still heard nothing from Washington. The unexplained silence exasperated the General, as months passed with nary a word. In fact, Jackson would not receive a response until January 17, 1815, shortly after the Battle of New Orleans. But mysteriously, the letter he did eventually receive was dated July 18, 1814, yet there was no explanation for the long delay. When Jackson read the reply at that late date Armstrong was as noncommittal as he could be. "The case you put is a very strong one," it said, but "there is a disposition on the part of the Spanish government, not to break with the United States. If that is true, the administration must be extremely careful in deciding a course of action. However, if the Spanish feed, arm and cooperate with the British and hostile Indians, we must strike on the broad principle of self-preservation-- under other and different circumstances, we must forbear." [491] Had Jackson received this letter in July instead of the following January he would have taken immediate action. His army would've been slammed into Florida without another moment's delay. How differently the War of 1812 may have been decided had the fate of these orders not hung in the balance.

Jackson arrived at Fort Jackson on July 10, 1814, and promptly notified the Indian agent, Benjamin Hawkins, that he was calling a general meeting of the Creek chiefs—both friendly and hostile—to meet with him at the fort on August 1. He wanted Hawkins to attend and use his influence with the Creeks that they might accept the invitation. And he made his mood perfectly clear. "Destruction will attend a failure to comply with those orders," Jackson told Hawkins.[492] He repeated this warning to General Coffee. "If they do not come in and submit,

---

[490] AJ to Armstrong, June 27, 1814, Jackson Papers, LC.
[491] Armstrong to AJ, July 18, 1814, Jackson Papers, LC; Quoted in Reid and Eaton, *Jackson*, pp. 196-197.
[492] AJ to Hawkins, Jackson Papers, July 11, 1814. LC; Merritt P. Pound, *Benjamin Hawkins*, Pg. pg. 236.

against the day appointed, which is the first of next month, a sudden and well directed stroke may be made, that will at once reduce them to unconditional submission."[493]

Jackson's intent was clear, and its tenor was fierce: to destroy the Creek Nation. Sensitive to western land greed and conditioned to disregard Indian rights, Jackson aimed to strip the Creeks of their property. Despite the alliance with the many friendly tribes who had assisted in his victory, Jackson acted on the belief that the savage and warlike nature of Native Americans in general was largely due to having too much land. He believed this was at the root cause of their "wandering habits of life." By restricting their activities, Jackson believed these habits would decline, prompting them to adopt industry and agriculture. Ultimately, he argued that seizing their property and restricting movement was necessary for the Creeks' safety and welfare. [494]

Negotiations began at Fort Jackson on August 1, though only in name. In reality, Jackson, sole representative of the United States, essentially dictated terms under which the Creek nation ceded some 22 million acres--most of present-day Alabama, and the lower fifth of Georgia. In the course of these "negotiations," Jackson permitted "precaution against revolt" to dominate all else. Much of the territory ceded belonged to Creeks allied to Jackson's forces. Their failure to control the Red Sticks, he claimed, validated the land grab. A preamble to the Treaty of Fort Jackson, drafted on the fifth and outlining his view of the situation concluded with the definitive, "The terms of peace will be read to you." Four days later nearly three-dozen exasperated chiefs signed the accord. The following day, Jackson confided to Coffee of having offered the Creek Nation "many who had fought by my side," no options other than removal or war. "I told them at last... Those who was our friends would sign it--and those who were not might go to the British, but I would furnish them with provisions to take them there, and then I would pursue and drive them and the British into the sea." The day following the treaty of Fort Jackson, the Creeks understood that the lean, bullying general was indeed aptly named, "Sharp Knife."

---

[493] Jackson to Coffee, July 17, 1814, Jackson Papers. LC.
[494] Rogin, *Fathers and Children*.

ANDREW JACKSON: THE POLITICS OF RESENTMENT

Though Jackson's approach was indeed ruthless to those tribes who had supported his army against the Red Sticks, the equivocal instructions from Washington only exacerbated matters. Two days before, President Madison had written Armstrong that he seemed open to the idea of preserving those Indian nations who fought on the United States' side. At the same time, the president agreed, "the hostile Creeks have forfeited all right to the territory we have conquered, justice to the friendly part of the nation requires that they should be left in the peaceful enjoyment of their towns and villages with a sufficient appendage of woodland." But then he added, "Still the grand policy of the government ought to be, to connect the settlement of Georgia with that of the Territory of Tennessee, which at once forms a bulwark against foreign [European] invasion, and prevents the introduction of foreign influence to corrupt the minds of the Indians. Invariably," he argued, "we must.... extend our settlements to the Mississippi to cut off all communication of the southern tribes with that of the north, and to give our citizens perfect safety in passing through their country." He concluded by predicting Indian removal's likely impact on race and regionalism in America: "This then will give strength to the southern section of the United States." [495]

Which is precisely what happened. Following the admissions of Mississippi and Alabama into the Union (1817 and 1819 respectively,) the old Virginia Dynasty of slaveholding presidents (Washington, Jefferson, Madison, and Monroe) evolved into a southwestern style of southern Republicanism, driven largely by advancing into former tribal lands. Between 1820 and 1844, the Democrats, linked to the protection of slavery, won five of seven national elections, with southern enslavers taking four. The 1814 Treaty of Fort Jackson led to the U.S. obtaining over 20,000,000 acres of Creek territory and initiated further land cessions, resulting in the removal of southern Native American tribes. Jackson significantly influenced this process as a military officer and negotiator.

In 1948 the Creek nation of Oklahoma filed a claim to obtain payment for the millions of acres lost in 1814. In 1952, the Creek nation east of the Mississippi received authorization to join this case as "petitioners by intervention." Six decades later, in 1962, the Indian claims

---

[495] Madison to Armstrong, May 20, 1814, LOC.

commission awarded the Creeks nearly $4 million (roughly $34 million in current dollars.)

In August of 1814, tasked with negotiating a peace treaty with the Creek Nation, following specific government instructions, Jackson was unbending in his terms to the Creek chiefs. By imposing upon them the Treaty of Fort Jackson, even friendly Creeks were forced to give up nearly twenty-three million acres of their ancestral lands and remove their settlements to a smaller area that American forces could more easily patrol. Ill-health or not, Jackson's dogged resolve remained intact, and at Fort Jackson, it was in full display. To the people of Tennessee, Jackson was more heroic than ever, but to those indigenous peoples who had supported Sharp Knife, his betrayal was the deepest cut of all. [496]

---

[496] Kendall, *Jackson*, p. 87.

CHAPTER

35

THE BRITISH MONSTER COMES SOUTH

"Who could brook a British tyranny, who would not prefer dying free, struggling for our liberty and religion, than live a British slave?

—Andrew Jackson

The treaty of Fort Jackson spurred Jackson's desire to extend America's conflict into the Gulf region. Upon learning that hostile Creeks, near the Georgia border, were receiving support from Spain and Great Britain, Jackson sought permission to enter Florida to verify these claims, expressing his opinion to Secretary Armstrong, "Whether these rumors are founded in fact, or not, we ought at least to be prepared for the worst." [497] The General of the Seventh Military District now planned to advance toward Fort San Carlos de Barrancas, which was built in 1797 to protect Pensacola, the capital of Spanish West Florida.

Around the time Armstrong communicated with Jackson, who had set his sights firmly on Pensacola, he began to develop a plan to protect New Orleans. In late July, he informed Louisiana Governor Claiborne of rumors regarding a significant British force that had reportedly unloaded arms at Apalachicola Bay, 175 miles east of Pensacola. He warned that Mobile and New Orleans were likely targets for the British, who could incite insurrection among the black population. Jackson urged Claiborne

---

[497] AJ to Armstrong, 1814, Jackson, *Correspondence*, II.

to organize a militia of 1,500 well-equipped men. He suspected Spain, with British support, sought to reclaim Louisiana, leading him to conceive a Gulf strategy that included securing Mobile and defending New Orleans.[498]

Jackson's swift actions prompted the British to accelerate their plans, shifting their focus from the European theater of war to North America. With the threat of Napoleon Bonaparte soon diminished and the Creek Confederacy defeated, the British Royal Navy redirected its attention to the Gulf coast. They aimed to replicate their previous success in Washington, with amphibious assaults targeting perceived vulnerabilities in the American coastline.

The attempts upon the part of England to invade Louisiana began with the abdication of the French emperor, the enigmatic Napoleon Bonaparte, when he fled Fontainebleau in the early summer of 1814 for the island of Elba. This temporary calming of the turbulent European waters enabled Great Britain to redirect the vast forces that had been operating against France. After the fall of Paris in 1814, one of the demands England posed, if France wished for peace, was the return of Louisiana to Spain. The territory, England claimed, had been fraudulently acquired by Napoleon, and England would take it back for its weakened ally on the Iberian Peninsula.

While England had been moderately successful in its campaign against the United States in the War of 1812, its chief triumph being the capture and burning of Washington, D.C. in August of 1814, the British cabinet resolved that future warfare against America could now be vigorously prosecuted. With the Napoleonic Wars seemingly over, the intention of victorious England with her hands now completely free in Europe was to give the United States a lesson and a military chastisement that the upstart Americans would never forget.

President Madison described the assault in Washington in a public proclamation as "a deliberate disregard of the principles of humanity and the rules of civilized warfare."[499] Already reeling from Washington having been so humiliatingly set ablaze, the Madison administration was determined to show its constituents that the government would never

---

[498] AJ to Claiborne, Aug. 30, 1814, Jackson Papers, LC.
[499] Madison Papers, National Archives, 1 September, 1814.

again be caught so unaware. Three weeks after Washington's torching, in fact, Britain's sea and land assault on Baltimore met with far less success, as American forces fended off the attackers at Fort McHenry after a twenty-four-hour bombardment. A young lawyer from Maryland, Francis Scott Key, witnessed the bombing while negotiating a prisoner exchange aboard the HMS *Tonnant*. Under the spell of America's resilient stand through the night and into the next morning, Key penned a poem he called, the Star-Spangled Banner. [500]

Admiral Sir Alexander Cochrane, commander of the North American Station, advised London to prepare for an occupation of the Gulf region near New Orleans, setting his forces on a collision course with Jackson's. In mid-August, British troops led by General Edward Nicholls, invited by Spanish governor Don Mateo Gonzalez Manrique, landed in Pensacola. Simultaneously, Jackson moved his army nearly two hundred miles to Mobile, previously taken by General Wilkinson's forces a year earlier, and sent a small group to occupy Fort Bowyer, a fortification to protect Mobile from British ships.

However, on August 8, 1814, three Englishman and five Americans met in the hotel des Pays Bas, in Ghent, Belgium. They were peace commissioners, and they were meeting there to draw up a treaty of concord between the warring nations of Great Britain and the United States. William Adams, a Doctor of Civil Laws, Henry Goulbourn, a member of Parliament, and Lord Gambier, an admiral of the Navy, represented the British. There to address the wrongs committed against the young United States were John Quincy Adams, James Bayard, Henry Clay, Jonathan Russel, and Albert Gallatin. Negotiations, though, would be difficult, slow and laborious. [501]

When the great military victor, the Duke of Wellington, refused the honor of the task, it had been agreed upon in London that Major General Robert Ross would be the commander of the expedition against New Orleans. It was Ross who was celebrated for the dramatic invasion of Washington. Earlier in the summer, after landing in the vicinity of Washington DC, General Ross began that campaign by leading a successful attack on the thin U.S. forces at Bladensburg, Maryland.

---

[500] Fort McHenry, National Park Service, 2020.
[501] Taylor, Alan (16 April 2014). *The War of 1812 and the Struggle for a Continent*", p. 258.

There, his army easily brushed the defending American militia aside. Ross's forces then began clearing the way for the remainder of the British army to enter the capital city of the United States. Following orders from Vice Admiral, Sir Alexander Cochrane, and Rear Admiral George Cockburn, Ross ordered the burning of the White House, the Capital building and the Library of Congress on August 24th, 1814. With the destruction (and America's humiliation) complete, Ross and his troops set out again on August 30th, sailing up the Potomac toward Baltimore.

Ross's forces landed at Northpoint, southeast of Baltimore, early that morning. The Americans had anticipated this move, however, and they had flooded the woods with militia men. Ross, who was later alleged to have arrogantly stated that he didn't care if it "rained militia," moved swiftly to disembark his troops and move inland. After a two-mile march, American sharpshooters unleashed a torrent of bullets at the Redcoats. Ross, mounted on horseback, turned in his saddle to signal the reinforcements when a bullet struck his right arm, passed through it, and entered his chest. A surgeon was called for, but Ross's wound was fatal; he died on the way to the ships; his eyes resting for the last time upon the sight of the sprightly oak trees along the banks of the Patapsco River.

The treaty of peace was still in the works in Ghent, Belgium more than a month later when the somber news arrived in London that General Ross had met his untimely end. This marked the first setback in the Crown's plans for the daring Louisiana operation. With the death of Ross, the British once again turned to the Duke of Wellington, who again refused to take part in any war in America. Thus, the choice of supreme commander fell upon his brother-in-law, Sir Edward Michael Packingham, and there can be no doubt that the later conqueror of the mighty Napoleon had a hand in this selection. [502]

On September 18th, English and Canadian newspapers boldly announced the departure, from England, of the victorious troops of Wellington's Army. This experienced force was now led by General John Keane and had at one time numbered as many as 18,000. Among them were officers and enlisted men who had bested Napoleon's forces, and many would end up on the plains of the Chalmette plantation in Louisiana. This heralded force, the newspapers predicted, would now

---

[502] Fortescue, Sir John, *History of the British Army,* London, 1899-1930, X, 151.

bring their formidable might to the American South, and New Orleans, particularly, as the central point of attack.

Another month passed as Goulbourne, along with Under-Secretary Bathurst continued to object repeatedly at the peace conference in Ghent, delaying the talks. On November 24th, a great fleet assembled at Negril Bay, on the island of Jamaica. The fleet not only carried sailors, but also thousands more of Wellington's seasoned veterans. These forces would later be joined by those that had taken Washington, as well as (quite presumptuously) an entire civil government staff to rule over "the Crown colony of Louisiana." General Keane was in command, as the ship bearing the youthful and ambitious Packenham was still in mid ocean. On October 24, 1814, Lord Bathurst had given Pakenham his commission and orders to proceed to Plymouth and embark there for Louisiana "to assume command of the forces operating for the reduction of that province."[503]

In New Orleans, the federal government had four companies of regulars, a half dozen light draught vessels, called by courtesy, gunboats. Colonel Ross of the regular army was there, as was Master Commandant David Patterson of the U.S. Navy. Jackson, who was still in Alabama at the time, seeking to punish any remaining Creeks. Louisiana was told to raise a thousand-man force. After making these preparations for defense, the federal government left New Orleans to cope as best it could with the heart of Britain's most elite troops, soon to descend upon it.

The people of New Orleans were laden with anxiety about the coming attack. Rumors had flown through the streets of the crescent city through various sources, like yellow fever. Yet, while there was a general idea of what was to come, there was no definitive knowledge as to the timing of the attack. That is until Jean Lafitte, the French privateer, sometimes referred to as the "Terror of the Gulf," sent a warning to the governor.

Prior to this, Governor W.C.C. Claiborne, the first American governor of Louisiana had exchanged several communications with Jackson, then in Alabama. As a result, immediate preparations were made to hold the state militias in readiness, and on the 8th of September, these home troops were ordered to "exercise twice a week." Governor Claiborne went further, recommending to fathers of families and men too old for active service in the field, to form themselves into a corps

---

[503] Riley, *British at the Gates*, 1974. p. 170.

of veterans, choose their own officers, acquire arms, and "exercise occasionally."[504]

Express riders were hurriedly dispatched along the road between the Gulf of Mexico and Mobile, where Jackson's troops were camped out. They were a motley mix of militia volunteers, regulars and a force of Tennessee riflemen, all huddled under the canopy of trees in the Alabama forest. The danger grew more real with each passing day, but still, no active show of force against New Orleans presented itself. At least not yet. To the people of Louisiana, however, the likelihood that just such a prospect was the main objective of a fleet of six war vessels now in the Gulf of Mexico, there was no doubt.

By the late summer of 1814, the war was over two years old, and it had not gone well for the United States. The country was reeling with division, economic stagnation, and a lack of confidence. The nation's morale was at an all-time low. Months before the Battle of New Orleans, President James Madison fretted over America's dwindling chances against England. A May 18, 1814, communication from peace commissioners Albert Gallatin and James Bayard warned him that, with Napoleon exiled in Elba, Britain could now focus all of its forces on the United States. Additionally, Gallatin and Bayard cautioned that the Crown might try to return Louisiana to Spain, its pre-Napoleonic ruler. As British naval power shifted from the Chesapeake to the Gulf, the fate of New Orleans appeared increasingly precarious.

Even those Americans who had led the shouts for war were growing despondent. "I've intended, my dear Rodney, twenty times to write you," Henry Clay wrote to an old friend during the first winter of the war, after a string of defeats in the northwest, "but really such have been the mortifying incidents of the last campaign on that theater where all our strength was supposed to lay, that I have not had the courage to portray my feelings to you." America's problems, Congressman Clay contended, started at the top. "It is vain to conceal the fact. At least I will not attempt to disguise with you, Mr. Madison is wholly unfit for the storms of war. Nature has cast him in too benevolent a mold. . . for the rough and rude blasts which the conflicts of nations generate." [505]

---

[504] Remini, 1977, Ch. 16.
[505] Henry Clay Correspondence, 1813, *Henry Clay Family Papers, 1732-1927*, LOC.

ANDREW JACKSON: THE POLITICS OF RESENTMENT

The war had divided the nation; more so than since the days of the "Tory War" during the last two years of the Revolution. A foreign visitor to Washington in early 1812, wrote of the startling gulf that had developed between Republicans and Federalists, "The opposite parties live separate from each other, and have but little intercourse except on business. I once asked Mr. Potter (Rhode Island's Federalist Congressman Elijah Potter), if it would not be better for the members of different parties to live more together and become more sociable with each other. He said they could not live in peace together, and that after the contentions they continually had in the Hall (Congress,) they required some rest and quiet when they got home. He said also that some of the Democrats (Republicans) are men of such unruly minds that is extremely difficult to be upon good terms with them." [506]

Typically, American wars, or all wars for that matter, have united people that fight on the same side, even factions that are usually separate, as they confront a common enemy. The War of 1812, however, was having quite the opposite effect. Federalists, especially in New England, driven further and further apart from their Republican rivals, despised the war as if it were a plague, particularly its devastating impact on trade, which New England merchants relied upon so heavily. The fragile economic ties to Britain the Federalists had so carefully rebuilt since the Revolution were now in tatters, and they placed the blame squarely on Republicans. Their criticism of the administration knew no bounds, and Federalists attempted to block all but the narrowest of defensive measures. [507]

In return, Republicans blasted back at the Federalists. In Baltimore, Jeffersonians took to the streets, rioting against Federalists while chanting tunes from the Revolution. "We'll feather and charr every damned British Tory, and that is the way for American glory." [508]The riot resulted in one death and nearly a dozen injuries. If the war had been successful and brief, the opposition might not have mattered, but that was not at all how the conflict had developed. One Republican

---

[506] Brands, 2005, Ch. 18.
[507] ibid.
[508] Paul A. Gilje. "The Baltimore Riots of 1812 and the Breakdown of the Anglo-American Mob Tradition." *Journal of Social History*, Vol. 13, No. 4 (Summer, 1980): 547-564.

newspaper likened the Federalists to traitors and Tories, "When war is declared there are but two parties: citizens, soldiers, and enemies. Americans and Tories."[509] The country needed a hero and needed it fast.

Instead, however, it looked as if things were about to go from bad to worse. In 1814, following Napoleon Bonaparte's defeat at the hands of the British, led by the indomitable Duke of Wellington, the United States suddenly faced an intensified threat of British might. Could the full force of the world's greatest military power now bear down entirely on North America? The thought alone gave shudders to an American public already reeling from wartime mismanagement. The potential of a singularly focused British military altered the military strategy of General Andrew Jackson in the South, particularly regarding the defense of Mobile and the Gulf Coast. Having received intelligence about Britain's newly available military reshuffle, Jackson recognized the threat of British forces potentially using Spanish Florida as a military base, and this suddenly became a very real and pressing concern. With this threat bearing down upon the Americans, Jackson sent Captain John Gordon to Florida to conduct reconnaissance of Spanish-held Pensacola.

After several days, Gordon returned to Alabama to report that British forces had indeed made forays into Spanish Florida and had established a supply base at the Apalachicola River. The captain confirmed that, as suspected, the British were in fact actively recruiting and training hostile Creek warriors. Spanish commander Don Mateo Manrique's response alluded to Spanish willingness to enter the fray; and to enter into potential conflict with the United States. Jackson identified Mobile as a likely target for an invasion by the Royal Navy, and thus, Fort Bowyer became a crucial defensive position. The fort's location on a boot-shaped peninsula commanded the water passage to Mobile, and Jackson was determined to ensure its fortification.

On August 22nd, 1814, Jackson marched into Mobile, at the head of the Third Infantry Regiment, with approximately 500 men, all regulars of the United States Army. Immediately, he sent Major William Lawrence and one-hundred and sixty men by boat to Fort Bowyer to occupy and restore the fort's defenses. During the next few days, Jackson's scouts sent in alarming reports that a British war fleet was

---

[509] Brands, 2005, Ch. 18.

actively gathering strength at Pensacola, located only fifty miles from Fort Bowyer. More British troops had arrived, and their commander, Colonel Edward Nicholls, had issued a proclamation to the "Natives of Louisiana," and arrogantly vowed that "all of Mobile would soon be in British hands." [510] Nicholls played on Native American disdain for the United States, calling on them to overthrow the American government.

As tensions escalated, Jackson arrived in Mobile just as the British advanced into American territory. Jackson's request for naval support from Patterson was denied, leading to a strained relationship between the Army and Navy, although, both branches eventually learned to cooperate, as each aimed to defend against the British threat.

Simultaneously, British forces sought to exploit the geopolitical landscape, considering attacks on American positions in Mobile and Pensacola. After a series of unsuccessful attempts to capture Fort Bowyer, British forces reevaluated their strategies, focusing on a combined operation against New Orleans, strategically vital for controlling the Gulf. As if these threats were not enough, rumors also ran rampant that another large British fleet was amassing in the West Indies. The fleet's purpose, so it was said, was to cut off the Mississippi Delta, assuring that the mouth of the river would be entirely in British hands. From there the British army would easily invade and capture New Orleans and return all of Louisiana to its rightful owners. The American people were nearing their wits' end, and to most, it appeared that the government was sitting on its hands, doing nothing to help the people. It was as if the Madison administration was concussed from the blows to the head the British had inflicted on Washington.

A strong advocate for national unity, the Irish-born publisher and economist Matthew Carey wrote in the magazine *The Olive Branch* that "The national vessel is on the rocks and quicksands, and in danger of shipwreck. There is moreover, a larger and more formidable vessel preparing all possible means for her destruction. But, instead of efforts to extract her, the crew are distracted by a dispute how she came into that situation. [Part of the crew criticizes, part defends the pilot.] A few individuals, who see that both parties have contributed to produce this calamitous event . . . implore them to suspend all enquiry into the cause

---

[510] Reilly, *British at the Gates*, p. 170.

of the danger till the ship is extracted. . . . At this awful moment, the horrible, the disorganizing, the Jacobinical idea was not infrequently advance in our coffee house, the streets, in our newspapers . . . [that the Republicans had started the war, and that they should finish it without any federal help." [511]

It was around this time that Jackson received worse news. The word had reached Fort Bowyer that the British had destroyed Washington, D.C. Both the White House and the Capitol Building had reportedly been burnt to ashes, and the President and Congress were forced to flee the city. When news of the invasion reached other coastal cities, panic ensued, just after the invasion of Washington, the *Republican and Savannah Evening Ledger* called "to ARMS, CITIZENS Prepare for defence . . . Apathy will prove fatal to us as [it] has to Washington . . . which is laid waste! . . . Let our city be placed in best possible defence."[512] Henry Clay's words embodied the indignation of the American public at this most distressing of humiliations, "[The loss of public property] gives me comparatively no pain. What does wound me to the very soul is that a set of pirates and incendiaries should have been permitted to pollute our soil, conflagrate our Capital, and return unpunished to their ships." [513]

On September 14, Jackson boarded a schooner to sail down Mobile Bay for an inspection of Fort Bowyer's defenses. While en route, they came across a small boat carrying a messenger sent by Major Lawrence. He carried even more troublesome news: the British had landed a force of marines and some of their Native American allies toward the rear of Fort Bowyer. [514]

Without delay, Jackson ordered the schooner to turn about and head with all possible speed to Fort Bowyer. Lawrence would need reinforcements, as the British would otherwise have the American entirely outgunned. Alarmingly, the forecast became ever more grim: his spies confirmed that the British fleet was rapidly en route to Fort Bowyer to reinforce the Royal Marines.

---

[511] Mathew Carey and "The Olive Branch," 1814-1818; Economic Nationalism and the War of 1812, *American System Now*, January 30, 2020

[512] *The Republican and Savannah Evening Ledger*, Aug. 1814, (Savannah, Ga.) 1807-1816; Savannah, Ga.

[513] Clay, LOC, August, 1814.

[514] Heidler, David S. and Heidler, Jeanne T., *War of the 1812*, 2004, p. 115.

CHAPTER

36

NEW ORLEANS

"Here we shall plant our stakes and not abandon them until we drive these red-coat rascals into the river, or the swamp."
-Andrew Jackson

In the thin air atop the earthen and wooden fortification at the mouth of Mobile Bay, Fort Bowyer, Major William Lawrence felt a rush of panic. In the distance he spotted them: four British warships fast approaching the channel. Within the hour the ships would be in the range of attack and Lawrence fought down an uneasy feeling in his gut, remembering his training. Below him, a battery faced Mobile Bay, and he put on an air of confidence with his men, assuring them that the fort's cannons could deter the British. However, Lawrence worried about the British Marines and their Creek allies behind the fort, preparing to launch a ground attack from the dense terrain. He felt time quickly ticking away.

After inspecting his 160 troops, who had practiced steadily with the fort's cannons for three weeks, Lawrence noted a weakness: the lack of protective casements for his gunners. When enemy forces were spotted, the British would likely recognize this and coordinate their assault with the advancing warships accordingly. But, despite being outnumbered, Lawrence prepared for battle, assuring his men by recalling Old Hickory's words of confidence in American resolve, uttered just days earlier, "One American could lick ten British men any day of the week!"

As the British soldiers attempted landings, Lawrence ordered his men to open fire. Their practice was paying off, as the gunners sprayed shells across the entire Bay, forcing the British to pull back. However, though the fleet raised their sails and pulled away, to the cheers of the men in Fort Bowyer, Lawrence knew they would be back before long. Sure enough, the British fleet regrouped overnight, and returned at dawn on September 15, re-emerging through the morning fog. The Major ordered his men to commence fire as the warships got within range. Soon, the battle became intensified, with both sides exchanging cannon fire while facing a barrage from British Marines on land.

Soon, Major Lawrence spotted a telltale sign; the British flag on the *Hermes* was no longer flying. Uncertain as to why, he gave the command to pause fire, and the Americans waited. An ominous hush settled over Mobile Bay. Just as the Americans were convinced the British would raise the surrender flag, they soon heard the faint command from the brig below the flagship to recommence the attack. Lawrence, in turn, commanded his men to fire away once again. The cannons appeared to just miss the *Hermes*, although it suddenly began to drift aimlessly. The American barrage had cut through the flagship's anchor cable. The fleet pulled back and was nearly out of sight of Lawrence's spyglass. There they remained, and the Americans withheld their celebration.

After many hours of waiting, as night fell, the British ships slowly turned and began to withdraw, but as they did, a fire erupted on the *Hermes*, causing a massive explosion on her main deck. Lawrence and the men inside the earthen and wooden fort were jubilant, and their cheers were deafening. [515]

General Jackson awaited news from the fort and dispatched Captain Laval for reinforcements. Laval reported that he had encountered a fierce fight in progress, and witnessed an explosion, fearing the worst for the fort. However, news soon reached Jackson that the explosion came from the British flagship, not the fort. Jackson, relieved and pleased with Major Lawrence's victory, planned to strike back against the British while the iron was hot.

On the 27th, Jackson wrote to Secretary Armstrong, expressing his regret that the government had not allowed the seizure of Pensacola, "I

---

[515] Horsman, *War of 1812*, pp. 232-233.

can but regret that permission had not been given by the government to have seized on Pensacola," Jackson wrote Armstrong on the 27th, "had this been done the American Eagle would now have soared above the fangs of the British lyon." [516] Instead, knowing that the British force (albeit only four ships) had failed to dislodge Americans from Fort Bowyer, Jackson resolved to invade West Florida and capture Pensacola, with or without orders, asserting that Spain was covertly siding with the British through its actions. "... as it has become our enemy covertly, if not openly," he wrote, "and is secretly carrying on a war with Great Britain, by means of their Indians from Pensacola against the United States—why will not the government order the British to be expelled from Pensacola and seize and garrison it with their troops?"

Secretary Armstrong would later criticize Jackson's high-handed maneuvers in Florida, "The general's attack and capture of the town on 7 November 1814, he wrote "was to say the least of it decidedly ill judged, involving at once an offense to a neutral power, and a probable misapplication of both time and force, as regarded the defense of New Orleans." [517] But by the time Armstrong received Jackson's communication, he had resigned as Secretary of War after the criticism heaped upon him for his failure to defend the nation's capital. Armstrong was replaced by Secretary of State James Monroe, who was forced to head both departments. In Monroe's efforts to caution the hard-charging General against provoking Spain, he was too late. On October 21, Monroe, having reviewed Jackson's correspondence with Armstrong, wrote to Jackson, "I hasten to communicate to you, the directions of the president, that you should at present take no measures, which would involve this government in a contest with Spain." But Monroe's letter did not make it in time, and Jackson went ahead on his own. He and his troops captured Pensacola on November 7, 1814, without much of a fight, before Monroe's warning arrived. The battle lasted two days, though it caused fewer than 40 casualties, leading to the withdrawal of the small British force in the area, and the surrender of Spanish troops under Governor Manrique. [518]

---

[516] ibid 3:123.
[517] Adams, *History of the United States During the Administration of James Madison*, page 1139.
[518] Monroe Papers, LC, 3: 122.

Jackson's invasion of Florida and capture of Pensacola was a strategically sound move, as it sealed off potential invasion routes more sensible than attacking New Orleans directly. However unauthorized, his success at taking Pensacola disrupted British efforts to support the Creeks, and it greatly diminished their operational base in the region. Jackson's decisive actions in Pensacola not only weakened British influence among their Native allies in the area irrevocably, but it was also a tremendous boost to American morale. Jackson framed his actions as "liberating Spain from British influence," despite previous American annexations of Spanish territories in 1810 and 1813. In fact, these annexations, encompassing an area extending roughly from Baton Rouge to the Perdido river, just west of Pensacola, which the Madison administration claimed as part of the Louisiana purchase, had played an important role in Spain's collusion with Great Britain. Jackson defended his army's actions— "I came not as the enemy of Spain," he maintained, but rather "to prevent a repetition of those acts [the occupation of Spanish force by Britain] ... so inconsistent with the neutral character of Spain." [519]

A successful dash from Mobile or East Florida across Louisiana could have cut off New Orleans from supplies, leaving it defenseless against the British fleet. By securing his eastern position, Jackson enhanced the country's security, even if it meant forcing an invasion through New Orleans, a formidable location for large armies due to its landscape. Jackson's earlier victories against the Creeks and the capture of Pensacola not only prevented the British from using it as an invasion route but shook their alliance with Spain. Long discouraged by Spanish indecision in Florida, Jackson's power play forced the British to abandon plans to cooperate with Spain entirely, while the Spanish distanced themselves from the British after witnessing what Splain considered their "abysmal" actions in their lack of assistance in Pensacola. This invasion also eliminated any Seminole support for the British.

After taking Pensacola, he returned to Mobile and commenced the defense of the city, while also considering plans for defending New Orleans, all while Monroe's later communications advised against his actions. Yet, Jackson's bold maneuvers in West Florida elevated his status within his region and improved his leadership within his army.

---

[519] Jackson Papers, III: 179-180.

The victories boosted troop morale to all-time highs and strengthened New Orleans' defenses by reducing the threat of a land invasion. Upon his return to Mobile, he learned rumors of a British assault on New Orleans, and thus, Jackson took steps to reinforce Mobile's defenses, with the intention of preventing British use of the city as a staging ground. In the meantime, he prepared for the impending conflict, soon to hit the Crescent City. [520]

In November 1814, Jackson directed his army's fortification of Mobile Bay, and he instructed his subordinate, Brigadier General James Winchester, to secure the area. At the same time, Jackson sent General Coffee ahead to New Orleans, to commence the protection of the city, while arranging for stout artillery placements at the mouth of the Mississippi. Meanwhile, doubts about his defiance of civilian authority in Florida may have begun to surface, and evidence suggests he viewed the upcoming campaign as potentially his last.

Anticipating British cooperation with landed troops, Jackson directed the coastal forts' defenses bolstered. As Jackson directed this effort, he received a rather frantic letter from Secretary Monroe. Monroe had received intelligence from Cuba on the movements of the British fleet; confirming the rumors that they were on their way to New Orleans. The fleet had set out under the command of Admiral Cochrane, and it would not be Mobile that they planned to descend upon. "Mobile is comparatively a trifling object with the British government. Your presence at such a point, on the river with the main body of your troops will be of vital importance." Monroe continued, "All the boasted preparation which the British government has been making through the year with veteran troops from France and Spain after having been gloriously foiled in attacks on other parts of our Union is about to terminate in a final blow against New Orleans. It will, I hope, close there its inglorious career, in such a repulse as will reflect new honor on the American arms."[521]

Monroe's assessment was accurate. On November 26, 1814, British Vice Admiral Alexander Cochrane's British fleet under the flagship *Tonnant*, along with nearly sixty other vessels, got underway. Setting sail from Negril Bay, Jamaica, the fleet carried a massive force of 14,000 troops

---

[520] Adams, Henry, *History of the United States during the administration of James Madison*, page 1139-1140.
[521] Monroe to AJ, Jackson, *Correspondence*, II: 110.

for the conquest of Louisiana. The ships which accompanied the flagship included frigates, gunboats and various other vessels of the Royal Navy; the soldiers on board were under the temporary command of General Keane. Cochrane could have chosen to strike Mobile, but he decided instead upon New Orleans as the preferred target. For it was in New Orleans where the money resided, along with its strategic importance, situated where it was. The fleet resembled that of a colonizing expedition, carrying not only the manpower, but many of their wives as well. It even included a newspaper printing press. The officers' wives on board ensured quality entertainment for the men en route, in the form of music, dancing and theater. The merriment belied the gravity of what the soldiers and sailors were soon to encounter upon their rude welcome in Louisiana.

Never before in her history had Great Britain fitted out an expedition upon such a grand scale. The regiments of British regulars on board were the choicest troops then on earth; and in the wars against Napoleon most of them had won laurels at Martinique, Badajoz, Salamanca, Vittoria, the Pyrenees, and Toulouse. Others were but recently transported from the fiery ordeals of Corunna, Busaco, and Ciudad Rodrigo.

Jackson wasted no time in following Monroe's directive, packing up his army's encampments to march on to Louisiana. The march itself was grueling. Jackson's troops, numbering around 4,000 men, trudged through the muddy swamps and dense forests of the Mississippi Territory. Writing to Rachel after leaving Mobile on November 22, Jackson requested she meet him in New Orleans, where he hoped to arrive by the end of the month, and to bring "my little son." He also told Rachel to bring beds, bedsteads tables, carriage, servants, and a nurse, but, inexplicably, not Lincoya. However, he needed her desperately; he was close to total physical collapse. Revealing his recent struggles, he added "Before I set out from here, I was taken verry ill.... the doctor gave me a dose of jallap and calamel, which salavated me, and there was eight days on the March that I never broke bread—my health is restored, but I am still very weak." Debilitated, but nonetheless determined to throw back the invasion, he set out west for New Orleans on November 22, 1814, with 2,000 troops, allowing himself time to assess potential British landing sites. Jackson struggled to his horse and headed towards the setting sun. [522]

---

[522] ibid, 3:194, 3:187.

ANDREW JACKSON: THE POLITICS OF RESENTMENT

On the road to New Orleans, described as gaunt and worn, Jackson's rugged face nevertheless portrayed an intense determination. His behavior seemed to align with speculation that the General was on a final mission, come what may. Neglecting his health to such an extreme begged the question for those around Jackson. Was the General sacrificing himself for one last ditch stand, accepting his road to death or decommission in a blaze of battlefield glory; a triumphant victory at New Orleans that would validate his legacy?

On horseback, trudging steadily through the forests of Alabama and Mississippi, Jackson thought long and hard about the city he was soon to enter, the city most vulnerable to Britain's planned coastal invasion. Though New Orleans was sparsely populated in 1814, it had grown exponentially since 1803, and as a result, there were deep divisions among its residents. With a diverse population, largely French-speaking, contentious suspicions of others ran high, particularly among the city's Anglo-Americans and Creoles, who harbored deep-seated mistrust towards one another, while a significant portion of the population consisted of enslaved individuals who many feared might side with the British. General Jackson was soon to face a complex situation, and it would take some clever political skill to navigate.

Fortuitously for Jackson, his adversaries were the British. The Creoles, individuals of French, Spanish, and/or African descent born in the Western Hemisphere, were ambivalent about being governed by Anglo-American Protestants but preferred them over the idea of rule by the hated Redcoats.

A description of Jackson by a woman on the streets of New Orleans upon the General's arrival testifies to the decline of his health. The Creole woman describes Jackson as "a tall, gaunt man, very erect, ... With a countenance furrowed by care and anxiety. His dress was simple and nearly threadbare. A small leather cap protected his head, and a short blue Spanish cloak, his body, whilst his... high Dragoon boots [were] long innocent of polish or blacking... His complexion was shallow and unhealthy; his hair, iron grey, and his body, thin and emaciated like that of one who had just recovered from a lingering sickness... But...[a] fierce glare... [lit] his bright and hawk-like eye.[523]

Normally, the charming and tranquil city of early New Orleans was a festive place. A melting pot of cultures, the Crescent City housed a diverse population including French, Spanish, African, and American influences. It was the kind of city typically bursting with joyful sounds, shouts, and lively celebration, especially in the famed French Quarter. But in those late fall days of war, a sense of impending doom settled across the city like the thick morning fog that rose up from the many bayous that surrounded New Orleans. Located just over 100 miles from the mouth of the winding Mississippi River, it stretches along the river's eastern bank in a swampy marsh filled with swamps and majestic trees draped in Spanish moss. The river is wide and nearly impossible to cross, making the city relatively safe from attacks from the west. Therefore, any invasion would likely have to come from the south or east.

As Jackson approached the placid, drowsy city of New Orleans, anxious concerns beat a furrow into his already well-lined countenance. Scanning the terrain, the variety of attack routes the British could take to invade the city swirled troubling scenarios in his mind. Disconcerting though these thoughts were, Jackson stayed transfixed on just one question: how to prevent the type of devastation the King's forces had wreaked upon the nation's capital just months before. All was on the line for the relatively untested major general from Tennessee. Just a simple militia man at the start of the war, having never before squared off against a European foe, this was Jackson's biggest moment. The potential British threats were immense. The Redcoats had all the advantages, combat experience, numerical advantage, superior mobility at sea. To make matters worse, all reports indicated that the local population was restless, and might easily welcome the invaders with open arms, rather than help Jackson resist. He should have been distraught. He should have been dismayed. But that was not Jackson's way. Although he couldn't change the strategic advantages the British held, his first order of business was to rally the people of New Orleans to the cause.

Approaching the Crescent City was relatively easy during peacetime. Strategically located over 100 miles upstream from the Gulf's main

---

[523] James, p. 201.

channel, there were several routes of invasion available to enemy commanders. A lengthy option involved landing at Pensacola or Mobile Bay and advancing north to Baton Rouge, which, if captured, could isolate New Orleans. Jackson believed the British had originally planned to take this longer route, and he now hoped his actions in Pensacola had thwarted their plans. Another option for the British was to move north from Barataria Bay, immediately south and west of the city, but this area was notorious for marauders, and piracy, and it meant crossing the Mississippi River or going around the powerful currents of its delta. Although crossing the Mississippi posed challenges, it offered a chance for surprise.[524]

That left two other options, both involved invading from the south and east. It was apparent that an invasion from the south would be difficult, although not entirely impossible. If a direct approach upstream from the Gulf was blocked, the British could land troops at Lake Borgne or exploit Lake Pontchartrain. However, that approach was often slow due to the river's numerous turns, which required sailing ships to halt and wait for favorable winds or tides. While a few hours of waiting were insignificant for merchant ships after long voyages, it could be critical for warships. Over the years, first the French, then the Spanish, and now the Americans had all recognized these bottlenecks and fortified them with mounted gun batteries, making it perilous for enemy fleets. The most perilous involved a sharp bend in the river known as "The English Turn." For hostile warships delayed at this turn, the enemy guns could engage in what amounted to a turkey shoot. This meant invading ships became vulnerable targets for the fort's cannons, which could easily pick them off as they sat idle.

In 1814, Fort Saint Philip, a military installation 65 miles downstream, protected this route. It was garrisoned by regular troops with twenty-eight 24-pounder cannons at the ready. That left the water route from the Gulf into Lake Borgne and Lake Pontchartrain. The former concerned Jackson the most. The lakes were connected by a narrow strait of shallows, called the Rigolets, just a few miles to the northeast of New Orleans. Bayou St. John flows out of Lake Pontchartrain and comes within 2 miles of the city limits, but Fort St. John guarded the entrance

---

[524] Coles, Harry L., *War of 1812*, Chicago, pp. 210-212.

to the bayou. Further up the river, Fort Saint Leon sat about 25 miles south of the city, positioned at the English Turn.

The land between the lakes and the city was flat, swampy and lined with a multitude of bayous. It was mostly void of roads. Northeast of the city were the Plains of Gentilly, a patch of dry land set atop a narrow ridge. A road known as the 'Chef Menteur' followed this ground and connected the Rigolets with the Crescent city. Most residents of the city felt confident that an assault would come from this route. They also believed the extensive swamps on either side of the plains would make defending it much easier. If the British chose not to invade along the Chef Menteur, they could choose among the myriad of bayous between Lake Borgne and the eastern banks of the Mississippi.

Jackson and his staff now rode into the Crescent City. It was the chilly morning of December 1st. With the General rode Robert Butler, his adjutant general; Major Howell Tatum, his chief topographical engineer, and his aide, Captain John Reid. As they approached the center of New Orleans, Jackson's army felt the anxiety more profoundly than anything they had experienced thus far. Their determination would soon be tested against the world's most powerful army. The stage was set for what would become one of the most decisive victories in American military history, though none of these weary soldiers could have predicted just how significant their march would prove to be.

Riding just ahead of the officers that made up his staff, Jackson sat tall in the saddle throughout the seven-mile route from Fort St. John—the small, rundown brick fort which overlooks New Orleans. The party of officers on horseback trotted along at a brisk pace. The twisting road they traveled along the bayou connected Lake Pontchartrain to the city, and it was in bad shape; low, muddy, and pitted. The mist of the early morning brooded over the swamp and still hung in the damp and uncomfortable air, as they wound their way along. The ragtag travelers, hardened and weathered from the many months on the campaign, were by now accustomed to exposure, and their purpose absorbed their concerns, enough to leave them unmolested by the external discomforts of war.

As New Orleans resident Alexander Walker later wrote in his 1856 book, *Jackson and New Orleans* upon witnessing the arrival of Jackson and his staff, "Though devoid of all military display, and even of the ordinary equipment of soldiers, the bearing and appearance of these men betokened their connection with the profession of arms. The chief of the party... was a tall, gaunt man, of very erect carriage, with a countenance full of stern decision and fearless energy but furrowed with care and anxiety. His complexion was sallow and unhealthy; his hair was iron grey, and his body thin and emaciated, like that of one who had just recovered from a lingering and painful sickness. But the fierce glare of his bright and hawk-like eye betrayed a soul and spirit which triumphed over all the infirmities of the body. His dress was simple and nearly threadbare. A small leather cap protected his head, and a short Spanish blue cloak his body, whilst his feet and legs were encased in high dragoon boots, long ignorant of polish or blacking, which reached to the knees. In age he appeared to have passed about forty-five winters — the season for which his stern and hardy nature seemed peculiarly adapted."[525]

Jackson had every reason to move briskly. He had just received a near-hysterical letter from Secretary James Monroe. Intelligence had been gathered from Cuba that a large invasion force under Admiral Cochrane had embarked the island headed for New Orleans. Monroe intimated that he expected Jackson to already have taken up a suitable position to defend the city. "Mobile is comparatively a trifling object with the British government," he continued. "Your presence at such a point, on the river, with the main body of your troops will be of vital importance. All the boasted preparation, which the British government has been making thro' the year, with veteran troops from France and Spain, after having been gloriously foiled, in attacks on other parts of our Union, is about to terminate in a final blow against New Orleans. It will, I hope, close there its inglorious career, in such repulse as will reflect new honor on the American arms." [526]

Upon his arrival, Jackson found the morale of the city's residents in a sunken state. Some were in a near panic over the impending invasion, others seemed indifferent to their fate, while even more seemed certain of defeat at the hands of the British. Others doubted his militia's ability to resist the seasoned British troops and said so publicly. Jackson found that the reports of disloyalty among the French and Spanish residents were not, in fact, entirely false. A few of the city's foreign born openly

---

[525] Walker, Alexander, *Jackson and New Orleans*, 1856, Kessinger, pp. 17-18.
[526] Monroe to AJ, Dec. 10, 1814, Jackson, *Correspondence*, II, 110.

wished for defeat, with hopes that a British victory would restore Spanish control over Louisiana. Others disguised their hopes and their defeatism, convinced that Jackson's pitiful force of militia and volunteers could never defeat the mighty, battle-hardened British troops. Gathering his informants, Jackson learned that some of the more irredentist of the city and the surrounding area not only wished for a British victory but would do what they could to assist the Redcoats.

It was becoming clear to Jackson that he needed to make an immediate impression. But how to boost the morale of a city full of seditionists? The British owned the sea, which gave them the mobility Jackson lacked. The army they were bringing from the Chesapeake with reinforcements from the Caribbean would outnumber his army severely. Additionally, the British held the upper hand in having the offensive, being able to choose their route to the city. And given the restlessness of the New Orleans inhabitants, the British command had reason to expect support or at least indifference from the locals. Jackson could not change the balance of power in the Gulf or the geography of the Delta. But he could hope to change the mood of the people he was charged to defend.

The General and his men were greeted by the thirty-nine-year-old Governor W.C.C. Claiborne, whose tenure was troubled by a running feud with the discontented Louisiana legislature, the threat of slave revolt, and the heightened tensions of the city's residents, anxious about the imminent invasion. With the Governor was the young Commodore Daniel Patterson, the short, stout commandant of the naval district; New Orleans Mayor Nicholas Girod, a pleasant Frenchman in his later years accompanied them; along with the brilliant lawyer Edward Livingston, who had served with Jackson in Congress back in 1796 and was the sharpest legal talent in New Orleans. Livingston quickly renewed his friendship with Old Hickory and won the General's respect for his wise counsel and countenance. He soon became Jackson's translator, secretary of sorts, and a confidant. Livingston found himself in the role of mediator between the prickly General Jackson and the haughty, headstrong citizens of New Orleans.[527]

Jackson, with the Governor alongside, addressed a large crowd who had gathered to welcome in the man some were already beginning to

---

[527] Walker, p. 17.

refer to as the "Savior of New Orleans." In front of the elegant estate of the deceased Congressman Daniel Clark, Jackson offered some words of encouragement to the furrowed brows and nervous faces, as Livingston translated to the mostly French inhabitants. In characteristic Jackson oratory, the General informed the people of the city that he was there for one reason: to save them and the city of New Orleans, and that if it was the last thing he did, he was going to drive the British into the sea. The crowd responded with enthusiasm at the fervor of the gritty silver-haired General Jackson, who went on to beseech the crowd to come together for their country, to bring honor to their city.

Faced with the residents' discontent, Jackson spoke in a confident, commanding voice, acknowledging their fears about the British threat. He assured them that with unity and determination, they could repel the invaders. He dismissed rumors of a British victory leading to Spanish restoration, emphasizing the peace between their government and Spain. For now, he reminded them, their true enemy was Britain. "Your government, Louisianians, is engaged in a just and honorable contest, for the security of your individual, and her national rights. The only country on earth, where man enjoys freedom, where its blessings are alike extended to the poor and rich, calls on you to protect her from the grasping usurpation of Britain--she will not call in vain. I know that every man, whose bosom beats high, at the proud title of freeman, will promptly open her voice, and rally round the eagles of his country, resolved to rescue her from impending danger, or nobly die in her defense. Who refuses to defend his rights, when called on by his government, deserves to be a slave, —deserves to be punished, as an enemy to his country--a friend to her foes."[528]

Perhaps it was the energy and resolve that Jackson resonated as he stood before the people on that chilly December morning, for at the conclusion of his speech, the hungry crowd roared with approval at Livingston's translation of the General's words. For the moment, the relieved crowd seemed to breathe deeply for the first time in months. And, although the sentiment would be short-lived, they took the General at his word and seemed to embrace him with gratitude. As Walker wrote in *Jackson and New Orleans*, "It produced an electric effect upon

---

[528] Reilly, *British at the Gates*, pp. 209-210.

all present. Their countenances cleared up. Bright and hopeful were the words and looks of all, who heard the thrilling tones, and caught the heroic glance of the hawk-eyed General." [529]

Impressed by the heroic entrance and the commanding presence of this rugged, iron-haired, worn but resilient general, the residents of New Orleans seemed injected with new life, buoyed by a new hope; perhaps their city could indeed be saved, despite all of the dangers and turmoil of the previous months. Jackson and his staff, eager to get down to the business at hand, then climbed back into their carriages. A parade was organized and made its way to 106 Royal Street, one of the few brick structures standing in New Orleans at the time. A flag was raised from the third floor, quickly signaling to the locals that this was to be the headquarters of the fierce General who had arrived, so quietly and unceremoniously, to assist them.

New Orleans, Lake Borgne de la Tour map, 1720, Public Domain

---

[529] Walker, p.18.

CHAPTER

37

CRESCENT CITY CLASH

"Oh, the side I choose will be the winning side!"
-Pierre LaFitte

The venerable Edward Livingston was chosen as chairman of the Committee of Public Safety in New Orleans, and he had been in communication with Jackson for several months in this capacity. As a result, he was assigned in the role of aide-de-camp. He invited Jackson to dine with him that evening in his home. Livingston's wife, a beautiful creole, and a gregarious woman, a leader in the cities. The social scene was distressed upon hearing the short notice of such an imminent guest coming to her home on Chartres Street. Livingston's wife, Louise, had in fact been in the middle of a dinner party for a small group of younger ladies. "What shall we do with this wild general from Tennessee?" the anxious group wondered. As the apprehensions and whispers flew among them, Jackson, dressed in a uniform of course blue cloth and yellow buckskin high-rising dragoon boots, scuffed up from the campaign, entered appearing to be "the very picture of a war-worn noble warrior and commander."

Unshaken by the unexpected social gathering, Jackson quickly assumed the role of a gentleman, bowing to the ladies around the room gracefully. The social mores of the time required an awkward acknowledgment of everyone in the room, which Jackson managed. Turning to Mrs. Livingston, the General took her hand and escorted her to the sofa, politely greeting her with conversation. The women of the room were astonished at the dignified and relaxed manner the general comported himself. Addressing them, he assured the ladies that he would indeed save their city, and to not trouble themselves any further about the matter. When it came to being in the presence of lovely females, Jackson was known to turn on the charm. When he finally turned to leave, getting up from the dinner table and excusing himself, he and Mr. Livingston took their exit politely. The moment they departed, the young ladies descended upon Mrs. Livingston, "Is this your backwoodsman? Why Madame, he is a prince!" [530]

Having returned to his headquarters on Royal Street, Jackson began preparing the city's defenses. New Orleans was certainly defensible to be sure, particularly due to its location, surrounded by swamps, bayous, and the wide, twisting Mississippi, but at the same time, the challenge was how to plan a precise defense in advance, with the many possible routes open to invasion. Like most residents of the city, Jackson believed, erroneously, that the Chef Menteur Road was likely the most certain invasion route. But until he knew the exact location the British would take, he kept his troops on the move. If there was one ability as a commander in which Jackson excelled, it was the ability to move his troops rapidly within a short window of time. Despite the difficulties the area posed, the General was confident he could concentrate his forces at the exact point of the British invasion.

The General gathered the engineers present in the city, including Major Latour, who later became the historian of the campaign. They discussed the city's vulnerable points and possible approaches, determining the most effective ways to defend each location. Orders were given to obstruct every bayou that connected the city to the nearby bays, and through them to the Gulf of Mexico, using earth and sunken logs. Guards were to be stationed at the mouths of these bayous to alert them of any enemy approach. It was also decided to invite local planters to assist in the various works with groups of enslaved individuals. Young gentlemen rushed to Jackson's headquarters, offering their services as aides to the General.

The army of the Seventh Military District would soon be bolstered by the addition of militia troops from both Tennessee and Kentucky. On

---

[530] Parton, *Jackson*, II, p. 31.

October 20th, 1814, Kentucky Governor Isaac Shelby issued a call for men for the New Orleans campaign, and under that call three regiments of Kentucky Detached Militia were brought into the field and organized for that campaign. Governor Shelby sent the force to New Orleans under the command of Major General John Thomas. But when would they arrive? Would they make it in time? Would he be able to mold these raw militia men into a fighting force capable of matching the hardened veterans of the Napoleonic Wars? These were the questions Jackson grappled with on a rainy, chilly December evening in the Crescent City.

The previous summer, about two-hundred miles west of Andrew Jackson's Mobile headquarters, a British sloop was approaching the green island of Grand Terre on the Louisiana coast. Captain Nicholas Lockyer stared at the yellow beach, and then beyond it. Through the steamy September haze, he spotted a small brick fort but saw no flag flying above the rampart. Moving quickly, Captain Lockyer ordered the signal gun to be fired. Within a few minutes of the blast, smiling with satisfaction at the sight of a boat putting out from shore with five men aboard, Lockyer turned to the man beside him, a Captain McWilliams, and ordered him to lower his gig and row him out to meet them.

McWilliams wore the uniform of the Royal Colonial Marines. He was well armed and pushed his black varnished hat down tightly on his head, warning Lockyer not to trust Jean Lafitte and his buccaneer crew. Lockyer scoffed, for he knew that Lafitte's Baratarian pirates, for all their scurrilous antics, respected the power of the British Royal Navy, and he stepped down toward the deck, undeterred. A hundred yards offshore, the captain's gig, and the pirates' boat met amid the gently rolling waves. McWilliams shouted to the men on the boat that they wished to see Monsieur Jean Lafitte, but the boatman replied in French that Lafitte was not on board, but onshore.[531]

Minutes later, the British sailors jumped into the surf and hauled the boat onto the beach. Lockyer and McWilliams stepped out on the damp sand and turned to face the Baratarians. There were five of them,

---

[531] Ramsay, Jack, *Prince of Pirates*, 1996. p. 47.

all deeply tanned. The tallest of the five, whose wavy brown hair was worn long, was barefoot and wore a faded green shirt and baggy trousers made of sailcloth. The look of these men seemed to mock the British sailors. The tall pirate bowed sarcastically, addressing them with "At your service."

In the meantime, over a hundred Baratarians, armed with knives and pistols began gathering on the beach behind them. Captain McWilliams, betraying a nervous glance, addressed the tall boatman and handed him a packet of letters for Lafitte. After a promise from the tall buccaneer to deliver the letters, McWilliams took a small canvas package from his coat pocket hesitatingly, and handed it to the pirate, who then took it with an exaggerated bow, commanding the British sailors to follow him toward the fort. In front of the fort was a low-roofed porch with several hammocks swung from ropes. The pirate motioned for the British officers to wait outside while he entered the fort. They waited for what seemed an eternity in the summer heat. Several minutes later, the man returned, swinging open the porch door. To the surprise of the Brits present, the tall pirate had changed his attire dramatically, donning dress clothes and neatly polished boots. With a wink, he revealed that he was, in fact, Jean Lafitte. He invited the men to be his dinner guests inside the fort.

Lockyer and the aim of the British was clear: to enlist Lafitte and the Baratarians to fight against the United States in New Orleans. Hopeful that Lafitte and his men would help the Royal fleet navigate through the many bayous that surrounded the city, they also promised the outlaws fair value for the use of their well-armed ships. Their offer was simple, they would pay Lafitte $30,000, grant him a captaincy in the British Navy, and amnesty for his many crimes. Intrigued, Lafitte requested two weeks to consider the offer.

Most of Jean Lafitte's life remains a mystery, including his name. He was born around 1780 in either France or Saint Domingue (modern-day Haiti). Lafitte, as historian H.W. Brands writes, "was French, Spanish or Jewish depending on who was asking."[532] Little is known about his early life, although he had at least two brothers, Pierre and Alexander (known as Dominique), who assisted in his smuggling operation. By 1810,

---

[532] Brands, 2005. Ch. 20

Lafitte was operating as a pirate, primarily smuggling African slaves into Louisiana, as the U.S. had outlawed international slave imports by 1808. He bought slaves in the West Indies, where they were cheaper, and smuggled them into Louisiana, where they were more expensive due to the federal ban. Lafitte also worked for the government of Cartagena (modern-day Columbia) to sabotage Spanish commerce, which aided in the colony's independence.

By the terms of his commission, Lafitte and his brothers could keep the goods they captured, but according to U.S. law, they were prohibited from their legal sale within the country. This did not deter the Lafitte brothers, who established their base in Barataria Bay near New Orleans. The bay's geography was ideal for smuggling, allowing them to launch into the Caribbean while evading Spanish warships. Lafitte's followers, known as Baratarians, faced consistent threats from U.S. customs officials and the Spanish Navy, but this did not persuade the brothers from ceasing their enterprises.

Lafitte considered the British offer made by Lockyer and McWilliams, and he pretended to be on board. On September 4, 1814, he informed Captain Lockyer that he would need two weeks to consider an offer, leaning towards acceptance. He also wrote to Mr. Blanque of the Louisiana House, sharing documents from the British officer and expressing his desire to join the American cause if a pardon for past offenses could be granted. Blanque delivered the letters to Governor Claiborne, who presented them to the Committee of Safety and Defence. They advised Lafitte to wait for their decision while under government protection.

After two weeks, Lafitte ignored Lockyer's signals, instead writing to Governor Claiborne informing him of the British intrigue. When Claiborne appealed to the legislature, Lafitte's offer was originally turned down. When Jackson first arrived in New Orleans at the start of December 1814, and was informed of Lafitte's offer of assistance, he too scoffed. The General held a strong prejudice against the Baratarians whom he called "a hellish bandetti" and of whom he said that he "would not call upon either pirates or robbers to join him in the glorious cause he had to defend." [533]

---

[533] Parson, p. 218.

The threat the pirates operating out of Barataria Bay posed had long been an elusive challenge for the defense of Louisiana. The Bay itself was located about seventy miles southwest of the city, and its sheer size meant that several options were open to the British should they be able to exploit the Bay. The previous September, the Louisiana government took steps to eliminate the Lafitte threat in early expectation of a pending British invasion. Commandant Patterson had led a force sent by Governor Claiborne to Barataria Bay to put an end to the freebooters once and for all. The cagey Lafitte, however, managed to slip away, along with some of his best ships. Patterson still managed to capture about 80 pirates, nine vessels, and half a million dollars' worth of valuable merchandise before destroying their lair.

Despite this ungracious treatment at the hands of American forces, Lafitte wished to assist Jackson's army against the British. Having been granted permission to meet with Jackson, Lafitte asked the General for "the honor of proving that if they had infringed the revenue laws, yet none were more ready than they to defend the country and combat its enemies."[534] Could the freebooter's promises of assistance be a ruse to avenge this discourteous act by the Americans? It was a gamble, but one that Jackson had to risk.

Local friends of the Lafittes tried to dissuade Jackson against his opposition to Lafitte's offer. Finally, Edward Livingston, the brilliant American advocate, having been made one of the aides to General Jackson, was also the personal counsel of the Lafittes, thus this opened a bridge. Soon Lafitte would set sail for New Orleans, at the behest of Livingston, whose influence began to sway the stubborn Jackson, who now saw the merits of adding this "banditti" to the cause. With Livingston's backing, a meeting with Governor Claiborne and General Jackson was arranged by mid-December. The General and Lafitte met in Governor Claiborne's office, through Livingston's clever, cogent persistence. Although there is no written account of the interview between Lafitte and General Jackson, Major Latour made a brief statement from the December meeting between the two men and simply noted that Jackson agreed to accept Lafitte's help. At last, Jackson relented, reconsidering Lafitte's

---

[534] Lafitte to Claiborne, no date, Latour, *Historical Memoir*, pp. xi-xii, xiii-xiv.

offer. Despite his initial concerns about the loyalty of the Baratarians due to their federal indictment, Jackson accepted their help.

The clincher in the General's decision came after the Louisiana legislature chose to suspend the privateer's indictment for four months. Recognizing the dire threat the British posed, Jackson could not ignore the value of the expertise Lafitte and his men could provide when it came to the bayous surrounding New Orleans. Governor Claiborne had also come to see the value of the addition of the Baratarians, and he suggested to the Washington government leniency towards the captives of the recent expedition associated with Lafitte. More specifically, the governor requested the U.S. District Attorney and Federal Court to 'nolle prosequi' the case against the Baratarians and pledged himself to ask for them a full pardon from the President of the United States in return for loyal service in the American cause. In the desperation of the pending British invasion, the Louisiana legislature passed conciliatory resolutions.

Claiborne proclaimed the decision of the Louisiana legislature, and hesitantly, each supported his request. The Committee of Defence accepted Lafitte's proposition, leading to an official proclamation inviting the Baratarians to join the U.S. forces, with promises of pardons for those who complied. Lafitte informed his followers, many of whom joined him, and his elder brother, who was festering behind bars in New Orleans, having previously been apprehended by the American authorities, was released, and permitted to join his brother once again. The freebooter Lafitte had promised his loyalty to Jackson's cause, but could he really be trusted?

Along with Major Reynolds, Lafitte and his pirates were soon manning the batteries below New Orleans, serving effectively alongside a company of marines, aiding American forces in securing the Barataria and Bayou Lafourche passes. The "cutthroats" proved adept as gunners and marksmen. From December 22 to January 1, several engagements occurred between the Americans and the approaching British vessels. Although none were decisive, the Royal Navy was kept at bay. [535]

Fortunately for Jackson, Lafitte was determined to serve at his utmost for the American cause, if for nothing else than to clear his name in his

---

[535] Latour, *Historical Memoir*, p. 72.

chosen country. The infamous marauders, the Lafitte brothers, would prove beneficial to the American cause. His bravery and enthusiasm for fighting had, like William Weatherford's, impressed Jackson. He appreciated Lafitte's aggressiveness, and the help the pirates could provide in defense, along with one thousand extra men, shot, powder, flint, and incomparable marksmanship and knowledge of the Bay. Jackson could not resist the offer. He ordered Lafitte to assist in defending the area between New Orleans and Barataria Bay. The Baratarians flocked to the standard of Jackson. The charges against Lafitte and his buccaneers would soon be dropped, as promised, in acknowledgment of their contributions and loyalty to the U.S. Ultimately, Lafitte and around fifty of his Baratarians would prove instrumental in their support of the American cause, and their efforts would help Jackson on his epic road to glory.

Presumed portrait of Jean Lafitte, anonymous source. Rosenberg Library

CHAPTER

38

THE BRITISH ARE COMING

"When they declared war they thought it was pretty near over with us, and that their weight cast into the scale would decide our ruin. Luckily they were mistaken, and are likely to pay dear for their error."
— *William Ward, 1st Earl of Dudley*

On December 8, Vice Admiral Cochrane's fleet reached the vicinity of Ship Island, located approximately 60 miles east of New Orleans. The hostile fleet landed at Ship Island a few days later, and their arrival initiated a series of indecisive land and naval engagements. The British believed their plans were unknown to General Jackson, expecting to surprise him and easily conquer the area. However, the Americans were well-prepared, thanks to an extensive network of spies, and aimed to surprise the British in return. Admiral Cochrane and General Keane later learned of Lafitte's subterfuge, and of his having informed Jackson of their plans.

The Jackson command now squared off with the main problem at hand, how to block the many bayous that served as avenues into the fringes of the city of New Orleans. Studying the maps that the city's chief engineer, Major Lacarriere Latour, had provided, Jackson and his fellow officers lost count of the number of bayous and coulees that the map showed surrounding the city, thus Jackson had Governor Claiborne close off all waterways to the city entirely. This task Claiborne assigned to his militia chief Jacques Villeré.[536] Jackson took the added step of assigning a guard at every bayou to be on the lookout for any British approach. He further added the protection of additional batteries at Fort St. Phillip. Unfortunately for Jackson, however, one step he failed to take was personally inspecting the execution of all orders to their fullest.

Jackson sought to cover all of his bases when it came to the city's defense. After inspecting the Rigolets firsthand, Jackson ordered alterations to Fort St. Phillip. Another concern of Jackson and his staff was the lack of defensive strength within New Orleans itself. The city's forces numbered only 700, and within that number, several were away from duty at the moment, and there was uncertainty as to either their return or reliability. Additionally, there was the issue of disloyalty among the French and Spanish inhabitants within the city. Who would they serve in the heat of the battle? Jackson was not entirely certain; and, as if to round out his anxieties, the city's legislature seemed intent on creating trouble, for the sole purpose of making life difficult either for Governor Claiborne or for Jackson himself, regardless of the dangers of the moment. This infuriated Old Hickory.

To ease his anxieties somewhat, Jackson welcomed the enlistment request of a large number of Louisiana free blacks.[537] The free men of color within the Crescent City had written Governor Claiborne, expressing their willingness to take up arms for the American cause. Claiborne had forwarded the request to Jackson, who responded affirmatively. Jackson needed all the help he could get, and he knew it. In writing to the Louisiana legislature, Jackson emphasized that the free men of color wished to be involved in the fight, and he urged trust in these men, rather than suspicion. "Our country," Jackson wrote, "has been invaded and threatened with destruction. She wants Soldiers to fight her battles. The free men of colour in your city are inured to the Southern climate and would make excellent soldiers. They will not remain quiet spectators of the interesting contest. They must be for, or against us–distrust them and you make them your enemies, place confidence in them and you engage them by every dear and honorable tie to the interest of the country who extends to them equal rights and priviledges with white men."[538]

---

[536] AJ to Villeré, Dec. 22, 1814, NA.
[537] AJ to Claiborne, Sept. 21, 1814, Jackson Papers, LC.
[538] AJ to W. Allen, Dec. 23, 1814, Jackson Papers, LC.

Yet, although he accepted the offer, Jackson ordered white officers to command the battalions. He did, however, ensure that colored troops received equal treatment via strict orders to his officers. Appointing Major Pierre Lacoste to lead the first colored battalion and Major Jean D'Aquin for a second battalion of Santo Domingo refugees that soon formed. He issued a proclamation promising 160 acres of land and $124 for their service, along with regular pay, rations, and uniforms. Some Louisianians were unhappy with Jackson's fair treatment of the free black volunteers, fearing it could incite rebellion. When faced with criticism from an assistant district paymaster, Jackson firmly rebuked him, insisting that troop payments should not depend on color.[539] "Be pleased to keep to yourself your opinion upon the policy of making payments of the troops with the necessary muster rolls without inquiring whether the troops are white, black or tea." [540]

Five days later—nearly 2 weeks after Jackson arrived in New Orleans—on Dec. 13, 1814, to be exact—the British armada was sighted off Cat Island at the entrance of Lake Borgne. As the British advanced westward into the lake, soundings warned against further penetration by the deep-draft vessels. But before landing troops, it was imperative to clear the lake of the small force of five American gunboats commanded by Lieutenant Thomas Catesby Jones that hovered ahead of them. Jones' fleet of five gunboats, under the direction of Commandant Patterson, carried twenty-three guns and 180 men, and it had been stationed at Lake Borgne under Jackson's explicit orders. Jones was instructed to retire if attacked and ensure the pursuit of the British. The aim was for his crew to ignite a chase that would lead the enemy directly into the Rigolets and Fort Petite Coquilles' line of fire.

The next morning, December 14th, the British advanced on Lake Borgne, seeking to remove Lieutenant Jones flotilla. Admiral Cochrane dispatched Captain Lockyer and an expedition of 45 boats, loaded with 42 cannons and 1,000 sailors and Marines to pursue the Americans. An unbroken line of barges, with six rows of oarsmen on each side, bore down on Jones's squadron, overwhelming the flotilla with their customary superior numbers and firepower. Jones unleashed a barrage

---

[539] To the Free Colored Inhabitants of Louisiana, Jackson, *Correspondence*, II: Pg. 59.
[540] AJ to W. Allen, Dec. 23, 1814, Jackson Papers, LC.

of gunpowder, but it did little to stop the British advance. The lieutenant then attempted to retreat as planned, but on this windless day, his fleet was becalmed, and many of his boats got stuck in the mud near Malhereux Island. By noon, all the American gunboats were captured, and the flagship was taken. The battle resulted in significant casualties on both sides, with Jones' forces suffering forty-one killed and wounded.[541] Jones' failed in his mission to draw the British into American hands.

The British victory at Lake Borgne shifted the initiative into their hands, and they sought to capitalize on it. Many within the British command hoped to seize the opportunity to land and advance towards New Orleans immediately. However, the process was far from straightforward, and the logistics of the landing caused headaches for both Admiral Cochrane and General Keane, as their chosen rendezvous point caused extreme challenges. They first needed to land thousands of troops on an island at the lake's entrance, Pea Island, thirty miles east of New Orleans, where they planned to transition to shallow draft boats for their journey into the lake and onward to the city.

One eyewitness, Ensign George Glieg would later write, "It is scarcely possible to imagine any place more completely wretched," recalled Glieg, who had previously admired the glow of the torching of Washington in the summer. In May 1814, George Robert Glieg was serving with the British Army in France when Napoleon surrendered into exile and the European war came to an end. Glieg and his unit were then shipped to North America to take part in the War of 1812. Participating in British raids at Chesapeake Bay, the Battle of Bladensburg, the capture and burning of Washington DC, the fighting at Ft. McHenry, the attack on Baltimore, the invasion of Mobile, and the Battle of New Orleans, before the war came to an end, Glieg wrote an invaluable account of his vast war experiences, *Narrative of the Campaigns of the British Army: At Washington, Baltimore, and New Orleans, Under Generals Ross, Pakenham and Lambert in the Years 1814 and 1815*.[542] Glieg provides us with vivid accounts from the British side of some of the key battles of the War of 1812, including the British debacle at New Orleans. "It was a swamp

---

[541] Brooks, *Siege of New Orleans*, pp. 92-96.
[542] Glieg, George Robert, *Narrative of the Campaigns of the British Army: At Washington, Baltimore, and New Orleans, Under Generals Ross, Pakenham and Lambert in the Years 1814 and 1815*, Reprinted, 2020.

with a small patch of firm ground at one end, almost entirely devoid of trees. The interior was home to wild ducks and other waterfowl, while the pools and creeks that crisscrossed the area were teeming with dormant alligators."[543] The alligators, which would later terrify the British soldiers as the campaign progressed, were dormant due to the unseasonably frigid Louisiana winter.

A driving rain drenched the soldiers all day. As night fell the rain stopped, and a heavy frost set in. The Britons in the battle force Used to the cold and wet suffered but survived. The West Indians, who had lately been added to the army, fared worse. "Many of the wretched Negroes, to whom frost and cold were all together new, fell fast asleep and perished before morning," Glieg wrote.

Within two hours of running off Jones' flotilla, thousands of British soldiers took command of Lake Borgne, came ashore, and began building a garrison on Pea Island. Their victory was a disaster for the Americans, and it cleared the lake of American forces, destroying Jackson's efforts to guard the lakes, and allowing the British to prepare for an invasion of the mainland. However, some of the American prisoners, upon interrogation, falsely inflated the size of Jackson's army, which worked in favor of the American cause. This information, however false,[544] gave the British pause, and their hesitation led to a command decision to delay the invasion, as Admiral Cochrane and General Keane resolved to transport the British infantry through the adjacent bayous instead, with the intent of approaching the city from the south.

Two days later, December 20th, the British completed their troop transfer on Pea Island, and shortly thereafter, Admiral Cochrane gained valuable intel as to a navigable route to the city, Bayou Bienville. The bayou was navigable for large barges and ran west off Lake Borgne to within just twelve miles east of New Orleans. Following orders, British personnel, engaged in the complicated troop transfer to the new garrison under construction on Pea Island, realized just how arduous the operation was, and just how costly. Moving the remaining troops to the island in the harsh weather and challenging conditions was slow

---

[543] ibid, p. 112.
[544] Likely, even the Americans taken were unsure of the actual size of their forces, which numbered ultimately between 3,500 and 4,000 troops.

and laborious, lasting nearly a week.⁵⁴⁵ Its results were unsatisfying to the British command as well, as it provided only a slightly improved position in relation to the city. The week-long slowdown was all the time Jackson needed to gather his forces in New Orleans.

When the news of the Battle of Lake Borgne reached New Orleans, it ignited a wave of panic among the residents. Although confidence in Jackson was on the rise, the alarming news caused no small amount of confusion and fear. Jackson had just returned from Chef Menteur when he received the news of the battle. Exaggerated versions of the disaster spread quickly, and by the time he arrived in the city, he had already learned that the gunboats had been lost, the enemy controlled the lake, and an unprecedented fleet had gathered in the waters near New Orleans. The city was in a state of panic upon receiving the disturbing news. Jackson's initial fury and finger-pointing soon gave way to a more pragmatic response, for there was one plus to the intel: the battle on Lake Borgne confirmed to him that New Orleans, and not Mobile, was indeed to be the target of the British invasion.

Jackson's first thought was to immediately declare martial law throughout the city. Governor Claiborne hesitated to endorse this, however, based on his concerns about the state legislature. Claiborne also worried about the possibility of spies infiltrating the city. The anxiety that filled the city was not forgotten, which had quickly spread throughout the countryside during the busy night that followed the general's return from the Chef Menteur. The wild rumors increased and circulated widely. It was commonly believed that the enemy's fleet consisted of three hundred ships. There were claims of treason brewing within the city. The old fear of a potential slave uprising resurfaced. To ease these concerns and instill fear in any potential traitors, a proclamation was issued on the morning of the 15th. This proclamation reflected a distinctly Jacksonian spirit, though it was likely written by Edward Livingston. Jackson had decided to act without the consent of the legislature and declared martial law throughout New Orleans and the surrounding area.⁵⁴⁶

---

[545] The ferrying operation ran from Dec. 17 to Dec. 22nd. Remini, 1977, p. 256.
[546] ibid, p. 257.

"To the Citizens of New Orleans: The Major General commanding has, with astonishment and regret, learned that great consternation and alarm pervade your city. It is true the enemy is on our coast and threatens an invasion of our territory; but it is equally true, with union, energy, and the approbation of heaven, we will beat him at every point his temerity may induce him to set foot upon our soil. The General, with still greater astonishment, has heard that British emissaries have been permitted to propagate seditious reports among you, that the threatened invasion is with a view of restoring the country to Spain, from a supposition that some of you would be willing to return to your ancient government. Believe not such incredible tales — your government is at peace with Spain — it is the vital enemy of your country, the common enemy of mankind, the highway robber of the world that threatens you, and has sent his hirelings among you with this false report to put you off your guard, that you may fall an easy prey to him; — then look to your liberties, your property, the chastity of your wives and daughters — take a retrospect of the conduct of the British army at Hampton and other places, where it has entered our country, and every bosom which glows with patriotism and virtue will be inspired with indignation, and pant for the arrival of the hour when we shall meet and revenge those outrages against the laws of civilization and humanity. The General calls upon the inhabitants of the city to trace this unfounded report to its source and bring the propagator to condign punishment. The rules and articles of war annex the punishment of death to any person holding secret correspondence with the enemy, creating false alarms, or supplying him with provisions; and the General announces his unalterable determination rigidly to execute the martial law in all cases which may come within his province. The safety of the district intrusted to the protection of the General, must and will be maintained with the best blood of the country; and he is confident that all good citizens will be found at their posts, with their arms in their hands, determined to dispute every inch of ground with the enemy; that unanimity will pervade the country generally; but should the General be disappointed in this expectation, he will separate our enemies from our friends — those who are not for us are against us, and will be dealt with accordingly." [547]

Later in the same day that this ominous proclamation appeared in the newspapers, the measure was made public. Faced with these difficulties, Jackson saw, first and foremost, the need to assert control over New Orleans to protect the city, thwart the invasion, and push the British back into the sea. The decree mandated that every individual entering the city must report to the general's office, and no one could enter the city, or leave without written consent from the general or his staff. Additionally, ships were required to possess passports to dock at the port, and a curfew was established at 9:00 PM. Any individual found in the streets after curfew without authorization would be arrested as a suspected spy.

Jackson essentially turned New Orleans into an armed camp, and required all citizens to accept military authority, suspending the local government's authority. This proclamation was met by no small amount of resistance by many of the residents of the city. But Jackson paid them no mind. His troops remained in good spirits, nonetheless. One letter, written by a member of the militia on the 16th, two days after the gunboat battle, describes the sanguine condition of the American camp, "We are weak here at present — say twelve hundred regulars and two thousand militia. We expect Coffee, with two thousand more, in a day or two, and ere long the Kentucky and Tennessee drafts. When they all arrive we are ready to stand against any number the British may send. As we are, they may outnumber us, but even if my Lord Wellington trained them they are not better soldiers. We will weather the storm like honest fellows, and if our weakness is taken advantage of, they shall at least have a fight in miniature. Our old General stands it nobly, and is full of fight. The French turn out handsomely."[548]

Jackson took command of the newly organized troops of the Louisiana militia. With prior experience in the Tennessee militia, he understood that transforming ordinary young men into soldiers would

---

[547] Parton, *Jackson*, p. 58.
[548] Parton, *Jackson*, p. 68.

be a challenge. The Louisiana militia presented a unique situation, and he must have questioned how to defend the city with such a diverse group of Americans, French, Spanish, whites, Blacks, and mixed-race individuals, ranging from the eager to the reluctant. Most simply wished to survive the impending battle against the world's top soldiers. Despite the motley appearance of his troops, Jackson knew he had to inspire their confidence.

His success in the Creek Campaign had already established him as a capable tactician, and the defense of New Orleans would elevate his reputation further. While Jackson's organizational skills were impressive, what truly distinguished him was his ability to motivate his men. Many soldiers admired him, some even loved their "Old Hickory," yet most feared him, remembering the would-be mutineers who he threatened with cannon fire in Alabama, or those who remembered the fate of John Wood.

Jackson had already threatened the militia men from Louisiana, now he appealed to them. To the native-born Americans, he described the enemy in terms of the American Revolution. "They are the oppressors of your infant political existence with whom you are to contend; they are the men your fathers conquered whom you are to oppose. Descendants of Frenchmen! natives of France! They are the English, the hereditary, the eternal enemies of your ancient country, the invaders of that you have adopted, who are your foes. Spaniards! remember the conduct of your allies at St. Sebastians, and recently at Pensacola, and rejoice that you have an opportunity of avenging the brutal injuries inflicted by men who dishonor the human race."[549]

Jackson's authority to declare martial law and take control of New Orleans, along with the Louisiana militia, was questionable at best. Yet, he certainly did not have the authority to invade Spanish Florida. While he may have been concerned about potential reprimands or punitive measures from Washington, he likely believed that his actions against civil liberties in New Orleans would be viewed as less severe than waging war against a nation that the government aimed to keep neutral. Regardless, Jackson often disregarded authority if he believed the outcome was

---

[549] Jackson's Address to the Troops in New Orleans, Jackson, *Correspondence*, II, pp. 118-119.

justified. He considered no cause more just than the defense of American liberty, and he was willing to employ various means to achieve it. As the attorneys debated and argued, he focused on preparing the defense of New Orleans. "The lakes, in complete possession of the enemy, will give me a large coast to watch and defend, and the difficulty of finding out their point of attack is perplexing." He wrote on December 16, "But I trust with the smiles of heaven, I will be able to meet and defeat him at every point he will put his foot on land." [550] Ever the optimist, Jackson trudged forward.

---

[550] AJ to Coffee, Dec. 16, 1814, Jackson Papers, LC.

CHAPTER

39

VILLERÉ'S PLANTATION

"But I am an American."
–Major Gabriel Villeré

To boost morale and confidence, as well as to reassure the public, Jackson organized a review of the militia on Sunday, December 18, at Place d' Armes, (now called Jackson Square) parading the troops in front of the multitudes who came out eagerly to cheer their defenders on.[551] The colorful ceremony was applauded enthusiastically by the crowd, dressed up in their Sunday best, and perhaps eager for something to cheer about. Jackson had come to value the two African American battalions and showcased them in a formal review, demonstrating his support for the men of color. He also reviewed the city militia, consisting largely of young men from affluent families, commanded by Major Jean Plauche. Setting the variously diverse units on equal footing, Jackson demonstrated the egalitarian nature of his army in the review. Whether men of color, or the young men of the city's wealthiest ranks, his command's treatment of all who were courageous enough to support the cause by putting their lives on the line was, to Jackson, equal in merit.

The residents of New Orleans watched anxiously and cheered as Jackson read a speech he had written for the occasion, which was translated into French by his Aide-de-Camp Edward Livingston. The speech is notable for the appeal to "free" African American men to join in the defense of New Orleans. The stirring address did much to

---

[551] Walker, *Jackson and New Orleans*, pp. 143-144.

rally the troops and citizens crowded into the square, and in it, Jackson emphasized the country's current fight, reminding the public that the cause was for liberty and the safety of their families. With each line, hearty applause followed, especially after Livingston's deep voice rang out the translation to the mostly French speaking crowd. Jackson recalled his days as a youth when he had been moved by reading tales of the ancient Greeks, and the speeches the great generals had roused their soldiers with on the eve of battle. Like the ancient days, Jackson's words were stirring, and the crowd embraced them.

"Fellow Citizens and Soldiers, the general, Commanding-in-Chief, would not do justice to the noble ardour that has animated you in the hour of danger... if he suffered the example you have shewn to pass without publick notice. Natives of the United States!... Fellow Citizens of every description! Remember for what and against whom you contend. For all that can render life desirable—for a country blessed with every gift of nature—for property, for life—for those dearer than either, your wives and children—and for liberty, dearer than all, without which country, life, property are no longer worth possessing: as even the embraces of wives and children become a reproach to the wretched who could deprive them by his cowardice of those invaluable blessings.

Soldiers! From the shores of Mobile I collected you to arms. I invited you to share the perils and to divide the glory of your white countrymen. I expected much from you, for I was not uninformed of those qualities which must render you so formidable to an invading foe. I knew that you could endure hunger and thirst, and all the hardships of war. I knew that you loved the land of your nativity, and that, like ourselves, you had to defend all that is most dear to man. But you surpass my hopes. I have found in you, united to these qualities, that noble enthusiasm which impels to great deeds.

Soldiers! The President of the United States shall be informed of your conduct on the present occasion, and the voice of the representatives of the American nation shall applaud your valor, as your general now praises your ardor. The enemy is near: his 'sails cover the lakes:' but the brave are united, and if he finds us contending among ourselves, it will be for the prize of valor and fame, its noblest reward."[552]

As Livingston translated the last line, the crowd erupted in emotional exuberance, and the soldiers beamed with pride. Jackson had once again moved the multitudes with his words. With that, the General dismissed the troops and gave them the rest of the day off to visit with their families.[553] Meanwhile, Jackson eagerly awaited the arrival of his Tennessee volunteers, still in Baton Rouge, as General Billy Carroll was en route to join them with 2,000 more men. These troops would not arrive until December 22nd. Jackson instructed Coffee to keep his brigade ready to march at a moment's notice, anticipating a potential encounter with Lord Hill during the Christmas holidays.[554] In an effort to address the situation further, Commodore Patterson suggested suspending habeas corpus to detain sailors to man his two armed vessels, the *Carolina* and the *Louisiana*. However, the legislature rejected this proposal and instead decided to offer a bounty to recruit volunteers. Exasperated, Claiborne recommended that the legislature take a brief recess of a couple of weeks, but again, they turned down the governor's suggestion.

The declaration of martial law proved extremely beneficial for Jackson. The panic diminished, public confidence returned, and a sense of security was revived. Factions were thwarted in their designs, and large-scale treason was rendered impossible. During the period of danger, no one dared oppose the action that united the populace as near to a single entity as Jackson could get against the invaders of their land. Although there were many in New Orleans who resented the suspension of civil authority, it was widely recognized as a necessary response to the crisis, and one that most felt was the best course to follow, given the crisis of the moment.

The following day brought the exciting news of General Coffee's approach with his mounted sharp shooters. Jackson's message found him near the Creole city of Baton Rouge, one hundred and twenty-nine miles from New Orleans, where he had gone in search of supplies. Late on the evening of the seventeenth, he received Jackson's urgent orders. Most of

---

[552] Past Now, History, Arts and Stuff, 2014. https://pastnow.wordpress.com/2014/12/18/december-1814-jacksons-address-to-the-men-of-color/

[553] Walker, *Jackson and New Orleans*, p. 144.

[554] AJ to Coffee, Dec. 19, 1814, Jackson Papers, LC.

his horses were fatigued and underfed; three hundred of his men were ill; all were weakened from prolonged exposure and relentless marching, with his troops scattered over several miles.

After spending the night preparing for the march, Coffee and his men forged on, despite their weariness. Early on the eighteenth, leaving his sick and poorly mounted troops in Baton Rouge, he set out for New Orleans with twelve hundred and fifty men. By the end of the day, he found it necessary to divide his force again, leaving four to five hundred of the slower-moving cavalrymen behind. He continued with a force of eight hundred, whose horses were in better condition. On the first day, he marched fifty miles; on the second day, seventy miles, reaching near New Orleans. By the morning of the third day, he camped just four miles from the city and rode ahead to meet his general and receive further orders.[555]

The arrival of General Coffee and his sharp shooters further boosted the morale of the people. As Alexander Walker describes Jackson's most trusted subordinate in *Jackson and New Orleans*, "Coffee was a tall, herculean man with a natural dignity and ease of manner. Though of great height and weight, his appearance on horseback, mounted on a fine Tennessee thoroughbred, was striking and impressive." Though hardened by the campaign and excellent marksmen, Coffee's men were not so pleasing to the eye of those who came out to assess them upon their arrival in the city. The British were not entirely inaccurate when they spoke of them as a '*posse comitatus*,' wearing broad beavers, armed with long duck guns."[556] But beneath their rough exterior were those exact qualities that Jackson valued more than any others: loyalty, courage and a strong sense of duty.

Colonel Thomas Hinds arrived around the same time, leading his regiment of roughly 150 Mississippi dragoons, who had marched an impressive two hundred and thirty miles in just four days. On the twenty-second, General Carroll's flotilla reached the scene, bringing with it another regiment of Tennessee soldiers and, even more crucially, a much-needed supply of muskets that had been causing the General considerable anxiety. The streets of the Crescent City were now filled with armed men.

---

[555] Coffee to AJ, Dec. 1814, Jackson Papers, LC.
[556] Parton, *Jackson*, p. 69.

Major Latour provided a colorful account of the activity and patriotism of so many of the New Orleans citizens as they prepared for battle, as well as Jackson's management of the proceedings. "Such was the universal confidence inspired by the activity and decision of the Commander-in-chief, added to the detestation in which the enemy was held, and the desire to punish his audacity, should he presume to land, that not a single warehouse or shop was shut, nor were any goods or valuable effects removed from the city. At that period, New Orleans presented a very affecting picture to the eyes of the patriot, and of all those whose bosoms glow with the feelings of national honor, which raise the mind far above the vulgar apprehension of personal danger. [557]

The residents of the city were preparing for battle as enthusiastically as if to distract themselves from the gravity of the dangers, each in his vernacular tongue singing songs of victory. The streets resounded with Yankee Doodle, the Marseilles Hymn, the Chant du Depart, and other martial airs, while those who had been long unaccustomed to military duty were furbishing their arms and accouterments. In the words of Major Latour, "Beauty applauded valor, and promised with her smiles to reward the toils of the brave. Though inhabiting an open town, not above ten leagues from the enemy, and never till now exposed to war's alarms, the fair sex of New Orleans were animated with the ardor of their defenders, and with cheerful serenity at the sound of the drum presented themselves at the windows and balconies to applaud the troops going through their evolutions, and to encourage their husbands, sons, fathers, and brothers, to protect them from the insults of our ferocious enemies, and prevent a repetition of the horrors of Hampton."[558]

By this time, the British command had discovered a most opportune route to the city. Bayou Bienvenue, a stretch of swampland that stretched roughly thirty miles west of Pea Island, could take them to within twelve miles of the city. A few disaffected Spanish and Portuguese fishermen, former residents of New Orleans now residing outside of the city at a place called Fishermen's Village, guided two of Admiral Cochrane's officers, Captain Robert Spencer, and Lieutenant John Peddie through the bayou. The officers were tasked with determining if the route was navigable for

---

[557] Latour, p. 167.
[558] ibid.

large barges. The Village was located a quarter mile from the bayou's stream, and the fishermen guided the two British officers from there to an unguarded path leading to the east bank of the Mississippi River, where Louisiana militia Major General Jacques Villeré's plantation house sat nestled quietly and relatively unguarded amongst the lush sugar fields of Chalmette.

General Villeré's elegant estate was named Conseil and taking it would allow the British a commanding position within just nine miles of the city. Spencer and Peddie thanked the fishermen and hurried back to camp to report their findings to General Keane. The two British officers reported enthusiastically that the bayou appeared navigable and largely clear of American defenses. Keane was elated, for the route was promising, and taking the plantation would provide the perfect launching point for the pending invasion of New Orleans; an attack which was certain to be a resounding victory, and one that was likely to land Keane's name in the British history books.

The oversight that allowed this route to remain unblocked posed a significant threat to Jackson and the city of New Orleans, and it remains unexplained to this day.[559] At 9 o'clock on the morning of December 22, British Colonel William Thornton promptly led 1,800 men to Bayou Bienvenue, accompanied by General Keane, whose poor decisions would later mar the expedition for the British. By dawn, they had successfully reached the mouth of the bayou, having quietly sailed through the reedy swamp in secrecy. When the sentinel on duty in the village realized this was no false alarm, he called his comrade and informed him that some boats were coming up the bayou. These boats composed the advanced party of the British, which had been sent forward from the main body of the flotilla, under Captain Spencer, to reconnoiter and secure the village.

The Americans, perceiving the hopelessness of defending themselves against such a superior force, concealed themselves behind the cabin, where they remained until the barges had passed by. They then ran out and attempted to reach a boat by which they might make their escape. They were spotted quickly, however, and the British, who advanced towards them, seized the boat before it could be dragged into the water, and captured four of the pickets. Four others were afterwards taken on

---

[559] Reid and Eaton, *Jackson*, p. 306.

land. Of the four remaining, three ran into the canebrake, and from there into the prairie, where they wandered about a day, until, worn down with fatigue and suffering, they returned to the village, happy to surrender themselves as prisoners. Only one escaped, and after three days of terrible hardships and constant dangers, wandering over trembling prairies, through almost impervious canebrakes, swimming bayous and lagoons, and feeding on reptiles and roots, got safely into the American camp.[560]

The prisoners were shut up in one of the huts and closely guarded. One of them, a native Louisianian by the name of Ducros, was separated from his companions and placed in a boat with Captain Spencer and other British officers. The boat returned to the lake, and near the mouth of the bayou was met by the main body of the British flotilla, when Captain Spencer introduced his prisoner to a tall, black-whiskered, youthful officer, as General Keane, and to another rough and stern-looking, white-haired old gentleman, in plain and much worn clothes, as Sir Alexander Cochrane. These two distinguished British officers then proceeded to interrogate Ducros very closely. But neither of them were able to extract any valuable or pleasing intelligence from the shrewd Creole. Although the information was not of much worth to the British, it proved to be invaluable to the Americans, as Ducros succeeded in convincing the enemy that Jackson had from twelve to fifteen thousand armed men to defend the city, and four thousand at the English Turn.[561]

These figures were alarming, and if true, they couldn't be certain of their numerical superiority, and if true, the number of defenders Jackson had at his disposal was disconcerting. As planned previously by the pickets, the remaining prisoners confirmed this estimate. It greatly surprised the general and admiral and led them to doubt the character and veracity of the fishermen, who had made so light of the defenses of the city, and rendered it necessary that the greatest caution and prudence should be observed in their movements. The timely fiction of the prisoners' account proved a shield for the city.

Yet the British commanders, unaware that one of the pickets had escaped, still believed they held the element of surprise, a factor that they were sure would lead to a rout of Jackson's defenses. Colonel Thornton's

---

[560] Gayarré, Charles, *History of Louisiana*, IV, Making of America Books, 1866, p. 219.
[561] DeGrummond, Jane Lucas, *Baratarians*, Legacy, 1979. pp. 75-76, 85-86.

advance force were sent ahead to exploit the fortuitous route, and he and his men continued to move up the bayou throughout the afternoon of December 22nd, until they discovered a thin strip of land along the bank. Quietly debarking at this point, the seasoned force moved steadily through the swampy terrain in single file, continuing until the swamps began to give way to more solid ground. Soon, they entered a forest of dwarfed cypress trees. These then began to give way to canebrakes, and before long the men stopped at the edge of broad, cultivated sugar fields. They had reached the Villeré plantation.

The next morning, December 23, the remainder of the British forces under General Keane woke up before dawn, intent on reconnoitering with Thornton's men. They decamped quickly, and quietly moved up the bayou, disembarking on solid land and advancing toward Villeré's plantation. The British command was aware of the absence of the estate's owner, the Major General, for the elder Villeré was indeed away, encamped with Jackson's troops. He had left behind a small force of militia men to guard his home, including two of his sons.

Following the same route, Keane and his veteran soldiers met up with Thornton's force and formed the men into companies. Given the order, the redcoats advanced on the plantation, surprising the small force, commanded by the elder Villeré son, Major Gabriel Villeré. According to the account written by Eualie Villeré Lanaux, the granddaughter of Major Gabriel Villeré, in 1924, Major Villeré was standing with his brother Celestin in the front hall smoking a cigar and conversing pleasantly with one of their neighbors when a servant came to announce that some men in red coats wanted to speak to him. Major Villeré, advancing on the porch, was confronted by several British officers. "We mean no harm to the French, nor to the Spaniards," remarked one of the officers, addressing Major Villeré.

"But I am an American" replied the Major.

"Then you are my prisoner," said the British officer.[562]

The Major suddenly turned and dashed away, running through the house and out the back door. In his haste, however, he ran straight into more Redcoats, including Colonel Thornton himself. Raising his arms

---

[562] Villeré Family History, *Account Written by Eualie Villeré Lanaux*, the granddaughter of Major Gabriel Villeré, 1924.

in surrender, and with bayonets pointed into the small of his back, young Villeré was forced back into the house, to await the arrival of General Keane. The remaining militiamen assigned to guard Conseil were quickly overwhelmed, and Keane's troops seized the main plantation house. The British were on the cusp of the destruction of the City of New Orleans, the gateway to the West.

CHAPTER

40

THE BRITISH HOLD THE CARDS

"O' say can you see, By the dawn's early light"
-Francis Scott Key

As the sun rose above the Gulf on the blustery morning of December 23rd, New Orleans' inhabitants prepared for what they hoped and prayed would be a peaceful Christmas. But soon the word was out: British forces had successfully made landfall south of New Orleans, and they were advancing on the city. Panic began to spread through the streets of the Crescent City, as the British victory at Lake Borgne now placed the initiative in the invaders' hands.

Detained by the British guards at gunpoint, and awaiting General Keane's arrival, Major Gabriel Villeré sat on the floor in shame, and thought about his humiliating circumstances, and how he would have to explain to his disappointed father that he had let him down. His father would never trust his eldest son again. It was he who had been assigned not only to defend the family estate, but also to defend the Bienvenue approach. The Major could not stand the thought. He resolved to act. Taking a deep breath, he waited until the guards began to converse, taking their eyes off their captive for just a moment. Suddenly, seizing his chance, the young Major, driven by a desperation of having failed at his duty to protect his father's house, sprang from the room, dodged his captors and leaped through a window in the house, running at full speed across the yard under a volley of musketry. Dodging the musket balls, he found a stableman along his way, and the Major ordered him to bring his horse to the outskirts of the woods, which he mounted and then penetrated the dense thicket for a distance of two miles or more.

"Catch him or kill him!"[563] Colonel Thornton called out as he ordered his men to fan out and find the fleeing Creole. Fearing that his trail might be discovered by the pursuing soldiers rapidly closing in on him, Major Villeré dismounted, and spurred his horse to run off. He then climbed a moss-draped tree for concealment. Waiting until the coast was clear, he climbed down, and resumed his escape, crashing through the cypress forests until finally he found a neighbor, Colonel de la Ronde. Together the two rushed to the banks of the river, where they found a skiff, and crossed to the opposite bank. The two continued on at a breathless pace and soon made their way to the home of Dussau de La Croix, a member of the New Orleans Committee of Public Safety. The three men quickly saddled horses and galloped towards the city.

Meanwhile, the British troops had formed along the Mississippi. When General Keane joined the column, he commanded the troops to assemble in battalion formation, then turned right onto the levee road, which ran parallel to the river. They marched past Villeré's house to the upper line of the plantation, where he halted between the river and a cypress swamp, establishing a strong advance toward New Orleans. Thornton urged Keane to continue the march and seize the certainly defenseless city. Having moved without opposition and without the awareness of the Americans, it appeared that a surprise attack on New Orleans could succeed with the troops at hand. Had he taken Thornton's advice, Keane and his troops could have continued up the river road, which was indeed largely undefended, to within cannon shot of New Orleans. Thornton had been correct; Jackson had no knowledge of the British forces' location and lacked sufficient defenses to thwart an attack. Such an assault would have forced him into guerrilla-style fighting in the streets, likely causing devastating effects on the city and its residents.

However, Keane was not sure as to exactly what level of defenses Jackson had placed in New Orleans. Remembering the words of the picket he had captured at Fisherman's Village, that the city was teeming with soldiers—perhaps as many as 20,000, Keane, who was by nature a cautious man, second guessed himself. The alarming claim as to Jackson's

---

[563] Brooks, *Siege of New Orleans*, pp. 133-134.

numbers was confirmed by prisoners previously interrogated, including those from the American gunboats on Lake Borgne, as well as some of Lafitte's men. Despite this, Keane was concerned about his supply lines and communication with the fleet. The Irishman, Keane, thought it wise to wait until the main body of his command caught up with the advance column. As Major John Eaton later recounted in his history of the battle, "Every word (of the American captives) was heard, and treasured, and not supposing there was any design, or that he presumed himself overheard, they were beguiled by it, and at once concluded our force to be as great as it was represented; and hence, no doubt, arose the reason of that prudent care and caution with which the enemy afterwards proceeded; for, as it was remarked by a British officer, the actual strength of General Jackson's army, though repeatedly sought after, could never be procured; it was a desideratum not to be obtained,"[564] Regardless of the delay, one in which so many would later question Keane for, the British now sat roughly ten miles from New Orleans, on the banks of the Mississippi, and appeared poised to take the city.

Jackson, back at his headquarters on Royal Street, was surrounded by his staff, busily studying maps of the city, trying desperately to determine the best possible defense strategy. It was around 1:30 in the afternoon of Friday, December 23, 1814, when Jackson's attention was drawn from the maps by the sound of horses galloping down the streets with more alarm than a city under martial law would normally contain. Dismounting hastily, a breathless de la Croix, de la Ronde, and Major Villeré ran up to the sentry on duty in front of the vast estate, anxious and out of breath, demanding to speak with the General. The sentry then entered the headquarters and notified Jackson that there were three gentlemen to see him about important information; the three Creoles were ushered into the room, flushed from their ride.

"What news do you bring gentlemen? "Jackson asked.

"Important! Highly important! The British have arrived at Villeré's plantation 9 miles below the city and are there encamped. Here is Major Villeré, who was captured by them, has escaped and will now relate his story."

---

[564] Eaton, *The Life of Andrew Jackson*, 1828. p. 293.

Villeré yammered rapidly in French, with De La Croix translating as he spoke. When he finished, the General rose, his eyes smoking with anger at the treason that had allowed the British to slip from the lake to the river undetected. "With an emphatic blow upon the table with his clenched fist," related one of his aides in a letter written shortly after the battle, "Jackson cried, 'by the eternal they shall not sleep on our soil!' His fury spent in that brief outburst, the general courteously invited his guests to join him in a glass of wine, at the same time summoning his secretary at eight. 'Gentlemen,' he said as the officers entered the room, "the British are below; we must fight them tonight.'"[565]

Unwelcome news though it was, Villeré's report helped solve the problem of knowing where the British force was located. As the defender, Jackson knew he could withstand a modest disadvantage when it came to troop strength, but he could not withstand being surprised and outflanked. Were that to happen, he would lose the advantage of defense and very possibly lose control of the city. The only way to avoid such a dilemma was to discover or guess where the enemy was. With the report from Villeré's plantation, he knew at least part of where the British were concentrated.

Keane's cautious decision had given Jackson the time he needed to plan a surprise counterattack that same night, using the warship guns of the *Carolina* and the hastily manned *Louisiana* for support from the river, commanded by Commodore Patterson, who was a distance away. Jackson sent messengers to him with his orders to prepare the *Carolina* for anchoring and move down the river. General Coffee's cavalry were encamped about four or five miles above the city, and Jackson had word sent to him as well to move south. Orders were quickly sent out to gather the regular troops, the city guard battalions, the Mississippi Dragoons, and the free Black battalions. The State militia, led by Governor Claiborne, was on the Gentilly road, three miles away, and the regulars were scattered throughout the city. General Carroll's Tennesseans appeared to still be in the boats that brought them down the river. Major Planche's battalion was stationed at Bayou St. John, two miles from headquarters.

---

[565] Latour, p. 88.

Calmly but quickly, General Jackson sent messengers to each corps under his command, ordering them to break camp and march to assigned positions: General Carroll to the upper branch of the Bienvenue, Governor Claiborne further up the Gentilly road, and the remaining troops to a plantation just below the city. Jackson also had his men build defensive earthworks along the Rodriguez Canal, about four miles south of New Orleans. According to historian Wilburt Brown, this decision was "the most decisive single factor in the campaign."[566]

After issuing these orders, General Jackson had a brief dinner of rice (about the only food his stomach could take at that point in the campaign) then rested on a sofa in his office. This would be his last sleep for over seventy hours. Before three o'clock, he mounted his horse and rode to the lower part of the city, where Fort St. Charles stood. As he rode along the levee, ladies waved handkerchiefs from the windows, hiding their anxiety behind smiles. Soldiers were recognized by their loved ones, and the hurried goodbyes exchanged would be the last for some.

In true Jackson style, a pincer attack was planned. Coffee was instructed to move his brigade through the cypress swamp to strike the British from the left flank, while the main force would target the British center. Jackson also arranged for Patterson's ship, the *Carolina*, opposite the British camp, to commence firing at precisely at 7:30 PM. Carroll's Tennesseans and the Louisiana militia under Governor Claiborne remained behind to guard the Chef Menteur, in case Jackson's initial suspicion was correct and the British were merely creating a distraction while advancing up the Mississippi.

As if matters weren't unstable enough, the vague and terrifying fear of a slave insurrection was revived. Congressman Charles J. Ingersoll, Pennsylvania District Attorney, wrote to President Madison that it was rumored in camp that a British officer, disguised, attended a ball in New Orleans, spreading Colonel Nichols' proclamation from Pensacola, urging slaves to revolt. The dread among the residents was so intense that Louisiana Supreme Court Judge Francois-Xaiver Martin described the anxiety of the old inhabitants on that same evening when General

---

[566] Brown, Wilburt, *The Amphibious Campaign for West Florida and Louisiana, 1814-1815: A Critical Review of Strategy and Tactics at New Orleans*, Hardcover, Univ. of Alabama Press, 1969.

Jackson prepared to confront the British at their landing on Villeré's plantation. They were alarmed by reports that Jackson had arranged to blow up the magazine and set parts of the city ablaze should the British breach his lines, and one could hear women openly weeping on the city's streets. Upon hearing this, Jackson turned to Livingston and told him to inform the women that "he was there, and that the British should never get into the city, so long as he held the command."[567]

As the sounds of musketry and artillery echoed, reminding them that their sons were in battle, they lamented Jackson's perceived inexperience shown by such hasty decisions. There were fears that British agents would incite slaves to ignite their owners' homes and march on the city, spreading terror, fire, and death, interpreting Jackson's firing as the signal to commence destruction. The thought of fleeing with their families from flames toward a devastating enemy, now allied with a vengeful slave population, haunted the minds of the inhabitants.

But Jackson was to prove the city's residents wrong. As a commander in the field, was neither so hasty, nor so reactionary. In fact, he was confident that he and his rugged troops could give the British the fight of their lives. As was his way, the more intense a situation, the more Jackson settled into a steely, calm resolve, and an assured constitution. It was four o'clock in the afternoon when the *Carolina* left her anchorage, and, having napped, Jackson rode away from the gates of Fort St. Charles.

By four o'clock in the warm afternoon of Friday, the 23rd, most of the American troops reached the Rodriguez Canal; others continued coming up with each passing hour. They were all on, or near the high road, which runs along the river's bank. The second division of the British army, consisting of the 21st, the 44th, and the 93rd Highlanders, was nearing the Fisherman's Village, at the mouth of the Bayou Bienvenue. On the Villeré plantation, the advance British force was preparing to eat dinner and bed down for the night, as the unsuspecting General Keane and Colonel Thornton were pacing the foyer of the Villeré mansion, Keane feeling confident in his position, Colonel Thornton distrusting it.

At 7 o'clock, it was dark in the *Carolina* as the men stood 300 yards from the British position. The enemy's campfires blazed brightly in the

---

[567] Nolte, Vincent, *Fifty years in Both Hemispheres or Reminiscences*, New York, Redfield, 1854, p. 209.

cold, creating a beautiful silhouette, making the British soldiers perfect targets for the American gunners. This was probably the first time in a week the Britons had the chance to try to get rested and warm. But it was not to be, as the tranquility was shattered suddenly and explosively at 7:30 pm precisely, when the *Carolina* opened fire with a broadside that roared over the Mississippi Delta, taking the British completely by surprise. For about ten minutes, Keane's men stumbled in total confusion, scrambling for their guns, extinguishing fires, and seeking protection along the levee. As the *Carolina* reduced its fire, the British were just beginning to regain their composure, when Jackson ordered a frontal assault on their ranks.

Down the high road near the river, the Americans advanced with the Seventh regiment, artillery, and marines. A light breeze carried the smoke from the *Carolina's* constant fire, mingling with the fog rising from the river. Illuminated by the flashes of guns and musketry, the General approached within a mile of the British headquarters when Lieutenant John A. McLelland's company faced a sudden attack from a British outpost hidden behind a fence. Colonel William Piatt, quartermaster-general, rushed to the front and, spotting the British by their gunfire, shouted, "Come out, and fight like men on open ground." Before they could respond, he directed a volley into their ranks, maintaining fire for several minutes. The British picket retreated, allowing Piatt's company to occupy the abandoned post, marking their first success.

However, this victory was short-lived. A large contingent of British, reportedly around two hundred, soon arrived to reclaim their position, renewing a fierce attack. Lieutenant John McClelland was killed, Colonel Piatt was wounded, and several men were injured as the situation grew dire. Just in time, two cannons were positioned on the road, delivering a vigorous barrage that forced the enemy to retreat. The Americans celebrated a brief success, but more British forces advanced, unleashing a devastating fire aimed at the artillery and marines. The marines faltered under the onslaught, and some horses were injured, causing chaos as one cannon toppled into a ditch.[568]

In the midst of this turmoil, Jackson charged into the fray with two aides, commanding fiercely, "Save the guns, my boys, at every sacrifice!"

---

[568] AJ to Monroe, Dec. 27, 1814, Jackson, *Correspondence*, II, 127.

His presence rallied the marines, and as another company from the Seventh arrived, they managed to protect the cannons from danger. All of this transpired within minutes, while other companies of the Seventh and the Forty-Fourth engaged in close combat with the British regulars.

For several hours, the fighting turned into a chaotic maelstrom of guerilla warfare, and hand-to-hand combat. The American line swayed back and forth as the British regulars pressed their attacks repeatedly. As Jackson would later report, the invaders benefited from a thick fog that suddenly rolled in from the river, causing confusion among the British corps. By 9:30 pm, the fog had thickened, and the moonlight had vanished, making visibility near impossible. Concerned about the implications of continuing a night attack with troops that were operating together for the first time, Jackson decided to withdraw his men several hundred yards from the enemy, along the road leading to the city, to wait for daylight.[569]

This was the right decision under the circumstances. Shortly after 8 o'clock, Keane began receiving reinforcements from Bayou Bienvenue. Fresh, disciplined troops would have posed a significant challenge for Jackson's inexperienced soldiers, who would soon find themselves outnumbered. It was clear that Jackson's men needed to retreat; again the General's battlefield instincts proving adept. According to American estimates, they suffered 24 killed, 115 wounded, and 74 missing or captured. The British reported 46 killed, 167 wounded, and 64 missing. Both sides faced over 10% casualties, which is a notably high count. Jackson managed to escape with a draw; however, the British could—and did—claim victory since the Americans failed to destroy their advanced guard. Nevertheless, the Americans had taken the offensive, responding to the surprise invasion with a counter-attack that startled the British into staying put. Always aggressive, Jackson brought the invasion to an abrupt stop. In fact, his swift actions saved New Orleans; had he not attacked so quickly and with such fervor, the British would have undoubtedly marched against the city after the arrival of reinforcements.

All told, the Battle of Villeré's plantation caused the British an unexpected setback and numerous injuries, while the Americans boosted

---

[569] Ibid; Robert V. Remini, ed. *Jackson's Account of the Battle of New Orleans*, THS, 1967, XXVI, 26-31.

their morale. This decision proved vital. Although Jackson did not destroy the British guard, his aggressive counterattack prevented them from advancing further. The men under Jackson's command had shown no hesitation in marching out to confront the advancing enemy head on, erasing any doubt the residents of the city had about Jackson's ragtag troops. Although they could not claim victory, the men gained a sense of confidence from having stood toe to toe, for the first time, with the mighty British.[570]

After the battle and Jackson's decision to disengage, he and his men retreated two miles north to the Rodriguez Canal, where some of Jackson's troops had already commenced the construction of an earthwork, which would later be designated as Line Jackson. This fortification extended perpendicularly from the Mississippi River for three-quarters of a mile toward a nearby cypress swamp. The Rodriguez Canal, once an old mill-race, had become overgrown and partially filled. In the early days of the colony, planters built mills on the levee, channeling river water to the swamp through canals, especially during seasonal river floods. This canal crossed the narrowest part of the plain, making it an ideal location for General Jackson's defense.

A marine battery was established on the right bank of the river to bolster defenses. Troops deepened the canal, creating embankments and using cotton bales as makeshift defenses. The batteries in Jackson's line were placed on wooden platforms over cotton bales to prevent sinking in the mud. The breastwork consisted of earth mounds with openings made from cotton bales. Jackson quickly seized on the idea of using cotton for protection, but when cannon fire struck, it became a liability, as the bales caught fire and produced thick smoke, and needed replacement. The British also miscalculated, using sugar to reinforce their batteries, only to discover it offered no real protection.

Meanwhile, Jackson sent over fourteen hundred Louisiana militia to the right bank of the river to prepare defenses, anticipating the main British assault would occur on the left bank, which ultimately proved correct. As dawn broke, the fog lifted, and Jackson's army was ready behind the canal. Supplies, including tools from New Orleans, arrived just in time for the digging and fortifying of their position. Rallying his

---

[570] Latour, *Historical Memoir*, p. 112.

troops along the waterway, Jackson called out to his men, "Here we shall plant our stakes and not abandon them until we drive these red-coat rascals into the river, or the swamp!"[571]

On December 24th, Jackson's forces completed a mile-long defense line, raising it to heights of four to five feet. The cotton error was swiftly corrected. Every bale of that deceptive material was taken away from the site, replaced by thick, black, spongy soil from the delta, which had proven to be an excellent defense during the Sunday cannonade; the cannonballs sank into it without disturbing the embankment. The fortifications were reinforced in every section, and new cannons were installed. Work continued on the second line of defense, located a mile and a half behind the first. A third line of defense was also planned and initiated, even closer to the city. On the opposite bank of the river, the existing fortifications were repaired, and new ones began. The exact number of artillery pieces Jackson had during the first engagements is unclear, but he added more guns throughout the battles.

By December 28, he had four batteries, increasing to eight by January 8. The initial four American batteries included two six-pounder field guns, a six-pound howitzer, and two naval twenty-four-pounders crewed by Laffite's Baratarians. In fact, by Christmas Day, Jackson had grown so fond of this Baratarian bandit that he appointed Lafitte as an aide.[572] This was a wise decision, as there was likely no one in New Orleans more knowledgeable about the unconventional routes to the city than Jean Laffite. The American line, forever-after remembered as Line Jackson, extended about three-fourths of a mile, with one-third located in the cypress forest.

On Christmas Day, the long-awaited thirty-seven-year-old General Sir Edward Michael Pakenham arrived to take command of the British expeditionary force. Accompanied by a significant number of reinforcements, the British army appeared revitalized. As Admiral Cochrane's fleet carried the new British commander to New Orleans, he was cheered heartily. Pakenham, however, was soon disappointed to find that he would not be celebrating Christmas in the city, as he hoped and expected. The esteemed Wellington brother-in-law, Pakenham,

---

[571] Borneman, Walter, R. *1812: The War That Forged a Nation*, 2005.
[572] Marigny, *Reflections on the Campaign of General Jackson*, p. 67.

considered one of the most skilled officers in the vaunted British army, found himself immediately dissatisfied with their current position, and he did not hide his displeasure. Some reports suggest that he considered withdrawing to launch an attack elsewhere; however, Admiral Cochrane persuaded him against this course of action. Cochrane's disdain for the American troops led him to believe that they would falter and retreat in the face of a direct assault.

Pakenham was a skilled officer who had risen rapidly through the ranks. He had suffered from a noticeable cock of the head from a wound at St. Lucia, but when he sustained another wound at Martinique, the defect corrected itself. During the Peninsula War against Napoleon, he achieved military distinction when he broke open the French line in a daring, but costly attack. But Pakenham had yet to prove himself on American soil, and as he surveyed the position of his troops along the Mississippi, his initial annoyance turned to cold fury, as he realized his army was cramped into a narrow strip of land between a swamp and a river. Before him was an enemy entrenched in a fortified position with armed river vessels, guarding the flank and catching his left column in crossfire whenever it attempted to move forward.[573]

Putting first things first, Pakenham decided he must silence the *Carolina* and the *Louisiana* or drive them away, before anything else. At his command, nine field pieces were dragged to the riverbank--29 pounders, firing hot shot, 46 pounders firing strap, 25.5-inch howitzers, and a 5.5-inch mortar—along with a furnace for heating shot. Once in place, the battery opened up on the *Carolina* in a devastatingly accurate display of fire power. On the second round of hot shot, the ship caught fire; because the shot lodged in her main hole under her cables and could not be removed, the fire soon raged out of control.

The crew tumbled over the sides. And none too soon. The *Carolina* suddenly blew up with a tremendous roar, shaking the ground for miles and raining burning fragments in every direction. Jackson, from his command post at the Macarté house 200 yards behind the mud rampart, ordered the *Louisiana* out of range--not that Patterson needed the advice. To move, the *Louisiana* sailors were piled into boats to assist in the operation, while hot shot fell hissing into the water all around them.

---

[573] Fortescu, *History of the British Army*, X, 161.

The sailors, with much exertion, succeeded in towing the ship out of the range of Pakenham's guns.

The escape of the *Louisiana* was an egregious error for Pakenham's forces. Had he fired his artillery at the *Louisiana* first, which was further away than the *Carolina*, he would have been able to destroy both ships. Yet, by going after the closer target, the heavier and better armed *Louisiana* was able to remove to fight another day, relocating on the other side of the river and out of the range of Pakenham's guns. To make matters worse, it was positioned to rake any enemy force that attempted to attack Jackson's barricade. Frustrated by the failure of his subordinate officers to defeat the Americans and seize New Orleans, Pakenham relocated his army to the Chalmette Plantation, approximately five miles southeast of the city, on December 27.[574]

Not waiting any longer, on December 28, Pakenham launched an attack at daylight, moving forward in two columns toward the American lines. The dreariness of the previous days had finally lifted, and the moment the morning sun poked its head over the edge of the water, the fog cleared. Amidst Congreve rockets and heavy artillery fire, the British troops advanced toward Jackson's rampart. The formation nearest the river, under General Keane, advanced to within 800 yards of Jackson's right and opened fire with two field guns. Keane's men took cover, when they reached within 600 yards, and waited for their bombardment to disrupt the American defenses, ready to pounce if the big guns battered a hole in the US fortifications. They did not. Despite the initial confusion the British bombardment caused in the American lines, it failed to breach Jackson's defenses, and his artillery soon regrouped and returned fire. The American batteries unleashed a tremendous cannonade, supported by fierce fire from the *Louisiana*. Keane's men were ensnared and could do little but wait until the Americans ceased fire.

Pakenham's hope for a successful assault was quickly dashed as his troops became caught up in a deadly crossfire, forcing them to dive for cover in ditches. After three hours of fighting, Pakenham's troops were repelled, suffering one hundred twenty casualties. Those near the river had to wait until nightfall to retreat, while others fled as best they could. The American losses were minimal, with only seven killed and eight

---

[574] Remini, ed. *Jackson's Account of the Battle of New Orleans*, THS, 1967, XXVI, pp. 33-35.

wounded. The British failure to breach Jackson's line forced them to move back two miles from the rampart and construct advanced redoubts. This cost the British their chance to breach Jackson's line and advance into New Orleans.[575]

Recognizing the ineffectiveness of his artillery, Pakenham ordered the guns to be moved to safety. Over the next five days, he made two attempts to thwart Jackson's defenses but was repelled both times. Convinced that additional cannons were necessary to counter the American artillery, Pakenham was stymied; to receive those additions, with the difficulties of logistics, continuing the attack would have to wait. Facing transportation delays, Pakenham's frustrations mounted.

Meanwhile, following the attack of December 28th, Jackson continued to improve the American breastworks. He also made a considerable addition to his artillery, mounting a thirty-two-pound naval gun at the center of his line. To the left of this he added another six-pounder, a twelve-pounder, an eighteen-pounder, along with an old brass carronade. All his guns except the carronade were manned by regular army gunners, naval gunners, Baratarians, and former French artillerists. In addition to the artillery on Jackson's line, Commander Patterson established a battery of two twelve pounders and a twenty-four-pounder on the west bank of the river, so positioned as to fire on the flank of any attack on Jackson's line. Once again, the combination of a British blunder, a British delay, and a Jackson opportunity, worked to the Americans' advantage, which Jackson and his men would make the most of, thoroughly reinforcing his position on both sides of the Mississippi.[576]

During the last few days of December, however, the British managed to pull off the laborious task; transporting ten eighteen-pounders and four twenty-four-pound carronades successfully to within a quarter of a mile of the main road. No small feat, these guns and their ammunition were moved by boat across Lake Borgne and up the canal. They were unloaded and placed on carts, then pulled by seamen to their positions. Four eighteen-pounders were positioned on the main road in a battery, aimed at the *Louisiana*, while another battery of six eighteen-pounders targeted the center of Jackson's line. Additionally, four twenty-four-pound

---

[575] DeGrummond, p. 106-107.
[576] Latour, pp. 126-27.

carronades, along with field guns and a howitzer, were set up to support the British advance. The positioning of the guns was completed on the night of December 31, and the British commenced bombardment on January 1, 1815, at ten o'clock am, just as the fog lifted to welcome in a new year. [577]

In the meantime, while General Jackson's army fortified their defenses against the British, peace negotiations were concluding across the Atlantic, underscoring the disconnect between the War of 1812's battlefield and diplomatic resolutions. News of the negotiations reached Washington during this period, but to that point, the word was that stubborn British representatives still stymied the talks. Both armies in New Orleans, unaware of any of the goings-on in Belgium, continued their preparations under the belief that war raged as continuously as ever. Word would not reach Louisiana for weeks, and in the city, unease festered.

---

[577] Journal of C.R. Forrest, Jan. 1, 1815.

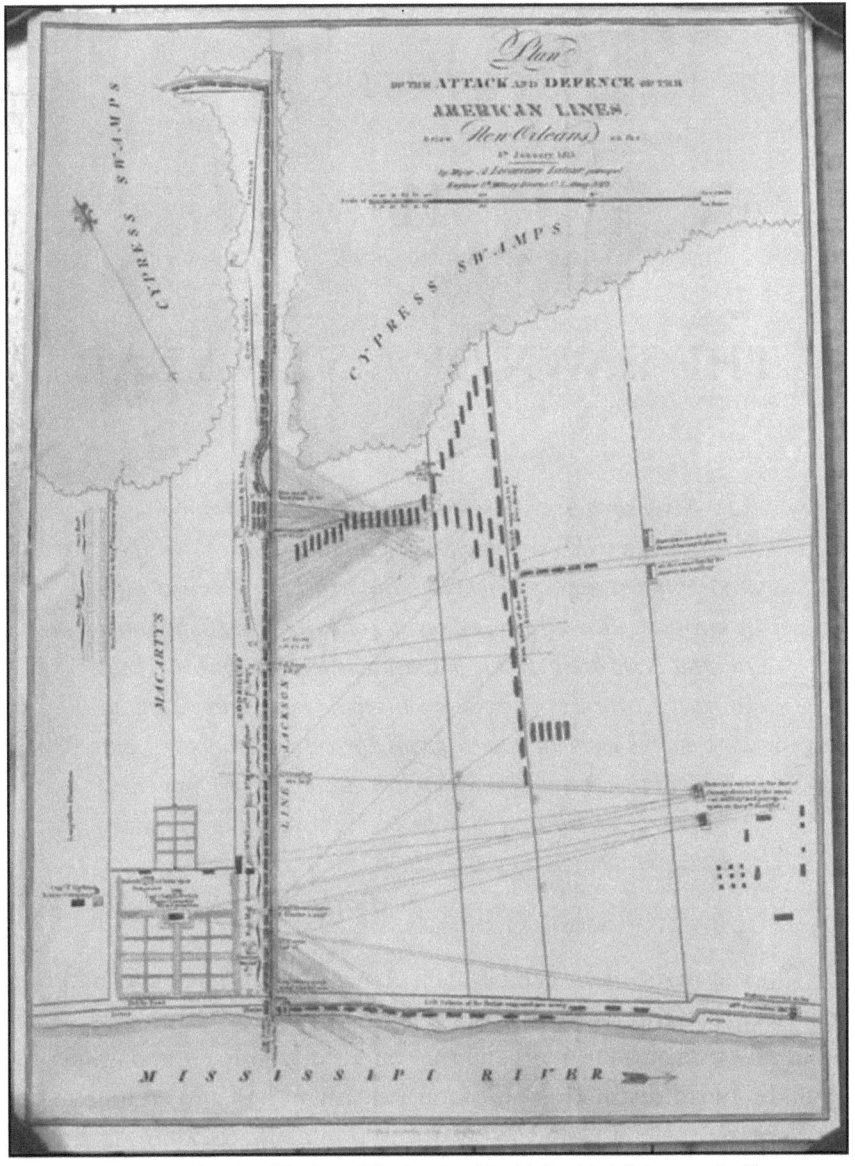

Plan of the Attack and Defence of the American Lines below New Orleans on the 8th January, 1815. A. Lacarriere Latour. Source: Alexandremaps.com, Item #M9691

CHAPTER

41

THE DAWN OF A NEW YEAR

"To have shrunk, under such circumstances, from manly resistance, would have been a degradation blasting our best and proudest hopes; it would have struck us from the high ranks where the virtuous struggles of our fathers had placed us, and have betrayed the magnificent legacy which we hold in trust for future generations. It would have acknowledged that on the element which forms three-fourths of the globe we inhabit, where all independent nations have equal and common rights, the American people were not an independent people, but colonists and vassals."

-President James Madison

On the night of December 31st, American sentinels and outposts reported that the entire British army had moved within five or six hundred yards of their lines, and the sounds of digging and hammering could be heard distinctly.[578] General Pakenham had agreed to give the artillery and navy a chance to turn the tide of the battle by trying to breach Jackson's defenses. Thus, on that same night last night of the year 1814, in the cold and the mist, twenty long cannons and ten shorter ones were brought to camp, along with enough ammunition for six hours of continuous cannon fire. The plan was not to toast holiday cheer,

---

[578] Dale, Matthew B., *The Staff Ride Handbook for The Battles of New Orleans, 23 December 1814 - 8 January 1815*. 2015. pp. 97-101.

but to build several redoubts close to the American lines and blast the Americans into submission.

As darkness fell, half of the British army was ordered to move forward quietly, passing by the pickets and stopping about four hundred yards from Jackson's camp. There, the soldiers stacked their arms and began working with shovels and picks under the guidance of engineering officers and Colonel Sir John Burgoyne, the British army's Inspector of Fortifications and Director of Engineering operations in Sevastopol, and the son of "Gentleman Johnny" Burgoyne of Revolutionary War fame. The men worked energetically, with the 85th and 95th regiments providing cover for the workers. The night was dark, and strict silence was enforced by the officers. Each soldier aimed to complete his task more quickly and efficiently than his neighbor. Even the officers joined in, and many hands that were unused to hard labor were toughened by the night's work. Everyone who was able managed a shovel or pickaxe, fully aware that they were working for their lives.

The task required caution and silence, as the "cunning Yankees" were alert, and any noise could ruin the surprise of their new operation. The British were focused on constructing several redoubts that would allow them to fire on the American entrenchments, which they believed would be easily destroyed. The engineers faced the difficulty of finding solid materials for the embankments. Everything that could provide resistance was used to strengthen the mounds, including hogsheads of sugar from nearby plantation ruins, which were believed to be just as effective as sand in stopping cannonballs. This resulted in the waste of several thousand dollars' worth of sugar.

By dawn, their hard work had paid off with the completion of three strong demilunes or crescent-shaped fortifications, positioned at nearly equal distances on the right, center, and left. These redoubts housed thirty heavy cannons, ready with ammunition. Manned by skilled artillerymen and seasoned gunners from the fleet, veterans of notable battles, this formidable battery was set to open fire on the enemy as soon as they became visible through the morning mist.

New Year's Day, 1815, dawned in thick fog that rose up from the river; a fog so dense that a man could discern nothing at a distance of twenty yards. The fog covered all the plain like a blanket. When the day broke, and the New Year was ushered in, not a sound was heard in the direction of the enemy's camp, nor did the American sentinels nearest their position hear or see anything to excite alarm. At eight o'clock the fog was still impenetrable, and the silence unbroken. As late as nine o'clock, the American troops, who were on slightly higher ground than the British, saw little prospect of the fog breaking away, still less of any hostile movement on the part of the enemy. The soldiers, therefore, did as they were ordered, and dressed up in their finest dress uniforms, and got ready to muster. The fog gradually cleared under showers of rain, which also obscured all view of the enemy positions. The British troops formed in two columns, ready for the assault. At 9 o'clock Pakenham's artillery opened fire.[579]

The first fire was aimed directly at the Macarté house, which the British knew was Jackson's headquarters. The General and his staff were finishing their breakfast when the house was suddenly shaken by the explosive and awe-inspiring sounds of Congreve rockets. Balls and shells crashed into the building, shattering masonry, splintering furniture, and tearing plaster from the walls. The General and his staff were in the house, but although it was struck repeatedly, remarkably, no one was injured, "Though for ten minutes after the batteries opened, not less than 100 balls, rockets, and shells struck the house."[580] The Macarté house was completely destroyed in the shelling.

When the bombardment began, great confusion appeared for a time within the American line. The army was conducting a parade review, decked out in their flying colors, and most ornamental dress to ring in the New Year. Jackson had ordered the review in another attempt to raise troop morale, and the decision might have been a total disaster as a result. All was pomp and circumstance, as the American regiments marched within their fortifications, as the different military bands bellowed forth those sweetly familiar tunes. But as the fog lifted, and the shots rang out, the men were suddenly scattered about and the parade dispersed. It was 9 am, and Line Jackson was suddenly broadsided by a cannonade that seemingly arrived out of nowhere. All the British clanging of the night before should have alerted the "Cunning Yanks," yet it had not.

---

[579] Glieg, *Campaigns of the British Army*, p. 173.
[580] Walker, pg. 256.

The Redcoats had been waiting at the ready for that very moment when visibility would finally be achieved. [581]

Dodging a certain death, Jackson hurried to the rampart, where the troops, after a brief moment of confusion, were gathering to fire back at the artillery. Despite the chaos, Line Jackson held firm. "Don't mind these rockets!" Jackson is reported to have cried, "They are mere toys to amuse children!" John Reid would report that the British would later acknowledge that "ours is the first army that was not thrown into confusion by their rockets." [582]

The heavy British barrage had not breached Jackson's mud wall, and within minutes, the American lines thundered its' response to the attack. For an hour and a half the cannonading was constant, the entire delta shaking from the impact of the explosions. Dominique You, the brother of Jean Lafitte, stood on the end of the embankment, shouting to his men to fire more rapidly, and to cram their pieces to the mouth with chain shot, ship cannister, and any other destructive missile they could find. As the firing continued, the Americans began to improve their accuracy by watching where their shots fell, adjusting the range to improve their marksmanship. "Too much praise," Jackson wrote to Secretary Monroe, "cannot be bestowed on those who managed my artillery." [583]

Ten guns were positioned in the American lines, with more across the river. When General Jackson arrived, he found his artillerymen ready to fire as the smoke cleared. He quickly inspected each battery, rushing to the left and waving his hat as the men cheered him on. "Jackson's first glance, when he reached the line" as Walker wrote, "was in the direction of Humphrey's battery. There stood this right arm of the artillery, dressed in his usual plain attire, smoking that eternal cigar, coolly leveling his guns and directing his men. 'Ah!' exclaimed the General, 'all is right; Humphrey is at his post, and will return their compliments presently.'" [584]

Walker was referring to Captain Enoch Humphrey, who was coolly directing his men while smoking a cigar. In the midst of the chaos, soldiers faced the danger with various reactions—some skillfully avoiding incoming fire while others remained unfazed by the relentless

---

[581] Tatum, *"Journal,"* p. 121.
[582] Reid to Elizabeth Reid, Jan. 10th, 1815, Reid Papers, LC.
[583] AJ to Monroe, Jan. 2, 1815, Jackson Papers, LC.
[584] Walker, p. 257.

bombardment. Captain Humphrey, commanding the number one battery, patiently straddled his targets to find the exact range and direction. Patterson's naval batteries located the British artillery mounted on the levee and knocked it out.

Jackson, accompanied by his aides, walked down to the left of the line, stopping at each battery to inspect its condition, and waving his cap to the men as they gave him three cheers. Colonel Butler, whom the General had seen prostrated at headquarters, came running up to the lines covered with dust. " Why, Colonel Butler," roared the General, "Is that you?" I thought you were killed." "No, General," Butler replied calmly, "only knocked over." [585]

Captain Humphrey soon caught a glimpse of the British batteries; structures of narrow front and slight elevation, lying low and dim upon the field; no such broad target as the mile-long lines of the American position. Adjusting a twelve-pounder with the utmost care, he quietly gave the word, "Let her off."

"Never," remarks Alexander Walker, "was work more completely done — more perfectly finished and rounded off. Earth and heaven fairly shook with the prolonged shouts of the Americans over this spectacle. Still the remorseless artillerists would not cease their fire. The British infantry would now and then raise their heads and peer out from the ditches in which they were so ingloriously ensconced. The level plain presented but a few knolls or elevations to shelter them, and the American artillerists were as skillful as riflemen in picking off those who exposed ever so small a portion of their bodies. Several extraordinary examples of this skill were communicated…by a British officer who was attached to Pakenham's army." [586]

A number of the officers of the British 93rd took refuge in a shallow hollow behind a slight elevation, and there it was proposed that the only married officer of the party should lie at the bottom, as it was deemed the safest place. Lieutenant Phaups was the officer indicated, and he assumed the position assigned to him. This mound had attracted the attention of the American gunners, and a great effort was made to hit this exposed target. Lieutenant Phaups could not resist the temptation to see what was

---

[585] Butler, *MSS 102. Butler Family Papers, 1778–1975.*
[586] Walker, p. 258

going on in front, and peered out, with not more than half of his head exposed. Immediately, Phaups was struck by a twelve-pound shot, and instantly killed. His companions buried him on the spot, in full uniform. In so doing, several officers and men were picked off in a similar manner as the fire continued all around them.

While the bombardment was at its height, word was brought to Jackson that a small British contingent was approaching to the left of his line along the edge of the swamp. Reacting quickly, Jackson turned to his most trusted man, Brigadier General John Coffee of Tennessee. The ever-steady Coffee was ready for this maneuver, having learned his lessons on December 28th. With just a nod of the head, Coffee and his cavalry dismounted and anchored their position knee-deep in the mud. Jackson had given special attention to this segment because of their experience three days earlier. Coffee ordered his men to drive the British into the swamp and then drown them. While his troops fell short of accomplishing this, they did manage to steer the British force back to the main body, assisted by the difficulties of the ground. [587]

It was nearly noon when the Americans became aware that the British fire was slackening. The American batteries were then ordered to cease fire, to allow their guns to cool and the smoke to roll away. As James Parton describes the sight, "What a scene greeted the anxious gaze of the troops when, at length, the British position was disclosed. Those formidable batteries, which had excited such consternation an hour and a half before, were totally destroyed, and presented but formless masses of soil and broken guns; while the sailors who had manned them were seen running from them to the rear, and the army that had been drawn up behind the batteries, ready to storm the lines as soon as a breach had been made in them, had again ignominiously 'taken to the ditch.'" [588]

Once the smoke cleared, it became apparent that the embankments of the British batteries were all beaten in, the guns exposed, and some of the artillerists killed. The infantry, which had been ordered to be ready for an advance when a breach was made in the American works, grew impatient, and became so exposed that it was deemed prudent to retire them again into the ditches. The British lines had been hurt, damaged,

---

[587] Brown, Wilburt S., *Amphibious Campaign*, 1969, p. 124.
[588] Parton, *Jackson*, pg. 161.

and disabled by the Yankee barrage. But the Americans took a pounding too, although at first the British seemed unconcerned about range and threw much of their fire beyond Jackson's line.[589] Still, the carriage of Dominique's 24-pounder was broken, the 32- and 12-pounders were put out of commission, and two caissons, one of which contained a hundred pounds of powder, blew up. When the ammunition exploded, the British infantry let out a cheer in the hope that the American line had finally been breached; but they soon learned otherwise when more intense fire from the rampart rained down on them.

Within two hours it was clear that the British had failed in their objective. Indeed, the bombardment was a poor demonstration of their usual professional standards. The use of hogsheads of sugar in the construction of their parapets had proven to be a great mistake. Many of the sugar casks stacked around the gun emplacements for protection burst and disabled the guns; the balls penetrated these hogsheads as if they were so many empty casks, dismounting the guns, and killing the men in the very center of the works. Sugar, it was clear, was no substitute for sand. Some batteries had inadequate flooring and after a few salvos drove themselves into the mud and out of operation. Several field pieces were damaged by the Americans, and casualties among British gunners were particularly heavy.[590]

"The largest British battery," wrote Vincent Nolte, cotton merchant, and a volunteer in the Louisiana militia, "had directed its fire against the battery of the pirates Dominique and Beluche, who had divided our company into two parts, and were supplied with ammunition by it. Once, as Dominique Avas, examining the enemy through a glass, a cannon shot wounded his arm; he caused it to be bound up, saying, 'I will pay them for that!' and resumed his glass. He then directed a twenty-four pounder, gave the order to fire, and the ball knocked an English gun carriage to pieces, and killed six or seven men. Our company lost that day but one man, our least, a French hatter, called Laborde. For pre-destinarians I would mention that the young notary, Philippe Peddesclaux, was standing exactly in front of Laborde, and the latter would not have been hit had he not been bending forward at the moment to light his cigar

---

[589] Coles, *War of 1812*, p. 224.
[590] Brown, *Amphibious Campaign*, p. 124.

by my neighbor, St. Avit's. When the latter turned he saw Laborde's scattered brains and prostrate body. The flash of a gun reaches the eye long before the report gets to the ear, and thus the ball can sometimes be avoided. I have watched both the flash and the report, and I have seen the best tried soldiers, both officers and men, even the utterly fearless Jackson himself, getting out of the way of the congreve rockets, which were sent in great quantities from the British camp. Others, again, either actuated by a different principle, or less prudently observant of danger and less anxious to avoid it, like my friend St. Avit for instance, remained confident in their fate in the same position, and stood quietly as if all the roar of the cannon and the hissing of missiles about their ears was entirely without interest for them." [591]

"On this day," Nolte continued, "which saw our whole line except the batteries exposed to the fire, my worthy friend, Major Carmick, who commanded the volunteer battalion, and was near the pirates' battery, was struck by a congreve rocket on the forehead, knocked off his horse, and had both his arms injured. I asked leave to accompany him to the guardhouse, and as we reached the low garden wall behind Jackson's headquarters, I saw, to my great amazement, two of the General's volunteer adjutants, Duncan, the lawyer, and District Marshal Duplessis, lying flat on the ground to escape the British balls. Livingston was invisible — writing and reading of proclamations kept him out of sight. The General during this cannonade was constantly riding from one wing to the other, accompanied by his usual military aides, Reid and Butler, and the two advocates, Grymes and Davezac.... The munitions were in charge of Governor Claiborne, who was so frightened that he could scarcely speak. On the 1st of January ammunition was wanting at batteries Nos. 1 and 2. Jackson sent in a fury for Claiborne." [592]

In exasperation, after three hours of fighting, Pakenham ordered the guns withdrawn to a safe position and wrote to his superiors that he required even more artillery for a successful attack. American losses that intemperate New Year's Day amounted to thirty-five, while the British lost as many as seventy-five. The year 1815 was shaping up to be another tough year for the Empire. Back at headquarters after his abysmal failure

---

[591] Parton, *Jackson*, p. 159.
[592] Nolte, Vincent, *Fifty years in Both Hemispheres or Reminiscences*, New York, Redfield, 1854, p. 211.

to penetrate the American line, Pakenham cursed the imbecility that had confined him to this narrow plane. One thing now struck him as crystal clear: since he could not move, he must punch his way straight ahead through Jackson's fortification if he was ever to reach New Orleans. And that required additional troops. That also necessitated massive power hurled directly forward, committing thousands of men to a frontal assault in such depth that the Americans would be overwhelmed by sheer numbers. That was, Pakenham determined, his only hope.

Glieg's reaction was typical of many of the British soldiers on the New Year's Day assault. "For two whole nights and days not a man had closed an eye, except such as were cool enough to sleep amidst showers of cannonball; and during the day scarcely a moment had been allowed in which we were able so much as to break our fast. We retired, therefore, not only baffled and disappointed, but in some degree disheartened and discontented. All our plans had, as yet proved abortive; even this, upon which so much reliance had been placed, was found to be of no avail; and it must be confessed that something like murmuring began to be heard through the camp."[593]

British dismay at the difficulties that beset them was beginning to mount. "The ground which we now occupied," Pakenham wrote frustratingly, "resembled in almost every particular that which we had quitted. We again extended across the plain, from the marsh to the river: no wood or cover of any description concealing our line, or obstructing the view of either army; while both in front and rear was an open space, laid out in fields and intersected by narrow ditches. Our out-posts, however, were pushed forward to some houses, within a few hundred yards of the enemy's works, sending out advance sentinels even further; and the headquarters of the army were established near the spot where the action of the 23d had been fought." [594]

Considering the low morale among some of the British troops, particularly those unprepared and ill-equipped for the Louisiana weather, the plan had built-in disadvantages. In any event, Pakenham decided to wait for the reinforcements under Major General John Lambert, that were expected daily. These troops included the crack Seventh Fusiliers,

---

[593] Glieg, George Robert, *Campaigns of the British Army*, p. 174.
[594] Reilly, pg. 272.

and the very able 43rd regiment. The two elite regiments had actually arrived at the fleet anchorage already and were on their way across the lake to join the main force. They reached Pakenham's position on January 6th.

To lessen the burden of the frontal assault and to support his attacking soldiers, Pakenham planned to catch Jackson in a crossfire. He proposed to ferry 1,500 troops, under the brilliant Colonel William Thornton, to the west bank of the Mississippi, capture Patterson's guns, and turn them on Jackson. This enfilade, timed to coincide with the assault by the main force on the east bank, would rake Jackson's position and with luck, wipe him out. Only one problem existed: the boats to ferry Thornton's men across the river. Barges were available, but they lay moored in Bayou Bienvenue. Admiral Cochrane suggested widening and deepening Villeré's canal to provide a navigable route from Bayou Bienvenue to the Mississippi. Once the canal had been improved and the levee breached, barges could move freely from their base to the river and then across the Mississippi.

In many respects, Pakenham's basic strategy had great merit. The American defense on the West Bank was dangerously thin, and could easily be captured, provided it was hit quickly and in strength. With Patterson's heavy guns trained on the American line, a murderous crossfire could be established and hole after hole drilled into Jackson's position. Unfortunately, the difficult work of extending, widening, and deepening the canal took many days, delaying the mission and giving Jackson additional time to reinforce his position. Not until January 7th was the canal ready for use. While inspecting it, Pakenham noticed that only one dam had been constructed to hold the force of the river, and he questioned his engineers about the advisability of a second dam as a precaution against the collapse of the first. The engineers dismissed his fears--and, sure enough, the dam collapsed, delaying the operation enough to thwart Pakenham's crossfire scheme.

Not surprisingly, the ever-energetic Jackson did not sit on his hands during the time so fortuitously provided by the British command. Again the ditch was deepened, the mud rampart heightened. Rodriguez Canal was lengthened and a high parapet constructed along the northern edge and revetted with fence nails to keep it from sliding into the canal. The American line ran for more than half a mile from the river to the swamp, extending into the swamp for a short distance, then turning in a right angle toward the city. The rampart averaged five feet in height; it was twenty feet thick in some places but was so thin in others that cannonballs could easily puncture it. On the left side, for example, the breastwork was only thick enough to withstand musket-fire. Reluctantly, Jackson agreed to construct an advance redoubt near the river, but it was still incomplete when the major assault began on January 8th. He had also begun the construction of two additional lines of defense behind the canal, one closer to the city by two miles and the third closer still by a mile and a quarter. To assist in the difficult and time-consuming construction, Jackson had the help of a task force of slaves—something the British desperately needed. [595]

Throughout these encounters, although the British did not deploy their most elite regiments, Jackson's troops faced many hardened veterans of the Napoleonic Wars. The conditions were as harsh as they come. That winter was unusually frigid for Louisiana standards, and many soldiers lacked proper winter clothing. Surviving on meager rations, often just cornbread and salted pork, the men faced the constant threat of disease, with many suffering from dysentery and malaria. Jackson himself did not shrink from these hardships, but shared in them right alongside his men, validating his reputation as "Old Hickory."

Hard as hickory themselves, Jackson's troops dug in through the New Year, which promised to decide the contest one way or another, once and for all.

---

[595] Walker, p. 256.

CHAPTER

42

THE EIGHTH OF JANUARY

"But remember, that without obedience, without order, without discipline, all your efforts are vain, and the brave man, inattentive to his duty, is worth little more to his country than the coward who deserts her in the hour of danger..."
-Andrew Jackson

On the 7th of January 1815, Commodore Daniel T. Patterson walked along the western side of the Mississippi River to a point directly across from the main British position. For several hours, the twenty-eight-year-old New Yorker, veteran of both the Quasi War and the Barbary Wars, stared across at the enemy's forces. What he observed left Patterson in a cold sweat. Villeré's canal had been extended to the river, and it now breached the levee. Floating ominously in the river were barges loaded to the hilt with cannons under a British flag, and the enemy was readying to carry a large contingent of soldiers to the west bank. Patterson felt his heart sink into his stomach when he saw the men assigned to defend this point in the line, General David Morgan's thin numbers would be no match for the British here. Patterson immediately sent sailing master Richard S. Shepherd to beg the General to reinforce Morgan's position.

"Hurry back and tell General Morgan that he is mistaken," Jackson told Shepherd, "The main attack will be on this side, and I will have no men to spare. He must maintain his position at all hazards. Gentlemen,"

Jackson told his aides, "Arise. We have slept enough, the enemy will soon be upon us in a few minutes. I must go and see General Coffee." [596]

Major General Andrew Jackson commanded a diverse army by the start of 1815; a remarkable mix of regular U.S. Army soldiers, local Creole, both white and free blacks, and Anglo-American militias had joined the ranks, Native American warriors, made up mainly of the Choctaws, and of course, the Lafitte pirates of Barataria, along with other smugglers used to running stealthily through the lines of authority. By late December, the Tennessee volunteers, and new additions of local Louisiana militia were added to Jackson's numbers. Jackson now commanded both regular infantry and artillery units; some were raw, some were veterans of previous engagements, including the Creek War. The ultimate result was a spirited force characterized by resilience and enthusiasm, though overall lacking in experience. His regular army units wore traditional blue uniforms, while the frontier volunteers were clad in homespun clothing and buckskin. The free Black soldiers, forming the 1st and 2nd Battalion of Free Men of Color, brought crucial local knowledge of the terrain. The Choctaws mainly served as scouts, and they proved invaluable, along with the Baratarians, for navigation through the treacherous bayous.

What made Jackson's force unique was its democratic nature - something unprecedented for its time. Wealthy merchants marched alongside humble farmers, while free black soldiers served next to frontiersmen. The pirates, led by Lafitte, brought their maritime expertise and knowledge of the local waterways. Despite their differences, Jackson molded them into a cohesive fighting force through strict discipline and his own unwavering determination. Their determination would soon be put to the test in the most audacious fashion on the 8th day of 1815.

It had been a brutal winter. Army reports revealed a series of cold fronts marked by rain, sleet, and cold blustery northerly winds. Constant frosts had caused frostbite, and the loss of toes to more than a few of the frigid soldiers. Mired in misery and mud, with little shelter, the troops struggled to survive the winter. Unbeknownst to even the most astute early-19th century weather recorders, the winter of 1814-15 was

---

[596] Walker, *Jackson and New Orleans*, pp. 318-319; Remini, 1977. p. 274.

particularly bad as a result of an El Niño in the Pacific, bringing cooler, wetter conditions than normal across the southern states of the US. Although the term was coined by fishermen in the 1600s, it referred solely, to that point, to the weak ocean current that seemed to arrive around Christmas time. Not until the twentieth century, would the current be connected to the gifts of cold, wet weather El Niño delivered.[597]

The week that followed the failed British attack of January 1st was marked by anxiety for all involved in and around New Orleans. Tensions simmered as both sides prepared for the inevitable clash that seemed to hang suspended in the thick air of an unseasonable cold front.

Jackson, now saddled with the Morgan question on the left bank, pondered what the enemy might attempt next, striving to discern Pakenham's intentions. Monday through Thursday passed without any movements from the hostile army that might hint at their plans, if they had any. Jackson began to believe that his lines would not be attacked again, and he communicated this to the Secretary of War. Outwardly, the General showed no signs of apprehension, and seemed entirely focused on strengthening his position, but, internally, as his letter indicated, he grappled with the fear of being surprised from another direction.

It was, indeed, a valid and natural concern. Yet, if thirty cannons could not breach his lines, and, as on January 1st, if the American position seemed impregnable, could it be any less so after three thousand men had continued to fortify it for nearly a week? After two failed attempts, would any general, even the brother-in-law of the great Duke of Wellington, risk his army and reputation on a third?

Reasoning along these lines, and after having already faced two false alarms of an enemy landing above the city, the General instructed his trusted friend and volunteer, the fearless pioneer and filibuster, Reuben Kemper—who held a strong dislike for Spaniards, having once been their prisoner—to lead a group of selected men around via canal and bayou to the mouth of the Bienvenue, where the enemy had landed, to assess their activities and intentions. After a grueling twenty-four hours of covert effort and danger, Kemper reached a vantage point overlooking the enemy's position. He observed that they did not seem to be on the

---

[597] Warren, Bob, "Cold adds historic touch to the Battle of New Orleans." *NOLA*, Jan. 7, 2010.

verge of relocating any time soon. On the contrary, the British were well entrenched, with sentinels stationed in trees, and others busy burning the prairies for a broader view. Based on all signs Kemper could gather, the British base of operations remained occupied with fears of an imminent American attack. [598]

Before retreating to the swamp, some of Kemper's men, deep in enemy territory, daringly (and perhaps foolishly) fired upon a small group of enemy troops guarding some boats. The enemy quickly turned the Americans on their heels, and pursued, capturing one American soldier. Kemper was the first to return to Jackson's headquarters, and despite the capture, the information he provided significantly alleviated the General's concerns. Jackson was now able to focus his forces and efforts on the lines.

However, the activities of the English soldiers near the Villeré mansion remained an enigma, and it was this very uncertainty that caused alarm among the General's many detractors in and around the city of New Orleans. Apprehension mounted among the residents of the city, many of whom skirted the stringent martial law mandate and flirted with the idea of collusion with the British.

As Jackson's men prepared for battle and labored with the construction of new defenses around New Orleans, the General's inability to repel the enemy rankled even the most loyal of Jackson supporters among the inhabitants of the Crescent City, growing ever more anxious with each passing day. Seeing the might of the British army camped just miles away, some believed Jackson doubted his own capacity to protect the city. Whispers spread that he would rather ignite New Orleans than let it fall, a notion he never denied.

Anxiety had peaked before the December 28th engagement when Abner Duncan, an aide to Governor Claiborne, relayed that the legislature considered surrendering to the British to save their properties. Outraged upon hearing this, Jackson reportedly urged Duncan to advise Claiborne to "blow up" the legislature if surrender was their intent. While Claiborne refrained from such reactionary destruction, he locked the doors and barred legislative meetings until further notice. Then a

---

[598] Andrew McMichael, "The Kemper 'Rebellion': Filibustering and Resident Anglo American Loyalty in Spanish West Florida", *Louisiana History*, vol. 43, no. 2 (Spring 2002), p. 133-165.

committee of the legislature confronted Jackson and demanded to know how he would respond, should a general retreat come about. Old Hickory Jackson laid into the committee. Believing that the legislators were more concerned about the safety of New Orleans than the destruction of the invading army, Jackson's response probably began to peel the paint on the walls. "If I thought the hair of my head could divine what I should do," he told the committee, "forthwith, I would cut it off; go back with this answer: say to your honorable body, that if a disaster does overtake me, and the fate of war drives me from my line to the city, they may expect to have a very warm session." His intent did not escape them. [599]

When news of Jackson's comments and obvious bluster reached the legislators, they reacted predictably. The outraged Louisiana Legislature sent the wealthy and influential councilman, Bernard Marigny, to the General and complained that he and his fellow legislators had been misunderstood, maligned and abused. He further stated that they had no intention of betraying their country or surrendering to the enemy. It was another attempt by Claiborne and his friends to discredit them, he argued. Ultimately, Marigny's defense was so spirited and sincere that Jackson accepted his word and ordered a halt to further interference in the body's functioning. It was a necessary and much needed defusing of the situation, and Marigny's sincerity convinced Jackson that the legislature did intend to resist the British. Satisfied, Jackson allowed the governing body to function, quelling further discontent, and quieting, at least for a time, the disorder in the city's internal operations.[600]

After the artillery clash on January 1, a stillness had settled over the battlefield. Jackson hedged his bets. Intent on patience, the General avoided confronting the main British force, knowing his troops were outnumbered. The American army remained outnumbered, even with the arrival of 500 Louisiana militiamen and 2,250 Kentucky soldiers. Additionally, most of the Kentuckians, who arrived on the morning of Wednesday, January 4th, led by Generals John Thomas and John Adair, arrived unarmed. The disheartening reality was that only one in ten was adequately armed, and only one in three had any weapons at all. Only

---

[599] Parton, *Jackson*, II, p.143.
[600] Marigny, "Reflections on the Campaign of General Jackson," p. 70.

500 bore weapons altogether, and Jackson had none to spare. Despite searching the city, he could arm only about 400.

The arrival of the long-awaited Kentuckians in New Orleans caused quite a stir, in fact. Their arrival had been eagerly anticipated, but it also brought intense disappointment. They were some sight to behold. Many of the Kentuckians were so tattered that, as they marched through the streets, they had to hold their garments together to hide their exposed skin. Moreover, This news was a bitter pill for General Jackson to swallow, as well as for those brave men who had hoped to find shelter and resources in New Orleans; the General had no muskets, blankets, tents, or clothing to offer them. In fact, the lack of adequate supplies had been plaguing the army for months, and Jackson was beside himself.

A group of Louisiana militia had also arrived a day or two earlier from Baton Rouge, but they were in an almost equally dire situation. With nearly three thousand men urgently needed, these men had rushed to the service of their country, only to be rendered immobilized and ineffective due to a lack of arms, the supply of which had been delayed for sixty days on its way down the river. Had the captain of the belated boat faced the irate General Jackson at that moment, he may not have lived to captain another voyage. In fact, Jackson gave orders, which were sent up the river to bring the culprit down in chains. Eventually, the unfortunate captain was brought to the General, but it was far too late. Jackson's staff retold the stories for years of the colorful nature of the General's remarks about the man, the nature of which could not be repeated in polite company.

A lack of weapons and ammunition had plagued Jackson's army for months; rifles requisitioned in August arrived in mid-January, well after the major battle had been fought. Covering himself, the General warned Washington that it was courting a disaster for which it would be solely responsible. "Depend upon it," he wrote Monroe, "this supineness, this negligence, this criminality, let me call it, of which we witness so many instances in the agents of Government, must finally lead, if it be not corrected, to the defeat of our armies, and to the disgrace of those who superintendent them." The Kentucky troops had just arrived, he added, but "not more than one third of them are armed, and those very indifferently. I have none to put in their hands." [601]

The Louisiana Legislature, along with many of the citizens of New Orleans responded with admirable generosity during the crisis. The legislature had been allowed back into their chambers after just one day of exclusion. Major Latour, a staunch defender of the Legislature, recorded the actions taken by them and the people to assist the destitute soldiers:

"Mr. Louaillier, the elder, a member of the House of Representatives, obtained from the Legislature the sum of six thousand dollars, which was put at the disposition of a committee formed for their relief. Subscriptions were also opened at New Orleans for the same purpose, and another sum of six thousand dollars was soon subscribed; and it is to be observed that the Orleans Volunteers and Militia, not satisfied with discharging their duty to their country by their presence in the camp, sent for a subscription list, and filled it with their signatures.....The whole sum thus obtained, including what was voted by the Legislature, amounted to sixteen thousand, one hundred dollars, and was laid out in purchasing blankets and woolens, which were distributed among the ladies of New Orleans, to be made into clothes. Within one week twelve hundred blanket cloaks, two hundred and seventy-five waistcoats, eleven hundred and twenty-seven pairs of pantaloons, eight hundred shirts, four hundred and ten pairs of shoes, and a great number of mattresses, were made up, or purchased ready made, and distributed among our brethren in arms, who stood in the greatest need of them. Though the gratitude of their fellow-citizens, and the consciousness of their patriotic service, be to Mr. Louaillier, and to Messrs. Dubuys and Soulie, who cooperated with him in his honourable exertions, a sufficient reward, yet I must be allowed to pay those gentlemen the tribute of applause so justly due to them. Over the course of the campaign, several fathers, or men who were the support of families, among the volunteers and militia of the state, having been killed or wounded, those who depended on them for support were left in the greatest distress; wherefore the legislature....enacted that the pay of wounded men should be continued till the end of next session, and that the families of those slain in the service of the country, should

---

[601] AJ to Monroe, Jan. 2, 1815, Jackson Papers, LC.

receive pay for the deceased, until the same period. With pleasure I take this opportunity to do justice to the patriotic and highly praiseworthy conduct of the legislature." [602]

Such words of praise were direly needed by those in the Jackson camp who could still view the legislature favorably. Up to that point, this body of men had come across as anything but patriotic and praiseworthy towards the presence of Jackson and the army. Yet, their contributions facilitated the Kentuckians' transition to assisting in the defense of the city. Soon, the additional troops would be desperately relied upon, and their mettle would soon be held to the fire.

As the British struggled to regroup, Jackson remained vigilant, sending troops to potential flanking sites and ensuring every position was defended. His relentless energy kept the American soldiers driven, and on their toes, even as they faced logistical challenges. Aware that his position could be flanked, Jackson and his aides crafted a layered defense. Once satisfied with the first line, the Americans constructed a second along the canal of the Dupree plantation, with a third beginning on the Montrevil plantation. The second line, potentially stronger than the first, was fortified by three batteries, ensuring overlapping fields of fire. The unarmed Kentucky militia held this second line, prepared to regroup should the British assault succeed.

Jackson, however, did not immediately recognize the danger to his right flank across the river, despite the preparations of the British in digging their canal and breaching the levee. He likely assumed that a British crossing of the river would require such a large fleet of boats, that their assembly would allow him plenty of time to act against it. Over the past week, he had already ordered Brigadier General David Morgan to abandon his post at the English Turn and set up a position on the west bank of the river. He had also sent Latour to help build a defensible line and an advanced position. These commands were carried out accordingly, but the location of Patterson's gun placement and furnaces required that Morgan advance further south, and that required the deployment of many more troops than Jackson felt he could afford.

The best Jackson felt he could do was to send Morgan 500 Kentuckians, only 250 of whom were armed. The rest of Morgan's troops

---

[602] Latour, pp. 100-101.

included 500 Louisiana militia men and a few hundred from the First, Second and Sixth regiments. This force, however, was not adequate to the task, as Patterson was so stridently pointing out; it was undermanned and under-armed. The exposed position of the west bank was approved by the commander, who refused to reinforce it adequately, even when made aware of the dilemma. Thus, the disaster that was soon to occur on the west bank of the river was largely the responsibility of General Andrew Jackson himself. [603]

When Patterson's subordinate officer, the sailing master Richard Shepherd arrived at Jackson's headquarters at 1 o'clock in the morning of January 8, he found the general lying on a sofa trying to catch a few hours' sleep. Shepherd repeated Patterson's instructions, ending with Morgan's information that the main attack would be made on the West Bank and his request for troops as quickly as possible.

Upon hearing Jackson's dismissals of Morgan's theory, a frustrated Shepherd recrossed the river with the General's answer, which could not have been very reassuring to Morgan and his inexperienced men, not a dozen of whom had ever been in action. [604] Morgan was beside himself, but Jackson was confident that the main thrust of the attack would be at the center of his line and not on the west bank. In that, he would be proven right, but by not reinforcing the far side of the river, Jackson left the city of New Orleans entirely vulnerable.

Seeing that it was 1 o'clock, the General went into action. One of Jackson's aides related the story in writing days later, "Jackson's order was obeyed very promptly. Sword belts were buckled; pistols resumed; and in a few minutes the party was ready to begin the duties of the day. There was little for the American troops to do but to repair to their posts."[605]

Repair to their posts they did, and each man found the situation all quiet, perhaps too quiet. "About three o'clock, or as soon as the modification of positions on the left of our line was completed," said General William O. Butler, in an 1874 reminiscence related to A. C. Buell, a newspaper reporter, "I went as fast as I could toward the Macarte house to report. I met the General, with a group of staff-officers, just

---

[603] Brown, *Amphibious Campaign*, p. 139; Latour, Historical Memoir, pp. 165-166.
[604] Arthur, Louisiana Anthology. 1915.
[605] Ibid.

descending from the porch. I reported simply — 'It is done, sir. General Adair is in the designated position."[606]

Jackson was right about the main attack coming on his side of the river, but he took the threat of the west bank too lightly, and it nearly cost him everything. Too many preparations bustled in front of him. Plus, he was not concerned, he had 4,000 men on the front line and another 1,000 men in reserve.[607] Besides the artillery set up in three groups: river, center, and swamp--the line consisted of the Seventh Regiment, commanded by Colonel George Ross, alongside the Mississippi; Plauché's battalion; Lacoste's and Daquin's battalion of black soldiers; the 44th regiment; the Tennesseeans under Carroll, supported by Adairs's Kentuckians; and General Coffee's cavalry on the left, with the Choctaws scouting in the swamp.

Against Jackson's impenetrable line Pakenham planned to send a column of 2,200 men (the Fourth, Twenty-First, and Fourty-fourth Regiments and three companies of the Ninety-fifth) under Major General Sir Samuel Gibbs to hit the American position, slightly left of center, accompanied by a second column of 1,200 men, the 93rd, two companies of the 95th, and two companies of the 43rd, under Major General Keane to strike Jackson's right along the river. Simultaneously, a West Indian regiment of 520 men would skirmish in the swamp to distract Coffee and slice through his line if possible, while Thornton, having crossed the river, would capture Morgan's batteries as Gibbs and Keane moved up. They were then to turn the batteries against Jackson. A third column of 1500 men, the Seventh Fusiliers, and the remainder of the 43rd under Major Lambert, was held in reserve near the center of the field.[608]

It was 3 o'clock in the morning when, after many cave-ins along the banks of the canal, Colonel Thornton and a third of his force started across the Mississippi. They were not long underway, however, when the river's current seized the flotilla and swept it a mile and a half further downstream. According to Pakenham's plan, Thornton and his men were expected to land three miles below the American line, move

---

[606] Ibid.
[607] Jackson to Monroe, Feb. 13, 1815, Remini, pp. 274-275.
[608] Lambert to Lord Bathurst, Jan. 10, 1815, in Latour, *Historical Memoir*, p. cl.; Horsman, *War of 1812*, pp. 245-246.

rapidly along the bank, and seize Morgan's and Patterson's position. But they landed further south than anticipated, which put them many hours behind schedule. It was nearly daylight when they finally got ashore on the west bank. The unfortunate Colonel Thornton knew he had no chance of capturing the American batteries before the general attack began. In dismay, he started across the river and saw the flashes of gunfire that told him the attack had already begun.

Around the same time his adversary was roused from his couch, General Sir Edward Pakenham, having slept an hour or two at the Villeré mansion, also rose, and rode immediately to the bank of the river, where Thornton had just embarked his diminished force. He was immediately informed about the delay and challenges faced by Colonel Thornton's flotilla and stayed at the spot, hoping to catch any sound that might reveal Thornton's location. However, no sounds reached him, as the swift Mississippi River had carried the boats far away. Surely, Packenham must have realized that a crucial part of his plan was thwarted that morning. He would likely hold back his troops from launching an attack until Thornton made his presence known. The unfortunate General, however, did not share that concern. It is said that he was provoked by a comment from Admiral Cochrane, who claimed that if the army couldn't take those mud banks defended by a ragtag militia, he could do it with just two thousand sailors armed with cutlasses and pistols. This had gotten up his gander, and he would not stand for such a scenario. Pakenham was confident that nothing could withstand the calm and determined advance of his troops. He had no intention of waiting for Thornton, unless it was perhaps until sunrise.

CHAPTER

43

ALL HAIL, THE SAVIOR

"We will expel the invader from every spot on our soil, and teach him, if he hopes for conquest, how vain it is to seek it in a land of freedom."

—Andrew Jackson

On the cold and foggy morning of January 8th, the American army awaited the British on the plains of Chalmette. The darkness of the early morning hours began to give way to an eerie orange fog that, once it lifted, revealed the entirety of the British army stretched out over two-thirds of the broad, open field. Then, a Congreve rocket rose with a shriek on the left, and another shot off from the right.[609] This signaled to all the battle was on.

The Americans had not had to wait long. Faced with limited alternatives and encouraged by the arrival of reinforcements, Major-General Sir Edward Michael Pakenham had resolved to initiate, at long last, a renewed assault on Jackson's lines. This time would be different, Pakenham believed. After careful study, the British commander felt strongly that he now held the formula that would push through Line Jackson. The climactic moment of the British army's mission to seize the American South had finally arrived.

General Gibbs's regiments would lead the main thrust of the attack, against the American left center. However, around 4 am, General Adair led a thousand Kentuckians to the back of General Carroll's position,

---

[609] Reid and Eaton, Jackson, p. 338.

directly in the area of Line Jackson for which Gibbs was headed. Adair stopped his men fifty yards away from the fortifications and moved ahead to join the line of soldiers peering over the embankment into the fog and darkness of the morning. The location of the reserve was very well chosen. It was almost directly behind the section of the line that a deserter from Jackson's army had informed General Pakenham was the weakest point. The deserter was partially correct; he had defected on Friday, before the reserve was even considered, and he neglected to mention that Coffee and Carroll's troops, numbering over two thousand, were some of the best marksmen and ablest sharpshooters in the army. His misleading information ended up setting Gibbs' column into a lethal trap.[610]

If Jackson was shaken as his untested men first glimpsed the organized ranks of the British army across the field in the pre-dawn hours of January 8th, he didn't let on. Before sunrise, the British launched their attack, but from start to finish, it was a debacle. At 4:00 in the morning, a column of Redcoats snuck forward to within half a mile of the mud rampart. This was the 44th Regiment, led by a particularly incompetent officer, Lieutenant Colonel, the Honorable Thomas Mullens, third son of Lord Ventry.[611] The men of the 44th were ordered out in advance of General Gibbs' column and instructed to carry fascines and ladders with them. The fascines were bundles of sugar cane to be thrown into the ditch in front of Jackson's line to fill it up. The sixteen ladders assigned for the operation were needed to scale the rampart.

The practice was known as escalading, and in the matter of Jackson's line, the British intended to use plank ladders "by raising them on end and letting them drop across the ditch for the assailants to run over them." The fascines and ladders had to be in place in order for the advance to move forward smoothly once the attack began. Yet, both the fascines and ladders had been forgotten and left behind. When the mistake was realized, three hundred men had to double-back to retrieve the equipment, a time-consuming operation at the critical moment the attack was supposed to begin. Furthermore, part of the troops got lost returning to the front, so that those farthest in advance had ladders instead of fascines, which were needed first. This produced hesitancy

---

[610] Lambert to Lord Bathurst, Jan. 10, 1815 in Latour, *Historical Memoir*, p. cl.
[611] Reilly, British at the Gates, p. 295.

and confusion, and the 44th did not make it back until the fighting had already commenced. If Pakenham believed in bad omens, he might well have been better served to quit right then and there. But quit they did not, for now there was no turning back.[612]

Daylight broke through the fog. Around six o'clock, both groups were moving forward at the steady, determined pace typical of British forces, with the 44th unit, crucial to the mission, lagging behind as they carried the fascines and ladders, cursing all the while. The advancing column soon encountered the American outposts, led by Hind's spirited Mississippi cavalry. Initially, the dragoons retreated slowly, but quickly picked up speed and charged back, spreading the important news and alerting every soldier in the fortifications. Each commander was eager to be the first to catch sight of the enemy and fire upon them.

Jackson gave the order to fire as soon as it was light enough for his gunners to see their targets. Lieutenant Spotts of Battery Number Six was the first person in the American lines to see, through the fog, the faint red line of General Gibbs' advancing column far down the plain, near the cypress forest. The thunder of his cannon shattered the eerie silence. Then, silence fell again as the fog shifted or the enemy's position changed, obscuring them once more. As the fog lifted, both divisions became visible, their detached companies covering two-thirds of the plain, presenting the Americans with a stunning military sight reminiscent of the spectacle they had witnessed on December 28th. Three cheers erupted from Carroll's men, followed by three cheers from the Kentuckians behind them. The cheers continued from the advancing column that had not yet reached the American lines. The band of the Orleans Battalion band began an energetic rendition of *Yankee Doodle*, and soon, three batteries were firing without pause, ignoring the return fire from the British guns, shaking the soft earth from the riverside plain and mixing plumes of powder smoke with the rising fog.[613]

If there was confusion in the advance column of General Gibbs, there was uncertainty in that of General Keane — at least, in that lost fraction of it where Captain Cooke was. "The mist," says Cooke, "was slowly clearing off, and objects could only be discerned at two or three hundred

---

[612] Ibid, p. 296.
[613] Reid and Eaton, p. 339.

yards distant, as the morning was rather hazy." Along the edges of the cypress swamp, just half a mile below the section where Carroll and his Tennesseeans stood at the ready, with Adair's Kentuckians prepared to assist, a strong force of nearly three thousand British soldiers arrived, led by General Gibbs. This group aimed to assault the lines where they seemed most vulnerable, staying close to the trees to avoid the crossfire from Commodore Patterson's artillery. This was the primary attack force. It consisted of three entire regiments, the 4th, the 21st, and the 44th, along with a brigade of sharp shooters, the 95th Rifles.

What was worse, in the dense darkness of the morning Mullens had gone by the redoubt where the fascines and ladders had been deposited and marched his men to the head of the column without any of them. It does not seem possible that Mullens could have forgotten what Pakenham had expressly ordered him to do. When the 44th returned to the forward position after picking up the ladders and fascines, Mullens was not with them. Mullens believed his regiment had been ordered to its execution and that the bodies of his men were intended to fill the ditch.[614] Whether this oversight was accidental or not, Mullens was blamed after the fact. For that and other military sins Mullens was afterward court-martialed for his negligence.

The column of General Gibbs continued to march steadily toward Batteries Six, Seven, and Eight, which fired upon it with occasional success—sometimes missing entirely or hitting the middle of the column, causing it to stagger and pause momentarily. As the enemy advanced, American batteries continued to fire away. Despite heavy losses, the British troops continued undeterred, pressing forward despite the lack of scaling ladders and fascines. The gaps in their ranks were quickly filled, and bravely, the column advanced. As they got closer, well-aimed shots caused more destruction, creating large gaps in their formation and sending men and parts of men flying. Eventually, still unbroken, they entered the range of small arms — the rifles of Carroll's Tennesseans and the muskets of Adair's Kentuckians, forming four lines of sharpshooters.

General Carroll, remaining calm, waited for the right moment to fire until the enemy was within two hundred yards, then commanded, "Fire!" Initially, the riflemen fired with deliberate precision, but as the

---

[614] DeGrummond, *Baratarians*, pg. 131.

battle intensified, their pace quickened, delivering deadly, if sometimes inaccurate shots. The top of the embankment erupted with fire, except where the large cannons belched flames. The sound was unique and indescribable—a rolling, bursting, echoing noise that would be unforgettable for anyone who experienced it. The whole line blazed with gunfire, while British batteries showered rockets onto the scene, and Patterson's batteries across the river joined in the chaos. It was a scene that defied description, one that words could hardly capture.[615]

"Fire! Fire!" ordered General Carroll to the Tennessee and Kentucky sharpshooters, responding to Jackson's command. The order was executed with calm precision. Hardly a shot was wasted as the skilled marksmen systematically shattered the British column. Major Harry Smith, an aide to Pakenham, commented that he had never witnessed such destructive fire directed at a single line of troops. It seemed every shot found its target; scores of British soldiers fell, many collapsing on top of each other. Seeing the British down, Captain Patterson, of the Kentucky troops, jumped onto the breastwork and shouted to his men, "Aim low, boys! Rake them! They're coming at us with everything they've got!"

Despite being mowed down by rifle fire, General Gibbs' column somehow continued to advance, with Gibbs at the forefront. As they neared the ditch, some officers shouted. After being reassured by General Gibbs, these courageous men pressed on despite the deadly fire. However, the situation could not continue. With half of their number fallen and all commanding officers except the general disabled, the ground littered with dead and wounded, the column began to falter, resembling a ship tossed on a troubled sea.

The confusion among the British forces spread as they neared 100 yards of the American line. Instead of rushing the rampart as planned, they instinctively paused at the first shots fired and returned fire. Before they could recover, the American cannons, particularly those in Batteries No. 6 through 8, poured forth its grape and canister into the uncertain ranks. Gibbs's column began lying down, then doubled back on itself as the shelling and musketry opened from Jackson's entrenchments. Rather than storm the works, the British obliqued left to avoid Battery No.8,

---

[615] Smith, Sir Harry, *The Autobiography of Lieutenant General Sir Harry Smith*, London, 1902, I, 236.

then halted, trying to fire at the line. Finally, within fifty yards from the works, the column wavered. The front ranks halted, throwing the column into disarray, while Gibbs shouted in frustration for them to regroup and advance. But under such fire, regrouping was impossible. Once halted, the column could only break and retreat in chaos.

With the mistake made by Mullens' 44th, the British advance had failed to approach the Americans closely enough before daylight revealed their presence. The soldiers also had to traverse the several water-filled drainage ditches, each four or five feet wide, although this was apparently accomplished with ease. But as the soldiers of the 4th and 21st moved forward in column, they became confused at seeing Mullens's disorderly men coming on their flanks from the rear bearing the implements that should have been well ahead.

In this area of the battle, Jackson's troops were nearly flawless. The destructive effect of the American fire on the British soldiers in the open field was appalling. The American gunners aimed low and each round cut a bloody, gaping hole in the British ranks. No army, it seemed, could endure such carnage. But somehow, the British did, continuing to move in disciplined ranks up the field, to the amazement of the Americans. "Every discharge opened the column and mowed down whole files." Latour recalled. "Which were almost instantly replaced by new troops coming up close after the first." [616]

"Stand firm!" Jackson shouted as he surveyed his troops. "Don't waste your ammo! Make every shot count!" The hesitation of the British 4th and 21st proved deadly. The 44th regiment mirrored this action, dropping their ladders and starting to shoot, leaving both groups vulnerable as volley after volley crashed into them from the rampart. With each volley, dozens of Redcoats fell to the ground. Within moments, the entire advance devolved into chaos, with troops reeling and losing their formation. "Give it to them, boys!" As the British troops began stumbling frantically toward the rear. To add to the confusion, an acoustical illusion took place when "the roar of musketry and cannon seemed to proceed from the thick cypress-wood . . ., whilst bright flashes of fire [on Jackson's line] . . . were not apparently accompanied by sound." [617]

---

[616] Latour, *Historical Memoir*, p. 130
[617] Cooke, *Narrative of Events*, Pg. 248; "Sir John Maxwell Tylden Journal," p. 59.

Captain lines: of the Twenty-first, later recollected the assault: "The Column advanced, composed, and perfectly steady, until we were within about 40 yards of the enemy's lines; during the time between our leaving the advanced Battery and getting to within 40 yards of the enemy's works, several individuals of the 44th Regiment passed to the front, on our Flank, in an hurried and irregular manner, bearing Fascines and Ladders, particularly our left flank, in groups of 3 or 4, and others individually. When we were within 40 yards of the enemy's lines, several straggling shots were fired on both Flanks, and I particularly saw one man of the 44th, throw away his Fascine, and take his firelock and fire. Cheering at this time had also commenced; I went to the rear of the 21st Regiment, in order to prevent men joining them, either in cheering or firing, several musket shots passed over while I was in the rear, and the men complained of being fired on very much by the rear; I returned in a few minutes to the head of the column and found it checked, and a great many men of the 4th and 44th intermixed with the head companies of our Regiment, which they said had fallen back on them; the head of the column was at this time in considerable confusion . . . ."[618]

Soon, British officers barked orders to advance, and the disciplined column began to move again. Some men scrambled into the ditch but found no way to scale the rampart. "Where are the 44th? If we reach the ditch, we have no way to cross and scale the lines!" General Gibbs recognized the disaster unfolding. He did what he could. "Here comes the 44th!" he shouted, cursing under his breath that if he survived, he would see Mullens hanged. "Here comes the 44th!"[619] Reassured, the column pressed on, but the 44th did not arrive in force, and there were not enough ladders or fascines. The columns halted again. Then it happened: the psychological collapse of the attack. The troops lost their nerve. "The horror before them was too great to endure," and they could no longer face the "flashing and roaring hell" ahead. They recoiled, and in that moment, the battle was lost.

Unable to move forward, the British ranks held for a few more minutes under the murderous fire of the Americans. But finally, they broke. Some of the men sought refuge in a ditch. Others simply ran for

---

[618] Benson Earle Hill, *Recollections of an Artillery Officer* (2 vols.; London: Richard Bentley, 1836), II, p. 11.

[619] Reilly, *British at the Gates*, p. 338.

their lives. British officers rode to the ditch and ordered the troops there to re-form. They did so reluctantly. "And now for the second time, the columns recruited with the troops that formed the rear, advanced." Latour wrote, "Again it was received with the same rolling fire of musketry and artillery, of having advanced without much order very near our line, it at last broke again and retired in the utmost confusion. In vain did the officers now endeavor as before, to revive the courage of their men. To no purpose, did they strike them with the flat of their swords to force them to advance. They were insensible to everything but danger and saw nothing but death which had struck so many of their comrades."

Captain Hill described this first retreat: "Rushing to the scene of confusion, we found many men falling back. We did everything possible to rally them; most of those retreating were wounded and all complained bitterly that not a single ladder or fascine had been brought up to help them cross the ditch. A strange illusion occurred as we got closer to the American lines: the roar of musketry and cannon seemed to come from the thick cypress woods on our right, while the bright flashes of fire in front of us were not accompanied by sound. This odd effect was likely due to the atmosphere and the terrain, but I'll leave the explanation of this mystery to time and the curious."[620]

While the situation on the Jackson's left and center was going encouragingly well, on the American right, closest to the river, the state of affairs started off quite the opposite. The British column facing Jackson's right was slightly ahead of the others in the advance. This was on the British left flank, part of Major General John Keane's infantry which had made the swiftest progress, and they soon managed to breach an unfinished American redoubt closest to the river. This advance column was made up of most of the 93rd, led by Colonel Robert Rennie. This especially fearless company pressed forward in close order along the left of the levee. They had launched their surprise attack immediately following the explosion of the first signal rocket and had snuck up on the American sentries at the outpost so suddenly that the pickets had to scramble for safety, with Rennie's men in close pursuit behind them. The chaos quickly brought the two forces into a melee of hand-to-hand

---

[620] Benson Earle Hill, *Recollections of an Artillery Officer* (2 vols.; London: Richard Bentley, 1836), II, p. 11-12.

combat, forcing American commander Captain Humphrey, of Battery One, to hold his fire to avoid hitting his own troops. After a few furious minutes the British force drove Jackson's men away. The Americans retreated from the hand-to-hand combat and managed to escape by running over a plank that spanned a ditch to the rampart. They were able to withdraw into the main line, having spiked the redoubt's two guns. Rennie's success encouraged his British comrades, who hoped it portended a larger break in the American line.[621]

Jackson feared what the British hoped, and he immediately determined that the redoubt must be retaken at all costs. Summoning fresh troops, both the New Orleans Rifles, and the 7th U.S. Infantry, he threw them against it. For a long moment, the whole battle centered on this little hillock of mud. Now the earlier roles were reversed. The British now defended and the Americans attacked. The numbers too were switched, the Americans outnumbered the British at this critical spot on the field. And it was the American numbers that finally made the difference. The British were forced to yield the position they had won so courageously. "Being opposed by overwhelming numbers," George Glieg wrote of his comrades, "they were repulsed. The Americans in turn, forcing their way into the battery, at length, succeeded in recapturing it, with immense slaughter."[622]

At that moment, Humphrey's artillery opened fire as Rennie, now slightly injured, led his men across the canal and up the parapet of the line, he and two of his men reached the rampart's top but were quickly shot down by one of Captain Thomas Beale's New Orleans sharpshooters, with Rennie suffering a musket ball to the eye, and falling, mortally wounded. More British soldiers tumbled into the ditch, either killed or wounded by Beale's riflemen or bayoneted by the marines. Others were captured. The militiamen and regulars of the 7th Infantry leveled volleys of musketry from the right and left until the British occupants of the redoubt were forced to secure themselves in the ditch awaiting relief by General Keane. Other members of the column retreated back down the levee road, many taking cover in the drainage ditches as Patterson's shore batteries and Humphrey's Battery No. 1 began a heavy fire directed at them. In the

---

[621] Brown, *Amphibious Campaign*, p. 148.
[622] Glieg, p. 114

meantime, Batteries No. 2, 3, 4, and 5 sent discharges at the British field guns, hoping to dismount them. Eventually, the American fire proved overwhelming, causing the remainder of the enemy to retreat.[623]

Patterson's artillery on the west bank likewise opened an enfilading fire of grape against the Redcoat columns moving in semi-darkness across the plain. Batteries No. 1, 2, and 3 directed their guns against Rennie's men. Only when the British came within a few hundred yards of the American position did gusting winds lift the fog and make them visible to Jackson's men. At one point, as they came closer, Jackson ordered his right batteries to cease firing so that the smoke could clear for his riflemen to take aim. At the outset of the action, amid the distant blare of British bugles could be heard in the distance, below the bellowing blasts from the guns.

Had the remainder of the British column followed Rennie's advance, Keane could have reached Jackson's line. The original plan had been that the troops on the British left were supposed to support Thornton's attack across the river. When that failed to occur on schedule, with Thornton's men landing in a far distant location, Pakenham directed Keane to lead his men in support of the column on the right under General Gibbs. The survivors of Rennie's assault force therefore had no further support but for the artillery. This decision proved to be a costly mistake as Keane led his men across the field, and directly into their demise. [624]

Colonel Dale, of the 93rd Highlanders, a highly respected veteran of many British engagements, was grave and depressed. "What do you think of it?" asked the physician of the regiment, when word was brought of Thornton's delay. Colonel Dale had no words in reply. Giving the doctor his watch and a letter, he simply said, "Give these to my wife; I shall die at the head of my regiment." [625]

"I will await my own plans no longer," General Pakenham informed one of his aides as he rode away from the bank. Instead, he rode to General Gibbs, who met him with another piece of ominous intelligence. "The 44th," Gibbs said, "had not taken the fascines and ladders to the head of the column; but I have sent an officer to cause the error to be

---

[623] Tatum, *Journal*, p. 126.
[624] Brown, *Amphibious Campaign*, pg. 148.
[625] Stanley Clisby Arthur, *The Story of the Battle of New Orleans*. Louisiana Historical Society. 1915. Ch. 21.

rectified, and I am then expecting every moment a report from that regiment." General Pakenham, without delay, sent Major Sir John Tylden to ascertain whether the regiment could still be positioned in time. Tylden found "the 44th just moving off from the redoubt, in a most irregular and unsoldierly-like manner, with the fascines and ladders. I then returned," adds Tylden, in his evidence, "after some time, to Sir Edward Pakenham, and reported the circumstance to him, stating that by the time which had elapsed since I left them they must have arrived at their situation in column." [626]

Without waiting to obtain absolute certainty upon a point so important as the condition of the head of his main column of attack, the impetuous Pakenham commanded, to use the language of one of his own officers, "that the fatal, ever-fatal rocket should be discharged as a signal to begin the assault on the left." A few minutes later a second rocket whizzed aloft — the signal of attack on the right.

As the attack began, General Jackson moved back and forth behind his line, particularly on the left side, to ensure all necessary precautions were taken. Rallying his men, as best he could, he was boisterous and encouraging. Jackson called, moving along the left side of his line to encourage his men. "Let's finish this today!"[627] The men cheered him as he passed, all the while loading and firing. Once the battle was in full swing, Jackson took a position on slightly elevated ground near the center of the line to have a clear view of the entire scene. He appeared calm and composed, exuding confidence, unrattled by the cacophony of blasts all around him, watching as if he had no doubt about the ultimate outcome of the battle. This was not half an hour since dawn.

Elsewhere on the field, the British's lack of ladders became a matter of life and death. General Gibbs screamed at the men to reform and advance, but his commands went unheeded. The troops began a general retreat. Pakenham rode forward from the rear. "For shame!" he cried. "Remember, you are British soldiers. This is the path you must take," pointing to the fiery chaos ahead. Gibbs rushed to him, his voice choked with emotion. "The troops won't obey me," he sobbed. "They won't follow me." Removing his hat and pack, he urged his horse to the front of the wavering column,

---

[626] Brooks, *Siege of New Orleans*, p. 239.
[627] *Niles Weekly Register*, Feb. 11, 1815,

shouting reassurances and pleading with them to follow. A hail of bullets from the rampart met his appearance. When his horse was shot out from under him, Gibbs mounted his aide's black Creole pony, and pursued the retreating column, calling for them to halt and reform.[628]

They heard him. Once out of range of the fierce Tennessee and Kentucky rifles, the column stopped and turned, spirits lifted as they saw the Highlanders, commanded by General Keane, marching rapidly to reinforce them. The Highlanders, 900 strong, had successfully feigned an attack on Jackson's right side and were ordered to cross the field to assist their comrades on the left. As the Highlanders advanced, the bagpipers began playing "Scotland the Brave," the regimental charge. The soldiers broke into a run at the sound. But the rampart also responded. Round shot, grape, musket fire, and buckshot rained down on the Highlanders, targeting both the front and left flank. The carnage was horrific.

"Order up the reserve," Pakenham called to his aide. Seeing the Highlanders still advancing toward the ditch despite the murderous fire, he saluted them with a wave of his hat and a shout of "Hurrah! Brave Highlanders!" In that instant, the American big guns returned his salute with a devastating blast of grapeshot that struck down everyone near the commanding general.

Seeing the charge, Gibbs' men dropped their knapsacks, reformed, and moved back toward the rampart. When they came within rifle range again, the mud ditch barked its command to halt. Round after round slammed into the British ranks. A 32-pounder, loaded to the brim with musket balls, struck the head of the column at point-blank range, leveling it. About 200 men were killed or wounded in that single barrage. General Gibbs himself was struck down in the devastating fire. He was carried from the field in agony and lingered for another day before death finally released him. General Keane was painfully wounded in the groin and was borne to the rear.[629]

As if the loss of Generals Gibbs and Keane wasn't disheartening enough for his majesty's troops, the death of their commander-in-chief was soon to follow. Not even Pakenham, audacious as ever, could stem the retreat. "Sir Edward saw how things were going" George Glieg

---

[628] Cooke, John Henry, *A Narrative of the Attack on New Orleans in 1814 and 1815*, London, 1835, pp. 234-235.

[629] Lambert to Lord Bathurst, Jan. 10, 1815, in Latour, *Historical Memoir*, p. cli.

wrote, "and did all that a general could due to rally his troops." Riding toward the 44th, which had returned to the ground, but in great disorder, he called out for Colonel Mullens to advance. But that officer had disappeared and was not to be found. "He therefore prepared to lead them on himself, in a desperate attempt to turn the tide of the battle, having put himself at their head for that purpose. Pakenham advanced with his staff but was struck by a volley from American forces. "One shot tore open Pakenham's thigh, killing his horse and throwing both to the ground. As his aides began to lift him, a second shot hit him in the groin. As he rose from the battlefield to mount another horse and continue riding forward he was hit again, this time in the arm and he instantly lost consciousness." Hit by a barrage of grapeshot for a second time, more fatally, he dropped into the arms of his aide-de-camp. He was carried to the rear, out of gun range, and propped up under an oak tree in the center of the field. Within minutes, Lieutenant General Sir Edward Michael Pakenham died.[630]

Jackson would later write a personal letter to President Madison regarding the death of his adversary at New Orleans. "Then, seeing the Highlanders advancing to the support of General Gibbs, he, still waving his hat, but waving it now with his left hand, cried out, amidst the deafening din of musketry: "Come on the tartan! Hurrah, brave Highlanders!"

"At that moment I heard a single rifle shot from a group of country carts we had been using, and a moment thereafter I saw Pakenham reel and pitch out of his saddle. I have always believed he fell from the bullet of a free man of color, who was a famous rifle shot and came from the Attakapas region of Louisiana." Jackson went on, "I did not know where General Pakenham was lying or I should have sent to him, or gone in person, to offer any service in my power to render. I was told he lived two hours after he was hit. His wound was directly through the liver and bowels."[631]

Pakenham's charge to the front had inspired his men, and now his death disheartened them, and rallied the Americans who could see him fall. "A great number of officers of rank had fallen," Arsend Latour remembered, "The ground over which the column had marched

---

[630] Lambert to Lord Bathurst, Jan. 10, 1815, in Latour, *Historical Memoir*, p. cli.
[631] AJ to Madison, Jan. 9, 1815, Jackson Papers, LC.

was strewn with the dead and the wounded. Such slaughter on their side, with no loss on ours, spread consternation through their ranks as they were now convinced of the impossibility of carrying our lines and saw that even to advance was certain death." Pakenham's death led to further disarray among his forces. For the British assault, after months of buildup, and even before they had fully begun this final push, the army's head had now been severed from its body. [632]

Out of the 3,000 soldiers commanded by Gibbs and Keane, 2,000 became casualties in under thirty minutes. A soldier from Kentucky later recalled, "When the smoke had cleared and we could obtain a fair view of the field, it looked at first glance like a sea of blood. It was not blood itself, but the redcoats in which the British soldiers were dressed. The field was entirely covered in prostrate bodies. Now, no senior officer remained in the forward position to take command and rally the demoralized troops."[633]

The destruction of the high command in one blow caused a wavering in the column that became irreparable, General Lambert reported later. The brave Highlanders, under Major Creagh, did not waver, but advanced steadily, though too slowly, directly into the heart of General Carroll's deluge of fire, until they were within one hundred yards of the rampart, absorbing round after round from the Americans. There, for unknown reasons, they halted and stood, a huge and glittering target, until five hundred and forty-four of their number had fallen. The remainder of the Scots then broke and fled in horror to the rear. Colonel Dale, of the Highlanders, fulfilled his prophecy, and fell at the head of his regiment. The column of General Gibbs did not advance after the fall of their leader.

On the extreme left of Jackson's line, Coffee and his men defended the cypress swamps while a group of British West Indian troops faced off with them in a series of skirmishes in the woods. Some of these troops managed to reach close to Coffee's position but ended up trapped in the muck of the swamp, either drowning or being captured. They were astonished by the Tennesseans' squirrel-like agility as they moved

---

[632] Latour, *Historical Memoir*, p. 131.
[633] Anderson, Sonja, "An Unlikely Army of Militia and Pirates Shocked the World by Defeating the British Army at the Battle of New Orleans," *Smithsonian Magazine*, Jan. 7, 2025; Latour, *Historical Memoir*, p. 132.

effortlessly from log to log and navigated through the water and mud. Once again, Coffee and his men displayed remarkable courage and skill.[634]

"Before they reached our small arms, our grape and canister mowed down whole columns," said General Coffee, "but that was nothing compared to the carnage from our rifles and muskets." Indeed, there was one moment, when that thirty-two pounder, loaded to the muzzle with musket balls, poured its charge directly, at point-blank range, right into the head of the column, literally levelling it with the plain; laying low, as was afterwards computed, two hundred men. The American line, as one of the British officers remarked, looked like a row of fiery furnaces. The Americans, on the other hand, faced very few casualties in comparison.

Still, the British refused to quit. Members of two British regiments braved the American fire and reached the base of the American wall. Some did manage to scale the parapet. To do so "without ladders was a work of no slight difficulty," Glieg observed. "Some few, indeed, by mounting one upon another's shoulders, succeeded in entering the works, but these were speedily overpowered, most of them killed, the rest taken. Whilst as many stood without, exposed to a sweeping fire, which cut them out by whole companies. It was in vain that the most obstinate courage was displayed. They fell by the hands of men whom they absolutely did not see. For the Americans without so much as lifting their faces above the rampart swung their fire locks by one arm over the wall and discharged them directly upon their heads."[635]

The British soldiers that remained out in the open were shot apart with grapeshot from Line Jackson, including the 93rd Highlanders, having no orders to advance further or retreat. Major Wilkinson, known as Wilky, was at the head of the 21st Regiment, one of the two regiments that reformed their lines and made a third assault. These were the regiments that Glieg described having reached the entrenchments, only to fall attempting to scale them. Wilkinson managed to make it to the top, but just as he raised his head and shoulders above the parapet, he was hit by a hail of bullets and fell. The Tennesseans and Kentuckians defending that section of the line, struck by his bravery, lifted his still-breathing body

---

[634] Walker, *Jackson and New Orleans*, pg. 337.
[635] Glieg, p. 115.

and carefully carried it behind the barricade. "Stay strong, my friend," said Major Smiley from the Kentucky reserve. "You're too brave to die." "Thank you from the bottom of my heart," the dying man reportedly whispered. "It's over for me. Please do me a favor: tell my commander that I fell on your parapet and died like a soldier and a true Englishman."[636]

Wilkinson was followed by Lieutenant Lavack and twenty other men as they raced toward the ditch. They struggled across it and climbed the breastwork. Lieutenant Lavack made it to the top of the parapet unscathed, despite having two bullet holes in his cap. He had heard Wilkinson shout as they crossed the ditch, "Why aren't the troops coming? The day is ours!" With those words echoing in his mind, and without looking back, he reached the breastwork and immediately demanded the swords of the first two American officers he saw. "Oh, no," one of them replied. "You're alone, so you should consider yourself our prisoner." It was then that Lavack looked around and recounted to his comrades later, "Imagine my outrage when I turned to see that the two leading regiments had disappeared as if the earth had opened up and swallowed them whole." [637]

"In a word, notwithstanding the repeated efforts of some officers to make their troops form a third time, they would not advance and all that could be obtained from them was to draw them up in a ditch where they passed the rest of the day." George Glieg observed.[638]

Facing devastating losses near Line Jackson, the remnants of the British forces retreated beyond the range of American artillery. Although Colonel William Thornton's attack on the marine battery along the right bank showed far better success, Pakenham's successor, Major General John Lambert, was unable to salvage the British campaign and initially ordered Thornton's forces to withdraw, although Colonel Dickson would convince Lambert to delay the withdrawal for the time being. At any rate, the main thrust of the battle was, for the most part, over. All told, it had lasted just thirty-seven minutes.

Many of Jackson's men went over the parapet after the retreat to assist the wounded British into their lines, often using planks and discarded ladders to transport the injured soldiers. Doing so was risky, for British

---

[636] Parton, *Jackson*, II, p. 199.
[637] Ibid, 199.
[638] Glieg, p. 115.

marksmen in the first ditch tried to dissuade the Americans from removing the wounded. During the afternoon, a company of Daquin's Free Men of Color advanced to rid the ditch of these British, a mission that succeeded despite several casualties.[639]

Some Americans now ventured over the plain, picking up muskets and other articles scattered over the ground. One observer commented, "When we first got a fair view of the field in our front, individuals could be seen in every possible attitude. Some lying quite dead, others mortally wounded, pitching and tumbling about in the agonies of death. Some had their heads shot off, some their legs, some their arms. Some were laughing, some crying, some groaning, and some screaming. There was every variety of sight and sound. Among those that were on the ground, however, there were some that were neither dead nor wounded. A great many had thrown themselves down behind piles of slain, for protection." [640]

It was all over but the crying.

Andrew Jackson as portrayed in 1815 by John Wesley Jarvis, present at the time of the battle. From the collection of Stanley Clisby Arthur.

Portrait of Sir Edward Michael Pakenham, after a lithograph of an original painting in England. Pakenham, a veteran of many wars, was only 36 years old when he met his death at Chalmette

---

[639] Dickson, "Journal of Operations in Louisiana," pp. 69-70, 71.
[640] "Sir John Maxwell Tylden Journal, 1814-1815," pp. 62, 64.

CHAPTER

44

THE AFTERMATH

"The ground was covered with dead and wounded lying in heaps, the field was completely red."
—*Unknown*

The January sun had erased any last remnants of fog from the field, as the British retreated, and General Andrew Jackson's officers congratulated him on an impressive victory. At 8:30 am, with no signs of a renewed attack and no enemies visible, orders were sent along the lines to stop firing with small arms. The General, along with his staff, walked from one end of the fortifications to the other, stopping at each battery and post to offer a few words of congratulations and praise to the defenders. It was a proud moment for these men, who, after two hours of hard work and covered in smoke and sweat, rejoiced in the General's praise, and saw the victory reflected in his expression. Jackson especially thanked and praised Beale's small group of riflemen, the companies of the 7th, and Humphrey's artillerymen for their bravery in repelling Colonel Rennie's forces. He also commended the prowess of General Carroll's and General Adair's divisions, while not forgetting General Coffee, who had courageously charged the skirmishers in the swamp.

Old Hickory was still anxious, however, glancing across the river. Expecting the roar of Morgan's guns, he was troubled by the eerie silence. Jackson had reason to be troubled. And it was fortunate that Lambert decided to call Colonel Thornton off, for, on the right bank, Morgan's line, in contrast to Jackson's, had fared poorly. In truth, Morgan was poorly positioned. This was largely due to the need to protect Commodore Patterson's batteries, which had been set based on the American and British locations on the opposite bank. Morgan was sheltered behind a sawmill race, but it was too long for the number of men available to defend it. Many of his men were poorly armed or not armed at all. The right side of Morgan's line was especially vulnerable, so another brigade of Kentuckians were assigned there. However, even with their presence, a section of the line extending to the swamp remained unprotected, except for a small picket guard of 18 men. Thornton quickly identified this soft spot, particularly the vulnerability of their right flank.[641]

Suddenly, General Morgan's artillery opened fire, providing Jackson with a sense of relief. He commanded his men, "Take off your hats and give them three cheers!" The order was obeyed and many of the main army watched the action with intense interest, not doubting that the gallant Kentuckians and Louisianians on the other side of the river would soon drive back the British column, as they themselves had just driven back those of Gibbs and Keane. Jackson with his staff and generals, hurried to the river side and across the muddy Mississippi, saw Thornton's column advancing to the attack and saw Morgan's men open fire upon them vigorously. Having become used to seeing British columns recoil and vanish before their fire, not a thought of disaster on the western bank crossed the elated minds of those who fought immediately under Jackson.[642]

As the harried soldiers tried to understand what was happening nearly a mile and a half away, the American command began to see a disaster unfolding. What was happening on that far right bank of the river was that the British were beating back the Americans. In fact, the defeat on the west side of the Mississippi would be as complete as the American victory on the east side. In this area, Jackson had not done his due diligence; in fact, Jackson seemed unaware of the vulnerabilities across the river, having failed to reinforce that position or even visit it during the more than two weeks the British were advancing toward the city, despite warnings from his subordinates. Convinced that the west bank of the river would not be a concern, he had not arranged for boats

---

[641] Latour, *Historical Memoir*, p. 167-168.
[642] Ibid, p. 167.

to facilitate crossing the three-quarter-mile wide river if reinforcements were needed. The defense on the west bank was easily overwhelmed by the British once their offensive began. It was an oversight of costly proportions, and, as noted, had the British recognized this opportunity, New Orleans may well have been theirs.

To prevent a landing on the west bank, 120 Louisiana militia men, led by Major Jean Arnaud, were sent three miles below Morgan's main position. They camped along the river road, and fell asleep, leaving only one sentry on guard. At dawn, Colonel Thornton, with 600 men and three-gun barges manned by 100 sailors, landed about one mile downstream from Arnaud's men. Despite planning for a larger force, only a third of the necessary boats were moved into position the night before, allowing Thornton to proceed with a smaller contingent. Upon reaching the opposite side, Thornton organized his men into columns, using the gun barges for cover, and advanced rapidly. When a bugler sounded the charge, British sailors and soldiers advanced in two columns, attacking both the center and the extreme right of the American line.

Thornton narrowly missed capturing the sleeping Louisianians, who quickly fled after the alarm was sounded.[643] About a mile from Morgan's line, they encountered a group of Kentuckians under Colonel John Davis, who had been sent to assist them. They combined forces to try and halt Thornton's advance, but the British officer easily outmaneuvered them, forcing the Louisianians into the swamp and routing the Kentuckians, who retreated in mass confusion toward Morgan's line. The Kentuckians had found themselves trapped between the two divisions, fired a few shots, and then fled their position. Morgan rode to the right and called out to Colonel Davis to stop his men. Davis claimed it was impossible. "Sir," replied Morgan, "I have not seen you try."

Turning to the fleeing Kentuckians, Morgan shouted, "Halt! Men, and resume your position!" An adjutant ran after them, urging, "Shame! Boys, stand by your general!"[644] But they did not listen. They ran in panic and confusion. Morgan followed on horseback, managing to bring a few back, but another barrage of rockets renewed their fears, sending them scattering in all directions. Meanwhile, the British stormed over

---

[643] Reid and Eaton, p. 345.
[644] Walker, *Jackson and New Orleans*, pg. 353.

the millrace, scaled the parapet, and attacked the left side of the line, forcing it to retreat. [645]

Commodore Patterson, stationed with his battery on the levee 300 yards behind Morgan, witnessed the retreat. In a fit of rage, he turned to a midshipman near a 12-pounder aimed at the road, shouting, "Fire your piece into the damned cowards!"[646] However, he quickly regained his composure and countermanded the order. Instead, he directed his guns to be spiked and the ammunition thrown into the river. Unfortunately, his orders were not properly executed, allowing the British to restore half of his guns to action. The American naval gunners abandoned the *Louisiana* and retreated into the river. Patterson fell back with an aide, alternating between cursing the Kentuckians and the British. Thornton paused his advance within 700 yards of the Americans, preparing for a general assault. [647]

The heartfelt American joy at the overwhelming victory achieved on one side of the river, was clouded by the disaster witnessed on the other. Following the mishaps on the west bank of the American lines, a debate ensued regarding the behavior of the Kentucky forces. The weakest part of the line, which was protected only by a slight ditch, was attacked by the greatest strength of the British forces: this was defended by 180 Kentuckians, who were stretched out to an extent of 300 yards, and unsupported by any artillery. Thus, openly exposed to the attack of a greatly superior force, and weakened by the extent of ground they covered, their much-maligned retreat can be seen in a more understandable light, in that they considered resistance ineffective, and abandoned their post, which they had strong reasons to believe they could not maintain.

General Morgan reported the circumstances of the Kentuckians' flight to General Jackson, attributing his defeat to the actions of those troops, who had also drawn along with them the rest of his forces. It is true, they were the first to flee; and equally true, that their example may have had the effect of producing general alarm among the ranks;

---

[645] Genl. David B. Morgan's Defense of the Conduct of the Louisiana Militia in the Battle of the Left side of the River, The *Louisiana Historical Quarterly*, January, 1926, IX, 16-29.

[646] Walker, *Jackson and New Orleans*, p. 354.

[647] Patterson, Daniel T. to the Sec. of the Navy, Jan. 13, 1815.

but in their defense they were exposed, some unarmed, unsupported and vulnerable in their situation. The British forces under Thornton, considerably superior in numbers, covered no greater extent of ground, were defended by an excellent breastwork, and several cannons; with this difference, the Kentuckians loss of confidence was not unreasonable.

Unaware of these facts, Commodore Patterson agreed with General Morgan. Both attributed the disaster to the flight of the Kentucky militia. Upon their information, General Jackson founded his report to the Secretary of War, by which those troops were exposed to censures that many believe they did not deserve under the circumstances. Had all the facts been disclosed, reproach would have been prevented. Many defenders of the Kentuckians argued that, at the millrace, no troops could have behaved better: they were well posted and bravely resisted the advance of the enemy. Nor had they considered retreating until an order to that effect was given.

The British, under Colonel Thornton, had gained an advantageous position on the far side of the American line, which they could well have taken advantage of and possibly destroyed the entirety of Jackson's army had things worked out differently. In short, the Americans dodged a bullet. Were it not for the quick thinking of Commodore Patterson, in spiking his guns, and destroying the ammunition, it would have been in the power of Colonel Thornton to have commandeered the *Louisiana* and turned it on Jackson's line. The guns might well have been unspiked and brought to operate against him. In fact, the men under Thornton's command were ordered to recross the river, just as they were about to unspike the guns, and release a cannonade on Jackson's men.

Unfortunately for the British, it all happened too late. The failure of the British force across the river to capture the guns of the *Louisiana* in time had already done its damage. "The whole of the guns likewise from the opposite bank kept up a well directed and deadly cannonade upon their flank. And thus, were they destroyed, without an opportunity being given of displaying their valor or obtaining so much as revenge." George Glieg pointed out. For all Thornton's valor, and that of his men, the point was moot. The mistake made by landing so far from the point of contact cost the British the battle.

Upon being made aware of the fiasco on the west bank, Jackson, to his credit, hastened to throw detachments across to the left side, with orders to regain it, at every hazard. But there was no need. The British had already called off the dogs. In regard to the crisis at the redoubt, facing Rennie and the 93rd's brutal assault, Jackson had made the right moves, at the right time, with the exact tone needed in those harrowing moments. If ever there was a question about Jackson's ability to coordinate movements in the heat of battle, it was answered on the Chalmette Plantation in the early hours of the morning. Exciting his troops to deeds of valor, with spirited words that lifted men to action, invigorating their courage, obtaining it, sparing the effusion of blood, Jackson, despite his mistakes pulled victory out of the jaws of defeat.

The overwhelming loss of British life, in the main attack, has been, at different times, variously stated, though all figures point to a disturbingly high death toll. The killed, wounded, and imprisoned, on the day after the battle, by Colonel Hayne, the inspector general, placed it at higher counts than any of the British high command could have imagined. The count was so high that the British were still counting the bodies, but there was no denying that among them were their commander-in-chief, and many of their most valuable and distinguished officers. On the other side of the coin, it was painfully clear that the Americans had lost but a fraction of their total.

In George Glieg's view, the critical event was the fall of Gibbs and Keane. "Riding through the ranks," Glieg said of the two generals' final effort to re-gather the troops, "They strove by all means to encourage the assailants and recall the fugitives until, at length, both were wounded and borne off the field. All was now confusion and disarray. Without leaders, ignorant of what was to be done, the troops first halted and then began to retire, till finally, the retreat was changed into a flight and they quitted the ground in utmost disorder."[648]

Yet the British spirit wasn't entirely broken. The retreat was covered in gallant style by the reserve, under General Lambert. "Making a forward motion, the 7th and 43rd presented the appearance of a renewed attack, by which the enemy were so much awed that they did not venture beyond their lines in pursuit of the fugitives."[649]

---

[648] Glieg, p. 116.
[649] Reid Papers, March 1814.

ANDREW JACKSON: THE POLITICS OF RESENTMENT

Jackson felt no intimidation or awe for the British, especially at this moment in the battle, which had exceeded his expectations. His inexperienced troops had withstood the force of the renowned British charge and had successfully pushed it back with great honor. In the moment of victory, although Jackson later attested that he felt the urge to chase after the retreating British and try to wipe out their entire army, he quickly regained himself, and reconsidered. It would have been a reckless move to pursue the Redcoats on open ground with inexperienced troops who had no knowledge of maneuvering. It was wiser to stay behind the defenses that had proven so effective for the Americans. Wisely then, Jackson and his counselors decided to sit behind their ditch and wait for the enemy's next move.[650] Just how effective those defenses were, and how harshly the British had suffered, became clear in the aftermath. The intense fighting wrapped up by 8:00 in the morning.

Soon after midday, some American troops who were walking about the blood-stained field in front of Jackson's position, perceived a British party approaching. It consisted of an officer in full uniform, Major Sir Harry Smith, aide-de-camp to General Lambert, a trumpeter and a soldier bearing a white flag. Halting at a distance of three hundred yards from the breastwork, the trumpeter blew a blast upon his bugle, which brought the whole army to the edge of the parapet, gazing with curiosity upon this unexpected approach. Col. Robert Butler was immediately dispatched by General Jackson to receive the message. After an exchange of courtesies, the British officer handed Col. Butler a letter directed to the American Commander-in-Chief, which proved to be a proposal for an armistice of twenty-four hours, that the dead might be buried and the wounded removed from the field. The letter was signed "Lambert," in an effort to conceal from Jackson the death of Pakenham.[651]

Concerned about the dire situation on the west bank, Jackson refused to accept this request as long as the British operation proceeded across the river. At the moment, Jackson and his staff were consumed with addressing a reinforcement of Morgan's troops on the far side of the river, while also ensuring that the British did not attempt to do the same. Jackson ordered 400 troops under General Jean Humbert to reclaim

---

[650] Brown, *Amphibious Campaign*, p. 159.
[651] Smith, Sir Harry, *The Autobiography of Lieutenant General Sir Harry Smith*, London, 1902, I, 237.

the Americans' lost ground there. Jackson, unaware that Pakenham was indeed mortally wounded, questioned whether Lambert had the authority to communicate directly with him, without going through the commander-in-chief. Flags passed between the commands through the afternoon until 4 p.m., after which Jackson renewed his cannonade, shortly to include mortar fire from the weapon on his right, besides that of five new gunboats placed under cover of the riverbank.

Jackson wrote again to General Lambert, who had not officially identified himself as the highest-ranking officer remaining. He agreed to Lambert's truce request, but only if both sides committed not to increase their forces on the west bank. Reluctantly, Lambert acknowledged Pakenham's death and requested time to assess Jackson's terms, having already approved Colonel Alexander Dickson's request to delay the withdrawal of Thornton's troops. After Dickson indicated the need for several thousand troops, Lambert ordered the withdrawal and accepted Jackson's truce terms. The British quickly vacated the west bank, which the Americans reoccupied, having dodged a very serious bullet. Lambert buried the dead in mass graves and prepared for the difficult withdrawal through the swamps.

Although George Glieg wasn't part of the British hospital crew, he wanted to see the extent of the damage his fellow soldiers had endured. "Prompted by curiosity, I mounted my horse and rode to the front," he explained. What he observed burned an image in his brain. "Of all the sights I ever witnessed, that which met me there was beyond comparison the most shocking and the most humiliating. Within the narrow compass of a few hundred yards were gathered together nearly 1,000 bodies, all of them arrayed in British uniforms. Not a single American was among them, all were English, and all were thrown by the dozens into shallow holes, scarcely deep enough to furnish them with a slight covering of earth." Despite the grief, some American troops displayed a troubling sense of exultation. An American officer, seemingly indifferent to the tragedy, counted the enemy's casualties while smoking a cigar, provoking anger among his peers. "An American officer stood by smoking a cigar. And apparently counting the slain. With a look of savage exultation, and repeating over and over to each individual that approached him that their loss amounted to only to eight men killed, and 14 men wounded. One soldier, feeling a mix of sorrow and indignation, chose to leave rather than confront the officer."[652]

Arsend Latour also visited the battlefield on that day, possibly passing by Glieg, though neither had any particular reason to acknowledge each other. "The whole plain on the left, as also the side of the river from the road to the edge of the water was covered with the British soldiers who had fallen." Latour wrote. "What might perhaps appear incredible were there not many thousands ready to attest the fact, were that a space of ground attending from the ditch to our lines, that on which the enemy drew up its troops to 150 yards in length by about 200 in breadth, was literally covered with men either dead or severely wounded." While Latour couldn't count the bodies, it was evident that the British losses were significant. "It cannot have amounted to less than 3000 men killed, wounded, and prisoners. Our loss was comparatively inconsiderable, amounting to no more than 13 in killed and wounded."[653]

Later a Frenchman tried to account for the staggering British losses. "Ah!" he exclaimed, after some moments of reflection, "I see how it all happened. When these Americans go into battle, they forget that they are not hunting deer or shooting turkeys and try never to throw away a shot."[654] Indeed it was massive fire power—a "most destructive fire, of ball, grape and musketry." — heavily concentrated at the precise point of the main enemy attack that accounted for the heavy toll among the British. British losses had, indeed, been exceedingly high. Jackson's inspector general, Colonel Arthur P. Hayne, accounted for 700 killed, 1,400 wounded, and 500 captured. The Medical Director of the British Army later reported that 381 British soldiers had been killed on the field and that 477 others died of wounds received, making a total of 858 killed. All told, total wounded numbered 2,468, bringing the grand total of British casualties to 3,326.[655] Yet another estimate placed British losses at 1,971 killed and wounded. These casualties, moreover, included "one lieutenant general, two major generals, eight colonels and lieutenant colonels, six

---

[652] Brands, 2005, Ch. 21.
[653] Latour, *Historical Memoir*, p. 169.
[654] Tatum, *Journal*, p. 125.
[655] Walker, *Jackson and New Orleans*, p. 341

majors, eighteen captains, and fifty-four subalterns." On the right bank of the Mississippi, British losses stood at 120 killed and wounded.[656]

When news of Jackson's stunning victory reached New Orleans, just hours after the battle on Chalmette Plantation, the streets rang with delirious joy. Through Rue Royale and Rue Chartres and Rue Burgundy and all the other narrow streets of New Orleans, horsemen, dashing from the field on exhausted horses, sent the cry of "VICTOIRE" echoing and re-echoing throughout the city. These were the moments in which the legend of General Andrew Jackson began, and his fame that the victory brought would grow from this moment on and remain throughout his life.

Jackson›s victory on the plains of Chalmette, like previous battles his army endured, could partially be chalked up to luck, and it could well have gone the other way. Even Jackson himself had to admit it. But, instead of using the word luck in his correspondence following the battle, he referred to his army's fortunes as "providence." In letters, Jackson expressed his belief that divine intervention seemed to protect his men during the battle. "It appears," he wrote Colonel Robert Hays, "that the unerring hand of providence shielded my men from the shower of Balls, bombs and Rocketts, when every Ball and Bomb from our guns carried with them the mission of death." [657]

However, Jackson also recognized that he narrowly escaped consequences for his mistakes in managing the west bank defenses, struggling with his pride to accept any responsibility for the near calamity. After hearing of the disaster across the river, he quickly blamed external factors, unfairly comparing his command to that of Morgan's. What Jackson escaped, with a little bit of luck, was the consequence of his own mistakes and oversight—blunders that nearly cost him the battle. His immense ego and pride prevented him from accepting responsibility for his failures.

Upon learning of the disaster on the opposite side, Jackson became irate, seemingly concerned above all else with tarnishing his victory and reputation. In his address to his troops on January 8, 1815, he made an unfair comparison between his command and Morgan's troops on the

---

[656] Contemporary Account of the Battle of New Orleans," pp. 14-15. See also Parton, *Life of Andrew Jackson*, II, pp. 208-09.
[657] AJ to Hays, Jan. 26, 1815, Jackson Papers, LC.

west bank. Blaming Morgan's men for issues largely stemming from his own shortcomings, lacking the grace to accept any blame, Jackson heaped the criticism on Colonel Davis and his Kentucky troops. This was similarly unwarranted, while he defended Morgan and Patterson for their bravery which had impressed him immensely during the battle. In his view, neither of the two commanders bore any responsibility for the defeat at the west bank.

In a letter of Jan. 9th to James Monroe, Jackson described the battle in florid detail, "Of mine, how many had been lost in the several engagements, from the 23d December to the 8th January, or how many, upon that day were upon the sick list. It would not however be deemed improbable that from ten to twelve thousand, were engaged, about double the effective force of Gen. Jackson. Early upon the morning of the 8th January,1815, a day which will forever be memorable in American and British annals, a tremendous "shower of bombs and Congreve rockets," from the British army, announced the battle begun. The result will be found in the following reports, of the American Conqueror, GEN. JACKSON TO HON. JAMES MONROE - Camp 4 miles below New Orleans, 9th January, 1815.

"Sir, During the days of the 6th and 7th, the enemy had been actively employed in making preparations for an attack on my lines. With infinite labour, they had succeeded on the night of the 7th, in getting their boats across from the lake to the river, by widening and deepening the canal on which they had effected their disembarkation. It had not been in my power to impede these operations by a general attack: added to other reasons, the nature of the troops under my command, mostly militia, rendered it too hazardous to attempt extensive movements in an open country, against a numerous and well-disciplined army. Although my forces as to number had been increased by the arrival of the Kentucky division, my strength had received very little addition; a small portion only of that detachment being provided with arms. Compelled thus to wait the attack of the enemy, I took every measure to repel it, when it should be made, and to defeat the object he had in view. Gen. Morgan, with the New Orleans contingent, the Louisiana militia, and a strong detachment of the Kentucky troops, occupied an intrenched camp on the opposite side of the river, protected by strong batteries on the bank, erected and superintended by Com. Patterson. In my encampment, everything was ready for action, when, early on the morning of the 8th, the enemy, after throwing a heavy shower of bombs and Congreve rockets, advanced their columns on my right and left, to storm my intrenchments. I cannot speak sufficiently in praise of the firmness and deliberation, with which my whole line received their approach—more could not have been expected from veterans inured to war. For an hour, the fire of the small arms was as incessant and severe as can be imagined. The artillery too, directed by officers who displayed equal skill and courage, did great execution. Yet the columns of the enemy continued to advance, with a firmness which reflects upon them the greatest credit. Twice, the column which approached me on my left was repulsed by the troops of Gen. Carroll, those of Gen. Codee. and a division of the Kentucky militia, and twice they formed again and renewed the assault. At length however, cut to pieces, they fled in confusion from the field, leaving it covered with their dead and wounded.

The loss which the enemy sustained on this occasion, cannot be estimated at less than 1,500 in killed, and wounded, and prisoners. Upwards of three thousand have already been delivered over for burial; and my men are still engaged in picking them up within my lines, and carrying them to the point where the enemy are to receive them. This is in addition to the dead and wounded, whom the enemy have been enabled to carry from the field, during, and since the action, and to those who have since died of the wounds they received. We have taken about 500 prisoners, upwards of 300 of whom are wounded, and a great part of them mortally. My loss has not exceeded, and I believe has not amounted to ten killed, and as many wounded. The entire destruction of the enemy's army was now inevitable, had it not been for an unfortunate occurrence, which at this moment took place on the other side of the river. Simultaneously with his advance upon my lines, he had thrown over in his boats a considerable force to the other side of the river. These having landed, were hardy enough to advance against the works of Gen. Morgan! And what is strange and difficult to account for, at the very moment when their entire discomfiture was looked for with a confidence approaching to certainty, the Kentucky reinforcements, ingloriously fled, drawing after them, by their example, the remainder of the forces; and thus yielding to the enemy that most fortunate position. The batteries which had rendered me, for many days, the most important service, though bravely defended, were of course now abandoned; not however, until the guns had been spiked. This unfortunate route, had totally changed the aspect of affairs. The enemy now occupied a position from which they might annoy us without hazard, and by means of which they might have been enabled to defeat in a great measure, the effects of our success on this side of the river. It became therefore an object of the first consequence to dislodge him as soon as possible. For this object, all the means in my power, which I could with any safety use, were immediately put in preparation.

Perhaps, however, it was somewhat owing to another cause, that I succeeded, beyond my expectations. In negociating the terms of a temporary suspension of hostilities, to enable the enemy to bury their dead, and provide for their wounded, I had required certain propositions to be acceded to as a basis; among which was this one–that although hostilities should cease on this side the river until 12 o'clock of this day, yet it was not to be understood, that they should cease on the other side; the but that no reinforcements should be sent across by either army, until the expiration of that day. His excellency Maj. Gen. Lambert, begged time to consider of those propositions until 10 o'clock of today and in the meantime re-crossed his troops. I need not tell you with how much eagerness I immediately regained possession of the position he had thus hastily quitted. The enemy having concentrated his forces, may again attempt to drive me from my position, by storm. Whenever he does I have no doubt my men will act with their usual firmness, and sustain a character, now become dear to them. I have the honour, &tc.,

-ANDREW JACKSON."

A subsequent court of inquiry led by General Carroll cleared the Kentucky troops of any wrongdoing, criticizing instead the retreat of his own men and Morgan's choice of defensive line. Despite the court's findings, Jackson maintained his stance on guilt, and his disparagement of the Kentucky troops not only sparked a newspaper backlash but also damaged his relationship with General John Adair, who commanded the Kentuckians at the Rodriguez Canal.

He questioned the abandonment of their lines, rejecting cowardice and instead blaming a lack of discipline. He insisted that these issues must be addressed or he would relinquish command, threatening severe consequences for breaches of orders. Never once did Jackson acknowledge his own role in the situation, and an inquiry later cleared Colonel Davis's troops of wrongdoing.

"While by the blessing of heaven directing the valour of the troops under my command, one of the most brilliant Victories in the annals of the war was obtained, by my immediate command; no words can express the mortification I felt at witnessing the scene exhibited on the opposite bank. I will spare your feelings and my own by entering into no detail on the subject. To all who reflect it must be a source of eternal regret, that a few moments exertion of that courage you certainly possess was alone wanting to have rendered your success more compleat; than that of your fellow citizens in this camp: by the defeat of the detachment, which was ration enough to cross the river to attack you."

"To what cause was the abandonment of your lines owing? To fear? No! You are the countrymen, the friends, the brothers of those who have secured to themselves by this courage, the gratitude of their Country who have been prodigal of their blood in its defence, and who our strangers to any other fear than that of disgrace. To disaffection to our glorious cause? No my countrymen, your general does justice to the pure sentiments by which you are inspired. How then could brave men abandon the post committed to their care. The want of discipline, the want of order, a total disregard to obedience, and a spirit of insubordination, not less destructive than Cowardise itself, appears to be the cause, which led to the disaster. And the Cause must be eradicated, or I must cease to command, and I desire to be distinctly understood, that every breach of Orders, all want to discipline, every distention of duty will be seriously and promptly punished."[658]

The general continually blamed his troops for failures largely resulting from his own shortcomings, refusing to accept any responsibility. His unjust criticism of Colonel Davis and the Kentucky troops contrasted sharply with his defense of Morgan and Patterson, whom he admired for their bravery. A later inquiry led by General Carroll cleared the Kentucky troops of any wrongdoing, yet Jackson maintained his negative assessment, damaging his relationship with General John Adair, who commanded the Kentucky troops.[659]

---

[658] "Jackson's Address to His Troops on the Right Bank," Jan. 8, 1815, in Latour, *Historical Memoir*, pp. lxiv, lxvi.

[659] Parton, *Jackson*, II, 383, ff.

CHAPTER

45

A HERO IS BORN

"Every breach of orders, all want of discipline, every disattention of duty will be seriously and promptly punished."
-Andrew Jackson

Beginning in the days after the battle at Chalmette Plantation, the rains fell heavily, and floods spread across the soft delta of the Mississippi, turning the camps of the two armies into muddy pits. No amount of rain could dampen the mood of Jackson's army, however, and on January 9th, even Jackson himself felt a sense of victory at what his men had accomplished. That day, a flag of truce arrived, signaling General Lambert's agreement to the terms of an armistice. Most of the day, however, was consumed with the grim task of collecting the dead and preparing graves, which were, out of necessity, shallow and hastily dug. In the evening, by the light of torches, in the presence of the whole British army, the remains of the deceased were laid ceremoniously in their inadequate graves, mired in the mud and muck. So numerous were the bodies, and so hastily were the graves prepared, that the rank field was later reported to be unbearable during the succeeding summer.

A melancholy scene unfolded as a line was established three hundred yards from the American position, where both armies gathered to honor their fallen soldiers. The bodies of the brave men who fought and died were brought to this line. The ladders initially intended for scaling the lines were repurposed as biers for the deceased.

Witnessing the somber task of identifying the bodies, Vincent Nolte noted, the sight of British Major Whittaker's body elicited tears and lamentations among the British soldiers. "I was present," says Nolte, "for a while, when they were trying to recognize the bodies, and when they found that of Major Whittaker the soldiers burst into tears, saying: 'Ah, poor Major Whittaker! he is gone, the worthy fellow." [660]

For ten days after the battle, General Lambert and the British remained in their encampment, deluged with rain and flood, and fired upon at intervals by the American batteries on both sides of the river. Hostilities remained and intensified when Admiral Cochrane attempted to maneuver his fleet past Fort Saint Philip on the lower Mississippi beginning on January 9th. The operation was poorly timed, and its execution was even worse, lacking coordination with the overall assault on the Rodriguez Canal. It was as if the British just didn't have it in them anymore. Cochrane's fleet caught no one by surprise, and the American bombardment was thorough, lasting until the 12th, prompting Major William Overton to request heavy mortars from the New Orleans Navy Yard, leading to the British withdrawal. Instead, the British persisted in their bombardment of Fort St. Philip, located at the mouth of the Mississippi River, for an additional week. [661]

Even while the battle raged on the river below, the British army under Lambert was making preparations to leave. Following the battle of January 8th, the army withdrew one and one-half miles back from Jackson's position, but the American guns, radically elevated, continued their harassing fire. Commander Patterson mounted 12- and 24-pounders at his batteries between the tenth and thirteenth of January, and soon he began erecting levee batteries opposite Lambert's encampment. There was some concern among the Americans that the British might still consider a renewed attack. But, following their catastrophic defeat, Lambert's forces refrained from launching another assault on Line Jackson. It soon became clear to Jackson's army that Lambert would withdraw his forces. The process promised to be complicated, what with the thick swamp, and a lack of boats for transport.

---

[660] Nolte, *Fifty Years*, p. 224.
[661] Brannan, John, *Official Letters*, 1923. p. 454.

The aftermath of the battle brought devastation, particularly in British hospitals. Captain Hill described the harrowing scene at de la Ronde's hospital, where the wounded and dying crowded every room. "The scene presented at de la Ronde's (hospital) was one I shall never forget; almost every room was crowded with the wounded and dying. The dead bodies of two gallant generals lay close to each other" (Pakenham and Gibbs) "and another was severely hurt" (Keane). Mortifying defeat had again attended the British arms and the loss in men and officers was frightfully disastrous."[662]

The American troops, though free from worries and labor, were forced to remain in the field indefinitely, and had no choice but to endure the inevitable hardships of their situation. Already homesick, some in recovery from their wounds, now faced the spread of disease. Illness began to take its toll; serious influenza, fever, and, most troubling of all, dysentery spread among the ranks. Major Latour estimates that, during the few weeks from January 8th until the campaign's end, five hundred of Jackson's beleaguered soldiers lost their lives to these various forms of pestilence—far more than those who died in battle. Yet, as long as the enemy was present, there was overall, very little complaining. The sick soldiers, pale yellow and gaunt, simply crawled into the field hospital when they could no longer stand at their posts, lying down, hoping to die in peace.

Despite the armistice, skirmishes continued as both sides maintained their positions, with British troops, especially, enduring endless discomfort. Conditions faced by the British soldiers, who were constantly on edge, never assured of peace, were abysmal. Lacking proper tents, many slept in the open or makeshift huts, enduring weeks without changing clothes. Heavy rains, coupled with storms and freezing temperatures, exacerbated their suffering, leaving them alternately drenched and chilled. The old way of annoying the enemy by cannonade in the daytime and by "hunting parties" during the night, was kept up while the armies still faced each other.

As John Henry Cooke explained, "Of the extreme unpleasantness of our situation it is hardly possible to convey any adequate conception. We

---

[662] Benson Earle Hill, *Recollections of an Artillery Officer* (2 vols.; London: Richard Bentley, 1836), II, p. 11-14.

never closed our eyes in peace, for we were sure to be awakened before many minutes elapsed, by the splash of a round shot or shell in the mud beside us. Tents we had none, but lay, some in the open air, and some in huts made of boards, or any materials that could be procured. From the first moment of our landing, not a man had undressed excepting to bathe; and many had worn the same shirt for weeks together. Besides all this, heavy rains now set in, accompanied with violent storms of thunder and lightning, which lasting during the entire day, usually ceased towards dark, and gave place to keen frosts. Thus were we alternately wet and frozen: wet all day, and frozen all night. With the outposts, again, there was constant skirmishing. With what view the Americans wished to drive them in I cannot tell; but every day were they attacked, and compelled to maintain their ground by dint of hard fighting. In one word, none but those who happened to belong to this army can form a notion of the hardships which it endured and the fatigue which it underwent." [663]

Amidst these challenges, even minor setbacks had serious implications. A cannonball knocked over a cooking kettle, spilling valuable soup, highlighting the dire straits of the soldiers who struggled to maintain supplies amidst harsh winter conditions. "The consequence was that the consumption was beyond the produce; on some days we did not taste food," Stanley Clisby Arthur writes, "and when we did it was served out in small quantities as only to tantalize our voracious appetites, so that between short rations and a perpetual cannonade we passed ten days after the repulse in as uncomfortable manner as could fall to the lot of most militaries to endure."[664]

The sailors, tasked with transporting the wounded and provisions, faced grueling weather, exhaustion and suffering. However jubilant the Americans who fought the Battle of New Orleans were, sorrow, hardship, and grief defined the aftermath of the battle among the soldiers of both sides. The tragedy of loss was everywhere, while the relentless conditions of the campaign, and the threat of desertion added layers of difficulty to an already grave situation.

---

[663] Cooke, p. 107.
[664] Arthur, Sir Stanley Clisby, *The Story of the Battle of New Orleans*. Louisiana Historical Society. 1915. Ch. 21.

Indeed, desertion became a serious concern for the demoralized British army. It was a temptation many homesick British soldiers not only considered; some acted upon. To increase desertion, there were concerted efforts made by the Americans to secretly coax their counterparts to abandon their ranks, attempting to entice British soldiers away with promises of land and money. Printed leaflets were thrown into British picket lines, and individuals approached sentinels, persuading them to abandon their posts. The frequency of desertions escalated, posing a real threat to whatever remained of British morale and strength. As Arthur attests, "Printed papers, offering lands and money as the price of desertion were thrown into the pickets, whilst individuals made a practice of approaching our posts and endeavored to persuade the very sentinels to quit their stations. Nor could it be expected that bribes so tempting would always be refused. Many desertions began daily to take place and became before long so frequent that the evils rose to be of a serious nature."

Facing a difficult retreat, the British attempted to construct a rough trail through the brush to the lake, from the head of Villeré's Canal to and along Bayous Mazant and Bienvenue to to expedite the passage of troops, ordnance, and equipment over the marshy terrain. The British 44th regiment spearheaded the work, perhaps to improve their standing, and a fascine-corduroyed road was engineered. The process was painfully slow, however, and the soldiers, weary and far from home, continued to face exposure to attack throughout the long days of road construction. "To obviate this difficulty, prudence required that the road which the British had formed on landing should be continued to the very margin of the lake; whilst appearances seemed to indicate the total impracticability of the scheme. From firm ground to the water's edge was here a distance of many miles, through the center of a morass where human foot had never before trodden. Yet it was desirable at least to make the attempt; for it if failed we should only be reduced to our former alternative of gaining a battle or surrendering at discretion."[665]

Having determined to adopt this course, General Lambert immediately dispatched strong working parties under the guidance of his engineering officers. Lengthening the road, directing it as near

---

[665] Glieg, p. 116.

as possible to the margin of the creek, their task was burdened with innumerable difficulties. In the marshy terrain, firm footing was hard to come by, nor were there many trees that could have been used for planks. "All that could be done, therefore, was to bind together large quantities of reeds, and lay them across the quagmire;" Arthur explains, "by which means at least the semblance of a road was produced, however wanting in firmness and solidity. But where broad ditches came in the way, many of which intersected the morass, the workmen were necessarily obliged to apply more durable materials. For these bridges, composed in part of large branches, brought with immense labor from the woods, were constructed; but they were, on the whole, little superior in point of strength to the rest of the path, for though the edges were supported by timber, the middle was filled up only with reeds."[666]

This work was completed by the royal engineers and three hundred men of the 44th. Bridges also had to be built over the numerous secondary streams emptying into the principal bayou. On January 11th, a rainstorm accompanied by thunder and lightning impeded the work. It required nine days of round-the-clock labor to complete the road. The British wounded were then sent on board, although there were eighty unfortunate souls who could not be removed. The abandoned guns were spiked and broken. Finally, on the evening of the 18th of January, under the cover of night, the main body of the army began its retreat. The British withdrawal from New Orleans had begun. The road was finished on the night of January 17th. Previously, on the eleventh, the wounded had left, and on the thirteenth, fourteenth, and fifteenth, the West Indian regiments, the Forty-fourth regiment, and the Marines departed. During the night of January 14th, a party of Americans came through the woods, took some slaves from de La Ronde's, and caused an alarm among the British pickets, but no engagement ensued.[667]

There remained nothing for Lambert to do but to complete his final negotiations with Jackson. These were mainly concerned with the continuous exchange of prisoners, but also included a heated argument about the return of slaves who had left with the British. In Latour's account, the British "carried off all the Negroes of the plantations they

---
[666] Arthur, Sir Stanley Clisby, *The Story of the Battle of New Orleans*. Louisiana Historical Society. 1915. Ch. 22.
[667] Tylden, p. 70.

had occupied. There were doubtless some amongst these, who were very willing to follow them; but by far the greater part, particularly the women, were decoyed, or carried off by force." Like much of Latour's memoir, this is an invitation fabricated to court popularity among Louisianians. Dickson, writing in his journal at the Fisherman's Village on January 19, after watching the rear guard of the army complete it's nine-mile march from Villere's plantation, noted: "a good many negroes, both men, women and children have taken the opportunity of the night to accompany the army down to the huts, which General Lambert was extremely displeased at."[668] Lambert's displeasure is scarcely surprising. His army assembled at the Fisherman's huts were critically short of food. Quite apart from the obvious inconvenience likely to be caused by these unwelcome guests on board the fleet, their transport to the ships would require the navy boats to make additional unnecessary journeys, and there was, meanwhile, no food for them. "For two whole days the only provisions issued to the troops were some crumbs of biscuit and a small allowance of rum." [669] Far from carrying any of them off by force, only Lambert's human concern for the plight of the slaves if their masters caught them again persuaded him to allow them room in the boats. Having done so, he did not feel obliged to return them against their will.

The argument continued through six long weeks. The Americans, insisting on the restitution of property and the British declining to force slaves to return to their masters. Latour notwithstanding, it was clear from the start that the British regarded the runaway slaves as a burden which only compassion persuaded them to carry. There was no underlying motive of financial gain to balance the American motive of financial loss. As Lambert wrote in his letter to Jackson dated February 8, "I did all I could to persuade them to return at the time, but none was willing, as will be testified by Mr. Celestin, a proprietor whom I had detained until the British forces had evacuated their last position: this gentleman saw the slaves that were present, and did all he could to urge them to go back."[670]

Later, when news of the ratification of the Treaty of Ghent had been received, and both sides had agreed on a cessation of hostilities. Lambert

---

[668] Latour, p. 295
[669] Ibid, 296
[670] Ibid, 297

again refused to concede that the clauses concerning removal of property could be applied to runaway slaves:

"If those negroes belong to the territory or city, we were actually in occupation of, I should conceive we had no right to take them away; but by their coming away, they are virtually the same as deserters. . . I am obliged to say so much in justification of the right; but I have from the first done all I could to prevent, and subsequently, together with Admiral Malcolm, have given every facility, and used every persuasion that they should return to their masters, and many have done so; but I could not reconcile it to myself to abandon any, who, from false reasoning, perhaps, joined us during the period of hostilities, and have thus acted in violation of the laws of their country, and besides become obnoxious to their masters. Presumably Celestin Lachiappella, shown in Latour's appendix 68, as having lost 43 slaves out of a total of 199 listed as taken by the British.

Latour's accusation that the British "repeatedly declare their intention to restore them to their owners on their coming to claim them," is another fabrication. The offer applied only to those slaves who were willing to return. When the British sailed, the slaves who had refused to return to their masters, went with them. They were landed at their request on colonial Islands, including Jamaica and Bermuda, where they settled in poverty, but freedom.

On the 18th of January, a prisoner exchange was carried out between the two armies. Upon written agreement, the uniform companies of New Orleans, with colors flying and the regimental band playing, marched down to the line of British outposts, and drew up to receive their friends and comrades who had been taken by the enemy in the night battle, nearly a month before. The prisoners, about sixty in number, were escorted by a party of the British 95th rifles. The roll was called and found to be correct. "Forward, Americans!" the British sentry called out. The prisoners marched along the line, saluted as they passed by the British troops, and then proceeded to the American camp, where cheers and congratulations greeted them and hundreds of their old friends rushed forward to embrace them.[671]

---

[671] Arthur, Sir Stanley Clisby, *The Story of the Battle of New Orleans*. Louisiana Historical Society. 1915. Ch. 24.

"In spite of our losses," Stanley Clisby Arthur explained, "there were not throughout the armament a sufficient number of boats to transport above one-half of the army at a time. If, however, we should separate, the chances were that both parties would be destroyed: for those embarked might be intercepted and those left behind would be obliged to cope with the entire American force. Besides, even granting that the Americans might be repulsed, it would be impossible to take our boats in their presence, and thus at least one division, if not both, must be sacrificed."

"Trimming the fires," continues Arthur, "and arranging all things in the same order as if no change were to take place, regiment after regiment stole away from the Villeré plantation, as soon as darkness concealed their motions; leaving the pickets to follow as a rear guard but with strict injunctions not to retire till daylight began to appear. As may be supposed, the most profound silence was maintained; not a man opening his mouth, except to issue necessary orders and even speaking in a whisper. Not a cough or any other noise was to be heard from the head to the rear of the column; and even the steps of the soldiers were planted with care to present the slightest stamping or echo."[672]

The final humiliation of the British army was their ill-fated retreat to Lake Borgne. In order to avoid attack from Jackson's army, the unfortunate British soldiers were forced to march all night through the swamps surrounding the Villeré plantation. While the first section of the hastily built path was relatively firm, skirting along the high road beside the bank of the river, once Lambert's troops arrived at the marsh, all comfort came to an end. The road they had hastened together was constructed of materials so light, resting upon a foundation so flimsy, that the tread of the first corps to move over it inevitably beat the path to shreds. Those that followed were therefore compelled to muddle through in the best way they could; and by the time those at the rear of the column reached the morass, all trace of a path had entirely disappeared. But not only were the reeds torn apart and sunk by the pressure of those who had gone before, but the bog itself, which at first contained a few spots of firm footing, was trodden into the consistency of mud. The result was that every step sunk the soldiers to their knees or higher. In the lowest ditches, many spots were so marshy that the troops found them entirely

---

[672] Ibid, Ch. 25.

impassable. To make matters worse, the moon was nowhere to be found on the night of the 18th, as the dark sky was mostly cloud covered. The few stars that poked through supplied the only light, and it was difficult for the soldiers to see where they stepped, or even to follow those just a few feet in front of them.

Three regiments--95th 43rd and Seventh--with the rear guard picket struggled through this lethal quagmire after Glieg had been saved from drowning in the mud by a canteen strap thrown to him by one of his soldiers. These last troops took more than 10 hours to cover the distance of 9 miles.

As soon as the rear guard had passed the landing point, Lambert and Admiral Malcolm followed down the bayou by boat. Dickson and Burgoyne were behind them in the armed barge of the *Asia*, which had been left to guard the vulnerable junction of the Mazant with the upper Bienvenue. In the rear of the retreating army, Lieutenant Peddie directed the destruction of all bridges. By about midday on the 19th the entire army was miserably camped in the area of the Spanish fishermen's village. The men were exhausted, cold, covered in mud, and hungry. By the time the last of them were embarked, they were nearly starving. Once more, Cochrane supply line showed themselves to be stretched to breaking point. For nine days the boats were sailed and rode between the fleet and the mouth of the Bienvenue. At 9 o'clock in the evening of January 27, the last company of the seventh and 43rd regiments reached their transports. There they remained for six days while fierce gales whipped up the sea and cut off all communication between the ships.

"Over roads such as these did we continue our journey during the whole of the night and in the morning reached a place called Fisherman's Huts upon the margin of the lake. The name is derived from a clump of mud-built cottages, situated in as complete a desert as the eye of man was ever pained by beholding." Arthur explains, "Here at length we were ordered to halt and perhaps I never rejoiced more sincerely at any order than at this. I threw myself upon the ground without so much as pulling off my muddy garments, and in an instant all my cares and troubles were forgotten. Nor did I wake from that deep slumber for many hours; when I rose I was cold and stiff, and creeping beside a miserable fire of reeds, addressed myself to the last morsel of salt pork which my wallet contained."[673]

The whole army had now arrived at the edge of the lake, having escaped without notice or at least without annoyance from Jackson's troops. Forming along the brink of the lake, a line of outposts were set up, and the soldiers were ordered to make themselves as comfortable as they could. But the few huts that the place was named for were occupied by the highest-ranking officers, so for the majority of the men, their bed was the morass. The remaining clothes the British wore were what had survived a month on the campaign. Cold and hungry, the soldiers' only hope was to make it to the boats.

A flotilla lay ready to receive Lambert's men, to transport them to the main fleet, some eighty miles away. Yet, these transport boats lacked food for the soldiers. They would have to reach the main fleet, some eighty miles away before they would be fed. Many of the British troops, some of whom were extremely ill from disease, feared the weather. If the winds did not cooperate, and the boats were delayed before they reached the fleet, they faced death by starvation.

George Glieg remembered the despair of the evacuation. "As soon as the boats returned regiment after regiment embarked and set sail for the fleet but, the distance being considerable and the wind foul, many days elapsed before the whole could be got off. Excepting in one trifling instance, however, no accident occurred and by the end of the month we were all once more on board our former ships. But our return was far from triumphant. We, who only seven weeks before had set out in the surest confidence of glory, and I may add, of emolument, were brought back dispirited and dejected. Our ranks were woefully thinned, our chiefs slain, our clothing tattered and filthy, and even our discipline in some degree injured. A gloomy silence reigned throughout the armament, except when it was broken by the voice of lamentation over fallen friends; and the interior of each ship presented a scene well calculated to prove the short-sightedness of human hope and human prudence."

With this ignominious wallow in the mire, "covered with mud from the top of the head to the sole of the foot" the Wellington heroes ended their month's exertion in the delta of the Mississippi. The retreat was

---

[673] Ibid, Ch. 25., 268-270

so well managed, however, that General Lambert was knighted for it soon after. [674]

Not until dawn on the 19th did Jackson realize that the British army had gone. The sun was high in the heavens that morning, one day after the British abandoned their camp, and rumors of the British retreat circulated more openly throughout the American camp. The British camps had been arranged to appear the same as they had been for days. Sentinels seemed to be posted as usual and flags still flew. It was, it is said, General Humbert, who remarked on the strangeness of enemy sentries standing motionless with birds perching on their heads. Despite British efforts to steal away covertly, local residents had also caught on to the British retreat. But rumors were one thing, and Jackson could not be sure. The American general and his aides, looking through a spyglass from the uppermost window at headquarters, scanned the British position and were inclined to think that the enemy were inactive, and only lying low, with a plan to draw the Americans out of their lines into the open plain.

A reconnaissance party was sent out to make sure to make certain that the move was not a ruse. Shortly after a British doctor arrived from Villere's plantation to deliver a letter from Lambert. In this, he informed Jackson that his army had evacuated the position and abandoned for the time the campaign against New Orleans. He recommended to Jackson's care some eighty wounded men who were too severely injured to be moved. American Surgeon General David C. Kerr was charged with making the necessary arrangements for the British wounded, who were later taken to New Orleans by steamboat, and Jackson turned his attention to the consolidation of victory. Colonel Hines was sent with the cavalry to follow Villere as far as possible toward the British landing place, and Lacoste formed a detachment of expert hunters to scour the woods for stragglers and escape slaves. Wanting to be certain, and to confirm the rumors, Jackson ordered a party out to investigate. Hind's Mississippi dragoons led the reconnoiter, accompanied by Colonel de la Ronde, who knew the terrain as well as anyone. While his men were forming the reconnoiter, a British medical officer, Dr. James Wadsdale, approached the line bearing a letter from General

---

[674] Arthur, *The Battle of New Orleans*, pp. 268-270.

Lambert which announced his departure and "recommended to the humanity of the American commander the eighty wounded men who had necessarily been left behind." The rumors of the British retreat were now confirmed, and the men became ecstatic, exploding in raucous cheers. But Jackson was still wary and restrained the men's celebrations. Instead, he expedited the men chosen to visit the abandoned camp, in order to verify Wadsdale's claims.[675]

Jackson and his staff soon rode over to inspect the enemy's camp themselves. Colonel de la Ronde was also given orders to harass the enemy's rear to vouchsafe the mission, along with Major Gabriel Villeré, who was to do the same in and around his father's plantation, which the British had continued to occupy as their headquarters. After sending David C. Kerr, Surgeon-General of the American army, with Dr. Wadsdale to the British field hospital at Jumonville, Jackson and his staff mounted up and rode to the British camp to assess the situation himself. Coming upon the scene, Jackson found fourteen pieces of large cannon, "many implements of war, and a great quantity of private as well as public property of the British army." [676]

At long last, the mighty Redcoats had cleared out, having failed in their mission to capture the Crescent City of New Orleans. Jackson's army had withstood the might of the world's great superpower. Andrew Jackson had finally met his destiny.

---

[675] Ibid, 270.
[676] Ibid, 302.

CHAPTER

46

A MAN FOR THE AGES

"To the victors belong the spoils."
-William L. Marcy

After visiting the abandoned British camp, Jackson made a visit to the hospital at Jumonville, himself, where wounded English officers were being treated. With a touch of humanity, and respect for his foe, he expressed his sympathy and assured the wounded that they would receive the necessary care. Among the injured was Lieutenant d'Arcy from the 43rd regiment, who had lost both legs to a cannonball just days after the 8th. The circumstances of these wounded men were made known to the residents of the city. Receiving word of the wounded, ill, and dying at Jumonville, a number of the leading women of New Orleans rode down in their carriages to tend to the wounded.

Having confirmed the British departure, after fully inspecting the area the enemy had abandoned, Jackson again considered pursuing the British retreat. To this question, his trusted friend and aide-de-camp, Edward Livingston spoke up. The ever-judicious Livingston had sway with Jackson, as the General highly respected his former Congressional colleague, and his advice was sound. "What do you want more? Your object is gained," Livingston argued. "The city is saved. The British have retired. For the pleasure of a blow or two you will risk against those fearless troops your handful of men, composed of the best and worthiest citizen, and rob so many families of their heads." After all, Jackson had already achieved his main goal, Livingston argued. He had saved the city. Still, concerned that his critics in Washington might question allowing the British to retreat unmolested. Jackson penned a letter to the Secretary of War, James Monroe. In it, he explained his reasoning, "Such was the situation of the ground which he [the enemy] abandoned, and of that through which he retired, protected by canals, redoubts, entrenchments and swamps on his Right, the river on his Left, that I could not, without encountering a risque which my true policy did not seem to require or authorize, annoy him much on his retreat." In short, the enemy's position, Jackson informed Monroe, was too fortified for a successful attack without putting his troops at risk. For all his faults as a commander, Jackson was learning to rein in his impetuous nature. He was also gaining the all-important leadership quality of knowing when to listen to his more sagacious cohorts.[677]

Jackson made no serious attempt to pursue or harass the defeated enemy. The retreat had been carried out with such skill and secrecy that by the time he was aware of it there was little he could do. He was always aware of the vulnerability of his unseasoned troops, if they were caught in the open, and he had no intention of allowing victory to be snatched from him by an injudicious change from defense to attack. However, two of Jackson's men, Surgeon Robert Morell and Purser Thomas Shields, were not satisfied to remain inactive while the British departed. No sooner were they released, in the exchange of prisoners, than they persuaded Commodore Patterson to authorize the recruitment of volunteers for an expedition on Lake Borgne. On the 19th, with 34 men and four small boats, they put out from Bayou St. John. At Fort Petites Coquilles, the next morning, they were reinforced by two more boats and nineteen men. On the 20th the small force passed into Lake Borgne by the Chef Menteur passage, and that night rowing with muffled oars, they surprised and boarded a transport carrying 40 dragoons and 14 seamen, whom they captured. [678]

By the 22nd, Shields and Morrell had taken six launches, a transport schooner, and more than 60 prisoners. The schooner was set on fire when it was found that she could not be brought over the bar at the rigolets, and a number of the prisoners were released for lack of sufficient numbers

---

[677] Remini, pg. 289.
[678] Brodine, Jr., Charles E., and Hughes, Christine F., *The Naval War of 1812, A Documentary History*, Volume IV, 2023, p. 940.

to guard them; but Lambert was obliged to send out boats and soldiers from the fleet to clear the lake. Shields was eventually captured again in February, leading a daring raid on Horn Island after the British fleet had left Lake Borgne. Cochrane was so impressed by the Purser's exploits that he invited him to dinner aboard the *Tonnant* to give a personal account of them.

Jackson believed "Admiral Cochrane is sore, and General Lambert, crasy (sic)" he still thought it possible that they might "attempt some act of madness--if their panic does not prevent it."[679] Jackson had come to New Orleans to defend it against an attack by the strongest British force ever sent against the American coast. That force, although maimed and bloodily repulsed, remained with a powerful fleet offshore. Jackson would not relax his vigilance until that fleet had departed, and until that time his tactics were unchanged: flexible, defensive, based on concentration and mobility. The extent of his victory on January 8th was to prove more of a handicap than an asset in his dealings with the people of New Orleans, who believed that the danger no longer existed.

Jackson finally deemed it appropriate to reposition most of his army from the Rodriguez Canal on January 21st. For General Jackson, with the assurance that the enemy had departed, he began making preparations for the return of his army to the city they had left behind on December 23rd, nearly a month earlier. It would be the first time he would be in the city proper since his arrival in Louisiana. The morning was sunny when Jackson ordered the army drawn up behind the rampart for the last time. An address was read to the troops that described, in glowing terms, the heroic events of the campaign. Effusively, Jackson praised his men for their bravery and skill.

The address had all the usual Jackson flair. Before the troops left the scene of their great victory, general orders were read at the head of each regiment. The words were Jackson's gratitude for his men, and he named every corps, every commander, and every officer on his gun batteries. To the Baratarians he gave "warm approbation," mentioning Dominique You and Renato Beluche for "the gallantry with which they have redeemed the pledge they gave… to defend the country" and promising "the brothers Lafitte, who have exhibited the same courage

---

[679] AJ to Monroe, Jan. 1815, Jackson Papers, LC.

and fidelity "that the government should be informed of their conduct."[680] Though no corps was excluded, the special attention given to the artillery shows that Jackson was fully aware of his debt to gunnery. He owed to the Baratarians, also, the vital supplies of ammunition. Altogether, his agreement with the "hellish banditti" had proved to be one of the most crucial decisions of his life. At the end of it, amid exultant shouts of praise and gratitude, the troops wheeled into marching order and began preparations to march back into the Crescent City.

Just two days earlier, he had written to Abbé Guillaume Dubourg, the apostolic administrator for the Diocese of Louisiana and the Floridas, that the army's return to the city should be marked by a public act of thanksgiving. He stressed in his letter that he wished for his men to be recognized, but also to give thanks to God for their astounding victory. Jackson was thinking of higher powers at play when he requested the public ceremony; not only for having allowed his men's safety in the victory, but also for what seemed to him to be assistance from a divine source. "The signal interposition of heaven," he wrote, "in giving success to our arms against the enemy, while it must excite in every bosom attached to the happy government under which we live, emotions of the liveliest gratitude requires at the same time some manifestation of those feelings. Permit me, therefore, to entreat you that you will cause the service of public thanksgiving to be performed in the cathedral and token at once of the greatest assistance we have received from the ruler of all events and of our humble sense of it." [681]

The Abbé was agreeable, readily approving of the idea, promising Jackson that he would begin immediately to "make the disposition for the ceremony, the brightest ornament of which will certainly be yourself, general, surrounded by your brave army." [682]

On the same day that he wrote to Dubourg, Jackson wrote to inform Monroe of the British retreat and added "there is very little doubt, but his last exertions have been made in this quarter, at any rate, for the present season."

The second Louisiana militia were left at Villere's plantation, and the seventh U.S. infantry guarded the Rodriguez canal line; but the

---
[680] Jackson's Address to his Troops, Jan. 21, 1815.
[681] Parton, *Jackson*, II, pg. 270.
[682] Abbé DuBourg to AJ, no date, Jackson, *Correspondence*, II, 150, Note 1.

rest of the army returned to the city. Those who left the battlefield for the city did so with considerable relief. Heavy rains had washed the shallow covering of mud from the hastily-dug graves, and the stench of death was overpowering. The danger of disease was a cogent reason for withdrawing the army, as soon as the British retreat was known to be final. On Saturday, January 21st, New Orleans welcomed the victorious troops. As Arsend Latour wrote of the army's return to the city, "The old and infirm, women and children all turned out to hail the noble rescuers of their city. Every contingent was expressive of gratitude. Joy sparkled in every feature on beholding fathers, brothers, husbands, and sons who had so recently saved the lives, fortunes, and honor of their families by repelling any enemy come to conquer and subjugate the country, nor were the sensations of the brave soldiers less lively on seeing themselves about to be compensated for all their suffering by the enjoyment of domestic felicity, how late, how trifling, how inconsiderable did their past toils and danger appear to them at this glorious moment. All was forgotten, all painful recollections gave way to the most exquisite sensations of inexpressible joy." [683]

Casualties had been so small that there was scarcely a family, whose joy was tempered by the sorrow of bereavement. Curfew was suspended, the celebrations went on all night. Pierre Favrot wrote to his wife at 8 o'clock the following morning that he had never seen such crowds, "Tomorrow they... will crown the general; twelve young girls will strew his path with flowers.... They are practicing at Madame Floriant's."[684]

The Abbé, with Jackson's approval, postponed the religious service until Tuesday, January 23 in order to have time to make the necessary preparations. It must have been an incredible celebration on the day of the ceremony. The streets were packed with people, and balconies and rooftops were buzzing with spectators. Crowds gathered everywhere in the large square in front of the cathedral by the river. Along the levee, uniformed members of Plauché's battalion lined up in two rows from the entrance of the square by the river to the church. In the middle of the square, right in front of the Cathedral Basilica's main entrance, a temporary arch stood tall, supported by six Corinthian columns. On

---

[683] Latour, *Historical Memoir*, pp. 197-198.
[684] Reid to Elizabeth Reid, Feb. 10, 1815, Reid Papers, LC.

either side of the arch stood two young women, one symbolizing justice and the other representing liberty. Under the arch, on a pedestal, were two children holding a laurel crown, positioned between the arch and the cathedral.

The 23rd had been set aside for the Thanksgiving service, and however Jackson might direct the gratitude of his mentor "the God of battles," the citizens of New Orleans were determined to honor the gaunt and haggard general from Tennessee. *Te Deum* was to be sung in St. Louis Cathedral, and the Place d' Armes was decorated for the parade. From the entrance on the Riverside, the brilliantly uniformed companies of Plauche's New Orleans volunteers line to the route to a triumph, full arch resting on six columns in the center of the square. From the arch to the cathedral, the way was marked with "young ladies, representing the different states and territories composing the American union, all dressed in white, covered with transparent veils, and wearing a silver star on their foreheads. Each... Held in her right hand, a flag, inscribed with the name of the state she represented, and in her left a basket trimmed with blue ribbons, and full of flowers. Behind each was a shield, suspended on a lance stuck in the ground, inscribed with the name of a state or territory." [685] Under the arch standing on two pedestals, two thrilled, children held crowns of laurel for the conqueror. Madame Floriant had a reason to be satisfied with her pupils.

A group of young women stood at equal distances apart, each symbolizing a different state or territory in the Union. They wore white outfits paired with delicate blue veils and had silver stars adorning their foreheads. Each girl carried roses and floral garlands, holding a flag with her state's name in her right hand and a basket of flowers in her left. Behind them, a lance was planted in the ground, showcasing a shield with her state's name. The shields were linked by garlands of evergreen and flowers, creating a beautiful display from the arch to the cathedral. [686]

Through the gate of the plaza walked the hero of the Battle of New Orleans, flanked by his staff and followed by a large chair that seemed to emerge from the crowd. People waved and called out his name. A cannon salute marked his arrival, honoring his astounding achievements. As he

---

[685] Latour, *Historical Memoir*, pp. 197-198.
[686] Ibid, 199-200. Reid to Elizabeth Reid, Feb. 10th, 1815.

entered the square, Jackson was asked to proceed along the path prepared for him, passing beneath an arch. Two children lowered a laurel crown onto his head. The eight-year-old daughter of Dr. David Kerr stepped forward to congratulate him on his victory. In honor of the people of Louisiana, a ballad written by Mrs. Ellery of New Orleans was sung to the tune of "Yankee Doodle." The general was so moved by the children's words and gestures that he paused to speak with the young ladies and requested a copy of the ballad, which he later sent to his nieces. As he continued toward the church, the young lady scattered flowers in front of him and recited a heartfelt ode:

> "Hail to the chief who hie'd at war's alarms!
> To save our threaten'd land, from hostile arms;
> Preserv'd protected by his gallant care,
> By his the grateful tribute of each fair;
> With joyful triumph, swell the coral lay—
> Strew, strew with flow'rs, the heroes welcome way.
> Jackson! all hail our country's pride and boast,
> Whose mind's a council and whose arms an host;
> Who, firm and valiant, 'midst the storm of war,
> Boasts unstained praise—laurels without a tear:
> Welcome blest chief! accept our grateful lays
> Unbidden homage, and spontaneous praise;
> Remembrance, long, shall keep alive thy fame,
> And future infants learn to lisp thy name. [687]

At the entrance of the cathedral, Abbé Dubourg, dressed in his ceremonial robes, warmly welcomed Jackson with a speech filled with gratitude to God for sending such a heroic savior to the country. "By proving yourself as a worthy instrument of Heaven's compassionate plans," the Abbé began, "your first instinct was to recognize the clear involvement of Providence. Your initial action was a profound acknowledgment of His blessings — eternal thanks to His supreme

---

[687] Reid and Eaton, *Jackson*, pg. 369.

majesty for granting us such a tool for His generous purposes." He then presented the general with a branch of consecrated laurel.[688]

Jackson, who was, by that time, something of a master at addressing crowds, responded to the Abbé's glowing salute in words of his own, crafted to sound both republican and imperial, praising the brave men under his command, while at the same time not diminishing his own exalted accomplishment. "General Jackson knew well how to do a pretty thing," said one observer.[689]

The crowd hushed to hear their General. "Reverend, sir," began Jackson with a stately bow, "I receive with gratitude and pleasure the symbolical crown which piety has prepared; I receive it in the name of the brave men who have so effectively seconded my exertions for the preservation of their country--they well deserve the laurels which their country will bestow. For myself, to have been instrumental in the deliverance of such a country is the greatest blessing that heaven could confer. That it has been affected with so little loss—that so few tears should cloud the smiles of our triumph, and not a cypress leaf be interwoven in the wreath, which you present, is a source of the most exquisite enjoyment."[690]

After he thanked the Abbé for the prayers offered for this happiness, Jackson added a few more sentences, concluding by wishing the city, "Wealth and happiness commensurate with its courage." Then, Jackson was escorted into the cathedral to a prominent seat near the altar. The cathedral was ablaze with light from 1,000 candles. The *Te Deum* boomed forth with impressive jubilation, after which a guard of honor attended the general to his quarters in the evening. The curfew suspended for a night, the town and its suburbs were brilliantly illuminated; all New Orleans—in its own inevitable way—gave itself over to pleasure and feasting. [691]

---

[688] Reid to Elizabeth Reid, Feb. 10, 1815, Reid Papers, LC; Address of Abbé Dubourg to A.J. Jan. 23, 1815, in Brannan, *Official Letters*, pg. 467.
[689] Parton, *Jackson*, II, p. 274.
[690] Jackson's Response, Ibid, p. 468.
[691] Latour, *Historical Memoir*, pp. 199-200.

CHAPTER

47

JACKSON VERSUS THE CITY OF NEW ORLEANS

"To silence opposition and satisfy the refractory and designing that judicial interference should not mark the execution of his plans, or for the screen, behind which treason might stalk unmolested. He did it to make the example factual, and to obtain, through fear, that security, which could not be had through love of country."

–John Eaton

The honeymoon between Jackson and the city of New Orleans did not last long. Celebrated as the savior of New Orleans, wined, dined and feted, Jackson should have been in his glory. Yet, in true Jackson form, he was not. Instead, he fretted. Despite the withdrawal of British forces, no amount of persuasion could convince Jackson that the threat was gone. Perhaps this level of anxiety lies at the heart of that special something that made Jackson an effective commander. Or perhaps he obsessed over security issues because he loved the power. To his many exasperated New Orleans detractors, the General was on a power trip, and a paranoid obsessive.

Despite the urgings of the local legislature to suspend habeas corpus, to rescind the city-wide curfew, to end martial law, Jackson simply would not. He would not hear of it. He would continue to demand vigilance, suspecting a return of the enemy at any moment, and therefore securing an indefinite perimeter around the circumference of the city, to the chagrin of those who longed for a return to peace.

As winter gave way to spring, 1815, in light of such stubborn refusal to hear the voices of the citizenry, Jackson's popularity in Louisiana plummeted considerably from the lofty heights the city held for him in his initial moments of victory. Challenges with the local inhabitants had intensified dramatically during the long, stagnant months of February and March. Weary of martial law, the demands of the citizens of New Orleans for a return to normality grew louder with each passing day. Early in February, whispers spread through the city that a peace treaty had been signed in Ghent, signaling the end of the war. This news, many believed, would surely lead to the lifting of the decree. The whispers grew louder, and it became clear to all that indeed, the war was over. All except one man, the only man that mattered. Without any official confirmation, Jackson stood his ground.[692]

Additionally, Jackson sought to suppress the circulation of this "inflammatory" report in the newspapers—a decision that only attracted more criticism for "muzzling" the press. By the month's end, the Louisiana militia was on the brink of mutiny. In desperation, Governor Claiborne urged Jackson to allow their discharge, but Jackson steadfastly refused, adding a layer of enmity now with his former ally Claiborne. But Jackson would not revoke the decree until March 13, when official word of the peace treaty's ratification finally arrived. [693]

In fact, the treaty had been unanimously ratified by both sides on Feb. 17th, and went into effect on that date. But the news took longer to reach New Orleans. In the meantime, Jackon was particularly hard on the French Creoles, whom he still distrusted. Federal judge Dominick Hall had a particular distaste for the General in his staunch refusal to end his strict control of the city.[694]

---

[692] Deutsch, Eberhard P., "The United States Versus Major General Andrew Jackson," Louisiana Bar, New Orleans, Sept. 1960, p. 967.
[693] Parton, *Jackson*, II, p. 311.
[694] AJ to Arbuckle, March 5, 1815,

On the other side of the lines, knowing nothing of the success of the negotiations at Ghent, General Lambert was obliged to consider his next move. It was inconceivable that his army should return to England without any attempt to efface the disaster at New Orleans. His men were despondent: "A solid carelessness, a sort of indifference as to what might happen" had followed defeat and exhaustion. A successful operation was essential to restore the men's spirits. On January 28th, at a conference on board the *Tonnant*, Lambert revealed his intention: he would land the army on Dauphine Island, at the entrance to Mobile Bay, and take possession of Fort Bowyer. From there "He would consider how far it would be of advantage to attack the town of Mobile." [695]

Contrary to the accounts of later historians, the British command still had no firm intention to renew the campaign against New Orleans. Nevertheless, the reinforcement of troops and artillery received before he quit Lake Borgne, might have tempted Lambert to make an attempt by the land route, if the war had continued.

On January 25, the British fleet, filled with wounded soldiers and the dead, left Lake Borgne. Nearby, some of the enslaved population gathered at Lambert's headquarters, hoping to be allowed to leave with the British, but in keeping with Lambert's approach to the issue, most of them were turned away. Cochrane's fleet did not go home and lick its wounds, however. As far as the Admiral knew, the war was still on. Instead, they headed for Fort Bowyer, commanded by Major William Lawrence. On February 7th, the British launched a second attack on Fort Bowyer, this time concentrating all their resources on the fort. Surrounding and bombarding the seaward side with warships, the British decimated the fort, but the Americans held out. The next day, General Lambert landed seven miles east of the fort with close to 5,000 troops and artillerymen. Almost immediately, Royal Engineer Colonel Burgoyne began constructing a 100-yard siege line, despite coming under constant fire from American defenders. Although they lost ten men, the British completed the line, which soon housed eleven guns and three Congreve rockets.

On February 6, the gales having died down, the fleet left the anchorage. Two days later, while Keane landed the remainder of the

---

[695] Arthur, 290.

army on Dauphine Island, Lambert led the second brigade against the fort. The choice of the 4th, 21st and 44th regiments for this task was clearly a deliberate effort to enable them to regain their confidence and to provide an opportunity for the 44th to redeem its tarnished reputation. By noon on the 8th, the three regiments had been put ashore on Mobile Pointe, a barren, sandy spit of land sparsely dotted with pine trees, about 3 miles from the fort.

A series of sandhills provided good cover to within 200 yards of the defenses and after a reconnaissance, Dickson began to land his artillery. Burgoyne set his engineers to dig formal siege works. Lambert intended to take his time, avoid unnecessary casualties, and take no risks of failure. Admiral Cochrane launched a renewed against the fort on the morning of the 11th. Dickson had four 18 pounders, two 6-pounders, two heavy howitzers, and eight mortars in position, and Burgoyne took his trenches to within 25 yards of the fort.[696] With the embarrassment and pain of Chalmette fueling them, the British sought to shake defeat from their minds.

At ten o'clock on Feb. 12th, after a fierce bombardment, General Lambert had the terms of surrender drafted and sent Harry Smith under a flag of truce to demand the capitulation of the fort and garrison. In the event of refusal, the women and children were to be allowed to leave under Lambert's personal guarantee of safety. Smith presented the terms to the American defenders of the fort and urged them to give up the fight, to prevent unnecessary bloodshed. The British remained in their positions with guns manned at the batteries.

The American commander, Colonel William Lawrence, asked for two hours to consider the terms. At 12 o'clock he accepted them. After valiantly resisting against a vastly superior British force, Lawrence, realizing his precarious situation, surrendered himself and his 400 men. At midday the American garrison, the majority of whom were from the second U.S. infantry, marched out and laid down their arms. Dickson reported, "They were very dirty, and both in dress and appearance looked much like Spaniards."[697] Among them were twenty women and sixteen children. Dickson took charge of the captured artillery, 22

---

[696] ibid, 292.
[697] Ibid, 293.

pieces including three 32-pounders. Later that day, a force of a thousand Americans was sent from Mobile to relieve the fort but withdrew on learning that it had been surrounded.[698]

Major Lawrence's surrender of the fort was an action which Jackson, upon hearing the news, unaware of the circumstances, condemned as an act of cowardice. But Lawrence's five-day holdout was actually quite a feat, considering the odds against him. And this feat turned out to be vital, for the fort held out long enough to delay the British plans for capturing Mobile, and the British soon discovered that their victory and capture of Fort Bowyer was futile. The following day, February 13th, the frigate *Brazen* arrived from England with the news; the peace had been signed at Ghent on December 24.[699] Just when the British were finally set to embark on another mainland invasion and advance into Mobile, news of the Treaty of Ghent signaled the end of hostilities between the Americans and the British.

The King's forces were headed home at long last, marking the conclusion of the final campaign of the War of 1812. By early March, the unfortunate expedition returned to England. Soon after, an American court of inquiry met, and Lawrence was cleared of any wrongdoing regarding the surrender of Fort Bowyer. Until confirmation arrived that the treaty had been ratified by Congress, the war was not officially ended, but no one doubted that official confirmation would soon follow.

Meanwhile, news of the British capture of Fort Bowyer on February 11th was more than enough justification for Jackson's safety concerns to be turned up a notch. Mercifully, news of the peace treaty signed between the British and the United States reached Jackson as well from the British fleet. While he communicated this to the citizens amidst a frenzy of cheers, he urged them not to become complacent and to remain alert to possible deception, reminding them that the treaty still required ratification by the President, Congress and the British Prince Regent. To Jackson, a continuation of martial law was simply not open for debate.

The restless volunteers in Jackson's army, however, had grown painfully weary of military life. Their three months of service had expired, and they sought to be discharged. But Jackson refused to consider their

---

[698] Heidler, 2004. p. 358.
[699] Tucker, 2012, p. 20.

request until word of the ratification came through. Imploring his men to maintain their vigilance and discipline, his entreaties began to fall on deaf ears increasingly as the days passed. The troops were done with war, they were tired of being away from home, they missed their loved ones, and their demands increased for a return to civilian life.

The situation became exacerbated further when rumors spread that Jackson would destroy property, even burn the city, to keep it from the enemy. The governor, legislature, and civil authorities grew fearful of what he might be capable of. They were particularly resentful of his continuation of martial law. The love between city and general had clearly dissipated, and as the days passed, civil discontent escalated from whispers to shouts. Soon, the once heroic Jackson was being labeled a tyrant and a despot. Tensions increased further as both Jackson and the civil government struggled with the issue of nearly 200 runaway slaves seeking refuge with the British army. Extensive correspondence between Jackson and General Lambert ensued over the matter, but the generals were unable to reach an agreement. When the generals could not resolve the matter, the governor and legislature decided to step in.[700]

To Jackson, this constituted an unnecessary intrusion into a military matter, and he made it clear that he would not stand for it. "I do hope that the legislature, nor yourself," he wrote Governor Claiborne "will not attempt anything like negotiating or having any communication with the enemy, that is the subject on which you nor the legislature as such has any power over… Be assured, if either of the assembly or yourself attempt to interfere with subjects not belonging to you, it will be immediately arrested."[701]

To prevent the legislature from forming a commission to negotiate with the British, Jackson urgently sent Edward Livingston, Manuel White, and R.D. Shepherd to General Lambert. Their mission was to reclaim the slaves and organize an exchange of prisoners. In the meantime, the legislature expressed its growing dissatisfaction with Jackson by passing a resolution on February 2, thanking all the prominent army officers involved in the Battle of New Orleans—excluding the commander-in-chief himself. Adair, Carol, Coffee, Hines, and Thomas received

---

[700] Jackson, *Correspondence*, II, 151.
[701] AJ to Claiborne, Feb. 3, 1815, Jackson Papers, LC.

the legislature's gratitude, delivered through Governor Claiborne. The General paid no attention to the snub. The blatant omission did not go unnoticed, however; its intention and impact were clear to all involved. This caused outrage among General Coffee and others, who expressed their disdain for the omission, emphasizing Jackson's leadership and the collective success achieved under his command.

By that time, Jackson was far too entangled in the jealousies, quarrels, and general public criticism which followed victory, to concern himself with the dubious rights of plantation owners. Local leaders then hit upon another scheme. Registering themselves as French citizens with the French consul, Chevalier de Toussard, they demanded discharge from military service for reasons of their foreign nationality. Many French subjects in the army, not yet naturalized as citizens, hoped this route would be their ticket out. When word of the sheer volume of discharge requests reached Jackson, however, alarm bells were set off, and his suspicions regarding the disloyalty of the French nationals returned. Jackson's Feb. 28th response was in keeping with his willful approach throughout the war; he issued an order expelling French nationals from the city, including Consul Toussard himself.

The reaction, of course, was widespread and immediate; it ignited no small amount of panic among the predominantly French-speaking population. According to the decree, the French-speaking population of New Orleans had three days to leave the city, and had to keep to a distance of 120 miles from the city until news of the ratification of the peace treaty had been officially published.[702] The voter registration lists for the last election were used to determine who were American citizens, and who were not. Those who had voted were compelled to serve in the militia; the others, claiming French citizenship, were ordered out of the city.[703]

The public outcry grew throughout New Orleans, culminating in a newspaper article urging citizens to seek justice through the civil courts rather than through military tribunals. The word was out that going through Jackson was no route to fairness. The article in question had appeared in the French language newspaper, *la Courriere de la Louisiana*,

---

[702] Extract from a General Order, Feb. 28, 1815, in Jackson, *Correspondence*, 181.

[703] Gayarre, *History of Louisiana*, IV, p. 585.

and it was signed by "A Citizen of Louisiana of French origin," which boldly and forcefully criticized Jackson's order of expulsion. "It is high time," the writer said, "the laws should resume their empire; that the citizens of this state should return to the full enjoyment of their rights; that, in acknowledging that we are indebted to General Jackson for the preservation of our city, and the defeat of the British, we do not feel much inclined, through gratitude, to sacrifice any of our privileges, and, less than any other, that of expressing our opinion of the act of his administration. Persons accused of crimes should be brought before civil judges," the writer continued, "not military or special tribunal. The moment for moderation has arrived. With the enemy gone, Jackson's acts of authority are no longer compatible with our dignity and our oath of making the constitution respected." [704]

Jackson was characteristically irate about the blatant challenge to his authority. He summoned the newspaper editor and demanded to know who wrote the controversial article. The editor revealed that it was Louis Louailler, a legislator and strong supporter of the war. Two days later, Jackson sent a group of soldiers to arrest Louailler for inciting mutiny and discontent within the army. The soldiers found him walking along the levee near the Exchange Coffeehouse. The officer in charge approached him, tapped him on the shoulder, and informed him that he was under arrest, urging him to comply peacefully.

Louailler did not go quietly. He shouted loudly to a group of onlookers that armed men were seizing him, claiming they were using police state tactics. A lawyer in the crowd heard his cries and stepped forward to help. The lawyer quickly went to the home of the federal district judge Dominic Augustine Hall and requested a writ of habeas corpus for Louailler. Like many others in New Orleans, Hall believed that an end to martial law was necessary, and he saw this as a chance to reaffirm civil authority. He quickly approved the petition, ordering Louailler to appear in court at 11 o'clock the following day.

When this writ was handed to him, Jackson responded with a scoff, and an order of his own. "Having received information that Dominic A. Hall has been engaged in abiding, abetting and inciting mutiny within my camp," he wrote Colonel Matthew Arbuckle, "you will forthwith

---

[704] Parton, *Jackson*, II, p. 311.

order from your regiment, a detachment to arrest and confine him, and make report of the same to headquarters."[705]

Jackson clearly overstepped his bounds in his response. To the people of the Crescent City, the General now bordered on the ludicrous, reactionary in the extreme. Still, the order was quickly executed, and by evening, Hall was confined in the same barracks as Louailler. From that day on until the end of his life, Jackson felt he was justified in locking up Judge Hall. Later on, in a biography that he was aware of and actively participated in, the General justified his actions through the words of the biographer. "He did it.... to silence opposition and satisfy the refractory and designing that judicial interference should not mark the execution of his plans, or for the screen, behind which treason might stalk unmolested. He did it to make the example factual, and to obtain, through fear, that security, which could not be had through love of country."[706]

On multiple occasions, to the disdain of the inhabitants of New Orleans, Jackson employed fear as a tactic to achieve his goals. With a shrill voice, and "hawk-like" demeanor in the stark penetrating effect of his eyes, Jackson was well-aware that his countenance was particularly effective at instilling terror in his victims. In New Orleans, there were several instances where his 'reign of terror' was evident; rumors of criticism prompted him to bring as many as one hundred soldiers to arrest individuals for insubordination and mutiny. This pattern repeated itself frequently. Jackson effectively established a police state, operating solely under his own authority, clearly overstepping his bounds.

The city had been transformed into an armed camp, even with so many aware—though not officially—that the war was over. The security in and around New Orleans turned a charming city into a military stronghold, guarded like Fort Knox. Each time the people demanded an end to Jackson's oppressive rule, he responded by tightening his grip further. Efforts to hold meetings protesting his violations of constitutional rights faced heavy repression, as Jackson deployed his troops to stifle these movements. Locals began discussing the idea of forming a secret military battalion to uphold judicial authority, but these talks remained

---

[705] AJ to Arbuckle, March 5, 1815, Jackson Papers, LC.
[706] Reid and Eaton, *Jackson*, p. 381.

nothing more than gossip in coffee shops, including an incident where a portrait of Jackson was destroyed in a public venue. [707]

The situation had deteriorated to the point in which a courier from Washington delivered semi-official news of the war's end—despite Jackson's personal belief that a treaty had indeed been signed—Old Hickory still refused to relinquish his military power, focusing on the "semi-official" nature of the news. The people were left with no choice but to endure the harshness of his 'unwavering sense of duty.' [708]

Louailler's court-martial ended in his acquittal. The legislator had challenged the authority of the military court since he was not a member of the militia or army, and the court accepted his argument. Regarding the charge of espionage, the court found it absurd that a spy would openly share his opinions in a newspaper. However, Jackson strongly disagreed with the court's ruling and chose to keep Louailler imprisoned, overruling the court's decision, fanning the flames against those who were already outraged by his "despotism" and abuse of power. Realizing that trying to convict Judge Hall was futile, Jackson ordered him out of the city with instructions not to return until peace was officially declared, or the British had left the southern coast. "I have thought proper to send you beyond the limits of my camp," Jackson informed Hall, "to prevent you from a repetition of the improper behavior for which you have been imprisoned and confined."[709]

On Sunday, March 12th, a small group of soldiers marched Judge Hall four miles beyond New Orleans—outside the limits of Jackson's camp—and set him free. Jackson's extreme militarism had reached alarming heights. His behavior was erratic at best, extremely dangerous in reality. While one could justify certain actions when defending a city facing clear danger, the General's blatant disregard for civil and judicial authority—especially when he knew the war was effectively over—was unjustifiable.

To the Creole population of New Orleans especially, Jackson's treatment seemed motivated by his resentments, ego, and a general dislike for the Creole lifestyle, or as some claimed, his nativist tendencies, his disdain for their "foreignness." At any rate, Jackson's approach reeked

---

[707] Nolte, *Fifty Years*, p. 599.
[708] AJ to Lambert, March 6, 1815, Jackson, *Correspondence*, II: p. 184.
[709] Jackson's Order to D.A. Hall, March 11, 1815, Jackson, *Correspondence*, p. 189.

of personal vendetta, and rather than defusing the hostilities between civil and military authority, Jackson threw gasoline on the fire. The only explanation lay in his belief that he was doing his duty, his due diligence, an obsessive allegiance to his own personal code, which dictated that he could only relinquish his power once he received official confirmation of peace or a replacement. His grip on control had reached almost comical proportions. It wasn't until he was officially relieved of that duty that he could step back and recognize authorities beyond his own.

Yet, Jackson's actions were far from humorous. He acted in an overbearing, bullying, reckless and bizarre manner, with a total disregard for civil and judicial authority—along with individual legal and constitutional rights. This is difficult to justify, especially when he had near certainty that the war was over. The people were inexorably at the mercy of one man.

CHAPTER

48

PEACE

"Dearly as I value peace, and much as I know it is needed and desired by our Country, I pledge myself to you that you shall never see my name to a treaty, no, nor to any one stipulation that shall give you cause to blush for your country or for your friend."

-John Quincy Adams

The following day, Monday, March 13, 1815, the long-awaited official confirmation of the peace treaty's ratification arrived from Washington, along with copies of the treaty and the ratification results. Shockingly to the people of New Orleans, Jackson let go of his dictatorial power without an instant's hesitation. Without a second thought, Jackson gave up his tyrannical control. Military law was lifted, trade was allowed to resume, military offenses were pardoned, and everyone held for military crimes were released. It was a strange contradiction in Jackson's character that he could take absolute power and then, moments later, surrender it with seemingly no self-awareness of the frustrations he had caused others. Somehow, fused within Jackson's personality, was the dichotomy of ruthless acrimony one moment, and then amity the next, with no sign of regret or guilt.

Apparently, Jackson felt he had made his point. His will had been proven, and now, perhaps sensing his grip on the city had grown to outlandish proportions, Jackson wished to show he was a man of his word. Louaillier was promptly released, Hall and Toussard were returned to the city amid cheers and acclaim. The next day, the dedicated militia and volunteers from Tennessee, Louisiana, Kentucky, and Mississippi were dismissed with heartfelt praise from their commanding officer.

"Go then, my brave companions," said Old Hickory, "... full of honor, and crowned with laurels, which will never fade... Farewell, fellow soldiers, the expression of your general's thanks is feeble, but the gratitude of the country of freemen is yours—yours the applause of an admiring world." [710]

It had a nice turn, this farewell address. Its sincerity was clear and heartfelt. As far as his soldiers were concerned, Jackson was a hero, a great leader who won battles and who always shared the credit of those victories with them. Even the Louisianians admired him for that. The officers of the city battalion extended Jackson a warm and glowing tribute, grateful that he had "allowed us the endearing title of your brothers and arms." They referred to the retention of martial law, although they sidestepped the issue by leaving it to others, they said, "the task of declaiming about privileges and constitutional rights; we are content with having fought in support of them."

Jackson's reply was carefully worded: "Whenever the invaluable rights which we enjoy under our happy constitution are threatened by invasion, privileges the most dear, and which, in ordinary times, ought to be regarded as the most sacred, may be required to be infringed for their security. At such a crisis, we only have to determine whether we will suspend, for a time, the exercise of the latter, that we may enjoy the permanent enjoyment of the former. It is wise, in such a moment, to sacrifice the spirit of the laws to the letter, and by adhering too strictly to the letter, lose the *substance* forever, in order that we may, for an instant, preserve the *shadow*? Private property is held sacred in all good governments, and particularly in our own, yet, shall the fear of invading it prevent a general from marching his army over a corn-field, or burning a house which protects the enemy? A thousand other instances might be cited to show that laws must sometimes be silent when necessity speaks." [711]

---

[710] Latour, *Historical Memoir*, p. ciii
[711] Ibid, cxvi.

Jackson's coldly pragmatic defense of his actions articulated a soldier's contention that the good of his country trumped all other considerations. It is the sort of argument that can justify egregious errors in judgment, but also noble acts of patriotism. It was Jefferson's argument in overcoming his constitutional scruples about purchasing Louisiana, and now it was Jackson's argument in defense of his treatment of the inhabitants of Louisiana. Clearly to Jackson, however, in times of war, military authority trumped civil authority in every scenario.

For the next few days, the city of New Orleans was finally able to celebrate fully, and it joyfully toasted its freedom, freedom from General Andrew Jackson, as well as from the British. Now that the hardship was over and Old Hickory had 'voluntarily' ended martial law, the people seemed to forgive him his harshness and reminded themselves that after all he had saved the city and brought honor to them and to the country. Let the worst be forgotten.

But one Louisianian who did not forget was Judge Dominic A. Hall. Tensions had continued to simmer since the judge's release, and now they would increase to a boiling point when Jackson was summoned to appear before Hall for contempt of court. Waiting until most of the rejoicing had ended, Hall issued the order on March 21st to show cause why Andrew Jackson should not be held in contempt for refusing to obey the writ of habeas corpus issued in the case of Louis Louallier. To Jackson and his counsel, Hall was clearly retaliating for his own arrest, imprisonment, and exile from the city. In this instance, Jackson had a valid complaint. By "becoming the prosecutor in arbiter of his own grievances," Hall placed himself directly in the situation, in a conflict of interests, "where reason could have but little agency, calculated to do injustice, and attached to his decision, suspicion and censure."[712] Jackson believed a trial by jury the better instrument of justice, considering the judge's own involvement in the case.

Nevertheless, on Friday, March 24, 1815, at 10:00 AM, as directed, Andrew Jackson, strode to the courthouse with a commanding presence surrounded by his legal team. Dressed in civilian attire, the General walked tall alongside his aide, Major Reid, and his legal counsel, Edward Livingston and Abner L. Duncan. The public's reaction was fierce, with

---

[712] Reid and Eaton, *Jackson*, p. 384.

a large crowd gathering outside the courthouse, with some of the largely pro-Jackson supporters even threatening violence against the judge. The boisterous crowd cheered Jackson's appearance and gave the judge cause for alarm. At one point, the pirate Dominique You even sidled up to the hero. "General," he whispered, "say the word and we pitch the judge and the bloody courthouse in the river." Jackson shook his head, then reassured the judge in a typical Jacksonian announcement. "There is no danger here," he intoned, "... The same arm that protected from outrage this city... will shield and protect this court or perish in the effort." [713] The former judge knew how to operate within the confines of a courtroom, and the celebrity in Jackson knew how to win in the arena of public perception.

So began the celebrated trial, *United States vs. Major General Andrew Jackson*. As soon as the court had come to order, the defense raised objections to the propriety and legality of the proceedings, all of which Hall overruled. Nor would the judge permit the reading of a prepared statement explaining why the General could not validly be held in contempt. "The ears of the court were closed against everything, of argument, or reason," Jackson complained. [714]

The case was continued on the following Friday, when Jackson again appeared before Judge Hall and was asked nineteen specific questions concerning his actions and his handling of the writ. The two strong minded, willful men glared at each other. Then, very deliberately, Jackson replied, speaking guardedly, but firmly.

"I will not answer interrogatories, "he said. "When called upon to show cause why an attachment for contempt of this court ought not to run against me, I offered to do so... You would not hear my defense.... Under the circumstances, I appear before your honor to receive the sentence of the court, and with nothing further to add. Your honor will not understand me as meaning any disrespect to the court by the remarks I make; but as no opportunity has been furnished me to explain the reasons and motives which influenced my conduct, so it is expected that censure will form no part of the punishment which your honor may imagine it Your duty to perform." [715]

---

[713] *Niles Weekly Register*, June 3, 10, 1815.
[714] Reid and Eaton, *Jackson*, pp. 386-387.
[715] Statement in John Reid's hand, Jackson Papers, LC.

It was a dignified and astute protest, one that revealed Jackson's legal background and experience, and it placated matters. It was an rational approach that the wise and urbane Judge Hall appreciated. The judge responded in like manner, skipping the formalities and imposing a fine of $1000--which he stated he found an unpleasant duty in view of the General's services to the country.[716] In consideration of the services, he would not send Jackson to jail. Then he said something fundamental about the institutions of the American government. "The only question," Hall said, "was whether the law should bend to the general or the general to the law."[717] But Jackson argued that he had never claimed the law should bend to his will. Under martial rule, he was the law, and he believed himself justified in declaring it. Period.

Jackson paid the fine, much as it may have distressed him to do so, and the principle of it was one he would never forget. He was not prepared to defy Hall; he did not wish to taint his victory any further with a petty quarrel that he was certain to lose. This business had already run on too long, and the General was anxious to have done with it. In the final display of spirit, he refused to accept $1000 raised by popular subscription and, in a gesture of good will, requested that the sum be distributed among the families of soldiers who died in defense of the city.

When the courtroom proceedings concluded, friends of Jackson crowded around him and hurried him to his carriage. A line of people formed, unhitched the carriage from his horses, and dragged the carriage to the coffee house "amidst the huzzas" and approving shouts of a large gathering of people who trailed behind him.[718] His brief role as tyrant had been forgotten by the frenzied crowd that now hailed him as their hero. Once again he was the savior of New Orleans.

Relieved by this display of the public regard and gratitude for his exertions in their defense, Jackson turned to the crowd and gestured for silence. "I have," he said, "during the invasion exerted every one of my faculties for the defense and preservation of the constitution and the laws. On this day, I have been called on to submit to their operation under the circumstances which many persons might have thought sufficient to justify resistance. Considering obedience to the laws, even when we

---

[716] *The Louisiana Historical Quarterly*, Oct. 1922, V, 511.
[717] *Niles Weekly Register*, June 15, 1815.; Bassett, *Jackson*, p. 229.
[718] Reid and Eaton, *Jackson*, p. 387.

think them unjustly applied, as the first duty of the citizen, I did not hesitate to comply with the sentence you have heard, and I can treat you to remember the example I have given you of respectful submission to the administration of justice."[719] It was sound, fatherly advice, but with none of the thunder the crowd expected.

When the administration in Washington learned of Jackson's brush with civilian authority, it mildly reproved him for it. "The president instructs me to take this opportunity," wrote the new acting secretary of war, Alexander J. Dallas, "requesting that a conciliatory comportment be observed towards the state authorities and citizens of New Orleans."[720] Jackson took no notice of this rebuke, and the entire matter was soon forgotten. Thirty years later a grateful and partisan Congress remitted the fund and Jackson was pleased to accept both principal and interest.

The General's final days in New Orleans, prior to his return home, were spent quietly in the relaxed company of his family. A few days after the announcement of peace, Rachel and their adopted son, Andrew, finally arrived in New Orleans, much to the General's delight. Rachel was now an extremely stout, dark complexioned, 47-year-old woman, religious to the point of fanaticism, yet warm and gently beguiling. During Jackson's long absence from the Hermitage, she had recently been forced to manage the plantation, and her appearance now reflected the many hours she had spent outdoors under the Tennessee sun. Homely dress and speech, every inch the farmer's wife, she hardly seemed the mate of so distinguished and commanding a figure as Andrew Jackson. On occasion, the General reminded her of her new status and its obligations. "You must recollect," he told her, "that you are now a Major General's lady--in the service of the U.S., and as such, you must appear elegant, and plain, not extravagant--but in such stile as strangers expect to see you."

Rachel felt uncomfortable and inhibited among the elegant Creole ladies of New Orleans; she confessed to Mrs. Livingston that she was "ignorant to fine clothes and fine company," for she had never before visited a city larger than Nashville. In time she came to regard New Orleans with some disdain, as a veritable "'Babylon on the Mississippi,'

---

[719] Gayarre, *History of Louisiana*, IV, p. 625.
[720] Dallas to AJ, April 12, 1815, Jackson, *Correspondence*, II, 204.

given over totally to dissipation, and the delights of the flesh. Oh, the wickedness, the idolatry of this place! Unspeakable the riches and splendor. So much amusement balls, concerts, Plays theaters, etc. but we don't attend the half of them" she told one of her relatives in Tennessee.[721]

Mrs. Livingston took Rachel under her wing and arranged a selection of suitable dresses for the wife of the city's distinguished hero. Shortly after Jackson lifted his censorship of the press, a derisive editorial cartoon depicted a short and stout Rachel standing on a table while Mrs. Livingston tugged at the strings of her stays, trying to create a waist where a waist had once existed. The fashionable ladies of New Orleans were rather amused by Rachel's country ways and tastes, but they later warmed to her gentle disposition and kindliness. Their conversion from sly amusement to genuine affection, was marked by their presentation to her of a set of topaz jewelry. To the General, the ladies awarded a handsome and quite valuable diamond pin. Gallant to a fault, Jackson gushed his thanks. "The world heaps many honors on me," he said to them, "but none is greater than this." [722]

At one grand ball, complete with transparencies, flowers, colored lamps, sumptuous dinner, and dancing, Rachel could scarcely believe such splendor possible. At dinner, she was placed opposite a transparency that read "Jackson and Victory: they are but one." When the meal ended, Jackson and his wife led the way to the ballroom and they treated the guests to "a most delicious 'pas de deux', country style. As one New Orleans editorial mockingly put it, "To see these two figures, the General, a long, haggard man, with limbs like a skeleton, and madame la General a short, fat dumpling, bobbing opposite each other, like half drunken Indians, to the wild melody of 'possum up de Gumtree,' and endeavoring to make a spring into the air, was very remarkable, and far more edifying a spectacle than any European ballet could possibly have furnished." [723]

These final days in New Orleans were relatively happy ones for Jackson. He could relax and enjoy playing the role of hero and savior. The old animosities toward the tyrant had dissipated with hardly a trace; only a few continued to harp on his former high handedness in ruling the

---

[721] AJ to Rachel, Aug. 10, 1814. Jackson Papers, LC.
[722] Parton, *Jackson*, II, pp. 323-324.
[723] Nolte, *Fifty Years*, p. 238.

city. The presence of little Andrew, Jr. also cheered him. Having been an absent father for so long, Jackson spent many leisurely moments with his son and of course denied him nothing. On one occasion, a crowd of soldiers congregated outside his headquarters and shouted to him to come to the window and acknowledge their cheers. Just then little Andrew, who had been asleep in an adjoining room, heard the noise outside and started to cry. The General, on his way to the window to greet the soldiers, heard his son's cries and paused for a moment, unsure which summons to obey. Then he rushed to the child's bedside, caught him in his arms, quieted his fears, and carried him to the window, where he bowed to his men, all the while distracting the child from his fright by laughing over the noisy actions of the soldiers below. [724]

Jackson undoubtedly felt guilty about his long absences from home and the limited time he could devote to the child when they were together. Already he had begun to spoil his son; in later years young Andrew had trouble developing into a mature, responsible adult. Jackson's own fatherless early life, the lack of sustained parental guidance, and the resulting aimlessness of his formative years, may have encouraged him to dote on the child, to spoil him with extravagances. Moreover, he was an older man, just turned forty-eight, away for most of the boy's young life, and probably struggled as a father. Then, too, Jackson was now a famous man, accustomed to command and deference, and surrounded constantly by aides and hangers on. To the child, his presence came was a happening everywhere he went, full of attention and scenes of agitation and activity, cheering crowds and saluting soldiers. Under these circumstances, a normal father-son relationship would be difficult to achieve at best. Andrew, Jr. was certainly awed by his father and was reportedly respectful and obedient. He found favor when "he behaved like a soldier "and he was always reminded to act like one.[725] But as with many children of famous fathers, the son could not always handle the notoriety in the obligations of distinction. For much of his adolescent and early adult year, Andrew Jr. proved to be irresponsible, and ambitionless, and was, for a time, a considerable disappointment to his father.

---

[724] Parton, Jackson, II, pp. 324-325.
[725] AJ to Coffee, April 24, 1815, Jackson Papers, LC.

Before leaving New Orleans, Jackson presented his aide, Edward Livingston, with a miniature of himself and a letter of appreciation for his personal services and his invaluable assistance in the defense of the city. To Livingston's daughter, the general presented a brooch and a pretty note full of gallant remarks about how much she had brightened his stay in New Orleans. There were other gifts expressive of his gratitude as he prepared to depart the city. Arrangements were made to turn over the detailed work of his command to Edmond P. Gaines, and on April 6, 1815, together with his family, Jackson boarded a ship and headed home.

It was difficult to leave New Orleans. The city was the scene of his greatest triumph, and the acknowledgments he had received for his stupendous feet and gratified his need for recognition and applause. "We left Orleans on the 6th amid the lamentations and benedictions of whites, blacks, and half breeds, of men, women and children," John Reid reported "One hundred dinners, tendered to the general and his staff, consisting of 40 dishes, each, and many and many a bottle of wine."[726] But the victory was over. It was time to move on.

Despite Jackson's delays in ending the state of war in New Orleans, mercifully, and at long last, the Second War of Independence (as many considered the War of 1812) was over. With Congress' ratification of the Treaty of Ghent, and with the people of New Orleans finally able to resume life as normal, wartime tensions finally ceased. After nearly three long and tumultuous years of bloodshed, the last ever armed conflict between the Mother Country and her former colonies was concluded once and for all.

Throughout the long and harrowing negotiations in the city Ghent, Great Britain had categorically refused to recognize any American claims to territory along the Gulf Coast. The British correctly disputed the legality of the Louisiana Purchase. According to the 1800 Treaty of San Ildefonso, which Napoleon forced Spain imperiously to accept, France couldn't sell Louisiana to the United States without first offering it back to Spain. When Napoleon ignored this agreement and sold Louisiana

---

[726] Reid to John Williams, April, 1815, Reid Papers, LC.

to the U.S., many nations, beginning with Great Britain, viewed this action as illegal and unjust.

From the British perspective, the lower Mississippi, New Orleans, and the Gulf Coast did not rightfully belong to the United States. By invading Louisiana and seizing New Orleans, Britain likely intended to give the area back to Spain, its rightful owner. The treaty of Ghent, which ended the war, did not imply any acceptance of the Louisiana Purchase's terms; in fact, Louisiana was not addressed in the treaty at all. Although the U.S. claimed West Florida as part of the Louisiana Purchase, they hesitated to take control until hostilities began.

Consequently, Mobile was not included in the treaty either, from the British viewpoint, and would likely have been returned to Spain if the invasion had established a strong presence on the Gulf Coast.[727] In fact, Spanish representatives claimed they were assured that all of Louisiana and West Florida would revert to Spain after the war.[728] Even as late as April 1815, Spain, believing that Pakenham had defeated Jackson at New Orleans, asked Britain to keep the areas they had occupied despite the Treaty of Ghent and return them to Spain. [729]

Jackson's role in the War of 1812 was vital for the future expansion of the United States. He not only helped prevent a significant loss of territory in the Southwest but also set the stage for the nation's growth in the years to come. Despite the mistakes he made in his command, in the end, Jackson prioritized protecting the city and repelling the British invasion. He displayed singular determination, courage and self-sacrifice for the cause. He had achieved a most significant victory, despite all the odds against him, inspiring his troops with his bravery and his pluck. Much of the command flaws he made could be chalked up to inexperience. No, he had not yet proven himself to be a master strategist, but he understood the bottom line, to get the job done, and he was willing to do whatever it took, within his power, to complete the mission.

Secretary of War James Monroe explained the situation in the southwest clearly to President Madison.[730] If Jackson's army had fallen to the British at New Orleans, the Crown would have ensured that the

---

[727] Rogin, *Fathers and Children*, p. 169.
[728] Ibid, p. 170.
[729] Jackson, *Correspondence*, II, 216-217.
[730] Monroe to Madison, May 3, 1815, Monroe Papers, LOC.

United States understood that the entire Gulf Coast was the rightful property of Spain. The British would have argued that the Treaty of Ghent did not apply in this region, since American claims were unlawfully gained, with Mobile having been illegally seized, and Louisiana illegally purchased.[731] The victory achieved by Jackson extended beyond the mere display of American military prowess on the battlefield. It served as a crucial barrier against the potential secession of the entire Gulf Coast region, and possibly even Louisiana, from the United States. Such a loss would have constituted a significant disaster for the nation. Thus, Jackson's triumph can be seen as not only a military success but also as a validation of the Louisiana Purchase, a transaction that many argued France had no rightful authority to undertake in the first place. Thus, Jackson's victory effectively legitimized the acquisition of territory that was fraught with controversy regarding its rightful ownership.

Fortunately, for the United States, the British did not capture Fort Bowyer until after the war had been concluded. The fort's seizure made the capture of Mobile an inevitability. The city could not have held out long under a British siege, much less a direct attack. General James Winchester, who was in charge of the Mobile forces, chose to resign with the news of the capture of Fort Bowyer, rather than risk another embarrassing surrender, especially since he had already surrendered one army to the British in Canada. The loss of Mobile would have allowed a significant British army, led by Lambert with over 6,000 trained soldiers, to establish a presence on the American continent. This could have led to further attacks into the interior of the country and potentially a renewed assault on New Orleans, this time over land. Furthermore, since Britain did not view Mobile as covered by the Treaty of Ghent, they could have opted not to surrender it, possibly keeping Mobile as a strategic stronghold similar to Gibraltar in the western hemisphere.

How different the American South might have been had any of this played out differently. The conclusion of the War of 1812 is often characterized as a stalemate; that neither side emerged as a clear winner or loser, with the peace treaty resulting in a return to the pre-war conditions, known as the status quo ante-bellum. However, this interpretation overlooks significant implications regarding territorial

---

[731] Brown, *Amphibious Campaign*, p. 166-167.

claims. Britain, for its part, did not consider Florida or Louisiana as territories included in the treaty's provisions. General Andrew Jackson's victory, therefore, was far from meaningless. Not only did it provide the psychological boost the country yearned for, but it held considerable importance for American territorial ambitions.

The reality was that a genuine status quo would have involved the restoration of New Orleans and Mobile to Spain. However, since the British did not occupy these regions and the United States continued to control them, one could argue that they were effectively acquired through the conflict. Mobile, in particular, poses an interesting case. The city was captured after the onset of hostilities—well over a year into the war. A true status quo would have necessitated its return to Spanish control. By maintaining possession of Mobile, the United States not only expanded its territorial boundaries but also fueled the nation's desire for further acquisitions, particularly in Florida, ultimately paving the way for the annexation of the entire Gulf Coast.[732]

Due to the lack of an established status quo and the United States' control over the western part of Florida, Spain divided the remaining territory into two sections: east and west, with the Suwanee River serving as the dividing line. The Perdido River became the western boundary of Florida, which is the state border to this day. Additionally, Spain struggled to protect this border area from further American expansion. Between 1810 and 1825, the Spanish Empire faced a series of revolutions in Central and South America, leaving Spain without the resources to maintain any significant authority along the American frontier.

The American victory at New Orleans had another major consequence: it led to the systematic destruction of Native American communities in the South and greatly intensified the loss of their land. This process had already commenced long before the war, but with Jackson's army victorious, and in occupation of much of the South, General Andrew Jackson's presence hastened the process. The war opened up vast tracts of Native American land for American settlers, and this trend of land acquisition would only accelerate once the peace was established.

---

[732] Owsley Jr., F. L., "The Role of the South in the British Grand Strategy in the War of 1812". *Tennessee Historical Quarterly*, 1972, 31 (1): 36.

In a scenario where the British had successfully established a presence along the Gulf Coast, even if only for a short duration, it is plausible that an indigenous buffer state would have been created in the southwestern region. This would have served to impede the westward movement of American settlers and offer a protective barrier for the Spanish territories in Florida. However, even in the absence of a coastal stronghold, the British provided significant military assistance to the Indigenous peoples, actively seeking their cooperation in the conflict against the United States.

To grasp the events that led to the decline of the indigenous peoples of the American South, and their eventual removal, we need to look back at a series of events that began in the spring of 1814. Admiral Cochrane directed Captain Hugh Pigot, serving on the frigate *Orpheus*, to take the vessel *Shelburne* to the mouth of the Apalachicola River. The goal was to establish communication with the Creek Nation in hopes of securing their support for an upcoming invasion. Pigot was also tasked with providing the Creeks with weapons and ammunition, bringing along 2,000 sets of arms and 300,000 rounds of ammunition.[733]

On May 10, 1814, the ships anchored, and a landing party explored the area. Within ten days, nearly a dozen Creek leaders agreed to meet with Pigot. The discussions led to an agreement to station George Woodbine, Brevet Captain of Marines, along with a sergeant and a corporal, on shore to organize the Native groups and distribute the weapons. In his official report to Admiral Cochrane, Captain Pigot highlighted the strong anti-U.S. sentiment among the Creeks and estimated that 2,800 of their brave warriors were ready to assist a British invasion. He noted there was a similar number of Choctaws and 1,000 others in the swamps around Pensacola, in addition to black slaves in Georgia. These groups were willing to offer their support if Britain guaranteed them the necessary arms and supplies.

With their assistance, along with a small contingent of regular troops, Pigot believed that Mobile could be easily captured, which would lead to a takeover of Baton Rouge and then New Orleans. He included a letter from the Creek chiefs in his report, confirming their intention to support a British invasion and push the Americans out of the coastal

---

[733] Mahon, *War of 1812*, pg. 341.

region. This letter was penned just two months after their devastating defeat at Horseshoe Bend, and two months before the signing of the Treaty of Fort Jackson.[734]

Upon receiving the report from Pigot, Admiral Cochrane dispatched Major Edward Nicholls, accompanied by four officers and a contingent of 108 marines, along with arms and ammunition, to the Apalachicola region. The mission was to initiate training for the Creeks and any other allies the British could recruit. Among Nicholls's directives was the task of recruiting as many enslaved individuals as possible, encouraging them to escape from their bondage. He was also charged with surveying the territory west of the Apalachicola River, identifying the challenges related to the capture of New Orleans, and facilitating the recruitment of more Native allies for the forthcoming invasion. Command of the operation was entrusted to Nicholls, with Woodbine serving as his subordinate.

Nicholls was met with great success in his mission concerning the indigenous peoples he encountered, eventually arming over 4,000 braves. He distributed approximately 3,000 muskets, 1,000 pistols, 1,000 carbines, 500 rifles, and more than 1 million rounds of ammunition to the Creek and Seminole tribes. This created a potent threat to the United States' efforts to shore up control of the area; a formidable combined Native American and African American force, armed and ready to fight for George III.

After the New Orleans campaign didn't go as planned, Admiral Cochrane returned his focus to the strategy of attacking through Mobile, aiming to join forces with the Indian Confederation he had been training and supplying for the past six months. However, upon learning that the peace treaty at Ghent had been signed, he called off the invasion.

Nonetheless, alongside supplying the Indian Confederacy with weapons and ammunition, Nicholls, acting on Cochrane's behalf, assured them that the King of England would protect their interests after the war.[735] This promise was included in the Treaty of Ghent. At the urging of the British government, an article was added to the treaty, ensuring

---

[734] Horsman, *War of 1812*, pg. 341.
[735] J. Leitch Wright, Jr. "A Note on the First Seminole War, As Seen by the Indians, Negroes and their British Advisors." *Journal of Southern History*, 1968, Pg. 569.

the rights of their Indian allies. Specifically, Article IX of the treaty stated that the United States had to cease hostilities with the Indians.[736]

It was quite specific. Article IX provided that the United States agreed to end hostilities with the Indians "and forthwith to restore two such tribes... All possessions... Which they have enjoyed or been entitled to in 1811 previous to such hostilities." This article effectively canceled the Treaty of Fort Jackson.[737]

Additionally, many Creek chiefs had refused to sign the Treaty of Fort Jackson (only one chief had actually signed it,) and many had fled to Florida, where they continued to resist. They were still technically at war with the United States. Neither the Red Sticks, nor the British ever recognized the legitimacy of the Treaty of Fort Jackson. However, now that the U.S. had agreed to end the war and both Washington and London accepted the restoration of Indian rights and property to 1811, Cochrane left Nicholls and a group of Marines at Apalachicola to support and protect his allies until the guarantees of Article IX were fully implemented. Moreover, Cochrane reassured the Creeks that the U.S. was obligated by treaty to restore all lands taken from them by Jackson at the end of the Creek War. With that, he departed. [738]

But the Iron General was not about to let the Treaty of Fort Jackson be nullified. That was *his* treaty. The Madison administration might yield to the Creeks, or to the influence of the British, but Andrew Jackson, Old Hickory, Sharp Knife, would not. Jackson insisted that the Creeks had reached a peace agreement with the United States based on his treaty and were therefore not bound by the Treaty of Ghent. He argued that Article IX did not pertain to them. Regardless of what others claimed, this was his perspective, and he was determined to stick to it.

Could Jackson justify such an interpretation? The administration was aware of its treaty obligations, and the Creek chiefs were already expressing their grievances. "I am also desired to say to you by the chiefs," wrote Nicholls to Benjamin Hawkins in May 1815, "that they do not find that your citizens are evacuating their lands, according to

---

[736] Owsley, *Struggle for the Gulf*, Ch. 17; Bradford Perkins, *Castlereagh and Adams, England and the United States*, 1812-1823, Los Angeles, 1968. pp. 71-72, 78, 82.
[737] Israel, Fred, *Major Peace Treaties of Modern History*, 1648-1967, pg. 704.
[738] Cochrane to Malcolm, Feb. 7th, 1815, Cochrane to Nicholls, Feb. 14, 1815, PRO, WO 1/143.

the Ninth Article of the treaty of peace." Reluctantly, the United States government recognized its responsibilities in June 1815, and Jackson was informed accordingly. "Enclosed are copies of the communications from the commissioners assigned to propose peace to the hostile Indians," the Secretary of War wrote to Jackson. "In pursuance of the stipulations of the ninth article of the treaty of Ghent... the President... is confident that you will cooperate with all means in your power to conciliate the Indians, upon the principles of our agreement with Great Britain." [739]

Did Andrew Jackson ever really consider conciliating with the hostile Creeks, or returning their land? Not at all. He disregarded the instructions given to him and believed he knew better about how to handle the situation. He felt the American government had certain responsibilities regarding the Treaty of Ghent, but he decided that the Secretary of War's intentions did not apply to his treaty. As a result, he continued to enforce the terms of the Treaty of Fort Jackson. Despite numerous objections from the Creek chiefs, Jackson persisted in removing the tribes from their territory, and no one intervened. The administration, fearing backlash from the western states and reluctant to rein in a national hero to appease the Native Americans or Great Britain, chose inaction. Thus, Jackson was allowed to carry on with his policy of removal without any interruptions. The outcome of the United States vs. the Creek Nation was dictated by the opinions of one man.

If Jackson's assertions held true, one must consider the implications for the Creeks who rejected the treaty of Fort Jackson in 1814. These individuals, who chose to continue their resistance against the United States, posed a significant question. Sharp Knife provided a clear perspective on this matter. He argued that these Creeks were not within the jurisdiction of the United States; instead, they were located in Florida. Therefore, according to his reasoning, they had not forfeited any property under the provisions established by the Fort Jackson treaty.

The response was flawless and entirely self-serving. It aligned perfectly with western perspectives and expectations, which the government was fully aware of. Consequently, the Madison administration had no choice but to give its official approval. As a result, the United States government accepted Jackson's interpretation and actions, despite breaching its treaty

---

[739] Carter, *Territorial Papers*, pg. 62.

obligations and breaking the law. The travesty of breaching the Treaty of Ghent was not merely a result of the administration acknowledging the western desire to seize Indian lands and the risk of alienating a beloved national figure. Rather, the administration actively endorsed the concept of expansion, choosing to turn a blind eye. It sought the removal of indigenous peoples from their territories and knew that their inactivity would mean an accomplishment of the goal. The nation's growth necessitated the backing of western claims, and national policy effectively barred the safeguarding of Indian property and rights. [740]

A significant issue arose as the government had promised Great Britain to uphold Indian rights and restore possessions taken after 1811. It was expected that the British would demand this guarantee and enforce Article IX of the treaty. However, they did not. England chose to prioritize its northern possessions, effectively betraying both the Spanish and the Indians in the South. To appease American expansionists, it was deemed more advantageous to allow the United States to expand into Spanish and Indian territories in exchange for American abandonment of claims to Canada. If the U.S. agreed to respect the northern border, Britain could overlook the dispossession occurring in the South.

The United States did agree. Within two years, Charles Bagot, the British envoy, and Richard Rush, the acting Secretary of State, signed an agreement on April 28, 1817, the Rush-Bagot Treaty, which neutralized the Great Lakes and established an unfortified border between Canada and the U.S. This agreement not only mandated disarmament on land and sea but also indicated Britain's acceptance of American expansion in the Gulf Coast and Mississippi Valley, signaling an end to any northern aspirations for the U.S. Canada was effectively relinquished.[741]

On October 20, 1818, the two nations further solidified their positions by signing the Anglo-American Convention in London, which established a boundary along the 49th parallel from the Lake of the Woods in Minnesota, to the Rocky Mountains. This agreement allowed joint occupation of the territory west of the Rockies and permanently

---

[740] Fort Jackson Treaty, "Archive of Native American Agreements and Treaties"; *First People Web*; accessed December 2022

[741] Radojewski, Christopher Mark, "The Rush–Bagot Agreement: Canada–US Relations in Transition." *American Review of Canadian Studies* 47.3, 2017: 280–299.

defined the boundary, marking the end of American ambitions in Canada following numerous failed attempts to annex the northern provinces.

The British realized they had betrayed their agreement with the Natives, and admitted that the United States had broken the treaty, and that they should protest. Lord Bathurst, the Secretary for War and Colonies, tried to support the interests of Native Americans, but was overridden. Likewise, Edward Nicholls, who had promised protections for the Creek Nation, urged his government to step in, although he eventually gave up in frustration as Britain ignored his pleas to honor the treaty. The British government refused, however. They had shored up their control of Canada, and the southern territories were thus sacrificed.

In contrast, Andrew Jackson firmly established his position in the South, adamantly opposing the enforcement of Article IX of the treaty by the government. His administration facilitated the seizure of Native American lands and refrained from advocating on their behalf. Jackson stayed committed to the cause, insisting that the expulsion of Spain from Florida, Texas, and Mexico was crucial for the security and expansion of the United States. This perspective indicated that while opportunities for northward expansion were curtailed, the drive to the South and West would persist.

Jackson's policies catalyzed the removal of Southern tribal populations, enabling their relocation beyond the Mississippi River. He dismantled a potential Indian buffer state that could have shielded Spanish interests in Florida, thereby further diminishing their influence. The Creek War culminated in a significant defeat for British and Spanish forces, decimating Indigenous communities and establishing a formidable American military presence in the Southwest, which ultimately paved the way for Jackson's ascendance.

Over the subsequent years, Jackson relentlessly pursued the removal of Indigenous peoples, negotiating treaties that resulted in the acquisition of extensive territories across Southern states. His efforts led to the United States gaining nearly one-third of Tennessee, three-quarters of Florida and Alabama, one-fifth of Georgia and Mississippi, along with portions of Kentucky and North Carolina, thereby forming what became known as the Cotton Kingdom.[742]

In a span of less than 16 months, Jackson achieved extraordinary outcomes, thwarting British resurgence in the southwest while securing American expansion and dismantling indigenous power. Despite facing seemingly insurmountable challenges with a relatively small army assigned to defend the Gulf Coast from potential invasions, his leadership ensured a successful defense. This culminated in the British retreat from their stronghold at Apalachicola, prompting Indigenous groups to vacate as well.

The abandoned Negro Fort, (as it was being referred,) occupied by armed African American men, both free and formerly enslaved, emerged as a significant point of contention. The Spanish were unable to capture it due to its heavily armed defenses, generating frustration among American settlers who urged Jackson to take action against it. The British withdrawal from the Gulf Coast and their indigenous allies incited outrage among the Spanish, who lost West Florida and their protective indigenous buffer state without engaging in hostilities.

General Jackson's ambitions for expansion into Florida and potentially Texas were unmistakable, as he perceived much of Spanish North America as territory rightfully belonging to the United States, following the Louisiana Purchase. He believed that mobilizing volunteers could swiftly dismantle Spanish authority, allowing American claims to what they viewed as their rightful land. But first, Florida is where he set his sights.

"He stands in grim relief against the dark
And bloody era of his troublous time
Like some stark pine, gaunt and of rugged bark
Etched on the red west of a Southern Clime...
He fought with valor and he fought with brain;
Rough-hewn, but modeled on a hero's' plan,
And thus posterity sums up his Fame —
A general — a soldier — and a Man!"
— Etta Bentley Arthur.[743]

---

[742] Waselkov, Gregory A., *A Conquering Spirit: Fort Mims and the Redstick War of 1813-1814*. University of Alabama Press. May 19, 2009, p. 2.
[743] Arthur, Ch. 30.

A man, indeed. And now very much America's man. But a man is mere mortal, and Jackson was as mortal as the next man. A great commander he had proven to be, one of strict discipline, and fearless mettle. Yet, for those who loved the Jackson rags to riches story, they would have him aspire far beyond the battlefield. They would have him one day sitting in the highest office in the land.

Battle of New Orleans, Jean Hyacinthe de Laclotte. New Orleans Museum of Art. 29 1/2 x 36 in. (unframed). Oil on canvas.

CHAPTER

49

NATIONAL HERO

"Well "Ole Hickory" said we could take 'em by surprise, if we didn't fire our muskets till we looked 'em in the eyes. We held our fire an we seen the British come, and there musta been a hundred of 'em beatin' on the drums. They stepped so high and they made their bugles ring; We stood behind our cotton bales and didn't say a thing. We held our fire till we seen their faces well, then opened up our squirrel guns an really gave em..."
- Jimmy Driftwood

The winter of 1814-15 was a dire time for America, one of the most distressing since the Revolution, during the frigid cold winter of 1777-78 at Valley Forge, Pennsylvania. Like then, the republic's very survival was at risk. Now, in its 40th winter as a nation, Federalists in Hartford were conspiring against the Madison administration, against the war, and even fulminating secession from the Union itself. A strong British force was preparing to invade the South, threatening to split the nation in two, and to wrest Louisiana out of American hands once and for all.

In Washington, ash still resonated in the air, and its stench was carried in the blustery winds. The remnants of the burned-out capital city contrasted sharply against the snowy winter landscape, leaving residents doubtful that a backwoods General at the head of an army of ragtag frontiersmen would be able to defend New Orleans against a real army; the very same army that had devastated Washington, and humiliated the American government just months before. Now their most hardened, seasoned veterans of the Napoleonic Wars were at large. What chance did America have?

In and around the torched buildings, gloom and despair pervaded the nation's capital. Locked in hushed resentment and apprehension since the new year of 1815 opened, the inhabitants were unhappily, tangibly conscious of the nation's shame. From the very start the war had gone poorly; now the capital was in ruins; burnt by the enemy, and the government humiliated by its disgraceful, cowardly flight from the British invaders. Congress indulged itself with ill temper, accusations of blame for the war, and misfortune. Worse, rumors abounded that representatives from the Hartford convention in Connecticut, which adjourned on January 5, 1815, were headed for Washington bearing constitutional revisions as the price of their continued acceptance of the Union. And what could the hapless James Madison, the poor "Appleseed Johnny" do but bow to their demands?

The *Boston Gazette* voiced these sentiments, questioning loyalty to leaders like Madison and Jefferson. "Is there a Federalist, a patriot in America, who conceives it his duty to shed his blood for Bonaparte, for Madison and Jefferson, and that host of ruffians in Congress who have set their faces against us for years and have spirited up the brutal part of the populace to destroy us? Not one. Shall we then any longer be held in slavery and driven to desperate poverty by such a graceless faction?"[744]

Amidst this turmoil, the Madison administration struggled to project optimism, with its spokesperson only able to express doubt about the situation in the Mississippi region. "Appearances justify the expectation that the British expedition will not be ineffectively resisted."[745]

News from Ghent suggested that the diplomats working to end the war were continually met with impossible British demands; demands that the Americans derided as aimed solely at dismantling the young nation. Increasingly, Americans were losing hope, and not many could foresee beyond the troublesome clouds on an ominous western horizon. Most who looked ahead, even the most sanguine, foresaw further disunity by spring, with New England seceding altogether, and western territories divided among European powers, and indigenous tribes. There

---

[744] *The Boston Gazette and Country Journal*, January 1815. Warof1812.net.
[745] Madison, Papers, LC. Dec.,1814. 1723-1859.

was yet another rumor, and if possible, a greater fear. It was generally known that an invasion force of monumental size had formed in the West Indies to strike a blow somewhere along the underbelly of the American Gulf Coast. Once New Orleans was picked off, and the West lost, nothing could stop the British from returning to the Chesapeake with Wellington's veterans, capturing Baltimore and Washington and marching onto Philadelphia and New York. A war that had begun with fantasies of conquest now appeared likely to conclude with defeat, humiliation and subjugation.

Toward the middle of January, the capital city learned of the invasion of New Orleans with news of the night battle of December 23rd. This was then followed by ten days of silence.[746] To add to the gloom, a severe snowstorm lashed Washington on January 23rd, and continued for three days, blocking roads in every direction until the last day of the month, when one mail delivery struggled through the snow drifts. But the mail was a disappointment; it brought only details of the gunboat battle on Lake Borgne, another British victory.

News traveled ever so slowly in 1815, and the rest of the nation had not yet heard of the warm winds of victory blowing up from New Orleans. The name Andrew Jackson was soon to be on the lips of patriotic Americans far and wide. Who was this heroic Tennessean who faced down the finest troops of the British Empire?

Yet, several more days passed with still no word. Then, on February 4th, came the report of the victory—and Washington went "wild with delight."[747] The city erupted from its gloom and fear, and general malaise. People thronged to the President's mansion. They invaded the homes of the cabinet officers and the leading advocates of the war, saluting all with shouts of congratulations. The mayor issued a proclamation for the illumination of the city. Newspapers broke out their largest type to announce: Almost Incredible Victory!!!! "Enemy... Beaten and repulsed by Jackson and his brave associates with great slaughter. The glorious news... Has spread around a general joy, commence it with the brilliance of this event, and the magnitude of our victory."[748]

---

[746] Brands, 2005. Ch. 22.
[747] Andrew Jackson Timeline, 1767-1845. LOC.
[748] Washington National Intelligencer, March 18, 1815.

"Glory be to God that the barbarians have been defeated, "shouted the *Niles Weekly Register.* "Glory to Jackson... Glory to the militia... Sons of freedom... Benefactors of your country... All hail!" [749]

The news shot further north as fast as it could be carried, "kindling everywhere the Madison enthusiasm. "Cities turned night into day with spectacular illuminations to celebrate the unbelievable news of the nation's triumph. In Philadelphia, parades were organized and transparencies constructed to depict the New Orleans battle as best they could conceive it. One man devised a transparency, showing Jackson on horseback at the head of his staff, in pursuit of the enemy, with the motto, "This day shall never go by from this day to the ending of the World, but he, in it, shall be remembered." [750]

Then, nine days later, and certainly before Americans could catch their breath over this ecstatic event came the announcement that the commissioners and Jen had signed a treaty of peace with their British counterparts that ended the war of 1812. Never did such happy news have such an immediate and electrifying impact on the entire nation. Men raced through the streets crying "Peace! Peace!" At night, the same deep throbbing anthem could be heard from town to town. No one wanted to be home alone so with a little preparation or organization, men and women lighted torches and lamps and marched through the streets, weeping with pride and happiness that this ugly war had, at last, been concluded.

The country had entered the war with a desperate need to prove it's right to independence, but the last two years seemed to prove the reverse, that the United States was only a temporary experiment in freedom, that its independence was undeserved. That is, until New Orleans. New Orleans demonstrated that the nation had the heart and the will and the strength to roundly defeat its enemies and defend its freedom. "The last six months is the proudest period in the history of the republic," asserted one newspaper. "We...*demonstrated* to mankind a capacity to acquire a skill in arms to conquer 'the conquerors of the conquerors of all'. As Wellington's *invincibles* were *modestly* stiled.... *Who would not be*

---

[749] Niles Weekly Register, Feb. 14, 1815.
[750] John Binns, *Autobiography,* quoted in Parton, *Jackson,* II, p. 248.

an American? Long live the republic!... Last asylum of oppressed humanity! Peace is signed in the arms of victory!" [751]

Andrew Jackson was now a celebrity of the highest degree, in bringing honor and glory to the nation, and he would remain a popular hero for the remainder of his life. His role in the War of 1812 was crucial to the future course of American expansion. Not only did he spare the nation an almost certain loss of territory in the southwest, but he prepared the way for the immediate future growth of the American nation. Jackson had restored the nation's faith and confidence in itself. To the public at large, he alone was responsible for giving the country back its self-respect. He had "slaughtered" a magnificent British army--over 2,000 victims, a figure that seemed incredible at that time--and repelled the greatest armada in history. The American people, their self-confidence restored, abandoned the need to prove their right to independence. Secure in the knowledge that their freedom had been permanently won, they turned to the important tasks of building a nation. The Union of the United States, from that time on, took on less of the character of a temporary experiment, something that might disappear in a stroke. The country had won respect abroad and was recognized in the family of nations as it had not been before. [752]

In the public mind, all of this was associated with Andrew Jackson—not simply because of the immensity of his victory over the British (although that was certainly important,) but because of the context and timing in which it occurred. The announcement of his enormous feat became publicly known almost immediately prior to the announcement of the conclusion of the war. The two events therefore became sequentially related in the mind of the American public. The tremendous boost to the public morale that his accomplishment on the battlefield provided when coupled with the news of the Treaty of Ghent, caused people (perhaps subconsciously) to fuse the two events together, especially when, prior to both, all seemed hopelessly lost. The result was the feeling that Andrew Jackson had ridden in on the tides of heaven, like some special messenger of the Almighty to rescue his people and preserve their freedom. It is no wonder, then, that Jackson's place in the pride and affection of the

---

[751] Denis, Matthew, 'New nationalism in an "Era of Good Feelings"', *National Park Service*, 2015.
[752] Remini, Robert V. 1977, p. 294

American people was established permanently, and would last until his death—and beyond. His popularity during the period after New Orleans surpassed that of Jefferson or Franklin, and even that of Washington himself.[753]

The accolades poured in. Congress, upon hearing the details of the victory, unanimously adopted a set of resolutions, honoring General Jackson with special commendations on him, and on all those involved in the New Orleans drama.

Resolved, by the Senate and House of Representatives of the United States of America in Congress assembled, That the thanks of Congress be, and they are hereby, given to Major General Jackson, and through him, to the officers and soldiers of the regular army, of the volunteers, and of the militia under his command... For their uniform gallantry and good conduct conspicuously displayed against the enemy, from the time of his landing before New Orleans, until his final expulsion therefrom, and particularly for their valor, skill and good conduct on the Eighth of January last, in repulsing, with great slaughter, a numerous British army of chosen veteran troops... And thereby obtaining a most signal victory over the enemy with a disparity of loss, on his part, unexampled in military annals.

Resolved, that the President of the United States be requested to cause to be struck a gold medal, with devices, emblematical of the splendid achievement, and presented to Major General Jackson, as a testimony of the high sense entertained by Congress of his judicious and distinguished conduct on that memorable occasion.[754]

George M. Troup, of Georgia, introduced the resolutions from the Committee on Military Affairs, and in his accompanying remarks, congratulated the House "on the glorious termination of the most glorious war ever waged by any people. To the glory of it, General Jackson and his gallant army have contributed not a little. I cannot, sir, perhaps language cannot, do justice to the merits of General Jackson...; It is a fit subject for the genius of Homer." [755]

---

[753] Sumner, William Graham, *Andrew Jackson*, Boston, 1882, p. 51.
[754] Annals of Congress, 13th Congress, 3rd Session, 1124, 1125, 1167; Calhoun Papers, II, 29.
[755] *Annals of Congress*, 13th Congress, 3rd Session, p. 1155.

Charles J. Ingersoll, of Pennsylvania, echoed these sentiments and repeated a question frequently asked in the newspapers. "Who is not proud to feel himself an American—our wrongs revenged–our rights recognized!" he asked. "For I repeat, that no matter what the terms of the treaty may be, (the terms of the treaty of Ghent had not yet reached Washington,) the effects of this war must be permanently prosperous, and honorable. The catastrophe at Orleans has fixed an impress, has sealed, has consecrated the compact beyond the powers of parchment and diplomacy... Let us pass, let us vote by acclamation, the thanks of Congress to General Jackson and his companions in victory."[756]

Nearly every state in the Union passed similar resolutions. "We consider your defense of... New Orleans," read one, "as the most illustrious among illustrious deeds." [757] The president dispatched his congratulations via James Monroe. "I am instructed by the President to convey to you in strong terms, "wrote the secretary, "his approbation of your conduct, and of that of the troops acting under you who have rendered such important services to their country. Your arrangements for the defense of the city, in selecting and fortifying the proper points at which to oppose the enemy, and in the disposition of your force in action; afford proofs of a talent for command which do you honor. By the example of your personal energy and distinguished gallantry in the field, the more necessary and commendable with your troops, it is believed that the happiest effect was produced. By these important services, you have merited in an eminent degree the approbation of the government and the gratitude of your fellow citizens." [758]

And it did not stop there. By mid-February, a number of songs had been composed to commemorate the great event. One of the most popular was 'Jackson is the Boy.'

Come all ye sons of freedom
Come, all ye brave who lead 'em
Come, all who say, God speed 'em
And sing a song of joy!
To Jackson ever brave,

---

[756] Ibid, p. 1161.
[757] Washington, *National Intelligencer*, March 18, 1815.
[758] Monroe to AJ, Feb. 5, 1815, Jackson Papers, LC.

who Noble did behave—
Unto Immortal Jackson,
the British turn'd their back on,
he's ready still for action,
oh Jackson is the boy…
Our country is our mother,
then let each son and brother,
stand firm by one another,
And sing a song of joy!
Let party spirit cease,
here's "victory and peace."
And here's "Immortal Jackson,"
The British turn'd their back on,
He's ready still for action,
o' Jackson is the boy. [759]

Even Jackson now knew he had ascended to the ranks of the immortals. He calculated correctly the impact of his victory on the country at large. And he had ego enough to see his triumph in fairly exalted terms. The "morning of the 8th of January," he wrote, "will be ever recollected by the British nation, and always hailed by every true American."[760]

Thereafter, for much of America, the white working class particularly, Jackson would always be the boy.

---

[759] Copy in Jackson Papers, LC.
[760] AJ to Robert Hays, Feb. 15. 1815, Jackson Papers, LC.

PART TWO

Image credit: The Hermitage Collection; thehermitage.com/military-life

CHAPTER

50

FAME GAME

"This day shall ne'er go by, from this day to the ending of the world, but He, in it, shall be remembered."

-John Binns

On April 6, 1815, Andrew Jackson and his family packed up and left New Orleans after a five-month stay. The General had been on the war front for over a year and a half. As Jackson prepared to head home, he handed over command responsibilities to Brevet General Edmund P. Gaines, a noted hero from the Battle of Lake Erie, in 1813. "We left Orleans on the 6th amid the sadness and blessings of Whites, Blacks, men, women, and children," reported John Reid. Despite the public acclaim, there were more than a few who were happy to see him go. During his time in the Crescent City, Jackson and his staff were honored guests at numerous dinners, each featuring multiple dishes and countless bottles of wine. But the victory was behind them, and it was time to move forward. Although, leaving New Orleans wasn't easy for Jackson. The city would always be tied to him as the place of his greatest triumph. The love and gratitude he received from the people he had helped defend fulfilled his appetite for recognition and acclaim. [761]

The first part of the journey brought him to Natchez, where he faced a brief delay due to a dispute with a man named Harman Blennerhasset. A shipwright, Blennerhasset had sued Jackson, claiming that he hadn't

---

[761] Reid to John Williams. April 1815. Reid Papers, LC. AJ to Coffee, April 28th, 1815, Jackson Papers LC.

received the remaining funds from the balance paid to the firm of Jackson and Coffee by Aaron Burr, which were meant for building several boats in 1806. However, Jackson and his partner Coffee proved in court that the money had already been returned, leading to the dismissal of the case. Aside from this minor issue, the return trip home was filled with celebrations, which brought Jackson immense gratitude, but also some unfamiliar exposure. Every town along the route competed to show their appreciation for the hero and his contributions to the country.[762]

"He is everywhere hailed as the saviour of this country," reported Reid. "He has been feasted, caressed, & I may say idolized. They look upon him as a strange prodigy; & women, children & old men line the road to look at him as they would the Elephant. This is the sort of business in which he feels .... very Awkwardly. He pulls off his hat-bows graciously, but as tho' his spirit was humbled & abashed by the attention that is shown him."[763]

After a tedious 800-mile journey, Jackson finally made it home. When he got back to Nashville, on May 15th, the homecoming was the most grandiose yet for the conquering local hero. Everyone turned out, as a frenzied, ecstatic procession escorted Jackson and his family into the public square, amid a chorus of joyous shouts. At the courthouse, Felix Grundy, the great War Hawk of Tennessee, welcomed him home with a long oration that praised the peak moments of the last campaign. When Grundy concluded, and the applause died down, there was a moment's pause when everyone looked to the General for his reaction. "I am at a loss," he finally stated, "The approbation of my fellow-citizens is to me the richest reward. Through you, sir," he said to Grundy, "I beg leave to assure them that I am this day amply compensated for every toil and labor."[764]

A group of Cumberland College students then delivered a short ode to the General, to which Jackson expressed his "lively feelings of pride and joy."[765] After the ceremony was over, Jackson was finally able to return to the Hermitage after so long away. Here, too, they faced a gathering, this one of family and friends who greeted Jackson heartily and paid him

---

[762] Reid to Sophia Reid, April 20, 1815, Reid Papers, LC.
[763] Ibid, April 20, 1815.
[764] Parton, *Jackson*, II, p. 329.
[765] Ibid.

a tear-filled tribute. But it was on May 22nd that the seminal event of his Nashville homecoming occurred. Presided over by Governor Blount, with the most prestigious Tennesseans in attendance, a grand banquet was held. Jackson was feasted and praised some more. In the ceremony, an elegant and ornate sword was presented to the General, voted by the Mississippi legislature the year before. With further speeches, Jackson was declared the first man of Tennessee, and the promise was that he would be so for life.

Jackson would spend the next five months at the Hermitage. These were some of the most pleasant months of his life.[766] At long last, Jackson was able to rest, recoup, and bring his shattered health back to a more normal state. After this period of recovery, and of the confidence that comes from being celebrated by the nation for his achievements, Jackson was in a strong state of mind and was once again eager for action. After selling his cotton crops, and restoring his plantation to its former efficiency, Jackson was suddenly out of debt for the first time in nearly twenty years. Always one to loathe debt, Old Hickory could breathe a sigh of relief. On top of all this success, the General had been asked to remain in the regular army at a high rank. The United States army was reorganized in the spring of 1815, into the Northern and Southern Divisions. Jackson was given command of the Southern District. Nationally appreciated for the first time, and respected for his talents, the General seems to have found himself more fully in this period. The conquering hero and iron warrior now had the perfect job. The salary was more than sufficient, and his duties during peacetime did not take up much of his time and energy. The army allowed Jackson to turn the Hermitage into his command headquarters, and he was able to spend many happy hours there with his wife, and now six-year-old son, Andrew Jr. Jackson now had the luxury that he had always sought, supplementing his income on a handsome government salary, while also being able to attend to his plantation first hand. Andrew Jackson, one could argue, had finally achieved the good life.

Even more conveniently, General Jackson's staff not only worked at the Hermitage, but lived with him on the estate as well. His officers and aides essentially became part of the family, for all intents and purposes.

---

[766] Andrist, p. 86.

This included Sam Houston, Richard Keith Call, Andrew Jackson Donelson, Robert Butler, James Gadsden, John and Samuel Overton, Dr. James C. Bronaugh, who was Jackson's personal doctor, and John H. Eaton.[767] Jackson also had his immediate family and a large number of extended family and close friends around him at all times. The General truly had no need to travel, although he often did anyway. As a national celebrity, he was invited to be recognized at banquets far and wide. Whenever Jackson did travel, men greeted the hero of New Orleans not only with enthusiasm, but also with encouragement to run for President at the next election. Originally Jackson shrugged off these suggestions, insisting that he had no interest in running for political office, but soon the talk of Jackson for president became louder and more frequent.

Every trace of past bitterness, hurt, anger, jealousy, resentment, or indignation caused by Jackson's earlier actions seemed to fade away in the summer sun. It was as if the warm feelings of love and gratitude that his fellow Tennesseans promised him would last forever. In every way, his homecoming was a victory, something Jackson both desired and deserved. To his credit, during this period of early fame and fortune, the hero remained genuinely humble in the face of the enthusiastic praise he received. At times, he sounded almost like a politician, but the many months he spent at war, where he raised, trained, and led an army on the field had taught him valuable lessons about diplomacy and politics.

In the ensuing months and years--again, like a politician--he nurtured his national reputation and kept himself visible in the public eye. The slightest criticism of his behavior at New Orleans, however, particularly from within the administration, Jackson would take immediate and alarming defense. When informed of such detractors, he sprinted to Washington to face down his critics. He also began touring the country to receive his due, accepting invitations from this town, or that, to attend a banquet or some other public activity commemorating the New Orleans victory. Always, the militia turned out to salute him and parade him in his honor. Militiamen acknowledged him as their chief and identified with him. If there was one organization that could be said to have formed the earliest base of his political strength throughout the

---

[767] Doherty, *Richard Keith Call*, pg. 14.

country, it was the militia. Every state had one, and the members almost universally acknowledged him as their head.

Some newspapers traced Jackson's movements around the country and detailed his activities, much to the delight of their readers. "Though I have not had the honor of hearing from you since your departure," wrote Edward Livingston to the general, "... Yet your progress has been so distinctly traced by the expression of public gratitude that your friends have not lost sight of you for a moment."[768] And it was not just the major cities that claimed him. "In every little town," John Reid reported, "the citizens seem exceedingly desirous to demonstrate their regard for the general."[769]

The headlines in the New York newspapers on the 6th of June proclaimed the big news of the summer of 1815. "The Allies in Paris! Napoleon fallen! The images of the idol smashed by the populace of the French towns! The Bourbons to be restored! Peace in Europe!"[770] While Jackson was capitalizing on his victory, and savoring the sweet results of his campaigns, another conqueror, one with an even stronger claim to such a title, went down in crushing defeat. The summer of 1815 was the summer of Waterloo and the end of Napoleon Bonaparte, at the hands of the Duke of Wellington. Jackson sympathized with the French emperor, perhaps in some ways he saw them as kindred spirits, fueled by Jackson's anglophobia or his admiration for Napoleon's military prowess. In any event, Jackson watched the declining fortunes of the emperor with regret. When the news arrived that Marmont had surrendered Paris, and Napoleon was forced into exile, he not only decried the betrayal, but revealed the full dimension of his own capacity for annihilation to serve a military end. "It was not Marmont that betrayed the emperor," he exclaimed; "it was Paris. He should have done with Paris what the Russians did with Moscow—burnt it, sir, burnt it to the ground, and thrown himself on the country for support. So I would have done, and my country would've sustained me in it."[771] As historian Robert V. Remini points out, "As a military commander, Jackson could be both ruthless and unyielding, and yet absolutely certain of his country's

---

[768] Livingston to AJ, Jan. 4, 1816, in Jackson, *Correspondence*, II, 224.
[769] Reid to Sophia Reid, Oct. 25, 1815, Reid Papers, LC.
[770] Parton, *Jackson*, p. 550.
[771] Ibid, II, p. 333.

approval for whatever he did. Another contradiction to which he seemed totally oblivious."[772]

This pleasant period at the Hermitage was soon disrupted, in the late fall of 1815, by a request from Washington that Jackson visit the capital, to be honored by the administration. Jackson dutifully accepted, and soon he was on his way there to receive official government recognition of his tremendous accomplishment. It was a great state occasion, with the President, the Cabinet, various other officials, and their ladies formally acknowledging the nation's pride in him at a magnificent reception in the presidential mansion. The attention and flattery heaped on Jackson signaled his arrival as the first man in America.[773]

Only one thing tarnished the triumph: Jackson's physical health. In fact, Jackson nearly died on the trip. President Madison was so alarmed that he insisted on summoning the celebrated Dr. Philip Physick from Philadelphia to attend the General. Jackson's arm caused him great discomfort during this crisis, and it took several weeks before the pain subsided. Probably, he suffered a general infection which accompanied the flareup of his old wound. In addition, he caught a particularly bad cold in the fall and could not shake it off. His incessant coughing racked his emaciated body. Each cough brought up blood. Each spasm frustrated him. Not until spring did he fully recover.

It was during this trip, prior to his collapse, that Jackson had occasion to ride through Lynchburg, Virginia, and the entire town turned out en masse to greet him. The militia proudly lined up for his inspection and approval, and prominent citizens congregated to extend their welcome. In the afternoon, a grand banquet attended by 300 people honored the conqueror, and among the distinguished guests was Thomas Jefferson, now 72 years of age, who lived a long day's ride from Lynchburg. Although Jackson harbored distinct reservations about the former president, he was profoundly impressed to learn that Jefferson had made the journey to participate in the tribute. It helped to wipe away all the acerbity of the past.

During the banquet, Jefferson was asked to give a toast and most willingly obliged. "Honor and gratitude," he said, "to those who have

---

[772] Remini, Robert V., 1977, p. 322.
[773] Reid Papers, Nov. and Dec. 1815 to his mother, Reid Papers, LC.

filled the measure of their country's honor." Jackson responded with both grace and clarity. He raised a toast to James Monroe, who was the Secretary of War during the Battle of New Orleans, a fellow Virginian and a close friend of Jefferson, as well as a recognized candidate in the upcoming presidential election. The attendees at the banquet found Jackson's humble toast to be gracious and modest. They were quite surprised to see that a man from the backcountry could be so sophisticated, aristocratic in his demeanor, and eloquent in his speech.[774]

It was becoming evident during this period that Jackson showed growth in his role of the modest hero. He genuinely seemed modest—unless of course someone else described his victory in less favorable terms. The few rumors that lingered about his actions in New Orleans after the battle, such as claims of him being a tyrant, faded away in the following months. What remained was an incredible image of an unattainable hero to whom the American people felt eternally indebted. There was "little doubt," he was told, that "with the right support from your friends, you could be elected to the highest office in the American government."[775]

Jackson did not take such early talk of entering politics too seriously, for his new position and head of the Southern Department of the Army demanded his attention. Jackson's main military focus after the British forces left American territory was to secure the southern border. This task was made more difficult by the ongoing aggression from the Creeks. Even though the Creeks had suffered a significant defeat, they were still supported by the Spanish, who remained in Florida. As long as the Spanish were there, the Creeks had an ally that would encourage and financially support their opposition to the Americans. However, Jackson believed he had already found a solution to this issue; he felt that it would not be long before the United States would be able to remove these "foreign" influences altogether. Of this he was confident.[776]

While the War of 1812 went tragically for Native Americans in the American South, the post-war period posed even more difficulties for the indigenous tribes. The United States government, eager to "deal with the Indian problem," commenced further white-settler expansionism

---

[774] Parton, *Jackson*, II, p. 334.
[775] Andrew Hynes to AJ, Oct. 24, 1815, Jackson Papers, LC.
[776] Parton, *Jackson*, II, p. 333.

through land cession treaties with the Cherokees and the Chickasaws. On March 22nd, 1816, the Cherokee Nation signed a treaty in Washington which was framed as an effort to compensate the tribe for a loss of land, but in actuality, led to the Cherokee Nation ceding away even more land, paving the way for the westward expansion of white settlers, and ultimately, the Trail of Tears.

A challenge to the Treaty of Fort Jackson was the continued British presence, in the form of two British officers, Colonel Nicholls and Captain Woodbine.[777] Keeping Creek hopes alive that their former lands would soon be returned to them according to the Treaty of Ghent, hostile Creek chiefs remained unrepentant, and undaunted by the agreement made at Fort Jackson. These ongoing frustrations only strengthened Jackson›s resolve—if it needed strengthening—to deal with the Indians in a strict and uncompromising way. [778]

The Creek Nation, facing removal, were desperate for any chance to avoid surveying the boundary line set by the Treaty of Fort Jackson. The idea offered a glimmer of hope. The northern and western edges of the land they ceded were unclear, perhaps intentionally, to enable white surveyors to cheat indigenous nations. Congress appointed three commissioners to define the boundary, and Jackson insisted that his close friend, General John Coffee, be one of them. Acting on behalf of Jackson himself, Coffee took a tip from his General and mentor and chose not to wait for the other commissioners to join him. Instead, the burly, rugged Coffee took it upon himself to mark the boundary line. With the strong commitment to strictly enforcing the Treaty of Fort Jackson from both Tennesseans, they effectively ensured the destruction of Creek landownership in the southwest. Consequently, the eventual removal of the indigenous nations posed little challenge.

One of the many arguments the Creeks advanced against the treaty of Fort Jackson was the claim that some of the lands appropriated by the United States under the treaty had been recognized in a treaty of 1806 between the federal government and the Cherokee tribe. Thus, some of the area was Cherokee land. This argument infuriated Jackson, possibly because it was all too true. A 50-mile-wide tract south of the Tennessee

---

[777] Rogin, *Fathers and Children*, p. 169.
[778] Remini, Robert V. 1977, Ch. 21

River in northern Alabama was the area in question, stretching from the Coosa River to what is now the Mississippi boundary. One of Coffee's outstanding accomplishments was the collection of affidavits from various individuals, both native and white, certifying that the land had been loaned to the Cherokee by the Creeks.[779] The gall of the tribes in daring to defy Jackson's iron will prompted the General to visit the various tribes (Creeks, Cherokee, Chickasaw, and Choctaws) in person. No longer willing to leave it to Coffee, Jackson arrived on scene to hold ceremonial talks and force their agreement to a land settlement once and for all. But to the Creeks, he sent a not-so-subtle threat.

Friends and brothers. You know me to be your friend, you remember when your nation listened to the advice of bad men and became crazy by the prophecies of your wicked prophets raised by the machinations of Great Britain and Spain.... You remember I destroyed your enemies, put those wicked profits to death and to flight, and by the capitulation and treaty at Fort Jackson gave peace to your nation...

Brothers listen, did I not send my men and warriors... and destroyed upwards of two hundred of the Hostile Indians, and did the British dare to land any men to protect them? Listen, did not the British, after exciting them to war, after promising them protection, flea like cowards and leave the Indians to perish, and is there any of your nation after all this so crasy as to listen to their wicked talks again.

Friends and brothers I hear with sorrow that some of your people has been listening to the wicked talks of Colonel Nicholls again, and that he has directed you to oppose the running of the line agreeable to the Treaty of Fort Jackson...

Brothers Listen did I ever tell you a lie? Listen I now tell you that line must and will be run, and the least opposition brings down instant destruction on the head of the opposers. Brothers, listen,

---

[779] Rogin, *Fathers and Children*, p. 170.

my men are ready to crush all the enemies of the US states I am your friend and brother.[780]

The treaty involved the Cherokee Nation relinquishing their claim and ceding all title to lands south and west of a designated line in South Carolina. In return for this land cession, the United States agreed to pay the Cherokee Nation an annuity of $6,000 for ten years, along with a one-time payment of $5,000 for improvements on the surrendered lands. The treaty granted the United States the right to lay out and use roads through Cherokee territory north of the established boundary, ensuring free passage between Tennessee, Georgia, and the Mississippi Territory. It also allowed citizens of the United States to freely navigate the rivers and waters within Cherokee territory. The Cherokee Nation agreed to establish and maintain ferries and public houses on the roads opened under the treaty to accommodate the needs of U.S. citizens. As part of a larger pattern of U.S. expansionism, where treaties were used to acquire land from Native American tribes, it set a precedent for future land cessions and the eventual forced removal of the Cherokee Nation during the 1830s.

The Chickasaw Nation, along with the Choctaw Nation, also signed a treaty with the United States to settle territorial disputes and ensure peace. On September 20, 1816, the Chickasaw ceded approximately six million acres in what is now southwestern Tennessee and northern and western Alabama. Jackson, along with other representatives, led the U.S. negotiations with the Chickasaw chiefs at Chickasaw Leader George Colbert's home. In return for the land cession, the Chickasaws received a $12,000 annuity for ten years. This treaty was another major step in the United States' westward expansion and the displacement of Native American tribes from their ancestral lands. Further complications arose, including the later Treaty of Pontotoc Creek in 1832, which formalized the Chickasaw removal from their homeland.

But to Jackson, the treaty's results were cause for celebration. "The whole southern country from Kentucky and Tennessee to Mobile," he wrote to William Crawford, "has been opened up by the late treaties and... I know of no situation combining so many advantages... As the

---

[780] Jackson's Talk to the Creeks, Sept. 4, 1815, Jackson, *Correspondence*, II, 216, 217.

lower end of the Muscle Shoals." [781] This area was prime real estate that provided, he said, clear navigation to the Ohio River in all seasons. Its falls could be "adapted to any machinery; it contained iron, salt and flint; and it allowed excellent military access to the lower country, the better to attack the Spanish."[782] What the tribal councils thought of the treaty goes unrecorded. The pattern of removal was becoming clear.

Consumed by treaties, Jackson did not actively involve himself in the 1816 presidential election, although he did support James Monroe, preferring him over all other candidates, particularly William H. Crawford, for whom Jackson held no small amount of disdain. A personal grievance stemming from Crawford's modification of Jackson's Treaty with the Creeks had grown into another of Jackson's bitter personal rivalries. Crawford's egregious mistake in altering what Jackson considered *his* treaty had caused him no small amount of irritation, and Jackson believed the Georgian was out to undermine him. The General resumed negotiations to reacquire land previously surrendered by Crawford's involvement, which, of course endeared him to the people of Tennessee, Georgia, and Alabama.

On November 12, 1816, Jackson wrote a letter to Monroe, urging the appointment of William Drayton as Secretary of War. This letter, drafted by Jackson's confidant William B. Lewis, included political suggestions that seemed out of character for Jackson. Drayton, a Federalist and part of the South Carolina elite, had no known ties to Jackson, who would later in 1816, claim to not know Drayton. Ultimately Crawford was appointed, and then later, was replaced by Calhoun. The Jackson letters lay dormant for seven years.

Intending it for Jackson's future biographer, William Lewis preserved the letters, believing them to be politically worthy of saving. When the letter resurfaced in 1824, it unexpectedly bolstered Jackson's reputation, helping him secure a significant electoral vote in both 1824 and 1828. His letters also discussed the theory of appointments, urging Monroe to move away from Federalist practices. In one part of the letter, Jackson characteristically informed Monroe that he would have executed the Hartford Convention leaders had he been in command in 1815.

---

[781] AJ to Crawford, Nov. 12, 1816, Jackson Papers, LC.
[782] Ibid.

These letters attracted the support of Democratic-Republicans ready to roast the Federalists, although some Democrats were wary of Jackson's overtures to appoint Federalists to office. Ultimately, the letters were full of contradictions and seemed staged for political effect. The letters did not appear to have been written by Jackson at all, but likely by William B. Lewis.

Meanwhile, the new President, James Monroe, destined to be the last of the Virginia Dynasty, faced conflicting pressures. Having to consider Jackson's appeal, Monroe also had to consider factions pressuring him to favor the Republican Party. In response to Jackson's advocacy, Monroe maintained a political theory more aligned with party needs, and ignored much of Jackson's suggestions, although he had to do so with kid gloves.[783]

As the Jackson-Crawford split increased, more enmity followed. On April 22, 1817, Jackson issued an order barring his subordinates from obeying orders from the War Department unless they came directly through him, a move that led to a public outcry. Jackson believed his right to do so was justified, citing chain of command issues, but the public nature of his order caused unnecessary scandal. It was clearly directed at Crawford, still the Secretary of War at the time, who had sent directives to some of Jackson's lieutenant generals without his knowledge. When John C. Calhoun replaced Crawford as Secretary of War, he acknowledged Jackson's concerns, but only under specific emergencies.[784]

In the five years after the War of 1812, the nation's economic troubles had become increasingly pronounced, particularly in the perpetually cash-strapped west. But in 1816, these struggles devolved into a national crisis. Gold flowed out of the country in droves, largely due to cheap banknotes. At the same time, silver became increasingly scarce. To fund the war, treasury notes were issued by the federal government, often not backed by gold or silver. As any cut-rate economist knows, printing more notes only speeds up the devaluation process. Even reliable banks struggled, as less stable institutions failed, leading merchants to prefer barter instead of notes, while rampant inflation discouraged potential lenders.

---

[783] Monroe Papers, NYPL, 1817; *ASPIA*, II, 89-91.
[784] Calhoun Papers, IV, 271-272.

The financial turmoil forced Republicans to adopt measures they would have never dreamed of in better times. Even fundamentally Federalist measures, a direct affront to the Jeffersonian creed were suddenly not out of the question. In 1816, Congress, under Republican control, reinstated the Bank of the United States. Originally created by Alexander Hamilton to connect wealth with political power by placing the federal government's financial activities in the hands of wealthy individuals, Republicans had criticized its chartering as unconstitutional. They chastised Hamilton and derided his bank as a Federalist tool for prioritizing profit over liberty. They were happy to see its charter expire in 1811, but James Madison, once an adamant opponent of the bank, called for its revival amid the financial crisis. Desperate times called for desperate measures, and consequently, Congress agreed, chartering a second Bank of the United States in April 1816.

Congress' next big step would also have long lasting impacts on the nation. On April 27th, 1816, it passed a measure to regulate commerce, including tariffs on imports. Tariffs were nothing new in American history; the difference was that before the war, low tariffs aimed to encourage trade, but disruptions during the war allowed domestic industries, such as iron and tools, to grow. These industries formed political alliances to push for protective tariffs, with an aim to enhance profits rather than maximizing government income. Congress ultimately passed the bill, and the outcome was the first protective tariff in American history.[785]

Andrew Jackson did not directly influence the creation of the new bank or the protective tariff, yet both would significantly affect his presidency in the decades to come. Even at the early stage of Jackson's role in national affairs, the General's actions were destined to fundamentally change American politics and the economy in the long term. Indigenous peoples had long been the main barrier to westward expansion, but Jackson's victories against the Creeks facilitated settlement in the Southwest. Following the British defeat at the Battle of New Orleans, migration surged into this region, transforming it into a center for America's burgeoning cotton industry. The Gulf coastal plain's rich

---

[785] Bancroft, Hubert H. The protective tariff, in *The Great Republic By the Master Historians*, 1902, Vol. III,

soil produced cotton exceptionally well, and an economy aided by Eli Whitney's cotton gin (1793) and Robert Fulton's steamboat (1807) meant the South now had a new money-maker. Alongside the labor of hundreds of thousands of Black slaves, the southern economy was well on its way to a total transformation. By the 1820s, the economic transition was complete, from the questionable future of slavery to a cotton empire driven on the backs of slaves and the ambitions of slaveholders, from Maryland to the Mississippi Valley.

CHAPTER

51

REMOVAL

"I have no motive, my friends, to deceive you."
-Andrew Jackson

The noted historian, H.W. Brands, sums up Jackson's affinity for conflict eloquently. "Some people seek danger as a way of making themselves feel alive. They scale mountains or explore jungles, when they feel existence becoming mundane, as they often do. Others seek confrontation for similar reasons. Jackson wouldn't have admitted that he sought confrontation, but that confrontation always found him because he stood on principle. But the number and gravity of his duels and shooting affrays, and the frequency of his ignoring and exceeding orders suggested that confrontation wasn't just a side effect of a boisterous personality. It was Jackson's raison d'etat."[786]

Andrew Jackson was poised and ready for another conflict and was eager for it. Seated again at the head of negotiations between the United States and the Native American tribes of the Southwest, Jackson, on July 8, 1817, watched as the Cherokee tribe signed the treaty prepared for them. The treaty they had agreed to ceded 2,000,000 acres of land in Tennessee, Georgia, and Alabama to the United States. In return, the Cherokee were promised "Acre for acre, land on the west side of the Mississippi with the understanding that the United States reserved the right to build factories, military posts, and roads within their new domain." Those who agreed to relocate would be given $6,000 over the

---
[786] Brands, Ch. 24.

next two years—along with one rifle and ammunition, one blanket, and one brass kettle or a beaver trap. In addition, flat bottom boats and provisions would be supplied by the United States for use in the removal. Those who remained on the east side of the river and "who may wish to become citizens of the United States," were to be granted 640 acres, which heads of families might hold permanently as freeholders. If they later moved, however, the land reverted to the United States.[787]

Another massive cession that land-crazed Americans were ecstatic with had been completed. Jackson, however, was not ecstatic about the amount of land ceded. Jackson was pleased with what he had accomplished with this treaty for another reason. "The cession of land is not important, but the Principle Established leads to great importance."[788] Jackson refers to the principle of removal. The idea of not only removing the indigenous out of the east, but removing the idea that tribes were autonomous nations, tribal governments immune to federal law within the territorial limits of the states. Jackson believed the treaty the Cherokee had agreed to in the summer of 1817 was the beginning of a new and more effective policy that was to end the conflict over jurisdiction and over sovereignty and domain now and forever. The status of 'Indians,' the assertion of supremacy of the American government over them, and the supremacy of the right of Congress to impose its sovereignty over *all* people living within the United States was now beginning. And he, Andrew Jackson, had been at the forefront of this generational change.

For Jackson, as for Westerners, removal was the only solution to the continuing problem of the 'Indian presence.' The treaty with the Cherokee, therefore, Jackson felt certain, was an excellent beginning to the process of subordination to every tribe residing east of the Mississippi.[789] The success of this convention strengthened Jackson's belief in the feasibility of the removal solution. To him it was the only practical solution, and ultimately, inevitable. Whether motivated by self-interest or not, Jackson spoke openly about the "security of all" the treaty guaranteed.[790]

---

[787] *ASPIA*, II, 130.
788 Commissioners to Graham, July 8, 1817, Jackson Papers, LC.
[789] Schmeckebier, *The Office of Indian Affairs*, 1927, pg. 30.
[790] Jackson Papers, LC, July 8th, 1817.

The indigenous who chose to assimilate, Jackson believed, and remain in the east would farm, build homes, schools for their children, gain citizenship, and become productive members of society. Those who relocated as directed would ensure their "national existence... on the Arkansas River." [791] Through removal, tribes would escape what Jackson felt was certain destruction, and their identity and culture would remain intact. Removal was the "the only means we have in preserving them as nations, and of protecting them." By 1820, Jackson convinced himself that the people of the Southern tribes themselves favored removal "if they had the means."[792]

In the mind of Andrew Jackson, removal was based on these essential tenets: that the two races could not live together harmoniously; that the tribal lands under protection were more than the tribes needed or would cultivate, and therefore the country was limiting its productive potential; that the tribes endangered the frontier and threatened not only settlers, but the country as a whole; that removal involved consent, but it was a limited, (unclear, and potentially non-consensus) type of consent. Individual natives, individual tribal families might choose to go or to stay, but the Indian nation, as a nation, could no longer stay in the east.

In theory and in practice, for legal and moral reasons, an indigenous nation was first asked to agree by treaty to the principle of removal, and then to the land exchange. Since an indigenous nation (in this case, the Cherokee) must give their consent, withholding it produced "presents" and secret deals to corrupt individuals within the tribe, influential chiefs, or others more amenable to consent that did not speak for the entirety of the tribe. This process, therefore, opened the door to fraud, corruption, trickery, and to bribes. Therein lied the rub.

Americans through the years have long believed that Andrew Jackson hated 'Indians.' Did he? Was Jackson bent on racial annihilation, was genocide his real objective? The key to understanding Jackson's attitude toward the natives of the Southeast seems to lie in the concept of Southern paternalism. In a similar manner in which Jackson viewed his enslaved people, he consistently took the view of father-figure to Native Americans he encountered, who he consistently referred as "children."

---

[791] Ibid.
[792] AJ to Calhoun, Sept. 2, 1820, Jackson Papers, LC.

The indigenous were children in the sense that they did not know what was good for them. His approach maintained that he himself knew, and he would enlighten them, and then, they must obey. If they did not obey, if they did not see the light, they could expect severe punishment from a disciplinarian, from their parent. [793]

As culturally domineering and ethnocentric as this notion sounds today, it was nothing extraordinary for the times. It is language Lewis and Clark were instructed to use by Jefferson in their communications to the tribes of the Great Plains in 1804, for instance. Most of Jackson's white contemporaries took this same approach toward indigenous peoples. It was the common mode of behavior. Particularly, it kept in keeping with the southern code of chivalry, so steeped in paternalism. Many within the indigenous population themselves adopted the language of paternalism and frequently spoke of themselves as children of their father, the president.[794]

Jackson, by most accounts, seems to have agreed with removal because he believed it was best for the American nation. Most important of all, removal meant the elimination of tribal government, tribal organization, and tribal sovereignty from white society. It was not the indigenous, per se, that Jackson was against, although that idea is sometimes debatable. It was their troublesome presence as a *nation*, as an independent unit, separate and distinct from the rest of the country, that Jackson opposed. Jackson had long despised the policies of a previous generation of government officials, those of the Northeast, and the Northwest Territory for example. The notion that an indigenous nation had a right to the status of a free, independent and sovereign state within the United States was one that Jackson could not and would not submit to. Instead, he was determined to clear away the "problem" to beyond the Mississippi. If the Indians wished to exist as tribes, let them go west. If they agree to homestead on a plot of land and obey the laws of the states, and the United States, then they may remain in the east. Old Hickory could not get his mind around any other possibility.[795]

---

[793] Rogin, *Fathers and Children*, 1991.
[794] Remini, 1977. p. 337.
[795] Faust, Richard H., "Another Look at General Jackson and the Indians of the Mississippi Territory," *The Alabama Review*, 1975, XXVIII, 202f.

On October 19th, 1818, less than one year after signing a treaty with the Cherokee, Jackson stripped the Chickasaws of all their remaining lands in Kentucky and Tennessee.[796] It was another gigantic cession that included an entire third of Tennessee as well as a large chunk of the state of Kentucky. The United States now controlled all western land still held by indigenous nations east of the Mississippi river in those states. Jackson had specifically sought permission from Monroe to participate in the negotiations due to the high stakes both economically and militarily such a cession involved. "Although it may be said that we have sufficient territory already, and that our settlements ought not to be extended too far, yet everything should be done too... consolidate our settlements." [797]

Jackson persuaded Monroe of the importance to the western region, that it would create a buffer between North and South, that it would boost trade and industrial opportunity on the Ohio and Mississippi. The lands would also enable stronger defense of white settlements on the Mississippi and Missouri rivers. He then added his most important provision; that all people living within the territorial limits of the United States were subject to its sovereignty and laws, and that no separate tribal governmental powers should exist. With both federal and state laws to consider, which everyone was subject to within these boundaries, separate laws and sovereignties only muddled the ability to keep law and order, he argued. The time had come, Jackson explained to the President when "their territorial boundary must be curtailed." The president needed no further convincing and granted Jackson's request. [798]

Jackson and Isaac Shelby were appointed the two commissioners who would arrange a treaty with the Chickasaw Nation. Knowing the importance of the negotiations, Jackson invited Shelby to stop at the Hermitage on his way to discuss strategy. During one part of their conversation, Jackson got down to brass tax, asking Shelby how a figure he was willing to offer the Chickasaw. In Jackson's version of the story, Shelby replied that he would not go more than $300,000, and Jackson agreed.[799]

---

[796] Kappler, *Indian Affairs*, II, p. 135-137.
[797] AJ to Monroe, Oct. 1818, Jackson Papers LC.
[798] Jackson to Monroe, March 4, 1817, Monroe Papers,
[799] Williams, Samuel C., *Beginnings of West Tennessee in the Land of the Chickasaws*, 1541-1841, Johnson City, Tennessee, pp. 86-89.

The two men were assisted as secretary of the negotiations by Colonel Robert Butler, Jackson's former ward and aide, as well as William B. Lewis, Jackson's friend and neighbor, who served as commissary. They arrived at the Treaty Grounds in Alabama shortly after 9:00 am on the morning of October 1, 1818. They found the Chickasaw in an unfriendly mood. The "bad humor" lasted throughout the negotiations, and for several days the Chickasaws were "very litigious and slow in their decisions,"[800] reported the commissioners in their secret journal. Jackson and the Commissioners felt they had only one option. They resorted to bribery. The Colbert brothers, Levi and George, who were of mixed white and Native American descent, were singled out for special consideration by the Commission, as they seemed to have great influence over the other Chickasaw. "Colbert," wrote one future commissioner, "is to the Chickasaw as the soul is to the body; they move at his bidding."[801] After negotiating their price, Levi and George Colbert ultimately received $8500 each; brother James got $1666.66; captain Sealy $666.66; and Captain McGilvery $666.66. The money was to be paid in cash or merchandise, and Jackson, to prove his good faith, posted a bond for the total amount of $20,000. Now the convention could begin.[802]

While giving his fatherly sermon to the Chickasaws, Jackson explained that the land he wanted from them had already been purchased by white men years earlier. The land was granted initially by England to the states of Virginia and North Carolina, he asserted. Later, Jackson went on, the land was conquered from England in the Revolution and made official by the treaty of 1783. Their father, the President, had protected their holdings, and kept white men away from it "so that his red children might Hunt on it; but the game is now gone, and his white children claim it now from him."[803] Jackson then laid out a map to show the Chickasaw which land specifically belonged to the white men. "It lies in Tennessee and Kentucky," he said, "and they have called on your father, the President, for it, and he cannot keep it from them any longer."[804]

---

[800] Ibid, p. 87
[801] Young, *Redskins, Ruffleshirts and Rednecks*, p. 40.
[802] Ibid, p. 86.
[803] Ibid, 286, 283-300.
[804] Calhoun Papers, III, 182-184.

"We hear that bad men in your nation threaten your chiefs with death," Jackson warned, "if they surrender this land... If this is true, we call you all to listen well—if the bad men of your nation do any active violence upon your chief for entreating with your father, the President, he will put them to death for it... He will not suffer such threats and insolent conduct to pass unpunished. If you refuse to sign the treaty, Jackson concluded, "your father will look on your conduct as an act of ill will and ingratitude."[805]

Levi Colbert then spoke up. For his part he would agree to cede the land to prove Chickasaw good will and gratitude. He only hoped their father, the President, by his commissioners, would be generous in his price. Jackson rose from the table to answer. He looked around at the chiefs and then said in a loud voice: "What do you ask for this land? "We don't know," replied the chiefs, "what will you give?"

Jackson began by offering $150,000 but was met with a resounding "No!" from the chiefs. Jackson and the chiefs then went back and forth haggling over the price, with Jackson eventually offering $300,000. When this sum was offered by Jackson, Shelby suddenly jumped from the table, outraged —he later said— by the exorbitant price Jackson offered. He would not participate further in the proceedings. The council broke up. Jackson stormed after Shelby, citing treason and villainy. When he caught up with Shelby he could barely contain himself. "God dammit," Jackson swore to Shelby, "did you say you would give $300,000?"

"No sir, "Shelby snapped, "I did not authorize you to make any such a proposition."[806]

Jackson stared at him, his hands fisted in anger. Shelby looked at those eyes and retreated. Within moments he was preparing to leave for home, but his son spoke to him and prevailed on him to stay. Too much was at stake. After he had calmed down, he agreed to return to the Council. He also agreed to the amount offered by Jackson. The $300,000 would be paid to the Indians at the rate of $20,000 a year for the next 15 years.[807]

Years later, during the Presidential election of 1828, Shelby would be reminded of this incident when it was printed in the newspapers. When

---

[805] Jackson Papers, LC, Oct.,1818.
[806] Journal of the Convention, Jackson Papers, LC.
[807] Kaplan, *Indian Affairs*, II, p. 135-137; 174-177.

asked, Shelby admitted he had originally agreed to the $300,000 prior to the Council but insisted that his meaning had been misunderstood. At any rate, the Chickasaws, under the direction of the Colbert Brothers, signed the treaty on October 19, 1818. The deal was done.

Secretary of War John C. Calhoun was so pleased with the treaty that he sent a special letter of commendation to Jackson upon hearing of it. "The notice of the conclusion of the treaty with the Chickasaws is received," wrote Calhoun, "and it affords much satisfaction that so valuable a cession has been obtained upon terms so favorable."[808] Later news of corruption clouded the agreement, however. Jackson was accused of allowing a salt lick to be leased to William B. Lewis, "before the ink was fairly dry."[809] In fact, Lewis had agreed to post a bond in case the government refused the land. The Indians, suspicious of the government, complained that past annuities had not been paid as promised and forced Jackson to send to Nashville for money to appease the chiefs and improve their trust in him. Ultimately, several factors in the negotiations seemed not entirely up front, if not disgraceful. Still, it was a magnanimous cession, and Jackson was celebrated as a hero once again.

---

[808] Carter, *Territorial Papers*, XVIII, p. 79.
[809] Abel, *Indian Consolidation*, p. 284.

CHAPTER

52

AND NOW FOR THE SEMINOLE

"I have caused them to be pursued and humbled."
-Andrew Jackson

The devastating impact on the Creek, Cherokee, and other Native American tribes caused by Andrew Jackson, with the backing of the United States government, has rightfully drawn criticism and outrage from contemporary Americans. However, to fully grasp the implications of Jackson's actions, it is essential to consider them within the 19th-century context rather than through a 21st-century lens. During Jackson's era, there was a widespread belief that it was necessary to subdue Indigenous populations and remove them from lands deemed vital for national expansion and security. Jackson was both a product of this mindset and a key figure in its execution. His military prowess and unwavering resolve led to the decimation of Native tribes and facilitated the westward movement of thousands of settlers. His policies decisively separated white settlers from Indigenous peoples, leaving tribes such as the Cherokee, Creek, Choctaw, Chickasaw, Catawba, and Seminole heartbroken and displaced. The principle of removal became firmly established, and many Americans celebrated this shift. By this time, the only remaining threat along the southern frontier was the presence of Spain, which became Jackson's next target.

Jackson was forever the warrior, never running from a challenge, always one to embrace controversy, much of which he created himself. In January 1817, the General learned of a topographical engineer,

Major Stephen Long's temporary reassignment from the southern command in Nashville to a northern Post. Acting Secretary of War George Graham had ordered the seemingly harmless move without first going through Jackson. Ever the stickler on points of courtesy, Jackson seethed, believing that a division officer such as Long owed allegiance to Division headquarters first and foremost, not the War Department. Jackson wasted no time writing an angry missive to Graham. In a courteous February 1st response, the acting Secretary assured Jackson that Long, "after having completed an engineering study in New York will be ordered to report himself to you in Nashville." He then went on to remind Jackson that "it is distinctly to be understood that this department at all times exercises the right of assigning officers to the performance of special duties at its discretion." This reply from Graham did not suit Jackson, who immediately went over the Secretary's head, taking his complaint "I cannot forbear," to newly-sworn-in President Monroe in a communication dated March 4th, the very day the incoming president assumed office. He insisted that the acting Secretary displayed in his interpretation of War Department prerogatives, "an inexperienced head, perfectly unskilled in military matters."[810]

"How," brayed Jackson, "did Monroe see matters?" Monroe indubitably wanted to see as little of this matter as possible, strapped to the hilt with an excessively large stack of requests and entreaties for appointments from office-seekers. Jackson, though, was still not satisfied that Washington would not repeat the oversight, and so he ordered his officers to disregard future directives from the War Department altogether, insisting that all communiques should flow only through him. "There is a chain of communication that binds the military compact. Which if broken, opens the door to disobedience and disrespect and gives loose to the turbulent spirits who are ever ready to excite mutiny." [811] Critics likened Jackson's stance to that of Caesar, whose unbridled ambition was seen as a real threat. To many, Jackson's martinet-like approach resembled military dictatorship far too closely, led by a man one could easily see tossing out the Constitution if it suited his purposes. For those already wary of a standing army during

---

[810] Brown, *The First Populist*, Ch. 20.
[811] Brands, H.W., 2005, Ch. 25.

peacetime, the questions flowed naturally: how far would Jackson go, and was he bent on undermining the government entirely?

Later that year, Jackson received an anonymous warning about enemies in the Northeast, particularly targeting Major General Winfield Scott, the Major General of the First and Third military districts, based in New York. "The war office gentry and their adherents, pensioners and expectants, have all been busy," the source asserted, "but no one, whose sufficient mark for your notice, more than Major General Scott, whom I am credibly informed, goes so far as to call the order in question an act of mutiny. In this district, he is the organ of government insinuations, and the supposed author of the paper enclosed, (an unsigned newspaper article critical of Jackson and his order). "Be on your guard."

Confronting Scott, Jackson presented the anonymous letter, seeking clarification. "I have not permitted myself for a moment to believe that the conduct ascribed to you is correct," Jackson lied diplomatically, "candor however induces me to lay them (the anonymous letter and the article) before you that you may have it in your power to say how far they may be incorrectly stated." Scott (Old Fuss and Feathers) was certainly not thrilled to be summoned based on the word of an anonymous someone not decent enough to even leave his name. Known for his insistence on strict military discipline and protocol, Scott denied authorship of the article, but he did not deny the article's point. Pointing out that Jackson's order created a compromising situation for his subordinates. "Suppose the President ordered one of Jackson's captains to take a certain action. If the captain obeys, you arrest him. But if in compliance with your prohibition he sets the commands of the president at naught, he would find himself in direct conflict with the highest military authority under the Constitution." Scott, not wanting any further involvement in the controversy, expressed his hope Jackson would reconsider his order.[812]

Scott's response set Jackson off, no matter how respectfully Old Fuss and Feathers tried to frame it, and Old Hickory's harsh reply to Scott had many questioning his health. Going so far as to question Scott's honor, accusing him of betraying a fellow soldier, Jackson accused Scott of having approached the issue "with the designs of an assassin lurking under a fair exterior." Jackson did not stop there, obviously feeling a

---

[812] Scott to AJ, Oct. 4, 1817, Jackson Papers, LC.

sense of betrayal, he went on, "is it due from a brother officer to assail in the dark the reputation of another, and stab him at a moment when he cannot expect it? I shall not stoop, sir, to a justification of my order before you, or to notice the weakness and absurdity of your tinsel rhetoric. To the intermeddling pimps and spies of the war department, who are in the garb of gentlemen, I hold myself responsible for any grievance they might belabor under on my account, with which you have my permission to number yourself."[813]

Jackson was so distraught over this feud that he threatened to resign over the issue. Fortunately, the onset of the Seminole War averted a potential duel between the two officers, sparing Americans the disgrace of such a spectacle. The calming intervention of President Monroe defused the situation. Monroe, appealing to Jackson's sense of duty and emphasizing the unresolved issues with Spain, calmed his hotblooded fellow Southerner. "It is my earnest desire that you remain in the service of your country," the President said. "Our affairs are not settled; the Spanish government has injured us and shows no disposition to repair the injury. Should we be involved in another war, I have no doubt that it will decide the fate of our free government."[814] Monroe's contemporaries, and historians after him often viewed the two-term Virginia President as somewhat naive, yet it was politically savvy of Monroe to recognize and exploit Jackson's major weakness: his inability to resist any opportunity to increase the glory and adulation military success would bring. Monroe knew the right buttons to push to keep Jackson in line.

The dispute with the War Department ended when John C. Calhoun became the new Secretary of War. Calhoun, acting in accordance with Jackson's wishes, announced that from thereafter, all department directives would flow through the commanding officers. Calhoun came in with a Southern swagger, and he reflected the belief that the country could benefit greatly from the services of General Jackson and allowing him a freer hand might facilitate even greater results, especially for like-minded Southerners. Calhoun assured just that in a letter to Jackson upon taking over as Secretary. "Permit me to say that to you individually, I participate in those feelings of respect, which any lover of his country

---

[813] AJ to Scott, Dec. 3, 1817, Jackson, *Correspondence*, II, 338-339.
[814] Monroe to AJ, Dec. 14, 1817, Jackson, Correspondence, II, 266.

has toward you. In any effort to add greater perfection to our military establishment, I must mainly rely for support on your weight of character and information. I cannot therefore conclude, without expressing the wish, that our country may long continue to be benefitted by your military services."[815] Jackson no doubt felt secure in his high-strung, opinionated approach based on the deference he received from the might John Calhoun.

Calhoun was not embellishing the popular feeling for Jackson, and it was not limited solely to the South. Around the country, the feeling was that if the country was to continue to grow and expand, the government needed Jackson on the front lines. And now the nation's eyes turned to the dangerous Southern frontier, the same frontier Jackson had been harping on for years. By 1817, the Spanish border in the South grabbed the attention of the nation. As Jackson had argued for years, developments in Spanish Florida were causing a new national crisis. Across the Florida border, one would encounter a 'rogue's harbor,' one that now provided safe haven for "savages" and runaway slaves. Spanish control of Florida had suddenly become untenable, and the issue had to be dealt with.

The cause of American intervention was ignited by the actions of the Seminole Nation during 1816 and 1817. The Seminoles refused to acknowledge American claims to lands acquired from the Creek War and fiercely resisted all efforts to remove them from those lands. The center of the threat revolved around a small group of Seminoles living just north of the Florida border near a village called Fowltown. It was here Jackson was soon to be called.

As early as the spring of 1816, Jackson, always with an eye on the lush lands of Florida, had written to Mauricio de Zuniga, the commandant of Pensacola, to address a problem that continued to rear its ugly head in late 1817. The issue at hand was that fugitive slaves were escaping to what he called the "Negro fort" occupied by blacks along the Apalachicola River. The fort was well-armed and well-manned, and the Spanish seemed unable or unwilling to police it. To Jackson, Zuniga's inaction gave runaway slaves an unspoken license to seek shelter at the Negro fort, and it was a situation that he wrote "will not be tolerated by our

---

[815] Calhoun to Jackson, Dec. 29, 1817, Jackson Papers, LC.

government, and if not put down by Spanish Authority will compel us in self-defense to destroy them."[816] A few months after Jackson's letter, the commander of the troops along the border, General Edmund Gaines, who had replaced Jackson in New Orleans in 1815, led an army in the fort's destruction. Tragically, Gaines' troops killed all 270 people inside the fort. [817]

Some of the black leaders that escaped were eventually captured, and in lieu of a trial, were turned over to the Seminole and brutally put to death. As rough as Gaines's tactics were, the raid took care of the first issue, although it worsened relations with the Spanish. The American approach to the "solution" of the Negro Fort offended many leaders of the Spanish government in Florida. The Americans did not take Spanish sovereignty into consideration when it went in and dealt with the fort. For those who cared about justice, the slaying of the inhabitants of the fort was also a crime for which there was to be no punitive measures. The entire situation was abysmal.

The Seminole towns were all in Florida except for Fowltown, just on the Georgia side of the line. The Seminoles living there were not generally hostile, nor warlike. The problem was that they simply refused to move from their lands. The Treaty of Fort Jackson, however, stipulated that Native Americans could not live in that part of Georgia, and thus these inhabitants were breaking the law. The 1814 treaty was clear on this point. Although these tribesmen were peaceful, General Gaines declared them in violation of the treaty and ordered them removed by a certain date. When that date passed, Gaines acted. On November 12, 1817, Gaines's troops attacked the village, driving the Seminoles away after a short but fierce battle. He and his men then burned Fowltown to the ground.[818]

The entire Seminole tribe, upon learning of the army's actions against this peace-loving band, rose up in outrage against what they perceived as an unprovoked violation. The Seminoles sought revenge, and this set off a series of raids against the Georgia towns along the border. The act that stirred the outrage of Americans occurred nine days after the burning of Fowltown, when a group of Seminoles attacked an open boat that carried

---

[816] AJ to Zuniga, April 23, 1816, Jackson, *Correspondence*, 241.
[817] Norman, *The Seminoles*, 1957, p. 77.
[818] Gaines to AJ, Nov, 26, 1817, in *ASPMA*, I, 686.

forty American soldiers, seven women and four children. The passengers on the boat were floated up the Apalachicola River toward Fort Scott when they were swiftly ambushed and then routed in a bloodbath. Worse yet, the Seminoles brutally slayed the children, and the details of their brutal murder was reported to the press by the few men and one woman who managed to escape. It was a national outrage.

Orders were then sent down to General Gaines from Washington to punish the Seminoles, even if he had to pursue them into Spanish Florida to do it. He was not, however, to attack any Spanish towns he encountered along the way. This made the task very difficult for Gaines and his troops, as the Seminole could escape into the thick Florida brush, and take refuge in a Spanish fort if threatened.

Georgia towns near the border now lived in fear, under the constant threat of terror. Meanwhile, as far as the public knew, the Seminole simply returned to the safety of Florida and the protection of villages across the border, while the Spanish did nothing. Legislators across the country, especially in Georgia, were up in arms and they demanded action. With this raised level of scrutiny the issue garnered, Monroe knew where he had to turn. The people had demanded Old Hickory, and their demands would be met.

The new crisis would bring General Jackson back into the field, and Old Hickory had to be licking his chops. The spiraling events in Florida meant the old hero of New Orleans was soon to be back into the field. The Seminole threat afforded Jackson the opportunity to once again command an army of men, and he relished the opportunity. Best of all, Jackson would have the chance to deal with two long-time foes at once, hostile natives, and the hated "Dons" of Spain. This meant, however, that Jackson would have to depart the Hermitage, and leave Rachel and his son behind, this time for a longer stretch, something that caused Rachel great consternation.

Yet, Andrew Jackson relished the opportunity. On the day after Christmas, 1817, he was ordered to the area to relieve Gaines on the Georgia-Florida border and take over the campaign himself. Characteristically, the moment a task of this nature was before him, Jackson became a whirlwind of activity. He turned to his 'Old Reliables,' a brigade of veterans from New Orleans, swore them in, and started marching south. He had already written to President Monroe stating that the instructions sent to Gaines respecting Spanish rights made it impossible to complete the mission. Limits could not be placed on the American army; they would have to be allowed the freedom to pursue the Seminole wherever they led them. Jackson proposed a simpler plan that he suggested would solve the whole problem: Take Florida away from Spain, period. [819]

The Spanish Empire had long struggled to manage its unstable borders and demands from land-hungry Americans who wanted to see Spanish control and the region's Native American populations replaced now became more intense than ever, especially as the population in the southwest surged; in 1810, Alabama and Mississippi had about 16,000 white settlers, but this number skyrocketed to nearly half a million by 1830 and close to one million by 1840. The growing plantation economy in the Gulf Coast region became a significant part of Jackson's support base. It was this economic system that drove the population boom, and with ever-increasing industrialization elsewhere, especially in the textile industry, migrants heading into these newly opened lands envisioned cotton 'fields of gold.'

All President Monroe had to do, Jackson promised, was to give him some hint that "the possession of the Floridas would be desirable.... And in sixty days it will be accomplished."[820] When Monroe did not answer the letter, Jackson decided to take this as silent approval. This issue, however, would be of much importance later. In the meantime, however, when it came to doing what he wanted, Jackson did not often need much approval anyway. General Jackson and his brigade of one thousand reached Fort Scott near the Florida border in March 1818, having traveled 450 miles in 46 days, despite heavy rains and bad roads. There, close to two thousand troops waited for them. He led them at once into the swamplands along Florida's Apalachicola River. News had reached Jackson that the Seminoles had gone to St. Marks to demand guns, thus, the General decided to lead his men there without delay. Upon arrival, he seized the town and accused the Spanish officials there of aiding the Seminole. But no Seminoles were found, although one prisoner was taken: a seventy-year-old Scottish trader named Alexander Arbuthnot.[821]

---

[819] AJ to Monroe, Jan. 6, 1818, Monroe Papers, LC.
[820] Ibid.
[821] *ASPMA*, I, 682, 726.

The flowing white-haired Arbuthnot had been a trader among the Natives of the area for many years. He had treated them fairly and did his best to defend them against those who took advantage of them. Arbuthnot had been outspoken in favor of the rights of native Americans and had vociferously spoken out against the way they had been cheated by both the Americans and the English. This meddlesome behavior was not taken lightly by the powers that be, and as a result, Arbuthnot had developed a reputation as something of a rabble rouser. Few frontiersmen in 1818 felt that especially the Seminole had any rights that white men should feel obligated to respect. Jackson referred to Arbuthnot as "that noted Scotch villain," and ordered that he be held for trial.

General Jackson then hustled his troops over to the village of the Seminole Chief Bowlegs. His village was located over one hundred miles away through swamps and tangled forests. Jackson had hopes that he could catch the enemy's main force by surprise. Coming up on the village, however, he did not encounter the enemy, in fact, the village was entirely deserted. Jackson was furious that he had been fooled, and he grew even more irate when he learned the Seminoles had slipped away after being warned by a message from Arbuthnot. The Scot had informed the Seminoles in his message that Jackson's army was too strong to fight, and that they should flee.

That night, Jackson's sentries captured Robert Ambrister, an ex-lieutenant of the British marines. He had arrived at Bowlegs' village unaware that the American army was in occupation of it. Ambrister was accused of helping the Seminoles wage war against the United States. He was taken back to St. Marks to stand trial along with Arbuthnot. On April 28, Arbuthnot was charged before a military court with "exciting the Indians to war," acting as a spy, and giving aid to the enemy. In truth, the only 'crime' Arbuthnot was guilty of was sympathy for the Seminoles. But this alone was enough to condemn him in the eyes of Andrew Jackson. Arbuthnot admitted that he had sold gunpowder to the Seminoles, but only enough, he said, for their hunting. He confessed to the crime of treating the Seminoles as friends and human beings.[822] Despite his plea for mercy, the court decided he was guilty of all the

---

[822] *ASPMA*, I, 734.

charges with the exception of spying. They sentenced him to death by hanging.

In Ambrister's case, the former British marine was charged with "taking command of Indians at war with the United States." There was proof that he had obtained arms for the Seminoles, and that he had actually sent one party of warriors against the Americans. He admitted his guilt and asked the court to show mercy. None was given, however. Ambrister was sentenced to death by firing squad. Then one of the members of the court, in admiration of Ambrister's soldierly manner, asked for reconsideration of the vote against him. The other members agreed and decided to change the verdict to fifty lashes on the bare back, and a year's hard labor with ball and chain. Jackson, however, upon hearing of the verdicts, approved Arbuthnot's sentence, but overruled the more lenient decision regarding Ambrister. The court was ordered to show no mercy and to carry out the first sentence. Ambrister was shot by firing squad.

As Arbuthnot swung by the neck from a rope, from a yardarm onboard his own ship, and Ambrister lay on the ground, his head a bulbous, bloody mess, a group of Seminoles arrived on the ship to ask for mercy. They stopped, speechless, however, at the sight of their executed friends. They now understood the full fury and vengeance of Andrew Jackson, the fabled Sharp Knife.

Ready to move on, and unconcerned about the fate of the two men, Jackson had already left before either man was executed. Leaving the Seminole problem behind, the General hurried west to Pensacola, and on May 24th, seized it from the Spanish without a fight. Leaving one of his officers in charge as military governor, he headed to Tennessee, feeling that his work in Florida was finished, as he believed it to be firmly under American control. Jackson had been on a rampage, acting the part of a conqueror. It was as though he envisioned himself in the spirit of the fallen Bonaparte, whom he idolized, although to many, he had summoned the ghost of Ivan the Terrible.

Jackson and his men continued on their rampage, and arrived in Pensacola on May 28, 1818, where only a smattering of Spanish resistance challenged them. Jackson quickly thwarted the meager resistance and captured the town. The Spanish governor of the town, Colonel Don Jose Masot, retreated to a nearby fort, Fort Carlos de Barrancas, outside of town to make a stand against the Americans. Jackson led his men directly to the fort and demanded its surrender. Masot made a small show of resistance by having his men fire their guns, but to little effect. Upon hearing Jackson demand Masot's surrender, the Spanish governor replied, "Your Excellency has violated the territory of Spain...I protest before God and man that my ardent wishes are to contribute to the peace and friendship of our respective nations...If your Excellent will persist in your intentions to occupy this fortress, I will defend it to the last extremity, opposing force to force." [823]

After Jackson had his men drag cannons to the mouth of the fort, Masot responded by raising the white flag. Recognizing the untenable situation, and the sheer size of Jackson's force, Masot did the only thing he could, he surrendered and marched his men out of the fort. "All I regret," Jackson wrote, "was that I had not stormed the works, dragged out the governor, put him on trial for the death of Stokes and his family, (recently killed in a Seminole raid) and hung him for the deed." [824] But in actuality, Jackson had agreed to allow Masot and his men to retire from the fortress with full honors of war, to transport them to Cuba, and respect Spanish rights and property. The American occupation, he decreed, would continue until Spain could provide enough support to police Florida effectively. "The articles of capitulation with but one condition amount to a complete cession to the u. states of that portion of the Floridas hitherto under the government of Don Josse Massot."[825]

With that small show of force, Jackson had virtually wiped out Spanish control of Florida. To Jackson, the cession of Florida to the United States had already been achieved. In later defense of his actions, he cited the helpless American women and children along the frontier who could now sleep a little easier. On June 2nd, the General informed Monroe that "the Indian War was now over." He alerted that the president that the war had taken a toll on his health and asked to be allowed to return to Tennessee. "I am at present worn down with fatigue and by a bad cough with a pain in my left side which produced a spitting of blood and has left me a skeleton....I have established peace and safety

---

[823] Masot to AJ, May 22, 1818, Calhoun Papers.
[824] Parton, *Jackson*, II, 492, 493.
[825] AJ to Calhoun, June 2, 1818, in *ASPFA*, IV, 602, 603.

and hope the government will never yield it."[826] He added that before he left, he would like, with the president's permission to take his men to seize St. Augustine as well as Cuba with a few more men and a boat or two.

Monroe, with good reason, declined Jackson's offer to continue rampaging Spanish Florida, and fortunately for Spain, thanks to ill-health, the General was on his way home to Tennessee. The First Seminole War was over, and it for nationalists throughout the country, Jackson at their head, it was about time. The conflict showed them just how easily the Spanish could be pushed out. Many swore it should have happened long ago, and that if Jackson had been sent to Canada in 1812, that frontier would be flying the stars and stripes as well.

---

[826] AJ to Monroe, June 2, 1818, Monroe Papers, NYPL.

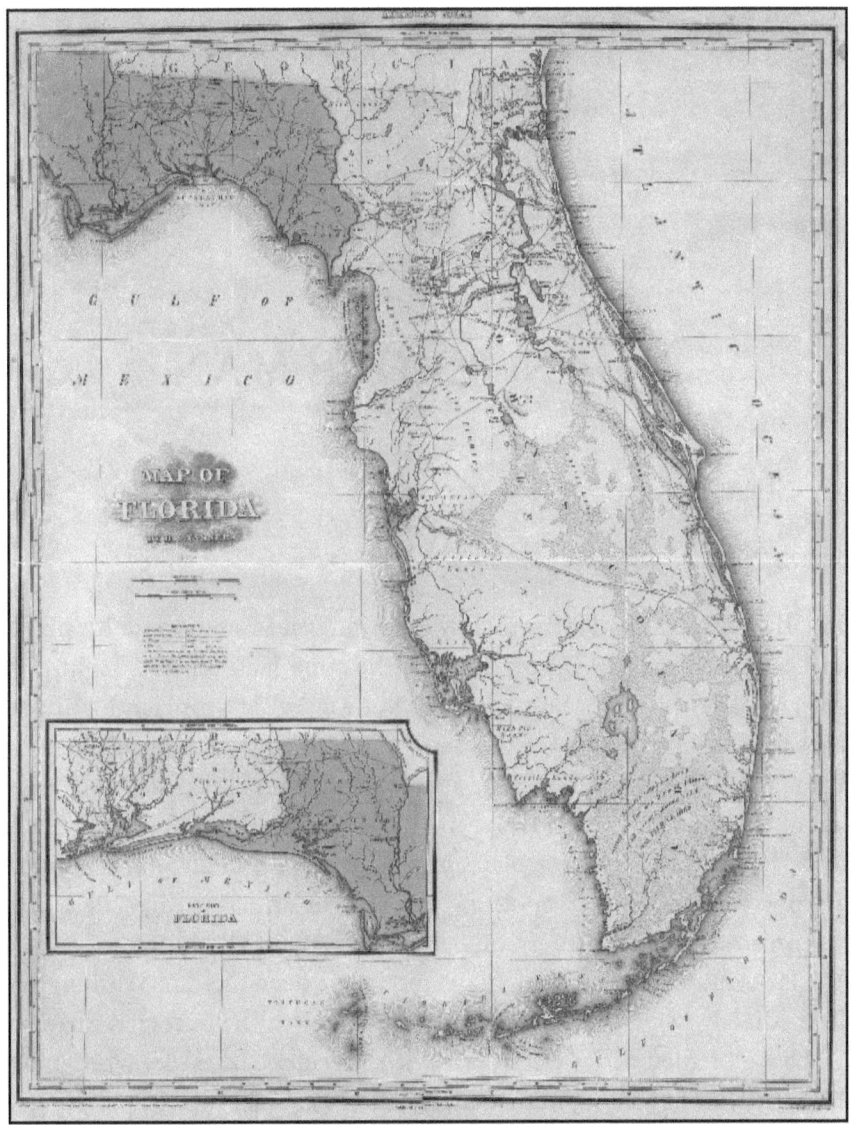

Map of Florida by H.S. Tanner (1823) Source: Floridamemory.com

CHAPTER

53

A DANGEROUS MAN

"Major, there is a combination in Congress to ruin me."
-Andrew Jackson

The president had conveniently gone into vacation mode at his home in Loudon County, Virginia right at the time Jackson was beginning his rampage through West Florida. Not a word of reproach had been sent to Jackson throughout the Seminole campaign as a result. Yet, all throughout April and May, the newspapers had printed raging stories about the capture of St. Marks, the trials of Arbuthnot and Ambrister, and the seizure of Pensacola. Only Secretary of State John Quincy Adams was on the job, enduring the rash of criticism directed at the administration by the international community in Washington.[827]

Jackson's actions in Seminole country were denounced in Washington immediately when word reached the capital city. The outraged Spanish ambassador filed a formal protest with President Monroe, who, upon his return from hiding, immediately called a cabinet meeting to discuss the issue. All those within the cabinet expressed their disapproval of Jackson's actions, all except one: John Quincy Adams. Adams, for reasons that were initially unclear, became Jackson's staunchest and eventually sole defender in the cabinet, motivated less by admiration for Jackson and more by animosity toward Crawford and Calhoun.

For John Quincy Adams, however, there was more reason than the other cabinet officers to criticize Jackson for his measures in Florida. The

---
[827] Adams Memoirs, IV, 102-107.

potentially dire fallout on the diplomatic front kept Adams busier that summer than he should have been. First, the British came at him with questions. Adams' diary entry for the 25th notes that British Ambassador Sir Charles Bagot somewhat dryly stated during their recent interview he would need to "say something to his London superiors about the execution of the two British subjects, Arbuthnot and Ambrister, and the occupation of Pensacola by General Jackson. Could Adams provide copies of the proceedings of the court martials?" Adams replied that he could not do so. Adams, however, did assure Bagot that Jackson's seizure of the Florida forts was unauthorized, and came as quite an unexpected surprise to the President and his cabinet. Bagot replied that he'd guessed as much and confessed "a complete ignorance on what circumstances might possibly have led to" the strange deaths of his countrymen. "He could," Adam's recorded, "not indeed imagine any." At this point in the meeting, the experienced Adams knew it was time to feint and said, "I was willing to change the subject of conversation."[828]

Two weeks later, the Spanish wanted their own answers to these questions, and of course they wanted their forts back. Spain's minister to the United States, Luis de Onís demanded to know what Jackson's punishment was to be. To this, Adams replied aggressively, and without a hint of apology or contrition, in defense of Jackson's action. He described the invasion as necessary and justified by Spain's unwillingness or ability to live up to the 1795 Pinckney Treaty, which stipulated that both contracting parties "shall maintain peace and harmony on their shared frontier." Spain had failed, he contended, to effectively keep is house in order. American citizens, he continued, had been "exposed to the depredations, murders and massacres of a tribe of savages, a greater number of them dwelling in the borders of Florida." Adams then seamlessly placed the blame for the invasion on the Spanish officers who refused to abide by the treaty and to the duties required of a neighboring country. This had forced Jackson, Adams argued, "to no recourse but to fall back upon the immutable principles of self-defense."[829]

Leaning into this tit-for-tat approach, Adams called upon "His Catholic Majesty for the punishment of those officers who the President

---

[828] Ibid, 107
[829] Adams to Onís, July 23, 1818, in *ASPFA*, IV, 496-497.

is persuaded have therein acted contrary to the express orders of their sovereign. Pensacola and Saint Marks would, of course, be returned as soon, in the latter's case, as a force strong enough to hold it from Indian incursion arrived." By taking the offensive himself, the Secretary of State effectively defused the Spanish outrage. Jackson's bellicose defense for occupying Spanish forts had now been backed by Adams and reinforced in an equally logical defense. Ironically, based on later events, Adams did much to boost Jackson's national prominence in this case by defending the quick-tempered General, the public now saw their heroic conqueror as legitimized by the highest echelons of government.

On July 14th, President Monroe wrote to Jackson for the first time since the Florida invasion, and as with the division order controversy, the president seemed eager to assert the commander-in-chief's authority without ostracizing the popular, but sensitive General, whom he well knew was not someone one wished to antagonize. The Virginia President knew from experience that the General would be quick to deny any hint of misconduct. Monroe's communication to Jackson exculpated the administration of wrongdoing. Adroitly, the President also omitted any glaring examples of finger-pointing blame at Jackson. "In transcending the limit prescribed by your orders, you acted on your own responsibility." Monroe acknowledged, however, that the General may have had good reason for his actions. "You acted on facts and circumstances which were unknown to the government when the orders were given." The note further justified sending troops into Florida. "It is not an act of hostility to Spain" while acknowledging "An order by the government to attack a Spanish post would assume another character. That of war. And only Congress," Monroe pointed out, "could, by our Constitution, make such a declaration."[830] This seemed a fine balance between admonishing Jackson and conciliating him. It also kept the critics from having weapons to use against the administration. Nonetheless, this would not prevent Jackson from eventually turning on Monroe as well before his Presidency was through.

Many Americans were in agreement with the Spanish ambassador, Luis de Onís. While the general public largely adored Jackson, many politicians were deeply suspicious of him. Some genuinely feared how far

---

[830] Monroe to AJ, July 19, 1818, Monroe, *Writings*, VI, 54-61.

he might take his power and control of the army. Others were concerned about the implications for the Constitution if a representative of the executive branch could initiate war without Congressional approval. Some, arguably many, viewed Jackson as a barrier to their own political aspirations. This latter group was notably present in Monroe's administration.

The decline of the Federalists, who offered little resistance to Monroe's 1816 election and had no candidate in 1820, did not end bipartisan politics in America; instead, their demise shifted political battles within the Republican Party. Aspirants to become Monroe's successor were positioning for advantage, and these were formidable men. William Crawford was open about his ambitions, creating tension with John Quincy Adams, who tried unsuccessfully to hide his own aspirations. John Calhoun, a master of political intrigue, also had ambitions for the presidency.

A report soon emerged that Jackson's motivations in Florida had been fueled by self-interest, based less on concerns over national defense, and more on a motive involving land in Pensacola. The report came with explicit contradictions by other participants in the corrupt allegations, defending Jackson's motivation in his seizure of the town. Jackson of course was stung by the report, and he grew angrier at hearing exaggerated rumors (not entirely false) that the source was William Crawford himself. The battle heated up, as each side went on the attack, and arranged its defenses. Crawford, aligned with Clay, also brought Thomas Cobb, a congressman from Georgia, and others threatened by Jackson, onto their side against the Tennessee general. Jackson's friends, as devoted as the disciples to the Messiah, rallied around him.

The bad blood between Crawford and Jackson goes back well before the Florida crisis. But that conflict provided the Georgian a fresh opportunity to attack the General. Crawford truly believed most of the vicious things he said about Jackson, but he also aimed to keep Jackson from becoming the successor to Monroe. Conceivably, Crawford hoped to undermine Monroe himself. But with the Presidency in play in 1820, this was a trickier maneuver since Crawford was a part of the administration. He could not take down the administration in the public's eyes without tainting himself. Those who knew him didn't put it past him. Jackson prepared to defend himself against Crawford in part by defending the president. "I am not insensible to the implacable hostility of Mr. Crawford towards me," he wrote Monroe in 1818, "nor have I any doubt of his hostilities toward you." Jackson suggested that Crawford had deliberately scrambled communications regarding the operations in Florida. "In this, he would have the double object of injuring both you and myself in the estimation of our country and more so than I calculated, to accomplish the object so desirable to himself and his colleagues, the injury, nay, the ruin of his country would interpose no barrier."[831]

But those who had voted in favor of censuring Jackson, who viewed him as a dangerous "man on horseback," including the aging sage of Monticello, Jefferson himself. Some were already very anti-Monroe and were so thoroughly outraged by the Florida campaign and its clear disregard for the constitution, as well as the president's lack of concern over Jackson's actions. Some voiced their fears over an executive branch that felt it conduct a war without Congressional approval. This view included states' rights groups who could not swallow such an extension of federal power. Virginia included many of the anti-Jacksonians, and their leading mouthpiece, the *Richmond Enquirer*, actively encouraged anti-Jackson sentiments around the country, and reprinted articles and editorials critical of the General.[832]

In January 1819, in response to the plethora of criticism, Jackson traveled to Washington to report on the Florida campaign and confront his accusers and defend his actions. One member of this group would create hostility with Jackson that would result in worse bad blood than Jackson held against Crawford. It would take years for Jackson to realize that he and Henry Clay were actually aligned on the same side when it came to many of the most significant political issues of their era. But Clay had made an enemy out of Jackson from the moment the General read Clay's speech, given on the Senate floor, critical of Jackson's actions in Florida. "I hope gentlemen will deliberately survey the awful isthmus on which we stand. They may bear down all opposition; they may even vote the General the public thanks; they may carry him triumphantly through this House. But, if they do, in my humble judgment, it will be a triumph

---

[831] AJ to Monroe, Dec. 7, 1818, Jackson, *Correspondence*, II, 404-405..
[832] Ammon, Harry, *James Monroe: The Quest for National Identity*, Univ. of Va. Press, 1990, p. 430.

of the principle of insubordination, a triumph of the military over the civil authority, a triumph over the powers of this House, a triumph over the Constitution of the land. And I pray most devoutly to Heaven that it may not prove, in its ultimate effects and consequences, a triumph over the liberties of the people."[833]

The most damaging claim that Clay made cut Jackson deeply, and it would tarnish his image for years to come. In a particularly hurtful comparison, Clay suggested that Jackson belonged in a "rogue gallery of historical despots; beware how you give a fatal sanction in this infancy of our republic, scarcely yet two score years old." Clay warned his audience, "remember that Greece had her Alexander, Rome her Caesar, England her Cromwell, and France, her Bonaparte." Looking ahead, Clay advised, "if we could escape the rock on which they split we must avoid their errors." Referring again to the gallery, Clay offered up his coup de grâce, judging the threat of the despotic Jackson as far more lethal than a war on the Gulf Coast.

However, Clay's words notwithstanding, most of the nation disagreed with him. Congress thought differently as well, judging Jackson's actions in Pensacola to be justifiable. Jackson's unprecedented popularity cannot be overstated; to the vast majority, he represented the nation's will and resilience as it expanded westward. In early February, Congress voted on the issue of a censure of the president. Various resolutions were offered up; condemning the seizure of Pensacola, the executions of Arbuthnot and Ambrister, but all were overwhelmingly rejected. The total was 94 nays to 54 votes of yea. The evidence was in: Did many Americans believe a loose cannon like Jackson needed to be reined in? Affirmative, but were there many more who believed he acted in the best interests of the country? Yes, there were. Jackson's capture of the Florida forts, the House declared, was not unconstitutional.

After Clay's efforts to censure Jackson failed in the House, the debate shifted to the Upper House. A Senate committee composed mainly of Crawford supporters conducted an investigation into the Florida campaign, filing a report denouncing the invasion and Jackson's execution of Arbuthnot and Ambrister. Just as in the lower house, however, multiple resolutions aimed at reprimanding the General were

---

[833] Clay's Address to the Senate, Jan.,1819, LOC

proposed but ultimately voted down. Feeling vindicated, Jackson left Washington.

He would never forget Clay's speech, however, nor the sting of his words. Despite the Speaker's efforts to meet with Jackson, to soften the blow, to explain himself to the General, he was rejected. Jackson ignored the overtures, having already decided that Clay was his enemy, and there was no going back. The General's knee-jerk reaction ignited a rivalry that would last for over a quarter of a century and would have implications on national politics for decades. Jackson's tendency to hold onto a grudge fueled his animosity to the Kentuckian. The animosity only festered over the years, preventing the chance of forming a strong political alliance between the two powerful westerners.

Before leaving the Capital, Jackson wrote home citing, "the combination formed was more extensive than I calculated, with Mr. Clay's anxiety to crush the executive through me." But Jackson was pleased to note that Clay's efforts were failing. "The whole Kentucky delegation except Clay, I am told, goes with me and Clay is politically damned." A week later, he wrote Rachel, "The insidious Mr. Clay will sink into that insignificance that all those who abandoned principal and justice and will sacrifice their country for self- aggrandizement, ought, and will experience."

Although Jackson was off-base on his Henry Clay prediction, who still had decades of influence ahead of him at the national level, he was correct in believing that he was not in the majority on the Florida issue. Willie Blount argued that anyone who didn't see the value in the Florida campaign was not worth notice. "What poor minded bitches are Messieurs Crawford and Clay, the government is on your side, the Floridas are at last ours."[834] Governor John Clark also detested his fellow Georgian, William Crawford. He claimed to have information linking Crawford and some others, including Andrew Erwin, to a slave-smuggling scheme and he offered to share that information publicly. Jackson was delighted. "I am happy to be informed that you are preparing a publication to give to the world a full portrait of Mr. William H. Crawford. If the painting is well drawn of my own knowledge of the

---

[834] Blount to AJ, Jan. 1819, Blount Papers, LC.

man, it will portray hypocrisy, surrounded with all its horrid deformity, depravity and baseness of human character."[835]

Jackson seemed energized by having political foes, as he no longer could count on military foes to pester. For months he spoke of Crawford, Clay, and Cobb, as 'an unholy cabal.' "Having labored from my youth to establish a character founded on uprightness of conduct," he told a supporter, "the only solitude I had upon the subject was that I should not be deprived of that character by the falsehood of a conspiracy formed by designing demagogues, of which I found Crawford, the chief surrounded by his minions Clay, Cobb and company, whom he wielded with the dexterity that a showman does his puppets, to exalt himself by prostrating the executive through me, and thereby raise himself to the Presidential chair."

But those who hoped to unseat Monroe in 1820 failed in their efforts. Monroe secured his reelection handsomely. Jackson delighted in Crawford and Clay's discomfiture. "Like Lucifer, they have politically fallen, never to rise again." On that note, however, Jackson was quite wrong. Both would continue to hound his own political efforts. As would others in Monroe's cabinet. "Mr. Calhoun is extremely dissatisfied with General Jackson's actions in Florida," John Quincy Adams noted after a series of heated cabinet meetings where Jackson and Florida were recurring themes. "He believes Jackson's goal was to instigate a war in order to lead an expedition into Mexico, which would undoubtedly lead to a conflict with Spain."[836]

The criticisms from his fellow Carolinian continued. "Calhoun claims he has heard that the court martial initially acquitted the two Englishmen, but Jackson sent the case back to them. He also mentioned that last winter a company in Tennessee sent Jackson's nephew to Pensacola to purchase lands in Florida, and that Jackson himself is rumored to have a stake in the speculation." The astute South Carolinian sensed Jackson's massive popularity among the people, and in an effort to dismantle the rise of a potential rival, he kept up his acrimony against the controversial General. Vocalizing his opposition to Jackson's high-handed actions in Florida, Calhoun had been one of the first to

---

[835] AJ to John Clark, 1819, Jackson, *Correspondence*, II.
[836] Adams, *Memoirs*, IV, 233.

recommend that the General be reprimanded and censured. President Monroe initially agreed with Calhoun, but hesitated to act, especially in light of Adams' adamant defense of Jackson.

While the President and many others readied themselves for the international fallout that Jackson's illegal actions were sure to engender, the fact was that the American people approved of the methods Jackson had employed in Florida. This, more than anything else, seemed to carry the most weight with Monroe, who soon became an emboldened defender of American rights in Florida, particularly affecting Congress's decision to veto censure. While the President saw to it that control of the seized Spanish forts were given back to Spanish authorities, Monroe warned Spain that if they could not keep order in Florida, then they should hand the territory over to the United States, who would.

Had Jackson shown even a hint of remorse, it would have eased Monroe's situation. However, Jackson felt no need for repentance. "I have destroyed the Babylon of the South, the hotbed of the Indian war and the depredations on our frontier. I have taken Saint Marks and Pensacola," he wrote to Rachel shortly after occupying Pensacola and weeks after comparing Saint Marks to Sodom and Gomorrah. He claimed to have delivered the "just vengeance of heaven," punishing those responsible for the Indian war and the horrific massacre of innocent women and children. To Monroe, he justified his actions as "absolutely necessary to put down the Indian war and provide peace and safety to our southern frontier." He believed his occupation of Florida was driven by noble ideals: "In all things, I have consulted the public good for the safety and security of our southern frontier."[837]

Monroe could only shake his head at his impulsive general. The questions continued from the Spanish minister, who pressed for clarification on whether the president had ordered Jackson's invasion of Florida. Monroe found himself at a crossroads. He couldn't honestly or politically claim he had given such an order, yet to disavow and censure Jackson would portray his administration as inept, while also risking the anger of Jackson and his considerable supporters. Monroe later confided to James Madison that had General Jackson faced trial, "I have no doubt that the interior of the country would have been much agitated

---

[837] AJ to Rachel, 1818, Jackson Papers, LC.

if not convulsed." Monroe chose the middle ground, return Florida to Spain but stand behind Jackson. It became evident that Monroe feared Jackson as much as he did Spain, given the lengths he went to appease the General. "If the executive refused to evacuate the posts, especially Pensacola, it would amount to a declaration of war, which is incompetent," Monroe told Jackson. "It would be accused of usurping Congress and delivering a deep and fatal wound to the Constitution." Publicly, Monroe defended Jackson by placing the blame on the Spanish for the chaos they had allowed in Florida, echoing Adams's sentiments.

In light of all this, and to rid itself once and for all of all the annoyance, the fading Spanish empire, in need of money to fund its counterrevolutions in Latin America, sold Florida to the United States for five million dollars on February 22nd, 1819. John Quincy Adams, well aware that what Spain couldn't defend on the ground they certainly couldn't claim at the negotiating table, was diplomatic enough not to leave Onís with nothing. While insisting on Florida, Adams felt compelled to give up Texas.[838]

Since the time of the Louisiana Purchase, the southwestern frontier remained vague. Thomas Jefferson believed the Rio Grande marked the border between the United States and Spanish territory. This made the region of Texas an American possession. Onís and Spain argued that the border was the Sabine River, which meant Texas was Spanish land. For 10 years, the Texas issue was not a major concern, since it was, at the time, remote, and largely uninhabited. But the war with Britain and especially the attack on New Orleans had changed things immensely. Now, the American focus was firmly pointed southward, and westward. Adams was hesitant to give up hopes for Texas in exchange for securing Florida, but with Spain agreeing to give up its claim to Oregon, the deal was still sweet. Acquiring Florida, Adams knew, would pay immediate dividends, rounding out the southeast. Oregon was a long-term investment when the United States would require an outlet to the Pacific. Texas was the sacrifice in 1819, although it would be highly desired later. Meanwhile, it would not remain in Spanish hands for long.

---

[838] John Quincy Adams, *Writings of John Quincy Adams, Volumes 1–7*, Macmillan, 1916, p. 488.

The question of whether General Jackson approved the surrender of Texas at that time became a contentious issue sixteen years later. It is now indisputable that he did. In 1820, President Monroe communicated with Jackson to clarify the reasons that led him to agree to give up Texas. "Having long known," Monroe wrote, "the repugnance with which the eastern portion of our Union ... have seen its aggrandizement to the West and South, I have been decidedly of opinion that we ought to be content with Florida for the present, and until the public opinion in that quarter shall ...change. I mention these circumstances to show you that our difficulties are not with Spain alone, but are likewise internal, proceeding from various causes, which certain men are prompt to seize ... their own ambitious views."[839]

Jackson agreed with Monroe on the Texas issue, although some years down the road, when the Texas issue came into the forefront, he would deny having ever seen the details of the treaty. But the proof is in the pudding: "The view you have taken of the conduct pursued by our government relative to South America, in my opinion, has been both just and proper, and will be approved by nine-tenths of the nation. It is true, it has been attempted ... by certain demagogues to the injury of the administration, but, like all other base attempts, has recoiled on its authors; and I am clearly of your opinion that... we ought to be content with the Floridas — fortify them, concentrate our population, confine our frontier to proper limits, until our country, to those limits, is filled with a dense population. It is the denseness of our population that gives strength to our frontier. With the Floridas in our possession, our fortifications completed, Orleans, the great emporium of the West, is secure. The Floridas in the hands of a foreign power, can be invaded, its fortifications turned, the Mississippi reached, and the lower country reduced. From Texas an invading enemy will never attempt such an enterprise; if he does, notwithstanding all that has been said and asserted on the floor of Congress on this subject, I will vouch that the invader will pay for his temerity."[840]

---

[839] Monroe to AJ, Jackson, *Correspondence*, II, 1819.
[840] AJ to Monroe, Ibid, 1819.

CHAPTER

54

GROWING PAINS

"A free, virtuous and enlightened people must know full well the great principles and causes upon which their happiness depends."

-James Monroe

The Era of Good Feelings that marked the post war period were beginning to sour. In some ways, things began to turn bad almost overnight. Just as John Quincy Adams and Luis de Onís wrapped up their 1819 boundary treaty. After a bumper crop in Europe, the price American cotton producers had been enjoying tanked. With Europe recovering from its postwar wounds, high cotton prices had been driving the settlement of the Gulf Coastal plain. But in 1818, when the British shifted to purchasing Indian cotton, American cotton was no longer in demand, what had been close to $0.40 a pound, soon plummeted to $.15 going down. The delay that had kept the armies fighting weeks after the signing of the treaty of Ghent, provided a grace period for American markets, but when the collapse finally did reach New York and other American cities, those involved in the cotton market faced sudden desolation. The catastrophic drop soon spread to Wall Street, where the situation had already faced an imbalance with adjustments to the new bank of the United States. The Bank had attempted to restore the strength of the currency by promoting payments by specie (gold, and silver) instead of paper currency. The American dollar faced deflation like it never had before, and the nation's economy was soon in a tailspin.

There seemed to be no end in sight to how far things might fall. The United States was in the midst of its first economic depression.

"The years of 1819 and 1820 were a period of gloom and agony" remembered Thomas Hart Benson, who served many years in the U.S. Senate representing the state of Missouri. Benton was also an avid trader of commodities himself and engaged in a lifelong obsession for finance. "No money, either gold or silver, no paper convertible into specie, no measure or standard of value left remaining, no price for property or produce, no sales but those of the sheriff and the marshal, no purchasers at execution sales but the creditor, no employment for industry, no demand for labor, no sale for the product of the farm. Distress, the universal cry of the people. Relief, the universal demand, thundered at the doors of all legislatures, state, and federal."

Amid the Panic of 1819, Americans facing struggles looked to the west, where land was cheap and people did not judge others on past failure, since most had come west for the same reason. Migrations westward were ignited by the Panic, and it pushed thousands of men, women and children into areas such as the Gulf Coast territories, soon to be states, of Mississippi, Louisiana and Alabama. Others pushed even further, streaming across the Mississippi into the lands of the Louisiana purchase. Arkansas filled with settlers, then Missouri. Some who dreamt of a cotton fortune left America entirely, following the invitation of the Mexican government to settle their northernmost outpost of "Tejas." Leading the way was one Moses Austin, a heavily indebted Missourian, now turned "Empresario."

An "Empresario" was a land agent or contractor contracted by the Mexican government to bring settlers to Texas and establish colonies in exchange for large land grants. Empresarios played a key role in the settlement of Texas under the Mexican government's colonization system. The idea was that Empresarios would establish colonies for Mexico, thus providing expansion, growth, and a tax-base. Empresarios were responsible for recruiting and settling families in the designated areas in the northeastern part of what is today the state of Texas. Prominent

Empresarios also included the likes of Green DeWitt, and Martín de León. [841]

After Moses Austin's untimely death, his son, Stephen F. Austin led the first group of 300 eager Americans into Texas. They arrived in December of 1821, and many of them brought their slaves with them. Mexico, like Spain before them, allowed slavery, at least for the time being. The newly arrived Americans knew of the Adams-Onís treaty, (which became Mexican territory after Mexican independence in 1821) but their presence in Mexico threatened to blur the boundary line the treaty had established. The Empresario system would lead to the widespread settlement of Texas and ultimately contributed to the Texan Revolution by the mid-1830s, and the eventual secession of Texas from Mexico.

For those who the Panic didn't drive west, another group did what Americans have also habitually done when times were tough, they sought litigation. In 1816, when Congress re-established the Second National Bank to help control the amount of unregulated currency issued by state banks, the faltering economy was expected to rebound. The bank of the United States had plenty of wealthy supporters, but also a long list of enemies who opposed it. Opposition to the bank included states-rightists who favored state banks, unapologetic Jeffersonians who seemed to despise all banks, and individuals damaged by the bank's contraction of the money supply. Many states questioned the constitutionality of the national bank, and Maryland set a precedent by requiring taxes on all banks not chartered by the state. But the cashier of the Baltimore chapter of the bank, James McCulloch, refused to pay the Maryland tax, and was summoned to county court, which confirmed the state's law. McCulloch appealed and the Supreme Court agreed to hear the case. The oral arguments took place in February 1819, just as the nation's economic foundation was crashing down.

The high court, still sharing a building with the legislature, faced a large audience in its cramped hearing room. The excitable crowd included many who hoped to see the Bank of the United States taken down entirely. Another faction wished to see it emerge victorious, and some

---

[841] Edmondson, J.R., *The Alamo Story-From History to Current Conflicts*, Republic of Texas Press (2000), p. 75.

were just there to hear what kind of oratorical magic Daniel Webster might regale them with this time.

Daniel Webster had been a Federalist in New Hampshire, and a congressman from that state for two terms. After the War of 1812, the future of federalism looked dark, and Daniel Webster took a step back from politics. He traded the Granite State for the bustling city of Boston, Massachusetts, where a man of talent and ambition could well reach new heights. There he made a fortune, and a name for himself defending wealthy clients, but he also earned respect by standing up for those in need, including his beloved Dartmouth College. "It is, sir, a small college," Webster argued in defense of his alma mater, "and yet there are those who love it." His argument was valid. The college's charter was protected by the contract clause in the Constitution, meaning the states couldn't just change it whenever they pleased. Chief Justice John Marshall was on his side, and so was most of the court. This ruling was a significant win for federal power and for the prestige of Daniel Webster. [842]

Almost immediately after the case of Dartmouth College vs. Woodward wrapped up, Webster dove into the McCulloch case. The Bank of the U.S. was a much less popular client than Dartmouth, but luckily for Webster, Chief Justice John Marshall wasn't too worried about party lines or popularity. After he had managed to thwart Jefferson's agenda in the Burr trial, he continued to fortify the judiciary, making sure it stood strong against both the executive and legislative branches. Thanks to Marshall's efforts, the federal government remained supreme over the states and would continue to empower well-heeled property owners against the general populace.[843]

While many Federalists who relied on elections started to drift away from their party, Marshall remained steadfast. As the head of the highest court in the land, he was not beholden to voters, or elections, thus he was largely untouchable. This gave him the freedom to steer the Republic in the direction he wanted, riding the favorable winds of federalism. In the landmark case of Maryland vs. McCulloch, there were two main questions legislators were buzzing about: Did Congress even

---

[842] *Dartmouth College v. Woodward*, 1819, 17 U.S. (4 Wheat.), 518.

[843] Newmeyer, R.K., *John Marshall and the heroic age of the Supreme Court*, Baton Rouge: Louisiana State University Press, 2001.

have the authority to create a bank? And if so, could the states tax it? The old Jeffersonian Republicans, always in favor of a strict interpretation of the Constitution if it meant limiting the Federal government, found themselves silenced by Marshall's arguments.

"The power to tax involves the power to destroy." If the states could tax a federal bank, they could potentially destroy any action or institution of the federal government. "This was not the intent of the American people. They did not design to make their government dependent on the states. Let the end be legitimate, let it be in the scope of the constitution, and all means which are appropriate, which are plainly adapted to that end, which are not prohibited, but consist within the letter and spirit of the constitution, are constitutional."[844] Republican critics of John Marshall lamented his decision making, but his role in the landmark cases of early American history cannot be overstated. Marshall ensured federal supremacy over the states at a time when the states' rights platform was riding high. The empowerment the federal government gained from Marshall and the Court's interpretation of the Constitution would pay huge dividends later on, as the nation headed toward future conflicts that would threaten to bring the country to its knees.

In 1820, America stood at a crossroads. The nation faced its first major crisis over the expansion of slavery, centered around Missouri's bid for statehood. The crisis, which foreshadowed storms on America's horizon, shed light on the growing tensions between North and South. It would also display to the country the political brilliance and astute maneuverings of the Speaker of the House, Henry Clay.

By 1820, Missouri had grown significantly, reaching the required 60,000 residents needed for statehood. However, what seemed like a straightforward process of admission to the Union quickly evolved into a national crisis that would test the very foundations of the American republic. The North's population had long surpassed the South's by 1820, and a power imbalance in the House of Representatives was the result. The South maintained its influence, though, through equal representation in the Senate, where slavery-related interests could still be protected. But with westward migration now increasing beyond the Mississippi, the

---

[844] *McCulloch v. Maryland*, 1819, 17 U.S. (4 Wheat.) 316.

Louisiana Purchase territories became the new battleground for this power struggle.

New York Congressman James Tallmadge proposed admitting Missouri as a state under the condition that the new state gradually eliminate slavery. This proposal gained support from Northern states seeking to limit slavery's expansion. Tallmadge proposed that Missouri be allowed slave state status, on the condition that Missouri planters gradually free their slaves. The proposed amendment was seen favorably by Northerners who wished to see the new West free, viewing it as a relatively painless step in that direction. However, the Southern reaction was starkly different. Tallmadge's proposals sparked intense opposition from Southerners, and it revealed the growing economic divide between the regions. The South's reaction was swift and severe. Representative Thomas Cobb of Georgia warned that such restrictions could lead to the dissolution of the Union, famously declaring that this conflict had "kindled a fire which all the waters of the ocean cannot put out."[845]

In the early 1790s, signs seemed to indicate that slavery was a dying institution. Some Northern states, led by Pennsylvania, enacted laws for the gradual abolition of slavery, and others followed suit. The Atlantic slave trade was steadily outlawed by individual states during the American Revolution and was banned by Congress in 1808. Abolitionist movements gained momentum, with state abolition societies forming a national association in 1794 to mobilize public consciousness and work towards ending slavery.

That is, until the cotton gin, which, as noted, ensured the economic viability of cotton production, and ignited the largest cotton boom the world had ever seen. No other area was more ideal for growing cotton than the Deep South, particularly the area of the Mississippi Valley, and soon, the rush was on.

After the Treaty of Fort Jackson, an entire new generation of migrants flooded into these lands eager to capitalize on the cotton craze. Most were land speculators and planters, hungry for lucrative profits. These were not your father's generation of planters, either, the moneyed slave aristocracy of the east, who had long since paid off their land. This new

---

[845] Cobb Papers, 1820.; Bailey, Matthew and Steven Nash. "Thomas R. R. Cobb." *New Georgia Encyclopedia*, last modified Mar 11, 2020.

generation, men in the mold of Andrew Jackson, had largely financed their property through these same land speculators, and they faced exorbitant debts as a result. Entire states had been settled on the premise that slaves would be available to tend the cotton. New manumission laws passed by a northern-dominated Senate would mean financial ruin for these upstarts, who would be left holding the bag, facing a much more difficult time absorbing the shock of a loss of their labor force. To them, the Southern way of life was at stake.

Southerners interpreted the Tallmadge amendment as a herald of trouble not just for Missouri, but for all of the South—a future of gradual emancipation of not only their slaves, but their way of life. This, the planter class simply could not accept. As Thomas Cobb forewarned Tallmadge ominously, "If you persist, the Union will be dissolved." Up to that point, Tallmadge had not intended to interfere with slavery where it already existed, but with Cobb's antagonistic words, he became less conciliatory. "Sir, if a dissolution of the Union must take place, let it be so! If civil war, which gentlemen so much threaten, must come, I can only say, let it come! My hold on life is probably as frail as that of any man who now hears me; but, while that hold lasts, it shall be devoted to the service of my country—to the freedom of man. If blood is necessary to extinguish any fire which I have assisted to kindle.....I shall forbear unity. Sir, the violence to which gentlemen have resorted on this subject will not move my purpose, nor drive me from my place. I have the fortune and the honor to stand here as the representative of freemen, who possess intelligence to know their rights, who have the spirit to maintain them. Whatever might be my own private sentiments on this subject, standing here as the representative of others, no choice is left me. I know the will of my constituents, and, regardless of consequence, I will avow it; as their representative, I will proclaim their hatred to slavery in every shape; as their representative, here will I hold my stand, until this floor, with the Constitution of my country which supports it, shall sink beneath me. If I am doomed to fall, I shall at least have the painful consolation to believe that I fall, as a fragment, in the ruins of my country."[846]

---

[846] James A. Tallmadge, Address to Congress, February, 1819.

Into the arena stepped Henry Clay. As the Speaker of the House, he had been hinting at retirement, burdened by debts he couldn't hope to repay with a congressman's salary. This placed him in a similar position as many new planters who couldn't afford to free their slaves. "No man is more aware of the evils of slavery than I, nor do I regret them more," he wrote to a friend. "If I lived in a state where slavery was not allowed, I would certainly fight against its introduction with all my strength."[847] However, Kentucky was a slave state, and Clay was a slave owner, which gave him a level of influence among other slaveholders that northern politicians lacked.

When tensions around the Missouri question intensified, Clay postponed his return to private law practice to work on legislation that could keep the Union intact amid threats from figures like Cobb and Tallmadge. The Tallmadge Amendment passed in the House through a sectional vote, prompting the debate to shift to the Senate, where discussions on slavery would continue for the next 40 years. The South stood firm, blocking the amendment and keeping Missouri in a state of uncertainty. Missouri might have remained in this limbo if Senate moderates hadn't tied its admission to that of Maine, which sought to become a free state after breaking away from Massachusetts. Hardliners in the House rejected the Senate's proposal, however, leading Clay to suggest forming a joint committee to address the various provisions.

Once his proposal was accepted, he filled the committee with fellow compromisers. The committee's report endorsed the Senate bill while promising separate votes on each part of the package, which now included a ban on slavery in the remaining territories of the Louisiana Purchase, north of the latitude line at 36° 30'. Some lawmakers, especially those who lacked Clay's long-term vision, questioned the Kentuckian's strategy, believing that hard-liners opposed to compromise would simply divide and conquer. But, Clay's approach was simple, yet effective. It allowed legislators to vote according to their conscience on different parts of the package while finding common ground on others. By crafting majorities, he aimed to push through the compromise while protecting their reputations with constituents back home. The results were brilliant;

---

[847] Clay Papers, 1819; Brands, H.W., *Heirs of the Founders: The Epic Rivalry of Henry Clay, John Calhoun and Daniel Webster, the Second Generation of American Giants*, November 13, 2018.

some would even refer to it as legislative art. The Missouri Compromise passed, and in so doing, it averted a Civil War, the likes of which testy politicians such as Cobb and Tallmadge were already threatening. It established a boundary between North and South across the Mississippi River and solidified Clay's reputation as a leader who could rise above regional divides for the sake of the Union.

Nationalism and sectionalism had long been in conflict with Federalists on one side and advocates for states' rights on the other. However, in the 1820s, what these labels actually meant began to shift. Throughout most of Jackson's career, the division was primarily East versus West, but now distinct factions were emerging in the North and South. Much of this change was due to Jackson's victory at New Orleans, which ensured the West would remain part of the Union. By gaining control of New Orleans and the Mississippi River, the gateway to the West was opened, inviting both the North and South to extend their differing economic systems into the new territories. However, the Western territories, which relied on both free and slave labor, could not coexist peacefully. This reality created a growing divide between Northern "free-soilers" and Southern slaveholders.

For Thomas Jefferson, the Missouri debate was "a fire bell in the night."[848] Jefferson, who had vowed equality for America and the world in 1776, was one of the few slave owners who actually reflected upon the moral implications of the peculiar institution of slavery. Jackson, on the other hand, suffered no sense of guilt and was slower to recognize the threat that the Missouri issue posed to the Union. For now, Clay had helped avoid civil war, but how long could the peace last?

---

[848] Thomas Jefferson to John Holmes, April 22, 1820, Jefferson Papers, LC.

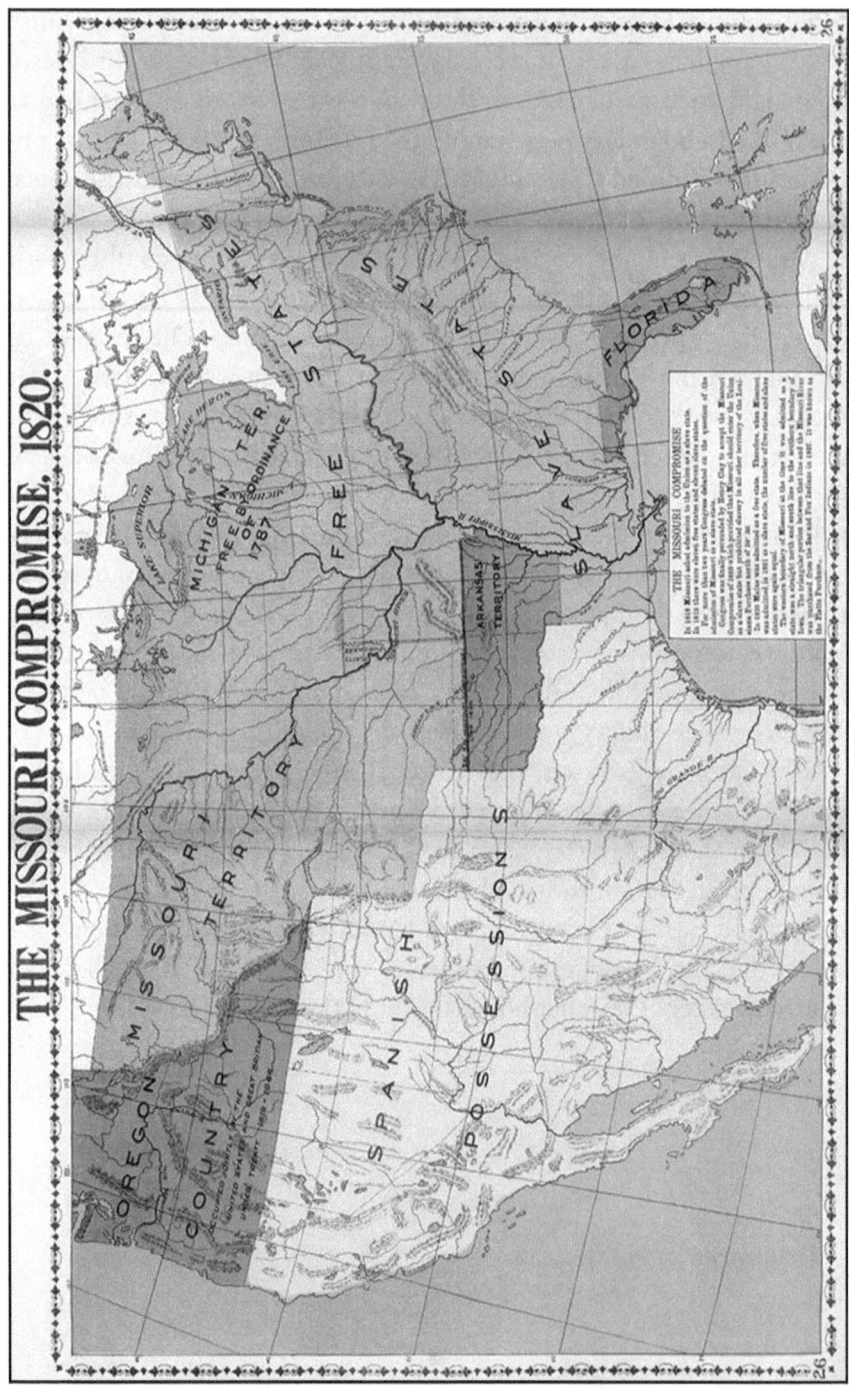
Map of the Missouri Compromise, 1820, Wikimedia Commons

CHAPTER

55

THE LIFE OF A PLANTER

"Our grandfathers were soldiers, so our fathers could be farmers, so we could be artists."
—John Adams

In the midst of the Panic of 1819, Andrew Jackson was back at the Hermitage, having returned to life as a planter. With a handful of black Tennessee soil in his hand, Jackson weighed his prospects. His land was holding up fairly well, but like most plantations, he knew, it would slowly wear out, and he would eventually have to cease depending on farming for his income. With the recession in full swing, the price of cotton was falling and the price of laborers was at an all-time high. Besides, Tennessee's limited growing season made it a risky proposition to begin with. Jackson once again was forced to ponder his age-old question: how to improve his estate.

To make matters more challenging, Jackson had made a promise to his wife, and he meant to keep it. Despite the hard times, he would build the home she had always dreamed of on the site, replacing the old log cabin he and Rachel had occupied since first moving onto the property, fifteen years earlier. As the General told his friends, he wasn't going to build it for himself, as he did not expect to be around for much longer. No, he would honor Rachel the way she meant to be honored. He would build the best mansion in Tennessee.

The General had returned ill, fatigued and weary from his escapades in Florida, and he was convinced that he was not long for this world.

He had to act fast, and so he did. The construction of the new estate house began in the summer of 1819, when the General returned from the Seminole War.[849] Major Lewis recounts how he rode out to the Hermitage one day while General Jackson was recovering from a severe illness. With slow and faltering steps, leaning heavily on his stick, the General took him to the site selected for the new residence— a very level spot in a large flat field, near the old block-house. Major Lewis recommended another site slightly elevated above the almost prairie-like level of the farm.

"No, Major," said the General, "Mrs. Jackson chose this spot, and she shall have her wish. I am going to build this house for her. I don't expect to live in it myself."[850] And there the house was built. Jackson could never have guessed then that he would have many years ahead of him in that new house.

In the throes of an economic panic, the finances of Andrew Jackson fared far better than most. Had he relied solely on his cotton plantation, he may well have been ruined. But somehow Jackson remained immune to the fallout, and this was largely due to his multiple land speculations. According to Jackson's many detractors, these were somewhat shady speculations at best. "The secret of his prosperity was that he acquired large tracts when large tracts could be bought for a horse or a cow bell," James Parton explains, "and held them until the torrent of emigration made them valuable."[851]

One titanic acquisition, however, sheds light on Jackson's employment of questionable tactics. The land grab following the Creek War shows the shrewd manner in which many land speculators, including Jackson, operated. It was the seizure of the Tennessee River Valley, where the great river bends in what is present-day Alabama. When General Jackson wrested control of the valley from the Creeks, he turned it into an explosive real estate opportunity. Jackson and several friends made off with a breathtaking 45,000 acres, colonized the area and were instrumental in founding the new city of Cypress, Alabama. They then established multiple cotton plantations run by enslaved laborers just as cotton prices were reaching record highs. All told, Jackson both created

---

[849] The Hermitage Collection, 2025, Andrew Jackson Foundation
[850] Parton, *Jackson*, II, p. 644
[851] Ibid, p. 557-558.

and scored in the greatest real estate bubble in the history of the United States up to that time.

The details of the partnerships formed for the speculations are hazy at best, even to this day. Also unclear were the speculations' profits. Jackson certainly made money in the boom-times, when the economy thrived, and lost money in the downturns. Yet, one thing is clear: during this period the General's standard of living went in only one direction, up. It did not hurt that he enjoyed a Major General's salary, even during the peaceful period where he was not expected to campaign and could focus on his plantation. To boot, the salary appreciated in value as prices fell during the Panic of 1819. Evidence of his sustained standard of living was the decision, as noted earlier, to take on the major construction project at the Hermitage that led to the columned mansion that stands today. Busy as he had been throughout the period with his various public efforts, he got around to seeking bids only around the time of the Panic. The timing proved fortuitous, for as economically strained as so many Americans were, contractors around the Cumberland were eager for work, and were not apt to haggle over price.

During the next several months, a federal-style brick house, built by skilled carpenters and masons from the local area, took shape. The enslaved on the property manufactured the bricks onsite. The central hallway's design was popular among Southern planters but was beginning to lose favor at the time in the more fashionable eastern areas. But for Jackson, his was now the best house in the neighborhood. The high ceilings, papered walls, and carved balustrades ornamented the interior, and tall, stately white columns adorned the facade. The first floor contained two parlors, a dining room and Andrew and Rachel Jackson's bedroom. On the second floor were four bedrooms. The house featured a basement kitchen, nine fireplaces, a fanlight above the front door and metal gutters. Later, Jackson added a simple exterior entry portico. By landed southern gentry standards, the house was nothing fancy, but for Jackson and his beloved, Rachel, it was a home much more befitting a Major General and national war hero.

Jackson's struggles with his health may have also prompted his desire for a more comfortable home setting. He had experienced physical strains since the end of the Seminole war, more so than he and others might have expected. The old injuries, the depravations of nutrition and rest during the war campaigns had taken a heavy toll. His increased pains and discomfort annoyed him, impacting his mental state as well, as was often the case when he was no longer on the war trail. "I reached Nashville in a bad state of health, much emaciated," Jackson wrote his nephew, Andrew Donelson in July 1818. "I am still much pestered by the bad cough and pain in my side and breast." A few weeks later, he wrote to Isaac Shelby, "My health is bad, I am much debilitated." A little relief came in the months after. "I was taken very ill and confined to my bed for 10 days," he wrote in September 1819, even after he managed to get moving again he felt the effects of the many previous ailments. "My hand shakes from debility and I cannot write with facility." He increasingly expressed his belief that his condition was beyond help and continued to declare pessimistically that he didn't have much longer. "My health is gone," he told Andrew Donelson, "my constitution I fear will never bear up under another campaign."[852]

On some days, when his health was less bothersome, Jackson dreamed of fighting again. The American Senate had ratified the Adams-Onís treaty at once, but the Spanish government, preoccupied with revolutions throughout much of their Latin American colonies, faced more than the loss of Florida, and put off ratification. "I never believed that Spain would ratify the treaty." Jackson wrote in the late summer of 1819, "I do not believe she will now." There was talk that Jackson and his army might have to again take the field in Florida to reconquer the area once again, and this seemed to galvanize the General. "Were you to see how much I am emaciated, you would scarcely believe I could ever again take the field. However, excitement has kept me alive and it might raise me quickly to the necessary strength. I am beginning to eat with a good appetite."

The prospect of war with Spain continued to loom on the horizon for several more months, and Jackson's health stayed tolerable throughout. If he had his way, however, he would have walked into Congress and convinced the hesitant men on the floor that only war would end the wait. Jackson couldn't understand why the government did not simply force Spain's hand. "What does Congress believe?" Jackson argued, "it

---

[852] AJ to Donelson, July, 1818, Jackson, *Correspondence*, II; AJ to Shelby, 1819, Jackson Papers, LC.

is consulting the feelings of the American nation when it is bearing with perfidy the insults of Spain? Are we thus to be humbled?" Jackson knew that his western compatriots would not suffer Spain's insults much longer. "Believe me, sir, the people in the west are prepared to live free or die. they are prepared to surrender the last cent before they will surrender their independence." Jackson was ready and willing to lead the army into the Floridas again, take St. Augustine, and as noted, sail for Cuba to culminate the campaign and oust Spain entirely.

President Monroe, however, facing enough criticism as it was, did not wish to see Jackson further discredit his administration with high-handed measures for a second time, and fortunately he didn't have to. Spain finally ratified the treaty in 1821. Jackson was disappointed, for he had his heart set on another campaign, maybe even one that would include Texas. But he would have to wait.

Spanish control of Florida since the 1500s had not come to much, overall, and most Americans living in the South celebrated the addition of what would become the Sunshine State. In 1821, the long negotiations involved in the drafting of the Florida treaty were finally concluded and ratified by Congress. Monroe, who had been reelected in 1820 in the only uncontested presidential race in American history, needed a man of stature to supervise the transfer, and Jackson was the natural choice. It made sense that the conqueror of Florida should accept the surrender, as the multitude of Jackson supporters expected. Monroe had worked hard to keep the fiery general content, and this provided him a way to continue doing so, without ruffling his feathers. Jackson would have to retire from the army to take on this position in Florida.

Another motive for Jackson's retirement from military service was Congress's decision to reduce the size of the military. Some anti-Jackson members of Congress argued that a smaller army wouldn't have room for him, nor any interest for the vainglorious General. Others were simply following the American tradition of downsizing the military during peacetime, still recalling the days when British soldiers patrolled American streets. Regardless of their motivation, the new army structure would accommodate only one major general, and Jacob Brown, due to his seniority, had priority over Jackson. A torn Monroe, seeing both the pros and cons of the extremist Jackson's efforts, and recognizing the practical value of the "no holds barred" approach Jackson employed, didn't want to let him go, but he felt he had little choice.

After the costly negotiations and purchase of Florida, President Monroe faced budget constraints, and pressure therefore to find ways to cut defense spending. This led to a decision to reduce the nation's military budget. In March 1821, Congress cut much of the army, reducing troop strength from 12,000 to 6,000, eliminating regiments, and scaling back the officer corps. In reducing the number of high-ranking officers, Monroe was forced to decide among his Major Generals as to who was to stay and who was to go. As a commander, Jackson, as noted, had given Monroe headaches more than once with his many conflicts with other military leaders, secretaries of war, and even the president himself. It's still unclear to what degree any of these groups and individuals viewed Jackson as a potential warlord for the Gulf Coast, but there were certainly such whispers. Secretary Calhoun's push for a more centralized hierarchy among officers hinted at the Reduction Act of 1821, which narrowed the army's high command to one major general and two brigadier generals. This meant that either Jackson or Jacob Brown, the only major generals in the army, would need to accept a demotion.[853]

While General Jacob Brown could not boast of a flashy battlefield victory like Jackson's heroic stand at the Battle of New Orleans, he had seniority over Jackson, and a distinguished military record. Appointed brigadier general of a New York militia in 1811, he quickly rose to major general in the regular army, participating in several key campaigns in the War of 1812. Brown's troops defeated the British at the Battle of Chippewa, and he suffered two wounds at the Battle of Lundy's Lane, later helping to defend against the British siege at Fort Erie. As a national hero, he earned a congressional gold medal a year before Jackson received the same honor.

As a believer in national military strength, Jackson could not have been more opposed to the reduction of the army. Adjutant General Gad Humphrey, of New York, describes a letter received by his brother from General Jackson. "The letter alluded to was written about the time when the last reduction of the army took place I will mention some of the most striking features it presents. Among other expressions he says,

---

[853] Adams, *Memoirs*, V, 322.

in express terms—'the government ought to be damned—instead of reducing the army in a republic like this, it should be increased tenfold.' He ridicules the idea of depending upon our militia, speaks of reducing them to a proper state of subordination as an impossibility, and of their utter inefficiency in cases of emergency! He dilates on the state of our frontier, and the extreme impropriety of leaving our remote posts with the inadequate garrisons to which they are necessarily reduced in consequence of the diminution of the army. In fact, the general tenor of the letter is that of decided and bitter animadversion upon the measures pursued by the general government."[854] Like it or not, Monroe stood his ground, and Jackson was forced to accept the end of his military career.

In Jackson's farewell address to his soldiers, given in June 1821 in Montpelier, Alabama, the departing General took one last jab at the government's decision to reduce the nation's military strength. "Under the present organization for the reduction of the army, agreeably to the act of Congress, many valuable officers who have served with me have been suddenly deprived of the profession which they had embraced and thrown upon the world. But let this be your consolation, that the gratitude of your country still cherishes you as her defenders and deliverers, while wisdom condemns the hasty and ill-timed policy which has occasioned your disbandonment; and that, too, while security was yet to be given to our extensive frontier, by the erection of the necessary fortifications for its defense, greatly extended as that frontier has been by the recent acquisitions of the Floridas." Additionally, Jackson warned against leniency when it came to desertion, and in other areas he felt that there was a want of discipline. This reprobation seemed directed at the remaining head of the Southern Department, Jacob Brown. Jackson was not one to go out quietly. [855]

Although Jackson did not agree with the downsize, the situation in Florida provided Monroe with the perfect solution for keeping the General at least a little less dissatisfied, while also ridding himself and the army of the controversies for which the General was renowned. The new territory needed a stern governor to ensure compliance from the Spanish, and as noted, someone with stature for the momentous occasion.

---

[854] Yurie, *American*, October, 1828; Parton, p. 590.
[855] Ibid.

Who better than Jackson, who had made the Florida grab possible. While Jackson's administrative approach was never to be mistaken for diplomatic, he was well-acquainted with Spanish Florida, and with the Spanish officials who ran it. Many still balked at the thought however, remembering his inept handling of martial law in New Orleans, among the many other occasions in which Jackson seemed to disregard civil authority. As a result, there were more than a few concerns about his appointment. Monroe reassured himself, though, that Jackson wouldn't remain in Florida for long. Monroe knew Jackson, and recognized that the job would not be a preferred assignment for the General. But Monroe saw the opportunity to frame the appointment as a great opportunity to celebrate his contribution to bringing Florida into the United States. He would ceremoniously raise the American flag over Pensacola gratifyingly. But the mundanity of peaceful administration of the territory, far away from Tennessee, Monroe believed, would not be to Jackson's liking, and that the General would soon wish to retire quietly as a private citizen.

Monroe was spot on. "Will you take it?" he asked, "the climate will suit you, and it would give me pleasure to place you in that trust."[856] After some hesitation, Jackson accepted the position of governor of the new territory. Not overly enthused with the idea of a governorship in the tropical climate, Jackson recognized the symbolic role he was to play. Reluctantly, the Jacksons headed south in the transfer of Florida to the United States. Traveling first to New Orleans, the General and his wife were celebrated in their return to the scene of the famous battle.

While the Jacksons enjoyed the celebratory welcome in the Crescent City, an interesting development occurred which would have a lasting impact on the relationship between Jackson and the National Bank, later to be a prime motivator against the bank, and a remote cause of important events of the 1820s and 1830s. The General came into conflict with the Bank of the United States while in New Orleans. Desiring to take with him to Florida a sum of money to defray the first expenses of organizing his government, he sent an aide-de-camp to the branch of the United States Bank at New Orleans to see if the bank would advance ten or fifteen thousand dollars on a draft to be drawn by Jackson accountable to the Department of State. His aide returned with

---

[856] Monroe to AJ, Jan. 24, 1821, Jackson Papers, LC.

disappointing news; the branch bank, he was told, had no authority to advance money upon drafts. The mother bank, the cashier had explained, had expressly forbidden drafts. The aide-de-camp argued his case and pointed out the inconveniences that might result from the refusal, but the cashier would not budge on the matter.

From the tone of the General's subsequent dispatch to Washington, it was clear that the General's disdain for the Bank grew tenfold in those moments. "From all this," he wrote to the Secretary of State, "you will discover that, without discount, money cannot be obtained here on drafts upon the government. No delay, however, shall occur in the transportation of the Spanish troops from the want of funds, as far as I can command them; nor will I ever consent to sell bills on the government at a discount to any, and more particularly to the Branch Bank of the United States, in which is deposited all the revenue of the government received at this place. I shall endeavor, at Mobile or Pensacola, to raise the necessary funds or drafts. Should I fail there, I trust, upon the receipt of this, the government will instruct the Branch Bank to furnish me with the amount that may be necessary."[857]

Jackson merges two complaints regarding the bank into a single issue. The Branch Bank did not ask for a discount; instead, it outright declined to negotiate the draft under any conditions. It was the street brokers who would only exchange the bank's notes for General Jackson's draft at the standard discount rate. The General soon resumed his journey toward Florida, but he would tuck this new resentment away for another time. The American financial system would one day pay the price for this refusal to accommodate the hero's immediate financial needs.[858]

They traveled in the latest style, via a river steamboat, arriving in Pensacola in early summer 1821. "All the houses look in ruins, old as time," Rachel wrote. "Many squares of the town appear grown over with thick shrubs, weeping willows and pride of China. All look neglected." The residents were a diverse group. "The inhabitants all speak Spanish and French, some speak four or five languages. There are few white people far than any others. Such a mixed multitude you or any of us ever had an idea of. Mixed with all nations under the canopy of Heaven."[859]

---

[857] Parton, p. 590.
[858] Ibid, 596.
[859] Rachel to Mrs. Eliza Kingsley, April 27, 1821, in Parton, *Jackson*, II. Pp. 595-596.

CHAPTER

56

THE GOVERNOR

"My fortune and constitution have already been much impaired in the service of my country...yet will I go on, and devote what remains of my strength to its best interests."
                                                            -Andrew Jackson

"Pensacola is a perfect plain." Rachel wrote to a friend in Tennessee from the Florida capital. "The land is nearly as white as flour, yet productive of the finest peach trees, oranges in abundance, grapes, figs, pomegranates, etc. Fine flowers growing spontaneously. The town is immediately on the bay, the most beautiful water prospect I ever saw, and from 10 o'clock in the morning until 10 at night we have the finest sea breeze. There is something in it so exhilarating, so pure, so wholesome, it livens the whole system." Rachel and the locals were on hand to experience the final days of Spanish control of Florida, a region that had been governed in the name of the Spanish monarch since the 1500s. By this time, General Jackson was staying outside the city, communicating with Spanish Governor Jose Maria Callava by note. "For three weeks, transports were bringing troops from Saint Marks so they could all sail to Cuba at the same time."[860] Rachel and some American officers urged Jackson to enter the town, but he refused to do so until the transfer was official. He wanted to enter under his own terms, marking the third time he would plant the flag there. So, he waited with a small entourage.

---

[860] Ibid, 596.

"At length, Tuesday, last, was the day. At 7 o'clock, at the precise moment, they hove in view under the American flag, and a full band of music. The whole town was in motion, they marched to the Governor's house where the two generals met in the location prescribed. Then his Catholic Majesty's flag was lowered and the American hoisted high in air not less than 100 feet." It was with great satisfaction that Jackson accepted the surrender from Colonel Callava. "Yesterday I received possession of this place with the whole of West Florida and its dependencies," he wrote John Coffee. "I will have the pleasure to lay the foundation of permanent happiness to the people and lasting prosperity to the city." And then for himself, sweet freedom from public life. "I am contented that this will terminate my political career and that I will have the pleasure to see you at your house in all the month of October, next fully satisfied with the Hermitage to spend the rest of my days."[861]

After the flags changed hands, General Jackson appointed David Brackenridge as the Alcalde of Pensacola. Part of this role involved collecting and safeguarding documents related to private property from the Spanish authorities, as the treaty required these papers to be handed over to the United States government. Elijius Fromentin was a newly arrived U.S. Judge for West Florida. Fromentin was originally from France and had been educated at a Jesuit college to become a priest. Now he found himself in Pensacola, serving as a federal judge, and was soon to find himself caught in the crosshairs of another Jackson tirade.

Jackson's obsession with propriety prevented him from leaving Florida without issue. Even after the formal transfer from Spain, settling affairs required extensive back-and-forth between Jackson and Callava by note, neither of whom was suited for the task. Jackson distrusted the Spanish and despised bureaucratic details, while Callava scorned Americans and resented their disregard for international law. Complicating matters further, there was the language barrier, as neither man spoke the language of the other. They relied on translators, which added uncertainty to their communications, which led quickly to suspicion and mistrust.

The origins of the conflict between Jackson and Colonel Callava seem almost absurd. A woman in Pensacola, one Mercedes Vidal, filed a lawsuit regarding an inheritance of land near the town. To support her

---

[861] AJ to Coffee, July, 1821, Jackson Papers, LC.

case, she needed documents held by Callava's subordinate, Domingo Sousa. She requested assistance from Alcalde Brackenridge, who deemed the request reasonable and brought it to Jackson. Jackson agreed, sending Brackenridge and two helpers to Sousa to retrieve the documents. Sousa refused to hand them over, however, stating he worked for Callava and couldn't comply without orders from the Colonel.

Jackson's men went to carry out the order, but by the time they reached Sousa's location, he had already given the documents to Callava's steward. When Sousa was arrested and questioned, he informed Jackson about what had happened. Jackson felt as though he was being played with, and his ire mounted. He sent Sousa, accompanied by guards, to Callava's place to get the papers back. On their way, they stumbled upon Callava having dinner with several Spanish officers, some Americans, and their wives. Souza and his guards entered the dining room and explained the situation to Callava. The Colonel assured him he would take care of it and sent an aide to Jackson requesting a written application for the documents. At this point, Callava seemed willing to surrender the documents; he just needed the proper paperwork to justify it to his superiors.[862]

Jackson was tired, and with his stomach churning, was not at or near his best. Looking forward to going to bed, he was interrupted by his men's arrival reporting Callava's insistence on a written request. More irritated now than ever, Jackson ordered Callava to hand over the papers. "It is further ordered," he continued, "that if the former governor Don Jose Maria Callava, or his steward Fullerta, fail or refuse to deliver the requested documents, they should be brought before me at my office to answer any interrogations that may be put to them."

Callava was also dealing with some ill health of his own, and had left the dinner party early to return home, when a group of Jackson's soldiers arrived, per Jackson's orders. Callava's intestinal troubles surely worsened at the sight of the armed Americans. Accounts of what happened next varied, reflecting the biases, translations and perspectives of those involved. An American colonel described Callava as verbally aggressive, as might be expected. "Colonel Callava repeatedly asserted that he would

---

[862] Callava's Protest, October 3, 1821, in *ASPFA*, IV, 769.

not be taken out of his house alive, but he seemed to act without much difficulty when the guard was ordered to prime and load."[863]

Accusing the Americans of abuse of power, Callava was irate. "A group of soldiers and commissioners assaulted my house, breaking the fence, notwithstanding the door was open, and entered my room," he testified. "They surrounded my bed with soldiers with drawn bayonets in their hands. They removed the mosquito net. They made me sit up and demanded the papers, or they would use their arms against my person." Callava was taken to Jackson's office, where the two irate men shouted at each other—Jackson in English and Callava in Spanish—while their interpreters struggled to keep up, trying to accurately convey the insults. A Spanish officer present described Jackson as furious. "The Governor Don Andrew Jackson, with turbulent and violent actions, with disjointed reasonings, blows on the table, his mouth, foaming and possessed of the furies, told the Spanish commissary to deliver the papers." Callava refused, according to Jackson, "out of pompous arrogance, and ignorance."

Jackson ordered Callava to be imprisoned. Upon hearing the translation, Callava protested that the order was unjust and dishonorable. "Rising to his feet," recalled the Spanish officer, "he addressed the Secretary, who was seated next to the Governor, loudly declaring that he protested before the government of the United States against the injustices done to his person and public character. Jackson responded to the protest, stating that he was accountable only to his government and that he didn't care about the consequences, even if Callava protested before God himself."[864]

The next day, Callava remained detained by the Americans while Jackson had the papers seized from his home. The situation might have ended there if the recently appointed Judge Fromentin hadn't issued a writ of habeas corpus for Callava. Jackson disregarded the writ, telling the Judge that it deserved nothing but disdain and contempt. Releasing the prisoners Callava, Sousa and Fullarat, Jackson then turned his full wrath onto Fromentin. "Elijius Fromentin, Esq., will forthwith be and

---

[863] Bronaugh to AJ, August 23, 1821, in Jackson, *Correspondence*, III, 112.
[864] Affidavit of Brackenridge, in *ASPM*, II, 830-831.

appear before me to show cause why he has attempted to interfere with my authority as Governor of the Floridas." [865]

A few days after his liberation Colonel Callava left Florida for Washington, to protest the indignity done to him. Several of his loyal subordinates who stayed behind published a statement of the late proceedings. "None of the interrogatories and highly offensive accusations of the General were faithfully interpreted to Colonel Callava, any more than the replies of the latter to the former. It was therefore out of the power of our chief, not knowing what was said to him, to make the auditory understand how innocent he was of the foul charges with which his unsullied honor was endeavored to be stained." They also observed that they " shuddered" at the violent and tyrannical course of General Jackson.[866]

Jackson had a response for them, which he wasted no time in communicating. "Whereas, the said publication is calculated to excite resistance to the existing government of the Floridas, and to disturb the harmony, peace, and good order of the same, as well as to weaken the allegiance enjoined by my proclamation, heretofore published, and entirely incompatible with any privileges which could have been extended to the said officers, even if permission had been expressly given to remain in the said province, and, under existing circumstances, a gross abuse of the lenity and indulgence heretofore extended to them:

"This is therefore to make known to the said officers to withdraw themselves, as they ought heretofore to have done, from the Floridas, agreeably to the said seventh article, on or before the third day of October next; after which day, if they, or any of them, shall be found within the Floridas, all officers, civil and military, are hereby required to arrest and secure them, so that they may be brought before me, to be dealt with according to law, for contempt and disobedience of this my proclamation." The Spanish officers were guilty of crossing General Jackson, and standing up for their commanding officer, Colonel Callava. They were forced out of Florida upon penalty of arrest, never to return. The scourge of Jackson was laying waste to what had been Spanish Florida for nearly 300 years.

---

[865] Parton, *Jackson*, II, 634.
[866] AJ to Adams, Sept. 30, 1821, *ASPM*, II, 814.

In the end, the only gain this standoff provided Jackson was more enemies. Callava soon left for Spain, making Fromentin's writ irrelevant, but the judge stayed behind.[867] With his now passionate animosity for the General, he was not reserved when it came to bashing Jackson's name, regaling friends with lurid tales of his uncontrollable temperament. "The first time General Jackson's authority is challenged," Fromentin asserted, "I wouldn't be surprised if he added 'grand inquisitor' to his list of titles. And if he discovered my library containing many books previously banned in Spain, including the Constitution of the United States, he might send me to the stake."[868]

Jackson dismissed the criticism, as was his lifelong habit. To the General, too much time and energy had been invested securing America's southern border to let someone he didn't respect (albeit a federal judge) undermine his sense of accomplishment. In Jackson's mind, he had earned the right to govern as he wished, having fought against Indians on the frontier, the British at New Orleans, and the Spanish in Florida to protect the American way of life. Finally, his mission was complete. If having personal enemies was the cost of his version of American liberty, he was more than willing to pay it, without batting an eye regarding right or wrong.

The questions remained, however: what was this brand of American liberty Jackson promoted? American liberty for whom? Andrew Jackson was never one to ruminate on the feelings of others, unless it was to take on anyone at any time who dared to question his actions. Perhaps he was not aware that there was another side to the argument, but more likely he didn't care. For his passions were always centered around one main goal: the betterment of America as he saw it. For many, the feeling was that he worked solely for the betterment of Andrew Jackson.

"There never was a man more disappointed than the General has been." Rachel wrote to one of her brothers back home in August of 1821, "In the first place he has not the power to appoint one of his friends, which, I thought, was in part the reason of his coming. But far has it exceeded every calculation; it has almost taken his life."[869] Jackson's

---

[867] *Niles Weekly Register*, XXI, 150.
[868] Martin, S. Walter, *Florida During the Territorial Days*, Athens, Univ. of Georgia Press, 1944, p. 31.
[869] Rachel to Mrs. Eliza Kingsley, July 23, 1821, in Parton, *Jackson*, II, 605.

disappointment was felt throughout Pensacola. He had hoped Monroe would commence the process Jackson himself would later perfect: that of the Spoils System—rewarding political supporters with government office—which would so revolutionize the American government that it would take years of Civil Service reform efforts to undo. Yet, Monroe had already appointed the important Florida positions to others, and Jackson's last great hope to salvage something from the reduction to the civilian office was thwarted. He and Rachel dreamed of returning to the lush lands of the Cumberland. But their departure was not set until the first of October.

On September 2nd, Jackson wrote to Senator Donelson in Tennessee, ruminating on the financial issue of the day, specie vs. paper currency. "I fear the paper system has and will ruin the State. Its demoralizing effects are clearly seen and spoken of everywhere, and I have but little doubt (at least I fear it) that it has predominated in your late elections, although I am unadvised how they have terminated. But from Dr. Butler's letter I learn that he is doubtful that Colonel Wood will lose his election. If this should be the case, let every honest man take care of himself, and have nothing to do with the new rags of the State; for, be assured, it will be a reign of immoral rule, and the interest of speculators will be alone consulted during the existence of the new dynasty."[870] Another momentous foreshadowing of Jackson's later financial reforms, which would become known as the infamous "Specie Curricular."

But Jackson was not yet finished in his mismanagement of Florida. An unfortunate affair occurred towards the end of his reign as Governor of Florida. "In the plenitude of his power he permitted a fatal duel to be fought in Pensacola, in the most public and notorious manner, when a single word from him would have prevented it!" David Brackenridge wrote of the fatal duel that ensued between two army officers. "I allude to the unfortunate affair of Hull and Randal, two young officers; the former just then reformed, the other still in the army. Randal came from Baton Rouge on purpose, it was generally said, to draw a challenge from Hull, who had thrown out threats against him. The challenge was accordingly given by Hull; the duel took place; Dr. Bronaugh, the bosom friend of General Jackson, acting as physician. I was present when the doctor

---

[870] AJ to Donelson, 1821, Jackson Papers, LC.

returned to communicate the result to the General, who was waiting impatiently to hear it. Poor Hull was shot through the heart; his pistol, which was a hair trigger, had stopped at half cock. The General was much displeased. 'Damn the pistol,' by God, to think that a brave man should risk his life on a hair trigger!' He was sufficiently generous not to arrest Randal but gave him an intimation instantly to quit the town, which might have been given before the affair had taken place."[871]

The Jacksons arrived back home on November 3rd, 1821, and General Jackson was fifty-four years of age, hoping, he insisted, on spending his golden years among his family and neighbors on the banks of the Cumberland. Essentially, he had already lived multiple lives in his 54 years. He had first worked to subdue the western wilderness and then taken the lead in defending it. He had led the charge in breaking the power of the southern tribes, and then, by a series of treaties, regulated the terms upon which they were to live either with or without the conquering society. He had managed to set himself and his family up in a handsome private estate, and then acquired, by his actions in war, national renown and intense popularity. He would be justified by many of his contemporaries to think he had done his part for the country, had borne his share of private and public burdens, and could now, with impaired health and strength, sit down under his own porch swing and rest.

The Monroe administration continued to support Jackson's actions, although John Quincy Adams discreetly remarked that he was anxious about the next mail from Florida. He was unsure of what General Jackson might do next, and he understood that whatever actions Jackson took, it would be the Secretary of State who would have to explain it to the Spanish government. But Adams would prove to be one of Jackson's strongest supporters, at least regarding his actions in Florida. Jackson would have reason to feel animosity toward every other member of the cabinet at one point or another, including eventually the chief executive himself.

But for now, Monroe read the room correctly. Jackson's bold actions in Florida were positively received by the majority of Americans, who had no love loss for Native Americans, and even less for the Spanish. "Since my arrival at home," Jackson wrote to David Brackenridge in November, "I have received a very friendly letter from Mr. Monroe, in

---

[871] AJ to Brackenridge, Jackson, *Correspondence*, II, Sept. 1821.

which he has expressed his satisfaction in my having placed you in the office of alcalde: and from the manner he speaks of you, I have no doubt but he is disposed to extend to you any kindness in his gift."[872]

But not everyone was pleased with Governor Jackson's actions, or his handling of the transition. "We feel," said the *National Advocate*, a New York paper, "toward General Jackson all the respect and gratitude which his great and eminent services deserve; and, without the least disposition to cavil or find fault, we cannot approve of the above proclamation any more than with the proceedings as to Colonel Callava. . . . What, then, has been the conduct of these officers? They have published a defense of their former commander, Colonel Callava, and under a government, and in a territory where the freedom of the press and of speech prevails; and for this they are prescribed, ordered to quit the territory, and if found in Florida after the 3d of October they are to be seized and brought before the American 'Captain General of Cuba,' and 'to be dealt with according to law.' We don't understand this new system of government and cannot conceive that there is danger in permitting these Spaniards to say what they think, or what they please."[873]

Most Americans exonerated General Jackson, especially those in the South and West, particularly those who had long eyed the lands the meddlesome Spanish had long held. They not only saw him as a strong-willed General who stood up for the rights of the country, but also as the defender of the weak against the powerful. "I did believe," Jackson wrote in his defense, "and ever will believe, that just laws can make no distinction of privilege between the rich and the poor. And that, when men of high standing attempt to trample upon the rights of the weak they are the fittest objects for example and punishment. In general, the great can protect themselves, but the poor and humble require the arm and the shield of the law. Colonel Callava's powers having ceased here with the surrender of the country, it was only a display, and so considered by me, of pompous arrogance and ignorance, in his claiming the privileges of diplomacy, which, in fact, he never possessed, and his powers having ceased, his commission accomplished, the pretension which he set up was an insult to the weakest understanding."[874]

---

[872] AJ to Brackenridge, 1821, Jackson, *Correspondence*, II. 611.
[873] *National Advocate*, New York, 1821.
[874] Parton, *Jackson*, II, p. 640.

CHAPTER

57

HOME AGAIN

> *"I have made no discrimination of persons. My house has been surrounded by no guards ... all have free admittance ... when they required my aid for the protection of their rights."*
> *–Andrew Jackson*

"Our place looks like it has been deserted for a season. But we have a cheerful fire for our friends and the prospect of living at it for the balance of our lives," Jackson wrote upon returning to Nashville with Rachel. At 54 years old, both he and Rachel were concerned about his declining health, which had not improved since returning home. He was already older than his parents at the time of their deaths, leading him to believe he had limited years left, and he wished to spend them surrounded by loved ones at home. Jackson also often felt guilty about the long absences from home, and how they affected Rachel, who suffered during his departures. When duty called, whether from threats posed by Indians, the British, or the Spanish, he justified prioritizing his country over Rachel. However, for less pressing obligations, such as administering Florida, he felt he could delegate those responsibilities to others.

A summer and fall in the swamps of Florida had nearly destroyed Jackson's vitality. He suffered from many ailments, particularly an excruciating bout with dysentery. "I am truly weary of public life," he wrote to Monroe when resigning the governorship. "I want rest, and my private concerns imperiously demand my attention. My duties have been laborious and my situation exposed me to heavy expense, which makes it more necessary that I should retire and resuscitate my declining fortune to enable it to support me in my declining years." ⁸⁷⁵

Unfortunately, domestic life did not improve his health. The richer home-cooked meals intensified his digestive issues, and the absence of responsibilities meant he had no way to distract himself from his ailments. "For four months, I have been plagued by a severe cough and costiveness," he wrote to James Gadsden in the spring of 1822. Gadsden had suggested a tour of the north and east to keep Jackson's name in the public eye and ease concerns about his past. However, Jackson declined, citing health issues. "I have been recently troubled by my old bowel complaint, which has greatly weakened me, with a constant flow resulting in over 20 occurrences in the last 12 hours." (Probably a bit too informative for Gadsden's preferences.) While his lungs showed some improvement, they were far from clear. "I continue to expel large amounts of phlegm. My health is poor, and I have little hope of recovery. Retirement and relaxation may prolong my life, but I fear they will never restore my broken constitution." ⁸⁷⁶

Jackson's finances were in better shape than his health but still not secure. This was another reason he declined Gadsden's offer for a northern tour, as financial constraints weighed heavily on him. Following the panic of 1819, the western states felt like a different country compared to the east regarding the money supply. By the summer of 1822, the exchange rate between the West and East, particularly the discounts on notes from Western banks, was unfavorable for Jackson. "The state of our paper money would preclude the possibility of procuring eastern funds, which I would need to travel in the east," he wrote to Gadsden.

In regular correspondence with Andrew Donelson, Jackson cautioned his nephew to be mindful of expenses. He had sent Donelson some money but warned he might not be able to send much more. "I remitted you $200, $100 in each letter of Nashville paper, which I hope has reached you and will cover your current needs. I will always be glad to send you amounts necessary to finish your education, but, my young friend, you must realize that I have no means of obtaining money other

---

[875] AJ to Monroe, 1822, Jackson Papers, LC.
[876] AJ to Gadsden, April,1822, Jackson Papers, LC.

than from my farm's produce or the sale of my slaves. I mention this so you can practice economy and keep your expenses within my limits."[877]

The Hermitage primarily produced cotton and corn by this time, having reduce its production of cotton after the Panic. The corn was used to feed the livestock and for corn meal and other foods for the enslaved. The cotton was sold at the market. Like any commercial farmer, Jackson closely monitored market prices as they fluctuated wildly, sometimes increasing 200%, or reducing to half the value at any given time. Those with perishable crops such as wheat struggled more than he did in the hard times of the post-Panic period. Jackson could store bales of cotton and wait for better market conditions, a luxury wheat-farmers were not afforded. However, storage was not cheap, and he couldn't pay his bills with his cotton crop sitting in a warehouse. The advent of steamboats improved access to markets for westerners, but the challenge of being so far from major markets remained. In 1822, Jackson inquired with his agents in New Orleans about the status of the cotton market. They reported that "the very best selections of prime Louisiana cotton will not command over 14 or 14.5 cents." This concerned Jackson, knowing that Tennessee cotton would likely sell for far less. "The prime and best of the new crop will not command over $0.10, with common crops selling for no more than $0.06 to $0.08."

Additionally, Jackson's Hermitage plantation was relatively modest compared to other cotton farms, with cotton yields varying year to year depending on weather and market conditions. In 1825, he planted 131 acres of cotton, producing 71 bales, each weighing about 500 pounds of clean, seeded cotton. Nonetheless, for all the troubles with varmints, critters, bad weather, fluctuating cotton prices, Jackson got the Hermitage into a condition that drew the attention of the neighbors. Willie Blount, who visited Jackson's plantation during this period, remarked on his favorable view of Jackson's operations. "Although I have ever considered him to be among the most industrious men of my acquaintance, both in public and private life, I was really surprised to find his farm in such excellent order and so productive. Under all the circumstances relating to his absence from home, attending the public relations during the late war and since. His farming land is as you know very fertile, very beautiful and

---

[877] AJ to Donelson, 1822, Jackson, *Correspondence*, II, 613.

eligibly situated for comfort. It is largely improved, handsomely arranged, with gratifying appearance to the visitors in his most hospitable house, open to all who have the pleasure of his acquaintance, and who travel through his neighborhood. None of whom passed that way without calling on him for social intercourse knowing him to be the polite gentleman at home and abroad and the friend of men everywhere." Blount's comments notwithstanding, there were quite a few who may have disagreed with his last line, but nonetheless, Jackson's plantation had become a squared away operation.

There are such plenty of reasons to believe that retirement was his sincere desire and real intention. Civil service he appears always to have accepted unwillingly and resigned gladly. Nothing but a summons to the field ever completely overcame his reluctance to leave his happy home; and now that the aspect of the world was such as to promise a lasting peace to his country, he had, doubtless, no thought but to pass his remaining days in the pleasant labors of his farm and the tranquil enjoyment of his home.

Yet, it was not to be. Far from it. For the American public was not done with Andrew Jackson, and he, in truth, was not yet done with them. One might argue that his life had yet to be lived.

By this time, The Hermitage had transformed into a stunning Southern mansion, in stark contrast to the simple log dwellings of the early Cumberland settlers. The Jackson home exuded Southern charm and resembled toned down versions of the antebellum plantation homes of which the South was renowned. The reputation of its owner attracted esteemed visitors from far and wide. The kindness and the down-to-earth generosity of his wife made it a gathering place for friends and family. Those they had supported, including young people who enjoyed the simple pleasures of the time, and ministers of the Gospel, whom the pious Rachel particularly welcomed. To honor his wife, the General built a small church on the Hermitage estate and respected the faith his wife devoutly built her life around. Although Jackson himself did not personally profess the faith to the degree his wife did, his unwavering loyalty to her was one of the most commendable aspects of his life. Mrs. Jackson, affectionately known as "Aunt Rachel" by the neighborhood's younger generation, was a straightforward, kind-hearted frontier woman. Having grown plump and matronly over the years, she stood alongside in great contrast to the polished figure of her husband. They often shared moments together, smoking reed pipes by the fire after dinner.

In the spring of 1825, the Marquis de Lafayette came up the Cumberland in a steamboat, for a visit to Nashville, and was received by General Jackson and enthusiastic crowds of people at the Nashville levee. The Marquis visited the Hermitage, and the two former military men connected on a range of topics. Lafayette discovered the pistols he had given to Washington, which were now in Jackson's possession, and declared that they had found a worthy new owner. Jackson was equally eager to show off another weapon, stating, "That is the pistol with which I killed Mr. Dickinson." At the banquet given in honor of the nation's guest at Nashville, General Jackson presided. Afterwards, Lafayette made the tour of Tennessee in his company. Auguste Levasseur, Lafayette's secretary, provides an interesting recollection of the Frenchman's time at the Hermitage:

"At one o'clock, we embarked with a numerous company to proceed to dine with General Jackson, whose residence is a few miles up the river. We there found numbers of ladies and farmers from the neighborhood, whom Mrs. Jackson had invited to partake of the entertainment she had prepared for General Lafayette. The first thing that struck me on arriving at the General's was the simplicity of his house. Still somewhat influenced by my European habits, I asked myself if this could really be the dwelling of the most popular man in the United States, of him whom the country proclaimed one of her most illustrious defenders; of him, finally, who by the will of the people was on the point of becoming her Chief Magistrate."

"Jackson took pleasure in showing off his home and proud memorabilia he had collected over the years to the famous Frenchman, particularly two handsome swords, and a pair of rustic pistols. The sword was presented to him by Congress; "The saber, I believe, by the army which fought under his command at New Orleans." Levasseur wrote. "These two weapons, of American manufacture, were remarkable for their finish, and still more so for the honorable inscriptions with which they were covered. But it was to the pistols that General Jackson wished more particularly to draw our attention; he handed them to General Lafayette and asked him if he recognized them. The latter, after examining them attentively for a few minutes, replied that he fully recollected them to be a pair he had presented, in 1778, to his paternal friend, Washington, and that he experienced a real satisfaction in finding them in the hands of one so worthy of possessing them. At these words the face of 'Old Hickory' was covered with a modest blush, and his eye sparkled as in a day of victory."

"'Yes, I believe myself worthy of them,' exclaimed he, in pressing the pistols and Lafayette's hands to his breast; 'if not from what I have done, at least for what I wished to do for my country.' All the bystanders applauded this noble confidence of the patriot hero and were convinced that the weapons of Washington could not be in better hands than those of Jackson."[878]

The General bid Lafayette adieu, hoping to see him again in the future, which he would. Jackson returned his attention to his family, particularly his adopted son, Andrew Jr. Jackson always loved the boy as his own but struggled to connect with him as he grew older. When the young man had grown to adulthood, the General established him upon a plantation near his own. Young Andrew, however, was often a poor judge of how best to increase his finances, and often made bad investments, tried costly experiments, and involved himself in failing enterprises. As a result, embarrassment often followed, along with hefty bills at the stores, which Jackson would often have to help settle. By the mid-1820s, with the economic scarcities that followed the Panic of 1819, Jackson's finances, while having improved somewhat, were not as well off as they could have been had he not had to bail out his son. The troubled Jackson later on as he considered how he take on the costs of the Presidency.

Early on in the 1820s, when Jackson was still insisting that he intended to spend his remaining years at the Hermitage, his friend John Eaton, who was at that point a Tennessee Senator, had already documented Jackson's life down to New Orleans. It had made Eaton a celebrity in Tennessee, and part of the reason for his political rise. Jackson likely would have been satisfied to let his greatest victory mark the end of his public career. However, Eaton, Major Lewis, and other friends, along with the vast public stirred by his actions, would not let

---

[878] Levasseur, *Lafayette in America in 1824 and 1825; Journal of a Voyage to the United States.* New York, 1829.

him rest. Within a year of his retirement, a group of supporters was strategizing to make him President of the United States.

Some tell a tale of the origins of the Jackson presidency as deriving from a simple mechanic in Pennsylvania in the summer of 1822, who amidst a discussion among his fellow villagers of the services Jackson had performed for the country, as well as the criticism he had suffered, exclaimed, 'Let us have him for our next president, and show his slanderers that we don't believe them!'[879] The proposal caught on with enthusiasm and was agreed upon with hearty acclaim among the villagers. It was soon in active circulation around the mechanic's home area of Harrisburg; for being approved of by every heart, it was repeated by every tongue. It made its way into the newspapers; the whole nation heard it; and millions who knew not whence the suggestion originated, responded to its propriety."[880] The legend of the General who carved his own path for the good of the country was spreading, and his many enemies had to shudder at the thought.

Much of Jackson's presidential rise involved Tennessean John Williams' opposition. In 1823, John Williams, an adversary of Jackson's, sought reelection to the United States Senate from Tennessee. Jackson's friends, determined to defeat him, found a solution: they would seek to elect Jackson to the Senate, with the idea of not only replacing Williams, but making the Senate a stepping stone to the presidency for Jackson. Major Lewis played a key role in this clever political maneuvering. As most Southern and Western states did, let alone Jackson's home state, Tennessee wholeheartedly supported the General's return to the political arena. The expectation was that his allies would face little trouble in the state after his nomination. However, this was not the case. The popular Colonel John Williams, who had served as a Senator from Tennessee for eight years, had increased his base of support as he faced the end of his term on March 3, 1823.

The Tennessee legislature, meeting in October that year, prepared to decide whether the incumbent Colonel Williams would stay in the Senate. Williams was, as noted, another of Jackson's personal and political rivals. The General's supporters aimed to defeat him unless

---

[879] Phillips, Kim T., The Pennsylvania Origins of the Jackson Movement, *Political Science Quarterly*, Volume 91, Issue 3, Fall 1976, Pages 489–508.

[880] Walsh, Robert, *The Jackson wreath, or, National Souvenir*, Philadelphia, 1829, p. 61.

he agreed to support Jackson's presidential bid, which he refused to do, having already pledged his support to William H. Crawford. With a fellow Tennessean blocking Jackson's bid for the White House, the General's hopes of overcoming Crawford in the 1824 election would have been doomed.

If Jackson's supporters hoped to place Jackson in the White House, they felt they had no choice but to work for the defeat of Colonel Williams. Yet, they recognized what a challenge this would be. East Tennessee claimed the Senator, and Williams was quite popular in that region. To further strengthen his position, he toured the state after the August elections, meeting with newly elected legislators and securing commitments from many to vote for him. Although many were reluctant to make such a commitment to Williams, most did, and were inclined to honor their promises, even if they recognized the damage it would do to Jackson's candidacy.

Despite this, Jackson's most dedicated partisans were determined to do everything possible to prevent Williams from being reelected. Several potential opponents were considered, but none could gather enough votes. Johnny Rhea, a longtime friend of Jackson, came the closest but still fell short by three votes. This situation was troubling; electing a known enemy of Jackson who supported Crawford for president could significantly harm Jackson's prospects. Even though the General had been nominated by the legislature some fifteen months earlier, sending an opponent to the Senate could undermine the state's genuine support for him, appearing inconsistent nationally, and weak at home. It could well nullify his nomination.

To prevent this, a bold plan was necessary. Since no other candidate could beat Williams, it was proposed that Jackson himself would run for the Senate. This idea caused anxiety among some members who feared Jackson could well lose to Williams. John Eaton and Major Lewis went to work to prevent such a scenario by first taking the initiative to nominate the General to the legislature. The reasoning was that if Jackson had to be politically sacrificed, it wouldn't matter how it happened—either by his own defeat or the election of his enemy. Major Lewis, however, was confident that a majority of Tennesseans would not dare vote against Jackson, believing it was impossible.[881]

In light of this situation, the correspondence between Jackson and a member of the Tennessee Legislature prior to the election sheds light on the tension. "All we want," the legislator declared, "is a belief that you will allow your name to be used." Jackson responded, "I earnestly request my friends, and beg of you, not to pressure me into accepting the appointment. If appointed, I could not decline, but in accepting it, I would go against my wishes and feelings. Given my long public service, I hope this request will be seen as reasonable."[882]

Despite his wishes, only twenty-five members of the legislature voted against Jackson for the Senate. His prominence in Tennessee was so strong that only three of those twenty-five were re-elected to the next legislature. His popularity wielded significant influence in many areas of the state, where being known as a Jackson opponent could be risky. Major Shaw Maury, a respected member from Williamson County, nominated Jackson, and he was ultimately elected by a substantial majority, just as Lewis had predicted.

Running for the Senate had been a risky move for Jackson's presidential ambitions, but the consequences were believed to be no worse than electing Colonel Williams under the circumstances. The effectiveness of the Tennesseans' strategic maneuvering meant Jackson was heading to Washington to serve in the United States Senate in the winter of 1823-24, a move some had misgivings about. Not only could it prove to be politically unwise, Jackson himself was not keen on the idea, recalling his previous unhappy time in the Senate. There were also fears that Jackson's performance in the Senate might, like before, be so mediocre that it could tarnish his potential as president. But, in the end, it was decided, and reluctantly, he agreed to it. General Jackson thus became both a Senator and a presidential candidate.

"General Jackson is elected to the Senate. He was the only man in Tennessee who could out turn John Williams. He has done it! The country may yet rue the change." — *Richmond Inquirer*, November, 1823. Jackson probably occupied no more than ten minutes of the Senate's time

---

[881] Brown, William Garrott, p. 102.
[882] AJ response to Tennessee Legislature, Jackson Papers, LC.

during the session, but his fame and candidacy made his votes on the tariff and internal improvements important to politicians.

By the time the successor to President Monroe needed to be chosen in 1824, Tennessee had declared its support for its most prominent citizen, and Pennsylvania surprisingly followed suit. The political landscape was shifting, with notable figures emerging from various states, including William H. Crawford from Georgia, John C. Calhoun from South Carolina, Henry Clay from Kentucky, and John Quincy Adams from Massachusetts. Yet, Tennessee stood out by offering a political outsider the post; a soldier, and not just any soldier, the people's soldier.[883]

It had been twenty-six years since Jackson first served in Congress, and although he struggled as a legislator, he would become a significant figure in the Senate. His rivals were not Senators; Clay was the Speaker of the House, while Adams, Crawford, and Calhoun held Cabinet positions. The country was entering a new phase where voters would choose their party based on positions on issues such as tariffs and internal improvements, rather than older issues of Jefferson's day. However, clear party divisions had yet to emerge, and the Federalist party had faded away and was no more. Personal politics were the sign of the times, with the main question up in the air: who would succeed Monroe?

Jackson arrived in Washington to find loyal friends awaiting him, and he quickly reconciled with some former enemies. Among his allies was Edward Livingston, now a Louisiana Congressman, while one of his previous adversaries, Senator Thomas H. Benton, former Tennessean now turned Missouri Senator, became friendly with him after Jackson made the first move to reconcile. General Winfield Scott also made overtures, and Jackson responded positively, although he maintained a courteous distance from Henry Clay, with whom he never formed a genuine friendship, although relations warmed between the two westerners for the time being. The ice was not entirely removed, however, and soon another heavy frost would polarize conditions between the two permanently.

---

[883] James, Marquis, p. 376.

CHAPTER

58

THE PRESIDENCY ROUTE

"It became necessary, now, to play a bold game"
-Major William B. Lewis

Ultimately, the essence of human experiences—our emotions and the actions they inspire—remains woven throughout history, even in the narratives of presidents. Jackson's narrative as an American President began in small ways from the moment he emerged so outstandingly victorious on the Chalmette Plantation that fateful day in 1815. Interest in a Jackson candidacy began to slowly bubble up from underneath. In that same year as his New Orleans ascendency, Anthony Wayne Butler, a recently retired colonel in the regular army informed the General, "On my way through Pennsylvania and Virginia, I had numerous conversations with people of the first consideration, and I found a strong disposition manifested to run your name for the presidency."[884] Whether or not the frenzied "Jackson-crazies," stunned by his outstanding achievement, truly believed a Jackson presidency was possible is uncertain, but what is certain is that the idea stayed in the minds of the people from that moment forward.

Aaron Burr was no fan of the congressional caucus. Like clockwork, the old caucus system had returned a Virginian to the executive mansion without fail. Exiled from national politics, he still kept a finger on the pulse of the nation. In 1816, although New York was far from Virginia, Burr could already feel the energy building among the Virginians to

---

[884] Brown, William Garrett, *Andrew Jackson*, Kessinger, 1900.

promote another of their fortunate sons for the Presidency. Burr was clearly not a fan of the then Secretary of State either, referring to 'the naturally dull and stupid and indecisive James Monroe.' Burr expressed his preference for what he felt would be a far better choice. "The moment is extremely auspicious for breaking down this degrading system," he complained. "If, then, there is a man in the U.S. who is of firmness and decision, and having standing enough to afford even a hope of success, it is your duty to hold him up to public view." Burr felt no need to hide his feelings on the issue, "That man is Andrew Jackson. Nothing is wanting but a respectable nomination, though it would probably take several more years and one final Virginia presidency to arrive."[885] Burr was onto something.

An important step in the rise of a Jackson president goes back to well before the Williams Senate race. It occurred in the winter of 1821 to 1822, when another tight political struggle in Tennessee resulted in Jackson's first candidacy nod. The John Overton faction, having lost their seats in the state government, believed that by nominating Jackson for President, it might galvanize the state's electorate in 1824. The idea was to create momentum and interest among voters that would help their faction unseat their eastern Tennessee rivals in both the gubernatorial and senatorial races. The Erwin party, something of a successor to the old Sevier faction, had dominated of late.

Many in the Overton camp actually wished to see Henry Clay become the western candidate for president, largely because they didn't believe Jackson had a chance to win, underestimating the General's appeal beyond the borders of Tennessee. Nonetheless, John Overton played a significant role in mobilizing support for Andrew Jackson's presidential campaign. He worked closely with Felix Grundy to organize the Blount-Overton faction within the Tennessee General Assembly to nominate Jackson for president. Additionally, Overton's involvement with the Nashville Junto—a committee formed to support Jackson—further illustrates his active participation in Tennessee politics during this time. His efforts were crucial in promoting Jackson's candidacy against opposition from rival factions.

---

[885] Burr Papers, 1824.

Months before the Tennessee house and Senate caucuses nominated Jackson in the summer of 1822, the *Philadelphia Columbian Observer* had already endorsed his candidacy.[886] When a group of Tennessee lawmakers then informed Jackson that they intended to nominate him for the presidency, the General's candidacy began to gain speed. The announcement from his Tennessee cohorts didn't come as a surprise to Jackson, as talk of the idea had long preceded it. It was in January of 1822 that the General's supporters began the more serious clamor to see him take the executive reins. The first demonstration of promoting Old Hickory was made in January 1822, in one of the Nashville papers. Soon afterward, the editor of the Nashville Gazette, Colonel George Wilson, took the field openly and boldly for the General, as his candidate for the Presidency. The proposal was well received by the people of Tennessee, and the momentum grew. The idea of a Jackson candidacy spread to other states. It was soon determined, therefore, that the necessary steps should be taken to bring him forward at the next session of the Legislature.

The Tennessee legislature had now made it official, they wanted Jackson in the top post, and therefore they needed an answer from the man himself. An initially hesitant Jackson drafted his answer carefully, noting that he did not seek the nomination. "I am silent, but the papers are not," he told his former aide Richard Keith Call, who was to inform the legislature of Jackson's response. "The voice of the people I am told would bring me to the presidential chair, and it is probable some of the legislatures may bring my name before the public... The people have a right to call for any man's services in a Republican government, and when they do, it is the duty of the individual to yield his services to that call." [887] Supporters of Jackson were decided, Jackson's response required no more encouragement, the General was on board. The Tennessee Republicans met in caucus later that summer and the vote was unanimous in support of Andrew Jackson's candidacy for the Presidency.

Sam Houston, not entirely recovered from the Battle of Horseshoe Bend, but certainly on the mend, was not only a rising star in Tennessee politics, but also one of the leading Jackson supporters for President. Jackson had long been one of Houston's leading mentors, and fondly

---

[886] Anonymous Letter, Archives of the *Philadelphia Columbian Observer*, 1825,
[887] AJ to Call, 1823, Jackson, *Correspondence*, II, 615.

recalled their days together in combat, and in Nashville. He thought of Jackson as a second father, and to Houston, Jackson was the embodiment of character. Like so many other Jacksonians, Houston loved the irascible General for his indomitable will, his uncompromising authority, his passion for his region, and he and the multitudes of Tennesseans would not let him tend his farm in peace.

James Gadsden, another of Jackson's former subordinates very much on the political rise, would not either. Gadsden was one of the earliest to plant the seeds of a Jackson Presidency in the minds of many, including the General himself. "The next president has, as you will perceive, been agitated in the papers," Gadsden wrote from Washington. "Crawford's friends are intriguing deeply, and in some quarters with success." Gadsden, one of Jackson's former lieutenants, shared Jackson's distaste for William H. Crawford. "To elevate him to the presidential chair would produce a chain of evils and entail a series of misfortunes on our country that would require a century to remedy."

Gadsden had written to Jackson to report on the prospects of the 1824 succession of Monroe, soon to complete his two-term presidency. He was both reporting the political forecast in his letter to Jackson, and also subtly suggesting that his former commander enter the Presidential race himself. "I know not your opinions as to who should be the next president, but believe you agree with me as to the total unfitness as to a certain aspiring personage. If in this case you deem me worthy of your confidence, you will give me your views on the subject. You will appreciate my motives on this request; the good of our country requires that all honest men who are in favor of a settled policy for the administration of our government characterized by honest independence and a freedom from intrigue should unite in elevating to the presidency the man who will be governed accordingly." Gadsden suggested no candidate for Jackson's endorsement, but he reiterated that the man with the current advantage was definitely not what America needed, a man that both he and Jackson despised: the current Treasury Secretary William H. Crawford. "Mr. Crawford is and has even been a most dangerous and unsettled politician."[888] Gadsden knew Jackson well enough to understand his former commander's personality. He knew

---

[888] Ibid.

Jackson was a strong ally to have in one's corner, but as an enemy he could be absolutely petrifying. He wished to recruit him to the anti-Crawford crusade and take on the mantle of a pro-Jackson crusade in 1824.

Gadsden knew the way to get Jackson into the race was to convince him that without his candidacy, William H. Crawford would win. Gadsden believed in Jackson. He respected his honesty and uprightness of character, as he saw it. The two men shared opposition to the Secretary of the Treasury, and Jackson could not agree more with Gadsden's harsh words against Crawford. Gadsden went on to explain that the alternative to the Treasury Secretary seemed, by some, to be the Secretary of State, John Quincy Adams, although Gadsden did not believe his chances were very strong. "Mr. Adams' friends are not so active and even in the quarters from where he should expect support appear lukewarm."[889] In New York, supporters were promoting their governor, Dewitt Clinton. "Clinton stands no chance, except within his immediate party. He is execrated by a large majority of the community." Gadsden judged.

Gadsden knew how devoted Jackson was to what he deemed the public good, and he was writing to Jackson in November of 1821, a time in which few people, Jackson included, seriously considered the idea of the former General for president. Yet, opponents like Crawford and Clay saw the massive popularity Jackson enjoyed with the American public at large, and they recognized the threat to their hopes Jackson posed. But a man of Jackson's humble origins had never come close to the White House before. In the early 1820s, it did not enter into the realm of possibility that a man not of the ilk of the wealthy, connected political elite could ever hope to be nominated, let alone elected, for the highest office in the land.

George Washington was the closest possible example among predecessors to Jackson's presidential hopes. The hero soldier of the Revolution led his country through war and devastation to peace and independence. But Jackson was not Washington, who was the most prominent citizen of the leading state in the Union, and had been at the head of national politics since even before the Revolution, when he served as a delegate to the First Continental Congress in 1774, representing Virginia, playing a key role in organizing the colony's response to British

---

[889] Gadsden to AJ, Jackson, *Correspondence*, II, 616.

policies, including helping train militias and enforcing the Continental Association boycott. He was the uncontested military leader of the war, and after the war, was voted president of the Constitutional Convention of 1787, where he oversaw creation of the federal government over which he was then elected.

The other presidents had all been members of the political elite, founding fathers of the Revolution (or the son of a Founding Father, in John Quincy Adams' case), well-connected lifelong politicians, groomed for service to their predecessors. The pattern had developed since 1800 in that Secretaries of State became the next President after serving their time in the cabinet. In the era when communication and travel was slow, gaining a national standing and renown took years to build and it was only built by years of experience in government. The men in the capital from the several states became familiar with each other over time, formed views of each other, and spread those views of their colleagues when they returned home, where the state legislatures chose electors. This interpersonal political networking led naturally to the massive role political parties have come to play in the nominating of candidates.

Since the fall of the Federalists, the Republican Party had essentially dictated the choice of president. Among the general public, the candidates on a ballot were often not much more than a name; it was party affiliation that determined how they might vote. People voted for those that had the support of their party, which was all that Monroe had needed to be elected President twice, the second time entirely uncontested. Monroe was a steady politician who had been in the midst of Revolutionary events since the war but was never an overwhelmingly charismatic leader. To gain the nomination he required the support of the Republicans in Washington.

Yet in the early 1820s, there were signs of change. Westerners were never fond of the exclusivity of the caucus system, which had the effect and intent of keeping the eastern hold on the federal government. As the population moved west, more western states entered the Union, and a new demographic resulted, where western views had to be taken into consideration. And the western states typically entered with fewer suffrage restrictions. Several supported the idea that voters, rather than the state legislatures, should choose the electors who chose the president. The result was that for the first time a westerner, and a man popular with the people, even if not within the party, might become president. The beginnings of the primary system were being planted in the American political system, although it would be some years before it would fully take root.

If Jackson dreamed of the presidency at that time, he kept his dream to himself, not sharing his political aspirations with anyone, not even telling Rachel, who liked to have her husband home and certainly would have objected. Perhaps this is why he kept any future political plans under wraps. He left Gadsden and various others (who would have spread the word quickly) unsure of his plans. It is possible that he had not considered the idea, had any desire to be President (although that is unlikely knowing how much Jackson relished power,) or think that he was qualified or capable of the job of President of the United States. His brief career in politics in the 1790s, as both a Congressman, and then Senator from Tennessee had convinced him that most of what Congress did was talk, have dinner parties, and balls.

By 1823, the 55-year-old Andrew Jackson was being hailed as the novel, fashionable choice of especially western voters for the upcoming presidential race in 1824, and the candidate was riding a wave of popularity rivaling that of George Washington himself.[890] Jackson's military conquests had propelled him to rock-star status throughout the U.S. and having the backing of the people, it set the stage for his later revolutionary ideas and actions as president. Many forward-thinking Americans envisioned a radical shift in leadership, assets and foreign affairs if they could push the iron-willed Jackson to the helm.

But then, as now, before one could consider a successful run at the Presidency, much work needed to be done. Rival interests need to be reconciled; competing egos calmed; unfounded pretensions set aside; local pride acknowledged or eased; and local biases identified and addressed, extensive correspondence written. There will be discussions in editorial offices, customs offices, country homes, law firms, and the cozy corners of major hotels, as well as in the hallways and committee rooms of legislative buildings.

Throughout this momentum building period of a Jackson candidacy, the General insisted that he was not interested in the presidency. He had

---

[890] Meacham, Ch. 3.

always maintained that he was never one to seek political office. Jackson wrote to a former aide, "I never have been an applicant for office. I never will. I mean to be silent. I have no desire nor do I expect ever to be called to fill the presidential chair." At the end, he continued with tranquility, "should this endorsement from the legislature be the case, contrary to my wishes, I am determined that it shall be without any exertion on my part. Of this unexpected event all that can be expected of me is to obey the call of the people."[891]

---

[891] Jackson to G.W. Martin, Dec. 1823, Jackson, *Correspondence*, III, 222.

CHAPTER

59

ERA OF SHADY DEALINGS

"Heaven smiled upon us and gave us liberty and independence. That same Providence has blessed us with the means of national independence and national defense. If we omit or refuse to use the gifts which he has extended to us, we deserve not the continuation of his blessings.
—Andrew Jackson

At his study at the Hermitage, Andrew Jackson picked up his pen and stared at the page before him. Struggling to find the right words that would provide a salve for his rage, Jackson was uncharacteristically drawing a blank. Frustrated at the hypocrites who sought to take him down with their accusations, Jackson thought of the ever-changing opera of public scandals and anxiously stared at the "memorandums" spread out before him. Finally, the words began to flow, slowly at first, and then like a flood. Jackson scribbled down each word as it popped into his head. The result was a jumble of Jacksonian wrath: "The case, of the opinion of the attorney general U.S. on which M. was removed, the charges as the Secretary of the T. swindling the government out of 25,500 and giving it to the Cherokee in violating the constitution, and employing a senator to travel over three states to examine the land offices that he might election year for him. The charges in the papers versus the post office department, etc. etc. etc. etc. The conduct of other nations towards their officers contrasted with that of our government towards me. The charges for preserving Orleans, the necessary, urgent, martial law declared, the country and the constitution saved by. The Seminole campaign, the conduct of Congress in that case, the members mutilated and distorted the evidence, their views and object—particularize them. The conduct of the committee of the Senate, the declaration of Eppes that he consented to the report without hearing the testimony, William H. Crawford charged with abiding in drafting it. The Sec of the T being publicly charged with interfering with the state election of those favorable to his views to the presidency."[892]

Noticeably, Jackson vented his frustrations directly at his personal vendettas against those he despised, or on acts of his own in his various campaigns. But on and on he went, releasing the anger and self-pity pent up inside him, alternating between serious charges of corruption in government, and the victimization he had suffered from Washington officials during his Florida tenure. Much of his vitriol was directed toward Treasury Secretary Crawford, whom he loathed. His disdain for Crawford had only worsened since the Secretary's criticism of Jackson, and his interference in the Treaty of Fort Jackson. But what was important–what he had decided, and of which he became convinced, was that he now knew the reason for the mistreatment. The administration was corrupt, simple as that. He had to feel better; he had to feel vindicated believing this. It had always been corrupt—"corrupt to the core"—and that accounted for its abuse of patriots like himself. He too could play the mud-smearing game.

Without knowing the specifics of Jackson's charges, which were a log of all the misbehavior of government agents during James Monroe's two terms in office, evidence does exist, both public and private, to prove that his administration was perhaps one of the most corrupt in the early history of the United States. The years 1816 to 1828 are generally known as the Era of Good Feelings, because it was a period in which one party ruled the nation, and it was believed, brought political peace and goodwill to the country. Not so well hidden under the surface, however, was the considerable quarreling and factious bickering within that party. But instead of an Era of Good Feelings this 12-year period of the Madison/Monroe years, some historians have argued could well be referred to as the nation's first "Era of Corruption."

---

[892] Jackson Papers, LC.

With the rise of corruption, the economic strains the country faced, the graft, the fraud, the threats from both within and without, one wonders if Jackson felt compelled by his sense of duty to seek the reins of government. The need for a new direction in government was apparent. The country had grown beyond its former capacities, the west was no longer the west of old, now it extended to the Oregon territory. Westerners, those without wealth, those with big dreams, and more means than ever before of pursuing those dreams, clamored to have their voices heard. No longer would a government controlled by the old establishment suffice. And Jackson embodied this rising tide more than any other. Thus, they sought him out.

Jackson read the papers religiously. He brooded over what was happening to the nation he had done so much to defend and protect. In letters to friends he blasted as criminal the incompetence of those in high office. Worse, he would angrily write, they were systematically robbing the people of the freedoms so much blood had been spilled to protect. Of course, Jackson coupled these criticisms with his usual themes: harping on the questioning of his Florida actions, and the abuse he'd suffered at the hands of the administration. His only purpose, he scribbled, had been a desire to ensure justice for every citizen no matter his rank. "I was determined to administer the government for the happiness of all, and prevent the poor and humble from the tyranny of wealth and power, this I have accomplished, I trust."[893] And what was the thanks he received? Criticism and vicious accusations from those same corrupt officials, whose personal immorality made them unable to see the right and true acts of patriots.

Even James Monroe, whose administration Jackson had always supported, had failed him. The president's appointments, his hypocritical affectations, his duplicitousness and lack of recognition of what Jackson achieved in Florida–all these and more kept the General up at night. "Strange to tell," he commented, "I have never from the first got a single line of instructions from the president during my Florida tenure. All my measures were supported," he fumed, "none of them... were disapproved of." Yet, in his annual message to Congress on December 3, 1822, Monroe galled Jackson by discussing Jackson's feud with Elijius

---

[893] AJ to Coffee, Jackson, *Correspondence*, III, 223.

Fromentin as "a misunderstanding of authority." Jackson was beside himself on hearing this. A misunderstanding?! What a typical Monroe dodge that was. "The manner in which he speaks of Fromentin and myself, when the facts were before him, proves that his statement was not true."[894] Jackson may have had a point. Monroe struggled to be straight with the testy General, and that had to be misleading to Jackson, a man who struggled to see the fault in his own actions.

Jackson, typically and characteristically, failed to see the argument from the viewpoint of another, even if that person was the President. President or not, to Jackson, Monroe had simply misrepresented the truth. Jackson now believed that the greatest fraud in the nation sat in the executive mansion in Washington. Only a few years before, Monroe shared with Jackson that he planned to have documentary evidence altered in regard to the seizure of Florida. It was no surprise to the General that the country was in the throes of an epidemic of corruption. At the very top of the administration in Washington, a friend of Jackson's swore, sat "a base, infamous hypocrite named James Monroe." Jackson found it hard to disagree.

Jackson was excessively agitated to be sure, but he had a point. It was becoming commonplace for government officials to be accused of corruption, involved in alleged questionable activities which usually involved enormous sums of money. From the President of the United States to various cabinet members and officials in Washington, as well as state officials, there was a growing revelation of misconduct in how official business was being handled. The level of corruption across the country was so widespread that it raised concerns among many about the safety of American institutions.

Throughout 1822 the newspaper headlines alerted the American people to scandalous swindlers almost on the daily. "That scandalous default locations in our public pecuniary agents, gross misapplications of public money," the New York Statesman observed in a summer news story, "and an unprecedented laxity in official responsibilities occurred and been suffered under our government for the past six or eight years are faults not to be concealed." The *Washington National Intelligencer*, the Monroe administration's apologist newspaper, admitted that "one of the

---

[894] Ibid.

charges brought against the present administration is a gross neglect and waste of public property," but assured the reader that there "has been less speculation in public affairs... than has been supposed." Washingtonian readers had to wonder how that qualified as a defense. The article went on to admit that "errors of judgment may have been committed by the president and his advisors as well as other men."[895]

Like all good politicians, Jackson was an avid reader of newspapers and he absorbed the details of the specific scandals as they appeared in the press over the next several years. "Enormous defalcation," the *Baltimore Federal Republican* bellowed in the spring of 1822, "involving naval agents, marine paymasters, pursers, and the like. And these," said the newspaper, made up only "one of the innumerable instances of corruption in Washington."[896] The situation was rapidly getting out of hand and people were beginning to worry that the pillars of government were rotting from the decay. "There has been no accountability in our public agents," said another newspaper, "from the highest to the lowest." There was no hiding the implication. The highest meant no other than the President of the United States, and the members of his cabinet.

Public and private misbehavior was nothing new, and could be expected, as it has habitually existed throughout American history, and the history of governments in general, for that matter. Monroe's presidency followed the War of 1812, and after all wars, as the historical record indicates, morality in American life and government tends to plunge. Also, and far more important, the country was entering an era of profound and revolutionary change that would permanently alter every aspect of national life. The Industrial Revolution had just taken hold and the process of converting a predominantly agrarian society into an industrial and heterogeneous one had already begun. The economy was expanding and diversifying, as was the population--and with it, the hopes and dreams of American citizens. The country's leadership was in transition, as the old Revolutionary generation was dying off, and a new generation of young leaders emerged. As the economy generated new and unprecedented amounts of wealth, men scrambled for gains in every way

---

[895] Archives of the *Washington National Intelligencer, 1822.*
[896] Archives of the *Baltimore Federal Republican*, Spring, 1822.

they could, caught up in the momentum of unheard-of profits. And none had more ability to ensure that for themselves than government officials.

Although some of the worst offenses never came fully to light, [897] and enough information about government corruption escaped into the courts and public prints to alarm men like Jackson, who concerned themselves about what this corruption might do to their free institutions (and possibly threaten to expose some of their own shadier land dealings,) its very ubiquitousness was particularly disturbing. It seemed to be everywhere, spreading from Washington--always at the epicenter of corruption--to state and local governments and even into the private sector. The entire nation seemed to be adrift in its moral and ethical compass.

Newspapers lamented the decline of public and private virtue, individual correspondence frequently addressed it, and diaries and journals that have survived the years give us insight into the details of the concerns. "Mr. West, Cashier of the US Branch Bank at this place," recorded one such journal in 1822, "... has lately been sent here in place of Mr. Latimer, who became a defaulter to a considerable amount—it is really lamentable and humbling to the pride of integrity--to look at the numerous instances of this kind of fraud which have occurred within the last three or four years--scarcely is there a large city, or indeed a small one, where there is a bank—that has not had cause to bewail the aberration from rectitude of some men of (before) unsuspected honesty, and one whom the people have delighted to honor- Even now as I passed through Richmond, a trial was pending against the State Treas. as defaulter for $120,000." [898]

Andrew Jackson, Old Hickory, the hero of New Orleans, was combative, often controversial, but as of yet, no one had any hard evidence that he, himself, was corrupt. The rumors were rampant, particularly of land fraud, but Jackson had ways of keeping his self-motivated land-grabs from becoming overtly scandalous. Jackson's harsh treatment of Southern tribal nations in the late 1810s was backed by a strong government presence, masking any potential fraud on the General's part. Questions arose about whether Jackson or his associates directly benefited from treaties during this time. In late 1817, just months before Jackson

---

[897] Bancroft to W.L. Marcy, Nov. 5, 1841, Miscellaneous Papers, NYSL.
[898] J. D. Steele, Manuscript Journal, 1820-1829.

entered Spanish Florida and took control of Pensacola to subdue the Seminole nation, several of his family members and friends established the Pensacola Land Company. Some accused Jackson of collusion, but the Secretary of State at the time, John Quincy Adams, defended him, claiming that the two actions were unrelated despite their timing. Was this simply a case of coincidence?

Additionally, a land company called Cypress, founded by Jackson's friend John Coffee in Northern Alabama, acquired 45,000 acres from the Cherokee in a treaty marred by allegations of fraud. Monroe had appointed Coffee as the surveyor general of public lands in early 1817. The following year, Jackson, who held shares in the Cypress Company, purchased some of this land with no competing bids. In one correspondence, Jackson advised Coffee on boundary negotiations, and that the government's goal was to bring the land to market and populate it, trusting that Coffee would use his judgment in any disputes.

As the end of Monroe's tenure neared, Jackson went from a dark horse to a potential frontrunner in the race for the highest office in the land. The 1824 election was shaping up to be one of the most highly contested races in the nation's history. To succeed Monroe, all four candidates had lined up their voter bases; each held a large coalition of supporters. But, after William Crawford withdrew from the race due to health reasons, there were but three left. The top three candidates that remained, Andrew Jackson, John Quincy Adams, and Henry Clay, were all from the Republican Party, the only party that existed at the time after the demise of the Federalists. But by no mean were the platforms on which each man stood even remotely the same.

Compared to Adams and Clay, Jackson was a political outsider. His reputation as a self-made man appealed to a large percentage of the American people, although early on, Jackson's political opponents failed to recognize this phenomenon. "Having come from virtually nothing there is a connection that people feel with him, and his great power base is going to be these newly empowered white male Americans from northern cities and also from western farms, and they're going to see him as their guy." Historian Edward T. O'Donnell explains.[899]

---

[899] O'Donnell, Edward T., *Visions of America*, Pearson, 2009.

The idea of Andrew Jackson becoming president changed the dynamics of the coming campaign, although not everyone recognized this shift. Not even the normally razor-sharp Henry Clay, "Harry of the West" the only other prominent candidate not from the east, who initially dismissed Jackson's chances. Clay viewed the General's candidacy as a mere acknowledgment of the hero's distinguished service to the nation, or perhaps as a strategy to create division in the West, to benefit a non-western candidate. He confidently asserted that no other western state would support Jackson and leaned on his "friends in Tennessee" for their unwavering backing, should Jackson be sidelined.

It was likely that the remainder of President Monroe's cabinet wished for Jackson to fade from the political scene altogether. For years, the three department heads, Secretary of State John Quincy Adams, Treasurer William Crawford, and Secretary of War John C. Calhoun had all vied for positions in a party that was rapidly splintering into various regional factions. The emergence of more candidates only added to the uncertainty. In an effort to narrow the field, Monroe, possibly with Adams' endorsement, had previously offered Jackson the role of minister to Mexico, a country enjoying newly won independence from Spain. While Adams reportedly received Jackson's name positively, concerns were raised about the General's infamous temper, his violent nature, questioning whether these traits made his appointment sensible. "I said that, although the language of General Jackson was sometimes passionate and violent, he always appeared, to me, calm and deliberate. And acting under responsibility, I do not apprehend that he would do anything to the injury of his country, and if he should commit any indiscretion, he would bear the penalty of it himself, for the nation would not support him in it."[900] This Adams claim is particularly befuddling, knowing what Adams knew of Jackson's conduct in Florida, where his improprieties were unparalleled. Yet it was through Adams' unwavering support that Jackson managed to avoid paying a price for his misconduct.

Adams did acknowledge that there were challenges regarding Jackson's potential diplomatic role. It was hard to envision Jackson in any diplomatic capacity, especially given his disdain for Spain, serving as an envoy to Mexico— a nation whose Spanish speaking population

---

[900] Adams to Monroe, *Adams Memoirs*, IV. 1824.

shared a controversial boundary on the U.S. frontier that Jackson wanted to see expanded further south and west. On March 15, 1823, Jackson, citing the "unfortunate, revolutionary situation in Mexico," turned down the appointment, citing among his reasons that no U.S. minister could negotiate a beneficial treaty during this tumultuous period. By then, Jackson had already publicly shown interest in running for the presidency.

Colonel John Williams, Source: Samuel G. Heiskell, Andrew Jackson and Early Tennessee History (Nashville, Tenn.: Ambrose Printing Co., 1921). Uncited artist.

CHAPTER

60

WHAT DOES JACKSON STAND FOR?

"In short, sir, we have been too long subject to the policy of the British merchants. It is time we should become a little more Americanized, and instead of feeding the paupers and laborers of Europe, feed our own, or else in a short time, by continuing our present policy, we shall all be paupers ourselves."

-Andrew Jackson

Washington had gone through a grand transformation since the end of the war, nearly a decade before. The burned and charred remnants left by the British invasion in 1814 had been rebuilt, repaired, or painted over. The Presidential mansion, once blackened and damaged by fire, had received a fresh coat of paint, and local residents, now referring to the mansion as the White House, enjoyed the presence of a large cannon on its lawn.

The new Capital building, situated on a 22-acre plot about a mile from the White House and surrounded by an iron railing, offered a stunning and expansive view of the city due to a major dip in the ground to the west. From this vantage point, one could admire the heights of Georgetown and the winding paths of the Potomac River extending as far as Alexandria.

The Jackson family would soon be experiencing a grand transformation of sorts themselves, for the year 1824 marked a significant moment in the lives of Andrew Jackson and his family. It was the year Jackson first campaigned for the presidency and the year Emily and Andrew Donelson celebrated their marriage.

Raised in a comfortable environment yet instilled with strong values, Emily and Andrew entered their married life with great aspirations. Jackson saw promise in Donelson's potential as a political leader, while Emily captivated those around her with her charm. "Emily, it is hoped, will make a fine woman, and I know her to be more than ordinarily smart," her sister remarked.[901]

Their lives were already deeply intertwined with the world of politics. Andrew Donelson, educated at prestigious institutions such as West Point, Transylvania University, and Nashville's Cumberland College, demonstrated his ambition by delivering speeches, including one on July 4th in Nashville during the summer of 1824. Though his speeches may have been somewhat lengthy and a bit ornate, his youth afforded him a pass, and the opportunity to refine his skills. With Jackson as a mentor, Donelson found guidance akin to that of a father figure, who aimed to prepare him for a promising future.[902]

Family tradition holds that Donelson was just 18 years old and on his way to West Point when he first felt a spark for the redheaded Emily, who was only 10 at the time. As she left her log schoolhouse on Lebanon Road to return home—a place the family affectionately called "The Mansion"—Donelson encountered schoolchildren attempting to cross a stream on a narrow log, a family historian wrote. "Other children got over as best they could, but not so princess Emily, for her Fairy Prince took her in his arms, restoring her to earth on the other side. In later years, Donelson admitted he realized then that he loved her." By 1823, Jackson had begun to express his affection for Emily in letters to Donelson. "Present me affectionately to Miss E.," he wrote in January 1824.[903]

"I sincerely thank you for your attention to my business," Jackson wrote his nephew from Washington in April 1824. "I assure you it gives me pleasure to find that my private concerns are kept so snug and all

---

[901] Meacham, Jon, Ch. 4.
[902] Armstrong, Zella, "Andrew Jackson Donelson," in *Notable Southern Families* Vol. 2, Chattanooga, TN: Lookout Publishing Co., 1922, p. 103.
[903] AJ to Donelson, Jan. 1824, Jackson, *Correspondence*, III, 231.

my debts paid, and accounts so nearly closed." Flattering Donaldson, Jackson told him: "I hold no correspondence with anyone but yourself… I will have to bring you on with me; I have been this winter at a great loss for some confidential friend to aid me." For Donelson, the excitement at these words were palpable, for this meant that he would very likely be accompanying this uncle to Washington, for Jackson's presidential prospects looked strong. In fact, it was this letter, according to family lore, that prompted Donaldson to propose to Emily in the spring of 1824.

Donelson was determined not to leave for Washington without Emily as his bride. After receiving the summons to come assist his uncle, he spoke with Emily at the mansion. It was clear that the two young lovers had reached a pivotal moment in their relationship. Rachel and Andrew Jackson played supportive roles in their romance. "Romance was not a stranger to Rachel's heart," a later family historian noted, "and she had watched with the greatest interest the growing fondness between Andrew and Emily and had encouraged its development." Rachel would send the couple out to stroll beneath the tall poplar trees at the Hermitage, or to sit together in her garden under the vine-covered arbor. It worked quite effectively, and their engagement took place in Rachel's garden, with a wedding date set for September.

Jackson was thrilled with the union. The Donelsons embodied the qualities he admired: virtue, intelligence, loyalty, and the fact that they made a handsome couple. As a wedding gift, he presented them with a sizable and appealing piece of land within a mile of the Hermitage. Following their wedding, which was officiated by Reverend William Hume at The Mansion, the couple embarked on a journey to Washington, accompanied by their aunt and uncle. If their travels at that early date were any indication, their married life was destined to be filled with politics, drama, and adventure.

Shortly after leaving Tennessee, they encountered a near-fatal carriage accident outside Harrodsburg, Kentucky. Emily recounted, "The tongue snapped at the top of a very steep and rocky hill, and it was by the interposition of Divine Providence that our lives were spared." Despite the frightening brush with danger, the following day brought joy as they attended "a splendid ball" in Lexington. Emily marveled at witnessing the Marquis de Lafayette and Jackson greet each other upon their arrival in Washington.[904]

Amidst the grand gatherings and bustling evenings, Emily found her life with her uncle enjoyable. She wrote to her mother in December 1824, stating, "We are very comfortably situated here, crowded with company, and boarding at an excellent house. We live very well and have everything in abundance. Everything was new and interesting to me."

On Sundays, Emily and Andrew opted not to join Rachel at the Presbyterian and Methodist services she preferred and instead attended the more fashionable Episcopal Church. To Rachel, this was yet another reflection of the capital's extravagant lifestyle. Emily's father noted the couple's social engagements, expressing concern that it might spoil them: "Much visiting in the grandest Circles in the City." Despite the indulgences, the Donelsons relished their experiences, attending performances such as *"Virginius; Or The Liberation of Rome,* and The Village Lawyer." Rachel remarked on the "extravagance in dressing and party-going," though Jackson, while quietly critical of the city's excesses, shared more in common with the young couple than with his wife's views.

In the years 1824-25, however, political matters weighed heavily on Jackson's mind, and he found himself at a disadvantage against his more experienced political rivals. Nevertheless, he placed great trust in his nephew, Donelson, believing in his capabilities.[905]

As the 1824 election neared, those not necessarily in favor of the controversial General Jackson wondered where he stood politically. It was one thing to have a strong willed, seemingly patriotic General fighting to extend American borders, but it was another to have someone at the head of the executive branch whose political philosophy was anathema to their own. To this, Jackson began to clarify what he stood for.

Jackson's correspondence throughout the 1820s echoed the philosophy of the founding fathers. "I weep for the liberty of my country," he wrote in response to the corruption in Washington since the war, "when I see in this early day of its 'successful experiment' that corruption has been imputed to many members of the House of Representatives, and the

---

[904] "Emily Donelson," The White House Historical Association. 2025.
[905] Meacham, *American Lion*, p 43.

rights of the people for promises of office."[906] He was growing old, he admitted, and did not feel he had too much more time in this lifetime, "but my fervent prayers are that our Republican government may be perpetual, and the people alone by their virtue, and independent exercise of their free suffrage can make it perpetual."

Jackson emphasized the importance of free elections and argued that anyone concerned with the preservation of freedom must therefore condemn a symposium of a congressional caucus to nominate the Republican candidate for president. "I do hope the one last held will put this unconstitutional proceeding to sleep forever, and leave to the people their constitutional right of suffrage. Should this not be the case, it will introduce into our government, a systematic system of intrigue and corruption… That will ultimately destroy the liberty of our country, central power will arise here; who, under patronage of a corrupt, and venal administration, will deprive the people of their liberties." [907]

Free elections, Jackson believed, were the antidote for government corruption. "The great constitutional corrective in the hands of the people against usurpations of power, or corruption by their agents," he said, "is the right of suffrage; and this when used with calmness and deliberation will prove strong enough. It will perpetuate their liberties and rights."[908] On this point Jackson so consistently relied, that the wide extension of voting rights became a key pillar of the idea of "Jacksonian Democracy."

Fundamentally, though, Jackson was still very much an old Jeffersonian; a state's rightist, as he believed the best way to check the power of the federal government was through the states. But Jackson was not as willing as the earlier Democratic-Republicans to allow that mentality to threaten the Union. He consistently wrote of the need for a delicate balance, one pillar of government not overtopping the other. "To keep the sovereignty of the states in the general government properly and harmoniously poised," Jackson wrote in 1824, "is the pivot on which must rest the freedom and happiness of this country." A delicate balance, though, would prove more and more difficult in the years to come. [909]

---

[906] AJ to Coffee, Coffee Papers, Feb. 15, 1824, LHS. 61. Quoted in Remini, 1977, p.32.
[907] Ibid.
[908] Ibid.
[909] AJ to John. Q. Adams, Nov. 20, 1821, Jackson, *Correspondence*, III, 139.

ANDREW JACKSON: THE POLITICS OF RESENTMENT

As a military man, Jackson understood the importance of the national government's ability to defend the nation from foreign enemies, while also operating within the limits of the Constitution. He believed in the supremacy of the federal government over the states, and he was very much against a state's secession. In fact, Jackson was a Unionist, and the first to take a clear public stand against secession. "There is nothing that I shudder at more than the idea of a separation of the Union. Should such an event ever happen, which I fervently pray God to avert, from that date, I view our liberty gone. It is the durability of the Confederation, upon which the general government is built, that must prolong our liberty, the moment it separates, it is gone. The State governments hold in check the Federal, and must ever hold it in check, and the virtue of the people supported by the sovereign states must prevent consolidations, and will put down that corruption engendered by executive patronage, wielded, as it has been lately, by executive organs, to perpetuate their own power; the result of the present struggle between the virtue of the people and executive patronage will test the stability of our government, and I for one do not despair of the Republic; I have great confidence in the virtue of a great majority of the people, and I cannot fear the result. The Republic is safe, the main pillars, virtue, religion and morality will be fostered via a majority of the people, the designing demagogues who have attempted to retain power by the most corrupt means will be driven by the indignant frowns of the people into obscurity." [910]

With these words, Americans alienated by the era of corruption took heart, reassured by Jackson, and turned to him to lead a preservation of their freedom, and a restoration faith in honest government. Jackson, in a sense, was restating the doctrines of the Founding Fathers of a generation or two earlier. It was strikingly similar to the democracy of the Revolution. His rhetoric resonated with the American people, and it would pay dividends.

The delegates who gathered inside Independence Hall in Philadelphia in the hot summer of 1787 were not overly concerned with establishing

---

[910] AJ to James A. Hamilton, Jr., June 30, 1828, Jackson, *Correspondence*, III, 412.

the rule of the majority. After the debacle of Shays' Rebellion in Massachusetts, where overburdened farmers were compelled to take up arms and shut down the state's courthouses, the country was trending in the opposite direction. The 85 essays that made up the Federalist Papers, as well as the heated debates on the floor of the Constitutional Convention centered on how the new nation might most effectively check the popular will. The 55 'framers' at the convention made certain to keep the proceedings entirely a secret for fear that unqualified people might somehow influence the important decisions being made. Hence the electoral college, the election of Senators by state legislatures, the caucus system, and limited suffrage, based on race, gender and property requirements. America's governing system was Federalism, but the philosophy of the Revolution was Republicanism—steeped in Enlightenment principles of checks and balances–counterweights that safeguarded the ability of powerful elites to ultimately maintain control. These elites would be elected by propertied white male farmers. "The people" were not to be trusted with too much power. Thus, in 1824, only 27% of the population of America's citizens actually voted.

As the election neared, the candidates got in their last licks at each other. Henry Clay brayed about his inability to see how Jackson was fit to become president based on a half hour battle at New Orleans. After the results of the election later on, Jackson would accuse Clay of being "certainly the basis, meanest scoundrel that ever disgraced the image of his God."[911]

For now, though, the General was in high spirits, encouraged by the support of so many who saw Jackson as their candidate, the hero who would surely prevail, and lead America to unprecedented heights. Jackson recognized his influence and appeal with the masses, enjoying their admiration, something he had always sought, whether he would admit it or not. Throughout the winter, Jackson made amends as well, reconciling with some of his former adversaries, including General Winfield Scott, who reached out to Jackson in a note expressing his hopes for a friendly meeting. "Sir, one portion of the American community has long attributed to you the most distinguished magnanimity, and the

---

[911] Henry Clay, the 'Great Compromiser', quoted in *Murray Ledger and Times*, by Duane Bolin, Ledger Columnist, 2013.

other portion the greatest desperation in your resentments — am I to conclude that both are equally in error? I allude to circumstances which have transpired between us, and which need not here be recapitulated, and to the fact that I have now been six days in your immediate vicinity without having attracted your notice. As this is the first time in my life that I have been within a hundred miles of you, and as it is barely possible that you may be ignorant of my presence, I beg leave to state that I shall not leave the District before the morning of the 14th instant."[912]

Jackson replied to his fellow General, "Sir, your letter of today has been received. Whether the world are correct or in error, as regards my 'magnanimity' is for the world to decide. I am satisfied of one fact, that when you shall know me better, you will not be disposed to harbor the opinion that anything like 'desperation in resentment' attaches to me. Your letter is ambiguous; but concluding from occurrences heretofore, that it was written with friendly views, I take the liberty of saying to you, that whenever you shall feel disposed to meet me on friendly terms, that disposition will not be met by any other than a corresponding feeling on my part."[913] The two "alpha males" later met and maintained civility for years.

Another significant reconciliation involved Mr. Clay, who described his initial friendly encounters with Jackson prior to the Seminole War controversy, when their relationship soured due to differing opinions on Jackson's military conduct. "I did not again see him until the session of Congress, at which the events of the Seminole war were discussed. He arrived at Washington in the midst of the debate, and after the delivery, but before the publication, of the first speech, which I pronounced on that subject. Waiving all ceremony, I called to see him, intending by the visit to evince, 'on my part, that no opinion, which a sense of duty had compelled me to express of his public conduct, ought to affect our personal intercourse. My visit was not returned, and I was subsequently told that he was in the habit of indulging in the bitterest observations upon most of those — myself among the number — who had called in question the propriety of his military conduct in the Seminole war." In time, during a session of Congress, it became evident that Jackson, or

---

[912] Scott to AJ, 1824, Jackson Correspondence, III, 368.
[913] AJ to Scott, *Correspondence*, III, quoted in Mansfield's *Life of General Scott*, p. 175.

at least Jackson's Tennessee entourage, was extending an olive branch by reconciling with various individuals, including Clay. They eventually dined together and began to develop a respectful rapport. [914]

"Such was the state of our relations, at the commencement of the session of Congress in 1823," Clay continued, "He became suddenly reconciled with some individuals, between whom and himself there had been a long-existing enmity. The greater part of the Tennessee delegation....called on me together, early in the session, for the express purpose ....of producing a reconciliation between us. By way of apology.... some of the gentlemen remarked, that he did not intend any disrespect to me, but that he was laboring under some indisposition. I stated that the opinions which I had expressed in the House of Representatives, in regard to General Jackson's military transactions, had been sincerely entertained, and were still held, but that, being opinions in respect to public acts, never had been supposed by me to form any just occasion for private enmity between us, and that none had been cherished on my part." The Tennessee delegation gave a dinner shortly thereafter on Capitol Hill. "We there met, exchanged salutations, and dined together. I retired from the table early, and was followed to the door by General Jackson and Mr. Eaton, who insisted on my taking a seat in their carriage. I rode with them, and was set down at my lodgings. I was afterward invited by General Jackson to dine with him, where I met Mr. Adams, Mr. Calhoun, Mr. Southard, and many other gentlemen, chiefly members of Congress. He also dined, in company with fifteen or eighteen members of Congress, at my lodgings, and we frequently met, in the course of the winter, always respectfully addressing each other."[915]

The most remarkable reconciliation was between Jackson and Colonel Thomas H. Benton, who still bore the bullet from their prior conflict. Despite their violent history, they found themselves sitting next to each other in the Senate. "Well," Benton wrote in a letter home, "how many changes in this life! General Jackson is now sitting in the chair next to me....Several Senators saw our situation, and offered mediation. I declined it upon the ground that what had happened could neither be explained, recanted, nor denied. After this, we were put upon the same

---

[914] Clay, Address to the Public, 1828, p. 22.
[915] Henry Clay Letters, 1823, Univ. of Kentucky.

committee. Facing me one day, as we sat in our seats, he said to me, 'Colonel, we are on the same committee; I will give you notice when it is necessary to attend,' (he was chairman, and had the right to summon us.) I answered, 'General, make the time suit yourself; it will be convenient for me to attend at any time." The two worked together on the Senate Committee on Military Affairs. The General knew how to politick after all, or he never would have reached his level of success. It was time to turn on the charm. Benton and his old commander began to communicate civilly once again, eventually dining together and establishing a friendly relationship. Soon, the two were old chums once again.[916]

However, Jackson had a more difficult time from some of his other critics, most notably Thomas Hart's brother, Jesse Benton, who still harbored ill will for Jackson all these years since their duel. Benton published a pamphlet accusing Jackson of numerous offenses, informing the public at large how unfit the General was for the Presidency. Aiming to tarnish Jackson's reputation and draw votes away from him, Benton listed thirty-two charges that ranged from political maneuvering to personal misconduct. The pamphlet was generally ridiculed in Tennessee, but in other regions it gained traction. Jackson supporters, not to be waylaid by anything other than praise for their man, robustly vilified the younger Benton, and wrote off his pamphlet as a work of fiction.

In a continued effort to woo constituents, Jackson, truly politicking for the first time, turned the Hermitage into a hub of activity during the summer months. Welcoming numerous guests drawn by curiosity, friendship, and political interests, Jackson and Rachel hosted a diverse range of guests to their home. Jackson was now in the game, handshakes, kissing babies, and throwing dinner parties were prerequisites of the political arena. Jackson played the gracious host, determined to charm, to show off his handsome estate, and above all, to appear Presidential.

However reluctant he may have been to return to the capital as a Senator, Jackson saw that he not only needed to mend some fences and maybe even build some more, but also to clarify his own political platform. Unlike many in the Republican Party, Jackson was not opposed to such revenue issues as the protective tariff, or federal money for internal

---

[916] Parton, *Jackson*, III, pp. 47-48.

improvements. His massive popularity allowed him the luxury of voting against the tide of his party, especially among southern and western legislators. On the flip side, his wide support base meant that by voting against the 'Southern grain,' Jackson cultivated a following in budding industrial states such as Pennsylvania, which tended to support protective federal tariffs on iron products and textiles. In this as in other respects, Jackson, becoming a shrewder politico by the day (when the need suited him,) made the most of his brief time in the Senate. Forging alliances and rebuilding important friendships in the capital proved both long lasting and strategic, and Jackson always delighted in the opportunity to play the gracious host, particularly to dispel an image held by those who expected to encounter a brute. "I am told the opinions of the minds of those who were prepared to see me with a tomahawk in one hand and the scalping knife in the other has greatly changed," he happily explained to a correspondent, "and I am getting on very smoothly."[917]

Favoring policies that read well in industrial states paid off for the General when, in 1824, a Pennsylvania convention meeting at Harrisburg nominated Jackson for President. Prior to this, the assumption was that Calhoun would get the nod from the Keystone State. Instead, the electoral landscape began to shift unexpectedly, against conventional opinions. "The movement in Philadelphia," Calhoun wrote, "was as unexpected to me as any of my friends. Had Pennsylvania decided favorably, the prospects would have been most fair. Taking the U.S. together, I never had a fairer prospect than on the day we lost the state."[918]

Before the Civil War, most Americans, no matter how far they lived from the coast or industrial centers, felt that the tariff would somehow, some way, have a huge impact on their lives. Some tied the tariff issue to whether or not their wages would remain high or their basic goods cheap. Others felt just the opposite. The desks in the House and Senate were never vacant when any tariff petitions Americans sent to the capital were being debated. Many of the petitions both for and against an increase or decrease in tariff duties contained hundreds, if not thousands of signatures. In fact, these debates brought even dying Congressmen, whose nearly lifeless bodies had to be carried into the chambers so that

---

[917] Brown, David S., *The First Populist*, Simon & Schuster, 2022. Ch. 25.
[918] Ibid.

their last act might be to cast a vote for or against a tariff bill. "It is a subject in which the whole population are concerned," a New England editor noted in 1832, "it affects not merely the wealthy, the monopolists, the joint-stock companies, but the industrious, hard-working classes, who earn their subsistence by their daily labor." [919]

Many aspects of Jackson's candidacy set him apart, and unlike before, the General was now a serious candidate for the executive chair. But this did not come without its challenges. The first of these was that it attracted a raft of detractors, who sought every angle to attack Jackson's temperament, judgment and past conduct. The Dickinson duel, executions of militiamen, and the imprisonment of Callava were all dragged out into the light, along with a host of other questionable actions. This print criticism incensed Jackson, who seemed to view it as a test of his strength. If it was to be a war of attrition, then he was up for it. In fact, the prospect cheered him. "I wish my name had not been brought before the nation as president," He tried to convince Donelson, "but as it has been," he continued, "and the radicals now heap upon me every scurrilous, slanderous abuse that falsehood can suggest I am glad." A prisoner to his penchant for confrontation, Jackson welcomed the fight in his endless quest for vindication.

---

[919] Bolt, William K., *The Tariff in the Age of Jackson*, 2009.

CHAPTER

61

A CORRUPT BARGAIN

"I weep for the liberties of my country, the rights of the people have been bartered for promises of office."
-Andrew Jackson

William H. Crawford had spent years building up his political image, along with his 1300-acre Georgia plantation known as Woodlawn. With its lush grounds, tilled by over three dozen slaves, Crawford had profited handsomely on the backs of human bondage. Politically, Crawford was a throwback, a relic of past politics. The most agricultural of the four candidates, he was very much cut in the Jeffersonian mold, leaning always on a steady states' rights stand. Crawford had given Monroe a run for his money in the Presidential race of 1816 and seemed a favorite for the 1824 Republican nomination. Born in the Old Dominion, he had the patterned Presidential lineage. As a boy, he had moved with his family first to South Carolina, and then to Georgia, where he enjoyed a stellar career in public service. He had served as a Senator, a minister to France, and he had run both the War and Treasury departments in two presidential administrations. Like most Southerners, he was not a believer in allowing excessive power to the national government. Many, especially those in the states' rights camp, liked Crawford's chances, but he also faced stiff opposition. Like Jackson, Crawford had made enemies, and as it turned out, this would prove to be insurmountable.

After nearly a quarter of a century, the Virginia Presidential dynasty was coming to an end. After Jefferson, Madison and Monroe, no lofty groomed Secretary from Virginia stood in the way. As an Amherst County Virginian by birth, Crawford was the next best thing to the heir apparent, but Adams, Clay, and even Jackson saw no reason why they should not throw their hat into the ring and feel favorably of their chances. The caucus system itself now appeared old-fashioned, an antiquated method of promoting a qualified candidate. Crawford was the 'caucus candidate,' so anyone who backed any candidate other than Crawford denounced it as "a gathering of oligarchs." A small number of powerfully connected men met and thrust a candidate upon the people. To protest the caucus, several state legislatures passed resolutions that condemned the practice as undemocratic. Change was in the air in America. Charles Fisher, a former North Carolina congressman, represented the shift in the winds when he complained during the campaign that Virginia "assumed an arrogant proprietorship of the presidency," and he called on the people of the Tar Heel state to "break the charm of Virginia influence and think and act for ourselves."[920]

If a fresh and politically wide-open political landscape didn't doom Crawford's candidacy, his health certainly did. The Georgian suffered a debilitating stroke in September 1823, having escaped the swampy Potomac for the cooler air of the Piedmont. But apparently, he had waited too long to leave, because by the time he reached his destination, he was gravely ill. Whatever the precise disease the Georgian was suffering from, the doctor summoned by Crawford's host James Barbour proceeded to misdiagnose it as a heart ailment. He prescribed an extremely dangerous remedy called digitalis. Well-meaning though the doctor was, digitalis, an extract of the poisonous foxglove plant, is an extremely toxic medicine if incorrectly dosed. Less than a drop of the drug separates a harmless from a fatal dose. The doctor gave Crawford too much, and his heart began beating out of control. As a result, Crawford suffered a massive stroke, and although he returned to some cabinet activities the following year, he never fully recovered.[921]

With Crawford's health-scare, the caucus candidate was no longer the frontrunner. Yet, his candidacy carried on, largely due to the shrewd maneuverings of New York's junior Senator Martin Van Buren. The short,

---

[920] Brown, David S., 2022. Ch. 25.
[921] Mooney, Chase, *William H. Crawford, 1772-1834*, Lexington, Kentucky, 1974.

stocky, politically brilliant Van Buren, the founder of the New York's Albany Regency, or the "Holy Alliance," a well-organized and disciplined political machine that had begun to dominate New York Democratic politics since 1820, had a receding hairline, strong, penetrating blue eyes and a penchant for successful political campaigns. Those detractors who sought to deride the man who didn't appear worthy of such talents, names like the "Little Magician," or the "Red Fox of Kinderhook" could not take away from the belief Van Buren possessed in himself and his political journey. Van Buren had gravitated to the Democratic-Republican party as a way to counter New England federalism. He had long entertained a desire to bring together northern Republicans and Southern planters, using the fallout from the controversies of the Panic and the Missouri Crisis. He had celebrated the 1800 election of Thomas Jefferson in one of his earliest political memories.

The "Revolution of 1800" was, to Martin Van Buren, "the triumph of a good cause over a federalist administration and party who I thought were subverting the principles upon which the Revolution was founded, and fastening upon the country a system, which, though different in form, was nevertheless animated by a policy in the acquisition and the use of political power akin to that which our ancestors had overthrown. I have ever since regarded the continued success of Mr. Jefferson's policy as a result of the superiority of the principles that he introduced into the administration of the government over those of his predecessor, and was sincerely desirous that they might continue to prevail in the federal councils."[922] A true Jeffersonian, the New Yorker Van Buren explained, "I announced in 1824 my intention to support Mr. Crawford." With his endorsement, New York joined Georgia and Virginia in support of the Treasury Secretary, hoping to dissuade competitors by making Crawford's victory seem inevitable.

While William Crawford's health took its unfortunate turn, Martin Van Buren's remained vital, as did his political ambitions. Van Buren, who opposed the anti-faction stance, stood out among the early founders by favoring political parties and embracing party spirit. He believed that political parties had the ultimate ability to organize, rally, and inform the public. To Van Buren, party discipline was the ideal substitute for the

---

[922] Foote, Henry S., *Casket of Reminiscences*, St. Louis, 1876, pp. 59-60.

earlier patrician system. He held a low opinion of James Monroe, citing Monroe's failed fusion policy as a catalyst for the contentious Missouri debates, the collapse of the caucus, and the House's controversial decision to promote Adams to the presidency in 1825. Van Buren felt that if a two-party structure had remained, these issues could have been avoided. He emphasized the critical importance of party discipline to prevent such pitfalls.

Two additional nicknames emerged for him: "the careful Dutchman" and "the great manager." These reflected his unconventional approach and the respect his colleagues had for him. Describing him as a master political strategist was not inaccurate. By 1826, he had put these skills into action, moving from Crawford's camp to align with Jackson. He reported that Jackson and Calhoun agreed with him on Monroe's party approach. "They understood too well my feelings on Monroe's partisanship policy to expect me to sustain it."

As a Jeffersonian who favored agrarian states' rights and concerned about the growing influence of finance and industry, Van Buren aimed to connect the old Republicanism with the rising Jacksonianism. He believed that the defining issues of the Jeffersonian era—such as economic development, central government power, and slavery's role in the Republic—still resonated with voters. In a letter to Jackson from Albany in 1827, he noted, "The politics of the state of New York, like those of Pennsylvania and most of the northern states, are yet governed by old party feelings."[923] He asserted that neither Monroe nor Adams could suppress the ongoing struggles between power and liberty, aristocrats and agrarians.

Leading the call for a quadrennial caucus, a notice appeared in the February 7, 1824, edition of the *National Intelligencer*. This notice, signed by several congressmen, invited their colleagues to convene the following week in the representatives' chamber to "recommend a presidential candidate."[924] However, another article in the same edition argued against holding a caucus under the current circumstances. On February 14, the caucus convened and nominated Crawford for president and Albert Gallatin for vice president. Yet, only 66 of the 240 Democratic-

---

[923] Van Buren to AJ, 1827, Jackson, *Correspondence*, III.
[924] *National Intelligencer Archives*, Feb. 7, 1824.

Republican members of Congress attended, viewing the caucus as a special interest group masquerading as the entire Democratic-Republican Party. The Massachusetts legislature subsequently nominated Adams as their favorite son candidate, while Clay received a nomination from the Kentucky legislature. John C. Calhoun chose to run for Vice President instead.

Jackson's following had become, to many in Washington, a frightful monolith, a cult of personality. Former Treasury Secretary, Albert Gallatin, who had not only been instrumental in the formation of the Republican party but had served as head of the Treasury for both Jefferson, and Madison. Gallatin led the charge among those who fell on the extreme end of dismay at the thought of Jackson as president. Gallatin was especially distraught over the popularity Jackson enjoyed in Gallatin's home state of Pennsylvania. In Gallatin's mind, the General embodied the antithesis of Republican government. "Whatever gratitude we owe him for his eminent military services," he wrote in a May, 1824 letter, "He is not fitted for the office of the first magistrate of a free people to administer a government of laws."[925] Perhaps unsurprisingly, Gallatin, a member of the old guard which Jackson rejected, embraced the caucus politics of the past, which Jackson often railed against. Accordingly, Gallatin condemned Jackson as an iconoclast intruding uninvited on cherished political institutions, of which the likes of Gallatin and others in the east spent years carefully crafting. "His doctrine of paying no regard to party in the selection of the great officers of government is not only in direct opposition to the principles of the Republican party, but it is tantamount to a declaration that political principles or opinions are of no importance to the administration of government."

Referencing more of the Jackson-Monroe correspondence, Gallatin spotlighted Jackson's bellicose attitude toward the Hartford Convention Federalists, who he had written about as deserving of a hanging. "Gen. Jackson has expressed a greater and broader disregard for the first principles of liberty than I have ever known to be entertained by any American. However hyperbolized Jackson's threats were in his correspondence with Monroe, Gallatin did not see the humor in it. "He entertains, no doubt very seriously, but very erroneously, the most

---

[925] Gallatin, Albert. *The Writings of Albert Gallatin, vol. 2*. J. B. Lippincott, 1879.

dangerous opinions on the subject of military and executive power. Whenever Jackson has been allowed free rein in martial authority," Gallatin added, "he seized more power than was granted legally. When he thought it useful to the public, he has not hesitated to transcend the law & the legal authority invested in him."[926]

The times were a-changing, however, in what had become an ever broadening, westward-creeping nation. The principles that Gallatin and his ilk had decided upon as manifestly 'right and proper' were now under threat from a massive new constituency. More forward-thinking politicians, quicker to read the writing on the wall of the new "populism" slowly starting to percolate around Jackson, adapted more quickly than Gallatin. Adams, always the sage diplomat, decided to hold a soiree for Jackson on the 8th of January 1824, the ninth anniversary of the Battle of New Orleans. Although his wife Louisa Catherine recognized the damage it would cause for her husband's presidential aspiration, there was no stopping the cocksure Adams. "I objected much to the plan, but was overpowered by John's arguments," the Secretary's wife lamented.[927]

The event would go on, and well it did. It was a smashing success, attended by far more than the 500 who had been invited. "The party of Mrs. Adams was the largest I ever witnessed at a private residence." Jackson later wrote with evident pride to one correspondent. "Every room was crowded." Some reports suggested as many as one thousand people piled into the Adams home on F Street. In anticipation of the excessive attendees, the Adamses felt compelled to install pillars to support the upper floors of their home. Wreaths, garland, and roses covered the walls, while delicate, chalked eagles and flowers graced the floors. Guests were treated to a sumptuous buffet. "Mr. Adams and I took our stations near the door that we might be seen by our guests and be at the same time ready to receive the General to whom the fete was given," Louisa recalled in her diary. "He arrived at nine o'clock and I took him round the Rooms and introduced him to the Ladies and Gentlemen whom we passed. . . . my Company dispersed at about half past one all in good humour and more contented than common with their entertainment."[928]

---

[926] Ibid.
[927] Louisa Catherine Adams to Charles Francis Adams, 1824.
[928] Adams, Louisa Catherine, edited by Margaret A. Hogan, and C. James Taylor, *A Traveled First Lady: The Writings of Louisa Catherine Adams*, 2014.

Dolly Madison's friend, Phoebe Morris reported after the reception, "Mrs. Adams' reception was really a brilliant party and admirably arranged." The ladies stood on whatever they could to see over the heads of the crowd to gawk at the heroic general. "Mrs. Adams, very gracefully, took his arm and walked through the apartments with him, which gratified the general curiosity."[929]

The following month, Daniel Webster wrote to his brother, and the subject of General Jackson came up, particularly his rather regal comportment, which Webster believed gave him a leg up in the race. "Jackson's manners are more presidential than any of the other candidates. He is grave, mild, and reserved. My wife is decidedly for him." [930] Jackson, to his credit, balanced war hero celebrity status with presidential candidate and wise man with aplomb. He acted as presidential as he could, even posing for a portrait by the American Neoclassicist, John Vanderlyn, as both Presidents Madison and Monroe had done. He was feted in Congress with a Congressional Gold Medal for war service, the highest civilian award bestowed by Congress. He was toasted at public dinners, where he smiled, shook hands, and regaled the crowds with war stories, and frontier humor. It was a lot to take on, and it took a toll on the more reserved Rachel Jackson. But Jackson, on the contrary, was in his element when he got to be the center of attention.

Relishing the attention, Jackson laughed along with the crowd, who poked fun at his renowned volatility, boasting that others should fear not for, "When it becomes necessary to philosophise and be meek, no man can command his temper better than I!" Evidently, Jackson was very much in his element, and he was looking more presidential by the minute.

In the late autumn, from October 26th to December 2nd, the long-awaited election finally took place, and as state legislatures prepared to cast their ballots, Jackson and his wife took rooms at Gadsby's Tavern in Alexandria. There they were steadily mobbed by over-friendly and overconfident crowds, who proclaimed Jackson's victory before the ballots were even cast. Soon, the electoral results began to pour in, and an interesting picture began to take shape. Jackson had won both the

---

[929] Miss Phoebe Morris to Dolley Madison, Jan., 1824 Correspondence.
[930] Daniel Webster letters and documents, 1824 correspondence, Manuscripts and Archives Division, The New York Public Library, compiled by Susan P. Waide, 2017.

popular vote (41%) and the electoral vote (99) over second place finisher Adams, who harnessed 31% of the popular vote and 84 electoral votes. Jackson outgained Clay and Crawford's combined totals of 24% of the popular vote and 78 electoral votes. A victory for Jackson! Or was it? The constitution requires that a candidate attain a majority of electoral votes, lest the decision goes to a vote in the House. Jackson failed to accomplish this, falling well shy of the necessary 131, but so did every other candidate. Only Calhoun, with the support of both Adams and Jackson backers, could claim a victory; as vice president. Yet, despite this, Jackson was the only candidate that proved to have the greatest national standing. Receiving votes throughout the North, South and West, Jackson supporters felt confident that Congress would award the national hero the victory. [931]

Exuberance reverberated among the Jackson supporters throughout the country. But, as per the 12th Amendment to the Constitution, nothing was yet decided. The letter of the law states that when no candidate wins a clear majority of electoral votes, the decision moves to the House of Representatives. The House would then hold a separate vote with each state receiving one vote, and Congressmen are under no obligation to vote according to anything but their own conscience. As Speaker of the House, Henry Clay immediately dropped out of the race, and his withdrawal meant it was now down to the final two. The decision would take months, well into the new year of 1825. But, at long last, the results went public. Clay, so influential in the House, had cast his vote for Adams, and many others followed suit. What was said during the proceedings remains a mystery to this day. In any case, as a result, Adams became the sixth President of the United States, not Andrew Jackson.

The date was the 9th of February 1825 when Adams was finally elected. That evening he and Jackson came famously face to face at a presidential reception. According to those present, it was the defeated Westerner who bore himself with far more grace than the victorious New Englander. Jackson had attended the party given by Monroe at the White House with Rachel on his arm. President-elect Adams was standing by himself in the crowded room. An observer at the gathering noted, "General Jackson had a large, handsome lady on his arm."

---

[931] Brown, David S., 2022, Chapter 26.

Encountering each other, neither Adams nor Jackson initially moved nor reacted, but simply held each other's stare. Here, within a few feet of each other, stood two of the most powerful men in the nation. Adams, the son of a president, the lifelong politician in his moment of glory, and the defeated Jackson, who'd risen from squalor and wretchedness, the defeated and spurned runner-up. Yet, it was reportedly Jackson who rose to the occasion.

"How do you do, Mr. Adams?" Jackson said cheerfully, holding out his free hand to Adams. "I give you my left hand, for the right, as you see, is devoted to the fair. I hope you are well, sir."

"Very well, sir: I hope General Jackson is well." A stunned Adams responded, but as one observer who overheard the exchange noted, Adams' spoke "with chilling coldness." The old courtier and diplomat was "stiff, rigid, cold as a statue." [932]

Jackson moved through the crowd and left the party with Rachel. The two returned to their hotel as Washington society buzzed with reports of his class and grace in the face of his opponent. "You have, by your dignity and forbearance under all these outrages, won the people to your love," a friend wrote the General. Nevertheless, while some solace may have been salvaged from the support he had received, in the end, it was a disappointing way to end the campaign. Soon, the Jacksons and the Donelsons left Washington for Tennessee. But, it would not be the last the capital would see of Old Hickory.

When rumors flew that Adams planned to appoint Clay as his Secretary of State, a traditional stepping-stone to the White House, the Jacksonians exploded with outrage. On January 28, 1825, an unsigned letter surfaced in the *Philadelphia Columbia Observer*, accusing Henry Clay of promising votes in the House in exchange for the position of Secretary of State. Just four days after the public announcement of this controversial arrangement, it was claimed that two unscrupulous politicians had colluded to undermine the American people's constitutional rights. Whether true or not, the accusations seemed credible enough that few felt the need for proof; the mere existence of the so-called "union" was seen as evidence. Clay vehemently denied the newspaper's allegations, labeling the author a "base calumniator, dastard,

---

[932] Goodrich, S.G., *Recollections of a Lifetime*, New York and Auburn, 1856, II, 403-404.

and liar," and demanded that the writer reveal his identity and face him. The anonymous author was later identified as Pennsylvania Congressman George Kremer, known for his eccentric clothing, yet recognized for a notable congressional record. A congressional committee investigated Kremer's claims but ultimately found no evidence to support them.[933]

Although the defeated General would later attest to be the most livid of all, he originally met the news calmly. Jackson was prepared to cry foul if the rumors were true, accusing the Clay-Adams team of defrauding the American public. Many of his constituents were already plotting revenge, with westerners declaring Clay a traitor to his region. A result such as the 1824 election would never happen again, Jacksonians swore, while they were alive to prevent it.

Snow blanketed Washington on February 9, 1825, as the House of Representatives convened to choose the president for the first time since 1801. Up to the last moment delegates scurried back and forth across the chambers for hurried conferences, and Clay had to call for order as the polling began. Each state then cast a ballot that was determined by its delegation, with a majority of ballots being required for election. Finally, Congress voted to settle the longest presidential race in history, at long last.

Five days later, Clay accepted Adams' offer to become the new Secretary of State, the office from which the president sprung habitually, further infuriating Jackson. Briefing William Lewis, Jackson called Clay "the Judas of the West" and added "his end will be the same." He became convinced that Clay had sold his vote out of an exchange for the cabinet appointment, and Jackson's fury at this alleged corruption never abated. "If at this early period of the experiment of our republic, men are found base and corrupt enough to barter the rights of the people for proffered office, what may we not expect from the spread of this corruption hereafter," Jackson told Lewis. Was any more proof needed, in Jackson's opinion, of the deterioration of the moral and ethical scruples of the politicians in control of America's political system?

Jackson seethed. This was the final straw.

---

[933] *National Intelligencer*, Jan. 31, 1825.

CHAPTER

62

REVENGE

"The Judas of the West has closed the contract and will receive the thirty pieces of silver."
                                                    -Andrew Jackson

Andrew Jackson was in a dark place. Having returned to Tennessee, the General was convinced that he had been cheated. The Jacksonians echoed this theme from the Atlantic to the West. The uproar over accusations against President-elect Adams and the new Secretary of State Henry Clay was becoming a tidal wave. Allegations had planned their secret deal all along flew as if spirited by the winds of the Potomac, to reward each other with high office: control of the State Department (the stepping stone to the presidency) in exchange for the executive chair. The label of "corrupt bargain" was born. Writing from the Senate floor, Jackson, with some bitterness, expressed his disdain: "it shows the want of principle in all concerned… It will give the people a full view of our political weather, Cox here, and how little confidence ought to be proposed in the professions of some great political characters."

Jackson vented in a memorandum to Lewis on Feb. 20th:

GENERAL JACKSON TO MAJOR WM. B. LEWIS.

"City of Washington, February 20th, 1825. " Dear Major: You have seen from the public journals that the rumors of union, and barter for office, between Mr. Clay's friends and Mr. Adams have been verified by the result of the presidential election. The information now is, that the contract, so far as Mr. Clay is concerned, is fulfilled, by the offer of Mr. Adams to Mr. Clay of the appointment of Secretary of State, which, it is said, Mr. Clay has agreed to accept. I have, as you know, always thought Mr. Adams to be an honest, virtuous man, and had he spurned from him those men who have abandoned those principles they have always advocated, that the people have a right to govern, and that their will should be always obeyed by their constituents, I should still have viewed him as an honest man; and that the rumors of bargain and sale was unknown to him. But when we see the predictions verified in the result of the presidential election — when we behold two men, political enemies, and as different in political sentiments as any men can be, so suddenly unite, there must be some unseen cause to produce this political phenomenon. This cause is developed by applying the rumors before the election, to the result of that election, and to the tender of, and acceptance of the office of Secretary of State by Mr. Clay." [934]

Yet, by all accounts, Clay had made up his mind long before that he would vote for Adams over Jackson. Before leaving home in November, before the result of the popular election was known, he declared to confidential friends that in no circumstances whatsoever would he vote for Jackson. He told Thomas Hart Benton so around the middle of December, and a few weeks later Benton passed the news on by letter to Francis Blair, "I left Washington," says Col. Benton, "on the 15th o------f December, on a visit to my father-in-law, Colonel James McDowell, of Virginia, where Mrs. Benton then was; and it was before I left Washington that I learned from Mr. Clay himself that his intention was to support Mr. Adams. I told this at that time to Colonel McDowell, and any friends that chanced to be present, and gave it to the public in a letter which was copied into many newspapers, and is preserved in *Niles' Register*. I told it as my belief to Mr. Jefferson on Christmas evening of

---

[934] AJ to Lewis, Feb. 20, 1825. Memorandum, Jackson Papers, LC.

the same year, when returning to Washington and making a call on that illustrious man at his seat, Monticello; and then that Mr. Adams would be elected, and, from the necessity of the case, would have to make up a mixed cabinet, I expressed that belief to Mr. Jefferson, using the term, familiar in English history, of 'broad bottomed,' and asked him how it would do? He answered: 'Not at all—would never succeed—would ruin all engaged in it.' Mr. Clay told his intentions to others of his friends from an early period." [935]

In a letter dated January 9, 1825, Henry Clay wrote to a friend back home in the Bluegrass State of the unpleasant decision he and his colleagues were required to make. "We are beginning to think seriously of the choice we must finally make. I will tell you then that I believe the contest will be limited to Mr. Adams and General Jackson, Mr. Crawford's personal condition, having suffered a stroke, precludes the choice of him, if there was no other objection to his election. As to the only alternative which is presented to us, it is sufficiently painful, and I consider whatever choice we may make will be only a choice of evils. To both those gentlemen, there are strong, personal objections. The principal difference between them is that by the election of Mr. Adams, we shall not, by the example, inflict any wounds on the character of our institutions. But I should much fear hereafter, if not during the present generation, that the election of the general would give to the military spirit, a stimulus and a confidence that might lead to the most pernicious results. I shall therefore support Mr. Adams." [936]

The final act in this "nefarious drama" was yet to unfold: the appointment of the Secretary of State, which everyone anticipated with bated breath. Five days post-election, the tension resolved when the two men met to discuss the election. "Mr. Clay... said that the time was drawing near when the choice must be made in the House of Representatives, of a president, from the three candidates presented by the electoral colleges. He wished me, as far as I might think, proper, to satisfy him with regard to some principles of great public importance, but of no personal considerations for himself. In the question to come

---

[935] Benton, Thomas Hart, *Thirty Years View*, New York, 1863, i. 48.
[936] Clay to Francis Brooke, Jan., 1825, *Clay Papers*, IV, 67.

before the House between General Jackson, Mr. Crawford, and myself, he had no hesitation in saying that his preference would be for me."[937]

In the end, Adams made it official, offering the position to 'Harry of the West.' Henry Clay hesitated only briefly, writing to his friend Francis Brooke of Virginia, "I am offered the State, but have not yet decided... What shall I do?"[938] After a week of contemplation and despite the warnings, Clay accepted the offer, effectively ending his own chances for the presidency.

Knowing what he knew, what everyone believed, whether right or wrong, Clay would have been better off to decline the offer. By this point, he understood the risks of acceptance. But this was the stepping-stone to the presidency; he was so close, and it was so tempting. He had worked too hard to let it slip through his fingers now. But was he willing to gamble everything for it?

Once Clay's decision became public, Colonel Richard M. Johnson hurried to inform Jackson. Although he maintained his composure while Johnson was present, the General erupted in anger once alone, "So you see, the "Judas of the West" has closed the contract and will receive the 30 pieces of silver. His end will be the same. Was there ever such barefaced corruption in any country before?"[939] Jackson had assumed Clay would reject the appointment, given all the talk of the "corrupt bargain." To Jackson, Clay's acceptance confirmed that, indeed, a secret agreement had been made. A dirty, selfish bargain to undermine the people's will. He expressed the sentiment shared by many when he remarked, "When we see the predictions are verified."

Sadly, the miscarriage of justice regarding the 1825 presidential election wasn't solely about whether Adams and Clay secretly conspired. Historians have debated this for years and have gotten nowhere over this moot point. The true corruption lay in the decision to hand the presidency to Adams in blatant disregard for what the public wanted. Individual interests overshadowed the will of the people, at least the largest percentage of the people who voted. Like Jackson or not, the will of the largest percentage of people should have been respected. It was

---

[937] Adams, John Quincy, *Adams Memoirs*, Vi, 518.
[938] Clay to Francis Brooke, Feb. 14 1825, in *Clay Papers*, IV, 67.
[939] AJ to Lewis, Feb. 14, 1825, Miscellaneous Jackson Papers, NYHS. Also in Jackson, *Correspondence*, III, 276.

clear that a significant portion of the American populace wanted Andrew Jackson as their president, a fact that was dismissed with contempt. To make Adams president, Kentucky had to be delivered to him, even though he received less than one percent of the popular votes there. Did the Kentucky delegation feel they knew better about what was best for the country than 41.3% of the American people who wished to see a Jackson Presidency? Perhaps.

Adams' election and Clay's appointment as Secretary of State initiated a movement that would reshape American political history. It solidified Jackson's belief in the necessity for reform and the restoration of Republican principles in government. Jackson recognized that he must lead this reform movement and rally the people to his cause. "There is no other corrective of these abuses," he declared, "but the suffrages of the people. If the electorate calmly and judiciously apply this corrective, they may preserve and perpetuate the liberty of our happy country. If they do not, in less than 25 years, we will become the slaves, not of a military chieftain, but of such ambitious demagogues as Henry Clay."[940]

Clay's decision was no surprise to those in the political circles of the time, of which Jackson stood more decidedly outside of. Although there had never been a large amount of love loss between them, Clay and Adams were not far apart on many of the major issues. A number of these same issues would one day fall under the banner of the Whigs: the American system for example (internal improvements, protective tariffs and a national bank.) Crawford was not only the unpopular caucus candidate, but his stroke had left him unable to perform the duties of state. Since Clay's hammering of Jackson's high-handed Florida actions in his infamous "military chieftain" speech, animosity had reigned between the two westerners, despite Clay's efforts to conciliate the General.

Setting aside his reservations about Jackson's unpredictable temperament, the Kentuckian Clay held serious skepticism about Jackson's commitment to republican government. Like many, the "Cult of Personality" that had reached fever proportions over the unorthodox candidacy of Jackson frightened many a liberty loving politician, Clay included. Ultimately, Clay would always see Jackson as the military chieftain he accused him of being. Politically, Clay viewed his fellow

---

[940] AJ to Lewis, Feb. 14, 1825, Jackson, Correspondence, III, 276.

western counterpart as a "Johnny-Come-Lately," inexperienced and unqualified, whose talents aligned much more within the military profession. "I cannot believe, Clay wrote home, rather flippantly in late January, that "killing 2500 Englishman at New Orleans qualifies for the difficult and complicated business of the chief magistracy."[941]

Yet, Jackson supporters saw Clay as the ringleader of a cabal of corruption. Thus, Jackson was not alone in his dissatisfaction with the hypocrisy of the Capital. His wife also became exasperated with the slander and the double-talk of Washington. "The pious here are not like those at home," Rachel Jackson wrote to her sister, "They are too much divided with the world…..Washington," she wrote, was a "terrible place."[942]

Shortly before the March swearing in ceremony, *The Allegheny Democrat* damned Henry Clay as "morally and politically a gambler, a black leg and a traitor."[943] Jackson mocked Clay's defense of the corrupt bargain charges as written in a "begging cringing tone … but he steers clear of denying this charge. The various papers are commenting on it. How little common sense this man has. Silence would have been to him wisdom."[944]

Adams' unconventional victory in the contested election placed a pall upon the proceedings, and the opposition's malcontent was palpable. The corrupt bargain rang in the ears of many Jackson supporters as Adams rattled on. Concerned over the nationalistic theme that resonated through Adams' words, Republicans saw a new Federalist torch bearer before them, as if the son was on a crusade to resurrect the lost throne of the father. Such perceptions called for firm resistance, and the soon to be "Democrats" dug in their heels.

On March 4th, 1825, President John Quincy Adams was sworn in before a full chamber. In his first annual message, the new President set forth his policies with passion. To many of those on hand, sitting bitterly in front of a man they felt had cheated his way into the Presidency, his words seem too bluntly to be the second coming of the Federalists. Despite

---

[941] Clay to Lucretia Hart Clay, 1825, Clay Papers, IV.
[942] Rachel Jackson to Katherine D. Morgan, May, 1825, Western Reserve Historical Society, Cleveland, Ohio.
[943] Quoted in Brown, David S., *The First Populist*, 2022, Ch. 26.
[944] AJ to Coffee, April 24, 1825, Coffee Papers, THS.

the elegant rhetoric and lofty ideals, in the end, the effect was alienating to many in Congress. Discussing the issue of internal improvements, Adams appeared much like his father, baring an entanglement of Federalist roots underneath a thin Republican veil. His ideas were lofty and ambitious, and the oratorical rhetoric was pleasant in hindsight, harkening back to New England's "City On a Hill" foundations, though it proved to be too much for his Republican audience.

Referring to the ancient Romans, Adams addressed the issue of internal improvements through a historical lens. "The magnificence and splendor of their public works are among the imperishable glories of the ancient republics. The roads and aqueducts of Rome have been the admiration of all after ages, and have survived thousands of years after all her conquests have been swallowed up in despotism, or become the spoil of barbarians. Some diversity of opinion has prevailed with regard to the powers of Congress for legislation upon objects of this nature. The most respectful deference is due to doubts, originating in pure patriotism, and sustained by venerated authority. But nearly twenty years have passed since the construction of the first national road was commenced. The authority for its construction was then unquestioned. To how many thousands of our countrymen has it proved a benefit? To what single individual has it ever proved an injury?"[945]

Adams willingly admitted the controversial circumstances of his ascension to the presidency, acknowledging that he was "less possessed of your (the electorate's) confidence in advance than any of my predecessors."[946] Similar to Jefferson, Adams attempted to unify the somewhat skeptical audience by asserting that the "dissension" that has risen is merely "founded upon differences of speculation in the theory of republican government" and that there exists "no difference of principle."

In a gracious gesture, the members of the Senate voted Jackson, as oldest member, (he was weeks away from turning 58) to swear in the vice president, John C. Calhoun. "The two men, tall and erect, stood facing each other, their brilliant eyes locked in a magnetic embrace."[947]

---

[945] Inaugural Address of John Quincy Adams, Friday, March 4, 1825, Yale Law School, Lillian Goldman Law Library.
[946] Pagliarini, Thomas, Rhetorical Democracy: An Examination of the Presidential Inaugural Addresses Senior Capstone Project, p.18.
[947] Remini, 1977, p. 102.

Only during the trip home from Washington had Jackson occasionally lost his grip. Along the way Jackson met supporters who assured him that he was in fact, the rightful president and that the will of the people have been bargained away by power hungry politicians. At Baltimore, there was a ball given in his honor. The following day a cavalcade escorted him beyond the town limits to demonstrate the city's appreciation for his visit. Everywhere he reviewed the troops drawn up for his inspection, and in most towns, the people turned out in mass to salute and applaud him. What touched him particularly was the almost universal expression of disappointment over his defeat. It was their defeat too, they told him, it was the defeat of a constitutional Republican government. At West Alexandria, Pennsylvania, the general met an old comrade by the name of Edward McLaughlin, who came up to him and offered his sympathy. "The voters by the free exercise of their suffrage had done all they could for their hero to elect him president," McLaughlin angrily asserted, "but the rascals at Washington cheated you out of it."

Perhaps it was hearing the word "cheated" put so bluntly by McLaughlin that resonated with a clang inside Jackson's head. "Indeed my old friend," the General blurted out, "there was cheating, and corruption in bribery too."[948] In each town he visited, the people received him with enthusiasm and vociferousness, shouting out their chagrin and disappointment that there will had been callously and contemptuously set aside by a "cabal" of politicians Jackson invariably replied, in not so calming tones, about the widespread corruption that now infected the entire government apparatus. "How it must be purged if the liberties of the people are to survive." Overly amenable to taking the low road and making no effort to help restore the people's trust in their government, Jackson ranted against his opponents. By the time he reached the Hermitage, he was in "'high dudgeon' about that poor devil H Clay and "how through corruption and intriguing maneuvers, he had procured the office of Secretary of State for himself."[949] He could hardly wait for the next election so that he could have his revenge. For the moment, however, he kept his peace. "My friends say," he told Lewis, "I should not answer whether I'll run in 1828 or resign my seat."[950]

---

[948] *Niles Weekly Register*, July 5, 1828.
[949] AJ to Lewis, Feb. 22, 1824, Jackson-Lewis Papers, NYPL.
[950] Ibid.

Jackson had just arrived at the Hermitage bitter and frustrated over his electoral defeat when a copy of Clay's address to his constituents reached him. As he scanned the pages he shook his head slowly and bitterly. Disregarding Clay's response to his own letter, the General concentrated instead on Clay's explanations, muttering his disdain. "The address was written," he said, "in a begging, cringing tone to free him of the (corrupt bargain) charge, but he steers entirely clear of denying it.... The various papers are commenting on it... How little common sense this man displays.... Silence would have been to him wisdom."[951]

Within a matter of days of the House election, the major issue of the presidential campaign of 1828 had already been made manifest. The "corrupt bargain" charge was all over the newspapers, as Jackson had predicted, and never left. It was repeated time and again over the next three years, ad nauseam. Over and over the Jacksonians repeated the phrase, determined to never let the people forget the sins of the opposition, and the need for reform. Pro-Jackson papers printed the charge incessantly, reminding Americans of the moral failures of their age. The politics of resentment were in full swing.

Old Hickory now settled into a three-year period of public dinners, ceremonial civic obligations, and the continued defense of his reputation. In addition, the time off provided the itinerant planter the ability to keep a careful eye on his farming affairs, and his family's financial concerns, truly a full-time occupation in the tenuous times of 1820s. A December 1825 note to his most trusted lieutenant, John Coffee, attests to Jackson's return to domestic concerns. "I suppose there will be some corn to spare from the little Hutchings farm, you will be the best judge as to how much and when to offer it for sale. The quantity that could be spared can be Best judged after the crop is housed and the hogs killed. As soon as the pork is fatted, direct that it be killed. This will save corn as well as ensure the safety of the pork, for I anticipate an open winter after this month, and a great deal of rain. If in this I should be correct, some danger may be expected in saving pork after this month. I have killed half of mine and upon the change of this moon, will slaughter the balance."[952] He continued on, directing such activities as clearing land,

---

[951] AJ to Richard Keith Call, March 20, 1828, CHS.
[952] AJ to Coffee, Dec. 1825, Coffee Papers, *THS*.

mending fences, when to plow the fields in arid weather, etc. With the General's diverse array of financial interests, which at that point included farming, land speculation, slaveholding, slave trading, tavern-keeping, operating a general store, and maintaining a track for racing horses, the General was accumulating the fortune he had long sought.

Apart from Jackson's sporadically violent past, as duelist, gambler, cockfighter, and all-around ruffian, what troubled the foremost political analysts of the period was the General's disregard for the law when it did not appear it would suit his purposes. Trampling on individual rights, constitutional guarantees, and the men in authority placed over him, much of Jackson's career seemed to contradict the most basic Democratic processes for which the country stood. Perhaps no man put it more clearly than Albert Gallatin when it came to the doubts and fears Jackson provoked. Gallatin, one of the early leaders and shapers of the Republican Party, was an able statesman who had also served with distinction as Treasury Secretary under both Jefferson and Madison. Gallatin had supported Crawford in the 1824 election, but eyeing the 1828 election, the former Secretary now recognized that the General was "the most formidable opponent" in his home state of Pennsylvania. Jackson's correspondence with Monroe, Gallatin wrote to Walter Lowrie, "the publication of which you have forced," proved beyond doubt that "whatever gratitude we owe him for his eminent military contributions, has been offset by his total disregard for Constitutional principles."[953]

Mrs. Jackson fretted. While the General's wife relished having her husband at home, his exalted level of celebrity meant unwanted and frequent intrusions upon her privacy that added to her anxieties. Her neurotic state had only worsened with age. Her husband's many extended trips away from the Hermitage had caused her to descend into a near state of temporary madness. In the past these had been short spells, but by the mid-1820s, it not only caused longer bouts of melancholy for the General's wife but came with the added anguish of physical pains as well. When Jackson departed the Hermitage for whatever

---

[953] Gallatin, Albert. *The Writings of Albert Gallatin*, vol. 2. J. B. Lippincott, 1879.

public obligation drew him away, Rachel's neuroses activated, which now included hysterical emotions, heart palpitations and high blood pressure. Following doctor's orders, she medicated herself with tobacco. Guests who visited the Hermitage, especially those from the east, were astonished to encounter Rachel enjoying her snuff, or lighting up a cigar with the men. "She was the first woman I ever saw smoke a cigar," noted one northerner who visited Nashville. After dinner at the Hermitage, he and some officers sat with the Jacksons by the fireplace. Mrs. Jackson, as was her custom, lit her pipe and offered it to one of the officers, saying, "Honey, won't you take a smoke?"[954]

Despite their differences in physical appearance, manners, and worldly experiences, the Jacksons were deeply connected. Their affection for each other was profound, as noted by an officer's daughter: "The General treated her always as his pride and glory, and words cannot describe her devotion to him." Rachel thrived at the Hermitage, and Jackson understood the toll the Adams press had taken on her during the campaign. "My savior has been my guiding support through all my afflictions, which I must confess have been many and unprovoked over the last four years. I have no doubt he will continue to aid and guide me in my duties, which I anticipate will be numerous and challenging."[955] Her anxiety did not lessen at the thought of a possible transition to Washington, and the tumultuous spotlight.

But those who commented on Rachel Jackson would invariably remark on her kindness in the same breath. "She was correct", he warmly added, "easy in her manners, playful in her conversations and fond of a joke." A depiction from the daughter of an officer who served under Jackson once commented on the odd pairing the two made. "Picture to yourself a military looking man, above the ordinary height, dressed plainly, but with great neatness, dignified and grave, I had almost said stern, but always courteous and affable with keen searching eyes, expressive of deep thought, and active intellect. Side-by-side with him stands a coarse-looking stout little old woman whom you might easily mistake for his washer woman. Her figure is rather full, but loosely and

---

[954] Brady, Cyrus Townshend, *The True Andrew Jackson*, J.P. Lippincott, Co., Cornell Univ., 1906, p. 171,

[955] Rachel to Elizabeth Watson, July 18, 1828, Jackson Papers, YUL.

carelessly dressed, so that when seated, she seems to settle into herself in a manner that is neither graceful nor elegant."[956]

To Jackson, Rachel could do no wrong. By all accounts, he truly loved her. Yet he had to have been given some pause as Rachel's anxieties grew during the years leading up to the election of 1828. There were two main reasons: Rachel's disdain for the thought of having to relocate to Washington, and due to the drubbing she took in the Adams' press. To see Rachel in discomfort bothered the always discomfited Jackson doubly.

Evidence consistently shows Jackson's devotion to his wife all through the years. But Jackson could not be content, even in the steady embrace of his wife, without his affinity for resentment and confrontation. Although he professed satisfaction with life at the Hermitage, surrounded by loved ones, Jackson still seethed at being cheated by his adversaries. Whether or not Clay and Adams had struck a deal, the American people who had rallied behind Jackson had been slighted. The time had come for change. How could their candidate, having won both the popular vote and the electoral vote, have lost the election? It just didn't add up, especially to the laymen unfamiliar with the electoral process, which was much of Jackson's constituency. Whether or not these voters understood the system, they wanted reform.

Determined to act and insulted by the coalition that seemed stacked against their 'man of the people,' Jackson supporters, led by Martin Van Buren, split off from the Republican Party and forged a new party. They called themselves the Democratic Party, and they claimed to be the party of the "common man", dedicated to individual rights, state sovereignty, and opposition to banks and high tariffs.

The two sides were now formed, spelling the end of any last vestiges of the postwar "Good Feelings" of non-partisan politics in America. The National Republicans who followed John Quincy Adams made up one side of the divide, representing the monied east, and the establishment, with Democrats and "The People" on the other. The Jackson camp was energized, it was galvanized, it was determined to upend the system for the first time, and to get their voices heard. Yet by and large these

---

[956] Toplovich, Ann. "This is the real story of Andrew and Rachel Jackson". *The Tennessean*. Retrieved June 5, 2024.

voices were those of rural, conservative white male farmers just as before, but farmers with a set of needs distinct from the eastern planters and merchants of their father's generation.

The Jacksonians sought to distance themselves further from the Adams camp as public outrage over the corrupt bargain continued to fester among ordinary voters. As president, Adams had failed to fully connect with the average citizen, largely due to the widespread belief that he and Clay were corrupt. This prevalent belief continued to boost Jackson's image among sympathetic voters even further. Four years since the fateful 1824 presidential campaign, the Democrats had all the motivation they needed to head a spirited campaign of revenge in the election of 1828. Facing off against John Quincy Adams for a second time, Jackson and his camp were on a crusade to win the outright majority.

John Quincy Adams shared Monroe's goal of ending partisan conflict, and his Cabinet included individuals of various ideological and regional backgrounds. In his 1825 annual message to Congress, Adams presented a comprehensive and ambitious agenda, calling for major investments in internal improvements as well as the creation of a national university, a naval academy, and a national astronomical observatory. His requests to Congress spurred the opposition, leading to the creation of an anti-Adams congressional coalition consisting of supporters of Jackson, Crawford, and Vice President Calhoun. Following the 1826 elections, Calhoun and Martin Van Buren (who brought along many of Crawford's supporters) agreed to throw their support behind Jackson in the 1828 election. In the press, the two major political factions were referred to as "Adams Men" and "Jackson Men".

The addition of Henry Clay to the Adams party, which he made no effort to conceal, made its success a near certainty. The old federalists, however, could never quite forgive Adams for deserting them, and thus many of them, based in New England, still hesitated. Having long been excluded from political office, the former federalists were anxious to know if Adams would continue their exclusion. It was through Daniel Webster, however, that the last few federalists still in the arena were given a fresh start. A telling Webster letter on this subject survives, addressed to a member of the House who had sought advice from the great ideologist. Webster replied that although he didn't know Adams intimately, he had confidence in his patriotism and ability and believed that he would pursue a liberal and conciliatory course toward Federalists. Webster's advice was that the Congressman should in fact vote for Adams, and to advise his friends to do the same.

When it came to Andrew Jackson, Daniel Webster held mixed feelings. In 1827, he stated, "General Jackson's friends have made, and are still making, great efforts to place him in the chair. He is a good soldier. And I believe a very honest man, yet some of us think him wholly unfit for the place to which he aspires. Military achievement, however, is very visible and has palpable merit, and on this account, the general is exceedingly popular in some of the states."[957] Jackson had no qualms as to whether he was fit for the Presidency. He was driven by one main force politically, a belief in the will of the people. Characteristically, he thought of himself as the perfect interpreter of that will. Were he to be elected president, his supporters knew they could count on a new direction, that of a strong executive, claiming a mandate from voters, who would act confidently and decisively according to his instincts, not those of his advisors. "As long as the government heeds the popular will, the republic is safe. The three pillars, virtue, wisdom, and morality will be fostered by the people."[958]

But would the imperious General Andrew Jackson heed the popular will? Would he respect the majority's will when it came to votes by those within the United States Congress? Time would tell, and in the meantime, the questions remained.

---

[957] Webster, Daniel, 1828, Online Library of Liberty.
[958] Bartleby Research, "How Did Andrew Jackson Represent The Common Man", 2025.

Daniel Webster, image courtesy of Wikipedia, photographer and date unknown/ Henry Clay (right) Photo: Library of Congress/Corbis/VCG via Getty Images

CHAPTER

63

MUDSLINGING

"The patronage of the government for the last three years has been wielded to corrupt every living thing that comes within its influence, and was capable of being corrupted, and it would seem that virtue and truth, has fled from its embrace."
-Andrew Jackson

Even for those who knew Jackson well, there were serious reservations about whether the man was cut out for taking on the highest office in the land. It was well and good to promote the iron-fisted General if you agreed entirely with him on all matters. For those "in the know" believed that given the keys to the kingdom, Jackson would pursue only one path, his path. Even if that meant eliminating any and all who stood in the way of that end. For reasons such as this, the opposition to the General decided it was time to turn up the heat.

Jackson never enjoyed more popularity than he did in early 1825, in the period immediately following his defeat. Over the next few weeks, Jackson's actions captivated most observers who witnessed him. Some called him the "Washington Marvel," this bad-tempered, easily excitable hothead, who had endured a "miscarriage of justice," while managing to keep his emotions in check. Who was this Jackson, taking the high road, and being a good sport in the face of trickery? Did he feel the presidency had been unfairly taken from him? Yes. Did he feel the people were being manipulated like "sheep" for the ambitions of demagogues? Yes, he did. But Jackson stayed calm, at least to the public, and professionally, he simply carried on. Instead of resorting to aggression or threats, he hosted a lavish dinner on February 18th for 22 loyal supporters, featuring drinks like apple toddy, punch, wine, brandy, whiskey, cider, and champagne. It was a night to remember. [959]

The talk around Washington was that General Jackson was simply "that guy." Was it charisma? panache? The classiness that comes from a show of grace? The papers seemed starry-eyed, gushing about the General's "manly style." His backers showed their adoration at every opportunity. At both private gatherings and public events, the General was applauded and received innumerable accolades. When it came to the victorious, newly minted President John Quincy Adams, however, the same enthusiasm did not apply. It was quite the contrary. Understandably, Adams was bitter. Having endured many years of political ups and downs; having diligently crafted his public persona through a sparkling diplomatic record, guiding the state through the trying times of the previous 8 years, this was supposed to be his moment, the moment he had dreamed of his entire career. And here he was, yet all anyone could talk about was how he and Clay had cheated America's greatest military hero.

To many, President John Quincy Adams had become an object of pity. During one theater performance, when Adams and his family appeared, the actors made jokes referencing the election. Adams reacted with what was described as "death-like silence" (according to John McLane, who was also present). Then, someone started singing "The Hunters of Kentucky," celebrating Jackson's victory at New Orleans. The audience erupted in cheers, and the message in support of Jackson was obvious. Adams was mortified. Observing all this, McLane wrote, "What will he feel, when he hears this shout, penetrating every part of the union? Well may he say, he would not take the office if he could avoid it."[960] The President-elect may well have wished, in that moment, that he had avoided the presidency altogether.

The scandal surrounding the election placed a dark cloud over Adams. The unceasing accusations of "corrupt bargain," diminished the president's achievement, and that of his family. His presidency seemed

---

[959] Bill dated Feb. 18, 1825 in Jackson, *Correspondence*, III, 277.
[960] McLane to Mrs. McLane, Feb. 12, 1825, McLane Papers, LC.

unpopular at best, fraudulent at worst. The laughter, mockery, and contempt surrounding it made it feel less like a win, and more like a joke.

Jackson had always respected John Quincy Adams. He considered him an "honest, virtuous man." Jackson had long held the belief that Adams followed a similar creed, that "the people have a right to govern, and that their will should always be obeyed by their constituents." However, the golden prize of the presidency proved that even Adams could abandon his principles and get in bed with demagogues, even if it meant betraying the people. "Would it not be well," Jackson proposed to his campaign manager in Tennessee, "that the papers of Nashville and the whole state should speak out with moderate but firm disapprobation of this corruption, to give a proper tone to the people and draw their attention to the subject? When I see you, I have much to say."[961]

Andrew Jackson didn't know it yet, but he had already begun campaigning for the 1828 election and had taken the helm of a historical movement that the history books would one day dub "Jacksonian Democracy." Rallying cries of the Jackson zealots were already beginning, and the fervor would only increase over the next four years: "Bargain and Corruption," "Huzza for Jackson," and "All hail Old Hickory. Aware of it or not, the General was now in command of the first populist reform movement in American political history.

Tennessee's nomination of Jackson in 1825 marked the end of a brief period of politics without strong party divisions that had characterized the Monroe years. Even during the recent contentious election, all candidates had played along with the script of Jeffersonian Republicans, although much of their words and actions belied this. While their differences appeared mostly regional at first, deeper sovereignty issues surrounding federal versus state power began to rear its head. This novel shift meant that more than ever, those who wished to win elections found it more necessary than ever to detect the public mood. Unfairly for Adams, Jackson already had the market cornered on this front.

The transition from a caucus-driven political system, favoring a bestowal of a Congressionally ordained 'crown' upon a single candidate, to a system with distinct political parties, saw two clear voting blocs vying for power. Even before inauguration day, keen observers were

---

[961] AJ to Lewis, Feb. 14, 1825, Jackson, *Correspondence*, III, 276.

noticing the change in the landscape. "A party is forming itself here to oppose Mr. Adams' administration," remarked the old Federalist and New York Senator Rufus King in 1825, upon hearing of a rumored dinner summit between Jackson and Calhoun. "This first step may serve to appease the malcontents," he added.[962]

The Democratic Party's early years were influenced first by the Virginia Dynasty, but equally as much by the "cult of Jackson." Nashville loyalists and the Tennessee legislature helped initiate this movement, which gained traction after the 1824 election, attracting support from the Crawford-ites and the followers of the "Cast-Iron Man" himself, John C. Calhoun. This collaboration would evolve into a most cohesive national organization. In 1826, Vice President John C. Calhoun shed his War Hawk nationalism that characterized his early career, to become the spokesman of the Southern perspective, focused on limited government and states' rights. He reached out for Jackson's aid, pulling no punches. "In my opinion, "he observed, "liberty was never in greater danger." In Calhoun's not so humble opinion, the next three years would determine the power dynamics of the American political system. Calhoun criticized the Adams-Clay coalition, with stern warnings that corrupt patronage could undermine elections and lead to hereditary, imperial power; that is, power in the hands of the wrong people. Appealing successfully to the General's vanity, Calhoun expressed his belief that it was a Jackson administration, "under Providence," that was capable of combatting these political machinations.[963]

Jackson responded positively, he had always admired Calhoun, believing throughout that the former Secretary of War had been Jackson's sole defender amid the Florida controversy. The General praised the people's virtue ("the virtuous yeomanry of the country,") and their common cause against Adams. He condemned the use of political appointments for patronage ("the enemies of freedom.") He asserted his desire to march hand in hand with Calhoun in the common cause of pushing Adams out of office. "An artful management of patriot patronage can never be abided in a people's republic." [964]

---

[962] Rufus King to John King, Feb. 27, 1825, King Papers, NYHS.
[963] John C. Calhoun to AJ, June 4, 1826, *Calhoun Papers*, X, 110.
[964] Remini, *Martin Van Buren and the Making of the Democratic Party*, New York, 1959, pp. 84-146.

In contrast, Adams advocated unity, discouraged factionalism, and expressed a willingness to let Jackson supporters retain their federal positions, potentially undermining his own authority by yielding partisan advantage. Clay criticized Adams for enabling enemies within his administration. But the president urged individuals to overcome party rancor and embrace unity for the nation's benefit, although his efforts were futile. "There still remains one effort of magnanimity, one sacrifice of prejudice and passion to be made by the individuals throughout the nation who have heretofore followed the standards of political party," Adams claimed, "it is that of discarding every remnant of rancor against each other, of embracing as countrymen and friends, and of yielding to talents and virtue alone that confidence which in times of contention for principle was bestowed only on those who bore the badge of party communion." Holding tight to the high road, and as well-meaning as he may have been, the opposition viewed the Massachusetts president as condescending and imperious.[965]

In December, in delivering his first annual message to Congress, Adams seemed to almost intentionally antagonize his opposition. His idealistic words emphasized to the central states the urgent need to improve the nation's commercial infrastructure, to enhance communication and interaction among different regions and populations. Adams promoted the idea of a national university and an astronomical observatory, referring to them—amid the mocking catcalls of critics—as "lighthouses of the skies." The new President's broad vision involved an active Congress recognizing the necessity of using all its constitutional powers to promote improvements in agriculture, commerce, manufacturing, the arts, and sciences. Failing to do so, Adams argued, would be a betrayal of a sacred, fiduciary trust. Concluding by urging his colleagues to "embrace the future, to steer the ship boldly, resisting any force among constituents who raise objections to this bold vision," Adams asked the question, "Were we to slumber in indolence, throw up our arms and declare that we are palsied by the will of our constituents...would we not proclaim to the world that we cast away the bounties of Providence, and doom ourselves to perpetual inferiority?" Considering the contentious atmosphere of

---

[965] Richardson, James D., *Messages and Papers of the Presidents*, II, Part 2, 1904, pp. 866-968, 872, 879, 882.

the recent election, a more cautious approach might have served Adams better in this opening address.[966]

In glowing oratory and high-minded ideals, Adams courageously attempted to convince his obstinate audience of the American potential for something greater. A national university, exploring expeditions, an astronomical observatory, and a refined infrastructure through the funding of roads and canals. "The spirit of improvement," he concluded, is abroad upon the earth. It stimulates the heart, and sharpens the faculties, not of our fellow citizens alone, but of the nations of Europe, and of their rulers. . . . While foreign nations, less blessed with that freedom which is power than ourselves, are advancing with gigantic strides in the career of public improvement, were we to slumber in indolence, or fold up our arms and proclaim to the world that we are palsied by the will of our constituents, would it not be to cast away the bounties of Providence, and doom ourselves to perpetual inferiority? In the course of the year now drawing to its close, we have beheld under the auspices, and at the expense of one State of this Union, a new University unfolding its portals to the sons of science and holding up the torch of human improvement to the eyes that seek the light. We have seen, under the persevering and enlightened enterprise of another State, the waters of our western lakes mingled with those of the ocean. If undertakings like these have been accomplished in the compass of a few years, by the authority of single members of our Confederation, can we, the representative authorities of the whole Union, fall behind our fellow-servants in the exercise of the trust committed to us for the benefit of our common Sovereign, by the accomplishment of works important to the whole, and to which neither the authority nor the resources of any one State can be adequate?"[967]

His speech was forward thinking. It was worthy of the reputation the intellectual Adams had earned throughout his life. Yet, the Democrats hated it with a virulent passion. Adams was in for a struggle, as these were contentious times, and the mood of his opponents was all too ripe for criticism. The old Jeffersonian-Hamilton controversy seemed to be resurrecting before their very eyes. Old wounds were reopened, new animosities forged. Federalism, believed to be dead, was living, rampant,

---

[966] Ibid.
[967] John Quincy Adams, 6th President of the United States: 1825 - 1829, First Annual Message, December 06, 1825.

and sitting in the seat of power. Or so they thought. To say that there was a real and fair ground of opposition to the new administration was an understatement, because looking at Adams' early addresses in hindsight, they were worthy of consideration, and deserving of praise. Adams' concluding paragraph is another eloquent example, in which he addresses the "elephant in the room" corruption charge:

"Fellow-citizens, you are acquainted with the peculiar circumstances of the recent election, which have resulted in affording me the opportunity of addressing you at this time. You have heard the exposition of the principles which will direct me in the fulfillment of the high and solemn trust imposed upon me in this station. Less possessed of your confidence in advance than any of my predecessors, I am deeply conscious of the prospect that I shall stand more and oftener in need of your indulgence. Intentions upright and pure, a heart devoted to the welfare of our country, and the unceasing application of all the faculties allotted to me to her service are all the pledges that I can give for the faithful performance of the arduous duties I am to undertake. To the guidance of the legislative councils, to the assistance of the executive and subordinate departments, to the friendly cooperation of the respective State governments, to the candid and liberal support of the people so far as it may be deserved by honest industry and zeal, I shall look for whatever success may attend my public service; and knowing that 'except the Lord keep the city the watchman waketh but in vain,' with fervent supplications for His favor, to His overruling providence I commit with humble but fearless confidence my own fate and the future destinies of my country."

All criticism aside, the administration of John Quincy Adams, although forgotten by most who look back at the early 19th century, or written off as ineffective by others, can be viewed today with a mix of pride and sadness. It was a respectable administration, symbolized by the adoption of the oak for their oaken-ly independent candidate. Though plagued by hostility and accusations from the opposition right from the start, Adams was more of a free-thinker than many gave him credit for. Many of these Adams-ites who served him were principled, educated men, who mirrored their commander-in-chief. That is, they showed compassion, a sense of right and wrong, and seemed to truly wish to do what was best for the country. The critics railed, however, how easy it was to promote such costly, high-minded goals when one is born with a silver spoon in one's mouth.

Nevertheless, in a show of good faith, President Adams sought to bring the factions together by avoiding wholesale replacements of federal officers. The practice of removing honest individuals from lower positions due to their name or party affiliation was not a part of John Quincy Adams' administration. He dismissed only two officeholders, and both were for justifiable reasons. In the third month of his presidency, he wrote insightfully: "The customs officials across the country were likely opposed to my election. They are now under my authority, and I've been strongly urged from various sources to replace my opponents with my supporters. I can only justify my refusal to follow this approach by remaining steady and consistent in my own beliefs. If I make an exception in one case, my friends will expect me to do the same in many others. A negative and intrusive examination of the personal views of public officials would spread throughout the entire country, igniting the most selfish and base instincts, leading to a distortion of behavior and a misrepresentation of the feelings of individuals whose positions might become targets of slander." [968]

Adams, as evidenced by his glowing vision for the United States of America founded on enlightenment principles, education and a quest for exploration and progress, made efforts to, in essence, pull the squabbles of partisan rancor out of the muck. Perhaps his efforts were doomed from the start. Perhaps the turbulent forces at work throughout the country, ignited by the nation's first severe recession, created such bitter resentment, such combative politics, that it was already too late. But to be labeled a corrupt bargainer, a fraudulent President, without the evidence, was unfair. Adams, ultimately, can be seen as something of a victim of the 'Cult of Jackson,' and his biggest mistake was his determination to be president, however the cost. For coming in second place in the election, the American people, probably correctly, saw him as a usurper. His grand vision would one day become reality, but one could argue, Adams was far ahead of his time.

As for Old Hickory, for the rest of this spring and summer, an easy pace set in, back in the hills of Tennessee. Jackson enjoyed a slower

---

[968] Quincy, Josiah, *Life of J. Q. Adams*, p. 147.

paced, celebratory political life, away from the hustle and bustle of Washington, with the running of his farm and the entertainment of his many visitors. The most distinguished of whom was the Marquis de Lafayette, as noted, followed later by the Scottish-born Francis Wright, the feminist reformer.

Lafayette's visit caught Old Hickory at a bad moment. As a result of too much sitting in Washington and too much horseback riding at the Hermitage he suffered "an inflammation in the rectum which communicated to the bladder and affected the prostate glands." Even so he roused himself from his bed to welcome the touring Frenchman and made him feel comfortable.[969]

By the end of the summer dozens of visitors had huddled with Jackson and advised him about his future. There was never any question about running in 1828. The General was told that he owed it to the country, that the people expected him to put down the men who had shown contempt for their will. Tennessee politicians demonstrated what they meant. In October, 1825, before the Adams administration had had a chance to address itself to Congress and propose a program of legislation, the Tennessee legislature passed a resolution that lacked unanimity by just three votes, but which recommended to the American people that Andrew Jackson by virtue of his public services and political qualifications merit election to the president presidency in 1828.[970] In other words, even before the Adams administration had an opportunity to begin, Tennesseans had already leveled a brickbat at it by declaring that it needed to be replaced at the earliest possible moment. This action officially launched the presidential election of 1828.

At approximately the same time, Jackson decided he would step down as U.S. Senator. His election to the post had come, after all, under very unusual circumstances. He had never really wanted the office in the first place and found himself in an awkward position when the presidential election landed in the House of Representatives. If he continued as Senator, now that he was again a presidential contender, that awkwardness could become painfully sharp. Besides, since he intended to give more of his attention to the campaign this time around,

---

[969] AJ to Swartwout, May 16, 1825, in *Some Letters of Andrew Jackson*, Henry F. DePut edited, Worcester, 1922, p. 20.

[970] Parton, *Jackson*, III, 95.

he was better off staying at the Hermitage, where he could meet with politicians relatively free from observation. His friends' efforts to organize a political party on his behalf would be much easier with his proximity and input. Jackson would never again serve as a legislator.

Upon notification of his nomination for the presidency, Jackson hurried off to the state assembly at Murfreesboro to announce his retirement. As soon as they learned of his coming, the legislators in both houses invited him to appear before them and address the assembled members. The General readily accepted. He could not pass up the opportunity to hammer at the theme of Washington's fraud, corruption and intrigue threatening the liberty of the American people, in front of a large public forum. He also wished to assure everyone that while so many others stooped to intrigue and malfeasance, he, Andrew Jackson, remained a forthright, pure, and unaffected 'man of the people.'[971]

The address came off without a hitch. The General showed all his now refined political arts. To start, Jackson carefully reminded his audience that he had never sought the position to which they had selected him and, of course, he would continue to serve if his "feeble aid "might in some way advance the "security of our Republican system." But he doubted that he was needed in Washington. Moreover, in view of the recent resolution of the legislature in "proposing again my name to the American people for the office of chief magistrate of the Union," he felt constrained "to ask your indulgence to be excused from any further service in the counsels of the country." With that said, he came right to his main point. Using the likelihood of a proposed amendment to the Constitution being brought before Congress to limit the tenure of the president to a single term of four or six years, Jackson leveled his sights on his target. He not only approved such an amendment so that "some new barrier to the encroachments of power or corruption in any of the departments of government" could be provided, but he suggested a provision "rendering any member of Congress ineligible to office under the general government for and during the term from which he was elected." It was clear to the assemblage of Tennesseans that his remark was intended for the Kentuckian, Clay. "The danger to

---

[971] To the Tennessee Legislature, Oct. 12, 1825, in Jackson, Correspondence, III, 293-296.

liberty is the breakdown of the system of checks and balances," he said, "and the proposed amendment would provide additional protection for that system. There is no truth more sacred in politics; and none more conclusively stamped upon all the state constitutions, as well as the federal constitution, than that which requires the three great departments of power, the legislative judicial, and executive, to keep separate and apart." Jackson then zeroed in on exactly what his candidacy would be bent on eliminating:

"But if this change in the constitution should not be attained, and important appointments continue to evolve upon the representatives in Congress, it requires no depth of thought to be convinced that corruption will become the order of the day, and under the garb of conscientious sacrifices to establish precedence for the public good, evil may arise of serious importance to the freedom and prosperity of the Republic. It is through this channel that the people may expect to be attacked in their constitutional sovereignty, and where tyranny may well be apprehended to spring up in some favorable emergency."[972]

The legislature accepted Jackson's resignation, recognizing the delicate situation that confronted him, and elected Judge Hugh Lawson White of east Tennessee to serve out the General's four remaining years. White was expected to be a useful member of the Senate, both to the state and to Jackson, who then returned to the care of his farm and children.[973] This in no way distracted him from his focus on a return run to the White House. He had crossed the Rubicon and was headed straight for the White House.

As the election of 1828 neared, to say the race for the presidency became ugly between John Quincy Adams, and Andrew Jackson would be an understatement. Mudslinging reached new lows in 1828, and the electorate developed an affinity for bare-knuckle politics. Most were aware that relations had gotten ugly the moment Jackson lost in 1824. But as time went on, the dirt and the grime tossed only increased. The Adams camp made the most of Jackson's controversial past. While Adams himself did not wish to stoop to gutter tactics, many of his backers were less squeamish, even going so far as: "Jackson's mother was

---

[972] Ibid.
[973] Statement by AJ, Dec. 30, 1825, Jackson Papers, THS.

a COMMON PROSTITUTE, brought to this country by the British soldiers! She afterward married a MULATTO MAN, with whom she had several children, of which number General JACKSON IS ONE!!!" When Jackson read this notice, he reportedly wept. [974]

The Jackson men also hit below the belt. President Adams had purchased, with his own money and for his own use, a billiard table and a set of chess pieces. To the Jacksonians, these items became "gaming tables" and "gambling furniture" for the "presidential palace." Critics also went after the large federal salaries Adams had received over the years of his diplomatic service, as well-earned and honest as they may have been. "We disapprove the kingly pomp and splendor that is displayed by the president incumbent." But that was mellow compared to other characterizations of Adams as a bigot, an alcoholic, an amoral sabbath-breaker. Adams journaled to ease the pain, writing of the abuse and referring to his detractors as "skunks of party slander."[975]

In response to criticisms and accusations, the General's campaign, in their most outrageous claim against the president, labeled John Quincy Adams a "pimp." This claim stemmed from Adams's role as an ambassador to the Russian Empire, where he employed a young woman as a personal assistant for his wife. Jackson's campaign exaggerated this situation, alleging that Adams had presented the young woman as a gift to Czar Alexander I. This humdrum story had no political appeal until it appeared in a short sketch of Jackson published by Isaac Hill in which Hill accused Adams of being a pimp who had procured a woman for the lascivious pleasure of the czar. Once the story appeared in the sketch, it spread throughout the Jackson press.

The distorted narratives enraged Adams, yet he chose not to directly counter the slanderous claims. Meanwhile, Jackson's team actively reached out to newspapers, providing them with specific guidelines on how to handle anti-Jacksonian narratives. But there was one ant-Jackson narrative that the General simply could not abide, although he had to. In desperation, and sensing the polls going against them, the Adams team took aim directly at Jackson's heart. They went after his heart and soul, Rachel Jackson.

---

[974] Remini, *The Election of Andrew Jackson*, New York, 1963, pp. 117-119; *National Journal*, Sept. 4, 1828.
[975] *Telegraph*, Jan. 26, Feb. 16, July 2, 23, 1828.

CHAPTER

64

WEATHERING THE STORM

"They have dipped their arrows at wormwood and gall and sped them at me."
—Rachel Donelson Jackson

In the election of 1828 "J. Q. Adams who can write" squared off against "Andy Jackson who can fight" in one of the most bitter campaigns in American history. If the two candidates had more issues that they differed on, the campaigns of 1828 might have been different. Things might not have grown so intensely bitter between the camps of Adams and Jackson, but their only distinct difference politically was how they viewed the funding of internal improvements, which Adams was for, and Jackson was against. But with the economic residue of 1819's Panic still heavy in the air nine years later, funding roads and canals was no longer held up as a serious consideration.

Both candidates were similar in most other areas. Both favored a nationalistic approach when it came to foreign policy. Both had done much to ensure the strength and defense of the nation, although in different ways. The most contentious issue during Adams' presidency was the question of protective tariffs, yet the complexity of the controversy left voters with little clear distinction between the two men.

With Jackson seemingly unable to make up his mind on the tariff issue, his position could be described as ambiguous during his time in the Senate, leaving many uncertain about his true stance on the issue that would rear its ugly head time and again throughout the antebellum period. Adams was similarly inconsistent regarding the tariff. Many politicians of the time, in fact, contradicted themselves often on this issue, with only Southern planters most decidedly against it. The state of South Carolina, particularly, was outspoken in its opposition to the tariff, for this group relied on the cost of its cotton exports. A high tariff, in the eyes of spokesmen like Calhoun and Robert Hayne, would likely bring high reciprocal tariffs from foreign nations, potentially causing troublesome waves in the trade of King Cotton.[976]

Unfortunately, this position did not translate well into effective election strategies. Vice President Calhoun was now part of Adams' administration, and although he eyed the collaboration with Jackson in the next election, he could not very well exploit this issue and save face. Thus, with a lack of a clear platform, Jackson's supporters relied instead on a campaign based on what they stood for symbolically. One area of focus which Jacksonians made a meal of was the obvious one, the charge of corruption and the taint of the corrupt bargain. For Adams and Clay, that was their bugaboo, and there would be no getting around it for the remainder of their careers. But the Jackson faction did not stop there, they implied a much deeper corruption at play that was pulling the rug out from under American liberty, stifling the voices of ordinary citizens, and preventing access to government.

The pattern of anointing presidential successors during the days of the Virginia Dynasty, the Republican caucus' efforts to control nominations, and the exchange of political support for office positions (re: Adams/Clay) were all seen as crystal clear examples of the nefarious nature of government barring the people from true democracy. To reclaim power, the people needed to dismantle this corrupt system, and the obvious answer to enable this was to vote for the candidate that truly was of the people: none other than Andrew Jackson.

Jackson's campaign was invested in the idea that the General need not utter a word. His life story resonated more loudly than words—hero of New Orleans, savior of the nation, and the standard bearer for the common man, supporting Jackson was the true patriot's path to rejecting corrupt government and replacing it with a democracy led by

---

[976] Freehling, William W., *Prelude to Civil War: The Nullification Crisis in South Carolina 1816–1836*. 1965. p. 143

the people. All across the campaign trail, Jackson committees trumpeted this consistent theme in rallies. Promoting the right of the people to choose a leader from amongst themselves, Jacksonian orators banged upon the podium with feeling, reiterating the company line. Newspapers aligned with Jackson published these speeches, amplifying the praise and countering criticisms from the Adams camp.

A dedicated group of Jackson supporters, including Sam Houston and William Lewis, established a committee to counteract the negative portrayals from the Adams side. Although having to concede to certain allegations, with a justifiable spin, they countered editorials and gathered mitigating testimonies for the General. Adams's supporters countered by digging up the ample dirt from Jackson's past. They called the general a slave trader, a gambler, and a backwoods buffoon who could not spell more than one word out of four correctly. The Adams' campaigners even went so far as to publish a piece claiming "cruel and deliberate murder," suggesting Jackson had killed up to 1,500 British soldiers on January 8, 1815, at Chalmette, simply because they wished to enter the city that night to eat[977].

The Jackson campaign in 1828 was the first to appeal directly for voter support through a professional political organization. Skilled political organizers, like Martin Van Buren of New York, Amos Kendall of Kentucky, and Thomas Ritchie of Virginia, created an extensive network of campaign committees and subcommittees to organize mass rallies, parades, and barbecues, and to erect hickory poles, Jackson's symbol.

Despite the attacks on his character, particularly regarding his wartime actions, Jackson was advised not to 'take the bait,' to stay above the mudslinging himself. Resentful though he was at what he deemed slanderous libel, outwardly he remained steadfast. In his writing, however, Jackson found his route to vent his frustrations in letters to friends and family. In one correspondence, playing upon his war record, Jackson questioned his critics' absence when the British came calling, "Where were they in times of peril?" Finding his voice through the pen, Jackson reminded friends that his critics could enjoy their freedom to attack his character because of his sacrifices, and those of other brave warriors. No stranger to personal slander, the slanders intensified. Still,

---

[977] The Presidency of Andrew Jackson, Digital History, ID 3544.

they were not unfamiliar to him, as these were the same regurgitated arguments he faced his entire career. The difference being that he was now forced to refrain from a public response. He reassured his friend Felix Grundy, however, that "Truth is mighty and will prevail."[978]

However, there was one degree of slanders Jackson could not overlook, and these he considered the basest of them all. To attack the General was one thing, but to go after his wife was another, and it was there where Jackson drew the line. It was much tougher in the early 19th century to gauge public opinion, but it was clear that Jackson's popularity had only grown since he finished first in the 1824 election. Jacksonians, unwilling to tolerate another stolen election, were worked up to a frenzy by 1828 for their hero. That John Quincy Adams must have been aware of the General's unprecedented upward trend became manifest when the Adams team resorted to the lowest strategy they could devise to provoke Jackson to lose his cool: attacking Rachel. The Adams camp had a field day using the controversial circumstances of the Jackson marriage to attack his opponent's character, questioning whether "a convicted adulteress and her paramour husband" should hold the highest offices in the land. One newspaper echoed this sentiment, amplifying the scandal. [979]

As the momentum of the presidential campaign accelerated in 1827, a growing entourage of political managers emerged to orchestrate a robust show of support for Old Hickory. Jackson faced significant pressure to fulfill their demands: providing information, clarifying his stance, and explaining his actions related to various events. Questions arose about his vote against George Washington in the House of Representatives in 1796, his involvement in the Burr conspiracy, and his decision to imprison Judge Hall in New Orleans after the battle. The execution of several militia members prompted a particularly aggressive propaganda effort from the opposition, requiring explanations from Jackson. He was challenged to clarify incidents such as the executions of Ambrister and Arbuthnot, the killing of Charles Dickinson, and the altercation with the Bentons. However, the most damaging accusation against Jackson as the campaign intensified revolved around the circumstances surrounding

---

[978] AJ to Grundy, 1827, Jackson Papers, LC.
[979] Alton Telegraph, 1828, Newspaper Archives.

his marriage to Rachel. Given that General Jackson had adopted a strong moral stance in his campaign, condemning corruption in Washington and beyond, his opponents revived allegations of an adulterous and bigamous union, demanding explanations for his actions in eloping with another man's wife.

Attacking Rachel and Jackson's marriage was a risky strategy, but to unsettle the people's uncharacteristically unflappable favorite, the opposition was desperate. Slowly at first, but then more intensely, the old charges of Jackson's controversial early relationship with Rachel were revived. Jackson was portrayed as a man of insatiable appetite who demanded instant carnal satisfaction; one who disrespected the sacred institution of marriage by "stealing" another man's wife. Rachel was depicted as an adulteress in milder reports, and an outright whore in the most severe. Some publications even crossed racial lines in their descriptions of Rachel, such as one in Kentucky that referred to her as a "dirty, black wench," a remark that was widely circulated in other papers.

This tactic was fraught with risk for Adams, as disgusted voters might well have reacted negatively to the public humiliation of Rachel. Yet, the Adams camp believed it would do the trick. They believed Jackson would lose his cool eventually and return to his former days of very unpresidential temperament. Jackson, indeed, was bubbling with provocation. "Such feelings of indignation I could scarcely control," he wrote to an associate, "when the midnight assassin strikes you to the heart, murders your family, and robs your dwelling, the heart sickens at the relation of the deed, but this scene loses all when compared to the recent slander of a virtuous female propagated by the minions of power for political effect."[980]

Had it been twenty years earlier, no doubt Jackson would have been on the road to some remote outpost, dueling pistols in tow. Yet, Jackson understood his enemies' aim, "It is evident that it is the last effort of a combined coalition to save themselves and destroy me," he told Richard Call. "It is calculated to arouse me to some desperate act by which I would fall prostrate before the people."

Jackson managed to hold himself together, understanding that the opposition wanted an irate reaction from him, and that reacting back

---

[980] AJ to Richard Keith Call, Jan. 1828, Jackson Papers, LC.

with vengeance would not only doom the campaign but would only make things worse for Rachel, by simply exposing her to additional insults. "For the present, my hands are pinioned" but he vowed that "the evil doers would be punished, the day of retribution and vengeance must come, when the guilty will meet with their just reward."[981] Jackson did not give the Adams people what they wished for. He believed that his revenge would come in the fall of 1828, politically at least. He believed there was no doubt that when the votes were counted, he would have his revenge.

As the 1828 campaign gained speed, a remarkably malicious partisanship targeting both candidates in the campaign took hold. Adams was denounced as a secret monarchist, enamored with European manners, and married to a foreigner. London-born Louisa Catherine Adams admitted to having an English mother.

Of course, Jackson, owner of a much more violent, colorful, and controversial past, attracted even greater attention for scandal. Portrayed by his supporters as a curative battling against the corrupt political behemoths in Washington, he found himself repeatedly attacked for complicity in adultery, accused of knowingly marrying an already married woman. The accusations were ceaseless. *Cincinnati Gazette* editor Charles Hammond, in an arrangement with Henry Clay, spread such charges starting in the winter of 1827. "I spuriously added for good measure that the General descended from a mixed raced father and a prostitute."[982] Hammond casually remarked. The Jackson camp, headed by John Eaton, responded alertly to the bigamy charge by putting together a labored narrative complete with documents and testimonials reporting to exonerate, sort of, the candidate and his wife. There is no doubt that Lewis Robards obtained a divorce in 1793, approximately two years after Rachel began living with Jackson. So, the Jackson defenders were forced to argue that Jackson was well-meaning but naive in assuming that Robards had received the dissolution prior to their marriage. This explanation reduced, among friendly ears, Rachel's embarrassing infidelity to being merely technical and unintended.

---

[981] Ibid.
[982] Hammond to Clay, Dec. 1827, Miscellaneous Clay Papers, DUL.

Jackson's dubious repute as a "violent chieftain" echoed among Republicans, based on past transgressions. The many transgressions and various recurring quarrels with civic officials over the years drew generous attention. One engraving by the Boston printmaker David Claypool Johnston made Jackson out to be a modern King Richard III, who ruled England from 1452 to 1485. Commemorated as cruel in deed, ruthless at heart, and monstrously ambitious, Jackson's face tattooed with the bodies of his victims, he wears a military tent for a hat, with an inscription at the bottom of the illustration quotes from the Bard "and he thought the souls of all I have murdered, came from my tent." [983]

A still even more direct accusation against Jackson came from the Dublin-born journalist John Binns, editor of the *Philadelphia Democratic Press*, who published an attack on the General under the heading "some account of some of the bloody deeds of General Jackson." Known as the 'Coffin Hand-Bill,'[984] it featured six caskets bearing the names of the Tennessee militiamen executed after the victory of New Orleans, and after reports of peace had reached Jackson. More than two dozen versions of Binns's handbill were printed. Other attacks alleged that Jackson indiscriminately exterminated Indian towns, murdered Indian women and children, and refused to pardon the "generous-hearted" John Woods.[985]

To the charge of putting to death mutineers at least, Jackson made no apologies. "It will be recollected in the Revolutionary War that in a time of great trial," he wrote one correspondent in an 1828 letter that subsequently appeared in the *Lexington Kentucky Gazette*, "General Washington ordered deserters to be shot without trial." In a memoir, newspaper publisher Thurlow Weed offered a glimpse into how the National-Republicans searched for new ways to exploit Jackson's not-so-honorable history. Only thirty-years old at the time, the lanky New Yorker would go on to become a key player in both the Whig and Republican parties. In 1828 he was an Adams man. "In August, 1828, I received from the National General Committee two large dry goods boxes containing campaigning documents. Upon opening which I found

---

[983] David Claypool Johnston, in Forbes Magazine, Harry T. Peters "America on Stone" Lithography Collection.
[984] Coffin Handbill, HL.
[985] Philadelphia Democratic Press, 1828, Newspaper Archives.

two pamphlets. One containing an account of the trial and execution of six militia men. This document was generally known and will be better remembered as the Coffin Hand Bill. The other document was entitled General Jackson's Domestic Relations and gave an account of the general's duel with Mr. Dickinson and his marriage. A letter from the committee advised me that these boxes contained valuable campaign documents, the distribution of which throughout the western counties of this state was entrusted to me, adding that if more were to be desired, they would cheerfully furnish them."

Offering some further insights into Jackson's victory, Weed contended that the "enlightened, enabled statesman, editors, etc., etc. who supported Mr. Adams were oblivious to the good portion of the country's attachment to General Jackson, the impression of the masses was that the six militia men deserved hanging, and any attempts to embarrass Jackson by ruthlessly invading the sanctity of his home via the bigamy charge would only damage the cause of their own candidate." [986]

If the executions of the militia men failed to gain purchase, and generate enough enmity to Jackson, neither did the killing of Jackson's slave Gilbert by an overseer. This, the National Republicans on the Adams side also attempted to utilize to Jackson's discredit. A Virginian by birth, purchased by the General and taken to his northern Alabama plantation, Gilbert ran away, only to be apprehended. He again fled in 1824, was captured, and escaped yet again in August 1827, only to be returned once again. Jackson ordered his overseer, Ira Walton, to whip Gilbert in front of the other slaves. According to Walton, he and Gilbert were walking toward a field to enact the punishment when Gilbert managed to free his bound hands and attack him with a piece of wood. Fearing for his life, so Walton claimed, he stabbed Gilbert several times. The man died a few hours later. Jackson called the death an unfortunate occurrence and seemed to back Walton. "I believe the fatal stab," he wrote the Davidson County coroner, "was given in self-defense." A local nine-man jury predictably agreed.

Jackson, however, perhaps sensing or alerted to the potential political damage that the incident could well cause, suddenly decided

---

[986] Weed, Thurlow (1883). Weed, Harriet A. (ed.). *Autobiography of Thurlow Weed.* New York, NY: Houghton, Mifflin and Company.

to pursue the matter. On August 30, he wrote Andrew Hays, the state prosecutor for the Fourth Circuit Court, suggesting that he investigate Gilbert's death. "I have discharged Mr. Walton from my service," he provocatively added. The following day, after examining Gilbert's body, Hays offered the following opinion, "There exists a considerable doubt as to the absolute necessity of killing the slave Gilbert. The wound in Gilbert's back afforded a strong presumption that he was stabbed from behind whilst running and not in the first scuffle, and among other circumstances, which induced me to think that it is not a case of justifiable homicide, is that his hands were tied." Hays advised Jackson "To have Mr. Walton brought before the circuit court to answer a bill of indictment for the death of Gilbert."[987]

In November, a grand jury discharged Walton from prosecution. The following year as the election neared, the *National Banner* and *Nashville Whig* published 'General Jackson's Negro Speculations and his Traffic in Human Flesh', which included a few sharp words on Gilbert's death.[988] This commentary soon circulated more generally as a pamphlet. Its author, long time Jackson critic Andrew Erwin, wrote in part, "I never had a slave brought before me for offending against whom I gave an unmerciful sentence, which is what you have said to have done at or near your own fireside at the Hermitage, in the execution of which your own slave was killed." The *Nashville Republican*, returning fire, exonerated Jackson. "Whatever might have been the conduct of the overseer, the General was entirely free from blame." Gilbert, like John Woods, the Florida Seminoles, and the six militiamen, would simply become a footnote of the campaign.

The personal attacks on both Jackson and Adams in 1828 underlined the growing influence of newspapers in America. Successful candidates were soon to grasp that editors can make strong allies in a campaign, shaping public opinion while offering ideas on which issues to accentuate. Amos Kendall, a Kentucky transplant and editor of the *Frankfurt Argus of Western America*, proved to be a tremendous asset to Jackson. Originally a Clay supporter, (and tutor of Clay's children) Kendall, an unprepossessing asthmatic with myopic vision and a slight stoop,

---

[987] Parton, Jackson, III, 144.
[988] *National Banner* and *Nashville Whig*, 1828, Newspaper Archives.

drifted into the opposition during the Panic of 1819, supporting the interest of debtors in what became known as the Kentucky Relief War. The Bluegrass State blamed the country's national bank, the cash and credit engine behind Clay's grand 'American System' vision, for the financial collapse. Kendall and his *Argus* associate Frances P. Blair, both Relief War veterans, and western defenders of hard money, would play important roles in fashioning Democratic Party economic policy under Jackson.[989] They would make the move to Washington and begin publication of the *Washington Globe*, the premiere Jackson mouthpiece throughout his presidency. Andrew Jackson has been word produced as a bloodthirsty tyrant, a murderer, and a dangerous aspirant, His adversaries have openly invaded his private sanctuary, and the innocent partner of his bed has been dragged forth with unblushing effrontery, To be made the subject of jest, suspicion, and slander. Their private history has been shamefully and wickedly, perverted, and trumpeted through the medium of obscene gazettes, and bandied about in the pestiferous breath of hollow hearted and treacherous demagogues."[990]

"Let the cry by Jackson, Calhoun, and Liberty!" The *Telegraph* shouted in October of 1828.[991] The message was reprinted in Democratic newspapers throughout the country. It was becoming evident that Jackson was steadily winning the publicity battle. "The Hurra boys were for Jackson...all the noisey, turbulent, boisterous Politicians are with him and to my regret, they constitute a powerful host."[992] The Hurra Boys worked around the clock for Old Hickory. They distributed hickory brooms, hickory canes and hickory sticks. They stuck them all over town in the most prominent places, such as steeples and signposts. The National Republicans scoffed.[993]

In 1828, the tariff question, the major economic issue facing the nation, became a major political tool. Congress, composed mainly of Jackson supporters, passed a bill in May designed to encourage support

---

[989] *Frankfurt Argus of Western America*, Frankfort, KY, 1808-1830, LOC.
[990] *Reflections on the Character and Public Services of Andrew Jackson with Reference to his Qualifications for the Presidency with General Remarks*. By a Native American. New York, 1828, p. 7.
[991] *Telegraph, Charleston Mercury, Richmond Examiner*, Oct. 20, 1828.
[992] Parton, Jackson, III, 144.
[993] *National Journal*, May 4, 1828.

for the General's candidacy. Presumed swing states Pennsylvania, New York, Kentucky, Ohio, and Missouri, stood to benefit from the new protective rates. 1828 was unique among election years in that for the first time the people would be voting to nominate candidates directly, rather than the old caucus system where the insiders alone controlled whose name would be on the ballots. Technically, the people still voted for electors, but a substantial variation existed as to how the electors were chosen. Some states devised a 'clean sweep' system, with a popular majority going to the winning candidate. This meant that the states' electors would vote unanimously for that candidate. Other states allowed a 'split decision.' Had the election results been close these differences might have mattered, but as things turned out, it was a wash.

At this point, no firm Jacksonian position on the tariff had come to manifest itself. Some of those in the Jackson camp favored higher rates, while others, especially in the South, rode the fence. Jackson, as noted, took no definitive stand for or against. His view on the issue remained open to interpretation. As part of the Blount faction, he tended towards an active economic outlook on issues such as the tariff, internal improvements, and land speculations. This was on par with Clay's American system ideology. His support in the Senate for the protectionist tariff of 1824 was proof of the General's flexibility on the issue. Jackson voted favorably for the tariff for reasons of national defense, as opposed to economic principle. But there were limits to his economic nationalism. He supported hard money in the Tennessee and Kentucky Relief Wars, and he had also shown support for Monroe's 1822 veto of the National Road/Cumberland Road. "My opinion has always been," he wrote Monroe, "that the federal government did not possess the constitutional power to oversee improvements, and that it was retained to the states' respectively and with great wisdom." [994]

Like most Jeffersonian Republicans, his view on the protection issue remained fluid. He seemed to casually accept federalism's disintegration and the near disastrous war with Great Britain. The National Bank, the protective tariff, and the Cumberland Road were all Republican proposals. But then with the Panic of 1819 and the Relief Wars, and the revitalization of a partisan system in which supporters of Clay and Adams

---

[994] AJ to Monroe, 1822, Monroe Papers, LC.

so conspicuously doubted internal improvements, he began to question these initiatives. Jackson never abandoned his belief, however, in the constitutionality of the tariff. He regarded the principle of protectionism as legal in the hands of the federal government and necessary to secure the republic against European rivals. The tariff's actual impact on the election is debatable as Jackson hardly needed it to claim victory. As it turns out, Adams never stood a chance.

"When Clay and John Adams a bargain first made, They took Sammy Southard their councils to aid, But Southard turned out to be a most consummate ass, As deficient in brains as abundant in brass . . . Ha! Ha! Ha!"[995]

---

[995] *United States Telegraph*, May, 1828.

CHAPTER

65

A TRAGIC VICTORY

"Now to my tent, O God, repair, and make thy servant wise, I'll suffer nothing near me there, that shall offend thine eyes. The man that doth his neighbor wrong, by falsehood or by force, the scornful eye, the slanderous tongue; I'll banish from my doors. I'll seek the faithful and the Just, and will their health enjoy, These are the friends that I shall trust, the Servants I'll employ.
—Author unknown

And finally, mercifully, election day arrived. "To the Polls, to the Polls! Duff Green ordered in his pro-Jackson United States Telegraph, "The faithful sentinel must not sleep, let no one stay home—let every man go to the polls--let not a voice be lost—let every Freeman do his duty—and all will triumph in the success of JACKSON, CALHOUN and LIBERTY!"[996]

Huzza for Jackson! "The political news from all quarters is of the most flattering kind," Jackson wrote to Richard Call, "New York is constantly believed to be well given against the administration, for thirty, if not thirty-three votes. Ohio and Kentucky are believed to be safe for the people's cause. But both sides are sanguine. New Jersey and Delaware are against the administration, and in Maryland, a majority. A few days more will test the result."[997] The results turned out to be overwhelming.

---

[996] *Telegraph*, Oct. 20, 1828.
[997] AJ to Richard Keith Call, Fall, 1828, Jackson Papers, LC.

As expected, New England voted for Adams, along with New Jersey and Delaware. New York and Maryland split between Adams and Jackson, but the rest of the country, all the West, and nearly all the South, voted for Jackson. The popular vote was 647,000 for Jackson to 508,000 for Adams.

These were much larger totals than in 1824, a result of the successful efforts in many states to remove the property requirement, and to promote 'universal manhood suffrage.' The results had clearly taken effect, as less than 400,000 people had voted in the previous election compared to over 1.1 million in 1828. The shift toward popular voting for electors in states had a major impact as well in getting the people to the polls. Jackson's victory in the electoral college was even more of a rout, as he garnered 178 electoral votes to Adams' 83. The Congressional elections went to the Jacksonians as well, who won heavily in the lower house, and took the win, though more narrowly, in the Senate. Jackson's administration could now count on support from both chambers of the legislature, with a large majority in the House of Representatives, and a small majority in the Senate. Jackson was satisfied with the results, and grateful for the people's overwhelming mandate. "The suffrages of a virtuous people pronounced the verdict of condemnation against their slanders. It has justified my character and my course" he wrote to John Coffey. The victorious Jacksonians, who were now beginning to call themselves Democrats, took to the streets to celebrate.[998]

Jackson received letters of congratulations from all around the country. "Providence has procured for us a verdict of the people which has condemned these wicked proceedings." Jackson wrote Coffee when he had a moment. "It has announced to an admiring world that the people are virtuous, and capable of self-government. The liberty of our beloved country will be perpetual." He mentioned as well to Coffee that he and Rachel were grateful that they had survived the wicked slanders during the campaign. "Providence has snatched us from the snares of the fowler."[999] Yet, Jackson intimated as well of feeling depressed, although he wouldn't say why. This coincides with Rachael beginning her decline. Little did the Jacksons know what was in store.

---

[998] AJ to Coffee, Nov. 1828, Coffee Papers, *THS*.
[999] Ibid.

The election results showed one thing for sure: Jackson's appeal ranged widely. This news was met with chagrin among the many who hoped for a more respectable political order. "In this state, as in Kentucky, the people en masse are favorable to General Jackson," Supreme Court Justice John Marshall complained to a nephew, "A great portion of the intelligent and unambitious are in favor of the reelection of Mr. Adams, but they constitute a decided minority."[1000] Elections took place over two weeks and this contributed to a wide array of discrepancies of participation across the various states. Virginia's limited voting requirements resulted in only 39,000 white men voting, while in Ohio the total was nearly 131,000. And yet, due in part to the constitution's infamous Three-Fifths clause, the 'Old Dominion' provided 24 electoral votes to Ohio's mere 16. It was a moot point in 1828, but in hindsight, an improbable shift of only 11.5 ballots in five states (Ohio, Kentucky, Indiana, Louisiana, and New York) would have produced a much closer result and an Adams victory, with the electoral vote count at 132-129. Adams' supporters fired out impassioned calls for a reform of the system based on what they deemed as inaccurate and unrepresentative results.

Perhaps sensing his defeat to Jackson, John Quincy Adams had ceased writing entries in his usually prolific journal since early August, but he picked it up again in December, postmortem. He included a theatrical entry on the third. "The sun of my political life sets, in the deepest gloom."[1001]

"When Jackson's victory became clear," Henry Clay reflected, "it occurred to me that no greater calamity had struck the United States since we were a free people." In the first weeks of 1829 Clay began thinking of his own camp and how to defeat Jackson in four years' time. "We are beaten," a despondent Henry Clay wrote to Daniel Webster, after seeing his own state of Kentucky go to the General.[1002]

Knowing that the democratic process had failed them, for just a moment Jackson's opponents thought that maybe Providence had saved them from the people's candidate.

There were reports that Jackson was sick, too sick, possibly, to live long. Rumors flew that Jackson had taken very ill in the anticipation

---

[1000] Marshall Papers
[1001] Adams, 1828, *Memoirs*, IV.
[1002] Clay to Webster, Nov. 20, 1828, Webster Papers, LC.

of his arrival in Washington to be sworn in. Some even went so far as to suggest that the General had died, along with his wife. Louisa Catherine Adams, John Quincy's wife, wrote to her son Charles Francis Adams, on February 1, "On Wednesday morning we awake with the rumor of the death of the hero, which put the city generally into a state of great consternation." However, Daniel Webster wrote to a friend, "Mrs. Adams' intelligence was wrong, the rumors of Mr. J.'s death has subsided. My own private opinion, however, still is that he is very ill and I have my doubts whether he will ever reach this place."[1003]

Jackson was not sick, but Rachel was. The strain of the campaign took its toll on Mrs. Jackson. The slanders and libels, the bespotting of her name, and that of her husband increased her anxiety, her discomfort, and eventually put an unbearable strain on her heart. Or perhaps it was an accumulation of poor eating habits, and lack of exercise. Either way, the defamation she endured from a very brutal press did not help. As if the trial of the campaign was not enough, Rachel was depressed at the thought of living at the capital, "I would rather be a doorkeeper in the house of God" she has reported to have said, "than live in that palace at Washington."[1004] She seems to have been, in the end, a collateral casualty of the General's career.

"I am denied maney pleasures and Comforts in this Life," Rachel wrote. It was her devout faith in God that kept her going. Rachel's devotion to the bible and to her religion sustained her through the hard times of the campaign. "I Can say my soule Can be a testimony to the truth of that Gospel, for who has been so cruelly tryed as I have my mind my trials have been severe." Rachel had been through the wringer emotionally, as the attacks on her past and her character caused severed episodes of racking tears and grief. "The persecution she has suffered" Jackson wrote, "has endeared her more if possible than ever to me." Jackson tried to shield his wife from the abuse at the hands of his enemies, but Rachel was aware of the vicious reports against her

---

[1003] Webster, Daniel, 1829, Webster Papers, LC.
[1004] Wise, Henry A., *Seven Decades of the Union*, Philadelphia, 1872, p. 113.

character. "Enemies of the Gen'ls," she wrote to a friend, "have Dipt their arrows in wormwood & gall & sped them at me almighty God was ther ever aney thing to equal it my old acquaintances wer as much hurt as if it was them selves or Daughters."[1005]

But Rachel didn't complain. "I could have spent at the Hermitage the remnant of my days in peace. And were it not that I would be so unhappy being so far from the General. No consideration could introduce me again to abandon this delightful spot," She wrote to a friend on December 1. "But since it has pleased grateful people once more to call him to their service and since by the permission of Providence, he will obey that call, I am resolved, indeed it is a duty I owe to myself and my husband to try to to forget at least for a time all the endearments of home and prepare to live where it is pleased heaven to fix our destiny."

Rachel, as it turns out, would never again leave the Hermitage. On December 17[Th], the toll on Jackson's wife reached its climax. According to James Parton's three-volume biography on General Jackson, published in 1860, he writes of hearing the story of Rachel's death from "Old Hannah," Rachel's faithful servant. According to the enslaved woman, Rachel drew her last breath in "Old Hannah's" arms. "It was Wednesday morning, December 17 (1828). All was going on as usual at the Hermitage. The General was in the fields, and Mrs. Jackson, apparently in tolerable health, was occupied in her household duties. Suddenly she heard a horrible shriek from Rachel, who placed her hands upon her heart, sunk into a chair, struggling for breath, and fell forward into Hannah's arms. While messengers hurried away for assistance, Old Hannah employed the only remedy she knew to relieve the anguish of her mistress, 'I rubbed her side,' said the plain-spoken Hannah, 'till it was black and blue.'[1006]

Rushing to her, the General lifted her up and carried her to bed. He called a doctor who arrived shortly thereafter. For three days she held her own. Unfortunately, lacking a cure, and running out of ideas, the doctor chose to bleed Rachel. This probably contributed to her death. On the fourth day, her condition became more critical. Mrs. Jackson continued to suffer, for the space of sixty hours, during which her husband never left her side for ten minutes. Rachel was concerned about him, knowing

---

[1005] Remini, 1822, pg. 143.
[1006] Parton, *Jackson*, III.

he had to attend a great banquet planned in Nashville to celebrate his victory. Jackson was uncertain as to what to do. Washington was also waiting, ready to inaugurate the new president. The journey would not be quick, but he could not leave his dying wife.

After several days in bed, On December 22, 1828, Rachel seemed to rally and felt well enough to get up. She begged Andrew to get some rest. The doctor remained in the house, and servants Hannah and George agreed to sit up with their mistress. The General bid his wife good night and retired to the next room. He was gone for only five minutes. At her bidding the servants lifted Rachel from her bed to arrange her sheets. While sitting in the chair, supported by Hannah, Rachel suffered another severe attack. She let out a long, loud cry. There was "a rattling sound in her throat." Her head fell forward onto Hannah's shoulder. Rachel Jackson's heart expired, and she passed away.

Two days later, on Christmas morning, a steady flow of carts and carriages, wagons and horses took to the roads leading to the Hermitage. "Thousands from the city and from all around the country flocked to her funeral," reported Henry Wise, a young Tennessee lawyer from Virginia. "The poor white people, the slaves from the Hermitage, and the neighbors crowded off the gentry from the town and country and filled the large garden in which the internment took place." Following the pallbearers, "General Jackson, with his left hand in the arm of General Carroll, holding his cane in his right hand, not grasping it with the hand over the head, nor with the thumb up, but with the back of the hand up and holding the point of the cane forward as he would have held a sword, and where he stopped at the pile of clay, it's point rested on the clods."

Burdened by the strains of the election, the anxieties brought on by her husband's enemies' cutting insults against her, and the stress of the impending move away from the life she loved to the spotlight of the White House, Rachel's heart had finally given out. She was sixty-one years old. Probably her condition was mainly caused by excess weight, a poor diet and lack of exercise, but to the General, his enemies had killed her. He would never forget.

Jackson did not wish to leave her. Observers reported that he held Rachel's lifeless body so tightly that she had to be pried from his arms to be buried. Friends say that it appeared Jackson aged twenty years in one night. Rachel was buried nestled in the corner of her beloved garden, in a gentle rain.

The sight of Rachel being lowered into the ground until she was covered up with dirt stayed in Jackson's mind until his dying day. "That I would withdraw from the scenes around me," he wrote from Washington, "to the private walks of the Hermitage, how soon would I be found in the solitary shades of the garden at the tomb of my wife there to spend my days in silent sorrow and in peace from the toils and strife of this world. Oh how fluctuating are all earthly things. At the time I least expected and could least spare her, she was snatched from me, and I am left here a solitary monument of Grief without the least hope of happiness here below." Jackson remained convinced that his enemies' accusations of bigamy and adultery had caused her health to fail. He was absolutely certain that his political opponents had done this, attacking him viciously, slandering, libeling, belittling him, and ultimately killing her. This belief would haunt the General for the remainder of his life. [1007]

The loss of Rachel hardened Old Hickory's heart more than it had ever been, shaping his demeanor in the years that followed, his years as the President of the United States. One wonders how things might have been different had Rachel been around to help guide Old Hickory through the tumultuous years in the hot seat as the Commander in Chief. "May God Almighty forgive her murderers," Jackson declared at Rachel's funeral, "I never can."

Jackson had Rachel's grave stone inscribed: 'Her face was fair; her person, pleasing, her temper, amiable, and her heart kind: she delighted in relieving the wants of her fellow creatures and cultivated that divine pleasure by the most liberal and unpretending methods: to the poor, she was a benefactor; to the rich, an example; to the wretched a comforter, to the prosperous an ornament, her piety went hand-in-hand with her benevolence, and she thanked her creator for being permitted to do good. A being so gentle, and yet so virtuous, slander might wound, but could not dishonor; Even death, when he tore her from the armes of her husband, could but transport her to the bosom of her God.'

[1007] Brands, HW, 2005, Chapter 30.

CHAPTER

66

KING MOB

"A triumph of principle over intrigue, of truth over falsehood; in one word, of the people over corruption."
—Robert Hayne

Andrew Jackson, the president-elect, was uncertain as to what he should do. A servant of duty throughout his life, he now had a duty to head to the nation's capital. But he had a hard time tearing himself away from the freshly dug grave of Rachel Jackson. "My heart is nearly broke, the partner of my life, my dearest Heart, assassinated by vile slanderers." Jackson, through tears, absorbed every shocking moment of his loss, "a loss so great, so sudden and unexpected. I need not say to you, can be compensated by no earthly gift. Could it be, it might be found in the reflection that she lived long enough to see the countless assaults of our enemies, disarmed by the voice of our beloved country?"[1008]

But Jackson did as he always did, he responded to the call of duty. He packed up and he went to Washington. He was accompanied by his nephew, Andrew Jackson Donelson, who was to be his private secretary; by Mrs. Andrew Jackson Donelson, Emily, who was to preside over the official mansion; by a beautiful and accomplished niece of Mrs. Jackson, who was to reside with him, and assist Mrs. Donelson to do the honors of his house; by Henry Lee, his scribe, who went with him to be appointed to an office; and, lastly, by Major Lewis, whose intention was merely to witness the inauguration and then return to his plantation.

[1008] AJ to Jean Plauche, Dec. 27, 1828, Jackson Papers, TSL.

"He was not entirely well," Emily said, "had a very bad cough and has been a good deal troubled with headache and fever." Preparations for an explosive welcome for the new President, which had included the firing of cannons, and a lively marching band, were all for naught, as Jackson managed to slip into town quietly and without fanfare around midmorning. Alfred Mordecai, a military academy acquaintance of Andrew Donelson, was in Washington on the day of the General's arrival and witnessed his carriage through his window that morning. "It was a humble train," wrote Mordecai, "a plain carriage, drawn by two horses followed by a single black servant." Mordecai was intrigued by the contrast between the excitement and anticipation the President-elect aroused, and his actual arrival, so ordinary and unheralded. "A man alternately hailed as a demigod and hero and announced as a tyrant," Mordecai recalled, "arrived without ceremony. What a spectacle this must present to those who have had opportunities of seeing the entrance of European potentates to their capitals to take possession of their throne."[1009] The date of his arrival was Wednesday, February 11, 1829.

"Sly Old Hickory," Davy Crockett wrote, had "stolen a march upon his friends, as he had always done upon his enemies."[1010]

Once in the capital Jackson was at the epicenter of a storm of office seekers at his suite at John Gadsby's National Hotel on Sixth Street. From across the city, Clay called them a motley host of greedy expectants. The new president, on the other hand, cut a dashing figure despite his grief–tall, lean, with bush iron-gray hair brushed high above a prominent forehead, rather craggy eyebrows, and vivid blue eyes. His irritability and emaciated appearance resulted, as noted, from his many war-time bouts with such maladies as dysentery, malaria, tuberculosis and lead poisoning from the two bullets his body still retained from his near-fatal duels. His life story was well-written within the lines of his face. As devastated as he was by Rachel's death, the General would have been forgiven for being inactive for the time being. Yet, with the press of office-seekers, Jackson showed patience and did the best he could.

[1009] Quoted in Meacham, Jon, An American Lion, Chapter 3.
[1010] Quoted in Miles, Edwin A., "First People's Inaugural--1829," THQ, XXXVII, p. 297.

The first president from the West, and only the second without a college education (along with George Washington,) Jackson was the most unique president-elect the country had ever seen. With a modest secondary education, and no college experience, he had risen from the masses, and the people, in turn, were infatuated with his story. Yet, despite the public's vision of this modest man from the most humble, log-cabin background, in truth, Jackson had essentially become something of an aristocrat. By this point in his life, the General held nearly one hundred slaves, cultivated broad acreage, and lived in one of the finest mansions in Tennessee. Having lived under the care of servants for decades either at his plantation, of within the military, he was used to being waited on. He had become one of the wealthiest men in the country. More westerner than easterner, more country gentleman than common clay, more courtly than crude, Jackson was hard to fit into a neat category, and his presidency would fit the same mold.

Jackson's inauguration, held on March 4th, 1829, seemed to symbolize the ascendancy of the masses. "Hickory-ites," as his many supporters were calling themselves, poured into Washington from far and wide, sleeping on hotel floors, hallways, tents. Some twenty-thousand people converged on the Capitol grounds. They were curious to see their hero take office and perhaps hoped to pick up a well-paying position for themselves. Many in the crowd filling the city felt that Providence was smiling on the country in general, and on Washington, D.C., in particular, for they believed that the resolute will of the people had swept from office a corrupt administration. "It was," Emily Donelson reported home, "by far the largest crowd that ever was seen in Washington."[1011]

President-elect Jackson left Gadsby's Hotel, met an escort of Revolutionary War and Battle of New Orleans veterans, and walked up Capitol Hill. The "common man" had come to the capital to revel in the installation of a popular champion as chief executive. Washingtonians, generally, were not so cheerful, deeming the admired champion a backwoods barbarian, his associates they considered his 'cronies,' and his followers an 'uncivilized horde.' After a brief ceremony at the Capitol that March day, at 61 years of age, Jackson was set to become the

---

[1011] Emily Donelson to Mary Eastin, March, 1829, Donelson Papers, LC.

ANDREW JACKSON: THE POLITICS OF RESENTMENT

oldest president of the United States to date. His enemies winced at the prospect.

One enemy that would not be in attendance was the outgoing president. Adams, snubbed by Jackson, who didn't give the customary call upon the president from his arrival in Washington, chose to sit the inauguration out. Jackson still seethed over the slander of the campaign that Adams failed to put a stop to. Jackson could have kept in mind that Adams had defended Jackson's actions after the Seminole War, when all others were turning against him. The two men handled it poorly and missed an opportunity to show the nation that politics did not have to be personal.

Jackson's followers, however, could hardly contain their glee, and, at least for a time, they did not try. The masses rode alongside Jackson as he made his way to the Capitol building. The town bulged with tourists, so much so that some likened it to the arrival of the Roman hordes. But the most memorable moment of the day, in fact, would not be the unadorned swearing-in. It was what followed back at the executive mansion that would be talked about for years to come.

On the steps of the Capitol building, Jackson commenced his address by expressing his gratitude that the will of the people had been heard: "Fellow citizens; About to enter upon the duties to which as President of the United States, I have been called by voluntary suffrages of my country, I avail myself of this occasion to express the deep and heartfelt gratitude with which a testimonial of such distinguished favor has been received. To be elected under the circumstances which have marked the recent contest of opinion to administer the affairs of a government deriving all its powers from the will of the people, a government whose vital principle is the right of the people to control its measures, and whose only object and glory are the equal happiness and freedom of all the members of the confederacy, cannot but penetrate me with the most powerful and mingled emotions of thanks, on the one hand, for the honor conferred on me, and on the other, of solemn apprehensions for the safety of the great and important interests committed to my charge."[1012]

[1012] Andrew Jackson's First Inaugural Address, March 4, 1829, American Treasures, Library of Congress

Jackson closed his address with a prayer to the almighty for order and guidance, for himself as well as for the Union. As the chief executive, he stated, he would depend "on the goodness of that Power whose providence mercifully protected our national infancy and has since upheld our liberties in various vicissitudes." His hopes, he said, were particularly "that He will continue to make our beloved country the object of His divine care and gracious benediction." Jackson then bowed to the people, and amid the roar of the crowd, after he took the oath of office from Chief Justice John Marshall, the new president kissed a Bible and bowed to the people, who could no longer contain their excitement.

The crowd in their ecstasy pushed forward, surging through the barricade to surround Jackson on the east portico, where the ceremony took place. Amid all the excitement and congratulations from the masses, the marshals did all they could to protect the new president, but the people pushed in anyway. Eventually, the marshals and Jackson's friends managed to wrest their man from the unruly mob, and Jackson mounted a white horse to ride down Pennsylvania Avenue to the White House. "Country men, farmers, gentlemen, mounted and dismounted, boys, women and children, black and white" followed him, Mrs. Smith said, "carriages, wagons, and carts all pursuing him to the President's House." [1013]

"The avenue was jammed as far as the eye could reach," reported Amos Kendall, "the sidewalks of the avenue were covered with people on foot and the centre with innumerable carriages and persons on horseback moving in the same direction. For a full half hour, I stood waiting for the stream to run by; but like a never failing fountain the Capitol continued pouring forth its torrents."[1014]

A public reception was scheduled in the White House, so the lofty words of the new president notwithstanding, the day's defining hour would be when "the majesty of the people"[1015] descended upon it to pay their respects to the new president. To the conservatives who stood aghast at what ensued, the "orgy of King Mob" that followed the inauguration would be long remembered, despite the wishes of many of the more prestigious Washingtonians who longed to forget it. Backwoods hicks

---

[1013] Meacham, Jon, p. 61.
[1014] Amos Kendall, *Argus of Western America*, March 18, 1829.
[1015] Margaret Bayard Smith, *First Forty Years in Washington*, 1906, p. 295.

mingled with notable gentlemen and ladies as the White House, which was, for the first time, thrown open to the multitudes. Jackson's arrival at the house amplified an already chaotic situation. Renowned visitors greeted him first, but ordinary folks soon rushed forward to shake his hand and offer their best wishes. Jackson shook so many hands that his were black and blue by the end of the evening. A milling crowd of "rubber-neckers, clerks and shopkeepers, hobnailed artisans, and grimy laborers surged in, allegedly wrecking the china and furniture, and threatening the "people's champion" with cracked ribs. Men with muddy boots sat on the damask furniture.

"What a scene did we witness," Mary Bayard Smith, "The *majesty of the people* had disappeared and a rabble, a mob of boys, negroes, women, children, scrambling, fighting, romping. What a pity, what a pity!" All told,

The surging crowd made mingling impossible, and as people pushed to get close to Jackson and lunged toward the refreshments, they collided with fragile furniture and shoved servants laden with punch bowls and trays of food. Waiters trying to maneuver with a large bowl of spiked orange punch crashed into a crowd and spilled it all on the carpet. Men in work boots, straining to see Jackson, stood on expensive upholstered furniture.

That such people were even present at so august an event represented the triumph of democracy to some. To others, the much-reported mayhem demonstrated the danger of giving the ungovernable rabble political rights. Both views were exaggerations. Senator James Hamilton of South Carolina, a Jackson supporter, struck a balance when he described the event as a "regular Saturnalia," but with the qualification that most of the damage was trivial.

The people had gotten out of hand—Jackson's opponents thought it an apt evaluation of the election as well as the inaugural reception—but whether they had done any real harm in either instance was a matter of opinion. At any rate, a legendary scene it was, and one that has forever linked Jackson with the image of a crude and unruly mob trashing the White House. "No arrangements had been made," Mrs. Smith noted, and "no police officers placed on duty and the whole house [was] inundated by the rabble mob."[1016]

"Here was the corpulent epicure grunting and sweating for breath," reported the New York Spectator, "they dandy wishing he had no toes–the tight-laced Miss, fearing her person might receive some permanently deforming impulse–the miser hunting for his pocket-book–the courtier looking for his watch–and the office-seeker in an agony to reach the President." The household staff's efforts to serve the multitude of guests only made things worse. "Orange punch by the barrels-full was made, but as the waiters opened the door to bring it out, a rush would be made," said one Congressman from Pennsylvania, "the glasses broken, the pails of liquor upset, and the most painful confusion prevailed."

Jackson, positioned in the back corner of the ballroom of the mansion, found himself nearly overwhelmed by the influx of visitors. His aides had to create a protective barrier around the president, and soon he had to be quickly escorted back to Gadsby's when word spread that the heavily spiked punch bowls had been set up on the lawn. This chaotic event led critics to label it "the inaugural brawl." Mrs. Smith, perhaps exaggerating, likened the scene to the sack of Versailles, although she conceded that the most significant damage she noticed was to "the carpets and the furniture." For some, it felt like the collapse of civilization. "King Mob" had claimed victory, as Jacksonian exuberance replaced Jeffersonian decorum. The more delicate, traditional residents of Washington recoiled, closed their blinds, shook their heads, and nervously recalled the initial moments of the storming of the Bastille. While the damage amounted to only a few thousand dollars, this incident served as further evidence, for those eager to criticize the new president, that the unruly masses had arrived in Washington, proudly displaying the Jackson banner.[1017]

Once in power, the Democrats, known for their skepticism toward big government, aimed to reorganize the system. However, they also engaged in political "bargains." Under Jackson, the spoils system—rewarding supporters with public office—was expanded. This practice, dating back to ancient politics, was famously summarized by New York Senator William Marcy in 1832: "To the victor belong the spoils of the

---

[1016] Margaret Bayard Smith Papers, 1829, quoted in *The First Populist*, David S. Brown, Ch. 30.

[1017] Hamilton to Van Buren, March 5, 1829, Van Buren Papers, LC.

enemy." The system had already thrived in cities like New York and Pennsylvania, where political machines distributed jobs.

Jackson understood that populations migrating westward sought representation not only in their interests, in suffrage, but in the actual administration of the government as well. Jackson hoped to provide that for his fellow westerners, long shut out of government by the east's bureaucratic monopoly. But, in so doing, inevitably, some mistakes occurred. A prominent example was the appointment of Samuel Swartwout, a notorious embezzler. Appointed Collector of Customs in New York, he oversaw significant revenue, estimated at $15 million annually (around $440 million today). Despite Van Buren's warnings, Jackson retained Swartwout, who eventually embezzled $1.2 million before fleeing to England. Jackson, who publicly condemned defaulters, paradoxically appointed friends with questionable integrity. Van Buren noted that they never discussed this issue, even during his visit to Jackson's home in 1842. Swartwout returned to the U.S. in 1841, avoided prison after forfeiting property, and died in 1856, buried near notable figures like Alexander Hamilton.

Despite unavoidable mistakes, lapses of judgment and errors, with Swartwout being the most infamous example, the rotation policy boldly confronted certain established class norms. It rocked the boat of American government in a way that wasn't always the most ideal, but it opened up another avenue of American social mobility. Its contribution to such a narrative has not perhaps received sufficient attention. By securing positions for groups that previously lacked representation in government administration, Jackson significantly challenged the perception of who was deserving of civic service, and who should be considered for such lofty positions. This notion was precisely what unsettled Jackson's critics. Prominent among them were the privileged, individuals such as Henry Clay, who hailed from an aristocratic Virginia slaveholding family. Clay viewed government office as his birthright and the realm of his social class, not meant to be shared with the masses.

Having been instructed by wealthy and powerful Virginians such as George Wythe, a prominent legal scholar and signer of the Declaration of Independence, at William and Mary College, Clay betrayed his elitist roots when in 1829, he opined to a friend that government misrule stemmed largely from the humble origins of its leaders. He stated, "I hope both you and I shall live to see the Jacksons, Eatons, and others of their kind driven back to their original stations and insignificance."[1018] Clay foresaw dark clouds of chaos if such individuals were permitted to wield governmental power.

The quiet class struggle that shaped the rotation debate didn't just fade away after the 1830s. Eventually, aristocratic types stepped up their efforts to put an end to the spoils system, a system that dared to disregard their standing, their college degrees and long family histories. In 1869, Henry Adams, who was the grandson of John Quincy Adams, wrote a sharp essay in the influential *North American Review*, advocating for a return to rule by the elite. His perspective aligns with Clay's, reflecting a collective unease among men who were wary and cynical about giving power to those who had previously been powerless. "It is one of the unfortunate but inevitable results of the situation," he wrote, "that the better class of politicians on whom a president ought to rely, men of dignity and self-respect, will not lower themselves to this struggle for patronage. Their suggestions or wishes, once expressed, and met by refusal and neglect, they retire, offended and mortified, but too proud to beg for favors. Not so with the baser type of professional politicians. These are never wearied and never absent." Adam's view is a variation of Clay's, the collective sigh of men equally fearful, suspicious, and cynical about seeing power in the hands of those hitherto powerless." This tension was at the heart of American politics in the 1830s. [1019]

Ultimately, despite the anti-Jackson fears of a "dictatorial mobocracy" only about 10% of officeholders lost their positions at the beginning of Jackson's presidency, a figure similar to Jefferson's removals in 1801. However, this percentage increased significantly for presidential appointments, which Jackson could influence more readily. Consequently, the turnover rate in federal positions, such as those in US Customs houses, land offices, and postal systems, reached approximately 50%. This means that one out of every two federal office workers lost their jobs.

Looking back, it can be viewed as Jackson's efforts to prevent the emergence of what might be referred to as a "shadow government." This term describes a scenario where a group of relatively permanent

---

[1018] Clay to Francis Brooke, Sept. 1829, *Clay Papers*.
[1019] Brown, David S., Chapter 31.

government bureaucrats and influential financiers effectively govern the nation, operating beyond the control of the populace. In opposition to this "unelected oligarchy," which some Democrats claimed was exemplified by the clandestine mechanisms that facilitated Quincy Adams's presidency and the considerable financial power of the National Bank, Jackson proposed a strategy of rotation in office. He believed that if incoming presidents adhered to this principle—removing what he termed "dangerous sentinels" over the public purse—the republic would remain robust. However, much to his frustration, Jackson quickly realized that many of these "sentinels" anticipated retaining their positions. "Now every man who has been in office a few years," he wrote in his Memoranda book shortly after taking office, "believes he has a life estate in it, a vested right, and if it has been held twenty years or upwards, not only a vested right, but one that should be passed on to his children, and if no children then to his next of kin. These are not the principles of our government. It is rotation of office that will perpetuate our liberty."[1020]

On March 10, 1829, Jackson moved into the White House, which had been rebuilt after its burning by the British during the War of 1812. Significant updates to the Executive Mansion were made by previous presidents, including John Quincy Adams, who designated the southeast rooms on the second floor as the president's domain. Jackson's presidency marked a transformation in the office itself, as he exercised unmatched executive authority.

Jackson initiated several changes to the White House. Upon his arrival, he completed the decoration of the unfinished East Room and made the Second Floor his private residence, bringing his extended family, including his nephew, (and adopted son) Andrew "Jack" Donelson and Jack's wife, Emily, (left) who acted as the official hostess. Their children added a lively atmosphere to the house. The Second Floor included various rooms

---

[1020] Brown, David S., Chapter 31.

for different purposes, such as the yellow bedroom for women to rest during events and the circular green room for receiving morning callers.

When Jackson assumed the presidency in March 1829, he controversially appointed his one-time biographer and fellow Tennessean, Senator John Eaton (right) as Secretary of War, infuriating many in Washington. The appointment was seen as cronyism and it brought outrage from many, including Jackson's own niece, Emily Donelson, who was essentially the surrogate first lady in the White House. But it was Floride Calhoun, the wife of Vice President John C. Calhoun, a powerful figure in Jackson's cabinet, who led the effort to alienate Peggy Eaton. Leading a group of cabinet wives (including at times, Emily Donelson) in ostracizing the Eatons, Floride and the others refused to associate with them, concerned with the taint of Peggy's tarnished reputation. This social exclusion was rooted in the societal norms of the 1830s, when concerns over women's morality were rigid, and highly magnified, especially in the political arena.

Jackson's leadership style was marked by a demanding and divisive personality. He required complete obedience from his cabinet. He was used to getting his way through the sheer will of his iron personality. What he wanted was peace and acceptance of his cabinet family. But, with the elite women of Washington committed to ostracizing Peggy Eaton, his good friend's wife, Jackson's sensitivities were inflamed. His extreme loyalty to his friends had always been part and parcel of the General's persona, and John Eaton was in the inner circle. He was basically family to Jackson, who was maybe just a little smitten himself by Peggy Eaton's charms. Moreover, Jackson could never forget the years of abuse and defamation from the many slanders against his own wife. Thus, Jackson steadfastly defended Peggy, and this ultimately became the cause that led to a full splintering of the Jackson cabinet. While some called it simply the Eaton Affair, the more colorful name hand-picked by the press, was "The Petticoat Affair."

From the start of his time as the nation's chief executive, Jackson expressed a heavy degree of distrust towards the "experts." Defying tradition would become his modus operandi. As president, he preferred a new direction, and it began with his own closest set of advisors. Indeed, Jackson's interactions with his cabinet were complex. He navigated through several cabinet phases, struggling with loyalty and political effectiveness. A notable strategy, which will be explored in more depth later, involved persuading Martin Van Buren to resign along with Eaton to clear the cabinet of tensions. Jackson's insistence on loyalty also led him to cycle through cabinet members, as he sought allies to support his policies on issues like the Second National Bank and Indian removal.

Setting a new precedent, Jackson created his own informal "kitchen cabinet," which he relied on heavily for advice. Rather than a reliance on the elite politicians, the insiders, who had always cornered these types of appointments, (and who had expected the same from Jackson) the General preferred to heed the counsel of his friends. As a result, Jackson increasingly relied on these men, those who his enemies referred to as his "cronies," but who comprised both official cabinet members and trusted associates. Van Buren stayed within this circle of trust, but even Eaton himself would eventually be forced out due to the fallout from the Eaton/Petticoat Affair.

Two influential members of Jackson's Kitchen Cabinet were Amos Kendall, and Francis P. Blair, two newspapermen who would play key roles in ensuring that pro-Jackson news reached the public early and often through their editorials. Kendall would later go on to his appointment by Jackson as Postmaster General after the resignation of William T. Barry. The Kitchen Cabinet, which also included William B. Lewis, a longtime aide and friend, provided the warmth and loyalty Jackson craved, and it was these individuals at the Blair House, with whom the president spent many an evening discussing political strategy and the affairs of the nation. Both Blair and Kendall (right) were invaluable as Jackson's 'ministers of propaganda.'

Were these men qualified for such important access to the chief executive? Many thought not. But Old Hickory was known to demonize certain groups, foremost among these were eastern bankers, and in a close second, know-it-all politicians in the traditional sense. Part of the reason was that, as noted, Jackson had held a very low opinion of the senatorial proceedings during his time in the upper house. Combining that view with Jackson's humble background, his rugged western approach, and his disdain for insiders such as Clay, Adams, Crawford, and (increasingly) Calhoun, surrounding himself with non-traditional political outsiders like himself was much more to the old man's liking.

While his appointed cabinet had been carefully selected, relations with his various department heads quickly soured. Among the likes of Martin Van Buren as Secretary of State, Samuel Ingham as Secretary of the Treasury, John Branch as Secretary of the Navy, John M. Berrien as Attorney General, John Eaton as Secretary of War, and William T. Barry as Postmaster General, only Van Buren, Eaton and Barry remained loyal and trusted by Jackson. With the others it felt like a mockery at his efforts for reform. Instead of unity and loyalty with the president, the department heads seemed to be conspiring with Calhoun against John Eaton, a universally unpopular choice as Secretary of War. Their conspiracy seemed, to Jackson, a combined effort "to put Major Eaton out of the Cabinet, & disgrace me, and weaken my administration… [and] lessen my standing with the people, so that they would not again urge my re-election." [1021]

Jackson's first cabinet choices, while not all political heavyweights, had been selected to create a sense of balance and control. He had chosen two New Yorkers for regional equity, but soon the entire cabinet was anything but in balance and feeling very inequitable indeed. Ingham, Branch and Berrien were now traitors to the president, he said, under the conniving influence of Vice President Calhoun. "A cabinet ought to be a unit," Jackson told Donelson, "Otherwise, like the interests of a divided house, it must fall. Ere long I will have my cabinet as it ought to be, a unit. The double-dealing of J.C.C. is perfectly unmasked." What had Calhoun done to lose favor with the president? A combination of disagreements had led to Calhoun's fall from grace in the mind of Jackson.

[1021] AJ to Donelson, Dec. 25, 1830, Miscellaneous Jackson Papers, NYHS, AJ to Emily Donelson, Jan. 20, 1831, Statement of Andrew Jackson Donelson, Nov. 21, 1830 in Jackson, *Correspondence*, IV, 227, 304.

By late 1830, Jackson had decided that he would, that he must, run for a second term, particularly to prevent Calhoun from taking the reins of the country and leading it in a direction he did not wish to see it go. He also hoped to rid himself of the troublesome members within his cabinet and start anew. But how to clean house without discrediting his administration?
(William T. Barry (right) of Kentucky was Jackson's first Postmaster General)

On Sunday, January 10, 1830, Jackson, who had been ill, rallied from his bed to host a White House levy. The cabinet was there and crowds of others packed in from five until nearly 10 that night. Guests came and went, as Jackson stood with Emily Donelson, and Mary Eastin, (the daughter of William Eastin and Rachel Donelson Eastin.) "The ladies were the picture of hospitality," one observer remarked on the hostesses approvingly, "steadily shaking hands with those who had just entered the room, or those about to retire from it." Congenial and smiling, happily playing the role of surrogate first lady, Emily Donelson, along with twenty-year-old Mary Eastin, represented the president's family. They were humbly "dressed in American calico, wore no ruffles and no ornament of any sort." Emily's descendent Pauline Wilcox Burke wrote, "The calico serves to show their loyalty to the Jackson party." In 1828, the Jackson partisans had worn it to show their support for Old Hickory's candidacy. Mrs. Burke added that "No doubt Emily's concession to this whim of fashion was at a personal sacrifice, for her choice in dress leaned rather to velvets, brocades and rich satins. [1022]

Emily Donelson and Mary Eastin were gracious with their guests. "They affected no superiority, showed no pride, and from their behavior, no one would suppose they belonged to the family of the chief magistrate of a great nation," an observer remarked, "their honor sat so easy on them they seemed not to know it. It was," he said, "an example of perfect good breeding, taught from their earliest infancy, both by precept, and by the

---

[1022] Pauline Wilcox Burke, Jan., 1830, Donelson Papers, LC.

example set by their aunt, the good, the amiable, and ever to be lamented, Mrs. Jackson." [1023]

Martin Van Buren worked the room, a political artist enamored with the social scene, the swirl, the Washington mingle. He also relished his favor with the president; that too was evident. "There is no scarcity of subjects for an epistle in the metropolis of the Union, as you know the inhabitants of Washington insist on having their city called," John Quincy Adams wrote his daughter-in-law, "it is the prevailing opinion that Mr. Van Buren is about to scale the presidency of the United States, by mounting upon the shoulders of Mrs. Eaton."[1024] Van Buren had been one of the few who had refused to alienate Peggy Eaton, and it was paying dividends with his relationship to Jackson, at the expense of Vice President Calhoun.

At the annual commemoration of Jackson's victory at New Orleans, the guests treated Peggy Eaton even more coolly than usual. "She is not received at any private parties, and since 8 January has withdrawn from public assemblies," Mrs. Smith added, "At the ball given for that occasion, she was treated with such universal neglect and indignity that she will not expose herself again to such treatment." Yet Peggy remains central in the public and political eye. "Our government is becoming every day more democratic; the rulers of the people are truly their servants, and among those rulers women are gaining more than their share of power." Margaret Bayard Smith wrote to a friend in January 1830. Referring to Peggy Eaton, Calhoun and the members of Jackson's cabinet, Smith went on, "One woman has made sad work here. To be or not to be her friend is the test of presidential favor. Mr. V.B. sided with her, and is consequently the right-hand man, the constant riding, walking and visiting companion. Mr. Calhoun, Ingham, his devoted friend, Branch and Berrian form one party, the president, VB, General E and Mr. Barry the other. It is generally supposed that, as they cannot sit together, some change in the cabinet must take place."[1025]

She was right, the cabinet nearly broke apart over the matter in early 1830. There were conversations and meetings, and finally a session between the president, Ingham, Branch, and Berrian. "I will not part

---

[1023] Meacham, Jon, Ch. 10.
[1024] JQA to Mary Hellen Adams, Jan., 1830, Adams, *Memoirs*, IV.
[1025] Margaret Bayard Smith Papers, Jan., 1830, LOC

with Major Eaton from my cabinet," Jackson told them, "and those of my cabinet who cannot harmonize with him had better withdraw, for harmony I must, and will have." A kind of compromise was reached. Jackson would not press the social question if his cabinet would agree not to add to the gossip mill circulating against the Eatons. But the compromise was only a temporary reprieve, as later events would prove.

John Quincy Adams, 1840s,
Brady-Handy Photography

Francis P. Blair, photo by
daguerreotype by Matthew Brady

CHAPTER

67

THE PETTICOAT AFFAIR

"I would rather have live vermin on my back than the tongue of one of these Washington women on my reputation."
—Andrew Jackson

What was all the hullabaloo about Margaret "Peggy" Eaton? What was brewing, however trivial the Eaton/Petticoat Affair seems today in hindsight, had long-term ramifications for the Jackson administration's early days, and would have important consequences for the United States as a whole. The entire issue provides insight into many aspects of 1830s American political society, and society as a whole. Particularly enlightening is how the affair sheds light on the social pressures women faced at the time, and how women were viewed in America, and what sort of expectations they faced in the 1830s. To call it an 'affair' does not do it justice, the controversy surrounding Secretary of War John Eaton's wife, Peggy, was a scandal of calamitous proportions, in that it divided a presidential cabinet irrevocably, and impacted the direction of the executive branch time and again from the start of Jackson's first term in office until 1831. The conflict over the Eatons would also dictate who was "groomed" by the president as his successor, as this depended on where they stood regarding Peggy Eaton. The many issues within the scandal demonstrates the type of repressive treatment women faced at the time from "polite society," as well as the competitive pressures of the American antebellum political scene.

Less than a year after taking office, Jackson's Secretary of War, John Eaton, married Margaret "Peggy" O'Neill, the daughter of William O'Neill, owner of the Franklin House, a popular Washington, D.C. boarding house and tavern. Located near the White House, Franklin House was a well-known social hub frequented by politicians. Well-educated for a woman of the era, Peggy had studied French, played the piano, and worked at her father's tavern. Despite these respectable characteristics, and while still young, Peggy's reputation suffered initially because of her employment in her father's tavern, frequented mainly by men. Her casual chatting with the tavern's often influential patrons was not something that respectable women were expected to do. In fact, polite society frowned upon women in taverns generally; this was a place for men. Yet, in her memoirs, Peggy recalled, "While I was still in pantalettes and rolling hoops with other girls, I had the attention of men, young and old; enough to turn a girl's head."

The tavern environment in which Peggy Eaton was brought up generated speculation regarding a somewhat lascivious reputation as both a harlot and adulteress, whether this was truly justified or not. The social ostracism the Eatons faced in Washington as a result, where such events often mattered more than one's job performance, was a dilemma that hampered John Eaton's political career, as well as his domestic life. Perhaps Jackson had designs for Eaton's future, perhaps he foresaw the younger Tennessean as his successor to the throne? Or perhaps, simply because Peggy and John had been kind to consistently kind and deferential to Rachel Jackson whenever she was in their presence. Whatever the reason, this was a snubbing that Jackson could not abide, and it weighed heavily on Peggy as well, a woman that Jackson seemed to care for deeply.

Familiar with politicians from a young age, Peggy became well-known among government officials and military personnel. She married John B. Timberlake, a Navy officer, who died on April 2, 1828, while serving on the USS Constitution. Contrary to expectations of mourning, Peggy married John Eaton shortly after Timberlake's death, raising suspicions about her fidelity during her first marriage. The Eaton's nuptials, just nine months after Timberlake's passing, sparked rumors that Peggy had been unfaithful and that John Eaton had a role in Timberlake's demise.[1026]

Timberlake's death occurred while his ship was anchored in Port Mahon, Minorca, as he served as part of the Mediterranean Squadron. He had been suffering from asthma and other health issues, with his death attributed to pulmonary disease, likely pneumonia or tuberculosis. Speculation arose that he may have taken his life due to distress over alleged infidelities involving Peggy (left) and John Eaton, who had been a close friend of Timberlake's. The rumors increased dramatically when Eaton was appointed to the high-profile position as Secretary of War. However, official records classified Timberlake's cause of death as pulmonary disease, and not as a result of a broken-hearted suicide.

Eaton's position as Secretary of War diminished support for Floride Calhoun's anti-Peggy faction. Additionally, Calhoun had alienated Jackson by opposing his re-election and then in his role in the rising debates over the protective tariff known as the "Tariff of Abominations," which appeared to heavily favor northern industries over southern interests. In response to the escalating conflict over the tariff, the Nullification Crisis emerged in 1832, where southern states, led by Calhoun, argued for their right to refuse compliance with federal laws deemed unconstitutional.

Jackson, sensitive to such slights from his own experiences with slander against Rachel, was sympathetic toward Peggy, and he thus viewed the attacks on her personally. Always a believer in conspiracies, Jackson not only took such attacks as a personal affront to himself, but also as politically motivated and generated by his enemies. He believed that any attempt to degrade Eaton was an indignity towards himself. William Barry, the Postmaster General and the Eatons' only ally in the cabinet, noted that opinions on Peggy remained divided.

[1026] Louis McLane to James A. Bayard, Feb. 19, 1829, Bayard Papers, LC.

Soon, Peggy began to strike back herself, particularly taking umbrage from the snubs received from Jackson's niece, Emily Donelson. Shortly before four o'clock on the afternoon of June 9, 1830, John Eaton came home from the War Department bearing an invitation from the president for the Eatons to dine at the White House. It was the moment, Peggy decided, for total war. Up to this point she had complained of the Donelsons to Jackson, but not so strongly that Jackson could not choose to avoid a showdown. Even the ablest of politicians, however, cannot always control the timing of a crisis, and as Jackson read a note from Mrs. Eaton, written that afternoon, he realized his tarrying strategy had come to an end.

"Circumstances, my dear General, are such that under your kind and hospitable roof I cannot be happy," Peggy wrote, playing to Jackson's instinct that his house should be a shelter against the world for those he loved and cared for, and Peggy was one of those people. Some argued that the widower Jackson may have fallen under Peggy's spell himself. "You are not the cause," she assured Jackson unnecessarily, "for you have felt and manifested a desire that things should be different." But things were not, and it appeared that Emily and Andrew Donelson were at fault. "I could not expect to be happy at your house for this would be to expect a different course of treatment from part of your family." Eaton had tried to talk her into going, arguing, she said, "that it may be a triumph to some if it may be said I were not invited, but what of that, it will only be another feast to those whose pleasure it is to make me the object of their censures and approaches." [1027]

Peggy blamed the Donelsons for her predicament and accused them of open hostility without much real evidence. Emily was often cooler than she might have been on the social circuit in Washington, but overall, the Donelsons had not been vicious, which seemed to be the impression Peggy was intimating to Jackson. And Margaret did not stop there. "I ask to say to you that whatever may be the cause of the unkind treatment I have received from those under your roof... I have done all in my power to avoid it." Professing her own innocence in the affair, she continued to stretch the truth. "I have spoken of your family in no other manner than a respectful one," she claimed, adding, "I have ever

---

[1027] Eaton Papers, LC, quoted in Meacham, p. 146.

endeavored to return good for evil."[1028] But Jackson, although arguably the most powerful man in America, was in Peggy Eaton's hands by this point. She had hit all the right notes to convince the president that his family was out of line—and had been unwelcoming to the wife of his friend.

Jackson was frustrated with the Donelsons, and he unleashed these frustrations on Andrew. The Donelsons owed their place in Washington entirely to the General, and if they could not follow his rules, then they needed to leave. Andrew Donelson was hurt, so much so that he could not muster the ability to put his feelings down on paper. Here was his guardian, essentially his father, telling him that he and his family might well be cast out. Donelson was beside himself, both at Jackson, and toward Peggy Eaton. Although they would eventually reconcile, Donelson held onto the memory of the hurtful disappointment for years to come. Writing in October 1830, Andrew told Jackson, "I have not forgotten the language you employed on that occasion, and the determination you then expressed of carrying us home and leaving us there."[1029]

Reflecting upon the situation, Jackson aimed to stabilize his domestic situation with a spirit of conciliation. The Eaton affair remained a persistent issue that seemed unsolvable, leaving the president frustrated and resentful. This conflict disrupted his life significantly, and it now threatened to result in a breakup of the president's once happy home life. Could the only solution be the expulsion of Andrew and Emily Donelson from the White House? In an effort to find a resolution, Jackson proposed a compromise to his nephew, one that he had already discussed with Secretary Eaton. As he prepared to return to the capital in late summer 1830, he expressed his willingness to have Donelson accompany him to Washington, while leaving Emily at home. Peggy Eaton would also remain in Tennessee.

Although it was not a perfect solution, it marked an important step toward future reconciliation. Donelson accepted this arrangement, much to Jackson's satisfaction. Once back in the White House, Jackson attempted to resolve the ongoing tensions by offering to welcome Emily

---

[1028] Margaret Eaton to AJ, June 9, 1830, with endorsement by Donelson, Donelson Papers, LC.

[1029] Donelson to AJ, June, 1830, Donelson Papers, LC.

back, provided she agreed to be cordial with Peggy Eaton and fulfill her social duties. However, Emily declined this offer. Both she and her husband were committed to their principles, just as Uncle Jackson was, and even as president, he could not compel them to abandon their beliefs.

The following months were marked by discord between Jackson and Donelson, uncle and nephew. "Altho we have been visited by a number of ladies and Gentlemen," Jackson wrote to Emily, "and inundated as usual by office hunters, still we have appeared loansome—several times I have been left to sup alone." The separation from his wife was also challenging for Donelson. "Pray," he wrote to his uncle, "let me know what challenges I need to address before my family can be allowed to live in the same house as I do." [1030]

Committed to the defense of the Eatons, but fraying from the toll of the endeavor, Jackson soon began to realize he would either have to give up the balancing act, or make some changes. Tired and weary from the dual battle of fighting to force Washington society to do his bidding, while at the same time keeping his house in order, Jackson was torn. Could he cut his beloved Emily and Andrew out of his innermost circle and his home permanently? Andrew defended his wife's actions toward Peggy. "The only unkind treatment which my family can have practiced towards Mrs. Eaton is their refusal to acknowledge her right to interfere with social relations. All else is imaginary or worse. This letter is abundant evidence of the indelicacy which distinguishes her character and is disgraceful to her husband." [1031] The Eaton affair had wreaked its havoc on Jackson's health, well-being and peace of mind. And soon the country itself would be tossed into the fray.

John C. Calhoun's grandiose vision of himself and his own abilities was on display in the critical early months of 1831. In Columbia, South Carolina, James Hammond rose early on the morning of Saturday,

---

[1030] AJ to Lewis, August 7, 1830. Jackson-Lewis Papers, NYPL. Donelson to AJ, November 9, 1830, Jackson Papers, LC; AJ to Emily Donelson, Jan. 20 1831, in AJ, *Correspondence*, IV, 187, 226; See also the exchange of letters between Donelson and Jackson, ibid, pp. 192-195.
[1031] Donelson to AJ, Jan. 1831, Jackson Papers, LC.

March 18th to meet with Calhoun at the home of the Charleston lawyer. Hammond's long account of the ensuing conversation shed some light on Calhoun's thinking at this juncture. "It was only 7 o'clock in the morning, but Calhoun immediately entered freely into the discussion of the affairs of the nation," Hammond recalled. "He said that great changes were taking place and had taken place in the political elements." As extraordinary as it had been unexpected, Calhoun believed that three-fourths of the members of Congress were with him as were Pennsylvania, Virginia, and Kentucky, which would have surprised Henry Clay to hear.[1032]

But then came the beginning of Calhoun's fall from grace. In the spring of 1831, Eaton would have his revenge against the vice president for the Calhouns' role in Peggy's public shunning. The now former Secretary of War Eaton retaliated against Calhoun by orchestrating public revelations that the South Carolinian had urged Congress to denounce Jackson during the First Seminole War, further straining an already turbulent relationship between the General and Calhoun.

The Eaton/Petticoat Affair placed a pall over Jackson's relationship with his vice president most of all. The rift with Calhoun, already stewing over differences of opinion on the tariff, but exacerbated by Floride Calhoun's animosity for Peggy Eaton, contributed to a shift in the Cabinet that favored Martin Van Buren.

[1032] James H. Hammond, Selections from the Letters and Speeches of the Hon. James H. Hammond, of South Carolina, 1831. New York, published 1978.

CHAPTER

68

AMERICA: FEDERAL VS. STATE

"The greatness of America lies not in being more enlightened than any other nation, but rather in her ability to repair her faults."
—Alexis de Tocqueville

On May 11th, 1831, a twenty-six-year-old man stepped ashore in New York City from France, beginning his fateful acquaintance with America in the Age of Jackson. For nine months, Alexis de Tocqueville visited the cities of the Atlantic seaboard from Washington to Boston. He then headed west, on a trek to Detroit, before voyaging down the Ohio and Mississippi Rivers to New Orleans, keenly observing the American scene. Four years later he published the first volume of his stupendous work Democracy in America, which remains today probably the most insightful analysis of 19th century American society ever penned. Tocqueville's writing provides an indispensable, panoramic view of both the nature of democracy and the American national character. Tocqueville highlights the unflagging connection between Jackson and the people at large. "Jackson is the spokesman of provincial jealousies." Tocqueville wrote, "It was decentralizing passions that brought him to sovereign power. He yields to its intentions, desires and half-revealed instincts, or rather he anticipates and forestalls them." Contrastingly, he pointed out that, "All the enlightened classes are opposed to General

Jackson."[1033] Nonetheless, Jackson imposed his priorities on the nation, a connection still relevant today as some contemporary Americans often view populism as a potential threat to constitutional democracy.

Tocqueville himself was born in the era of the French Revolution, witnessing the so-called July Revolution in France in 1830, which resulted in a widened French electorate. He followed Britain's landmark Reform Bill of 1832 closely and was also interested in the several independent and burgeoning democratic republics in Latin America, as the disruption of the Napoleonic Wars weakened the imperial grip Spain had long held. Venezuela, Argentina, Chile, Mexico and Peru had all claimed independence from Spain in the years between 1811 and 1821, with Brazil declaring its independence from Portuguese rule in 1822 (although it would remain a monarchy until becoming a republic in 1889.) These dramatic changes convinced the Frenchman that democracy was the irresistible wave of the future, with Jacksonian Democracy becoming its own unique brand. He was less certain, however, about what that democratic future would mean for the happiness, political stability and social equality of the human race. Tocqueville, therefore studied America intently to understand the rest of the world's (especially his home region of Europe's) fate. "In America," he wrote, "I saw more than America. I sought there the image of democracy itself….in order to learn what we have to fear or to hope from its progress." [1034]

Tocqueville began his book with his main insight: "Among the novel objects that attracted my attention during my stay in the United States, nothing struck me more forcibly than the general equality of condition among the people." While he of course recognized the "elephant in the room" of slavery, he considered it to be peculiar to America, not to democracy itself. He contended that the primary fact of equality affected "a prodigious influence on the whole course of society." This impact on Tocqueville is certainly understandable given that mass democratic participation was already a well-established reality upon the Frenchman's arrival. This point specifically characterizes the core of the Age of Jackson. Almost 1.2 million voters, almost half of adult white males in the nation, had voted in the election in Jackson's first presidential victory

---

[1033] Charles Lane, Arthur Goldhammer, *The Tocqueville Review/La revue Tocqueville*, University of Toronto Press, Volume 42, Number 1, 2021, pp. 177-184

[1034] Kennedy, David and Cohen, Lisbeth, *American Pageant*, 16th Edition, 2015.

in 1828. By comparison, France's July Revolution had given suffrage to less than 200,000 propertied males, less than one percent of the total population in 1830. A similar contrast appears when viewing the Reform Bill in Great Britain in 1832: voting rights were extended to just 800,000 male property owners in a country with 50 percent more people than the United States.

In one of Tocqueville's arguments, he offers the concerning potential of a suffering conformity that might be bred by the type of equality that America seemed to offer. But he also suggests that it could go in another direction, that of radical individualism. In the former, the state, he argued, would be compelled to invoke its power to enforce a rigid control; a type of consensus that he calls the "tyranny of the majority" that had concerned many of the Founding Fathers. Tocqueville thought he recognized such signs already emerging. "I know of no country in which there is so little independence of mind and real freedom of discussion as in America." In the self-proclaimed "land of freedom," the irony was not lost on the Frenchman.

Yet, on the other hand, in Tocqueville's offered alternative of American equality, he noticed a unique psychology everywhere in America that lent optimism. "As social conditions become more equal, people acquire the habit of always considering themselves as standing alone, and they are apt to imagine that their whole destiny is in their own hands." Yet, even in this more hopeful scenario, Tocqueville shades the potential results as a gnawing loneliness of the individual, and even social anarchy that could well define America's future. "Democracy makes every man forget his ancestors" he argues, "It throws him back forever upon himself alone and threatens in the end to confine him to entirely within the solitude of his own heart." [1035]

Yet, both of those grim prospects, Tocqueville noted, could, and likely would be mitigated by several factors that would hold American democracy in a healthy balance. The absence of hostile countries on its borders was one. A robust and free press was another, along with strong voluntary associations, particularly within political parties and churches. Lastly, and Tocqueville stressed this factor most of all, "habits of the heart," which he argued, sustains a sense of civic belonging and

---

[1035] de Tocqueville, Alexis, *Democracy in America*, New York, 1899, p. 58.

responsibility that thrived across the bountiful fields and communities of America. Still, however, Democracy in America raised troubling questions about whether such mitigating factors would prove to be enduring, and if not, then what would be the fate of democracy for the rest of the world?

English novelist Charles Dickens traveled to the United States just a few years after Alexis de Tocqueville, Dickens was at the height of his popularity on both sides of the Atlantic and, securing approval from his publishers, Chapman and Hall, determined to visit the young nation to see for himself this haven for the oppressed which had righted all the wrongs of the Old World. His views were not quite as complimentary on the implications of America's much-acclaimed "equality." Dickens wrote of his experiences, "The people are all alike. . . . There is no diversity of character. They travel about on the same errands, say and do the same things in exactly the same manner, and follow in the same dull cheerless round. All down the long table there is scarcely a man who is in anything different from his neighbor." [1036]

Charles Dickens came away from his American experience with a sense of disappointment. To his friend William Macready he wrote "this is not the republic I came to see; this is not the republic of my imagination."[1037] On returning to England Dickens began an account of his American trip which he completed in four months. Not only did Dickens attack slavery in American Notes, he also attacked the American press whom he blamed for the American's lack of general information. In Dickens' next novel, Martin Chuzzlewit, he sends young Martin to America where he continues to vent his feelings for the young republic. American response to both books was extremely negative and passions flared. Yet, the United States contained a 21-percent higher rate of eligible voters than did the United Kingdom, Dickens' home country. Dickens made amends during his second visit to America in 1867-68 with a conciliatory speech in New York.

Jackson stood at the helm of the present and future that Tocqueville and Dickens observed for America, and the president positioned himself as the voice of, and the voice for, the people: the nation's farmers, mechanics,

---

[1036] Kennedy and Cohen, pg. 253; Forster, 1899, v. 1, p. 196.
[1037] Charles Dickens Letters, 1974, v. 3, p. 156.

and laborers specifically; more specifically. On behalf of the interests of the working class, (the white working class that is) or so Jackson argued, the time had come to ensure that the machinations of government were no longer monopolized by the monied elite. Like the working class, Jackson's main education had been adversity, and a desire to rise above his early disadvantages of circumstance. But also like the majority, he shared many of the prejudices of his age. Yet, like the America that Tocqueville so eloquently described, Jackson was tough to fit into a neat category. This would make for a dramatic presidency, and it would come to define this new brand of democracy in America, and a new age.

As America industrialized, Jackson navigated the chaotic realignment as well as he could, and whether he understood all the changes or not, he became a defining figure of his time. The nation was caught between the industrial and transportation revolutions, which disrupted traditional notions of community and economy. Many citizens, eager for a new political order, rallied around Jackson, viewing him as both a hero and a villain. He possessed a unique ability to resonate with the aspirations and frustrations of emerging constituencies in a country ready for change.

Jackson operated outside the established eastern political mainstream, reshaping the electoral landscape. Groups eager for popular politics prepared to elevate him as their champion. In his own words, "I will recollect when I was left an orphan," reflecting his personal connection to the American populace.[1038]

By 1828, the U.S. was transitioning from an agriculture-based economy toward a larger industrialized system, with railroads, canals, and roads connecting disparate regions. The growth of factories and manufacturing was notable, as evidenced by the expansion of the cotton textile workforce, which more than tripled from 1820 to 1840. Wage earners increased five-fold during this period, and immigration from Britain and Ireland rose significantly, from 27,018 in 1828 to 80,000 by 1837. Regular transatlantic steamship travel began in 1838.

Jackson's presidency also coincided with significant conversations and controversies surrounding race, religion, and the role of women. In 1829, David Walker, the son of a slave, published Appeal to the Coloured Citizens of the World, alarming Southern slaveholders and inspiring

---

[1038] Jackson, *Correspondence*, 1843.

early abolitionists. He expressed the despair of Black Americans, stating, "The blacks of the United States are the most degraded, wretched, and abject set of beings that ever lived... If an attempt was made by blacks for liberty, slaves should feel justified to take up arms."[1039]

From 1829 to 1837, there were numerous slave disturbances and revolts across several states. Laws prohibiting slaves from learning to read and write were enacted, and in 1831, William Lloyd Garrison published The Liberator, the first abolitionist newspaper. This period saw a surge in reform movements and critical thinking; for instance, the first tract on birth control in North America was published in 1830, and Oberlin College opened its doors to Black and white students, men and women alike.

The American Journal of Science and Arts explored various scientific fields, marking a distinction between scientists and philosophers. During Jackson's tenure, liberal arts colleges were established at more than twice the rate of the previous decade.

The era was characterized by a clash of faith and atheism, with evangelical fervor converting thousands to Christianity. In upstate New York, Joseph Smith claimed an angel instructed him to restore the church, leading to the birth of the Mormon faith. Tocqueville noted, "There is no country in the world where the Christian faith remains of greater influence over the souls of men than America."[1040] He observed that skeptics and doubters utilized the nation's liberty of conscience to challenge prevailing beliefs, exemplified by a public debate in Cincinnati in April 1829 between evangelist Alexander Campbell and atheist Robert Owen.

In domestic politics, the divisions between Federalists and Republicans had dissolved, leaving the Republicans a diverse coalition of competing interests. By 1820, the Federalists failed to nominate a presidential candidate for the first time, leading to James Monroe's unopposed reelection. But by the late 1820s, all that had changed, and the country was about to enter into one of the most fractious periods in the nation's political history.

As president, Jackson sought to implement lasting changes to the federal system. He aimed to eradicate corruption through a "rotation

---

[1039] Walker, David, *Appeal to the Coloured Citizens of the World*, 1829.
[1040] Brown, Frederic K., *Letters from America*, Yale University Press, 2010.

in office" policy, which, while politically motivated, often resulted in the appointment of unqualified individuals. Some argued that instead of preventing corruption, it fostered it. Notable instances of corruption from this approach caused Jackson's critics to unleash a maelstrom of opposition, particularly, after the fallout from the previously mentioned Customs collector Samuel Swartwout. The situation in New York worsened when Van Buren replaced Swartwout with another Jackson crony, Jesse Hoyt, who soon faced similar allegations of embezzlement. Controversy also arose over Jackson's removal, in just one year, of over 400 postmasters, many with good service records, who were replaced to make way for Jackson's supporters. The system's potential for abuse seemed more and more evident, especially as time passed.

Yet, Jackson's rotation of office became a hallmark of his administration, intended to foster partisanship and involve the public in governance. However, it also perpetuated a culture of patronage that favored loyalty over competence. Critics pointed to the inefficiency and corruption that had characterized government positions for years.

In economic matters, Jackson shifted from supporting internal improvements to opposing Henry Clay's "American System," particularly its high protective tariffs. Soon, anything proposed by Clay became adamantly anti-Jackson. In 1806, Congress authorized construction of the Cumberland Road. To replace the old foot and wagon traces that connected the Potomac and the Ohio rivers. Built between 1811 and 1837, the road ran from Baltimore, Maryland, all the way to Vandalia, Illinois, seventy miles east of St. Louis. Thomas Jefferson found the route an essential piece of infrastructure that would do much to unify an ever-increasing nation. Despite the obvious benefits the road provided, however, the use of federal monies to improve America's roads, canals, and waterways remained controversial. States' rights politicians pointed out, both within Congress, and without, that the federal government did not possess the Constitutional authority to pay for such improvements. Previous presidents were somewhat ambiguous on this issue. On his way out of office in early 1817, James Madison, concerned with the surge of nationalism after the War of 1812, had put a stop to the Bonus Bill with one of his rare vetoes. The Bonus Bill had passed Congress, promoted by those who hoped to utilize the presumed revenue bonus generated from the recharted National Bank for internal improvements. Five years later, James Monroe, in his one and only presidential veto, shot down a bill authorizing the introduction of tolls to pay for repairs along a government financed thoroughfare. Monroe believed projects of this sort should be handled by private individuals or state governments, and that federal sponsorship would set a pattern in motion that would increase the power of the federal government to an extent he did not wish to see.

No presidents prior to Jackson, however, were consistent on the issue. As David S. Brown points out, though "Madison had signed bills extending the Cumberland Road and Monroe believed that the Constitution's general welfare clause might be massaged so as to permit federal money to be channeled towards such improvements. Two generations into the life of the Republic, in other words, the government's relationship to public works remained uncertain and inconsistent."[1041] Frontier states such as Tennessee, Ohio and Kentucky, most in need of the infrastructure the east had long established, often lacked the funding needed to catch up, especially in the cash-deprived west during the perpetual boom and bust cycles of the early 19th century. Seeing the necessity of expediting development, a nationalist approach to improvements was largely embraced by many in the west.

In that spirit, Kentucky congressman Robert P. Letcher, a Clay ally, introduced a bill in May of 1830 to extend the Cumberland Road from the Kentucky town of Maysville, on the Ohio River, to the Kentucky town of Lexington, 60 miles to the southwest. After three days of debate in the House, the bill passed, 102 to 85. Anticipating that it would likely pass the Senate as well, President Jackson prepared his stance on the subject. On the fence as to whether or not he would veto the 'Maysville Road Bill,' he consulted Van Buren to ascertain his opinion on the legislative debate. The Secretary of State responded with a long written report laying out his views against the bill. The president was impressed, and agreed with Van Buren. He replied to the Secretary on May 4, "I have been engaged today....pouring over the manuscript you handed me. As far as I have been able to decipher it, I think it one of the most lucid expositions of the Constitution, and historical accounts of the departure by Congress from its true principles that I have ever met with. It furnishes clear views on the constitutional powers of Congress;

[1041] Brown, David S., *The First Populist*, Ch. 33.

the inability of Congress under the Constitution to apply the Funds to private not National purposes I never had a doubt of. The Kentucky Road Bill involves this very power and I think it right to boldly meet it at the threshold." [1042]

Van Buren, well-versed in Jackson's views, expressed gratitude for Jackson's favorable opinion but cautioned that the bill represented a conspiracy aimed at pressuring the president. He argued that the bill would either force Jackson to approve local improvement projects without national significance or risk alienating supporters of public works. The strategy, as Van Buren outlined, involved "drawing you into the approval of a bill most emphatically local," referring specifically to the Maysville Road project, the entirety of which was in Kentucky alone. This would compel Jackson to oppose internal improvements more broadly, rallying support for numerous schemes that had emerged in recent years. He reassured Jackson that a carefully crafted veto would send a clear message to all involved, stating, "I think I see land."[1043]

Just under two weeks later, on May 15, the Senate approved the Maysville Road Bill with a vote of 24 to 18. In the following days, President Jackson, along with Van Buren and Congressman James Polk from Tennessee, worked on a response to the anticipated veto. Many western Democrats, eager for improvements in their states, sought to persuade Jackson not to veto the bill. Some even visited the White House to advocate for their position. However, Jackson remained resolute. Since the bill was linked to Henry Clay, he felt it necessary to oppose it, even though it contradicted the types of internal improvements he had previously endorsed. He ultimately vetoed the bill, citing as his reasons his belief that such expenditures fostered corruption.

The Maysville Road veto bridged the gap between the competing generations. Jackson's decision was within the parameters of the traditional Constitutional approach, and it was in keeping with precedents set in earlier administrations. But the rest of his veto statement read to Congress took precedence to task. With his assertions in his veto message, the president commenced the movement to undermine traditional principles he disagreed with and prepare the nation for broad reform.

[1042] Ibid.
[1043] Van Buren to AJ, May, 1830, Jackson Papers, LC.

CHAPTER

69

THE HATED TARIFF

"Their object is disunion, but be not deceived by names; disunion, by armed force, is TREASON. Are you really ready to incur its guilt?"

—Andrew Jackson

Tensions over the federal tariff continued to escalate in South Carolina. Senator Robert Y. Hayne, scion of one of the state's wealthiest families, and related by marriage to the former governor, Charles Pinckney, took the floor of the Senate on January 19, 1830. Hayne was responding to a resolution from Connecticut Senator Samuel A. Foot to limit the sale of western lands. Hayne rose immediately and urged that state issues should take precedence over national political matters. Unbeknownst to anyone at the time, Foot's resolution, and Hayne's adamant response would provoke a raging debate in the Senate that would last until May.

The arguments encompassed various hot topics and issues, including slavery, states' rights, and executive power, capturing the attention of both lawmakers and the public. One could argue that this was a turning point in relations between north and south, and the beginning of the regional divide that would ultimately culminate in "a house divided," as a famous Illinois Republican would later assert.

As the debates unfolded, Vice President Calhoun presided over the sessions, which drew the attention of the masses as they raged on. Soon, the chambers were filed with citizens, including many women, eager to witness the legislative proceedings. The discourse that Calhoun presided over embodied the profound societal and political tensions of the era.

Jackson's right-hand man, William B. Lewis, monitored the speeches closely, always on the move, hurrying from the Capitol building down Pennsylvania Avenue to update the president. The debate commenced on Monday, January 18, when Thomas Hart Benton criticized Foot's resolution, labeling it an unjust attack on the West. Representing the perspective of his state of Missouri, Benton asserted that lower prices for public lands were essential. He emphasized the importance of balancing not only the nation's demographics but also the distribution of power. According to Benton, the movement of people would enable power to spread across the continent. A proposal like Foot's, Benton contended, posed a threat to the safety of the West, as it favored the northeast solely at the expense of others. If the national government was going to target public lands now, "then every part of the country would be at risk in due time." Benton argued. "The whole country may be alarmed, agitated, and enraged with mischievous inquiries, the South with its slaves and Indians, the West with its lands, and the Northeast on the subject of its navigation and fisheries, lighthouses and its manufactories."[1044]

Hearing the trigger words of 'the South and its slaves', Hayne recognized an opportunity and began to articulate the 'states' rights manifesto.' If embraced, his viewpoint, he believed, could very well safeguard the institution of slavery. Charismatic and vigorous, Hayne was influenced by the environment of Charleston, where he was educated in the prevailing attitudes of the antebellum South, and the planter aristocracy particularly. "Yankees were never in great credit here, even their consummate impudence could not gain them admission into society. But now they are in worse odor than ever." Alexander Garden, a revolutionary war hero in South Carolina, wrote to Charlestonian planter Charles Manigault in 1828.[1045]

Hayne held many of these same feelings. "Viewing the United States as one country, the people of the South might almost be considered as strangers in the land of their fathers." Hayne expressed his concerns, warning that the tariff was fostering a "spirit of jealousy and distrust."

[1044] Thomas Hart Benton, Digital History UH, 3546.
[1045] Alexander Garden to James Manigault, 1829, Garden Papers, SCHS.

For many Southerners, the tariff was also seen as a precursor to abolition. Calhoun, as always, led South Carolina's efforts to nullify the tariff. The Yale-educated former nationalist and unionist viewed nullification as a means to uphold the Union while also preventing the secession of southern states. In his perspective, he remained a unionist, even as he embraced southern sectionalism. "I never use the word 'nation' in speaking of the United States," Calhoun wrote, "I always use the word 'union' or 'confederacy.' We are not a nation, but a union, a confederacy of equal and sovereign states."[1046] Both Hayne and Calhoun would more accurately be called Unionists with an asterisk.

The touchy issue of the protective tariff had long been a headache for United States presidents. Since Jefferson, and particularly for Yankee President John Quincy Adams, the issue often threatened to bring down their administrations. Now, Andrew Jackson began to feel the pain of his predecessor when it came to this regionally divisive bill. Tariffs protected American industry from competition with European manufacturers by driving up prices for foreign goods. This extra cost to buy British or French goods meant that the products made in the country's manufacturing region of New England, by comparison, became an American consumer's best bet. Yet, by driving up prices for all Americans, Southerners saw none of the tariff's benefits.

The tariff, southerners argued, invited retaliatory tariffs from foreign nations as well, threatening to disrupt the vital cotton industry, on which the southern 'plantocracy' relied so heavily. The middle states of Pennsylvania, New York and New Jersey had long been supportive of protectionist tariff measures. In the 1820s, Webster, the voice of New Englanders everywhere, had given up his traditional defense of free trade to support higher tariffs. The wool and textile industries were producing like never before, and industrious northerners envisioned a future of factory, rather than maritime, success.

In 1824, Congress passed a measure to significantly increase the general tariff, but not enough to satisfy wool manufacturers, who wished to see even higher protections against foreign competition. Ardent southerners, largely made up of Jacksonian Democrats, responded with

---

[1046] William W. Freehling, *Prelude to Civil War: The Nullification Controversy in South Carolina, 1816–1836* (New York: Harper and Row, 1965; reprint, New York: Oxford University Press, 1992).

a risky political gamble, cynically promoting a high-tariff bill, expecting it to be heavily defeated in Congress. Hoping to give a black eye to President Adams in having the bill rejected, to their dismay, the tariff passed in 1828, just in time for Jackson to inherit the unsavory issue, which Adams gladly tossed over to his successor as though it were a hot potato.

Wealthy Southerners had money to burn, particularly the planter class that made up the top tier of American wealth during the antebellum period. Yet, they lacked liquid funds, and at the same time, they had little manufacturing of their own. Thus, they became heavy consumers of manufactured goods. Goods, that is, that were manufactured elsewhere which meant that whatever liquid money planters did have was usually on its way out, usually into British hands. With a long-standing, world-renowned manufacturing industry, no one knew how to produce more cost-effectively than the British. Booming English factories relied on southern cotton, enjoying ready markets in the American South, and they offered quality products at reasonable prices for their favored region in return. But suddenly, New England sought to stand in the way of these cushy deals by daring to develop a competing industry of its own.

Southerners were particularly shocked by what they regarded as the outrageous rates of the Tariff of 1828. Southern hotheads labeled it the "Black Tariff, or the infamous "Tariff of Abominations." Several southern states protested vehemently and organized formal rebukes. In South Carolina, to voice their displeasure, flags were lowered to half-mast. "Let the New England beware how she imitates the Old," warned one rather expressive South Carolinian.[1047] Anti-tariff protestors in Charleston took to wearing palmetto blossoms, real or sewn from fabric, to symbolize their defiance of the federal tariff, indicating their adamant support for the right of nullification.

The always outspoken agitator Thomas Cooper, who had once been imprisoned for his opposition to President John Adams in the Sedition Act purges of the 1790s, now spoke out heavily against the protectionist system. Then a professor at the University of South Carolina, Cooper, an Englishman by birth had come to favor the views of his adopted region and became one its strongest spokesmen. He had once held a positive

---

[1047] Kennedy, Ch. 13.

outlook towards the country saying he preferred America because, "There is little fault to find with the government of America, either in principle or in practice... we have no animosities about religion; it is a subject about which no questions are asked... the present irritation of men's minds in Great Britain, and the discordant state of society on political grounds is not known there. The government is the government of the people and for the people."[1048]

By 1831, however, Cooper's views on the government of the United States were not so rosy. In 1832, he was formally tried for infidelity. Before his college classes, in public lectures, and in numerous pamphlets, he constantly preached the doctrine of free trade, and tried to show that the protective system was especially burdensome to the South. His remedy was state action. Each state, he contended, was a sovereign power and was in duty bound to protest against the tyrannical acts of the Federal government. In a speech, he described the South as the perennial loser in an "unequal alliance." Cooper predicted that South Carolina would be compelled, in the near future, to calculate the value of our Union. "The idea that the South should withdraw received its first extensive advertising as a result of that speech." [1049]

Not entirely without logic, southerners believed that the "Yankee tariff" discriminated against their region. The bustling Northeast was in the midst of a manufacturing boom, the West was prospering in its early development with rising property values and an ever-increasing population. The energetic region of Jackson's Southwest was expanding into virgin cotton lands. The General had been instrumental in opening space for such expansion. So where did that leave the Old South? Older, tobacco based southern states such as Virginia and Maryland, those not of the rich, fertile Deep South cotton lands, had fallen on hard times. In search of a scapegoat, the tariff was an easy target.

Having heard the passionate words of Thomas Hart Benton on the 18th, Robert Hayne decided it was time to speak up, and he did so on the 19th. That day, Daniel Webster happened to be a floor below, in the Supreme Court chamber, arguing a case before chief Justice Marshall.

[1048] Malone, Dumas, "Thomas Cooper and the State Rights Movement In South Carolina, 1823-1830, *The North Carolina Historical Review*, Vol. 3, No. 2 (April, 1926), pp. 184-197.

[1049] Malone, Dumas, 1926. p. 309.

Once his work there was done, Webster, who had no particular business in mind, walked upstairs to the usually chilly court in the Senate with, as he said "my court papers under my arm just to see what was passing." Amid a long address in the context of discussing the merits of a national treasury, states' rights advocates feared that the concentration of federal funds would lead to corruption, Hayne painted an emotional portrait of the South under the tariff. "The fruits of our labor are drawn from us to enrich other and more favored sections of the Union. The rank grass grows in our streets; our very fields are scathed by the hand of injustice and oppression." The answer, Hayne said, was local, not central, control. "I am one of those who believe that the very life of our system is the independence of the states and that there is no evil more to be deprecated than the consolidation of this government. It is only by a strict adherence to the limitations imposed by the constitution on the federal government that this system works well and can answer the great ends for which it was instituted."

Listening, Webster began to feel the hairs on his neck stand up. "I did not like it." he frankly declared. In the same way South Carolina saw New England's hand behind all of its troubles, New England was still absorbing Thomas Cooper's July 1827 declaration that it was time to "calculate the value of the Union." On this windy winter Tuesday, Webster thought of Cooper's threats as he heard Hayne's words. Rising the next day, Webster took the debate to a more momentous plain, that of the nature of the Union itself. That had not been Haynes' chief point, but just as he had seen an opportunity in Benton's words, so Webster saw an opportunity in the words of Hayne.

Alluding to the "firebrands of South Carolina, the "hotheads," Webster questioned their loyalty to the Union, "They significantly declared that it is time to calculate the value of the Union and their aim seems to be to enumerate and magnify all the evils, real and imaginary, which the government under the Union produces. The tendency of all these ideas and sentiments is obviously to break the Union into discussion as a mere question of present and temporary expediency. Nothing more than a mere matter of profit and loss." In a passage devoted to the prospect of a passing civil war, Webster said "I am a Unionist. I would strengthen the ties that hold us together. Far indeed, and my wish is very far distant be the day when our associated and fraternal stripes shall be severed asunder, and when that happy constellation under which we have risen to so much renown shall be broken up and be seen sinking star after star into obscurity and night." [1050]

Five days later, Hayne replied to Webster, whose speech had successfully lured his adversary into the larger discussion. Defending slavery, laying out the arguments for nullification, singing hymns to the glory of his native state, Hayne was articulating Calhoun's world view (and there were even reports that the vice president went so far as to hand down notes to his colleague from South Carolina.) The exchanges as the debate went forward were substantive and sincere, and both Hayne and Webster acquitted themselves well. An admiring 19th-century Webster biographer said that Hayne was 'deficient in that weight and impressiveness, which alone belong to men of greater caliber; though, while speaking, few men could exceed him in the hold with which his fluent and graceful declamation retained the attention and thrilled the feeling of an audience.'[1051]

What had started out as a simple, rather innocuous discussion about whether the federal government should reduce the sale of public land quickly transformed into a confrontation over nullification. Hayne argued that states had the right to nullify federal laws deemed unconstitutional to safeguard their citizens. In contrast, Webster asserted that only the Supreme Court held the authority to determine a law's constitutionality. He considered nullification to be heretical at best and treasonous at worst, as it implied that state sovereignty could override federal authority, potentially leading to disorder. Webster contended that the states did not form a compact known as the Constitution; rather, they represented a national union of the American people.

The exchange of rhetoric persisted for eight days between the South Carolinian and the articulate New Englander. Historian James Schouler asserts, "South Carolina nullification was now becoming evident, and the renowned debate... [of] the first session revealed its claims and shortcomings to the nation. The chosen venue for this initial impression was the Senate, where the main figure, the arch-heretic, presided and

---

[1050] Sheidley, Harlow W. "The Wester-Hayne Debate: Recasting New England's Sectionalism" *New England Quarterly* 1995 67(1): 5–29.
[1051] Meacham, Jon, Ch. 10.

directed the proceedings with keen observation." [1052] This arch-heretic was none other than Vice President John C. Calhoun.

Senators who spoke after the personal encounter between Webster and Hayne had been concluded were conscious of the historical significance of the debate. Edward Livingston expressed the purpose of the extraordinary deliberation in observing: "The publication of what has been said, will spread useful information on topics highly proper to be understood in the community at large. The recurrence which has been had to first principles is of incalculable use. The nature, form, history, and changes of our Government, imperceptible or disregarded at the time of their occurrence, are remarked; abuses are pointed out; and the people are brought to reflect on the past and provide for the future." [1053]

Much deeper issues underlay the southern outcry against the tariff—in particular, the growing anxiety about possible federal interference with the institution of slavery, that peculiar institution, that remained forever embedded as the thorn in the side of the Union. The congressional debate on the Missouri Compromise had kindled those anxieties, and they were fanned even more demonstrably by an abortive slave rebellion in Charleston in 1822, led by a free black named Denmark Vescey. The South Carolinians, still closely tied to the British West Indies, also knew full well that their brethren, the slaveholders of the West Indies were becoming more and more weighed down by the pressure of the British abolitionist movement on the government in London. Abolitionism in America might use a similar government power approach from Washington to suppress slavery south of the Mason-Dixon line. If that should be the case, now was the time to take a stand on principle against all federal encroachments on states' rights; and the tariff was just the issue.

South Carolina's legislature, in protesting against the "Abominable" tariff published, though without formal endorsement in 1828, a pamphlet called The South Carolina Exposition. Though unknown at the time and kept a secret from all except those in his close circle, its author was none other than John C. Calhoun himself. Calhoun, one of the top-flight political theorists America ever produced, would live out the

---

[1052] Schouler, *History of the United States under the Constitution*, 1789–1877, pp. 101-114.
[1053] Edward Livingston, 1832, Livingston Papers, LC.

remainder of his years attempting to reconcile strong states' rights with a strong Union. The Exposition denounced that recent tariff as unjust and unconstitutional. Going a step beyond Jefferson and Madison's Virginia and Kentucky resolutions of 1798, it bluntly proposed that states should nullify the tariff–that is, they should declare it null and void, and thus to be ignored within their borders. Calhoun, by secretly expressing his views to the nation, put South Carolina in the lead among southern states against the Tariff of Abominations.

The stage was now set for a showdown of epic proportions. Through Jackson's first term, the "Nullies" as the nullifiers of the South became known, made strenuous efforts to muster the necessary two-thirds majority for nullification in the South Carolina legislature. But they were blocked by a determined minority of Unionists, derisively labeled "submission men." Back in Washington, Congress tipped the balance by passing the new Tariff of 1832. Though it trimmed back the worse of the "abominations" of 1828, it was still too protective of Northern interests, and did not do enough to mollify the most hotheaded Southerners. Falling short of southern demands, it had a disquieting feeling of permanence about it, which seemed to worsen the mood in the south, particularly in South Carolina. Thus, the Nullification Crisis deepened.

Calhoun, Jackson's vice president, now led South Carolina more openly, and nerved his home state for more drastic measures. Nullies and Unionists clashed head on in the state's election of 1832. With their palmetto ribbons on their hats to mark their loyalty to nullification, the Nullies emerged with a two-thirds majority in the state. The South Carolina legislature then called for a special convention. Several weeks later, the delegates met in Columbia and solemnly declared that the existing tariff was null and void with their state. As a further defiant act, the convention threatened to take South Carolina out of the Union if Washington attempted to collect the duties by force.

South Carolinian George McDuffie, in a dramatic burst of rhetoric, addressed the South Carolina assembly, "the Union, such as the majority have made it, is a foul monster which those who worship, after seeing its deformity, are worthy of their chains."[1054] Reading about McDuffie's remarks, Duff Green, editor of the influential publication the *United*

[1054] Ellis, p. 7.; Freehling, *Road to Disunion*, p. 256.

States Telegraph, thought the South Carolinians were going too far. Such hot rhetoric put Calhoun in a precarious position nationally. Green's fear, fellow South Carolinian James Hamilton Jr. attested, was that the southern extremists intended to start into open rebellion and ensure the empire of the "Whore of Washington" (re: Peggy Eaton,) Hamilton told him on Saturday, June 11, 1831.

Worried about Jackson's more precarious political position, and disturbed by McDuffie's words, the Unionists in South Carolina hastily arranged a day-long Fourth of July rally in Charleston. Congressman William Drayton spoke vividly, "In a civil struggle," he said, "all the kindly feelings of the human heart would be eradicated, and for them would be substituted those burning and savage passions, which wore rancor into the bosom of friends and which in the end could lead to the spectacle of brother armed against brother, the parent against child, and of the child against his parent."

Though he was secluded at the Rip Raps in Hampton Roads, Jackson had the last word of the day. In a letter that was read aloud at the meeting, the president warned, "Every enlightened citizen must know that a separation, could it be affected, would begin with civil discord, and end in colonial dependence on a foreign power, and obliteration from the list of nations." Before any of these calamities could come to pass, Jackson he said would "hurl all the strengths at his command at all hazards in order to present an insurmountable barrier to the success of any plan of disorganization."[1055]

Anxiety about civil war was widespread. "I fear, from my observation to the south, that our Union is in danger." Stephen Van Renssalaer, a former congressman from New York, wrote Clay. "I had no idea of the violence of the planters; they are deluded by their ambitious leaders."[1056] Renssalaer, a northern Federalist, viewed the South Carolinians as though they were from a foreign land, and saw their states' rights approach as akin to the days under the Articles of Confederation that had limited the national government's effectiveness in the earliest years of the republic.

From his study in South Carolina, Calhoun, the most ambitious of the planters, was in the midst of a particularly vigorous summer. On

---

[1055] President Jackson's Proclamation Regarding Nullification, December 10, 1832.
[1056] Renselaar to Clay, 1832, Clay Papers, LC.

Tuesday, July 26, 1831, he delivered what became known as his 'Fort Hill Address'. The South Carolinians' speech did not incite rebellion or call for the South to immediately pursue disunion. Instead, in a dense philosophical manner, Calhoun argued that the Union could only endure if the states—being the original parties to the Constitution—had the authority to nullify a law while the Constitution was specifically amended to correct the defective statute. While this was an elegant theory, it was neither constitutional, nor practical. The appropriate venue for such disputes was Congress, where the Framers of the Constitution ensured that minority voices could be heard, primarily through equal representation in the Senate, regardless of state population. Additionally, the courts were established to provide checks on both executive and legislative powers.

The most extreme southern secessionists, often referred to as the "fire-eaters," argued that their actions were rooted in the tradition of the Kentucky and Virginia resolutions of 1798. These resolutions had been adopted to protest the Alien and Sedition Acts and the federalism represented by John Adams. However, the resolutions of 1798 did not support the more radical measures South Carolina sought to implement. A draft from 1832 revealed that Thomas Jefferson did indeed make strong arguments, but ultimately, the Kentucky legislature approved a more moderate version. In his retirement at Montpelier, James Madison clarified that the Virginia resolutions were not intended to endorse the threats now being made by South Carolina. Madison had then asserted that states had the right to seek reform, but only through the national government. Citing Calhoun's Fort Hill address, Madison argued, nullification would provide a mechanical means for states to exert more power over national laws than the nation could over them. This was contrary to a true federalist system.

The objections from most Americans at the time, including President Jackson, were less about the broader issue of states' rights. Even while defending the Union, Jackson spoke favorably of the old Republican ideology, as did many "Unionists." Their concerns were primarily about the implications of Calhoun's doctrine, which would bring about a confederacy rather than a truly cohesive nation, allowing member states to selectively follow laws as they pleased. Proponents of nullification contended that Calhoun's theory would only suspend the objectionable law until the Constitution could be amended.

However, this interpretation overlooked a crucial reality: amending the Constitution required a supermajority of states to agree, making it virtually impossible for the minority to protect its interests through constitutional amendments. This fundamental flaw in Calhoun's logic, combined with growing tensions between state and federal authority, set the stage for an even greater crisis. As the summer of 1832 approached, South Carolina's stance hardened, and a showdown between state and federal power seemed increasingly inevitable. The question that hung in the air was not just about tariffs or states' rights, but whether the American experiment in self-government could survive the growing storm of sectional discord.

Amidst the poetic tableau of low country charm, South Carolinians stewed in their discontent. Loathing the tariff he referred to as abominable, John Calhoun held firm to his principles. Remembering the Virginia and Kentucky Resolutions of a generation earlier, the South Carolinian firmly believed that nullification was the answer to the federal government imposing the interests of one region on another.

Along the gentle curve of the South Carolina coast, the planter class decried the injustice of the tariff. As they took to Charleston's cobblestone streets, the salty air carrying the scent of the sea, Palmetto state leaders bellowed the exaggerated claim that "forty bales" out of every hundred were lost due to the tariff. Over time, they argued, this heavy burden would lead to the collapse of the entire cotton economy. Since the price of cotton was directly linked to the value of enslaved people, the destruction of this economy would bankrupt slaveholders, whose fortunes were deeply tied to the wealth generated by cotton and slavery. Ensconced in their luxuriant mansions nestled below the moss-draped trees, South Carolina slaveholders feared for their wealth. Reluctant to depend on new legislation to safeguard their riches, especially given that South Carolina's enslaved population surpassed the white population, they also feared for their lives. Thus, in the words of the historian Sean Wilentz, slaveholders viewed the tariff as "but a means to effect 'the abolition of slavery throughout the southern states," even predicting a race war if abolition occurred: these prophecies lay at the heart of the "abominable" effects of the tariff."[1057]

To nullify laws they viewed as unconstitutional, Calhoun recommended that states hold conventions through which "effectual protection is afforded to the minority against the oppression of the absolute majority."[1058] With Andrew Jackson's inauguration on the horizon, Calhoun also wrote of the hope that "this eminent citizen" would restore the "pure principles of our government."[1059] Calhoun was profoundly mistaken. Between the publication of the Exposition and the Jefferson Birthday dinner, the heated Webster-Hayne debates had raged.

Three months after the Webster-Hayne debates, President Andrew Jackson, Vice President Calhoun, and other notable figures gathered for a dinner celebrating Thomas Jefferson's birthday on April 13, 1830. Robert Hayne himself helped organize the event and requested no fewer than 24 toasts beforehand. However, the attendees were unaware that the evening would end in failure on multiple fronts and be long remembered for one of the most tense, awkward standoffs at a presidential dinner table in American history. The first setback came from the Pennsylvania invitees, who left after seeing the list of toasts. They deemed the toasts excessively partisan, reflecting southern interests. The toasts included fervent declarations of states' rights, such as "the support of the State Governments in all their rights" and "the bane of the Union: oppression of minorities; unequal taxation; unequal distribution of public benefits." Senator Hayne lamented during his toast that South Carolina's stance on the tariff had been "misrepresented, and her position reviled," while the 20th toast clearly stated, "the States: Their harmony, and overriding consideration in the minds of all patriotic statesmen."

This contradictory toast sought to balance state sovereignty with the supremacy of the Union, though it leaned more towards the former at the expense of the latter. President Jackson endured each of these irritable toasts, feeling a quiet rage building within him. The now-known

---

[1057] Drago, Elliott, "The Birthday Dinner," *The Jack Miller Center*, 2022.

[1058] Kelley, Lucas, "The Nullification Crisis," Essential Civil War Curriculum.

[1059] John C. Calhoun, *The South Carolina Exposition and Protest*, in *The Papers of John C. Calhoun*, ed. Clyde Wilson and Edwin Hemphill (Columbia, SC: The University of South Carolina Press, 1977), X, 444.

authorship of the South Carolina Exposition by Calhoun, the audacity of the states' rights advocates' toasts, and their presumptuous attempt to commandeer Jefferson's birthday to legitimize nullification all disgusted Jackson. Thus began the row and the second significant failure of the evening.

With composed restraint, Jackson complied when the master of ceremonies called for volunteer toasts. Raising his glass and locking eyes with Vice President Calhoun, he declared: "Our Federal Union: It must be preserved." This succinct toast reflected Jackson's commitment to the Union, which should not be trampled by the desires of individual states. The Vice President then rose to his feet and responded with a counter toast: "To the Union, next to our liberty, most dear."[1060]

[1060] John C. Calhoun, April 30, 1830, quoted in the *Connecticut Herald*, Digital History, 354.

*A Civil **War**-era political cartoon depicting Andrew Jackson (aka the Union) triumphing over **John C. Calhoun** (aka states› rights proponents) during the Nullification Crisis. The cartoon was meant as a critique of presidential candidate George B. McClellan›s plan of making peace with the Confederate States of America. From Pendleton›s Lithography, 1864.*

CHAPTER

70

THE FALL OF CALHOUN

"They must be either for us or against us."
-Andrew Jackson

It had long been a question whether Calhoun or Van Buren should lead the Jackson party at the end of the one term which Jackson had declared to be the limit of his stay in the White House. Calhoun's friends in the Cabinet, and General Duff Green, of "The Telegraph," were active in his interest. Van Buren, however, was constantly growing in favor with the President. In fact, it was now Van Buren, not the South Carolinian Calhoun, who was being groomed as the successor to the president.

But then a shock reverberated through the capital. President Jackson announced that he would run for a second term. The decision jolted Washington because of its suddenness. Having insisted he would serve but one term, everyone had taken the old man at his word. Now, the shake up was palpable. Trying to read into the decision some larger political meaning, some saw it as a ploy to block any movement in Pennsylvania for John McLean. In truth, the belief was that building support for Martin Van Buren's candidacy as Jackson's heir apparent would take four more years.

Calhoun's friends, however, assumed the aim was to get rid of the vice president and that Van Buren had conceived it. They always saw the Magician as the conspirator behind most Jackson maneuvers. Under the circumstances, there was only one course of action for them to take: a reconciliation between Jackson and Calhoun had to be arranged, and somehow a truce negotiated. Since the General was desperate to restore peace to the cabinet, perhaps he might be receptive to the idea. The Calhoun team decided it was worth a try.[1061]

The vice president Calhoun had not yet returned from South Carolina to begin the new commercial session, so mutual friends, Senator Felix Grundy of Tennessee and Richard A. Johnson of Kentucky along with Samuel Swartwout, felt compelled to take it upon themselves to facilitate the now necessary reconciliation. Swartwout. who knew of Van Buren's opposition to his appointment, decided they would have to initiate the matter immediately, and make the first move. On behalf of the vice president, they proposed to patch things up with Old Hickory.

Jackson sat in a room of the White House that had been converted into a studio by Ralph Earl, while the painter worked at one of his many portraits of the president. A servant entered to announce that Swartwout was in the president's office and wanted to speak with him. Upon returning Jackson expressed to Van Buren "the whole affair was settled." He recited the terms of the reconciliation, but Van Buren could later not recollect what those terms were. "He did not appear entirely satisfied with what he had agreed to," reported Thomas Hart Benton, who was also present at the time, "but said the matter was done with, and he would think no more about it."[1062]

The Magician embraced the decision with his typical calm demeanor, even expressing his satisfaction to Jackson about the outcome. Coincidentally, around the same time, Van Buren hosted a grand soiree. One guest described it as "a splendid state dinner," attended by a diverse mix of political figures. As is often the case, some invited guests did not show up. Suddenly, to everyone's surprise, the Vice President entered the room. Calhoun had made a most unexpected appearance.

In response to the Vice President's unexpected visit, the Magician reciprocated with utmost courtesy, and the dinner unfolded splendidly. They began dining at 6:30 and did not rise until 9 o'clock.[1063] The full details of the subsequent reconciliation remained undisclosed. Some evidence hints that part of the agreement involved the destruction of correspondence between Jackson and Calhoun regarding the Seminole

---

[1061] Edward Everett to Alexander Everett, Jan. 21, 1831, Everett Papers, MHS.
[1062] Van Buren, *Autobiography*, 377.
[1063] Everett to his wife, Jan. 19, 1831, Everett Papers, MHS.

controversy, though this remains uncertain.[1064] It is believed that the two men agreed to never speak of the matter again. Another aspect of their arrangement included Calhoun's visit to leave his card for the President, which would lead to an invitation to dine at the White House.

Regrettably, the reconciliation quickly fell apart. For reasons known only to him, Calhoun chose to publish the Seminole correspondence, directly violating their agreement to destroy it. This reckless decision obliterated any hopes for reconciliation, and became the death knell of amity between Calhoun, and the Kitchen Cabinet. Perhaps he believed that revealing the correspondence would expose a conspiracy against him or demonstrate Van Buren's deceitfulness. Perhaps he simply wished to embarrass Van Buren, and that publishing the documents public would improve his standing with the president, but such a miscalculation was astonishingly foolish. Jackson was notoriously sensitive about his actions in Florida, and any publication of documents that contradicted his claims would surely provoke a catastrophic backlash. Calhoun's actions were nothing short of sheer folly, an inexplicable blunder of monumental proportions.[1065]

Senators Grundy and Johnson, both Calhoun supporters, approached Francis P. Blair with a request to publish certain documents in his newspaper. Blair outright refused, warning them that such publication would likely cause a rift with the president and could lead to Mr. Calhoun's dismissal.[1066] This warning may have alarmed the two senators, prompting them to consult John Eaton. They showed him the material that the vice president intended to publish, seeking his advice on any content that might provoke a strong reaction or be misinterpreted.[1067] After reviewing the documents and noting several of Eaton's suggestions, Grundy inquired whether there was anything that might compel a response from Jackson. Eaton believed there was not, although he expressed concern about how the newspapers might handle the information. As they were about to leave, Grundy made a final request: "Will you see General Jackson and explain to him what is

---

[1064] Van Buren, *Autobiography*, 379.
[1065] Hugh Hamilton to James Buchanan, Feb. 20, 1831, Buchanan Papers, PHS.
[1066] Blair to Van Buren, Dec. 9, 1858, Van Buren Papers, LC.
[1067] Van Buren, *Autobiography*, 378.

taking place? I will see Mr. Calhoun, and if the course we have taken is approved, you shall be informed."[1068]

However, Eaton chose not to discuss the matter with the president. After some contemplation and likely influenced by Lewis's advice, he deemed it inappropriate to do so. The following day, Eaton received a note from Grundy indicating that "all was right..." and that his suggestions had been adopted. Eaton did not respond, leading Grundy to assume that Jackson had also given his approval. Eaton's silence represented a calculated deception.

A pamphlet featuring the Jackson-Calhoun letters and the preparatory address was prepared for publication by Duff Green's *Telegraph* between February 18 and 26, 1831. On the evening prior to its public release, a complete copy was sent to Eaton, with a request that he share it with Jackson for his review. However, Eaton took no action. As the vice president was believed to be behind the scheme to ostracize and humiliate Peggy, he allowed Calhoun to assume that Jackson supported the pamphlet and its publication. Revenge is, after all, a dish best served cold.

Like a fox in the hen house, Jackson was not blind to what Calhoun was up to. He may have been toying with Calhoun, feigning support for a reconciliation while playing his true cards close to his vest. Jackson harbored suspicions about Johnson and Grundy's motives, recognizing their concerns regarding Calhoun's political ambitions. What particularly worried Jackson was the circulating gossip in Washington, suggesting that Calhoun was compiling correspondence related to the Seminole affair, which could potentially embarrass the administration. Lewis was aware of this as early as January 13, indicating that Jackson was likely informed as well.[1069] "The gossip of Washington," said Van Buren, spread the rumor about the correspondence in the newspapers, and "gave loose and contradictory accounts of its contents." [1070]

In his defense, Jackson sought evidence and reached out to Overton for help in his inquiry. On January 22, Overton responded with two letters that seemed to provide exactly what Jackson needed. In a reply dated February 8, Jackson stated, "I am now fully prepared for defence should it become necessary to make one--Mr. Calhoun's conduct has

---

[1068] Ibid.
[1069] Lewis to Overton, Jan. 13, 1831, Overton Papers.
[1070] Van Buren, Autobiography, pg. 376.

been truly astonishing; he has been growling and grumbling, and petto, and his friends intimating that he has written a pamphlet, others of his friends deny this. He has shewn the correspondence between himself and myself has been cutting his own throat as fast as he can politically. My own opinion is that the whole affair has been a political movement, without any intention of comeing out before the public—be this as it may, I am prepared for defence, and will make him understand the old adage, 'O that my enemy would write a book.'"[1071]

Jackson must have been a hell of a poker player, for Jackson was well aware of the pamphlet all along. In fact, the rumors surrounding Calhoun's plans were so widespread that it was impossible for him not to know what was happening. Additionally, Blair had conversations with him about it. Later, Blair confessed he wasn't sure if he had discussed the Johnson-Grundy proposal when he was first approached—"when the thing was in petto"—but he was certain he had before Green published it. Blair recalled telling Green—just days before the pamphlet's release—that it would likely incite a conflict between General Jackson and Mr. Calhoun.[1072]

There were even whispers that Calhoun would blame Van Buren for reigniting the controversy to advance his political ambitions. The evidence suggests that Jackson not only knew the timing of the pamphlet's release but also its main focus. Nevertheless, he opted to feign ignorance, allowing Calhoun to undermine himself. As Frances Granger of New York mentioned to Thurlow Weed just days before the publication, "it will make a devil of a buzzing, but my own opinion is that Calhoun will suffer more by it than anyone else. . . . The thrusts at Van Buren will be very direct & undisguised. . . . Matty will use the claws of others to take his own chestnuts from the fire." Granger also knew the exact date of publication.[1073]

"The city is all agog about the controversy between Mr. Calhoun and Van Buren," wrote Edward Everett to his wife on February 11; "the rupture is supposed to be impending. At the French minister's, Van Buren went up to Calhoun & offered him his hand. Calhoun turned on his heel & went off; and it said that a very angry pamphlet is to be published by Calhoun in a day or two." [1074]

[1071] AJ to Overton, Feb. 8, 1831, Overton Papers, THS.
[1072] Blair to Van Buren, Dec. 9, 1858, Van Buren Papers, LC.
[1073] Granger to Weed, Feb. 15, 1831, Granger Papers, LC.
[1074] Everett to his wife, Feb. 11, 1831, Everett Papers, MHS.

The explosive pamphlet reached the American public on February 17, 1831, nine days after Jackson penned the portentous words, "O that my enemy would write a Book." In fifty pages entitled "Correspondence between Gen. Andrew Jackson & John C. Calhoun... On the subject of the course of the latter, in the cabinet of Mr. Monroe, on the Occurrences in the Seminole War" Calhoun tanked any hopes he ever had of reaching the White House. In the introductory address, the vice president explained to the American people his purpose in publishing the correspondence. "I have come before you, as my constituents, to give an account of my conduct in an important political transaction, which has been called into question, and so erroneously represented, that neither justice to myself, nor respect for you will permit me any longer to remain silent; I allude to my course, in the deliberations of the cabinet of Mr. Monroe, on the Seminole question." Copies of James A. Hamilton's letter to John Forsyth followed, along with Forsyth's letter to Crawford, a few letters of Jackson's about Crawford accusations that Calhoun had called for the general's censure on account of his supposedly unauthorized invasion of Florida, and of course, many letters of Calhoun that spoke to his defense. To Jacksonians it was a smoking gun.

Readers of the publication quickly discerned two main objectives: to defend Calhoun's actions within Monroe's cabinet and to suggest that there was a conspiracy aimed at derailing Calhoun's political career, orchestrated by Martin Van Buren. Although Van Buren's name was not explicitly mentioned, it was clearly evident who was implicated in this alleged scheme of political sabotage. The insinuation was so obvious that Van Buren felt compelled to request that Green publish a statement in the February 25 issue of the Telegraph, firmly denying any involvement in a plot against the vice president. He declared that any "assertion or insinuation" suggesting he aimed to undermine Calhoun in the President's eyes was "unfounded and unjust."

The explosion reverberated not just through Washington, but across the entire nation. In a letter to Van Buren, John Williams from Tennessee remarked, "Mr. Calhoun's pamphlet has become the focal point of discussions in this region. The reactions from the pamphlet and the *Telegraph* have significantly impacted public opinion." What made Calhoun's work so objectionable was its mockery of the Jackson administration, exposing the personal feuds that had plagued the cabinet over the past two years. This revelation was not something the public had fully grasped until now, leaving them both shocked and disheartened. While most Democrats acknowledged that Calhoun presented his argument effectively, they also recognized that he had done a disservice to himself, the President, the party, and the nation. He had aired their dirty political laundry for everyone to witness, an inexcusable act. Across the Northern, Middle, and Southern states—all but South Carolina—Calhoun's "Attack on the President" faced widespread condemnation.[1075]

"Mr. Calhoun's publication was wholly uncalled for. It is a firebrand wantonly thrown into the [Democratic] party. Mr. Calhoun will be held responsible for all the mischief which may follow." So the party line read, and the White House had not taken long in sending it. "Calhoun is a dead man. He must be shunned by all loyal Democrats as a disturber of party harmony. War, open war, is now the cry," Amos Kendall bawled on February 21 in his *Globe* editorial, which was then repeated in hundreds of other pro-administration newspapers around the country. Calhoun and Green were to be "put down," and support for Green's *Telegraph* was now a thing of the past, and for Jacksonians, deservedly so. Kendall predicted that it would only take Blair a few short weeks to "torpedo Green with a few short hits." With no love loss for Green, Blair admitted the pleasure to do so would be all his.[1076]

The two newspapers engaged in a fierce exchange of salvos, igniting a titillating controversy. Similar to Jackson, Blair flourished in contentious situations, delivering editorial strikes that were spot on. With the dismissal of the *Telegraph*, the administration recognized the need for more than just a semiweekly publication to combat its challenges. Consequently, the *Globe* was upgraded to a daily newspaper. To support

---

[1075] The complete work can be found in the Telegraph, Feb. 17, 21, 23, 26, 1831; the essential parts are reprinted in Remini, ed. The Age of Jackson, New York, 1972, pp. 33-43; Williams to Van Buren, March 22, 1831, Van Buren Papers, LC; Henry Storrs to Abraham Van Vechten, Feb. 1831, Miscellaneous Storrs Papers, NYHS; Parton, Jackson III, p. 345; Marcus Morton to Calhoun, March 7, 1831, Miscellaneous Papers, MHS; Edward Everett to his wife, February 17, 1831; AJ to Charles J. Love, March 7, 1831, in Jackson, Correspondence, IV, 1831.

[1076] Kendall to Welles, March 19, 1831, Welles Papers, LC; Blair to Van Buren, December 9, 1858, Van Buren Papers, LC.

this transition monetarily, "the President's allies in Washington and beyond" were urged to "showcase their loyalty."[1077]

The newspapers blasted it out, front and center, in broad type: "Mr. Calhoun's attack on the President!" Condemns unequivocally Mr. Calhoun and the nullifiers!" The publication of this provocative headline sparked intense reactions, condemning Mr. Calhoun and the nullifiers without reservation. It raised the question: Were politicians misguided in claiming that "General Jackson's popularity could withstand anything?"[1078] In response, the President acted swiftly and decisively. Within a month of Congress adjourning, he removed three cabinet members—Ingham, Branch, and Berrien—who were allies of Calhoun. This timing was strategic; it allowed enough time for Mr. Calhoun's pamphlet to be effectively ridiculed in administration publications, making the issue appear to be less urgent. This typically firm Jackson move came during a relatively calm period ahead of the upcoming presidential election, nine months before any potential Senate confirmation challenges. It was a historically important moment when it came to the powers of the presidency.

Jackson claimed ownership himself of the choice to oust Calhoun and Duff Green from the Democratic Party came from Jackson himself, calling the vice president's publication an act of self-destruction. "They have cut their own throats, and destroyed themselves in a shorter space of time than any two men I ever knew. Without my consent," he complained, "they published part of my private letters. Surely, they deserve the fate that awaited them."[1079]

Despite how things seemed, these events were ideal for Jackson. They provided him with an opportunity to remove Calhoun and his associates without being seen as influenced by Eaton and his wife. This allowed him to restore unity within his cabinet by eliminating Calhoun's supporters.[1080] In fact, just five days after the announcement, it became clear that Samuel D. Ingham, the treasury secretary and a close ally of Calhoun, would be dismissed. Edward Everett wrote to his wife on February 2, 1831, stating, "Ingham and Green were the two most

---

[1077] Kendall, *Autobiography*, p. 379.
[1078] Parton, *Jackson*, III, 343.
[1079] AJ to Charles J. Love, March 7, 1831, in Jackson, *Correspondence*, IV, 246.
[1080] William S. Archer to Van Buren, March 12, 1831, Van Buren Papers.

dangerous and disloyal members of the administration, and once they are removed, a degree of harmony will be restored."[1081]

Most in Washington believed that Van Buren, the Little Magician, was responsible for the remarkable events unfolding at the time, for only he could craft such schemes. In a scathing accusation, Senator Samuel Bell of New Hampshire described Jackson as "an ignorant, weak, superannuated man, scarcely fitter for the office he holds than a child of ten years old would be," asserting that "Van Buren is president de facto"[1082] The belief that Van Buren was the master manipulator of events became so prevalent that Van Buren assumed Jackson and Calhoun had reconciled at his expense. In response, James A. Hamilton felt compelled to write to Jackson, assuring him of Van Buren's innocence. Hamilton, a key figure in initiating the revelations regarding the Seminole controversy, understood that Van Buren had not engaged in any deceitful actions. Regarding Calhoun's publication, Hamilton informed the General, "I have the best evidence to prove that Van Buren determined... to have no concern in the matter. It is manifest that he is the object of attack." Meanwhile, the wrongly accused Van Buren even believed that Jackson and Calhoun had reconciled.[1083]

The publication troubled the Secretary of State to no small degree, causing him to worry about its long-term implications for his career. His friends often wrote to inquire about the public's reaction, and their responses deeply unsettled him.[1084] He was aware of the gossip circulating but felt powerless to refute it. As a result, he reverted to his usual behavior: remaining silent and attempting to maintain an air of calm. He avoided making any comments and, when attending social gatherings, would often sit down at a card table to play whist for the evening, which helped him steer clear of company he disliked. Van Buren was truly a political magician.[1085]

[1081] Edward Everett to this wife, Feb. 2, 1831, Everett Papers, MHS.
[1082] Samuel Bell to William Plumer, Jan. 22, 1831, Samuel Bell Papers, NYHS.
[1083] Hamilton to AJ, February 24, 1831, in Hamilton, Reminiscences, page 196; Van Buren, Autobiography, page 377.
[1084] Henry L. Ellsworth to Van Buren, March 10, 1831; William S. Archer to Van Buren, March 12, 29, 1831; Van Buren to John Van Buren, March 27, 1831, Van Buren Papers, LC.
[1085] Edward Everett to his wife, Feb. 2, 1831, Everett Papers, MHS.

CHAPTER

71

A SECOND CABINET

"War, open war, is now the cry!"
–Amos Kendall

The intra-party divide put Van Buren in a difficult situation. The Little Magician from New York was forced to take on the role of scapegoat, becoming the perceived villain. He understood that, once the initial shock of the vice president's revelations faded, public sympathy would shift towards Jackson and Calhoun. Ultimately, Calhoun would be viewed as a wronged and innocent victim of a cunning plot, while Van Buren would be left to face the criticism alone. He would bear the "long-lasting" blame for the situation. Van Buren later reflected, "The offense charged against me was, in every respect, a heinous one... It would have been hard to imagine a case better suited to provoke the unmeasured condemnation of all good citizens." To many, Van Buren was soon to be a political ghost.[1086]

To protect himself and his career, the New Yorker had to turn things around. He had to win public sympathy, and the only thing he could think of was resignation. Nothing else would suffice. But the thought of it depressed him further. During the spring of 1831 he was noticed as "looking pale & spiritless—he has been much secluded of late and has not appeared at the fetes as heretofore."[1087]

[1086] Van Buren, Autobiography, p. 384; Henry Storrs to Abraham Van Vechten, Feb. 22, 1831, Miscellaneous Storrs Papers, NYHS.
[1087] McCall to Cadawalader, April 20, 1831, Cadawalader Papers, PHS.

Throughout all of these happenings, Jackson thought seriously about issuing a defense of the Seminole War and his actions in it. In it he would directly accuse Calhoun for misleading him intentionally into thinking he had supported him within the Monroe cabinet.[1088] Wisely, prudence dictated that he decide against it, which he did. The massive political cost of such a gratuitous endeavor, he realized, would be too much,[1089] and he put the idea to bed. Jackson began to see that the only solution was to remake his official family of advisors, something he had determined upon months before. But it would not be easy, fraught with public ridicule and scandal, for the purge of a cabinet by a president usually brings with it the loss of popular confidence in his ability to lead the nation. Still, he reasoned, he had to have a united cabinet, and this was the only way.

Although the decision to purge the cabinet was Jackson's, the way it happened resulted from Van Buren's need to withdraw himself from the awkward position the Calhoun downfall had placed him in.[1090] The "unmeasured condemnation" of him by "all good citizens" for his involvement in the vice president's situation seemed to leave him just one option: that he retire from his position. To do so might be seen as an active self-sacrifice to spare Jackson further humiliation. Maybe then he might inherit a measure of public sympathy. Also, Jackson would certainly interpret his martyrdom as undying loyalty, and the president's appreciation for such acts meant long-term security with the General. Thus, it only required a moment's thought for Van Buren to decide what he must do. He later convinced himself that his resignation was submitted to restore the general's peace and comfort, but make no mistake, Van Buren did it for himself. This was political survival.[1091]

Van Buren explained his reasons for resigning to his son Abraham, who totally agreed with him. The only real hurdle, as they both recognized, was the problem of explaining it to the president. It must be done carefully to avoid giving a wrong impression about his motivation. Several times Van Buren started to tell the president but fell silent at the crucial moment. His son teased him about his timidity. On one such occasion, Van Buren and Jackson were out horseback riding when a severe

---

[1088] Memorandum, Feb. 1831, Jackson Papers, LC.
[1089] Lewis to Overton, Jan. 13, 1831, Overton Papers, THS.
[1090] Edward Everett to his wife, Everett Papers, MHS.
[1091] Van Buren, *Autobiography*, 402

thunderstorm developed, and they took shelter in a small tavern near a racetrack. They were confined for several hours. Jackson's spirits were low. Donelson had returned to Tennessee to induce his wife to return to Washington under their uncle's conditions, and William B. Lewis was his only companion in the White House.[1092] Emotionally, Jackson was drained. He just sat there, saying nothing, looking morose. It was one of the lowest points in his life. Finally, the storm abated. The two men remounted and headed home on the wet roads, riding at a risky canter. Suddenly Jackson's horse slipped in the mud and almost threw his rider. Van Buren quickly seized the bridle, and the horse regained his footing.

"You have possibly saved my life, sir!" said Jackson. Then he muttered something to the effect that he wondered whether his escape from death had been fortunate or not. Seeing how depressed the president was, Van Buren could not bring himself to speak of resigning.[1093]

A few days later, the secretary tried again. It was a bright, sunny day and as usual the two men went riding. Passing Georgetown, Van Buren noticed he had lost his glove. He told the president to go on while he turned back to look for it. After finding it, Van Buren put his horse to a gallop to catch up. As he rode, he felt exhilarated. This is the moment, he thought. He caught up to Jackson, and just as they were turning from the Potomac toward Tenleytown, the president said something about feeling better once his niece and nephew returned. Their return, he felt, would provide some relief from his domestic troubles.

"No!" Cried Van Buren. "General, there is but one thing can give you peace.

"What is that, Sir?"

"My resignation!"

The words jolted the old soldier. Van Buren could never forget to look on Jackson's face as he pronounced the words. "Never, Sir!" Jackson responded in solemn tones, "even you know little of Andrew Jackson, if you suppose him capable of consenting to such a humiliation of his friend by his enemies."[1094]

The response was exactly as Van Buren feared. After all, what was the Eaton problem but a mistaken notion about friendship? Van Buren

---

[1092] Ibid, 402-403,
[1093] Ibid, 403.
[1094] Van Buren, *Autobiography*, 403.

fell silent for a moment. After collecting his thoughts, he pleaded that Jackson surely knew he would sooner "endure any degree of personal or official injustice and persecution" then appear to desert a friend. But the president had the nation to think about, said Van Buren. If he would just hear him out, he thought he "could satisfy him that the course I had pointed out was perhaps the only safe one open to us." [1095] For four hours Van Buren talked, and the president listened, his mind a cauldron of concern. Then he suddenly interjected a question for the New Yorker. What would Van Buren do if he accepted his resignation? Oh, Van Buren shrugged, return to the law.

"Out of the question," responded Jackson. That would be an admission of defeat. It would provide a "triumph to our enemies," and that he would never suffer without a fight.[1096] They talked of other possibilities. The English ambassadorship was mentioned. Not only would it provide a suitable situation for the New Yorker, but it would get him out of the country for a spell.

When the interview finally ended, Jackson said he would think the matter over, telling Van Buren to return the next day for further discussions. Jackson knew Van Buren must go. His resignation would simplify things by allowing the president to discharge Ingham, Berrien, and Branch, and improve the quality of the entire cabinet. Still, it would be hard to lose such a loyal, and capable man. Or was the little fellow deserting a sinking ship? He would soon find out.

Van Buren arrived at the White House early the next morning. He could tell from Jackson's appearance that he had put in a sleepless night. When he spoke, the president showed no emotion. He was "unusually formless and passionless." 58. Obviously something had not sat right with what Van Buren had tried to explain the previous day.

"Mr. Van Buren," said the General, "I have made it a rule through life never to throw obstacles in the way of any man who, for any reason satisfactory to himself, desires to leave me, and I shall not make your case an exception."[1097]

The words struck Van Buren like a sledgehammer. The secretary jumped from his chair before the president could say another word. This

---
[1095] Ibid, 404.
1096 Ibid.
[1097] Van Buren, *Autobiography*, 405.

was precisely what he feared, he cried, and he swore his motives were selfless. If only Jackson could pee into his heart and examine his quote in most thoughts," he would know the truth. "Now, Sir!" he declared, "Come what may, I shall not leave your Cabinet, not until you say "you are satisfied that it is best for us to part. I shall not only stay with you but… Stay with pleasure."[1098]

Jackson seized Van Buren's hand. The little man had responded with all the melodrama and sentimental gush the old man needed to hear. "You must forgive me, my friend," Jackson declared, "I have been too hasty in my conclusions–I know I have–say no more about it now, but come back at 1 o'clock-we will take another long ride and talk again in a better and calmer state of mind."[1099] Obviously, Jackson did not need convincing about the wisdom and necessity of Van Buren's resignation. What he needed was assurance that Van Buren acted out of loyalty. Otherwise, he would never have responded so emotionally and quickly to Van Buren's protests of devotion and fidelity.

By the time the two men met again, the matter was settled. Jackson asked Van Buren's permission to discuss the matter with Eaton, Lewis, and Barry--has only other trustworthy associates. That night he thrashed the matter out with his friends. Lewis had long championed Van Buren's cause and like everyone else he quickly saw the necessity of letting him go. It would ease the difficulty of demanding the resignation of the others. In the final discussion, Van Buren joined the group. When this parley ended, Van Buren invited them all to his house for supper to mark the occasion. As they were walking down the street, Eaton suddenly stopped them.

"Gentlemen," he exclaimed, "this is all wrong! Here we have a cabinet so remarkable that it has required all of the General's force of character to carry it along. There's but one man in it who is entirely fit for his place, and we were about consenting that he should leave it."[1100]

Everyone laughed, but Eaton persisted. Addressing Van Buren, he said: "Why should you resign? I am the man about whom all the trouble has been made, and therefore the one who ought to resign." Van Buren remained silent. What could he say? And no one else tried to talk Eaton out of it. Later they ask Peggy. Would she consent to his resignation? He

---

[1098] Ibid, 405-406.
[1099] Ibid. 406.
[1100] Van Buren, *Autobiography*, 406.

thought so, but he was asked to consult her first. When he reported back that she supported his decision, Jackson agreed to accept both resignations.

Many historians have assumed that Van Buren executed a "masterpiece"[1101] of manipulation in convincing Jackson to accept his resignation and of prompting Eaton to submit his own. Actually, there was no manipulation, and Van Buren has been vastly overrated as the precipitator of the cabinet dissolution. What he did came out of necessity. He was in a very awkward and dangerous position. Van Buren himself swears he never thought of inducing Eaton's resignation and there is every reason to believe him.[1102] Once the New Yorker resigned the obvious thing for Eaton to do was follow suit. Their departure then lightened the burden of dismissing the others.

In the final discussion, Eaton said he wished to submit his letter first, to which Van Buren cheerfully exceeded. On April 7, 1831, Eaton tendered his resignation and gave us as his reason his wish to retire to private life. On April 11 Van Buren followed as scheduled, but his letter alluded to the suspicions in charges brought against him and his desire to spare Jackson further distress from these unfounded accusations. The president responded graciously to both men, but his reply to Van Buren conveyed a real sense of loss. "In the most difficult and trying moments of my administration," he wrote, "I have always found you sincere, able, and efficient-- anxious at all times to afford me every aid."[1103]

The resignation of John Eaton from Jackson's cabinet members put an end to the Eaton/Petticoat Affair, but the residual damage lingered throughout most of 1831. The resignations of Eaton and Van Buren prompted Calhoun's allies within the cabinet, particularly Branch, Ingham and Berrian, to follow suit. Jackson set out to appoint a new Cabinet and later assigned Eaton roles away from Washington. Ultimately, Jackson agreed to dismiss nearly all his Cabinet members, dissolving almost an entire presidential cabinet for the first time in American history. Only William Barry remained on as the Postmaster-General, and preparations for replacements were already made before the dissolution became official. Jackson's first move was to call on longtime

---

[1101] James, *Jackson*, p. 557.
[1102] Van Buren, *Autobiography*, 406-407
[1103] Van Buren to AJ, April 11, 1831, AJ to Van Buren, April 12, 1831, in Jackson, *Correspondence*, IV, pp. 257-258, 260-263.

friend and colleague Edward Livingston, so instrumental during the Battle of New Orleans, and now Louisiana Senator, to offer him the position of Secretary of State, which Livingston readily accepted. He had recently settled a personal financial debt with the government, removing any threat of potential objection.

A new figure soon emerged in the President's cabinet, as Lewis Cass took on the role of head of the Department of War in July. At that time, Cass was relatively unknown to the broader public, despite having served in government for nearly a quarter of a century. His political career began in 1806 as a member of the Ohio legislature and he took part initiating measures against Aaron Burr, effectively thwarting Burr's ambitions in Mexico. Born in New Hampshire to a Revolutionary War veteran father, Cass embarked on a journey at the age of seventeen, walking across the Allegheny Mountains in search of opportunities in the western frontier. After studying law, he became a prominent figure in Ohio, gaining recognition from President Jefferson for his vigorous opposition to Burr, which led to his appointment as U.S. Marshal. Cass's service was marked by both ability and distinction, and he would later go on to become a Democratic presidential nominee.

Louis McLane, Minister to England, was recalled back to the states and Jackson offered him the position of Treasury Secretary, replacing Ingham. This would allow the Little Magician, Van Buren, to accept the English post. Judge Hugh L. White, Tennessee Senator, was to replace Eaton as Secretary of War. Eaton, then, was expected to be appointed as White's replacement in the Tennessee Senate. Levi Woodbury was chosen to become the new Secretary of the Navy.

Risky as it was, these bold measures aimed to achieve several goals. Most importantly to the president, he wanted a united cabinet, with unquestioning loyalty in advancing his agenda. Additionally, relocating Van Buren to a secure position abroad seemed the best choice not only to get him away from the controversy over the Calhoun feud, but to set him up for a later return as Jackson's successor. The President had expressed his intention that no cabinet member would succeed him. Another goal was to assist Eaton in overcoming his embarrassing situation and return him to the Senate.

On April 7, 1831, Eaton wrote to the president, "Dear Sir: Four days ago I communicated to you my desire to relinquish the duties of the War Department, and I now take occasion to repeat the request which was then made. I am not disposed, by any sudden withdrawal, to interrupt or retard the business of the office. A short time will be sufficient, I hope, to enable you to direct your attention toward some person in whose capacity, industry, and friendly disposition you may have confidence, to assist in the complicated and laborious duties of your administration. Two or three weeks—perhaps less—may be sufficient for the purpose. In coming to this conclusion, candor demands of me to say that it arises from no dissatisfaction entertained toward you— from no misunderstanding between us, on any subject; nor from any diminution, on my part, of that friendship and confidence which has ever been reposed in you. I entered your Cabinet, as is well known to you, contrary to my own wishes; and having nothing to desire, either as it regards myself or friends, have ever since cherished a determination to avail myself of the first favorable moment, after your administration should be in successful operation, to retire. It occurs to me that the time is now at hand when I may do so with propriety." [1104]

A dissolution of the cabinet, except at the end of a presidential term, had never happened before in the United States and has only occurred once since. This unexpected event caught the general public off guard, as they had no prior knowledge of the Eaton scandals and did not immediately see the link between the cabinet upheaval and the Calhoun pamphlet. Within three days of Van Buren's resignation announcement, a minor rumor of an impending change was repudiated in the Jackson papers. The event caused quite a stir, as at that time, official titles were highly regarded, and a cabinet member was held a lofty status. Washington seemed to tremble with anxiety. Adding to the impact of this dissolution was the fact that leading editors refused to provide a clear explanation, while other editors were unable to do so. Some vague references to 'Madame Pompadour' surfaced in print, but the Jackson papers fiercely refuted such claims.

The various administration newspapers, particularly *The Courier* and *Enquirer* tried their best to portray the dissolution as a boost for Van Buren, as it appears they were instructed by Jackson. At the time, Berrien's

---

[1104] Eaton, John. Resignation Letter to Andrew Jackson, Library of Congress Manuscript Division.

resignation had not yet taken place due to his absence from Washington. "What has Mr. Calhoun gained by the firebrand he has thrown into the democratic ranks? Mr. Van Buren, it is true, has retired from office, but he returns to a State where his political knowledge and consistency are invaluable—a State that can and will support him for the highest office when the proper time arrives. Mr. Calhoun has strengthened Mr. Van Buren by his violent opposition—he has returned from the cabinet and is thrown back on the people with a higher reputation for disinterested zeal. and upright principles. In this movement, however, Mr. Calhoun has sacrificed Mr. Ingham and Mr. Branch, his two friends; and the members of the new cabinet are not assailable on any point. How stands the case, then? General Jackson has lost two friends in his cabinet and gained four. Mr. Van Buren becomes a private citizen, and mingles again with his political friends in an energetic support of the President. On all sides General Jackson is strengthened and his enemies discomfited; well indeed, may Mr. Van Buren be called the 'great Magician,' for he raises his wand and the whole cabinet vanishes. What will Mr. Calhoun now say to this new order of things? His friends will not venture to declare that Mr. Van Buren rules General Jackson—they can not say that Mr. Van Buren at Albany manages the affairs of the administration at Washington. All motives for assailing Mr. Van Buren are at an end; trouble and difficulty have been produced, but on whom does it fall— who suffers, who almost staggers under the blow? Mr. Calhoun and his impudent advisers."

A short time later Jackson and Van Buren took a walk and suddenly found themselves in front of the home of the Eatons. On the spur of the moment, they decided to pay the lady of the house a visit. But their reception was distinctly "formal and cold." Peggy made it very clear that she was deeply disappointed in the president over the resignation of her husband. They stayed long enough to know that her attitude was no "passing freak," but rather a "matured sentiment." A few moments after they left the house, Van Buren turned to Jackson and expressed his surprise at her attitude. "There has been some mistake here," he said.

Jackson shrugged. "It is strange," he muttered, and turned away.[1105]

[1105] Van Buren, *Autobiography*, pp. 407-408.

CHAPTER

72

EXECUTIVE STRUGGLES

"He asserts a right of individual judgment on constitutional questions, which is totally inconsistent with any proper administration of the government, or any regular execution of the laws."

-Daniel Webster

To so many Jacksonians, Andrew Jackson, President of the United States, was larger than life. Jackson was, ultimately however, just a man. Throughout his first term, he struggled with poor health, and at times, it seemed unlikely he would survive. Old wounds plagued him, and on one occasion, he exposed his shoulder while gripping his cane, as a surgeon removed a bullet from Jesse Benton's pistol. The procedure, by Dr. Harris of Philadelphia was swift. Jackson held out his arm, grit his teeth, and said, "go ahead."[1106] The surgeon made an incision, squeezed the arm, and out popped a half ball of metal, mangled on one end from the contusion with the bone. Jackson, although ill with influenza, had the dressing applied and went right back to work. Still, though, due to the flu, he was too ill to complete his tour of New England and hastened back to Washington.

However, his opponents had little cause for celebration regarding his condition. Before long, he resolved to undertake one of the boldest actions of his public career. Although he was opposed to a new charter for the Bank, it remained intact, still holding the public funds and

---

[1106] Parton, Jackson, III, p. 415.

wielding significant influence in the business world. He suspected that the Bank's president, Nicholas Biddle was using money to oppose him and believed that eventually, Biddle would achieve his goals in Congress. Consequently, he considered ways to weaken the Bank, one that Jackson began to contemplate at this time was a drastic one. By withdrawing public deposits and redistributing them among various banks across the country, Jackson could dismantle Biddle's Bank, and hence, his power. But this was tantamount to a Bank War. On that though, Old Hickory smiled.

Biddle, known for his handsome appearance, eloquent writing, and cleverness as a financier—was usually very cautious in his financial dealings. His sharp writing skills initially led to his downfall, however. Democratic Senators Isaac Hill and Levi Woodbury from New Hampshire lodged complaints against Jeremiah Mason, an old Federalist and president of the Branch Bank in Portsmouth. Their allegations varied, but they fueled Jackson's belief that the Branch Bank was misusing its influence to undermine his supporters and assist the Adams faction.

Biddle was tasked with investigating these claims. He thoroughly examined the situation and staunchly defended Mason against all accusations. This led to an extensive correspondence, during which Biddle traveled from Philadelphia, the headquarters of the Bank, to Portsmouth. His letters to the Secretary of the Treasury were not only polite and well-articulated but also assertive. He argued that it was Jackson's allies attempting to politicize the Bank, which had consistently maintained its neutrality.

Biddle presented a compelling case; however, as the correspondence continued, Jackson's conviction that the Bank was entangled in political affairs grew stronger. He believed it was actively opposing him, corrupt, and a threat to the freedoms of the common people who had elected him to the presidency. Biddle had unintentionally vilified the Jackson family in his efforts to defend his Bank branch. Meanwhile, he solidified that enmity by seeming to ally himself with Jackson enemy number one, Henry Clay.

Henry Clay and his supporters had smarted since Jackson had destroyed the Maysville Road with his veto. The fire-eaters of Calhoun's home state now branded Jackson a traitor, and number one on their hit list, and for New Englanders who had wished to see Adams or Webster in charge, Jackson was, and always would be, a dolt who could barely spell his name. Many who felt his tactics were a bit too reminiscent of George III, now took to referring to him sarcastically as King Andy. What was brewing was the formation of a new political party, dedicated to the opposition of King Andy, and they would call themselves the Whigs.

To add more fuel to the growing fire of conflict between Jackson and Congress, Van Buren's nomination as the new minister to England came before the Senate, where Vice-President Calhoun, just prior to leaving office, cast the deciding vote on an arranged tie against the nomination. It was a great session for the orators, particularly Thomas Hart Benton, who argued for the Jackson nomination. Ultimately Clay, Webster and Calhoun had their way. Rejected for the post, Van Buren, who had already assumed his station abroad, now came home as a political martyr, Jackson's choice for vice-president in 1832, and his heir apparent to the presidency. Some have argued that Congress' rejection of the diplomat post was the best thing that ever happened to the Little Magician.

The vacant attorney-generalship was eventually conferred upon Roger B. Taney, then Attorney-General of Maryland, and later to become the Chief Justice of the Supreme Court. Taney was an accomplished lawyer in his native state and was one of the Federalists who had given zealous support to General Jackson in 1828.

McLane, who arrived back in the United States in the late summer of 1831 to take the mantle of the Treasury department, was a native of Delaware, where he studied law under James A. Bayard, known in political history as the friend and correspondent of Alexander Hamilton. McLane, like Hamilton, was initially a Federalist, and a friend to the Bank of the United States. He had distinguished himself, in London, by the zeal and ability with which he conducted important negotiations and was said to be one of the numerous aspirants to the presidency.

As the disruption of the Cabinet occurred in April, and McLane did not return to the country until August, there was an interregnum in the Treasury Department of more than three months. It was during this time in which tumultuous events took place. A few weeks after Jackson's dissolution of his cabinet, the scandalous stories of Peggy Eaton hit the newspapers, and, at length, the various accounts of Ingham, Branch, and Berrien appeared. John Eaton, driven to near outrage by all the negative publicity, wrote an angry, and very discrediting letter to Samuel Ingham that resulted in a back-and-forth exchange of hostile letters between the two.

In the letter, Eaton vented his frustration over the alleged defamatory remarks published in the U.S. *Telegraph*, which he has tried to disregard while confirmation of the truth of Ingham's accusations against him and his family.[1107] A specific claim made by his wife regarding the refusal of key government officials to associate with her, questioning whether the recipient of the letter endorses or disavows this publication, given its appearance in a paper purportedly supportive of him. "In that paper of this evening is contained the following remark of my wife: 'It is proved that the Secretaries of the Treasury, and of the Navy, and of the Attorney-General refused to associate with her.' This publication appears in a paper which professes to be friendly to you, and is brought forth under your immediate eye. I desire to know of you, whether or not you sanction, or will disavow it." Eaton demanded an immediate response from Ingham.[1108]

Ingham replied in impudent fashion, according to John Eaton: " Sir: I have not been able to ascertain, from your note of last evening, whether it is the publication referred to by you, or the fact stated in the Telegraph, which you desire to know whether I have sanctioned or will disavow. If it be the first you demand, it is too absurd to merit an answer. If it be the last, you may find authority for the same fact in a Philadelphia paper, about the first of April last, which is deemed to be quite as friendly to you as the Telegraph may be to me. When you have settled such accounts with your particular friends, it will be time enough to make demands of others. In the meantime, I take the occasion to say, that you must be a little deranged, to imagine that any blustering of yours could induce me to disavow what all the inhabitants of this city know, and perhaps half the people of the United States believe to be true. I am, sir, respectfully yours, S. D. Ingham."[1109]

The very same day, an infuriated Eaton replied, "Sir: I have received your letter of to-day, and regret to find that to a frank and candid inquiry brought before you, an answer impudent and insolent is returned. To

---
[1107] *United States Telegraph*, editorial, June, 1831. Green, Duff, editor,
[1108] Eaton to Ingham, June 17, 1831, Parton, *Jackson*, III, pp. 364-365.
[1109] Ingham to Eaton, June 18, 1831, ibid, III, 365.

injury unprovoked, you are pleased to add insult. What is the remedy! It is to indulge the expectation that, though a man may be mean enough to slander, or base enough to encourage it, he yet may have bravery sufficient to repair the wrong. In that spirit I demand of you satisfaction for the wrong and injury you have done me. Your answer must determine whether you are so far entitled to the name and character of a gentleman as to be able to act like one. Very respectfully, J. H. Eaton.

Ingham's reply came two days later, "Sir: Your note of Saturday, purporting to be a demand of satisfaction for injury done to you was received on that day; company prevented me from sending an immediate answer. Yesterday morning your brother-in-law, Dr. Randolph, intruded himself into my room with a threat of personal violence. I perfectly understand the part you are made to play in the farce now acting before the American people. I am not to be intimidated by threats, or provoked by abuse, to any act inconsistent with the pity and contempt which your condition and conduct inspire. Yours, sir, respectfully, S. D. Ingham."

Eaton scribbled off another hasty reply that same day, "Sir: Your note of this morning is received. It proves to me that you are quite brave enough to do a mean action, but too great a coward to repair it. Your contempt I heed not; your pity I despise. It is such contemptible fellows as yourself that have set forth rumors of their own creation, and taken them as a ground of imputation against me. If that be good cause, then should you have pity of yourself, for your wife has not escaped them, and you must know it. But no more; here our correspondence closes. Nothing more will be received short of an acceptance of my demand of Saturday, and nothing more be said to me until face to face we meet. It is not in my nature to brook your insults, nor will they be submitted to. J. H. Eaton.

The next day Eaton attempted to carry his threat into execution. In a letter to the President, Mr. Ingham gave a version of the events of that day: "It is not necessary for me now to detail the circumstances which have convinced me of the existence of vindictive personal hostility to me among some of the officers of the government near your person, and supposed to be in your special confidence, which has been particularly developed within the last two weeks, and has finally displayed itself in an attempt to waylay me on my way to my office yesterday, as I have reason to believe, for the purpose of assassination. If you have not already been apprised of these movements, you may perhaps be surprised to learn that the persons concerned in them are the late Secretary of War and the acting Secretary of War; and that the Second Auditor of the Treasury, Register of the Treasury, and the Treasurer of the United States, were in their company; and that the Treasurer's and Register's rooms, in the lower part of the building of the Treasury Department, and also a grocery store between my lodgings and the office, were alternately occupied as their rendezvous while lying in wait—the former affording the best opportunity for observing my approach. Apprised of these movements, on my return from taking leave of some of my friends, I found myself obliged to arm, and, accompanied by my son and some other friends, I repaired to the office to finish the business of the day, after which I returned to my lodgings in the same company. It is proper to state, that the principal persons who had been thus employed for several hours, retired from the Department soon after I entered my room, and that I received no molestation from them, either at my ingress or egress."[1110]

On Monday morning, June 20th, 1831, Eaton and his group of cronies, who happened to be men of some of the loftiest positions in the United States government, including Lewis, Randolph, Colonel John Campbell (the Treasurer of the United States), and Major Thomas L. Smith (the register of the Treasury), searched the city high and low for the former Secretary of the Treasury Samuel D. Ingham, who believed that they were "lying in wait" for one purpose: assassination. The Eaton party positioned themselves outside of the Treasury and at a nearby grocery store close to Ingham's lodging on F Street. Duff Green informed William Cabell Rives that the suspicious movements of the group prompted Ingham's son to warn his father. Upon learning of the danger, Ingham armed himself and, with the help of his son and a few friends, was able to go to work and return home safely. The presence of daylight likely deterred Eaton's forces, and Ingham's unexpected show of strength likely played a key role as well. Duff Green wrote that Ingham's "firmness ... backed by his friends" frightened Eaton, who "felt his courage oozing out of his fingers' ends and immediately left the building without noise or bloodshed."[1111]

[1110] Ingham to AJ, June 18, 1831, AJ to Ingham, June 23, 1831, in Jackson, *Correspondence*, IV, 231.
[1111] *United States Telegraph*, June, 1831.

However, this momentary retreat did not last long. By nightfall, Eaton had regrouped and gathered additional forces. Ingham recalled, "But having recruited an additional force in the evening, they paraded until a late hour on the streets near my lodgings, heavily armed, threatening an assault on the dwelling I reside in." Seeking intervention, Ingham appealed to President Jackson, emphasizing Jackson's duty to maintain order in the District of Columbia. Ultimately, Ingham concluded that it was unwise to rely on Jackson's support, knowing his loyalty to his fellow Tennessean, and considering that guessing wrong could mean life or death.

That same day, the President immediately addressed a letter to each of the officials charged with "waylaying" Ingham, enclosed to each a copy of Ingham's letter, and asked to be informed whether "you, or either of you, have had any agency or participation, and if any, to what extent, in the alleged misconduct imputed in his letter herewith enclosed." Every man of them denied in full Ingham's accusations and Eaton had an article published in the paper exonerating his friends and playing the wholly innocent victim himself.

"From the moment" said Eaton, "that I perceived Mr. Ingham was incapable of acting as became a man, I resolved to pursue that course which was suited to the character of one who had sought difficulties and shunned all honorable accountability. I harbored no design upon the heart of one who had shown himself so heartless. Having ascertained that his sensibilities were to be found only upon the surface, I meant to make the proper application. On the 19th I notified him that unless the call I had made upon him was promptly and properly answered, he might expect such treatment as I thought his conduct deserved. My note of the 20th also advised him of my intention. Accordingly, it appeared a matter of duty for me to dissolve all connection with the administration of the government. How, then, can Ingham suppose that I would involve those gentlemen in a disgraceful conspiracy against him; one in which, as public officers, they could not engage even if inclination had sanctioned it. Their own characters are a sufficient answer to the accusation, unaided by their positive denial of its truth. I did endeavor to meet Mr. Ingham, and to settle our differences. Unattended by anyone, I sought after and awaited his appearance during the accustomed hours for business, openly and at places where he daily passed to his office. He was not to be found!

I passed by, but at no time stopped at or attempted to enter his house, nor to besiege it by day or by night."[1112]

The next day Ingham, finding the city of Washington neither a safe nor a comfortable dwelling place, left it in disgust, unwilling to risk his luck any further, he took a stagecoach to Baltimore, as the *Globe* reported, in terror. He took the "whole of the four o'clock stage," said the *Globe*, and induced the driver to make excellent time to Baltimore."[1113] Ingham sought refuge at his home in Bucks County, Pennsylvania. Meanwhile, Jackson departed for a vacation at the Rip Raps, and Eaton's plans remained uncertain. A correspondent of Henry Clay's reported that Eaton's actions were "most ridiculous and even crazy," and reason appeared to be absent from Eaton's decision-making. Eaton lingered in the city, according to Duff Green, who reported rumors about the Eatons' intentions to leave for Tennessee circulated, with Green suggesting that Peggy would resist any attempts to exile her from Washington.

John Eaton eventually dragged his wife away from Washington, and the two returned home. Eaton ran for the Senate back in Tennessee and lost, but soon Jackson appointed him Governor of Florida, where he had lands and lots believed to be valuable. Less than two years later, the President sent him to represent the United States at the court of Spain. Upon his return home, Eaton had a falling out with his old chief, and the two remained unreconciled until the day of his death.

Ingham's escape on that harrowing June day likely saved his life. Rather than protecting the district or reprimanding officials like Lewis, acting Secretary of War, Jackson seemed to take perverse pleasure in Ingham's plight, ridiculing Ingham's flight as cowardly, while rewarding his old friend John Eaton with a new political post. In response to Ingham's concerns, Jackson dismissed the allegations about the confrontation, simply insisting the men Ingham mentioned denied any wrongdoing.

However, to Andrew Donelson, Jackson was more candid. He confirmed that Eaton had indeed sought Ingham, spending time in a grocery store after wandering the streets. Jackson suggested that Ingham's guards posed a greater threat than anyone, claiming they were prepared to shoot Eaton if he attacked. It is quite revealing for the president of

---

[1112] Eaton to AJ, in Parton, Jackson, III, 368.
[1113] *The Washington Globe*, editorial, June, 1831, Washington, FP Blair. 1830-1845.

the United States to have such a blase attitude about a department head seeking to kill another on the streets.

It was an abysmal summer for the administration. The Telegraph ran daily stories ridiculing the shenanigans of the fallout from the "Eaton malaria." While Blair's Globe editorials defended the administration, National Republicans spoke confidently about the slim chance Jackson had of being reelected. "To what new developments are these things to lead? Governor John Floyd of Virginia lamented, "Step after step our degradation seems hurrying on." [1114]

Meanwhile, as the turbulent waves of Jackson's cabinet dramas were unfolding, two former presidents met up in New York City at Prince and Marion Streets, not far from the Bowery. John Quincy Adams visited the Dutch roof house of Mr. and Mrs. Samuel Gouverneur. Mrs. Gouverneur was the daughter of former President James Monroe, who had come to live with her in his old age. General Lafayette often visited there as well, and a boy who frequented the Gouverneurs' home recalled President Monroe in satin knee breeches, sitting by a grate in the Gouverneurs' "dingy" parlor.

During Adams' visit, Monroe, now elderly and nearing death, relished the opportunity to discuss politics and foreign affairs with a fellow former president. With Washington, the senior Adams, and Jefferson all deceased, only Madison remained alive at Montpelier. The incumbent president, Andrew Jackson, dominated the conversation as the two men shifted from discussing the latest European violence to what Adams termed "the recent quasi revolution at Washington." The chaotic events within the Jackson administration profoundly offended the orderly sensibilities of the two former presidents, who had once pursued peace and tranquility. Adams remarked to another friend, "If other revolutions partake of the sublime, this one entirely and exclusively belongs to the next step"—the ridiculous. Ridiculous it was, and the absurd theater begs the question of the Jackson administration: Were the inmates running the asylum?

[1114] Floyd to John Barbour, June 24, 1831, Miscellaneous Floyd Papers, LC.

CHAPTER

73

THAT ABOMINABLE TARIFF

"Disunion by armed force is TREASON."
-Andrew Jackson

On December 28, with only a few months remaining in his second term, John C. Calhoun, seeing the writing on the wall, resigned as vice president and returned to South Carolina. The fiery "Cast-Iron Man" did not sit idle for long, however, as the hero of the Palmetto State was soon elected to the United States Senate, which he had presided over for years. Now hardened, and more guarded than ever, he was determined to become the nation's leading advocate for states' rights and slavery. Calhoun's departure from Jackson's fold set up the ensuing discord over the tariff issue that would threaten to disrupt the harmony of the nation. "The amber waves of strain" that the growing rift between north and south, federal and state, Jackson and Calhoun caused was a powder keg set to ignite, and disunite the nation, and the impacts it would lead to, nullification and secession, would continue to be felt for years to come.

Yet, although his pride had been wounded, Calhoun was feeling confident. After an energetic day of rallying North Carolinians in Raleigh, the state capital, to support nullification, he arrived back in Washington and checked into Brown's Hotel. Edward Livingston had not replied back to his vice-presidential resignation letter. From his hotel, he tried again to coax a letter from Livingston, hoping for some sort of salve for his wounded ego. He asked Livingston "to inform me by the bearer whether it has been received."[1115] Despite what he felt was Livingston's lack of manners, Calhoun believed that events were moving favorably for him. With Jackson's annual message on states' rights being so poorly received, as well as the nationalist proclamation, things did not seem, for once, to be going Jackson's way. "Our cause is doing well," Calhoun wrote on January 10, 1833. "Let our people go on; be firm and prudent; give no pretext for force, and I feel confident of a peaceable and glorious triumph for our cause and our state."[1116]

Tensions between Andrew Jackson and John C. Calhoun did not end with Calhoun's resignation as vice president. Nor did tensions over South Carolina's disdain for the tariff. On the contrary, the conflict would only increase as the months and years passed, and soon these tensions had a name: the Nullification Crisis. A crisis of epic proportions, it was, one that would foreshadow the conflicts of the late 1850s that would lead the Civil War, and nearly the demise of the Union.

Throughout, as he did with his stern toast against any attempts to undermine federal authority, Jackson would reinforce his dedication to the Union, when Calhoun and South Carolina would make the consequential decision to adopt an "Ordinance of Nullification." This ordinance aimed to nullify the tariffs of 1828 and 1832, arguing that they were "unauthorized by the Constitution of the United States, violate its true meaning and intent, and are null, void, and no law, nor binding upon this state."

In response, Jackson issued one of the boldest proclamations from any president: "Strict duty" required him to uphold the Constitution to maintain the Union, a Union established during the Revolution to unite the states for their "common interest" and not the "impractical absurdity" of a single state defying the others. Jackson further stated: "I consider, then, the power to annul a law of the United States, assumed by one State, incompatible with the existence of the Union, contradicted expressly by the letter of the Constitution, unauthorized by its spirit, inconsistent with every principle on which it was founded, and destructive of the great object for which it was formed."

[1115] Edward Livingston Papers Collection (1764-1836), 1832, Princeton University.
[1116] Calhoun Papers, IV, Jan. 10, 1833, National Archives.

Old Hickory emphasized his point by referencing his own South Carolinian heritage: even as a native of that state (sort of), he prioritized the common good of the Union over the specific interests of his home state. Hoping to forge a common bond with South Carolinians, Jackson was still compelled to candidly address the significant issue: South Carolina's nullification efforts brought the state to the "brink of insurrection and treason."

Since his childhood hiding in the Carolina countryside on the lookout for British soldiers, Jackson loved being in on secrets. As president, he was no different, maintaining both a formal and informal network, gathering bits and pieces of political intelligence. In the South, Joel Poinsett, a diplomat, world traveler, and firm Unionist who was Jackson's main source of information in the region, was hearing talk of conspiracy and rebellion. "I know not how things are moving over in Charleston, but with us the nullifiers are in motion and are endeavoring to rally their scattered forces for a new contest in 1832. Alexander Speer, a former comptroller general of South Carolina, wrote to Poinsett early in 1831 from church Hill in Abbeville, near the western edge of South Carolina, "I will not be at all surprised if at the next election, Mr. Calhoun's name shall be brought forward as a candidate." A repeat of 1824 with Calhoun and Henry Clay in the villainous roles was under consideration, Speer said. And he thought his information was bulletproof. "The understanding appears that Mr. Calhoun's name is to be run as a candidate, not because it is expected that he can be elected, but to defeat the election by the people and thus, throw it into the House of Representatives, where it can be managed as to their best interests. This junto are making open declarations of hostility to the Union and expect roundly that civil war must and shall be the consequence. As to General Jackson, their hostility is unequivocal."[1117]

Such strong-armed measures might have intimidated the likes of John Quincy Adams (although Adams proved his resilience through years of legislative battles in Congress post-presidency), or another less oppositional president, but Andrew Jackson was the wrong man to stare down. The cantankerous Jackson was not a die-hard supporter of the tariff, but he was a strong Unionist, and he would not tolerate defiance

---

[1117] Speer to Poinsett, 1831, Joel Poinsett Papers, NYPL Archives,

or disunion. His military instincts kindled, Jackson privately threatened to invade the state and have the nullifiers hanged. In public he was only slightly less bellicose. In early 1833, declaring that states did not have the right of nullification, Jackson urged Congress to pass the Force Bill, which would empower the commander-in-chief to use military force to collect the tariff from South Carolina, if necessary. Congress responded supportively, putting forward a motion to allow the president to relocate customs houses and to require that customs duties be paid in cash. The Force Bill was approved, and it authorized the use of armed forces to protect customs officials and enforce collection of tariffs.

Calhoun and the South Carolinians welcomed the opportunity to extract themselves from this precarious situation without losing face. To the dismay of Calhoun supporters, no other southern state had come to the aid of South Carolina in their stand against federal power. Though Georgia and Virginia considered an alliance with the Palmetto State, in the end, each state decided against it. Furthermore, a substantial Unionist minority amidst the palm-fronds of South Carolina was gathering weaponry and nailing the Stars and Stripes to flagpoles in a show of support for Jackson's government.

Meanwhile, Jackson dispatched naval and military reinforcements to the Palmetto State, while quietly preparing a sizable army. Making good on his threats, Jackson also issued a ringing proclamation against nullification, to which Hayne, now the governor of South Carolina, responded with a counter-proclamation. The lines were drawn. If civil war was to be averted, one side was going to have to back down, or both would be forced to compromise. Yet, in the end, cooler heads prevailed, and civil war was averted, largely (and ironically) through the diplomatic efforts of one of Jackson's worst enemies, Henry Clay, who, despite not being an ally of Calhoun's either, negotiated a compromise tariff with the fierce South Carolinian. Although a supporter of tariffs himself, the brave Kentuckian threw his weight behind a compromise bill that gradually reduced the Tariff of 1832 by roughly ten percent over a period of eight years. By 1842, the rates would be back to the mildly protective level of 1816. The ensuing Compromise Tariff of 1833 narrowly squeezed through Congress after bitter debates. Naturally, most of the opposition came from New England and the Middle States. Both the "Force Bill" and the Compromise Tariff were passed on the same day, allowing

Jackson's executive power as Commander-in-Chief to stand while also addressing the tariff issue through Congressional action.

Neither Jackson nor the nullifiers won an outright victory in 1833. Much to the consternation of the president, it was Henry Clay who came out of the crisis smelling like roses. Hailed in Charleston and Boston alike for saving the country, and defusing what looked like an incendiary situation, Clay was the true hero of the hour. The reduced tariff compromise was credited almost entirely to Clay, who was now in the Senate, and more than ever the great conciliator, adding another notch to his belt.

Riding in on his white horse, Clay had again stepped forward in the nation's hour of need, much as he had during the Missouri crisis. An unforgiving adversary of Jackson's, Clay had no desire to see his old enemy win new accolades by trouncing Calhoun publicly, nor did he wish to see Jacksonians swoon to Old Hickory's heroic return from South Carolina with scalps hanging from his belt. Calhoun and the South favored the compromise, so it was very evident that Jackson would not have to use the firepower he had prepared and pointed directly at Charleston. Yet, both Jackson and Congress did not wish to look weak, so in light of the Compromise Tariff, partly as a federal effort to save face, Congress passed the Force Bill that Jackson had asked for. South Carolinians referred to this measure as the "Bloody Bill," as it authorized the president to use the army and navy, if necessary, to collect federal tariff duties.

While the nullifiers in South Carolina convened a week later to nullify the "Bloody" Force Bill, an even more dangerous idea took root among some southerners: nullification was no longer a viable option within the Union. Consequently, less than a generation later, their perceived last resort became a fundamental principle of the Confederacy's political philosophy: the right to secede. The seeds of secession had now been planted. Fortunately for the Union, all parties involved (Jackson, Clay, Calhoun, and ultimately Congress) favored the Compromise Tariff, and given this reduction, South Carolina repealed its nullification of the tariff laws. But, sending an ominous message for future consideration, the Palmetto State also spitefully voted to nullify the Force Bill, though its provisions were no longer necessary, as the bite had been taken out of the protective tariff.

As noted, not everyone in South Carolina favored nullification, let alone secession. The eyes on the ground for Jackson, the afore-mentioned Joel Poinsett, a strong supporter of Jacksonian democracy, was a Unionist leader in South Carolina during this period. For two months during the heat of the crisis, Poinsett wrote long, impassioned letters to Jackson, without getting the type of response from the president that he sought. Finally, on November 29th, 1832, he wrote to Jackson, this time practically begging him for reassurance. "We had rather die than submit to the tyranny of such an oligarchy as J.C. Calhoun, James Hamilton, Robert Y. Hayne and McDuffie, and we implore our sister states and the federal government to rescue us from these lawless and reckless men." Poinsett pointed out that other Unionists in South Carolina believed that "Congress will say to us, 'Let South Carolina go out of the Union if she will go .... if such a course should be adopted, the Union must be dissolved in all its parts and foreign and domestic wars necessarily ensue. Whereas if these bad men are put down by the strong arm, the Union will be cemented by their conduct and by the vigor of the government, and you will earn the imperishable glory of having preserved this great confederacy from destruction."[1118]

Jackson certainly understood Poinsett's sentiments and could sympathize with the South Carolinians. Thus, on December 2nd, the president made his own opinion clear. "I fully concur with you in your views of nullification. It leads directly to civil war and bloodshed and deserves the execration of every friend of the country." While he assured Poinsett that the government would ensure Unionist support in the case of an armed struggle, he cautioned "calmness and firmness." The law, Jackson asserted, would be "duly executed, but by proper means."[1119] While the president wished to flatten Charleston with force, his more cool-headed advisors won the day, reminding the General that he did not want to strike the first blow that might cause an explosion of civil war.

Two days later, Jackson had his nephew Andrew Donelson, his most trusted assistant, carry his newly penned annual presidential message to Capitol Hill. The tone was conciliatory, "This is all we want, peaceably to nullify the nullifiers." Jackson told Van Buren. Keeping his

---
[1118] Poinsett to AJ, Nov. 29,1832, Jackson Papers, LC; Quoted in Meacham, pg. 225.
[1119] AJ to Poinsett, Dec. 2, 1832, Jackson Papers, LC.

temperament under control, Jackson, with the help of the talented mind of Edward Livingston, crafted a message very Jeffersonian in spirit. Opposing nullification, it also advocated tariff reform, and at times resembled a states' rights defense. Overly high protective tariffs, Jackson insisted, created "discontent and jealousy dangerous to the stability of the Union."[1120] Jackson had promised to eliminate the national debt, and he spoke of the impacts this positive step would have on the crisis, as the theoretical necessity of the tariff would become obsolete as the need for great sources of federal revenue would be eliminated in the process.

Bringing to mind images of simpler Republican virtues of earlier generations, Jackson's annual presidential message of late 1832 offered an assuaging vision of life and governance: "not calculated to restrict human liberty, but to enforce human rights, this government will find its strength and its glory in the faithful discharge of these plain and simple duties." Initially the message was to many in Congress, perplexing, and incongruous to Jackson's maneuvers behind the scenes. Congressman John Quincy Adams considered it "a complete surrender to the nullifiers of South Carolina."[1121] Yet, Jackson's supporters saw it for what they believed it was: a rhetorical strategy designed to isolate South Carolina by showing the federal government to be fair and reasonable in regard to the issues at hand. Simultaneously, though, those who knew of his not-so-secret military preparations recognized that Jackson had the leverage that came with strength, which shored up the spirits of the Unionists in South Carolina, knowing the federal government could fight and win if needed.

On December 7th, just three days after Jackson's message was read to Congress, Poinsett received assuring news from Secretary of War Lewis Cass. "The president has instructed me to inform you that 5,000 stands of arms and 1,000 rifles, the propriety of placing which in depot at Charleston was suggested by you, have been ordered to that place, and that directions have been given to General [Winfield] Scott for issuing them for the use of any portion of the citizens of South Carolina for

---

[1120] AJ to Van Buren, Nov. 31, 1832, Jackson Papers, LC.
[1121] JQA, *Adams Memoirs*, IV, 1832.

the defense of the laws of the Union."[1122] In other words, Jackson was demonstrating that the Force Bill was more than just words; he meant action.

In the end, Jackson's actions in pushing forward the Force Bill were seen by nationalists as a heroic move that preserved the integrity of the Union. His forceful stand, though rankling the pride of many South Carolinians, underscored the primacy of the federal government. Yet dodging the bullet of secession and war in 1833 would prove to be only a temporary reprieve. Once again, the government of the United States failed to address the real dilemma, the differing views on the necessity of slavery between north and south.

Jackson was alone in his office, standing at his desk when he started writing what would later be known as the famous "Nullification" document. With a steel pen in hand, he moved swiftly from page to page—so swiftly, in fact, that it was later reported that Jackson had to spread the pages across his desk to allow them to dry: "A gentleman who came in when the president had written 15 or 20 pages observed that three of them were glistening with wet ink at the same moment."[1123] In a rush of inspiration, Jackson outlined his stance on states' rights and nullification, intent on conveying to the American people the importance of Union and critiquing the concept of nullification. The pages of the document were sent across Lafayette Square to the prominent Decatur House, where Edward Livingston was tasked with polishing up Jackson's rough draft. Refined by Livingston, the final version was a collaborative effort between Jackson and Livingston, with input from William H. Drew, on the ideas that Livingston had outlined in the Senate in 1830. These ideas centered around affirming the concept of union and a strong critique of nullification. The document ran to approximately 8,700 words.

As the document was being prepared for publication, William Lewis suggested a change. His suggestion was aimed at appealing to Americans who believed in states' rights, but did not support nullification. Jackson, too, did not wish to alienate the states' rights folks, the majority of whom were his own constituents, so he was open to hearing Lewis out, but

---

[1122] Cass to Poinsett, Cass Papers, LOC; "Force Bill of 1832". Law, March 02, 1832. From Teaching American History. https://teachingamericanhistory.org/document/force-bill-of-1832/ (accessed July 18, 2025).

[1123] AJ Donelson to Emily Donelson, Dec. 9, 1832, Donelson Papers, LC.

ultimately, he stated that there would be no compromise or quarter given on the issue. "Those are my views, and I will not change them or strike them out," Jackson said. The final version of the document, therefore, remained steadfast in its support for the Union and its opposition to nullification, and became a notable aspect of the Jackson presidency.[1124]

Jackson's views were intensely nationalistic. Nullification, he said, was "incompatible with the existence of the Union, contradicted expressly by the letter of the constitution, unauthorized by its spirit, inconsistent with every principle on which it was founded, and destructive of the great object for which it was formed." Jackson argued that if a single state veto had been permissible at an earlier time, "the Union would have been dissolved in its infancy." He emphasized that the War of 1812, which served as his true trial by fire and the battleground from which occurred his dramatic ascent to power, would have been a lost cause. "The war into which we were forced in order to support the dignity of the nation, and the rights of our citizens might have ended in defeat and disgrace, instead of victory and honor, if the states who supposed to a ruinous and unconstitutional measure had thought they possessed to the right of notifying the act by which it was declared and denying supplies for its prosecution." The constitution, he said, "forms the government, not a league... It is a government in which all the people are represented."

No, Jackson granted, the system was by no means perfect. There were, however, "two appeals for an unconstitutional act passed by Congress—one to the judiciary, the other to the people in the states" through constitutional amendment. Jackson argued that "We the People" had formed the Union that produced the Constitution, as opposed to the Calhounites' theory that the Constitution was a compact between the states in which the individual states were paramount. To Jackson, the people were supreme, and the American system of government was, in his opinion, not only equal to the task of reconciling the competing interests of modern life, but more capable of doing so than any other human institution.

Jackson addressed the people of South Carolina with a mixture of both firmness and gentleness. He depicted a nation on the rise, emphasizing its path to greatness, and how it could only be hindered by

---

[1124] Andrew Jackson and the Nullification Crisis, The Hermitage Collection.

the efforts of a single interest trying to take power from the collective. "Contemplate the condition of that country of which you still form an important part. Consider its government, uniting in one bond of common interest in general protection, so many different states, giving to all their inhabitants the proud title of American citizen. Protecting their commerce, securing their literature and their arts, facilitating their inter-communication, defending their frontiers, and making their name respected in the remotest parts of the Earth. Consider the extent of its territory, its increasing and happy population, its advance in arts, which render life agreeable, in the sciences, which elevate the mind! See education spreading the lights of religion, morality, and general information into every cottage in this wide extent of our Territories and States. Behold it as the asylum where the wretched and the oppressed find refuge and support. Look on this picture of happiness and honor and say, we too are citizens of America."[1125]

The price of ignoring the benefits of the Union that had taken America so far, Jackson argued, would be egregious. Not hesitating to invoke the fears of disunion, he reminded anyone who considered secession a viable option of the threat to liberty. "Carolina is one of these proud states; her arms have defended, her best blood has cemented, this happy Union... For what do you throw away these inestimable blessings? For what would you exchange your share in the advantages in honor of the Union? For the dream of a separate independence – a dream interrupted by bloody conflict with your neighbors and a vile dependence on a foreign power. If your leaders could succeed in establishing a separation, what would be your situation? Are you united at home? Are you free from the apprehension of civil discord, with all its fearful consequences? Do our neighboring republics, every day suffering some new revolution or contending with some new insurrection, do they excite your envy?"

To Jackson, the answers to these questions were so obvious that he did not even await a reply. Instead, he continued to hammer home his point, "But the dictates of a high duty oblige me solemnly to announce that you cannot succeed. The laws of the United States must be executed. I have no discretionary power on the subject; my duty is emphatically pronounced in the Constitution... Disunion by armed force is treason.

[1125] Ibid.

Are you really ready to incur its guilt?... On your unhappy state will inevitably fall all the evils of the conflict you force upon the government of your country. It cannot accede to the mad project of disunion, of which you would be the first victims. Its First Magistrate cannot, if he would, avoid the performance of his duty... Declare that you will never take the field unless the Star-Spangled Banner of your country shall float over you; that you will not be stigmatized when dead, and dishonored and scorned while you live, as the authors of the first attack on the Constitution of your country. Its destroyers you cannot be."

Among the radicals in South Carolina, the publication of the proclamation prompted fury. To James Henry Hammond, Jackson's words were "destined to bring about another reign of terror." to the Union, poinsettia said, the proclamation was considered "wise, determined and firm." James A. Hamilton, a son of Alexander Hamilton, told Jackson: "I pray God to preserve your life... That you may preserve this Union." According to Joseph Story, John Marshall became one of Jackson's "warmest supporters" after the proclamation. Henry Clay, on the other hand, could not get over the contrast between this and the annual message: "one short week produced the message and the proclamation, the former ultra, on the side of state rights-- the ladder ultra, on the side of consolidation." to another friend, he complained: "who can have confidence in any man that would put forth two such contradictory papers?"[1126]

Still unable to see the calculation behind Jackson's confrontational approach, Clay was unwilling to acknowledge what in hindsight appears clear enough: that the two messages, while different in tone—understandably, since they were written to serve different purposes in the same cause—were ideologically and philosophically compatible. The cumulative effect of the two documents was, first, to define the ideal shape and scope of the federal government, and second, to defend the existence of that government as the best means yet devised to reconcile contending forces in a peaceful and enduring way. The annual message was about the brushstrokes and the colors, the shading. Jackson sought

---

[1126] Robert Y. Hayne Letters, 1832, Hamilton to AJ, Jackson, *Correspondence*, III, 247; Clay Papers, LC.

to use the art of American politics and governance. The proclamation explained the size and importance of the canvas.

Nonetheless, despite it all, the core issues remained unresolved. When the Nullies confronted the Union again, the Great Conciliator would no longer be there to mediate. In the ensuing decades, as southerners sought to define their 'liberty' through the oppression of enslaved individuals, they acted on Calhoun's ideas, igniting a brutal civil war over slavery that claimed over 750,000 American lives. While Jackson's forceful stance was hailed for its heroism at the time, what was the opportunity cost of a blind allegiance to holding the Union together, while steadfastly ignoring efforts to cleanse the Union of its most glaring stumbling block?

Nearly thirty years later, another Union man, President Abraham Lincoln, embodied Jackson's principles during the turmoil of a true secession crisis. Following Jackson's commitment to a strong, unbreakable Union, Lincoln deployed troops to the South—not just to reclaim land or property after South Carolina's unprovoked attack on Fort Sumter but to initiate a renewed era of freedom for the United States—a Union "of the people, by the people, and for the people."

CHAPTER

74

THE QUESTION OF REMOVAL

"What then? Do you believe that you can live under these laws? That you can surrender all your ancient habits, and the forms by which you have been so long controlled? If so, you're a great father has nothing to say or to advise."
—*Andrew Jackson*

The cabinet breakup ignited a debate throughout the nation regarding Andrew Jackson's leadership. It had been three years since he had taken the reins, and the question was kicked around as to whether or not he deserved a second term. At this point, with the next election not far down the road, Jacksonians, Calhounites, Clay-ites, and others all discussed the unprecedented mass resignations. Was Jackson right to allow the dismissal of his department heads? George Woolf, Pennsylvania governor wrote the dismissed Ingham discussing allegations that "Jackson had turned you and Branch out because he detected you in conspiracy to turn him out and put Calhoun in his place." [1127]

The opposition continued to fear Jackson's mysterious power over so many people. "His administration is absolutely odious, and yet there is an adherence to the man." John Sergeant, a former congressman from Pennsylvania wrote to Clay, "it remains to be seen, whether this will not yield to the conviction that his continuance must be destructive of everything that is worthy to be cherished."[1128] Civility in Washington,

---
[1127] Quoted in Meacham, *American Lion*, p. 178.
[1128] Sergeant to Clay, 1832, Clay Papers, LC.

rare enough since the election of Adams by the House in 1825, disappeared. Writing to her son Charles Frances Adams, Louisa Adams called the battles within the Jackson administration "Altogether as mean and scurvy a piece of business as I have ever seen."[1129]

"The Jackson party is a good deal dispirited in the week of the resignations, General Jackson will not get on as successfully as many are inclined to think, " Supreme Court justice John McLean of Ohio (appointed by Jackson in 1829) wrote Ingham in May, "the General's qualifications for the office begin to be questioned by many, who believed him capable of managing the office by the superior powers of his own mind." In some states that were once fully Jacksonian in character, McLean claimed Jacksonians "have lost the enthusiasm they once possessed in the cause."[1130]

From the safety of his home in Pennsylvania, Samuel Ingham struck back. Hearing of Jackson's ridicule at his flight from Washington, Ingham turned his anger on his former boss. He told a friend that when, "the people know but a small part, they will dispose of General J. The magic of General J.'s popularity is all a delusion. He has more unbearable points about him than I have ever seen in a public man." James Hamilton, Jr. of South Carolina wrote to fellow South Carolinian James A. Hammond of Charleston, "The administration at Washington cannot recover from the retreat precipitate of the late Cabinet, and consequently Jackson's reelection is placed in such hazard as scarcely to be a probable event."[1131]

But Jackson, once again, would somehow prove the doubters wrong. And much like teflon, nothing seemed to stick to Jackson. In fact, Old Hickory came out of the cabinet resignation scandal stronger than ever, much to the dismay of his critics. The Democrats, too, seemed more willing and able to commit to western expansion, regardless of the consequences. Such expansion meant, however, that there would be a need to confront the current inhabitants of the land. More than 125,000 Native Americans lived in the forests and prairies east of the Mississippi in the 1820s. There were a variety of federal policies in place towards these groups of indigenous Americans, but by the late 1820s, popular

---

[1129] Louisa Adams to Charles Frances Adams, August, 1832, *Adams Memoirs*, IV.
[1130] McLean to Ingham, May, 1832, McLean Papers, LC.
[1131] Hamilton to Hammond, July, 1832, James Henry Hammond Papers, 1774-1875.

opinion was unconvinced that these policies were, any longer, in the best interests of the country.

President Jackson now contemplated his plans for the removal of the Indians living east of the Mississippi. It was a policy largely followed by those of his predecessors, the difference being that Jackson now possessed the military authority to follow through with such plans. The State of Georgia argued that an 1802 agreement from the federal government under the Jefferson administration had promised to extinguish all Indian titles within their state once Georgia ceded its western lands to the federal government, which later became the states of Alabama and Mississippi. John C. Calhoun, the Secretary of War in 1825, had proposed such a removal plan during the Monroe presidency, yet his proposal received such little support in Congress that the policy was not put into motion.

A small group of Creek chiefs agreed to a land cession in the treaty of Indian Spring in 1825. The very unrepresentative minority of chiefs gave their consent to sell their lands east of the Chattahoochee River to the states of Georgia and Alabama for an equal amount in the west for an allocation of $400,000 (approximately $11 million in today's currency). Representing only eight of the 46 Creek chiefs, these individuals, some of whom accepted bribes, had no authority to engage in such dealings. Having caused a forfeit of tribal lands by operating in collusion with their white allies, several of the signatories were executed shortly thereafter by an outraged group of fellow Creeks. Though he had signed the Indian Springs accord, once President John Quincy Adams was made aware of the fraudulent nature of the agreement, he called for renewed negotiations.

Several months later, in the Treaty of Washington, which nullified the previous agreement, an authorization for cession of some Creek lands in the state of Georgia occurred. The treaty further recognized others, primarily a thin strip along the Alabama-Georgia border, as belonging to the Creeks. Unwilling to accept native sovereignty in his state, Governor George Troup ignored the new accord however. He then ordered a survey of the treaty lands, including those reserved for the Creeks. Threatening to employ the state militia if Adams sent soldiers to enforce the treaty, the governor got his way. By 1826, Georgia's efforts had largely achieved the forced removal of the Creek nation. Having dealt decisively with their "Creek problem, the Georgia assembly then turned its attention to the state's Cherokees.

A half century earlier, George Washington, like Jackson, a land speculator, and Indian fighter, argued that "the gradual extension of our settlements will as certainly cause the savage, as the wolf, to retire." Officially, the Washington administration recognized tribal rights, and loosely embraced a program of civilization, attempting to persuade Indians to become Christian farmers, and live in nuclear families as opposed to large tribes or clans. In practice, however, it continually pressed upon Indian sovereignty, and indigenous rights. The treaty of Holston in 1791 prompted the Cherokee to sell off a large section of their territory in eastern Tennessee in return for an annual payment and a promise of "perpetual peace with the United States."

George Washington, both in and out of government service, the historian Colin G. Calloway explains, had "spent a lifetime turning Indian homelands into real estate for himself and his neighbors in land speculation."[1132] Washington, referred to as "Town Destroyer" by Seneca chiefs in 1790, saw land as the southern hope, and the indigenous peoples as an obstacle to Southern prosperity. Native perceptions' of Washington as an Indian killer were justifiable and based largely on his orchestration of military campaigns during the Revolutionary War, particularly against the Iroquois nations. Washington's actions were part of a broader strategy aimed at subduing Native American resistance to colonial expansion. In 1779, he ordered General John Sullivan to conduct a campaign against the Iroquois, which involved the total destruction of their settlements and crops. The objective was not only to defeat them militarily but also to devastate their ability to sustain themselves and prevent future resistance. Washington's orders explicitly called for "the total destruction and devastation of their settlements" and aimed at capturing prisoners of every age and sex." [1133]

Thomas Jefferson also believed that the future of the republic depended upon acquiring native lands. Though intellectually interested in the culture and history of Native Americans, as evidenced by his

---

[1132] Colin G. Calloway, *The Indian World of George Washington*, Oxford Univ. Press, 2018. p. 24

[1133] Washington to the Seneca Chiefs, Washington Papers, LC, 1 December, 1790. *Founders Online*.

1781 book, Notes on the State of Virginia, in which Jefferson wrote extensively on the forms of Native American government. Still, Jefferson, as president, worked to undermine Indian autonomy. In advising William Henry Harrison on how to use indebtedness as a tool to extract territory belonging to native peoples, Jefferson unmasked his cards on the subject. "By the decrease of game, rendering their subsistence by hunting insufficient, we wish to draw them to agriculture; to spinning and weaving. When they withdraw themselves to the culture of a small piece of land, they will perceive how useless, to them, are their extensive forests, and will be willing to pare them off from time to time in exchange for necessaries for their farms and families. To promote this disposition to exchange lands, which they have to spare and we want, they will trade for necessaries, which we have to spare and they want. We shall push our trading houses and be glad to see the good and influential individuals among them run into debt, because we observed that when these debts get beyond what these individuals can pay, they become willing to lop them off by a cession of lands."[1134]

In correspondence, Jefferson sometimes seemed open to the idea of whites and Native Americans in peaceful coexistence, though his words on this subject do not inspire confidence. Perhaps more indicative of his true feelings comes from a letter to John Adams in 1812, where Jefferson argues there will always be a "backward contingent of natIves, and we will be obliged to drive them, with the beasts of the forest, into the stony mountains." From the Treaty of Ghent onwards the United States negotiated from a strong position, as those Indian peoples formerly tied to the British were now without allies. "They have, in great measures, ceased to be an object of terror." Secretary of War John C. Calhoun informed the House of Representatives in an 1818 report on Indian trade, "and have become that of commiseration. The time seems to have arrived that we should undergo an important change." Anticipating Jackson's position, Calhoun said of the natives, "They neither are, in fact, or ought to be considered, as independent nations"[1135]

Many white Americans felt respect and admiration for the Indians and believed that they could be assimilated into white society. Much

---

[1134] Brown, David S., Ch. 34.
[1135] Calhoun, John, Report on Indian Trade, Address to Congress, 1818.

energy, therefore, was spent in such efforts to "civilize" and Christianize the Indians. The Society for Propagating the Gospel Among Indians was founded in 1787, and many denominations sent missionaries into native villages. In 1793, Congress appropriated $20,000 for the promotion of literacy and agricultural instruction, along with vocational training among the Indians.

Although many tribes violently resisted the encroachment of whites, some did indeed follow the path of accommodation and assimilation. The Cherokees of Georgia had made remarkable efforts to learn the ways of the whites. In July 1827, the Cherokee nation, eager to prove false the stereotype of Indian savagery, drafted a constitution modeled on that of the United States, complete with three branches, checks and balances, and popular sovereignty. Gradually abandoning their semi-nomadic lifestyle, the Cherokee adopted an agrarian system of sedentary farming, along with embracing a form of private property. Missionaries opened schools among the Cherokees, and a prominent Cherokee, Sequoyah, devised a Cherokee alphabet. In the year 1808, the Cherokee National Council created a legal code. Some Cherokees became prosperous cotton planters, even taking on slave ownership. Some thirteen thousand blacks worked on the plantations of their Native American masters in the Cherokee nation in the 1820s. William Bartram reported on the Cherokee: the Cherokees in their disposition and manner are grave and steady; dignified and circumspect in their deportment; rather slow and reserved in conversation; yet frank, cheerful and humane; tenacious of their liberties and natural rights of men; secret, deliberate, and determined in their councils; honest, just and liberal, and are ready always to defend their territory and maintain their rights. For their efforts, the Cherokees, along with the Creeks, Choctaws, Chickasaws and Seminoles, were referred to by whites as the "Five Civilized Tribes."

The Cherokees' assimilation, symbols of tribal sovereignty and civilization, rather than generating respect from the white population of Georgia, was met mostly with derision and resentment. In response, Governor Troup and the Georgia assembly soon passed resolves designed to extend the state's legal powers over the Indians. Three months later, Jackson was sworn in as president. Confident that they would receive Jackson's support, the Georgians approved the Cherokee Code, which, among other things, annexed Cherokee lands, barred Cherokees testimonials against whites in court, and prohibited the Cherokee from meeting in groups. Yet despite such efforts to embrace "civilization," the strides made by the tribes was apparently not good enough for white Americans. In fact, the remaking of native communities along white lines is exactly what many whites resisted, for, if tribes were to become "civilized", their forced removal would expose decades of deceit and anglocentric policies. Under the fallacy that whites and Native Americans could not live peacefully together, the only option remaining to those who desired unoccupied Indian lands would be left with no leg to stand on. That Presidents such as Jackson failed to mention thousands of other native tribes who had managed to coexist in or near white settlements is a sad and perplexing omission.

The United States efforts to educate, and to elevate the presumably uncivilized, were losing steam by 1830, with the prevailing view, especially among land-hungry whites of the South and West, that this approach was untenable, beginning to take its place. Monroe, and his successor, John Quincy Adams, faced great pressure from the state of Georgia, which removed most of its Creek population during the latter's presidency. Adams complained about Georgia's actions but chose not to interfere. "The Cherokees in Georgia have now a written constitution, but this imperium of a state within a state is impractical and in the instance of the New York Indians removed to Green Bay, and Cherokee Indians removed from elsewhere, in my own opinion, is that the most benevolent course would be to give them the rights and subject them to the duties of citizens as a part of our own people." [1136]

Historians tend to view Adams as equivocal when it came to his Indian policy. Michael D. Green writes in regard to removal, "Adams' sensitivity required that it be done legally, but there was no disagreement between him and the state of Georgia on the goal." Robert Remini observes that, to Adams, Indian removal was the only solution possible, but he could not bring himself to commence the process. Historian David S. Reynolds argues that "Although Adams later criticized Jackson's Indian policy as ruthless, Adams' own resolutions had the same goal as Jackson's, but not the same firmness: the removal of natives from their

---

[1136] JQA, *Adams Memoirs, IV*, 1828.

ancestral lands."[1137] Two of Adams' most decisive actions on this subject were very much unsympathetic. He refused, while mediating the Treaty of Ghent, to consider an independent state for Indians, and as noted, he subsequently aided and abetted Jackson's destruction of Seminole villages in Spanish Florida.

In truth, the logic of United States Indian policy up to 1830 leaned heavily towards the expulsion of the indigenous peoples to the West. It was a project well underway politically, culturally, and economically, by the time of the Indian Removal Act's passage. That many American political leaders truly believed that the Indian education process would work, or wished to see it work, is doubtful.

Both John Ross and William Hicks, Cherokee chiefs, recognized the hypocrisy of government policies, with the combined approaches of expulsion and education and assimilation. Both were mixed-race, educated and active in efforts to improve the rights of the Cherokees. John Ross especially resembled Jackson in many respects. He was a land speculator, he had bought slaves, he had taken on the life of a southern gentleman. Ross and Hicks had appealed to the government under President Adams in 1825, asking for federal intervention against the state of Georgia, in order to keep the state from confiscating lands belonging to the "Cherokee people whom we represent." They insisted that unlike other tribes in the South that had engaged in a process of resistance (which had led only to degradation and extinction,) the Cherokees had successfully adopted white standards. It was now incumbent upon the government, Ross and Hicks asserted, to make good on their promise to respect this achievement. "If Indian civilization and preservation is sincerely desired, and is considered worthy of the serious attention of the United States, then," Ross wrote, "it must become the policy of the United States to resist all talk of removal of those tribes who are now successfully embracing the habits of civilized men within their limits."[1138]

[1137] Michael D. Green, *The Politics of Indian Removal*, Nebraska, 1985, Remini, Robert V., *The Course of American Empire*, 1977, David S. Reynolds, "The 'Ruinous Betrayal' of Indians and Black Americans: David Reynolds in NYRB," CUNY, December 6, 2016

[1138] Evans, Tony T., "The Cherokee Leader Who Tried to Prevent the Trail of Tears," History.com, Nov. 2023.

Such well-crafted arguments, however, meant little to Andrew Jackson. As president, he reduced the complexities of removal to a simple certainty. Neither Alabama or Georgia would allow a separate Cherokee nation to exist within their borders. Accordingly, he counseled the Deep South Indians in his first address to Congress "to emigrate beyond the Mississippi or submit to the laws of the states." Of course, he knew that those states showed little interest in allowing their native peoples to remain. To those still adamant on an Indian policy of education and assimilation, Jackson declared that removal was the only solution to outright annihilation and destruction. "It is too late to inquire," he stated, "as to whether it was just, in the United States, to include the Indians and their territories in the bounds of the new states whose limits they could control. That step cannot be retraced." Identifying the Narragansett, the Delaware, and the Mohican among the "dead tribes in the north," he maintained that the same fate, presently faced the Creek, Cherokee and Choctaw. He did not mention those thousands of supposedly "dead" Iroquois living peacefully in New York in the midst of white settlements. Jackson explicitly suggested to Congress "for your consideration, the propriety of setting apart an ample district west of the Mississippi." He offered this direction, "without the limits of any state there formed, to be guaranteed to the Indian tribes as long as they should occupy it. Each tribe having a distinct control over the portion designated for its use."[1139]

In under twenty years, the populations of the new southwestern states had tripled. In light of this rapid increase, Jackson addressed Congress in December 1829, arguing against the pursuit of such self-defeating policies, by previous federal administrations, in trying to both introduce assimilation to the native peoples, while striving to purchase their lands, at the same time, at every opportunity, thrusting them farther into the wilderness. Those Indians "seeking progress," he continued. "now pursued erecting independent governments within the limits of Georgia and Alabama." Appealing to the constitution, Jackson referenced the clause in which 'No new states shall be formed or erected within the jurisdiction of any other state.' He found the Indians' claim of autonomy to be ineffective as a result, and therefore, he declared,

---

[1139] Andrew Jackson First Annual Address, Dec. 8, 1829, The American Presidency Project.

unacceptable. Jackson sought new precedent and Northern consent in his attempts to justify the "southern right of removal," identifying several northern states who were "justly jealous" of their own authority. "Would the people of Maine," he asked, "permit the Penobscot tribe to erect an independent government in Bar Harbor?" Claiming that continued contact with whites only doomed the Indian to destruction, he argued for their relocation. This migration should be voluntary," he stressed in a statement now seen in all its shameful disingenuousness, "for it would be as cruel as unjust to compel the aborigines to abandon the graves of their fathers and seek a home in a distant land." [1140]

Georgia now knew that it could count on Jackson's support. There were roughly. 25,000 Georgia Creeks in the 1820s. The state claimed that as one of the original 13 colonies, it preserves a charter right to deal peremptorily with its domain." It noted further that in exchange for ceding its western territory to the federal government in 1802, much of which became Alabama and Mississippi, that the government had promised to extinguish Indian titles in the state.

In 1828, the Georgia legislature passed a bill placing all lands in their state under Georgian judicial jurisdiction, which, as they interpreted it, included the Cherokee territory. Also, in December 1828, they passed a resolution, intended to be a warning, a testing of the waters: "That the policy which has been pursued by the United States toward the Cherokee Indians has not been in good faith toward Georgia. . . . That all the lands, appropriated and unappropriated, which lie within the conventional limits of Georgia belong to her absolutely; that the title is in her; that the Indians are tenants at her will . . . . and that Georgia has the right to extend her authority and her laws over the whole territory and to coerce obedience to them from all descriptions of people, be they white, red, or black, who may reside within her limits."[1141]

The resolution further stated that Georgia would not use force to exercise her authority "unless compelled to do so." Despite Jackson professing his amity toward the Cherokee, his actions had belied such friendship since before being sworn in as president. A bitter Jackson set

---

[1140] ibid.
[1141] United States Congress. House. *Resolutions of the Legislature of the State of Georgia, in relation to certain lands occupied by the Cherokee Indians, belonging to the said state. Referred to the Committee on Indian Affairs.* [Washington, D.C., 1828]. Library of Congress.

his sights on the removal of the Indians as early as his days as President-elect, when he sent this message to a Georgia congressman: "Build a fire under them. When it gets hot enough, they'll move."

In July 1829, an event occurred that deeply unsettled the Cherokees' faith in their ability to govern their lands. It was more shocking than an earthquake or devastating flood. The first hint of this news came when a young Black slave discovered an unusual stone and presented it to his white master, who immediately showed keen interest. When asked where he had found it, the slave revealed it was about thirty miles east of New Echota.

Subsequently, another rumor emerged, claiming that an Indian youth residing near Ward Creek sold his pebble to a white trader, a Yankee, who recognized it as gold. For a generation—dating back to at least 1804—the gold mined in the United States had primarily come from North Carolina, totaling around twenty million dollars; however, this new discovery was mainly located south of the North Carolina border, much of it within Cherokee territory in Georgia. Many of the elders, upon hearing news of the discovery, rather than reacting that should have been met with jubilance among the tribesmen, portended trouble for the Cherokee nation.

Miners flocked to Georgia in large numbers, driven, tough, and convinced of their rights, often reckless and indifferent. In 1829, opportunities for wealth were scarce. There was no stock market, no franchises for sale, and few factories in the South. The primary avenues for making money were gambling or finding gold. Gold was a powerful force in elevating fortunes. With luck and gold, a man could attain status and respect, gaining favor among friends and rivals alike. Gold was the key to unlocking all possibilities; nothing else held such immediate persuasive power.

This gold strike was the largest since North Carolina's. The precious metal lay on the ground's surface and in the streams, readily available for anyone willing to take it. A man's fortune could change in an instant in the Georgian fields. Each day brought more miners, discovering gold and expressing their joy. Communities of huts began to rise in the muddy fields of Auraria and Dahlonega. One reporter noted: "The dust became a medium of circulation, and miners were accustomed to carry about with them quills filled with gold, and a pair of small hand scales, on which they weighed out gold at regular rates; for instance, 3 – ½ grains of gold was the customary equivalent of a pint of whisky."

The autumn of 1829 saw an influx of men and mules, leading to the devastation of streams and riverbanks, along with thefts, deceit, and questionable deals. Gold miners were not good neighbors. The Cherokee council convened, overwhelmed and disheartened by issues too vast to manage. They avoided confronting the problem and postponed decisions. William Hicks and Alexander McCoy, still wounded from the previous year's losses, were the focus of the chiefs' attempts to appease them and their supporters. A few new measures were proposed. The full-bloods sought a new law, and John Ross, John Ridge, and Elias Boudinot, along with other mixed-blood leaders, welcomed the opportunity to satisfy them.

Their initiative aimed to formalize an ancient law and strengthen it: "Whereas a Law has been in existence for many years, but not committed to writing, that if any citizen or citizens of this nation should treat or dispose of any lands belonging to this nation without special permission from the national authorities, he or they shall suffer death; therefore, resolved, by the Committee and Council, in General Council convened, that any person or persons who shall, contrary to the will and consent of the legislative council of this nation in general council convened, enter into a treaty with commissioner or commissioners of the United States, or any officers instructed for this purpose, and agree to sell or dispose of any part or portion of the national lands defined in the constitution of this nation, he or they so offending, upon conviction before any of the circuit judges of the Supreme Court, shall suffer death; and any of the circuit judged aforesaid are authorized to call a court for the trial of any such person or persons so transgressing. Be it further resolved, that any person or persons, who shall violate the provisions of this act, and shall refuse, by resistance, to appear at the place designated for trial, or abscond, are hereby declared to be outlaws; and any person or persons, citizens of this nation, may kill him or them so offending, in any manner most convenient, within the limits of this nation, and shall not be held accountable for the same."[1142]

[1142] Ramage, Noah Isaac, "Phoenix on Fire: The Cherokee Nation from Reconstruction to Denationalization," Dissertation, University of California, Berkeley, Summer 2024.

All council members who spoke supported the measure. Chief Womankiller gave a particularly moving speech: "My sun of existence is now fast approaching to its sitting, and my aged bones will soon be laid underground, and I wish them laid in the bosom of this earth we have received from our fathers who had it from the Great Being above. When I shall sleep in forgetfulness, I hope my bones will not be deserted by you. I do not speak this in fear of any of you, as the evidence of your attachment to the country is proved in the bill now before your consideration. I am told that the Government of the United States will spoil their treaties with us and sink our National Council under their feet. It may be so, but it shall not be with our consent, or by the misconduct of our people. We hold them by the golden chain of friendship, made when our friendship was worth the price, and if they act the tyrant and kill us for our lands, we shall, in a state of unoffending innocence, sleep with thousands of our departed people. My feeble limbs will not allow me to stand longer. I can say no more."[1143]

Despite intense debates within the council regarding the impact of white gold miners and the oppressive laws enacted by the state of Georgia, the Cherokees reached very few conclusions. "Depend on national influences to force Georgia to relent," missionaries privately advised. "Take no rash action yourselves, either against Georgia or the miners. It's too big a problem for piecemeal measures or for resolutions." Several weeks later, on December 8, President Jackson sent to Congress his first message, and in it he endorsed the removal of Indians from the eastern part of the United States. The removal, Jackson stated, should be "voluntary, for it would be cruel and unjust to compel them to abandon the graves of their fathers and seek a home in a distant land." Jackson explicitly referenced the Cherokees and the state of Georgia, indicating that the United States would now uphold Georgia's claims to jurisdiction, just as it had during President Jefferson's administration. If the Cherokees did not choose to relocate willingly, they would face the prospect of being absorbed by the state.

Confident in the support Jackson's government would surely provide, Georgia took steps toward the removal of the Cherokees. However, some

---

[1143] Cherokee Council Meetings from 1829; Chief Womankiller, 2021. National Park Service.

residents expressed caution, warning that hasty actions could jeopardize the respect Georgia had earned from its neighboring states over the past few generations. Despite these concerns, Georgia's lawmakers ultimately decided to move forward with their plans. It passed laws forbidding any Indian to engage "in digging for gold in said land, and taking therefrom great amounts of value, thereby appropriating riches to themselves which of right equally belong to every other citizen of the state."

A law was enacted that further restricted the rights of Indians in court. It stated that an Indian could not testify in trials involving white men, that no Indian testimony would be considered valid without the presence of at least two white witnesses, and that any contract made by an Indian would require at least two witnesses to be deemed valid. They voted through a bill making it unlawful "for any person or body of persons. . . from selling or ceding to the United States, for the use of Georgia, the whole or any part of said territory." The penalty for the offense was a sentence to the Georgia penitentiary, where individuals would serve hard labor for up to four years. Legislation was passed that made it illegal for any person or group to use force or threats to prevent Cherokees from agreeing to emigrate or relocating to the West. This bill also included a provision that prohibited all meetings of the Cherokee council and any political gatherings of Native Americans in Georgia, except for those convened for the purpose of ceding land. These measures were set to take effect in June 1830, just six months later.

By this time, Jackson had determined to settle the issue of removal forever. Working with his fellow Democrats in Congress, the president pushed through the Indian Removal Act in 1830. It cleared the Senate 28 to 19 in late April, and then squeaked through the House, 102 to 97. Jackson signed the bill into law on May 28, endorsing the establishment of lands west of the Mississippi for the Indian tribes. Several Indian districts were to be created in Indian Territory (modern-day Oklahoma) and given in exchange for the tribal lands in the east. It further promised assistance and protection for all tribes who agreed to relocate. Money was to be provided for those forced into the removal process as well.

That the Indian Removal Act ignited rigid sectionalism was abundantly clear. 61 out of 77 Southern congressmen voted for it, with more than 80 northern legislators against. Jackson understood the bill's controversial nature, and avoided specifically asking for the removal of the Indians. By omitting any language in the act permitting the government to take land unless ceded by treaty, Jackson could claim he was simply continuing his predecessor's pursuit of land by treaty; a harmless trade of western for eastern land. Future Democratic president James Buchanan of Pennsylvania, the chairman of the House Judiciary Committee, duped his colleagues by insisting, in the removal debate, that Jackson had no intention of "using the power of the government to drive that unfortunate race of men across the Mississippi." All political assurances aside, the criticism poured in.

59-year-old Vermont native Jeremiah Evarts, one of the great moral figures of the early nineteenth century, was determined to thwart Jackson's wish to remove the Five Civilized Tribes. The Yale graduate and son of a farmer, Evarts was to the rights of the indigenous peoples as William Lloyd Garrison was to abolition. Since Jackson's arrival in the capital, Evarts had ramped up his enduring efforts to battle against removal. "The Great Arbiter of Nations never fails to take cognizance of national delinquencies," Evarts once wrote, "In many forms and with awful solemnity, he has declared his abhorrence of oppression in every shape; and especially of injustice perpetrated against the weak by the strong, when strength is in fact made the only rule of action."[1144] In reviewing Cherokee treaty history, Evarts touched on one of the bills' glaring contradictions, for though Jackson insisted on the erroneous nature of treating the Indians as sovereign entities, he had himself done so many times as a military officer. In such parlays, Evarts pointed out, General Jackson had represented a government that recognized Cherokee autonomy.

New Jersey Senator Theodore Frelinghuysen, a devout Christian who opposed Jackson in favor of Evarts' argument, led the opposition against "The Bill for an Exchange of Lands with the Indians Residing in Any of the States and Territories, and for Their Removal West of the Mississippi." The Indian Affairs Committee of the Senate met on Monday, February 22, 1830, debated an essential point of contention whether the Jackson administration could legally ignore the covenant of previous agreements in order to remove the Indians. Frelinghuysen held the floor for nearly 3 days, correctly identifying the true intent of

---

[1144] Meacham, pg. 142.

the bill as a forced removal of the Cherokees, rather than a voluntary relocation program. Like Evarts, the Senator argued that the rights of the Cherokee in Georgia were clearly protected by the previous treaties with the U.S. government. He further raised the obvious issue of racism embedded in the legislation. "Do the obligations of justice change with the color of the skin?" he asked. "Is it one of the prerogatives of the white man that he disregard the dictates of moral principle where an Indian is concerned?" Frelinghuysen appealed directly to Jackson, "Mr. President, if we abandon these aboriginal proprietors of our soil–these early allies and adopted children of our forefathers, how shall we justify it to our country, to all the glory of the past and the promise of the future? . . . How shall we justify this trespass to ourselves?"[1145]

Perhaps the most dramatic moment came when Congressman Henry R. Storrs of New York spoke on the House floor on May 15th, 1830. Storrs insisted that past treaties obligated the United States to protect Cherokee lands from illegal incursions by whites. He told the House "The treaties of this Government, made with them from its first organization and under every administration, to which they have solemnly appealed for their security against these fatal encroachments on their rights, have been treated as subordinate to the laws of these states, and are thus virtually abrogated by the Executive Department. The president has assumed the power to expose of the whole question, and . . . proposes to us little more than to register this executive decree." Jackson had "shocked the public feeling and agitated the country."

Storrs went even further in his distaste for Jackson's bid for wide authority. The government, he told the House, "was to be a government of law, and not of prerogative, and especially not of executive prerogative; for if his will was to have the force of law, that [would be], to a certain degree, despotism." Storrs then compared Jackson to Napoleon, and suggested that if the president should succeed in Indian removal, America would more closely resemble imperial France than a democratic republic: "The eye of other nations is now fixed upon us. Our friends are looking with fearful anxiety to our conduct in this matter. Our enemies, too, are watching our steps. They have lain in wait for us half a century, and

---

[1145] Meacham, pg. 142.

the passage of this bill will light up joy and hope in the palace of every despot."[1146]

United States Senator Wilson Lumpkin, of Georgia, sought to implement the President's Indian policy by proposing a bill that would allocate fertile land west of the Mississippi for the five Southeastern tribes, ensuring they would have it permanently in exchange for relinquishing their eastern territory. The bill included funding to cover transportation costs, reimburse the tribes for their horses and other improvements, compensate for any livestock losses, and provide subsistence for the first year while they established new fields for crops and constructed homes. The bill faced intense debate, drawing both fervent support and opposition, with the press actively engaging in the discourse. The Cherokees, noted for their advanced society and their issues in Georgia, were often at the center of the discussion, but the other four tribes—Creeks, Chickasaws, Choctaws, and Seminoles—also found themselves with both defenders and critics.

Edward Everett of Vermont gave as his view that the move "cannot, as it professes, elevate the Indians. It must and will depress, dishearten, and crush them." He called on Georgia to yield: "If Georgia will recede, she will do more for the Union, and more for herself, than if she would add to her domain the lands of all the Indians, though they were paved with gold." Everett asked his fellow senators not to stain the country's name. "Our friends will view this measure with sorrow, and our enemies alone with joy." He asked how Americans of the future will view it "when the interests and passions of the day are past," and replied, "I fear, with self-reproach, and a regret as bitter as unavailing."[1147]

Senator John Forsyth struck back at the opposition, accusing those against Indian Removal of "victimizing the South." Insisting that nothing in the Act authorized a forced deportation, Forsyth stated that to suggest otherwise revealed among some of his Northern colleagues "ugly anti-southern prejudice." Northerners, he contended, were hypocrites when it

---

[1146] H.W. Brands, *Andrew Jackson His Life and Times*, New York: Anchor Books, 2006. Ch. 38.
[1147] Ehle, John. *Trail of Tears*. Pg. 235.

came to the relocation issue, considering their own convenient expulsions of the Pequot, Hurons, Senecas and Erie among many other tribes.[1148]

Jackson's supporters made the usual arguments for removal. The states were sovereign, the Indians were irredeemable in current conditions, and a fresh start beyond the Mississippi under the protection of the president was the only way to ensure the survival of the tribes. The Senate vote was not particularly close with the measure passing 28 to 19. The House, though, was a different story. God, justice, and presidential power dominated the debate which began on Thursday, May 13, 1830. The efforts of Frelinghuysen and case resonated more in the house than in the Senate. The Indian issue had become an emotional one. Congressmen were more likely to be roiled by popular passions. Pro-Jackson lawmakers had begun attacking the anti-removal forces, arguing that religious fervor was trumping deliberate judgment.

Evarts was a key cog in the engine of opposition, and he too complained of the 'spirit of party at work in Congress' saying that a Jacksonian and congressman from Alabama had told him he believed in the Indians' cause but would not cross the White House. "Now what can we do when men will act in this manner," Evarts said, "the question is already as plain in the Senate as any question of human conduct can possibly be. Not one question of theft, robbery, or murder in ten thousand is so perfectly free from all doubt... Yet it is expected that men will vote by platoons in regular rank and file, according to party drilling on this question of public faith. I have never before seen such a commentary on human depravity." [1149]

In the House, Congressman Wilson Lumpkin of Georgia dismissed the Evarts contingent as fanatics who were unjustly accusing his people of being atheist, deists, infidels and sabbath breakers. Jackson supported Georgia's stance, criticizing the courts' "wicked decision" and seemingly gave the green-light to any state to feel it within their rights to create laws that challenged tribal sovereignty. After making his argument, and to prevent turning Worcester and Butler into martyrs, Jackson urged Governor Lumpkin to release them. The two missionaries were set free

---

[1148] Goss, George William, "The Debate over Indian Removal in the 1830s," University of Massachusetts Boston, 2011. Ch. 4.

[1149] Andrew, John A., *From Revivals to Removal: Jeremiah Evarts, the Cherokee Nation, and the Search for the Soul of America*, Publisher: University of Georgia Press, 2007.

in January 1833. By then, the relentless process of removal had begun, and the machine, once started, would prove difficult to turn off.

The Indian Removal Act was passed by Congress on May 26, 1830, and signed into law by President Jackson two days later, despite emotional appeals against it. This initiated a long and challenging process that ultimately led to the forced relocation of over 100,000 indigenous people. Jackson justified the Act as a means to rescue "this much injured race," believing that Native Americans could maintain their cultures in the vast lands of the West. The Act included a provision for Congress to facilitate the relocation of all Indian tribes east of the Mississippi River. Ironically, the Five Civilized Tribes faced the most severe consequences.

In 1830, the Cherokee Nation fought against their removal by filing a lawsuit for a federal injunction against laws passed by Georgia that aimed to strip them of their rights. Attorney William Wirt, a native of Virginia, and a neighbor of Thomas Jefferson, offered to represent the Cherokees. The former attorney general under James Monroe, Wirt was familiar with the Indians' legal status and previous treaties. He spent three days going over the legal problems the Cherokee faced, particularly the financial situation that threatened to bring them financial ruin. Jackson's government had altered the Cherokee annuity, the tribe's main income. They were now receiving only small payments proportionally to each Cherokee, and only when they traveled to one central place to receive their share. The Cherokee Council objected and voted to retain Wirt and his associates as their principal council.

Wirt argued that the Cherokees possessed the right to self-government as a distinct entity, a status long recognized by the United States through various treaties with Native peoples. Although the court heard the case, it declined to rule on its merits. However, Wirt and the Cherokee were fighting an uphill battle, and it had only just begun.

CHAPTER

75

ENFORCEMENT MATTERS

> *"Our property may be plundered before our eyes, violence may be committed on our persons, even our lives may be taken away, and there is none to regard our complaints. We are denationalized; we are disfranchised. We are deprived of membership in the human family!"*
>
> —Chief John Ross

Major John Ridge was a prominent Cherokee leader, known for his military service, having fought in the Creek War, earning the rank of major, and later became a key figure in the Cherokee Nation's decision-making during this turbulent period of white encroachment and removal that defined the early 1830s. Major Ridge owned 250 acres of cleared land, consisting of eight fertile fields in which he grew the traditional three-sisters: corn, beans and squash, along with indigo, potatoes and oats for his many animals. There was enough indigo alone to fill his wife Susanna's dye pots and sell the rest at a profit in the market. Ridge owned a ferry, and a general store to boot, both of which prospered. His orchard contained over a thousand peach trees, hundreds of apple trees, and a number of plums. His ship had truly come in, more than most Cherokee, as Ridge was wealthy beyond counting. Yet, even so, he saved every penny, and lived as sparingly as possible, a minimalist to the end. His only luxuries were his fine horse, and his grand two-story colonial house, painted white to match the picket fences and out-buildings on his property. His estate was a marvel to travelers who happened to be passing.

The Ridges had escaped the pattern of retreat, hiding, skirmishing with whites, and then retreating. They were luxurious, with many friends and family to call loved ones.

They could boast of the success of their elder son as well, had they been the type to. John was a lawyer–a greenbag–a writer of great renown, a powerful public speaker and negotiator for the Creek Nation. He was so successful in this latter role that the federal government had recently informed him that he could no longer continue as a diplomat for the Creeks, refusing to ever receive him again. Only by such means could the government neutralize his powerful influence with the Creek chiefs, and in Washington, bring about negotiations that would result more favorably for the government. Thus, John Ridge became the leading member of the Cherokee delegation in Washington, meeting with President Jackson and his Secretary of War, writing a memorial for Congress, and conferring with New England lawmakers.

While in Washington, Ridge moved into the Brown's Indian Queen, decorated with a portrait of Pocahontas over the doorway. Representing the Cherokee delegation, John wrote home to his parents that delegations from other tribes were in Washington, for the same reason: lobbying Congress on behalf of the nation. The Choctaw, Creek, Iroquois, Quapaw, and other tribal representatives met often together, to eat and drink together, and to listen to the orations of the Senators and Congressmen debate over the fate of their people. Hoping to hear their favored representatives challenge their colleagues to be fair to the Native peoples, they heard one Senator speak on this topic for three days, only to lose the vote in the end.

Susanna Ridge and the Major discussed the oratory efforts day and night, they learned of the speech by dear Congressman Edward Everett, which had brought tears to many of the chiefs in attendance in the gallery. Following this defeat, all the chiefs of the several tribes met back at Brown's to lament, and to either find another savior, a new strategy, or a solution to their problems that might finally lead to an escape. It was March 1831, and the Ridges, the Ross's, Elias Boudinot, and the missionary Samuel Worcester followed the ups and downs of the action as the public, the press, and Congress debated the heated topic of the day: Indian matters. The actions of the Supreme Court they watched most closely that month, their legal team, led by William Wirt appeared before the court, along with Philadelphia lawyer, John Sergeant, argued: "We know that whatever can be properly done for this unfortunate people will be done by this honorable court. Their cause is one that must come home to every honest and feeling heart. They have been true and faithful to use and have a right to expect a corresponding fidelity on our part. Through a long course of years they have followed out counsel with the docility of children. Our wish has been their law. We asked them to become civilized, and they became so. They assumed our dress, copied our names, pursued our course of education, adopted our form of government, embraced our religion, and have been proud to imitate us in every thing in their power. They have watched the progress of our prosperity with the strongest interest, and have marked the rising grandeur of our nation with as much pride as if they belonged to us. They have even adopted our resentments; and in our war with the Seminole tribes, they voluntarily joined our arms, and gave effectual aid in driving back those barbarians from the very state that now oppress them. They threw upon the field, in that war, a body of men who descend from the noble race that were once the lords of these extensive forests—men worthy to associate with the "lion," who, in their own language, "walks upon the mountain tops." They fought side by side with our present chief magistrate and received his personal thanks for their gallantry and bravery." [1150]

On July 18, 1831, Chief Justice John Marshall was to read the court's opinion on the constitutionality of the recently amended Georgia law. Marshall was old, his hair gray, his body bent, and his voice feeble. John Ridge had to strain intently to hear him, as the Chief Justice expressed his sympathies for the Cherokees for nearly a half an hour. Admitting that he had been moved by their appeal, he regretted to inform the tribesmen that the Court had not been able to accept their claim to be a foreign nation. Though, he argued, they were a separate state, the court considered the Cherokee to be a "domestic, dependent nation," and one that was in a "state of pupilage" and therefore the court had no jurisdiction over a domestic, dependent nation. Marshall, speaking

---

[1150] Arrell M. Gibson, *Constitutional Experiences of the Five Civilized Tribes*, 2 Am. Inrlu L. Rev. 17, 20 (1974).

for the majority, noted that the Indian tribes resided within the borders of the United States and accepted its protection. Consequently, they lacked the right to initiate legal action in U.S. courts. Dissenting voices came from Justices Smith Thompson of New York and Joseph Story of Massachusetts, who contended that the Cherokees did indeed constitute a foreign nation and state. The Cherokee were thus subject to the laws of the state of Georgia. Case-closed.

William Wirt had been rejected by his old friend, and fellow Virginian, John Marshall, and the defeat was galling. Yet the loss was devastating to the Cherokee, who were now more desperate than ever. They had been struck down by both the Supreme Court and Congress, and Ridge's delegation but to seek a face to face with Jackson himself. They received an affirmative answer from the president, and the delegation headed to the White House.

Jackson received the Cherokees with friendly and hospitable charm. Inviting them into the drawing room, the gaunt president recalled his campaigns with the "Keetowah" against the rebellious Creeks and the Seminoles. He reminded the delegation that he was supportive of the Cherokee and favored them over all other tribes. He assured Ridge and his associates that he had a "disposition to do them good."[1151] Ridge, however, noticing the lines on the president's lean face, pressed there by the stress of office, saw in those eyes the mark of a dangerous, cornered animal, aware of being hunted. "I am particularly glad to see you at this time," Jackson told the visitors, saying that he had known all along that the Marshall Court would not take the side of the Cherokees, blaming Wirt and the high-priced lawyers of Philadelphia in general. "I blame you for suffering your lawyers to fleece you. They want your money, and will make you promise even after this, perhaps, that they can make you safe. I have been a lawyer myself long enough to know how lawyers will talk to obtain their clients' money."

Reportedly one of the Cherokee delegation spoke up at that point, declaring, "We don't believe you would blame the Cherokee for their effort to maintain their rights before the proper tribunal."

"Oh no," Jackson replied, followed by a hacking cough that seemed to hang in the air a bit too long. "I only blame you for suffering the lawyers

---

[1151] Ehle, *Trail of Tears*, pg. 242.

to fleece you," Old Hickory repeated, but then changed his approach. He returned to bridge building, speaking again of his friendship with the Cherokee, remembering their fighting for the country. "I know well that the Cherokee have shed their blood with the blood of my soldiers."[1152]

Yet, as much as Ridge and the others tried to steer the conversation to the situation of the Cherokees in Georgia, the President chose to discuss the 1783 treaty with the British that had ended the Revolution. As irrelevant as that was to the delegation, the president went even further off track when he wandered into considerations of the Catawba nation, who had been powerful when Jackson was a boy living in Monroe, North Carolina. "At one time, they took some of the Cherokee warriors prisoners, threw them in the fire, and when their intestines were barbecued," the president explained all too graphically, "they ate them." He compared the Catawba's former position of power to their present prostrate status, "poor and miserable and reduced in numbers, and such will be the condition of the Cherokees if they remain surrounded by white people." At that descending note, a Georgia politician was announced and was invited to come in and join the conversation. The Cherokees, having heard enough, rose to leave, each shaking Jackson's hand. He delayed them, though, holding each of their hands as he tried to assure them of his friendship, his high regard for their people, and told them, "You can live on your lands in Georgia if you choose, but I cannot interfere with the laws of the state to protect you."[1153]

The Cherokees knew now that they had exhausted their hopes for support from all three branches of the federal government. They left Washington shattered, returning to Georgia, the tribesmen faced new legislation that further reduced their rights. New Georgian laws were passed aimed at white missionaries who resided on Cherokee lands. In an effort to end missionary efforts to assimilate Indians, and to stop public dissent. All white men living within the Georgia portion of the Cherokee nation were required to be licensed by the state or suffer four years imprisonment. Some of the missionaries knew the law was aimed at them. Yet, most remained, carried on their work, and awaited the

---

[1152] Jackson to the Cherokee Chiefs, Washington, DC, Jackson Papers, LC.; Perdue, Theda; Green, Michael D. (2007). *The Cherokee Nation and the Trail of Tears*. The Penguin library of American Indian history. New York: Viking. P. 178.

[1153] *The Papers of Chief John Ross*, Volume I, 1807–1839, p. 78.

consequences. Two of these missionaries who did just that were Samuel A. Worcester and Elizur Butler.

Unsatisfied with his own decision, Marshall sought a "proper case with proper parties." During the summer, he contacted Wirt, suggesting he find someone whose rights had been denied by a Georgia court. After ruling against Wirt and the Cherokee in their challenge of the Georgia statute, Marshall felt uneasy about his decision. Expressing sympathy for the Cherokees, he reiterated the court's reasoning to his fellow Virginian and friend, Wirt. Marshall explained that the Cherokee case could be revisited by the court if "someone of standing" challenged the Georgia law. In September of 1831, such a case arose.[1154]

In September 1831, the missionary, Samuel Worcester, Elizur Butler, and several other non-Native Americans were indicted in the Supreme Court for Gwinnett County, Georgia. They faced charges for "residing within the limits of the Cherokee nation without a license" and for not having taken an oath to support and defend the Constitution and laws of Georgia. This indictment was based on an 1830 act of the Georgia legislature, titled "An Act to Prevent the Exercise of Assumed and Arbitrary Power by All Persons, Under Pretext of Authority from the Cherokee Indians."

Worcester contended that the state could not pursue the prosecution, arguing that the statute infringed upon the Constitution, treaties between the United States and the Cherokee Nation, and a Congressional act known as "An Act to Regulate Trade and Intercourse with the Indian Tribes." Despite his arguments, Worcester was convicted and sentenced to four years of hard labor in the penitentiary. The U.S. Supreme Court under John Marshall later received the case through a writ of error.

In an opinion issued by Chief Justice John Marshall, the Court determined that the Georgia act, which led to Worcester's prosecution, was in violation of the Constitution, treaties, and laws of the United States. Chief Justice Marshall noted that "the treaties and laws of the United States consider the Indian territory as entirely separate from that of the states; and stipulate that all interactions with them shall be conducted solely by the federal government." He asserted, "The Cherokee nation, therefore, is a distinct community residing in its own territory

---

[1154] Marshall to Wirt, August, 1831, John Marshall: Writings, Library of America.

where Georgia's laws hold no authority. All interactions between the United States and this nation are, according to our constitution and laws, entrusted to the federal government." Consequently, the Georgia act infringed upon the federal government's jurisdiction and was deemed unconstitutional. Justice Henry Baldwin dissented based on procedural grounds and the merits of the case.[1155]

In short, the Supreme Court overturned the convictions on the basis that states lacked criminal jurisdiction in Indian country. Marshall emphasized that, as the inheritor of British rights on former British lands, the United States government, not those of the states, held the exclusive right to negotiate with Indian nations.

The order for the release of the detainees, who were held in a prison in Milledgeville (then the state capital), was issued on March 5, 1832. Twelve days later, the court went into recess and would not reconvene for several months. During this break, Justice Story accurately assessed the situation, expressing concerns that Georgia might ignore the court's decision. He wrote to a colleague, stating, "Georgia is full of anger and violence. What she will do is difficult to say. Probably she will resist the execution of our judgment, and if she does, I do not believe the president will interfere unless public opinion among the religious of the eastern, western, and middle states should be brought to bear strongly upon him. The rumor is that he has told Georgians he will do nothing. I, for one, feel quite easy on this subject, be the event what it may. The court has done its duty. Let the nation now do theirs."[1156]

"The Democracy", the Democratic Party, made up of Jackson supporters continued to grow. Jacksonians in the House and Senate found themselves the objects of wooing and lobbying. Those who backed Jackson stood to be rewarded by favorable coverage in administrative newspapers and might be heeded on matters of local patronage. The political machine conceived by Van Buren and being built and maintained by Kendall and others would be at the disposal of law makers, who voted with Jackson on key matters. On April 6, John Quincy Adams told his diary. "General Jackson rules by his personal popularity, which his partisans in the Senate dare not encounter by opposing anything that

---

[1155] The Marshall Decision, Worcester v. Georgia, 31 U.S. 515 (1832). LOC.
[1156] Story to Marshall, 1832, Joseph Story Papers, 1794-1851.

he does. While that popularity shall last, his majority in both houses of Congress will stand by him for good or evil. It has totally broken down in the Senate both the esprit de corps and the combination against the executive, which from the last session of Mr. Jefferson's administration had presided in many of their deliberations and governed many of their decisions."[1157] With such a fortified backing, Jackson was to have his way on removal, regardless of the opposition.

Shortly thereafter, Jackson confirmed Story's prediction on the subject in writing to John Coffey, "The decision of the Supreme Court has fell stillborn and they find that it cannot coerce Georgia to yield to its mandate." Indeed, feeling vindicated by the president, the Georgia Superior Court refused to submit to the Supreme Court's decision, refusing to reverse its ruling and free Worster and Butler. The stubborn Governor Wilson Lumpkin swore he would prefer to "see the missionaries hanged" before going so far as to "submit to this decision made by some superannuated life estate judges."[1158]

Jackson argued that the indigenous peoples were being asked to make a difficult choice. The tribes had to either adopt the customs and laws of the white settlers or relocate. Remaining in their traditional ways was not an option. Jackson, familiar with the frontier communities from his own experiences, understood that the settlers would not allow the native peoples to maintain their lands, which were highly valuable and only lightly occupied, nor continue to live free from state rule. He believed the current situation was unsustainable and that the "aborigines" faced the risk of annihilation. While Jackson's policy served his own interests, it was consistent and never wavered. He generally deferred to state authority in matters not affecting the Union's integrity, and in this instance, he chose not to intervene between the states and the tribes. The Cherokees would have to either find peace within the states where they were living (as individuals) or relocate. The situation had not changed much, although the frontier certainly had. It had been pushed much further west. Georgia was not a much more densely populated place, and no longer on the fringes of "settlement." Whenever white settlers

---

[1157] Diary of John Quincy Adams, *Adams Memoirs*, IV.
[1158] Brown, *The First Populist*, Ch. 34.

encountered Indigenous peoples living separately in tribes, old tensions resurfaced.

Settlers resented tribal immunity from state laws and coveted their lands. Despite Congressional legislation and judicial rulings, the struggle that began with the arrival of Europeans in North America as early as the 1500s would continue until the descendants of those Europeans claimed all of the continent. Despite his critics' accusations, Jackson did not hate the Cherokees, the Creeks, or the Choctaw. His adoption of Lincoya and other Indian children that he and Rachel took into their home demonstrated the good intentions he held toward the tribes, and he said the right words at least indicating he wanted to see them thrive. But he was certain that could not and would be in the east, and he would not budge on this issue.

Jackson had never been friendly with John Marshall. The Chief Justice was, to Old Hickory, a misguided, stubborn, old Federalist, married to outdated Federalist principles: prioritizing property rights, and diminished state authority. He had mixed feelings about Marshall's handling of the Burr trial. His opinion of Marshall had not improved since he became president, even though the Chief Justice's history of nationalism had eased Jackson's defense of the Union against nullifiers, much more so than a similar defense by John Adams had been against the would be Virginia and Kentucky nullifiers in 1798. Jackson was put off by Marshall's authoritative demeanor, however, and the seemingly undemocratic nature of the court's decisions. Though he usually deferred to the court's rulings, he particularly disagreed with Marshall's judgment in the 1832 Cherokee case. However, as he became increasingly convinced that the future of the tribes in the settled areas of the United States depended on their migration west of the Mississippi, he reported to Congress in 1832, during the Worcester court case, that he was eager for all necessary arrangements for their removal and improvement to be executed without delay.

Marshall's ruling was seen as just such a delay, fostering unrealistic hopes among reluctant indigenous families and their advocates. Jackson reiterated that he intended to treat all Native Americans similarly to other inhabitants of Georgia and neighboring states, and had offered to cover their relocation costs. Those who chose not to accept the removal offer were free to stay, but they would have to live under the laws and regulations set by the states in which they resided. In his 1832 annual address, several months after the Supreme Court's decision, Jackson glaringly omitted the ruling. He told Congress that the wise and humane policy of transferring the remnants of the tribes from the eastern to the western side of the Mississippi was steadily progressing toward completion. Defending his offers to the Georgia Cherokees, Jackson asserted that whatever disagreements existed about their claims, he hoped there would be none regarding the generosity of his proposals or the urgency of their acceptance.

In reality, there was significant disagreement about the generosity of Jackson's propositions. Advocates for Indigenous rights criticized Jackson for defying the Supreme Court and allowing removal to continue, alleging that he was acting on behalf of greedy Georgian land speculators and rewarding his political allies in that state. Politicians and editors who opposed Jackson for other reasons suddenly became allies of the Cherokees. Reality tended to defy Jackson's assertions that the president's policy was generous. He presented the option for the Cherokees to remain in Georgia and live according to white customs but considering how much the Cherokees had already adapted to white ways and the little respect their dutiful assimilation had generated among their neighbors, accepting this alternative would have required an enormous leap of faith.

"Our children by thousands yearly leave the land of their birth to seek new homes in distant regions." Jackson argued that the Indians were being asked to do no more than Americans had done for generations (though voluntarily, and not by forced removal.) The tribes must either adopt the ways of the whites, including the laws of the states in which they lived, or move. To stay where they were, under their own customs, was not an option. Jackson knew the Indians' neighbors well, having lived on or near the frontier for most of his life, and he knew they would not leave the Indians alone, or let them keep the lands that were worth so much, and sat so lightly occupied. The status quo was simply unsustainable, the president argued. The Indians risked utter annihilation, he insisted. "I am anxious that all the arrangements necessary to the complete execution of the plan of removal, security and improvement of the Indians should be made without their delay," Jackson told Congress.[1159]

The Supreme Court upheld the rights of the Cherokee twice more before all was said and done. But Jackson was dead set on opening Indian lands to white settlement, and he never acknowledged the court's ruling publicly. In not following the constitutional protocol he had sworn to do upon taking office, he took presidential prerogative further than any previous president had heretofore.

In the following decade, countless Indigenous people perished during forced marches, notably the Cherokees along the infamous Trail of Tears, toward the newly designated Indian Territory (present-day Oklahoma), where they were promised to be "permanently" free from white encroachments. A survivor of the grueling forced march during the harsh winter of 1838-1839 recalled the ordeal vividly. "One each day, and all are gone. Looks like maybe all dead before we get to new Indian country, but always we keep marching on. Women cry and make sad wails. Children cry, and many men cry, and all look sad when friend die, but they say nothing, and just put heads down and keep on toward west....She [his mother] speak no more; we bury her and go on."[1160]

There are various estimates and several arguments regarding the social, cultural and physical damage caused by the 1838 removal. The main portions of all five tribes were uprooted and the people became socially disoriented, their town and clan organizations disrupted. Families dwindled and were divided; many people died. It was sometimes true that those too feeble to travel were left with a kinswoman in the Qualla Cherokee band in North Carolina, but only a few of these handicapped, aged individuals were protected that way. Most elders had been sent along and, weakened by the traveling, assaulted by a different diet of meal and pork, had fallen into illnesses unknown by name to doctors of the time. Traveling five to ten miles daily was not of itself deadly, but the diet, the filth of the camps, the flies feeding at the slit trenches, and visiting the food and hands of the people proved to be. Then, too there was the mosquito, carrying malaria, which struck in summer seasons. And there was smallpox, which struck the Choctaw and became

---

[1159] Jackson's Address to Congress, 1830, *Teaching American History*.
[1160] Kennedy and Cohen, pg. 260.

an epidemic among them. There was gonorrhea, a complication for many. And finally, there was the old reaper, who could be relied on to make everyday, standard visits, selecting travelers for that other western journey.

The official figures for the trail, those of government and Cherokee officers including John Ross, became available soon thereafter. While the United States government's official figure puts the death total at 424, Ross's count numbered in the thousands. Historian James Mooney, in 1900, stated in Myths of the Cherokee, "it is asserted, probably with reason, that over 4,000 Cherokee died as the result of the removal."[1161] Whether one accepts the government figures, or those of Ross and Mooney, deaths were needless and numerous, and suffering was intense, and of equal importance the government of the Cherokees, once promising, was destroyed. These losses place in context an extraordinary message to both houses of Congress by Jackson's successor, President Van Buren: "It affords me sincere pleasure to be able to apprise you of the entire removal of the Cherokee Nation of Indians to their new homes west of the Mississippi. The measure authorized by Congress with a view to the long-standing controversy with them have had the happiest effect, and they emigrated without any apparent resistance."[1162]

The Bureau of Indian Affairs was established in 1836 to administer relations with America's indigenous peoples. But as the land-hungry "palefaces" pushed west faster than anticipated, the government's guarantees went up in smoke. The "permanent" frontier became temporary very quickly, lasting only about fifteen years.

Suspicious of white intentions from the start, Sauk and Fox braves from Illinois and Wisconsin, ably led by Black Hawk, resisted eviction. They were bloodily crushed in the Black Hawk War of 1832 by regular troops, including Lieutenant Jefferson Davis of Mississippi, and by volunteers, including Captain Abraham Lincoln of Illinois.

In Florida the Seminole Indians, joined by runaway slaves, retreated to the swampy Everglades. The removal of the Seminoles from Florida had been contentious and violent, was it was about to become even more so. Osceola led the Seminole war party, and the conflict had the usual

---

[1161] Ehle, pg. 391.
[1162] Van Buren's Second Annual Message to Congress, December 3, 1838, The American Presidency Project.

elements: white greed, internal Indian divisions (Osceola had murdered a rival Seminole who had chosen to comply with removal), and for whites, alarming word that escaped slaves were finding sanctuary among the Seminoles.

On Friday, December 18, 1835—a week before Christmas—Osceola attempted a Florida militia wagon train at Kanapaha. Ten days later a force of 180 Seminoles routed an advance guard of Major Francis Dade's force near the Fort King road. By the time the fighting was over, Dade's soldiers—-roughly a hundred—were all dead.

The conflict that followed, which became known as the Second Seminole War, would last seven years, from 1835-1842. It was to become the nation's longest and most expensive Indian War, as the Seminoles waged a bitter guerilla war that took the lives of some fifteen hundred American soldiers. Jackson grew impatient and angry with the American commanders who lost battle after battle to the Seminoles, he never doubted that total victory was the only acceptable answer, no matter how costly. "I have been brooding over the unfortunate mismanagement of all the military operations in Florida, all of which are so humiliating to our military character, that it fills me with pain and mortification—the sooner that a remedy can be afforded the better." Without security—from Indians, from Mexico, from Spain, from Britain, from whomever—-Jackson believed that everything else about the American republic was at risk. He was anguished about the Seminole success. In a meeting with Florida's territorial delegate, the president denounced the people of Florida. "Let the damned cowards defend their country," Jackson said of Florida's militia. He fumed that if five Indians had come into a white settlement in Tennessee of Kentucky—Jackson's territory —-"not one would have ever got out alive." Yet the war went on.[1163]

In fact, the spirit of the Seminoles was broken in 1837, when the American field commander treacherously seized their leader, the fierce Osceola, under a flag of truce. The war dragged on for five more years, nonetheless, but the Seminoles were doomed. Some fled deeper into the Everglades, where their descendants now live, but more than three-fourths of them were moved to present-day Oklahoma, where several thousand of the tribe survive to this day.

[1163] Meacham, p. 317.

Historian H.W. Brands points out that, at the end of the day, "Jackson adamantly believed the harsh fact of the matter was Georgia was determined to take the Indians' land. "Jackson knew this, and did not prevent it."[1164] He was on firmer ground in declaring his policy inescapable, although even that can (and should) be questioned. The defenders of the Cherokees were few and mostly far away from Georgia. Their persecutors were many and near at hand. Given the racist realities of the time, Jackson felt certain that for the Cherokees to remain in Georgia risked their extinction. To preserve the Cherokee as a tribe; to enforce Marshall's decision, would have required raising and sending federal troops to Georgia, stationing them there indefinitely, and ordering them to shoot white Georgians who threatened the Indians. Jackson believed American democracy simply wouldn't sustain such a policy. It was one thing to use force to preserve the Union. In such an endeavor, he could expect broad support from the people who would actually do the fighting. It was another thing to ask white citizens to risk death protecting Indians. They wouldn't do it."

Horace Greeley, the famous newspaper man who founded and co-edited the New Yorker magazine beginning in 1834, was responsible for the now famous, but apocryphal quote attributed to Andrew Jackson. The quote, "John Marshall has made his decision; now let him enforce it," was first printed in Horace Greeley›s 1864 book, *The American Conflict*, which was an account of the Civil War.[1165] While it was Greeley who actually printed those words, and not what Jackson actually said, he certainly said something similar, and his actions in the early 1830s showed it is how he felt regarding, as noted, his decision not to enforce the Marshall Court's decision. The words Greeley printed thirty years later perfectly captured Jackson's attitude. The Chief Justice would have to enforce the decision, because Jackson would not, which meant that there would be no enforcement, and no support for the Cherokees.

During his travels across America, Alexis de Tocqueville observed from the banks of a frozen Mississippi River as a group of Choctaw people, displaced from their lands during an unusually harsh winter, gathered for a brief moment in Memphis. "They came in families, Some

---
[1164] Brands, 2005, Ch. 38.
[1165] Greeley, Horace, *The American Conflict*, 1864. Chapter 1.

ill, some old, some near death. They took what they could and renounced the rest. "All the Indians had got into the boat that was to carry them across," Tocqueville wrote, "as soon as their dogs finally realized that they were being left behind forever they altogether released a terrible howl and plunged into the waters of the Mississippi to swim after their masters."[1166]

Jackson began a new era of Indian removal, and presidential power, when he sided with his Southern brethren of Georgia rather than fulfilling his executive responsibilities of enforcing the decision of the Supreme Court. However, an unexpected side effect of this decision made him, and future presidents vulnerable in interaction with other Southern states. The precedent had been set, and it was an example of which other Southerners were eager to follow: for the first time, a state had successfully resisted the decree of a branch of the federal government and had gotten away with it. South Carolinians remained consistently outspoken against what they viewed as the federal tariff's unconstitutionality, and Georgia's successful refusal to comply with Marshall's ruling only emboldened the Palmetto State all the more. The successful stance made by Georgia sent the message: a determined Southern legislature could effectively nullify federal law, especially if that law threatened slavery in any way. What other dissatisfied parties would follow suit in the years to come?[1167]

Often, in the debates over the constitutionality of Indian Removal, the cruelty of the events can be overlooked, or forgotten entirely. Thus, it is imperative to close out this review of the events of the late 1830s by exploring what Jackson's reversal of Worcester v. Georgia meant to its victims. The Cherokee were no longer protected by any legal authority, and therefore, they were basically thrown to the wolves. General Winfield Scott informed the tribe's leaders that "the president of the United States has sent me, with a powerful army" to enforce removal.[1168] As federal and state troops entered Cherokee territory, the process of gathering the Cherokee population for removal commenced. Families were startled by

---

[1166] Tocqueville, Alexis de, New Haven [Conn.]; London: Yale University Press, 2010. Pp.2-32.
[1167] Brown, David S., *The First Populist*, Ch. 34.
[1168] Military Orders and Correspondence on the Cherokee Removal, *Journal of Cherokee Studies 3*, 1978: 145.

screaming soldiers who broke into their homes with guns and bayonets to force-march these families from their homes with minimal notice and were subsequently marched to designated internment camps. These camps, established as temporary holding facilities, housed the Cherokee under guard before their westward journey. "Families at dinners were startled by the sudden gleam of bands in the doorway, and rose up to be driven with blows and oaths along the weary miles of trail that led to the stockade, where they were locked up like cattle."[1169] On their way out, "they saw their homes and flames fired by the lawless rebels that followed on the heels of the soldiers to loot and pillage."[1170] Of the 18,000 Cherokee who were shipped West along the "Trail of Tears," about 4000 died.[1171] One militia man later said that "I fought through the civil war and have seen men shot to pieces and slaughtered by thousands, but the Cherokee removal was the coolest work I ever knew."[1172]

Looking back on the Removal, Martin Van Buren wrote that "unlike histories of many great questions which agitate the public mind in their day. This issue will in all probability endure as long as the government itself, and will in time occupy the minds and feelings of our people."[1173] In the immediate aftermath, his predictions proved incorrect. Worcester accompanied the Cherokees into their forced removal. His arguments went unheard in the corridors of authority, and the Supreme Court would not reference his case in its rulings regarding Native American law. However, this exile was not a temporary situation. History has demonstrated that the territory to which the Cherokees were relocated would not remain exclusively theirs, despite Jackson's assurances. The opposition from Chief Justice Marshall would persist among a small yet increasingly vocal faction of dissenters—the abolitionists. Their involvement would soon become crucial in the ongoing struggle against the dominant majority in America.[1174]

[1169] Garrison, *Legal Ideology*, 1
[1170] ibid; Remini, 1822-1832, p. 302
[1171] Ibid.
[1172] Satz, *American Indian Policy in the Jackson Era*, p. 101.
[1173] Van Buren, *Autobiography*, pp. 275-276.
[1174] Magliocca, Gerard M., *Andrew Jackson and the Constitution: The Rise and Fall of Generational Regimes*, 2007. University Press of Kansas. P. 73.

In his 1832 annual message, several months after the Supreme Court's decision, Jackson ignored the ruling, acting as though it had never happened. "I am happy to inform you," he told Congress, "that the wise and humane policy of transferring from the eastern to the western side of the Mississippi, the remnants of our own aboriginal tribes with their own consent and upon just terms, has been steadily pursued, and is approaching, I trust, its consummation." Jackson made just one vague reference to the Marshall Court's decision, "With one exception, every subject involving any question of conflicting jurisdiction, or of peculiar difficulty has been happily disposed of, with that portion of the Cherokees however living in the state of Georgia, it has been found impracticable as yet to make a satisfactory adjustment." Jackson considered his approach more than generous. "Whatever difference of opinion may have prevailed respecting the just claims of these people, there will probably be none respecting the liberality of the propositions, and very little respecting the expediency of their immediate acceptance." [1175]

There was indeed much more difference of opinion over Jackson's defiance of the Supreme Court. The outcry was widespread, and Jackson's claims were seen instead as self-serving, taking on the role agent of grasping Georgia land speculators. The harsh fact of the matter was that Georgia was determined to expel the Cherokee, and Jackson saw that as a battle he did not wish to fight. To Jackson, the Cherokees remaining in Georgia risked their extinction. Could American democracy sustain such a policy?

[1175] Quoted in Brands, HW, 2005. Ch. 38.

CHAPTER

76

THE MONSTER MUST BE KILLED

> *"I intend to rout you out, and by the eternal God, I will rout you out. If the people only understood the rank injustice of our money and banking system, there would be a revolution by morning."*
>
> —*Andrew Jackson*

At this peak of his career, Andrew Jackson, the once skinny 'Andy of the Waxhaws,' enjoyed unmatched popularity by the summer of 1833. No other American had wielded such influence over his fellow countrymen since Washington had dismissed any notions of that he be made a king. Having established the precedent of federal power over nullification by the states, having removed the indigenous and opened up land for the hungry masses of westerners, Jackson emerged as a national hero like never before. His journey to the Northeast, including New England, was met with a warm reception, even in a region that traditionally despised the man. Although many Bostonians were skeptical, Harvard College honored Jackson with an honorary Doctor of Laws degree. As he rode through the streets of Boston, a merchant, rooted in Federalist traditions and initially closing his windows in protest, was reportedly so moved by Jackson's presence that he sent a child to wave a handkerchief at the former president.

This story, like so many others from the time period, must of course be taken with a grain of salt, as the Jacksonian press controlled much of what was printed to the masses of Jackson supporters during this period.

But the enemy's press was revving up again, this time determined to take the battle to the Democrats.

Buoyed by the "success" of Indian Removal, and the ecstasy that comes with getting your way, President Andrew Jackson now set his sights on his next target: The Bank of the United States. Jackson did not hate all banks, nor was he against all businesses, but he distrusted eastern money, especially monopolistic banking and overly large corporations. The Jacksonians who followed him religiously felt the same way. A man of many venomous resentments, he came to embrace Western prejudices against the "moneyed monster" known as the Bank of the United States. He was very Jeffersonian in this view, but unlike Jefferson, Jackson was less willing to compromise. Why was the Bank such a monster to Jackson? That is a question that cannot be answered in just one sentence. The reasons for Jackson's visceral disdain for a centralized bank are many. Primarily, like many westerners who struggled over the years with the lack of hard currency in the west, Jackson blamed the 'Eastern Establishment,' embodied by the National Bank, as the culprit.

No bank in America had more power than the Bank of the United States. In many ways, the bank acted like a branch of the federal government. A source of credit and stability, the bank was an important and useful part of the nation's expanding economy. The national government minted gold and silver coins in the mid-1800s but did not issue paper money. Paper notes were printed by private banks, and the value of these notes rose and fell with the bank's health, and the health of the economy as a whole. The amount of money printed gave private bankers considerable power over the nation's economy. As the Bank of the United States was a private institution, accountable not to the people, but to its elite circle of wealthy investors, Jackson felt it should not have such an integral role in a government by "the people." To Jackson, the Bank, for one, had too many foreign investors. He also strongly believed that it favored the rich over the poor. Regionally-speaking, he believed, without real proof, that the Bank purposefully resisted lending funds to develop commercial interests in America's western territories. As noted, Jackson was not fond of the Bank's president, Nicholas Biddle, who had been elected by the Bank's board in 1823. Biddle held an immense (and to many, unconstitutional) amount of power over the nation's financial affairs. Enemies of the bank dubbed him "Czar Nicholas I" and considered the Bank a serpent that grew new heads whenever old ones were cut off. Along with paying off the national debt, the Bank question, Jackson believed, needed to be settled before he left office.

A scion of a wealthy and politically connected Pennsylvania family, and a financial savant, Nicholas Biddle was a formidable adversary. The bank president was also very resourceful in many ways, but particularly in the fact that the resources he controlled, available to the Bank of the United States included a significant portion of the nation's money supply. If Biddle chose to use these resources against the Jackson administration, he could cripple the economy. However, he hoped it wouldn't come to that. Even after Jackson vetoed the bank's renewal bill and won reelection, Biddle believed that the bank remained in a strong position. The key issue for both the bank and Jackson was control over the federal government's deposits. These deposits were the bank's main source of financial strength, providing the capital for loans that would generate interest for the government. Because it was the main depository of the Washington government, and controlled much of the nation's gold and silver, its notes, unlike those of smaller banks, remained stable. Yet, they were managed by the Treasury, which meant they were, ultimately, under Jackson's authority. If the president decided to withdraw these deposits, he could easily undermine the National Bank of the United States, leading to its destruction. However, doing so would disrupt financial systems established over the bank's sixteen-year existence, severely inconvenience both the government and the public, and destabilize the economy. Biddle felt confident, and in fact, far too over-confident. "They will not dare to remove them," Biddle wrote to Daniel Webster. "If the deposits are withdrawn, it will be a declaration of war that cannot be recalled."[1176]

War, though, was Andrew Jackson's element, the environment in which he thrived, and war was just what he had in mind in this case, if need be. Jackson argued that a Bank War was one that Biddle and the Bank's big money supporters brought on themselves. In February 1832, the president received a distressing report of what, to the president, exemplified the bank's continuing 'designs against democracy.' "I am informed by a gentleman whose knowledge of the U.S. Bank is second

---

[1176] Biddle to Webster, Jan., 1832, Webster Papers, LC.

only to that of its president, that the Bank counts upon being rechartered." James Hamilton wrote. "Its purpose is for the next two years to fortify itself beyond all hazard by calling in its responsibilities gradually. This operation will be performed under the avowed idea that it is necessary and preliminary to winding up its concerns at a proper time, about the expiration of the period referred to. It will by withholding bills and by other means within its power, cause exchange to advance so as to cause the exportation of specie, and thus occasionally a run upon all the monied institutions. This, it will be prepared for, and the affairs of the state banks will consequently be so deranged as to compel them to stop specie payments. The immense injury to the whole nation resulting from that event, it is believed, (and not without foundation) will generate a strong public feeling in favor of the rechartering of the bank as the only means of restoring a sound currency."[1177]

Whether or not this was Biddle's true intention, it was congruent with his expectations of banks and bankers. The president was no expert on currency issues, nor was he a financial expert, as evidenced by his earlier struggles as a businessman in Nashville, yet his experiences led him to distrust those managing the money supply. This was a very western viewpoint by the 1830s. The reality that a small group of men in eastern cities (or abroad) controlled the nation's fate were anathema to Jackson's democratic principles. Nicholas Biddle represented a 'deep state' problem, he was unelected, and not subject to the democratic process, but yet he held the reins of the money supply for the entire nation. Jackson simply could not abide by this. Only Biddle's associates on the Bank's board had placed him in that position, and their interests, Jackson believed, were not aligned with those of ordinary citizens. Even if the money power had the best of intentions, Jackson would have opposed it, but he was certain of the fact that their intentions were harmful. Jackson described the Bank as a many headed serpent, "a hydra of corruption" in a private letter, reflecting his ever-growing opposition. And the fact that it now seemed to be a personal stand-off between himself and two men he despised, in Clay and Biddle, Jackson was even more resolute.

Elizabeth Bayard Smith had been onto something when she had once speculated about the possibility of Louis McLane turning into trouble

---

[1177] Hamilton to AJ, Feb. 1832, Jackson Papers, LC.

for Jackson. The larger cause, as usual, was the Bank. McLane was a supporter of the Bank, and believed the institution should be reformed, not abolished, and was open about his views. A former Congressman who had chaired the House Ways and Means Committee, McLane was, his cabinet colleague Roger Taney said, "an ambitious man who loved power, and had an eye on the presidency, which he confidently expected to reach." McLane's time as Minister to England had confirmed his long-time support for the Bank. He had, Taney said, "a close intimacy with Mr. Biddle, and with Barings in England. He came to the Treasury in late 1831 with a plan to save the Bank and accomplish much else besides."[1178] Linking most of the questions of the day, McLane proposed to pay off the national debt, as Jackson had long planned, and to sell the government's stock in the bank, sell the federal lands to the states, and modify the tariff. Then in future years, recharter a reformed bank. The trade-off would be to somehow convince President Jackson to stay silent on the Bank issue in the annual presidential message so McLane could introduce his broad proposals himself in his annual Treasury report to Congress. These would include the Bank's eventual recharter. If he could persuade Jackson to go along, McLane believed he could rescue the Bank. He did not feel it was too unreasonable to believe this outcome possible. [1179]

When McLane met with Jackson and the rest of the cabinet, Andrew Donelson read a draft of Jackson's annual message aloud, the mild language on the Bank issue startled Roger Taney, who took the message as Jackson's willingness to "defer to the representatives of the people and abide by the decision of Congress" on the Bank issue, as though Jackson was in favor of the Bank's recharter. Taney recalled the wording as: "Having conscientiously discharged a constitutional duty I deem it proper without a more particular reference to the subject to leave it to the investigation of an enlightened people and their representatives."[1180]

Although the "newbie" of the cabinet, and not personally acquainted with the president, Taney felt the need to voice his concerns. Knowing it would irritate McLane, and possibly Jackson, Taney made his objections

---

[1178] Taney to AJ, 1832, Jackson Papers, LC.
[1179] 1831 Louis McLane Correspondence, 1795-1894, LOC.
[1180] Draft of Jackson's message to Congress, 1831, Donelson Papers, LC.

anyway, compelled by "the duty of making this objection I felt to be an unpleasant one," he said.

When McLane rose to defend his wording as it was written, and "objected strongly to any changes to the message, no one else in the cabinet seconded Taney's recommendations. "The discussion continued for some time," Taney said. "The president was worried and desired it to end." Taney was a subordinate to McLane in the pecking order, and Jackson did not wish to undermine McLane in front of the other cabinet members. It was clear "from the earnestness and tenacity with which Mr. McLane defended this paragraph [that] he himself had prepared it.... The President I am sure was the more unwilling to make alterations because he saw that Mr. McLane would be dissatisfied and perhaps a little hurt if the paper was materially changed."[1181]

After further discussion in front of a roaring fire in Jackson's office, it seemed that McLane had carried the day. He was an accomplished diplomat after all, and as though he were at a foreign court, he displayed his powers of negotiations with aplomb in Washington. "He had great tact," Taney said, "and always knew whether he should address himself to the patriotism, the magnanimity, the pride, the vanity, the hopes or fears of the person on whom he wished to operate. And he thus always had a clique about him wherever he was in power over whose opinions he exercised a controlling influence." But Jackson was one to pull away the moment he sensed that someone was attempting to control him. McLane's mistake, Taney later observed, "was in underrating the strength and independence of the President's mind; and the extent of his information. He expected to manage him .... He evidently believed that he would be able to change [Jackson's] opinions, and induce him to assent to the continuance of the charter with some slight and unimportant modification, as a salve to the President's consistency."[1182]

But events unfolded in a way that hindered McLane's plans. Taney persuaded Jackson that McLane's proposal was merely a rebranding of the old Federalist agenda. Furthermore, he insisted that McLane's proposals contradicted Jackson's previous positions. At that time, Jackson was somewhat open to discussion, and McLane still hoped

---

[1181] Roger Taney Correspondence, Dec., 1831, Taney Papers, LC.
[1182] ibid.

he would delay the decision until after the 1832 presidential election. However, with Henry Clay's efforts to thrust the issue into the election spotlight, through a "defeat Jackson strategy" of an early renewal of the bank charter, Harry of the West convinced Biddle to advocate for an immediate re-charter. This was the death knell to McLane's plans as it solidified Jackson's opposition to the re-chartering, leading to his subsequent veto when it passed through Congress.[1183]

In the spring of 1832, the president meticulously prepared his anti-bank strategy. He hinted at the potential creation of a new national bank limited to the District of Columbia, while simultaneously consulting his cabinet secretaries about the practicality of utilizing state banks for the federal government's financial operations. This survey served a dual purpose: to evaluate his ideas and gauge the loyalty of his cabinet members. He understood, just as Biddle did, that withdrawing government deposits would spark conflict, and he wanted to ascertain if his lieutenants were as committed to this cause as he was.

To many, the Bank's very existence was perceived as a violation of American equality and democratic ideals, a belief central to Jackson's opposition. The Bank was particularly detested in the West, especially after the Panic of 1819, when it foreclosed on numerous western farms and redirected wealth to the East. Its priority was profit, not public service. The infamous Bank War erupted in 1832 when Daniel Webster and Henry Clay introduced a bill in Congress to renew the charter of the Second Bank of the United States. Although the charter wasn't set to expire until 1836, Clay advocated for its early renewal to make it a central election issue that year. Clay aimed to defeat Jackson in the upcoming election and believed he could benefit from the president's stance against renewing the Bank's charter. Fatefully, however, Clay was blind to the extreme popularity that Jackson enjoyed, and instead he looked upon the bank issue as a "surefire winner."[1184]

Clay aimed to push a recharter bill through Congress and then forward it to the White House. If Jackson approved it, he risked alienating his loyal western supporters. Conversely, if he rejected it, which seemed likely, he could lose the presidency in the upcoming election by

---

[1183] Kahan, Paul, *The Bank War: Andrew Jackson, Nicholas Biddle and the Fight for American Finance*, WesHolme Publishing, 2022, Ch.1.

[1184] Kennedy and Cohen, pg. 261.

upsetting wealthy and influential groups in the East. However, Clay underestimated the power of the newly enfranchised majority of regular citizens. The wealthy elite, once seen as the "best people," were now just a minority and generally wary of Jackson.

On July 3rd, 1832, the recharter bill passed smoothly through Congress as planned but was ultimately killed by a strong veto from Jackson. The "Old Hero" declared the monopolistic bank unconstitutional. Although the Supreme Court had previously ruled it constitutional in the case of McCulloch v. Maryland (1819), Jackson's actions seemed to many as if he believed the executive branch was superior to the judicial branch, provoking outrage among his critics. He privately remarked, "The Bank… is trying to kill me, but I will kill it."[1185]

Jackson's veto message had significant constitutional implications. It not only defeated the bank bill but also greatly increased the power of the presidency. Previous vetoes had primarily focused on constitutional issues. However, Jackson argued that he was vetoing the bill because he personally deemed it harmful to the nation. Essentially, he claimed for the president a power equivalent to two-thirds of the votes in Congress. By suggesting that the legislative and executive branches were partners in government, he implied that the president was clearly the senior partner.

To explain his decision to the nation, Jackson issued this veto message on July 10, 1832. "I sincerely regret that in the act before me I can perceive none of those modifications of the bank charter which are necessary, in my opinion, to make it compatible with justice, with sound policy, or with the Constitution of our country. . . .It is maintained by the advocates of the bank that its constitutionality in all its features ought to be considered as settled by precedent and by the decision of the Supreme Court. To this conclusion I can not assent. Mere precedent is a dangerous source of authority, and should not be regarded as deciding questions of constitutional power except where the acquiescence of the people and the States can be considered as well settled. . . .The opinion of the judges has no more authority over Congress than the opinion of Congress has over the judges, and on that point the President is independent of both. The authority of the Supreme Court must not, therefore, be permitted to control the Congress or the Executive when acting in their legislative

---

[1185] ibid, 261

capacities, but to have only such influence as the force of their reasoning may deserve.... It is to be regretted that the rich and powerful too often bend the acts of government to their selfish purposes. Distinctions in society will always exist under every just government. Equality of talents, of education, or of wealth can not be produced by human institutions. In the full enjoyment of the gifts of Heaven and the fruits of superior industry, economy, and virtue, every man is equally entitled to protection by law; but when the laws undertake to add to these natural and just advantages artificial distinctions, to grant titles, gratuities, and exclusive privileges, to make the rich richer and the potent more powerful, the humble members of society—the farmers, mechanics, and laborers—who have neither the time nor the means of securing like favors to themselves, have a right to complain of the injustice of their Government. There are no necessary evils in government. Its evils exist only in its abuses. If it would confine itself to equal protection, and, as Heaven does its rains, shower its favors alike on the high and the low, the rich and the poor, it would be an unqualified blessing. In the act before me there seems to be a wide and unnecessary departure from these just principles.... Nor is our Government to be maintained or our Union preserved by invasions of the rights and powers of the several States. In thus attempting to make our General Government strong we make it weak. Its true strength consists in leaving individuals and States as much as possible to themselves—in making itself felt, not in its power, but in its beneficence; not in its control, but in its protection; not in binding the States more closely to the center, but leaving each to move unobstructed in its proper orbit."

"Experience should teach us wisdom. Most of the difficulties our Government now encounters and most of the dangers which impend over our Union have sprung from an abandonment of the legitimate objects of Government by our national legislation, and the adoption of such principles as are embodied in this act. Many of our rich men have not been content with equal protection and equal benefits, but have besought us to make them richer by act of Congress. By attempting to gratify their desires we have in the results of our legislation arrayed section against section, interest against interest, and man against man, in a fearful commotion which threatens to shake the foundations of our Union. It is time to pause in our career to review our principles, and if possible revive that devoted patriotism and spirit of compromise which distinguished the sages of the Revolution and the fathers of our Union. If we can not at once, in justice to interests vested under improvident legislation, make our Government what it ought to be, we can at least take a stand against all new grants of monopolies and exclusive privileges, against any prostitution of our Government to the advancement of the few at the expense of the many, and in favor of compromise and gradual reform in our code of laws and system of political economy."[1186]

Henry Clay's political instincts continued to fail him. Delighted with the financial fallacies of Jackson's message but blind to its political appeal, he arranged to have thousands of copies printed as a campaign document. The president's sweeping accusation may indeed have seemed demagogic to the moneyed interests of the East, but they made perfect sense to the common people. The bank issue was not thrown into the noisy arena of the presidential contest of 1832. This election was unique in that it was the one and only time in the nation's history that a major issue was submitted to the electorate in the form of a popular referendum. Jackson insisted that voters got to decide for themselves their feelings on the Bank. Old Hickory was that confident, and he had reason to be. Most Jacksonians knew banking from a hole in the ground.

Nicholas Biddle was also feeling good about Jackson's veto message, particularly because he too was certain that those who understood money would see the economic problems his views would ignite. The negative impacts he expected the veto message would take time to materialize, however, and the more immediate impact was that the president's words on equality of opportunity inspired the masses, and increased his support. Unlike Henry Clay, who should have known better, Biddle was not a politician, and while he was a fiscal mastermind, he lacked the instincts of the politico, and he was wanting when it came to a true understanding of the political arena. On August 1, 1832, Biddle wrote to Clay expressing his satisfaction: "I have always deplored making the Bank a party question, but since the President will have it so, he must pay the penalty of his own rashness. As to the veto message, I am delighted with it. It has all the fury of a chained panther biting the bars of his cage. It is really a manifesto of anarchy... and my hope is that it will

---

[1186] Jackson's Bank Veto Message, July 10, 1832, Yale Law School Online, Lillian Goldman Law Library, *The Avalon Project*.

contribute to relieve the country of the domination of these miserable [Jackson] people."[1187]

Nicholas Biddle (1786-1844), portrait courtesy of the Frick Art Reference Library

---

[1187] Kennedy and Cohen, pg. 262.

CHAPTER

77

MANDATE OF THE PEOPLE

"The opposition you will see are reckless, with all kinds of slander, but the virtue of the people will meet the crisis and resist all the power and corruption of the Bank."
-Andrew Jackson

Daniel Webster rose from his seat on the Senate floor. Frustrated over the president's veto, and no longer able to sit back and listen to the arguments of the Jacksonians, Webster took the shiny wooden floors of the hall on July 11, 1832. Webster spoke vehemently in opposition to Jackson's message as the debates in Congress raged following the president's veto. "Should presidents," Webster argued, "be bound by the constitutional interpretations of past Congresses, presidents, and courts? If a president sincerely believes that a previous interpretation was constitutionally incorrect and followed it because of Webster's reasoning, would he violate his oath of office?" Webster recognized that the president had the authority to veto bills based on policy considerations. However, he disputed Jackson's assertion that he could reject a bill on constitutional grounds. Initially, Webster's stance resembled departmentalism—the belief that all three branches of the federal government share the responsibility to interpret the Constitution. Nevertheless, he argued against the president's ability to veto a law on constitutional grounds after it had been passed by Congress and signed into law. Webster contended that by dismissing the constitutional reasoning of Congress, previous presidents, and the Supreme Court, Jackson was claiming a "universal power" that amounted to "pure despotism." (It is important to note that Jackson had vetoed a new law, not one from 1816, regardless of the validity of Webster's argument.) Once a bill is passed and signed, Webster maintained, questions of constitutionality fall exclusively within the jurisdiction of the Court. Therefore, Webster ultimately articulated a position that granted the Supreme Court the final authority on constitutional matters. The very thing that Jackson argued the Court should not have.

Webster's masterful oratorical skills were in full display:

"No one will deny the high importance of the subject now before us, Congress, after full deliberation and discussion, has passed a bill, by decisive majorities, in both houses, for extending the duration of the Bank of the United States. It has not adopted this measure until its attention had been called to the subject in three successive annual messages of the president. The bill having been thus passed by both houses, and having been duly presented to the president, instead of signing and approving it, he has returned it with objections. These objections go against the whole substance of the law originally creating the bank. They deny, in effect, that the bank is constitutional; they deny that it is expedient; they deny that it is necessary for the public service."

Webster's voice rose as he continued on, emphasizing that the president's stance challenges the authority of both Congress and the Supreme Court, suggesting he can individually judge the constitutionality of laws. This claim, if upheld, Webster argued, could undermine the rule of law and lead to despotic governance, as it would allow the president to selectively enforce laws based on personal judgment, contrary to established constitutional principles.

"... But if the president thinks lightly of the authority of Congress in construing the Constitution, he thinks still more lightly of the authority of the Supreme Court. He asserts a right of individual judgment on constitutional questions, which is totally inconsistent with any proper administration of the government, or any regular execution of the laws. Social disorder, entire uncertainty in regard to individual rights and individual duties, the cessation of legal authority, confusion, the dissolution of free government—all these are the inevitable consequences of the principles adopted by the message, whenever they shall be carried to their full extent. Hitherto it has been thought that the final decision of constitutional questions belonged to the supreme judicial tribunal. The very nature of free government, it has been supposed, enjoins this; and our Constitution, moreover, has been understood so to provide, clearly and expressly. It is true that each branch of the legislature has an undoubted right, in the exercise of its functions, to consider the constitutionality of a law proposed to be passed. This is naturally a part of its duty; and neither branch can be compelled to pass any law, or do any other act, which it deems to be beyond the reach of its constitutional power. The president has the same right, when a bill is presented for his approval, for he is, doubtless, bound to consider, in all cases, whether such bill be compatible with the Constitution, and whether he can approve it consistently with his oath of office. But when a law has been passed by Congress, and approved by the president, it is now no longer in the power, either of the same president or his successors, to say whether the law is constitutional or not. He is not at liberty to disregard it; he is not at liberty to feel or to affect "constitutional scruples," and to sit in judgment himself on the validity of a statute of the government, and to nullify it, if he so chooses. After a law has passed through all the requisite forms; after it has received the requisite legislative sanction and the executive approval, the question of its constitutionality then becomes a judicial question, and a judicial question alone. In the courts that question may be raised, argued, and adjudged; it can be adjudged nowhere else.

"The president is as much bound by the law as any private citizen, and can no more contest its validity than any private citizen. He may refuse to obey the law, and so may a private citizen; but both do it at their own peril, and neither of them can settle the question of its validity. The president may say a law is unconstitutional, but he is not the judge. Who is to decide that question?" [1188]

Such a position as Jackson's, Webster insisted, threatened the foundational structure of the government and calls for a reevaluation of power dynamics between the branches, insisting that the judiciary alone should determine the constitutionality of laws. Ultimately, the

---

[1188] Daniel Webster, "Speech on the Presidential Veto of the Bank Bill," July 11, 1832, TeachingAmericanHistory.org

New Englander warned, embracing the president's reasoning could lead to the downfall of the Constitution itself.

"It remains now for the people of the United States to choose between the principles here avowed and their government. These cannot subsist together. The one or the other must be rejected. If the sentiments of the message shall receive general approbation, the Constitution will have perished even earlier than the moment which its enemies originally allowed for the termination of its existence. It will not have survived to its fiftieth year."[1189]

Jackson's veto of the bank recharter bill is recognized as one of the most significant and debated vetoes in United States history. His decision sent the bill back to Congress, where it failed to secure the necessary two-thirds majority to pass. As a result, the Supreme Court's ruling in McCulloch v. Maryland, which had validated the bank's existence, was effectively disregarded. The Bank of the United States ultimately ceased operations four years later when its original 20-year charter expired in 1836.

This veto also played a crucial role in Jackson's 1832 presidential campaign, for it won him favor with the people, although those in Congress who opposed him were anything but impressed with his leadership. Supporters of the Bank, including figures like Clay and Biddle, along with the rising Whig Party, believed that the veto could be unpopular enough to threaten Jackson's reelection prospects. Clay and Jackson emerged as the primary contenders in the upcoming election. Although Jackson had previously advocated for a one-term presidency and the rotation of officeholders, he was convinced by his allies to seek re-election. The allure of presidential power proved difficult to resist.

The campaign that followed was tumultuous. Supporters of the "Old Hero" rallied around the hickory pole, chanting, "Jackson forever: Go the Whole Hog!" Meanwhile, Clay's admirers proclaimed, "Freedom and Clay," while his opponents criticized his lifestyle choices, including dueling, gambling, cockfighting, and other excesses. Clay characterized the Democratic Party as "the Jackson party," suggesting it was merely a personal faction. As the 1832 election approached, Clay's "Coalition," in its second national election, could not boast of the popularity and prestige

---

[1189] Kennedy and Cohen, pg. 263.

that President Andrew Jackson commanded.[1190] Historian David S. Brown asserts that "The President seemed to will even his opposition into existence."[1191] The National Republicans criticized the Indian Removal Act and Jackson's veto of the national bank, emphasizing the threat of executive tyranny and denouncing his use of what they considered high-handed and unconstitutional actions. No single figure had a greater capacity to mobilize both supporters and detractors.

Henry Clay and his swaggering, overconfident National Republicans enjoyed impressive advantages. Ample funds flowed into their campaign chest, including $50,000 in what was referred to as "life insurance" from the Bank of the United States. Most newspaper editors, some of them "purchased" by Biddle's bank loans, dipped their pens in acid when they wrote of Jackson.

During this contentious period, political parties seemed to form almost out of thin air. Another emerging faction, the anti-Masonic Party, fielded a candidate in former Cherokee defender William Wirt. The Anti-Masons were primarily opposed to secret societies that influenced political agendas, viewing the Freemasons similarly to how Jackson perceived the national bank—as an elite group seeking to control government direction. As historian David M. Kennedy points out, "The Anti-Masonic party appealed to long-standing American suspicions of secret societies, which they condemned as citadels of privilege and monopoly–a note that harmonized with the democratic chorus of the Jacksonians. But since Jackson himself was a Mason, and publicly gloried in his membership, the Anti-Masonic party was also an anti-Jackson party." [1192] Anti-Masons gained the backing of various evangelical Protestant groups aiming to leverage political influence for moral reform and to advance their religious objectives, such as banning mail delivery on Sundays and maintaining the sanctity of the Sabbath. Economically, the Anti-Masonic Party supported internal improvements and a protective tariff, aligning with Clay's National Republican coalition. However, despite their efforts to organize Wirt's campaign, the Anti-Masonic Party was in decline by 1832, and by 1840, its remaining members had merged into the Whig Party. Established in 1834 as a response to

---

[1190] ibid
[1191] Brown, David S., *The First Populist*, Ch. 25.
[1192] ibid

what they called "King Andrew Jackson," the Whig Party, led by Clay, represented a progression from the National Republicans, encompassing others who felt that the executive branch had become too dominant in national politics. "Every engine is at work to batter down the reputation and popularity of Uncle, "Andrew Donelson wrote to his brother-in-law in 1832. "but as far as I can perceive, he is gaining new strength in the affection and love of the people."

The 1832 presidential election introduced several new elements, including the emergence of multiple third parties, such as the States' Rights party, primarily composed of southerners and individuals from border states. Additionally, this election saw the organization of three national nominating conventions to select candidates. Another significant development came from the Anti-Masons and a faction of National Republicans, who implemented formal platforms to clearly communicate their stances on various issues.

The 1832 election was a significant moment in the democratization of the nation. It was marked by political cartoons, barbecues, and various campaign strategies, which highlighted a shift away from serious discussions about crucial public issues. These tactics reflected politicians' efforts to connect with the masses by appealing to what they believed would garner popular support. One commentator noted the influence of striking pamphlets and well-run newspapers on voters, stating, "a hickory pole, a catchy cry, a transparency, and a display of fireworks hold more sway over a significant portion of our electorate than printed eloquence ever could." An Ohio editor aptly remarked, "there is no resisting such arguments."[1193]

The election spanned several weeks, and it ultimately resulted in a decisive victory for Jackson. The people had given Jackson a mandate for a second term. "Old Hickory" garnered 54.2% of the popular vote and 76% (219 to 49) of the electoral vote, winning 16 states compared to Clay's six. Wirt managed to secure only Vermont, while the states' rights candidate, Virginian John Floyd, also won one state (South Carolina). Clay proved to be a poor candidate, trailing three states and six percentage points behind John Adams' already lackluster performance four years earlier. Jackson, now more than ever, claimed a strong national

---

[1193] Remini, *Election of 1832*, I, 514.

following, receiving support from nearly every region. He performed significantly better in New York and New England, areas that had previously shown little support. His party also improved its standing, gaining three additional congressional seats. Unsurprisingly, Jackson excelled in the South, swept the Northwest, and captured much of the Mid-Atlantic states. In Maryland, one of the eight states where Jackson lost, the vote difference was a razor-thin margin of just four votes out of 38,000 cast.

Although Jackson did not set any historical records for popularity—several presidents, including Jefferson, Lincoln, Grant, Teddy and Franklin Roosevelt, Eisenhower, Nixon, and Ronald Reagan received higher percentages of popular support—he did secure a notable victory. Jackson actually received a smaller percentage of the vote than in 1828, becoming one of only four presidents to experience such a decline. With one percent less support than four years earlier, he joined Madison, FDR (twice), and Barack Obama in this unusual statistic. The presence of third-party candidates detracted from Jackson's popular vote, and while the Democratic Party gained some congressional seats, they ultimately lost control of the Senate during the 1832 election. These shifts in Senatorial power certainly had a detrimental effect on Jackson's results, but nevertheless, Old Hickory was riding high by renewing the people's mandate, defeating the big-money Kentuckian. A new Jacksonian wave swept over the West and South, surged into the Middle States, and even washed into the rocky coasts of New England.

While such electoral developments were not uncommon in American election politics, they illustrated voters' ability to distinguish candidates from their parties. Blair, Kendall and the Jackson propagandists had made the election a moral issue, with Jackson as their moral champion. To the masses, Jackson was more than a candidate or a symbol to them, he appealed to their moral values, to what they considered right and wrong. The dignity with which they viewed Jackson added to their own moral dignity, as they sought social equality with the elites they had long been placed below on the class pyramid. Jackson's appeal was that he was the answer to the corruption of Washington. He was not one to pander for votes, or to make corrupt bargains. He represented the conscience and patriotism of the common voter, he was their standard-bearer. Andrew Jackson epitomized this dynamic and vibrant democracy. His appeal extended beyond his military achievements; by 1832, he was perceived not just as the "hero of New Orleans," but as the "Man of the People." As one politician put it, "Democracy and Jackson are one."[1194]

John Quincy Adams' son, Charles Francis Adams, expressed his dismay over the election results, stating, "The disastrous result of the presidential election throws a gloom over the political affairs of the country, which is deeper and darker than it ever has been before. The fate of our currency is sealed and the judiciary is in imminent danger. Office ceases to be honorable and is everywhere triumphant."[1195] In defeat, Clay expressed another concerning lament, "The dark cloud, which is suspended over our country, instead of it being dispelled as we had hoped it would be, has become more dense, more menacing, more alarming."[1196]

[1194] Dallas to Edward Livingston, May 30, 1831, Livingston Papers, JRDF.
[1195] JQA to Charles Francis Adams, Nov. 1832, Adams Memoirs, IV.
[1196] Clay to Hammond, Nov. 17, 1832, Clay Papers, PHC, VIII, 199.

CHAPTER

78

PET BANKS

"Nothing but widespread suffering will produce any effect on Congress."
—Nicholas Biddle

Having already won the Congressional battle against the Bank of the United States and knowing that its charter was set to expire in 1836, President Jackson was now determined to see it dismantled without any further delay. He believed he had gained significant support from the public, which motivated him to take action against the bank once and for all. To prevent the bank's president, Biddle, from attempting to manipulate the situation for a recharter, Jackson decided in 1833 to eliminate the bank entirely. On Sept. 17, Jackson announced to his cabinet his plans withdraw the federal deposits from the Bank's vaults. Jackson proposed that no new funds would be deposited with Biddle and that existing deposits would gradually be reduced by using them for the government's daily expenses. This strategy would effectively drain the bank's resources and ensure its downfall.

Removing federal deposits from the Bank of the United States was a nasty and complicated business. Even the president's closest advisors opposed this seemingly unnecessary, possibly unconstitutional, and certainly vindictive policy. Jackson's cabinet officers, particularly Duane, Cass and Woodbury, walking a very thin line, argued against such a risky step. From Jackson's viewpoint, the situation worsened on March 2, when the House voted 109 to 46 against selling the government's shares in the

Bank, implicitly rejecting his concerns about its solvency. In reaction to these challenges, Jackson expressed his anger toward his congressional adversaries, particularly Clay and Calhoun. He confided to a friend that they "wield the United States Bank, and with its corrupting influence, they calculate to carry everything, including its renewed charter by a two-thirds vote in Congress, against the veto of the executive. If they can do this, they calculate with certainty to put Clay or Calhoun in the presidency, and I have no hesitancy to say that if they can recharter the bank with this hydra of corruption they will rule the nation, and its charter will be perpetual and its corruptive influence will destroy the liberty of our nation."[1197]

Jackson, lacking self-reflection, saw any opposition to his policies as evidence of corruption and a personal attack that warranted, nay, demanded, a ferocious response. Consequently, his allies targeted journalists and politicians who were deemed insufficiently supportive of Jackson's agenda. A notable instance was Roger Taney's fierce critique of the *New York Courier and Intelligencer*, a newspaper that had previously backed Jackson during the election but now opposed his Bank policies. Taney alleged that the newspaper's editors had "secretly received $50,000 from Mr. Biddle, the president of the bank."[1198]

These fierce attacks proved effective, as many who had once supported Jackson and the Bank now began to openly oppose it. The conflict over the Bank became a defining issue for the Democratic Party. Consequently, being a Democrat meant embracing Jacksonian principles, particularly a strong opposition to the Bank. Those who did not, faced irrelevance within the Party.

Determined to win at all costs, a frustrated Jackson was forced to reshuffle his cabinet twice before he could find a Secretary of the Treasury who would comply with his strong will.

Although Jackson had a personal fondness for Louis McLane and preferred not to make divisive changes in his Cabinet hastily, he removed the bank issue from McLane's responsibilities. However, when the moderately pro-Bank McLane declined to withdraw government deposits from the Bank, Jackson felt compelled to replace him with someone willing to do so, offering McLane the esteemed position of U.S.

[1197] Kahan, Paul, *The Bank War*, Ch. 5.
[1198] ibid

Secretary of State instead, in order to free up Edward Livingston to take the desired position as minister to France. By reshuffling his Cabinet, Jackson aimed to retain the capable McLane without burdening him with the task of dismantling the Bank. McLane was appointed U.S. Secretary of State in a recess appointment and served from May 29, 1833, until June 30, 1834. He quickly undertook the first major reorganization of the department, establishing seven new bureaus.

On May 29th, 1833, Jackson chose William J. Duane as McLane's successor, but Duane was equally reluctant to remove the deposits. This appointment proved embarrassing for Jackson, with many placing the blame on McLane for the situation. But it was Jackson whose moves were greatly controversial. Irate with Duane, Jackson struggled to find the right man for the job. Eventually, Jackson realized that the man he needed was already in his cabinet, and was the guiding voice behind much of the Bank War maneuvers from the start, Roger B. Taney.

Under Taney, the deposits were steadily and systematically removed. Duane defended his own position in his book *Narrative and Correspondence Concerning the Removal of the Deposites, and Occurrences Connected Therewith*, published in 1838.[1199] Jackson biographer James Parton writes of Duane's courage in standing up to Old Hickory. He lauds the Treasury Secretary for refusing to yield to a position that he could not in good conscience accept, therefore preserving his integrity and honor. "In not yielding," Parton says, "he displayed a genuine moral heroism."[1200] Later Jackson biographer Robert V. Remini treats Duane far less favorably. He faults both Jackson and Duane for the turmoil that characterized Duane's brief time in office. He criticizes Jackson for not adequately screening Duane before nominating him, for allowing members of his administration to treat him poorly upon taking office, and for his dismissal of Duane. He continues: "But Duane is not without fault. When all is said and done, he placed his own judgment above that of the President. All because of wounded pride, he challenged not only Jackson's policy but his authority to make that policy. He was a small-minded, inconsequential bureaucrat, and he deserved to be sacked." [1201]

[1199] Duane, William J., *Narrative and Correspondence Concerning the Removal of the Deposites, and Occurrences Connected Therewith*, Philadelphia, 1838.
[1200] Parton, *Jackson*, III, p. 433.
[1201] Remini, *Andrew Jackson and the Bank War*. 1984, pp. 115-124.

In light of Jackson's decision to withdraw federal deposits from the Bank of the United States, Biddle became desperate. In a last-ditch effort, Biddle called in his bank loans, seemingly trying to demonstrate the Banks' importance by creating a minor financial crisis. Several unstable banks faced dire consequences due to "Biddle's Panic," but Jackson remained resolute. If anything, the chaotic behavior of the dying bank seemed to confirm the earlier claims made by its opponents.

However, the real victim here in Jackson's win at all costs show of force embodied by the withdrawals was the American economy. The central banking system that Biddle managed prevented regional banks from handing out risky loans on ventures that Biddle and the board did not feel confident in. Therefore, the demise of the Bank of the United States created a financial void throughout the United States, initiating a turbulent cycle of booms and busts. As surplus federal funds were funneled into various state institutions—known as "pet banks," selected for their loyalty to Jackson, the nation was soon flooded with paper currency, and speculation ran amuck. Without a reliable central bank to provide oversight, these pet banks, along with smaller "wildcat banks"—often consisting of little more than a few chairs and a suitcase filled with printed notes—were determined to right the wrongs of the past, especially in the west, by handing out speculative loans at an alarming rate. These state banks, which were not backed by gold or silver, issued only paper money in their lending practices. Deflation was another result of these shoddy lending practices.

The term "pet banks" emerged because many banks were selected not for their financial stability, but rather through the spoils system, which favored Jackson's friends and political allies with government positions. Having secured reelection in an overwhelming victory in1832, largely due to his campaign advocating the dissolution of the Second Bank of the United States, Jackson decided he had the approval he needed to go forward with the dismantling of the "Monster" Bank of the United States. He instructed Taney to oversee the transfer of government deposits to these pet banks. The state-chartered banks that were favored with federal monies were those which demonstrated their undying loyalty to his administration.

By 1833, through the combined efforts of Jackson and Taney, there were 23 of these pet banks holding U.S. Treasury funds. The establishment of these banks resulted in a significant increase in land speculation, as their managers struggled to effectively manage the nation's finances. During this time, the country experienced a remarkable rise in banking capital, loans, and currency circulation, compounded by the inefficacy of the banks' management.

However, most pet banks ultimately faced financial losses and failed in their investments. The 23 banks were inadequate to handle the entire public's money. Both the pet banks and smaller "wildcat" banks inundated the nation with paper currency, leading to a decline in its reliability. In response to this instability, Jackson issued the Specie Circular, which will be discussed further in the next chapter.

As a result of the dispersal of government funds through pet banks, it became nearly impossible to mobilize the remaining specie reserves of gold and silver. It became evident that Nicholas Biddle's role in the economic stability of the nation was underestimated. Soon, a financial disaster was very much in the making, and one that would make the Panic of 1819 look like a walk in the park.

As the 1830s progressed, new political parties began to take shape. By 1828, the Democratic-Republicans, led by Andrew Jackson, proudly adopted the name "Democrats," previously disdained by many. In response to Jackson's czar-like use of presidential power, his opponents labeled him "King Andrew I" and began to unite in the name of anti-Jacksonian belief[1202]. In the 1833-1834 session, led by Henry Clay, Jackson's congressional foes who had converged in their anti-Jacksonian coalition made it official: the new Whig Party was formed. The use of the name Whigs was intentional, borrowed from Revolutionary-era American and British opponents of royal prerogative.

The Whigs had been forged in the turbulence of the early Jackson years, although they had not yet coalesced officially until now. Initially criticized as "an organized incompatibility" due to the extremely diverse elements among their membership, their primary unifying factor was a shared disdain for Andrew Jackson and his perceived "executive

---

[1202] Cole, Donald B., *The Presidency of Andrew Jackson*. University Press of Kansas, 1993, pp. 211-213.

usurpation." The Whigs became a recognizable group in the 1834 Senate surrounding the Clay-Webster-Calhoun triumvirate collaboration to oppose Jackson for what they considered the unilateral and unlawful removal of federal deposits from the Bank of the U.S. Thereafter, the Whigs quickly grew into a powerful national political force by attracting the many various groups disillusioned with Jackson: supporters of Clay's American System, southern states' rights advocates upset with Jackson's stance on nullification, northern industrialists, merchants, and eventually many evangelical Protestants associated with the Anti-Masonic party. The Whigs were a diverse amalgamation of all of the various interests.

Although the Whigs considered themselves conservatives, they were progressive in advocating for active government programs and reforms. Instead of pursuing extensive territorial acquisitions, they focused on internal improvements within the existing U.S. territory. This included federal funding for canals, railroads, and telegraph lines, as well as government-supported institutions such as prisons, asylums, and public schools. The Whigs embraced the market economy, garnering support from manufacturers in the North, planters in the South, and merchants and bankers across the nation. However, contrary to the Democratic portrayal of the Whigs as merely a party of wealthy elites, by incorporating anti-Masonic supporters, Jackson's opposition increased their appeal to the common man. The anti-Masons depicted Jackson and his New York successor, Martin Van Buren, as arrogant aristocrats. This shifted the narrative, with the Whigs positioning themselves as champions of the common man and branding the Democrats as a party of cronyism and corruption. The tides were turning.

The Whigs rode the tide of Jackson's controversies. What had happened to the promises of preserving liberty, they asked. Thanks to the efforts of the increasingly relevant Whigs, many former Jackson supporters began to believe that he was gradually, whether intentionally or unintentionally, undermining this concept. He had altered the very definition of liberty, many argued, in which government would leave individuals alone to enjoy their natural rights. Governments were to be on standby, ready to protect any infringements on those freedoms when necessary. People could enjoy the benefits of their labor without government interference, a notion that persisted to some extent during Jackson's time.

ANDREW JACKSON: THE POLITICS OF RESENTMENT

In the early stages of the Bank War, Jackson returned to this idea. However, as his era progressed, liberty became equivalent to majority rule; to be considered free, one had to conform to the will of the majority. This Locke-ian ideology seemed a divergence from the liberty Jefferson had spoken of in 1776. Since Jackson claimed to represent the people, his agenda of "reform, retrenchment, and economy" was seen as their collective demand. Rejecting this agenda was viewed as rejecting majority rule. Opposing the majority was said to threaten the liberty of everyone, or so the argument went.

By 1834, relations between the Senate and President Andrew Jackson had gone beyond simply souring, they had become putrid, to the point in which the president chose to postpone submitting his recent cabinet appointees for confirmation until the last week of the congressional session. Even before the formation of the Whigs was official, and despite Jackson's landslide victory in 1832, the Clay-ites had taken control of the Senate. The Bank War marked the clear dividing line, and by March it came to a head. On March 28, 1834, Jackson became the first president to suffer censure for his actions in the Bank War. This formal disapproval from Congress, from having dismantled the Bank of the United States, and having found a friendlier source of funds for his western expansion plans, Jackson, ever the Wild West frontiersman, had made innumerable enemies in Congress for his adamant opposition to the Bank. Reaction against the president's move was swift. Congress could not charge Jackson with a crime, per se, so the censure was their way of condemning the president's actions in the Bank crisis. Congress declared, as their reasoning, the president's refusal to hand over classified documents from an 1831 meeting with his cabinet, in which he discussed his Bank veto.

With Clay at its helm, the senators demanded to see the 1831 meeting documents. By June 1834, the Senate was evenly split between Jackson's supporters and his opponents. When Jackson refused their release, Clay retaliated by introducing a resolution to censure the president in the Senate, declaring Jackson's actions unconstitutional. This unprecedented remedy of censure, rather than impeachment, was again dictated by circumstance. Clay later said that "No senator believed, in 1834, that, whether the President merited impeachment or not, he ever would be impeached... by a majority of his political friends in the House of Representatives."[1203] Since no impeachment would be forthcoming, given the balance of political forces, a censure resolution was the only way to express the Senate's views in framing the campaign for the 1834 elections. In Thomas Hart Benton's view, censure was "purely and simply for popular effect. Great reliance was placed upon that effect. It was fully believed... That a senatorial condemnation would destroy whomsoever it struck—even General Jackson."[1204]

Congress debated the proposed censure for 10 weeks. Jackson protested, saying that since the Constitution did not provide any guidance regarding censure of a president, the resolution to censure him was therefore unconstitutional. The Senate chose not to publish his message in its journal, though, and Congress ignored him, voting on March 28 in favor of censure. This largely symbolic wrist-slap of the president amounted to no more than a public scolding for assuming authority and power not conferred by the Constitution.

Censuring Jackson only fueled the president's ire however, and it failed to stop Jackson from revamping the federal banking system. Democrats regained the majority in the Senate in 1837 and would seek to expunge Jackson's censure from the record. Characteristically, Jackson took the reprimand personally. A biographer later attested that when Jackson retired from the presidency, the only regret he expressed was not being able to shoot Henry Clay.[1205]

To better understand the context of all the financial and legal maneuverings, it's important to zoom out just a little more. The bank veto emerged in the early 1830s at a pivotal moment, and it became the issue that exposed internal divisions within the Democratic Party; divisions that had previously remained concealed. While the majority of President Jackson's supporters opposed the bank, a faction—primarily those who had endorsed the Maysville "Turnpike"—advocated for traditional financial practices and federal spending. In 1830, Jackson struggled to maintain this coalition, and now, Clay sought to compel Jackson to take

---

[1203] Henry Clay, 1834-1844, Henry Clay Papers, 1834-1844, Univ. of North Carolina Libraries.

[1204] Thomas Hart Benton, 1834, Thomas Hart Benton Papers, Missouri History Consortium.

[1205] Article in *The Columbus Dispatch*, Jan. 15, 2023.

a definitive stance. As Clay was the presidential candidate opposing Jackson in 1832, he perceived a real campaign opportunity.

Nine months prior, Jackson appointed Roger Taney, the architect of his anti-bank strategies, as Secretary of the Treasury. Many senators, already exasperated with Jackson for what they considered blatant abuse of executive power, argued that Taney was illegally holding his office without confirmation. As Jackson biographer Robert Remini noted, "Whether this was true did not disturb Jackson one whit."[1206] However, Jackson was aware that he eventually needed to present Taney's nomination to the Senate, knowing that senators would fiercely oppose it as retribution for the removal of the deposits, and that Taney would likely suffer greatly as a result.

The Supreme Court became a focal point during the lame duck congressional session of 1835. Although the Democrats celebrated substantial victories in the midterm elections, a conservative majority persisted in the Senate. Following the death of Justice Johnson in Autumn 1834, Jackson nominated a fellow slaveholder, Representative James Wayne of Georgia, to succeed him. Wayne's bipartisan support stemmed from his unionist position during the nullification crisis, leading to his confirmation. Subsequently, Justice Duval's resignation prompted Jackson to nominate Taney as his successor.

In stark contrast to Wayne's appointment, Taney's nomination incited significant controversy. His actions related to the removal of deposits from the bank positioned him as a radical figure. One opposition publication criticized the appointment, stating, "The pure ermine of the Supreme Court is sullied by the appointment of that political hack, Roger B. Taney." The Senate had previously rejected Taney's nomination for treasury secretary, and there was a concerted effort to block his advancement. Instead of outright opposition, Webster devised a strategy illustrating the lengths to which Jackson's opponents would go to undermine his constitutional authority.

To understand the unfolding of the Taney nomination, one must consider the judiciary's structure in the 1830s. During this era, the nation was divided into various judicial circuits, with circuit courts consisting of a

---

[1206] Remini, Robert V., *Andrew Jackson and the Course of American Empire*, 1822-1832, p. 373.

district judge and a Supreme Court justice who rode circuit to hear cases. Each justice was assigned to a circuit, ensuring familiarity with relevant state laws. Consequently, when a vacancy arose in the Supreme Court, it also created an opening in the corresponding circuit, necessitating that the number of circuits match the number of justices. This arrangement placed significant constraints on the president's ability to fill vacancies, as nominees had to originate from the circuit of the previous justice.

As the nation expanded, the need for new circuits became evident. By the 1830s, approximately one-fourth of the states, primarily in the West, were outside the circuit system. Congress attempted to address this by allowing a single district judge to exercise jurisdiction over both district and circuit courts, though this solution was far from ideal, granting considerable power to a lone judge. Efforts to create new circuits for western states encountered political resistance, as expanding the Supreme Court would grant Jackson additional justices.

Faced with Taney's nomination to replace Justice Duval, Webster proposed legislation merging two smaller eastern circuits while establishing a new western circuit. This approach aimed to maintain the number of circuits and court seats while extending judicial access to underserved areas. However, if successful, the vacancy would shift westward, forcing Jackson to withdraw his nomination. Webster expressed his intent to a colleague, indicating that the measure aimed to remove Taney without appearing overtly political.

"Court tampering" has been a tactic employed by various generations, often justified by technical arguments rather than overt political motives. The Jeffersonians' repeal of the Judiciary Act of 1801, which eliminated Federalist judges, was defended on the grounds of a reduced need for judges given the limited federal docket. Conversely, during the New Deal, proposals for court packing were rationalized by claiming justices were overwhelmed by their caseloads. Rarely did such measures occur without an efficiency rationale. Despite Webster's claims of impartial statesmanship, Jacksonians recognized the underlying intentions and ultimately rejected his bill.

When the insulted Jackson had resubmitted Taney's name for the position of associate justice of the Supreme Court a year before, opponents stalled a vote on the final day of that session and attempted unsuccessfully to reduce the number of seats on the Court. When the

ANDREW JACKSON: THE POLITICS OF RESENTMENT

Senate reconvened in December 1835, with the narrow Democratic majority, Jackson nominated Taney again, following Chief Justice Marshall's death that summer, this time for the Chief Justice position. After prolonged negotiations and intense debate, the Senate ultimately confirmed Taney. The composition reflected increased public support for Jackson and his party, and the new Democratic Senate confirmed him. With Taney in the Chief Justice role, Jackson capitalized on his political momentum, successfully passing a circuit reform bill that established two new western circuits and expanded the number of justices from seven to nine. This reform was not only necessary to address the exclusion of western states from the circuit system but also allowed Jackson to consolidate control over the judiciary.

This instance marked the first successful example of court packing in American history and represented a significant achievement for the Jacksonian generation. Reformers would henceforth pursue their agenda through judicial channels rather than through formal constitutional amendments. Despite this pragmatic approach, it would be erroneous to conclude that the movement did not seek constitutional alteration; rather, the means of affecting change were redefined.

As new constitutional generations often encounter resistance from the remnants of the old establishment, the Jacksonian era illustrates an exception. Figures like Clay and Webster continued their opposition despite electoral defeats, remaining steadfast until their efforts culminated in the rise of the Whig Party in 1840, which temporarily displaced the Democrats.[1207]

However, this resurgence was short-lived due to the untimely death of President William Henry Harrison shortly after his inauguration, leading to the ascension of Vice President John Tyler. Tyler's presidency represented a return to state rights principles, complicating the Democratic agenda and temporarily stalling Jackson's legacy.

Ultimately, the bank endured until the expiration of its charter in 1836, subsequently acquiring a state charter as the Bank of the United States of Pennsylvania. This long-standing conflict, known as the Bank War, effectively precluded any substantial regulation of private banks

---

[1207] Kennedy and Cohen, p. 264.

in the United States for nearly 80 years, until the establishment of the Federal Reserve System in 1913.

At the start of 1837, as Jackson prepared to leave office, he expressed to a friend his eagerness to see his loyal supporter, president-elect Martin Van Buren, sworn in by Chief Justice Taney. Whether or not this was motivated by spite, the ironic protagonists of Jackson's appointment rejections, now redeemed for all to see, had to have bathed the old General in a sense of schadenfreude in the presence of Clay, Calhoun, Webster and others of the outgoing president's many detractors. The satisfaction of witnessing the heralded ceremony of two recipients of the loftiest positions in the land, head of the Supreme Court, and chief executive, both placed there by the mighty arm of the Populist King Andrew Jackson. The chagrin of the Whigs was palpable, and one could almost detect its acrid scent in the winds blowing off the Potomac.

On July 2, 1834, a dramatic event unfolded involving anti-Jacksonians in the historic city of Boston, Massachusetts. Contrary to what many may have hoped at the time, it was not the President himself who was beheaded, but rather his figurehead onboard the famous ship, the U.S.S. Constitution. This incident was believed to be linked to the ongoing Bank War, which had begun in the summer of 1832. The U.S.S. Constitution had sustained damage during the War of 1812 and had fallen into disrepair. Plans were made to dismantle the ship, but public outcry led President Jackson to order its repair at the Charlestown Navy Yard in Boston. During this process, the original figurehead, a sculpture of Hercules, was removed. Commodore Jesse Duncan Elliott, a protégé of Jackson, commissioned a new figurehead depicting the President himself, commemorating Jackson's warm reception in Boston after receiving an honorary doctorate from Harvard University in 1833. However, by 1834, Jackson's popularity in Boston had significantly declined, primarily due to his opposition to the Second Bank of the United States.

It had been two years since Congress, led by Senator Henry Clay, sought to renew the charter of the Second Bank of the United States, set to expire in 1836. Jackson's veto of the bill was widely detested throughout much of New England, especially in prominent urban areas such as Boston. While Jackson still viewed the Bank as unconstitutional and detrimental to southern and western farmers, he remained outspoken in his belief that Biddle's bank favored the economic elite at the expense of the agricultural sector. To diminish the Bank's power, Jackson had gone through two Treasury Secretaries before finding one amenable to his instructions, which were initiated on October 1, 1833. By the summer of 1834, the transfer of federal funds to various state banks was well underway.

In response, Nicholas Biddle's self-imposed "Panic" was ignited to demonstrate the need for a central bank. This strategy backfired, as noted, leading to public outrage and providing support for the Anti-Bank Jacksonian Democrats. The move negatively impacted Boston merchants, many of whom had outstanding debts with the Bank, threatening east coast trade.

By April 1834, Laban Smith Beecher had completed the new figurehead, which was then placed aboard the Constitution under heavy guard. However, on the stormy night of July 2, the figurehead was decapitated. Samuel Dewey, an 18-year-old captain with the West Indies Company, later confessed to the act, claiming the storm helped him conceal his actions. He sawed off the head below the nose, leaving the mouth and chin attached to the body. Dodge & Son was commissioned to create a new head for the figurehead, and the Constitution set sail for New York in 1835, where the new head was attached to the original body.

After hiding the severed head for some time, Dewey decided to return it to Andrew Jackson. However, Jackson was too ill to meet him, so Dewey handed it over to Vice President Martin Van Buren. Van Buren advised Dewey to take it to Secretary of the Navy Mahlon Dickerson, who attempted to arrest Dewey. However, there was no law against the beheading of figureheads, and most media outlets were skeptical of Dewey's confession, as it lacked political motives. Ultimately, the original head and body were reunited in a collection, though they remain separate to this day.[1208] The Bank War had claimed another victim.

[1208] Hazelwood, Madeliene; Associate Registrar, Museum of the City of New York. Sunday, May 14, 2017.

CHAPTER

79

PLANTING THE SEEDS OF RECESSION

"The president has promulgated a rule of action for those who have taken the oath to support the Constitution of the United States, that must, if there be practical conformity to it, introduce general nullification, and end in the absolute subversion of the government."

—Henry Clay

The financial chaos only worsened throughout President Andrew Jackson's second term in the executive chair. Playing bully ball with the economy for the sake of personal resentments would ultimately bring calamity to the nation. In the middle of 1836, the year Biddle's bank collapsed entirely, Jackson signed a bill that increased the number of banks that received government deposits. This Deposit Bill led to the distribution of the federal surplus to banks in the states and fed speculation in the wild market for public lands. The economy soon burst into a frenzy of out-of-control speculation. In an attempt to rein in the unbridled economy that same summer, Jackson used an executive order authorizing the Treasury to issue the infamous "Specie Circular" on July 11th. Wildcat currency had become so unreliable, especially in the West, that Jackson felt the decree was necessary. The Specie Circular mandated that all public land purchases were to be made with "hard" or metallic money, known as specie (gold and silver) as payment for public lands over 320 acres. The executive order's secondary goal was to quash the enormous growth of paper money in circulation as well. The Treasury, pet banks and other receivers of public money were to accept only specie after August 15.

The Specie Circular marked Jackson's knee-jerk reaction to fears of another "panic," as the rapid rise in speculation too closely resembled the lead up to the Panic of 1819. This time around, the recession was largely driven by the Bank War and the removal of Native Americans. The Bank War removed important regulatory measures on soft currency, which included notes that could fluctuate in value, while the Indian Removal opened up extensive new lands for sale. Slamming the brakes on the speculative boom, this hairpin turn would ultimately contribute to another panic just a year later, as the circular, by seriously curtailing the use of paper money, was highly deflationary, and at least in part produced the ensuing credit crunch in the economic crisis called the panic of 1837. This was exactly the downturn Jackson had hoped to avoid by enacting the measure. By the time the fallout fully took hold, Jackson had returned to his Nashville home, celebrated as the hero of his era, leaving his successor to address the Panic.

In response to the Specie Circular, many investors rushed to snap up as many western lands as they could using quickly-depreciating paper money from state banks, which was, far too often, not backed by hard currency. Not wishing to leave office in the midst of a potential repeat of the Panic of 1819, Jackson sided in favor of restricting credit. For most Whigs, and even some Democrats, the Specie Circular reinforced their belief in the president's financial incompetence. They found the whole scheme entirely unreasonable, primitive, and risky to replace a limited supply of precious metals with paper currency in an ever-expanding nation. Daniel Webster spoke in the Senate on this matter. "An exclusive circulation of gold and silver is a thing absolutely impracticable, and if practicable, not at all to be desired in as much as its effect will be to abolish credit, to repress the enterprise and diminish the earnings of the industrial classes, and produce faster and sooner than anything else in this country, a class of monied aristocracy." [1209]

[1209] Daniel Webster's Address to the Senate, 1836, *The Writings and Speeches of Daniel Webster*, Univ. of California, 1903, Vo. 14.

A group of concerned Democrats aligned with Webster on the issue, crossing party lines to collaborate with Whigs to pass a bill several weeks later that effectively nullified the order. An enraged Jackson criticized those Democrats who had defected the ranks over the circular. "I must express that the actions of some of our friends in the Senate regarding this paper currency are completely incomprehensible to me. Despite being self-proclaimed advocates of states' rights and hard money, they still voted for and passed a bill that incorporates banknotes into our currency."[1210] He formally expressed his disapproval by vetoing the bill just days before leaving office in 1837.

On May 21, 1838 a joint resolution of Congress repealed the species circular, once and for all.

The Jacksonian era was a time of fierce change in America. The nation was growing out of its infancy and into a buoyant adolescence, soon giving way to eager young adulthood. It was defined by strong personality and a wave of westward migration driven by increasing mobility, materialism, and a push for popular democracy. In 1835, William Ellery Channing, the foremost Unitarian preacher in the United States in the early nineteenth century, described American society as filled with "jarring interests and passions, invasions of rights, resistance of authority, violence, and force....older paternalistic patterns were in decline while urban growth and immigration, riots, poverty, sectionalism and slavery, suggested to some a coming upheaval."[1211] The various reform movements that grew out of the Second Great Awakening signaled a shift away from older rural, paternalistic patterns and toward urban growth, immigration, and political upheaval. One's America of Fathers and Mothers was slowly, and for the first time, giving way to the America of the Sons and Daughters. Reform movements of the antebellum period, particularly temperance, abolitionism, and women's rights, emerged from a mix of hope and anxiety, seeking to reshape the nation's evolving republican culture.

[1210] AJ to Coffee, July, 1836, Jackson Papers, LC.
[1211] Channing, 1835, William Ellory Channing Papers, 1791, 1892, Massachusetts Historical Society.

ANDREW JACKSON: THE POLITICS OF RESENTMENT

Amid the turbulence of the times, it seems rather appropriate in hindsight that Andrew Jackson, renowned far and wide for his confrontational and self-righteous demeanor, became the first U.S. president targeted for assassination. The intense partisanship that brought him to power is a direct result of the increased number of Americans who moiled in the midst of the vast changes of the period. While it could be argued that the 1790s were just as contentious a period politically, by the 1830s, an entire new generation of upstart westerners had now added to the complex and diverse fabric of American political discourse, and Jackson was at the helm of this demographic. The targeting of Jackson appears in a sense to be somewhat foreseeable, if not grimly fitting. Often aggressive, self-righteous and bellicose, at times even to the point of bullying, he could invite the animus of others. Many viewed his duel with Dickinson as a calculated act of cold-blooded murder. He bore the weight of bullets fired by men motivated by a mix of honor, resentment, and fear.

The General's contentious presidency was fodder for personal encounters, the first of which took place in May 1833 when Robert P. Randolph, a disgraced former naval purser, discharged on Jackson's discretion for the crime of stealing, found himself in close proximity to the president. In a cool act of defiance, Randolph would gain a measure of revenge on the steamboat Signet while it was docked in Alexandria, Virginia. The president and his entourage were en route to Fredericksburg, Randolph's home, to take part in a ceremony honoring Martha Washington. The unexpected closeness to the president offered a swift and opportunistic moment of vengeance for the disgruntled Randolph. James Parton documented the incident in his epochal Jackson biography. "Excuse my rising, sir, I have a pain in my side which makes it distressing for me to rise." Randolph made no reply to this courteous apology but appeared to be trying to take off his glove.

"Never mind your glove, sir," said the General, holding out his hand. At that very moment, Randolph thrust his hand violently into the president's face, intending as it appeared, to pull his nose. The captain of the boat who was standing nearby instantly seized Randolph, and drew him back. A violent scuffle ensued during which the table was broken. Randolph's friends onboard clutched him and hurried him ashore before any of the passengers knew what had occurred, and thus he affected his escape. Jackson's nose was reportedly bloodied and his pride predictably wounded. "I am not much hurt," he reportedly commented on the Cignet, while a few days later he complained to Van Buren of "the dastardly and cowardly insult offered me." John Quincy Adams saw the incident as a case of 'vicarious, cold revenge" for many of the long list of the general's victims over the years. "A president of the United States pulled by the nose is a new incident in the history of this country." Adams wrote, "And as he himself has countenanced personal violence against members of Congress, he will not meet with much sympathy." [1212]

But the insult onboard the *Cignet* paled in comparison to the first ever assassination attempt of a sitting U.S. president in the nation's history just two years later. In January, 1835, while the young republic had endured internal rebellions, intense partisanship, and increasing sectional divides, it had yet to experience an assassination attempt on the life of a sitting president, but that was about to change. After a memorial service for a South Carolina congressman in the large House chamber, Jackson and a small group were walking through the Capitol building toward the east portico when Richard Lawrence, a 30-year-old unemployed house painter, confronted the president just a few feet away. Lawrence drew a pocket pistol and fired, which, according to John Quincy Adams, who was nearby, sounded "like a squib." Fortunately for Jackson, the gunpowder in the barrel failed to ignite, prompting the panicked Lawrence to whip out a second pistol with his left hand. In response, Jackson, perhaps driven by a mix of alarm, anger, and self-preservation, drew his walking stick as if to defend himself. Lawrence fired again, but again the cap did not ignite the powder. A struggle ensued, and the would-be assassin was quickly subdued by a group of men and taken into custody. The writer Harriet Martineau, who witnessed the incident, noted that "the attack threw the old soldier into a tremendous passion."

Jackson's narrow escape, along with his history of surviving duels, battles, and various forms of political opposition, led his supporters to perceive a hint of divine intervention in the event. This perception was reinforced when it was later revealed that Lawrence's pistols, when tested after the fact, fired successfully on each pull of the trigger. Lawrence,

---

[1212] John Quincy Adams Correspondence, May, 1833, LOC.

exhibiting signs of mental illness, claimed that Jackson was a tyrant who was responsible for his father's death. He was ultimately found not guilty by reason of insanity and confined to institutions for the remainder of his life. Following the assassination attempt, Jackson himself was convinced of a conspiracy plot behind the attack, as were many Democrats, who suspected involvement from opposition figures. Blair's *Globe* too saw the divine in the assasination attempt, insisting "Providence has ever guarded the life of the man who has been destined to preserve and raise his country's glory and maintain the cause of the people." A skeptical Daniel Webster saw no such apotheosis, instead he feared that "thousands of ardent Jacksonians will believe there was a plot in it to remove this populist Messiah from his masses" and that "many more thousands will see in it new proof that he is especially favored and protected by heaven."

Critics of the Democrats argued that the incident was merely a ploy to garner sympathy. The variety of conspiracy theories shed light on the culture of distrust and partisanship so prevalent throughout the turbulent period. When Lawrence was later questioned as to his motive, he stated that he "could not rise unless the president fell, and that the mechanics would all be benefited and have plenty of work, and that money would be more plenty." When asked why there would be additional money, he replied "because it would be more easily obtained from the bank," and when asked which bank, he replied, "the Bank of the United States." For good measure, Lawrence called the president "a tyrant." And how did he form this conclusion, "it was a common talk among the people," he observed, "an opinion repeated in all the papers."

Visiting the United States to gather materials for a book she later published on American Society, Harriett Martineau sat down with Jackson the day after the assassination attempt. She later wrote of the president's conviction that the incident was part of a conspiracy, and his strident insistence upon it made her feel uncomfortable. "He protested that there was a plot, and that the man was merely a tool. And at length quoted the Attorney General as his authority. It was painful to hear a chief ruler publicly trying to persuade a foreigner that any of his constituents hated him to the death, and I took the liberty of changing the subject as soon as I could." [1213]

Jackson's suspicions reflected the politics of resentment on both sides of the divide that wished to make of Lawrence's effort something grander and more sinister. Such corrosive posturing indicates the depths to which partisanship was beginning to poison the nation. Rather than bringing the Americans together, Jackson's leadership was having just the opposite effect. The actions of a single delusional man had set into motion a reactive season of allegations, bickerings and bellowings among the country's chosen officials. Ever since the old corrupt bargain charge of 1824, government service seemed to correlate with corruption and distrust, and the effects continued to create reckless acrimony in a restless age. Mississippi senator George Poindexter, a Jackson critic, for having hired Lawrence for a house painting a few weeks prior to the assassination attempt, was accused by Jackson and numerous Democrats as being the chief conspirator, an accusation that dogged Poindexter and probably cost him reelection. Not only were these a byproduct of an impassioned and often inflammatory political discourse that continued well past 1835, but the unfounded accusations were the kind of irresponsible condemnations that in other nations, both past and present, led to brutal suppression.

In the midst of such a destructive spirit, the persistent thorn in the side that marked an even more divisive issue, and its peculiar place in the republic, began to generate an even deeper source of dispute that brought with it greater attention and moral interest. The divisive issue that grew out of this era of bitter partisanship which would threaten to bring the nation—one forged on the anvil of freedom—to its knees, containing the added emotionally charged element of the sanctity of human flesh and blood, was that of slavery.[1214]

Bank issues and internal improvements were the primary focus of Jackson's two terms in office. But he did engage in foreign affairs on occasion, interacting with major European powers through his State

---

[1213] Boissoneault, "The Attempted Assassination of Andrew Jackson," Smithsonian Magazine, March 4, 2017.
[1214] Brown, David S., Ch. 46.

Department appointees. Unlike his predecessors—Jefferson, Madison, Monroe, and Quincy Adams—who had all served as Secretary of State, Jackson did not have formal experience in international diplomacy. Critics often derided Jackson's lack of diplomatic savvy, with concerns over his actions in Florida still resonant, and the opposition questioned whether the irascible General had the temperament necessary to maintain peace in the country.

In his office at the State Department on Wednesday, March 28, 1832, Edward Livingston issued a revealing directive to American diplomats around the globe. From Rio to Saint Petersburg, envoys were instructed to inform foreign governments regarding a change in the long-standing protocol of the usual form of address in letters between nations. Though the order affected only six words, it represented a dramatic and symbolic power shift in the opening months of 1832. "It is observed that official communications from foreign powers intended for the executive of the United States have been usually addressed to the president and Congress," Livingston wrote, such a convention was fine in the pre-1787 days of the Articles of Confederation, but now Livingston said, "Its inaccuracy is apparent, the whole executive power, particularly that of foreign intercourse being vested in the president, you will therefore address a note to the minister for foreign affairs, apprising him that all communications made directly to the head of our executive government should be addressed to the president of the United States of America without any other addition."

Dropping the Senate and the House of Representatives from diplomatic correspondence was ceremonial but telling. Jackson was consolidating presidential power, and the fight at hand against the Bank of the United States was the catalyst. In this struggle against the big money interests, Jackson appealed to the people for support on the grounds that he, more than Congress, more than the courts, more than anything or anyone else, represented them. He was sending a message to Congress, the Senate, and to governments abroad, that he, and he alone, had the mandate of the people, and he would use this mandate to promote his agenda; an agenda that was characterized by prestige for America. More specifically, as any Whig worth their weight in salt would point out, this was clearly an attempt by Jackson to ensure the world that he was in charge, and he was White America, and White America was the world's royal family, as long as he was king.

Whether it was due to the ministers Jackson had selected to lead the charge in diplomacy with the two strongest nations of Europe, or his own reasonably adept statesmanship, when it came to international relations, Jackson's administration proved surprisingly effective. Especially considering that this success came about throughout two terms marked by a high rate of turnover. The State Department, headed by no less than five different men during Jackson's two terms, lacked traction, but secured enough footing to hammer out two seemingly favorable treaties. The Department was aided considerably by the culmination of the Napoleonic Wars, which seemed to have sapped much of the fight out of previously incendiary European rivalries.

A generation-long struggle that bedeviled Jeffersonian statecraft, the series of struggles ignited by the narcissistic Napoleon Bonaparte essentially brought European warfare to American shores. In their wake, the United States determined, with the Monroe Doctrine of 1823, to warn the Old World away from any attempts at future New World colonization. With this bold declamation, the walled off Western Hemisphere had mastered its geopolitical fate. As president, Jackson's first significant diplomatic success involved a new trade agreement with Great Britain. This achievement, considering the president's deeply rooted loathing of British power, gives some suggestion of the pragmatic qualities of leadership Jackson sometimes employed. Following the War of 1812, a series of British Navigation Acts, followed by retaliatory American measures, combined to seriously limit American exports to the lucrative West Indies trade.

The situation festered for several years until finally, in 1825, American shipping was banned entirely from British colonial ports. Naturally, Jackson supporters hammered away at then President Adams, renowned as a master of international politics, for failing to find a way to open this commerce. The impasse, stemming in part from the poor relations between Adams and British Secretary of Foreign Affairs George Canning, improved dramatically once Adams left office and Canning conveniently died. Determined to set aside all the issues dividing the powers, Louis McLane, the successor to Adams as American minister to the United Kingdom, negotiated a treaty in October 1830 which reopened West Indian seaports to American trade, and granted British ships most-favored-nation status in American ports. "The trade will be placed upon a footing decidedly more favorable to this country than any on which it ever stood," the President confidently informed the nation in his annual address. "Our commerce and navigation will enjoy in the colonial ports of Great Britain every privilege allowed to other nations." The New York Jacksonian James A. Hamilton boasted accurately enough, regarding the treaty, that "all ranks and parties, except the factious cavillers" are satisfied.[1215]

Feeding off this success, Jackson refused to let another chance at international acclaim slip away, especially when it involved the potential to "best" another mighty European power; France. Even more appealing to Jackson was the reward: French payment for past "injuries" against the United States. Jackson's State Department addressed a dispute with France regarding the "Spoliation Claims" resulting from French privateers' attacks on American ships during Napoleon's reign. In 1832, France had agreed to compensate the United States for shipping losses that accumulated from the late 1790s to 1815, but successive French governments failed to allocate the necessary funds, despite their intent to do so.

Jackson, eager to resolve the matter, collaborated with Louis McLane on a firm policy to confront France. However, Vice President Martin Van Buren, without consulting McLane, intervened and persuaded Jackson to grant France additional time. This action infuriated McLane, who seared at his obvious diminished authority with Jackson, leading to his resignation. The incident not only undermined McLane's efforts to orchestrate a deal with France, but also severed his friendship with Van Buren, resulting in them never speaking again. In the following year, Jackson appeared to have finally broken through in regard to the French situation, thanks primarily to the persistent efforts of one of McLane's trusted ministers, American diplomat William Cabell Rives. Appointed to France by Jackson in 1829, Rives received a rejection by the French government in June 1830, but in July, revolution brought Louis Phillippe to the French throne, and he proved more amenable to compromise. A

[1215] Wilcoxson, Samantha, *James Alexander Hamilton: Son of the American Revolution*, Pen and Sword History, 2025. p. 222.

Franco-American commission decided that France would pay 25 million francs in settlement of the claims. In July 1831, Rives and the French concluded a treaty, which was proclaimed a year later. [1216]

Through Rives' efforts, France agreed to pay the United States nearly $5,000,000 from damages inflicted on American shipping. Under the terms of the treaty, France was to pay the claims in six installments beginning in 1833. In return the United States agreed to pay a significantly smaller sum for the Revolutionary War claims of the Beaumarchais family, whose polymath patriarch Pierre Beaumarchais—inventor, spy, and author of the Barber of Seville, among other Figaro plays—provided arms, money supplies, munitions, and covert support for the American cause from both France and Spain to further the Revolution. Beaumarchais's estate, headed by his daughter Eugenie de Beaumarchais, had petitioned the United States for payment. In 1803, a Virginia court had ruled in favor of Beaumarchais, and the state agreed to pay his estate, with interest. After years of further legal and political battles, Beaumarchais's heirs finally received a settlement of 800,000 francs in 1835. Additionally, mutual adjustments on American long staple cotton and French bottled and casked wines were part of the compact.

Two months later, the Senate unanimously approved the treaty and in early February both nations exchanged ratifications. Jackson thought the accord and the one signed the previous year with Great Britain marked a real turning point in American international affairs. "Thus in two years," he wrote John Coffey shortly after receiving the French treaty, "we have been able to reach agreements with all foreign nations which had been the subject of negotiations for many years." But the sanguine president spoke too soon, for France's Chamber of Deputies took no positive action on the treaty until April of 1834, when the French received the United States' draft for the first payment, they balked; the French Parliament made no appropriation for payment.

Word of the French decision to refuse to repair American damages reached the United States via the ship *Liverpool* in early May 1834. Edward Livingston arrived with the insulting news, and as Jackson took it in, along with Treasury Secretary Louis McLane, Louis Barbe

---

[1216] Feller, *Andrew Jackson, Foreign Affairs*, UVa., Miller Center, p.101.

Charles Serurier squirmed in the hot seat. As the French minister in Washington, Serurier had promised the United States government that the matter would soon be settled, and he now struggled to figure out a plan to appease the Jacksonites who wanted answers as to why the French had chosen to ignore its obligations to the United States. With Jackson's temperamental disposition in mind, which Serurier described as "fiery character, his cruel disappointment, and his own personal political situation at the moment"[1217] (in light of the recent censure vote just weeks earlier), Serurier hurried to discuss the matter with McLane at the State Department.

"I was informed that the President and the Secretary of State had received the dispatches....that the President was incensed, and that they were talking about a message to Congress on the following Monday concerning our legislature's decision," Serurier wrote Paris on Sunday, May 11, 1834. "It would no longer be discussed on a purely monetary basis, but would be treated as a question of national honor and injured pride."[1218]

Jackson finally lost patience and asked Congress to authorize reprisals if the money was not paid. The French government then demanded retraction of this insult as a condition of payment. Jackson responded in effect that what he said to Congress was none of a foreign government's business. [1219]

The impasse deepened through 1835; ministers were recalled and military preparations were put into motion. American dander was up. Finally, under British urgings (the Brits had offered to mediate the situation), the French agreed to construe a conciliatory passage in a later message of Jackson's as sufficient apology, much to the relief of Louis Serurier. With their own sensitivities assuaged, the French finally agreed to pay the four installments past due and pay the remainder when due. Yet, ultimately, despite France's agreement to pay the entire sum back, there continued to be delays. Finally, the payments began to filter

---

[1217] Nester, William, *The Age of Jackson*, 2013, Chapter 13.
[1218] Meacham, Ch. 25.
[1219] Remini, Robert V., *Andrew Jackson and the Course of American Democracy*, 1833-1845 Volume III (New York: Harper & Row, 1984), 201-10, 217-18, 274-75; Erik McKinley Eriksson, "French Spoliation Claims," *Dictionary of American History* rev. ed. (New York: Charles Scribner's Sons, 1976, 3:121-22.

in, although the American claimants received less value per dollar for the total amount awarded. Fifteen hundred and sixty seven American claimants received money; the final settlement was at a rate of fifty-nine cents on the dollar, as the amount awarded by the special commission totaled $9,352,193, while the six installments from France plus interest totaled $5,558,108.

Although the remainder of the debt was never entirely paid in full, neither was Beaumarchais's money by the United States. France defused the crisis by promising to pay off the debt at a later time. As a result, the crisis passed without repercussions, until it was largely forgotten with changes in regimes over time. The world continued to turn, and peace was restored. The same, however, could not be said of Jackson›s dealings with Mexico.

The Beaumarchais, Pierre and daughter Eugenie

CHAPTER

80

WE MUST HAVE TEXAS

"Texas, with peace, could exist without the United States, but the United States can not, without great hazard to the security of their institutions, exist without Texas."
—Sam Houston

"Let a listening ear, a silent tongue, and a steadfast heart, the three jewels of wisdom, guard every advance which you make on the subject of Texas." Jackson wrote to Anthony Butler, the ambassador to Mexico in 1829. "The acquisition of that Territory is becoming every day an object of more importance to us, and if any reliance can be placed on the illiberal speculations which they already ascribe to us, in connection with it, a still stronger argument, for the cession, can be based upon them: for it is obvious, if they really believe that we have ten thousand troops on that frontier, watching an opportunity for the conquest of the Territory, any attempt to chastise the Indian hostilities thereafter, may endanger the peace of the two countries."[1220]

Jackson craved the Mexican border province of Texas for the United States and he made its purchase the first priority of his presidential diplomacy. During the turbulent period of the Bank War, Andrew Jackson received an unexpected visit from an old friend, the rugged veteran from Tennessee and the Creek War, Sam Houston. With his long black hair and sturdy build, Houston appeared revitalized after a period of personal turmoil. Jackson's one-time "surrogate-son," he

---

[1220] AJ to Butler, Oct. 10, 1829. The Papers of Andrew Jackson, 1980, pp. 487-488.

had risen to the rank of governor of Tennessee in 1827 and was serving in that position in 1829 when his fortunes took a sharp turn for the worse. His life had been temporarily shattered that year when his bride of a few weeks left him, and he took up transient residence with the Arkansas Indians, who dubbed him "Big Drunk." He still drank, as did most men in those days, especially with the limited amount of potable water available, but not to the degree "Big Drunk" had. In early 1832, Houston had traveled to New York for business before continuing to Washington, D.C.

While in the capital, Houston heard news of Ohio Congressman William Stanbery's openly critical rant against both Jackson and Houston; for Stanbery remembered Houston as a loyal supporter of the president. During a speech, Stanbery directed his ire at Houston, using him as a means to attack Jackson's character. Upon hearing of Stanbery's disparaging remarks, Houston confronted him on Pennsylvania Avenue and turned his cane on the Congressman violently in anger. In retaliation, Stanbery filed charges against Houston in the House. However, Jackson, who long viewed Stanbery with animosity due to his consistent opposition to Jackson's bank policies, felt that Stanbery deserved what he received. He was not only supportive of Houston's actions but also appreciative of Houston's choice of a hickory cane for the confrontation.

Jackson invited Houston to the White House to express his gratitude and provided him with money for a new suit for his trial. He also offered advice: "When you make your defense, tell those infernal bank thieves that when an American citizen is insulted by one of them, he has some privileges too."[1221] During the trial, Houston defended himself eloquently, acknowledging the beating but citing extenuating circumstances. He argued that Stanbery had insulted him beyond what any man could bear and had refused an honorable duel. Houston concluded his defense with a stirring oration that drew comparisons to the great Daniel Webster. He proclaimed, "So long as that flag shall bear off its glittering stars, I trust that the rights of American citizens shall be preserved and transmitted as a sacred legacy." Despite winning rousing applause from the gallery, Houston was found guilty, reprimanded by the House, and later convicted in a criminal court, resulting in a $500 fine.

[1221] Quoted in Brands, Ch. 40.

Nonetheless, he felt vindicated in the eyes of Jackson and his supporters. Houston reflected, "I was dying out, and had they fined me $10, it would have killed me. But they gave me a national tribunal for a theater, and that set me up again."[1222]

Jackson agreed, and Houston's passionate defense restored their relationship. Jackson criticized the House's actions as "the greatest act of tyranny and usurpation ever attempted under our government." The Constitution prevented the president from overturning Congress's decision, but he could remit Houston's fine imposed by the Washington District Court. Although Jackson would have supported Houston in any political sphere, Tennessee was less welcoming of Houston's return from disgrace, and he felt personally conflicted about going back. Instead, he set his sights on Texas.

Having dreamed of acquiring Texas, especially since the Aaron Burr plot nearly 30 years earlier, Jackson's ambition was to free the Mexican province from Spanish control and add it to the American empire. However, after Burr's disgrace, Jackson had to momentarily set aside his dream. With pressing matters in Mississippi, Louisiana, and Florida, he had little attention to spare for Texas. Like Thomas Jefferson, Jackson believed Texas was part of the Louisiana Purchase and opposed John Quincy Adams's decision to exclude it from the Adams-Onís Treaty of 1819. At the time, he did not object, as the treaty granted Florida to the United States, and he and Adams were allies at the time, especially given Adams's defense of Jackson's actions in Florida.

When Mexico gained independence from Spain in 1821, the situation regarding Texas became more complex. While Texas had previously been under Spanish rule, the annexation could be framed as a move to spread democracy and self-rule. An independent Mexico, initially flirting with imperialism, adopted republicanism and modeled its constitution after that of the United States. As noted, following Mexican independence, American empresarios, led by the Austins, migrated to Texas, bringing multitudes of American families (and often their enslaved people) seeking land for cotton plantations.

Americans, always greedy for land, continued, like their president, to covet the vast expanse of Texas, which, as mentioned, the United States had

---

[1222] ibid,40.

abandoned to Spain, in 1819. The Spanish authorities wanted to populate this virtually uninhabited area, but before they could carry through their contemplated plans, the Mexicans won their independence officially in 1821. A new regime in Mexico City thereupon concluded arrangements in 1823 for granting a huge land tract with Moses Austin, who became the first of these many 'empresarios' who accepted the invitation to immigrate to Texas from the United States. The understanding was that the Austins, and others given these grants would bring into Texas three hundred American families each. Immigrants were to be either of the Roman Catholic faith or were expected to convert. This was step one in becoming properly Mexicanized; step two was following Mexican authority, which meant becoming Mexican citizens, and following the decrees made in Mexico City.

However, these stipulations were largely ignored by the Americans who made the journey to settle in Texas. Hardy Texas pioneers remained largely American at heart, as Jackson understood, and they resented the restraints imposed by the "foreign" government of Mexico. They were especially concerned with the presence of Mexican soldiers patrolling in Texas, many of whom were ex-convicts.

Falling just three families short of recruiting the three hundred households that his father had contracted to bring to Texas, Stephen Austin felt like he had done what was asked of him, and he became a proud Mexican citizen and leader of the Anglo-Texans, often referred to as Texians. He settled his colony on a lush spot between the Brazos and Colorado Rivers. Austin chose this area, which included land that is now part of 19 Texas counties, in 1821. The first settlers arrived during 1821 and 1822, transforming the area from wilderness into a sparsely populated rural community. Despite numbering only 297 households, the original settlers were dubbed the "Old Three Hundred," and they became renowned as the Texas equivalent of New England's Mayflower Pilgrims, or the "First Families of Virginia." Mostly Scots-Irish southerners from the trans-Appalachian frontier, the Old Three Hundred were cultured folk by frontier standards; all but four of them were literate.

Other settlers followed, from Europe as well as America. Within ten years, the "Anglos" (many of them French and German) outnumbered the Mexican residents, or *tejanos,* ten to one and soon evolved a distinct

"Texican" culture. The wide-ranging horse patrols organized to attack Indian camps became the Texas Rangers; Samuel Maverick, whose unbranded calves roamed the limitless prairies, left his surname as a label for rebellious loners who refused to run with the herd; and Jared Groce, an Alabama planter whose caravan of fifty covered wagons and one hundred slaves arrived in 1822, etched the original image of the larger-than-life, big-time Texas operator.[1223]

The original Anglo-Texans brought with them the old Scots-Irish frontiersmen's hostility to authority. They ignored Mexican laws and officials, including restrictions against owning and importing slaves. When the Mexican government tried to impose its will on the Anglo-Texans early in Texas history, the Texicans usually responded by taking up their guns.

Jackson believed Texas should become an American state, considering its proximity to the Mississippi and its vast lands. American settlers in Texas, who were naturalized citizens of Mexico, Jackson believed, still identified as Americans. The General's attitude toward Texas mirrored his earlier views on Florida; he wished to see the United States annex Texas, especially given what he felt was a true power vacuum in the region. He knew he couldn't force the annexation, but he feared that if the U.S. did not act, a European power might seize the opportunity. Spain had attempted to reconquer Mexico in 1829, but thanks to the efforts of Generalissimo Antonio Lopez de Santa Anna Perez de Labron, it had failed. However, Jackson worried they might just try again.

More worrisome to the president was that Great Britain might exploit Mexico's vulnerabilities, just as they had in Florida. He also considered the French, recovering from the Napoleonic era, who might attempt to reclaim lost territories. Additionally, Jackson was concerned about Texas as a refuge for both fugitive slaves, and groups of tribal nations fleeing the southwest in search of freedom, who would be tempted to cross into Texas as they had once done in Florida. The president wanted the vast state of Texas in American hands, but saying so directly, he knew, would alienate northern constituents. The now savvy politician understood this, so as much as he wished to extend the slavery kingdom into Texas, he

---

[1223] "Groce, Jared Ellison (1782–1839)". *Handbook of Texas*. Retrieved 2021-06-04.

had to proceed with tact, which was not always the most reliable tool in the Jackson wheelhouse.

Given the instability of Mexico's government and its suspicions of American designs, a Texas negotiation required great discretion and patience. Border disputes have always posed challenges, which was a key reason Jackson sought to expand that of America's. During his first presidential term, he aimed to purchase Texas from Mexico. To facilitate negotiations, he dispatched Anthony Butler, an army colonel, to Mexico City. Jackson praised Butler's straightforwardness but was wary of his trademark impulsiveness, which sometimes required Jackson to intervene and calm him down. "In addition to his many merits is that of frankness and honesty, which are so well taught in the school of war." When Butler reported on the political unrest in Mexico City and hinted at supporting those loyal to republicanism, Jackson advised him to refrain from interference. "No contingency can authorize your interference with her concerns," the president said. "Let them take what form they may in setting up and pulling down rulers, friendly or unfriendly to free government. Yours is the part of neutrality, this is the course of duty as well as prudence."[1224]

Butler was determined to fulfill Jackson's trust, noting the absence of Mexican troops in the disputed territory, with all forces deployed further west. He highlighted Nacogdoches as a key location, and one that would be very beneficial for negotiating the Texas issue. "The occupation would therefore be unopposed. And with troops on the ground, the United States government would be in a favorable position to enforce the settlement of the whole Texas question." [1225]

Jackson preferred to see the acquisition of Texas as a diplomatic adjustment of the U.S.-Mexico border, a narrative that might resonate better with the nationalistic sentiments of Mexicans than the outright occupation of territory as a result of what would be deemed an American invasion. However, his intentions became clearer when he specified the desired border location, envisioning a line in the arid region southwest of American settlements in Texas. The rich prize of Texas would ensure American security on the southwestern border, and for that reason,

---
[1224] Brands, HW, 2005, Ch. 40.
[1225] Butler to AJ, April, 1832, Jackson Papers, LC.

Jackson was not entirely against the idea of some pecuniary support to coax Mexico their way. "The informed intimations you so appropriately gave to the secretary of foreign affairs, devising ways and means, should their pecuniary distresses become pressing, were happy and opportune," he told Butler. Jackson said he had begun to seek the money, "your private letter was submitted confidentially to the chairman of our committee on foreign relations."[1226]

Butler had more than a loan or grant in mind for the Mexican government. Those millions he spoke of to help move the deal along would include something personal for certain Mexican officials. In the summer of 1832, he thought he was making progress with the intellectual Lucas Aleman y Escalada, a prominent Mexican official who had resigned from the cabinet but retained influence over foreign affairs. "He still directs the Department, and in fact is as much the minister as at any period before."[1227] Butler explained to Jackson. The fact that he wasn't formally in charge apparently made it easier for him to negotiate, and Butler thought they were close to a deal. The purchase price for Texas, however, remained undetermined.

Jackson was no expert on Texas geography, and his information was cloudy at best; he likely aimed for a boundary between the Rio Grande and the Nueces, a desolate area he assumed would remain uninhabited. His goal was to create a buffer zone between American settlements and Mexico, providing a geographical guarantee for peace. "The Grand Prairie," he told Butler, "would be a boundary that would give permanent peace to the two republics." Jackson was more concerned about American encroachment than Mexican expansion. "The citizens of the United States will never be contented until this boundary is acquired," he said, and he enjoined Butler to use his "best exertions to secure it."[1228]

Jackson wrote to Butler, "Provided you keep within your instructions, and obtain the cession, it is not for your consideration whether the government of Mexico applies the money to the purchase of men or to pay their public debt." Obviously, Jackson didn't want to be compromised by any public allegations of bribery, which would tarnish his reputation, and perhaps spoil a Texas deal. "I admonish you to give these shrewd

---

[1226] AJ to Butler, May 1832, Jackson Papers, LC.
[1227] Butler to AJ, June 1832, Jackson Papers, LC.
[1228] Jackson to Butler, 1830, Jackson Papers, LC.

fellows no room to charge you with tampering with their officers or obtain the cession through corruption," he sternly instructed. By now Jackson had settled on no more than five million as his price for Texas. Butler was instructed to offer that, and no more. What the Mexicans did with the money was their own business. "We are not interested in her distribution of the consideration," but he added, crucially, "we are deeply interested that this treaty of cessions should be attained without any just imputation of corruption on our part."[1229]

But Butler suggested any payment from the United States would "very probably be in part applied to facilitate the negotiation. "That part of the arrangement should be provided for by a secret article." Butler added that he would bring the treaty home himself for the purpose of making explanations in regards to the contemplated 'secret article.' In other words, Butler himself would explain the bribe to Congress.[1230]

Unfortunately, for Butler and Jackson, the revolving door of Mexican politics kept rotating, and thus it became nearly impossible to pin down any one regime as the guaranteed authority. In the autumn of 1832 Aleman, with the rest of the regime, fled the capital. The new man of the hour was Antonio Lopez de Santa Anna, who, after repulsing the Spanish re-conquering effort, could immediately have made himself president of the country, but preferred to let his competitors eliminate each other fighting over the position, so that he could ride in and save the day. He did so in October 1832 at Puebla, where his followers routed government troops and opened the pathway to Mexico City. Santa Anna entered the capital in triumph in the beginning of 1833, beginning his rule in Mexico about the time Jackson was commencing his second term in the United States. Perhaps not surprisingly, given their common backgrounds as soldiers, Jackson thought Santa Anna's succession would mark a positive turn for Mexico's republic. "Soldiers are natural patriots," Jackson assumed. But he was off the mark on this call. Things happened slower in Mexico than he anticipated, but Jackson still kept up hope. "I still hope the General Santa Anna's patriotism and good fortune may succeed in tranquilizing that unhappy country," Jackson told

---

[1229] ibid
[1230] Butler to AJ, 1830, Jackson Papers, LC.

Butler, "giving it peace, a true republican government not executed by the bayonet, but by the wholesome administration of just and equal laws."[1231]

Butler, on the ground in Mexico City, did not share Jackson's optimism. "The new regime might've restored order to Mexico, but it evidently had not ended the corruption of Mexican politics." Yet this might work to the advantage of the United States regarding Texas, he conjectured. But reported "a very singular conversation." With an official he declined to name lest his letter fall into the wrong hands, but who "is one of the most shrewd and intelligent men in the country, holds, at the present time, a high official station, and has much influence with the President General Santa Anna." This unnamed individual told Butler that the Texas question might be reopened under the right conditions. "There is but one man who must be brought over to us, without whom we can do nothing, but with him, everything." The official didn't name Santa Anna as the individual, and neither did Butler, but he was the only one in Mexico City who fit the description. The official went on, "Have you command of money?" Butler said he had. "There will be a large sum necessary," the official said, "Half a million or upwards. This man, so important for us to gain, must have himself 200 or $300,000. There are others among whom it may become necessary to distribute three or $400,000 more. Can you command that sum?" Butler nodded. "Assure me of the object and the money will not fail." [1232]

During the same period Jackson was seeking to acquire Texas, he was trying to settle a long-standing dispute with France regarding debts left over from the Napoleonic Wars. France had agreed to pay these reparations but still had not done so. Jackson was casting the issue as a matter of American honor. "Ask nothing but what is right and admit nothing that is wrong,"[1233] he instructed Edward Livingston, who handled the negotiations in Paris. The conflict ended amicably, but not before Jackson threatened to seize French ships and ask Congress for money to expand the Navy. Had the United States been caught bribing Mexican officials in an official capacity during the drawn-out French negotiations, it would certainly undermine American honor that Jackson made such a show of upholding.

[1231] AJ to Butler, Jan., 1833, Jackson Papers, LC.
[1232] Anthony Butler Papers, LOC, 1833.
[1233] AJ to Livingston, 1833, Jackson Papers, LC.

Would bribing Mexican officials really work? Jackson was not certain and was certainly not confident in the integrity of the officials Butler described. He had concerns: what would keep Mexico from taking the money and then refusing to hand over Texas? What recourse would the United States have in such a scenario? If the U.S. "bought" one Mexican government, what could they do to prevent that regime from being overthrown, and the new leaders demanding money themselves? The exposure of the bribery could not only tarnish the Jackson administration, but the regime's successor could, and probably would, disavow the deal. The United States would have lost the money, been embarrassed, and still would not have control of Texas. But if bribery wouldn't work, what other methods might?

As Butler's initial attempts yielded no results, Jackson's anxiety grew. In August 1831, he expressed his concerns to Butler regarding the border with Mexico, especially upon learning that a group of Americans planned to settle 10,000 new colonists in Texas. With the already established American settlements, this influx would exert significant pressure on the existing situation. "When these get possession and become permanently fixed they will soon avail themselves of some pretext to throw off the Mexican authority and form an independent government of their own. This would beget great disquietude and might eventually endanger the peace and tranquility of both countries." The prospect of an independent Texas worried Jackson more than the idea of Texas remaining with Mexico. With South Carolina causing him headaches, the last thing he wanted was a new independent nation of Americans outside the Union. Hoping that $5 million could convince the Mexicans to part with their northwestern outpost, Jackson would be disappointed. Butler was even more aggressive in pursuing the annexation of Texas, and convinced that Jackson had given him ample latitude, still considered the offer of a large bribe to Mexican officials. ("A. Butler: What a scamp," Jackson wrote on one of Butler's letters.) [1234]

Despite originally encouraging Butler to use whatever monetary means were necessary, Jackson now made a sudden about-face, expressing astonishment at Butler's willingness to resort to bribery. Butler had to have been scratching his head at Jackson's mixed messages, as well as

---

[1234] Jackson to Butler, Aug. 1831, Jackson Papers, LC.

his chastisement at his talk of bribery. Something had changed. "This must be an honest transaction," Jackson informed his charge d'affaires, but did add, "I never knew a Spaniard who was not a slave of avarice, and it is not improbable that this weakness may be worth a great deal to us, in this case."[1235] Yet, despite Butler's many efforts, Mexico continued to resist its powerful northerly neighbor's offers.

Butler thought Jackson naïve for rejecting bribery, "What you advise of being cautious proves how little you know of Mexican politics, and the Mexican character," he wrote, with the frankness that Jackson had come to admire. "I can assure you, sir, that bribery is not only common and familiar in all the ranks and classes here but ... freely spoken of." If Jackson wanted Texas peacefully, there was only one way, Butler argued. "Resort must be had to bribery, or by 'presence,' if the term is more appropriate." But Jackson still resisted, refusing (at least in writing) to be associated with bribery in any fashion. It would make him, and the United States government look corrupt, and with Jackson's many enemies seeking to expose his corruption, he had to make it appear that he was squeaky clean in that regard. Jackson also argued that such offers to Mexico would complicate various other diplomatic deals. Butler, however, found Jackson's stance on bribery naive, arguing that bribery was commonplace in Mexican politics and asserting, "What you advise of being cautious proves how little you know of Mexican politics and the Mexican character."[1236] He contended that if Jackson wanted a peaceful acquisition of Texas, resorting to bribery or a strong military presence was necessary.

According to the 1819 Adams-Onis Treaty between the United States and Spain, the eastern boundary of Texas was the Sabine River. There was no chance of changing the treaty, but Jackson hatched a plan that might change the meaning of what was the Sabine River. The president sought to reinterpret this boundary by redefining the river itself. He argued that the western river, known as the Natches, should be considered the true boundary due to confusion surrounding the naming of the rivers. Two streams empty into Sabine Lake, which then feeds the Gulf of Mexico. Ordinary usage called the eastern stream

---

[1235] Meacham, p. 316.
[1236] Butler to AJ, 1832, Papers of Andrew Jackson, Univ. of Tennessee Press, 1980.

the Sabine, and the western river was the Natches. The Sabine River is named after the Spanish word "Sabinas," which means "cypress," yet that added to the confusion of the two rivers, especially since Sabina/Cypress trees were more common on the Natches than along the Sabine. This gave Jackson the justification for calling the Natches River the western Sabine and declaring it the true boundary between the United States and Mexico. This reasoning, though flimsy, (nor honorable) served as a tactic to intimidate Mexico into relinquishing control over Texas.[1237]

Negotiating in Texas required careful discretion and patience. However, Butler lacked these essential qualities. Jackson's own vague instructions further encouraged Butler's awkward involvement in bribery and personal influence in his rugged brand of diplomacy. These actions, coupled with the influx of American settlers into Texas, heightened Mexican fears regarding American intentions in the region. Soon, both Butler's and Jackson's clumsy attempts to acquire the territory would contribute to a growing mutual distrust.

Jackson needed someone else, someone he knew, someone he could trust, and someone with a little more pluck than Anthony Butler. If it could be someone who was like a son to him, even better. That man was Sam Houston.

[1237] Quoted in Brands, HW, 2005. Ch. 40.

CHAPTER

81

TEXAS REVOLUTION

"I shall never surrender or retreat. Then, I call on you in the name of Liberty, of patriotism, and everything dear to the American character, to come to our aid with all dispatch."
-William Travis

While Jackson's woes over Butler's ineffectiveness in Mexico increasing by the minute, he began to work more closely, although quietly, with Sam Houston. Houston had previously made a drunken boast about conquering Texas. "I was really deranged to believe that you had so wild a scheme in contemplation," Jackson lectured Houston at the time. And while the purchase of Texas remained a possibility, Jackson didn't want any American filibuster making the Mexican government angry. But now, as Jackson's hopes for a peaceful acquisition diminished, he reconsidered Houston's ambitions. During a meeting at the Hermitage in 1832, Jackson discreetly supported Houston's journey to Texas, providing him with financial assistance and a little cover to facilitate his passage. From Tennessee, Houston traveled to Arkansas, where he obtained a federal passport requesting "All the tribes of Indians, whether in amity with the United States or as yet not allied to them in treaties, to permit general Sam Houston, a citizen of the United States, 37 years of age, 6'2" in stature, brown hair, light complexion, and in case of need to give him all lawful aid and protection."[1238]

[1238] ibid

Houston's mission, ostensibly to investigate Native American affairs, held broader implications for Texas acquisition. The Americans in Texas, frustrated and discontented under Mexican rule, particularly following a 1830 law that prohibited U.S. immigration and the introduction of slaves, increasingly disregarded Mexican authority. Although the law went unenforced, it created tensions and fostered an environment ripe for rebellion. "It has been my first, and most important object, to obtain all the information possible relative to the Pawnee and Comanche Indians," Houston reported en route, "To reach the wild Indians in this season is difficult and the only practicable way of reaching San Antone."[1239]

Houston exaggeratingly reported that a significant majority of the Texas population favored U.S. acquisition, as well as how capable it was of defending itself against Mexico. "19/20ths of the population," he said, "wanted the United States to acquire Texas. They are now without laws to govern or protect them, Mexico is involved in civil war. The federal constitution has never been in operation. The government is essentially despotic and must be so for years to come. The rulers have not honesty and the people have not intelligence, Texas was "halfway to independence from Mexico," Houston said "she has already beaten and expelled all the troops of Mexico from her soil, nor will she permit them to return. She can defend herself against the whole power of Mexico, for really, Mexico is powerless and penniless."[1240]

Houston warned that U.S. inaction would surely lead to European intervention in Texas. He argued, "if the United States does not press for it, England will most assuredly obtain it by some means." And if that strategy did not persuade Jackson to act, Houston figured a little hyperbole on the wonders of the Texas environment might. "I've traveled near 500 miles across Texas, and I have no hesitancy in pronouncing it the finest country to its extent upon the globe. The greater portion of it is richer and more healthy in my opinion than West Tennessee. There can be no doubt that the country east of the river Grande of the north (the Rio Grande) would sustain a population of ten millions of souls."[1241] But

---

[1239] The Texas Revolution, Key Events and Impacts, TSHA.
[1240] Writings of Sam Houston, 1813-1863, Texas History Trust, Edited by Amelia W. Williams and Eugene C. Barker, Vol. 6.
[1241] Quoted in American Imperialism in the Southwest 1800-1837, Stenberg, Richard Rollin, Austin, TX, 1933. Thesis, Univ. of Texas.

Houston was not being very forthright. While there was some serious discontent among Texans, they were not yet determined to become American citizens again.

Stephen F. Austin, and most of his fellow Texans, simply hoped for a separate Mexican state of Texas within the Mexican federation. Despite what Houston argued, they were not crying out for American support. But that did not match with what Sam Houston wanted. What he had learned in his short time in Mexico caused him to conclude that the Mexican government would never approve of a separate statehood for Texas within the Mexican government. Its refusal rendered full separation the only viable option and the inevitable option. Events soon made Houston a prophet. General Santa Anna, for reasons having little to do with Texas, gathered more and more power for himself in Mexico City, alarming Republicans throughout Mexico, and especially advocates of states' rights. Mexicans around the country objected to Santa Anna, to the point of rebellion, in such places as Zacatecas, whose revolt was soon crushed brutally by Santa Anna, who attempted to send a message to all of Mexico that any opposition to his authority was not only futile, but would be met with bloody force. Rather than intimidate the Texans, however, it convinced that their only security lay beyond the reach of Santa Anna, which was to say, beyond the authority of Mexico. By the autumn of 1835, Texans were forming into militias and drilling. While they drilled, they talked more openly of independence.

During this time Jackson received a curious letter from Sam Houston and six other Texas leaders. The seven men introduced themselves as a 'Vigilance and Safety Committee' for the Department of Nacogdoches. Houston had informed them of Jackson's claims regarding American sovereignty over Natches. Essentially, Nacogdoches was considered by Jackson to be part of American territory. Consequently, it was not difficult to convince the committee of the necessity of stimulating action on the disputed region. The Committee hatched a plan: to notify the American president about reports indicating that a 'large group of Creek Indians, numbering at least 5,000,' was preparing to settle in the contested area. The Texans reminded Jackson of a treaty between the United States and Mexico, which permitted both nations to prevent unauthorized Indian movements along their shared border. They urged the president to take action on behalf of themselves and their fellow residents. "A sparse and comparatively defenseless population, unprotected from the evils which were so tragically manifested on the frontiers of Georgia and Alabama, evils which can only be remedied by the skill and generalship of a Jackson."

Houston and the committee added that the government of Mexico would show the Texans no support or assistance. "The unhappy distractions of this government as to command the attentions of the president, Santa Anna, to the interior condition of the country."[1242] Yet, not only did any Creek invasion ever take place, there were no signs whatsoever that the Creek had ever planned anything of the sort. The letters had but one intended purpose: to remind Jackson of the lack of Mexican troops anywhere in Texas, and to signal that American Texans looked eagerly to Washington for protection.

The letter complimented intelligence from Butler, who reported escalating tensions and skirmishes between Mexican troops and Texan riflemen. "You have heard of the revolt in Texas, where it is said there has been some skirmishing between the Mexican troops and the Texas riflemen, always resulting in favor of the latter," Butler wrote in November 1835. "The course pursued by the people of Texas has greatly exasperated General Santa Anna as we hear, and he vows to chastise the insolence of these borderers even if he goes in person to do so."[1243] By the time Jackson received Butler's communication, the Texans' revolt had intensified, and a critical juncture in the struggle for Texas was at hand.

Jackson had wished to see Texas a new American state but was not keen on an independent Texas Republic. His objections to Texas independence paralleled his resistance to South Carolina's secession; he believed that multiple autonomous political entities increased the likelihood of conflict. While he supported self-governance within the Union, he viewed self-governance outside it as a potential threat. Jackson hoped to persuade the Mexican government to consider his perspective, arguing that unrest in Texas would ultimately harm Mexico more than the United States. "I cannot but think that a thorough examination of the whole subject will satisfy Mexico. Their true policy recommends a cession of the province," he told Butler. Urgency was essential; Jackson

---

[1242] Houston to AJ, 1832, Jackson Papers, LC.
[1243] Butler to AJ, Nov. 1835, Jackson Papers, LC.

warned Butler that a Texas rebellion could permanently jeopardize its settlement and permanently destroy the friendly relations between the two nations. "A revolt in Texas may close the door forever to its advantageous settlement and may eventuate not merely in the loss of that province to Mexico with much blood and treasure, but break up the friendly understanding which is now established between this government and hers, and lead to a train of events that may obscure for a long period the sun of liberty in that quarter."[1244]

Mexican officials, however, were resistant to Jackson's reasoning, primarily due to the instability of their government and the frequent turnover in leadership. Since gaining independence, Mexico had suffered from various insurrections and unstable administrations. Even if Jackson could convince the Mexican leadership that relinquishing Texas was in their national interest, they were unlikely to compromise their territorial integrity, as doing so would jeopardize their political position, and in fact, could well prove suicidal given the nature of Mexican politics. Thus, no official felt compelled to expedite such a process. Frustrated, Butler suggested offering financial incentives. A $600,000 loan from Mexican capitalists sustained the government, but it was merely a temporary solution. "This is but a drop and will very soon be exhausted," Butler wrote, "and as I am confident that the experiment cannot be successfully repeated, I shall be ready to offer a supply to their necessities the moment they are found to be pressing."[1245] Yet, soon what became pressing for Santa Anna was a show of military force in Texas, and while Mexico became more and more distracted by the troubles in Texas, Butler's schemes remained just talk.

Energetic and productive, Texan Americans numbered around thirty thousand by 1835.[1246] Most of them were law-abiding, God-fearing people, but some of them had left the states to escape punishment from the law. G.T.T. (Gone to Texas) became current fashionable slang, to describe the escape from law and order. Among the adventurers were Davy Crockett, the famous rifleman and former soldier under General Jackson, and the rugged Kentuckian Jim Bowie, the presumed

---

[1244] AJ to Butler, Dec. 1835, Jackson Papers, LC.
[1245] ibid
[1246] Kennedy and Cohen, *American Pageant*, "Makers of America: Mexican or Texican", pp. 270-271.

inventor of the murderous knife that bears his name. Bowie's blade was widely known in the Southwest as the "genuine Arkansas toothpick." By the spring of 1835, Bowie had shaken off his lethargy following the death of his wife and resumed his interest in land. A third well-known frontiersman soon to arrive on the scene as a latecomer was the rejuvenated Sam Houston.

The pioneer individualists who came to Texas were not easy to push around. Friction rapidly increased between Mexicans and Texans over issues such as slavery, immigration, and local rights. Slavery was a particularly touchy topic. Mexico outlawed slavery and emancipated its slaves in 1830, and prohibited the further importation of slaves into Texas, as well as further colonization by troublesome Americans. No longer did they wish to see American families pouring in over the border. The Texans refused to honor these decrees. They kept their slaves in bondage, and new American settlers continued to arrive, with their own slaves shamelessly in tow. When Stephen Austin went to Mexico City in 1833 to negotiate these differences with the Mexican government, the dictator Santa Anna slapped him in irons and stuck him in jail for eight months for daring to advocate for separation. The explosion finally came in 1835, when Santa Anna wiped out all local rights and started to raise an army to suppress the upstart Texans.

In 1835, Mexican officials had a lot on their plate, not least of which was its troublesome Texas province, which was part of the northern region of Coahuila y Tejas. Residents of Texas sought to establish their own statehood separate from Coahuila within the Mexican confederation.

Their aspirations put them in a precarious situation, especially since their leader, Stephen Austin, still languished in a Mexican prison. The sentiment in Texas was divided: some people wanted to maintain a peaceful relationship with the Mexican government, while others demanded more assertive actions toward independence. These differing viewpoints eventually led to the formation of two distinct groups known as the "Peace" and "War" parties.

In the spring of 1835, the legislature of Monclova, capital of Coahuila y Tejas, appointed Bowie as a commissioner to oversee the distribution of 1,771,200 acres around Nacogdoches, Texas, with the money raised to go to the defense of the region against Indian attacks. As incentive to Bowie, 420,660 acres of this land went to him, with other acreage going to his cronies at rock-bottom prices before the land hit the market. As tensions between Texas and Mexico increased, President Santa Anna sent General Martin Perfecto de Cós to Monclova to rein in the land speculators and the local government. Bowie joined the Monclova militia and forced Cós to back off without bloodshed, but the general returned in late May and arrested Bowie and others before they crossed over into Texas. Bowie escaped with a companion several weeks later and returned to their state.

That April, Sam Houston had set up shop in Nacogdoches, Texas, where, in good faith to Mexico, he embraced Catholicism. A strong incentive to his enthusiastic conversion was an entitlement to 1,480 acres of land. In January 1835, Davy Crockett, then a Tennessee congressman, was present in Washington when a would-be assassin, Richard Lawrence, attempted to shoot President Andrew Jackson. Crockett helped subdue Lawrence after he fired two pistols that both malfunctioned. He was among the bystanders who helped ensure the president's safety and transport him back to the White House.[1247] Yet, Crockett's political career soon faltered after a defeat in Congress, and he decided to venture to Texas. He departed on November 1, 1835, and after a series of events, reached Texas, where he enjoyed celebrity status while unaware of the brewing conflict.

Meanwhile, a young Texas attorney, William Barret Travis was occupied with his legal practice in Anahuac, a port of entry on the eastern end of Galveston Bay. He also dabbled in the Texas slave-trade. Having obtained land from Stephen Austin, Travis wondered about Austin's fate and gave up any hope of the Texas leader's release by June. "Let them sacrifice him if they dare," he declared. "A thousand of their contemptible 'red skins' shall be sacrificed to his name." Travis also pondered the increasing tensions with the Mexican government and impending conflict. "The rumor of troops coming to Texas in great

---

[1247] Solly, *Smithsonian Magazine*, 2024.

numbers must be false. Such a measure would kindle a flame in Texas that would burn in twain the slender cords that connect us to the ill-fated Mexican confederation."[1248]

Soon, Travis mistakenly came to believe that Austin had been released in June, leading him to sign "The San Felipe Pledge" with twenty-five others to disarm the Mexican military at Anahuac on June 22. They managed to achieve a quick and bloodless surrender from Captain Antonio Tenorio. However, public reaction among Mexicans and Americans of the Peace Party was extremely unfavorable toward the War Party, and toward Travis, with fears that his actions could provoke war. Mexican authorities, including Colonel Ugartechea and General Cós, called for the arrest of Travis, offering a $1,000 reward. Evading Mexican authorities, Travis rallied Texans to unite in defense of their rights.

Jim Bowie emerged as a leader in Nacogdoches, seizing weapons without a fight, and securing intel on Mexican plans to arrest Travis. Travis, though, continued to evade capture, and decided to pull back on his aggressive approach, instead advising caution and a defensive strategy. Meanwhile, Sam Houston was appointed to negotiate with local Indian tribes, and he warned them of impending attacks from Mexico. Calling for militia organization, Houston hoped to establish friendly alliances with the tribes to bolster the Texas cause.

Austin, finally freed on July 11, returned to advocate for stronger American influence in Texas. As tensions rose, Travis rallied Texans with calls for liberty. Austin, when writing to Jim Bowie on July 30 expressed his concerns as to the pace of the revolt, "The people are much divided here," he declared. "Unless we could be united, had we not better be quiet, and settle down for a while?" Travis later suggested a more defensive approach, when declaring, "If we are encroached upon, let us resist until our bodies and our property lie in one common ruin, ere we submit to tyranny."[1249]

"Huzza for Texas!" William Travis wrote in response to orders for his arrest and execution for the Anahuac expedition on August 31. "Huzza for Liberty, and the rights of man!" News of a "convention of all Texas, to

---

[1248] Groneman, "The Kindled Flame," *True West Magazine*, Feb., 2025.
[1249] ibid

declare our sentiments, and to prepare for defense, if necessary," rendered Travis almost giddy. On the same day, General Martin Perfecto de Cós wrote to Colonel Ugartechea announcing his plans of coming into Texas in person. Austin's return led to plans for a consultation to unite against a military government. By late September, Austin warned that war was unavoidable. Indeed, he was not wrong.[1250]

The first conflict occurred in Gonzales on October 2 when Texan forces resisted Mexican troops attempting to seize a cannon. The Battle of Gonzales, fought on October 2, 1835, was the first official military engagement of the Texas Revolution, occurring between Texian settlers and Mexican soldiers near Gonzales, Texas. The conflict arose when Colonel Domingo de Ugartechea requested the return of a cannon loaned to the settlers for protection against Comanche raids, which they refused. On September 29, Mexican troops attempted to retrieve the cannon but were delayed by the settlers, who sought support from nearby communities. By October 1, around 140 Texians rallied to defend their claim, leading to an armed confrontation the following day, where Mexican soldiers retreated after firing on the approaching Texians. Although the skirmish had minimal military impact, it symbolized the growing divide between the colonists and the Mexican government, marking the beginning of the Texas Revolution and earning the nickname "the Lexington of Texas." Two days after the battle, Austin declared to the San Felipe de Austin Committee of Public Safety that war was underway against a military despotism, and the news of the skirmish, initially called "the fight at Williams' place," spread throughout the U.S., inspiring many to support the "Texas Revolution." The Texas Revolution was now underway, and Sam Houston stepped up his efforts to encourage volunteers from the U.S. to support the Texan cause. Houston circulated posters to advertise for Americans to join in the cause, and he wrote to Isaac Parker in San Augustine on October 5: "... war in defense of our rights, our oaths, and our constitution is inevitable, in Texas!... If volunteers from the United States will join their brethren in this section, they will receive liberal bounties of land... Let each man come with a good rifle, and one hundred rounds of ammunition, and to

---

[1250] Dixon, Sam Houston, *The Men Who Made Texas Free*, Texas Historical Publishing Company, 1924, p.160

come soon... Our war-cry is "Liberty or death... Our principles are to support the constitution, and down with the Usurper!!!" [1251]

In October, a Volunteer Texas Army formed, with Austin as commander and Bowie as his aide. They besieged San Antonio, leading to the Texas Consultation on November 3, which appointed Henry Smith as governor and reassigned Austin to diplomatic duties. Just a month later, in November, when Texians, in response to the Battle of Gonzales, decided to create a provisional government separate from Mexican authority, Sam Houston was named Major General and Commander-in-Chief of the Texas Army:

"To Samuel Houston Esqr.--In the name of the People of Texas Free and Sovereign,

We reposing special trust and confidence in your patriotism valour conduct and fidelity do by these presents constitute and appoint you to be a Major General and commander in chief of the Army of Texas and of all forces....."[1252]

News of the fighting sent Mexico into a "perfect tempest of passion in consequence of the Revolt in Texas and all breathe vengeance against that devoted Country." Butler informed Jackson. General Antonio Lopez de Santa Anna was "perfectly furious, mad, and has behaved himself in a most undignified manner." As if taking his cues from General Jackson himself, Santa Anna told various European diplomats in Mexico that the Americans, he was convinced, had incited the rebellion. Butler added that the Mexican leader would "in due season chastise us .... Yes sir, he said chastise us." Bowing to the British ambassador in a brazen allusion to the summer of 1814, Santa Anna declared that he would "march to the capital and lay Washington city in ashes, as it has already been once done."[1253]

From December 5–9, the dissatisfied Texan forces attacked San Antonio, then called Bejar, driving the Mexicans into the Alamo, originally the Mission San Antonio de Valero, built by the Spanish. General Cós surrendered on December 9, marking the first stage of the Texas Revolution. The Texans commandeered the Alamo for themselves and fortified its defenses.

[1251] Groneman III, "The Kindled Flame," *True West Magazine*, 1835, Feb. 21, 2025.
[1252] From Sam Houston Memorial Museum & Republic of Texas Presidential Library.
[1253] Butler to AJ, 1835, Jackson Papers, LC.

In 1836, Santa Anna further centralized his authority and monitored the developments in Texas closely. While Austin remained in custody, he awaited a new amnesty law that would secure his release. He maintained correspondence with his allies, however, reassuring them that Texas had supporters among Mexican officials. Austin also expressed optimism about Santa Anna's favorable stance toward Texas, believing that it would soon achieve statehood within the confederation. Soon, Santa Anna, upon learning of the Rebels under Travis, led an angry force of Mexican soldiers to lay siege to the Alamo, by this time defended by nearly 180 Americans. The siege began on Feb. 23, 1836.

At the Alamo, the Texas rebels, led by William Travis, continued their stand against Santa Anna's vastly superior Mexican army. On the second day of the siege, February 24, 1836, Travis called for reinforcements with this message: "Commandancy of the Alamo—Bejar, Fby. 24th 1836—To the People of Texas & all Americans in the world—Fellow citizens & compatriots—I am besieged, by a thousand or more of the Mexicans under Santa Anna—I have sustained a continual Bombardment & cannonade for 24 hours & have not lost a man—The enemy has demanded a surrender at discretion, otherwise, the garrison are to be put to the sword, if the fort is taken—I have answered the demand with a cannon shot, & our flag still waves proudly from the walls—I shall never surrender or retreat. Then, I call on you in the name of Liberty, of patriotism & every thing dear to the American character, to come to our aid..."[1254]

This historic letter was carried from the Alamo by 30-year-old Captain Albert Martin of Gonzales, a native of Rhode Island. On the afternoon of the 25th, Martin passed the dispatch to Lancelot Smither, who had arrived from the Alamo the day before with an estimate of Mexican troop strength. Both Martin and Smither added notes to Travis›s letter. That evening, fighting an icy wind, Smither departed for San Felipe. In less than 40 hours he delivered the appeal to the citizens› committee in that town. Several copies were made, and transcripts of the letter began to appear in newspapers as early as March 2.

[1254] Travis' Victory or Death Letter, Feb. 24, 1836, Texas State Library and Archives Commission.

On March 2nd, 1836, in response to the Alamo situation, the Texans declared their independence at Washington-on-the-Brazos, and unfurled the Lone Star flag. The Texas Declaration of Independence, signed by 59 delegates, established the Republic of Texas. The fort had held out for 11 days, being defended by Travis, Crockett, Bowie, and roughly 185 others, both Anglo-Americans and Tejanos. On Friday, March 4, 1836, Santa Anna ordered a staff conference at his headquarters near San Antonio's Military Plaza. The rebels had held out for 11 days now, and Santa Anna's patience—never great when his prestige was at stake—was wearing decidedly thin.

Santa Anna had actually stepped down as president of Mexico in mid-February to assume this command, but so far he had failed to win the fresh laurels he had hoped for. He had envisioned a lighting-fast campaign that would throw the norteamericano "land pirates" off Mexican soil once and for all. After a promising start, he found himself bogged down before a ramshackle mission and the sheer frustration was starting to tell on his nerves.

The conference was held in a squat adobe building not far from the looming towers of San Fernando Church, the peacock brilliance of the officers' uniforms standing in stark contrast to its whitewashed drabness. Major General Santa Anna appeared, a tall and handsome man of 43 whose height was made even more imposing by a cocked hat that sprouted red, white, and green plumes. Doffing this headgear, Santa Anna motioned to the officers and the conference began.

Santa Anna came right to the point, saying he wanted to discuss the possibility of launching an all-out assault on the Alamo. Normally, his officers rarely revealed their true feelings, especially if they ran counter to the dictator's will, but the sheer audacity of the statement caused passive façades to drop. The Alamo served no strategic purpose and part of its north wall had recently crumbled into rubble. The Alamo rebels were short on provisions; sheer famine would soon compel them to surrender. Santa Anna listened to these arguments with an air of bemused condescension. Encouraged by the fact that Colonel Francisco Duque had arrived with three full battalions of the First Infantry Brigade, Santa Anna breathed a sigh of relief. He had vented his irritation with the fact that Duque's superior, Brig. Gen. Antonio Gaona, had granted the First Infantry Brigade five days of rest before pressing on. Gaona ignored

Santa Anna's express command to make haste, but now bygones could be bygones. Duque's arrival boosted the Mexican Army's numbers to about 2,500—more than enough to make an all-out attack.[1255]

Staff officers conceded these facts but pointed out that a crucial element of the First Infantry Division had not yet arrived. The remainder of Gaona's command, some 700 men and five guns, would not arrive for two or three more days. Two of those guns were 12-pounders, whose heavy cannonballs would knock down the Alamo's already crumbling walls in short order. The Alamo garrison was isolated and there was no evidence of any reinforcements coming to their aid. Why waste lives on a fort that was bound to fall in a very short time? These were sound arguments, but Santa Anna brushed them aside. "Against the daring foreigners opposing us," his Excellency declared in his usual bombastic way, "the honor of our nation and our army is at stake." No prisoners would be taken; Santa Anna intended to teach these "foreigners" a lesson.[1256]

General Joaquin Ramirez y Sesma, never missing an opportunity to curry favor with his chief, enthusiastically agreed. Other sycophants on the staff joined in the chorus of approval. Those who doubted the wisdom of the attack—and they were probably the majority—lapsed into tactful silence. Colonel Juan Nepomuceno Almonte, an aide who had been educated in the United States and spoke good English, reminded His Excellency that there would be heavy casualties. No matter, Santa Anna tersely replied, the nut must be cracked.

The matter settled, it was determined that March 4 and 5 would be devoted to planning the affair. The general assault would take place at dawn the morning of March 6, 1836. Santa Anna would later call the Alamo a "small affair," not realizing his rash and bloody actions would create an American legend.

In the meantime, Santa Anna had his men position his guns ever closer. Some artillery was placed a mere 250 yards from the north wall. At this range, even relatively light caliber guns were effective. The north

---

[1255] Hubert Howe Bancroft, *History of the North Mexican States and Texas* (2 vols., San Francisco: History Company, 1886, 1889). John Henry Brown, *History of Texas from 1685 to 1892* (2 vols., St. Louis: Daniell, 1893).

[1256] Niderost, Eric, "No Mercy, Remembering the Alamo," *History Warfare Network*, Feb. 2004.

face was so weakened by the constant pummeling that part of it finally gave way and collapsed. Feverish repairs managed to plug the gap, but it was clear the Alamo could not hold for much longer. It was obvious that Santa Anna was making preparations for a final assault and the beleaguered Alamo garrison prepared as best they could.

During a time when hyperbole was common in military communications, characters such as the likes of William Travis were known to showcase their intense devotion to the cause, to rally support, proclaiming "Victory or Death!" In the case of the fiery Travis, there was true passion in every word. He positioned Davy Crockett and the Kentuckians' trusted riflemen at the Alamo's most vulnerable point, while he commanded artillery on the north wall. The garrison was thinly held, and retreat plans were made for a last stand in the Long Barracks, which had been fortified for defense.

Santa Anna wasted no time bombarding the Alamo with an immense artillery setup, subjecting the garrison to unrelenting fire that initially caused mental strain more so than physical casualties. Although brief moments of morale-boosting occurred, such as Davy Crockett playing a heartrending number on his fiddle, as another defender broke out the bagpipes in accompaniment, the reality of dwindling ammunition and resources loomed large. On March 1, reinforcements arrived, momentarily lifting the defenders' waning spirits, but messages for aid continued to be met with grim news.

As the siege progressed, Santa Anna's artillery drew closer, weakening the north wall significantly. Travis distributed the remaining ammunition while sending out a final appeal for aid. The Mexican bombardment paused on March 5, but it was soon clear that a full assault was imminent. In an attempt to negotiate surrender, Travis sent a local woman as a messenger; however, Santa Anna, eager for victory, rejected the proposal outright.

The Mexican guns fell silent on the evening of March 5. It was an ominous sign, but for the moment all the exhausted Alamo defenders could think of was sleep. The men were ragged, many of them having worn the same clothes for weeks or months and also half-starved from scanty rations. Red-rimmed eyes peered out from beard-stubbled faces and nerves were stretched tight from days of ear-shattering bombardment.

Most of the garrison was asleep by midnight, but Travis continued to visit the various sentry posts until almost 4 am.

Ammunition was all but gone among the American defenders, so Travis distributed his last remaining stocks to the men. Sentries posted along the walls were given two or three additional muskets or rifles. Travis also penned a final appeal to Fannin, concluding the missive in the usual bombastic style of "God and Texas! Victory or Death!"[1257] About dusk in the evening of March 5, 1836, courier James L. Allen took the dispatches and managed to slip past the Mexican lines. Only 16 years old, Allen was the last messenger from the Alamo.

On the morning of March 6, the Mexican assault began at dawn, with Santa Anna's forces attacking simultaneously from multiple directions. The Alamo defenders, despite fierce resistance, suffered heavy losses. Travis was one of the first to fall, but the defenders fought valiantly, utilizing makeshift weapons in the brutal hand-to-hand combat that ensued within the compound. The Texans refused to give in, and in an hour and a half of brutal combat, they would fight to their death.

As Mexican troops continued to breach the walls, the Alamo transformed into chaos, with defenders overwhelmed and fighting for their lives. The battle concluded with Santa Anna's forces securing victory, leading to the execution of surviving defenders. Ultimately, Santa Anna ordered the massacre of every last defender of the fort, despite the protests of some Mexican officers. With these mass killings, the aftermath was gruesome, with the battlefield strewn with corpses, each bloody remains embodying the horrifying nature of the conflict.

Although the Alamo's defenders faced a disastrous fate, their sacrifice inspired a thirst for vengeance among Texian settlers. This sentiment ultimately fueled a decisive Texian victory at the Battle of San Jacinto less than two months later, where the rallying cry "Remember the Alamo!" became a unifying chant for Texas independence. Santa Anna's actions at the Alamo would later be viewed as a monumental blunder that ignited a fierce resolve among the Americans and Tejanos alike.

Two weeks later at Goliad, the Mexican dictator's ruthless killings continued. In what became known as "The Goliad Massacre," it marked a tragic conclusion to the Goliad Campaign of 1836 and stands as

---

[1257] The Travis Alamo Letters, Yallogy.com, 2020.

one of the most infamous events of the Texas Revolution.[1258] Although overshadowed by the Battle of the Alamo, the massacre rallied support for the Texan cause both within Texas and across the United States. This increased momentum ultimately contributed to the Texan victory at the Battle of San Jacinto and secured the independence of the Republic of Texas.

The massacre was ordered by Santa Anna, of course, who claimed to operate within Mexican law. This context is essential, as the massacre was not an isolated incident but part of a broader strategy to deter American support for the Texas colonists. Following the attack on Tampico by General José Antonio Mexía in late 1835, Santa Anna executed captured soldiers as pirates, establishing a precedent for severe treatment of future prisoners.

General José de Urrea, commanding Santa Anna's right wing, was tasked with executing the decree that mandated all foreign combatants be treated as pirates. Although he preferred to treat prisoners humanely, Urrea reluctantly complied with orders leading to the execution of captured Texan soldiers after their defeat in various battles, including the Battle of Refugio.

The pivotal moment came after the surrender of James W. Fannin and his troops at Coleto. Fannin had negotiated terms that promised humane treatment, but Santa Anna's orders were clear: the Texans would be executed. Urrea communicated his concerns to Santa Anna, advocating for clemency, but received a direct order to carry out the executions.

On March 27, 1836, the unwounded Texans were marched out and executed in groups. Many were killed immediately, while others were hunted down and slaughtered. Fannin and about forty wounded men remained in the presidio and were executed separately. In total, approximately 342 Texans were executed, with only a few managing to escape.

After the massacre, the bodies were left unburied until General Thomas J. Rusk organized a proper burial in June 1836. The Goliad Massacre significantly impacted the perception of Santa Anna,

---

[1258] Roell, Craig H., *Matamoros and the Texas Revolution*, Denton: Texas State Historical Association, 2013, p. 64

transforming him from a cunning leader into American public enemy number one; a cruel and unforgiving dictator. This shift galvanized support for the Texan cause, ensuring ongoing aid from both the United States and other nations. The brutality of the massacre, along with the fall of the Alamo, fueled outrage and contributed to the eventual success of the Texas Revolution.

In mid-April 1836, Stephen Austin reached out to Jackson for assistance. These developments placed the U.S. government in a precarious position. Although courageous, the Texans relied heavily on American support for men and supplies. The Mexican government voiced strong complaints about the U.S. obligation under international law to maintain neutrality, rendering federal authorities under Jackson powerless. However, American public opinion favored the Texans. Slain heroes Jim Bowie and Davy Crockett, well-known frontiersmen in life, became legendary martyrs in death. Texan war cries–"Remember the Alamo" and Remember Goliad!" along with "Death to Santa Anna!"- -swept through the United States.[1259] Multitudes of Americans with vengeance on their minds grabbed their guns and rushed to Texas and to the aid of relatives, friends, and compatriots.

Vengeance was now the word on Texian minds, but more importantly was the question of how to either force Santa Anna back to Mexico City, or end him once and for all, while simultaneously culminating the Texas Revolution. As noted, the Texas provisional government had named Sam Houston commander in chief of the Texas army back in November. Houston's campaign was one of calculated strategic withdrawal, in waiting for an opportune moment to strike back at the Mexicans. He avoided immediate engagement with Santa Anna's larger, better-trained force, instead focusing on building his own army and gaining an advantage. This involved a series of retreats eastward to avoid immediate confrontation and build strength. Having adopted this more defensive strategy, Houston gave the Texans the advantage of shorter supply lines from the United States, while simultaneously lengthening Santa Anna's lines. The Mexicans were forced to bring up supplies by land because

---

[1259] Klein, Christopher, "The Goliad Massacre—The Other Alamo," The History Channel online. May 26, 2015.

the Texas navy controlled the sea. This force consisted of only four small ships, but it was big enough to do the job.

Finally, on April 20 and 21st, 1836, at the junction of Buffalo Bayou and the San Jacinto River, Sam Houston struck. Houston's small army of "Texians," numbering just over nine hundred strong, had retreated to the east, luring General Santa Anna to San Jacinto, near the site of the city that now bears Sam Houston's name. The Mexicans under Santa Anna numbered over 1,300 men, but Houston rallied his smaller force for what became a final victory. His Texians encountered Santa Anna's men taking their siesta on the banks of the San Jacinto. Taking full advantage, the 900 Texians charged after a single volley, overrunning the groggy Mexicans who, taken by surprise, rushed for their weapons. Breaking ranks, Houston's men swarmed over the Mexican breastworks, yelling "Remember the Alamo! Remember La Bahia (Goliad)!", to engage in hand-to-hand combat. Santa Anna, his lieutenants, Manuel Gonzalez Castrillón, and Juan Almonte yelled often conflicting orders, attempting to organize their startled men into some form of defense. The Texian infantry forces advanced without halt until they had possession of the woodland and the Mexican breastwork; the right-wing of Colonel Edward Burleson's and the left-wing of Lieutenant Colonel Henry Millard's forces took possession of the breastwork. Within 18 minutes, Mexican soldiers abandoned their campsite and fled for their lives. The killing lasted for hours.

"Victory is certain! Trust in God and fear not! And remember the Alamo! Remember the Alamo!" Houston cried out as he rallied his men in what became forever known as the Battle of San Jacinto. Mexican soldiers, facing annihilation, retreated in a desperate rush through the marsh. Texian riflemen stationed themselves on the banks and shot at anything that moved. Many Texian officers, including Houston, attempted to stop the slaughter, but they were unable to gain control of the men, incensed and vengeful for the massacres at the Alamo and Goliad, while frightened Mexican infantry yelled "Me no Alamo!" and begged for mercy, but to no avail. In what historian David Brion Davis called "one of the most one-sided victories in history,"[1260] 650 Mexican

---

[1260] Davis, David Brion. "The Central Fact of American History Archived 2009-10-04 at the Wayback Machine," *American Heritage*, Feb/March 2005.

soldiers were killed, 208 wounded, and 300 captured. Only eleven Texians were killed and mortally wounded, while 30 others, including Houston, were wounded but survived.

As darkness fell, a large group of prisoners were led into camp. Houston initially mistook the group for Mexican reinforcements and reportedly shouted out that all was lost. Santa Anna had escaped towards Vince's Bridge. Finding the bridge destroyed, he hid in the marsh and was captured the following day, wearing the uniform jacket of a private. Confronted with thirsty bowie knives, this subterfuge was uncovered when other Mexican prisoners cried out in recognition of their commander. The quaking dictator was brought before Houston, who had been shot in the ankle and badly wounded. Texian soldiers gathered around, calling for the Mexican general's immediate execution.

Bargaining for his life, Santa Anna suggested that he order the remaining Mexican troops to stay away. In a letter to Vincente Filisola, who was now the senior Mexican official in Texas, Santa Anna wrote that "yesterday evening [we] had an unfortunate encounter" and ordered his troops to retreat to Béxar and await further instructions.[1261] Santa Anna was then speedily induced to sign two treaties. Faced with the Texans' determination, General Santa Anna quickly signed the treaties, agreeing to withdraw Mexican troops and recognize the Rio Grande as Texas's southwestern boundary. Upon his release, he claimed the treaties were illegitimate, having been signed under duress, repudiating the agreement.

These events put the U.S. government in a sticky situation. The Texans, though courageous, could hardly have won their independence without the help in men and supplies from their American cousins. The Washington government, as the Mexicans bitterly complained, had a solemn obligation under international law to enforce its leaky neutrality statutes. But American public opinion, overwhelmingly favorable to the Texans, openly nullified the existing legislation. The federal authorities under Jackson were powerless to act, and the pro-Texas Jackson even hesitated to extended the right hand of recognition to the Lone Star Republic, led by his old comrade-in-arms against the Indians in the Creek War, Houston. This non-recognition would not last long, however.

[1261] Davis, 2006, p. 273.

Many Texans sought not only recognition of their independence but also full union with the United States. They reasoned that no nation would refuse such a generous offer. In 1837, the eager Texas "bride" formally requested annexation, presenting herself for marriage to the United States. However, the prospective groom, Uncle Sam, was pulled back by the contentious issue of slavery, which was becoming more divisive by the day. Antislavery advocates in the North increasingly opposed annexation, arguing that the entire plan was merely a scheme devised by the southern "slavocracy" to expand slavery into new territories.

At first glance, a "slavery plot" charge seemed plausible. With a slaveholder in the White House, and most of the early settlers in Texas, as well as American volunteers during the revolution, coming from the states of the South and Southwest, it seemed highly probable. Most scholars have concluded, however, that no proslavery plot existed. Most of the immigrants came from the South and Southwest simply because these states were closer. The explanation was proximity rather than conspiracy. Yet the fact remained that many Texans were slaveholders, and admitting Texas to the Union inescapably meant enlarging American slavery.[1262]

Officially, Jackson had maintained the appearance of neutrality in the Texas conflict. When Austin wrote asking for help in what he told, Jackson was "a war of barbarism against civilization, of despotism against liberty, of Mexicans against Americans," Jackson demurred, noting on the letter "the writer does not reflect that we have a treaty with Mexico, and our national faith has pledged to support it. The Texans, before they took the step to declare themselves independent, which has aroused and united all Mexico against them, ought to have pondered well."

But to his young nephew, Jackson Donelson, Great Uncle President Andrew Jackson betrayed his true feelings of patriotism when it came to the dramatic tale of the Texans' last stand at the Alamo. Having received a letter from boarding school in Chantilly, Virginia, young Jackson has expressed his enthusiasm for the heroes of Texas. On Friday, April 22nd, 1836, the president replied: "Your sympathies expressed on hearing of those brave men who fell in defense of the Alamo displays a proper

---

[1262] Gibbons, Brendan, "Historian says slavery 'cannot be dismissed' but wasn't main cause of Texas Revolution," *San Antonio Report: Nonprofit Journalism for an Informed Community*, Feb. 9, 2021.

feeling of patriotism and sympathy for the gallant defenders of the rights of freemen, which I trust will grow with your growth....and find you always a strong votary in the cause of freedom."[1263]

Meanwhile, Andrew Jackson's achievements in foreign affairs began to beg notice. Jackson's flexibility when it came to foreign policy surprised many who expected the iron-willed General to dictate terms to foreign powers. Yet, his approach did not align with such expectations, and it showed his willingness to compromise—his ability to seek common ground and find middle solutions to challenges. It showed his growth as a politician, and his ability when it came to ministerial appointments as well.

After four years of clashes between Mexican and Texian residents, the Revolution of Texas ended. Texas and Mexico signed the Treaties of Velasco, and the Republic of Texas was born. The Texas Republic adopted its iconic lone star flag on May 11, 1836, by the Convention held at Washington-on-the-Brazos shortly after the victory at San Jacinto. Texas was now independent, and they expressed their desire to be annexed into the United States. Surely Jackson would immediately and happily accede to this request. Yet, Jackson declined. He even refused to recognize the new republic without prior Congressional approval. Looking back this seems to be contradictory of both Jackson's and America's desire. Especially considering that Americans had volunteered their blood, sweat and gold to help Texas gain their independence, so much so that the Government of Mexico accused America of not sufficiently enforcing neutrality between the nations.

Jackson had shown time and again that he was a bold man, and a bold president. Despite being known as one to never back down from a fight, Jackson backed away from embracing the annexation of Texas. In his 1836 State of the Union address, the president acknowledged the desire of Texans to become part of the United States and the desire for Americans to embrace their lands. To do so now, he explained, would in the eyes of the world make America appear too ambitious and open the country up to accusations of embracing harmful policies towards their neighboring nations, including both the Mexicans and the Cherokee. It's an accusation that history would nevertheless level on both Andrew

---

[1263] AJ to Jackson Donelson, April 22, 1836, Jackson, *Correspondence*, LC.

Jackson and the United States. But in 1836, Andrew Jackson was in his final year as president, having grappled with Congress, and faced a rash of criticism for non-constitutional acts. Perhaps, a shift against his expected Texas proposal was a way to counter such allegations. Moreover, in 1836, the United States was not prepared for war, not one that made the United States appear to be the aggressor against its republican neighbor, and certainly not one that could well induce Spain to get involved. In his final State of the Union address in 1836, Jackson explained his thinking:

"No danger is apprehended, however, that they will not be peacefully, although tardily, acknowledged and paid by all, unless the irritating effect of her struggle with Texas should unfortunately make our immediate neighbor, Mexico, an exception. It is already known to you, by the correspondence between the two Governments communicated at your last session, that our conduct in relation to that struggle is regulated by the same principles that governed us in the dispute between Spain and Mexico herself, and I trust that it will be found on the most severe scrutiny that our acts have strictly corresponded with our professions. That the inhabitants of the United States should feel strong prepossessions for the one party, is not surprising. But this circumstance should of itself teach us great caution, lest it lead us into the great error of suffering public policy to be regulated by partiality or prejudice; and there are considerations connected with the possible result of this contest between the two parties of so much delicacy and importance to the United States that our character requires that we should neither anticipate events nor attempt to control them. The known desire of the Texans to become a part of our system, although its gratification depends upon the reconcilement of various and conflicting interests, necessarily a work of time and uncertain in itself, is calculated to expose our conduct to misconstruction in the eyes of the world. There are already those who, indifferent to principle themselves and prone to suspect the want of it in others, charge us with ambitious designs and insidious policy."[1264]

Just before leaving office in 1837, however, Jackson recognized the Lone Star Republic, led by Sam Houston. Even this move was controversial, as it was sure to ignite discord with Mexico. In March 1837,

---

[1264] Wagner, Dennis, 1835, *Andrew Jackson-Texas Revolution*; Miller Center, 2022.

Jackson made it official, recognizing the Republic of Texas, appointing Alcée La Branche as the first U.S. diplomat to the new republic. This act was one of Jackson's last as president. While he recognized Texas's independence, Jackson was cautious about annexation, fearing potential war with Mexico and concerns about the expansion of slavery. For now. For Jackson was not about to give up on the Texas question.

This painting of the Alamo by artist Theodore Gentilz, a French immigrant, is considered the most accurate image of the mission and presidio complex ever rendered. Gentilz interviewed eyewitnesses and had access to the Alamo ruins before they were rebuilt by the United States Army in 1850. The original painting was owned by C.H. Mueller of San Antonio and was destroyed by fire circa 1906. Image Source: Texas State Library and Archives Commission.

CHAPTER

82

LEGACY & FAMILY

"Your trial is approaching. The spirit of freedom and the spirit of slavery are drawing together for the deadly conflict of arms. The annexation of Texas to this Union is the blast of the trumpet for a foreign, civil, servile, and Indian war, of which the government of the United States, fallen into faithless hands."

-John Quincy Adams

President Andrew Jackson advised a supporter in 1835 on how to tell the difference between Democrats and "Whigs, nullies, and blue-light federalists." In doing so, he neatly summarized the Jacksonian philosophy: "The people ought to inquire [of political candidates]--are you opposed to a national bank; are you in favor of rotation of office; do you subscribe to the republican rule that the people are the sovereign power, the officers their agents, and that upon all national or general subjects, as well as local, they have a right to instruct their agents and representatives, and they are bound to obey or resign; in short, are they true Republicans agreeable to the true Jeffersonian creed?"[1265]

The silver-tongued and keen-witted vice president, Martin Van Buren was Jackson's choice to be his successor in 1836. By this time, the hollow-cheeked Jackson, now nearing seventy years old, was becoming too old and frail to consider a third term. But the ever-defiant Jackson was not about to allow the likes of Henry Clay to take his place in the

---
[1265] Kennedy and Cohen, Ch. 13.

executive chair, as long as he had the ability to prevent it. And Jackson did have such ability, and the popular support to, in essence, serve a third term through the somewhat sycophantic Van Buren. Not taking any chances, Jackson rigged the Democratic nominating convention with care and rammed his favorite down the throats of the delegates assembled in Baltimore in May of 1835. Van Buren was supported by the Jacksonians without the type of wild enthusiasm they had shown for Old Hickory, even though he had promised to "tread generally" in the footsteps of the General.

The strife about the next presidential election (the first in a dozen years in which Jackson would not be taking part), was already moving quickly. For years now, Jackson had dreamed that Martin Van Buren would succeed him, and the Democratic Convention in Baltimore in May 1835 had duly nominated the vice president. But Jackson's fellow Tennesseans, unhappy with the prospect of a Van Buren presidency, had nominated one of their own, Judge Hugh Lawson White, a former Democrat, for the White House. Jackson was furious, but he could do nothing about it—except ensure that the Democratic Party he was building was behind Van Buren, not White. The Whigs in the North ultimately settled on William Henry Harrison as their nominee (Daniel Webster was also in the field), and White was the candidate in the South.

The reaction to Van Buren's rise had been vicious. "He is not one of the race of the lion or the tiger," Calhoun said of Van Buren; rather, he "belongs to a lower order—the fox."[1266] Van Buren, said fellow New Yorker William Seward, was "a crawling reptile, whose only claim was that he had inveigled the confidence of a credulous, blind, dotard old man."[1267]

Jackson, who had long argued for the people's right to choose their president, found himself limited in how overtly he could support Van Buren, having essentially tied his own hands when it came to ensuring his vice president's victory. Therefore, Jackson could not help Van Buren too overtly. Since the will of the voters had been thwarted with Adams's victory in 1825, Jackson became convinced of something he had

---

[1266] Grosvenor, Edwin S., "The Rise of the Little Magician," *American Heritage Magazine*, June, 1962, Volume 13, Issue 4.
[1267] Mackenzie, William Lyon (1846). *The Life and Times of Martin Van Buren*. Cooke & Company. pp. 21–22.

suspected: that Nicholas Biddle and his allies manipulated elections and had been doing so for some time.

In his first inaugural address, the memories of Clay and Adams still fresh, Jackson had said: "The recent demonstration of public sentiment inscribes on the list of Executive duties, in characters too legible to be overlooked, the task of reform, which will require particularly the correction of those abuses that have brought the patronage of the Federal Government into conflict with the freedom of elections."[1268]

In the Jackson years, in other words, the only kingmakers would be the people. A fine expression of principle—but politics has a way of complicating the application of such principles. As the election neared, the still ineffective organization of the Whigs showed in their inability to nominate a single presidential candidate. Their-long shot strategy was instead to run several prominent "favorite sons," each with the popular support of a different region of the country and hope to scatter the vote enough to throw the fate of the election into the hands of the House of Representatives. "Upon the supposition of there being three candidates, it would of course be sound policy to cultivate the best relations of amity between the 2 sections north and south of the Whig party since they might find it necessary to cooperate if the election were to evolve on the house." Henry Clay wrote in 1835.

The Whigs ended up with two main tickets: William Henry Harrison for president and Francis Granger for vice president in the North and Kentucky, and Hugh Lawson White for president and John Tyler for vice president in the middle and lower South. As Clay suggested, rather sprightly, to another correspondent, "If White can get the South, and another candidate can get Pennsylvania, should there be no popular election winner, as will be probable, V. Buren would enter the House the lowest candidate."

The Whigs' decision not to hold a convention reflected their determination to have multiple candidates in the mix. Among all the Whig nominees, William Henry Harrison garnered the most support. Hailing from a prominent Virginia family (his father, Benjamin, was a member of the Continental Congress and signed the Declaration of

---

[1268] Jackson, Andrew. Inaugural Address, March 4, in Jackson›s hand. March 4, 1829. Manuscript/Mixed Material. Retrieved from the Library of Congress.

Independence,) Harrison sought political opportunities in the expanding West, representing Ohio in both the House and the Senate, and serving as governor of the Indiana Territory. He gained national recognition during the War of 1812 when his forces defeated a combined British and Native American army at the Battle of the Thames in Upper Canada near Chatham. Harrison's reputation suggests that Andrew Jackson's influence extended beyond his own party; both men shared similar life stories, something the Whigs were eager to capitalize on. Like Jackson, Harrison had left the Old South for the New West, seeking public office on the frontier, and gaining popularity through military engagements against Native Americans and the British. In many ways, old "Tippecanoe" mirrored Old Hickory, even earning a homespun nickname of his own.[1269]

In order to have the election decided in the House, the Whigs' hope was predicated on ensuring that no one candidate received a majority of the votes. The deadlock would then have to be broken by Congress, where the Whigs might have a fighting chance. With Henry Clay rudely elbowed aside this time around, the leading Whig "favorite son" was the heavy-jawed Harrison. The fine-tuned schemes of the Whigs came to nothing, however, as the "Little Magician" squirmed into office by the close popular vote of 765,483 to 739, 795, but by the more comfortable margin of 170 to 124 in the electoral college. The dapper Martin Van Buren would indeed be headed to the White House as the eighth president of the United States.

In the summer of 1836, Emily Donelson's emotional distress began to foreshadow her physical decline. Having arrived in Nashville on June 26 she worked until August to ready Poplar Grove while she waited for her husband and eldest son, Jackson to make it home to her. The two left Washington on July 10th, hoping to make it home in swift accord, but severe rains that turned the already rough roads into mud caused delays. Jackson's horses suffered greatly during the journey and had to be rested longer than usual.

[1269] Kennedy and Cohen, *American Pageant*, Ch. 13.

From Salem, Virginia (which Jackson always spelled "Salum"), Andrew informed Emily a week later that their travel had been some of the worst they had endured, and that their progress had been limited to around 18 miles a day. He reassured her that their son, Jackson, was in good health, and was quite the little traveler. Unfortunately, July brought news of the death of Mrs. Mary Ann McLemore, a family friend, while their two-year-old daughter Rachel was ill, adding to Emily's strain.

The president, along with Andrew and Jackson Donelson, finally reached the Hermitage on August 4. Despite his fatigue, Jackson quickly resumed his political activities. Three weeks later, he was campaigning for Van Buren, shaking hands with thousands among the vast Democratic crowds. Andrew returned home to Poplar Grove, wisely choosing to stay with his ailing wife, who was later diagnosed with the dreaded consumption, tuberculosis.

Emily's condition worsened, and Andrew grew more deeply concerned. On September 17, Jackson wrote to Andrew Jr., expressing his anxiety over Emily's health. Six days later, he received distressing news from Nashville. Jackson's letters were intermixed with both his personal worries and his perpetual political duties, revealing the interconnectedness of their lives, and his inability to escape the draw of politics.

Despite the decline of Emily's health, Jackson could not help but to remain forever a politician, even with the obvious personal concern he felt for the ailing Emily. "I have no doubt of every Republican state going to Van Buren," Jackson told Donelson, in the midst of Emily's rapid decline. The old man so yearned for the vindication Van Buren's election would bring with it, as his chosen successor. For this desired outcome, and for Andrew's sake, he willed himself into an optimistic state of mind. "I can say to you that the political horizon is bright and cheering."[1270]

Yet while his letters conveyed his sympathies, he also remained consistently focused on political realities. The election was shaping up to be close, much closer than was comfortable, and therefore his anxiety for both Emily and his 'legacy' grew exponentially together. In the face of the grim reality, the president urged Andrew to remain strong for their children and expressed hope for Emily's recovery. By October 1, Jackson

---

[1270] Meacham, Ch. 32.

received confirmation that Emily's condition had deteriorated further. He reassured Andrew while preparing him for the harsh possibility of loss. While Andrew Donelson had to wonder how the Van Buren race had any importance at all, considering what was at stake with his wife, to Jackson, the two concerns were one and the same.

Andrew, who had despaired of leaving Emily ten days earlier to return to Washington, now changed his tune, deciding to leave her alone with her mother and their children. The pull of Washington and that of Jackson were too strong. The president was needy, and all around him were well aware of it. Jackson, himself, made no effort to hide the fact of his neediness. Mulling over a farewell address, Jackson asked Taney for help. "I am so harassed with business and company, and deprived as I am of the aid of Major Donelson, that I am compelled to ask the aid of friends in maturing the address I have in contemplation." But as this letter was written, Donelson was already on the road, having left Nashville behind for Washington, even as Emily's condition worsened. As he sat around the fire each evening after a long day of travel, Donelson would take pen to paper to assure his beloved and assuage his own guilt at having left her.

"Words cannot express the pain which the separation from you at this time has occasioned me," Andrew wrote Emily. But, in truth, the pain was not so severe that it kept him from returning to his Uncle's service. "Be assured, my dear Emily, that not a moment will be lost that can hasten my return." He wrote. "From what Dr. Laurence has told me I feel the strongest hopes that your strength will be gradually recovered. . . . Remember me affectionately to your Mother who is so good and kind to you and our dear children. Her remaining with you places me under obligations which I can never forget."[1271]

Perhaps prodded by Donelson, Jackson wrote Emily also, trying to underscore the importance of Donelson's mission in the White House, arguing that Andrew would have been subject to attack had he not come on to Washington. "The major is working night and day to get his work in signing patents so that he may return to you. He had upwards of 40,000 when he reached here all prepared for his signature. He will be with you the first moment after he can close this absolutely necessary

---

[1271] ibid.

duty, and my dear Emily you must bear his absence with patience as it is a very necessary one......as these grants without his signature would have been entirely lost to the public and he subject to the censure of a vindictive world for the same."[1272] Jackson's neediness was evident to all those around him, and Jackson made no attempt to cover it up. Finally, a date of departure was fixed, Andrew was to leave Washington for Nashville on November 22nd.

Meanwhile, the war over slavery, which was intensifying, continued to be fought by proxy. Particularly since slave preacher Nat Turner's revolt in Virginia in 1831, the same year William Lloyd Garrison began printing his abolitionist newspaper *The Liberator*, the abolitionist movement had gained momentum and did not appear to be slowing down. In his first term, Jackson had the tariff as his pretext. Then in 1835, the battleground question was if states would be allowed to dictate terms to postmasters regarding abolitionist mailings. But, as the wheels of time took the country into Jackson's final full year as president, the question had become one of the right of citizens to appeal to Congress in favor of emancipation, particularly in the District of Columbia.

To put a stop to slavery debates in Congress, and to avoid the difficulty of having to decide on the future of slavery in America, Congress began to employ what was called the "gag rule," which represented the slaveholders' attempt to pretend as though–at least in the halls of Congress–there was no dispute over the question of slavery in America. In a practice generated by South Carolina congressman Henry Pinckney, the House would "table" —the parliamentary term for ignoring—abolitionist petitions, effectively denying constituents the right to be heard on what had already become the most controversial issue in American life. While the Senate did not officially vote to "gag" abolitionists, it simply did so any time they tried to speak on the issue.

As 1836 dragged on, a number of Jacksonian decrees came into direct collision with one another. There was his tacit (and at times not so tacit) support for the Texas Revolution against Mexico; having long dreamed of an independent Texas becoming part of the United States, which put an end to any lingering discussion of British imperial designs on Texas. There was the ongoing situation with Indian removal, which,

---

[1272] AJ to Emily Donelson, 1836, Jackson, *Correspondence*, VI.

if the Seminole case proved any indication, could continue to frustrate American removal efforts further. "Mr. Chairman, are you ready for all these wars? A Mexican War? A war with Great Britain, if not France?" John Quincy Adams, recognizing the many tensions, asked the House of Representatives in May 1836, "A general Indian War? A servile war? And as an inevitable consequence of them all, a civil war? From the instant that your slaveholding states become the theater of war, civil, servile, or foreign, from that instant the war powers of Congress extend to interference with the institution of slavery in every way by which it can be interfered with.

CHAPTER

83

A TRAGIC LOSS

"The People, sir, the People will set things right."
-Andrew Jackson

From her sickbed in Nashville, Emily Donelson was sentimental about the flow of good wishes and prayers from Washington, all while fits of coughing and fever wracked her body and spirit. Yet, she had remained strong all throughout the fall, refusing to give in to self-pity, knowing that her husband would soon be on the road back to Tennessee before the holiday season set in. But, on November 19th, Jackson suffered his own bout of hemorrhaging, and Donelson felt compelled to delay his return while his uncle recovered. "My dear Emily, do not allow yourself to be disturbed by the delay…it will only be a few days of pain and anxiety for me—but if prayers can avail anything—they will be days of returning power and strength to you."[1273] But as had always been the case, dying wife or not, Jackson came first.

With tuberculosis ravaging her body, Emily, hemorrhaging from her lungs, waited patiently, but still Andrew did not leave his uncle's side. On Thursday, December 1, Jackson wrote in a note to Emily and Andrew's son Jackson, "Your dear papa was to have left here this morning, but owing to my own debility remains today and tomorrow to have my message copied well and prepared for transmission to Congress next Tuesday—say to your dear mama that I regret that he should be thus

---

[1273] AJ Donelson to Emily Donelson, Nov., 1836, Donelson Papers, LC.

one moment detained from her."[1274] Emily, whose condition grew worse every day, had to have known by early December that she would never see her husband again.

Donelson, who had been delayed a second time when Jackson insisted on his address being edited once more, did not leave Washington until Saturday, December 3rd, and did not arrive in Nashville until Wednesday, December 31st. Unfortunately, he was too late. Emily died on Monday, December 29th, 1836. She was twenty-nine years old.

The news of Emily's passing did not reach the White House until New Year's Day, 1837. Politics in Washington ran their usual tempestuous course. In November, people cast their votes for the next president, and it was indeed a close race. As the votes were trickling in, it looked for a moment like Van Buren would go down in defeat. Had the vote gone to the House, as the Whigs had hoped, he would likely have been defeated by either Harrison or White, but as it turns out, despite the popular margin measuring in only the hundreds in some states, Van Buren won a majority of electoral votes. Jackson gained his measure of vindication after all.

Distracted though he was with the transition process of becoming president, Martin Van Buren, (Matty to his friends,) attempted to console Andrew Donelson with a reminder that Emily's spirit had consoled even the most cynical Washingtonians. He would "never cease to admire her excellent character….It will I am sure be grateful to your feelings to learn how extensively this sentiment is entertained here where such feelings are, you know, not apt to take deep root—it is much more than I have witnessed on any former occasion." [1275]

In his grief, as he had been forced to do nearly eight years earlier when Rachel passed, Jackson pressed on. In those days, he had taken comfort in fighting what he saw as a war for the people. Now, in the last days of his presidency, he hoped to win one final battle for his presidential legacy; what he thought was the one blot on his record, the one dark spot on his presidential honor: He hoped to expunge the 1834 Senatorial censure of his actions in his removal of the federal deposits.

[1274] AJ to Jackson Donelson, 1836, Jackson, *Correspondence*, VI.
[1275] Meacham, p. 334.

Thus, the White House days of Andrew Jackson were to end as they had passed all along, with thumping backslaps from his supporters, and with deignful and resonating resentments from his enemies. The Age of Jackson, the eight years, so full of drama and melodramas, would now culminate in a series of speeches in the Senate chamber, among Senators either strongly for the president, or adamantly against him. The business at hand was whether or not to erase the censure from the record–undoing the Senate's denouncement of Jackson's unilateral decision to destroy the Bank of the United States in effect. Thomas Hart Benton led the President's cause, but the now older, more sarcastic, more bitter and resigned Henry Clay led the opposition. It would be one final battle between the two western warriors. Benton ordered a supply of cold ham, turkey, wine and hot coffee for the chamber, but as one page, Captain Isaac Bassett, remarked perhaps ironically, perhaps not, "The great part of the Senate was not in a humor to eat."[1276]

Clay opened the proceedings: "The decree has gone forth. It is one of urgency, too. The deed is to be done—that foul deed which, like the blood-stained hands of the guilty MacBeth, all ocean's waters will never wash out. Proceed, then, by the noble work which lies before you, and like other skillful executioners, do it quickly. And when you have perpetrated it, go home to the people, and tell them that you have extinguished one of the brightest and purest lights that even burnt at the altar of civil liberty. Tell them that, henceforward, no matter what daring or outrageous act any President may perform, you have forever hermetically sealed the mouth of the Senate. Tell them that he may fearlessly assume what powers he pleases, snatch from its lawful custody the public purse, command a military detachment to enter the halls of the Capitol, overawe Congress, trample down the constitution, raze every bulwark of freedom; but that the Senate must stand mute, in silent submission, and not dare to raise its opposing voice….. And, if the people do not pour out their indignation and imprecations, I have yet to learn the character of American freemen." [1277]

Calhoun then spoke up in opposition as well. "No one, not blinded by party zeal, can possibly be insensible that the measure proposed is a

---

[1276] Benton, *Thirty Years View*, p. 416.
[1277] Cong. Globe, 23 Cong., 1 Sess., 54, December 26, 1834.

violation of the constitution." Calhoun said. "The constitution requires the Senate to keep a journal; this resolution goes to expunge the journal. If you may expunge a part, you may expunge the whole; and if it is expunged, how is it kept?" Like Clay, however, he knew that his was a futile argument, for "this act originates in pure, unmixed, personal idolatry. It is the melancholy evidence of a broken spirit, ready to bow at the feet of power. . . . An act like this could never have been consummated by a Roman Senate until the times of Caligula and Nero."[1278]

Benton's words carried the day, however, and Clay and Calhoun had already known their argument was futile. Jackson and Benton had the votes they needed, but Benton painted a portrait of grand exultation. "History has been ransacked to find examples of tyrants sufficiently odious to illustrate him by comparison," Benton said of Jackson, "Language has been tortured to find epithets sufficiently strong enough to paint him in description. Imagination has been exhausted in her efforts to deck him with revolting and inhuman attributes. Tyrant, despot, usurper, destroyer of the liberties of his country; rash, ignorant, imbecile, endangering the public peace with all foreign nations; destroying domestic prosperity at home. . . .' Benton scoffed at all of these. "He came into office the first of generals; he goes out the first of statesmen. His civil competitors have shared the fate of his military opponents; and Washington city has been to the American politicians who have assailed his lines. Repulsed! Driven back! Discomfited! Crushed! has been the fate of all assailants, foreign and domestic, civil and military. At home and abroad, the impress of his genius and of his character is felt."[1279]

Like Calhoun said of those "Expungers" who ultimately won the vote, amid a "storm of hisses and groans" from the left side of the Circular Gallery, who had 'bowed at the feet of power,' the record of Jackson's censure for abuse of power was marked out of the journal by the secretary of the Senate. Jackson had prevailed once again.

Thrilled by the vote, Jackson invited the senators who had become known as "the expungers" to sup at the White House with their spouses. Feeling too ill to sit at the table, the president greeted the guests before bowing out. He made sure that Benton, "the head expunger," sat in the

---

[1278] ibid, 175 (January 28, 1835.
[1279] Benton, *Thirty Years' View*, I, p. 423.

presidential chair. The happy mood the Jackson team enjoyed after this final victory was reflected in a letter Andrew Jackson, Jr. wrote to his cousin, Stockley Donelson at the end of January, 1837, "All is going well here, and the President will go out triumphantly after all."

"My own race is nearly run, advanced age and a broken body warn me that before long I must pass beyond the reach of human events and cease to feel the vicissitudes of human affairs." Jackson had written in his farewell address. "I thank God that my life has been spent in a land of liberty and that He has given me a heart to love my country with the affection of a son." With that, he turned his eyes west, eager for the day soon beckoning when could depart for the hills of Tennessee, and home.

Saturday, March 4, 1837, was a beautiful day in Washington, with a light, warm breeze and not a cloud in the sky. The air was calm, and cool, and the day itself proved rather uneventful. Jackson and Van Buren arrived in a carriage pulled by four gray horses, entering the House chamber filled with public officials gathered to witness Johnson take the vice presidential oath. Watching the inauguration from a fine window view that overlooked the east front of the Capitol, the head expunger himself, Thomas Hart Benton, found the audience "profoundly silent.... It was the stillness and silence of reverence and affection; and there was no room for mistake as to whom this mute and impressive homage was rendered. For once," continued Benton, "the rising was eclipsed by the setting sun."

Shortly afterward, Van Buren addressed a crowd of around 20,000 people from a wooden platform set up in the east portico. His voice was remarkably distinct, according to one observer, as he delivered a 30-minute speech. Van Buren appeared to sense, too, that this was as much, if not more, about Jackson's farewell march, as his own moment. He would have had to be politically naive to not be aware that his big day was surely to be overshadowed by the political giant whose powers of appeal he could not hope to compare with. "I tread in the footsteps of illustrious men, whose superiors it is our happiness to believe are not found on the executive calendar of any country." [1280]

Referring to his predecessor, Van Buren hailed his chief, "In receiving from the people the sacred trust twice confided to my illustrious

---

[1280] Van Buren, First Inaugural Address, March 4, 1837. National Park Service.gov.

predecessor, and which he has discharged so faithfully, and so well," Van Buren said in his inaugural address, "I know that I can not expect to perform the arduous task with equal ability and success." Van Buren, looking short, slender, bland and bald as he gave his address, took wistful note of the end of an era. "But....I may hope that somewhat of the same cheering approbation will be found to attend my path."

Van Buren concluded with aplomb, unaware of the panic that was soon to ravage the country's economy. "But united as I have been in his counsels, a daily witness of his exclusive and unsurpassed devotion to his country's welfare, agreeing with him in sentiments which his countrymen have warmly supported, and permitted to partake largely of his confidence, I may hope that somewhat of the same cheering approbation will be found to attend upon my path. For him I but express, with my own, the wishes of all, that he may yet long live to enjoy the brilliant evening of his well-spent life; and for myself, conscious of but one desire, faithfully to serve my country, I throw myself without fear on its justice and its kindness. Beyond that I only look to the gracious protection of the Divine Being whose strengthening support I humbly solicit, and whom I fervently pray to look down upon us all. May it be among the dispensations of His providence to bless our beloved country with honors and with length of days. May her ways be ways of pleasantness and all her paths be peace!"[1281]

This was followed by a brief second swearing-in ceremony. Afterward, the former and new president descended the steps of the Capitol and got into a phaeton. Leaving the capital for the last time, Jackson, as was his habit, bowed to the people, then continued down Pennsylvania Avenue. Accompanied by blue-coated dragoons, the vehicle then took them to the White House.

Martin Van Buren, as Jackson had hoped, was now the eighth president of the United States. This was the thirteenth inauguration since the nation's founding, and it marked the commencement of the only four-year term of both Van Buren and Richard Mentor Johnson as his vice president. This was the first time the outgoing and incoming president rode together to the Capitol.

[1281] ibid

Van Buren's four years overflowed with toil and trouble. A pair of short-lived rebellions in Canada in 1837, mostly over political reform but aggravated by unregulated immigration from the United States, stirred up ugly incidents along the northern frontier and threatened to trigger war with Britain. The president's attempt to play a neutral game led to the wail "Woe to Martin Van Buren!" The antislavery agitators in the North were also in full cry. Among other grievances, they were condemning the prospective annexation of Texas. Worst of all, Jackson bequeathed to Van Buren the makings of a staggering depression. Much of Van Buren's energy had to be devoted to the purely negative task of battling the panic, and there were not enough rabbits in the "Little Magician's" tall silk hat. Hard times ordinarily blight the reputation of a president, and Van Buren was no exception.

Van Buren promised to continue Jackson's policies but faced significant challenges from the outset. As a candidate crafted by political machines, he faced resentment from various Democrats, who had so often railed against such corrupt practices. Ever the showman, Jackson's dynamism contrasted sharply with Van Buren's reserved demeanor, and those who hoped for a continued version of the old general were disappointed in the Little Magician, no matter how hard he tried. Moreover, Van Buren inherited Jackson's long list of enemies, making matters worse for the New Yorker.

With only one exception, Matty Van Buren kept the same cabinet in place left over from the last of Jackson's. But from the outset, the new president was fighting a losing battle. As a machine-made candidate, Democrats hammered against what they called a "bastard politician," one they considered "smuggled into office beneath the tails of the old general's military coat." Jackson's administration had resounded with 'furious quarrels and cracked heads,' while mild-mannered Van Buren seemed to rattle about in the military boots of his trusted predecessor.

Van Buren faced widespread turmoil throughout his four years in the White House, including unrest in Canada that risked war with Great Britain, and intense antislavery sentiments in the North. The economic hardships, which had been passed down from Jackson, made for an angry citizenry. In a similar vein to the troubles Herbert Hoover would face nearly a century later, Van Buren bore the brunt of the economy's gasping struggles, as well as the people's often venomous rage.

Van Buren's detractors felt he lacked the qualities of a president, and his detractors were many. The criticism he faced was rampant, and derisive, and probably made him, at times, wish he was back as President of the Senate. He was the first president born under the American flag. Short and slender, dull and unpossessing physically, but adroit and crafty, Van Buren has been described as a "first class, second-rate man."[1282] Van Buren, 'The Wizard of Albany,' was a statesman of wide experience in both lawmaking and administrative life. He possessed a unique ability as a political strategist, and as something of a "spoilsman" or someone who seemed to prioritize his own advancement at the expense of broader public interests. As far as his intellect, education and political training, Van Buren was above average among the presidents since Jefferson, but his mediocre reputation that developed over the years stemmed from a series of misfortunes over which he had very little control.

Shortly before his successor's early March inauguration, Jackson wrote to a colleague of the splendid vindication that day promised. Clearly the old curmudgeon warmly retained his catalogue of complaints and took some delight in leaving Washington with loyalists at the helm. "Tomorrow ends my official career forever," he noted with satisfaction. "On the 4th I hope to be able to go to the capital to witness the glorious scene of Mr. Van Buren (once rejected by the Senate,) sworn into office by Chief Justice Taney (also being rejected by the fracture Senate.)"[1283]

Three days later, Jackson, suffering, so he said, from "advanced age and a broken frame," left Washington for good. Accompanied by a small party made up of immediate family, his friend, the painter, Ralph Earle, and an army physician. Traveling by rail to Ellicott's Mills, on the Patapsco, Jackson and his entourage then traveled by carriage and steamboat to Wheeling, Cincinnati and Louisville. In Kentucky, when Jackson had a moment to pause, he wrote to Van Buren. "From the time I left you I have been, literally, in a crowd. Such assemblages of my fellow citizens I have never before seen on my passage to or from Washington." On the twenty-fourth of March, Jackson finally made it home, arriving at the Hermitage, to the welcome arms of his remaining family.

[1282] Kennedy and Cohen, *The American Pageant*, pg. 265.
[1283] AJ to Trist, March 2, 1837, Jackson, Correspondence, V, p. 462.

As a final public act, Jackson had left behind a farewell address, becoming just the second president, following George Washington in 1796, to issue a formal valediction. Principally authored by Justice Taney, the document both reviewed what Jackson regarded as his administration's cardinal achievements and warned readers to remain vigilant against the nation's internal enemies, namely bankers and abolitionists. Summarizing the financial questions on both currency and credit, the outgoing president cautioned the nation against the rising power of paper money to lift a privileged, financial elite unfairly, at the expense of others. "It is one of the serious evils of our present system of banking," Jackson warned, "that it enables one class of society, and that by no means innumerous one, by its control over the currency, to act injuriously upon the interests of all the others, and to exercise more than its just proportion of influence in political affairs." [1284]

On the other key point of his address, when speaking against the rising tide of abolitionism, Jackson seemed to mire down much in short-sighted dogma. Having dodged this troublesome debate throughout his eight years in office, Jackson might well left this contentious issue alone, as it played no role in his presidency in comparison with Indian Removal, the Nullification crisis, or the Bank War. Instead, Jackson spoke as would a founding member of the southern plantocracy, in language that seemed straight off the pages of Calhoun's old 'Exposition and Protest.' "Every state must be the sole judge of the measures proper to secure the safety of its citizens and promote their happiness. And all efforts on the part of people of other states to cast odium upon their institutions, and all measures calculated to disturb their rights of property, or to put in jeopardy their peace and internal tranquility, are in direct opposition to the spirit in which the Union was formed, and must endanger its safety." [1285]

"Weak men," so Jackson went on, referring derisively to opponents of slavery, "only "persuade themselves for a moment that they are laboring in the cause of humanity." This, despite the fact that half of the states in the Union by 1837 had either outlawed slavery or instituted gradual emancipation laws. A vast majority of the nation's population resided in

---

[1284] Jackson's Farewell Address, Mar. 4, 1837, The American Presidency Project.
[1285] Brown, David S., Ch. 50.

such areas, and Jackson certainly boasted of being a man of the majority. He took it upon himself, rather, however, to guide Northern public opinion away from such emancipation trends, both scorning abolitionism and condemning it in such a way that some might be encouraged to carry out acts of violence against those brave enough to challenge slavery. "But everyone, upon sober reflection, will see that nothing but mischief can come from these improper assaults on the feelings and rights of others. Rest assured that the men found busy in this work of discord are not worthy of your confidence and deserve your strongest reprobation." [1286]

A key point on which the outgoing president focused in his address is summed up in one of Jackson's concluding statements. Capitalizing one last time on the fears of the American public, Jackson offered this blanket warning mired in paranoia: "Knowing that the path of freedom is continually beset by enemies who often assume the disguise of friends, I have devoted the last hours of my public life to warn you of the dangers......It is from within, among yourselves--from cupidity, from corruption, from disappointed ambition and inordinate thirst for power--that factions will be formed and liberty endangered. It is against such designs, whatever disguise the actors may assume, that you have especially to guard yourselves." Enemies in the disguise of friends. Many of Jackson's critics were certainly of a mind to point out Jackson's hypocrisy on this point. Yet as always, it was vintage Jackson; forever on guard, on the lookout for those, like the Waxhaw boys who set out to get a rise out of young Andy so many years before, who were out to get him, to tear him down, to tear down his name. In this case, Jackson extended his fears to the nation, by association. Jackson warned, it was those same enemies forever at the gates, out to get the freedoms of his people.

The retired General attracted commentators and critics in inevitable swarms, those eager to assess the meaning of his presidency. In *The American Democrat*, 1838, James Fenimore Cooper, author of the epic tale, *The Last of the Mohicans*, wrote of Jackson's "imperious governing style," which he believed a product of "popular impulses that often work injustice." Former New York Mayor Phillip Hone, whose diary proved to be one of the foremost histories of the first half of the 19th century, considered Jackson's rule "more absolute than that of any hereditary

---

[1286] Jackson's Farewell Address, March 4, 1837. The American Presidency Project.

monarch of Europe," but considered the behavior of the nation's majority even more startling. "That the people should not only have submitted to it, (Jackson's rule) but upheld and supported him in his encroachments upon their rights and his disregard of the Constitution and the laws, will equally occasion the surprise and indignation of future generations."[1287]

One New Yorker, by contrast, thought the people "the true, evident, and unassailable spirit behind the era." This gentleman, one John Lawson, praised Jackson in verse for defying the odds, and overcoming so much, leading the "rise of the peasantry and bearing up through the example of his own obscure origins, the condition of commoners." He ruled in their good name, Lawson supposed. "Raised by the voice of freemen to a height sublimer, far, than kings by birth may claim."[1288] While the sentiment is heartfelt, note that Lawson clearly uses the term freemen pre-1865 in this case.

Once the seventy-year-old Jackson left the White House, on Tuesday, March 7, 1837, the pilgrimage south was filled with the anticipated cheers and hurrahs among the throngs and hordes of supporters who wished him well, as he made his way slowly back to Nashville. Taking his time, stopping after gradual steps and resting frequently, the now ex-President Jackson made his way back to the Hermitage. He stopped to visit Chief Justice Taney in Maryland. In Cincinnati, he stayed for two weeks as the guest of General Robert Lytle, a Democratic member of Congress. During his journey, he reportedly spoke openly about politics and people. While in Cincinnati, Jackson expressed regret over his estrangement from Henry Clay. Clay and himself, he said, should have been friends and would have been, if not for the slander and cowardice of a person he referred to as "that Pennsylvania reptile."[1289] He stated that he would have "crushed" this individual if friends had not intervened on his behalf. This statement, however, appears not to have evidential backing, in fact, upon digging deeper, there is some evidence that Jackson regretted not having become friends with Clay.

His friends at Nashville gave him an impressive and hearty welcome home as they had been inclined to do for many years upon his return

---

[1287] Cooper, James Fenimore, *The American Democrat*, 1838. Ch. 2.
[1288] Brown, David S., Chapter 50.
[1289] Parton, In Jackson, III, quotes this source as: *N. Y. Evening Post*, March 21st, 1859, Communication.

from his long absences. Andrew Jr. recalled, "The day of his return stands out as one of the most memorable of my life. We met him amidst the cedars near Lebanon. The old men were gathered in front, while the boys stood behind. When he exited his carriage, he listened attentively to Judge Campbell's address, responded with joy, and greeted his old friends with hearty handshakes. As he approached us, I stepped forward, offering a few words of kindness. I concluded by saying, 'The children of your old soldiers and friends welcome you home and are ready to serve under your banner.' His body trembled, and he bowed his head as tears streamed down his aged cheeks. He replied, 'I could have endured everything but this; it is too much, too much!' The crowd encircled him, and for a brief moment, there was a collective outpouring of sympathy and tears. I may live a hundred years, but no future event can ever erase that poignant scene from my memory."[1290] For all of his many enemies, Jackson inspired a deep and heartfelt love among his many supporters.

Yet, he had become a very frail old man, rarely free from pain for even an hour and never for an entire day. Despite owning a lavish and productive farm along with a hundred and fifty slaves, he still considered himself poor, upon returning to the Hermitage. "I returned home," he wrote to Mr. Trist, "with just ninety dollars in cash, having spent all my salary and most of the profits from my cotton crop. Everything was in disrepair; I needed to buy corn and other essentials for my farm. I had only one tract of land left, besides my homestead, which I sold, allowing me to begin the new year (1838) free of debt. I relied on our hard work and frugality to provide for us, trusting in a kind Providence for favorable seasons and a successful crop."[1291]

In the following years, he lived as a planter, carefully overseeing the operations of his farm and enjoying the process. He enjoyed the company of his adopted son, and his son's amiable wife, Sarah. They and their children were the solace of his old age. The still grieving Major Donelson and his family were near at hand and often cheered him by their presence at the Hermitage.

Surrounded by a large and affectionate circle, Jackson passed many days in relative contentment; and most of his later days might have

---
[1290] Quoted in Galloway, Linda, Andrew Jackson, Jr.: son of a President;: A biographical study (An Exposition-Lochinvar book) Hardcover – January 1, 1966.
[1291] AJ to Trist, Jan. 1838, Jackson Papers, LC.

been the same had it not been for the accumulation of his years of ill health that slowly turned the old general into something of an invalid. Nonetheless, his early tastes remained with him. He still took keen interest in a flourishing cotton field and loved a fine horse as much as he did when he brought home Truxton from Virginia thirty years before. William Henry Milburn, in his 1859 book *"Ten Years of Preacher Life,"* gives us a momentary glimpse of the General in these tranquil years, which shows us how he exulted in the mere sight of a superior horse. "The only time," wrote Milburn, "I ever saw Andrew Jackson, was early on a bright summer morning, when he came into my father's yard to look at some blooded animals that had just been imported from England. And well do I remember how the patriarch's face glowed and his eye shone as he gazed upon the noble creatures, and spoke in excited tones of the exquisite blending of beauty and strength in their mold. Never shall I forget the impressive appearance, the tall, spare figure, the glittering eye, and the commanding presence of the erect old man."[1292]

Jackson remained a dedicated letter-writer, and in his retirement, he stayed busy with his correspondence after returning to the Hermitage. His mailbox overflowed daily with letters, newspapers, and documents. He responded to most letters requiring an answer, unless he was too weak to sit at his desk. His letters to friends focused on his plantation affairs and his ongoing health issues.

The Hermitage remained a hub of hospitality, attracting numerous friends and visitors who came to pay their respects to the old man. Dr. William A. Shaw, a devoted admirer of Jackson, shared his memories of a lengthy stay at the Hermitage in 1839, particularly recalling conversations with the ex-President. "With regard to the quelling of the mutiny, during the Creek War, by presenting a pistol to Major Hart's breast, as reported by Eaton, the General stated to me, while we were alone at his fireside, that it was with an empty gun, which he took from a sentinel pacing his rounds before his tent, that this mutiny was quelled. Hart told his men to stop, and observed to a subordinate officer, 'd — d if I don' t believe the old fellow will shoot.' The mutiny being quelled, the sentinel, while reclaiming his gun, observed to General Jackson, 'Why, Gineral, that gun ain't loaded—not even primed.' The General scoffed,

---

[1292] Milburn, William Henry, *Ten Years of Preacher Life*, Cornell, 1859, p. 176.

'Never mind,' Jackson replied, 'it has answered my purpose as well as if it had been loaded and primed to the muzzle.'[1293]

"His description of the surrender of the British to our troops, 'Five hundred men, without a single wound, rising up from their prostrate position slowly and solemnly, as it were, out of the ground,' he declared, 'reminded him more of the resurrection at the last day than any thing he had ever read or conceived of.' He stated that he had only six killed and seven wounded in that battle, and only one of the seven wounded died.' Is there such another battle,' I inquired, 'where the loss was so inconsiderable on the victorious side, allowing for the numbers engaged?' 'Not one, so far as my researches have gone,' said he. Indeed, the victory at New Orleans was the old hero's greatest pride, as it was his greatest exploit.

Dr. Shaw was surprised at Jackson's energy as he spoke on such a sweeping array of topics. Jackson addressed the skepticism surrounding him during his election, asserting that he read at least three chapters of the Bible daily for thirty-five years, which surpassed the conduct of his detractors. He impressed Shaw with his insights on global commerce, comparing New Orleans to Constantinople, noting that New Orleans would become the largest commercial hub due to its fertile Mississippi Valley. Jackson predicted that the next significant war would be with Russia, despite the current friendship between the nations, citing the inherent conflict between a monarchy and a democracy. He expressed confidence that the U.S. could defeat Russia, emphasizing the effectiveness of flying artillery as revolutionary in warfare, as demonstrated in the Mexican Civil War. He lamented the misrepresentation of his character as reckless, arguing instead that his quick decision-making was often misunderstood as impulsiveness, highlighting his political acumen and judgment.

Shaw described Jackson as a thorough Union man in his feelings and principles, through and through. "He loved his whole country, without sectional bias. The Federal Union embraced all the States in his large-hearted comprehensiveness. He expressed a contempt for nullification and secession. In regard to his removal of the Indians to the west, he defended it on the ground of its absolute necessity as well as humanity to

---

[1293] Parton, *Jackson*, III, pp. 632-633.

the whites and the Indians. ‹Every war,› said he, ‹we had with the Indians was brought on by frontier ruffians, who stole their horses, oppressed, defrauded, or persecuted the Indians. This caused them to unbury the hatchet, and their massacres of the whites plunged innocent people in all the horrors and cruelties of war."

Shaw even reports of Jackson, in allusion to his early history, quoting the Bard: "There is a tide in the affairs of men, which, taken at the flood, leads on to fortune.' 'That's true, sir,' said he, with emphasis, 'I've proved it during my whole life.'"[1294]

[1294] Parton, *Jackson*, III. p. 655.

CHAPTER

84

RETIREMENT AT LAST?

"The decree has gone forth, it is one of urgency too, the deed is to be done, that foul deed, which like the blood-stained hands of the guilty Macbeth, all oceans' waters will never wash out. Proceed then by the noble work which lies before you, and like other skillful executioners, do it quickly, and when you have perpetrated it, go home to the people, and tell them what glorious honors you have achieved for our common country. Tell them that you have extinguished one of the brightest and purest lights that ever burnt at the altar of civil liberty, tell them that you have silenced one of the noblest batteries that ever thundered in defense of the Constitution, and bravely spiked the cannon."

-Henry Clay

A financial panic, followed by depression, struck the country only months after Jackson left office. There's much historical debate over whether it was Jackson's policies, crop failures, international forces, or some combination of all three that contributed to the hard times. Those critics who had long derided Jackson's lack of financial understanding were soon vindicated, although, like everyone else in the country, there was not much to celebrate. Although Jackson's destruction of a central bank, a steadying rampart against unbridled speculation, certainly did not help the already struggling economy, the main culprit was an international downturn in the cotton market.

There is plenty of blame to go around in the drama that was the Panic of 1837, from the White House to both the Democrats and Whigs in Congress to the bankers, and the speculators, even to British demands for specie. One lesson, learned belatedly, may be that the American economy had already become so complex, so overgrown, and so sufficiently subject to global forces, that even the most attentive of presidents would find managing it a daunting and often disappointing task. Unfortunately for Martin Van Buren, the country's first depression all but tanked his one and only term in the White House.

No matter what happened after Jackson left the White House though, his legend only grew. In January 1840, Mrs. C.M. Stevens passed along a rumor to Stockley Donelson's wife, Phyla Ann, from Cuba, "it was reported that General Jackson was expected at Havana and it created quite a sensation. There are many here who would delight to see him." In June of that year, Leonidas Polk, now the Episcopal missionary bishop in the southwest, wrote to his mother from Ashwood, his plantation in Maury County, Tennessee, "I was in Nashville the other day... where I met General Jackson. He looks very well and is very spirited yet." George P.A. Healy, an American artist living in Paris, had been sent to the United States to paint Jackson and other notable politicians--including Henry Clay, whom the painter was to meet after finishing the image of Jackson. Healy overstayed his time at the Hermitage. When he did finally arrive at Clay's estate, Ashland, Clay said "I see that you, like all who approached that man, were fascinated by him."[1295]

Throughout his presidency, Jackson yearned for a quiet retirement at The Hermitage. However, when the time came, he found it difficult to let go of politics. Jackson was eager to see his policies implemented and his legacy vindicated. Martin Van Buren, his chosen successor as President, became his closest political ally. During Van Buren's term, Jackson frequently offered him advice, encouragement, and warnings. He devoted his remaining energy to supporting Van Buren's Independent Treasury financial plan and his unsuccessful reelection campaign in 1840.

The ex-President's interest in the fortunes of his party was scarcely diminished by his retirement from public life. He corresponded

---

[1295] Parton, Jackson, III, 551; Clay Papers, IV.

frequently with President Van Buren, whose leading measures he heartily approved, and whose firmness against the pressures brought to bear against his administration he could not help but admire. When, in 1840, the economic struggles of the people and the re-nomination of William Henry Harrison threatened the Democratic party with defeat, General Jackson threw his efforts behind his friend's reelection. Early in the campaign, Jackson wrote an ill-advised letter on behalf of Van Buren, which had the effect of creating an uproar among Van Buren's critics, and among Harrison's supporters. "In respect to the statements which have been made in several of the newspapers of the day that I disagree with many of my political friends in the estimate they have formed of General Harrison's military merits, I am not aware of having said anything to justify them. Having never admired General Harrison as a military man, or considered him as possessing the qualities which constitute the commander of an army, I have looked at his political relations alone in the opinions I have formed or expressed respecting his pretensions to the presidency, and the consequences which would result to the country, should the suffrages of the people place him in that high office." [1296]

When the letter was printed in the major newspapers throughout the country, Jackson's words were not well-received. To many, it appeared to be a cheap shot against a man who had dedicated himself bravely to the defense of the country throughout his career. Van Buren, by comparison, whose military contributions to the nation were non-existent, lost favor with many at Harrison's expense. Some began to question the General's capacities.

In August 1840, Henry Clay, in compliance with a pressing invitation, visited Nashville and addressed a large assembly of political notables. Much to Jackson's dismay, Clay's reception was hearty and enthusiastic, consisting of an extended standing ovation. "such as have seldom been given to any man in this country except to Henry Clay, greeted his rising."[1297] Clay's references to Jackson were appropriately respectful, but were, some said later, calculated, and, perhaps, were designed to be exclusively offensive to him. "It was true,' said Mr. Clay, "that he had some reluctance, some misgivings, about making this visit

---

[1296] The *Washington Globe* Article, Jackson, Oct. 1840.
[1297] Parton, *Jackson*, p. 637.

at this time, which grew out of a supposition that his motives might be misconstrued.

The relations which had, for a long time, existed between himself and the illustrious captain in this neighborhood, were well understood. He feared, if he accepted the invitation to make the visit now, that it might be thought by some that his motives were less patriotic than sinister or selfish. But he assured that great assemblage, that toward that illustrious individual, their fellow-citizen and friend, he cherished, he possessed no unkind feelings. He was a great chieftain; he had fought well and bravely for his country; he hoped he would live long and enjoy much happiness, and, when he departed from this fleeting vale of tears, that he would enter into the abode of the just, made perfect." [1298]

So Jackson was still a mere chieftain to Henry Clay. And to how many others? Did it matter anymore? Was the damage already done and irreversibly so? Were Jacksonians still as giddy over their hero as they were on the White House lawn in 1829? What had Old Hickory done for the country? Had he sent the ship of state down a peaceful current? Had he brought together North and South in one united and happy country? Had he sowed the seeds of peace and accord, and done all he could to help his fellow man? Henry Clay was applauded for his speech in Jackson's hometown. It was a speech that while it did not call out the General specifically, made a mockery of Van Buren's appointments, (and in effect those of Jackson's) for the exceeding number of defaulters that resided in high office at the hands of the current administration. Jokingly satirical, Clay implied that the President perhaps was not aware of the implications an appointment of a defaulter such as Edward Livingston would have on the country. Jackson was outraged.

The following day, Aug. 18, 1840, Jackson struck back, in a letter to the editor of the *Nashville Union*,

"Sir: Being informed that the Hon. Henry Clay of Kentucky, in his public speech at Nashville yesterday, alleged that I had appointed the Hon. Edward Livingston Secretary of State when he was a defaulter and knowing him to be one, I feel that I am justified in declaring the charge to be false. It is known to all the

---

[1298] Henry Clay, Aug. 1840, Clay Papers.

country that the nominations made by the President to the Senate are referred to appropriate committees of that body, whose duty it is to inquire into the character of the nominees, and that if there is any evidence of default, or any disqualifying circumstances existing against them, a rejection of the nomination follows. Mr. Livingston was a member of the Senate from the state of Louisiana when he was nominated by me. Can Mr. Clay say he opposed the confirmation of his nomination, because he was a defaulter? If so, the journals of the Senate will answer. But his confirmation by the Senate is conclusive proof that no such objection, if made, was sustained, and I am satisfied that such a charge against him could not have been substantiated. I am also informed that Mr. Clay charged me with appointing Samuel Swartwout collector of the port of New York, knowing that he had been an associate of Aaron Burr. To this charge it is proper to say, that I knew of Mr. Swartwout's connection with Aaron Burr, precisely as I did that of Mr. Clay himself, who if the history of the times did not do him great injustice was far from avoiding an association with Burr when he was at the town of Lexington in Kentucky. Yet Mr. Clay was appointed Secretary of State, and I may say, confidently, with recommendations for character and fitness not more favorable than those produced to me by the citizens of New York in behalf of Mr. Swartwout. Mr. Clay, too, at the time of his own appointment to that high office, it will be recollected, was directly charged throughout the Union with having bargained for it... "Under such circumstances how contemptible does this demagogue appear, when he descends from his high place in the Senate and roams over the country, retailing slanders against the living and the dead." [1299]

Clay made an immediate reply to Jackson's accusations, giving a correct outline of his speech, and asserting that he had spoken of General Jackson and his measures only in proper and becoming terms. "With regard,' he concluded, "to the insinuations and gross epithets contained in General Jackson's note, alike impotent, malevolent, and derogatory from

---

[1299] Editorial, *Nashville Union*, Aug. 18, 1840.

the dignity of a man who has filled the highest office in the universe, respect for the public and for myself allow me only to say that, like other similar missiles, they have fallen harmless at my feet, exciting no other sensation than that of scorn and contempt."[1300]

It was clearly time for Jackson to step away, as his repeated efforts were doing neither him nor Martin Van Buren any good. While he was still being applauded from one region to another among Jacksonians, it was as though a seminal shift had occurred, and that Jackson had just ever so slightly begun to overstay his welcome. The Whigs' day had come, and the Jacksonians, reeling from the financial disasters of the Panic, were no longer riding high.

Toward the close of the 1840 campaign, Jackson made one last ditch effort to ensure his chosen successor's reelection. The old man embarked on a considerable tour in the western part of Tennessee, designed to aid the Van Buren cause. A Whig newspaper reported of Jackson's tour with scathing mockery "On authority to be relied upon' that the ex-President, in a bar-room filled with people, expressed the opinion "that Webster was sent over to England to negotiate a great mammoth bank in America, and that the dukes and lords and ladies of England were to be the stockholders, and that the Whigs of the United States had defrayed the expenses of their conventions and barbecues with British gold, 'which had been sent over to this country for these purposes."[1301]

William Henry Harrison's victory over Van Buren shocked Jackson, but he soon found a reason to celebrate with Harrison's unexpected death and the shift of his successor, John Tyler, back to Democratic policies on banking and tariffs. To Jackson's delight, he was once again able to influence events, this time advocating for the annexation of Texas. He supported this cause enthusiastically, and when Van Buren opposed it, Jackson helped initiate the movement to replace him with Tennessean James K. Polk for the 1844 Democratic nomination. Jackson lived long enough to see his loyal follower Polk take office and continue his work. Their difference of opinion on this issue caused the final rift in the longstanding political partnership between Jackson and Martin Van Buren. Jackson now had a new successor hand-picked in the young Polk.

[1300] Clay Papers, IV. Aug. 1840.
[1301] Parton, pg. 640.

ANDREW JACKSON: THE POLITICS OF RESENTMENT

The annexation of Texas was the final political ambition that preoccupied Andrew Jackson. Even at seventy-seven, he pursued this significant goal with a vigor and determination rarely seen in politicians of his age. As noted, for over forty years, Jackson had longed to push the Spanish further away from the western borders of the United States, and now by extension, the people of Mexico. He had strongly supported Colonel Burr's filibustering plan in 1806, which aimed to conquer Texas. However, he agreed to the Spanish treaty of 1819, which granted Florida to the U.S. but relinquished Texas. As previously noted, he maintained this stance until he became president in 1829, when an attempt to negotiate for Texas failed.

In 1830, when General Sam Houston arrived in Washington, having lost both his fortune and reputation, he lived temporarily in a boarding house with Dr. Robert Mayo, a once-prominent figure in the capital city. Houston confided in Dr. Mayo his ambitious plan to seize Texas from Mexico and establish an independent republic. Unfortunately, Mayo, who was then seeking a government position, betrayed Houston by revealing the details to the President in a lengthy letter. Using the secret codes employed by Houston's group, he informed the President that Houston was organizing an expedition against Texas, disguising himself as an Indian to gain support. Mayo suggested that conquering Texas could be easily achieved with the help of Arkansas Territory Indians and American recruits, without the need for direct confrontation.[1302] Recall that as noted previously, Jackson had issued Sam Houston the perfect cover to operate freely in Texas Indian country, the passport signed by the president himself to authorize Sam Houston as Indian agent among the tribes of Texas.

Another conspirator, known only as "Hunter," confirmed Mayo's information, stating that several thousand recruits had already enlisted along the East Coast. They were to travel to Mississippi under the guise of travelers and board steamboats to rendezvous in Arkansas or Texas.

This plan mirrored Aaron Burr's 1806 scheme. Given Jackson's relationship with Houston, it's hard to believe that he was unaware of these designs. Yet, his presidential role required him to publicly oppose them. Jackson noted on the back of Mayo's letter the need for a confidential

---

[1302] Mayo, Dr. Robert, *Eight Years in Washington*, 1839, p. 567.

981

communication to the Secretary of the Arkansas Territory, indicating his concern. A letter was drafted, marked "strictly confidential," relaying Mayo's information but claiming it was "erroneous." The message read: 'Dr. Mayo on the contemplated invasion of Texas, private and confidential — a letter to be written confidential, to the secretary of the Territory of Arkansas, with a copy of confidential letter to Wm. Fulton, Esq., secretary to the Territory of Florida.' This endorsement seems to indicate either confusion or anxiety in the mind of its issuer, for the "Wm. Fulton, Esq.," mentioned in it was not the " secretary of the Territory of Florida," but the secretary of the Territory of Arkansas.

However, Fulton was instructed to watch for any suspicious movements in the southwestern region, ensuring the utmost secrecy. Eventually, Houston began executing his plan without significant interference from the U.S. government, and Jackson seemed to follow his progress with interest. By the end of Jackson's presidency, Houston had taken control of Texas, and Santa Anna was captured. Santa Anna was released under the condition that he would advocate for Texas's independence, but he faced resistance upon his return. In spring 1837, he met with Jackson multiple times, with the details undisclosed, and returned home aboard a national vessel. Was Jackson the mastermind of the Houston scheme?

Before leaving office, Jackson spent hours burning unnecessary documents and returning letters. Dr. Mayo received back his letter from 1830, along with a copy of Jackson's letter to Mr. Fulton. The latter's inclusion likely was an accident, but Mayo showed it to opposition members, including John Quincy Adams, who read it to the House of Representatives. Jackson claimed Mayo had stolen the Fulton letter, while Mayo insisted he received it alongside his own correspondence. Regardless, Jackson was justified in calling it "purloined."

With these happenings behind the scenes, the Texas events stirred the aging Jackson and prompted him to take action. General Harrison had passed away, and Vice President Tyler had taken over. The 1844 presidential election loomed. Henry Clay, beloved yet disappointed time and again from reaching the top office, was the Whig candidate. Mr. Van Buren, who had been defeated in 1840 for his steadfast party loyalty, was expected to be the Democratic nominee. However, a faction led by Mr. Calhoun aimed to replace him, devising a new "issue"—the immediate annexation of Texas. As Mexico had not recognized Texas's independence, such a move would amount to a declaration of war.

In early 1843, Thomas Walker Gilmer of Virginia, a Calhoun ally, published a detailed argument for immediate annexation, claiming British interest in Texas posed a threat.[1303] This letter was forwarded to Jackson by Congressman Aaron V. Brown for his opinion. The aim was to secure a strong endorsement from Jackson for immediate annexation, to keep it secret until Van Buren's contradictory opinion was published and then reveal Jackson's support at the Democratic convention to undermine Van Buren's candidacy. Jackson, unaware of the plot, responded promptly and thoroughly to Brown.

As previously mentioned, Jackson had only tabled the Texas annexation issue upon leaving office in 1837. Six years later, as one of his post-presidential letters indicates, this one addressed to Congressmen Brown in 1843, Jackson's advice was still actively sought, and he was more than willing to offer it, especially when it came to the one carrot that got away, the annexation of Texas. In his correspondence with Brown, it is clear the old General remained on the front lines of the Texas annexation issue: "Great Britain has already made treaties with Texas, and we know that far-seeing nation never omits a circumstance, in her extensive intercourse with the world, which can be turned to account in increasing her military resources. May she not enter into an alliance with Texas? .... and reserving, as she doubtless will, the north-western boundary question as the cause of war with us whenever she chooses to declare it, let us suppose that, as an ally with Texas, we are to fight her! Preparatory to such a movement, she sends her 20,000 or 30,000 men to Texas; organizes them on the Sabine, where her supplies and arms can be concentrated before we have even notice of her intentions; makes a lodgment on the Mississippi; excites the negroes to insurrection; the lower country falls, and with it New Orleans; and a servile war rages through the whole South and West. In the meanwhile, she is also moving an army along the western frontier from Canada, which, in cooperation with the army from Texas, spreads ruin and havoc from the Lakes to the Gulf of Mexico. Who can estimate the national loss we

---

[1303] Thomas Walker Gilmer, *Baltimore Republican and Argus*, Jan., 1843.

may sustain, before such a movement could be repelled with such forces as we could organize on short notice?"[1304]

The points of view Jackson laid out in this correspondence are shown in stark contrast with those the General held in 1820. In a previously noted communication to Mr. Monroe from that year, he stated: "With the Floridas secured, and our fortifications established, New Orleans, the principal hub of the West, remains secure. ... An invading enemy from Texas would never attempt such an endeavor; should they try, I assure you they would pay dearly for their audacity." Unless he was simply talking out of both sides of his mouth, clearly General Jackson firmly believed in 1820 that "for the time being, we should be satisfied with the Floridas," as his endorsement of the treaty indicated. But things had changed by 1844, the nation had grown and would only continue to stretch its legs west.[1305]

For eleven months, the letter to Congressman Brown remained confidential, shared only among a select few prominent individuals associated with the conspiracy. During this time, Van Buren expressed his support for annexation, provided it could be achieved honorably and without provoking unnecessary conflict with Mexico. However, he justifiably opposed immediate annexation that disregarded Mexico's rights. In March 1844, conspirators, after fraudulently altering the date of General Jackson's letter from 1843 to 1844, publicized it in the *Richmond Inquirer*. This alarmed Van Buren's supporters, and Jackson was made aware of the deception. Reports indicated that a young Benjamin F. Butler, later to gain Civil War fame as a Union general, visited the Hermitage to inform Jackson of the situation.

Unable to retract his position, Jackson issued a second letter regarding Texas, reaffirming his original stance while also praising Van Buren. In closing this letter, the former President remarked: "I cannot conclude these observations without expressing my deep regard for Mr. Van Buren, and my trust in his patriotism, which has only grown through our long and close association. Any disagreement on this matter will not alter my opinion of his character. He has evidently drafted his letter based solely on the circumstances at the end of his administration,

---

[1304] AJ to Brown, Jackson, 1843, *Correspondence*, Vol. III. p. 2; Parton, *Jackson*, 653.
[1305] AJ to Monroe, 1820, Monroe Papers, LC.

without knowledge of recent disclosures that indicate a potential foreign interference in Texas affairs."

Despite this letter, Van Buren could not escape defeat in the nominating convention—such was the strength of the opposition against him. Jackson, ultimately chose to turn his back on his strongest ally, Van Buren, instead playing a significant role in securing the nomination of James K. Polk at the 1844 Democratic National Convention, held in Baltimore. The Tennessean Polk, who had scarcely been mentioned as a contender for the presidency, ultimately received the nomination. Polk, who had become nearly family to Jackson, was an ardent proponent of immediate annexation, willing to support even the most controversial measures if they served the party's interests; he represented the New York political ethos, generating northern support that should have by rights gone to the New Yorker Van Buren. Jackson's influence was considerable within the party, and he strongly supported Polk as a compromise candidate after Van Buren's candidacy began to stall. Jackson's endorsement helped propel Polk to victory on the ninth ballot. Van Buren was at a loss, and the betrayal from his old chief had to sting.

In General Jackson's initial Texas letter, he made several allegations regarding James Monroe's administration that were destined to ignite scrutiny. He accused that administration of unnecessarily ceding Texas. John Quincy Adams was prepared to confront this accusation and did so in a manner that ignited the ire of his long-standing rival. He denounced General Jackson's claims as absurd, implausible, and unfounded, reiterating a prior statement made in the House of Representatives, asserting that General Jackson had indeed approved the treaty of 1819. Adams produced his diary as evidence, clarifying how General Jackson had endorsed the treaty despite being absent from Washington at the time of its signing. "I have not suggested," Adams remarked, "that General Jackson was consulted on the day the treaty was signed. That would have been too late for consultation. The discussions with General Jackson occurred on February 2nd and 3rd, 1819, prior to the final proposal of the Sabine as the boundary to Mr. Onis. Had General Jackson expressed opposition, I believe Mr. Monroe would have proceeded regardless. He was not genuinely focused on acquiring land west of the Sabine, then a desolate wilderness, which he believed would weaken us by extending a defenseless coastline vulnerable to foreign naval attacks."

Adams' address provoked a vehement response from General Jackson, whose reaction was controversially published in the newspapers, at Jackson's demand, despite being directed toward a private individual. Among other insinuations, Jackson referred to Adams as having "a diseased mind." The following is an excerpt of the letter which was written to General Robert Armstrong on Oct. 22nd, 1844: "I trust I shall never deserve the shame of mistaking the path of duty where my country's rights are involved. I believed, from the disclosures made to me of the transactions of 1819, that Mr. Adams surrendered the interests of the United States when he took the Sabine River as the boundary between us and Spain, when he might have gone to the Colorado, if not to the Rio del Norte. Such was the natural inference from the facts stated by Mr. Erving; and there is nothing in the account now given of the negotiation to alter this impression. The address, on the contrary, does not at all relieve Mr. Adams. It proves that he was then, as now, an alien to the true interests of his country; but he had not then, as now, the pretext of cooperation with Great Britain in her peaceful endeavors to extinguish slavery throughout the world."[1306]

In a pivotal moment of early regional bashes over westward expansion, the very heart of which would ignite the American Civil War under twenty years later, here was Jackson, now deified in his declining years, sending a letter to the sycophant Francis Blair of the *Globe*, urging him to publish it along with commentary that would reveal former president John Quincy Adams "in his true colors to the American people." Reflecting on Adams' reading of the Fulton letter to the House of Representatives, General Jackson challenged Mr. Blair: "Has there ever been such dishonorable conduct from anyone claiming respectability? This act of betrayal comes from one who once held the presidency. Although he attained that position through intrigue, deals, and corruption, one would expect some regard for public honor, even if he himself lacks it."[1307]

Adams, too, responded with indignation, stating, "I presented to the youth in Boston my diary, which contains entries from that consultation. I reaffirm before God and my country that the published extracts are

---

[1306] Parton, *Jackson*, Armstrong's General Orders to Jackson to disband, 373; to Jackson, upon British in Florida, p. 593.
[1307] AJ to Blair, Nov.,1844, Jackson Papers, LC.

true copies of those entries, and the facts therein are accurate. Andrew Jackson has reacted to my summons, yet he does not confront the country regarding our mutual charges. He blusters but ultimately retreats; he hurls insults but avoids accountability."[1308] In contrast to the reconciled correspondences between two earlier combative presidents, Jefferson, and the senior Adams, Jackson and Quincy Adams' discord had only grown more hostile and reactionary over the years. And many dismissed the back and forth in that vein, but in hindsight, Jackson's true role in the Texas question, right or wrong, cannot be overstated.

In the wake of these tensions, Jackson actively worked to secure the election of James K. Polk (and Pennsylvanian George M. Dallas as his running mate.) The fiery General, perhaps sensing that his long road was nearing its end as his health continued to collapse, revived his accusations of bargain and corruption against Polk's opponent Henry Clay, maintaining his beliefs on the Kentuckian entirely unchanged and as hostile as ever. His numerous endorsements of Democratic nominations were widely circulated. It is not an exaggeration to assert that Jackson's opposition played a significant role in Henry Clay's surprising defeat in 1844. Despite having left office more than 7 years earlier, the stubborn, fiery General still thrust out his last few power strokes all the way until the very end. Even as his body failed him externally, Old Hickory's spirit was still as alive and combative as ever.

The election of James K. Polk brought Jackson great joy, who celebrated the event with a grand dinner for two hundred guests at the Hermitage. However, his concerns regarding annexation only intensified after the election. On the first day of the final year of his life, he penned another lengthy letter to his friend Francis Blair, urging him to leverage his influence to prompt Congress to act swiftly on the issue. Yet, unbeknownst to Jackson, one of the secret agreements that secured Polk's support from the Calhoun-led nullifiers was that the *Globe* would not serve as the administration's voice. This revelation left Jackson bewildered and outraged as he observed the sidelining of his old friend and ally. In a letter dated April 9, 1845, he expressed, "It is repugnant to see an old friend cast aside, with principles of justice and friendship forgotten for the sake of political maneuvering. The great Democratic

---

[1308] JQA, *Adams Memoirs*, IV, 1844.

Party is threatened by such policy. Upon reflection, every aspect of this turns to harm and division, yielding no beneficial outcomes. I await the results anxiously. If harmony is restored and the Globe is reinstated, I will rejoice; if sold, I wish to know to whom and for what purpose. Ensure the purchase money is secured. This may be my last letter to you; yet, live or die, I remain your loyal friend, never one to abandon a comrade for policy, and I entrust my papers and reputation to your care."[1309]

Jackson never learned the reasons behind Mr. Polk's unexpected actions. Thankfully for himself, Mr. Blair retreated from public life, while the editor of the *Union* took his place, leading to the fragmentation of the Democratic Party.

In the spring of his final year, Jackson engaged in a notable correspondence with Commodore Jessie Elliot regarding a sarcophagus believed to hold the remains of the Roman Emperor Alexander Severus. On March 18, 1845, the blunt old sailor and fellow veteran of the War of 1812 wrote, "Last night, I made a speech at the National Institute in Washington, D.C., offering the sarcophagus I obtained in Palestine, suggesting it be reserved for your final resting place. I implore you, General, to live with reverence; a soldier's death awaits you, and an emperor's coffin is prepared."[1310]

The General's response sheds light on Jackson's philosophy regarding republicanism, even if his actions often belied these sentiments. Writing in his waning days, the General expressed his desire to be buried humbly alongside Rachel. "With the deepest gratitude, I must decline this honor. I cannot allow my body to rest in a place designated for an emperor or king. My republican values and principles prohibit it; the simplicity of our governmental system forbids it. Every monument for our heroes and statesmen should reflect the economy and simplicity of our republican institutions, honoring the plainness of our citizens, who are the true sovereigns of our Union. I have arranged for a humble resting place beside my beloved wife, where I wish to be laid without ceremony when my time comes, awaiting the last trumpet that will summon the dead to judgment, hoping we will rise together, clothed in the heavenly

---

[1309] AJ to Polk, 1845, Jackson Papers, LC.
[1310] Elliott to AJ, March 18, 1845, Jackson, *Correspondence*, IV. 566.

body promised to those who believe in our Redeemer, who died for us so we might live, and through whose atonement I seek a blessed immortality."[1311]

Jackson's retirement was filled with honors and tributes. He became a living symbol of democracy, attracting a steady stream of admirers to The Hermitage. While he accepted public accolades with modest humility, he never seemed to tire of them. In 1840, he traveled to New Orleans to celebrate the twenty-fifth anniversary of his significant achievements. Aware of his importance and protective of his reputation, Jackson spent considerable time organizing his papers and preparing for Amos Kendall's planned biography.

In the spring of 1845, a niece wrote to Stockley Donelson of "our poor old gray-headed Uncle Jackson." As time passed, the burdens of age and illness weighed heavily on Jackson. His health had been fragile for many years, yet he had repeatedly recovered from serious ailments, leading friends to jokingly question his mortality. Jackson, however, was aware of his condition, although he couldn't name what it actually was. Doctors eventually diagnosed the old General with severe edema, or "dropsy" in the parlance of the day, a type of congestive heart failure. Jackson had, as noted, long anticipated his death.

Sarah Jackson, the wife of Andrew Jr., took care of the old man in his dying days. "He is swollen all over, sometimes his face is out of all shape and his sufferings are very great," she wrote to Emma Donelson, her cousin on Wednesday April 30, 1845. Jackson was forced to take an amanuensis in his final months, "My health is very low....not being able today to sit up much." On Sunday, May 25, 1845, Jackson was too ill to attend the church service on the Hermitage, so he requested the minister come to him to take first holy communion. Jackson had finally full embraced his faith in his waning days. The old wariior "When I have suffered sufficiently, the Lord will then take me to himself. But what are all my sufferings compared to those of the Blessed Savior, who died upon that cross of tree for me. Mine are nothing, not a murmur was ever heard from him. All was borne with amazing fortitude."

The last words of Andrew Jackson, seventh president, who died on June 8, 1845, at age 78, were uttered at the Hermitage in Nashville,

---

[1311] AJ to Ellott, April, 1845, Jackson, Correspondence, IV, 567.

Tennessee. As historian Cyrus Townsend Brady eulogizes, "When I think of the end of that life, the storm-tossed old warrior entering the haven where he would find that rest that had been denied him all his life, I am minded to voice an ancient prayer which runs, "Let me die the death of the righteous, and let my last end be like his." As to Jackson's last words, there have been many variations from historians as to what the General uttered upon his last breaths on this Earth. Brady believes the broken sentences of the dying man, "Don't cry. Be good. We shall meet....."[1312] Others have professed that Jackson provided a message of equality to those in the room, both slave and free, who witnessed his passing: "I hope to meet you all in heaven, both black and white. Be good children, all of you, and strive to be ready when the change comes." Whatever Old Hickory's last message was, he died the way he lived, on his own terms. He was surrounded by family and friends and was buried in his garden next to Rachel.

[1312] Brady, Cyrus Townsend, *The True Andrew Jackson*, p. 388.

CHAPTER

85

A MIXED MOURNING

"The shock is great, and grief universal."
-Francis P. Blair

When the news of the death of General Jackson reached Washington, the President of the United States, James K. Polk, ordered the departments to be closed for one day, and public honors were to be paid to the memory of the ex-President, at all the military and naval stations. In every large town in the country there were public ceremonies in Jackson's honor, consisting usually of an oration and a procession. In the city of New York, the entire body of the uniformed militia, all the civic functionaries, the trades and societies, joined in the parade. Martin Van Buren was invited to deliver the eulogy, but he declined. No one had had better opportunities than himself, he asserted, to observe the late General's character, and no one, among the millions who mourned his death, would cherish his memory longer or more reverently. He announced his intention "to prepare, at a proper time, a suitable memoir of his conduct and principles."[1313]

For the army of Jacksonians who had long worshipped Jackson as a deity, the gushing praise for the deceased now poured out from every corner of the country. Not least of these was the sycophant, the Chief Justice. Taney poured forth a canonizing commemoration of the man he had partnered with in the destruction of the Bank of the United

---

[1313] Martin Van Buren Papers, Manuscript Division, Library of Congress, Washington, D.C. 1845.

States. "The whole civilized world already know how bountifully he was endowed by Providence with those high gifts which qualified him to lead, both as a soldier and a statesman. But those only who were around him in times of anxious deliberation, when great and mighty interests were at stake, and who were with him also in the retired scenes of domestic life, in the midst of his family and friends, can fully appreciate his innate love of justice, his hatred of oppression in every shape it would assume, his magnanimity, his entire freedom from any feeling of personal hostility to his political opponents and his constant and unvarying kindness and gentleness to his friends." [1314]

Early on Tuesday morning, June 10, the day of his funeral, throngs of people who had procured every available vehicle in Nashville and surrounding towns gathered at the Hermitage, Andrew Jackson's home. Friend and foe alike gathered to take one last look at "Old Hickory." Some came out of respect and admiration, while others came to be sure he was mortal and was truly gone forever. Businesses throughout Nashville closed and "the city had all the appearance of a Sabbath." From 11:00 a.m., the time his funeral began, until 1:00 p.m., people fired "minute guns," guns fired at the top of each minute, and the bells of all the churches in the city tolled. Reverend Dr. Edgar presided over the funeral at the Hermitage and preached a sermon which, by all accounts, was most impressive and eloquent. Following the funeral, Andrew Jackson's body was interred in the vault next to his beloved wife, Rachel.

The former president's visitation, funeral, and burial was completed according to his wishes, quietly and peacefully...well, sort of. While the crowd was gathering at the visitation before the funeral, one who had been a constant companion of "Old Hickory" for nearly 20 years, an African parrot named Poll, "got excited and commenced swearing so loud and long" that he upset the others in attendance and had to be physically removed from the house.[1315]

Amidst the innumerable and lengthy orations of overeffusive eulogies for the departed ex-president, there were some comments of the press upon the character of the deceased that were not all of a flattering nature. Many of the Whig editors could not refrain from again deploring the

---

[1314] Roger B. Taney's Eulogy for Andrew Jackson, June 1845, LOC.
[1315] *Tri-Weekly Nashville Union*, June 10, 1845, p.2.

"fatal popularity" of a "military chieftain," who had brought unexampled woes upon a too-confiding people. A remarkable scene played out in opposition to the memory of the man who many felt had done everything in his power to dilute American democracy. In concluding this discourse on the Politics of Resentment it deserves its place in summation of the damage that resentful leadership can wreak. The scene occurred at the June meeting of the New York Historical Society. On this occasion, the well-attended meeting was packed with substantial intellectuals, and honorable individuals in the audience, with Daniel Webster among them, along with many other politicians and dignitaries present. Prosper M. Wetmore began, offering a series of resolutions, eulogizing General Jackson, and "lamenting, in common with our fellow-citizens throughout the Union," his death. Benjamin F. Butler seconded the resolutions, and Webster supported them with a few half-hearted words of his own.

The President of the Society, Governor Bradish, was about to put the resolutions forward, when, to the shock of the assembly, Mr. Fessenden rose and delivered a diatribe of his own on the subject of the late president. James Parton recorded the account of the proceedings in his Jackson biography as follows:

"I don't see, Mr. President, why such a society as this should be called on to put forth resolutions commendatory of the life and character of General Jackson. (Murmurs of disapprobation. A voice, 'Who's that?' Hon. Mr. Bokee—'Pooh! it's only a Yankee lawyer!'—a laugh.) It is true, he was a President of the United States, and a Major-General in the army, but what has that to do with this society—with historical literature? I don't agree at all with many of the opinions put forth in the address of the gentleman who seconded the resolutions. I can not sanction the resolutions themselves. (Applause and hisses.) I say I can not approve of those resolutions, and I will oppose them, though I stand alone. For thirty years I have sincerely and fervently opposed General Jackson, and I can not consent now, because he is dead, to approve of his conduct. General Jackson certainly never contributed anything to the Historical Society, nor to any other that I know of. He was not a literary man. Why, then, should a literary society be called on to pass such resolutions? Again, did he exhibit the pure motives and self-sacrificing devotion of the first Presidents? No, I don't believe he did. Why, then, pay him this mark of honor? Truth should come from societies like this. (Applause and hisses.) On his accession to office, General Jackson put a political enemy in jail, because he had been a defaulter under the previous administration; and he said he would keep him there till the money was paid, or he humbled himself before him. This led me to expect that he would carry out this stern administration of justice. But did he do it? No. There was more defaulting under Jackson than there was under all the Presidents; but because the defaulters had voted for him, he let them escape. Again, he gave the lie to John Quincy Adams about his approbation of the Florida treaty; and even when his own letter was produced in evidence, he still swore it was all a lie. Well may they call him 'the man of the iron will,' for he was determined to make it the sole arbiter of truth and falsehood. (Laughter, applause, hisses, and confusion.) But he has gone to a land where neither his will nor the behests of his party will determine what is right and wrong." (Applause, hisses, and confusion, in the midst of which the Hon. Mr. Bokee and the great Dody of the members of the Court of Errors, who had been invited to be present, rose and left the room.)

"I hope he has repented of his sins, and gone to a better state of existence. (Loud hisses.) We ought to recollect that we are not the first in this business; the Empire Club has gone before us. I don't want to make myself notorious— (shouts of laughter)— but when, as a member of this society, I was called on as a literary society— (a laugh)— to approve of the conduct and character of General Jackson, I have only to say that I approve of neither."[1316]

Mr. Charles King, of the New York American, vehemently supported the sentiments advanced by Mr. Fessenden. After a desultory debate, the resolutions were put and carried, only three gentlemen voting against them— Mr. Fessenden, Mr. King, and another. Obviously, the majority either approved of Jackson, or to the office he held, or simply to the principle of doing no dishonor to the dead. Or there was also very likely the fear that comes with standing against the majority. And in a divided national atmosphere that some politicians cultivate, the pressure of standing against the majority can be an intimidating prospect, and not many have the spine to take that one. Fessenden himself faced alienation as a result of his words, but like many determined to ensure

---

[1316] Report in *New York Herald,* June 20, 1845.

that America continued to be a country in which the freedom of opinion and expression did not come with asterisks, he stood up anyway.

Ultimately, as history has proven, people will hold a wide spectrum of varying opinions regarding Andrew Jackson. In the end, the legacy of President Andrew Jackson is mixed at best, and very possibly, his actions as a leader of this country may well have done more harm than good. But, regardless of one's opinion on the man, no one can deny the power of his popularity, and the impact he had on American history, and on the American system of governance. That impact is still felt today.

EPILOGUE

On June 23, 2020, protesters attempted to pull down a statue of Andrew Jackson, the seventh U.S. president, near the White House, marking it with "killer scum" before police intervened. Jackson, a slaveholder who signed the Indian Removal Act, is associated with racism, notably the Trail of Tears. President Trump, a supporter of Jackson, condemned the act as "disgraceful vandalism."

Historian James Parton highlights that Jackson's Scotch-Irish heritage shaped his tenacity and confrontational nature. Orphaned and self-reliant, Jackson transitioned from teaching to law and gained notoriety in the Cumberland Valley. His aggressive temperament led to violent incidents, yet his military successes earned him fame. However, his presidency saw the rise of a patronage system, often criticized for his lack of understanding of the process of governance.

Jackson's legacy is complex. While he defended the Union during the Nullification Crisis, his leadership style was marked by personal grievances and impulsivity. Supporters celebrate his populism and fiscal conservatism, while critics point to his overreach, support of slavery, and treatment of Native Americans. Despite mixed views, Jackson remains a symbol of American character and democracy.

Debates about his legacy continue, particularly regarding his image on currency. Plans to replace him on the twenty-dollar bill with Harriet Tubman have faced reconsideration. Jackson's memorials are fewer than those of other presidents, and he is notably absent from Mount Rushmore. Yet, at the same time, there are more places throughout the country named Jackson than any other president.

Over the course of nearly two centuries, historians have shifted perceptions of Jackson from a symbol of barbarism to a heroic figure defending the common people against elite interests. Schlesinger Jr.

framed Jacksonianism as a class struggle, while later scholars explored various interpretations of his impact on democracy and capitalism. Regardless of controversies, Jackson symbolizes the American spirit, prompting ongoing reflection on his strengths and flaws in shaping national identity.

—∞—

During Andrew Jackson's presidency, the American Democracy party emerged as the longest-lasting political party in U.S. history. Jacksonian Democracy saw electoral changes that fostered a more democratic political culture. Alexis de Tocqueville's *Democracy in America* highlighted democracy and equality as defining traits of the nation, contrasting the U.S. with Europe's aristocratic past. Jackson's supporters claimed this democratic identity, opposing the Whig Party's aristocracy.

The Democratic Party, shaped by Jackson's 1828 election, adopted a laissez-faire approach, advocating for minimal government intervention and opposing favoritism toward the wealthy. They supported the separation of church and state, attracting diverse religious groups. Under Jackson and Martin Van Buren, the Democrats innovated party organization, establishing local and national committees to engage voters, although often directed from Washington.

Jackson's Democrats presented themselves as champions of the common man, benefitting from expanded voting rights for white men. The intense competition with the Whigs led to high voter turnout and transformed campaigns into public spectacles. However, many Democratic positions were anti-egalitarian, particularly regarding abolition and social inclusion. Despite not fully embodying democratic ideals, Jackson's Democrats reflected the democratic spirit of the age. Jackson represented a shift toward equality and the common man, leaving a profound impact on American politics. Over his two terms, he established the Democratic Party as a model for future political organizations while prompting the formation of the Whig Party in opposition.

Similar to Donald Trump's second term as president, Jackson's presidency focused on blocking legislative agendas rather than advancing one, resulting in minimal significant laws passed, while igniting controversy. He connected directly with voters, positioning himself as their advocate against Congress. His assertive leadership style led to criticisms of executive overreach, earning him nicknames like "King Andrew." In 2025, the No More Kings movement spread across the United States; a series of demonstrations that took place on June 14, protesting Donald Trump's policies and actions during his second presidency. These actions included his purported fascist tendencies and associated democratic backsliding. The protests took place on the same day as the U.S. Army 250th Anniversary Parade.

While Jackson held a pragmatic political philosophy, his policies showcased a belief in minimal government intervention. He opposed nullification and secession, viewing the national union as indivisible. His personality shaped his presidency, leading to polarized opinions about him. Jackson's legacy is also marked by controversial actions, particularly the Indian Removal Act, which resulted in the Trail of Tears, an event that significantly impacted Native American communities, and continues to be a dark spot on American history to this day.

Many historical narratives have oversimplified the complexities surrounding the Indian Removal Act. Opposition existed, particularly from Northerners, including Jeremiah Evarts and Catharine Beecher, who argued against the act on moral grounds. The Senate passed the bill with a strong majority, but the House vote was much closer, indicating a divided sentiment. If the legislation had failed in 1830, alternative approaches to Indigenous relations might have emerged, yet advocates for removal, particularly in Georgia, would likely have persisted.

The Cherokee Nation's struggles, including court cases like Cherokee Nation v. Georgia (1831) and Worcester v. Georgia (1832), highlight their resistance to removal. Ultimately, the U.S. Army forcibly relocated 19,000 Cherokees in 1838, leading to significant suffering. Other southeastern nations also faced removal, underscoring the widespread impact of these policies.

The Indian Removal Act had catastrophic effects, displacing around 88,000 Indigenous people with a death toll estimated between 12,000 and 17,000. Some historians label this as ethnic cleansing or even genocide due to its devastating consequences and underlying intent. While policymakers claimed removal benefited Indigenous peoples, the destruction faced by communities suggests a more sinister motive.

While Andrew Jackson prioritized its enactment starting in 1829, he framed it as a culmination of a policy influenced by Thomas Jefferson's earlier advocacy for relocating Indigenous peoples to the Louisiana territory. Jackson was not in office during the Cherokee Trail of Tears; it was Martin Van Buren who oversaw the event in 1838-39. Focusing solely on Jackson risks implying the policy originated with him, while it was a broader national issue with significant support. Yet, Jackson, who professed to be a true believer in the United States Constitution, and its system of checks and balances, essentially nullified the act of the Supreme Court following the Worcester v. Georgia case, ensuring the removal of the Cherokee, and setting a precedent of disunion within the federal government.

Despite the tragedies, many Native peoples demonstrated resilience, rebuilding their communities. The Eastern Band of Cherokee Indians, descended from a group that avoided forced relocation, now thrives in North Carolina. They own the Qualla Boundary, a 57,000-acre area not classified as a traditional reservation. With a vibrant community of around 14,000 members, they maintain cultural and political autonomy, focusing on education, governance, and economic development. Their story encapsulates both the struggles and resilience of Indigenous nations in American history.

Jackson's promises of the Indian Territory remaining free from white encroachment were misguided. The exclusive ownership by Indigenous peoples lasted less than fifty years. However, the resilience of the Cherokee people, who faced the Trail of Tears and had to rebuild in a new land, is remarkable. The Cherokee Nation in Oklahoma not only survived the hardships of the 1830s and the Oklahoma land rush of the late 1880s but thrived. They have achieved significant economic and political development, becoming a powerful force in Oklahoma. The Nation focuses on providing services like health care, education, and infrastructure while pursuing economic ventures, countering the 1830s belief that Indigenous Peoples could not coexist with whites.

Jackson's presidency, marked by patronage and controversial policies like Indian removal, reflected tensions between educated elites and the working class. Historians debate whether Jackson transformed the presidency or merely maintained its existing power dynamics. Supporters praise his populist approach and fiscal conservatism, while critics highlight his high-handed overreach, and dictatorial disregard for the Constitution. Jackson's direct communication with voters and expansion of presidential power set new precedents.

Despite the controversies surrounding his presidency, Jackson remains a symbol of American democracy, as seen in the ongoing debates about his legacy and representation on currency. The 21st-century discussions reflect the enduring complexities of his impact on American history, particularly regarding race relations and governance. The dangers of the Age of Jackson, in which a popular figure is promoted by his supporters to the highest office in exchange for patronage jobs, brought the country to a place where political debate meant political warfare. Those placed in positions in which they were not qualified caused a diluting of the American government. Strong institutions and practices that had been put in place were dismantled. In foreign policy, a policy of jingoism and paternalism became prevalent.

A repeat of such deleterious patterns in the United States of the 21st century is a harrowing thought. History's cyclical nature reveals itself in stark relief as we witness the haunting parallels between Jackson's era and our contemporary political landscape. Like shadows cast by time itself, the dangers of populist fervor, institutional erosion, and the elevation of loyalty over competence threaten to replay their somber performance on our modern stage. Yet, in recognizing these patterns, we hold the power to chart a different course, to strengthen rather than weaken our democratic foundations, and to ensure that the lessons of the past serve not as prophecy, but as protection against the repetition of history's darkest chapters. The question remains: Will we heed the whispers of our past, or are we destined to dance once more to the dangerous rhythm of history's recurring refrain?

INDEX

Adair, John: Revolution 29, 33, Adairville, 237, 240, 243, Sharpshooters, 410-413, Rodriguez Canal, 425, Commanding Kentucky Troops, 435, New Orleans campaign, 458

Adams, John Quincy, Jackson opposes his nomination to Sweden, 182, negotiations at Ghent, 339, Quoted 463, Quoted, 463, Defending Jackson in Florida, 516-517, Mentioned, 554, During Seminole War, 547, Accused as pimp, 610, Reelection bid starts, 611, Slander of Rachel, 613, Denounced as secret monarchist, 615, Personal attacks, 618, Reelection bid, 620-621, Defeat, 622-623, Giving up Texas, 623, Slanders, 630, Updates to White House, 635, mentioned, 636, On Van Buren, 639, Photo, 640, On tariff bill as president, 656-658, mentioned, 684, Visiting Governeurs, 689, Visiting Monroe and commenting on cabinet purge, 690, Mentioned, 693, Reaction to Jackson's Nullification Ordinance, 695, Indian Springs Accords, 702, Indian Removal policies as president, 706, Commenting on Indian Removal, 722

As Sec. of State during Seminole Controversy, 516, Mudslinging Rachel, 598, Indian Policy, 607, Reacting to Jackson reelection, 745, Issues with British, 764, Adams-Onis Treaty, 770, 776, Corrupt bargain charge 798, Questions Jackson's policies to Congress, 802, candidate, 824, approbation of Florida Treaty, 830.

Adams, John, Federalist candidate 146, won presidency, 149, Blount Conspiracy, 176, Hatred for the west, 177, Quasi War, 180, Tensions with France, 183-184, revised Indian treaty, 185, Sedition of Lyon, 216, quoted, 533, Imprisoning Cooper, 658, Adams's federalism, 683, Mentioned, 690, 701, Correspondence with Jefferson, 704, mentioned, 724, relationship with Jefferson, 824.

Adams-Onis Treaty: made, 525-526; ratified, 535.

Avery, Waightstill: Turns away AJ, 54; court case, 82; challenged to duel, 83; duel, 84, 85.

Blair, Francis P.: 636; photo, 640; role in Calhoun fiasco, 669; Globe, 672, 689, 761 propaganda for AJ, 745; ; sycophant, 824; Writes critically of Adams, 824; Globe dropped by Polk, retreats from public life, 825; Quoted, 828.

Biddle, Nicholas: AJ suspicious of, 683; elected as Bank president, 732; AJ sees him as deep state problem, 733; response to veto message, 738; portrait, 739; Quoted, 746; missing Biddle's role in economy, 749; starts Biddle Panic, 756; AJ believes manipulating elections, 798. **Blount, William:** Appointed territorial governor, 112; transformed by Revolution, 113; frustrated with federal inaction, 134; leads TN statehood, 141; become Republican, 146; Land Grab, 155-156; Stewart's agent, 159; at odds with Sevier faction, 180; AJ mentor, 174; scandal, 176; financial difficulties, 182; helps AJ become judge, 191; AJ writes him, 192; death, 209.

Blount, Willie: takes over for brother William, 209; helps AJ save face, 209; visits Hermitage, 219; commissions AJ, 274; correspondence with AJ for soldiers, 275; recognizes Creek threat, 281; criticizes critics of Seminole campaign, 521; comments on Hermitage, 551.

Burr, Aaron: mentioned in Hamilton duel, 243; Quoted, 245; background, 246-247; leaves for West, 247; final day as VP, 248; sends Jackson money, 250; conspiracy, 251; trial, 252-253, returns to Nashville, 254; supports AJ presidency, 555.

Burr, Jeff: 238

Calhoun, John C.: Warhawk, 270; becomes Sec. of War, 496-497; praises AJ's treaty, 504; as Sec. of War, 516-517; presidential ambitions, 518, 554; wants censure of AJ, 522; army reduction, 537; splitting off of Democratic Party, 566; dines with Clay and AJ, 577; loses Pennsylvania, 578; aligns with AJ and VB, 582, 604; runs for VP, 583; wins VP, 585; sworn in by AJ, 594; supports AJ, 1828, 599; criticizes Adams-Clay coalition, 603; As Adams VP, 612; AJ ticket, 619, 621; insider, 637; troubles with AJ, 638, 639, states rights, 643; fall from grace, 646, presides over Webster-Hayne debates, 656-662; Fort Hill Address, 663, nullification theory, 664-666, Jefferson Birthday dinner, 665; SC Expo., 665; toast and political cartoon, 666; wants reconciliation, 667; releases Florida letters, 668; fall from grace, 667-674; opposes VB minister nomination, 684; resigns as VP, 691; visits Raleigh, 691; nullification crisis, 691-700; mentioned, 702, 704; quoted on Removal of Cherokee, 705; AJ adversary, 746; triumvirate with Clay, Webster, 750; AJ detractor, 755; insults VB, 798; anti-expungement argument, 805; mentioned, 806; Exposition and Protest, 810; faction to replace VB, 821; gets Polk's support, 825.

Calhoun, Floride: troubles with Peggy Eaton, 635, 643

Cherokee: Uprising, 17. During Revolution, 38; sold land to Transylvania Land Co., 71; fights with Franklinites, 75; against Nolichucky Jack, 80; trade network, 106; Mero raids, 109; Blount Superintendent of, 113-116; Knox ignores issue with, 133; band of Chickamauga, Treaty of Holston, 134; Battle of the Narrows, 137, Nickajack Expedition, 138; Friendly relations, 140; Hostilities with Blount, Robertson, 142; Tenase, Cherokee Chief, 144; vs. Sevier, 168; rising tensions, 1811, 269; helped by Tecumseh, 278, Creek War, helping Jackson, 300; Friendly Cherokee at Fort Leslie, 302; Mentioned in 1813 Jackson letter to Blount, 310; On map, 314; Fighting at Horseshoe Bend, 317-319; Casualties at Horseshoe Bend, 321; Treaty of Fort Jackson, 493-499; Jackson strips Chickasaw lands, 501; Jackson separates Nation from whites, 505; Crawford Deal, Jackson criticizes, 563; Cypress Land Co. deal, 565; Tsali, 707; Removal, 700-707.

Clay, Henry: As Burr's attorney, 252, Warhawk, 270, 276; oratory skills, 279; at Ghent, 339; laments war, 341; writes of Washington burning, 344; criticizes Jackson in Florida, 520-521; Speaker, 528; Missouri question, 530; presidential ambitions, 554; Overton supports candidacy, 556; Harry of the West, 566, election of 1824, 566; criticizes AJ, 575; failed meanest scoundrel, 575; drops out of race, 586; corrupt bargain charges begin, 587, 598; explains Adams decision, 590; Sec. of State offer, 591; called demagogue by AJ, 592; black leg, 593, Adams party, 599; photo, 600; gets Hammond to slander AJ, 615; laments AJ victory, 623; bothered by AJ spoils system, 633; mentioned, 646; American System, 652; Maysville Road bill, 654; AJ enemy #1, 684; criticizes Eaton, 689; 1832 candidacy, 692; compromise tariff, 693-694; criticizes AJ's Nullification address, 699; Bank recharter, 735-736; instincts, 738; mentioned 739; election campaign, 743; forms Whig Party, 750; AJ wants to shoot Clay, 752; mentioned 756; Quoted, 757; AJ wants to block Clay presidency, 757; hopes to throw 1836 election into House, 799; opposes expungement, 804; AJ professes regret on relationship with, 812; Quoted, 815; talks about AJ with Healy, 815.

Crawford, James: 13, 15, 16, as Lieutenant, 32, 36; imprisonment, 44; 47, 49

Crawford, Jane: 16

Crawford, Robert: 16, 21, 24; Major, 26, 61; field commander, 34, Lord Rawdon confiscates house, 36, 38; financial difficulty, 55

Crawford, William: (cousin) 44, 55, 58

Crawford, William H.: 495, 518, 521, withdraws from election, 566, 582.

Crawfords: family, 10-11, 13, 14, 16, 28, 39.

Creek War: 294; Red Sticks, 297; Fort Mims Massacre, 297; Weatherford Quotes, 300; Lyncoya, 302; forges AJ mettle, 307; Horseshoe Bend, 318; ends, 322.

Davie, William R.: Revolution, Lieutenant, 24, 32; Colonel, 31; at Hanging Rock, 32-33; Camden, 34-35; surprised British at Walkup farm, 39-40; mentioned 51, 52, 54, 61; set example militarily, 171.

Daviess, Joseph Hamilton: D.A, 252, 253.

Duke of Wellington: 339; refuses post, 340; mentioned 343; 403; Waterloo, 491.

Eaton, John: Describes Battle of N.O., 381; Quoted, 454; member of AJ military staff at Hermitage, 490; As Senator, promotes AJ candidacy, 553; helps AJ defeat Williams, 568; tries to reconcile AJ and Clay; 577; defends AJ from Hammond's bigamy charge, 615; Clay derides, 634; appointed Sec. of War, 635; photo, 635; gossip against, 639; marriage, 641; Eaton Affair, 644; resigns as Sec. of War, 681; AJ visits home, 682; driven to outrage, 685; publishes defense of Peggy, 685; Fight with Ingham, 685-688; "Eaton malaria," leaves Washington, 689; Mentioned, 813.

1005

Eaton, Margaret (Peggy): 635; ostracized, 636; VB kind to, 639; influence within cabinet, 641; background and photo, 642; has AJ in her hands, 644; tensions with Emily, 645; enmity with Floride shifts cabinet, 646; called "Whore of Washington," 662; her scandal hits newspaper, 685.

Erwin, Andrew: Allison land conflict, 217-218; slave smuggling scheme, 521, Erwin faction, 556, criticizes AJ slave dealings, 618.

Everett, Edward: correspondence with wife: 671, 673; speaks on removal, 714; brings tears to Ridges, 718.

French Spoliation: 765-767

Green, Duff: Supports AJ as candidate, 621; editor of Telegraph, 662; Supports cabinet, 667, 669; sides with Calhoun, ousted, 673; mocks Eaton, supports Ingham, 687; reports on Eatons, 689.

Gadsden, James: part of AJ staff at Hermitage, 490; offers AJ northern tour, 550; plants seeds of AJ presidential candidacy, 557; persuades AJ, 558-559.

Felix Grundy: defense of Anderson, 261, Warhawk, 270, praises AJ in Congress, 329; welcomes AJ home, 489; helps nominate AJ, 556; corresponds with AJ, 613; fails to reconcile AJ and Calhoun, 667-668.

Houston, Sam: Fights at Tehopeka, 320; part of Jackson military staff at Hermitage, 490; supports AJ presidency, 557; assists in slander campaign, 612; Quoted, 768; visits AJ in White House, 768; AJ seeks assistance from Sam in Texas, 777; AJ works more closely with in regard to Texas, 778; gets pass to travel to Texas from AJ, 778; en route to Texas, 779; role in Texas Revolution, 779-785; photo, 783; mentioned 819; Indian agent, 820.

Ingham, Samuel: Appointed Treasury Secretary, 637; mentioned, 678; resigns, 679; replaced as Treasury Sec,; 680 "sacrificed," 681; resignation articles in paper, 685, Eaton conflict, 684-688; ridiculed by AJ, 689; Woolf letter, 701; denounces AJ, 702.

Jackson, Andrew: AJ: Photo, 4; in schoolhouse, 5; "laugh and I'll kill you, 4-5; legacy, 6; birth, 15; says where he was born, 16; describing childhood, 18, 30; Revolutionary period, 18; 22; Hanging Rock, 30-32, respect for Davie, 32; conversation with Susan Smart, 36; returns to Waxhaws, 38; assists Davie, 40; Meeting House chase, 41-42; "clean my boots," 43; POW, 43-44; loses mother, orphaned, 45; lives with T. Crawford, 49; fight with Gallbraith, 50, saddler, 50, Charleston days, 51, returns to Waxhaw, 51; teacher, 52; heads to Salisbury, 54; seeks legal training 54, 55; law training with S. McCay, 56; trains with Stokes, 63; begins practicing law, 67; McNairy offers western post; 70; heads west, 80; stays in Jonesborough, 81, buys first slave, 81; challenges Avery to duel, 83; first duel, 84; shows poise in woods, 87; arrives in Nashville, 87; builds reputation, 89; Meets Rachel, 90-91; meets Overton, 91, moves in with Donelson, 90-91; Conflicts with Lewis Robards, 92; moves into Mansker's Station 94; solicitor job, 96-99; falls in love, 100; fights with natives,

ANDREW JACKSON: THE POLITICS OF RESENTMENT

101-102; vouches for Fagot to Smith, 106; mercantile interests begin, 108; allies with Blount faction, 112; AJ reputation in Nashville grows; lands speculations take off, 118; est. Natchez trade network, 120; slave trading, 121; Rachel and AJ go to Natchez to wed,122; hears of Robards not getting divorce, 124; purchases land in Natchez, 125; marries Rachel officially, 126; Davidson Academy board post, 127; return to Nashville via Natchez Trace, 129; conflict with McGary, 130; Robards divorce official, 131; he and Rachel move into Poplar Grove, 132; perspective on marriage, 133; accumulates wealth, 133-134; appeals to federal government over frontier attacks, 134; delegate to TN statehood convention, 143; become TN Congressman, 146; opposes Jay Treaty, 153; land deals with Allison, 156; Allison debt, 158; hears Washington's Farewell Address, votes against it, 161-162; criticizes Washington, 163; petitions for TN militia funds, 164-167; returns to TN, 168; seeks Major-Generalship in TN militia, loses; 171; conflict with Sevier begins, 172; finds out Sevier in land fraud, 175; wins Senate seat, 178; conflict with Cocke, 179; dissatisfied with the Senate, 181; resigns from Senate, 185; returns home, 186; Buys Hunter's Hill, 189; judgeship begins, 190; performance as judge, 190-194; conflict with Russell Bean, 194; AJ Donelson becomes AJ's ward,198; renewed Sevier conflict, 199; becomes Major-General of militia, 201; Knoxville encounter with Sevier, 203; duel with Sevier, 205-207; conflict in Jonesborough, 210; rallies militia to oversee Louisiana transfer, 214; seek La. Territory appointment, 215; travels to Washington, 216; resigns as judge, 217; Allison land debacle, 217; travels to Allison heirs in Ga., 217; buys Hermitage property, 218; death of slave Gilbert, 222; expands mercantile interests, Jackson, Coffee & Hutchings, 223; buys Clover Bottom, 222; sells shares of mercantile interest, 225; expands horse racing interests, 226; buys Truxton, 228; Dickinson affair, 221-242; Hermitage party host, 245; Burr conspiracy, 250-257; goes to Burr trial, 257; birth of Andrew Jackson, Jr., 259; drunken tirade, 261; Silas Dinsmore conflict, 262; anger over *Chesapeake* Affair, 266; AJ issues call for volunteers, 273; Blount appoints AJ to regular army commission, 274; Armstrong vouches for Jackson, 275; delivers TN call to action, 276-277; AJ rallies citizens with pro-war broadside, 280; ordered to join Wilkinson in New Orleans, 283; leaves for Natchez, 284; ordered by War Dept. to disband, 285; leads troops home, 288-289; arrives heroically in Nashville, 289; Benton feud, 290-293; Responds to Fort Mims Massacre, 298; heads to meet Red Sticks, 300; Tallushatchee, 301-302; leads troops at Talladega, 304; becomes Sharp Knife, 305; supply crisis, 306-309; blocks deserters, 309; leads troops at Emuckfaw and Enotachopco, 312; growth as commander, 315; Woods execution, 316-317; Horseshoe Bend, 319-322; talks with Weatherford, 323-324; rebuilds Fort Jackson, 327; returns home a hero, 329; Madison appoints AJ commander of 7th Military District, 332; takes charge of Creek negotiations, 333; arrives at Fort Jackson, 334; Treaty of Fort Jackson, 336; camped out in Mobile, 341; sends Gordon to FL, 343; sails to Mobile Bay, 345; resolves to invade West FL, 347; captures Pensacola, 348; fortifies Mobile, 349; sets out for New Orleans, 350; neglects health, 351; arrives in Crescent City, 353; Addresses New Orleans residents, 355; parade up Royal Street, 356; Livingston's wife's party, 359; establishes Royal Street headquarters, 359; meets with Lafitte, 362; hires on Lafitte, 363; develops N.O. defense, 365; enlists free blacks, 366; martial law declared, 369-370; takes command of La. militia; 371; addresses militia, 371; troop review, Place d'Armes, 373; addresses troops and crowd, 374; commences Villere planation battle, 382; Battle of Villere Plantation, 382-386; sets up line at Rodriguez Canal, 386; fortifies Line Jackson, 386-390; Dec. 31/Jan. 1 battle, 390-391; Battle of New Orleans, tells Morgan he is mistaken, 401; threatens to blow up legislature, 404; arms Kentucky troops, 405; neglects right flank, 407; Battle of New Orleans begins, 408; encourages troops, 414; orders retaking of redoubt, 416; cool under fire, 418; honors Pakenham, 420; praises defenders of line, 425; unaware of right flank, 426; finally reinforces west bank, 429; orders Humbert to regain lost ground, writes Lambert, 430; writes Hays with news of victory, 432; blames Morgan's men for west bank debacle, writes Monroe, 433; damages relationship with Adair, 435; appreciates victory, 436; inspects enemy camp, 446; visits Jumonville hospital, 447; fears return attack 448; returns army to city, 449, addresses troops, 449; requests ceremony from Abbe Dubourg, 449; Addresses New Orleans residents in victory ceremony, 453; conflicts with residents over martial law, habeas corpus, 455-460; Louailler arrest, 460, Hall deportment, 461; peace treaty ratified, ends martial law, 463; farewell address to soldiers, 464; Appears before Hall, 465; pays fine; reproved by Dallas, 467; dancing at ball with Rachel, 468; relationship with Andrew Jr, 469; leaves New Orleans, 470; role in war, 471; refuses to accept Article IX on treaty of Ghent; 475; Removes Creek, 477; ambitions for FL, 478; Arthur poem, 479; Jimmy Driftwood song on Ole Hickory, 480; AJ fame goes nationwide, 482; Congress recognizes AJ, 484-485; song Jackson is the boy, 485-486; portrait in uniform, 487; Leaves city, 488; Nashville homecoming, 489; given command of Southern District, 490; visits Washington, 492; meets with Creeks, 494; 'Friends and Brothers,' 495; Crawford praises Jackson treaty, 495; supports Monroe, promotes Drayton, 1816, 496; Jackson-Crawford split, 497; Cherokee treaty, 499; discusses removal principle, 500; did he hate indigenous, 501; meets with Chickasaw, 502-504; accused of salt lick corruption, 505; Indian policies, 506; conflicts with War Dept., Scott, 506-508; Calhoun assures Jackson, 509; Goes to FL; 511; First Seminole War, 511-514; denounced in Washington, 516; Adams defends AJ, 517; reactions to Seminole War, 516-523; no guilt over slavery, 532, builds Hermitage, 533; finances, 534; health struggles, 535-536; retired from Army, 537; becomes governor of FL, 539; governorship, Callava conflict, 540-548; back in TN, 549; life at Hermitage, 549-553; Eaton begins AJ presidential bid, 553; elected Senator, 554; Burr supports AJ candidacy, 555; Philadelphia endorses, 555-556; Tennessee legislature nominates for presidency, 556; Gadsden and Houston support, 557; compared to George Washington, 558; political outsider, 559-561; Monroe galls Jackson, 561; pens rage at detractors and corruption in government, 563; Aj stays ahead of corruption charges, 564; Cypress Land Co. involvement, 565-567; become serious presidential

AJ continued: contender, 568; rejects Mexican diplomat post, 569; flatters Donelson, recuits as aide, 572; carriage accident, Donelson nuptials, 573; lays out political views, 574-575; enjoys rising popularity, reconciles with Gen. Scott, 576; Clay criticizes AJ candidacy, 576; dines with Clay, 577; reconciles with T.H. Benton, 578; politicking, 578-579; clarifies platform, 579; faces detractors, 580; Cult of Jackson grows, 584; bellicose toward Federalists, 584; criticized by Gallatin, 585; Adams party for AJ, 585; receives Congressional gold medal for war service, 586; receives most votes, 1824

ANDREW JACKSON: THE POLITICS OF RESENTMENT

election, 586; loses election, encounters Adams at ball, 587; reacts calmly to corrupt bargain, 588; calls Clay Judas, 589; Back in TN, angry about corrupt bargain, 590-592; feels cheated, 595; rants over Clay's response to corrupt bargain charge, 596; disregard for Constitution, 597; relationship with wife, 598; Dem party formed, 599; Webster criticizes, 600; hosts party for supporters, 602; expresses respect for JQA, 603; leads first populist movement, 604; teams with Calhoun, 604-605; At Hermitage, Lafayette visit, 608; resigns from Senate, address at Murfreesboro, 609; AJ's mother called prostitute, 610; slander against Adams, 611; Platform similarities to Adams, 612; Mudslinging campaign, 1828, 612-618; Coffin Handbill, 617; Gilbert Scandal/Walton trial, 618-619; Links up with *The Globe*, 619; Tariff stance, 620; Election results, 1828, 622-623; Reacts to Rachel illness, 624; Reacts to Rachel's death, 626-627; will never forgive enemies, 627; funeral, 627; arrives in Washington, 629; storm of office-seekers, unique president-elect, 629; inauguration, 630; post-ceremonial reception at White House, 631-633; spoils system Swartwout mistake, 634; forces rotation of office, 635; moves into White House, 636; leadership style, 636-637; Kitchen Cabinet, 637; appoints regular cabinet, 638; White House levy, 1830, 639; VB cozies up, 640; sympathy for Peggy, 644; frustrated with Donelsons over Peggy, 645; sends Emily home, 646; Tocqueville comments on AJ's appeal to the people, 648; Jacksonian Democracy/Age of Jackson, 649-650; recalls days as orphan, 651; reforms federal government, 652; rotation of office, 654; Maysville Road veto, 655; Lewis informs AJ of Webster-Hayne debates, 656-662; vacations at Rip Raps, 663; Nullification crisis brews, 664-665; Jefferson Birthday dinner toasts, 666-667; Political cartoon on toasts, 667; announces he will seek a 2nd term, 668; speaks with Swartwout about Calhoun, 669; harbors suspicions about Calhoun, 671; reacts to Calhoun pamphlet, 671-672; dismisses Green's *Telegraph*, 673; Cabinet purge, 675-684; cuts off tour of New England due to illness, 684; considers Bank War, 684; offended by Biddle, 685; appoints Taney, McLane, bothered by news stories of Petticoat Affair, 686; ignores Ingham's plight, 689; appoint Eaton to FL, then Spain, 690; rift with Calhoun intensifies, 692-693; opposed Calhoun's Nullification; 693-694; pushes Force Bill through, 694-695; helps frame Compromise Tariff, 695; assures Poinsett, 696; "nullify the nullifiers, 696; Nullification Address, 697; Nullification document points, 698-700; oppositions fears AJ's power, 702; Ingham attacks, 703; Teflon AJ, 703; contemplates Indian removal, 703; declares removal only solution, 708; addresses Congress on removal, 709, 712, 726, 731; supports Ga. against Cherokees, 710; pushes thru Indian Removal Act of 1830, 713; urges Gov. Lumpkin to release missionaries, 716; receives Cherokees at White House, 720; ignores Supreme Court ruling, 723; anguishes at Seminole success in 2nd Seminole War, 728; John Marshall has made his decision, let him enforce it, 729; enormous power, 732; Bank as a monster, 733; James Hamilton letter ignites Jackson's animus for Bank, 734; "Hydra of Corruption, 735; McLane fails to sway AJ, 736; Taney persuades AJ, 737; "Bank is trying to kill me...738; veto/veto message, 738-740; veto message gains support of people, 743; 1832 election, 744-746; removing deposits, 747-749; replaces McLane, then Duane, with Taney, 749; Pet Banks, King Andrew I, 750; Whig Party forms against AJ, 751; Senate discord, 752; censure, 753-754; nominates Taney to Supreme Court, 754; court-packing, 755; satisfied to see VB sworn in by Taney, 756; Deposit Bill and Specie Circular, 758; Randolph attack,

1009

760; Lawrence assassination attempt, 761-762; Martineau interview, 762; Foreign affairs, 763-767; attempts to purchase Texas, 769-778; advises Butler in Mexico, 770-777; hires Houston as Indian agent, 779; receives letter from Houston, 781; Austin reaches out to AJ, 792; hesitates to recognize independent Texas, 794; appears neutral re: Texas, support Alamo defenders, 795; refuses annexation, 796; recognizes Texas independence, 797; summary of Jacksonian philosophy, 798; supporting VB, 799; deals with Emily's decline, 801-802; lung hemorrhaging/keeps Donelson from returning to dying Emily, 804; laments Emily's death, 805; censure expungement, 806-808; writes farewell address, 807; attends VB inauguration, 809; leaves Washington, 810; Farewell Address sent to Congress, 810-811; critics and admirers weigh in on AJ legacy, 812; welcome reception in Nashville, 813; retirement life, 813-816; AJ letter discredits WH Harrison, 817; strikes back at Clay in newspaper, 818-819; supports VB reelection bid; 820; supports Polk, 820; Mayo-Houston scheme, 821; writes of desire to foil British interest in TX, 822; chooses Polk over VB, 823-824; accuses Monroe administration of losing Texas in 1820; 825; Assists Polk victory; 826; celebrates Polk victory with party at Hermitage, 826; speaks of republican simplicity and values, 827; living symbol of democracy, 827; final days due to dropsy, death, 827; post-death reactions, 828-830; Taney eulogy, 829; funeral, 830; Gov. Bradish at NY Historical Society criticizes AJ's memory, 831-832.

Jackson, Andrew, Sr.: background story, 7; buys land, 14; death and final journey, 15.

Jackson, Hugh: leaves for Stono, 24; death, 25.

Rachel Robards Jackson, 89; Meets AJ, 90-91; introduced 72; death of father, 73; appearance, 89; meets Lewis Robards, leaves Robards; back in TN, 90; reconciles with Robards, 91; attractions to AJ, 92; Robards marriage struggling again, 93; Robards leaves, 94; love grows with AJ, 95; full bloom love, 100; mentioned, 116,118,119, 628, 629, 639, 644, 724, 805; Robards threatens to return, she and AJ leave for Natchez, 122-123; settles in Natchez, 124; "unofficial" wedding, 125; hears of Robards not obtaining divorce, 126; AJ correspondence, 160, 286, 302, 318; distraught over Alexander Donelson's death, 318; describes Pensacola, 540; describes AJ's FL disappointment, 545; describes "terrible" Washington, 594; neuroses, 597; snuff habit/kindness/character, 598; slandered, 598, 611, 614-616, 623; Quoted, 612; sick, depressed, 624; fatal illness, 625; death, 626; funeral, AJ grief, 627; Peggy Eaton was kind to her, 643.

Jackson, Robert: baby, 11; Revolutionary War, 12,15, soldier, 25; fights, 30; serves at Hanging Rock, 32; reunited with Betty, 34; serves with Sumter, 34; fights with Crawford relatives, 38;, captured by British, 43; death, 44.

Jefferson, Thomas: Aj compared to, 6; Quoted, 38, 58; states right-ist, 111; Blount names Jefferson County for TJ, 114; envisions agrarian West, 120; questioned morality of slavery, 121; mentioned 145; loses TN electoral votes, 146; as Sec. of State, 149; voices opinion on French Rev., 149; influenced Madison, 150; quoted, 155; ends practice of direct addresses to Congress, 162; pro-French ideology emulated by AJ, 163; negative impression of AJ, 182; offers to buy Louisiana, 184; speaks of importance of New

Orleans, 211; criticized by Federalists for Purchase, 212; La. Purchase mentioned 213; Orders AJ's militia to be ready to march to Louisiana, 214; AJ seeks appointment from, 215; denies AJ, 216; AJ becomes anti-Jefferson, 216-217; Burr trial, 256; "Fire bell in the night", 531.

Knox, Henry: Sec. of War 114; Knoxville named for him, 114; informs Blount to bide his time on Indian issues, 115; Blount badgers, 116. Madison, James: Federalist, 111; wants to impose sanctions on British, 150; criticizes Jay Treaty, 153; Congress leader, 161; supports AJ stance on TN militia funds, 166; inability to address British problem, 251; Burr trial animosity to AJ, 258; AJ against, 259; faces demands for war, 266; inaugural address, 268; addresses impressment, 269; Quoted, 270; Mr. Madison's War, 270; Asks Congress for Declaration of War, 271; struggles to lead in wartime, 272, 341; does not want Jackson, 274; mentioned, 275; administration, 276, 313, 344, 348, 475; photo and political cartoon, 277; brushes off AJ, 281; AJ letter, 288; wartime stress, 294, 326; responds to Fort Mims, 297; mentioned by AJ, 310; critics deride Mr. Madison's War, 331; finally promotes AJ, 334; writes to Armstrong on Indian treaty, 335; Virginia Dynasty, 336; burning of Washington, 338; Clay derides, 341; Ingersoll warns of British spy, 384; Quoted, 392; AJ letter, 420; Monroe explains New Orleans situation, 471; approves Treaty of Fort Jackson, 476; Federalists conspiring, 480; Appleseed Johnny, 481; AJ visits, 491-492; mentioned, 492; calls for Bank's recharter, 497; mentioned, 523; 564; end of Va. Dynasty, 581; mentioned, 584, 586, 597.

Marshall, John: Sent to France, 183; XYZ Affair, 184; rivalry with Jefferson, 257; Burr trial, 257; TJ blames, 258; Dartmouth case, 527; Stays Federalist, 528; McCulloch v. Maryland; comments on presidential race, 623; swears in AJ, 631; mentioned, 660; praises AJ's nullification proclamation; reads Court's opinion against Cherokee, 720; advises Wirt, 722; Jackson's disdain, 724; AJ ignores Marshall's decision, 728-729; death, 755.

Monroe, James: In France, 212; As Sec. of War, 348, 350, 354, 471; AJ writes, 394, 405, 433, 447, 450; Congratulates AJ, 485; AJ backs for president in 1808, 1816, 259; part of Va. Dynasty, 336; Cautions AJ, 349; accurate assessment of British strategy, 350; explains to Madison, 471; AJ toasts, 492; As president, 496, Quoted, 524; Era of Good Feelings, 557; treats AJ with kid gloves, 497; AJ persuades, 502; AJ involves in Army disputes, 507; calms AJ, 508; calls up AJ for Seminole War, 511; turns a blind eye (FL), 512; allows AJ to return home, 515; discusses AJ's actions in FL, 516; writes AJ ambiguously, 518, does not censure AJ, 519; reelected, 522; has to rein in AJ, 523; explains giving up TX, 524; forces AJ retirement from Army, 536; appoints AJ FL gov., 538-539; AJ disappointed in, 540; supports AJ despite criticism, 547; mentioned, 556; Burr ridicules, 557.

Story, Joseph, 700, 720, 723

Thompson, Smith, 720

Washington, George: Rev. War, 23; hero, 48; elected president, 76; appoints Blount, 112; Thomas Paine remarks to, 148; Farewell Address, 161; AJ disagrees with, 162; AJ votes against farewell address, 163; AJ compared to, 560, 562, 629, 810; mentioned, 615; treatment of indigenous, 704; Town Destroyer, 704; Administration, 134, 138, 162, 704.

www.ingramcontent.com/pod-product-compliance
Lightning Source LLC
Chambersburg PA
CBHW030327240426
43661CB00052B/1553